ECONOMIC GROWTH
AND DEVELOPMENT

Second Edition

ECONOMIC GROWTH
AND DEVELOPMENT

Second Edition

Hendrik Van den Berg

University of Nebraska, USA

World Scientific

NEW JERSEY · LONDON · SINGAPORE · BEIJING · SHANGHAI · HONG KONG · TAIPEI · CHENNAI

Published by

World Scientific Publishing Co. Pte. Ltd.

5 Toh Tuck Link, Singapore 596224

USA office: 27 Warren Street, Suite 401-402, Hackensack, NJ 07601

UK office: 57 Shelton Street, Covent Garden, London WC2H 9HE

Library of Congress Cataloging-in-Publication Data
Van den Berg, Hendrik, 1949–
   Economic growth and development / by Hendrik Van den Berg. -- 2nd ed.
   p. cm.
  ISBN-13 978-981-4374-64-4 (pbk)
  ISBN-10 981-4374-64-4 (pbk)
  1. Economic development--History.   2. Economic development--Mathematical models.   I. Title.
 HD78.V363 2012
 338.9--dc23

                       2012004864

British Library Cataloguing-in-Publication Data
A catalogue record for this book is available from the British Library.

In-house Editor: Alisha Nguyen

Printed in Singapore by World Scientific Printers.

About the Author

Hendrik Van den Berg is Professor of Economics at the University of Nebraska–Lincoln, where he teaches economic growth and development as well as international economics. He received B.A. and M.A. degrees in economics from the State University of New York at Albany in 1971 and 1973, respectively, and M.S. and Ph.D. degrees in economics from the University of Wisconsin–Madison in 1987 and 1989. Between studying in New York and Wisconsin, Hendrik served as a Foreign Service Officer at the United States Embassy in Managua, Nicaragua in the position of Commercial Officer, and at the U.S. Trade Center in São Paulo, Brazil, as Market Research and Promotion Officer. He left the United States Department of State to manage the São Paulo office of Marsteller Advertising, and later worked as Planning Manager for Singer of Brazil, also in São Paulo. Hendrik traveled widely for Singer and experienced the challenges of living and managing businesses in developing economies. In 1985, Hendrik decided to return to his first love, economics, and enrolled at the University of Wisconsin.

Hendrik has published many articles on exchange rates, international trade, alternative estimates of economic growth, the empirical relationship between international trade and economic growth, and, most recently, the determinants and consequences of immigration on source and destination countries. Currently, he is examining the biases of neoclassical economics and the influence of the neoclassical paradigm on the fields of international economics and economic development.

Hendrik also regularly writes for general audiences, including monthly articles on economic policy, peace, and social justice in *Nebraska Report*, the newspaper of Nebraskans for Peace. He also writes for the *Nebraska Worker*, the newsletter of the Nebraska Industrial Workers of the World. He is often invited to speak on immigration, foreign trade, and international finance.

Hendrik has written several economics textbooks, including *Economic Growth and Development*, 1st Edition (McGraw-Hill, 2001), *International Economics* (McGraw-Hill, 2003), *International Trade and Economic Growth* (M.E. Sharpe, 2006), *The Economics of Immigration* (Springer, 2009), *International Finance and Open-Economy Macroeconomics* (World Scientific, 2010), and *International Economics: A Heterodox Approach* (M.E. Sharpe, 2011).

Preface

In the first edition of *Economic Growth and Development*, which I wrote more than ten years ago, I used orthodox models to provide an answer to what I believed to be the most important question in economics: Why do some economies provide their citizens with high standards of living while others just do not seem to be able to satisfy the most simple human wants nor offer people very many options for change? This completely new *Economic Growth and Development* textbook takes a much more holistic approach to answer that same question more thoroughly.

Why I Wrote This Text: A Personal Note

When, in 1974, I left graduate school with a master's degree in economics and began my new job as a Foreign Service Officer with the United States Department of State, I thought I was well-prepared for my new job. My first assignment was Commercial Officer at the U.S. Embassy in Managua, Nicaragua. I had taken a number of courses on economic growth and development, and I had written my master's thesis on the Central American Common Market. Yet, I quickly discovered that my academic background provided little guidance for understanding why Nicaragua was poor. Of course, reconciling the real world with what one learns in academia is a common problem for recently-employed graduate students, no matter what field or university they come from. But, I still think I should have gotten more understanding from my two courses in mathematical growth theory and the four courses in development economics.

The mathematical models from my growth theory classes predicted that Nicaragua's reasonably high rate of savings should have caused respectable economic growth. But, instead, I saw abandoned children in Managua's shantytowns, cotton pickers who worked long hours only to suffer illness from the massive use of DDT, and blatant corruption throughout the dictatorial government. I saw very rich Nicaraguans shopping in Miami in the United States, while for the great majority of the population, a cold bottle of Coca Cola was a rare luxury.

My courses in economic development did not help much either. Many development economists cited in my college textbooks called for more foreign aid, but I noticed that there was plenty of foreign aid in Nicaragua. When I lived in Nicaragua in the mid-1970s, large amounts of foreign assistance were flowing into the country for the reconstruction of Managua, the capital city that had been leveled by an earthquake in 1972. Much of this aid ended up in the pockets of Nicaragua's dictator Anastasio Somoza, who owned the country's largest construction company, the largest equipment distributor, the country's only cement plant, the country's only shipping line, the country's largest bank, and, of course, the only luxury hotel for foreign aid officials to stay in while "overseeing" the theft.

Two years later, I was transferred by the U.S. Department of State to become the Market Research and Promotion Officer at a new U.S. Trade Center in São Paulo, Brazil. We thus moved from one of the least developed countries in Latin America to the highly industrialized South of Brazil. This U.S. Trade Center in São Paulo was built by the U.S. Department of Commerce to promote U.S. exports to Brazil, a country that actively prevented imports from entering the country in order to protect its own industries. "American jobs depend on you," a letter from the U.S. Secretary of Commerce told me. Not entirely sure that Brazil really needed gas guzzling Ford Galaxies or American fast food franchises to replace Brazil's Volkswagen "fuscas" and numerous family restaurants, or that these imports actually created jobs in the United States, I left the State Department two years later and took a job in the private sector. My friends joked that I had become addicted to Brazilian soccer and could not bring myself to leave. In 1980, I took a job as Marketing/Planning Manager for the Singer Company in Brazil, which employed over 10,000 people manufacturing and marketing sewing machines. Business crumbled in 1982 when the debt crisis hit Brazil and the other Latin American and African markets served by Singer's Brazilian subsidiary. Rather than planning new projects, I was planning layoffs and plant closings. Seeing the devastating effects of the debt crisis and the economic collapse that followed naturally led me to ask how a fast-growing economy like Brazil's could come to such a sudden, grinding halt in 1982. What could be done to remedy the situation? My ten years' experience in the real world had not prepared me to answer those types of questions any better than my growth theory and development economics courses had prepared me to understand poverty and exploitation. So I went back to school.

I enrolled in the economics Ph.D. program at the University of Wisconsin–Madison. I applied to Wisconsin in part because I had spent a wonderful summer there back in 1969 in an intensive Portuguese language program. While the State University of New York at Albany had not prepared me for what I encountered in developing countries, Madison's Economics Department may have done a poorer job. By 1985, the Economics Department at the University of Wisconsin–Madison had decided to maintain its status as a top-ten economics department by confirming its commitment to the culture of mainstream economics and teaching exclusively the neoclassical paradigm. The first year of Ph.D. study was a wholesale indoctrination in rational expectations and efficient markets. When I left for the University of Nebraska four years later I did not realize I had been converted into a disciple who was expected to go out into the world to spread the word of the neoliberal doxa that now dominates the culture of economics. It took another twenty years of research, experience, and thinking to discover the many *anomalies* between what the orthodox culture of economics suggests and what we actually observe in the real world. Not long after my first *Economic Growth and Development* textbook became the target of many subtle and direct criticisms, I realized it was time for what Thomas Kuhn (1962) calls paradigm shift.[1] This new book is the result of nearly ten years of search for a better paradigm.

Joseph Stiglitz wrote not long ago: "Changing paradigms is not easy. Too many have invested too much in the wrong models."[2] At the personal level, changing paradigms was not easy. I was very human and I resisted change all along the way. It was hard to come to the conclusion that many of my most beloved teachers were wrong. It was harder to admit that I was wrong. My experience is perhaps best captured by the words of my favorite economist, John Maynard Keynes, in his Preface to his monumental *General Theory of Employment, Interest, and Money* (1936:viii):

> The composition of this book has been for the author a long struggle of escape, and so must the reading of it be for most readers if the author's assault upon them is to be successful — a struggle of escape from habitual modes of thought and expression. The ideas which are here expressed so laboriously are extremely simple and should be obvious. The difficulty lies, not in the new ideas, but in escaping from the old ones, which ramify, for those of us brought up as most of us have been, into every corner of our minds.

As this book will explore from many different angles, culture plays a dominant role in human society. The orthodox neoclassical culture has a tight grip on economists.

This book definitively rejects the orthodox neoclassical paradigm as the exclusive framework within which economists should think. At the same time, this textbook also rejects the sharp division between orthodoxy and heterodoxy

---

[1] Thomas Kuhn (1962), *The Structure of Scientific Revolutions*, Chicago: University of Chicago Press.
[2] Joseph Stiglitz (2010), "Needed: A New Economic Paradigm," *Financial Times (USA)*, August 20.

that we often see in the literature. Instead, in what I see as the true spirit of heterodoxy, I have tried to follow a multi-paradigmatic approach that includes many useful neoclassical models. If we can compare a paradigm to a language, then it is fair to say heterodoxy enables economists to speak many languages. Such multilingual abilities enable economists to discover many viewpoints, discuss issues with many different interests, and uncover more information and evidence to support or refute many more hypotheses. As will hopefully become clear as you read this book, there is a compelling logic to heterodoxy that goes well beyond merely rejecting the generality of the neoclassical paradigm.

I mentioned that the reactions to my first *Economic Growth and Development* textbook helped to push me to what I think is a much more accurate and useful discussion of economic development. I therefore strongly urge readers and teachers to respond critically to this book. Given my experience, I am quite certain that the current state of knowledge does not include all the answers. In fact, I am certain that as one person, I have not come close to capturing all the relevant knowledge related to the issues I bring up. I look forward to your help to further the discussion of how economies develop.

Acknowledgements

In closing, I would like to thank the many people who played various roles in bringing this book about. First of all, I want to thank my teachers. At the State University of New York at Albany, I must mention Fred Dickey, who taught me principles of economics and inspired me to major in economics, Helen Horowitz, who inspired me to become a teacher of economics, Franklin Walker and Pong Lee, who introduced me to the cutting edge of economic thinking at the time, and Marvin Sternberg, who introduced me to the radical economic thinkers that I returned to for inspiration in writing this new edition. At the University of Wisconsin–Madison, I owe a special debt to Arthur Goldberger, who taught me to be critical of technical approaches to economics. His courses in statistical methods, or what economists call econometrics, demanded critical thinking and a heavy dose of skepticism. I must also thank the professors I worked with most closely at Wisconsin, Robert Baldwin, J. David Richardson, Rachel McCullough, and Kenneth Rogoff. While I have now embraced heterodoxy in place of the orthodox neoclassical analysis they taught, they nevertheless showed me many broad perspectives that prepared me well for my growth as an economist. Their endless energy in research and teaching made it clear that we never stop learning and revising our thinking.

I also want to thank several of my colleagues here at the University of Nebraska. Above all, I thank Greg Hayden and Ann Mari May, who did not hesitate to challenge me as I struggled with the neoclassical paradigm. They also provided great insight into heterodoxy. And, of course, I thank all the students who asked difficult questions and wrote unconventional answers to standard test questions. The current focus on research in academia incorrectly diminishes teaching; there is no advance in knowledge without teaching.

My wife Barbara, who makes my life so wonderful, provided the most comprehensive editing throughout the many stages of development that the manuscript for this book passed through. She added many ideas and perspectives from her reading and community activism. I also want to thank our three sons, Paulo, Matthew, and Tom, who continually challenged my reasoning while also proofreading. Matthew, who now also teaches economics, provided many detailed ideas, concepts, and additions that substantially expanded the book's heterodoxy. Finally, Rossitza Todorova provided the stunning artwork for this book's cover that so well represents the complexity of economic development.

Hendrik Van den Berg
Lincoln, Nebraska

Contents

PART I

Thinking About Economic Development

In 1998, the *Wall Street Journal* ran a story on how economic growth had transformed a small Indonesian village named Begajah on the Island of Java in Indonesia. The writer of the article compared Bagajah in 1998 to what he remembered from a previous visit in 1971:

> People walked everywhere then. Of 768 families who lived here in 1971... fewer than one in five owned even a bicycle. They had a few battery-powered radios but no electricity, telephones, or TV. Warnings of fire, thieves, bad spirits and such were banged out on slit-log drums... They lived in houses made of woven palm fronds and bamboo, slept on mats on dirt floors, cooked on open wood fires, and washed in the river. Cholera, malaria, and dysentery thrived. Children died early and often.
>
> ... Today, nearly three decades later, Begajah is barely recognizable. Its footpaths are asphalt streets with names, fluorescent street lights and speed bumps. Bicycles now are child's play: the 1,391 families who now call Begajah home own more than 550 motorbikes and motorcycles, and 54 automobiles and sport-utility vehicles.... Most houses are brick or stucco-covered, with teak doors and window frames and white porcelain floors. All have electricity. In their kitchens are Magic Jar electric rice cookers and Sanyo electric pumps that supply running water. Kerosene stoves have replaced wood fires. Begajahans own more than 700 television sets; they get five channels.[1]

The article describes the tremendous improvements in nutrition, health, and education that Begajahans enjoyed in 1998, compared to 1971. A modern clinic had replaced the common practice of giving birth at home in unsanitary conditions, and infant mortality had dropped drastically. While only half of the village's children attended any school before 1971, in 1998 full primary education was mandatory for all. Also before 1971, most children were infested

---

[1] James P. Sterba (1998), "A Village Transformed by Suharto's Politics Now Frets and Waits," *The Wall Street Journal*, July 22, p. A1.

1

with hookworm, an internal parasite that saps needed nutrition. Hookworm made 12-year-old children look no older than eight. "But nobody in Begajah noticed because every 12-year-old looked eight."[2]   During his 1998 visit to Begajah, however, the reporter wrote that "babies were so fat and healthy that visitors remarked that they looked bigger than their grandmothers."[3]

In the case of Indonesia, gross national product (GDP) grew at close to 8 percent per year between 1971 and 1998. Even when Indonesia's rapid population growth of around 2 percent per year is accounted for, GDP per capita grew at nearly 6 percent per year.[4] These high annual growth rates, compounded year after year, quadrupled the average material wealth of Indonesians over the quarter century preceding the reporter's visit to Begajah. No wonder things looked different since his earlier 1971 visit.

For development economists, stories such as this one on Begajah are inspiring. Indonesia had been one of the poorest countries in the world. In 1950, Indonesia's per capita GDP was less than one tenth that of the United States.[5] By the late 1990s, Indonesia's per capita GDP had grown to more than one-ninth of U.S. GDP per capita in real terms. This may seem like a small relative improvement, but after nearly two centuries of very unequal economic growth, a reduction in relative disparity of income levels was seen as a significant accomplishment. Indonesia's income per capita had declined from just half that of the United States 200 years ago to one-tenth in 1950, an outcome not uncommon among the less developed economies of Asia, Africa, and Latin America. The growth of Indonesia's GDP in the latter part of the twentieth century reversed a long-running trend of growing income disparity.

Begajah in 1998

Of course, the story of Begajah does not end in 1998. Later in that year, the Indonesian economy suffered a sharp downturn as a result of a financial contraction triggered by the fall in the value of the Indonesian rupiah in the foreign exchange markets. After maintaining a stable currency value for many years, the collapse of the currency took the Indonesian economy by surprise.

Over the years prior to 1998, many of Indonesia's banks, governments, and firms had borrowed heavily in the international financial markets to finance the housing, infrastructure, and business expansion in the thousands of cities and towns like Begajah throughout the country. This meant that much of Indonesia's debt was denominated in U.S. dollars, Japanese yen, or other foreign currencies. In 1998, when Indonesia's currency, the rupiah, depreciated by

---

[2] Sterba (1998), op. cit., p. A8.
[3] Sterba (1998), op. cit., p. A8.
[4] The numbers given as examples in this paragraph are from the World Bank's *World Development Report* and its *World Development Indicators*.
[5] We refer here to the estimates of real GDP per capita by Agnus Maddison (2001), who adjusts for many differences in prices, quality, tastes, and measurement problems across countries and time.

about two-thirds relative to the U.S. dollar and Japanese yen, Indonesia's foreign debt in terms of rupiahs suddenly became three times as large. Many Indonesian firms were surprised to find that their liabilities exceeded their assets, and they often stopped servicing their loans to Indonesia's banks. Many Indonesian banks had themselves also borrowed overseas to make more loans to domestic firms in the booming economy. Thus, banks' liabilities also rose in value while their assets lost value, and many banks found themselves with insufficient reserves to support their loans and other investments. To protect their remaining capital reserves, they stopped lending. As a result, investment plummeted and the Indonesian economy fell into a deep recession.

Indonesia's real GDP per capita fell by 15 to 20 percent in late 1998, reaching a low point in 1999. Unemployment soared in Indonesia's cities, and families in small towns like Begajah experienced a sharp decline in income. Housing construction stopped, some of the motorcycles and appliances purchased on credit were repossessed, and even school attendance dropped because children were forced to seek work to support their families. The residents of Bagajah and all other Indonesians, who had come to see the growth of income and material consumption as the normal course of events, asked: How could this suddenly happen?

According to economists, the rupiah lost value in the foreign exchange markets in 1998, in part, because of the economic policies of another Asian economy: China. Just a few years earlier, China had intentionally devalued its currency, the yuan, in order to give Chinese exporters a competitive edge in world markets. Other East Asian economies like Indonesia suddenly found it more difficult to keep their exports growing at the same rate as they had for much of the previous 25 years. Many people began to realize that countries like Indonesia would eventually have to also let their currencies decline in value, so many holders of rupiahs began to shift their wealth to assets denominated in other currencies. This *speculation* against the rupiah increased the supply of rupiahs on the foreign exchange market, depressing the value of the currency. The Indonesian central bank initially tried to neutralize the speculation by using its holdings, or "reserves," of dollars to demand those extra rupiahs and thus keep the exchange rate from falling. But, as fears grew that the rupiah would soon have to be allowed to fall in value, the shift to foreign assets turned into a mad rush. The Indonesian central bank soon ran out of dollar reserves, and the feared depreciation occurred sooner rather than later.

As the residents of Begajah saw their economic circumstances deteriorate, they felt betrayed. The sudden end to their good fortune seemed rather unfair. What did they do to deserve such a sudden and large decline in income? Who caused this economic disaster? The Prime Minister of Malaysia, a neighboring East Asian country that suffered a similar currency depreciation and financial crisis in 1998, publicly blamed international currency speculators and called them the "highwaymen of the global economy." He failed to mention that the "speculators" were mostly ordinary citizens and businesses who noticed that their national currency had become somewhat overvalued and, fearing a future depreciation, shifted their wealth overseas to protect themselves from possible losses. But, who *was* to blame for Begajah's economic downturn? Was it China's devaluation?

It was indeed tempting for Indonesians to blame China. Indonesians noticed that while Indonesia and many other East Asian economies were experiencing bankruptcies and economic stagnation in 1998, China's per capita real GDP continued to grow at annual rates exceeding 8 percent right on into the early 2000s. Mobs in several Indonesian cities burned and plundered businesses owned by ethnic Chinese-Indonesians, a relatively wealthy minority that had achieved a privileged economic position under the protection of the Dutch colonial government that ruled Indonesia for several centuries before it regained its independence after World War II.

China's impressive economic growth

China's rapid economic growth in terms of GDP per capita has been widely touted as the major economic development success of the last 25 years. Beginning with a sharp shift in economic policy, effectively reducing the role of central planning in favor of markets in many parts of its economy, China has since the late 1970s reported annual economic growth rates of over 8 percent. Chinese per capita income was doubling every ten years. It had quadrupled in less than one generation. Given that China contains one-fifth of the world's population, its rapid growth in material output suggests that a very large portion of the world's poor people have experienced large improvements in their standards of living.

In reality, the changes in China are more complex than the simple compounding of annual growth rates of GDP suggest. The town of Jinfeng, situated along the lower Yangtze River in China, provides an interesting example of the complexities of recent Chinese economic growth.[6] In the early twenty-first century, every morning more than 30,000 of Jinfeng's workers walked or bicycled to an array of industries paying wages equal to about US$0.50 per hour. Compared to working on small farms in their villages, these wages constitute a substantial increase in real income. This gain in income is why so many workers were flocking to cities like Jinfeng. Among Jinfeng's many industrial firms, there is the Shagang steel mill, which opened in 2002 after being transported, piece by piece, from Dortmund in the Ruhr Valley of Germany.

---

[6] The case of Jinfeng, is taken from Joseph Kahn and Mark Landler (2007), "China Grabs West's Smoke-Spewing Factories," *New York Times*, December 21; and James Kynge (2006), *China Shakes the World*, Boston: Houghton Mifflin Company.

The Ruhr Valley was the center of Germany's steel industry. In the early 2000s, the German steel conglomerate ThyssenKrupp AG faced strong foreign competition and tightening local environmental regulations. It therefore began selling off many of its ageing steel manufacturing plants. But it did not sell the plants to new owners who would continue operating the plants in Germany. Rather, the plants were sold to bargain-hunting Chinese entrepreneurs, who sent work crews to dismantle the equipment and pack it off to China, where labor costs were a tiny fraction of Germany's.

An interesting side note to this story is that Shagang sent its own work crew to Dortmund to dismantle and ship the plant. ThyssenKrupp had estimated it would take three years to dismantle the plant, but the Chinese work crews finished the job in one year. They worked seven days a week for many more hours per day than German labor law allowed but, somehow, the German government looked the other way.

Today, the plant produces steel at much lower cost in Jinfeng, and this steel is used to produce the many Chinese products that are shipped all over the world, including the wealthy German market. Because of the relocated steel plant in Jinfeng and dozens more like it throughout the country, China is now the world's biggest steel producer, well ahead of the once-dominant German steel industry.

So is Jinfeng, like Begajah, a development success story? The full story of Jinfeng must include the fact that China's steel mills have produced more than steel. The steel mills and the coal-fired power plants that provide their electricity have also produced massive greenhouse gas (GHG) emissions. This type of industrial growth helped China overtake the United States in 2007 as the largest emitter of the GHGs that cause global warming. In effect, German GHG emissions were transferred to China. While Germany proudly confirmed that it was on schedule to reduce its greenhouse gas emissions by 40 percent by 2020, its former steel mills were now increasing China's emissions. By 2005, China was also releasing more than 26 million tons of sulfur into its air, about two and a half times as much as the United States. One study attributes 400,000 premature deaths in China to air pollution. Furthermore, evidence shows that China's sulfur emissions and other pollutants travel across the Pacific Ocean and now account for 10 to 15 percent of California's air particles allowable under U.S. environmental laws.[7] We live in an integrated international economy.

Air quality is only one of many environmental problems caused by China's rapid economic growth. Around the town of Minqin in the Western Chinese province of Gansu, irrigation projects intended to expand agriculture to feed China's growing population, have emptied a river, eliminated a lake, and let the encroaching desert take over about 1,500 square miles of formerly fertile land each year. Desperate measures to drill over 11,000 wells and plant deep rooted

---

[7] Keith Bradsher and David Barboza (2006), "Pollution from Chinese Coal Casts a Long Shadow," *New York Times*, June 11.

trees at the edge of the desert have made matters worse by lowering the water table. The head of the project to stop the encroaching desert wants to move people out, stop agricultural production, and let the land heal itself: "Minqin is not going to get more water. It needs fewer people."[8]

China's rapid growth has not provided all 1.3 billion Chinese with comparable improvements in well-being. Some regions have grown faster than others, and some people in each region have captured greater income gains than others. According to standard measures of income inequality published by the World Bank, China's income is now much less equally distributed than before the beginning of its growth spurt three decades ago. Many workers' willingness to work long hours in Jinfeng's dirty industries for low wages means that incomes must still be even lower in the Chinese countryside.

China's spectacular growth slowed in late 2008 and 2009 because the world economy, where the Jinfeng steel plant and all of China's many industries sold their products, fell deep into recession. The global recession started in the United States, where a bubble in housing prices burst. The collapse of U.S. housing prices affected the rest of the world because the derivative assets based on the underlying mortgages had been acquired in other countries. These purchases of U.S. mortgage securities were just the latest acquisitions of U.S. assets by foreign investors since the United States began running large trade deficits with China and many other countries in the 1980s. As the default rate on U.S. mortgages shot up and securities that contained those mortgages were suddenly worth much less than their fraudulent AAA ratings had suggested, balance sheets deteriorated and bankruptcies spread across the economies of Europe, Asia, and other continents. As economic recession spread, China's exports tumbled, and growth slowed drastically. Not unlike towns such as Begajah in Indonesia a decade earlier, many Chinese asked themselves why the growth of income and employment had suddenly come to an end. At the start of 2009, news reports estimated that 20 million workers in Jinfeng and elsewhere in China had lost their jobs and were returning to their family homes in the countryside.[9]

The Chinese economy never saw its growth rate turn negative, however. In fact, Chinese GDP quickly resumed growing. Unlike Indonesia, Chinese firms and banks did not carry high amounts of foreign debt. China's large trade surpluses had permitted it to accumulate huge reserves of foreign currencies. As a result, there was a tendency for the Chinese yuan to appreciate, not depreciate. To prevent such appreciation, and the negative effect it might have on employment in the export industries, the Bank of China printed more yuan and used them to demand U.S. dollars in the foreign exchange market. This

---

[8] Joseph Kahn (2006), "A Sea of Sand Is Threatening China's Heart," *New York Times*, June 8.
[9] See, for example, Simon Elegant (2008), "China's Worst Nightmare: Unemployment," *Time*, October 3, or Tan Yingzi (2009), "China's Unemployment Rate Climbs," *China Daily*, January 21.

stimulative monetary expansion was supplemented by the Chinese government's acceleration of infrastructure projects and other fiscal expenditures. While much of the world economy was still experiencing high unemployment rates and several countries, most notably Britain and Japan, had entered a second recessionary phase in 2011, the Chinese economy was again growing at its customary rapid rate of the past three decades.

The complexity of economic development

These examples make it clear that the growth of economic activity affects broader aspects of human society and the natural environment. They also show how economic development generally implies more complex economic relationships within and across countries. The globalization of economic activity is very much a characteristic of modern economic development, but the international trade, investment, and financial flows that we observe have a broad range of effects, not all of which are positive. Together, these complexities mean that the study of economic development must deal with very difficult economic, social, and natural phenomena.

The complexity of economic development and its intimate relationship with our social and natural environments also calls into question the common focus on the gross domestic product (GDP) in the field of development economics. GDP per capita is simply the average per person production of a set of goods and services produced in the formally organized sectors of the economy. The common practice of assuming the growth of GDP per capita translates directly into improvements in the welfare of humanity biases discussions of economic development and the design of development policy. Political leaders and policymakers certainly never hesitate to use data on the growth of GDP to justify their continuation in office, and few political leaders have demanded alternative measures of economic development. However, the reality of economic development is not so simple. For every happy story of economic change, such as Begajah before 1998 and the continued rising incomes of a substantial share of China's 1.3 billion citizens, there are stories of economic change generating job losses, disruption of communities, and environmental damage.

An interesting exception to the widespread acceptance of GDP growth as the measure of economic success or failure is Bhutan's adoption of Gross National Happiness (GNH) in place of GDP. GNH was established as the goal of Bhutan's economic development policies by King Jigme Singye Wangchuck in 1972. GNH is a conceptual measure that reflects four general policy goals: (1) equitable and sustainable social and economic development, (2) preservation of cultural (Buddhist) values, (3) conservation of the natural environment, and (4) good governance.

It is difficult, however, to come up with useful and workable metrics that reflect the full complexity of economic development. And, GDP is very convenient: bureaucracies are set up to calculate it, and it is a simple number for economists to plug into their statistical programs. Some heterodox economists argue that GDP is intentionally emphasized in order to justify policies that favor private business groups whose income is directly related to the continued growth of material output in the market economy. GDP does not account for household activity, leisure, or the costs of environmental destruction, for example.

The way forward

The challenge is for humanity to enhance its capacity to deal with complexity. Unfortunately, most economists have not yet come to accept the complex nature of economic development, preferring to limit their models and analyses to certain economic phenomena while keeping other "non-economic" influences outside their analysis. Worse, many economists have ignored social and environmental issues altogether. Nothing reflects economists' limited vision more clearly than the continued acceptance of GDP as an appropriate measure of human progress. It does not take much reflection to come to the realization that the field of development economics has not yet satisfactorily answered the question: What kind of long-run economic change and development should humanity strive to achieve? Humanity seems to be traveling along a path that is not sustainable, and yet economists have hardly begun to ask themselves where humanity is headed. By embracing complexity, this textbook shows the way towards a more holistic and realistic approach to analyzing human progress. The next 18 chapters take you on a fascinating journey through the human experience and the accumulated knowledge about our existence and economic progress. The upcoming chapters go well beyond the field of economics; complexity demands that we venture into the other fields of social science as well as the natural sciences. As the examples of Begajah and Jinfeng suggest, humanity has created a complex global society. To understand life in Begajah or Jinfeng, people must know what is happening elsewhere and how their local community is linked to the rest of the world. More important, humanity's society of 7 billion people must understand that it is a large integral component of the natural environment.

Fortunately, beyond the narrow field of economic growth and development there is a huge body of knowledge and experience that we can draw on to begin formulating a useful understanding of humanity's current existence. This textbook's broad historical and inter-disciplinary perspectives not only bring us much closer to finding the path to sustainable economic development, but you will find the broader subject matter extremely interesting and intellectually satisfying. There is beauty in complexity, especially when you begin to make some sense of its order.

The first part of the book

The first leg of our journey, that is, the first section of the book, consists of three chapters. The first chapter introduces *the power of compounding, the scientific method, complexity, holism,* and many other useful concepts that will help you understand the process of economic development. The first chapter also provides a very brief history of thought on economic growth, and it defines *sustainable economic development.* The second chapter discusses how economists and other social scientists have traditionally defined and measured economic development. Despite the use of measures such as GDP and GDP per capita throughout orthodox economic analysis and the economic development literature, the fact is that these measures are woefully inadequate as measures of human economic progress. The chapter therefore also discusses some of the more comprehensive measures of economic development that have been suggested over the past several decades. Chapter 3 discusses the concept of economic development more holistically by bringing in several inter-disciplinary perspectives. That chapter presents the cutting edge research from interesting fields of economics such as happiness studies and behavioral economics, as well as from other disciplines such as neuroscience, psychology, and sociology.

We recognize that students often approach the early "definitional" chapters of a textbook with less than full concentration, saving their reading effort for the more substantial later chapters. That would be a huge mistake in this case. The three chapters that follow will open your eyes to the diverse and fascinating perspectives of the field of development economics. Most students find these chapters to be quite liberating. By the end of Chapter 3, you will be ready to think outside the confining box of orthodox economics, as you must if you are to grasp the complexity of economic development and the social and environmental changes with which it is intertwined.

CHAPTER 1

The Complexity of Economic Development

A wider or more altruistic attitude is very relevant in today's world. If we look at the situation from various angles, such as the complexity and inter-connectedness of the nature of modern existence, then we will gradually notice a change in our outlook, so that when we say "others" and when we think of others, we will no longer dismiss them as something that is irrelevant to us. We will no longer feel indifferent.

(Dalai Lama)

Economic development is a complex process. It is complex because a modern economy is a complex system that links millions of people, firms, organizations, and government agencies. Adding to the complexity is the fact that the economy is an integral component of even larger and more complex social and natural systems. Humans interact and carry out our economic activities within a **society**, and our economic and social systems operate within a natural environment that we call the **ecosystem**.

Economics has always recognized that an economy is characterized by a pattern of relationships. But economists have often limited their analysis to economic relationships. The environmental economist Herman Daly (1998) points out that the conventional methods of analysis used by mainstream economists today ignore the fact that "the macroeconomy is not the relevant whole, but is itself a subsystem, a part of the ecosystem, the larger economy of nature." From his perspective as an environmental economist, Daly explicitly links the economy to the ecological system, or ecosystem, of the Earth.

This textbook takes the additional step of placing the economy within human society, which is then linked to Earth's ecosystem. We will often refer to the three systems as, respectively, the economic, social, and natural spheres of human existence. Figure 1.1 illustrates the human economy as positioned within the social and natural spheres. The economic sphere is linked to the social sphere in many complex ways, and human society interacts with the

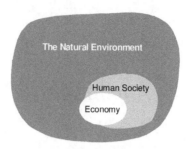

Figure 1.1 The Economy's Position in Society and the Natural Environment

natural sphere in many more complex ways to form a large interdependent system. Figure 1.1 shows the economy located mostly within human society, but it is also positioned to interact directly with nature at some points to reflect the fact that some economic events directly impact, or are impacted by, the ecosystem.

Figure 1.1 serves to remind us that the economy is not a self-contained system free from social and natural constraints and influences. It also illustrates that economic activity cannot be assumed to have no impact on the social and natural spheres of human existence. In fact, the process of economic development affects, and is affected by, what goes on in the larger environments that humans inhabit. Especially important for long-run economic development are the stresses that develop between the three **spheres of human existence**.

This chapter explains why this textbook rejects the orthodox notion that economic analysis can ignore social and natural events. It is simply unrealistic to treat social and natural events as independent outside shocks to the economic development process. Individual human beings are, and always have been, completely dependent on the rest of human society and the ecosystem for their economic well-being. At the same time, humanity's economic activity on Earth has grown so large that it is no longer realistic to refer to all things that happen outside the economic sphere as independent "non-economic" events that can be taken as givens rather than related events.

Chapter Goals

1. Present a brief history of economic growth, with emphasis on the apparent acceleration of the growth of material output over the past 200 years.
2. Discuss compounding, structural change, and other characteristics of growth.
3. Explain complexity, holism, science, and the practice of modeling.
4. Outline the perspectives that economic thinkers have taken in studying economic change and development.
5. Introduce the concept of heterodoxy and discuss its advantages for analyzing a complex phenomenon like economic development.

1.1 The Economic, Social, and Natural Environments

Since human economic activity occurs within broader social and natural environments, it is not possible to describe or predict human activity according to hypothesized economic relationships within only the economic sphere. Humans perceive their well-being in reference not only to economic outcomes, but also in terms of changes in their social and natural environments. Therefore, if we define economic development as the process that changes human well-being, then, clearly, we must study the process across all three spheres in which humans live and act.

1.1.1 Economic activity and the three spheres

China's per capita real gross domestic product (GDP) grew at an annual rate of nearly 8 percent between the mid-1980s and the first decade of the 2000s. The fast GDP growth in China was largely the result of the rapid growth of industrial production, and this required a rapid increase in energy usage. China's largest source of energy is coal, which fires most of its power plants and factories. In 2008, China passed the U.S. economy as the single largest emitter of the greenhouse gases (GHGs) that contribute to global warming.

The construction of a steel mill in China, as in the case just described in the Introduction to this section of the book, thus increases economic growth in China if we measure such growth simply as output counted in GDP. However, the environmental impact has been highly negative. The Chinese coal-fired power plants that provide the electric power to the transplanted steel plants emit more GHGs than do current German power plants, which increasingly consist of natural gas plants, wind farms, and solar panels. Therefore, the shipment of steel mills from Germany to China increased global GHG emissions. Can we really say, therefore, that the rapid growth of Chinese GDP represents an unequivocal improvement in human well-being?

Perhaps the overall effect of Chinese economic growth on human well-being is indeed positive, but clearly it is not as positive as suggested by the growth of Chinese GDP. To get to the whole truth of the matter, economic analysis must include the effects of increased steel production on the natural sphere. Since humans depend on the natural environment for countless resources, economic analysis must explicitly recognize the relationships between human economic activity, human society, and the capacity of the natural environment to provide the resources and services that are critical to human existence.

The example of the Chinese steel mill is not meant to give the impression that the natural environment is an inevitable barrier to the future growth of economic output. Nor does it suggest that China bears the major blame for climate change. The example is merely intended to serve as a reminder that the economic and natural spheres are closely related. In general, we economists must improve our understanding of the relationship between the economy and the other spheres of human existence.

1.1.2 Economic change and human society

It is difficult to envision solutions to the world's problems of poverty, hunger, oppression, and violence without increasing economic production. But even as increased production of goods and services improves human lives, the growth of production, or **economic growth**, also brings about fundamental changes in all three spheres of human existence. Some of these changes can affect people's lives in unexpected, and sometimes unpleasant, ways. Economic growth results in more complex and interdependent societies. The expanded interrelationships among people, businesses, organizations, social groups, governmental agencies, and other groups brings about very complex economic and social structures that can generate an almost infinite variety of outcomes. We have conquered diseases, reduced the incidence of famine, and tripled average life expectancy. But the economic, social, and natural changes that accompanied economic growth also caused repeated financial failures, devastating world wars, and rising economic inequality. Today, persistent social and political conflicts among seven billion people, militaristic governments with nuclear arsenals, and rising greenhouse gas emissions directly threaten not only humanity's existence, but also the existence of a great portion of Earth's plant and animal species that humans depend on for their survival.

Recall from the Introduction to Part I of this book that the financial crisis that suddenly caused incomes to fall by 15–20 percent in Indonesia in 1998 was caused, in part, by a devaluation of its currency, the yuan, by the Chinese government in order to promote Chinese industrialization and GDP growth. The $0.50 per hour wages paid in Shinfeng may be attractive for Chinese workers with few options in China's rural communities, but elsewhere in the global economy that now links all economies, the low Chinese wages have put downward pressure on wages in many other countries.

Working conditions in manufacturing plants in Chinese factories affect working conditions elsewhere. According to Cafod, the British-based Catholic development charity, Chinese workers producing high-tech computer products often work in factories with dangerous toxic chemicals, unclean air, excessive noise, and long hours sometimes totaling 16 hours per day. Workers in many Chinese plants live in company dormitories because they are migrants from rural areas, and as a result they do little more than work and sleep for months on end. In short, Chinese manufacturers have extremely low labor costs, and Mexican factories producing for the U.S. market have to compete with Chinese factories.

A Mexican labor activist complained: "Last year, the average pay for production line workers was a not very generous 500 pesos [about US$45 a week]. This year, most people are being offered 450 pesos."[1] Also, Mexican working conditions are deteriorating because workers can be threatened with dismissal by firms that could just as easily outsource manufacturing to China. According to a psychologist who used to work for one of the employment agencies used by manufacturers in the Guadalajara region, firms seek workers with little self-esteem or aspiration. The applications of workers involved with labor unions, those with relatives in government, or who have worked in the U.S. are rejected out of hand. Prospective workers are sometimes required to strip naked so they can be checked for tatoos (a sign of rebelliousness), and they are often given pregnancy tests. Such pre-employment tests are illegal under Mexican labor laws, but the law is routinely ignored. In practice, complaining immediately disqualifies a job applicant. Employers in Mexico can get away with these practices because Chinese competition has left Mexico with many more workers than jobs.

Many workers in Mexican manufacturing plants come from small towns and villages, where agricultural jobs were lost after the 1994 North American Free Trade Agreement (NAFTA) went into effect. NAFTA opened the Mexican market to imports of U.S. grain. U.S. grain is very inexpensive because not only are U.S. farmers highly efficient, but they are also heavily subsidized by the U.S. government. Because small Mexican farmers have neither the capital nor the technology to compete with the subsidized U.S. agricultural producers, most have given up farming. Without options, unemployed workers from rural towns and villages are willing to accept whatever the manufacturers are willing to offer. Another alternative is to migrate illegally to the United States, which millions of Mexican workers have indeed done. In this case, Mexican families are split up, children are not cared for, and rural communities come to consist disproportionately of children cared for by grandparents living on money sent from migrants in distant cities in other countries.

In the United States, cheap imports pressure U.S. producers to reduce labor costs. And, as described just above, free trade agreements like NAFTA and the Central American Free Trade Agreement (CAFTA) have created large pools of illegal immigrant workers, driven north after U.S. grain exports destroyed small family farms in Mexico and Central America. These immigrants compete directly with some U.S. workers in the U.S. labor market; for example, George Borjas (2003) estimates that the wages of low-skilled native U.S. workers were reduced by the large influx of low-skilled foreign workers between 1980 and 2000. The wage gains by immigrants are not as large as they could be, however, because illegal status subjects immigrants to abuse, exploitation, insecurity, and effectively second-class social status. Many U.S. employers exploit illegal workers because, similar to insecure workers in Mexican plants, illegal workers are unlikely to complain or join a union. Many people question whether this type

---

[1] Quoted in Authers and Maitland (2004), "The Human Cost of the Computer Age," *Financial Times*, January 26.

of **economic change** constitutes **economic development**. GDP has risen in China, Mexico, and the United States, but has human welfare improved?

In sum, both in the case of the natural environment and the social environment, the interactions with economic growth are complex and difficult to grasp. Who could have accurately predicted that a free trade agreement would result in massive flows of illegal immigrants to the United States or that the shift of a steel mill from Germany to China would increase greenhouse gas emissions? Fortunately, this textbook will show that many, but not enough, economists and scientists do understand the complexity of the overall system. Still, the complexity of the economic, social, and natural spheres that humans inhabit make it very difficult to come up with, and apply, consistent policies that can promote the economic development necessary to give all of the world's people high standards of living such as the citizens of, say, Canada, Norway, and Singapore currently enjoy.

1.2 The Conventional View: The Great Acceleration

In terms of GDP, recent economic growth is truly exceptional. Figure 1.2 illustrates the stunning explosion of real per capita output since the early 1800s. This graph is based on data compiled by the economic historian Angus Maddison (2006). His estimates of per capita world GDP from the year 0 to the present are given in Table 1.1.

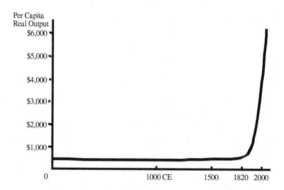

Figure 1.2 Economic Growth: 0–2000

Maddison estimates **gross domestic product (GDP),** a measure that is intended to approximate the total value of the goods and services produced in the economy. Table 1.1 also provides **GDP per capita**, which is total GDP divided by the world's population. Maddison puts the figures in *real* terms by adjusting the values for inflation so that the numbers represent true changes in output, and not just inflated money values. Official GDP numbers are easily obtained from government statistical agencies today, but such numbers were not available before the twentieth century. Hence, to compile his historical estimates, Maddison used a great variety of sources of information on output, consumption, prices, population, international trade, government tax revenues, etc., some from official government publications, others from independent historical studies.

Maddison's estimates of real per capita GDP going back through the centuries come with a sizeable margin of error. But the increase in output per person over the past 200 years is so large, compared to earlier periods, that there is little doubt that something extraordinary happened to economic production after 1800. If GDP per capita accurately captures the economic activity that improves well-being, then we are indeed lucky to be living at this very unique time in human history.

Table 1.1 World Population, Real GDP, and GDP per Capita: 0–2009

Year	World Population	World GDP	GDP Per Capita	Period	Population	World GDP	GDP Per Capita
	(millions)	*(billions 1990 $)*	*(1990 US$)*		_(Annual percent growth rates)_		
0	231	103	445				
1000	267	117	436	0–1000	0.01	0.01	0.00
1500	425	240	565	1000–1500	0.10	0.15	0.05
1820	1,068	695	651	1500–1820	0.29	0.33	0.04
1870	1,260	1,128	895	1820–1870	0.33	0.97	0.64
1913	1,772	2,726	1,539	1870–1913	0.79	2.05	1.26
1929	2,047	3,696	1,806	1913–1929	0.90	1.90	1.00
1950	2,512	5,372	2,138	1929–1950	0.97	1.78	0.80
1973	3,896	16,064	4,123	1950–1973	1.91	4.76	2.86
2009	7,614	50,974	7,614	1973–2009	1.60	2.92	1.44

Source: Angus Maddison (2006), *Historical Statistics for the World Economy: 1–2003AD*, Statistical Appendix; this document was downloaded on August 19, 2006 and updated through 2009 on June 2, 2011 from the website (http://ggdc.net/maddison/) maintained by the Groningen Growth and Development Centre at the University of Groningen, Netherlands. Growth Rates are from Angus Maddison (2003), Table 8b.

1.2.1 Rapid GDP growth only began after 1800

Figure 1.2 only depicts economic growth over the last 2,000 years. Human history extends back more than one million years, when humans and their immediate ancestors became distinguishable from other primates. Humans lived as hunters and gatherers at close to a **subsistence** level of income, which is the level that provides just enough consumption to maintain the species and, perhaps, permit some very slow growth in numbers. According to Lant Pritchett (1997), the subsistence level of output at Maddison's 1990 U.S. dollar prices cannot have been lower than about $250 per year, or $.68 per day, per person. Life is not sustainable with food, clothing, and shelter worth less than that (at today's prices), no matter how benign the climate and how simple the food and shelter. By the year 10,000 BCE, the line of humanoids from which present-day humans evolved had already existed for over 99 percent of its total presence on Earth, but the total human population was probably still less than five million according to estimates of historical population trends.[2] Population growth accelerated with the transition from hunting and gathering to farming, a shift in technology that occurred in much of the world between 10,000 and 5000 BCE.

Table 1.1 shows that even at the height of the Roman Empire, there were just over 200 million people on Earth. At $445 in 1990 U.S. dollars, average per capita output in the year 0 was less than double the bare minimum for the human race to simply survive. During the following millennium, there was practically no growth in per capita output. Notice also that average per capita output in the world was about the same in 1000 as it was in the year 0. By 1500, average output in the world was still little more than what it was 500 years earlier, although the rate of population growth had accelerated somewhat. Population growth accelerated further between 1500 and 1820, but still real output per capita barely changed. And even the accelerated population growth was less than 0.5 percent, a very slow rate by recent standards.

In the last 200 years of our existence as humans, a period proportionately equivalent to the last two centimeters of the 100 meter dash, things appear to have changed radically. Since 1820, real per capita output grew by a factor of nearly twelve, while the human population grew more than seven-fold. In 2003, the total production of real output was 70 times as great as total GDP in 1820.

1.2.2 A new acceleration in the twentieth century

The sharp increase in the *level* of per capita real GDP after 1800 is the result of increased *rates of growth* of real output. Using the estimates of population, real GDP, and real per capita GDP from the left side of Table 1.1, the right half of the table presents the corresponding rates of growth of population, GDP, and per capita GDP from 0 to 2009. The slope of the curve in Figure 1.2 reflects the rates of growth in Table 1.1. The higher the rates of growth of per capita output in Table 1.1, the steeper the curve in Figure 1.2.

Population, output, and per capita output all reached their highest growth rates over the period 1950–1973. The last period, 1973–2009, saw somewhat lower rates of growth for all three, although growth rates were still higher than any other period prior to 1950–1973. It is too early to tell whether this decline is the beginning of a gradual decline in population and output growth. One of the biggest mistakes analysts have made in the past was to project recent short-term trends in complex evolutionary processes into the future. Just think how

---

[2] See the survey of population estimates in Michael Kremer (1993).

inaccurate the projection of pre-1800 growth trends forward into the nineteenth and twentieth centuries would have been. We had better learned more about the complex process of economic development before we just project the past 50 years' growth rates into the future.

1.2.3 There have been many growth collapses

Humanity's impressive gains in per capita real GDP over the past 200 years should not be allowed to obscure the fact that not everyone has enjoyed the same gains in material well-being. First of all, many economies have not grown as rapidly as the average country. The average growth rates in Table 1.1 are just that: *worldwide averages*. In some countries, per capita incomes have actually declined since 1980. Among the worst performers in terms of economic growth were, according to World Bank estimates of real GDP per capita, the African countries of Cameroon (−6.9 percent per year), Rwanda (−6.6 percent), and Cote d'Ivoire (−4.6 percent). There were economic disasters elsewhere in the world as well. In Central America, for example, Nicaraguans' average real consumption of goods and services fell by 6.1 percent per year between the mid-1980s and the mid-1990s.

Some of the biggest declines in per capita real output occurred in newly independent countries that became independent after the Soviet Union broke up in 1990. For example, Armenia, Azerbaijan, and Tajikistan are estimated to have experienced nearly 10 percent per year declines in real per capita output between 1990 and 2000. It proved to be very difficult to establish new viable national economic organizations to replace the centralized communist system under the Soviet Union.

Not only have rates of growth varied greatly from one country to another, but most countries have also experienced greatly different rates of growth during different periods of time. For example, at the end of the nineteenth century Argentina was one of the fastest-growing economies in the world, and in 1913 only the four resource-rich countries settled by Europeans, Australia, New Zealand, Canada, and the United States, and just five European countries, Belgium, Germany, Switzerland, the Netherlands, and the United Kingdom, had higher per capita GDPs than Argentina. Argentina's 1913 per capita real GDP exceeded that of all other European economies in that year, including all the Scandinavian countries. Today, Argentina is classified as a *middle-income* developing economy by the World Bank. On the other hand, in 1900 Japan had a per capita real GDP on par with contemporary Latin American countries such as Brazil, Colombia, or Mexico. Japan's real per capita GDP at the turn of the century was little more than one-third that of Argentina. But, by 1990, Japan's real per capita GDP was more than three times as great as Argentina's and on par with the United States and Western Europe.

The economic fortunes of some countries have changed in recent decades. We have described above how rapidly the Chinese economy has grown since the

1980s. Less than two decades earlier, however, the Chinese economy had suffered a decline in per capita GDP under the Cultural Revolution, the disruptive social upheaval that included the mandatory transfer of urban residents to the countryside in order to promote ideological purity. Before that, there were the disruptive political revolution that brought the communist government to power in 1949 and the invasion/occupation by Japan at the start of the twentieth century. China had also isolated itself from the rest of the world and its new technologies for many centuries, a factor to which historians attribute China's loss of the technological leadership it had enjoyed before the year 1000. By 1970, China's per capita income had fallen so low that even the fast growth of GDP per capita over the past three decades still leaves the country classified among the poor countries of the world.

Among the most extraordinary examples of recent economic growth are Korea and Taiwan, whose per capita GDPs in 1950 were less than half that of Peru, at the time one of the poorest countries in Latin America. Today, per capita real GDP in Taiwan and South Korea are about five times as high as Peru's. Today, South Korea is considered to be among the more developed countries of the world.

These variations in economic performance show that a country's rate of economic growth and its relative level of GDP per capita can change rapidly. On the positive side, Taiwan and Korea show that it is possible for a very poor country to substantially narrow the gap with developed countries in little more than one generation. On the other hand, output per capita can stagnate or even fall when policies and circumstances change. Past development does not guarantee future development.

1.3 Small Differences in Growth Have Large Consequences

The great variety of growth experiences over time and across countries has created huge gaps between standards of living across countries. The real GDP of the average Ethiopian is between one-fortieth and one-fiftieth of the real income enjoyed by the average resident of Australia, Japan, or France. Because some countries grew quickly over the past 200 years while others did not, the measured incomes of countries today are much less equal than ever before.

The huge income inequalities that developed across countries over the past 200 years are not the result of large declines in per capita GDP in some countries and large increases in other countries. Rather, the inequality is the result of unprecedented high rates of economic growth in some of the world's countries and stagnant or very slow rates of growth elsewhere. It is important to note that most of today's poorest countries have experienced some growth of average material output over the past 200 years, although, as noted above, a few countries experienced negative economic growth rates.

Figure 1.3 illustrates the discrepancies in per capita real income across regions of the world. Based on Angus Maddison's historical data, these regional averages actually still understate the differences in incomes across countries. Since regional incomes are averages of individual country income levels, we should expect the differences between regional averages to be smaller than the differences between the most successful and least successful individual countries. Still, Figure 1.3 shows how unequal average incomes have become over the past 200 years even between entire regions. The ratio of average per capita output in the group of wealthiest countries, the so-called *Western offshoots* Australia, Canada, and the United States, to the lowest average income group, Africa, has risen from just 3:1 in 1820 to over 16:1 today. Compared to the huge differences in per capita GDPs today, people throughout the world had rather similar standards of living before 1800.

The relative equality of per capita incomes throughout the world before the nineteenth century is not necessarily something to be nostalgic about, however. The apparent equality of material wealth 200 years ago was mostly the result of little economic growth anywhere. The dark curve labeled *World* shows that, on average, there has been a substantial increase in material well-being over the past 200 years.

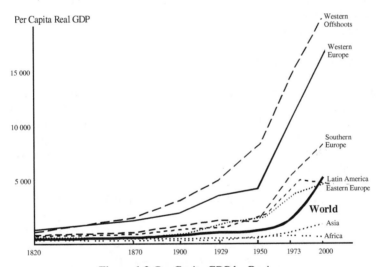

Figure 1.3 Per Capita GDP by Region

1.3.1 The power of compounding

It is impossible to fully appreciate the implications of economic growth without an understanding of the concept of **compounding**. Paul Romer, who has been one of the leading economists in the recent revival of the field of economic growth, provides an interesting example of the surprising power of compounding.

Suppose that an economics major, who has just graduated from college and started a good job, wants to buy a new home. She goes to her local bank to seek a loan for $200,000, fully aware that such a sum of money is going to take many years to pay off. To her surprise, the bank's loan officer makes her a strange, but seemingly attractive, offer: the bank will issue her a check for $200,000 today if she signs a contract obligating her to return in ten years with a chess board and enough pennies to place one penny on the first white square of the board, two on the second white square, four on the third white square, eight on the fourth, and so on until all of the white squares are covered. Should she accept the bank's offer?

Romer (1998) claims that "we systematically underestimate how fast things grow," and many people would thoughtlessly jump at the opportunity of filling a chess board with "just pennies." If the economics major had taken a course in economic growth, she would have understood that with 32 white squares on a chess board, the repayment scheme is equal to one cent that grows by 100 percent *thirty-one* consecutive times. The total payment is therefore 1 cent plus 2 cents to the thirty-first power, which adds up to about $21.5 million. The bank's strange offer is not such a good deal! The **power of compounding** transforms very small quantities into very large ones much faster than most people think possible.

1.3.2 Examples of compounding

For a more relevant economic growth example, suppose a country's per capita GDP (PCGDP) grows at the rate of 10 percent per year. We note this by defining the rate of growth as R and setting it equal to 10 percent. We thus assume that $R = 0.1$. If per capita GDP is equal to $1,000 at the start, which we denote as $PCGDP_{t=0}$, then such a growth rate implies that, after one year, per capita GDP would be equal to

$$PCGDP_{t=1} = PCGDP_{t=0}(1 + 0.1) = \$1000(1.1) = \$1100 \qquad (1.1)$$

If 10 percent growth continues for two years, the level of $PCGDP_{t=2}$ will be

$$PCGDP_{t=0}(1 + R)(1 + R) = \$1000(1.1)^2 = \$1,210 \qquad (1.2)$$

In general, after T years with 10 percent growth:

$$PCGDP_T = PCGDP_{t=0}(1 + R)^T = PCGDP_{t=0}(1.1)^T \qquad (1.3)$$

Using equation (1.3), ten years of economic growth of 10 percent growth causes per capita income to rise from $1,000 to

$$\text{PCGDP}_{t=10} = \$1000(1 + .10)^{10} = \$2594 \tag{1.4}$$

After ten years of 10 percent growth, GDP has grown not by ten times 10 percent, or 100 percent, but by nearly 160 percent. Compounding is a powerful process.

Economies do not often grow at ten percent per year, although a few countries such as Botswana, Brazil, China, Singapore, and Taiwan have achieved such annual growth rates for extended periods of time. The power of compounding is also apparent at low rates of growth. For example, suppose there are two economies, each with a per capita real output level of $1,000. Assume, also, that one country grows at just one percent per year, and the other grows at 2 percent. After ten years, the slow-growing economy has a per capita output of $1,105 because

$$\text{PCGDP}_{t=10} = \$1000(1 + 0.01)^{10} = \$1000(1.01)^{10} = \$1,105 \tag{1.5}$$

The slightly-faster growing economy, on the other hand, will have increased its per capita output to

$$\text{PCGDP}_{t=10} = \$1000(1 + 0.02)^{10} = \$1000(1.02)^{10} = \$1,219 \tag{1.6}$$

Thus, after 10 years, the economy with 2 percent annual growth will have a per capita output level a little more than $100 higher than the economy growing at 1 percent per year. "Not much," you may say. True, but a period of 10 years is very short in terms of human history.

Let's extend our time horizon from 10 to 100 years, a mere century in the course of human history. Using the same formulas, after one century of 1 percent growth, the slowly-growing economy's per capita output will be

$$\text{PCGDP}_{t=100} = \$1000(1 + .01)^{100} = \$2,705 \tag{1.7}$$

An annual growth rate of just 1 percent results in a per capita output is 2.7 times as great after 100 years. On the other hand, after 100 years 2 percent per year growth raises per capita GDP to:

$$\text{PCGDP}_{t=100} = \$1000(1 + .02)^{100} = \$7,245 \tag{1.8}$$

After 100 years, the per capita GDP of the country growing at two percent per year is 2.7 times as great as the per capita GDP of the country growing at 1 percent. In the long run, 1 percent makes a huge difference.

Now, let's add another 100 years to the time horizon for a total of 200 years, the amount of time that elapsed between the year 1800 and the turn of the millennium in 2000. Starting at the same level of $1,000 in 1800, by the year 2000 the slow growing economy will have increased its per capita output to

$$\text{PCGDP}_{t=200} = \$1000(1 + .01)^{200} = \$7,316 \qquad (1.9)$$

On the other hand, the economy that grows at 2 percent per year for 200 years reaches a per capita GDP of:

$$\text{PCGDP}_{t=200} = \$1000(1 + .02)^{200} = \$52,489 \qquad (1.10)$$

This is 7.2 times higher than the slower-growing economy's per capita output.

This latter multiple is not unlike the multiples we observe today when we compare developed and less-developed countries. For example, Mexican real income per capita has grown at an average rate of one percent since the early 1800s, while the United States, whose real income per capita is about 7 times that of Mexico, has grown at about two percent per year over that same period. The difference in measured per capita GDP between Mexico and the United States is a mere one percent per year. In general, annual growth of 2 percent doubles output in about 35 years, quadruples it in 70 years, and increases output eight-fold in little more than one century. The Appendix provides more details and examples of the power of compounding.

1.4 Structural Change and Economic Growth

If you have ever traveled in countries with very different levels of per capita GDP you have no doubt noticed that the ways people live, work, and go about their daily lives are different. It is not true that the only difference between people living in rich countries and those living in poor countries is that the former have more money than the latter. People living in high-income economies hold different jobs and consume different goods and services than do people living in economies with low per capita levels of output. High-income economies have a different **economic structure** than low-income economies.

1.4.1 Patterns of structural change

Table 1.2 shows data on how output and employment are divided between the three major sectors of the economy: agriculture, industry, and services. Part A of Table 1.2 shows how output shares varied over time for 16 economies that today have the highest per capita levels of output. Note that as today's wealthy economies evolved and increased their average output per capita over the past two centuries, the value of agricultural output shrank as a percentage of total output, and the service sector grew relative to the other two sectors. Also, the share of industrial output first grew and now seems to be declining.

Table 1.2 The Changing Structure of a Growing Economy: 1700–2000

		Agriculture	*Industry*	*Services*
A. Share of GDP: 16 OECD Countries[1]				
1870		39%	26%	35%
1900		28	31	41
1950		15	41	44
2000[4]		4	29	68
B. Share of Employment: Netherlands, United Kingdom, and United States[2]				
1700	Netherlands	40%	33%	27%
	United Kingdom	56	22	22
1870	Netherlands	43	26	31
	United Kingdom	37	33	30
	United States	70	15	15
1890	Netherlands	36	32	32
	United Kingdom	16	43	41
	United States	38	24	38
1998	Netherlands	3	22	75
	United Kingdom	2	26	72
	United States	3	23	74
C. Share of GDP: Low, Middle, and High Income Economies[3]				
Low-Income Economies:				
1980		31%	38%	38%
2000		24	32	44
Lower-Middle-Income Economies				
1980		15	41	44
2000		13	41	45
Upper-Middle-Income Economies				
1980		11	42	47
2000		7	32	62
High-Income Economies				
1980		3	37	58
2000		2	29	68

[1] Angus Maddison (1989), Table 1.4, p. 20.
[2] Angus Maddison (2001), Table 2.24, p. 95.
[3] World Bank (2002), *World Development Indicators*, Washington, D.C.: World Bank, Table 4.2.

Part B of Table 1.2 shows much older data on employment shares for the Netherlands, the United Kingdom, and the United States. The Netherlands was the country with the highest per capita real income in the 1700s, the United Kingdom had the highest per capita income in the 1800s, and the United States was the richest country in the last century. We see similar patterns of **structural**

change for these countries, with agriculture's share shrinking over time and the services sector's share growing.

Section C of Table 1.2 presents the shares of GDP for four groups of economies classified by the World Bank as low income, lower-middle income, upper-middle income, and high income economies in 1980 and 2000. The higher the level of per capita output, the smaller is the relative size of the agricultural sector of the economy, and the larger is the service sector. When an economy begins to grow and raise its level of per capita output above traditional subsistence levels, the industrial sector, which includes manufacturing, mining, construction, and utilities (water, electricity, gas, etc.), increases its share of the total value of output. But, when income levels approach those of today's highest income economies, the *relative* size of the industrial sector again declines.

The structural economic changes that accompany economic development occur for several reasons. First of all, as people's incomes rise, their consumption pattern changes. People with very low incomes acquire mostly basic food, clothing, and shelter, and they have little left for entertainment, consumer durables, or vacation travel. In high-income countries, people do eat more and better food, but most gains in income above the basic subsistence level are allocated to acquire goods and services not consumed at all at low incomes. Restaurant meals, movie tickets, tourist travel, and automobiles receive greater shares of total income as people's incomes rise.

Second, economies also change their structure because economic growth is usually accompanied by technological change. As will be explained in detail in later chapters, in the long run economies grow precisely because people, firms, organizations, and government agencies learn to do things differently. Output grows when people use more tools and equipment to supplement their labor. For example, in Lagos, Nigeria, a street cleaner works with a crude broom consisting of a stick with a bunch of straw attached by a piece of string. He cleans only one or two blocks in a day. On the other hand, in Toronto, Canada, a street cleaner drives a $100,000 piece of equipment and cleans fifty kilometers of streets in a day. Production methods often change life in more subtle ways, such as better working conditions and more vacation time.

Finally, when economies get wealthier they tend to alter the pattern of international specialization by importing more labor-intensive products and exporting more capital-intensive and technology-intensive products. As will be shown in later chapters, international trade tends to accentuate the structural change that accompanies economic growth.

1.4.2 The cost of structural change

Structural change underlies many of the controversies surrounding the process of economic development. As an economy develops workers first have to shift from agriculture to either the industrial or service sectors of the economy. Later on in the development process, industrial employment seems to fall again relative to service sector employment. For workers, these shifts involve substantial transportation costs, breakups of extended families, and moves from one part of the country to another or even from one country to another. Accumulated human capital, such as task-specific work skills, and technological knowledge do not always carry over to new and different jobs. The accumulated experience in operating a sewing machine is not very useful for programming video games. Economic change may also make physical capital obsolete. For example, a clothing factory cannot produce pharmaceuticals. Old factories are usually abandoned and replaced with new ones.

Fundamental changes in lifestyles over the past two centuries occurred as people moved from rural to urban communities in pursuit of jobs that opened up in the manufacturing and services sectors. In 1800, only about 10 percent of the population of Europe lived in towns and cities with populations over 10,000.[3] In Asia and Africa the percentage of the population living in urban areas was even less. Today, in high income countries about three-fourths of all people live in urban areas. A similar pattern emerges when we observe the urban-rural distribution of populations across different countries. Only 30 percent of the populations of the low-income countries of Africa and Asia live in cities and towns today, but the percentage of urban residents exceeds 70 percent for middle-income developing economies such as Argentina, Chile, Mexico, and Korea.[4] The year 2007 marked the first year that more than half the world's population lived in urban communities.

The shift from a rural to an urban society is welcomed by many people who are attracted by the challenges and bright lights of the city. But for many people in developing economies, urbanization means long working hours and poor housing, not bright lights. The fact that many people do *not* move despite often-large income differences between rural and urban areas suggests that there is a considerable cost to changing lifestyles or losing friends and family.

Mark Twain once wrote, "I'm all for progress; it's change I don't like." Indeed, economic development inevitably brings both progress and changes in work and lifestyles. An economy cannot provide people with more goods, services, health, lifestyle choices, and other desirable things if everyone insists on consuming, producing, and generally living life in exactly the same way they always have. A growing and changing economy tends to clash with social institutions and culture, and there is often increasing friction across generations and between social groups. Perceptions of what is and what "ought to be" will more often diverge in the rapidly developing economy than in a stagnant economy.

---

[3] J. De Vries (1984).
[4] United Nations (2008), *Human Development Report 2008*, New York: United Nations.

This conflict between the status quo and a more promising future is problematic. Economic growth and welfare-enhancing economic development are not possible if there is widespread social conflict. Complex economies and societies require high degrees of cooperation and coordination among the many people, organizations, firms, and governments that make up society. The inherent conflict between progress and change is thus a potential barrier to economic development. If we view economic development more broadly as an improvement in people's satisfaction with life, the disruption of life caused by the economic changes necessary to increase output per capita may actually diminish true economic development. We will return to this issue in Chapters 2 and 3, where we discuss the meaning of economic development.

1.4.3 Definitions of terms

The terms *economic change*, *economic growth*, and *economic development* cannot be used interchangeably. To avoid later confusion, it is useful to establish the following definitions:

- **Economic change** is any change in the performance or structure of an economy.

- **Economic growth** is an increase in material output per capita.

- **Economic development** describes the full range of changes in humanity's economic, social, and natural environments that are perceived by people as making life more pleasant and satisfying.

Not every economic change results in economic growth, although economic growth generally does cause changes in the structure of an economy and society. Improvements in human well-being are only partially and imperfectly related to the growth of production of goods and services, and some types of output growth actually reduces human well-being. Economic development is more broadly defined to include all the changes that occur in the social and natural environments we inhabit.

Given the constraints we face in our economic, social, and natural environments, the economic challenge is to manage economic change, growth, and development so that it becomes **sustainable economic development**, that is, to continue making life more enjoyable and satisfying. Sustainability is closely related to compatibility of economic activity with the social and natural spheres of human existence. When the growth of economic production damages the country's social organization or its natural environment, economic growth is likely to suffer because economic activity depends on human activity as well as many inputs from nature.

1.5 Holism and the Scientific Method

The complexity of the process of economic development and its interactions with our greater social and natural environments requires us to move beyond the familiar economic relationships studied by orthodox, or mainstream, economics. Gaining an understanding of our complex human existence is a difficult task. To be successful, we need to formally recognize the interdependence of social and natural phenomena. And, we need to adopt an efficient method for increasing our knowledge about this complex reality. The perspective we take in this textbook is called **holism**, our approach to economic modeling is **heterodox**, and our method of analysis seeks to follow the steps of **the scientific method**. These terms are defined in this section and the next.

1.5.1 Holism and economics

By viewing the growth of economic well-being as part of the dynamic evolution of our society and its ever-changing relationship to our natural environment, we are effectively embracing an intellectual approach called *holism*. The term is derived from the Greek word *holos*, meaning *entire, total, whole*. The term was initially used in the early twentieth century to describe new dynamic theories in the physical sciences, such as Charles Darwin's theory of evolution, Henri Becquerel's theory of radioactivity, and Albert Einstein's theory of relativity. These new theories described the world as evolving dynamic systems, in which the parts are related to all other parts in complex ways that effectively condition how each observed part actually functions. Holism is the explicit recognition that the component *parts* cannot be understood in isolation and their functions cannot be predicted without knowing the *whole* environment in which they exist. Overall, the outcomes of the whole system are a function of both its parts and the *systemic* interactions.

Figure 1.4 In Chinese philosophy, the diagram of Yin and Yang describes how different forces and phenomena are dynamically interconnected and interdependent in a balanced natural world.

An interesting example of why a holistic approach to understanding human activity is necessary is the near-meltdown of the Three Mile Island nuclear power plant in Pennsylvania. On March 28, 1979, the second reactor of the Three Mile Island nuclear plant released radioactive water. Soon thereafter, radioactive gas was detected near the plant. Something was clearly going dreadfully wrong at the plant, but no one seemed to know what the problem was. "I think it's safe to say chaos was the best way to describe it," wrote Samuel Walker, the U.S. Nuclear Regulatory Commission's historian.[5] The governor of Pennsylvania was not given any information for days, and he did not order a limited evacuation until three days after the initial indications of a problem at the Three Mile Island plant. "I needed facts, and we simply weren't getting them," the governor said later in an interview.[6] Only later was it apparent that the plant had come very close to a total meltdown that would have devastated the entire region, including perhaps even Washington D.C. One scientist in the U.S. Nuclear Regulatory Commission later admitted that among the many experts the commission had consulted to try to understand what had gone wrong, not one fully understood the whole Three Mile Island plant. No one was able to grasp why the separate parts of the plant, each performing as expected, could interact in a way that nearly destroyed the whole system.

The example of Three Mile Island reminds us of how difficult it is to monitor and manage complex systems. Clearly, complex systems cannot work unless each of its components works well. It is also true, however, that even when each of the complex system's components is managed well, the whole system may still fail if the parts are not well integrated or the linkages between them are not understood.

"This is true for atomic power plants, large enterprises operating in many countries and sectors, and the international financial system," writes the international economist Vito Tanzi.[7] Indeed, the failures of the international financial system during the Great Depression of the 1930s or the recent 2008 financial meltdown in the developed economies caused high unemployment, lost savings, and sharply lower incomes. In 1933, nearly 25 percent of all workers in the United States were unemployed as a result of the actions of bankers and financial markets during the 1920s. In 2010, Irish unemployment surged when the Irish government cut government expenditures sharply after its debt suddenly rose from a very manageable 25 percent of GDP to nearly 100 percent of GDP and it was unable to borrow in the bond markets. The debt rise occurred when the Irish government decided to assume the debt of its private banking sector after the Irish housing price bubble popped in 2008. Fintan O'Toole (2010) describes how this crisis was caused by the corrupt behavior of those

---

[5] Quoted in "Three Mile Island Nuclear Fears Revealed," BBC News, Website, June 17, 2006.
[6] Ibid.
[7] Vito Tanzi (2006), "Things Will Fall Apart But It Is the Aftermath that Matters," *Financial Times*, February 24.

same banks, government officials, and their friends in the construction industry. Holistic analysis is necessary to explain such systemic economic failures.

The holistic approach to understanding, that is, a simultaneous focus on the parts and the systemic interactions of those parts, has been pursued in many fields. In sociology, Emile Durkheim argued against the notion that society was nothing more than a collection of individuals. He showed that a community can take on many different forms depending on how the individuals who make up the community organize themselves and behave within the organization. In medicine, the holistic approach to healing analyzes how the emotional, mental, and physical elements of each person work together. Most psychologists recognize that a person's relationship to society shapes behavior. The International Electrical Engineering Association has published guidelines suggesting engineers should take a holistic approach to their work in order to avoid incompatibilities between specific projects and the societies in which the projects are carried out. And, of course, holism is fundamental to the field of ecology.

These holistic perspectives from other fields imply that economists are in good company when they embrace holism. This is not to say that holism is new to economics. The economist Kenneth Boulding described holism over half a century ago as the approach that links "the specific that has no meaning and the general that has no content."[8] Boulding and many current heterodox economists notwithstanding, however, it is fair to say that current orthodox economic thinking is not holistic.

The need to understand the parts and the way the parts interact and function as a whole is obvious when we examine the process of economic development. As described above, different countries have experienced different levels of growth, and current income levels differ greatly from one country to another. Yet, each country has similar component parts, such as people, land, natural resources, capital, and well-established cultures. And increasingly, countries are linked to a global economic system through trade, investment, immigration, and the flow of knowledge and ideas. Why do some countries achieve continuous economic growth and high standards of living while others fail to generate consistent economic growth? Why are natural resources not managed and exploited as well in some countries as in others? Why do people save, invest, and innovate in some countries but not in others? We know people are fundamentally similar, but individual societies evolved differently and their economies perform differently. Clearly, the explanation for these differences lies beyond the pure realm of economics. To grasp this complex "whole," we have to embrace knowledge from all fields of the social and natural sciences.

---

[8] Kenneth Boulding (1956), p. 197.

1.5.2 Homeostatic systems

Another characteristic of holism is that it views phenomena as dynamic, evolutionary processes. This is certainly appropriate for our study of economic development. While certain measures of economic development, such as per capita real output, only began to increase rapidly over the past 200 years, other aspects of economic development have been occurring, off and on, since the origins of humanity. Over the past several hundred thousand years, humans have gradually increased the number of people they deal with. They have also expanded their exploitation of their natural environment, they have increased their use of capital (tools), and they have improved their technology (their methods, knowledge, and understanding of their surroundings). Humans have developed very sophisticated social organizations. It now appears that the latest episode of rapid economic growth is changing human society's interaction with the natural environment. The recent acceleration of human activity on Earth has raised concerns that human society is threatening the stability of Earth's ecological system, or ecosystem.

There is a debate about whether the natural sphere humans inhabit is stable, or, more specifically, whether the ecosystem is characterized by **homeostasis**. This term is credited to Claude Bernard, who used it in 1865 to describe a living organism that automatically regulates its internal environment in order to survive within varying external environments. A typical example of homeostatic adjustment is the maintenance of constant body temperature by endothermic (warm blooded) animals like mammals and birds in response to changes in external temperatures. Exothermic (cold blooded) animals like reptiles and some sea creatures survive in different environments by letting their body temperatures change with the external temperature. Both mechanisms, internal regulation or conformism, have advantages and disadvantages. One important disadvantage of internal regulation is that it takes more energy. Snakes eat once a week or less often; many mammals and birds spend much of their lives seeking food. Biologically, humans are endothermic, and given the slow reaction to obvious changes in the natural environment, it appears as though humans' collective society is also endothermic.

James Lovelock's (1972) **Gaia hypothesis** states that the planet Earth functions as a large homeostatic organism that actively adjusts its internal natural conditions. For example, plants absorb carbon dioxide from the air, effectively reducing the amount of carbon dioxide in the atmosphere. And, when some event increases the carbon in the atmosphere and raises temperatures, plants grow faster and absorb more carbon, thus reducing the amount of carbon in the air. The term Gaia refers to the Greek goddess Gaia, who personified Mother Earth.

Peter Ward (2009), on the other hand, counters with his **Medea hypothesis**, in honor of Medea, the mythological Greek sorceress who killed her own children in a fit of rage against her husband.   Ward contends that Mother Earth's self-regulating procedures do not always provide individual species with stable natural environments.   The paleontological record suggests that the natural environment is occasionally driven to extremes that result in massive losses of life and the extinction of many species.   Because humans evolved in an ecosystem that has changed little over the past few million years, they are not likely to survive substantial changes in their natural environment.   There is evidence that the natural environment may be approaching just such a substantial change.

1.5.3 Holism and science

Holism accepts that complex systems that can only be understood by looking at the manner in which the parts operate together.   For this reason, holism is sometimes described as the opposite to **scientific reductionism**.   The latter assumes that we can understand the whole if we understand each of its parts, or that in effect "the whole is the sum of its parts."   Holistic scientists, of course, realize that in order to understand a complex process or system, one must also understand how the parts interact.   Scientific reductionism is not "scientific" if there are good reasons to suspect that the interactions between the components of the system determine the outcomes of the overall system.   To explain why holism is, and reductionism is not, scientific, we must review what we mean by the **scientific method**.

Strictly speaking, **science** is the practice of the scientific method.   The scientific method consists of the following steps:

1. Observe some world phenomenon or fact.

2. Use reason to invent a **hypothesis** (an untested idea) that clearly and logically explains the facts you observe.

3. Confront the hypothesis with real world outcomes or perform experiments to generate outcomes that can be compared to the hypothesis' predicted outcomes.

4. Prudence suggests that you perform many experiments or observe large amounts of real world outcomes in order to gather **empirical evidence** (objectively accumulated real world observations) under a variety of circumstances in order to avoid being misled by spurious outcomes driven by the selectivity of experiments or observations.

5. Record everything you do and observe.

6. Objectively examine whether all the observed outcomes consistently conform to your hypothesis.

7. If these tests of your hypothesis reveal that the real world outcomes or experimental outcomes are not consistent with your hypothesis, modify your hypothesis and return to step 3.

8. If your experiments consistently confirm your hypothesis, your hypothesis becomes a **theory** (a confirmed hypothesis). At this point you must publish your results, accompanied by all the details of the tests that confirm your hypothesis so that others can replicate your experiments and confirm your methods and results.

Those who follow these steps in their quest for knowledge in any field are **scientists**. When we apply the scientific method to gain understanding about social phenomena, we can call ourselves **social scientists**.

With regard to the steps of the scientific method, a few important points are in order. First of all, the popular definition of the word *theory* does not match the scientific definition of a theory. Most people think of a theory as some vague or fuzzy idea. In science, however, a theory is a precise conceptual framework that has been shown to consistently explain existing facts and accurately predict new facts. A theory is a "proven" hypothesis. A *hypothesis* is an unproven conceptual framework that the scientist confronts with data, direct observations of real phenomena, or a series of carefully designed tests. A hypothesis occupies the space between what we know and what we don't know.

Because a theory must have withstood the challenges of tests and accurate observations of reality when it was still a hypothesis, a scientific hypothesis must be **falsifiable**. For example, the economic theory that the continued expansion of the money supply in excess of the growth of economic activity will cause inflation is truly a theory because we can observe prices and output that could, potentially, falsify it. Repeated and careful examination of the evidence suggests that this hypothesis relating inflation to excessive money creation is *confirmed* by the evidence and thus worthy of the term *theory*. We may even say that the theory or model is *true*. But, we must be careful to avoid talking about **truth** because all scientific theories may be falsified when we engage in further scientific activity and discover new evidence and we learn more. An interesting example is Isaac Newton's theory of gravity. Newton's theory that gravitational force between two objects is directly proportional to the bodies' mass and inversely proportional to the square of the distance between them was confirmed repeatedly by a great amount of evidence. Then, in the nineteenth century, more accurate instruments revealed that the planet Mercury did not orbit quite the way Newton's theory predicted. Albert Einstein's theory of relativity seemed to more accurately explain what was observed in the universe.

More recently, however, experiments using a set of satellites orbiting the earth uncovered some slight variations in the orbits predicted by either Newton's theory of gravity or Einstein's theory of relativity. Truth is hard to find.

An important feature of the scientific method is that it raises the efficiency with which we accumulate knowledge. By providing full information about how the new knowledge was achieved, knowledge is permanently available to be built upon by later scientific activity. This is why the careful compilation of tests and results is so important. The scientific method depicts the advancement of knowledge as a systematic step-by-step process that builds knowledge and prevents losses of previous knowledge. Albert Einstein wrote:

> Creating a new theory is not like destroying an old bar and erecting a skyscraper in its place. It is rather like climbing a mountain, gaining new and wider views, discovering unexpected connections between our starting point and its rich environment. But the point from which we started out still exists and can be seen, although it appears smaller and forms a tiny part of our broad view gained by the mastery of the obstacles on our adventurous way up.[9]

1.5.4 Holistic science

Note that the scientific method is perfectly compatible with holism. Hypotheses about how complex systems interact must be tested and verified the same way all hypotheses must be objectively confronted with real world observations. The compatibility of holism and science suggests a new term: **holistic science**. Holistic science (1) studies **complex systems**, (2) recognizes the presence of **dynamic feedback** within complex systems, and (3) takes an **interdisciplinary perspective** in order to achieve an understanding of complex systems.

From our holistic perspective of growth, the scientific method can be seen as a method to overcome the all too common persistence of old ideas that are inconsistent with observed evidence. Perhaps the best known example of the persistence of bad ideas was the ancient Greek assertion, argued most elegantly by Aristotle and Ptolemy, that the Earth is the center of the universe. Despite growing evidence that it was incorrect, this hypothesis was so entrenched in human thinking that it became a central tenet of Christianity. When Galileo convincingly questioned this hypothesis, he was convicted for heresy and placed under house arrest for the rest of his life. Galileo also ruffled feathers when he used logic and reason to dispute Aristotle's widely accepted claim that heavy objects fall faster than lighter ones. Galileo was apparently so confident of his reasoning, however, that he did not see the necessity for testing the hypothesis. It was the defenders of Aristotle who actually conducted tests in an effort to prove Galileo wrong.[10] They dropped a set of different weights from the leaning

---

[9] Quoted in Gary Zukav (1979), *The Dancing Wu Li Masters: An Overview of the New Physics*, New York: William Morrow & Co., Inc.

[10] This incident is described in John Gribbin (2002).

tower of Pisa to see which ones would hit the ground first, and to their disappointment, the weights all hit the ground simultaneously, proving Galileo's reasoning to have been correct. To their credit, these critics of Galileo followed the scientific method by confronting opposing hypotheses with evidence. Galileo's reliance on his reasoning rather than carefully testing his conclusions reflects the tendency for people to skip steps of the scientific method. For psychological reasons that we will explain in Chapter 3, human beings tend to latch onto ideas and refuse to acknowledge that their reasoning could be wrong.

To some people, it is discouraging that our ignorance about our natural, social, and economic environments is still enormous despite large amounts of scientific research by many scientists. The true scientist modestly accepts that science is a work in progress, and it always will be. Those who do not understand science demand too much from it and often end up rejecting it.

1.5.5 Kuhn's revolutionary view of science

On the positive side, the human species stands out for having evolved a high level of intelligence. Apparently, the humans and human ancestors who were better at finding solutions to life's problems were more likely to survive, and so the genes of humans with relatively larger brains were more often passed on to later generations. Human brains thus evolved to become more and more powerful. Humans use their evolved brains to actively seek explanations for what they observe, and they accordingly feel good when they find an explanation that seems reasonable. However, because finding solutions and expanding knowledge are difficult, humans often take convenient shortcuts. Before we condemn such "unscientific" behavior, we should be glad that our ancestors did often just wing it rather than engaging in time-consuming research to figure out everything about a problem. Humans would have starved or been eaten by one of their many predators had they not made quick decisions. So, in today's complex societies, humans continue to wing it because they simply do not have time to contemplate a situation. The sheer complexity combined with humans' evolved desire to mentally justify their actions often lead them to embrace unproven hypotheses, to ignore observable facts, and to reason unsoundly. The economic historian Douglass North (2005) writes that humans often accept "half-baked" ideas as truth. However, while quick decisions and rules of thumb can be useful, knowledge suffers when the scientific method is not followed. Sometimes problems are so big that we simply have to stop and think, perhaps for a long time.

Thomas Kuhn's (1962) *The Structure of Scientific Revolutions* became one of the best read books on science because it qualified the popular conclusions about the scientific method. Kuhn argued that "science does not tend toward the ideal that our image of its cumulativeness has suggested. Perhaps, it is another sort of enterprise."[11]   He observed that while many scientific advances indeed followed a cumulative path, truly revolutionary scientific changes were often completely incommensurable with earlier knowledge, that is, they have no common standard of measurement.   Even their axioms, or common accepted truths, may differ.   Kuhn suggested that revolutionary science involved a shift in **paradigms**, by which he meant a completely new way of observing the world, analyzing the evidence, and reaching conclusions.   We sometimes refer to a paradigm as a **school of thought**.   Because paradigm shifts imply new perspectives and thus different interpretations of what scientists observe, paradigm shifts do not generate cumulative knowledge.   Revolutionary scientific discoveries imply sharp breaks with the past, and the completely new paths of research that they stimulate are not necessarily logically related to earlier knowledge.   Kuhn defined **revolutionary science** as a shift from one school of thought to another.   After each shift, however, **normal science** again takes over and follows a well-defined path over which the possibilities opened up by the revolutionary new paradigm are hashed out and expanded upon.

We will discuss how human knowledge advanced throughout this textbook. Note, however, that the sheer complexity of humanity's current existence and the need to embrace the holistic approach in order to understand it complicates the application of the scientific method.   First of all, it is difficult to apply the scientific method to generate revolutionary scientific advances because, as Kuhn suggests, they are not simple steps up from earlier knowledge. Second, it is notoriously difficult to understand how an overall cultural and intellectual perspective shifts, much less how to guide such a process.   Holism thus recognizes that specific hypotheses are likely to hold only under the restrictive circumstances pertaining to a specific paradigm.

Third, it is generally difficult to accurately test specific relationships among the components of a system because other things do not remain constant while the scientist examines a particular part of the system.   For example, we will see in Chapter 14 that there are good reasons why free international trade increases economic growth.   Our holistic approach will also make it clear that economic development requires many other conditions to be satisfied, and international trade, by itself, cannot guarantee gains in human well-being.   This implies that we need a more complex hypothesis to test, namely that trade together with other conditions promote economic development.   Note that if we did not take a holistic approach in this case, we might end up rejecting the hypothesis that trade is good for development for the simple reason that we happen to test it when the other conditions are not present.   Or, we might end up accepting the simple hypothesis that international trade is always good for humanity because, as was more often the case in the latter half of the twentieth century, we tested it when the many other conditions happened to be favorable to growth.

---

[11] Thomas Kuhn (1962), p. 2.

All these difficulties complicate our quest to advance knowledge. Absolute truth remains out of reach. Nevertheless, the more consistent application of the scientific method has clearly enabled us to accelerate the accumulation of knowledge, even if we still remain far from understanding everything about our economic, social, and natural environments. We can continue to satisfy our human desire for knowledge by seeking further answers to our questions, confirming new hypotheses, and gaining insights that inspire ever more ambitious hypotheses. Hopefully, we humans will more often engage in revolutionary science so that scientific activity will not be restricted by specific paradigms.

1.6 How Economists Study Complex Systems

The overwhelming complexity of our world inevitably means that social scientists must develop hypotheses that are simplified representations of that complexity. In economics, we refer to such simple hypotheses as **models**. We will often describe and use models in this textbook because they often do help us understand the process of economic development. It is useful, therefore, to review what models are, why we use them, and how they help us understand complex phenomena.

1.6.1 Economic models

Without realizing it, people use models all the time in order to make decisions in their lives. For example, suppose you and two friends are waiting at the clubhouse to begin a round of golf. A third friend, Mary, has not yet arrived, which leads one of your other two friends to comment: "Mary is not going to show up because it is raining." This seemingly straightforward statement effectively reflects the application of a model that describes a specific aspect of Mary's behavior, namely that she dislikes rain more than she likes to play golf with her three friends. Perhaps this model was inspired by the fact that Mary did not show up for golf the last few times it rained. In this case, we say that the model of Mary's behavior was supported by empirical evidence consisting of actual observations of Mary's behavior. Or, perhaps the statement is based on logical reasoning and observations of Mary's reactions to rain under similar circumstances. Perhaps Mary failed to show up at a company picnic when it rained; in this case, your friend is hypothesizing that Mary will treat the picnic and golf similarly. There is no guarantee that the hypothesized model of Mary's behavior is correct, of course. Mary could falsify the hypothesis by walking in the door with her golf clubs. The important point here is that we often deal with complexity by simplifying and focusing on what we think are the relevant relationships by which we can predict or explain some phenomenon of interest.

In economics, a model is a simplification of reality that explicitly highlights key relationships that we deem important to understanding and analyzing certain economic issues. The term *model* can apply to both the hypotheses that we make about economic phenomena and the confirmed theories that remain after systematically confronting the hypotheses with real world evidence.

1.6.2 The dangers lurking behind models

Economic modeling should follow the scientific method. This means that when an economic model is hypothesized, economists confront the model with unbiased observations or carefully designed objective tests. In practice, economists often use statistical data to test models, which means models must be represented in mathematical forms that can be tested using statistical methods.

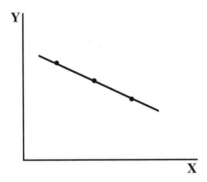

Figure 1.5 A Linear Hypothesis?

Suppose that we want to test the relationship between Y, the economy's per capita GDP, and X, the proportion of a country's production that is exported. Specifically, we want to test the hypothesis that economies that engage in more international trade have higher standards of living than economies that trade less, all other things equal. Suppose, also, that we have three observations of GDP and exports, which are shown as three points in Figure 1.5. Such observations could be from one country at different times, in which case the statistical data is called **time-series data**, or from three different countries at the same point in time, in which case we have **cross-section data**. Since the three points all lie right on a single line, we will be tempted to hypothesize a linear relationship between exports and per capita income represented by an equation of a line: Y = a + bX, where a is the Y-intercept and b is the slope of the line. The three observations shown in Figure 1.5, say for three different countries in the year 2010, suggest that there is a negative relationship between international trade and per capita GDP. That is, the model hypothesizes that the greater are a country's exports, the lower its per capita GDP.

Suppose that another researcher gathers more data for more time periods or for additional countries. This larger sample of observations is shown in Figure 1.6. It appears that the relationship between GDP and trade was not exactly the linear model represented by the line in Figure 1.5. Suppose a statistical method for finding a linear relationship that best reflects scatter of points in Figure 1.6 results in the upward-sloping dashed line. This suggests that the greater the proportion of its output that a country exports, the higher is its per capita GDP. The simple matter of adding some observations thus completely changes the conclusion about how international trade affects human welfare. Trade goes from being a negative factor to a positive factor.

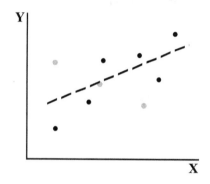

Figure 1.6 A More Complex Relationship

This example suggests that economic models based on a small number of observations should not be accepted as definitive evidence supporting or refuting a hypothesis. A holistic perspective on the matter would suggest that, because the scatter of points do not all lie on a simple straight line, the relationship between international trade and per capita income depends on other variables, perhaps many other variables. This is likely when a relationship between two variables, trade and GDP in this case, occur within a complex social system in which many other variables influence the two variables in question. Perhaps by adding more observations on more countries, the slope of the regression line can be more reliably calculated.

More sophisticated statistical regression models, which include more variables and thus control for the influence of other variables, effectively look at more dimensions beyond the simple two-dimensional relationship shown in Figures 1.5 and 1.6. In the case of international trade and GDP, there seem to have been other factors at play that caused several countries to end up with lower per capita GDPs despite trading more. Of course, models do not have to be linear, and statistical methods have been developed to fit the most likely non-linear shapes to scatters of points like those in Figure 1.6. In general, complexity makes it unlikely that observations on two isolated social phenomena seldom line up neatly along a straight line as shown in Figure 1.5.

1.6.3 Economic models, holism, and the scientific method

Economic models need not all be stated in mathematical form or graphic form. Relationships can also be represented verbally.   Many of the models of economic development detailed in this textbook were originally presented without equations or diagrams by their authors. In fact, it was not until the late 1800s that graphic illustrations became popular in economics, and mathematical models did not become popular until the middle of the twentieth century. In this textbook, in order to make the logic of the model clear to you, models will be represented using words, graphs, and mathematics. The scientific method can, and must, be followed regardless of how a model is represented. For complex issues, a verbal model can often describe observations of real phenomena better than mathematical or graphic models. The latter are constrained by practical mathematical forms and the number of dimensions that can be depicted on a flat screen, respectively. Nevertheless, evidence to test hypotheses is not easily presented verbally. Remember, a single case represents just one point on the graph shown in Figure 1.6, and it is impossible to determine the slope of the line from one observation. Statistical data is often the only evidence economists have with which to confront their hypotheses, and the field of statistics provides unbiased methods to interpret such data. Mathematics and statistics are useful tools, provided they are used with a holistic mindset and the assumptions behind the models and methods are fully understood.

Hopefully, the discussion so far makes it clear that holism is not a radical idea at all. Holism has actually been widely embraced in science. Universities often actively encourage inter-disciplinary research projects, and, more fundamentally, education experts have for centuries promoted the idea of general education to give people a broader insight into their existence. In fact, we tend to admire intellectuals who are able to transcend their own narrow fields and enlighten us on humanity's wider interests and issues. Who does not admire Galileo's success as a scientist, artist, and social activist willing to confront the dominant religious myths of his time? Today, there are even think tanks devoted to promoting holism, such as the well-known Santa Fe Institute. The two distinguishing features of research at the Santa Fe Institute are its multidisciplinary approach and its emphasis on studying complex systems. The Santa Fe Institute's stated goal is to counter the inevitable narrowing of interests as our knowledge about the world increases. Research at the Santa Fe Institute covers the design of computer systems that enable the analysis of complex systems, the interaction between economics and other social sciences, the robustness of natural and social systems in the face of disruptions, the role of networks, and cognitive neuroscience.

The growth of the field of **institutional economics** within the discipline of economics has also been important for the wider adoption of holism in economic research. One example of how institutional economists have embraced holism is Gregory Hayden's **social fabric matrix (SFM)**.[12] The SFM is a tool for evaluating alternative economic and social policies using a schematic model of how the economy interacts with the rest of the social system and with the natural environment. One specific form of social fabric matrix described by Hayden contains sets of variables that reflect cultural values, personal attitudes, social beliefs, the ecological system, technology, and social institutions, each of which influences, and is influenced by, all of the other variables. The SFM effectively prevents social scientists from isolating themselves in narrow perspectives when predicting the outcome of a certain policy. Hayden leaves it up to the analyst to decide precisely what to put into the SFM for a particular policy issue. The important aspect of the method is that it firmly pushes the analyst towards a holistic approach to examining every policy issue.

1.7 A Very Brief History of Thought on Economic Development

As important as economic growth and development have been for human well-being, economists have over the past 200 years been rather inconsistent in analyzing the process of economic change. Over the past century, macroeconomists were often much more concerned with short-run policies to deal with unemployment and inflation than policies to promote sustainable economic development. Microeconomists have focused almost exclusively on the allocation of resources. There have been extended periods during the past two centuries when economists paid little or no attention to the extraordinary rates of growth human society was achieving. Fortunately, there were many economists who *were* intrigued enough by the economic changes occurring around them to seek an understanding of technological change, factor accumulation, structural change, education, specialization, innovation, investment, and government policy. A brief description of the key ideas follows here. Part II of the textbook provides much more detail.

1.7.1 Economic thought before 1900

At the start of the Industrial Revolution in the late 1700s and early 1800s, Adam Smith, David Ricardo, John Stuart Mill, Thomas Malthus, and Karl Marx, among many noted economists, were very much interested in how an economy

---

[12] The social fabric matrix is thoroughly explained in F. Gregory Hayden (2006) and applied in Tara Natarajan, Wolfram Elsner, and Scott Fullwiler, eds. (2009).

grows and how the many economic and social changes that accompany economic development affect the welfare of people. This is not surprising, given the rapidly changing world these economists observed before their eyes.

Chapter 4 details some of the growth models presented by Smith and the **Classical economists** of the early nineteenth century. They are quite insightful, and many of the ideas contained in these models are still prominent concepts in modern economic thought. Among the ideas forwarded by the Classical economists are the importance of technological progress, the diminishing returns to investment, and the role of social, political, and economic institutions to guide human behavior in a complex society. The Classical economists also often took a holistic approach to economic development by enthusiastically delving into the fields of political science, sociology, and history to frame their hypotheses and seek supporting evidence. Marx is well known for linking economic change to political and social change, but Smith, Malthus, and Mill provided equally broad, holistic views of the changing world they observed.

1.7.2 Fading interest in development in the late 1800s

In the latter half of the nineteenth century, when the world economy was firmly embarked on its unprecedented path of growth and change, economists moved in a different direction and followed Alfred Marshall and other microeconomists to focus on economic efficiency and the allocation of resources. These economists are now known as the **Neoclassical school** because they borrowed some key ideas from the Classical school. In contrast to the holistic and evolutionary vision of the Classical school, however, they focused on specific categories of economic activity and took a scientific reductionist approach to the economic system: if the component parts were understood, then the overall system would also be understood. Also, unlike the Classical economists, who tended to range into topics that extended well beyond the economic sphere, neoclassical economists focused almost entirely on the economic sphere. Neoclassical economists developed models of how individual markets worked, usually under the assumption that the overall economy was a fixed system, a simple sum of its component markets.

Another fundamental shift in economic thinking in the late nineteenth century was the neoclassical economists' increasing reliance on **static models**. Static models are designed to generate an equilibrium without explicit reference to the path followed in moving the economy toward that equilibrium over time. That is, there is no concept of time in a static model other than *before* and *after*. The standard neoclassical economic problem was one of maximizing welfare subject to a given set of scarce resources. This approach to economics focuses attention on the allocation of resources in the economy under the static *all other things equal* assumption, but it completely ignores the long-run evolution of an economy. Such microeconomic analysis is of little use for development economics because over time other things do not remain the same. Within the economic sphere, the relative scarcities of resources vary, technology changes, and, as shown earlier, the economy's entire structure changes. Holistically, the complex interactions between the economic, social, and natural spheres further guarantee that virtually nothing stays the same in the long run.

The Great Depression of the 1930s caused another major shift in economists' priorities towards finding remedies for unemployment, overcapacity, and deflation. The British economist, John Maynard Keynes, led the way with a macroeconomic model that showed why an economic system may fail to reach an efficient general equilibrium in which product and labor markets clear. Keynes was holistic because his famous macroeconomic model focused on both the entire economic system and how the interrelationships among key macroeconomic variables determined the overall outcome of the system. However, with his short-run emphasis on bringing the world's economies back to their full capacity, Keynes' model was not often used to analyze long-run economic change. This is not to say that Keynes did not think about the long run; as we will discuss below, at the start of the Great Depression, Keynes (1930) produced a very insightful essay on future economic change. However, at the depth of the Great Depression, he focused on solving the immediate economic crisis. Thinking about long-run economic development would have to await the end of the Depression.

1.7.3 Renewed interest in growth after World War II

After World War II, economic growth indeed began to attract the attention of more economists. The independence of many former colonies in Africa and Asia in the 1950s and 1960s increased interest in raising the standards of living in the so-called **less developed economies**. Also, the Cold War and the ideological competition between capitalism and communism further heightened interest in economic growth: Which of the two rival economic systems would generate faster rises in people's standards of living and thus claim victory in their ideological contest? Unfortunately, the interest in economic growth evolved into two separate fields that came to be known as **development economics** and **growth theory**, with each one giving the other little recognition. The former was largely concerned with understanding how the poor economies of Africa, Asia, and Latin America could develop and raise the standards of living of their citizens. Growth theory emerged from the field of macroeconomics, and it mostly focused on explaining the growth of GDP per capita in the developed economies of North America and Europe. Growth theory was in large part motivated by the Cold War and the rivalry between the United States and the Soviet Union; growth theory sought to explain how the capitalist economies could grow faster and avoid being overtaken by the socialist economies.

1.7.4 Development economics and growth theory

The practitioners in the two fields, development economics and growth theory, took very different analytical approaches to modeling the phenomenon of economic change and development. Growth theorists made use of existing macroeconomic theory to develop elegant mathematical models that seemed to bear little resemblance to the real world economy. In 1956, Robert Solow published what has since become the most often-used model for analyzing economic growth. Solow would later earn the Nobel Prize in economics. The **Solow model** closely reflected the orthodox neoclassical approach in which functions were smooth and calculus could be used to solve for stable equilibria. Also, mathematical simplicity was maintained by assuming many of the key variables development economists were interested in were exogenously determined outside the model. Also, because so many things were assumed rather than explained, the Solow model gave policymakers few explicit roles to play in the process of economic development. This contrasts sharply with the Keynesian macroeconomic model, which gave policy makers very clear and critical roles in directing economic activity. Therefore, even as mainstream macroeconomic thinking after World War II definitely favored government action to solve problems such as unemployment, slow job growth, and inflation, the Solow model stealthily supported the gradual shift in mainstream economics away from Keynesian advocacy of government involvement in the economy.

During the decade following the publication of Solow's model, there was a flurry of new models that exploited a variety of mathematical forms to reach additional conclusions about the growth process. But, this research quickly reached diminishing returns, and interest in growth models faded. Charles Plosser's (1992, p. 57) description of the dominant view of growth theory before its recent revival is probably quite accurate: "... many economists interested in positive economic theories came to view growth theory as a rather sterile, and uninteresting branch of economics through most of the 1960s and 1970s." Still, Chapter 5 will show that the Solow model does have a lot to tell us about economic growth. And, an extension of the model will prove very useful for understanding the interaction between the economic and natural spheres. Growth theory was again revived in the 1990s with the emergence of new models based on the thinking of the early twentieth century economist Joseph Schumpeter. As will be detailed in Chapter 8, Schumpeter focused on the process of technological change, perhaps the most important variable in the process of economic development.

1.7.5 The biases of growth theory

Many, if not most, mainstream economists who have focused on economic growth over the past half century combined Neoclassical models of economic growth like Solow's with a strong bias towards free markets, free international trade, and unrestricted finance. This combination came to be known as the **neoliberal paradigm**. International institutions such as the International Monetary Fund (IMF), the World Bank, and regional development banks funded by the United States and European governments adopted the neoliberal paradigm for prescribing and analyzing economic development policies and programs. The neoliberal paradigm directly extends recent microeconomic and macroeconomic models that assume, among other things, that all economic transactions pass through competitive markets. Generally, neoliberal economists tend to favor market solutions over government regulation, free international trade over protectionist trade policies, private and unregulated financial sectors over regulated financial regimes, and private investment over public projects. The policy prescriptions generated within the neoliberal paradigm are often referred to as the **Washington Consensus** because they were actively pushed by the IMF and World Bank, both located in Washington, D.C.

Many development economists rejected the neoliberal paradigm, and they continued to address wide-ranging concerns like poverty, hunger, famine, oppression, colonialism, income inequality, population growth, discrimination, ethnic conflict, corruption, and many more issues that were not easily incorporated into orthodox economics' simple mathematical models. Many development economists tended to deal with the many aspects of economic growth on a piecemeal and disjointed basis, in large part because mainstream economics offered no models that permitted an integrated analysis of complex systems. Many development economists, in trying to make sense of the complexity of economic change and development, embraced broader intellectual paradigms such Marxism, structuralism, dependency theory, and **heterodox economics**. These efforts were not always appreciated or even recognized by mainstream economics, which embraced elements of the neoliberal paradigm.

Other disciplines and fields also contributed toward our understanding of economic development. For example, as economic historians amassed large amounts of evidence and cases, they began to offer more inter-disciplinary analysis to explain their historical data on economic development. Institutional economists stressed the importance of economic and social **institutions**, the formal and informal rules, customs, laws, traditions, organizations, etc. that guide and shape individual economic behavior. Other institutional economists expanded the scope of economic analysis towards more dynamic models of technological change in which institutions played critical roles in generating innovative activity.

Policymakers in developing countries often rejected standard microeconomic and macroeconomic analysis on the grounds that it did not apply to the economic situation faced by less developed economies. We will argue elsewhere in this textbook that the hypothesized models embraced by intellectuals, policymakers, and the public are indeed strongly influenced by culture, political hegemony, and economic power. Perhaps policymakers rejected traditional economic theory because they saw it as part of the culture of the developed economies, which were the same economies that had colonized them, exploited their resources, and imposed Western cultures on them. Unfortunately, the competing economic paradigms often led to inconsistent policies. The economic performances of developing countries over the past 50 years ranged widely between impressive successes and utter failures. Economic models played major roles in both the failures and successes.

1.7.6 Heterodoxy

After several decades of the Washington Consensus, neoliberal policy prescriptions are being gradually abandoned in many countries after they were found to generate undesirable consequences across the economic, social, and natural spheres. The recent success of China, India, Brazil, Korea, Malaysia, Chile, among others, suggests the superiority of a more flexible approach to economic development. Applying development policies that more closely reflect each country's particular economic and social conditions seems to work out better than the mechanical application of identical Washington Consensus policies across different economies. With development economics now taking new turns away from **orthodox** neoclassical economics, there is no longer as much discussion of a synthesis between growth theory and development theory in the field of development economics.

In recognition of the variety of approaches to the complex process of economic development, this textbook takes a *heterodox* approach to the study of economic development. To grasp the meaning of the term *heterodox economics*, note first that the prefix *hetero* has its origins in ancient Greek, where it meant *other* or *different*. The word *doxy* refers to a doctrine, a framework of analysis, or what many social scientists would call a paradigm. Heterodoxy thus suggests a set of ideas, perspectives, and models that are in some way different from the normal, or orthodox, framework for economic analysis. The relationship between heteroxy and orthodoxy is not always a comfortable one. To understand the conflict, note that the word element *ortho*, which also comes from Greek, means *straight*, *right*, or *correct*. In today's mainstream economics the terms orthodox and heterodox, respectively, are usually interpreted as referring to the mainstream paradigm and the alternative viewpoints that fall outside the accepted mainstream culture of economics. The linguistic origin of the term orthodoxy suggests mainstream economics is the correct framework within which to conduct economic analysis.

This textbook rejects the division between orthodoxy and heterodoxy. We define heterodoxy simply as a **multi-paradigmatic approach**, or a form of economic "multiculturalism." Heterodox economists do not reject neoclassical models, but they do diminish them to the status of just one of the many alternative approaches that must be considered in addressing the complexity of human economic, social, and natural existence. Heterodox economists firmly reject the idea that economic phenomena can be accurately understood and analyzed entirely from within the neoclassical paradigm, or any single paradigm for that matter. If you think of a paradigm as a language, heterodoxy enables economists to speak many languages, which enables them to discover many viewpoints, discuss issues with many different interests, and uncover more information and evidence to support or refute many more hypotheses.

There is a compelling logic to heterodoxy that goes well beyond merely rejecting the generality of the neoclassical paradigm. Heterodoxy accepts complexity, and, through its willingness to analyze a situation from multiple perspectives embraces holism in order to deal with that complexity. Heterodoxy recognizes that economic activity takes place within broad spheres of human behavior and therefore often uses models from different fields and specializations. Heterodox economists reject any reliance on just one set of related models generated under one uniform paradigm or restricted to analyzing activity within just one sphere.

Of course, heterodoxy's broader perspective makes it more difficult to arrive at precise conclusions. But precision is not necessarily a positive attribute for a model or a paradigm in a complex world. The complexity of economic development implies that economists often operate in a state of **uncertainty**. Development economists generally lack full knowledge and understanding of circumstances, options, and potential outcomes of policies. The orthodox neoclassical approach in economics normally assumes away uncertainty and imposes an artificial framework of analysis that translates specific decisions into firm outcomes. But reality is too complex to assume certainty, especially the reality of the dynamic complex process of economic development. Heterodoxy accepts complexity and the uncertainty that accompanies it. Accordingly, heterodoxy often seeks economic strategies that minimize the risk of income losses, rising unemployment, or environmental damage rather than those that simply maximize long-run average income gains. Also, heterodox economists prefer policies that can be adjusted if things do not work out exactly as planned. They expect to have to make revisions, adjustments, and corrections to their suggested policies.

1.8 What Will Future Economic Development Look Like?

Economic development, defined as the improvement in living conditions and the satisfaction with life for all people, is accepted by economists to be a worthy goal for policymakers. However, economic development is too often simplified to mean increases in income and/or output. Policymakers never hesitate to tout their government's success in bringing about the growth of income or output.

And, if they happen to be holding office when economic growth falters, our political leaders make certain to blame their predecessors and to be seen working hard to restore growth. Some economists have seriously questioned the need for further growth of human consumption of goods and services. And environmental concerns have led some people to oppose further economic growth. We thus conclude with a brief discussion of whether further increases in income are a realistic, or even a worthwhile, goal.

1.8.1 Is further economic growth necessary?

There is extensive evidence showing that per capita GDP is, at best, only partially correlated with human happiness and life satisfaction. As will be detailed in Chapter 3, some evidence suggests that in rich countries there is no relationship at all. And, if it is true that the mere growth of output of goods and services does little for human well-being or life satisfaction, then we must also question economic policies solely designed to expand the production of goods and services.

Reflecting a bit on the evolution of human culture suggests that the idea of economic progress, which so easily takes us to the corollary idea of economic growth, is actually a very recent human concept. As depicted in Figure 1.1, for most of human history life consisted essentially of slight variations around an unchanging level of income barely above basic subsistence and survival. People died pretty much in the same economic state as they were born into, and they expected little change for their children and grandchildren. Long run change was too slow for any generation to perceive, and there was no recorded information with which to make comparisons over time. Were people less happy thousands of years ago, when there was no apparent upward trend in life's condition? Are we really happier today in our world of rapid economic change and growing consumption?

Many orthodox economists argue that because humanity has apparently figured out how to expand output consistently over time, it should try to accelerate the process. They see growth as the normal state of affairs. Growth has become part of the culture of most societies. In a sense, most people have become addicted to it. This suggests that people would be miserable if output and income stopped growing and people could no longer look forward to having more stuff in the future and seeing their children achieve even greater levels of consumption. The fact remains, however, that until the past several hundred years, economic growth was not necessary for humanity to thrive on Earth.

1.8.2 The superfluity of economic growth

John Maynard Keynes, who was discussed above as the developer of a macroeconomic model that helped to explain how an economy gets stuck in a depression, incidentally also provided an insightful perspective on the desirability of yet another century of rapid growth of GDP per capita. In a short essay published, ironically, in the year the world fell into the Great Depression, Keynes (1930) wrote:

> Now it is true that the needs of human beings may seem to be insatiable. But they fall into two classes — those needs which are absolute in the sense that we feel them whatever the situation of our fellow human beings may be, and those which are relative in the sense that we feel them only if their satisfaction lifts us above, makes us feel superior to, our fellows.

That is, Keynes recognized that personal well-being depends on both the absolute amount of stuff we have and how much more we have than our neighbor. Keynes then argued from his 1930 perspective that if world output grows another ten-fold, humanity's absolute needs would be abundantly satisfied, but because it is impossible for everyone to do better than everyone else, *relative* gains for everyone would remain as impossible as ever. A ten-fold increase in real income was indeed achieved in developed economies by the start of the twenty-first century. Here in the twenty-first century, it is not obvious that humans feel over-abundantly satisfied as Keynes predicted.

Keynes was convinced in 1930 that the eventual solution to the traditional economic problem of scarcity would create a unique opportunity for humanity:

> Thus, we have been expressly evolved by nature — with all our impulses and deepest instincts — for the purpose of solving the economic problem. If the economic problem is solved, mankind will be deprived of its traditional purpose.
>
> Will this be a benefit? If one believes at all in the real values of life, the prospect at least opens up the possibility of benefit. Yet I think with dread of the readjustments of the habits and instincts of the ordinary man, bred into him for countless generations, which he may be asked to discard within a few decades.
>
> Thus for the first time since his creation man will be faced with his real, his permanent problem — how to use his freedom from pressing economic cares, how to occupy the leisure, which science and compound interest will have won for him, to live wisely and agreeably and well.

Chapter 2 explains the conventional ways in which we measure economic growth and development, Chapter 3 embraces Keynes' perspective and looks at the desirability of economic growth from a psychological perspective and the possibility for people to change the way they live.

1.8.3 Environmental limits to growth

It may not be the satiation of human wants and desires that brings economic growth to an end, however. An increasingly urgent reason why we must question the desirability of economic growth is that the continued expansion of production of goods and services may already be doing more harm than good. We may be doing little more than generating what Herman Daly (1998) calls **uneconomic growth**, where increases in the value of final output require the consumption of a greater value of nature's resources and the destruction of nature's capacity to provide services such as fresh water, pollination, fertile soils, warmth, food, etc. Evidences by Wackernagel *et al.* (2002) and the World Wildlife Fund (2008) show that the human economy's load on the ecosystem exceeds the earth's capacity to replenish and maintain the natural services and renewable resources. Scientists also estimate that human activity is causing global warming that is on track to raise atmospheric temperatures by several degrees by the end of this century, the consequences of which are potentially catastrophic for humanity. Our excessive use of resources seems to be condemning future generations to lower levels of GDP per capita than we enjoy today. Chapters 6 and 18 detail the environmental costs and sustainability of our unprecedented growth of population and production.

1.8.4 Sustainable economic development

Scientific evidence suggests that the growth of material production is raising the risk of an environmental disaster, and the continued growth of economic activity is not sustainable. Sustainable development is typically defined as:

> Economic change and development that maximizes the needs and aspirations of the current generations without sacrificing the ability of future generations to meet their needs and aspirations.

Scientific evidence shows that economic growth has already led humans to exploit Earth's resources and its natural services faster than they can be replenished. In this case, a commitment to sustainable development calls for a period of negative growth. Such a conclusion clashes head on with orthodox economic thinking and cultures in most of the world's countries, not to mention evolved human behaviors and instincts.

Perhaps humanity will find ways to keep expanding output without destroying the natural environment while also making life more satisfying. Or, perhaps humans will change the way they live, as Keynes (1930) hoped:

> The strenuous purposeful money-makers may carry all of us along with them into the lap of economic abundance. But it will be those peoples, who can keep alive, and cultivate into a fuller perfection, the art of life and so not sell themselves for the means of life, who will be able to enjoy the abundance when it comes.

So far, most people in developing economies are still far from satisfying all of their basic needs. And in developed countries like the United States, corporate advertising and economic policies to promote indebtedness have sustained humans' consumption binge. So Keynes' new economic problem of satiation has been postponed for now. On the other hand, the French have succeeded in increasing vacation time and reducing the number of hours in the average workweek while maintaining their global lead in worker productivity and public health. Perhaps the only certain prediction we can make is that future economic growth and development, whatever form it takes, will have to be sustainable. Remember, something that is not sustainable will, by definition, come to an end.

Key Terms and Concepts

Classical economists
Complex system
Complexity
Compounding
Cross-section data
Development economics
Dynamic feedback
Economic change
Economic development
Economic growth
Economic model
Economic structure
Ecosystem
Empirical evidence
Falsifiability
Gaia hypothesis
Gross domestic product (GDP)
GDP per capita
Growth theory
Heterodoxy
Heterodox economics
Holism
Holistic science
Homeostasis
Hypothesis
Institutional economics
Institutions
Interdisciplinary perspective
Less developed economies
Medea hypothesis

Model
Multi-paradigmatic approach
Neoclassical school
Neoliberal paradigm
Normal science
Orthodoxy
Paradigm
Power of compounding
Revolutionary science
Rule of 72
School of thought
Science
Scientific method
Scientific reductionism
Scientist
Social fabric matrix (SFM)
Social scientist
Society
Solow model
Spheres of human existence
Static models
Structural change
Subsistence income
Sustainable economic development
Theory
Time-series data
Truth
Uncertainty
Uneconomic growth
Washington Consensus

Questions and Problems

1. Discuss the relationship between Table 1.1 and Figure 1.2. Specifically, focus on the relationship between levels of income, rates of growth of income, and the slope of the long-run curve in Figure 1.2.
2. Define economic growth, and carefully explain your definition. How might your definition of the term *economic growth* differ from the term *economic development*? Discuss.
3. In the field of economics, the level of economic development is often described in terms of gross domestic product (GDP) per capita or gross national product (GNP) per capita. How accurately do these measures of output represent the true levels and growth of human well-being? (Hint: Recall from your principles of economics course what is included, and not included, in GDP and GNP.)
4. In a short essay, describe economic growth over the past 2000 years. What major trends and shifts stand out? What is the relationship between population growth and economic growth? (Hint: Use the data in Table 1.1 and Figures 1.2 and 1.3.)
5. This chapter and its appendix describe the power of compounding and provide some convenient formulas for calculating growth rates, doubling times, and predicted future income levels. Use these formulas to answer the following problems:
    a) If per capita GDP is $1,000 and the annual growth rate is a steady 2 percent, what will GDP per capita be after 5 years? After 72 years?
    b) If per capita GDP is $1,000 and the annual growth rate is a steady 3 percent, what will GDP per capita be after 5 years? After 72 years?
    c) Contrast the results in questions a) and b) above. What general conclusion can you draw?
6. This chapter and its appendix describe the power of compounding and provide some convenient formulas for calculating growth rates, doubling times, and predicted future income levels. Use these formulas to answer the following problems:
    a) If GDP per capita grows at a steady 1 percent per year, how long wwill it take for GDP per capita to double?
    b) If GDP per capita grows at a steady 10 percent per year, how long will it take to double GDP per capita? To quadruple GDP per capita?
    c) Contrast the results in questions a) and b) above. What general conclusions can you draw?
7. The textbook describes the growth of GDP per capita since the year 0, and Table 1.1 shows how this growth accelerated after 1950 and then slowed somewhat after 1972. Do you think that economic growth will continue to raise per capita output in the twenty-first century? Could growth accelerate further? Or, do you foresee the rate of economic growth falling in the future? Clearly state and explain your prediction.
8. If you are like most people in the world, you are living in an economy that has grown over the past century. Describe how you perceive this economic growth to have affected (1) your life, (2) the lives of your parents and grandparents, and (3) the lives of other people in your country. Has economic growth been good for the well-being of all the people in your economy? Why or why not?
9. Figure 1.1 shows the three spheres of human existence. Do you think this illustration of the complexity of our existence is accurate? Would you shape or position the spheres differently? What would you add or delete?

10. Define *holism*. Also, explain how holism embraces systems, dynamic evolutionary processes, and inter-disciplinary perspectives.
11. This chapter describes the near meltdown of the Three Mile Island nuclear power plant in Pennsylvania in 1979. Can you think of other cases in which a system of apparently well-functioning parts failed? Describe and explain.
12. Detail the steps of the scientific method. What are the specific advantages of the scientific method for humanity? Explain.
13. Describe *homeostasis*. Is the natural environment on Earth homeostatic? Do you think the Gaia hypothesis or the Medea hypothesis applies?
14. Explain the difference between *orthodox economics* and *heterodox economics*. Which approach is more appropriate for studying economic development? Why? Explain.
15. The last two sentences of the next-to-the-last paragraph of Section 1.8.1 ask: Were people less happy thousands of years ago, when there was no apparent upward trend in life's condition? Are we really happier today in our world of rapid economic change and growing consumption? Write a brief essay answering these two questions.
16. As later chapters will make clear, technological change is a fundamental element of economic development. In reference to Thomas Kuhn's hypothesis of paradigm shifts described in Section 1.5.5, do you think that knowledge and technology grow continually and smoothly or more erratically with jumps and stops? Explain.

Appendix 1.1: The Mechanics of Economic Growth

Equation (1.3) shows that if we start with per capita GDP in year $t = 0$, $PCGDP_{t=0}$, then after T years of R percent annual growth, per capita GDP in the year t, $PCGDP_T$, will be

$$PCGDP_{t=T} = PCGDP_{t=1}(1 + R)^T \qquad (A1.1)$$

In the case of 10 years of 10 percent growth, per capita income rises from $1,000 to

$$PCGDP_{t=10} = \$1000(1 + .10)^{10} = \$2594 \qquad (A1.2)$$

With this example, you can see the power of compounding. 10 years of 10 percent growth causes per capita GDP to grow by nearly 160 percent.

There are some additional exercises that we can perform using variations on equation (1.3) in the main text. These exercises help you answer questions such as: How fast must developing economies grow if they are to "catch up" to the developed economies in the next century? Or, if China continues to grow at 10 percent per year, as it has for the past three decades, and the U.S. continues to grow at 2.5 percent per year, how long before its per capita income is equal to that of the United States?

Calculating "doubling time"

Doubling time is the time it will take for some variable to double in value if it grows continuously at the rate of R percent per year. Suppose we want to find out how long it will take for a country to double its GDP if it grows at an annual rate of 10 percent. To find the answer to this question, we first divide each side of equation (A1.1) by $PCGDP_{t=1}$:

$$PCGDP_{t=T}/PCGDP_{t=1} = (1 + R)^T \qquad (A1.3)$$

A doubling of per capita GDP implies the left hand side of (A1.3) equals 2. Since we also assume $R = 10$ percent, we thus want to find the value of T which makes

$$(1.1)^T = PCGDP_{t=T}/PCGDP_{t=1} = 2 \qquad (A1.4)$$

The variable we seek is an exponent, which requires the use of logarithms. Taking the natural logarithms of both sides of the equation gives us

$$T \ln(1.1) = \ln(PCGDP_{t=T}/PCGDP_{t=1}) = \ln 2 \qquad (A1.5)$$

The natural logarithm of 2 is .69314, and $\ln 1.1 = .09531$. Therefore,

$$T(.09531) = .69314 \qquad (A1.6)$$

and, solving for T:

$$T = .69314/.09531 = 7.2725 \qquad (A1.7)$$

Thus, if an economy grows at a steady rate of 10 percent per year, it takes about 7.27 years to double per capita output.

This result can be approximated using the **rule of 72**. This simple rule states that the time for a variable growing at a constant rate to double in value is equal to $72/r$, where r is the growth rate in terms of percentage points. That is, if the growth rate is 10 percent per year, then $r = 10$. Applying this rule to the above example, $72/10 = 7.2$, or a constant growth rate of 10 percent implies that it takes about 7.2 periods to double the value of a variable.

Alternatively, a growth rate of 5 percent per year means that

$$\ln(1 + R) = \ln(1.05) = .04879 \qquad (A1.8)$$

and, therefore, the time it takes to double per capita GDP is equal to

$$T = .69314/.04879 = 14.2067 \qquad (A1.9)$$

Using either the formulas or the rule of 72, you should be able to confirm that if the annual growh rate is just 2 percent, it will take about 35 years to double PCGDP.

We can of course also find how long it takes to triple, quadruple, or cut in half PCGDP by taking the natural log of 3, 4, or .5. For example, at a 10 percent growth rate, per capita income will quadruple, that is a fourfold increase in PCGDP, in a little more than 14 years:

$$T = \ln 4/\ln(1.1) = 14.5451 \qquad (A1.10)$$

Thus, for two countries that start off at the same level of per capita GDP, if one grows at 10 percent while the other grows at 5 percent, after just 14 years the first will have four times its initial per capita GDP, or twice as great an increase in per capita GDP than the slower-growing country, which only doubles its initial per capita GDP.

Finding a "target" growth rate

We can alter the above formulas to find what rate of annual growth is necessary to achieve a certain level of PCGDP at a certain time in the future. In general, if we want to know the required annual rate for an economy starting with $PCGDP_1$ to attain $PCGDP_2$ in T years, we can use the following variation of equation (A1.1):

$$PCGDP_2/PCGDP_1 = (1 + R)^T \qquad (A1.11)$$

We now need to solve for R. Raising both sides of (A1.11) to the power $1/T$ then gives us

$$(PCGDP_2/PCGDP_1)^{1/T} = (1 + R)^{T/T} = 1 + R \qquad (A1.12)$$

Therefore:

$$R = (PCGDP_2/PCGDP_1)^{1/T} - 1 \qquad (A1.13)$$

For example, suppose we want to know how fast PCGDP must grow in order to double PCGDP in 10 years. Setting $T = 10$ and the ratio $PCGDP_2/PCGDP_1 = 2$, (A1.11) becomes:

$$2 = (1 + R)^{10} \qquad (A1.14)$$

Raising both sides of (A1.14) to the power $1/T = 1/10$, or

$$2^{1/T} = 2^{1/10} = (1 + R)^{T/T} = 1 + R = 1.0717 \qquad (A1.15)$$

Hence, $R = (1 + R) - 1 = 1.0717 - 1 = .0717$, or $R = 7.17$ percent. That is, it takes an annual growth rate of 7.17 percent for PCGDP to double in ten years. We conclude, therefore, that the R required to double per capita income in ten years is approximately 7.2 percent (this is another version of the **rule of 72**).

The power of compounding again

The power of compounding means that small differences in per capita output are quickly magnified. Or, looked at from the opposite side, large differences in per capita output can be eliminated much more quickly than is often imagined. For example, back in the 1990s, when people first started looking at China's impressive rate of GDP growth, people began wondering how long it would be before China overtakes the United States in per capita income. You now can answer this question, provided you are willing to make some assumptions about future growth rates.

For example, in 2000 the United States had a per capita real GDP of about $21,000. China, on the other hand, had an adjusted per capita real GDP of $3,000, one-seventh that of the United States.   Suppose that the United States grows at modest 2 percent throughout the twentieth century. As will become apparent as you read the rest of this textbook, it is unlikely that China will continue growing at 10 percent per year for an entire century. So you might assume conservatively that China will grow at "a mere" 4 percent per year. What would the per capita real GDPs be for each country at the end of the century?

In the case of the United States:

$$PCGDP_{2100} = \$21,000(1.02)^{100} = \$152,138 \tag{A1.16}$$

In the case of China,

$$PCGDP_{2100} = \$3,000(1.04)^{100} = \$151,515 \tag{A1.17}$$

Thus, if China's GDP per capita grows just two percentage points faster than that of the United States, the citizens of the two countries will have similar per capita incomes in the year 2100. That is only a bit more than three generations from now.

If you think that it is unrealistic for China to maintain even a 4 percent rate of per capita output growth for a whole century, you might ask what a mere 2 percent annual rate of growth would do for Chinese per capita output. Using the above equations, it is easy to show that China, with a current average per capita income of about $3,000, could raise the welfare of its 1.3 billion citizens to the very high level of income enjoyed in the United States in 100 years.

$$\$3,000(1.02)^{100} = \$21,734 \tag{A1.18}$$

Certainly, given the experience of so many countries in the twentieth century, a growth rate of 2 percent does not seem so difficult to achieve.

Of course, this book will discuss some of the difficulties that the world faces in providing growing numbers of people with ever-larger amounts of goods and services. Can we simply extrapolate the recent 200 years of economic growth into the future when many economic, social, and ecological conditions are likely to change? Recall the discussion of models in the main text of this chapter.

References

Boulding, Kenneth (1956), "General Systems Theory, the Skeleton of Science," *Management Science* 2(3):197–208.

Daly, Herman E. (1998), "Uneconomic Growth," Clemens Lecture 11, Saint John's University, October 25.

De Vries, Jan (1984), *European Urbanization 1500–1800*, London: Methuen.

Gribbin, John (2002), *Science: A History*, London: Penguin Press.

Hayden, F. Gregory (2006), *Policymaking for a Good Society: The Social Fabric Matrix Approach to Policy Analysis and Program Evaluation*, New York: Springer.

Keynes, John Maynard (1930), "Economic Possibilities for Our Grandchildren," in *Essays in Persuasion*, New York: W.W. Norton & Co., [1963], pp. 358–373.

Kremer, Michael (1993), "Population Growth and Technical Change, One Million BCE to 1990," *Quarterly Journal of Economics* 108(3):681–716.

Kuhn, Thomas (1962), *The Structure of Scientific Revolutions*, Chicago: University of Chicago Press.

Lovelock, James E. (1972), "Gaia as Seen through the Atmosphere," *Atmospheric Environment* 6(8):579–580.

Maddison, Angus (1989), *The World Economy in the 20th Century*, Paris: OECD.

Maddison, Angus (2001), *The World Economy: A Millennial Perspective*, Paris: OECD.

Maddison, Angus (2003), *The World Economy: Historical Statistics*, Paris: OECD.

Maddison, Angus (2006), *Historical Statistics for the World Economy: 1–2003AD*, Statistical Appendix; this document was downloaded on August 19, 2006 from the website (http://ggdc.net/maddison/) maintained by the Groningen Growth & Development Centre at the University of Groningen, Netherlands.

Natarajan, Tara, Wolfram Elsner, and Scott Fullwiler, eds. (2009), *Institutional Analysis and Praxis: The Social Fabric Matrix Approach*, Heidelberg: Springer.

North, Douglass (2005), *Understanding the Process of Economic Change*, Princeton, NJ: Princeton University Press.

Plosser, Charles I. (1992), "The Search for Growth," in *Policies for Long-Run Economic Growth*, Kansas City: Federal Reserve Bank of Kansas City.

Romer, Paul M. (1998), "Economic Growth," in David R. Henderson (ed.), *The Fortune Encyclopedia of Economics*, New York: Warner Books.

Wackernagel, Mathis, *et al.* (2002), "Tracking the Econological Overshoot of the Human Economy," *Proceeding of the National Academy of Sciences* 99(14):9266–9271.

Ward, Peter (2009), *The Medea Hypothesis*, Princeton, NJ: Princeton University Press.

World Wildlife Fund (2008), *Living Planet Report 2008*, Gland, Switzerland: World Wildlife Fund for Nature.

CHAPTER 2

Measuring Economic Development

... the years have been good for humanity.

(Julian Simon, 1995)

There are many alarming ways in which individuals will be able to trigger catastrophe.

(Martin Rees, 2003)

A 2005 article in *The Economist* compared the lives of two people: Mbwebwe Kabamba, a prominent surgeon in the main public hospital in Kinshasa, the capital of the Democratic Republic of Congo, and Enos Banks, an unemployed miner living in a mobile home in rural Kentucky in the United States. What is most interesting about the article in *The Economist* is that it compares a poor person in a rich country and a relatively well-off person in a very poor country:

> Mr. Banks makes $521 a month in a country where median male earnings are $3,400 a month. Dr. Kabamba earns $600 a month in a country where most people grow their own food and hardly ever see a bank note. The two men's experiences could hardly be less similar. But which of the two would one expect to be happier?[1]

This question addresses a very important issue in the field of economic development, which is how we measure economic development. Economists normally measure economic development in terms of the growth of average gross domestic product (GDP). But will average GDP in Mr. Banks' and Dr. Kabamba's home countries tell us much about their individual happiness?

While there is general agreement among economists that human welfare is the "bottom line" by which we should judge the performance of an economy, there is still no consensus on exactly what constitutes human welfare. And even when economists usually agree that human welfare is in some way related to the

---

[1] *The Economist* (2005), "The Mountain Man and the Surgeon," December 20.

conditions in which people live and the satisfaction with which they view their lives, measuring such conditions and satisfaction is not a simple matter. Human welfare is a difficult concept to pin down.

Economists have worked for more than a century to define a national **welfare function** that can be used to judge the performance of economies and to shape government policies. The field of economics known as **welfare economics** deals with this issue, of course, and development economists take advantage of many of the contributions of orthodox welfare economics when they analyze economic development. But, they have also sought to improve on orthodox economics' representation of human welfare, which has consisted of rather narrow measures such as income or the market value of goods and services produced. Recent research in experimental economics, psychology, behavioral economics, and neuroscience, among other fields, suggests that human well-being depends on more than the conventional national income accounting measures of *national income* or **GDP**. Orthodox welfare economics, therefore, does not provide a useful modeling framework for analyzing the complex process of economic development.

This chapter begins by describing the measures that economists and social scientists most often use to quantify the growth or development of the world economy. These measures of course include GDP per capita. GDP data suggest that standards of living have improved at unprecedented rates over the past 200 years, and we should be very happy that we are living today and not at some time in the past. However, a comparison of Mr. Banks and Dr. Kabamba, two people living in very different social and economic circumstances in today's wealthier world, suggests that simple per capita income numbers may not be closely correlated with individual feelings of well-being. Therefore, this chapter also presents several alternative measures of economic and social outcomes that are often associated with human well-being. The next chapter explains some more radical alternatives to the standard measures used by mainstream economics.

Chapter Goals

1. Describe gross domestic product (GDP) and its close relative, gross national product (GNP).
2. Explain why a single summary measure like GDP cannot accurately quantify human well-being.
3. Discuss what GDP leaves out, including household production and leisure.
4. Discuss other data that could be used to describe human well-being, such as health, longevity, education, leisure time, and freedom.
5. Detail several more complex alternative measures that have been suggested, such the Human Development Index (HDI) and lifetime GDP measures.
6. Present ideas for the holistic analysis of human welfare in the next chapter.

2.1 Real GDP Per Capita

Simon Kuznets (1966), the Nobel Prize-winning economist who played a major role in developing national income accounting, wrote that economic growth "is a sustained increase in per capita or per worker product."[2] A similar definition is suggested by the economic historians Douglass North and Robert Paul Thomas (1973): "Economic growth occurs if output grows faster than population."[3] Indeed, economists most often measure economic growth in terms of *real income per capita* or *real output per capita*.

Development economists have long discussed the shortcomings of standard macroeconomic measures of income and output. Yet, economists continue to use the readily available data on gross domestic product (GDP) and national income to describe and analyze economic development and development policies. Students of economics see few alternative development indicators being used in published economic analysis. This first section looks at this standard measure of economic development in detail so that you can judge its legitimacy for yourself.

2.1.1 Gross domestic product (GDP)

The *MIT Dictionary of Modern Economics* defines **economic development** as:

> The process of improving the standard of living and well-being of the population of developing countries by raising per capita income.[4]

This definition is compatible with the orthodox practice of defining economic development as an increase in **GDP per capita**. The reference to the standard of living does not really expand the definition of economic development because elsewhere in the same dictionary, the **standard of living** is defined as:

> The level of material well-being of an individual or household. In economic analysis, the standard of living is usually held to be determined by the quantities of goods and services... consumed.[5]

The concepts of economic development and GDP per capita appear to be caught in circular reasoning: economic development is defined as the growth in GDP per capita, and the growth of GDP per capita is assumed to imply an improvement in the standard of living.

The popularity of GDP as a measure of human welfare is in part due to the fact that GDP data is readily available. National accounting measures like GDP

---

[2] Simon Kuznets (1966), p. 1.
[3] Douglass C. North and Robert Paul Thomas (1973), p. 1.
[4] *The MIT Dictionary of Modern Economics* (1986), Cambridge, MA: MIT Press, p. 119.
[5] *The MIT Dictionary of Modern Economics* (1986), op. cit., p. 400.

are compiled by all countries' official statistical agencies in accordance with standardized procedures developed over the past 50 years by various working groups under the auspices of the United Nations. These procedures have helped to standardize economic data from around the world. However, not all countries' GDP data are accurate. It is costly to gather information, and shortcuts are often taken. Some governments intentionally distort their data.

It is important to note that GDP's widespread use as an indicator of national welfare is not only due to its availability and convenience. GDP is also used by economists because it is compatible with how orthodox economics models human welfare. GDP can be derived from some basic assumptions of the neoclassical economic model.

Orthodox economists usually assume that people have well-defined and stable **individual welfare functions** in which an individual i's welfare, w_i, is a function of the products consumed, such as

$$w_i = f_i(x_1, x_2, \ldots, x_n) \tag{2.1}$$

in the case of n products, denoted as x_1 through x_n.

Orthodox economics makes even stronger assumptions when it builds an aggregate welfare function to quantify society's well-being. A standard version of such a **social welfare function** for a population of k individuals is assumed to be equal to the sum of all individual welfare functions. The total aggregate welfare of all k individuals, W, is thus written as:

$$W = \sum_{i=1}^{k} w_i \tag{2.2}$$

Economic analysis uses this type of function of total, or *social*, welfare to find the most efficient allocation of products among people by solving for the maximun W subject to specific supplies of the economy's n products $x_1, x_2, \ldots$, and x_n. In short, this model assumes that when people consume more, they become better off. This social welfare function can also be used to estimate the marginal gain in social welfare from increasing the availability of one or more of the n products.

In practice, products can only be compared in terms of their monetary values, calculated as quantity times price. Individual welfare is thus quantified as the sum of the money values of the products each individual consumes:

$$w_i = p_1 x_1 + p_2 x_2 + \ldots + p_n x_n = \sum_{j=1}^{n} p_j x_j, \tag{2.3}$$

where p_j is the price of good j.

In addition to the assumption that there are n goods, suppose there are k people in the population. Then the total welfare of society, or total **social**

welfare, can be conveniently calculated as the sum of the values of all n products consumed by each of the k people in the total population:

$$W = \sum_{i=1}^{k} \left(\sum_{j=1}^{n} p_j x_j \right) \qquad (2.4)$$

This is fundamentally how we define GDP: the sum value of all goods and services produced in the economy. Per capita GDP is thus W divided by the total population, or

$$W/k = \left[\sum_{i=1}^{k} \left(\sum_{j=1}^{n} p_j x_j \right) \right] /k \qquad (2.5)$$

Nearly all economists implicitly accept GDP as a useful measure for quantifying the level of economic development. The popularity of GDP is evidenced by how often GDP per capita is used in economic research and teaching.

2.1.2 GDP versus GNP

Gross national product (GNP) is frequently used in place of gross domestic product (GDP). A country's gross *national* product (GNP) measures the value of output produced by the citizens and domestically-owned factors of production, regardless of the country in which the production actually takes place. Thus, that part of domestic output produced in a foreign-owned factory is added to the foreign country's GNP and is excluded from the GNP of the country where the factory is located. Gross *domestic* product (GDP), on the other hand, measures the total value of output within a country's borders regardless of the nationality of the owners of the factors of production. In our global economy, in which the share of productive assets owned by foreigners continues to increase in almost every country, the differences between GDP and GNP have become larger. GDP has become the more often-used measure of output for the simple reason that it is easier to keep track of activity within a certain geographic area than it is to accurately allocate the value of the activity within a country to specific productive factors and company owners classified according to their nationality.

2.1.3 Adjusting for price differences

Statisticians have struggled for decades to accurately account for price changes when calculating GDP. They normally use **price indices**, which are weighted averages of the prices of representative samples of goods and services consumed or produced in a country, to convert **nominal GDP** to **real GDP**. Production and consumption patterns depend on levels of income, country size, culture, geographic location, and many other factors unique to individual countries and time periods. Price indices, therefore, differ across countries, and international comparisons of GDP are likely to be biased.

Historical time-series of price indices tend to *overstate* inflation because price indices are usually calculated for constant samples of goods and services. Such unchanging samples fail to reflect (1) the substitution of cheaper products for more expensive products as relative prices change and (2) changes in consumption patterns as the economy grows and incomes rise, and (3) improvements in product quality and performance.[6]   An overstatement of inflation causes estimates of real GNP or GDP to understate real output growth.

Comparisons of countries' real per capita GNP or GDP are also distorted by the common practice of translating different countries' real measures into a common currency using nominal exchange rates. For example, when comparing the GDPs of Uruguay and Argentina, the GDPs stated in each national currency are normally converted to U.S. dollars so that both countries' figures are expressed in the same unit of account. Obviously, it would make little sense to compare Uruguay's per capita GDP in Uruguayan pesos with Argentina's per capita GDP denominated in Argentinian pesos, since the two currencies do not have the same purchasing power. But, putting all national figures into a common currency like the U.S. dollar introduces a new distortion: exchange rates seldom accurately reflect the relative purchasing power of currencies. Exchange rates are determined by a variety of forces that determine the overall supply and demand of currencies in the foreign exchange markets, and deviations from purchasing power parity are often very large. Also, exchange rates change from day to day, so relative GDPs depend arbitrarily on the day that comparisons are made. When comparing *growth rates* of real GDP or GNP, rather than *levels*, the exchange rate problem is not as serious because growth rates are given in percentage terms and the unit of account does not matter. But, when we compare levels of GDP, which we often do, exchange rates can distort our impression.

2.1.4 Adjusting for purchasing power

The World Bank's *World Development Indicators* data bank provides comparative measures of real per capita gross national product (GNP) for a large number of the world's economies, translated into U.S. dollars using exchange rates and detailed information on what can actually be purchased with each currency, that is, the currency's true purchasing power. Called **purchasing power parity** estimates of GNP, these measures give us a more accurate picture of differences in people's standards of living across countries. For example, in 2003 the World Bank reported that Bangladesh's per capita real GNP not

---

[6] A thorough discussion of the comparability of national accounts is provided by Irving Kravis (1984), who was one of the original designers of the national accounting procedures at the United Nations. See also Oskar Morgenstern's (1950) classic critique of GDP as a growth measure.

adjusted for actual purchasing power of money was $360, which was about one-hundredth of U.S. per capita income of $35,060 in that same year. Adjusting for the real purchasing power of money in each country changes the ratio to just 1 to 20, or $1,720 in Bangladesh to $35,060 in the United States.[7] That is, detailed analysis by the World Bank and others suggested that US$360 converted to Bangladeshi currency would buy a set of goods and services valued at $1,720 in the United States. Either way, the difference in average income between Bangladesh and the United States is staggering, but a factor of 20 seems more reasonable than 100.

In order to compare the growth of per capita real GNP or GDP of different countries or at different times for the same economy, comparable annual measures extending over many years are needed. The first attempt to compile national output measures comparable across both a large set of countries and over a long period of time was the *United Nations International Comparison Project*. This project brought together a team of economists in the late 1960s to compile a data set of GDP for 130 countries covering the post-World War II years. The first data were made available in an article by Irving B. Kravis, Allan Heston, and Robert Summers (1978). There have been several updates prepared by Summers and Heston. These data are called the *Penn World Tables* because they are maintained at the University of Pennsylvania.[8]

Because the Penn Tables' comparable GDP data only extends back to 1950, it does not permit us to analyze the last 200 years of accelerating output growth or for more distant periods of human history. Data compiled by Angus Maddison, already noted in the previous chapter, is more useful for long-term historical analysis. Maddison (2003, 2006) provides estimates of per capita real GDP back to the year 0. Because our holistic approach to economic development suggests that we examine economic development throughout history, Maddison's data is used throughout this book. Maddison states GDP in terms of 1990 U.S. dollars after adjusting for the purchasing power of each country's national currency.

Maddison estimates GDP for periods well before countries actually compiled such data. He draws on research by historians, anthropologists, archaeologists, and other scholars in order to evaluate how people actually lived in different parts of the world throughout history. His data for the post-World War II period are nearly identical to the Penn Tables. His estimates for earlier periods are approximations of what real per capita GDP would have been had governments actually compiled such data. Maddison estimates GDP, not actual human well-being, for the same reasons that statistical agencies of governments today focus on measures such as GDP: it is easier to count material wealth and consumption than to quantify feelings of happiness and life satisfaction.

---

[7] The World Bank (2004), *Selected World Development Indicators 2003*, CD-ROM.
[8] See the latest Penn Tables available online at http://pwt.econ.unpenn.edu.

Table 2.1   Real GDP for the World: Selected Countries and Regions: 0–2003
(1990 purchasing power parity dollars; bold numbers are period highs)

	1	1000	1500	1600	1820	1870	1913	1950	1973	2003
Austria	425	425	707	837	1,218	1,863	3,465	3,706	11,235	21,235
Belgium	450	425	875	976	1,319	2,692	4,120	5,462	12,170	21,205
Denmark	400	400	738	875	1,274	2,003	3,912	6,955	13,945	23,133
Finland	400	400	453	538	781	1,140	2,111	4,253	11,085	20,511
France	473	425	727	841	1,135	1,876	3,485	5,271	13,114	21,861
Germany	408	410	688	791	1,077	1,939	3,648	3,881	11,960	19,144
Greece	500	400	433	483	641	880	1,592	1,915	7,655	13,677
Ireland	-	-	526	615	877	1,775	2,736	3,453	6,867	24,739
Italy	**771**	450	**1,100**	1,100	1,117	1,439	2,564	3,502	10,634	19,150
Netherlands	425	425	761	**1,381**	**1,838**	2,657	4,049	5,996	13,494	21,479
Spain	498	450	661	853	1,008	1,207	2,056	2,189	7,661	17,021
Sweden	400	400	695	824	1,198	1,662	3,096	6,739	13,494	21,555
Switzerland	425	410	632	750	1,090	2,102	4,266	9,064	**18,204**	22,242
U.Kingdom	400	400	714	974	1,706	**3,207**	4,921	6,939	12,025	21,310
All W. Europe	560	427	772	889	1,202	1,960	3,457	4,578	11,417	19,912
Eastern Europe	412	400	496	548	683	937	1,695	2,111	4,988	6,476
Australia	400	400	400	400	518	3,273	5,157	7,412	12,878	23,287
Canada	400	400	400	400	904	1,695	4,447	7,291	13,838	23,236
U.S.	400	400	400	400	1,257	2,445	**5,301**	9,561	16,689	**29,037**
Former USSR	400	400	499	552	688	957	1,488	2,841	6,059	5,397
Argentina	-	-	-	-	-	1,311	3,797	4,987	7,962	7,666
Brazil	-	-	400	428	646	811	839	1,672	3,882	5,563
Mexico	400	400	425	454	759	1,732	1,467	2,365	4,853	7,137
China	450	450	600	600	600	530	552	439	839	4,392
India	450	450	550	550	533	533	673	619	853	2,160
Japan	400	425	500	520	669	737	1,387	1,921	11,434	21,218
Iran	500	**650**	600	-	588	719	1,000	1,720	5,445	5,539
Iraq	500	**650**	600	-	588	719	1,000	1,364	3,753	1,023
Turkey	500	600	600	600	643	825	1,213	1,623	3,477	6,731
Egypt	550	500	475	475	475	649	902	910	1,294	3,034
All Africa	456	425	414	422	420	500	637	890	1,410	1,549
World	461	450	566	596	667	874	1,526	2,111	4,091	6,432

Source: Angus Maddison (2006), Statistical Appendix.

2.1.5 The picture that Maddison's data paint

The high levels of consumption currently enjoyed by most residents of the developed economies of the world are a very recent phenomenon, a reflection of the dramatic economic growth experienced over the past 200 years. Maddison's data, presented in Table 2.1, help us to understand how we arrived at our present economic conditions. The world averages at the bottom of the table were used in drawing part of Figure 1.1 in the previous chapter, which so vividly illustrates the recent explosive rise in per capita GDP. Table 2.1 covers the years 0 through 2003, the latest year for which a consistent 2,000-year set of Maddison's data is available. This long period is broken down into sub-periods that reflect historical breakpoints such as the start of globalization after 1500, the post-Napoleonic period after 1820, the gold standard period after 1870, the start of World War I after 1913, the post-World War II period that began in 1950, and the fall of the Bretton Woods financial regime in 1973.

Table 2.2 Annual percent Growth Rates of Real Per Capita GDP: 0–2003

	0–1000	1000–1500	1500–1820	1820–1870	1870–1913	1913–1950	1950–1973	1973–2003
Austria	-	-	0.17	0.85	1.45	0.18	4.94	2.12
Belgium	-	-	0.17	1.44	1.05	0.70	3.54	1.95
Denmark	-	-	0.17	0.91	1.57	1.56	3.08	1.83
Finland	-	-	0.17	0.76	1.44	1.91	4.25	2.19
France	-	-	0.14	1.01	1.45	1.12	4.04	1.71
Germany	-	-	0.14	1.08	1.66	0.17	5.02	1.60
Italy	-	-	0.00	0.59	1.26	0.85	4.95	2.10
Netherlands	-	-	0.28	0.81	0.90	1.07	3.45	1.83
Spain	-	-	0.13	0.36	1.25	0.17	5.60	2.59
Sweden	-	-	0.17	0.66	1.46	2.12	3.06	1.52
Switzerland	-	-	0.17	1.32	1.66	2.06	3.08	0.72
United Kingdom	-	-	0.27	1.26	1.01	0.93	2.42	1.86
Western.Europe	−0.0	0.13	0.14	0.98	1.33	0.76	4.05	1.88
Eastern Europe	0.0	0.04	0.10	0.63	1.39	0.60	3.81	0.68
United States	-	-	0.36	1.34	1.82	1.61	2.45	1.86
All Latin America	0.0	0.01	0.16	−0.03	1.82	1.56	2.45	1.84
China	0.01	0.06	0.00	−0.25	0.10	−0.62	2.86	5.32
India	0.00	0.04	−0.00	0.00	0.54	−0.22	1.40	3.01
Japan	0.01	0.03	0.09	0.19	1.48	0.88	8.06	2.14
Total Asia	0.00	0.05	0.00	−0.10	0.42	−0.10	2.91	3.55
Total Africa	0.00	−0.01	0.00	0.35	0.57	0.92	2.00	0.19
World	*0.00*	*0.05*	*0.05*	*0.54*	*1.30*	*0.88*	*2.92*	*1.41*

Source: GDP per capita are from Angus Maddison (2006); Growth Rates are from Angus Maddison (2003), Table 8b.

Overall, the growth of world GDP per capita was fastest during the period 1950–1973. 1973–2003 was the second-fastest growth period, albeit growth just half as fast as the prior period. The latest period is often noted for its shift in economic policies towards free markets, privatization, and reduced government regulation. The data suggest this policy shift did not increase economic growth.

There were many differences in growth among individual countries. For example, Japan began to grow only after it abandoned its long isolation from the rest of the world midway through the nineteenth century. The data also show Japan's sharp decline in per capita income right after World War II, followed by several decades of exceptionally rapid growth. A growth rate of about 8 percent per year brought Japan's real per capita income up to the level of the most developed economies of the world, an example of the power of compounding.

Argentina offers a different growth pattern. There are no estimates of real per capita GDP for Argentina before 1870 because it was a sparsely-populated territory for which Maddison could find no data. After 1870, Argentina achieved a world-leading growth rate of 2.5 percent per year. By 1913 its per capita real GDP exceeded that of many European countries. But Argentina's growth of GDP slowed dramatically after 1973.

Table 2.3 Fastest and Slowest Growing Economies
(Average annual percentage growth rates)

1870–1913	1913–1950	1950–1973	1973–2003
Fastest Growing Economies:			
Argentina (2.5%)	Venezuela (5.3%)	Japan (8.0%)	South Korea (6.9)
Canada (2.2%)	Peru (2.1%)	Taiwan (6.2%)	Taiwan (6.2%)
Mexico (2.2%)	Norway (2.1%)	Greece (6.2%)	Thailand (5.3%)
United States (1.8%)	Sweden (2.1%)	Spain (5.6%)	China (5.3%)
Germany (1.6%)	Switzerland (2.1%)	Portugal (5.7%)	Egypt (3.8%)
Slowest Growing Economies:	Burma (−1.3%)	Bangladesh (− 0.6%)	Zaire (− 3.9%)
	China (− 0.3%)	Morocco (0.1%)	Cote d'Ivoire (−2.2%)
	India (− 0.2%)	Ghana (0.2%)	Ethiopia (− 1.7%)
	Philippines (− 0.2%)	Zaire (0.8)	Peru (− 1.7%)
	Korea (− 0.2%)	Chile (1.2%)	Romania (−1.6%)

Source: Angus Maddison (2003).

A closer look at Maddison's estimates suggests that growth performances changed frequently. Table 2.3 lists the five fastest-growing economies for five different historical periods. Several countries appear on both the fastest-growing and slowest-growing lists. Peru's economy grew rapidly in the first half of the twentieth century, but declined over the last decades of the twentieth century. The Chinese and Korean economies improved from their dismal performance in the first half of the century to unprecedented GDP growth in the latter part of the century. Cases of rapid and slow growth occurred in all parts of the world. Note that during 1950–1973 only one country actually experienced negative growth; global economic growth during this period was the highest ever experienced.

2.1.6 Are standards of living becoming more equal?

Table 2.1 suggests that differences between countries' per capita real output levels have been getting bigger over the past 200 years. In 1820, per capita income in the highest income country, the Netherlands, was little more than four times that of the lowest income country for which Maddison provides an estimate, Egypt. There may, of course, have been countries with lower levels of per capita output in 1820, but not enough data is available for reliable estimates for all countries in that year. As in the previous chapter, we can use Lant Pritchett's (1997) estimate that humans cannot survive on per capita real output of less than $250 per year in 1990 prices. Thus, at most, per capita real output in the Netherlands was seven times that of the poorest country of the world in 1820. In 2003, per capita real output adjusted for purchasing parity in the highest income country, the United States, was 72 times that of Sierra Leone, the country with the lowest GDP included in Maddison's (2006) data set.

Table 2.4 Average per Capita Real GDP by Region

A. Levels (1990 U.S. dollars)	1820	1870	1900	1929	1950	1973	2003
Western Europe	1292	2110	3092	4385	5126	12289	17387
Western Offshoots[1]	1205	2440	4022	6653	9255	16075	20850
Southern Europe	804	1108	1572	2153	2021	6015	8287
Eastern Europe	772	1085	1373	1732	2631	5745	4665
Latin America	679	760	1077	1832	2487	4387	4820
Asia	550	580	681	858	765	1801	3252
Africa	450	480	500	660	830	1311	1284
World	651	895	1263	1806	2138	4123	5145
Highest/Lowest Ratio	*2.9*	*5.1*	*8.0*	*10.1*	*11.2*	*12.3*	*16.2*

B. Growth Rates	1820–70	1870–00	1900–29	1929–50	1950–73	1973–03	1820–00	1900–2003	1820–2003
Western Europe	1.0%	1.3%	1.2%	0.7%	3.9%	1.8%	1.1%	*1.9%*	*1.5%*
Western Offshoots[1]	1.4	1.7	1.8	1.5	2.4	1.4	1.5	*1.8*	*1.7*
Southern Europe	0.6	1.2	1.1	−0.3	4.9	1.7	0.8	*1.8*	*1.4*
Eastern Europe	0.7	0.8	0.8	2.0	3.5	−1.1	0.7	*1.3*	*1.1*
Latin America	0.2	1.2	1.8	1.5	2.0	0.5	0.6	*1.6*	*1.1*
Asia	0.1	0.5	0.8	−0.5	3.8	3.2	0.3	*1.7*	*1.0*
Africa	0.1	0.1	1.0	0.9	2.0	−0.1	0.1	*1.0*	*0.6*
World	0.6	1.2	1.2	0.8	2.9	1.4	0.8	*1.5*	*1.2*

Source: Maddison (1995), Table G-3, p. 228; growth rates calculated by the author. See Table 2.1 for the names of the countries included in each group.

[1] Western offshoots include Australia, Canada, New Zealand, and the United States.

Recall from Figure 1.3 in the previous chapter how differences in economic growth rates have caused output per capita to vary greatly across countries over the past two centuries. In Table 2.4, Maddison's estimated growth rates are split according to the major regions of the world. Notice that the ratio of average per capita output in the highest output region, the so-called Western Offshoots, to the lowest, Africa, has risen from just 2.9 in 1820 to over 16 today. This widening of the differences in per capita GDP across countries is referred to as the **divergence** of real per capita output. A narrowing of per capita output differences is called **convergence**. Tables 2.1, 2.2, and 2.4 and the graphic trends in the previous chapter's Figure 1.3 suggest that economic growth over the past 200 years has been diverging, not converging.

Trends over the past several decades are not so clearly divergent, however. A number of economies, such as China, Korea, Chile, and Taiwan, are rapidly converging to the highest per capita levels of GDP. Charles Jones (1997) points out that the proportion of countries with per capita incomes that are converging to the most developed economies, relative to the number of countries that are diverging, has been increasing in recent decades. Furthermore, Jones shows that if we weigh country growth rates according to population size, then average per capita real output in developing economies has been growing at 3.7 percent compared to developed country GDP growth of about 2 percent since 1980. This result reflects the surge in GDP growth of China and India: China, a country with 1.3 billion people, and India, with 1 billion people, together account for one-third of the world's population. Jones also finds, however, that about half of all developing countries exhibited negative rates of per capita income growth in the 1980s and 1990s. Hence, the difference in standards of living gap between the highest-income countries and the lowest-income countries continued to grow.

The great variance in the per capita GDP growth across countries during the past two centuries means that development economists are challenged not only to explain the surge in *average* worldwide GDP growth after 1800, but they must also explain why growth experiences have differed so much across individual countries. Why did Argentina grow so fast and then stagnate? How was Japan able to grow at 8 percent per year after its economy was completely destroyed during World War II? What caused the declines in per capita real GDP in many African countries after 1973? Before we proceed to seek answers to these questions, however, we must ask whether the trends in GDP per capita over the past 200 years accurately reflect how true human welfare has evolved.

2.2 Finding Better Measures of Economic Development

The previous section has already highlighted some of the problems with making GDP and GNP data compatible across countries and time periods. Maddison's data makes use of many diverse bits of evidence on price levels, product quality, and consumption patterns to make his GDP estimates from the past compatible with current GDP numbers and to make each year's estimates compatible across 150 different countries. But, Maddison's many adjustments do not solve other fundamental weaknesses in GDP data.

First of all, GDP does not include all the things that affect human welfare. That is, we need to add more x's to the welfare function in equations 2.3 and 2.4. Also, some of the goods and services included among the x's in equation 2.3 may have a negative effect on welfare, and they should be subtracted from, not added to, a measure intended to serve as an indicator of total well-being. There are a number of further adjustments that can be made to equations 2.3 and 2.4 in order to arrive at a more satisfactory measure.

2.2.1 Household production

It is well known that GDP and GNP do not include all of a country's production. GDP and GNP were designed to provide policymakers with a coherent set of easily available information on the performance of an economy. Speed in compiling the data was of the essence in order to enable policy makers and central banks to react to economic conditions as quickly as possible. It makes little sense for a central bank to design its current monetary policy according to information on how the economy was growing several years ago. For data to be timely, shortcuts must be taken. Specifically included in GDP and GNP are market transactions and the estimated value of shelter provided by the country's stock of housing. Market transactions can be estimated using tax collection data, transportation data, banking data, and firms' accounting records. The value of the housing stock can be found from local tax records, publicly recorded deeds, and real estate records. However, not included in GDP are the services and products produced in the household. This latter information is difficult to collect because it would have to be provided by a very diverse set of household units who keep no formal records of most of their activities. Hence, home-cooked meals, parental childcare, and the tomatoes grown in the community garden for home consumption are not included in GDP.

The omission of household production can cause GDP to differ greatly from the economy's true level of production. For example, in traditional societies, where many women work in the home, men and women tend gardens and small farming plots, many people produce artisan products, and many people assist relatives and friends without immediate remuneration, the total services and products produced in the economy can be undercounted by as much as 25 to 50 percent. Furthermore, the rate of growth of the output in the economy will be distorted if, over time, activities traditionally performed in the household are gradually transferred to the market. For example, as more women have entered the formal labor force over the past century, household tasks such as sewing, food preparation, and the early education of children are increasingly purchased outside the home in the form of ready-made clothing, processed foods, and public and private schools. The latter are counted in GDP where the former household production was not. Hence, market activity substitutes for household production, GDP grows even though the newly measured activity merely substitutes household production.

The Levy Economics Institute has compiled a measure of U.S. economic well-being that includes household production as well as public consumption of public goods (GDP only includes the cost of producing public goods). Edward Wolff, Ajit Zacharias, and Thomas Masterson (2009) use the Levy Institute's measure to estimate that the rate of growth of economic well-being in the United States between 1959 and 2004 was just one-third of the rate suggested by the growth of real GDP per capita. A similar revision of the rate of economic growth may be called for in less developed economies that have undergone major shifts in production from households to market activities.

2.2.2 Accounting for informal production

GDP also fails to count **informal economic activity**, which is production of services and goods outside the normal legal labor and product markets. Obviously illegal services and products like certain drugs and gambling fall into this category. But in most developing economies, informal services and products are perfectly normal and legal products and services that are provided off the record in order to evade taxes, regulations, supervision, licensing fees, or the cost and bother of registering their activities. Informal activities include such things as street selling, maid and childcare services not reported to the tax authorities, small manufacturing plants that do not pay taxes or minimum wages, taxis that have not paid licensing fees, home construction without official building permits, and assorted cash transactions not reported to the tax authorities.

Table 2.5 presents some recent International Labour Office (ILO) estimates of informal activity in developing economies. Informal economic activity is most prevalent in developing countries. It also occurs in developed countries, but the percentages are usually much lower. According to Friedrich Schneider and Dominik Enste (2000), informal activity accounts for up to 15 percent of production in developed economies.

Scott Fuess and your author (1996, 1998) estimated total output including both household and informal activity in the United States and Mexico, respectively. We then used our estimates to recalculate economic growth in these countries. Our estimates show that economic growth between the 1950s and the 1990s was slower than the growth rates of reported GDP. Traditional GDP overstated the growth of output because as economies grow, more economic activity is carried out in the market economy and less is produced in the household and informal sectors of the economy. Thus, GDP erroneously shows an increase in the economy's production when, in fact, some of that new production was merely transferred from households and the informal sector to the formal sector where GDP is measured.

Our adjusted estimates of GDP also confirm that when countries experience sharp recessions, household and informal activity grows relative to the formal sector of the economy. Therefore, in times of recession, the true decline in human production is most likely not as low as the official GDP data suggest. For example, our study of Mexico finds that during the recession following the 1982 debt crisis, true per capita output in Mexico declined by about 1 percent per year, not the 2.5 percent shown in official GDP figures. The recession left more people unemployed, and they engaged in more household production and informal activities such as street selling and odd jobs paid for in cash.

Table 2.5 Informal Economic Activity: Selected Developing Countries 1994/2000

Country	*Informal Workers as % of Able Working-Age Population*		
	All Workers	*Women*	*Men*
North Africa	48	43	49
Algeria	43	41	43
Morocco	45	47	44
Tunisia	50	39	53
Egypt	55	46	57
Sub-Saharan Africa	72	84	63
Benin	93	97	87
Chad	74	95	60
Guinea	72	87	66
Kenya	72	83	59
South Africa	51	58	44
Latin America	51	58	48
Bolivia	63	74	55
Brazil	60	67	55
Chile	36	44	31
Colombia	38	44	34
Costa Rica	44	48	42
El Salvador	57	69	46
Guatemala	56	69	47
Honduras	58	65	74
Mexico	55	55	54
Republica Dominicana	48	50	47
Venezuela	47	47	47
Asia			
India	83	86	83
Indonesia	78	77	78
Philippines	72	73	71
Thailand	51	54	49
Syria	42	35	43

Source: Prepared by Jacques Chames for the ILO (2002), *Statistics on the Informal Economy*, Geneva: ILO.

2.2.3 The value of leisure

GDP measures only market production, which means it fails to account for the value of leisure. If people value an additional hour of leisure more highly than the goods and services they can acquire with their earnings from an additional hour of work, then human welfare rises when people choose to work less. But, because GDP does not count the value of leisure, GDP declines when people opt for more leisure.

The economic historian Robert Fogel (1999) estimated the changes in what he calls **earnwork** and **volwork** in the United States since 1880. Fogel uses these terms in order to avoid misunderstandings about the word *leisure*, which connotes rest and inactivity. Time off from paid work in fact often involves activities such as volunteer work, sports, or home improvement projects. Fogel defines *earnwork* as activity undertaken primarily to earn a living; the second term refers to voluntary leisure activity or rest. As Table 2.6 details, lifetime hours spent on earnwork and volwork have changed drastically in the United States since 1880. Volwork now exceeds earnwork. Earnwork has declined by over 50 percent, and volwork has increased more than fourfold. Volwork increased not only because people reduced their earnwork, but also because longer lifespans give people more years of retirement for doing volwork. Because it omits volwork, GDP presents a distorted picture.

Similar long-run patterns in the amount of leisure time are found for other countries. Table 2.7 shows the annual hours worked for a number of developed and several less developed economies from 1870 to 1998. For many developed economies, annual hours of work fell by as much as 50 percent in little more than one-hundred years. Notice that today's high income countries have fewer work hours than less developed economies, although work hours fell everywhere. This reduction in hours is largely the result of the political acceptance of basic labor standards such as the 8 hour workday and five day workweek.

Table 2.6 Trends in Time Used: The United States, 1880 and 1995

Activity	1880	1995	Activity	1880	1995
Sleep	8	8	Lifetime hours	225,900	298,500
Meals and essential hygiene	2	2	Lifetime earnwork	182,100	122,400
Chores	2	2			
Travel to work	1	1	Lifetime volwork	43,800	176,100
Work	8.5	4.7			
Illness	0.7	0.5			
Subtotal	22.2	18.2			
Residual for leisure	1.8	5.8			

Source: Robert W. Fogel (1999), Tables 2 and 3, pp. 5 and 6.

Table 2.7 Annual Hours Worked Per Person Employed, 1870–1998

Country	1870	1913	1950	1973	1990	1998
Austria	2,935	2,580	1,976	1,778	1,590	1,515
Belgium	2,964	2,605	2,783	1,872	1,638	1,568
Denmark	2,945	2,553	2,283	1,742	1,638	1,664
Finland	2,945	2,588	2,035	1,707	1,668	1,637
France	2,945	2,588	1,926	1,771	1,539	1,503
Germany	2,841	2,584	2,316	1,804	1,566	1,523
Ireland			2,250	2,010	1,700	1,657
Italy	2,886	2,536	1,997	1,612	1,500	1,506
Netherlands	2,964	2,604	2,208	1,751	1,347	1,389
Spain			2,200	2,150	1,941	1,908
Sweden	2,945	2,588	1,951	1,571	1,508	1,582
Switzerland	2,984	2,624	2,144	1,930	1,644	1,595
United Kingdom	2,984	2,624	1,958	1,688	1,637	1,489
Australia	2,945	2,588	1,838	1,708	1,645	1,641
Canada	2,964	2,605	1,967	1,788	1,683	1,663
United States	2,964	2,605	1,867	1,717	1,594	1,610
Japan	2,945	2,588	2,166	2,042	1,951	1,758
Argentina			2,034	1,996	1,850	1,903
Brazil			2,042	2,096	1,879	1,841
Chile			2,212	1,955	1,984	1,974
Mexico			2,154	2,061	2,060	2,073
Peru			2,189	2,039	1,930	1,926
Venezuela			2,179	1,965	1,889	1,931

Source: Angus Madisson (2001), Table E-3, p. 347.

The relationship between human well-being and work is not always negative, however. As Helena Lopes (2011) documents, people often enjoy working, and they "earn" more than wages from being employed. As discussed in the next chapter, research from behavioral economics and psychology shows that unemployment reduces overall human happiness very significantly, and the lost wages are just part of the reason.

2.2.4 Counting the "bads" as well as the goods

One of the most serious shortcomings of conventional GDP data is that some of the things counted as production clearly diminish human welfare. Kenneth Boulding (1966) referred to such production as "bads," as opposed to goods.

An example of such a "bad" is provided by the nineteenth century French economist and writer Frédérique Bastiat. He describes the case where a young man is dismissed by his employer, a local shop. Upon departing, the angry young man heaves a rock through the front window of the shop, shattering the expensive glass pane. An observer on the street declares: "Well, this is a good day for the glazer." And so it was, for the glazer was well paid to repair the window. In fact, French GDP went up by the value of the glass and the glazer's services. That makes little sense, of course, because the day ends with the same window place. The problem, of course, is that the destruction of the glass is not subtracted from GDP. The time spent by the glazer could have been spent actually putting in a window where there had been none before; fixing the destroyed window clearly has an opportunity cost. But conventional GDP measures are not designed to capture all opportunity costs.

There are many modern equivalents of Bastiat's example. Countries spend enormous amounts of money on their militaries, and this entire cost is added to GDP. If the military never does a thing, GDP still goes up by the amount the military and all its equipment costs for the year, and there is no accounting of what could have been accomplished with the labor and other resources taken by military. And, if the military goes to war, destroys another country and its soldiers die, those losses are not deducted from any country's GDP either. On the other hand, if some soldiers return injured and require expensive medical attention for the rest of their lives, GDP increases each year by the cost of the medical care.

Another example of adding bads along with the goods is the case of a person who is diagnosed with diabetes. The doctor advises the patient to go on a strict diet to lose weight instead of prescribing heavy doses of medications. The doctor might even suggest that she stop eating in restaurants where she cannot monitor the content of her food and, instead, buy food in bulk and prepare her own healthy meals. If she ignores the advice and continues to eat her corn-fed beef and caloric desserts at drive-through fast food restaurants, she will likely require ever-increasing doses of expensive drugs to deal with her deteriorating health. In this case, GDP goes up. On the other hand, if she takes the doctor's advice, GDP declines because she eats less, prepares her own meals, and no longer buys the pharmaceutical companies' expensive patented drugs. Indeed, GDP may not always have a positive relationship to human welfare.

2.2.5 Adjusting GDP for environmental costs and benefits

Environmentalists and ecologists argue that GDP is an inaccurate measure of human welfare because it fails to accurately account for the environmental damage caused by the production of goods and services. For example, the production of goods (and bads) uses non-renewable resources as inputs. Also, some production damages the ecosystem and reduces nature's capacity to provide renewable resources and critical life-sustaining services. Some environmental economists contend that GDP should be expanded to include the many goods and services that our natural environment provides, and then any reduction in nature's services can be deducted from such as expanded GDP.

Our natural environment provides us with heat from the sun, fresh water, air, fertile soil, wood from trees, bees for pollination, lakes for fishing, and beautiful scenery, among many more things. Very few of these natural products, so very critical to our human existence, show up in our measures of GDP because they are not provided through markets where they are priced and thus easily countable. A team of environmentalists and economists led by Robert Costanza (1997) estimated the value of nature's services using a variety of methods, such as calculating the cost of replacing nature's services or taking the values of substitutes for what nature provides. They calculated that in 1997 the total value of the goods and services provided by our natural environment was probably between $16 and $54 trillion, an average of $35 trillion, per year. Since measured world GDP for 1997 was about $18 trillion, a full accounting of the value of what nature provides us every year would, on average, about triple our current measure of world GDP.

Some of the benefits provided by the earth's ecosystem do show up in GDP. For example, when property rights are established and someone can charge for water, fish, minerals in the ground, or scenic views, some value of these goods and services of nature does end up in GDP. For example, the iron ore dug up by mining firms who supply the steel industry, the water purchased by a city water company from land owners who hold the water rights, and the payments by farmers to professional beekeepers are counted in GDP. Furthermore, benefits of "natural production" sometimes enter GDP when we explicitly take measures to protect nature's products. When production generates sewage and the government requires the sewage to be treated, the cost of sewage treatment becomes a cost that determines the price of the goods that are included in GDP. The cost of sewage treatment is unlikely to accurately represent the true environmental benefits of sewage treatment, however. The long-run environmental and health benefits from treating sewage can be many times greater than the cost of building and operating the treatment plants.

The wide range of Costanza *et al.*'s estimate of nature's services reflects the difficulty in estimating the real value of nature's services to humanity. Most economists agree, however, that we must do a better job of accounting for nature's services. Our holistic view of economic development clearly mandates taking our natural environment fully into account. Chapter 6 discusses nature's services and the depletion of non-renewable resources in greater detail.

Note that in the adjustments for household production, leisure, informal activity, and nature's services, we are effectively adjusting the number of x's in equation 2.5. The following subsection looks at changing that equation.

2.2.6 Welfare and lifetime consumption

Another weakness of real GDP per capita is that it measures output over some arbitrary brief period of time, usually one calendar year. To understand why an annual number is problematic, suppose two countries have the identical annual per capita real GDP of $10,000, but in one country everyone lived for only 30 years while in the other country everybody lived to the ripe old age of 80. Since GDP only measures output over one year, it effectively suggests that these two countries provide their residents with the same levels of welfare. That is absurd. Individuals normally live longer than one year, and most people judge the value of their lives by what happens to them over their lifetimes, not during just one calendar year. An accurate measure of an economy's capacity to satisfy human wants and provide people with well-being must reflect not only *how much* people have at some moment or period of time, but also *how long* the economy can keep people alive to experience the annual flows of goods and services.

The most direct approach to deriving a measure of lifetime individual welfare is to calculate the product of annual real GDP per capita and average life expectancy. **Life expectancy** in a given country at a given point in time is normally defined as the average age that newborns would reach if they are subject to the age-specific death rates prevailing in that country at the time of birth. Annual real GDP per capita reflects the amount of goods and services that the economy is capable of providing the average person in the year of their birth. The product of the two measures thus represents the economy's capacity in a certain year to (1) provide material welfare and (2) sustain an individual life.

Frank Lichtenberg (1998) defined expected lifetime real per capita GDP as $y_L = y_A \cdot E$, where y_A is average annual per capita GDP, and E is life expectancy. In Van den Berg (2002), I calculated historical series of Lichtenberg's measure for a large number of countries using data from Maddison (2001). I called this multiplicative measure **expected individual lifetime welfare (EILW)**. For example, Table 2.8 shows that the Indian economy in 1998 provided the average person with $1,746 worth of goods and services. Economic and social conditions in India kept the average person alive to enjoy this level of consumption for 60 years. Thus, 1998 Indian EILW was $104,760. In the United States in 1998, the economy provided each resident, on average, with $27,331 worth of goods and services, while economic and social conditions enabled people to live, on average, for 77 years. Thus, U.S. EILW in 1998 was $2,104,487. U.S. annual real GDP per capita was a little less than 16 times as great as that of India, but expected individual lifetime welfare per capita was over 20 times as great because the average American got to enjoy his or her higher annual income for 17 more years than the average Indian got to enjoy his or her lower real per capita GDP.

Table 2.8 shows that the growth of EILW was faster than real GDP per capita growth in *all* countries. In the case of China, EILW growth was positive during the period 1900–1950 even though real per capita GDP shrank. The rigid communist regime did not raise per capita GDP much before 1980, but health and life expectancy improved rapidly. In the case of India, EILW growth was nearly twice as fast as real per capita GDP growth. Only in Russia during 1950–1998 did EILW growth differ little from real per capita GDP growth; Russia experienced virtually no improvement in life expectancy over this period.

Table 2.8 Expected Individual Lifetime Welfare (EILW): Levels and Growth Rates — 1820–1998

A. Levels:

	Annual Real GDP per Capita				Life Expectancy at Birth				EILW			
	1820	1900	1950	1998	1820	1900	1950	1998	1820	1900	1950	1998
France	1,230	2,849	5,270	19,558	37	47	65	78	5,101	33,903	342,550	1,525,524
Germany	1,058	3,134	3,881	17,799	41	47	67	77	43,378	47,298	260,027	1,370,523
Italy	1,117	1,746	3,502	17,759	30	43	66	78	33,510	75,078	231,132	1,385,202
Nether.	1,821	3,533	5,996	20,224	32	52	72	78	58,272	183,716	431,712	1,577,472
Spain	1,063	2,040	2,397	14,227	28	35	62	78	29,764	71,400	148,614	1,109,706
Sweden	1,198	2,561	6,738	18,685	39	56	70	79	46,722	143,416	471,660	1,476,115
U.K.	1,707	4,593	6,907	18,714	40	50	69	77	68,280	229,650	476,583	1,440,978
U.S.	1,257	4,096	9,561	27,331	39	47	68	77	49,023	192,512	650,148	2,104,487
Japan	669	1,135	1,926	20,413	34	44	61	81	22,746	49,940	117,486	1,653,453
Russia	689	1,023	2,834	3,893	28	32	65	67	19,292	32,736	184,210	260,831
Brazil	740	704	1,672	5,459	27	36	45	67	19,980	25,344	75,240	365,753
Mexico	760	1,157	2,365	6,655	-	33	50	72	-	38,181	118,250	479,160
China	600	540	439	3,117	-	24	41	71	-	12,960	17,999	221,307
India	531	625	619	1,746	21	24	32	60	11,151	15,000	19,808	104,760
World	667	1,263	2,114	5,709	26	31	49	66	17,342	39,153	103,586	376,794

B. Annual Growth Rates:

	Per Capita Real GDP			Years of Life Expectancy at Birth			EILW		
	1820–00	1900–50	1950–98	1820–00	1900–50	1950–98	1820–00	1900–50	1950–98
France	1.06%	1.24%	2.77%	0.30%	0.65%	0.37%	1.36%	2.17%	1.90%
Germany	1.37	0.43	3.22	0.17	0.71	0.28	1.54	1.14	3.52
Italy	0.56	1.40	3.44	0.45	0.86	0.34	1.01	2.31	3.80
Nether.	0.83	1.06	2.57	0.61	0.65	0.16	1.45	1.72	2.74
Spain	0.82	0.32	3.78	0.28	1.15	0.48	1.10	1.48	4.28
Sweden	0.95	1.95	2.15	0.45	0.45	0.25	1.41	2.41	2.41
U.K.	1.24	0.82	2.10	0.28	0.65	0.22	1.53	1.47	2.33
U.S.	1.49	1.71	2.21	0.23	0.74	0.25	1.72	2.46	2.48
Japan	0.66	1.06	5.04	0.32	0.66	0.58	0.99	1.73	5.66
Russia	0.50	2.05	0.66	0.17	1.42	0.06	0.66	3.52	0.73
Brazil	−0.06	1.75	2.50	0.36	0.45	0.82	0.30	2.20	3.35
Mexico	0.53	1.44	2.18		−0.83	0.76	-	2.29	2.96
China	−0.13	−0.41	4.17		−1.08	1.13	-	0.66	5.37
India	0.20	0.00	2.18	0.17	0.58	1.29	0.37	0.56	3.53
World	0.80	1.04	2.09	0.22	0.92	0.61	1.02	1.96	2.73

Sources: Angus Maddison (2001), Table 1-5a, Table B-21; Because Maddison (2001) does not have per capita real GDP for 1900, we used Angus Maddison (1995), Table D, which, in most cases, corresponds to Maddison (2001); the few differences were not judged to be significant.

The growth of economies' capacity to provide *both* more things every year as well as a longer life span within which to enjoy the annual flow of goods and services seems to strengthen the conclusions provided by Maddison's per capita GDP estimates, namely that human welfare has surged ahead over the past 200 years. Note, however, that EILW is just a variation on per capita GDP. In terms of the notation used in equation (2.5) *expected individual lifetime welfare* defines average per capita real welfare as annual GDP multiplied by life expectancy E:

$$(W \cdot E)/k = \left\{ \left[\sum_{i=1}^{k} \left(\sum_{j=1}^{n} p_j x_j \right) \right] \cdot E \right\} /k \tag{2.6}$$

EILW measures the economy's combined capacity to produce a year's worth of goods and services, multiplied by the number of years that the economy is able to keep the average person born in that year alive to enjoy the output.

There are some possible extensions and refinements of the EILW that should be pursued. For example, the *Disability Adjusted Life Expectancy* (DALE) data published by the World Health Organization (WHO), which measures the number of years that a person is "healthy and in full possession of his or her mental and physical capabilities," is probably a better measure with which to measure a person's lifetime welfare than simple life expectancy. However, the WHO has only compiled this measure for a few years, so it is not yet possible to construct a long time-series. The EILW could also be adjusted for other shortcomings of GDP by accounting for leisure, informal activity, and the contributions of nature to human welfare. More broadly, it would be interesting to account for economic growth's relationship to the natural environment within the lifetime focus of the EILW, since climate change and specie extinctions have accelerated to where changes in the natural environment are becoming very noticeable over one person's lifetime.

2.2.7 Adjusting for variety

More troublesome for measures such as GDP is the likelihood that individual welfare is not a simple sum of x's in a function such as equation 2.3. For one thing, how much one product adds to our welfare depends on what other products we consume. Hence, the welfare function is probably not linear.

The Federal Reserve Bank of Dallas (1999) points out that GDP fails to measure the value of variety. Because GDP is a measure of aggregate output, a simple sum of products consumed, it effectively assumes that it makes no difference for your welfare whether you eat the same $5.75 lunch consisting of a hamburger, French fries, and a soda every day of the week or you eat the $5.75 hamburger only on Monday, a $4.50 Mexican taco platter on Tuesday, a $4.00 spaghetti dish on Wednesday, a $5.00 Chinese tofu stir fry on Thursday, and a $9.50 Japanese sushi lunch on Friday. In reality, even though the value of the five lunches is $28.75 in either case, the five different meals most likely provide greater welfare than the identical hamburger platter every day of the week. "Variety is the spice of life."

The value of variety is an important consideration when studying long-run economic development. Since the Industrial Revolution, production has become more standardized. For example, clothes were increasingly made on assembly lines in factories according to a limited number of patterns rather than custom tailored to each consumer's precise measurements and choices of cloth, design, quality, etc. Food was increasingly processed in large plants that produced standardized portions and flavors. Of course, the economies of scale that characterize industrialization also resulted in greatly decreased costs of production, and manufactured clothing and prepared food products could be purchased with smaller and smaller fractions of family incomes. Henry Ford was rightfully praised for drastically reducing the cost of mass-producing automobiles, making them affordable to the average U.S. consumer. But he was criticized for giving consumers "any color they want as long as it is black." If variety is important to people, it is very well possible that the increases in real per capita output brought about by industrialization *overstates* the actual gains in human welfare. In the future, perhaps modern programmable machinery can reverse the trend in uniformity of design and the loss of variety.

It should also be noted that more variety and more choices do not always increase human welfare. Too much choice may worsen human welfare by making transactions more complicated. More choices require the evaluation of more information, and there is an increased risk of making a bad choice. Beginning marketing courses often present the case in which shoe salespeople are instructed to avoid showing a customer more than two pairs of shoes at a time because too much choice increases the likelihood that the customer becomes confused and buys nothing. A recent study by two psychologists shows that people buy less candy and jelly when the choice for those items increases in the supermarket.[9] Perhaps people's fear of making a mistake comes into play; numerous psychological studies have found that, all other things equal, people are risk averse.[10]

There are likely to be other types of interrelationships among the x's in the welfare function, further suggesting that the welfare function is not linear as in the case of equation 2.3. For example, the enjoyment of eating pizza may depend on how much beer is consumed along with the pizza. An automobile is of little value if we have no gasoline. Microeconomics has developed models that analyze the effect on prices when two different products are *substitutes* or *complements*, that is, when an increase in the consumption of one product diminishes or enhances, respectively, the value of the other product.

In sum, not only are the x's on the right hand side of the equation interdependent, but, as the discussion of nature's services, leisure, and household production makes clear, there is also substantial uncertainty about the x's that should be included. The next section begins to examine alternative measures of human welfare that have been suggested.

---

[9] Barry Schwartz (2004), "Nation of Second Guesses," *New York Times*, January 22.
[10] See, for example, Cass Sunstein (2005).

2.3 Beyond Adjustment: New Measures of Economic Development

Table 2.9 presents several alternative indicators that most people would agree are important for the **quality of life** in a country. Included are life expectancy at birth, the infant mortality rate, the adult literacy rate, the percentage of children who attend primary and secondary school, and the percentage of the population that uses the Internet.

At first sight, the alternative measures in Table 2.9 appear to give us a picture that is not that much different from that provided by Maddison's GDP estimates, which are also shown in Table 2.9. Between 1973 and 2003, life expectancy rose, infant mortality fell, school enrollment rose, and literacy improved. For the most part, these measures also varied as expected depending on countries' per capita income levels. This suggests that GDP may not be such a bad summary measure of human well-being. On closer inspection, however, the variations in infant mortality rates, life expectancies, and years of schooling do not exactly parallel GDP. Many Eastern European economies have quality of life measures that exceed those of countries with higher per capita real GDPs. Perhaps some of the Eastern European economies are not as poor as their lower real GDPs per capita suggest. You can no doubt find other discrepancies between countries' GDP rankings and the other measures of the quality of life in Table 2.9.

2.3.1 Improvements in human health

10,000 years ago in the primitive hunter-gatherer societies, about half of all children died before reaching the age of five. As late as the 1500s, one quarter to one-third of all children died before reaching the age of five in countries that are highly developed today, such as England, Sweden, and Switzerland.[11] Very few countries have infant mortality rates over 100 per thousand births today. Overall, worldwide infant mortality is about 50 per 1,000 births, one-tenth the level of the pre-agricultural world before 10,000 BCE and one-fifth the level in the most advanced countries just 200 years ago.

Life expectancy was between 20 and 30 years from prehistoric times until about 1500. For example, George Acsadi and J. Nemeskeri (1970) used skeletal remains from northern Egypt to conclude that during the Neolithic period (6,000-3,000 BCE), life expectancy at birth was 21 years. John Hatcher's (1986) data on the lives of Benedictine monks in Canterbury, England during the period 1395–1505 shows that their average life expectancy was just 22 years.[12] In the mid-1700s, life expectancy in London was still just 25 years.[13]

---

[11] From evidence presented in Kenneth Hill (1995).

[12] Many studies on life expectancy are discussed in Samuel H. Preston (1995).

[13] Theodore Dalrymple (1999), "Taking Good Health for Granted," *Wall Street Journal*, March 31.

Table 2.9 Some Alternative Measures of the Quality of Life

	Per Capita Real GDP 1990US$ 2003	Life Expectancy (years) 1973	Life Expectancy (years) 2003	Infant Mortality (Deaths per 1,000) 1970	Infant Mortality (Deaths per 1,000) 2003	Adult Literacy (%) 2003	School Enrolment 2003 % Prim.	School Enrolment 2003 % Sec.	Internet Users (per 1,000) 2003
Austria	21,235	71	79	26	4	99	90	89	4
Belgium	21,205	71	79	21	4	99	100	97	386
Denmark	23,133	74	77	14	3	99	100	96	541
Finland	20,511	71	79	13	4	99	100	95	534
France	21,861	72	80	18	4	99	98	94	366
Germany	19,144	71	79	22	4	99	83	88	473
Italy	19,150	72	80	30	4	99	100	91	337
Netherlands	21,479	74	78	13	5	99	99	89	522
Norway	26,033	74	79	13	3	99	100	96	346
Sweden	21,555	75	80	11	3	99	100	100	-
Switzerland	22,242	74	81	15	4	99	99	87	398
United Kingdom	21,310	72	78	18	5	99	100	95	-
Australia	23,287	72	80	17	6	99	97	88	567
Canada	23,236	73	80	19	5	99	100	98	-
New Zealand	17,564	72	79	17	5	99	100	97	526
United States	29,037	72	77	20	7	99	92	88	556
South European Countries									
Greece	13,677	72	78	24	5	91	99	86	150
Ireland	24,739	71	78	20	6	99	96	83	317
Portugal	13,807	68	77	53	4	93	100	85	-
Spain	17,021	73	80	27	4	98	100	96	239
Turkey	6,731	57	69	150	33	90	86	42	85
East European Countries									
Bulgaria	6,278	71	72	28	14	98	90	88	206
Czech Republic	9,728	70	76	21	4	99	87	91	308
Hungary	7.947	69	73	36	7	99	91	94	232
Poland	7,674	71	74	32	6	99	98	83	232
Romania	3,510	69	71	46	18	97	89	81	184
Russia	6,323	70	65	29	16	99	90	-	-
Ukraine	3,547	70	66	22	15	98	100	69	-
Latin American Countries									
Argentina	7,666	67	74	59	17	95	94	81	-
Brazil	5,563	63	71	95	33	88	97	75	-
Chile	10,950	63	78	78	8	96	85	81	272
Colombia	5,228	62	72	69	18	94	87	55	53
Mexico	7,137	62	75	79	23	90	99	63	120
Peru	4,007	56	70	115	26	88	100	69	104
Venezuela	6,988	66	73	47	18	93	91	59	60

Table 2.9 (Continued)

	Per Capita Real GDP 1990US$ 2003	Life Expectancy (years) 1973	2003	Infant Mortality (Deaths per 1,000) 1970	2003	Adult Literacy (%) 2003	School Enrolment 2003 % Prim.	Sec.	Internet Users (per 1,000) 2003
Asian Countries									
Bangladesh	939	45	63	145	46	41	84	45	2
Myanmar	1,896	50	60	122	76	90	84	35	1
China	4,392	63	72	85	30	91	97	-	63
India	2,160	50	63	127	63	61	87	-	99
Indonesia	3,555	49	67	104	31	88	92	54	38
Iran	5,539	55	70	122	33	77	86	-	72
Japan	21,218	82	83	14	3	99	100	101	483
Malaysia	8,468	63	73	46	7	89	93	70	344
Pakistan	1,881	52	63	120	81	49	59	-	-
Philippines	2,536	58	70	60	27	93	94	59	-
South Korea	15,732	69	77	43	5	98	100	88	610
Syria	7,698	57	73	90	16	83	98	43	35
Thailand	7,195	61	70	74	23	93	85	-	111
Viet Nam	2,147	50	70	55	19	90	94	65	43
African Countries									
Cote d'Ivoire	1,230	50	46	158	117	48	61	21	14
Egypt	3,034	52	70	157	33	56	91	81	44
Ethiopia	711	44	48	160	112	42	51	18	1
Ghana	1,360	50	57	111	59	54	59	36	-
Kenya	998	54	47	96	79	74	67	25	-
Morocco	2,910	53	70	119	36	51	90	36	33
Niger	518	38	44	197	154	14	38	6	-
Nigeria	1,349	43	43	140	90	67	67	29	6
South Africa	4,311	54	49	-	53	82	89	68	44
Uganda	850	51	47	100	81	69	53	17	5

Sources: Maddison (2006); United Nations (2005), *Human Development Report 2005*, Tables 1, 10, 12, and 13.

After virtually no improvement for thousands of years, suddenly, after about 1750 or 1800, life expectancy grew rapidly. It tripled over the past 200 years. You should be able to envision a diagram of life expectancy that looks very similar to that of Figure 1.1, consisting of a horizontal path stretching over thousands of years and then, suddenly, shooting up during the last two centuries.

The data in Tables 2.9 and 2.10 suggest a direct relationship between per capita real output and the level of health after 1800. The direct relationship between per capita real output and health has been confirmed by many authors using statistical methods. In one such study, Lant Pritchett and Lawrence Summers (1996) summarized their results in their title: "Wealthier is Healthier."

The same forces that led to the economy's ability to produce more goods and services also led to improvements in nutrition, medicine, and hygiene.

Table 2.10 Life Expectancy: 1750–2000

Country:	1750	1800	1850	1900	1950	2000
Australia	n.a.	n.a.	49a	55	70	80
England(U.K.)	37	37	40	47	69	78
France	28	34	40	47	66	80
India	n.a.	n.a.	n.a.	24	n.a.	63
Japan	n.a.	n.a.	35	44	59	82
Mexico	n.a.	n.a.	n.a.	33b	n.a.	75
Netherlands	n.a.	32	37	50	72	78
Sweden	37	37	43	54	71	80
Russia	n.a.	n.a.	28a	32	64	65
United States	n.a.	n.a.	42	47	77	77

a) 1880; b) 1930. Sources: Maddison (1995), Table 1.7, p. 27 and United Nations, Human Development Report 2005 (2006), Washington, D.C., Table 1, pp. 219–222; Also, Table 4.1 from Massimo Livi-Bacci (1997), p. 121.

2.3.2 The relationship between output growth and health

The improvement in health is a result of the same technological progress and institutional changes that caused per capita output to begin growing so rapidly after 1800. Health has improved because the application of the scientific method led to better medical practices. According to one physician, "The principle of the controlled trial of treatments is one of the most momentous discoveries of our age, which has revolutionized medicine and for the first time turned therapeutics into a genuine science."[14] The scientific method led doctors to stop using ineffective techniques like bloodletting to reduce fever or prescribing deadly arsenic to treat asthma when monitored experiences made it clear that such treatments did not work. As a result, many major human diseases like smallpox, polio, and tuberculosis have been eliminated. The scientific research that led to the development of antibiotics has greatly reduced deaths from infections, which were the leading cause of death before the twentieth century.

The advances in medicine over the past 100 years are exemplified by the death of President Garfield of the United States after being shot in 1881. Had he lived in the second half of the twentieth century, Garfield would almost certainly not have died from his gunshot wound. In the nineteenth century, the best medical experts could not agree on where the bullet had lodged in his body. There were no X-rays or any other means to see inside a person's body. Exploratory surgery had not yet been developed as a viable medical option. As the country's leading doctors could not figure out what to do, Garfield

---

[14] Theodore Dalrymple (1999), op. cit.

developed a severe infection, which also could have been dealt with using antibiotics today. Garfield died from infection three months after being shot.

Human health also benefited from economic development. For example, David Landes (1999) explains how the introduction of cotton clothing to Europe improved personal cleanliness and, thereby, reduced the incidence of gastrointestinal infection, another one of the major causes of death before 1800. In pre-industrial northern Europe, most people wore wool underwear. Woolens, as underwear was generally called in England, were difficult to wash, and this led to uncleanliness and the spread of germs. Only the wealthy could afford easier-to-wash linen underwear, although the soap for washing clothing was not very effective.

The Industrial Revolution in the late eighteenth and early nineteenth centuries made cotton clothing available at reasonable prices. Improved transportation and international trade gave Europeans access to raw cotton, which was grown in warm climates. The development of large-scale industrial production, in turn, greatly reduced the cost of converting raw cotton into cloth and, subsequently, into underwear. Cotton clothing was much easier to wash than woolens. At the same time, the Industrial Revolution also brought better and cheaper soap with which to clean the more washable cotton. The improved technologies for producing and transporting goods caused the frequency of gastrointestinal infection to fall and life expectancy to rise.

David Cutler and Grant Miller (2004) found that the sharp decline in mortality rates that the United States experienced during the late nineteenth and early twentieth centuries was largely due to clean water technologies such as better delivery systems, filtration, and chlorination. After examining all the relevant changes that might have influenced the mortality declines, they conclude that "clean water was responsible for nearly half of the total mortality reduction in major cities, three-quarters of the infant mortality reduction, and nearly two-thirds of the child mortality reduction."[15] New medicines, medical procedures, and health services played a secondary, albeit substantial, role.

Public investment in infrastructure such as water systems and the public administration of the technologies used in these investments such as filtration and chlorination are integral components of the process of economic development. Peter Temin (2006) makes these points when he compares life in the Roman Empire with life during the Dark Ages in Europe after the fall of Rome. The Dark Ages were a period characterized by fragmented political jurisdictions, declines in education and literacy, and less scope for collective government action on a large scale. He notes that after the fall of Rome, the planning that had created elaborate infrastructure projects to bring fresh water to cities and to carry sewage out of the cities was often abandoned. Temin (2006, p. 149) concludes that the "economic growth that resulted in the prosperity of

---

[15] David Cutler and Grant Miller (2004), abstract of the paper.

the early Roman Empire... was not to be equaled in the West for almost two millennia thereafter."

These historical examples illustrate the importance of social and political institutions. The fall of the Roman Empire led to the deterioration of the social and political institutions that had made possible the organization of large-scale infrastructure projects, education systems, and personal security that enhanced human life. Recent improvements in health and life expectancy, similarly were the result of an improvement of humanity's ability to organize collective government actions and policies to address complex issues such as sanitation, education, and infrastructure.

2.3.3 Life expectancy and life's order

The improvement in health affects human welfare in several ways. Recall that the rationale behind our measure of expected individual lifetime welfare (EILW) was that increased life expectancy raises the average amount of time that people get to enjoy life. Longer life expectancy may also enhance human well-being in more subtle ways.

The rise in life expectancy documented over the past several centuries reflects primarily reductions in infant mortality and the discovery of remedies for diseases that attacked people of all ages. Economic development and medical advances did not increase the maximum life span for humans. A few people lived to the age of one-hundred in ancient times. Rather, economic development has enabled a much higher percentage of people to live until old age. The lower likelihood of dying prematurely constitutes a gain in human welfare. According to Frank Lichtenberg (1998):

> People tend to live longer than they used to, and there is also less uncertainty about the age of death... If people are risk averse, they are made better off by the reduction in the variance, as well as by the increase in the mean, of the age at death.

The demographer Massimo Livi-Bacci (1997) described the reductions in infant mortality and the medical remedies as adding "order" to life. This order fed back into economic growth because the reduction of mid-life death rates made it less likely that investments in education and work experience would be lost. People became more long-run oriented because they could plan their lives much more efficiently. Longer lives also give people more time to correct for bad decisions, and there are more second chances to grasp missed opportunities.

2.3.4 Education, technology, and what else?

Education is closely correlated with economic development because it adds to the economy's stock of **human capital**, that portion of an individual's productive capacity which is acquired after birth. Human capital is created through family upbringing, formal education, and life experience. In a modern economy, education is important for human productivity because the amount of knowledge needed to function in a modern economy is very large. Today, most people remain in school for at least twelve years before entering the labor force.

Education is more than a productive resource, however. Education itself contributes to human welfare because educated people live more rewarding lives. It can be argued that educated people have a better understanding of their options, and they, therefore, make better choices and achieve more valued economic and social outcomes. Measures of educational achievement are thus good measures of human welfare. Measures of educational opportunity can serve as indicators of future welfare improvements.

Table 2.9 also shows the spread of the Internet. Later chapters will highlight the importance of technology for living standards. One of the most popular and useful models of economic development distinguishes technological progress as the fundamental driving force of economic development.

Beyond the health, education, and technology variables presented in Table 2.9, many other important determinants of human welfare have been suggested. For example, Amartya Sen (1999, pp. 358–359) argues "in favor of judging individual advantage in terms of the respective capabilities, which the person has, to live the way he or she has reason to value." This suggests that personal freedom to decide what to consume, where to work, where to live, and how to conduct one's life in general are important for human welfare.

To test the hypothesis of a positive relationship between personal freedom and personal welfare, we need to be explicit about what we mean by freedom. It is not easy to quantify personal freedom. Some studies have focused on political freedom, which is the ability people have to participate in the political process. Others have focused on social freedom and **civil rights**, which give people the freedom to shape their own lifestyle. Finally, there is **economic freedom**, which includes the freedom to choose where and how much to work, what and how much to consume, and what to accumulate for future use.

Sen specifically argues that personal freedom is dependent on economic development because without income and some level of wealth, people are not free to make choices. A hungry person can more easily be forced to accept undesirable economic, social, or political conditions than a well-endowed and economically secure person. This close link between human rights and economic rights was recognized in the **Universal Declaration of Human Rights**, unanimously signed by all United Nations members in 1948. Given equal weight in the *Declaration* are, for example, Article 1, "All human beings are born free and equal in dignity and rights," Article 5, "No one shall be subjected to torture or to cruel, inhuman or degrading treatment of punishment," Article 17, "Everyone has the right to own property alone as well as in association with others," and Article 25, "Everyone has the right to a **standard**

of living adequate for the health and well-being of himself and of his family, including food, clothing, housing and medical care and necessary social services, and the right to security in the event of unemployment, sickness, disability, widowhood, old age or other lack of livelihood in circumstances beyond his control."

2.3.5 The Human Development Index

In recognition of the shortcomings of GDP as a measure of human well-being and the need for a broader-based measure, the United Nations Development Programme (UNDP) has for over three decades annually published its composite **Human Development Index** (HDI). The HDI is a weighted average of (1) real per capita income, (2) life expectancy, (3) the literacy rate, and (4) school enrollment rates. The weights of the four components of the index change with the level of real per capita income, however. Before the UNDP revised its methodology in 1999, the UNDP gave increases in per capita real output substantial weight only for low income countries. The UNDP assumed that the relationship between income and welfare looks like the solid "kinked" line in Figure 2.1, where increases in per capita GDP up to the world average of about $5,000 have a strong effect on human welfare, but after a per capita GDP of $5,000 was reached further increases in output were assumed to matter very little for human welfare. Thus, the huge difference in per capita real output between Japan and Brazil mattered almost nothing for the two countries' HDI indices, but the difference between the average per capita GDP of Brazil and Sierra Leone did matter a lot for those two countries' relative HDI rankings.

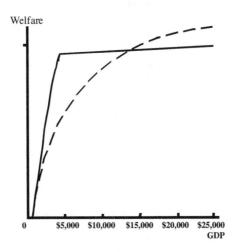

Figure 2.1 Welfare and GDP according to the United Nations HDI

In 1999, the UNDP assumed the more "curved" relationship between income and welfare in weighing real per capita income in the HDI illustrated by the dashed line in Figure 2.1. This change was in response to arguments such as Amartya Sen's that a rising per capita GDP provides not just more material things, but it also provides more choices, better health, more education, and a more secure life. The revised HDI index still assumed that the marginal effect on human welfare of increasing income is diminishing.

Table 2.11 lists the countries listed in the top 10 and bottom 10 of the 2010 HDI. Contrast the HDI ranking with the simple GDP per capita rankings; notice there are similarities and differences. A broader HDI is not perfectly correlated with GDP. Qatar and the United Arab Emirates, two countries whose oil exports have given them high GDPs, lag well behind many other countries in terms of education and health, the other two elements in the HDI. Note Dr. Kabamba's Congo near the bottom of both of the first two columns.

Table 2.11 Country Rankings under Alternative Measures of Economic Development (The top ten and bottom ten countries for each measure)

GDP per Capita[1] *(IMF — US$2010 PPP)*		*Human Development Index (UNDP)*[2]	*Corruption Index*[3]	*Environmental Performance Index*[4]
1. Qatar	$88,559	1. Norway	1. Denmark	1. Iceland
2. Luxembourg	81,383	2. Australia	2. New Zealand	2. Switzerland
3. Singapore	56,522	3. New Zealand	3. Singapore	3. Costa Rica
4. Norway	52,522	4. United States	4. Finland	4. Sweden
5. Brunei	48,892	5. Ireland	5. Sweden	5. Norway
6. United Arab Em.	48,821	6. Liechtenstein	6. Canada	6. Mautritius
7. United States	47,284	7. Netherlands	7. Netherlands	7. France
8. Hong Kong	45,736	8. Canada	8. Australia	8. Austria
9. Switzerland	41,663	9. Sweden	9. Switzerland	9. Cuba
10. Netherlands	40,765	10. Germany	10. Norway	10. Colombia
....		....	....	....
174. Togo	858	160. Mali	169. Equatorial G.	154. Benin
175. Malawi	827	161. Burkina Faso	170. Burundi	155. Haiti
176. Sierra Leone	807	162. Liberia	171. Chad	156. Mali
177. Niger	753	163. Chad	172. Sudan	157. Turkmenistan
178. Cen. African Rep.	745	164. Guinea-Bisau	173. Turkmenistan	158. Niger
179. Eretrea	681	165. Moçambique	174. Uzbekistan	159. Togo
180. Zimbabwe	434	166. Burundi	175. Iraq	160. Angola
181. Burundi	411	167. Niger	176. Afghanistan	161. Mauritania
182. Liberia	392	168. Congo	177. Myanmar	162. C. African R.
183. Congo	328	169. Zimbabwe	178. Somalia	163. Sierra Leone

[1] International Monetary Fund, World Economic Outlook database, June, 2011.
[2] UNDP (2010), Human Development Report 2010, New York: United Nations, Table 1.
[3] Transparency International's Corruption Perceptions Index 2010; downloaded June 7, 2011.
[4] Yale Center for Environmental Law & Policy and Center for International Earth Science Information Network at Columbia University, available at http://research.yale.edu/envirocenter/.

Table 2.11 also lists two other alternative indicators of economic development. One is an index of corruption, which reflects the quality of governance, and the other ranks countries by their environmental footprint, which reflects their efforts to make development sustainable. There are some surprising absences and presences in the latter columns compared to the first two. In sum, there are many ways to rank countries and quantify economic development. There is no single measure of human welfare that is universally accepted, and the debate on how to best quantify human well-being goes on.

2.4 Summary and Conclusions

This chapter began by describing the most popular measure of economic development: GDP per capita. The historical data on GDP gives us a truly stunning picture of recent economic growth. If we define economic development simply as an increase in real GDP per capita, then nearly all economic development occurred during just the last 200 years of the 200,000 years of human history. This cannot be true, however. Surely there has been human progress throughout history. At the same time, some of the recent increases in GDP have been, in the words of Kenneth Boulding, bads rather than goods. The GDP numbers are probably not giving us a very accurate measure of true economic development.

The discussion of this chapter described various alternative measures that have been proposed either to correct for the biases in the GDP data or to supplement GDP with other indicators of human welfare. Many suggested alternative measures of development do not seem to alter the impression that most economic progress occurred very recently in human history. While world GDP per capita increased nearly ten-fold between 1820 and 2005, life expectancy tripled in most countries after having probably remained within the range of 20–30 years for most of human history. Over the past 50 years, many diseases were wiped out, death before old age became a rare occurrence, and most people gained more education and more career choices. Whether we look at health, longevity, education, political freedom, or just plain GDP per capita, therefore, we indeed appear to be very lucky to be alive today rather than during one of the other thousands of centuries that humans have populated the earth.

Of course, not all people of the world experienced similar increases in their welfare. Recall from Chapter 1 that income and wealth inequality in the world increased over the past 200 years. Recall, also, that the structures of economies have changed as well. Most people live very different lives today compared to their ancestors, and that makes comparisons with the past difficult. The growing inequalities across and within countries imply that individual people's lives vary greatly depending on which country they live in and what social class they fall into in their country.

This varied evidence brings us back to the question introduced at the start of the chapter: Who is better off, Mr. Banks in Kentucky or Dr. Kabamba in the Democratic Republic of Congo? In terms of absolute real money income, Mr. Banks is clearly better off. Remember, Dr. Kabamba has to share his income with many family members, but Mr. Banks gets to keep all of his income for himself. However, from a psychological perspective Dr. Kabamba is likely to be the *happier* person of the two precisely because he has an extended family to share his income with. Also, Dr. Kabamba enjoys considerable stature in the Republic of Congo, but Mr. Banks is at the bottom of the social structure in Kentucky and the United States. On the other hand, Dr. Kabamba has to live in a very poor country, one ranked at the bottom of the income and human development lists in Table 2.11 while Mr. Banks can enjoy the better infrastructure, government services, and opportunities of a high income country.

Human happiness and social status are not accurately captured by measures such as GDP or any one of the alternatives discussed in this chapter, including the HDI. Fortunately, research outside the mainstream of economics provides very useful insights into human happiness. The next chapter examines this inter-disciplinary research. In reference to the quotes at the start of this chapter, we still have some work to do in order to determine whether the rapid growth of GDP has been "good for humanity," as the economist Julian Simon suggested, or whether economic growth has pushed people dangerously close to "triggering catastrophe," as the scientist Martin Rees warned.

Key Terms and Concepts

Civil rights
Convergence
Divergence
Earnwork
Economic development
Economic freedom
Expected individual lifetime welfare (EILW)
GDP per capita
GDP
Gross domestic product (GDP)
Gross national product (GNP)
Human capital
Human Development Index (HDI)
Individual welfare function

Informal economic activity
Life expectancy
Nominal GDP
Price index
Purchasing power parity
Quality of life
Real GDP
Social welfare
Social welfare function
Standard of living
Universal Declaration of Human Rights
Welfare economics
Welfare function
Volwork

Questions and Problems

1. Write a brief essay describing the advantages and disadvantages of using the growth of GDP per capita to represent economic development. Why do you think economists use this measure so often? What else should they use?

2. Describe the Human Development Index developed by the United Nations. Is this a better measure of social welfare? Why or why not?

3. Explain in detail the measure called *Expected Individual Lifetime Welfare (EILW)*. Is this an improvement on GDP per capita or not? What are its shortcomings as a measure of human well-being?

4. We introduced a measure that combines per capita real GDP and Life Expectancy, which we called *Expected Individual Lifetime Welfare*. Can you think of any other combinations of measures of economic development that, together, give a different picture from those given by the individual components of the combination? Find data for the measures you select and calculate the growth rate of the combination. (Hint: you might try years of schooling and life expectancy, as suggested in the text.).

5. While walking home after a wild party on a Saturday evening, you suddenly see a vision. The vision is a strange, nebulous figure who makes you the following offer: You will be reincarnated one hundred years from now, and you have the choice of beginning a new life in one of two countries: (1) a developed economy with a per capita income of $20,000, which will grow at a very respectable rate of 2.5 percent per year over the next century or (2) a developing country with a rather low per capita income of $2,000, which will grow at a rate of 5 percent per year for the next one-hundred years. Which country should you choose? Show exactly how you reached your conclusion.

6. Discuss the assumption about the relationship between per capita income and human welfare that lies behind the Human Development Index calculated by the United Nations. Specifically, explain how the assumption changed with the 1999 index. (Hint: use Figures 2.5 and 2.6 to illustrate your answer.)

7. How would you define *happiness*? Use this definition to explain how much a doubling of your income would contribute to your happiness. How well do your perceptions of what makes you happy coincide with the description of findings from happiness studies and psychology?

8. Recall the two quotes by Martin Rees and Julian Simon at the start of the chapter. Which of the two more accurately describes the past 200 years of economic development? Bring into your discussion all the alternative measures of economic development discussed in the chapter.

9. Do you think people have economic rights, such as the right to healthcare, education, or employment? Why or why not? Does your answer influence which of the available measures of economic development you would prefer to use? Explain your thinking.

10. Explain the terms Earnwork and Volwork introduced by Robert Fogel. Are both of these categories of human activity included in GDP? Which should be included in the measure of human well-being that we use to calculate the rate of growth of economic development? Explain.

11. From the GDP data presented in this chapter, are incomes throughout the world diverging or converging? Explain.
12. After reading this chapter, who would you say is better off, Mr. Banks in West Virginia or Dr. Kabamba in the Democratic Republic of Congo?
13. Explain Frédérique Bastiat's example of the disgruntled employee who throws a stone through his employer's window. How is this a criticism of the popular measure of GDP?
14. Table 2.9 presents several alternative indicators that most people would agree are important for the quality of life in a country. First explain why these indicators are included in the table. Then offer other indicators that you think are appropriate for measuring human well-being. Explain your choices.
15. In comparing Tables 2.2 and 2.9, many Eastern European economies have quality of life measures that exceed those of countries with higher per capita real GDPs. Perhaps some of the Eastern European economies are not as poor as their lower real GDPs per capita suggest. You can no doubt find other discrepancies between countries' GDP rankings and the other measures of the quality of life in Table 2.9.

References

Acsadi, George, and J. Nemeskeri (1970), *History of Human Life Span and Mortality*, Budapest: Akademai Kiado.

Boulding, Kenneth (1966), "The Economics of the Coming Spaceship Earth," in *Environmental Quality in a Growing Society*, Baltimore, MD: Johns Hopkins University Press.

Costanza, Robert, *et al.* (1997), "The Value of the World's Ecosystem Services and Natural Capital," *Nature* 387:253–260.

Costanza, Robert, *et al.* (2002), "Tracking the Ecological Overshoot of the Human Economy," *Proceeding of the National Academy of Sciences* 99(14):9266–9271.

Cutler, David, and Grant Miller (2004), "The Role of Public Health Improvements in Health Advances: The 20th Century United States," NBER Paper 10511, May.

Daly, Herman E. (1998), "Uneconomic Growth," Clemens Lecture 11, Saint John's University, October 25.

Federal Reserve Bank of Dallas (1999), "The Right Stuff, America's Move to Mass Customization," *1998 Annual Report*, Dallas: Federal Reserve Bank.

Fogel, Robert W. (1999), "Catching Up with the Economy," *American Economic Review* 89(1):1–21.

Fuess, Scott M., Jr., and Hendrik Van den Berg (1996), "Does GNP Exaggerate Growth in 'Actual' Output? The Case of the United States," *Review of Income and Wealth* 42(1):35–48.

Fuess, Scott M., Jr. and Hendrik Van den Berg (1998), "Does GDP Distort Mexico's Economic Performance?" *Southern Economic Journal* 64(4):973–986.

Hatcher, John (1986), "Mortality in the Fifteenth Century: Some New Evidence," *Economic History Review* 39(1):19–38.

Hill, Kenneth (1995), "The Decline of Childhood Mortality," Chapter 3 in Julian L. Simon (ed.), *The State of Humanity*, Oxford: Blackwell, pp. 37–50.

Jones, Charles I. (1997), "On the Evolution of the World Income Distribution," *Journal of Economic Perspectives* 11(3):9–36.

Kravis, Irving B. (1984), "Comparative Studies of National Incomes and Prices," *Journal of Economic Literature* 22:1–39.

Kravis, Irving B., Allan Heston, and Robert Summers (1978), *International Comparisons of Real Product and Purchasing Power*, Baltimore, MD: Johns Hopkins University Press.

Kuznets, Simon (1966), *Modern Economic Growth*, New Haven: Yale University Press.

Landes, David S. (1999), *The Wealth and Poverty of Nations, Why Some Are So Rich and Some So Poor*, New York: W.W. Norton & Company.

Lichtenberg, Frank L. (1998), "Pharmaceutical Innovation, Mortality Reduction, and Economic Growth," NBER Working Paper 6569, May.

Livi-Bacci, Massimo (1997), *A Concise History of World Population* (2nd Ed), Oxford: Blackwell.

Lopes, Helena (2011), "Why Do People Work? Individual Wants Versus Common Goods," *Journal of Economic Issues* 45(1):57–73.

Maddison, Angus (1995), *Monitoring the World Economy 1820–1992*, Paris: OECD.

Maddison, Angus (2001), *The World Economy: A Millennial Perspective*, Paris: OECD.

Maddison, Angus (2003), *The World Economy: Historical Statistics*, Paris: OECD.

Maddison, Angus (2006), *Historical Statistics for the World Economy: 1–2003AD*, Statistical Appendix; this document was downloaded on August 19, 2006 from the website (http://ggdc.net/maddison/) maintained by the Groningen Growth & Development Centre at the University of Groningen, Netherlands.

Morgenstern, Oskar (1950), *On the Accuracy of Economic Observations*, Princeton, NJ: Princeton University Press.

North, Douglass C., and Robert Paul Thomas (1973), *The Rise of the Western World, A New Economic History*, Cambridge: Cambridge University Press.

Preston, Samuel H. (1995), "Human Mortality Throughout History and Prehistory," Chapter 2 in Julian L. Simon (ed.), *The State of Humanity*, Oxford: Blackwell, pp. 30–36.

Pritchett, Lant, and Lawrence Summers (1996), "Wealthier Is Healthier," *Journal of Human Resources* 31(4):841–868.

Rees, Martin (2003), *Our Final Hour: A Scientist's Warning: How Terror, Error, and Environmental Disaster Threaten Humankind's Future in This Century — On Earth and Beyond*, New York: Basic Books.

Schneider, Friedrich, and Dominik H. Enste (2000), "Shadow Economies: Size, Causes, and Consequences," *Journal of Economic Literature* 38(1).

Sen, Amartya (1999), "The Possibility of Social Choice," *American Economic Review* 89(3):349–378.

Simon, Julian (1995), "Introduction," Chapter 1 in Julian Simon (ed.), *The State of Humanity*, Oxford: Blackwell.

Summers, Robert, and Alan Heston (1988), "A New Set of International Comparisons of Real Product and Price Levels Estimates for 130 Countries, 1950–1985," *The Review of Income and Wealth* (34):1–25.

Summers, Robert, and Alan Heston (1991), "The Penn World Table (Mark 5): An Expanded Set of International Comparisons, 1950–1988," *Quarterly Journal of Economics* 106(2):327–368.

Sunstein, Cass (2005), *Laws of Fear: Beyond the Precautionary Principle*, Cambridge, U.K.: Cambridge University Press.

Temin, Peter (2006), "The Economy of the Early Roman Empire," *Journal of Economic Perspectives* 20(1):133–151.

Van den Berg, Hendrik (2002), "Does Annual Per Capita Real GDP Overstate or Understate the Growth of Individual Welfare over the Past Two Centuries?" *The Independent Review* 7(2):181–196.

Wolff, Edward N., Ajit Zacharias, and Thomas Masterson (2009), "Postwar Trends in Economic Well-Being in the United States, 1959–2004," Report issued by the Levy Economics Institute of Bard College, February.

CHAPTER 3

Holistic Measurement
of Economic Development

It's better to win the lottery than to break your neck, but not by as much as you'd think.
(Jonathan Haidt)[1]

In the previous chapter, you were introduced to two people: Mbwebwe Kabamba, a surgeon in the main public hospital in Kinshasa, the capital of the Democratic Republic of Congo, and Enos Banks, an unemployed miner living in a trailer in rural Kentucky in the United States. Their situations were compared in the British weekly news magazine *The Economist*, which then asked "which of the two would one expect to be happier?"[2] The previous chapter discussed GDP, the most often used indicator of economic welfare and economic growth. Also discussed were several alternative indicators of economic development that economists have built in order to overcome the most glaring shortcomings of GDP. But, both GDP and the alternative indicators of economic development were largely measures of human production. GDP and the alternative indicators did not directly address the concept of human happiness. This is a serious issue: Why pursue further growth of production and consumption if the additional material wealth does not make people any happier and more satisfied with their lives? In this chapter, we look beyond the adjustments to per capita real GDP described in the previous chapter and more directly focus on human happiness. We will seek answers to questions that mainstream economics has largely ignored.

Fortunately, recent research in several different fields of the social and natural sciences, plus a willingness by economists to think outside the box of

---

[1] Jonathan Haidt (2006), *The Happiness Hypothesis*, New York: Basic Books.
[2] *The Economist* (2005), "The Mountain Man and the Surgeon," December 20.

mainstream economic models, has moved us closer to an understanding of what determines true human well-being and happiness. For example, research in economics and many other fields of the social and natural sciences shows that individual welfare depends not only on the products consumed by one individual, but also by what others consume. Humans are social animals, and human happiness is determined by people's interactions with others within a social environment. National welfare is not the simple sum of individual welfare functions. Rather, people's satisfaction with their lives depends on how they see themselves relative to others in society. People are status conscious, and they seek to maintain their dignity.

Because human happiness is not exclusively, or even largely, an economic phenomenon, GDP and its various modifications are inadequate metrics with which to judge economic development. Further complicating the measurement of economic development is the fact that humans are conscious of the natural surroundings they evolved in. In general, whenever something in the social or natural sphere of human existence changes, human happiness or satisfaction with life changes as well. Human welfare thus depends on how the economy and society interact with the natural environment, and welfare functions based exclusively on economic variables cannot accurately describe human welfare. Indeed, behavioral economists have documented the instability of orthodox welfare functions based exclusively on economic production. Experiments and observations of human behavior show that, in general, the material consumption that made people happy yesterday will not make them happy at a later time under different social and natural conditions.

Orthodox economists may view this chapter as controversial. But it is important to keep in mind that indicators like GDP are popular because they are

---

Chapter Goals

1. Discuss the concepts of happiness and life satisfaction.
2. Describe the happiness surveys and their statistical analysis.
3. Examine the evidence from neuroscientific studies of the human brain and link these results to the happiness studies.
4. Compare the results of happiness studies to neuroscientific research and experiments from behavioral economics and psychology.
5. Relate all of the evidence to the measures of economic development presented in the previous chapter.
6. Discuss the weaknesses of orthodox economic analysis in light of this chapter's broader perspective on economic development.
7. Discuss how economists can better measure an economy's performance.
8. Make the case for a heterodox approach to development economics.

readily available and easy to use, not because economists really think they are highly accurate measures of human well-being. Economists often use GDP for no other reason than that everyone else uses GDP; it is part of the "culture" of orthodox economics. Holistically, the discussion that follows brings us closer to meaningful, albeit less convenient, indicators of human well-being.

3.1 Thinking About Happiness

To determine whether Mr. Banks or Mr. Kabamba is happier, we first examine the meaning of **happiness**. The search for the source of happiness has, of course, occupied philosophers for ages. In his *Rhetoric*, Aristotle wrote:

> We may define happiness as prosperity combined with excellence; or as independence of life, or as the secure enjoyment of the maximum of pleasure; or as a good condition for property and body, together with the power of guarding one's property and body and making use of them. That happiness is one or more of these things, pretty well everyone agrees. From this definition of happiness it follows that its constituent parts are: good birth, plenty of friends, good friends, wealth, good children, plenty of children, a happy old age, and also such bodily excellences as health, beauty, strength, large stature, athletic power, together with fame, honour, good luck and excellence.

Note that not all of Aristotle's determinants of human happiness can be achieved by simply increasing the economy's material output or average income. His definition of happiness includes some of the alternative measures of economic welfare introduced in the previous chapter, such as health, education, and longevity.   Some of these latter alternatives are actually closely related to national production; a more productive economy can provide people with better health, longer lives, and more education with which to achieve Aristotle's "excellence." However, it is not obvious that the growth of output as measured by GDP increases fame or friendship. And how do we improve our luck?

3.1.1 Changing perceptions of the ideal life

An interesting way to find out what makes people happy is to examine their fantasies and dreams.   For example, Herman Pleij (2001) surveys the arts, literature, and popular culture to reconstruct **Cocagne**, the mythical, ideal place that existed in the minds of Medieval European writers and artists.   During Medieval times, life in Europe was not nearly as comfortable as it is today. People were much more impacted by extreme cold and heat of the changing seasons. Without advanced technologies of food storage and preservation or modern transportation systems to carry food from one part of the world to another, people were forced to greatly vary their diets over the seasons.

Starvation was always a threat.   Europe's dominant religion, Christianity, offered one channel of relief from the hardship and toil, namely the possibility of attaining eternal bliss in the afterlife. Heaven had its entrance requirements, however: it was open only to those who behaved well. And, of course, a person had to die before they could seek entrance to heaven. There were thus other popular fantasies about paradise. In Medieval Europe, none was more popular than the fantasy of Cocagne:

> It was a country, tucked away in some remote corner of the globe, where ideal living conditions prevailed: ideal, that is, according to late-medieval notions... Work was forbidden, for one thing, and food and drink appeared spontaneously in the form of grilled fish, roast geese, and rivers of wine. One only had to open one's mouth, and all that delicious food practically jumped inside... The weather was stable and mild — it was always spring — and there was the added bonus of a whole range of amenities: communal possessions, lots of holidays, no arguing or animosity, free sex with willing partners, a fountain of youth, beautiful clothes for everyone, and the possibility of earning money while one slept.[3]

Pleij's description of Cocagne makes it clear that our fantasies about what constitutes "paradise" have changed somewhat since Medieval times. If we were to fantasize about paradise today, roast goose would probably no longer appear on many people's wish lists. It might be replaced by sushi, steak, or vegetarian cuisine.   People today would probably include things like automobiles, home entertainment centers, and a luxury home on their wish lists. As work has become more pleasant, many people today might replace Cocagne's ban on work with options for a more interesting career. On the other hand, nice clothes are still a desirable luxury for many today, as they were 500 years ago. And, current spending on cosmetic surgery and dietary supplements suggests people are still searching for a fountain of youth.

There is one important similarity between Cocagne and Aristotle's sources of happiness: both cases suggest people do not find happiness alone! Aristotle's fame and friendship requires the cooperation of other people. And in Cocagne, the mention of sex, communal possessions, and social harmony suggests that happiness was largely determined by one's social environment.

3.1.2 Psychology and life satisfaction

Some psychologists have defined happiness more generally as an assessment people arrive at by comparing their actual life to their expectations of what life should be like.   A. C. Michalos (1985), for example, proposes a **multiple discrepancy theory of happiness** based on the difference between five main categories of people's desires, hopes, and expectations relative to what they

---

[3] Herman Pleij (2001), p. 3.

actually achieve in life.   Specifically, Michalos hypothesizes that individual happiness depends on the gap between expectations and the satisfaction of:

1. Basic needs and wants.
2. What one was accustomed to having earlier in life.
3. What one expects to have later in life.
4. What others in society have.
5. What one deserves.

Michalos' multiple discrepancy theory implies that happiness is a complex state of human consciousness that depends on how well we meet our basic needs and how we evaluate the past, predict the future, compare ourselves to others, and determine what we deserve.   Michalos' hypothesis suggests that happiness is a variable concept that changes over time, across cultures, and over the course of a lifetime.   Also, the difference between expectations and actual outcomes in life is not obviously related to absolute levels of income.   This suggests that happiness also is not systematically related to the orthodox measures of income that social scientists like to use to measure economic growth.   Note, finally, that Michalos' multiple discrepancy theory is holistic because the term "wants" is general enough to include much more than material wants.   Michalos' wants can include Aristotle's "fame, friendship, or good luck."

The twentieth century behavioral psychologist Abraham Maslow explained happiness in terms of a **hierarchy of needs**, depicted in the form of a pyramid in Figure 3.1.   Maslow (1943) argued that, first of all, happiness is fundamentally related to the physiological needs for human survival.   The process of evolution has translated such a basic need for survival into a psychological sense of happiness when these basic needs for survival are satisfied.   The second most important need associated with human happiness is safety and security.   Third in Maslow's triangle is people's need to feel they belong in the community they reside in.   Fourth, people value the love and respect of others.   These latter two levels reflect the fact that the survival and expansion of the human species has depended on group behavior.   Those who were unable to relate to others and preferred isolation to cooperating with others were also less likely to survive. But more importantly, the need for others' respect and self-esteem was probably important for efficient group behavior.   Those who "played well with others" were more likely to have contributed to the genes present in today's humans; therefore, modern human beings are happier when they are loved and respected in their communities.

Maslow's fifth, and top, category of human needs for happiness is **self-actualization**, which is the conscious feeling that you have become everything that you are capable of becoming.   Exactly how this human need can be satisfied depends on a person's character, innate abilities, world view, and societal constraints.   Creativity, innovation, art, and intellectual activity no doubt help

Figure 3.1 Maslow's Hierarchy of Human Needs

people lead more fulfilling lives, but some people would no doubt argue that in a materialistic culture owning a nice car also contributes to self-actualization.

Maslow's first level of physiological needs are strongly and directly related to real per capita GDP. Safety and security may also be related to income in the sense that wealth provides people with insurance against unexpected disasters. Maslow's top three categories of human needs have very little to do with average or absolute income levels like real per capita GDP. Self-actualization is clearly a relative concept that depends on expectations based on a person's current situation and the perceived possibilities for the future. Feelings about what one deserves are more complex still, closely related to people's sense of justice as well as the general distribution of income and status in society.

These insights from psychology, philosophy, literature, and the arts strongly suggest that traditional measures of economic growth like GDP are not accurate reflections of human happiness. But, how do we translate these observations on happiness into a practical indicator of economic development?

3.2 Happiness Studies

Some social scientists have measured human happiness by simply asking people how happy they are. The results of various opinion surveys have been converted to numerical measures and used in statistical tests of hypothesized determinants of happiness. Surveys of people's satisfaction with life have been carried out for many years in many countries, and it is now possible to compare happiness across countries and over long periods of time. Research studies using this data are referred to as **happiness studies**. This research was pioneered at the Center for Happiness Studies at Erasmus University in the Netherlands.

3.2.1 Surveys of life satisfaction

Many happiness studies have used the results from surveys by the University of Michigan's Survey Research Center (SRC), which asked people the question:

> *Taken all together, how would you say things are these days — would you say that you are (1) very happy, (2) pretty happy, or (3) not too happy?*

Another source of happiness data are *The World Value Surveys*, conducted every few years across a large sample of countries, which ask the question:

> *Taken all together, how happy would you say you are: (1) very happy, (2) quite happy, (3) not very happy, or (4) not at all happy?*

Finally, the level of happiness in Europe is revealed in the annual *Eurobarometer Survey* conducted in the European Union, which asks:

> *On the whole are you (1) very satisfied, (2) fairly satisfied, (3) not very satisfied, or (4) not at all satisfied with the life you lead?*

The average values of these surveys take the form of a number between 1 and 3 for the three-option question by the University of Michigan, and between 1 and 4 for the latter two surveys. These numbers represent a ranking, not an absolute measurement of happiness, because there is no way of knowing precisely how, for example, *very happy* compares to *pretty happy*. These survey results are useful for social scientists because they allow us to relate changes in the happiness number to hypothesized determinants of happiness such as income, health, age, marriage status, gender, educational achievement, and myriad other human conditions.[4]

Table 3.1 Life Satisfaction in the United States and Europe: 1972–1998

United States	*1972–1976*	*1977–1982*	*1983–1987*	*1988–1993*	*1994–1998*
Not too happy	14%	12%	12%	10%	12%
Pretty happy	52	54	56	58	58
Very happy	34	34	32	33	30
12 European Countries[1]		*1973*		*1983*	*1997*
Not at all satisfied		4%		6%	5%
Not very satisfied		16		16	17
Fairly satisfied		58		59	59
Very satisfied		22		19	19

[1] Belgium, Denmark, France, West Germany, Greece, Ireland, Italy, Luxembourg, Netherlands, Portugal, Spain, and United Kingdom.
Source: Eurobarometer; taken from David G, Blanchflower and Andrew J. Oswald (2000).

[4] Results of these surveys are in the *World Database of Happiness*, Center for Happiness Studies, Erasmus University, Rotterdam, Netherlands, available at http://www.eur.nl/fsw/research/happiness.

3.2.2 What surveys of happiness tell us

Table 3.1 presents data from surveys on happiness in Europe and the United States. This data shows how average happiness changed over the period. Notice how the proportions of people in each of the categories barely changed at all between 1972 and 1998. If anything, Table 3.1 suggests that the proportion of people who classify themselves as *very happy* or *very satisfied* declined slightly from 1972 to 1998 while real per capita GDP increased substantially. There certainly is no indication that people became happier as their incomes rose over three decades.

Also interesting are the findings from happiness studies of post-World War II Japan. According to survey responses, Japanese citizens did not reveal any increase in personal happiness over the four decades between 1950 and 1990, when the Japanese economy increased per capita real GDP sixfold. This period is still referred to as the Japanese "economic miracle." The survey results are illustrated in Figure 3.2: As Japanese per capita real GDP consistently increased, the average life satisfaction index remained about the same. These findings for Japan are similar to what Table 3.1 reveals for the United States and Europe.

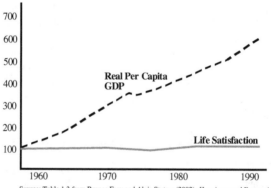

Source: Table 1.3 from Brunos Frey and Alois Stutzer (2002), *Happiness and Economics*, Princeton, NJ: Princeton University Press, p. 9.

Figure 3.2 Happiness and Real Per Capita GDP (1958 = 100) in Japan: 1958–1991

Studies that have looked at a large sample of different countries at a given point in time do seem to suggest that life satisfaction or happiness is positively related to income. However, the relationship is not linear. Figure 3.3 from Frey and Stutzer (2002) suggests a clear direct relationship between income and happiness for countries with average annual incomes under $5,000. Yet, once average income exceeds $5,000, the surveys do not show much variation in how satisfied people are with their lives. People's life satisfaction in the average country with an average per capita income of $7,500 is not much different from the average reported life satisfaction in a country with an average per capita income of $30,000. A broad study of a large number of countries for an extended period from 1960 through 2005 by Rafael Di Tella and Robert MacCoulloch (2008) confirms the lack of effect of income on happiness after basic needs are met, which it estimates occurs at a level of GDP per capita that prevailed in Europe at about 1960. Maddison estimates 1960 European GDP per capita at $7,000 in 1990 dollars.

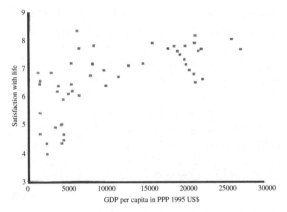

Figure 3.3 Life Satisfaction and Real Per Capita GDP Across the World in the 1990s

The time-series data on happiness does not give the complete story, however. Cross-section studies comparing people across different income groups within one country in any given year suggest that rich people are, on average, happier than poor people. Table 3.2 shows that average levels of happiness differ across income groups within individual countries. The lowest income *quartile* (25 percent of the population at the bottom of the income distribution) contains the highest proportion of people reporting they were *not too happy* in the United States and *not very happy* or *not at all happy* in a group of European countries. Nearly 20 percent of the poorest Americans were *not happy*, but only 5 percent of wealthy Americans were *not happy*. Less than 25 percent of poor Americans, but over 40 percent of wealthy Americans, were *very happy*. All other things equal, rich people are more likely to be happy than poor people. In sum, happiness studies reveal that:

- At a given point in time within the same country, people with higher incomes are happier, on average, than people with lower incomes.

- In the long-run, in high-income developed countries average human happiness does not change much as real average per capita income grows.

- Cross-section studies that compare average national levels of happiness for low-income developing and high-income developed countries show that overall happiness rises with average per capita income only until real per capita income reaches about $10,000.

In wealthy societies, where basic economic needs are usually satisfied, relative social status seems to be the predominant cause of variations in happiness.

Table 3.2 Life Satisfaction in Europe and the United States: 1975–1994

	Income Quartiles:			
United States	*Lowest*	*2nd*	*3rd*	*Highest*
Not too happy	18.28%	13.20	8.56	5.81
Pretty happy	57.43	58.07	57.53	52.48
Very happy	24.28	28.73	33.91	41.71
12 European Countries[1]				
Not very/not at all satisfied	28.58%	21.10	16.48	12.47
Fairly satisfied	49.52	54.54	56.71	54.96
Very satisfied	21.90	24.36	26.81	32.58

[1] Belgium, Denmark, France, West Germany, Greece, Ireland, Italy, Luxembourg, Netherlands, Portugal, Spain, and United Kingdom.
Source: Eurobarometer; taken from David G, Blanchflower and Andrew J. Oswald (2000).

3.2.3 The Human Development Index again

The above findings were effectively embraced by the United Nations Development Programme (UNDP) when it designed its *Human Development Index* (HDI). Recall from the previous chapter the United Nations' Human Development Index (HDI) is a weighted average of (1) real per capita income, (2) life expectancy, (3) the literacy rate, and (4) school enrollment rates. Before 1999, the UNDP gave increases in per capita real output substantial weight in the HDI only for low income countries. That is, the relationship between income and welfare was assumed to look like the solid "kinked" solid line in Figure 3.4. According to this function, increases in per capita GDP up to the world average of about $5,000 have a strong effect on the value of the overall HDI index, but after a per capita GDP of $5,000 was reached further increases in output were assumed to only weakly affect human welfare.

Beginning in 1999, the UNDP assumed a gradually diminishing relationship between income and welfare in weighing the role of real per capita income in the HDI, as illustrated by the dashed line in Figure 3.4. This new curve implies well-being continues to rise with higher incomes, albeit at a diminishing rate. It is not clear which of the two curves in Figure 3.4 better approximates the relationship between real per capita GDP and happiness suggested by the scatter of observations in Figure 3.3.

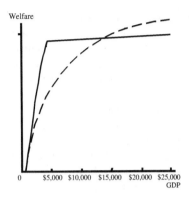

Figure 3.4 Welfare and GDP: UNDP

3.2.4 *Statistical studies of happiness*

Many studies have used happiness survey data in statistical regression equations in order to test which hypothesized determinants of human happiness are correlated with the variation in happiness survey results. Typical of such happiness studies is the paper by David Blanchflower and Andrew Oswald (2000), who use survey data from the Michigan Survey for the United States and from the Eurobarometer survey for the United Kingdom over the period 1972–1998 to explain the variations in happiness across different types of people. Their statistical regressions estimate whether (1) age, (2) gender, (3) race, (4) marital status, (5) employment status, (6) student status, and (7) the presence of a spouse have an effect on individual happiness. Table 3.3 presents the regression results for both countries.[5]

In both the United Kingdom and the United States, people are less happy, all other things equal, when they are unemployed, not married, older, male rather than female, retired, or have lost their spouse. Blanchflower and Oswald's statistical results suggest that, in order to achieve greater happiness, people should get married, stay married, stay employed, become educated, never retire, and males should contemplate a sex change. Dolan, Peasgood, and White (2008) identify an even longer list of living conditions that are statistically related to individual happiness, which includes a) gender, b) friendship, c) age, d) marital status, e) education, f) health, g) relative income, h) self-employment, i) blood pressure, j) regular sex with the same partner, k) political leaning,

---

[5] A survey of many happiness studies for other countries, time periods, and data sets by Dolan, Peasgood, and White (2008) confirm Blanchflower and Oswald's findings. Among the many authors surveyed are Ruut Veenhoven (1988), Richard Easterlin (1995), Ed. Diener, Marissa Diener, and Carol Diener (1995), Oswald (1997), and Bruno Frey and Alois Stutzer (2000). This growing literature has, so far, strengthened the conclusions outlined in the text above. Few anomalies have been uncovered, although much research remains to be done in this still-young field.

l) religious belief, m) membership in organizations, n) volunteer work, and o) regular exercise. In fact, nearly all happiness studies confirm that people value marriage, status, respect of others, and participating economically in their societies. In short, the results confirm that people are social animals.

The negative coefficients shown in Table 3.5 for being widowed, divorced, or separated reflect the human need for friendship and company. The large negative coefficients for unemployment need an explanation. Helena Lopes (2011, p. 70) provides some insight: "... if organized in the right way, work provides people with the opportunity to satisfy needs essential for well-being, such as the need for self-realization, the need for relatedness and the need to live a meaningful life." She cites evidence from behavioral economics showing that consumption is not the sole purpose of work. For most people, being productive and contributing something of value to society gives meaning to life.

Table 3.3 Marginal Influences on Happiness: 1972–1998

	United States	*United Kingdom*
Age	−0.0220	−0.0424
Male	−0.1595	−0.1555
Black	−0.4494	-
Unemployed	−0.8321	−1.1337
Retired	−0.0410	−0.0371
Student	0.1245	0.0141
2nd marriage	−0.1063	-
Widowed	−1.1109	−0.2894
Divorced	−0.9874	−0.6061
Separated	−1.2523	−0.6531
Never Married	−0.7384	−0.7830
Married	-	0.3972
Education	0.0482	

[1] Belgium, Denmark, France, West Germany, Greece, Ireland, Italy, Luxembourg, Netherlands, Portugal, Spain, and United Kingdom.
Source: Eurobarometer; taken from David G, Blanchflower and Andrew J. Oswald (2000).

3.3 Neuroscientific Evidence on Happiness

Happiness studies look for statistical correlations among self-declared happiness and various hypothesized determinants of happiness. For social scientists to have full confidence in the statistical results, the correlations must be supported by scientific evidence on how people really think and behave. This section looks at evidence from the field of neuroscience.

Fundamentally, a person's satisfaction with life or state of happiness are determined in the human brain. Happiness is the brain's interpretation of human circumstances, which means that the new techniques for monitoring brain activity can be used to evaluate human happiness. In order to interpret the results from neuroscientific studies, a quick review of the process of evolution is presented in the first sub-section below. The subsequent section explains what neuroscience has discovered about the human brain and how we can use this knowledge to interpret what brain signals tell us about human happiness.

3.3.1 *Linking brain activity to human happiness*

Evolution is the process by which a species changes as genes are selectively passed from generation to generation and as genes mutate. The genes of individuals who have the greater number of offspring show up more often in later generations than the genes of individuals who have fewer offspring. In the case where certain genes give individuals an advantage in generating offspring, a compound process sets in that eventually causes those individuals' genes to dominate and become characteristic of the species. Recall from Chapter 1 the compound process of economic growth, which caused the faster growing economies to account for ever-increasing portions of global material output.

Once a certain genetic structure becomes dominant in a population, the process of evolution does not stop. Two fundamental sources of evolutionary change continue to operate. First, genes are not always passed on from one generation to the next without occasional modifications or "copying mistakes." That is, genes are not always replicated perfectly. Such **mutations** are rare, but when they occur they result in new genes and new forms of human behavior. Sometimes the new behavior proves to be more successful in generating offspring, and when the random mutations in genes prove to be "successful," they will eventually dominate the genetic structure of the evolving species.

Secondly, the environment in which a species lives continues to change. Climate, atmospheric conditions, geological conditions, the rotation of the earth, the shifting of the continental plates, and other physical changes in our natural environment continually alter the success and failure of specific gene structures. And, of course, all the other living things that share the natural environment with humans also continually evolve, mutate, adapt, and change. Individual species must adapt to all these changes, or they will go extinct.

Patricia Churchland (2002) explains the distinctive way in which the evolution of human ancestors led to the development of today's large brains:

> The brain's earliest self-representational capacities arose as evolution found neural network solutions for coordinating and regulating inner-body signals, thereby improving behavioral strategies. Additional flexibility in organizing coherent behavioral options emerges from neura models that represent some of the brain's inner states as states of its body, while representing other signals as perceptions of the external world. Brains manipulate inner models to predict the distinct consequences in the external world of distinct behavioral options.[6]

---

[6] Patricia S. Churchland (2002).

Human brains have evolved to where they can now interpret signals about smell, light, sound, touch, and taste from sensors located throughout the body in ways that permit humans to formulate sophisticated behavioral reactions to their economic, social, and natural environments. We refer to this continual evaluation of, and reaction to, our changing circumstances as **consciousness**. The conscious feelings of satisfaction or dissatisfaction, contentment or discontent, pleasure or displeasure, and comfort or discomfort can be summarized as a person's level of happiness. The feeling of happiness is thus a cerebral control mechanism that humans evolved in order to deal with their natural and social environments.

Humans are not unique in having a sense of consciousness. Nearly all living things can in some way sense their surroundings, and most have some capacity to react to what their senses perceive. For example, there is an extensive literature on elephants' complex feelings of empathy, joy, and anger.[7] A tree senses its natural environment, and it uses this information to direct its roots to where it detects the presence of water in the ground and extends its branches towards the light of the sun.[8]

What is important for our discussion here is that the human brain evolved to react in a positive manner, by sensing pleasure or happiness, to conditions that were favorable to human survival in the past. The positive sensual signals that humans tend to equate with *happiness* are effectively the brain's evaluation of the body's performance and its likelihood of success in the natural and social environments humans and human ancestors lived in.

3.3.2 The discoveries of neuroscience

Neuroscientists have developed methods to monitor brain activity. These methods have made it possible to directly measure the brain's reaction to hypothesized determinants of happiness.

The most popular neuroscientific tool at the present time is **brain imaging**, which detects the flow of blood through the brain. This method usually compares how the brain is activated when people are performing two different tasks. The differences in the signals provide insight into which parts of the brain govern different functions. A related process is *diffusion tensor imaging*, which exploits the fact that water flows rapidly through the neural axons that transmit impulses from a brain cell. Brain imaging and diffusion tensor imaging make it possible to observe how specific tasks and situations affect the flows between

---

[7] For a general introduction, see Charles Siebert (2006), M. Goodman *et al.* (2008), or Jeheskel Shoshani, William J. Kupsky, and Gary H. Marchant (2007).

[8] For a clear explanation of plant consciousness, see Natalie Angier's (2009) article entitled "Sorry, Vegans: Brussels Sprouts Like to Live, Too," *New York Times*, December 22. For a very readable scientific paper on how plants consciously sense dangers and react to those dangers, see Nina Fatouros *et al.* (2008).

neural regions. Neuroscientists also use *electrical brain stimulation* techniques that intentionally stimulate specific parts of the brain to see how behavior is affected. These and other new techniques have enabled scientists to distinguish the distinct functions of specific parts of the brain and revolutionized our understanding of the active processes of the human brain. Neuroscience has determined that the distinct sectors of the brain work together in many different combinations that depend on the type of decision to be made and the circumstances under which the decision is made.

The brain's **automatic processes** are faster than conscious deliberations, and they occur with little or no awareness or feeling of effort. Reactions to pain, danger, and physical trauma, for example, are mostly automatic. These evolved automatic brain processes, and the behavior they trigger, do not follow normative axioms of inference and choice. They are more like constants than behavioral variables. Humans share these automatic processes with many other living creatures and organisms. The area of the brain where the automatic processes originate is called the *reptilian* sector of the brain, and it is at the base of the human brain.

Human behavior is also influenced by the brain's **affective** or **emotional processes**. Emotional processes occur in the neocortex, a part of the human brain that is of more recent evolution. Hence, many emotional processes are unique to humans and more recent mammals. Note that by "more recent" we still mean many millions of years, although admittedly, this is a very short period within the three billion or more years that life has existed on earth. Affective processes are often linked to what we commonly refer to as **instinctive behavior**. These systems also do not generate decisions predicted by economic models of rational choice, which assume a deliberative process that weighs options and compares all potential outcomes.

Finally, there are the brain's **cognitive**, or **deliberative, processes**. Deliberative brain activity potentially delivers what economists would define as rational decisions. Neuroscience has determined that cognitive behavior emanates from the prefrontal cortex, a part of the brain that has developed in nearly all animals but is especially well developed in human beings. Humans are thus not unique in their ability to reason and think abstractly, but arguably humans stand out among living species in how well they reason and think abstractly.

The brain's activity thus consists of the simultaneous automatic, emotional, and deliberative responses to circumstances. Neuroscientists have found that the three types of brain functions interact with each other, and the interactions vary with circumstances. The brain performs an enormous number of different computations in parallel in a very dense network of neural connections, and it specializes by allocating different tasks to different parts of the brain as it confronts different situations. According to Joseph LeDoux (1996), "the wiring of the brain at this point in our evolutionary history is such that connections from the emotional systems to the cognitive systems are stronger than connections from the cognitive systems to the emotional systems." The faster automatic and affective processes thus end up dealing with the most urgent issues first.

This dominance of the automatic and emotional processes over the cognitive process in the case of emergencies makes perfect sense from an evolutionary perspective. We humans are most likely the descendants of people who overreacted to the potential downside of dangerous events. Long-run visionaries engrossed in deep thought were more often overcome by predators and natural disasters and did not as often live to have descendants and pass on their genes. When life is insecure, as it always was, one misstep implied death and the end of the line for the embodied genes. This evolutionary development of the human brain means that today, although we face few wild bears and other natural dangers that could shorten our lives, we still let short-run annoyances that matter little for our long-term welfare dominate our thoughts while we just can't find the time to set up our retirement plan.

3.3.3 Homeostasis, empathy, learning, and other findings

Recall that in Chapter 1 we used the term *homeostasis* to describe the set of self-correcting feedback processes that maintain stability in Earth's ecosystem. The human brain is also characterized by homeostatic responses. When the senses tell the brain that something is different or not familiar, reactions are triggered that attempt to restore equilibrium, or what some psychologists have called a **set point**. Homeostasis in the brain's processes explains why humans react much more intensely to changes in their circumstances than they do to a continuation of familiar circumstances, but it also explains why humans are very adaptable in the long run.

Despite the short-term overreactions to changes in circumstances, people eventually adjust to their changed circumstances. The cognitive system of the brain, where deliberative thinking occurs, eventually kicks in to try to explain the situation after the automatic and emotional systems signal that something important has changed. And as time passes after the event, the cognitive processes become stronger relative to automatic and emotional processes. For example, Jonathan Haidt (2006) studied lottery winners and found that one year after the elation of being rich, lottery winners fall back to their former level of life satisfaction. Oswald and Powdthavee (2008) found that people who become permanently disabled recover much of their pre-injury level of happiness over time. "It's better to win the lottery than to break your neck, but not by as much as you'd think," concludes Jonathan Haidt. These conclusions may surprise you, but think about what would have happened to our ancestors over the millions of years of economic hardships, accidents, natural disasters, and violence if they had not been able to adjust and get on with their lives.

Another neuroscientific discovery is that specialization within the brain is changeable. People learn to change their instinctive behavior by altering the sequence in which different parts of the brain are activated in response to external events. Experiments show that in the case of an unfamiliar problem, many more areas of the brain activate than in the case of familiar and well-understood problems. Experiments have determined that as a person gains experience with a certain situation, the brain's reactions to that situation become more precise and organized. For example, one study that tracked the brain activity of floor traders in foreign exchange markets showed that seasoned traders reacted calmly to the same events that agitated novice traders. In sports, a team with some older experienced players often performs better than a young physically superior but less experienced team. And experienced parents do not react nearly as emotionally to their children's cries as do brand new parents.

The fact that seemingly instinctive behavior can be changed with training and practice explains the important role that culture has in shaping human behavior. Culture consists of the language, traditions, rituals, religious beliefs, and other social behaviors that people view as normal in the society they place themselves in. Through years of upbringing, peer pressure, education, and tacit human interaction, people learn instinctive reactions to complex economic, social, and natural events, just like the floor traders who learned to operate in an environment that inexperienced traders found confusing and taxing.

These findings therefore support what happiness studies suggest: income has a diminishing effect on human welfare the farther income rises above what is necessary to deal with the basic problems of survival. At very low real incomes, people encounter repeated crises and dangers, and they receive many unpleasant signals from the brain, such as hunger, discomfort due to the lack of shelter, and illness. At higher incomes, the changes in life that further increases in income bring are less about survival than adjusting life styles. The greater role of cognitive brain functions in the long run permits humans to learn, adapt, and adjust to new lifestyles. Therefore, just as the happiness studies suggest, the human brain's signals suggest that differences in per capita incomes across middle-income and high-income countries have little effect on overall levels of happiness.

Neuroscientific research on the human brain's reaction to other people also confirms the finding from happiness studies that people are conscious of their status in society. Maël Lebreton *et al.* (2009) used brain imaging techniques to detect the brain's reactions to social interaction with other people. They found that the portion of the brain that is stimulated by individual rewards and pleasures is the same portion of the brain that is stimulated by a person's *share* of social rewards and pleasures.

There are more complex interactions between individuals that further invalidate the orthodox practice of using social welfare functions that are simple combinations of individual welfare functions. For example, humans exhibit empathy, which is the ability to experience and understand what others feel. Empathy also affects an individual's sense of happiness. For example, Jean Decety and Claus Lamm (2006) find that when humans take time to conceptualize another person's situation, their own brain's response to their own first-hand experience is reduced in favor of processing the feelings of pain and happiness experienced by others. In sum, neuroscientific evidence reveals clearly that individual happiness depends, to some extent, on the welfare of others.

Feelings of empathy are not constant or predictable. They depend on the level of familiarity with other people, whether there is visual contact, and whether the other people behave in culturally familiar ways. Foreigners generally receive much less empathy than people belonging to the same community. And people's sense of empathy has to compete with negative feelings of envy, revenge, and fear, among many other mental reactions. Even parental behavior towards children varies with a broad range of circumstances. For example, a study by Quy-Toan Do and Tung Phung (2010) finds that parents' treatment of children who were planned was significantly different from their treatment of children who were not planned. People's behavior toward others is determined by many factors, but all research confirms that individual behavior takes the welfare of others into consideration to varying degrees.

Another very important finding from neuroscientific research is that short-term and long-run happiness do not depend on the same set of variables. Because our short term automatic and emotional reactions to changing circumstances are very different from the more deliberative long-run reactions, economic policies designed to deal with people's immediate desires and fears do not generally maximize humans' lifetime happiness. This evidence shows that welfare functions, if they can be determined at all, are not stable over time. Interesting in this regard is the article by Irena Grosfeld and Claudia Senik (2010) on Poland's transition from a communist government to a market economy. At first, Poles accepted the growth in inequality as a sign of wider economic opportunities, and the happiness score for the country rose. But eventually the growing inequality became a cause of Poles' dissatisfaction with their economic situation, and happiness surveys showed a decline in Poles' overall satisfaction with life. This study make a case for adding income equality to measurements of well-being.

These findings make simple summary measures like GDP or even the Human Development Index inappropriate for judging the benefits of economic development over time. The social welfare function is clearly not a simple sum of independent individual welfare functions. Economic development tends to be an unbalanced process that alters the distribution of income as well as the various economic and social interactions in society. The dependence of individual happiness on one's participation in society and one's share of social welfare suggests that it is extremely difficult, if not impossible, to accurately specify a social welfare function in a growing, changing economy.

3.3.4 Behavioral economics and the neuroscientific findings

The field of **behavioral economics**, in which economists and psychologists combine their knowledge to improve our understanding of human economic behavior, has engaged in human experiments to test the neuroscientific findings reported above. For example, in a now-classic study in behavioral economics, Daniel Kahneman and Amos Tversky (2000) conducted a series of experiments that confirmed that people almost always disproportionately value their current situation over other options. That is, people tend to shun change and cling to the status quo, even when such change represents a potential improvement in well-being.

In one of their experiments, Kahenman and Tversky show people two products of roughly equal value, A and B, and they inform each person that one of the two belongs to them while the other belongs to someone else. When everyone was given object A, the great majority valued it over the object B that they did not possess. But when they were informed that, contrary to what they were told earlier, object B was theirs and object A belonged to someone else, a majority then claimed to prefer the object B to object A. Richard Thaler (1980) first referred to this phenomenon as the **endowment effect**. This result implies that people are loss averse, and that they will fight harder to hold on to what they have than to acquire something new. Many animals exhibit this kind of behavior, and we refer to it as **territoriality**. People justify their aversion to loss by convincing themselves they like what they possess more than some other territory or set of possessions, even when there is no apparent rational reason for this preference. This behavior must have an evolutionary advantage, given the frequency it is observed across living species, probably related to the the preservation of the group or community.

Kahneman and Tversky also directly examined the **risk aversion**, or more precisely, **loss aversion**, exhibited by most people in uncertain circumstances. They found people seldom take an even bet. Instead, people must expect a substantial premium over a guaranteed outcome before they select a uncertain outcome over a guaranteed one. In one experiment, they asked people to choose between an instantaneous gift of $2 held out to them by a person standing right in front of them and an even chance of gaining $0 or $10 in a coin throw to be held on the other side of the room. The majority took the $2 although the expected value of the even bet was $5. As the popular saying goes, a bird in hand is worth two in the bush!

In summary, as the neuroscientific studies broadly confirmed what the happiness studies reported, experimental and behavioral economics have confirmed neuroscientific results. In the next section, we examine what the findings imply for economic development.

3.4 Economic Development and Human Happiness

Many of these findings about human behavior are problematic for orthodox economics and mainstream modeling of economic growth. As a review of what you have just read, some of the most disruptive findings are:

- There are great variations in how the automatic, emotional, and cognitive processes of the human brain interact under diverse circumstances. This implies individual welfare functions that are not stable.

- The brain's short-run bias means the human brain does not operate in accordance with orthodox economists' predicted rational behavior.

- Depending on recent experiences, people's happiness continually changes as they gradually adjust to changes in their circumstances, the circumstances of their fellow human beings, and their relationships with those fellow human beings.

- People's welfare functions contain much more than the goods and services counted in GDP.

- People relish recognition, prestige, and love; they are saddened by uncertainty, loss of status, and loss of friendship.

- People also judge their well-being by what they anticipate for the future or what they enjoyed in the past.

- Humans tend to ignore long-run issues because short-run problems tend to hog their attention.

It is nearly impossible to quantify many of these influences on human happiness, which may explain why mainstream economists effectively throw up their hands and continue using inaccurate individual and aggregate welfare functions. There is no scientific excuse for this intellectual surrender in the face of complexity, however.

In the more holistic field of development economics, some of the complexity has been explicitly dealt with, and the dependence on GDP per capita as a measure of economic development has been abandoned. In fact, there are interesting intepretations of economic development that take into consideration the evidence from happiness studies, neuroscience, and behavioral economics.

3.4.1 Is economic growth just a hedonic treadmill?

David Lykken of the University of Minnesota studied a sample of identical twins who grew up apart from each other, and he found that the twins' stated levels of happiness were very closely correlated, regardless of the differences in lifestyles they experienced. He concluded that, in the long run, happiness is 90 percent genetic, and only minimally influenced by environmental factors. In the short run, however, environmental factors could alter happiness substantially. Lykken (1999) suggests that each person has a happiness set point around which his or her happiness fluctuates. That is, people experience variations in happiness over their lifetimes, but in the long run they can, at best, only be marginally happier than their genetically determined set point of happiness.

Lykken's set point hypothesis, along with the vast evidence from happiness studies and neuroscience showing that people adjust to changes in life and income to where they eventually feel no different than they did before the change, begs an interesting question: Why do politicians continue to push policies that promote more economic growth? This question is very relevant today now that we know such growth has environmental consequences that potentially endangers the future of humanity.

Philip Brickman and Donald Campbell (1971) coined the term **hedonic treadmill** to describe the seemingly paradoxical urge for people to increase their material wealth even though it has little long-term effect on their happiness. People are very concerned with their relative status in society, and a capitalist society defines status in terms of material wealth. Brickman and Campbell argue that people work hard to raise their income because they know others are working hard to increase their incomes. Individuals who choose to work less will fall behind and suffer a psychological welfare loss. Each individual, therefore, ends up working hard in a never-ending struggle to keep up with the rest of society. Because everyone does the same, individuals' relative status, and thus their happiness, changes little.[9]

The political columnist Michael Prowse (2003) provocatively used the concept of the hedonic treadmill to describe modern consumerism as the way in which a capitalist system exploits workers. Prowse appeals to Maslow's pyramid when he argues that workers could achieve a higher level of happiness with less hard work and more leisure and non-work activity. The former only provides income for more material consumption, but the latter leads to self-actualization. He thus argues that the only gainers from the hedonic treadmill are capitalists, who, because of the hard work of the hedonically-trapped individual workers and consumers, are able to maintain the high profits that

---

[9] David Neumark and Andrew Postlewaite (1998) show that concerns about social status are the main reason why hours worked have not fallen in countries like the United States despite large increases in real income.

keep them wealthier and, because relative status is important, happier than those consumer/workers afraid to get off the treadmill.

3.4.2 Mandeville's "Fable of the Bees"

The concept of the hedonic treadmill actually dates back to the Dutch eighteenth century philosopher Bernard de Mandeville (1714). Mandeville's famous "Fable of the Bees" describes two different beehives, one where the bees have developed a pleasant cooperative society in which individuals have no desire to be better off than their hive-mates, the other where the bees are very status conscious. The first beehive is happy, but it does not grow very rapidly. Mandeville describes how the happiness of the first beehive comes to a sudden end when it is taken over by the second beehive, in which hedonically-trapped bees ended up making their hive larger and stronger as each bee worked, futilely of course, to "get ahead" of others.

Mandeville's fable effectively suggests that a society where people actively toil on the hedonic treadmill is less happy than in a society where people arrange for a social system with more leisure and freedom from the hedonic treadmill. However, he also provocatively points out that if the two different societies inhabit the same world, the happy society will eventually be conquered and colonized by the unhappy society chained by fear to their hedonic treadmills! Interestingly, this colonization of the happy society by the unhappy society ends up boosting the happiness of the latter because after conquest, the people in the colonizing society now see that they are relatively richer than the poor people of the conquered colony. And, after the conquest, the formerly happy people in the colonized society now find themselves relatively poor and, therefore, less happy than before. This is quite a reversal of happiness.

Mandeville's fable suggests that colonial conquest, post facto, justifies the seemingly senseless toil on the hedonic treadmill. He was, of course, writing in Holland, which in the 1700s was one of the major colonial powers. Perhaps he was seeking a justification for Holland's brutal and exploitative colonialism.

A more far-sighted observer might wonder if there is not some way to arrive at a cooperative global solution, say an international **economic disarmament treaty** under which all countries agree to scrap their hedonic treadmills. Such a worldwide agreement would cause conventionally-measured economic growth to slow. But, if more leisure enables more self-actualizing activities or simply reduces unpleasant work, overall happiness would rise. These observations add a whole new meaning to the traditional revolutionary slogan: "Workers of the World, Unite!"

How much would human welfare improve if all countries responded to worker pressure and instituted a 30-hour workweek? Or, a 20-hour workweek, as John Maynard Keynes (1930) predicted we would have adopted by now? The New Economics Foundation (2010, p. 2) explains their call for a 21-hour workweek as follows:

A normal workweek of 21 hours could help to address a range of urgent, interlinked problems: overwork, unemployment, over-consumption, high carbon emissions, low well-being, entrenched inequalities, and the lack of time to live sustainably, to care for each other, and simply to enjoy life.

So, some people are seriously thinking about the issues brought up by Mandeville 300 years ago. There has been little progress, however.

Life-changing collective actions, like a workers' revolution or an economic disarmament agreement such as the one suggested above, are very difficult for societies to negotiate and put into effect. For example, Mandeville suggested that if one country failed to join the scheme and kept its population chained to their hedonic treadmills while other countries enjoyed their greater leisure, the former country would eventually take over the world and raise its happiness at the expense of everyone else's happiness. The wealthy capitalists that dominate the economic and political systems, as well as the news media and entertainment industry, in most countries effectively shape cultures that keep individuals narrow-mindedly seeking greater status by working harder and thus preventing any revolutions or political groundswell for welfare-improving international agreements. So far, few countries have followed France in mandating even something as moderate as a 35-hour workweek.

Revolutions and collective movements for substantial social change are also rare because people tend to resist change. Recall the vast evidence from neuroscience and behavioral economics showing that people prefer a bird in the hand to two in the bush. It is therefore not as difficult as it might seem for those who favor a failing status quo to prevent change. It often takes exceptionally dismal circumstances to get people to accept major changes in their lives.

3.4.3 Growth, inequality, and happiness

The idea that economic growth does little for human happiness may not be an entirely accurate interpretation of the evidence on happiness. There is some evidence that people like manageable and predictable changes that improve their personal well-being relative to what they recently experienced. For example, in a recent study workers were given the choice of earning the same real wage every year of their lives or experiencing gradually increasing wages that average out to the same real level as the constant lifetime wage.[10] The majority selected the rising wage option even though it meant starting with a lower wage. Economists found the majority's choice surprising because standard economic theory mandates discounting future earnings relative to current earnings. Discounting the future means the constant wage provides a higher present value of lifetime income than a rising wage that starts with a below-average wage. In fact, a third choice that was also offered to the study participants, namely an

---

[10] George F. Loewenstein and N. Sicherman (1991).

identical average lifetime income that begins with a relatively high wage that gradually declines over time, provides the highest present value of income when people discount the future. But almost no one selected that option! Therefore, even though happiness may not be influenced by the level of income per se, people apparently would like to see things getting better over time.

These results suggest that people may not be as short-run oriented as some studies suggest. Another interesting implication of the results is that the standard economic practice of discounting future income may not be appropriate for making decisions that maximize long-run human happiness.

3.4.4 Individual happiness and economic growth

Happiness studies and Lykken's set point hypothesis suggest that, in the long run, there is little that individuals can do to alter their level of happiness. Should we, therefore, stop trying to improve our lives and just accept life as it comes?

The economic historian Richard Easterlin (2003) emphasizes the findings from happiness studies that suggest life-changing events such as marriage, divorce, widowhood, and physical disability can have a lasting effect on well-being even if increases in income and material consumption have no lasting influence on life satisfaction once basic needs are taken care of. Easterlin recognizes the danger of getting stuck on the hedonic treadmill, and he therefore argues that we need a better set of policies to maximize happiness:

> A better theory of well-being builds on the evidence that adaptation and social comparison affect utility more in the pecuniary than nonpecuniary domains. The failure of individuals to anticipate that these influences disproportionately undermine utility in the pecuniary domain leads to an excessive allocation of time to pecuniary goals at the expense of nonpecuniary goals, such as family life and health, and reduces well-being. There is need to devise policies that will yield better-informed individual preferences, and thereby increase individual and societal subjective well-being.[11]

Easterlin effectively urges people to stop and smell the roses. Or better yet, make sure you have lots of friends who will join you in the rose garden.

The psychologist David Lykken, who derived the set point hypothesis, in fact agrees with Easterlin that there *are* some things that people can do to keep their levels of happiness permanently above the average level mandated by their particular set points. Lykken offers a simple formula for personal happiness:

$$H = S + C + V, \tag{3.1}$$

---

[11] Richard A. Easterlin (2003), abstract at the start of the article.

where H stands for personal happiness, S is the set point as determined by an individual's genes, C represents the social and natural environment or "life conditions," and V represents work and participation in society. The V captures humans' apparent need to feel they are active and esteemed participants in the social group they think they belong to.[12] As shown earlier, happiness studies have found "belonging" relationships like marriage to enhance reported happiness. The positive influence of education on happiness revealed by happiness studies suggests that people enjoy learning, perhaps because they gain an understanding of the world around them and improve their ability to function well in their society. Humans evolved an extraordinary brain, at least compared to other living creatures, so it is not surprising that people find satisfaction in using this mental capacity.

It is not clear how we can affect the variable C in equation (3.1). Perhaps individual happiness improves if people can focus on doing things they like or are good at doing. For example, the psychologist Mihaly Csikzentmihalyi continually monitored how happy or satisfied people were as they went about their daily activities. His experiments showed that people were happiest when they were totally immersed in an activity in which they used their abilities and talents.[13] Jonathan Haidt (2006) also presented data confirming that people are happiest when they are deeply absorbed in what they are doing.

Of course, focusing on specific goals and tasks also leads people to tune out those things that could enhance happiness. There are potential conflicts between focusing on specific goals and the psychological need for friendship, social acceptance, and family relationships. In terms of Maslow's hierarchy of human needs, pursuing specific personal goals may clash with the need for approval of other people and acceptance in society. For example, Carol Nickerson, Norbert Schwartz, Ed Dieener, and Daniel Kahneman (2003) find that, all other things equal, a focus on financial goals increases human happiness. But they also find that all other things are not equal; the potential gains in happiness from a focused pursuit of financial goals are offset by lower satisfaction from relations with family and fellow workers. That is, people who are more focused on getting rich are less happy overall because the gains in wealth reduced their success in maintaining family and workplace relationships. Happiness and psychology research has shown these latter relationships to be very important for personal happiness. It matters, therefore, what people focus on and what they sacrifice when they focus on one potential source of happiness.

Many social scientists have interpreted the evidence on happiness as confirming the need for government action to change the social and natural environments we reside in. To what effect collective government actions can improve C is, of course, the focus of a lively political debate in every country.

---

[12] Lykken's ideas are presented in John Lancaster (2006), "Pursuing Happiness: Two Scholars Explore the Fragility of Contentment," *The New Yorker*, February 27.

[13] Reported in John Lancaster (2006), op. cit.

But there is no doubt that some form of collective action or a major shift in a society's institutions is necessary in order to bring about real changes in its social and economic environments. For example, policies that make societies more inclusive, more participatory, and more tolerant could raise average personal happiness above the average set point level. Such policies probably require new laws, regulations, taxes, subsidies, and public programs such as education, child care, retirement benefits, and other forms of social insurance. The finding that we react most negatively to the loss of a spouse and close friends and relatives suggests that better healthcare will raise average human welfare. And, the finding that people have difficulty coping with sudden job loss strengthens the case for good macroeconomic policy and a competently run central bank. The many examples of governments actually reducing expenditures on these types of social programs in many countries show that it is not easy to get people to think and act collectively to institute welfare-enhancing economy-wide programs.

3.4.5 Checking in with Kabamba and Banks

Now, after this discussion of human happiness, it is time to get back to Mbwebwe Kabamba, the Congolese surgeon, and Enos Banks, the unemployed former miner who lives in a trailer in rural eastern Kentucky. Recall that both Mr. Banks and Dr. Kabamba enjoy similar monthly incomes, but they live in countries at the opposite ends of the per capita GDP standings. According to International Monetary Fund data reported in Table 2.11 of the previous chapter, real per capita GDP in the United States was about 140 times that of Congo. These are two very different countries. But there are other reasons the incomes of the two men are not the same. Dr. Kabamba supports an extended family of 12 with his income. Enos Banks' ex-wife and three sons have their own income and receive some types of public assistance. Banks claims he and his wife divorced so that she could claim her own government welfare payments.

Our discussion on the distinct effects on human happiness of relative versus absolute income is quite relevant to the comparison of Mbwebwe and Enos, who live in very different social environments. According to the story in *The Economist*:

> ... whereas the poor in Kinshasa complain about the price of bread, the poor in Kentucky complain about the price of motor insurance. Fair enough, they need to drive to work. Granted, the poor in America do not starve. But their relative poverty can hurt in other ways. To be poor in a meritocracy implies failure. Eastern Kentucky is one of America's least meritocratic enclaves, but failure still carries a stigma. Though few Americans say that the poor have only themselves to blame, many believe it. Many of the poor believe it, too. For a Congolese peasant, there is no shame in living in a hut made of sticks. Everyone you know does too. In America, by contrast, the term "trailer" denotes more than a mobile home, and

the people who live in one know it. They are also acutely aware of how the richer folk live, because they watch so much television.[14]

Banks' understanding of where he fits into his own society remind us of the findings that happiness is related to people's need to feel they belong in their community and that they need to perceive they have the respect of others. Banks lacks dignity:

> Dr. Kabamba, though hard up, enjoys the respect that doctors receive in all societies... those who know Dr. Kabamba treat him with deference. When your correspondent was detained by the police outside his hospital, for the crime of appearing to possess a wallet, one telephone call to the doctor was enough to fix the problem. The officers even apologized. Mr. Banks, by contrast, has no illusions about how other Americans see people like himself.[15]

The fact that Dr. Kabamba supports an extended family of 12 may actually increase his happiness even though it greatly dilutes his personal income; he has the continual company and respect of a close family.

The question of who is happier is, therefore, not easy to answer. Clearly, Dr. Kabamba satisfies certain human needs better than Mr. Banks. On the other hand, Banks more easily satisfies his material wants. Kabamba and his family are more likely to suffer a debilitating illness or early death. Also, civil war in Congo has complicated life in Kinshasa, something Banks need not worry about in Kentucky.

The difficulty in comparing welfare across countries is compounded by the difficulty in comparing people's views of life across different cultures. The article explains that Dr. Kabamba hinted that he would not be as happy in another country with another culture. But, Mr. Banks is not sympathetic to other cultures or people from other cultures either:

> In eastern Kentucky, as in Congo, those with marketable skills often leave as soon as they graduate. Unlike Congo, however, Kentucky can attract doctors from poorer parts of the world, such as South Asia. Mr. Banks does not think much of these immigrant medics. He fears they may give him the wrong medicine, perhaps deliberately, and threatens to "shoot them plumb between the eyes" if they try. He is not serious about this threat, one assumes, but his sense of grievance is no less real for being incoherent.[16]

Mr. Banks' attitude toward foreigners reflects an attitude common to insecure people: "I may be at the bottom of my society, but I'm still better than those foreigners!" Recall that people are more attuned to relative income and status

---

[14] *The Economist* (2005), "The Mountain Man and the Surgeon," December 20.

[15] *The Economist* (2005), op. cit.

[16] *The Economist* (2005), op. cit.

than absolute income, so by extending the comparison to foreigners, Mr. Banks can effectively view his low social position in his local Kentucky community more favorably. He gets pleasure out of positioning himself above another person.

Before you condemn Banks for his attitude, remember that a similar sentiment keeps Dr. Kabamba in Congo. Kabamba could earn a much higher real income as a doctor in Europe or North America, but he chooses to stay in Congo where he enjoys superior status and authority over others.

3.5 How Economists Study Economic Development

The lesson from the discussion of this and the previous chapter is that comparing the average per capita real GDP of countries does not clearly decide the question of which country provides its people with more satisfying lives. The many other characteristics of life in different countries must be examined before we can even begin to calculate who is better off. The complexity of human happiness presents a challenge to the field of economic development. The orthodox paradigm that accepts using per capita real GDP and a few other closely correlated indicators to frame discussions and guide development policies must be amended or replaced.

Recent research in economics and many other fields of the social and natural sciences undermines many established economic models and hypotheses. Biology, zoology, ecology, and physics, among other natural sciences, clearly document the deterioration of our planet's valuable natural services and the stress that further growth of material output will put on our natural environment. At the same time, other social sciences make it clear that human well-being depends on much more than the money value of market production. The simple welfare function used in neoclassical economics, which takes individual welfare as a specific positive function of the sum of some finite set of consumption items, cannot even begin to capture important determinants of long-run human well-being like social peace, friendship, security, good health, a benevolent natural environment, and a sense of belonging. In short, GDP per capita, by itself, may not be very useful for framing discussion and economic analyses of economic growth and development.

3.5.1 How did economics become such a narrow field?

Given the vast evidence that is available from happiness studies, psychology, neuroscience, and behavioral economics, it is useful to briefly reflect on how economics developed the unrealistic models and hypotheses that currently dominate the field. Economics provides a lesson for all fields of science, which have all, at one time or another, fallen into the same trap of myopia and self-satisfaction. The inherent complexity of the world almost inevitably leads to a narrow focus on specific issues and the development of analytical tools (ways of thinking) geared to analyzing those specific issues. Soon, those tools and that narrow focus begin to define the field, and the quest for truth suffers even as the field's intellectuals increasingly believe they are improving their understanding of the world. The recent advances in neuroscience and behavioral economics discussed above may be the outside shock that finally leads to the substitution of more realistic models of economic behavior for the welfare models that currently dominate orthodox economics.

Interestingly, economics and psychology were considered to be closely related disciplines in the nineteenth century. They only parted company at the start of the twentieth century. It was, in part, psychology's narrow focus at that time that forced economists to seek their own model of human behavior. At the start of the twentieth century, psychology's approach was mostly to observe behavior. Because psychologists did not structure their observations within the framework of specific models, there were few hypotheses to test. Psychological research was mostly directed at explaining abnormal rather than normal human behavior. Economists needed models of the latter for their analysis of economic behavior.

Economists thus built their own models of economic behavior. These models consisted of the welfare functions we detailed in the previous chapter, which depicted welfare as a simple function of inputs of goods and services as counted in GDP. These models also assumed that individual welfare functions were completely independent of other people's income and consumption so that they could be summed, or aggregated, into a national welfare function. Economists occasionally adhered to the scientific method by confronting their models with evidence of human behavior, and the evidence on observed human behavior frequently contradicted the implicit assumptions that lie behind the standard preference functions. However, for lack of better models, economists continued to explain welfare and the economic choices people make using models that included a small number of variables in surprisingly simplistic mathematical functions.

But this historical view does not explain why economists continue to use their unrealistic models, especially now that the fields of psychology and behavioral economics have developed much more useful models of normal human behavior. The explanation for mainstream economics' reluctance to drop its unrealistic welfare functions may lie with Thomas Kuhn's (1962) description of paradigms, which was discussed in Section 1.5.5 of Chapter 1. Interestingly, the same experimental results from psychology, behavioral economics, and neuroscience that undermined the orthodox welfare functions also suggest why it is so difficult for the field of economics to free itself from the dominant neoclassical paradigm.

3.5.2 *Models and the human brain's preference for patterns*

In addition to the results discussed above, neuroscientific experiments also confirm that the cognitive part of the human brain can only handle a limited amount of information at one time. Unlike the automatic processes, which seem to be able to respond to enormous amounts of information sent by the senses from all over the body and make many simultaneous decisions, the brain's cognitive processes slow down very quickly as the amount and complexity of information increases. Therefore, a complex or confusing situation slows the cognitive processes and results in people's behavior being directed almost entirely by the brain's faster automatic and emotional processes. Thus, even the most intelligent people, that is, those with relatively well developed pre-frontal cortexes, cannot handle more than one or just a few problems at any one time. In very difficult or unfamiliar situations, people with high IQs have little advantage over less intelligent people. In such situations, the sheer speed of instinctive reactions, which as noted above depends in part on experience and training, is most important.

Research by Robin Aimee Lebeouf (2002), Douglas Medin and Max Bazerman (1999), Patricia Churchland and Paul Churchland (2002), and many others confirms that the automatic and emotional processes in the brain depend largely on the recognition of patterns. Another finding is that the brain becomes agitated when unfamiliar patterns emerge or familiar patterns cannot be found. The everyday word for such agitation is *confusion*. When the brain is confused, it ends up making mistakes.

Shane Frederick (2005) carried out experiments that showed clearly how people misinterpret a problem or an observation by placing it in a familiar pattern that does not quite match the problem at hand. Effectively, people routinely distort the sensual signals to the brain by effectively distorting the reality they observed. Surprisingly, cognitive processes are often inaccurate even when people have time to focus.

In his experiments, Frederick asked people questions that required all three of the brains' processes. He thus avoided questions such as finding the exact square root of 19,163, for which everyone knows an emotional response is useless. Nor did he ask whether a person likes a particular song or book, which is an emotional question of taste that does not require a carefully calculated rational response. He instead designed a short test with the following three questions that require some, but not too much, rational thought to figure out:

(1) A bat and ball cost $1.10 in total. The bat costs $1.00 more than the ball. How much does the ball cost? _____ cents

(2) If it takes 5 machines 5 minutes to make 5 widgets, how long would it take 100 machines to make 100 widgets? _____ minutes

(3) In a lake, there is a patch of lily pads. Every day, the patch doubles in size. If it takes 48 days for the patch to cover the entire lake, how long would it take for the patch to cover half of the lake? _____ days

You will notice that each of these questions evokes an impulsive answer that is wrong, but that the correct answer is not really very difficult to figure out.

Frederick posed these questions to nearly 3,500 students and other people in a variety of universities in the United States. Table 3.4 summarizes the results. Scores vary from 0 to 3, depending on how many of the three questions were answered correctly. The results suggest either that the human brain's emotional processes still exert influence even when there is time to think or human cognitive processes are not as accurate as we would like to believe. Human cognitive processes often take shortcuts by incorporating complex realities into familiar patterns. Note that the three questions suggest patterns that lead to wrong answers.

An important economic implication of this research is that human behavior does not always reflect rational deliberation and accurate assessment of circumstances. People will often make bad decisions and choose the options that are not in their best long-term interest. The way people answered the three questions posed by Frederick suggest that people instinctively recognize patterns, and they use those patterns to make decisions. When the perceived patterns are not accurate, human conclusions based on the false patterns will be inaccurate. Our Chapter 1 discussion of the usefulness of economic models should come to mind here.

Table 3.4 Frederick's Cognitive Reflection Test

Locations (No. of participants):	Mean Score	Percentage Scoring 0	1	2	3
MIT (61)	2.18	7%	16%	30%	48%
Princeton University (121)	1.63	18%	27%	28%	26%
Boston fireworks display (195)	1.53	24%	24%	26%	26%
Carnegie Mellon University 746)	1.51	25%	25%	25%	25%
Harvard University (51)	1.43	20%	37%	24%	20%
University of Michigan, Ann Arbor (1267)	1.18	31%	33%	23%	14%
Online sample (525)	1.10	39%	25%	22%	13%
Bowling Green University (52)	0.87	50%	25%	13%	12%
University of Michigan, Dearborn (154)	0.83	51%	22%	21%	6%
Michigan State University (118)	0.79	49%	29%	16%	6%
University of Toledo (138)	0.57	64%	21%	10%	5%
Overall Results	1.24	33%	28%	23%	17%

Source: Shane Frederick (2005), p. 29.

Frederick's results are very relevant to the field of economics. They are especially relevant for the sub-field of development economics, which explicitly studies economic change within the also evolving social and natural spheres. First of all, this research implies that orthodox economic models that assume rational behavior are wrong. Not only does the human brain rely on automatic and emotional processes that often overwhelm the more rational cognitive processes, but even the cognitive processes often make mistakes. We are not as smart as we like to think we are.

Secondly, the apparent carelessness with which we interpret real world observations of complex processes should raise concerns about how economists use models to make sense of the complex economic phenomena they observe. Frederick's results suggest that economists, like all people, are likely to make mistakes because they will be prone to interpret economic phenomena using models (patterns) that they are familiar with rather than thinking up new models that accurately apply to the problem at hand. Because economic development implies continual changes in the economic, social, and natural environments in which people find themselves, it is almost inevitable that economic models do not perfectly fit every new circumstance. But, like the students in Frederick's study, economists will tend to carelessly fit what they think they see into models that they are familiar with.

The physicist Garrett Lisi provides an interesting insight into how his profession became enamored with models to the point where they blatantly violate the scientific method. Specifically, Lisi criticizes physicists who have embraced *string theory* as their "unifying theory" of the universe. String theory is a complex model that is logically consistent. But, because many of the variables it includes cannot be detected or measured with current equipment, the hypotheses generated by string theory have not been scientifically tested. The large Hadron Collider in Switzerland may yet provide scientific support. But in the meantime, Lisi attributes string theory's popularity purely to the model's elegance. Says Lisi sarcastically: "If a figure is so beautiful and intricate and clear, you figure it must not exist for itself alone... It must correspond to something in the physical world."[17]

3.5.3 The need for reflexivity

As the example from physics suggests, all intellectual fields tend to develop their own cultures, or paradigms, and these cultures then shape and influence research and analysis within these fields. The influential sociologist Pierre Bourdieu urged his fellow sociologists to actively embrace **reflexivity**, which he described as a systematic and rigorous self-critical analysis of their own field. Bourdieu devoted his career to describing how societies developed cultures that perpetuated social structures that, from an objective perspective, were clearly not optimal for human development. He came to conclusion that sociologists, who he argued should know better, were also biased by their cultures. Bourdieu

---

[17] Quoted in Benjamin W. Wells (2008), "Surfing the Universe," *The New Yorker*, July 21, p. 34.

(1990) prescribed a *sociology of sociology* that would reveal sociologists' own tendency to let the social culture of their field bias their analysis:

> I believe that if the sociology I propose differs in any significant way from the other sociologies of the past and the present, it is above all in that it *continually turns back onto itself the scientific weapons it produces.*[18]

Bourdieu's prescription is equally valid for all intellectual fields. Economists, too, should follow Bourdieu's suggestion and be more critical of the culture of their own field. We need an objective sociology of economics.

The **neoclassical economic paradigm**, which includes the assumptions of stable individual welfare functions, rational expectations, efficient markets, and competitive markets with full information, conveniently supports the capitalist economic culture of the Western world. The neoclassical paradigm is increasingly embraced by the intellectuals from other parts of the world who have been educated at Western universities. Orthodox economists thus continue analyzing economic policies and economic outcomes using the value of market production as their principal guide. They effectively also continue ignoring non-market outcomes, externalities, the distribution of income, discrimination and other forms of exclusion, not to mention the unrecorded services that nature provides outside markets. These latter effects and consequences are not easily analyzed using the current set of economic models that economists are familiar with. Economists are thus in a type of vicious cycle in which they use GDP data in growth models that assume economic development is the same as the growth of GDP. Reflexivity demands that economists examine existing hypotheses and models from "outside the box" of their narrow paradigm.

3.5.4 The Happy Planet Index

The way to avoid the growing irrelevance of mainstream economics in our complex world is to embrace holism. A useful metric of economic development must capture the interrelationships, and especially the incompatibilities, between human economic activity and humanity's social and natural environments. And it must capture how the human brain and the human consciousness powered by the brain translates its full social and natural circumstances into feelings of happiness and life satisfaction. If humanity's position is becoming more sustainable in the sense that people feel a greater security and compatibility with the social and natural environments, we can be more confident in saying that economic development is occurring. On the other hand, if humanity's position is becoming less sustainable and there is greater fear of disruption, conflict, or even the collapse of society, then there is clearly no economic development no matter what GDP may be telling us.

---

[18] Quoted in Loïc J. D. Wacquant (1989), p. 55.

Unfortunately, our better understanding of human happiness does not point to an obvious or easy alternative measure of an economy's performance. The Human Development Index (HDI) is an improvement on GDP per capita, but it does not capture all of the psychological determinants of happiness discussed in this chapter. Worse yet, it does not capture the effect of economic growth on the natural sphere. An interesting new composite measure that does seek to capture the quality of human life across the economic, social, and natural spheres is the New Economics Foundation's **Happy Planet Index (HPI)**.

The HPI measures how well the economy provides people with lives that are happy and satisfying relative to the impact of the economy to the natural environment. To measure how the economy enables people to live satisfying lives, the HPI uses a measure first introduced by Ruut Veenhoven (1996) called **happy life years**. This consists of the happiness data discussed in this chapter augmented by life expectancy. The rationale for the multiplicative measure is the same as was presented in the previous chapter to justify the **expected individual lifetime welfare** (IEILW) measure. In the case of happy life years, a happiness index is used in place of the EILW's GDP per capita. Then the happy life years are divided by an estimate of the economy's ecological footprint, that is, the level of exploitation of nature's resources and services:

$$\text{HPI} = \frac{\text{Happy Life Years}}{\text{Ecological Footpring}} \qquad (3.2)$$

The HPI measure is scaled to a 2050 target of 87 years longevity, a happiness score of 8.0, and a footprint of 1.7. Note that this is an efficiency measure in that it shows how many life years are achieved per unit of environmental impact.

The HPI uses standard sources of information. For example, life expectancy data is from the United Nations, and it is given in Table 3.5 as the expected number of years people born today are expected to live. The happiness data are from the *World Database of Happiness* described in footnote 4 of this chapter; the replies are converted to an index that ranges from a low of 1 (completely dissatisfied with life) to a high of 10 (very satisfied with life). The environmental footprint is an often-used measure that quantifies a country's impact on the environment in terms of how many Earths would be needed if the entire world consumed natural resources at the rate of the country in question. For example, a footprint of 5 means that the country uses five times as much of nature's services and exhaustible resources as Earth can sustain in the long run. A long-run sustainable footprint is equal to one or less.

The HPI brings the economy, society, and the natural environment together into one index. Of course, many of the criticisms of any single index still apply. For example, the HPI is an average measure, and there is no indication of how the happiness is distributed among the population of a country. On the other hand, the hope is that since people's happiness has been shown to depend on

Table 3.5 The Happy Planet Index

Top Ten Countries	Life Exp.	Life Sat.	Foot-print	HDI	Bottom Ten Countries	Life Exp.	Life Sat.	Foot-print	HDI
1. Costa Rica	78.5	8.5	2.3	76.1	134. Benin	55.4	3.0	1.0	24.6
2. Dom. Rep.	71.5	7.6	1.5	71.8	135. Togo	57.8	2.6	0.8	23.3
3. Jamaica	72.2	6.7	1.1	70.1	136. Sierra L.	41.8	3.6	0.8	23.1
4. Guatemala	69.7	7.4	1.5	68.4	137. C. Af. R.	43.7	4.0	1.6	22.9
5. Vietnam	73.7	6.5	1.3	66.5	138. Burkin F.	51.4	3.6	2.0	22.4
6. Colombia	72.3	7.3	1.8	66.1	139. Burundi	48.5	2.9	0.8	21.8
7. Cuba	77.7	6.7	1.8	65.7	140. Namibia	51.6	4.5	3.7	21.1
8. El Salvador	71.3	6.7	1.6	61.5	141. Botswana	48.1	4.7	3.6	20.9
9. Brazil	71.7	7.6	2.4	61.0	142. Tanzania	51.0	2.4	1.1	17.8
10. Honduras	69.4	7.0	1.8	61.0	143. Zimbabwe	40.9	2.8	1.1	16.6

Some Other Countries									
17. Bhutan	64.7	6.1	1.0	58.5	75. Japan	82.5	6.8	4.9	43.3
20. China	72.5	6.7	2.1	57.1	88. Norway	79.8	8.1	6.9	40.4
35. India	63.7	5.5	0.9	53.0	89. Canada	80.3	8.0	7.1	39.4
36. Venezuela	73.2	6.9	2.8	52.5	102. Australia	80.9	7.9	7.8	36.6
53. Sweden	80.5	7.9	5.1	48.0	114. U.S.A.	77.9	7.9	9.4	30.7

Source: New Economics Foundation (2010), *Happy Planet Index 2.0*, downloaded from: http://www.neweconomics.org, June 7, 2011.

their society's economic and social equality, the level of inequality in society is captured in people's replies to the happiness surveys used to calculate the life satisfaction index. By using happiness data directly in the index, the creators of the index hope they are capturing many other determinants of human happiness.

Table 3.5 shows that the ranking of countries under the HPI differs substantially from the tables in Chapter 2. You may be surprised that the top of the list is dominated by Latin American countries, which are normally classified as developing, not developed, countries. The high ranking here reflects the HPI's emphasis on the natural environment. The countries listed near the top of the HPI index all have low environmental footprints, so their happy life expectancies are divided by small footprint numbers. Their relatively low levels of GDP actually reduce their carbon emissions, water usage, and resource usage. At the same time, many Latin American countries have life expectancies of over 70 years, and most Latin Americans claim to be fairly happy, as evidenced by happiness scores between 6.5 and Costa Rica's world-leading 8.5 out of 10.

Table 3.5 lists a sampling of other countries from the complete ranking of the HPI. Note that Norway, the country ranked at the top of the 2010 Human Development Index (HDI), is only ranked in eighty-eighth place in the HPI list despite its 79.8 years life expectancy and 8.1 happiness score because it has an environmental footprint of 6.9. It would take 7 planets for all people to live like Norwegians. The United States is ranked below Norway because its footprint is even greater than Norway' while it does not achieve Norway's life expectancy or average life satisfaction. Bhutan, a poor country whose government claims to focus policies exclusively on happiness, is ranked seventeenth. You can download the HPI from the website listed at the bottom of Table 3.5 to get the complete country rankings as well as a full description of the methodology.

You may be reluctant to accept the ranking of countries under the HPI, but realize that your reluctance is driven by the anthropogenic bias of human culture. When the "rights of nature" are taken into consideration, we must accept that human happiness is not the only factor in determining whether the natural sphere is happy. Note that the HPI puts the human footprint, which is largely determined by GDP, in the denominator.

3.6 Concluding Thoughts

If there is any one point you will want to carry forward from this chapter, it is that humans are social creatures whose individual welfare depends on the welfare of the whole society and their position within that society. The research from behavioral economics, neuroscience, and psychology clearly suggest that the welfare functions used explicitly by microeconomists and implicitly by macroeconomics are woefully misleading. Policies designed with those welfare functions are unlikely to lead to true human progress. In studying the process of economic development, therefore, it is necessary to focus on how economic change alters the overall organization of society and the relative positions of individuals within the changing society. The growth in material output and the technological changes of the past 200 years have made human life longer and more pleasant for most people, but the past 200 years of economic change have also brought new economic and social stresses that made life less satisfying. The Nazi holocaust, Soviet gulags, and the Cambodian genocide are but a few examples of recent human-made disasters.

The second major theme of this textbook is that the near-tripling of life expectancy and the ten-fold increase in per capita material wealth over the past 200 years has put humanity on course to destroy the ecosystem within which humanity evolved. Unless we humans change the way we live and work, environmental catastrophe threatens our very existence. It is the task of development economics to determine how our ever-changing human society will alter human happiness under alternative policy scenarios. There are always economic, social, and ecological stresses regardless of which economic policies humanity chooses to implement, but some choices are more likely than others to make humans satisfied with their lives. The difficulty is that humans have to make the choices in a state of uncertainty while under the influence of a complex combination of fear, status consciousness, compassion, and resistance to change. Oh, and did we mention that humans' capacity to think abstractly and rationally is not as great as we like to believe?

The plot of our story of economic development is thus much more complicated than you may have imagined. Complexity has its fascination, however. You will find that the true story of economic development is much more interesting and exciting than what the sterile neoclassical paradigm suggests. Fundamentally, the study of economic development is nothing less than the search for the meaning of life and human happiness. So, embrace complexity, and read on.

Key Terms and Concepts

Affective brain processes
Automatic processes
Behavioral economics
Brain imaging
Cocagne
Cognitive brain processes
Consciousness
Deliberative brain processes
Economic disarmament treaty
Emotional behaviors
Endowment effect
Evolution
Happiness
Happiness studies
Happy life years

Happy Planet Index (HPI)
Hedonic treadmill
Hierarchy of needs
Homeostasis
Instinctive brain processes
Loss aversion
Multiple discrepancy theory of
    happiness
Mutation
Neoclassical economic paradigm
Reflexivity
Risk aversion
Territoriality
Self-actualization
Set point

Questions and Problems

1. Describe the meaning of the term *hedonic treadmill*. Do you agree that humanity is stuck on a hedonic treadmill? Explain your answer.
2. Why have hours worked not fallen very much in countries like the United States despite large increases in real income?
3. Interpret Mandeville's Fable of the Bees in a modern context. (Hint: Draw on the discussion of the hedonic treadmill and the conclusions of happiness studies.)
4. Explain the *endowment effect*. What does this effect imply about how economic growth affects human welfare?
5. Many social scientists have interpreted the evidence on happiness as confirming the need for government action to change the social and natural environments we reside in. Is such an interpretation correct? Precisely explain your yes or no answer.
6. What is the secret to happiness? Base your answer on the available evidence from behavioral economics, psychology, happiness studies, neuroscience, and any other scientific sources you can find.

7. Compare how an orthodox economist measures human welfare and how happiness studies and supporting evidence from neuroscience and behavioral experiments would measure human welfare. Then suggest how the different perspectives of orthodox welfare economists' and behavioral economists would influence the policies each would recommend for improving human welfare.

8. Who would you rather be, Dr. Kabamba or Enos Banks? Explain using the information and measures presented in this and the previous chapter.

9. Relate the results from Shane Frederick's three simple questions to the Chapter 1 discussion of economic models. (Hint: Frederick' experiment showed that when perceived patterns are not accurate, human conclusions based on the false patterns are also inaccurate.) How economists should use models?

10. Review the main finding of the happiness studies that calculated the correlations between reported happiness and various hypothesized causes of happiness. Do these results make sense to you? Are they compatible with orthodox welfare models?

11. Is work a cost or a benefit? What does orthodox economic theory suggest? What do happiness studies suggest?

12. Describe the three categories of brain processes that neuroscientists have distinguished. How do these processes interact and combine to influence economic behavior? Provide some examples from the text of this chapter.

13. How do the results of psychological, neuroscientific, behavioral, and happiness studies conflict with the social welfare function normally assumed by orthodox economists? (Hint: Begin with equation (2.4) from the previous chapter and confront it with the various findings reported in this chapter.)

14. This chapter mentions that a "hedonic disarmament treaty" might be a feasible institutional mechanism for dealing with the hedonic treadmill. What might such a treaty say? What specific measures would countries have to institute? (Hint: You might look at government regulations and policies, including taxes, maximum work hours, public investment, education, infrastructure, etc.)

15. What could individuals do to be happier and satisfied with life? What could people do collectively through government actions to increase national happiness?

16. How does the use of GDP per capita bias the study of economic growth and development? (Hint: Begin by defining GDP per capita in the precise terms of the equations in Chapter 2, and then relate the inter-disciplinary results of Chapter 3 to those equations.)

17. When the 2007–2008 financial collapse and global economic recession were developing, many economists predicted that the neoliberal economic paradigm would be replaced by a more "Keynesian" paradigm. By 2010 and 2011, such a paradigm shift appeared less likely, and most mainstream orthodox economists had quietly abandoned their interest in heterodox perspectives. Does this sequence of economic thought confirm or contradict Thomas Kuhn's hypothesis? Explain.

18. "Social connectedness" shows up as a positive contributor to human happiness in the many happiness studies. For example, people who are married and employed are happier than single and unemployed people. How could measures of social connectedness be incorporated into summary measures of social well-being?

19. In Section 3.3.3, the text concludes: "In sum, neuroscientific evidence reveals clearly that individual happiness depends on the welfare of others." If this is true, then how do you explain theft, hooliganism, and oppression? How do you explain the reductions in social spending by governments seeking to reduce budget deficits?

20. Do you think the HPI is an improvement on GDP per capita and the HDI? Explain why or why not.

References

Ariely, Dan (2008), *Predictably Irrational: The Hidden Forces that Shape Our Decisions*, New York: HarperCollins.

Blanchflower, David G. and Andrew J. Oswald (2000), "Well-Being Over Time in Britain and the USA," NBER Working Paper No. w7487, January.

Bourdieu, Pierre (1990), *In Other Words: Essays Toward a Reflexive Sociology*. Stanford, CA: Stanford University Press.

Brickman, Philip, and Donald Campbell (1971), "Hedonic Relativism and Planning the Good Society," in M. H. Appley (ed.), *Social Comparison Processes: Theoretical and Empirical Perspectives*, New York: Wiley.

Camerer, Colin, George Lowenstein, and Drazen Prelec (2005), "Neuroeconomics: How Neuroscience Can Inform Economics," *Journal of Economic Literature* 43:9–64.

Churchland, Patricia S. (2002), "Self-Representation in Nervous Systems," *Science* 296(April 12):308–310.

Churchland, Patricia S., and Paul M. Churchland (2002), "Neural Worlds and Real Worlds," *Neuroscience* 3(November):903–907.

Dawkins, Richard (1976), *The Selfish Gene*, Oxford: Oxford University Press.

Decety, Jean, and Claus Lamm (2006), "Human Empathy through the Lens of Social Neuroscience," *The Scientific World Journal* 6:1146–1163.

Di Tella, Rafael, and Robert MacCoulloch (2008), "Happiness Adaption to Income beyond 'Basic Needs'," NBER Working Paper 14539, December.

Diener, Ed, Marissa Diener, and Carol Diener (1995), Factors Predicting the Subjective Well-Being of Nations," *Journal of Personality and Social Psychology* 69:653–663.

Do, Quy-Toan, and Tung D. Phung (2010), "The Importance of Being Wanted," *American Economic Journal: Applied Economics* 2(October):236–253

Dolan, P., T. Peasgood, and M. White (2008), "Do We Really Know What Makes Us Happy? A Review of the Economics Literature on the Factors Associated with Subjective Well-Being," *Journal of Economic Psychology* 29:94–122.

Easterlin, Richard A. (1995), "Will Raising the Incomes of All Increase the Happiness of All?" *Journal of Economic Behavior and Organization* 27:35–47.

Easterlin, Richard A. (2003), "Building a Better Theory of Well-Being," IZA Discussion Paper No. 742, March.

Fatouros, Nina E. *et al.* (2009), "Male-Derived Butterfly Anti-Aphrodisiac Mediates Induced Indirect Plant Defense," *PNAS* 105(29):10033–10038.

Frederick, Shane (2005), "Cognitive Reflection and Decision Making," *Journal of Economic Perspectives* 19(4):25–42.

Frey, Bruno, and Alois Stutzer (2000), "Happiness, Economy and Institutions," *Economic Journal* 110(446):918–938.

Goodman, M., *et al.* (2008), "Phylogenomic Analyses Reveal Convergent Patterns of Adaptive Evolution in Elephant and Human Ancestries," *Proceedings of the National Academy of Sciences* 106(49):20824–20829.

Grosfeld, Irena, and Claudia Senik (2010), "The Emerging Aversion to Inequality," *Economics of Transition* 18(1):1–26.

Haidt, Jonathan (2006), *The Happiness Hypothesis*, New York: Basic Books.

Kahneman, Daniel, and Amos Tversky (2000), *Choices, Values and Frame*, Cambridge, UK: Cambridge University Press.

Keynes, John Maynard (1930[1963]), "Economic Possibilities of Our Grandchildren," in *Essays in Persuasion*, NewYork: W.W. Norton.

Kuhn, Thomas S. (1962), *The Structure of Scientific Revolutions*, Chicago: University of Chicago Press.

Lancaster, John (2006), "Pursuing Happiness: Two Scholars Explore the Fragility of Contentment," *The New Yorker*, February 27.

Lebreton, Maël, *et al.* (2009), "The Brain's Structural Disposition to Social Interaction," *European Journal of Neuroscience* 29(11):2247–2252.

Leboeuf, Robyn Aimee (2002), "Alternating Selves and Conflicting Choices: Identity Salience and Preference Inconsistency," *Dissertation Abstracts International* 63(2–B):1088.

LeDoux, Joseph E. (1996), *The Emotional Brain: The Mysterious Underpinnings of Emotional Life*, New York: Simon and Shuster.

Loewenstein, George F., and N. Sicherman (1991), "Do Workers Prefer Increasing Wage Profiles?," *Journal of Labor Economics* 9:67–84.

Lopes, Helena (2011), "Why Do People Work? Individual Wants Versus Common Goods," *Journal of Economic Issues* 45(1):57–73.

Lykken, David T. (1999), *Happiness: What Studies on Twins Show Us about Nature, Nurture, and the Happiness Set Point*, New York: Golden Books.

Maddison, Angus (2001), *The World Economy: A Millennial Perspective*, Paris: OECD.

Mandeville, Bernard de (1714), *The Fable of the Bees*.

Maslow, Abraham H. (1943), "A Theory of Human Motivation," *Psychological Review* 50(4): 370–396.

Medin, Douglas, and Max H. Bazerman (1999), "Broadening Behavioral Decision Research: Multiple Levels of Cognitive Processing," *Psychonomic Bulletin and Review* 6(4):533–47.

Michalos, A. C. (1985), "Multiple Discrepancy Theory (MDT)," *Social Indicators Research* 16:347–413.

Neumark, David, and Andrew Postlewaite (1998), "Relative Income Concerns and Rise of Married Women's Employment," *Journal of Public Economics* 70:157–183.

New Economics Foundation (2010), *Happy Planet Index 2.0*, downloaded from: http://www.neweconomics.org.

Nickerson, Carol, Norbert Schwartz, Ed Diener, and Daniel Kahneman (2003), "Zeroing in on the Dark Side of the American Dream: A Closer Look at the Negative Consequences of the Goal for Financial Success," *Psychological Science* 14(6):531–536.

Oswald, A. J. (1997), "Happiness and Economic Performance," *Economic Journal* 107(445):1815–1831.

Oswald, A. J., and N. Powdthavee (2008), "Does Happiness Adapt? A Longitudinal Study of Disability with Implications for Economists and Judges," *Journal of Public Economics* 92:1061–1077.

Pleij, Herman (2001), *Dreaming of Cockaigne*, New York: Columbia University Press; translation by Diane Webb; original title: *Dromen Van Cocagne*, Amsterdam: Uitgeverij Prometheus, 1997.

Prowse, Michael (2003), "Why Capitalism Will Never Permit Us to Live A Life of Leisure," *Financial Times*, August 9/10.

Siebert, Charles (2006), "An Elephant Crack Up," *New York Times*, October 6.

Shoshani, Jeheskel, William J. Kupsky, and Gary H. Marchant (200?), "Elephant Brain Part I," *Brain Research Bulletin* 70(2):124–157.

Thaler, Richard (1980), "Toward a Positive Theory of Consumer Choice," *Journal of Economic Behavior and Organization* 1(1):36–60.

Veenhoven, Ruut (1988), "The Utility of Happiness," *Social Indicators Research* 20:333–354.

Veenhoven, Ruut (1996), "Happy Life-expectancy: A Comprehensive Measure of Quality-of-Life in Nations," *Social Indicators Research* 39:1–58.

Wacquant, Loïc J. D. (1989), "Toward a Reflexive Sociology: A Workshop with Pierre Bourdieu," *Sociological Theory* 7(1):26–63.

PART II

Models of Economic Development

This part of the book surveys the past 250 years of thinking on economic growth and development. These chapters are both respectful and critical of the models that the best minds in economics and social science developed to guide economic analysis. We must acknowledge the huge debt we owe those thinkers who came before us.

This part of the book comprises five chapters. Chapter 4 covers the period from Adam Smith in the late eighteenth century, through the Classical school and Marx in the nineteenth century, and concludes with the Harrod-Domar model of the mid-twentieth century. The variations in the models reflect the overall development of economic thought in general as well as the variation in the intensity of thinking about economic development. Chapter 5 details Robert Solow's 1956 neoclassical growth model, which still dominates the economic growth literature. Despite the limits of this model's neoclassical foundation, it offers insights that are very helpful in our more holistic analysis of economic development. Chapter 6 expands the Solow model to analyze the current environmental problems caused by the past 200 years of rapid economic growth, such as climate change and the loss of biodiversity.

The Solow model highlights the role of technological change in the process of economic development. Chapter 7 discusses the characteristics and complexity of technological change and the growth of knowledge. The chapter also outlines some of the early attempts by economists to model technological change and the advance of knowledge within a neoclassical framework. Chapter 8 details and extends Schumpeter's dynamic model of technological change. Development economists have found that a general version of Schumpeter's model provides a useful framework for analyzing technological change.

In reading this part of the book, recall Pierre Bourdieu's (Chapter 3) point that intellectual fields tend to develop cultures that effectively end up shaping and biasing the research and social analysis conducted in these fields. Bourdieu urged his fellow sociologists to actively embrace *reflexivity*, the systematic and rigorous self-critical analysis of their own field. Hopefully, this section provides a sufficient dose of reflexivity with regard to past economic thinking and the culture of economics so that we can, in subsequent chapters, make efficient use of past models of economic development without also becoming captives of the cultures associated with those models.

CHAPTER 4

The Evolution of Growth Models:
From Smith to Harrod-Domar

The greatest improvements in the productive powers of labour, and the greater part of the skill, dexterity, and judgement with which it is any where directed, or applied, seem to have been the effects of the division of labour.

(Adam Smith, 1776 [1976], p. 7)

Thanks to the division of labour, this labour power becomes specialised, is reduced to skill in handling a particular tool. As soon as the handling of this tool becomes the work of a machine, the use-value and the exchange-value of the worker's labour power disappears. The worker becomes unsalable, like paper money which is no longer legal tender.

(Karl Marx, *Capital*, Vol. 1, p. 470)

This chapter examines the models of economic growth and development that were popular among economists before the middle of the twentieth century. We will begin with several models that were developed as the world was just beginning its 200-year surge in material output. These models were suggested by Adam Smith and the nineteenth century Classical economists. We then relate the ideas of Karl Marx to these early economic thinkers, and show how Marx expanded Classical ideas into a broad model of social evolution. We conclude with a discussion of how economic thinking and economic culture in the late nineteenth century eventually culminated with the popular Harrod-Domar growth model in the twentieth century. This chapter's historical review of growth models prepares you for the subsequent four chapters, which examine today's most popular growth models.

The models in this chapter reflect a keen awareness of the complexity of human society. A reading of the principal works of the early economists reveal some dominant themes among the many issues covered:

- The growth of economic production goes hand in hand with increased *specialization* and *exchange.*

- Economic change is related to *saving,* the act of refraining from consumption, and *investment,* the use of economic resources and factors to produce new productive factors. We will refer to economic growth caused by increased saving and investment as *growth by factor accumulation.*

- Economic growth by factor accumulation will slow down because of *diminishing returns* if only some, and not all, factors can be increased.

- Economic growth and change is also related to *innovation* and the creation of *new ideas,* which we will refer to as *technological progress.*

Many of these themes reappear in today's most popular models of economic growth and development. Adam Smith detailed the role of innovation and new ideas in the growth process, even if he did not illustrate the relationship in as neat and logical a model as Robert Solow or Paul Romer did in their popular twentieth century models. The principle of diminishing returns figured

---

Chapter Goals

1. Introduce the economic thinking of the Physiocrats and Mercantilists.
2. Describe Adam Smith's concepts of the division of labor (specialization) and exchange.
3. Present a simple Smithian model of economic development that relates occasional breakthroughs connected by increasing rates of innovation.
4. Explain diminishing returns and the role it played in the growth model of Thomas Malthus, David Ricardo, and John Stuart Mill.
5. Explain Malthus population function and why it condemned humanity to eternal poverty.
6. Discuss the Classical economists' emphasis on the dynamic evolution of income shares and how this dynamic influenced economic growth.
7. Detail Karl Marx's model and his explanation of the collapse of capitalism.
8. Explain Marx's insight into capitalism's inherent problems in maintaining demand for its growing output.
9. Explain the development of neoclassical economics and its scientific reductionist perspective.
10. Present John Maynard Keynes' macroeconomic model as a reaction to the reductionist neoclassical model, and its debt to Marx and the Classicals.
11. Detail the full Harrod-Domar model.

prominently in the early nineteenth century models of the Classical School, a century and a half before Robert Solow built his well-known growth model around that same principle. Factor accumulation plays some role in nearly all growth and development models, although the roles vary greatly.

The growth of economic knowledge has been an erratic process influenced by social events and shifting intellectual paradigms. This chapter traces the erratic dynamic path of economic understanding of the development process. The next section begins with models from the eighteenth century.

4.1 Adam Smith's Model of Economic Change

Some early social thinkers linked economic development to the expansion of certain industries or sectors of the economy. They often advocated special policies to promote or benefit those special industries or sectors, always claiming to have the overall welfare of the nation in mind, of course. In a number of European countries in the 1700s, it became popular to subsidize, protect, and otherwise favor certain industrial and commercial activities. According to one such group of thinkers referred to as **Mercantilists**, the growth of industry was synonymous with economic development.[1] National wealth, they argued, is increased by transforming raw materials into final products. The more transformation takes place at home, the more prosperous are the industrialists. How the overall population fared under this industrial protectionism was left unanswered, although the mercantilist literature often suggested that a wealthy industrial sector would somehow benefit the nation.

The idea that transformation of raw materials into final products was an important source of national wealth led the Mercantilists to favor protective barriers to industrial imports from other countries. Protectionism was seen as the best way to maximize the amount of transformation, and thus wealth, within a country. Buying industrial, or transformed, products from other countries was equated with a loss of national wealth. Mercantilists supported colonialism because they viewed the conquest of foreign territories as necessary to secure sources of raw materials for the industries that generated national wealth. Mercantilists in England, France, Spain, and Portugal went so far as to ban industrial production in their colonies and, instead, required colonies to buy all industrial products from the mother country. Mercantilist policies have rightfully been blamed for obstructing economic development in the colonies. But, Adam Smith and many other late eighteenth century economists went further and argued that such protectionist policies were not optimal for either the colonies or the colonialist countries. They argued that free and voluntary

---

[1] What is now classified as the **Mercantilist school** of economic thought covers a very diverse and complex literature. The popular description of Mercantilists as advocates of protection and favorable policies toward industry deals with just one aspect of mercantilist policies before 1800.

international trade was a positive sum game in which all countries gained welfare. Colonialism and the monopolization of manufacturing by a few European countries was thus seen as harmful to all countries, including the European colonialist countries. The idea that industrialization is inherently good for a country's economic welfare is still embraced by many people today.

The eighteenth century school of French economic thinkers associated with the French Enlightenment, known today as the **Physiocrats**, argued that the wealth of a nation was derived from agriculture. They saw the natural order, what they termed the *physiocracy*, of the economy as a steady interaction between the **productive class** (farmers), the **sterile class** (industrial workers and artisans), and the **proprietor class**. They argued that farmers were the source of all wealth and true production; the other two classes appropriated part of what the productive class produced. In a sense, they were the polar opposites of the Mercantilists: the latter claimed the transformation of raw materials drove economic growth, the former claimed transformation added nothing to the economy's basic production of agricultural products. The Physiocrats generally favored *laissez-faire* economic policies because they saw the government as part of the sterile class that appropriated rent from the productive class.[2]

In a sense, the Physiocrats were holistic because they saw the economy as a complete system of interrelated parts. François Quesnay, perhaps the best known member of the school, developed his *Tableau Économique*, which was the first known diagrammatic model of an economic system. The Physiocrats failed to see that all of the parts were to some degree productive in the sense that they were necessary parts of the overall economic system that produced the economy's final output. Physiocrats argued that the economic system consisted of various "unproductive" economic sectors superimposed on productive agriculture in order to appropriate part of the latter's "fundamental" output. The Physiocrats were almost certainly wrong on the insignificance of transformation for economic development, but their point that some sectors of the economy are more productive than others is quite important. In fact, a popular theme in development economics that we will see in later chapters is that development policies should prioritize certain types of economic activities over others. In the twentieth century, industrial production was again a favored target.

In this chapter, we begin our historical survey of development models with Adam Smith, who in 1776 published *An Inquiry into the Nature and Causes of the Wealth of Nations*, or *The Wealth of Nations* for short.[3]   As the title of his work suggests, Smith attempted to explain how economies became

---

[2] Many of the early leaders of the United States identified closely with the Physiocrats. Thomas Jefferson's idealized *yeoman farmer* is also a Physiocratic ideal. Many Americans still identify with the concepts of individuality and self-sufficiency that were fundamental to Physiocratic economic thought. Of course, other early American leaders, Alexander Hamilton for example, embraced protectionism in order to stimulate industrialization.

[3] For more on Smith's writings on economic growth and development, and the popularity of his work, see J.M. Letiche (1960).

wealthier. The popularity of Smith's work in the late 1700s was in large part due to his ability to capture the economic changes that Scotland, Britain, and other countries were beginning to experience at that time. Smith explicitly criticized the Mercantilists' view of economic interaction as a zero-sum game in order to distinguish his arguments for free trade and free markets. Smith's work became the basis for the Classical and Neoclassical schools of economic thought that followed, and those schools have repeatedly come under criticism as misrepresenting how international trade and other human interaction actually works. Free markets can also be the channel through which one group exploits another.

4.1.1 Specialization and exchange

Adam Smith identified many important characteristics of growing economies. For example, in the quote at the start of this chapter Smith suggested that the **division of labor** was a fundamental characteristic of economic growth. Today, we call the division of labor **specialization**. There are at least three ways in which specialization is linked to the growth of economic output. First of all, at the early stage of the Industrial Revolution Smith noticed that specialization led to **economies of scale** in production. One of the advantages of industrial production was that resources are more productive when they are brought together in a single large production facility rather than being spread among a large number of small production units. In Chapter 1 of his *Wealth of Nations* (pp. 8–9), Smith describes the efficiency of a contemporary pin factory over a traditional pinmaker:

> One man draws out the wire, another straights it, a third cuts it, a fourth points it, a fifth grinds it at the top for receiving the head; to make the head requires two or three distinct operations; to put it on, is a peculiar business, to whiten the pins is another; it is even a trade by itself to put them into the paper;... But if they had all wrought separately and independently, and without any of them having been educated to this peculiar business, they certainly could not each of them have made twenty, perhaps not one pin a day...

Smith thus argued that, in order to specialize and exploit economies of scale, production had to be organized into larger business organizations.

The second way in which specialization increases economic efficiency is by permitting individual resources to be allocated among different tasks according to their peculiar abilities and capacities. Smith used the idea to advocate free trade and international specialization across countries. He suggested that each nation should concentrate on producing those goods for which it is best equipped or endowed rather than seeking to do everything for themselves. Later economists, notably David Ricardo early in the next century, extended Smith's idea to develop the concept of **comparative advantage**. This concept is so highly regarded in the field of economics that it is now referred to as the *principle of comparative advantage*. The principle logically leads to the conclusion that trade is a positive-sum activity that benefits all countries.

Comparative advantage and economies of scale together provide the foundation of the process of specialization and the division of labor. Output increases through specialization because factors of production are used where they are most productive. Productivity is further enhanced because people's focus on a single task permits them to gain experience in that task more rapidly, and they also do not have to spend time and effort switching gears, so to speak.

Specialization, whether based on comparative advantage or increasing returns to scale, requires the exchange of goods and services. The benefits of specialization are only realized if people and firms can exchange the goods and services they produce for those produced by others with different comparative advantages or economies of scale. To facilitate the necessary exchanges, Adam Smith advocated policies to liberalize markets and international trade. Smith is today most often remembered for having written that market prices serve as incentives that, like an "invisible hand," guide everyone's self-interested behavior towards those activities that most improve society's total welfare. Smith did in fact use the words *invisible hand*, but his description of markets and international trade was more subtle than those words suggest. Smith devoted great attention in his *Wealth of Nations* to the social and economic institutions he deemed necessary for markets to function efficiently. He did not trust free markets to magically arise, and he explicitly criticized the continual attempts by industrialists to collude and monopolize markets.

Smith is, of course, not the only economist whose contributions to economic thinking were subsequently oversimplified and misrepresented. Knowledge is a cumulative process in which new ideas build on earlier ideas. The task of dealing with such a massive body of accumulated knowledge often leads to a selective, recognition of earlier thought.

4.1.2 Specialization and technological progress

A third way in which specialization may increase economic efficiency is if it promotes technological change. Adam Smith's writings indicate he viewed specialization, or the division of labor, as a potential contributor to long-term technological progress:

> ... the invention of all those machines by which labour is so much facilitated and abridged, seems to have been originally owing to the division of labour. Men are much more likely to discover easier and readier methods of attaining any object, when the whole attention of their minds is directed towards the single object, than when it is dissipated among a great variety of things...[4]

---

[4] Adam Smith (1776 [1976]), p. 13.

Smith's suggestion has been incorporated into several recent growth models and is now commonly referred to as **learning by doing**. The longer one performs a task, the more productive one gets at doing it.

Smith also recognized that technological improvements were created as a result of intentional efforts to innovate:

> All the improvements in machinery, however, have by no means been the invention of those who had occasion to use the machines. Many improvements have been made by the ingenuity of the makers of machines, when to make them became the business of a peculiar trade; and some by that of those who are called philosophers or men of speculation, whose trade is not to do anything, but to observe everything; and who, upon that account, are often capable of combining together the powers of the most distant and dissimilar objects. In the progress of society, philosophy or speculation becomes, like every other employment, the principal or sole trade and occupation of a particular class of citizens... Each citizen becomes more expert in his own peculiar branch, more work is done upon the whole, and the quantity of science is considerably increased by it.[5]

These "philosophers and speculators" refer to two groups of people who are very important for the process of innovation: inventors and **entrepreneurs**. The latter are the driving force in the development model by Joseph Schumpeter, which we will study in Chapter 7.

In the above quote, Smith also suggests that new technologies, developed by inventors and put into practice by entrepreneurs, are often *embodied* in the machines provided by the capital goods sector of the economy. This suggests that investment and technological change are intimately linked, a possibility that has been recognized in some modern models of economic growth.

4.1.3 The importance of institutions

While Smith has been frequently criticized for suggesting a simplistic policy of **laissez faire**, his writing makes it very clear that he was aware of the difficulties associated with his growth recipe. Smith was not as dismissive of government as, for example, the Physiocrats were. Smith understood that there was a need for collective action and, therefore, a role for government in the economy. Smith also fully recognized the general role of **institutions** in a system of markets. By *institutions* we mean such things as laws, regulations, customs, legal systems, religions, and social pressures that encourage or constrain people in their quest to maximize welfare. Smith wrote that the protection of person and property, the maintenance of law and order, limitations on government's power to interfere in people's activities, and a fair and predictable legal system were necessary ingredients in an environment where innovation and specialization

---

[5] Adam Smith (1776 [1976]), pp. 13–14.

could flourish. Smith recognized government's role in establishing patent protection for innovations.

Among the many examples of institutions that Smith discussed was the institution of money, which facilitated the exchange of goods. Barter is a very costly form of exchange, requiring all traders to exactly balance their trade with each trader and in every period of time. Money, on the other hand, permits sellers to temporarily store their wealth acquired by selling goods or service before they use it to purchase other goods or services. And individual buyers and sellers need not exactly balance trade between themselves. If Mary buys goods from John, John can use the money earned to buy goods from Jim if Jim's goods are more desirable according to John's tastes. By making the exchange of products easier, money permits a greater amount of specialization and, hence, greater improvements in human welfare.

Smith described the **monetization** of the Dutch economy in the early 1500s as an important step towards its economic development. Much of the land that now comprises the Netherlands lies at or below sea level in the deltas of the Rhine and Meuse rivers. Settlers in the region learned early on to build dams, dikes, canals, and windmills to restrain and pump out the water seeping into the low lands. As described by Jan de Vries and Ad van der Woude (1997), originally, the Dutch settlements operated in communal fashion, with each resident providing labor to the cooperative drainage authorities that maintained the infrastructure. However, there was a constant problem of neglect and poorly-performed work, especially during the planting and harvesting seasons. Rather than resort to heavy handed methods to force citizens to contribute their time, in the 1500s the Dutch instead authorized the drainage societies to tax residents and employ a permanent staff to maintain the infrastructure. The tax system required farmers to sell their produce for money because the tax authorities did not permit payment in kind, and soon the entire Dutch economy used money for interpersonal transactions.

The spread in the use of money throughout the entire economy played an important role in the subsequent development of the Dutch economy. According to the economic historians Douglass North and Robert Paul Thomas (1973, p. 145), Holland "was the first country to achieve sustained economic growth." No longer restricted by the inefficient practice of barter, Dutch traders soon extended specialization beyond their borders to become world traders. Of course, monetization also increased the banking industry and the frequency of financial crises.

4.1.4 Transportation and communications

Smith also emphasized the importance of transportation for expanding specialization and exchange. Since specialization was limited by "the extent of the market," a reduction in transport costs that effectively increased the size of the market by making it easier to move goods between buyers and sellers located in different regions would be supportive of economic development. To emphasize the universal importance of transportation for specialization, Smith wrote:

> The sovereigns of China, those of Bengal..., and those of Egypt, are said accordingly to have been extremely attentive to the making and maintaining of good roads and navigable canals, in order to increase, as much as possible, both the quantity and value of every part of the produce of the land, by procuring to every part of it the most extensive market which their own dominions could afford.[6]

Smith also devoted many pages to discuss how roads, harbors, and canals could be financed and maintained. He observed that, under some circumstances, government should undertake to construct and maintain transportation projects.

In mentioning China in the quote above, Smith was referring to China under the Sung Dynasty between the eighth and twelfth centuries. To unify the vast territory that was China, the government during the Sung Dynasty constructed a 30,000 mile-long network of canals, which transformed the Chinese economy. Historical evidence suggests that the Chinese economy grew rapidly with the construction of the waterways.[7] Regional trade increased exponentially, money came into general usage, and the resulting specialization increased industrial productivity to levels not seen again in the world until the Industrial Revolution in Europe beginning in the 1700s. Infrastructure, by itself, did not guarantee continued economic development, however. Angus Madisson (1998) estimates that China's per capita income peaked in 1100, after which foreign invasions by the Mongols from the north caused specialization to decline. Chinese government institutions also deteriorated with the invasions, making collective decisions more difficult.

4.1.5 National welfare

Another of Adam Smith's contributions to economic development theory is his discussion of what constitutes the economic welfare of a nation. Prior to the writings of Smith and some of his contemporaries in the post-Enlightenment period, a nation's welfare had almost always been viewed in terms of the strength of a nation's military, the health of certain sectors of the economy, or the size of a nation's population or territory. Smith made it very clear that it is the standard of living of the entire population that matters for the welfare of the nation: "The causes of this improvement, in the productive powers of labour, and the order, according to which its produce is naturally distributed among the different ranks and conditions of men in the society..."[8] This concern with the general welfare of the whole population was radical in Smith's day, but it is

---

[6] Adam Smith (1776 [1976]), Book 2, p. 364.
[7] Morgan Kelly (1997).
[8] Adam Smith (1776 [1976]), p. 2.

fundamental to the welfare analysis of economics today. Our focus in the previous chapters on how to measure national welfare and the difficulty in measuring economic development owe much to the Adam Smith's emphasis on national welfare.

4.1.6 The Smithian model

Adam Smith never presented a detailed, integrated model of economic development in his masterwork, *An Inquiry into the Nature and Causes of the Wealth of Nations*. His intent clearly was to explain how a nation's economy could increase the wealth of its citizens, however. Directly and indirectly, economic development is discussed throughout the book. It is possible to summarize his wide-ranging but consistent analysis in the form of a simple growth model.

Smith hypothesizes two distinct sources of economic development, one directly linked to the *increase* in specialization, the other related to the *level* of specialization. First, when specialization *increases*, there are new gains from exchange as individuals, firms, and entire countries exploit the gains from comparative advantage and increasing returns to scale. The increase in specialization may be due to changes in institutions, transportation improvements, or sudden breakthroughs in human knowledge. Secondly, Smith suggests that as the *level* of specialization increases, individuals and firms are more likely to "discover easier and readier methods of attaining any object, when the whole attention of their minds is directed towards the single object, than when it is dissipated among a great variety of things..." Learning by doing and innovative effort increase with more specialization, and the rate of technological change thus accelerates. And, gains in technology, in turn, permit further specialization, thus creating a *virtuous cycle*.

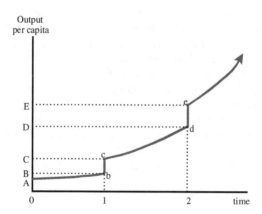

Figure 4.1 The Smithian Growth Model

The **Smithian development model** is illustrated graphically in Figure 4.1. Suppose the level of per capita income at time t = 0 is equal to A, the result of previous increases in specialization and innovation. As time passes, innovation, research, discovery, and learning by doing are continually taking place. Between t = 0 and t = 1 per capita income grows to B as the economy traces out the **growth path** Ab. At t = 1, suppose that the introduction of money permits a sudden increase in specialization, which raises per capita output (and income) to C. Then, innovation, research, discovery, and learning by doing continue at a higher rate because specialization is greater and, thus, allows for an even greater "direction of the minds towards single objects." Note that the segment cd of the economy's growth path rises more steeply than it did before the increase in specialization.

Suppose that there is a second institutional change at time t = 2, say the elimination of war between neighboring countries, which permits international trade where none had been possible before. There will be another sudden jump in specialization, which will cause per capita income to rise from D to E. The economy's growth path then rises at an even more rapid pace after t = 2.

Smith's optimistic view of future economic development thus consists of a series of discrete jumps and a gradually-increasing underlying rate of technological progress. The sudden discrete rises in per capita output are the result of increases in specialization caused by improved transportation infrastructure, some new breakthrough technology, or major institutional changes. The increased slope of the smooth sections of the curve represent continuous innovation, research, and learning by doing, which is a function of the degree of specialization. Increases in specialization drive technological development, and technological development, in turn, drives further specialization. Institutional improvements, which are really new forms of social or economic "technology," such as money, legal protection of property rights, and more personal freedom to make economic choices provide further boosts to the growth of per capita income.

4.1.7 Adam Smith's legacy

In summarizing Adam Smith's work, it is difficult to overestimate his influence on economic thought in general and development theory in particular. Some of the key points Adam Smith makes in his *Wealth of Nations* are:

- Specialization and exchange must increase if the economy is to grow.

- Competitive markets act like an "invisible hand" to guide selfish behavior toward enhancing the common good.

- There is a close association between specialization and the creation of new technology and knowledge because specialization promotes what we would now refer to as learning by doing and intentional R&D investment.

- The bottom line in judging the performance of an economy is the welfare of all members of society.

In addition to his broad analysis and many insights, Adam Smith introduced an interesting dilemma that economists have wrestled with ever since. On the one hand, Smith described how the *invisible hand* of competition serves to guide self-interested individual behavior toward maximizing total economy-wide welfare. But Smith's concept of *increasing returns to scale* and his example of the pin factory suggest that competition will tend to decline as fewer and larger firms come to dominate markets. How can an economy sustain competition among firms when increasing returns favors the growth of firms and the likely result that a small number of large firms will dominate the market for their products?

The incompatibility between free markets and economies of scale constitutes one of the most difficult issues in economics. Markets are not competitive when production is in the hands of a few large firms. Concentration of production in the hands of a few large businesses permits their owners to raise prices above marginal costs, capture larger shares of the gains from trade, and effectively change the distribution of income in their favor. The next two sections of this chapter explain how the Classical and Marxist schools of economic thought addressed the issue.

4.2 The Classical Economists and Diminishing Returns

The Industrial Revolution accelerated the growth of output in Europe during the late 1700s and early 1800s. The economists who followed Adam Smith, the so-called Classical economists, wrote extensively about economic development. The Classicals agreed on many things, which is why they are lumped together in the **Classical school**, but there are also important differences among them. This section focuses on the similarities, but we also highlight some differences that reveal important complexities of the process of economic development.

4.2.1 Malthus' theory of population

Thomas Robert Malthus, the early nineteenth century British economist, is best known for his theory of population. Malthus (1798) hypothesized that "the passion between the sexes" would cause population to grow in a *geometric* progression, but food production was constrained to grow only in *arithmetic* progression because of the limited "power of the earth to produce subsistence." Table 4.1 illustrates Malthus' geometric and arithmetic progressions.

Table 4.1 Malthus' Geometric Progression of Human Population and the Arithmetic Progression of Food Production

Years:	1	25	50	75	100	125	150	175	200
Population:	1	2	4	8	16	32	64	128	256
Food Supply:	1	2	3	4	5	6	7	8	9

Notice that in the case of population, Malthus was talking about nothing other than the power of compounding under a constant rate of growth. He assumed that the food supply would not grow at a constant rate because a fixed quantity of land would result in ever smaller gains in output as the additional people sought to grow more food for their subsistence.

Malthus's more complete model of economic development illustrated the conflict between population growth and the limited resource availability. First, he hypothesized a function linking population growth directly to real income. If people are well off, he reasoned, they can afford to eat well, live longer, and have more surviving children. Decreases in real per capita income, on the other hand, increase the death rate due to increases in starvation and disease, and shortened life expectancy reduces the birth rate. Adam Smith had suggested such a population function in *The Wealth of Nations*: "Every species of animals naturally multiply in proportion to the means of their subsistence."[9] It was Malthus, however, who gained fame for this population function because he made it central to his model of economic development, which was accepted by most other Classical economists of his day.

The **Malthusian population function** is illustrated in Figure 4.2. Population growth, which is the change in population P over the level of P, or $\Delta P/P$, is given on the vertical axis. Note that the symbol "Δ" signifies *the change in*. Real per capita income, $y = Y/P$, is shown on the horizontal axis. If real per capita income is above y_2, say at y_3, the death rate is less than the birth rate and the population grows. If real per capita income is below y_2, such as at y_1, the death rate is greater than the birth rate and the population shrinks. At real per capita income y_2, the death rate is equal to the birth rate, and the result is "zero population growth" or **ZPG**.

---

[9] Smith (1976), Book 1, p. 89. Smith actually credits Richard Cantillon, an Irish-born French banker and economic thinker/writer, for this idea.

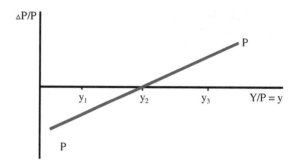

Figure 4.2 Population Growth

4.2.2 The "Classical" model

The Classical school of economic thought, or simply the *Classicals*, of the early to mid-nineteenth century, accepted Malthus' population hypothesis as a basic premise. When they combined it with the seemingly obvious observation that there was a finite, limited amount of land and other natural resources available on Earth, the Classicals were logically forced to conclude that humanity was doomed to eternal poverty.

To capture the influence of the resource scarcity hypothesized by the Classicals, we begin by building a general model of production. For simplicity, suppose that output is a function of labor and land, where the amount of land is fixed in quantity but labor can grow or contract depending on birth and death rates. Suppose also that output is determined by how much labor is combined with a fixed stock of arable land. This implies a **production function**, which is a mathematical construct that links output to varying sets of inputs, of the general form

$$Y = f(L, N) \tag{4.1}$$

where Y is real output, L is the variable amount of labor, and N is the fixed amount of arable land. If land is fixed in quantity, output can be increased only by increasing the amount of labor used to work the land. The classical economists hypothesized that, in the case where variable labor supply is combined with a fixed supply of land, labor is subject to **diminishing returns**. That is, for each additional worker employed, output increases by less and less because each additional worker has less and less land to work on.

4.2.3 An example of diminishing returns

Suppose that the production function, as specified in equation (4.1) above, takes on the specific form

$$Y = L^{.5} N^{.5} \tag{4.2}$$

In words, equation (4.2) says that output is the product of the square roots of Labor and land (Natural resources). This is a convenient formula because it results in diminishing returns to any one input, but if *all* inputs are doubled, output also doubles. Such a production function is said to exhibit both **constant returns to scale** and *diminishing returns* to individual factors.

Table 4.2 presents the results of inserting alternative values for the quantities of labor and land into the production function (4.2). Column (1) shows quantities of labor ranging from zero to ten, column (2) shows a fixed amount of land equal to 100 (acres). Column (3) gives the output levels; and column (4) gives the marginal increases in output as labor is increased by increments of one. The marginal increases are called the **marginal product of labor**. The constantly diminishing marginal increases in output given in column (4) reflect diminishing returns. Column (5) introduces an alternative example by assuming land is equal to 200 acres; this leads to total and marginal outputs as given in column (6). Column (7) shows that labor again exhibits diminishing returns, but the marginal returns are not the same with 200 acres of land as when labor was added to 100 acres of land.

Table 4.2 A Production Function with Diminishing Returns $Y = L^{.5}N^{.5}$

(1) Labor	(2) Land	(3) Total Output	(4) Marginal Product Of Labor	(5) Land	(6) Total Output	(7) Marginal Product Of Labor
0	100	0.0		200	0.0	
1	100	10.0	10.0	200	14.1	14.1
2	100	14.1	4.1	200	20.0	5.9
3	100	17.3	3.2	200	24.5	4.5
4	100	20.0	2.7	200	28.2	3.8
5	100	23.4	2.4	200	31.6	3.3
6	100	24.5	2.2	200	34.6	3.0
7	100	26.5	2.0	200	37.4	2.8
8	100	28.2	1.8	200	40.0	2.6
9	100	30.0	1.7	200	42.4	2.4
10	100	31.6	1.6	200	44.7	2.3

Table 4.2 also illustrates constant returns to scale. If we increase both labor and land by the same proportion, total output increases proportionately. For example, when we double labor from 2 to 4 and land from 100 to 200 (both 100 percent increases), total output doubles from 14.1 to 28.2. Or, if we double labor from 4 to 8 and land from 100 to 200, output doubles from 20 to 40.

Figure 4.3 illustrates diminishing returns and constant returns to scale graphically. The lower curve in Figure 4.3 represents the production function in the case of a fixed quantity of 100 acres of land, the higher curve the case of 200 acres of land. There are clearly diminishing returns to labor: the production functions always slope upward, but their slopes become less steep the more labor is added to production. Average output per worker depends on the ratio of output to labor. In Figure 4.3, output per worker is represented by the slope of the dashed lines that connect the origin and specific production points such as A or B. As more and more labor is added to the production process, diminishing returns causes the slope of the dashed line to become less steep, which means average output per worker declines. As already noted in Table 4.2, when both labor and land are doubled from 2 to 4 and 100 to 200, respectively, then output also doubles from 14.1 to 28.2. We move along the straight dashed line from A to C and the average productivity of workers remains the same at $14.1/2 = 28.2/4 = 7.05$. On the other hand, if only the quantity of labor increases from 2 to 4, then the economy moves from point A to point B, and the average productivity per worker declines, as illustrated by the lower slope of the line from the origin to B compared to the original average productivity of labor line through the point A. In sum, the production function $Y = N^{.5}L^{.5}$ clearly displays constant returns to scale and diminishing returns to labor.

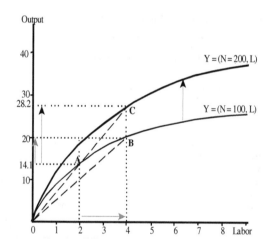

Figure 4.3 Diminishing Returns

4.2.4 The Classical equilibrium

The Malthusian growth model combines Figures 4.2 and 4.3. The basic logic of the model is that any improvement in technology that raises the average product of labor causes the population to rise, which in turn leads to diminishing returns and a decline in per worker output. Hence, if land is fixed in quantity, any fortunate increase in income will inevitably be canceled out by population growth and diminishing returns.

This result is illustrated in Figure 4.4. The production function is designated as Y(wP), which is shorthand for Y(N, L) under the assumption that N is fixed in quantity, and thus not a variable, and L = wP, under the assumption that a constant fraction w of the population P is in the labor force. In Figure 4.4, the straight lines from the origin represent different average levels of output/income per worker. The steeper the line, the greater the Y/P ratio and per capita output.

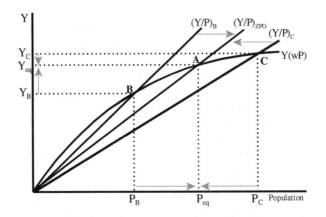

Figure 4.4 Equilibrium in the Malthusian Model

For example, the line $(Y/P)_{ZPG}$ represents real per capita income y_2 from Figure 4.3 when population growth is exactly zero. If real per capita income is greater than the ZPG level, say $(Y/P)_B$, the population grows and, all other things equal, the number of workers wP increases. As the number of workers increases, output rises. But, diminishing returns causes output to grow more slowly than population, and per capita income falls. The Y/P ratio thus gets smaller, and the slope of the line from the origin declines toward the line $(Y/P)_{ZPG}$. Alternatively, if real per capita income Y/P is less than the ZPG per capita income, which would be the case if the economy produced at a point like C on the production function Y(wP), then population declines. As the population shrinks, average product per capita rises, and the Y/P line shifts up and towards the line $(Y/P)_{ZPG}$. The population level P_{Eq} thus represents a **stable equilibrium** in that whenever P differs from P_{Eq} it will tend to return to P_{Eq}.

The Malthusian model thus suggests that humanity is destined to remain at subsistence levels of real per capita income, where we just reproduce ourselves. Future generations cannot expect to be better off than their parents, and technological breakthroughs have no lasting effect on living standards.

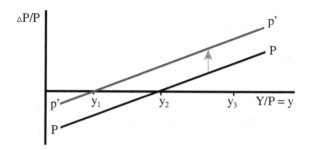

Figure 4.5 A Dismal New Equilibrium

In fact, the model leads to an even more dismal conclusion. For example, the discovery of the smallpox vaccine early in the twentieth century is viewed as a great advance in human welfare, but the model does not show the medical discovery in such a positive light. Because the vaccine reduces the death rate, all other things equal, the population function shifts upward from PP to p'p', as shown in Figure 4.5. There is, therefore, a fall in the ZPG real per capita income. This implies a long-run equilibrium at a higher population, say at P_C in Figure 4.4, as the entire ZPG line tilts to a lower slope and a lower per capita output. Thus, a reduction in smallpox deaths leads to an increase in population, diminishing returns causes real per capita income to fall, and poverty increases. Ironically, smallpox is replaced by starvation as a cause of death, and per capita income decreases to boot. With its models predicting outcomes like this, it is no wonder so many people refer to economics as the *dismal science*!

4.2.5 An evaluation of the Classical model

Benjamin Higgins' (1968, p. 68) describes of Malthus' model and those of other Classical economists of the early 1800s as follows:

> ... the development of the capitalist economies was a race between technological progress and population growth, a race in which technological progress would be in the lead for some time but which would end in a dead heat, or stagnation.

The Classical economists' predictions of eternal poverty are now viewed as disproved hypotheses, superseded by models that include the continuous improvement of living standards among the long-run outcomes. Indeed, things have fortunately not gone the way the classical model predicted they would. However, the classical model was not necessarily out of touch with reality, at least not the reality as it existed before 1800. The fear that population growth would undermine economic development was quite justified by the evidence available to Malthus and other classical economists in 1800.

We know from the Chapter 2 that there was very little growth in GDP per capita before the nineteenth century. Population growth was also slow before 1800, but it was not zero. There were several significant jumps in population growth, such as after the spread of agriculture between 10,000 and 5,000 BCE and during the relative peace and stability of the Roman Empire. In Table 4.3 we repeat data from Chapter 1, which shows that between the years 1000 and 1820 per capita output barely grew at all while total output nearly quadrupled over the same 820-year period. The simple classical model explains exactly why this happened: The gradual increases in the productive capacity of the world resulted in population growth, which fed back through diminishing returns to prevent per capita real incomes from rising in the long run. So total output grew, but per capita output remained largely unchanged.

Table 4.3 Annual Growth Rates of Real per Capita GDP: 1500–1992

	World Population	*World GDP*	*World GDP Per Capita*
0–1000	0.01	0.01	0.00
1000–1500	0.10	0.15	0.05
1500–1820	0.29	0.33	0.04
1820–1870	0.33	0.97	0.64
1870–1913	0.79	2.05	1.26
1913–1929	0.90	1.90	1.00
1929–1950	0.97	1.78	0.80
1950–1973	1.91	4.76	2.86
1973–2003	1.60	2.92	1.44

Source: See Table 1.1 in Chapter 1.

For the Classical economists writing at the start of the nineteenth century, there was little in history that hinted at the huge increases in per capita output that were about to dispel the fear of eternal poverty. Table 4.3 shows that Malthus' prediction of population growth turned out to be quite accurate, but the classical model failed to anticipate that world output would grow faster than population and permit per capita real output to grow continually for 200 years.

An accurate explanation of the past is useful, but historical accuracy, by itself, does not make a model useful for designing good policies for the future. Many Classical economists stuck to their predictions of permanent poverty well into the 1800s even as it was becoming obvious that people's incomes in many economies were rising rather than reverting to subsistence levels. In his history of how economists thought about economic growth, David Warsh (2006) writes:

> So powerful was the logic of their new tools — Ricardo's corn model, Malthus' table comparing geometric and arithmetic growth rates — that economists lost interest in countervailing tendencies, despite the evidence all around.[10]

---

[10] David Warsh (2006), p. 58.

Could it be that the Classicals were so influenced by their own models that they saw the world as their models described it, not as it actually was?

4.2.6 *Income distribution according to the Classicals*

The simple Classical model described above does not reflect everything that Thomas Malthus, David Ricardo, John Stuart Mill, and other Classicals had to say about economic development. Classical economists, in fact, reached more dismal conclusions about the inevitability of economic stagnation and human poverty when they explicitly added capital to the production function.

To understand their additional insights, suppose that the economy's production function contains capital, denoted as K, as well as labor and land:

$$Y = f(L, K, N) \qquad (4.3)$$

Suppose also that capital and labor are variable, but land (natural resources), N, is in fixed supply. Suppose, furthermore, that the Malthusian population function still accurately describes the variations in the supply of labor. Finally, assume that the capital stock increases with investment. This latter assumption enabled the classical economists to link growth of the capital stock to saving, since investment must be funded by saving elsewhere in the economy.

Many Classical economists saw income from the Industrial Revolution spreading unevenly throughout society, and they became very interested in how economic development was changing the distribution of income. They wanted to know how economic growth would affect the incomes of the different types of factors and how that would, in turn, impact investment and future economic development. The classical economists therefore began to specifically account for the wages, profits, and rent that the owners of labor, capital, and land earned in the process of production. If we define wages, profits, and rent in terms of rates w, π, and ρ, respectively, then total income Y is divided among the factor owners as follows:

$$Y = wL + \pi K + \rho N \qquad (4.4)$$

The classical economists reached various conclusions about the long-run effects of economic development, depending on their assumptions about how the stocks of factors and their returns change as the economy grows.

As they analyzed the Industrial Revolution that was unfolding before them, the Classical economists observed that many owners of industries were clearly becoming quite wealthy. The Classicals suggested that it was profit that stimulated, and paid for, the investment in factories, machines, tools, and other capital that were fundamental to the Industrial Revolution. The Classicals predicted that investment would raise output and, hence, the incomes accruing to the factors of production. The rise in output would at first also raise the wages of the workers who operated the machines, and the rise in income would cause the population to grow. With both population and capital stocks increasing, but land remaining constant, there would be diminishing returns to both labor and capital, and wages and profits would decline. As detailed above, the Classical population function would eventually cause wages to fall back to subsistence levels. This meant that wages could no longer serve as a source of saving from which to fund investment or as the source of demand for industrial output. Industry profits would, therefore, fall. Indirectly, declining population growth would cause diminishing returns to capital, which further reduces profits in industry. Industry thus stops growing. Only the rents to the fixed resource, land, would increase when the stocks of capital and labor grew. But most Classical economists assumed that land owners, the landed aristocracy, would not save their extra income, preferring to simply live more ostentatiously. Therefore, when profits diminish, the economy has no other source of saving and investment, and output growth eventually ceases. In the end, the capitalists are bankrupt, the increased numbers of workers are as poor as ever, and landowners enjoy higher but stagnant, incomes.

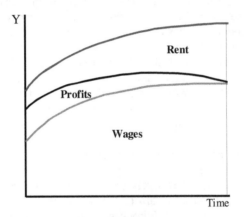

Figure 4.6 A Dismal New Equilibrium

The Classical economists' prediction of how the Industrial Revolution would play out is illustrated in Figure 4.6. At the beginning of the time period, say the start of the eighteenth century, new technologies like the steam engine, textile machines, and canal transportation created new profitable investment opportunities. The Classicals predicted that the new investment would increase output, and the capitalist owners would earn profits, which they could then use to invest in more projects. Initially, the increased stock of capital raises the wages and rents accruing to the other factors of production, labor and land, and the total earnings of labor and land thus rise. The higher wages and living standards cause population growth, however, and wages begin to fall again as diminishing returns to land set in. Eventually, with the workers' wages falling back to subsistence, population growth stops, total wage income also stops growing, and rents to the fixed quantity of land also stop growing albeit at a higher level given the increased capital and population. Only the landed aristocracy seems to gain from the growth predicted by the Classical model.

4.2.7 John Stuart Mill's recognition of technological progress

Recall that in the conclusion to our discussion of Adam Smith's contributions to economics we mentioned the potential conflict between the increasing returns to scale that characterized the Industrial Revolution and the difficulty of maintaining competition as large firms tended to dominate industries. This issue was taken up by John Stuart Mill in the middle of the nineteenth century. Mill largely accepted the Classical model, but living later during the Industrial Revolution and having seen the consequences of some 100 years of continued technological progress, he hypothesized that increasing returns to scale can delay the slowing of economic growth predicted by the classical economists. Mill thus sought to bring technological progress into his model. As you will see later in this textbook, increasing returns to scale is a form of technological progress that increases the amount of output derived from a given amount of inputs. Note, however, that Mill was not arguing that technological progress could forever overcome diminishing returns. In his popular textbook on economics entitled *Principles of Political Economy*, first published in 1848, Mill continued to suggest that diminishing returns would raise marginal costs and cause economic growth to falter.

4.2.8 Assessing the contributions of the Classicals

The Classical economists effectively predicted that the Industrial Revolution would eventually end with a return to the traditional aristocratic and unequal society that had characterized European societies for centuries. Mill only suggested that the growth slowdown could be delayed for a while. In short, the impressive spurt of economic growth and change during the Industrial Revolution was nothing more than a temporary improvement in living standards that population growth would eventually undermine. A generous interpretation of the Classical school would be that it is still not too late for the dismal forecast to come to pass; it has only taken a bit longer than most classical economists suggested. Many environmentalists contend that the deterioration of our ecosystem, which provides critical inputs such as water, air, drainage, etc., may yet trigger exactly the diminishing returns to investment and population growth that the Classicals predicted.

The Classicals showed that changes in the distribution of income are important for the long-run sustainability of economic growth. Income determines the demand for the production that generates income in the first place. Since demand for output depends on who earns the income from production, changes in the distribution of income influence overall economic activity. If workers' wages fall, demand for output also falls. The growth in output is only profitable for producers if demand for their output also grows. The Classicals were correct in focusing on both the demand and supply sides of the economy.

The Classical school's predictions of eternal poverty clashed with many other thinkers of their time. The Enlightenment had also bred the idea that human society could continually progress through reason and the scientific discovery of truth. For example, the French philosopher and economist Marquis de Condorcet (1795) wrote:

> Observations on what man has been and what he is today lead immediately to the ways of assuring and accelerating the further progress for which man's nature permits him to hope.[11]

Condorcet's statement actually goes beyond just linking human progress to technological progress and increased knowledge: He explicitly called for active measures for "assuring and accelerating" human progress. Many scientists, politicians, and activists took this challenge seriously and tried to bring change to human society. One nineteenth-century economist reached "revolutionary" conclusions when he combined the Classicals' focus on income shares with other Enlightenment philosophers' enthusiasm for promoting social change. That economist, a contemporary of John Stuart Mill, was Karl Marx.

4.3 Karl Marx

Many nineteenth-century intellectuals, including some students of Classical economics, rebelled against the increasingly uneven distribution of income during the Industrial Revolution. They observed that workers in the new factories received low wages and had to work long hours in unhealthy conditions. Child labor was also widespread throughout industry

Because the study of economics directly focuses on how a society uses its resources to enhance human welfare, it was inevitable that some philosophers and thinkers began to call for a *socialization* of economies. Many believed that the inequalities in income and living conditions in mid-nineteenth century England, Scotland, and other industrializing countries could be reduced by

---

[11] Marquis de Condorcet (1795).

means of spreading the ownership of the factories to those who worked in the factories.   This *socialist* movement soon grew to include a wide range of thinkers who advocated various types of changes in the economic organization of society in order to more equally spread the gains of economic growth to workers and peasants.

The suggested changes in the economic system did not always involve a government takeover of factories. One well-known socialist was Robert Owen, a wealthy industrialist who established private company-owned towns in Scotland and the United States that operated along communal principles. Most advocates of **socialism**, however, anticipated a shift toward a more communal society under the auspices of a democratic form of government. Most socialists saw socialism as a natural progression toward higher states of human development, even if their enthusiasm for socialism was at the same time a direct response to the economic and social upheavals caused by the uneven economic development that they experienced during the Industrial Revolution.

One student of the Classical school of economics who was especially perceptive in his thinking about the Industrial Revolution and the capitalist economic system that was emerging was Karl Marx. Marx was a German-born social scientist whose radical ideas about religion, economics, and political development forced him to leave Germany. He first went to Paris, then to Brussels, and finally to London. In Britain, he was free to write and develop his radical ideas. Marx combined Classical economic thoughts with many other ideas circulating in France, Germany, and Britain in the mid-1800s to build a holistic model of evolutionary economic development.

4.3.1 Karl Marx and the Classical School

Karl Marx studied Smith and Ricardo after going into exile in Paris. Marx's view of economic development builds on the Classical economic model described in the previous section. Marx, too, saw society as evolving and changing over time. And, like the Classicals, he built his model around the class distinctions he observed in Europe and in his adopted home, London. The split of income into wages to the workers (the **proletariat**), profits to the owners of capital (the **bourgeoisie**), and rent to the **landed aristocracy** is the centerpiece of Marx's thinking. Marx diverged from the classical school, however. Instead of predicting that society would revert back to the familiar and traditional aristocracies of earlier centuries, Marx predicted that the growth-induced changes in the distribution of income would eventually result in a political revolution that would put a completely new social order in place. Marx viewed capitalism and the Industrial Revolution as a temporary stage on a long-term path toward a better world, not a temporary surge in growth that would eventually stop and leave people no better off than before. His inclusion of social and political processes in an economic model differentiated Marx from the classical school. Marx was much more inter-disciplinary and holistic.

To understand Marx's reasoning, we need to note some assumptions that he made in framing his holistic model of economic evolution. First of all, he described economic growth as the result of investment by the bourgeoisie. The capitalists thus controlled the principal **means of production** in the economy. Also, Marx gave no explicit role to agriculture, perhaps because he wrote in London, a large city in a country whose agricultural sector had by 1850 been eclipsed by the manufacturing and service sectors. Marx did place agriculture at the center of an earlier stage of economic development, but industry was central to the current economy.

Marx acknowledged the role of capitalism in generating economic growth. He especially admired capitalism's role in fomenting technological innovation. He favorably contrasted the capitalist period of the nineteenth century with the primitive collectivism and feudalism that had preceded it:

> The bourgeoisie, during its rule of scarce one-hundred years, has created more massive and more colossal productive forces than have all preceding generations together. Subjection of Nature's forces to man, machinery, application of chemistry to industry and agriculture, steam navigation, railways, electric telegraphs, clearing of whole continents for cultivation, canalization of rivers, whole populations conjured out of the ground — what earlier century had even a presentiment that such productive forces slumbered in the lap of social labor?[12]

Despite capitalism's ability to foster economic growth, however, Marx also argued that the system had serious internal inconsistencies that would eventually cause it to be replaced by a social revolution. In effect, Marx argued that capitalism did not generate sustainable economic and social development.

The presence of inconsistencies within economic and social systems played an important role in Marx's model of economic development. He adopted the German philosopher Georg Wilhelm Friedrich Hegel's philosophical approach to history, which Hegel called its **dialectic**. The dialectic referred to an ancient Greek philosophical form of debate, in which two people with different views would alternatively critique and correct each other's arguments and, in successive stages, use logic to arrive at a reconciliation of views. Hegel applied this succession of "theses" and "antitheses" not just to philosophy or social thinking, but to the development of actual social systems. According to Marx, each successive social system was an improvement on earlier systems, improved through the application of logic, reason, and the acquisition of new knowledge. Marx idealized the communal nature of pre-capitalist societies as more closely reflecting basic human behaviors evolved from prehistoric times. He also pointed out that while pre-capitalist societies were more "human," this earlier stage of development was not very productive.

---

[12] Karl Marx and Frederick Engels (1948 [1848]).

Marx ranked capitalism as a superior response to earlier social stages of primitive collectivism and feudalism because he observed that capitalism generated much more new technology and material progress. Because Marx holistically viewed the economy as a dynamic, ever-evolving system, he grasped the strength of the capitalist system as a generator of technological progress:

> This is the law for capitalist production, imposed by increased revolutions in the methods of production themselves, by the depreciation of existing capital always bound up with them, by the general competitive struggle, and the need to improve production and expand its scale merely as a means of self-preservation and under penalty of ruin.[13]

In Chapter 8, this dynamic description of capitalism as a system that generates rapid technological change is discussed within the framework of Joseph Schumpeter's model of creative destruction. Schumpeter's model owes a lot to Marx.

Marx, however, also saw capitalism as dehumanizing because the private profit-driven ownership of the means of production resulted in a production system that turned people into mere labor machines. This he called the **commodification of labor**. This commodification of labor, along with the system's tendency to generate huge income inequalities, would effectively sow the seeds of its own destruction, despite the technological progress.

4.3.2 Marx's model of capitalist development

A simple outline of Marx's model of the capitalist economy must begin with his assumption that capital accumulation by the bourgeois capitalists was driven by profit. This was not a radical assumption, and most economists today would be perfectly comfortable with Marx's assumption that profits were both the motivation for, and the result of, investment. However, Marx also viewed profit as a form of exploitation. Specifically, he referred to profit as a **surplus**, denoted as R in

$$R \equiv Y - wL \tag{4.5}$$

where Y is total output, w is the wage rate, and L is the supply of labor. The surplus is thus what is left over after paying the workers. Like the Classical economists, Marx explained that the long run rate of growth of output depends on the income of the bourgeoisie, the surplus, which provides the savings to fund capital investment. He also followed the Classicals in hypothesizing that the ratio of surplus to output would decline over time. Marx's original contribution was his description of how the bourgeoisie's attempts to maintain

---

[13] Karl Marx (1967), *Capital*, Vol. 3, pp. 244–245.

profits in the face of declining demand would end up triggering a social revolution that replaces the capitalist system with a **communist system** whose key feature was the "abolition of private property."[14]

In the middle of the nineteenth century, it was clear to Marx that technological progress was driving the growth of output. Recall that even John Stuart Mill, one of the key members of the Classical school, had introduced technology into his 1848 economics textbook. However, where Mill explained the improved efficiency as a general process of increasing returns to scale, Marx linked technology specifically to capitalists' intentional investments in new equipment, machines, and factories. Marx argued that to increase their profits, the bourgeoisie introduces more efficient production methods by investing in new and better productive facilities. Investment, of course, requires saving, and that comes out of the capitalists' surplus. Marx's prediction of a declining ratio of profit was not based on diminishing returns to capital, as in the Classical model. Rather, Marx's prediction of declining profit would be caused by capitalists' own success in replacing labor with machines and technological improvements in productive efficiency. Marx hypothesized that the capitalists' surplus falls because demand for output falls with the increase in unemployment caused by the capitalists' substitution of machines for labor.

The essence of Marx's model can be grasped by using equation (4.5) above to define the capitalists' rate of return on output, R/Y, as

$$R/Y = (Y - wL)/(wL + \mu K) \tag{4.6}$$

Our definition of output as $Y = (wL + \mu K)$ reflects Marx's focus on industry and his neglect of agriculture. Land, so prominent in classical analysis, is ignored by the urban Marx. The symbol μ represents the cost of using capital, which Marx assumed to be a constant.

Equation (4.6) suggests that capitalists' profit share on output increases if (1) the wage declines, (2) the amount of labor employed declines, (3) the cost of capital declines, or (4) the amount of capital needed to produce output declines. Capitalists therefore want to keep wages low. But Marx recognized that there are limits to how far capitalists can reduce wages. People have to eat if they are to be productive workers. Once wages have been reduced to subsistence levels, the cost of the labor used in production can only be reduced by replacing workers with machines, that is, by increasing K relative to L. Marx therefore argued that technological advances that reduced the amount of capital needed to produce output were like a double-edged sword: labor-saving technologies lower the wage bill and thus increase R/Y by reducing L in the denominator of equation (4.6), but the introduction of more capital required to apply the labor-saving technologies causes an offsetting increase in K in the denominator of

---

[14] Karl Marx and Frederick Engels (1948 [1848]), p. 23.

(4.6). The effect of substituting capital for labor may, therefore, not increase the rate of return at all.

Marx assumed the cost of capital µ to be constant, largely because he could find no reason why its costs would fall. Marx noted that capital depreciates; the more capital is employed, the more capital depreciates and must be replaced in order to maintain production. This depreciation effect was used by Marx to justify his default assumption that the cost of capital was proportional to the stock of capital. Finally, note that equation (4.6) specifies that the rate of return to capital increases when technological progress raises Y. Marx, of course, hypothesized that capitalists sought technological advances to raise productivity in order to gain more profit.

Marx's hypothesis that employment was determined by the demand for output would later by embraced by the twentieth century macroeconomist John Maynard Keynes. During the Great Depression of the 1930s, Keynes advocated aggressive government fiscal and monetary policies to directly boost aggregate demand. Marx argued that full employment could not be maintained by letting wages decline because wages could not fall below the basic subsistence level at which labor could function productively. Classical economists generally assumed that workers would work regardless of how little they were paid, and that there was always some wage at which full employment could be achieved.[15] In Marx's nineteenth century London unemployed workers were visible everywhere despite wages that could barely sustain life in London. This unemployment had to be explained, it could not be assumed away, so Marx made it part of his model.

Marx thus argued that unemployment was a natural outcome in a capitalist system:

> The whole system of capitalist production is based upon the fact that the worker sells his labour power as a commodity. Thanks to the division of labour, this labour power becomes specialised, is reduced to skill in handling a particular tool. As soon as the handling of this tool becomes the work of a machine, the use-value and the exchange-value of the worker's labour power disappears. The worker becomes unsalable, like paper money which is no longer legal tender.[16]

According to Marx, the rising unemployment that accompanies capitalist development creates a **reserve army of labor** that prevents wages of those still working from rising, thus condemning workers to eternal poverty.

Finally, Marx argued that unemployment also rises because of the tendency for the ownership of capital to become more concentrated in the hands of fewer and fewer capitalists. This concentration of ownership of the means of

---

[15] Malthus also gave demand a prominent role in the dynamics of economic systems. The increasing complexity of economic system in the nineteenth century was clearly causing occasional factor market failures, and insufficient demand obviously came to mind as a cause.

[16] Karl Marx (1867 [1906–1909]), *Capital*, Vol. 1, p. 470.

production, like the technological progress that replaces workers with machines, is also the result of the capitalist quest for profit. According to Marx, the tendency of the capitalist surplus to shrink in the face of rising unemployment and declining demand inevitably leads the wealthier capitalists to buy the means of production controlled by less wealthy capitalists. In the mid-1800s, Marx observed the rising frequency of buyouts and mergers of business firms. Marx described the mergers and acquisitions as a desperate reaction by capitalists to the declining demand for industrial output. The growing industrial concentration thus drives increasing numbers of *bourgeois* capitalists into the ranks of the reserve army of the unemployed, which further depresses demand for output in a vicious downward spiral.

Marx predicted a natural alliance between three groups: those stuck in the reserve army of the unemployed, the employed but underpaid workers who lived in fear of also falling into the reserve army, and the bankrupt former capitalists. Marx thought that, once the proletariat realized that the capitalist system was the cause of their misery, people would revolt and overthrow the capitalists and begin organizing an advanced state of socialism called **communism**, in which everyone collectively owns the means of production and equitably shares the work and gains from production.

4.3.3 An assessment of Marx and Marxism

Karl Marx is accurately described as a social scientist rather than just an economist. Modern-day Marxists have continued this tradition, often intentionally rejecting precise and simple economic models in favor of more holistic, interdisciplinary models that incorporate ideas and structures from all the social sciences. This is not to say that Marxist models have predicted human history more accurately than less holistic economic models. Because of their holistic nature and the inherent complexity of building a unified model of broad social change, there were many variations and interpretations of Marx's analysis. These complex models were difficult to test against the available evidence. The models' holistic complexity often made it difficult to even prove their logical consistency. And, of course, Marx' prediction that the proletariat in an advanced capitalist country would revolt to form a new communist society has proved to be inaccurate. The communist revolutions that the world did experience, such as those in Russia and China, occurred in near-feudal or more traditional agricultural societies. So far, no communist revolution has been a transition from an advanced capitalist society.

The advanced capitalist societies of the nineteenth century, such as Britain, the United States, and other European countries found ways to spread the wealth, thus preventing a slowdown in investment and innovation. Instead, rising levels of education and the spread of democracy resulted in higher incomes for the proletariat and thus greater demand for output, which generated more savings to fund further investment, innovation, and technological progress. A cycle of rising human welfare, not a collapse towards poverty, seems to have arisen in most industrial societies. There were, of course, the frequent claims by right-wing ideologues that "creeping socialism" was taking over in many industrial countries, and they viewed this alleged political shift with great alarm. In their *Communist Manifesto*, Marx and Frederick Engels (1948 [1848], p. 38) warned that the capitalist bourgeoisie would seek to mitigate the worst social grievances of capitalism "in order to secure the continued existence of bourgeois society."

Two present-day economists, Oded Galor and Omer Moav (2006), hypothesize that increased incomes, higher levels of education, and the blurring of class lines were, in fact, the natural outcome of capitalism's quest for profit. Where Marx assumed that capitalists would use investment and technology to replace workers, Galor and Moav hypothesize that capitalists actually demand more educated workers because they see their salvation in innovation rather than investment in more physical capital. Capitalists thus support increasing education for the entire population. As a result, workers endowed with ever greater amounts of human capital gradually cause class distinctions to become blurred, and the threat of revolution disappears. Galor and Moav may be a bit premature in predicting an end to economic inequality, however.

Income disparities across the world and within countries seem to be growing again. For example, in the United States the median hourly wage in the private sector of the economy in 2008 was, in real terms, exactly the same as it was in 1968, forty years earlier.[17] The minimum wage in terms of real purchasing power was nearly 25 percent higher in 1968. Household income did grow slowly until 1999 as more household members joined the labor force. But since 2000, the incomes of the lower 90 percent of U.S. households failed to grow at all despite further increases in labor market participation.[18] Total real GDP per capita in the United States did grow consistently over the past forty years, however, which means that recipients of a small segment of the labor market and recipients of non-labor income received nearly all of the gains from output growth. Indeed, data show that the distribution of income in the United States has become much less equal in recent decades. U.S. households in the top 10 percent wealth bracket own nearly 99 percent of all stocks and bonds. The wealthiest 1 percent of U.S. citizens own two-thirds of all privately owned U.S. businesses.

Income and wealth inequality has also been growing in many other countries, including the rapidly growing emerging economies such as China and India. And, as Chapter 17 will detail, global inequality across countries is today

---

[17] Bureau of Labor Statistics (2011), *Current Employment Statistics*, available at www.bls.gov.
[18] See the official labor statistics published by the U.S. government in the Statistical Abstract of the United States (2010), Washington, D.C.: U.S. Department of Commerce or the thorough statistical analysis by Atkinson, Piketty, and Saez (2009).

at an all-time high level despite rapid GDP growth in several large developing economies. Marx's focus on the shares of income is apparently still quite relevant. But, you might ask: Where is the revolution?

Marx has been condemned for his role in promoting the twentieth century communist societies that, in nearly every case, deteriorated into autocratic and oppressive states. Some writers argue that this is why, despite recent rises in income inequality, few people are calling for the proletariat to unite and rise up against the capitalists. There are, no doubt, many more complex reasons for the absence of socialist revolutions. Later chapters will discuss income inequality and its connection to political change. For our discussion here, we should point out that it is not correct to blame Marx for the oppressive communist states of the twentieth century. Marx's analysis focused on detailing the evolution and inconsistencies of capitalism. His descriptions of communism, on the other hand, were more idealistic visions than detailed predictions.

Marx described communism as a system that would develop in reaction to capitalism:

> ... the positive transcendence of private property, or human self-estrangement, and therefore as the real appropriation of the human essence by and for man; communism therefore as the complete return of man to himself as a social (i.e., human) being — a return to become conscious, and accomplished within the entire wealth of previous development.[19]

Marx apparently saw communism as a consolidation of the gains from capitalism in a more attractive social state. He envisioned a social return to the more ideal "human" community of pre-capitalist society in order to enjoy the economic wealth of capitalist development.

Humorists have suggested that Marx was an instant hit because he offered something even better than religion, namely nirvana right here and now. Marx's ideas appealed to those brought up on the rationalist philosophies of the Enlightenment. Like the Enlightenment thinkers, Marx embraced the scientific method, and he rejected the arbitrariness and cruelty of religious authorities. Above all, Marx appealed to those who felt they had been exploited or left behind by the rapid changes the world was experiencing under the Industrial Revolution and global colonialism. Socialism's promise of a better life is still attractive to many people throughout the world, as evidenced by the free choice of socialist governments by people in recent elections in Nepal, Bolivia, Venezuela, Ecuador, Nicaragua, and many European countries. But, the fall of the Berlin Wall in 1989 and the collapse of many of the communist governments in Eastern Europe and Central Asia suggest that a revolution to destroy capitalism does not automatically lead to a realization of Marx's vision of a "workers' paradise."

---

[19] Karl Marx (1964), p. 135.

Objectively examined, Marx's model of the economic and social evolution of capitalism was no less accurate than the Classicals' predictions of eternal poverty or Adam Smith's invisible hand as the generator of universal prosperity. Marx's focus on income distribution and the potential for shifts in the distribution in income to instigate social and political change was an important contribution to our understanding of the process of economic development. His designation of profit as the driving force of capitalist innovation and investment was an insight that has been used in later models of economic growth and technological change. His recognition of the relationship between the supply and demand sides of the economy was incorporated into modern macroeconomics. Above all, Marx's model was holistic, that is, systemic, dynamic, and multi-disciplinary.

Marx described a system in which economic, political, technological, and cultural forces interact to drive the evolution of human society. At the same time, he described how evolving economic, social, political, and cultural forces cause the feedback that pushes human society from one broad phase towards the next. That is, Marx described the economy as a component of a larger and more complex social system that was in a constant state of change. Where the Classicals focused largely on economic forces, Marx explicitly linked the development of the economy to social class conflicts, political shifts, and cultural change. Marx's model was an ambitious attempt at developing a complete model of human economic and social development.

4.4 The Growth of Neoclassical Economics

In the latter half of the nineteenth century, when much of the world economy was firmly embarked on its unprecedented path of persistent growth and change, economists added only marginally to our understanding of the process of economic development. As we outlined in Chapter 1, economists responded to the accelerating economic growth in Europe, North America, Australia, and elsewhere by paying little attention to it. Economists rejected the holism of Smith, Marx, and the Classicals, and instead they effectively embraced the unsound strategy of **scientific reductionism**, discussed in Chapter 1, by concentrating on individual markets and how they determined the economy's allocation of scarce resources. They implicitly assumed that a good understanding of the system's component parts would be sufficient for designing the policies and institutions necessary to support the economic system. Scientific reductionism ignores the possibility that the whole may not be equal to the simple sum of its component parts. **Holism**, on the other hand, recognizes that the interrelationships among the parts are as variable as the individual parts.

4.4.1 Scientific reductionism

Textbooks in the late nineteenth and early twentieth centuries often used the *ceteris paribus* (all other things equal) assumption in order to focus on specific markets and sectors of the economy without having to worry about more complex relationships and feedback. The best-selling economics textbook at the end of the nineteenth century was Alfred Marshall's *Principles of Economics*, the eighth edition of which was published in 1920. It reflected the belief that a market economy would always move toward a stable equilibrium.

Of special interest is the mathematical model of a complete economic system developed by the French-born, Swiss-based economist Léon Walras in the late nineteenth century. Walras' modeled the economy as a huge system of equations representing each of the markets in which transactions simultaneously occur. There were equations for each of the consumers who purchase a great variety of goods and services from producers, equations for the government agencies that purchased goods and services from producers, and more equations for the producers who purchase capital goods from other producers. To complete the circle, there were equations representing the producers who purchase labor from individuals and rent land from landowners.

Specifically, Walras hypothesized m products, n productive services, m product prices, n productive services prices, and mn technical coefficients. The latter specified how many of each of the n productive services were used to produce each of the m products. There were thus $2m + 2n + mn - 1$ unknowns, since according to Walras' law, one of the products served as *numeraire*, the measure in which all other variables are valued. Money was usually the numeraire product. In general, a system of linear equations can be solved if the number of unknowns equal the number of equations. And, indeed, there are $m - 1$ demand equations for products, m cost equations for products, n quantity equations and n supply equations for productive services, and mn technical coefficients in the Walrasian system.

In a sense, Walras' model is holistic because it shows every part of the economy related to every other part. However, for practical reasons, Walras' mathematical model specified the system as a set of equations with fixed parameters that did not permit the relationships among the component parts to vary. Although he was never able to find a mathematical solution to his system, he intuitively reasoned that if all markets automatically tend to move toward their respective equilibria, then the entire system would also automatically move towards an overall stable equilibrium. The impossibility of actually solving the system of equations encouraged economists to focus on the system's individual markets and refrain from trying to analyze how the overall economic system performed. Walras' intuition that some solution must exist was accepted as obvious, although it was only in the latter half of the twentieth century that a new math called topology was used to prove that a solution to Walras' rigid system even existed. The impossibility of actually solving the **Walrasian system** seems to have led economists to increasingly focus on individual markets rather than the interconnections and the overall system.

These reductionist tendencies that slowed the study of economic development, which demands a more holistic approach, were only reversed when the world economy plunged into the Great Depression during the 1930s. At that point, mainstream economists recognized that a system of individual product markets, factor markets, asset markets, and money markets does not always result in an equilibrium where human welfare is maximized. Also, the Great Depression showed that an economy's equilibrium could change drastically even when the component parts, such as the number of workers, the capital stock, and natural resources, remained the same. The Great Depression of the 1930s shifted economists' focus from the component parts to how the overall system performed.

In 1936, the British economist, John Maynard Keynes, published his *General Theory of Employment, Interest, and Money*, the work that effectively created the field that is today known as macroeconomics. He developed a model that explicitly showed how the major components of the economy interacted to determine the total levels of output and employment. Keynes' macroeconomic model helped policymakers design policies to address the obvious failure of the world's major economies to reach efficient general equilibria in which product and labor markets cleared. Keynes, therefore, restored interest in looking at an entire economic system rather than just its individual components.

4.4.2 Some observations on Neoclassical economics

The school of economic thought associated with Walras, Marshall, and other late nineteenth-century economists is now referred to as the Neoclassical school.[20] Neoclassical analysis provided a framework that was useful for analyzing many short-term economic processes, especially those related to the short-term allocation of resources. Neoclassical economics dropped the Classical and Marxian assumption that all value was derived from human labor, what is known as the **labor theory of value**. Neoclassical analysis distinguished between the marginal values of all productive inputs, a very necessary step for determining the optimal allocation of society's scarce resources. This was an important step in the history of economic thought. It was sometimes argued that Classical and Marxian analysis gave human labor too great a role in the economy.

---

[20] The neoclassical paradigm is not the same as the modern day neoliberal paradigm, but the two paradigms have much in common. Neoliberals advocate policies of free trade, free markets, privatization, and limited government. These policies are usually justified by analysis that follows from Neoclassical economic analysis.

In order to develop practical approaches to solving allocation problems, neoclassical analysis almost always assumes a comparative static modeling framework in which resource supplies are taken as given. And, as mentioned in previous chapters, neoclassical economists implicitly accepted the unsound strategy of scientific reductionism in order to focus their analytical attention on individual producers, consumers, and markets. As discussed in the previous chapter, Neoclassical economists also have adopted a rather unrealistic social welfare function with which to judge alternative allocations of society's productive resources. Within the limits imposed by their assumptions of diminishing returns, the Neoclassicals developed an elaborate modeling structure that largely supports Adam Smith's idea that the invisible hand operates through free markets to channel self-interest into an optimal level of human welfare. Such nice outcomes are largely the result of the practice of specifying smooth functions with gradually changing marginal values so that consumers and producers act in ways that always move the economy towards a well-defined stable equilibrium.

Because neoclassical analysis mostly focused on allocating existing stocks of productive factors and resources efficiently within a static set of circumstances, it provided little insight into the process of economic growth and change. Under assumptions of perfect competition, neoclassical models could not explain capitalist profit and the unequal wealth accumulation, as Marx could in his model with distinct economic classes. Nor can neoclassical analysis provide useful insight into economic instability, as Keynes could with his macroeconomic model from the Great Depression era. Keynes of course argued that stable employment, income, and growth are policy goals precisely because economic systems cannot be assumed to smoothly adjust towards stable equilibria.

This is not to say that neoclassical economists did not occasionally try to use their framework to address issues such as economic growth. The next chapter will, in fact, present a growth model that has solid neoclassical roots. But we conclude this chapter with a popular growth model that is derived from Keynes' macroeconomic modeling framework of the 1930s.

4.5 The Harrod-Domar Model

After World War II, there was renewed interest in economic development. Per capita incomes were low at the close of the war, and people in the war-torn countries expected policymakers to generate economic growth that would raise standards of living above the levels experienced during the Great Depression and World War II. Secondly, during the Cold War communist leaders publicly challenged the capitalist economies to a contest among economic systems to see which would provide its citizens with higher standards of living. Thirdly, the independence of former colonies in Africa and Asia after World War II increased awareness of the huge income differences that existed in the world. Western governments publicly acknowledged the obligation of rich countries to provide foreign aid to the world's poor countries. Regardless of whether this aid was altruistic or merely a cover for payoffs to foreign leaders for siding with the capitalists in the Cold War, economists sought to justify the economic programs funded with the foreign aid. They needed a model to frame their analyses.

4.5.1 The "Keynesian" Harrod-Domar model

Roy Harrod (1939) and Evsey Domar (1946) independently developed a growth model that was particularly popular with economic planners immediately after World War II. Their model is now known simply as the **Harrod-Domar model**. That two economists would independently produce the identical model was not surprising: their model is a logical extension of John Maynard Keynes' macroeconomic model. At the time, economists relied heavily on the Keynesian macroeconomic model to frame their analysis of various economic issues.

Harrod and Domar developed a dynamic model that revealed a potential long-run source of instability in the demand-driven Keynesian macroeconomic model. In analyzing how macroeconomic policy could restore full employment, Keynes had focused on investment as a major category of aggregate demand for the economy's output. Dynamically, in addition to contributing to aggregate demand for output today, investment also increased the economy's potential output in the future. Thus, investment has both demand and supply effects. More important, full employment can be maintained in the long run only if investment and the other sources of aggregate demand grow just fast enough to exactly absorb the increased output that the investment makes possible. Both Harrod and Domar reasoned that if aggregate demand does not grow over time, investment would cause aggregate supply to exceed aggregate demand, and unemployment would rise. Wrote Domar (1946, p. 138): "The idea that the preservation of full employment in a capitalist economy requires a growing income goes back (in one form or another) at least to Marx."

To capture the potential inconsistencies between investment's effect on aggregate demand and its effect on the growth of the economy's productive capacity, Harrod and Domar specified separate demand and supply sides to their model. They used a simplified version of the **Keynesian macroeconomic model** for their demand side, and they hypothesized a very simplistic process by which investment determined the economy's supply side. Unfortunately, economists often used only the supply side of model, ignoring the demand side of the complete Harrod-Domar model.

4.5.2 The supply side of the Harrod-Domar model

In setting up the supply side of their model, Harrod and Domar make several simplifying assumptions. The first is that the marginal product of capital is constant; each additional unit of capital increases final output by the same amount. Implicitly, they assume that capital does not suffer diminishing returns because unemployed labor is always available to accompany the increases in capital and keep factor inputs changing proportionately. Output is thus a constant function of the stock of capital; the **capital-output ratio**, which is the amount of capital needed to produce a unit of real output over some period of time (usually a year), is a constant.

A second assumption is that there is no depreciation, so that the constant capital output ratio implies that output varies in direct proportion to new investment in capital. Finally, the Harrod-Domar model assumes that productive investment is always equal to saving. These assumptions simplify the formula for increasing the rate of economic growth. Since the model assumes that each additional unit of capital increases output by a fixed proportion and every increase in saving directly increases investment, an increase in saving must increase the rate of growth in output.

The formal Harrod-Domar model is usually presented in mathematical form, and we will do the same here because the mathematics are really quite simple. We begin by assuming that the economy's supply of output (Y_S) is split between two categories of commodities, consumption goods (C) and investment goods (I). That is,

$$Y_S = C + I \tag{4.7}$$

Harrod and Domar represented investment with the change in the stock of capital, ΔK, where the symbol "Δ" again signifies "the change in." If we substitute ΔK for I in equation (4.7) we get,

$$Y_S = C + \Delta K \tag{4.8}$$

Note that this assumption, that the change in the capital stock is equal to investment, implies that the stock of existing capital does not suffer any **depreciation**, that the existing capital stock never wears out or becomes obsolete. Hence, investment always increases the total stock of capital.

As mentioned above, Harrod and Domar assumed that the economy exhibits a constant capital-output ratio γ:

$$K/Y_S = \gamma \tag{4.9}$$

Moving both Y and γ to opposite sides of the equal sign makes it clear that this assumption makes output proportional to the stock of capital, as in

$$Y_S = (1/\gamma)K = AK \tag{4.10}$$

when we define $A \equiv (1/\gamma)$.

The linear relationship, $Y = AK$, leads to the Harrod-Domar model's conclusion that the rate of growth in output is exactly proportional to the economy's rate of saving. To see why, note first that the constant capital-output ratio implies that the change in the supply of output is directly related to the change in the stock of capital, or

$$\Delta Y_S = (1/\gamma)\Delta K \tag{4.11}$$

For the economy to invest in capital, it must save. Under the assumption that all savings, S, are invested productively, savings generate output in accordance with equation (4.10). From these assumptions, it follows that the change in the capital stock is equal to

$$\Delta K = I = S = \sigma Y_S \tag{4.12}$$

If we now put equations (4.11) and (4.12) together, it follows that

$$\Delta Y_S = (\sigma/\gamma)Y_S \tag{4.13}$$

Dividing both sides of equation (4.13) by Y and recalling that the growth rate of a variable is equal to the ratio of the *change* in the variable to the *level* of the variable, we derive a temptingly simple formula for the rate of growth of the economy's output, or supply, of goods and services, denoted as g_{Ys}:

$$\Delta Y_S/Y_S = g_{Ys} = \sigma/\gamma \tag{4.14}$$

That is, the rate of economic growth is a constant function of the savings rate. An increase in the rate of saving increases the rate of economic growth.

4.5.3 The popularity of the partial Harrod-Domar model

The supply side of the Harrod-Domar model only determines the growth in the economy's capacity under specific assumptions about the saving rate and the capital-output ratio. In order to determine whether a given rate of investment is compatible with long-run demand for goods and services, the demand effects of investment must be brought into the model. This is what Harrod and Domar did, but this aspect of Harod's and Domar's models was ignored in the field of economic development. The simple supply side model got a life of its own.

The Harrod-Domar model was popularly interpreted as showing that the rate of economic growth depends on the economy's rate of savings, σ, and the capital-output ratio, γ, shown in equation (4.14). To illustrate, suppose that the savings rate is 20 percent of income. Suppose also that every $100 of annual output requires installed capital valued at $500, which means γ equals 5. According to equation (4.14), output grows by $\sigma/\gamma = .2/5 = .04 = 4$ percent per year. If the savings rate σ is 30 percent, then output growth is $.3/5 = 6$ percent.

Table 4.4 Capital-Output Ratios for Selected Countries: 1970–1998

Country	*1970–1980*	*1980–1990*	*1990–1998*
United States	6.6	5.6	9.6
Japan	7.4	5.1	7.5
South Korea	3.3	4.0	4.4
Indonesia	2.6	5.5	5.2
India	6.0	5.7	4.7
Argentina	13.3	8.3	9.1
Brazil	2.8	4.8	7.2
Côte d'Ivoire	4.2	8.2	10.7
Kenya	4.0	5.9	6.6

Source: World Bank, *World Tables*, 1983, 1993, 1999.

If the capital-output ratio is indeed a technical constant, we can figure out exactly what the savings rate must be for the economy to achieve some target rate of output growth. Every beginning student of economics could instantaneously become an economic planner! The problem was that the model was dangerously inaccurate as a planning tool. First of all, evidence shows that capital-output ratios vary widely from country to country and year to year. It is anything but constant in the long run. Table 4.4 shows that estimate of capital-output ratios vary greatly not only among countries but across different periods of time for each country.

4.5.4 The incremental capital-output ratio (ICOR)

Equation (4.10) above showed that the constant $A = (1/\gamma)$ links the *change* in the capital stock with the *change* in output. It became the accepted practice in development economics to refer to the term γ as the **incremental capital-output ratio**, or in development jargon, the *ICOR*. The idea behind adding the word *incremental* to the capital-output ratio was to recognize that the capital-output ratio was not necessarily a constant. But, in practice, economic planners estimated the ICOR using economy-wide data on investment and output, which made their estimates technically an *average* capital-output ratio rather than an *incremental* one. In effect, despite the name change, economic planners were applying the simple Harrod-Domar model presented above.[21]

In sum, the supply-side Harrod-Domar model made growth predictions easy to calculate, but, given that they were based on past evidence of saving behavior and capital-output ratios, they were inherently inaccurate predictions of the future productive capacity of an economy. Even more damaging than the assumption of a constant capital-output ratio, however, was the use of the supply side of the model without its demand side counterpart.

4.5.5 *The demand side of the Harrod-Domar model*

Harrod and Domar also specified a demand side to their model. As they did on the supply side, they again left out government and foreign trade and defined aggregate demand, Y_D, in the economy simply as

$$Y_D = C_D + I_D \qquad (4.15)$$

Consumption goods demanded are thus equal to actual income not saved, so in the case where σ is the desired rate of saving:

$$C_D = (1 - \sigma)Y \qquad (4.16)$$

Textbook versions of the Keynesian macroeconomic model usually assume that investment is an inverse function of the interest rate, which measures the opportunity cost of investment. The interest rate is usually assumed to be the price that clears the financial markets that channel savings to investment. If $S = I$, then all income not spent on consumption is instead spent on investment, and aggregate demand equals aggregate supply. However, in his *General Theory of Employment, Interest, and Money*, Keynes viewed investment as a much more complex function, driven by a great many variables, including volatile expectations of the future. Keynes argued that the decision to invest was not the result of a precise decision process that compared future returns to the opportunity cost of investment. In reality, no one has enough information about the future to perform such a deterministic exercise. "Only a little more than an expedition to the South Pole, is it [investment] based on exact calculation of benefits to come," he wrote.[22] Rather, Keynes suggested that investment was driven by "animal spirits," by which he meant the complex combination of confidence, optimism, and unsubstantiated faith in the future growth of the economy. Sentiment, faith, and confidence are inherently volatile because we

---

[21] For an interesting discussion of the survival of the ICOR see William Easterly (1999).
[22] John Maynard Keynes (1936), p. 162.

have no firm information about the future. Keynes concluded that it was the volatility of investment that caused the ups and downs of economic growth. Keynes surmised that as long as most investors' expectations were approximately validated, investment would continue to occur despite the lack of any "exact calculations of benefits to come." If a large proportion of investments fail to meet expectations, however, confidence in the "benefits to come" erodes and investment collapses. Keynes hypothesized that continued investment depends on how fast aggregate demand grows relative to output (aggregate supply), and thus validates or invalidates investors' animal spirits.

In the light of Keynes' discussion of how investor confidence depends on whether recent economic outcomes were consistent with investors' animal spirits, Harrod and Domar hypothesized that investment demand is a function of recent growth in the demand for output:

$$I_D = b(\Delta Y_D) \tag{4.17}$$

In equation (4.17), b defines the function that relates new investment to the change in total actual output demanded, Y_D. According to equations (4.15) and (4.17) and assuming a constant rate of saving σ:

$$Y_D = (1 - \sigma)Y_S + b(\Delta Y_D) \tag{4.18}$$

That is, total demand for output is the income not saved and investment demand as determined by sentiments based on recent output increases.

Suppose that the economy starts out at full employment, and that $Y_D = Y_S$. Full employment depends on maintaining equality between desired investment and actual savings:

$$b(\Delta Y_D) = \sigma Y_S \tag{4.19}$$

This implies that shifting b and Y to the other side of the equal sign and setting $Y_D = Y_S$, the demand side model shows that under full employment the growth of demand is equal to

$$\Delta Y_D/Y_S = \Delta Y_D/Y_D = \sigma/b \tag{4.20}$$

Hence, in a state of full employment demand growth is equal to supply growth, given as $\Delta Y_S/Y_S = \sigma/\gamma$ in equation (4.14), only if

$$\Delta Y_D/Y_D = \sigma/b = \Delta Y_S/Y_S = \sigma/\gamma \tag{4.21}$$

Thus, a continuous growth path at full employment requires that $b = \gamma$. The problem is that, first, γ is not as constant as is often assumed (See Table 4.4

above), and, second, the parameter b is dependent on the volatile state of investor confidence, on Keynes' animal spirits. Why would these two parameters remain equal over time?

Suppose that after many years of consistent growth during which b remained equal to γ because things generally turned out as expected and there were no diminishing returns to capital, a financial crisis suddenly develops and banks stop lending to investors, as happened in 2008 in many countries. Investment falls, which means that actual investment is less than the amount of savings available to fund investment:

$$I_D = b(\Delta Y_D) < \sigma Y_S \qquad (4.22)$$

Aggregate demand therefore does not rise enough for it to absorb the increased output created by last period's investment, and investors' animal spirits are not validated. Thus, in the next period of time, there is likely to be a further decline in desired investment, which will reduce the demand for output even further. A cumulative downward spiral in aggregate demand results, unemployment grows, and economic growth declines. Harrod and Domar thus concluded that, if for any reason aggregate demand falls below the full employment level, the disequilibrium grows and the economy moves farther and farther from full employment.

Alternatively, if a sudden surge in optimism causes the demand for capital to rise above savings, then aggregate demand will exceed the economy's production capacity because actual investment falls short of what is needed to expand aggregate supply enough to meet aggregate demand next period. Hence, the next period aggregate demand will rise even further as investors attempt to make up for the missing capital investment, which generates an even larger production shortfall, which raises investment demand even further, and the economy will enter an inflationary spiral.

The complete Harrod-Domar model has been described as a **knife's edge model**: once the economy falls out of its full employment equilibrium, the economy spirals out of control. This suggests that when the economy falls off the *knife's edge*, there is a need for active economic policies that can raise or reduce aggregate demand in order to keep the growth in demand and the growth in the economy's supply side more or less in line. Also, the model shows that deviations from full employment can be large and last for a long time. The complete Harod-Domar model is a dynamic model based on the logic of Keynes' macroeconomic model. It is not surprising, therefore, that the model illustrates a need for active policy interventions to raise or lower demand for output and keep aggregate demand in line with the economy's capacity and thus keep the economy on its knife's edge. In sum, active stabilizing macroeconomic management of the economy is necessary for an economy to achieve constant growth.

4.6 Summary: What the Models Tell Us about Development

Our examination of the theory of economic development in this chapter covered a very large body of literature over a very long period of time. Taken together, the models provide a very thorough picture of the process of economic development. Among the important points made in this chapter are:

- Adam Smith highlighted the growth roles of specialization, technological progress and innovation, institutions, and national welfare.

- Smith also viewed economic development as a continual process, not necessarily subject to any inherent limitations or reversals.

- The Classical economists' development models were the first attempts in building rigorously logical models to explain the economic growth of the Industrial Revolution that was just beginning when Malthus published his population model.

- The Classicals emphasized diminishing returns, and they made population growth an endogenous element of their models, something which few other development economists have done since.

- The Classical model did not address technological change or how it could overcome diminishing returns.

- Marx pointed out that economic growth affects different groups in society differently, and he predicted that the unequal growth of income would stimulate conflict, economic stagnation, and, ultimately, revolution.

- Marx described the mechanics of capitalist economic development, the concentration of wealth, the growth of unemployment, the stagnation of income accruing to workers, and the collapse of demand for output.

- The popular partial "supply side" Harrod-Domar model is not a useful model of long-run development because it assumes key variables remain constant, contrary to all available evidence, and it ignores the demand side of the economy.

- The full Harrod-Domar model shows that the supply and demand sides of the economy must remain in balance in order to avoid economic instability.

The next chapter details Robert Solow's model, which addresses several shortcomings of the Harrod-Domar model. He drops the assumption of a constant capital-output ratio in favor of a neoclassical production function with variable inputs of labor and capital. Permitting one factor to vary relative to others reintroduces the problem of diminishing returns, which characterized the Classical models. In the Solow model, however, it is capital, not labor, that faces diminishing returns. Chapter 6 will explain to what extent economic activity in the economic sphere is subject to diminishing returns because of constraints imposed by the natural sphere of human existence. In short, a more holistic perspective suggests that the world has not yet definitively overcome diminishing returns. The next chapter on the Solow model shows that diminishing returns can be overcome by technological change, which consists of the advancement and application of new knowledge, new ideas, and innovations. Chapter 6 expands Solow's model to show that technological change must occur in all sectors of the economy if diminishing returns is to be avoided. This is very difficult in a real economy that does not have well developed markets in all spheres of human existence. How to achieve the broad range of technological change needed for continued economic development will be the focus of Chapters 7 and 8 in Part II of this textbook.

Key Terms and Concepts

Bourgeoisie	Learning by doing
Capital-output ratio	Malthusian population function
Classical model	Marginal product of labor
Classical school	Marxist model
Commodification of labor	Means of production
Communism	Mercantilists
Comparative advantage	Monetization
Constant returns to scale	Neoclassical economics
Depreciation	Physiocrats
Dialectic	Population function
Diminishing returns	Production function
Division of labor	Productive class
Economies of scale	Proletariat
Entrepreneur	Proprietor class
Growth path	Reserve army of labor
Harrod-Domar model	Scientific reductionism
Holism	Smithian development model
Incremental capital-output ratio (ICOR)	Socialism
Institutions	Specialization
Keynesian macroeconomic model	Stable equilibrium
Knife's edge model	Sterile class
Labor theory of value	Surplus value
Laissez-faire	Walrasian system
Landed aristocracy	ZPG

Questions and Problems

1. Who is correct: the Mercantilists, who said industry determined the wealth of the nation, or the Physiocrats, who saw agriculture as the source of national wealth?

2. According to the Harrod-Domar model, calculate the rate at which the economy can grow if:
   a. The saving rate is 10 percent and the capital-output ratio is 2.
   b. The saving rate is 10 percent and the capital-output ratio is 4.
   c. The saving rate is 20 percent and the capital-output ratio is 2.
   d. The saving rate is 20 percent and the capital-output ratio is 4.

   Then, describe the pattern that emerges as you calculate the effects of each of the four different sets of saving rates and capital-output ratios above.

3. Describe the policy implications of the Harrod-Domar model of economic growth. Specifically, what does the model suggest government policymakers could do to increase the rate of growth of the economy? (Hint: Distinguish the demand and supply sides of the Harrod-Domar model.)

4. Karl Marx built on the economic analysis of the Classical economists to predict social revolution. Briefly explain Marx's reasoning. Why do you think the social revolutions predicted by Marx did not occur in the industrialized capitalist societies of the world?

5. Thomas Malthus assumed that population growth was directly related to people's income. Today we observe that population growth is highest in low-income countries, lowest in high-income countries. Why would Malthus conclude that there was a direct relationship between population growth and per capita income? How could you explain the apparent inverse relationship between population growth and per capita income that we observe in many countries of the world today?

6. Adam Smith suggested that innovative activity, carried out by producers who act in their own interest, is important for economic development. Go back and read the descriptions and quotes of Smith, and briefly discuss whether his explanation of the intentional innovation by "entrepreneurs" covers what is known today as research and development (R&D) activity by firms?

7. Listed below are several different production functions, in which Y is output, and the X's are inputs. In the case of each of the following production functions, explain whether there are diminishing returns to any single factor:
   a. $Y = X_1 + X_2$
   b. $Y = X_1^{.5} \cdot X_2^{.5}$
   c. $Y = 2X_1$
   d. $Y = X_1 + X_2 + (X_1 \cdot X_2)$

8. In 1384 an epidemic of bubonic plague, also known as the *black death*, spread throughout Europe. This plague may have killed as much as one-third of the population of Europe. For centuries, new outbursts of the plague occurred every ten or fifteen years after that. Many economic historians have debated the economic effects of the plague, and many disagreements still exist as to how the plague affected the rate of economic growth in Europe. The interpretation of the plague of course depends on the particular economic model that is used.

    a.   Use the Smithian model to analyze the effects of the plague on economic growth.

    b.   Use Malthus' model to analyze the effects of the plague.

    c.   Contrast the results of the two models used in parts A and B of this question.

9.   Describe the Smithian development model, using both words and a diagram.

10. Describe equilibrium in the Malthusian model and explain exactly why this equilibrium is stable, which is to say, why the economy moves toward equilibrium if it is not already at equilibrium.

11. Are Adam Smith's suggestion that markets act as an invisible hand to direct the efficient allocation of resources and his focus on the pin factory's increasing returns to scale contradictory or complementary? Explain.

12. Explain the differences in perspective between the Physiocrats and the Mercantilists. How do you interpret their differences? How might their differences be reconciled?

13. A modern economy exhibits an astounding degree of interdependence between individual people, groups, business firms, and governments. How is this high degree of complexity possible? Should we be surprised at the occasional systemic crashes of this highly interdependent economic system? Discuss.

14. What were John Stuart Mill's contributions to Classical economic thinking? Explain his ideas and place them in the history of economic thought.

15. The distribution of income has attracted the attention of economists over the years. Explain how each of the major schools of economic thought treated the issue. Compare and contrast. Which school of thought do you think made the most relevant contributions to this subject?

16. Marx predicted that the capitalist economic system would eventually collapse because he said it was internally inconsistent. Precisely, what were the internal inconsistencies that Marx saw in the capitalist system? Explain.

17. According to Marx, why does unemployment tend to rise in a capitalist system? Explain.

18. In light of Marx's analysis, would the capitalist system become sustainable if mechanisms to redistribute income could be incorporated into the institutional structure that accompanies the system? Begin your answer by explaining how Marx described the evolution of the distribution of income in a capitalist system and why the changing shares of income undermined the system.

19. Why did neoclassical economists succumb to scientific reductionism in the late nineteenth century? Why does orthodox economics continue to frame its analysis in static and scientific reductionist frameworks?

20. Why was the Harrod-Domar model so popular among economists charged with formulating policy? Did they interpret the model correctly? Explain.

21. Why is there such a strong implicit belief in the stability of the economy in orthodox economics? (Hint: This is a conjectural question, and you may wish to draw on both the history of economic thought, the psychological behaviors discussed in Chapter 3, and the political influences that drive economic policy.)

22. In Section 4.3.3, the text states: "Galor and Moav hypothesize that capitalists actually demand more educated workers because they see their salvation in innovation rather than investment in more physical capital. Capitalists thus support increasing education for the entire population. As a result, workers endowed with ever greater amounts of human capital gradually cause class distinctions to become

blurred, and the threat of revolution disappears." Do you agree with the hypothesis of Galor and Moav? Explain. (Hint: You may wish to draw on current evidence on education and income distributions.)

23. Adam Smith is not known for a model of economic development. In fact, one has to piece together his thoughts from various parts of his work to create a cohesive model of economic development. Nevertheless, he did present more than enough consistent ideas that comprise a logical model of economic development. Outline how Smith described the process of economic development.

References

Atkinson, Anthony, Thomas Pikety, and Emmanuel Saez (2009), "Top Incomes in the Long Run of History," NBER Working Paper 15408, October.

Condorcet, Marquis de (1795), *Esquisses d'un tableau historique des progrès de l'ésprit humain*, Paris.

Domar, Evsey (1946), "Capital Expansion, Rate of Growth, and Employment," *Econometrica* 14:137–147.

Easterly, William (1999), "The Ghost of Financing Gap: How the Harrod-Domar Model Still Haunts Development Economics," *Journal of Development Economics* 60(2): 423–438.

Harrod, Roy F. (1939), "An Essay in Dynamic Theory," *The Economic Journal* 49:14–33.

Galor, Oded, and Omer Moav (2006), "Das Human-Kapital: A Theory of the Demise of the Class Structure," *Review of Economic Studies* 73:85–117.

Higgins, Benjamin (1968), *Economic Development*, New York: W. W. Norton & Company.

Kelly, Morgan (1997), "The Dynamics of Smithian Growth," *Quarterly Journal of Economics* 112(3):939–964.

Keynes, John Maynard (1936), *The General Theory of Employment, Interest, and Money*, New York: MacMillan.

Letiche, J. M. (1960), "Adam Smith and David Ricardo on Economic Growth," in Bert F. Hoselitz (ed.), *Theories of Economic Growth*, New York: The Free Press.

Maddison, Angus (1998), *Chinese Economic Performance in the Long Run*, OECD, Paris.

Malthus, Thomas (1798), *An Essay on the Principle of Population*, London: W. Pickering.

Marx, Karl (1967), *Capital*, Vol. 3, New York: Progress Publishers.

Marx, Karl (1906–1909), *Capital*, Vol. 1, Ernest Untermann (trans.) and F. Engels (ed.), Chicago: Charles Kerr.

Marx, Karl (1964), in Martin Milligan (trans.) and D.J. Struik (ed.), *Economic and Philosophic Manuscripts of 1844*, New York: International Publishers,

Marx, Karl, and Frederick Engels (1948 [1848]), *The Communist Manifesto*, New York: International Publishers Co., Inc.

Miller, Merton H., and Charles W. Upton (1974), *Macroeconomics: A Neoclassical Introduction*, Homewood, Illinois: Richard D. Irwin, Inc.

North, Douglass C., and Robert Paul Thomas (1973), *The Rise of the Western World*, Cambridge, U.K.: Cambridge University Press.

Quesnay, François (1991), *Physiocratie: Droit Naturel, Tableau Économique et Autres Textes*, Paris: Flamarion.

Saez, Emmanuel (2010), "Striking It Richer: The Evolution of Top Incomes in the United States (Update with 2008 Estimates)," Stanford Center for the Study of Poverty and Inequality, July 17.

Smith, Adam (1776 [1976]), *An Inquiry into the Nature and Causes of the Wealth of Nations*, Chicago: University of Chicago Press.

de Vries, Jan, and Ad van der Woude (1997), *The First Modern Economy*, Cambridge, U.K.: Cambridge University Press.

Warsh, David (2006), *Knowledge and the Wealth of Nations — A Story of Economic Discovery*, New York: W. W. Norton & Company.

CHAPTER 5

Solow's Neoclassical Growth Model

The verb "to grow" has become so overladen with positive value connotations that we have forgotten its first literal dictionary denotation, namely, "to spring up and develop to maturity." Thus the very notion of growth includes some concept of maturity or sufficiency, beyond which point physical accumulation gives way to physical maintenance; that is, growth gives way to a steady state.

(Herman Daly)[1]

Robert Solow responded to the popularity of the truncated supply-side Harrod-Domar growth model by developing an alternative model based on the principle of diminishing returns. In two articles in the mid-1950s, Solow showed why economic growth is not a straightforward function of investment as the supply-side version of Harrod-Domar growth models suggested.[2]

Solow explains the rationale for his growth model as follows: "A remarkable characteristic of the Harrod-Domar model is that it consistently studies long-run problems with the usual short-run tools. Instead one thinks of the long run as the domain of the neoclassical analysis, the land of the margin."[3] Solow permits the capital-output ratio to vary in response to changes in investment, in contrast to the Harrod-Domar model's linear relationship between investment and economic growth. Note that when Solow criticizes the Harrod-Domar model, he is criticizing the simplified supply-side version that had become popular in the development literature, not the full dynamic version that we described in the previous chapter.

The new **Solow model** was not immediately embraced by everyone. Many economists felt it was too simple and that a much more sophisticated model was

---

[1] Herman Daly (1977), Chapter 5.
[2] Robert Solow (1956, 1957).
[3] Solow (1956), p. 66.

needed to accurately model the complex process of economic growth. Non-economists simply had difficulty accepting the Solow model's conclusion that the economy's rates of saving and investment have no effect on an economy's long-run rate of growth. The fundamental logic of the model has held up well, however, and Solow's model remains prominent in the economic development literature fifty years later. This chapter explains Solow's growth model in detail.

Chapter Goals

1. Explain the production function of the Solow model.
2. Introduce the simple two-factor Solow model.
3. Discuss the saving function and its equivalence to the investment function.
4. Explain the Solow model's steady state.
5. Examine the effects of varying the model's parameters.
6. Introduce technological change as a shift in the production function.
7. Show why only continuous labor-augmenting technological change can sustain constant growth in output.
8. Present case studies that apply the Solow model.
9. Discuss the extreme case in which all factors are variable.
10. Discuss the model's inability to explain technological change.

5.1 Introduction to the Solow Model

Solow differentiated his model from the simplified Harrod-Domar model and its fixed capital-output ratio by defining a production function that permits factors to be continuously substituted for each other. Such continuous substitution means that the marginal products of each factor vary, depending on how much of the factor is used in production and how many other factors it is combined with. Solow also assumes that each factor of production is subject to **diminishing returns**. That is, as equal increments of one factor are gradually added to fixed amounts of other factors of production, output gains diminish in size. Recall that Classical economists like Thomas Malthus and David Ricardo modeled labor as subject to diminishing returns because it had to work with a fixed stock of agricultural land.

It is easy to grasp how diminishing returns to capital undermine the Harrod-Domar model's conclusion that a constant rate of investment brings constant increases in output. Less obvious is the Solow model's conclusion that economic growth will cease entirely even when investment continues as a constant percentage of output. Solow obtains this result by including capital depreciation in his model; recall that the Harrod-Domar assumed capital did not depreciate. Capital in fact continually wears out and must be replaced.

Therefore, a growing capital stock means that ever larger amounts of an economy's savings must be diverted from investing in additions to the capital stock to maintaining the economy's existing capital stock.

With these assumptions, Solow concluded that it was impossible to generate continued growth in output by maintaining a constant rate of saving and investment, no matter how high the savings rate. With that conclusion, the Solow model undermined what many development economists were advising policy makers to do in the post-World War II years, which was to take measures to increase saving and investment. Solow convincingly showed that something more than just saving and investment are needed to keep per capita output growing in the long run. This chapter will examine both the Solow model's conclusions and its implications for long-run economic growth.

5.1.1 The Neoclassical production function

The main component of the Solow model is a **production function** in which output, Y, is a function of several inputs or factors of production. To keep matters simple, suppose that there are just two factors of production, capital and labor. Therefore, Y is a function of the quantity of capital, K, and labor, L, as follows:

$$Y = F(K, L) \tag{5.1}$$

Solow assumed that this production function generated **constant returns to scale**. This means that if *all* inputs in the production function (5.1) are increased by the same multiple, say a constant c, then output will increase by c as well:

$$cY = F(cK, cL) \tag{5.2}$$

For example, if c = 2 and all inputs are doubled, then output Y also doubles.

A constant returns to scale production function means that, if we assume a constant supply of labor and let c = 1/L, we can write equation (5.1) as

$$Y/L = F(K/L, 1) \tag{5.3}$$

Then, if we redefine Y/L and K/L as y and k, respectively, and the function f(k) as F(k,1), we can conveniently rewrite equation (5.3) as

$$y = f(k) \tag{5.4}$$

Equation (5.4) describes output per worker as a function of capital per worker. This representation of the production function in *per worker* terms is attractive because it brings us closer to the popular definition of economic growth as a rise

in *per capita* output.   Granted, the number of workers in the economy is
generally not equal to the total number of people in the economy because the
population includes children and retired people who do not work.   But, if the
number of workers is a constant proportion of the overall population, POP, in
the long run, then the long-run rate of growth of Y/L is the same as per capita
output, Y/POP.

In addition to assuming constant returns to scale when all inputs are varied
proportionately, Solow also assumed diminishing marginal returns to any single
input. This means that equal additions of one input, all other things equal, cause
successively smaller and smaller increases in output.   In the case of Solow's
assumption, of just two variable inputs, if the supply of labor remains the same
while investment causes the capital stock to grow, diminishing returns implies
that output will increase in diminishing amounts.   Graphically, such a
production function looks like the curve in Figure 5.1. Note the similarity of
Figure 5.1 and Figure 4.3, which accompanied the discussion of Thomas
Malthus' diminishing returns to population. In the Solow model, output always
rises with an increase in the amount of capital relative to labor, but the slope
of the production function continuously decreases because of diminishing
returns.[4]

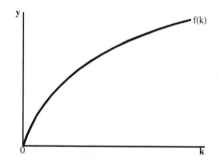

Figure 5.1 The Solow Model's Production Function

The production function f(k) represents the productive capability, or the
supply side, of the economy. The economy's capital stock depends, in part, on
society's willingness to save and invest, which depends on people's willingness
to refrain from consuming all of their income. The Solow model therefore also
recognizes a role for consumer behavior.

---

[4] For those familiar with calculus, the assumptions of diminishing returns to each factor for the
production function y = f(k) implies that the first derivative of output with respect to k is f'(k) > 0
and the second derivative is f"(k) < 0.   The first derivative tells us how much the value of the
function, f(k), changes when k changes. The second derivative tells us how the "change" changes;
therefore a negative second derivative implies diminishing returns.

5.1.2 Consumption and saving

In the simplest version of his model, Solow made saving a simple function of income, determined by the saving rate, σ:

$$S = \sigma Y \qquad (5.5)$$

In his model, Solow also assumes away complications such as government or foreign borrowing. This means consumption is simply income minus saving:

$$C = Y - S = Y - \sigma Y = (1 - \sigma)Y \qquad (5.6)$$

Solow also assumed that savings always flowed to productive investment, and:

$$S = I \qquad (5.7)$$

This assumption could be construed as a weakness of the model, the same weakness we noted for the Harrod-Domar model of the previous chapter.

There are actually many reasons why, in the real world, saving does not automatically translate into an equal amount of productive investment. The people, firms, and organizations that do the saving are not the same people, firms, and organizations that do the investing. Nor are saving and investing in new productive capacity driven by the same incentives. And, financial sectors do not always allocate savings efficiently. Large amounts of saving may not be productively invested; savings can be used to fund consumer debt, subsidize well-connected private businesses, pay for military aggression and war, and be directed to investments that have negative public returns. We will return to this issue in Chapter 11, when we discuss the important role played by the financial sector in the economy. For now, the discussion follows Solow in assuming that saving flows directly into new productive capital.

Putting equations (5.6) and (5.7) together gives us a simplification of the traditional macroeconomic relationship for national output:

$$Y = C + S = C + I \qquad (5.8)$$

Similar to equation (5.4), if we define $y \equiv Y/L$, $c \equiv C/L$, $s \equiv S/L$, and $i \equiv I/L$, we can put all the variables in *per worker* terms:

$$y = c + s = c + i \qquad (5.9)$$

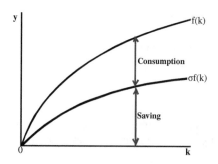

Figure 5.2 The Saving Function

Figure 5.2 shows the economy's per capita saving function as a function of the capital/labor ratio, or k. Since saving is assumed to be a constant ratio σ, the saving function is a diminished reflection of the production function f(k):

$$s = \sigma y = \sigma f(k) \tag{5.10}$$

With s = i, the savings function is effectively also the investment function.

5.1.3 The capital stock

As mentioned, Solow assumed that the stock of capital in the economy wears out over time. Solow assumes that a constant proportion of the existing capital stock depreciates in each period of time. This proportion of capital that wears out in each period of time is referred to as the **rate of depreciation,** represented by the Greek letter delta, δ.

When there is depreciation, the *change* (denoted by the symbol "Δ") in the stock of capital depends on the difference between investment and depreciation:

$$\Delta K = I - \delta K \tag{5.11}$$

Investment increases the capital stock of capital only if the former exceeds the amount of capital that depreciates.

Again, if we divide all the variables used in the equations above by the total number of workers, L, then we can state equation (5.11) in per worker terms. We again use lower case letters to designate such per worker variables. Equation (5.11) can be written in per worker terms as:

$$\Delta k = i - \delta k = \sigma y - \delta k = \sigma f(k) - \delta k \tag{5.12}$$

If σf(k) is greater than δk, then Δk > 0 and the capital-labor ratio k increases. If σf(k) < δk, then Δk < 0 and k declines. That is, if depreciation of existing capital exceeds new investment, the capital stock declines. The inclusion of depreciation differentiates the Solow model from the Harrod-Domar model.

5.1.4 The Solow growth equilibrium

The simple Solow model presented here predicts that if the parameters and assumptions of the model remain the same, the economy will, in the long run, settle at constant and stable equilibrium levels of k and y. That is, the growth of k and y will stop. To understand why, note first that the assumption of diminishing returns for the production function y = f(k) implies that the saving/investment function σf(k) also increases at a decreasing rate. Second, depreciation, δk, is represented by a rising linear function of k.

Figure 5.3 illustrates both the curve σf(k) and the line δk. As already noted just above, if investment, σf(k), is greater than depreciation, δk, then the per worker capital stock k increases. On the other hand, when σf(k) < δk, then k declines. The economy's equilibrium changes in response to differences between investment σf(k) and depreciation δk. The investment curve lies above the depreciation line when k is small, and thus the capital stock grows. The saving curve lies below the depreciation line when k is large, in which case the capital stock shrinks. The model thus has a **stable equilibrium** at the level k*; the economy automatically moves toward equilibrium if it is not already at that equilibrium. Because k tends toward a stable equilibrium and y is continuously related to k by y = f(k), y also tends toward the stable equilibrium level at y* = f(k*). Solow designates these equilibrium values of k and y as the model's **steady state**, the point where all variables in a model are constant.

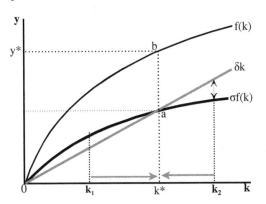

Figure 5.3 The Solow Model's Steady State

In Chapter 1, the term **homeostasis** was used to describe the process by which a living organism automatically or instinctively regulates its internal environment in order to survive within a variable external environment. If we view the economy as an organism that is accurately described by the Solow model, then the investment process, which is quantified as the difference between depreciation and savings, is a homeostatic process that reestablishes stable levels of capital and output if changes in the savings rate, the depreciation rate, or the production function upset an initial equilibrium.

In sum, the Solow model concludes that if (1) the production function is a fixed function that (2) exhibits constant returns to scale and diminishing returns to any single input, (3) the values of the parameters σ and δ are constants, and (4) the supply of labor L is constant, then in the long run the capital-labor ratio and per capita output settle at the steady state values k^* and y^*, respectively. The stunning conclusion of the model is that the rate of growth in per capita output in the long run is zero no matter how much people save and invest.

It should now be clear how these conclusions are arrived at. First, the need to replace depreciating capital changes in direct proportion to the size of the capital stock. Output, income, and savings, on the other hand, do not grow in direct proportion to the stock of capital because diminishing returns to capital reduce the marginal product of capital as k increases. The adjustment of k stops when marginal savings are just large enough to fund the marginal investment needed to replace the capital stock that depreciates each year.

5.2 The Rate of Saving and the Steady State

You should be skeptical of the conclusion that economic growth slows and eventually stops when the economy reaches its steady state. This result is obviously not reflective of the real world. Many countries have been able to increase per capita incomes year after year for extended periods of time. The simple version of the model above does not exhaust what Solow had to say about growth, however. We now examine whether the model generates continued growth in output by increasing the economy's rate of saving.

5.2.1 The rate of saving and output growth

Figure 5.4 illustrates how the long-run steady state equilibrium of the economy depends on the rate of saving. The higher the rate of saving, all other things equal, the greater the steady state stock of capital per worker and, hence, the higher is the steady state level of per capita income. If the saving rate is initially equal to σ_1, the economy's long run equilibrium steady state occurs where per worker capital stock is equal to k^*_1 and per worker output is y^*_1.

Suppose now that the saving rate increases to σ_2. This causes the $\sigma f(k)$ curve to shift up in proportion to the rise in the rate of saving, and the new intersection between the $\sigma f(k)$ curve and the unchanged δk establishes a new steady state where the capital stock k^*_2 and per worker output is $y^*_2 = f(k^*_2)$.

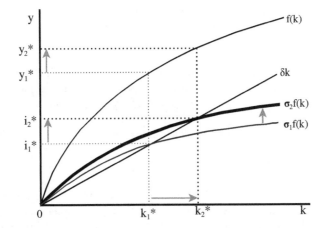

Figure 5.4 The Medium-Run Growth Effect of an Increase in the Saving Rate

The Solow model thus predicts that, all other things equal, a country with a higher savings rate will enjoy a higher standard of living than an otherwise similar country with a lower rate of saving. But, unless there are further changes in the saving rate or other parameters, each economy eventually settles in its steady state where the growth rate is zero. A rise in the saving/investment rate generates growth only until the new steady state is reached. This temporary growth predicted by the Solow model is often called **medium-run growth** of output per capita. According to the Solow model, an increase in saving does not generate **permanent growth** in output per capita.

5.2.2 Comparative statics

We derived the conclusion about the effect of a change in the rate of saving on the steady state levels of y and k by following an analytical procedure economists call **comparative statics**. We first built a model of the economy by making assumptions, such as a constant returns to scale production function, two inputs each subject to diminishing returns, consumers who save a constant fraction of their income, the equality of saving and productive investment, a constant depreciation rate, and a constant labor force (population). The second step of our comparative statics exercise was to use the model, plus logical reasoning, to determine how a change in one of the **exogenous variables** affected the final values of two **endogenous variables** y and k. We changed the rate of saving while holding all other exogenous variables and assumptions constant. We were able to conclude that, all other things equal, an increase in the rate of saving raises the steady state levels of y and k.

The word *comparative* in comparative statics reflects the practice of only comparing the beginning and end points of a process, while paying no attention to the path the economy follows in shifting from one equilibrium and another. Comparative statics describes only the direction and size of the final changes. It is thus important to establish that the equilibria are stable, which eliminates the possibility of diverse paths of adjustment. Note also that comparative statics analysis frequently uses the *all other things equal* assumption to isolate the effects of a change in a single variable. In Figure 5.4, this assumption isolated the effects of a change in the saving rate on the endogenous variables k and y.

5.2.3 Dynamic analysis

Comparative statics does not tell us how long it takes the economy to adjust to a change in a variable or exactly what the levels of per capita output and other relevant variables are at each stage of the adjustment process. Will the transition take one year or two generations? Does most of the eventual change occur early on in the transition process, or does it occur toward the end? Is the transition a smooth and straight path, or does it take some roundabout route to reach its new steady state? To answer these of questions, we need the **growth path** that the economy follows during its transition from one comparative static equilibrium to another. That is, we need **dynamic analysis**.

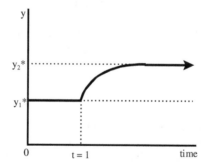

Figure 5.5 The Dynamic Adjustment of an Increase in Saving

Figure 5.5 illustrates the dynamic growth path of per worker output prescribed by the Solow model when the rate of saving alters the steady state. Time is shown on the horizontal axis and per worker output on the vertical axis. Suppose that the savings rate suddenly rises at time t = 1. As already shown in Figure 5.4, steady state per worker income increases from y_1^* to y_2^*, but actual income per worker increases only gradually to the new steady state as increased investment gradually raises k to its new steady state level.

The growth path in Figure 5.5 shows that the increases in per worker income are largest right after the rise in savings. Medium-term growth is faster early in the transition period for two reasons: (1) at the beginning of the transition depreciation is relatively small because the capital stock has not yet grown much, and (2) the marginal product of capital is still relatively large because marginal returns to capital have not yet diminished as much as they will when k becomes larger. Specifically, equation (5.12) showed that $\Delta k = \sigma f(k) - \delta k$, which implies that the magnitude of the change in k in each period depends on the difference between the savings curve and the depreciation line. In Figure 5.4, the distance between $\sigma_2 f(k)$ and k is greatest immediately after the shift in the saving rate when k is still close to k_1^*. Figure 5.5, therefore, shows the growth of per capita income to be fastest immediately after period $t = 1$. Then, as the capital stock approaches the new steady state at k_2^*, the slope of the growth path declines as the growth of capital slows and eventually stops when the economy reaches its new steady state.

5.2.4 What the Solow model reveals

The simple Solow model we have now constructed predicts that:

- The economy will move toward a *steady state* equilibrium, which is a *stable* equilibrium.

- There is no growth in per worker output or the capital-labor ratio when the economy reaches its steady state.

- As the economy moves from one steady state to another, *medium-term growth* in per capita output and the per capita capital stock can occur.

- In the long run, increasing the rate of saving does not cause a permanent acceleration of growth in per capita output.

As mentioned earlier, the conclusion that an economy cannot experience permanent economic growth does not fit the real world's experience over the past 200 years. So, if higher saving cannot produce long-run growth in output, what can? The next sections, we examine the roles of population growth and technological change. So far, both variables have been assumed to be constants rather than variables.

5.3 Population Growth and the Solow Model

Unlike what the simple Solow model of the previous two sections assumed, population growth has been positive through much of human history. Population growth rates vary greatly over time and from one country to another.

In Africa, annual population growth still exceeds 3 percent per year in some countries. In the fast-growing East Asian economies, population growth rates have fallen to less than 1 percent.   In several European countries, natural population growth is now negative. Clearly, population and the labor force are not constants, nor do they grow at uniform rates in all countries or over time.

In this section, we relax the assumption of a constant labor force. We examine whether a growing population and, therefore, an expanding labor force, can cause the Solow model to generate permanent economic growth.

5.3.1 Population growth and the steady state

Suppose that population growth causes the labor force to grow at the constant rate of ω. Specifically, $\Delta L/L = g_L = \omega$. Equation (5.12) thus no longer correctly describes the change in the capital-labor ratio. For $k = K/L$ to remain constant when the labor force, the denominator of k, grows, investment must both cover the capital that depreciates and it must equip with capital the new entrants to the labor force. Thus, for the per capita level of capital, k, to remain constant, the rate of investment must equal the sum of the rates of depreciation and population growth, $\delta + \omega$. The change in the capital-labor ratio k will thus be:

$$\Delta k = i - \delta k - \omega k = \sigma f(k) - (\delta + \omega)k \tag{5.13}$$

Figure 5.6 illustrates that, all other things equal, when $\omega > 0$, the intersection of $(\delta + \omega)k$ and $\sigma f(k)$ occurs at a lower level of k than if $\omega = 0$. The steady state is determined by the intersection of $(\delta + \omega)k$ and $\sigma f(k)$. In general, the higher the

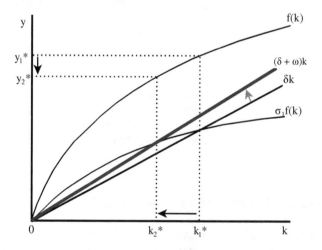

Figure 5.6 The Steady State with Population Growth

rate of population growth, the lower the steady state k. And, because y = f(k), the Solow model also predicts that, all other things equal, countries with higher rates of population growth have lower *levels* of per capita output and income. In practical terms, if an economy with a higher rate of population growth is not willing to save more, it cannot maintain the same per capita stock of capital as the economy with the lower population growth rate. Hence, all other things equal, average income is lower in an economy with the faster population growth.

5.3.2 Population growth increases total output

Compared to an economy with no population growth, an economy where $\omega > 0$ experiences continuous increases in *total* output in the steady state. A constant k in the steady state, plus our assumption of a constant returns to scale production function, imply that both capital and total output must grow at the rate of growth of the labor force. Another way to look at this result is that investment in effect does not suffer from diminishing returns if it causes the capital stock to grow in exact proportion to the labor force, the other factor of production. Recall the assumption by Solow that the production function exhibits constant returns to scale. Thus, output grows in line with population; that is, $g_Y = g_K = g_L$. But, in *per worker* terms, the steady state with population growth results in $g_y = g_k = 0$. Population growth does not generate long-run positive economic growth when economic growth is defined as an increase in per capita output.

Solow's growth model does suggest that policies to slow down population growth would raise the steady state level of per capita income, ceteris paribus. The model therefore is in accord with the many demographers, economists, environmentalists, social scientists, and politicians who have suggested that population growth does not raise human well-being. Note, however, that when the Solow model is taken to its logical conclusion, it suggests that society would enjoy an even higher level of per capita income if population growth were negative. The model thus seems to justify population control policies. Chapter 9 examines the role of population growth in the growth process in greater detail and provides some answers to these types of questions. For now, keep in mind that population growth creates the cost of providing new members of the population with the tools and equipment they need to be as productive as current members of society.

5.4 Technological Change

If population growth cannot explain the growth in per capita output that the world economy has experienced, then what can? The remaining candidate is

technological change. Technology is represented by the production function, which defines how the economy transforms inputs, such as capital and labor, into output. Technological change, therefore, consists of a change in the shape or position of the production function. Graphically, positive technological change shifts the production function upward so that for a given quantity of inputs, output increases.

Authors have alternatively referred to technological progress as an increase in know-how, the creation of new ideas, or an increase in economic efficiency. All of these suggestions describe why the economy's production function can shift. Here we assume that, regardless of precisely what specific form the technological change takes, technological change only affects labor efficiency. This is referred to as **labor-augmenting technological change.** By focusing exclusively on labor-augmenting technology, we can redefine all variables in terms of **effective labor**, the product of labor and an index of labor efficiency, E. We can rewrite the production function as

$$Y = F[K, (L \cdot E)]. \tag{5.14}$$

5.4.1 Technical change and the steady state

The level of capital per effective worker, $K/(L \cdot E)$, will grow only if the capital stock grows more rapidly than the labor force and the level of technology. That is, in addition to the effect of depreciation on the stock of capital per worker, the amount of capital stock per effective worker can grow only if investment per worker is greater than the sum of (1) the amount of capital that depreciates, (2) the amount of new capital needed to equip additional workers in the labor force, and (3) the amount of capital needed to match technological change's effect on labor's ability to produce.

In order to simplify the notation, we state effective per worker variables in italics. Specifically, the amount of capital per effective worker $K/(L \cdot E) \equiv k$, income per effective worker $Y/(L \cdot E) \equiv y$, and investment per effective worker $I/(L \cdot E) \equiv i$. We define the rate of labor-augmenting technological change as z. These new definitions permit us to use the equations we used earlier for the simpler versions of the Solow model, and the analysis looks similar to what you have already seen. For example, the capital stock per effective worker changes according to

$$\Delta k = i - (\delta + \omega + z)k = \sigma f(k) - (\delta + \omega + z)k \tag{5.15}$$

Figure 5.7 depicts the steady state equilibrium when $\omega > 0$ and $z > 0$. Note that the steady state is again stable. If $k < k^*$, then $\sigma f(k) > (\delta + \omega + z)k$ and k increases. But, if $k > k^*$, then $\sigma f(k) < (\delta + \omega + z)k$ and k decreases.

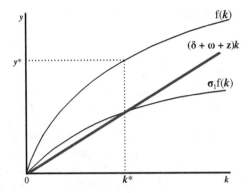

Figure 5.7 The Steady State with Technology Growth

5.4.2 Technological change generates permanent growth

The question is now whether there is economic growth in the steady state as shown in Figure 5.7. Note that the steady state values of y and k are constant, but economic growth depends on whether the per capita values of y = Y/L and k = K/L are growing. Indeed, it should be obvious that when the effective per worker terms y and k are constant, the per capita terms y and k must be growing. Some simple mathematics show why.

First of all, the rate of growth of a fraction is equal to the growth of the numerator *minus* the growth of the denominator. Thus, the growth of y = Y/L, denoted as g_y, is

$$g_y = g_Y - g_L \tag{5.16}$$

Second, the growth rate of the product of two variables is equal to the *sum* of the growth rates of each of the variables. Thus, the growth rate of the product L·E is $g_{(L·E)} = g_L + g_{E·} = \omega + z$. Putting these two mathematical results together shows that the growth rate of $y = Y/(L·E)$ is equal to

$$g_y = g_Y - g_L - z = g_y - z \tag{5.17}$$

Thus, in the steady state, when $g_y = g_Y - g_L - z = g_y - z = 0$, the growth of per worker output y = Y/L is

$$g_y = z \tag{5.18}$$

In words, in the steady state the rate of growth of per capita output is equal to the rate of labor-augmenting technological change.

5.4.3 The steady state with technology-driven growth

Figure 5.7 does not seem to show anything changing, but equation (5.18) tells us that there is economic growth occurring behind the scenes. In the steady state, per worker capital k and per worker output y are continually growing at a constant positive rate z. This implies that when the model is illustrated using only the k and y variables, the steady state from Figure 5.7 appears as a continual upward shifting of the production function, as in Figure 5.8.

To understand Figure 5.8, suppose the economy begins in the steady state with per capita output of y_1, where y_1 corresponds to y_1^* and k_1 corresponds to *k** in Figure 5.7. Technological change causes the entire production function to shift up from $f_1(k)$ to $f_2(k)$, and if the saving rate remains the same at σ the rise in the production function causes a proportional rise in the saving function. The steady state levels of per capita capital and income thus rise to k_2^* and y_2^*, respectively. Continuous technological change continues to shift the production function $y = f(k)$ upward, and this raises the economy's steady state levels of per worker capital and output to k_3^* and y_3^*. Since both y and k grow at the same rate of technological change z, the steady state combinations of k and y in the growing economy all lie along the straight arrow in Figure 5.8.

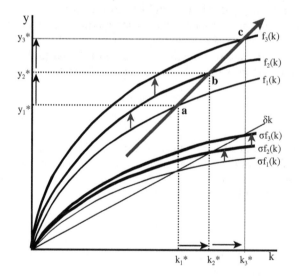

Figure 5.8 Technological Progress and the Solow Growth Model

5.4.4 Correlation does not imply causation

This proportionate growth of y and k could be interpreted by the unsuspecting researcher as proof that the growth of capital causes continued output growth, as the Harrod-Domar model from the previous chapter suggests. The Solow model warns us that such a conclusion may not be correct. Diminishing returns means that a steady stream of increases in k will not cause the proportional increases in y. However, technological change can generate a seemingly linear correlation between k and y. Specifically, the Solow model hypothesizes that the increase in k is the *result* of changes in the economy's steady state *caused* by technological change.

In Figure 5.8, the points a, b, and c seem to lie nicely along a straight line. If you were a researcher collecting evidence to test the validity of the Harrod-Domar model, you could use statistical methods to estimate the slope of this line. All you would have to do is enter the values for k_1^*, k_2^*, k_3^*, and the rest of the k values along with y_1^*, y_2^*, y_3^*, and the other successive observations of output into a statistical regression program on your computer, for example. The program would find that, indeed, y and k move closely together, and you could conclude that the evidence supports the hypothesis that increased values of k *cause* higher levels of y.

This example highlights one of the shortcomings of statistical analysis: Correlation does not *prove* causation! The apparent linear pattern of k and y could have been generated either by an economy with a positive rate of saving as modeled by the Harrod-Domar model or an economy with permanent technological change as modeled by the Solow model. The simple regression analysis produces statistical results compatible with both hypothesized models. The noted growth economist Paul Romer therefore noted: "We could produce statistical evidence suggesting that all growth came from capital accumulation with no room for anything called technological change. But we would not believe it."[5] The scientific method mandates that economists examine much more detailed evidence in order to confirm, or reject, the hypothesized Harrod-Domar and Solow models.

5.4.5 Technological change and the growth path

The effect of technological change can also be illustrated using a growth path diagram. Figure 5.9 shows the economy's growth path in the case of a constant rate of growth. A constant rate of growth results in a growth path that gradually slopes ever steeper. Compare Figure 5.9 to Figure 5.5. The latter illustrated the growth path for a Solow economy without technological change following a rise in the saving rate. The rise in saving resulted in a medium run growth of per capita output, but in the long run the economy's growth path approached a horizontal line along which the rate of growth is zero. The former illustrates continuous growth in y over time.

---

[5] Paul Romer (1993), p. 562.

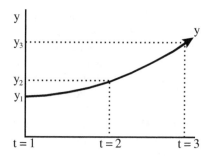

Figure 5.9 Growth with Technological Progress

5.4.6 Summarizing the Solow model

In Figure 5.10, we show the production function simply as $Y = f(K)$ under the assumption that the quantity of other factors is fixed. The resulting diminishing returns therefore implies that in the absence of technological progress, the first unit of capital results in 100 units of output being produced, but because of diminishing returns the second unit adds only 40 units of output. But, if the doubling of capital is combined with positive technological change and, therefore, a shift in the production function from $f_1(K)$ to $f_2(K)$, then output can double to 200. Thus, technological progress effectively reduces or eliminates diminishing returns.

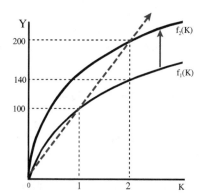

Figure 5.10 Technological Progress

The continually-rising standards we have experienced in most countries over the past 200 years have been the result of both more tools and machines, as illustrated by ever larger K's in Figure 5.10, and better tools, machines, knowledge, and production methods, as illustrated by the ever-rising production functions. Had the world only accumulated more of the same capital, our growth would have long-since stopped and we would not have achieved our current standards of living. The Solow model tells us that if we give a worker more and more identical shovels to work with, his or her ability to dig holes in the ground will not increase in proportion to the number of shovels. But, if additional capital comes not in the form of more shovels but in the form of, say, a diesel-powered mechanical backhoe, then diminishing returns can be avoided. Diminishing returns can be overcome because, despite costing 500 times as much as a shovel, the backhoe permits a worker to dig much more than 500 times as big a hole as she could dig with a shovel. Replacing shovels with a backhoe implies technological change; a worker with a backhoe digs holes very differently than a worker with a shovel.

To drive home the reason why investment in more of the same tools and machines does not generate permanent economic growth, imagine what our standard of living would be today if after 1800 we had increased the number of horses rather than inventing farm tractors, continued to give sick people more cod liver oil instead of developing antibiotics, and just made more quills and ink rather than inventing word processors. Can Earth support twice as many coal fired power plants, twice as many cars using gasoline engines, and twice as many acres devoted to grow our food? We will have to do things differently.

5.5 Applying the Solow Model

The popularity of the Solow model is only partly based on its simplicity. The model has also proven useful for examining real observed economic growth. In this section, we use the Solow model to examine two recent cases of economic growth: the rapid growth of the Asian tigers and the collapse of economic growth in Russia after the fall of the U.S.S.R.

5.5.1 The Asian "economic miracle"

Hong Kong, Korea, Singapore, and Taiwan experienced extraordinary rates of economic growth during the latter half of the twentieth century. These four *Asian tigers*, as they came to be called, have raised the average per capita incomes of their citizens from among the lowest in the world some fifty years ago to developed country levels today. According to Maddison's (2003) comparative income data, by 2000 Hong Kong and Singapore enjoyed real per capita incomes well over $20,000, placing them ahead of most European countries. Korea increased its real per capita income from less than $1,000 in 1950 to over $13,000 by 2000. Taiwan similarly raised its per capita income from $900 in 1950 to over $15,000 in 2000.

By the 1990s, many writers extrapolated recent growth trends to conclude that East Asian economies would soon enjoy per capita incomes above those of the United States and Europe. The power of compounding and the rapid growth suggested that Hong Kong and Singapore would pass U.S. per capita income as soon as 2015. In a popular article entitled "The Myth of Asia's Miracle," Paul Krugman (1994) argued against such an outcome. He applied the logic of the Solow model to argue that simple extrapolation was inappropriate and that the rapid economic growth of the Asian tigers would inevitably slow down.

Krugman emphasized the fact that factor accumulation was extraordinary in East Asia. For example, savings rates were about 40 percent of income in Singapore. Furthermore, the labor force grew exceptionally rapidly because the labor force participation rate of women increased. And, the productivity of the labor force improved with increased schooling; from an average of less than three years of elementary school education in the early 1950s, today the average years of schooling of workers entering the labor forces in Taiwan, Singapore, South Korea are at developed country levels. Krugman (1994, p. 78) thus concluded:

> The newly industrializing countries of the Pacific Rim have received a reward for their extraordinary mobilization of resources that is no more than what the most boringly conventional economic theory would lead us to expect. If there is a secret to Asian growth, it is simply deferred gratification, the willingness to sacrifice current satisfaction for future gain.

The "boringly conventional economic theory" that Krugman referred to was obviously the Solow growth model. The Solow model showed how East Asia's large jump in saving and factor accumulation indeed would have caused a great amount of medium-term growth. But, because the Asian tigers cannot continue to increase savings rates, women's labor force participation, or education levels forever, diminishing returns would kick in and the steady state would stop shifting out as rapidly as it had been. Eventually, the rate of economic growth would approach the rate of technological change, which Krugman claimed was not estimated to be very high in East Asia. Krugman therefore concluded that the East Asian economies were unlikely to catch up to and surpass the United States and Western Europe.

Table 5.1 Growth of Total Factor Productivity: G-7 Countries and the Asian Tigers

Country	Years	Growth Rate	Country	Years	Growth Rate
Canada	1960–1989	0.5% per yr.	Hong Kong	1966–1991	2.3%
France	1960–1989	1.5	Singapore	1966–1990	0.2
Germany	1960–1989	1.6	South Korea	1966–1990	1.7
Italy	1960–1989	2.0	Taiwan	1966–1990	2.1
Japan	1960–1989	2.0			
United Kingdom	1960–1989	1.3			
United States	1960–1989	0.4			

Sources: The G-7 countries estimates are from John C. Dougherty, "A Comparison of Productivity and Economic Growth in the G-7 Countries," Ph.D. Thesis, Harvard University, 1991. The Asian tiger estimates are from Alwyn Young (1995).

5.5.2 The reaction to Krugman's analysis

Krugman's article was severely criticized in many Asian countries. It also stimulated a great deal of research, some of which contradicted Krugman's conclusions. Krugman had relied on research by Alwin Young (1992), who had estimated that the rate of technological change was near zero in Singapore.[6] Not all the Asian tigers experienced such slow technological change. Table 5.1 presents data on total factor productivity for the G-7 countries as well as Young's data for the Asian tigers. **Total factor productivity** is the difference between the growth of total output and the growth of a weighted average of factor inputs. Young's estimates suggest that technological change was actually relatively fast in three of the four Asian tigers. More recent estimates of technological change using more appropriate methods show productivity growth in East Asia, including Singapore, to be quite high. Annual growth in technology in all of the four Asian tiger economies has been estimated at between 3.4 to 3.8 percent over the period 1960–1995. These are very high rates of technological progress compared to other developed economies, as shown in Table 5.1.[7]

At the same time, recent policy shifts by the government of Singapore suggest that it is quite aware of the need for technological change to support continued rises in per capita real income. Singapore has created a Ministry for Entrepreneurship to oversee its efforts to stimulate technological change. Now, even elementary education in Singapore, long noted for its efficient teaching of basic skills and rote learning, has been urged to change its teaching methods in order to foster more original thinking and risk taking. According to a 2004 *Wall Street Journal* article:

> Singapore is hammering the message to its youngest citizens. Schools emphasize group projects, debates and assignments with open-ended questions, and have mandatory courses on entrepreneurship. An eight-hour module requires 13-year-olds to write business plans and market products such as friendship bracelets. Authors of the best plans win a one-week trip to Silicon Valley in California.[8]

The government of Singapore has also begun providing incentives not only for high technology industries to locate in the city state, but especially for firms that build "innovation infrastructure" in the country. For several years, the official web site has promoted Singapore as the center of stem cell research and genetic engineering. Singapore has also sought the relocation of corporate headquarters

---

[6] See also Alwyn Young (1995) for a later refinement of Young's estimates of East Asian total factor productivity.

[7] See, for example, Iwata, Khan, and Murao (2002), Klenow and Rodriguez-Clare (1997), Rodrigo (2000), and Easterly and Levine (2001).

[8] Cris Prystay (2004), "Singapore Encourages Entrepreneurial Grit," *Wall Street Journal*, January 21.

with generous corporate tax policies in the hope of also attracting more research and management activity to the city state.

5.5.3 *The Soviet Union and the Solow model*

In his article on East Asia, Krugman (1994) refers to the Soviet Union as another example of how high rates of investment eventually lost their ability to generate economic growth because diminishing returns set in when technological progress slowed. Indeed, the Soviet Union is another excellent case study for the Solow model because its rate of technological change varied so much over time.

When Joseph Stalin established himself firmly in power in the late 1920s, the Soviet Union had begun to achieve rapid economic growth. The Soviet development strategy was based on the socialist model of state ownership of all means of production. Stalin introduced a system whereby all major economic decisions were made by central planners. What was to be produced, how it was to be produced, and who was to receive the output were all determined by Moscow bureaucrats according to a national plan. This was the socialist model that Stalin boasted would become a model for the world.

The growth of Soviet output was indeed rapid in the early years. When much of the capitalist world was mired in the Great Depression, the Soviet Union greatly expanded industrial production. Upon examination of the details, the rapid growth was essentially driven by very high rates of saving and investment. The saving was not necessarily voluntary. Central planners decided that consumer goods would be produced in limited amounts, and thus consumers had few alternatives to saving. But the forced saving did, for several decades, rapidly expand per capita total output by making resources available for producing physical capital.

Table 5.2 presents data on the Soviet economic performance from a study by Gur Ofer (1987). The numbers presented in Table 5.2 may be somewhat optimistic, since it is based on communist-era information. But, despite the fact that the old data may paint too bright a picture, it still shows how the Soviet model of economic development was unable to generate lasting economic growth. Notice that the rates of growth of output per capita declined steadily from the 1950s to the 1980s. But, notice also that the rate of growth of total factor productivity declined and eventually turned negative. By the late 1970s, inputs were growing more rapidly than output, which implies that it was taking increasing amounts of labor, capital, and other resources to produce the same amount of output. The return to capital fell over time: for most periods, the amount of output per unit of capital declined. This is, of course, nothing other than diminishing returns. As the growth of capital exceeded the growth of other inputs, as must be the case because the growth of capital, given in line 2 of Table 5.2, exceeded the average growth of all inputs in line 3, the marginal return to capital fell. Thus, when technology stopped improving and diminishing returns to capital set in, growth slowed down just as the Solow model predicts. Predictions back in the 1950s that the Soviet Union would eventually overtake capitalist economies such as the United States and Western Europe completely missed the mark.

Table 5.2 Annual Growth Rates of GNP, Inputs, and Technology: U.S.S.R., 1928–1985

	1928–1940	1940–1950	1950–1960	1960–1970	1970–1975	1975–1980	1980–1985
1. GNP	5.8%	2.2%	5.7%	5.2%	3.7%	2.6%	2.0%
2. Capital	9.0	0.4	9.5	8.0	7.9	6.8	6.3
3. Combined Inputs	4.0	0.6	4.0	3.7	3.7	3.0	2.5
4. Total Factor Prod.	1.7	1.6	1.6	1.5	0.0	−0.4	−0.5
5. GNP/Capital	−2.9	3.4	−3.5	2.6	−3.9	−3.9	−4.0

Source: Table 1 in Gur Ofer (1987).

The fact that Soviet efforts to generate economic growth through "brute force" capital creation ran into diminishing returns is compatible with the Solow model. But, that is just one aspect of the Soviet Union's economic performance. The hypothesis that the stagnation could have been avoided had there been technological progress has led economic historians to examine why the Soviet command economy failed to sustain technological change in the long run. Was the technology slowdown a specific planning failure or the failure of **central planning** in general?

5.5.4 Recent Russian economic growth

The collapse of the Soviet system in 1990 and its replacement by a more market-oriented economic organization has, so far, not improved the growth performance of most of the former Soviet Republics. To the contrary, economic growth has slowed even further. In fact, between 1991 and 1997, output in Russia fell by at least 40 percent, and it has recovered only gradually and erratically since 1997. Only thanks to exceptionally high oil and other commodity prices in the early 2000s has Russia been able to recover it former levels of output. In most of the former Soviet Republics, however, most people are still not as well off as they were in the 1980s.

Irina Dolinskaya (2002, p. 156) acknowledges that "Russia's growth performance had already worsened before the beginning of economic transformation due to the over-investment in physical capital and the failure of the central planning to provide the incentives needed for active innovation and technological progress." But she shows that the poor post-transition economic performance was not just a continuation of the past downward trend in per capita output growth. "The output collapse during the transition was far too dramatic," writes Dolinskaya.

Dolinskaya finds that after 1990 there was both a steep decline in the employment of factors and a decline in the overall productivity of the factors of production still employed. Each of these two effects accounted for about half of the overall decline in output between 1991 and 1997. The reasons for the declines in factor employment and productivity were all related to the economic reforms and the transition of the Russian economy from a centrally planned economy to a market economy.

Russia's state firms struggled, and many collapsed, when the support of the central government disappeared, but new private firms were slow to emerge. A market oriented financial sector was not in place, entrepreneurs were discouraged by the uncertainty of the reform process, and potential profits from investing in new firms were dubious because the incomes of consumers spiraled downward with rising unemployment. Unemployment grew rapidly because labor was slow to move from state firm employment, which traditionally included pensions, stable salaries, and job tenure. The shift in factors of production was further hampered in Russia by the fact that workers often required additional training before they could enter new jobs and professions. Also, capital from the state sector was not immediately useful in the private sector. In fact, Dolinskaya wrote in 2002 that "part of the capital stock inherited from the socialist era is so outmoded it will never be used again and thus has to be replaced, which requires time and resources."[9] Yet another reason for the slow transition from state firms to new private firms was the breakdown of production networks caused by the transition from central planning to a market economy. Also disruptive of production networks was the breakup of the Soviet Union into separate countries and the shift by the former Eastern European Soviet satellite countries towards developing trade with Western Europe.

Olivier Blanchard and Michael Kremer (1997) called this breakdown of economic relations among firms **disorganization**. There was a long delay between the collapse of traditional relations between suppliers, manufacturers, and distributors after the U.S.S.R. disintegrated and the establishment of new relationships between newly established private firms. Also preventing new relationships from developing was the failure of the legal environment after 1990. The collapse of Soviet legal institutions without first building new legal institutions undermined the enforcement of contracts, and thus it became difficult to carry out long-term market transactions among firms that had little experience dealing with each other. Production in the private sector grew slowly and absorbed few of the economy's factors of production. Even when new private firms employed resources more efficiently, they could not replace production by state firms fast enough to offset the declining productivity of state firms, and the combined productivity of state and private firms fell sharply.

---

[9] Irina Dolinskaya (2002), p. 156.

Russia's financial crisis in 1998 further undermined economic growth and the transition to a market economy dominated by private firms. Since 1998, however, the sharp depreciation of the ruble, the renegotiation of debt, and the general rise in the prices of oil and other raw materials exported by Russia have caused Russian GDP per capita to grow again.

Another lesson from the collapse of the Soviet Union is that a regime change that shifts an economy's resources from a state-owned sector to a new private sector is a difficult institutional transition that cannot be undertaken quickly. The analysis based on the logic of the Solow growth model can only highlight how some economic variables changed over the course of the transition. The combined paradigm shift and institutional regime change was much too complex a process to describe using a simple model like Solow's neoclassical growth model. And, of course, changes in GDP per capita do not accurately reflect changes in true human well-being. A broader examination of welfare indicators suggests a less optimistic story than does the recent resumption of GDP growth.

5.6 Economic Growth Paths with Technological Change

The issue of whether some fast-growing East Asian economies will "catch up" to high income economies such as the United States has been a popular topic in the press, at least before the Asian financial crisis drastically slowed economic growth in East Asia after 1997. At the same time, many policy makers and development economists have expressed their frustration over the inability of many developing economies to narrow the gap between high income and low income countries. This section looks at what the Solow model has to say about narrowing differences in per capita output across countries, or what economists call income convergence.

5.6.1 Long-run growth vs. transitional growth

Several examples will illustrate long-run growth paths that are compatible with changes in the rate of technological change and shifts in the steady state variables in the Solow model. For example, Figure 5.11 illustrates the growth paths of two countries that start with identical steady states and identical levels of per capita output, say y_1. But if technological change is faster in country C than in country D, then the growth paths will diverge. Thus, despite having the same saving rates, depreciation rates, and population growth rates, the two economies diverge. Figure 5.11 shows that the growth paths start out at the same level of income at time $t = 1$, but at time $t = 2$ and $t = 3$, the growth path of country D falls ever farther below the growth path of country C.

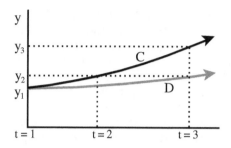

Figure 5.11 Variations in z

Figure 5.12, on the other hand, depicts the growth paths of two countries, A and B, that have been experiencing identical positive rates of technological change z; the different height of the growth paths reflects different steady states caused by differences in other variables. Perhaps country A has a higher saving rate or it started at a lower level of technology. Growth path A obviously represents a set of higher levels of output. Note that, with identical rates of technological change and, therefore, identical rates of economic growth, there is neither convergence nor divergence. The relative levels of per capita output remain the same over time; the growth path of B is always at the same *relative* height to growth path of A.

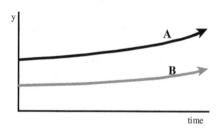

Figure 5.12 Growth Paths with Different Steady States

5.6.2 How countries "catch up"

If technological change has been the same in both countries since the beginning of time but differences in the rates of saving, depreciation, or population growth have put two countries on different growth paths, complete convergence can still occur if one country, say country B, somehow changes its saving rate, depreciation rate, or rate of population growth to match those of the other country, country A. Suppose that country B, after years of saving less or lagging in technology, suddenly at time t raises its saving rate to country A's level and imports country A's technology so that it matches A's steady state. This case is shown in Figure 5.13, which is similar to Figure 5.5 earlier in the chapter.

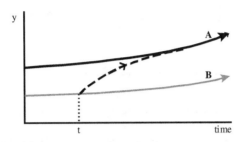

Figure 5.13 Convergence to a Higher Growth Path

Beginning at time t, country B's growth path diverges from its former long-run growth path and transitions along the dashed line in Figure 5.13. Country B's rate of economic growth will be faster than country A's as it moves toward its new steady state and a higher long-run growth path, as evidenced by the steeper slope of the dashed path compared to the slope of growth path of country A. Country B thus catches up to country A.

The Solow model is said to predict **conditional convergence**: When a low-income country achieves the same rates of saving, depreciation, population growth, and technological change as high-income countries, it will converge to the high-income country's standard of living. But complete convergence also requires that both countries have the same steady states *and* they have accumulated the same levels of technology so that they have the same production functions. This important point requires some further elaboration.

Suppose countries have the same steady states but enjoy different rates of technological change, as illustrated by Figure 5.11. In this case, catch-up is not as simple as matching steady states. For example, suppose that country D has been growing at a slower pace than country C because its technological progress has been slower, but, as shown in Figure 5.14, at time t the country suddenly manages to increase its rate of technological change to the same rate enjoyed by country C. The new growth path then becomes the path labeled D'. Perhaps country D accomplishes this by adopting policies that stimulate more innovation and invention. In this case, country D begins to grow at the same rate as country C. Country D thus stops diverging from country C, but as in the case of Figure 5.12, it does not converge. Despite having the same rate of technological change, because country D started out at a lower level of technology at time t, it does not approach the growth path or the level of per capita output of country C. Convergence requires that D also catch up to C's level of technology, as we assumed in Figure 5.13.

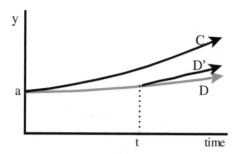

Figure 5.14 An Increase in the Rate of Technological Change

Figure 5.13 helps to explain the case of the Asian tigers. During the transition to their new steady states, raised by their increased saving rates, their rates of growth were sharply higher. But, as Krugman suggested, this growth rate will fall as the transition ends and the economies approach their growth paths. The economies may or may not surpass the levels of per capita output in the most developed countries, depending on whether the Asian tigers' higher steady states compensate for their lower levels of accumulated technology. The Asian economies' convergence will depend on their achieving higher rates of technological change than developed economies.

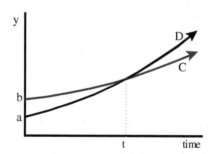

Figure 5.15 Catching Up and Passing a Slower Growth Country

Recent evidence suggests that the Asian tigers have been able to achieve high rates of technological progress. If Singapore's efforts to foment creativity and stimulate more entrepreneurship are successful, then Krugman's prediction that the Asian tiger economies will slow down may not turn out to be accurate. Figure 5.15 illustrates how a faster rate of technological progress over an extended period of time lets one economy catch up to and pass another economy even though the former begins with a lower level of accumulated technology or a lower steady state as determined by the rates of saving, population growth, or depreciation. Even though it starts at the lower initial point a, country D's per capita output rises along a steeper slope than country C's, and country D's per capita output level overtakes country C's at time t. Perhaps one or more of the Asian tigers will be able to create conditions favorable to continued innovation and technological change that carries their economies past the world's current leaders in per capita output.

5.7 Rebelo's AK Model: A Special Case of the Solow Model

We earlier concluded that, in the absence of technological change, the Solow model cannot generate permanent growth. That conclusion is not entirely correct. There is a special assumed case in which the Solow model *can* generate growth indefinitely. An understanding of this special case is important for linking the Solow model to the models of technological change and economic growth that we will study in Chapters 7 and 8.

5.7.1 The production function and the capital share α

The strength with which diminishing returns causes medium-run growth to slow down depends on how fast the marginal product of capital falls. In graphic terms, the strength of diminishing returns depends on the curvature of the production function. The slope of the production function represents the marginal product of capital, and thus when the slope declines rapidly, the marginal product of capital declines quickly.

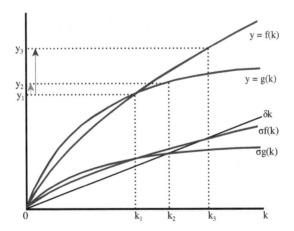

Figure 5.16 The Importance of α for Transitional Growth

Figure 5.16 illustrates two production functions, y = f(k) and y = g(k). The production function y = f(k) is closer to a straight line than y = g(k), which implies it is less subject to diminishing returns. Suppose the two economies represented by y = f(k) and y = g(k), respectively, initially have the same capital-labor ratio of k_1. In Figure 5.16, this capital-output ratio gives them both the same per capita output level of y_1. These levels of k and y are less than the steady state levels of k and y in both economies, so saving and investment cause the capital stock to rise. Notice, however, that because one country is able to expand more of its resources and is, therefore, less subject to diminishing returns than the second country, the two economies do not move to the same steady state. An economy in which the marginal product of new investment is less constrained by fixed supply of certain critical inputs enjoys a longer transition to the higher steady state value of k at k_3 and steady state per capita output is y_3.

5.7.2 *The special case of no fixed factors*

Suppose that all factors of production and resources are variable, like capital in the two factor model we have used so far. Specifically, suppose that all factors can be increased by means of investment. In this case the production function can be represented as

$$y = F(k) = Ak \tag{5.19}$$

where A is a constant that translates the stock of capital into output and k represents the stock of capital per capita. For obvious reasons, this model has become known as the **AK model** of economic growth. Sergio Rebelo (1991) is often credited as the originator of the AK model because he arrived at a model just like equation (5.19) by assuming that all factors were **reproducible**.

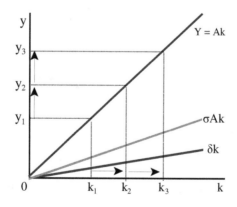

Figure 5.17 The "AK" Model

Figure 5.17 illustrates the AK model. So long as $\sigma f(k) > \delta k$, k continues to grow. With a straight-line production function, savings can continue to expand the capital output ratio indefinitely because savings grows linearly, just like depreciation. Because there are no diminishing returns, output grows fast enough to generate enough savings to cover both depreciation and the growth of the capital stock. The AK model is reminiscent of the Harrod-Domar model, which can also be described by the function $Y = AK$. There is a difference between the AK model described here and the Harrod-Domar model, however. The AK model still assumes, as does the Solow model, that capital depreciates. The Harrod-Domar model, as you may recall, ignored depreciation altogether. The matter of depreciation is important because it makes economic growth somewhat more difficult than the simple Harrod-Domar model suggests. Investment has to be at least large enough to replace the capital that wears out, otherwise there can be no growth. But, so long as the saving rate is greater than the depreciation rate, per capita output can grow forever.

5.7.3 *What does the AK model tell us about growth?*

The special case of the AK model is useful for several reasons. First of all, it is always a learning experience to examine how models behave under alternative assumptions. Among other things, the Harrod-Domar model is really just a special, and very extreme, case of the Solow model in which diminishing returns sets in so slowly that it can be ignored. More important, however, the AK model will take on new relevance once we examine technological change in detail in Chapters 7 and 8. While the world surely does not have an AK production function, once we build technological change into the Solow model it becomes possible for the economy to behave *as if* it does have an AK production function and investment can permanently cause per capita output to grow.

This discussion helps to clarify why, in Section 5.4, we introduced technological change as labor-augmenting technological change. Recall that in Section 5.4 we defined the effective labor force as the number of workers multiplied by an efficiency factor E, and our production function became $Y = F[K, (L \cdot E)]$. The AK model avoids diminishing returns to investment by assuming all inputs can grow, and Section 5.4 showed that positive labor-augmenting technological change can increase the effective labor supply. On the other hand, capital-augmenting technological change, which only expands the effective capital stock by some efficiency factor, would only quicken the appearance of diminishing returns to capital in the Solow model.

The AK model suggests another even more subtle requirement for permanent economic growth: The technological change that can maintain long-run economic growth must be the type of technological change that augments those factors of production that cannot be increased through investment. In short, permanent growth cannot proceed on just any technological change;

rather, a delicate mix of targeted technological changes is needed so that all effective factor inputs can expand in tandem. The next three chapters deal with the complexity of technological change and the difficulties in bringing forth the right mix of technological changes to sustain the continued growth of output in the economic sphere.

5.8 Smith to Solow: Some Conclusions

It is time to take stock of what the Solow model tells us about economic growth and development. First of all, it predicts that:

- The economy will move toward a *stable steady-state* equilibrium.

- In the steady-state equilibrium, there can only be *permanent economic growth* if there is *technological change*.

- But, when the economy *transitions* from one steady state to another, *medium-term growth* in per capita output can occur.

The Solow model's prescription for achieving a high standard of living is straightforward:

- *All other things equal*, an economy will transition toward a higher steady state if there is an increase in its rate of saving or a decrease in its rate of population growth.

- An economy experiences higher permanent economic growth if there is an increase in its rate of *labor-enhancing technological change*.

The Solow growth model thus permits us to logically derive a number of potentially important conclusions about the growth of output in the economic sphere of human existence. The question that we now need to address is whether these conclusions are accurate, and if they are, whether these conclusions are useful for designing economic policy. The next chapter looks at the Solow model again, but from a broader perspective that covers both the natural and economic spheres of human existence.

5.8.1 Comparing the Solow model with earlier models

Our examination of growth and development theory has now covered a great variety of models. We have learned about diminishing returns in the Classical and Solow models. The Solow model effectively avoids the eternal poverty trap described by Malthus and the classical economists because it does not permit population growth to be influenced by per capita income. Malthus assumed that gains in per capita income would cause population growth and, disappointingly, a subsequent reversal in per capita income. Marx, in the Classical tradition, gave population growth a negative role as well. Specifically, Marx hypothesized that population growth helped to increase the reserve army of the unemployed that kept wages low and caused average income to decline to where it no longer generated sufficient demand to absorb the economy's output. Treating population growth as purely an exogenous variable constitutes a clear weakness in the Solow model, although, as Chapter 9 will explain, the relationship between population and economic output is not as straightforward as Malthus described it either. On the positive side, the Solow model draws on Marx in giving the depreciation of capital an important role in slowing down the gains from investment. Capital stocks must be maintained and replaced as they depreciate, and they thus constitute a burden as well as an asset. Finally, the Solow model permits technology change to increase per capita income, although, like population growth, it treats technology as an exogenous variable.

Adam Smith explained technological change in part by linking it to the process of specialization. He argued that as people concentrate more and more on specific tasks and products, learning by doing and efforts to improve products become more likely. Marx linked technological change to the efforts of capitalists to expand profits. Note that, in one way, Solow's model is similar to Smith's model in that it highlights technological change as a source of long-run economic growth. On the other hand, Solow embraced diminishing returns, which makes his model more like that of Malthus and Marx. Marx took a less optimistic view of technological change. He attributed the huge expansion of industrial output in the 1800s to investment and technological change, but he also saw technological change as a futile effort by capitalists to maintain profits at the expense of workers. He argued that technological change would only hasten the revolution by the growing ranks of the poor and unemployed.

Solow's model, as we applied it in this chapter, is actually quite sterile. Unlike Smith, who talked a great deal about how technology develops, and Marx, who discussed the profit motive of innovation, Solow treated technology as an exogenous variable determined outside the model. Perhaps we can most kindly evaluate the Solow model as follows: The Solow model complements other models by pointing out why technological change is critical to long-run economic growth. Smith and Marx, among others, provide some insights into why technological change occurs. Chapter 8 focuses on a model by Joseph Schumpeter (1934) that provides a more useful framework for analyzing the fundamental causes of technological change.

Finally, the Harrod-Domar and Solow models both highlight the role of investment in the growth process, but they predict very different effects of investment on the long-run rate of growth. Remember, Solow developed his model in large part as a response to the simplistic use of the supply side of the Harrod-Domar model as an economic planning tool. Because the supply side of the Harrod-Domar model assumed a linear relationship between investment and output, it effectively permits investment to cause the economy to expand output forever. The Solow model suggests that diminishing returns prevents investment from permanently generating output growth.

In evaluating the early models of economic development and change, it is important to focus on what variables are endogenous, or determined within the model, and which ones are exogenous, or determined outside the model and taken as given. A truly holisitc perspective of our existence suggests that nothing is exogenous, but modeling, by nature involves simplification and, therefore, cannot make every possible variable endogenous. The real challenge is to find the most reasonable mix of endogenous and exogenous variables for the task at hand. This is, of course, why heterodox economists mix and choose from among many different models. But in order to make good modeling choices, it is absolutely necessary to keep close tabs on precisely what is endogenous and exogenous in the various models we have described.

5.8.2 Evidence supporting the Solow model

A recent test by William Easterly and Ross Levine (2001) confirms the Solow model's key prediction, namely, that technological change drives economic growth. Easterly and Levine begin by noting five general characteristics of economic growth over the past two centuries: (1) improvements in productivity explain most of the variation in growth rates across countries, (2) per capita income diverges over time, (3) factor accumulation has been much more similar across countries and over time than have growth rates, (4) economic growth is highly concentrated with all factors of production flowing to the countries that already have the highest incomes, and (5) national economic policies and institutions are closely correlated with national growth rates. Easterly and Levine then show that each of these characteristics is compatible with technological change, as the Solow model predicts, and not factor accumulation.

First, Easterly and Levine find statistical evidence that technological change is indeed closely correlated with economic growth, which is a very direct verification of one of the implications of Solow's model. The second characteristic of growth provides more subtle support. Because an additional unit of capital will have a larger effect on output in a poor capital-scarce country than in a rich capital-abundant country, all other things equal, a poor country should grow faster than a rich country if factor accumulation was all that mattered for growth. The fact that per capita income has diverged implies that something other than factor accumulation is driving growth. The third characteristic of economic growth that Easterly and Levine confirm with the data is that growth rates are not linearly correlated with capital accumulation. This suggests that it is not the capital stock alone that influences income levels. Fourth, the finding that returns to all factors of production are higher in rich countries clearly implies that technology in rich countries is not the same as in poor countries. Hence, the higher incomes in the rich countries are due, at least in part, to their having generated more technical change in the past. Finally, the fifth growth characteristic noted by Easterly and Levine is perhaps the most complex evidence suggesting that technological change plays a large role in increasing output per capita. The upcoming three chapters of this book will show clearly that policies and institutions are critical determinants of technological change. Specifically, it will be shown that the types of activities needed to generate new ideas and technologies are especially sensitive to a country's social and economic institutions.

5.8.3 Weaknesses of the Solow model

Despite its popularity in mainstream economics, however, the Solow model has many serious weaknesses that must also be acknowledged. As already mentioned, the Solow model does not tell us where technological change comes from. All the model says is that the production function must continually shift up if the steady state is to be compatible with ever increasing levels of per capita output. Fortunately, there are other models that provide useful insights into the process of technological change. Chapters 7 and 8 will detail what economists and social scientists have learned about the process of technological change.

Another serious problem with the Solow model is its focus on output in the economic sphere. Chapter 3 made it clear that simple output does not accurately reflect how humans judge their personal satisfaction with life. If we take human happiness as the goal of human economic activity, are there still diminishing returns to investment? Is human happiness related to investment at all? And what about social harmony, peace, and the fairness of economic outcomes? Clearly, the Solow model's focus on production and capital investment limits its usefulness for a holistic analysis of economic development.

The aggregation of all output into a single production function also limits the Solow model's usefulness for analyzing economic development. It does not take very long to think of different sectors of the economy where production functions and depreciation functions are very different. For example, in sectors of the economy that depend more heavily on the services and resources provided by the natural eco-system, such as agriculture or the tourist industry, the concept of depreciation takes on a very different meaning compared to, say, the personal services and education sectors. Also, investment in human capital is very different from investment in physical capital; yet, the simple Solow model presented here does not distinguish between types of capital.

Finally, the Solow model represents only the supply side of the economy. Recall our discussion of the Harrod-Domar model, which was distorted by growth economists who only applied that model's supply side. Like the Harrod-Domar model, the Solow model simply assumes that savings are instantaneously and efficiently converted into investment. Marx and Keynes have clearly taught economists that Say's law, the idea that supply creates its own demand, does not generally hold. Sustainable economic development requires the continued compatibility between aggregate supply and demand.

5.8.4 The importance of diminishing returns

With some extensions, the Solow model's embrace of diminishing returns does enable the model to provide useful insight into humanity's clash with the natural environment. Solow deserves credit for reviving the Classical economists' concern about how to sustain continued economic development in the face of limited resources. Humanity today faces serious environmental challenges as it attempts to continue increasing per capita output as it has over the past 200 years.

Some natural resources are fixed in supply, such as carbon energy sources and iron ore. Furthermore, humanity faces more complex limits to growth in the form of the atmosphere's capacity to absorb greenhouse gases without raising temperatures on Earth and our biological system's capacity to maintain the diverse living organisms that are critical to human survival. There are limits to nature's capacity to replenish itself and to sustain its supply of services, such as fresh water, clean air, absorption of rainfall, reverse osmosis, and the decomposition of waste. Solow correctly pointed out that to sustain their rapid expansion of material output, humans will have to continue generating new knowledge, ideas, and technologies at a rapid pace. The simple aggregate model with a single economy-wide production function presented in this chapter does not really make it clear that the required technological changes vary greatly across the economic, social, and natural spheres in which economic development takes place. Innovative activities will have to be appropriately targeted at sustaining the effective supplies of the exhaustible and renewable natural resources in the natural sphere. Humanity's economic, political, and cultural institutions are not currently capable of guiding individual and collective human activity towards developing the appropriate new technologies and social organization necessary to avoid costly clashes between humanity and the natural environment.

The fact that humans seem to have been very adept at making increasingly efficient and innovative use of the earth's fixed resources does not imply that humans will be able to continue expanding output at the extraordinary rate of the past two centuries. The ample evidence that humanity is over-exploiting the natural environment has led some economists and many other scientists to question whether the growing incompatibility between humanity and the natural environment will not trigger an economic and social decline. The Solow model predicts that, in the absence of technological change to augment the fixed set of natural resources on Earth, the growth of per capita output will stop.

The next chapter examines the relationship between humanity and the natural environment in detail. The basic logic of the Solow model and its focus on depreciation and saving will be used to analyze the current relationship between production and nature.

Key Terms and Concepts

AK model
Central planning
Comparative statics
Conditional convergence
Constant returns to scale
Diminishing returns
Disorganization
Dynamic analysis
Effective labor
Endogenous variable
Exogenous variable
Growth path
Homeostasis

Labor-augmenting technological
    change
Medium-run growth
Permanent growth
Production function
Rate of depreciation
Reproducible factors
Solow growth model
Stable equilibrium
Steady state
Supply side
Technological change
Total factor productivity
Transitional growth

Questions and Problems

1. The Solow model discusses how population growth affects the steady state of the economy and the rate of growth. As a realistic example, suppose that immigration increases sharply and continues at that higher level for many years.
    a. Use the Solow model to show how the increased inflow of people into the economy affects the economy's rate of economic growth in the short run, the medium run, and the long run.
    b. Suppose that all the immigrants come from a single other economy. What does the Solow predict will happen to rate of economic growth in the economy that sends the immigrants in the short run, the medium run, and the long run?
2. If there are no restrictions on capital movements between countries, then a country's level of investment need not be exactly equal to domestic savings. Suppose the citizens of the country of Spendmore do not save much of their income, but the citizens of the neighboring country, Frugalia, have a high propensity to save.

Suppose also that, because the Frugalian government taxes the earnings of new investment at a very high rate, Frugalians prefer to lend their savings to Spendmorians for new investment projects. According to the Solow growth model, what will be the effect of such capital flows on (1) Frugalia's steady state level of output and its growth rate and (2) Spendmore's steady state level of income and growth rate?

3.   The Solow model takes the rate of technology growth as given. Do you believe that technology just "happens" or is technological change a function of specific causes? What might cause the rate of technological change to increase? What might cause it to decrease? Are there government policies that can affect the rate of technology growth?

4.   Paul Krugman claims that the East Asian tigers grew because, among other things, they greatly increased the levels of education of their labor forces. But, he then shows that this investment in human capital will not permanently increase the rate of growth of the Asian economies. What are the effects of increased education according to the Solow model? Explain precisely what changes and what does not change as a result of increases in human capital, using both graphs and words.

5.   Illustrate clearly, using diagrams and words, how an increase in the depreciation rate affects an economy. Set up the Solow model, and clearly state the assumptions you are making about σ, ω, and z. Intuitively, explain why an increase in depreciation, δ, has the effect on k^* and y^* that you illustrate in your diagram.

6.   In his "AK" model, Robelo assumes that all factors are "replaceable" through investment. How realistic is that assumption? How do we "replace" resources that are forever depleted?

7.   In Section 5.4, technological change was introduced as "labor-augmenting" technological change, specifically in the form of an efficiency factor, E, that multiplies the supply of physical labor, L, in the production function $Y = F[K, (L \cdot E)]$. Explain why technological change must be "labor-augmenting" in order for technological progress to overcome diminishing returns to capital and enable permanent growth in per capita output.

8.   Since 1800, both economic output and human population have grown much more rapidly than ever before. Does this prove that one caused the other? Illustrate clearly, using diagrams and words, how an increase in the rate of population growth, ω, affects an economy according to the Solow model. Set up the Solow model, and clearly state the assumptions you are making about the saving rate σ, ω, and technological change z. Intuitively, explain how an increase in population growth, ω, effects k^* and y^*, all other things equal. Conclude by explaining the Solow model's prediction and its relationship to the observed positive correlation between output and population growth over the past 200 years.

9.   After reading about the declining rate of economic growth in the Soviet Union, what do you think the Soviet central planners could have done to avoid the growth slowdown? Use the Solow model to frame your answer.

10. Since the available evidence on capital investment and growth rates seems to be compatible with either the Harrod-Domar model or the Solow model, can't we just use either model to explain growth? Discuss.

Appendix 5.1: The Cobb-Douglas Production Function

The Solow growth model specifies a neoclassical production function of the general form Y = F(K, L), in which Y is output, K is capital, L is labor, and F represents the functional relationship between output and the inputs. The Solow model further assumes that the production function is characterized by constant returns to scale and diminishing marginal returns. A functional form that matches the assumptions of the Solow model and also has very convenient mathematical properties is the so-called *Cobb-Douglas* production function

$$Y = AK^{\alpha}L^{1-\alpha} \tag{A5.1}$$

in which Y is output, A represents the level of technology, K is capital, L is labor, and $0 \le \alpha \le 1$. The sum of the exponents of the inputs K and L, α and $1-\alpha$, is equal to one: $\alpha + (1-\alpha) = 1$.

The Cobb-Douglas production function can also be converted to *per worker* terms by dividing equation (5-14) by L, which gives us

$$y = Y/L = AK^{\alpha}L^{1-\alpha}/L = AK^{\alpha}L^{1-\alpha}L^{-1} = AK^{\alpha}L^{1-\alpha-1} = AK^{\alpha}L^{-\alpha} = Ak^{\alpha} \tag{A5.2}$$

where $k \equiv K/L$. It should be clear that for any $0 < \alpha < 1$, the function Ak^{α} looks like the function in Figure 5.1. If you are not convinced, you can use your calculator and insert any positive value for A, a value between 0 and 1 for α, and several values for k, and graph the result for $y = Ak^{\alpha}$.

Constant returns to scale

A few mathematical manipulations make it clear that that the Cobb-Douglas production function exhibits constant returns to scale. First, multiply each factor by a constant c and enter those new quantities into the Cobb-Douglas function in equation (A5.1):

$$(cK)^{\alpha}(cL)^{1-\alpha} = Ac^{\alpha}K^{\alpha}c^{1-\alpha}L^{1-\alpha} = c^{\alpha+1-\alpha}AK^{\alpha}L^{1-\alpha} = cy \tag{A5.3}$$

The Cobb-Douglas function exhibits constant returns only when the coefficients α and $(1 - \alpha)$ add up to exactly one. If the coefficients of K and L in equation (A5.1) were α and β, and $(\alpha + \beta) > 1$, then $A(cK)^{\alpha}(cL)^{\beta} = c^{\alpha+\beta}y > cy$. This represents the case of *increasing returns to scale* because a given percentage increase in each of the inputs results in a more than proportional increase in output. On the other hand, if $(\alpha + \beta) < 1$, the economy is subject to decreasing returns to scale. This could happen if the organizational costs of managing a more complex society expand faster than the overall output of the economy, or if the excessive exploitation of the natural sphere causes the availability of nature's services to decline. For the Cobb-Douglas production function to fit the Solow model, therefore, the coefficients must be specified as summing to one.

Diminishing marginal returns

The marginal products of the inputs can be found by taking the *partial derivative* of Y with respect to labor and capital:

$$\partial Y/\partial L = A(1 - \alpha)K^{\alpha}L^{-\alpha} > 0 \qquad (A5.4)$$

$$\partial Y/\partial K = A\alpha K^{\alpha-1}L^{1-\alpha} = A\alpha K^{\alpha-1}L^{1-\alpha} > 0 \qquad (A5.5)$$

Diminishing returns requires that the second derivatives $\partial^2 Y/\partial L^2$ and $\partial^2 Y/\partial K^2$ be negative:

$$\partial^2 Y/\partial L^2 = -A(\alpha - \alpha^2)K^{\alpha}L^{-\alpha-1} < 0 \qquad (A5.6)$$

$$\partial^2 Y/\partial K^2 = A(\alpha^2 - \alpha)K^{\alpha-2}L^{1-\alpha} < 0 \qquad (A5.7)$$

Since $0 < \alpha < 1$, the terms $(\alpha - \alpha^2)$ and $(\alpha^2 - \alpha)$ are greater than and less than zero, respectively, thus making each equation above less than zero. In *per worker* terms, the partial derivatives are:

$$\partial y/\partial k = A\alpha k^{\alpha-1} > 0 \qquad (A5.8)$$

$$\partial^2 y/\partial k^2 = A(\alpha^2-\alpha)k^{\alpha-2} < 0 \qquad (A5.9)$$

Thus, the Cobb-Douglas function matches the assumptions of the function drawn in the graphic version of the Solow model used in this chapter.

Constant factor shares

The Cobb-Douglas function has another characteristic that is particularly convenient. To uncover this characteristic, we first need to go through the intermediate step of rewriting total output as a function of L and k. Following equation (A5.2):

$$Y = AK^{\alpha}L^{1-\alpha} = LAK^{\alpha}L^{1-\alpha}L^{-1} = LAK^{\alpha}L^{-\alpha} = LAk^{\alpha} \qquad (A5.10)$$

Under perfect competition in the factor markets, each factor is paid its marginal product. This means that the *share* of total output that is earned by capital is equal to the amount of capital times its marginal product, all divided by total output Y. Using equations (A5.5) and (A5.10) and remembering that K/L = k, capital's share of total product is therefore

$$K(\partial Y/\partial K)/Y = [K(A\alpha K^{\alpha-1}L^{1-\alpha})]/Y = [K(A\alpha k^{\alpha-1})]/(LAk^{\alpha})$$
$$= A(A)^{-1}\alpha(k)(k)^{\alpha}(k)^{-\alpha}(k)^{-1} = \alpha \qquad (A5.11)$$

And labor's share is the amount of labor multiplied by its marginal product, all divided by Y. Using (A5.4) and (A5.10), labor's share is easily found:

$$L(\partial Y/\partial L)/Y = L(A\alpha K^{\alpha-1}L^{1-\alpha})/Y = LA(1-\alpha)k^{\alpha}]/(LAk^{\alpha}) = 1 - \alpha \qquad (A5.12)$$

Thus, the exponents of the inputs in the Cobb-Douglas production function turn out to be equal to capital and labor shares of total output. And, because α is a constant, the factor shares are constants in the Cobb-Douglas model.

An example: Thailand's rising savings

For simplicity, suppose that in equation (A5.1) A = 1, so that the per worker Cobb-Douglas production function is

$$y = k^{\alpha} \qquad (A5.13)$$

To make things even easier, suppose also that $\alpha = 0.5$. Therefore,

$$y = k^{0.5} = \sqrt{k} \qquad (A5.14)$$

In the Solow model, the steady state implies $\Delta k = 0$ and $\sigma f(k^*) = \delta k^*$. Therefore:

$$k^*/f(k^*) = \sigma/\delta \qquad (A5.15)$$

Note, however, that

$$k^*/\sqrt{k^*} = \sqrt{k^*} \qquad (A5.16)$$

Therefore,

$$k^* = (\sigma/\delta)^2 \qquad (A5.17)$$

If we know the values of σ and δ we can calculate k* and the steady state income y* = f(k*). Let's assume that depreciation is 10 percent, or $\delta = 0.1$.

Let's use Thailand as an example. According to World Bank data, Thailand increased its savings ratio from 21 percent in 1970 to 35 percent in 1997. Inserting these values for σ into (A5.17), we see that in 1970 $k^* = (.21/.1)^2 = 4.41$. And, in 1997, $k^* = (.35/.1)^2 = 12.25$. Then applying equation (A5.14), in 1970 $y^* = 2.1$ and in 1997 $y^* = 3.5$. With the assumptions for δ, α, and the production function as specified in equation (A5.16), the model predicts that Thailand should have experienced a $(3.5 - 2.1)/2.1 = 67$ percent increase in per capita output as, all other things equal, its economy went through the transition from the steady state in which the saving rate was 21 percent to the one where the rate was 35 percent.

Actually, Thailand's real per capita income grew by over 200 percent between 1970 and 1997. The increase in the rate of saving thus accounts for only part of Thailand's actual 1970–1997 growth of per capita income. What caused such a large discrepancy? Perhaps the specific Cobb-Douglas production function that we assumed in this example is incorrect. Perhaps the entire Solow model is not correct. More likely, the production function did not remain constant, as we implicitly assumed in the example above. No doubt, there was substantial technological change during the 28 years between 1970 and 1997; technological change would have shifted the production function up.

You may also wonder why we analyzed the period 1970–1997 and did not extend the analysis to include more recent years. Thailand suffered a severe financial crisis and its economic growth was sharply negative in 1998. Only in 2005 did Thailand recover its 1997 per capita income level.

A final note

This appendix on the Cobb-Douglas production function is provided for two reasons: (1) The model is very often used in the economic development literature, and (2) it is an example of how convenience takes precedence over the scientific method. The model is, obviously, a very special case of economists' more general hypothesized relationship between factor inputs and national output known as the production function. While it is convenient to have a model that is easy to manipulate, as we did above, it must be understood to be a very special case of a more general relationship (of course, even the more general relationship is not accurate from a holistic perspective). The conclusions of these mathematical models that specify a Cobb-Douglas equation should not be taken as more than an illustrative example of the fundamental logic of Solow's model. The precise estimates we derived above for Thailand are not credible. We have no idea what true production function for Thailand looks like. More fundamentally, it is unlikely that we can even depict the relationship between inputs and national output in the form of a national production function, much less in the form of a simple equation such as the Cobb-Douglas equation.

References

Blanchard, Olivier J., and Michael Kremer (1997), "Disorganization," *Quarterly Journal of Economics* 112(4):1091–1126.

Daly, Herman (1977), *Steady-State Economics*, San Francisco: W. H. Freeman and Co.

Dolinskaya, Irina (2002), "Explaining Russia's Output Collapse," *IMF Staff Papers* 49(2):155–174.

Easterly, William, and Ross Levine (2001), "It's Not Factor Accumulation: Stylized Facts and Growth Models," *The World Bank Economic Review* 15(2):177–219.

Iwata, Shigeru, Moshin S. Khan, and Hiroshi Murao (2002), "Source of Economic Growth in East Asia: A Nonparametric Assessment," IMF Working Paper WP/02/13, January.

Klenow, Peter, and Andres Rodriguez-Clare (1997), "The Neoclassical Revival in Growth Economics: Has It Gone Too Far?" in Ben S. Bernanke and Julio J. Rotemberg (eds.), *NBER Macroeconomics Annual 1997*, Cambridge, MA: MIT Press, 73–103.

Krugman, Paul (1994), "The Myth of Asia's Miracle." *Foreign Affairs* 73(6):62–78.

Kuhn, Thomas (1962), *The Structure of Scientific Revolutions*, Chicago: University of Chicago Press.

Maddison, Angus (2003), *The World Economy: Historical Statistics*, Paris: OECD.

Mankiw, N. Gregory (1995), "The Growth of Nations," *Brookings Papers on Economic Activity* 1995(1).

Ofer, Gur (1987), "Soviet Economic Growth: 1928–1985," *Journal of Economic Literature* 25:1767–1833.

Rebelo, Sergio (1991), "Long-Run Policy Analysis and Long-Run Growth," *Journal of Political Economy* 99:500–521.

Rodrigo, G. Chris (2000), "East Asia's Growth: Technology or Accumulation?" *Contemporary Economic Policy* 18(2):215–227.

Romer, Paul (1993), "Idea Gaps and Object Gaps in Economic Development," *Journal of Monetary Economics* 23(3):543–573.

Schumpeter, Joseph (1934), *The Theory of Economic Development*, Cambridge, MA: Harvard University Press.

Solow, Robert (1956), "A Contribution to the Theory of Economic Growth," *Quarterly Journal of Economics* 70(1):65–94.

Solow, Robert (1957), "Technical Change and the Aggregate Production Function," *Review of Economics and Statistics* 39:312–320.

Young, Alwyn (1992), "A Tale of Two Cities: Factor Accumulation and Technical Change in Hong Kong and Singapore," in Olivier Blanchard and Stanley Fischer (eds.), *NBER Macroeconomics Annual 1992*, Cambridge, MA: MIT Press, 13–54.

Young, Alwyn (1995), "The Tyranny of Numbers: Confronting the Statistical Realities of the East Asian Growth Experience." *The Quarterly Journal of Economics* 104:641–679.

CHAPTER 6

Economic Development and the Natural Environment

[T]he macroeconomy is not the relevant whole, but is itself a subsystem, a part of the ecosystem, the larger economy of nature.

(Herman E. Daly, 1998)

The expansion of human knowledge and technology accelerated sharply in the nineteenth century. There was a ten-fold increase in the per capita output by a population that grew six-fold between 1820 and 2000. The Solow model shows that this economic growth was not brought about by increasing the number of sailing ships, horse-drawn carts, and shovels. Rather, the huge increase in material output was mostly the result of people learning to do things differently and more efficiently. Sailing ships, horse-drawn carts, and shovels were replaced by steamships, railroads, and bulldozers.

This apparent victory of human ingenuity over diminishing returns has led many economists, social scientists, political leaders, and most everyone else to expect GDP to continue growing in the future. After all, technological change drives long-run growth, and there is no obvious limit to people's ability to think, learn, and develop new ideas. Richard Tomkins looks back into history, however, and suggests that some scepticism may be in order:

> In the industrialized west, we assume that the "normal" rate of economic growth is 2–3 percent a year because it is what we have experienced in our lifetimes. For most of human history, however, "normal" — in terms of per capita growth — has meant more or less zero.[1]

---

[1] Richard Tomkins (2003), "Economic Progress Was Quite Nice While It Lasted," *Financial Times*, January 24.

Are the past 200 years indeed nothing more than a brief exception, a special episode that will soon end? Or, is humanity on a new long-run growth path? To answer such questions, we must first analyze how we have been able to generate the recent technological advances that have enabled human society to avoid diminishing returns to growing population and its expanding cities, factories, and farms. Second, we have to understand the potential barriers to continued economic growth in the future. The Solow model is very useful for analyzing past and future diminishing returns.

This chapter focuses on one of the most daunting challenge that humanity faces today, which is the destruction of the natural system that provides humanity with the vital services, such as fresh water, air, fertile soil, and a stable climate, that humans depend on for survival. There is strong scientific evidence that human activity is causing global warming, a complex natural and economic phenomenon that humanity has, so far, been unwilling to deal with in a consistent manner. And, there is equally alarming evidence of a sharp acceleration in species extinctions and the accompanying decline in biodiversity.

According to Mathis Wackernagel *et al.* (2002):

> Sustainability requires living within the regenerative capacity of the biosphere. Our accounts indicate that human demand may well have exceeded the biosphere's regenerative capacity since the 1980s. According to this preliminary and exploratory assessment, humanity's load corresponded to 70 percent of the capacity of the global biosphere in 1961, and grew to 120 percent in 1999.

The World Wildlife Fund (2008, p. 2) estimates that "humanity's demand on the planet's living resources... now exceeds the planet's regenerative capacity by about 30 percent." In other words, we are not generating the technological advances needed to overcome the ecosystem's limited capacity to provide the natural services that humanity has depended on for its survival.

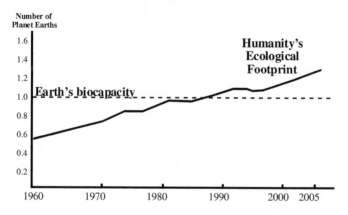

Figure 6.1 Humanity's Ecological Footprint: 1960–2005

The World Wildlife Fund defines humanity's global **ecological footprint** in terms of **global hectares (gha)**. The former is effectively the total human consumption of nature's services, including all the forest, grazing land, cropland, and fishing grounds required to produce the food, fibre, and timber humanity consumes, all the land, water, and air to absorb the wastes emitted when humans use energy and other resources, and all land and water required for humanity's living space, production, transportation, and storage. The latter is the average capacity of one hectare of the Earth's surface to produce nature's services and absorb waste. According to the World Wildlife Fund (2008), the total productive area of the Earth is equal to 13.6 billion gha, or 2.1 gha per person in 2005. In that year, however, the global ecological footprint was estimated to be 17.5 billion gha, or 2.7 gha per person. Hence, the WWF's conclusion that exploitation of the Earth's resources exceeds the planet's regenerative capacity by about 30 percent. Figure 6.1 illustrates the estimated path of ecological sustainability since 1960. It was during the 1980s that the human population began using the earth's services at a rate that exceeded the capacity of the Earth's ecological system to replenish itself.

Recall Figure 1.1 from Chapter 1 and Herman Daly's (1998) point that the economy is an element of human society, and human society in turn exists within the natural environment consisting of Earth and the universe. Once we recognize that the economic sphere is an integral component of a system that also consists of natural and social spheres, it is no longer possible to assume that humans will continue generating technological advances to overcome diminishing returns. Humans have only a very limited control over their natural environment, and as Jianguo Liu *et al.* (2007, p. 1513) explain, the relationships between the economic and natural spheres are complex:

> ... couplings between human and natural systems vary across space, time, and organizational units. They also exhibit nonlinear dynamics with thresholds, reciprocal feedback loops, time lags, resilience, heterogeneity, and surprises. Furthermore, past couplings have legacy effects on present conditions and future possibilities.

This description fits the anthropogenic (human-made) natural phenomena of global warming, the decline in ecosystem services, and the acceleration of species losses that we examine in detail in this chapter.

Since the economic sector is dependent on nature's services and resources, the apparent limits to these crucial services and resources imply that the natural environment is a source of diminishing returns to investment in the economic sphere. The Solow model provides a useful perspective with which to analyze these issues, provided we expand the model to include both the economic and natural spheres. This chapter thus expands the Solow model into a two-sphere model that is useful for examining the economic impact of global warming and the loss of biodiversity. This chapter concludes with a discussion of **sustainable**

economic development, which is the rate of economic change that is compatible with humanity's capacity to generate all the technological and structural economic changes necessary for humanity to overcome the adverse effects of diminishing returns and the depreciation/destruction of our stocks of productive resources across all the spheres of human existence.

Chapter Goals

1. Discuss human survival in light of pending resource scarcities.
2. Discuss whether there are limits to economic growth.
3. Examine how technological change can mitigate the exhaustion of exhaustible resources and damage to the natural sphere.
4. Show how effective resources can be sustained even as real physical resources are depleted.
5. Detail the evidence on the causes and consequences of global warming.
6. Analyze how economic growth has caused losses in biodiversity, and discuss the consequences.
7. Introduce a two-sphere Solow model, and use it to show why environmental destruction will ultimately cause damage in the economic sphere.
8. Discuss the technological change necessary for sustainable development.

6.1 Limits to Growth

Economists are very comfortable assuming limits to economic activity. After all, economics is usually defined as the study of how people can best employ their **limited resources** to satisfy their **unlimited wants**. Economics studies **scarcity**, and it has developed a set of tools for making decisions that reflect the opportunity costs of the available choices. Traditional economic analysis assumes that the limits to how many goods and services we can produce depend on the quantity of our resources and the technology we use to transform those resources into output. Therefore, economists address the question of whether there are limits to growth by examining whether, in the short run, we can find more resources or, in the long-run, we can develop better technologies that permit us to produce increasing amounts of goods and services from our limited resources.

6.1.1 Optimists, skeptics, and scientists

The current global warming, biodiversity losses, and other damages to Earth's natural environment are not the first examples of natural limits to economic development. Past concerns about limits to economic development were also often related to the natural environment.   Recall, for example, that Thomas Malthus and the Classical economists explicitly incorporated into their models the stress between the fixed amount of agricultural land on Earth and the need to feed growing numbers of people.   More generally, predictions of impending doom and warnings that the world will end have been made for at least as long as we have written records.   Thinkers from all disciplines and schools have taken up the issue.   For example, 250 years ago Benjamin Franklin worried about the price of firewood: "Since Fuel is become so expensive and will of course grow scarcer and dearer; any new proposal for saving may at least be thought worth Consideration."[2]   It seems logical that when we use up a resource that is not renewable, we will end up with fewer resources and prices will rise.   But, after two centuries of rapid economic growth and an accelerating use of resources, many resources still seem to be readily available.   We found oil and coal to replace firewood, and these energy sources proved to be much easier to use than the bulky and dirty firewood used to heat homes and cook food in centuries past.   New technologies further extended these new sources of energy; for example, the use of electricity effectively delivered coal's energy to homes and factories through copper wires.   In the early 2000s, as oil was becoming less accessible and the environmental effects of coal and oil were clear, the newly developed process of hydraulic fracturing (popularly called *fracking*) made available vast shale gas deposits that were long considered unexploitable.   The price of natural gas plummeted in 2010 as a result of this technology.   The press widely touted this natural gas as a less environmentally-damaging source of energy for electricity generation.

The last 200 years' experience, therefore, suggests that humans have the ability to overcome barriers to development.   Yet, noted scholars repeatedly warned about imminent disasters.   For example, in 1972 a widely-read book entitled *The Limits to Growth* came to an alarming conclusion:

> If present growth trends in world population, industrialization, pollution, food production, and resource depletion continue unchanged, the limits to growth on this planet will be reached sometime within the next one hundred years.   The most probable result will be a rather sudden and uncontrollable decline in both population and industrial capacity.[3]

Paul Ehrlich (1972, p. 13) described the future in equally dismal terms:

> Agricultural experts state that a tripling of the food supply of the world will be necessary in the next 30 years or so, if the 6 or 7 billion people who may be alive in the year 2000 are to be adequately fed.   Theoretically such an increase might be possible, but it is becoming increasingly clear that it is totally impossible in practice.

---

[2] Quoted in William J. Baumol, Sue Anne Batey Blackman, and Edward N. Wolff (1989), p. 211.
[3] Donella H. Meadows *et al.* (1972), p. 23.

These predictions from 40 years ago turned out to be overly pessimistic, but in 2008 and again in 2011, food prices rose rapidly and hunger increased in many countries. Humanity struggled to raise food production to match population growth in the social sphere and income growth in the economic sphere.

6.1.2 This time we should be concerned

There are today many reasons to be concerned about the future. First, there is clear evidence that the rate of species extinction has accelerated sharply over the past two centuries. Evolution predicts a continual loss of species accompanied by the development of new species, of course. But scientific evidence shows that the rate of species extinction is today probably at least 500 times as fast as its historical rate. Scientists attribute the rise in species extinctions and the fall in plant diversity to the increase in the human population, which, in turn, was enabled by the spread of agriculture and animal husbandry. Most farm land is now devoted to growing a very small variety of cereal crops or raising just a very small variety of animal species. To grasp the danger of the spread of **monocultural farming**, recall the Irish potato famine of the 1840s. Because the specific type of potato grown throughout Ireland was not resistant to one specific disease, the entire potato crop perished. One million Irish died of starvation, and several million migrated to the United States, Canada, and England to escape a similar fate. Such a devastating famine would not have happened had Ireland grown a greater variety of food crops, or even a greater variety of potatoes. Today, the entire world depends on a small number of strains of rice, corn, and wheat for most of its nutrition. A disease that wipes out one of these crops would cause mass starvation in poor countries where people do not have enough income to compete with wealthy consumers in high income countries for the limited supplies of food.

At the same time, anthropogenic **greenhouse gases (GHGs)** are warming the earth's atmosphere, a phenomenon often referred to as **global warming**. Scientists who participated in drawing up the 2007 report by the Intergovernmental Panel on Climate Change (IPCC) agreed that it is "nearly certain" that current trends in energy usage will result in the temperature of the earth's surface rising by 2 to 3 degrees centigrade this century. The IPCC report also points out that there is a realistic possibility that such a two or three degree rise in temperatures will thaw the Arctic tundra and release enough methane gas to cause the earth's temperature to spiral upwards by 10 to 15 degrees centigrade. Such temperature rises will melt most ice at both poles of the earth and cause sea levels to rise by as much as twenty meters. More worrisome is the fact that humans have never experienced average temperatures that high.

As for the natural gas made available with the new fracking technology, Robert Howarth, Renee Santoro, and Anthony Ingaffea (2011) point out that natural gas captured by means of hydraulic fracturing emits just as many greenhouse gases as burning coal to generate an equivalent amount of electricity. They specifically write (p. 679): "Natural gas is composed largely of methane, and 3.6 percent to 7.9 percent of the methane from shale-gas production escapes to the atmosphere in venting and leaks over the lifetime of a well." Finding better alternatives to dirty coal and dwindling oil is not easy.

6.1.3 Must we stop economic growth to survive?

The likelihood of further species extinctions and global warming suggest that continued economic growth may not be possible. Such a conclusion is based on at least three assumptions: (1) the earth's resources are finite, (2) humans will not be able to find new technologies that improve the efficiency with which we use those fixed resources, and (3) the human population will continue to grow.

The hypothesis that the earth's resources are finite was introduced to the field of economics by the economist Kenneth Boulding, who wrote a widely read article entitled "The Economics of the Coming Spaceship Earth." Boulding (1966) described the world economy as a closed system, similar to a spaceship, where resources were limited to what was "on board:"

> The closed economy of the future might... be called the 'spaceman' economy, in which the earth has become a single spaceship, without unlimited reservoirs of anything, either for extraction or pollution, and in which, therefore, man must find his place in a cyclical ecological system which is capable of continuous reproduction of material form.[4]

Boulding borrowed the idea of Earth as a **spaceship** from Buckminster Fuller's 1963 book entitled *Operating Manual for Spaceship Earth*, which admonished humans for carelessly using up resources, such as fossil fuels, that had taken millions of years to accumulate and could not be renewed.

Supporting the second implicit assumption is the vast evidence showing that the rapid growth of output and population over the past two centuries was achieved in large part by using up more of the earth's non-renewable natural resources rather than by increasing the efficiency with which the economy used Earth's resources. What has been perceived as technological progress was often nothing more than the development of new methods to more quickly use up the earth's natural resources. Dirty air, polluted rivers, exhausted soils, eroded farmland, deforested river basins, the surge in extinctions of animal species, and global warming are just a few of the many signs suggesting that the human population and its per capita production have expanded beyond the levels that the natural environment can sustain.

The third assumption reflects the reality of recent population growth. With recent declines in death rates, which make high birth rates unnecessary for

---

[4] Kenneth E. Boulding (1966), p. 9.

human survival, birth rates have fallen, but not far enough to stop the human population from continuing to grow. Resistance to birth control remains strong, largely due to well-ingrained instincts and cultures. Official United Nations (2010) forecasts suggest the global population will certainly approach, and possibly surpass, ten billion before it stabilizes near the end of this century.

6.1.4 Stopping growth is also problematic

If we are indeed living beyond the earth's means we will have to stop the growth of human production in the economic sphere. But, without further output growth, it will be difficult to eliminate the huge discrepancies in per capita output and income around the world.

One of the intellectuals promoting the idea that we had reached the limits to growth, Paul Ehrlich (1968), claimed that the richest countries were "overdeveloped" and that the earth's resources could not support all countries having such high levels of per capita output and consumption. Ehrlich called for the developed economies to "de-develop" so that the developing economies of the world could "semi-develop." In many less developed economies, Ehrlich's advice was seen as a justification for rich countries to protect their large share of the economic pie. H. W. Arndt (1978) observed in his history of economic development: "It is not surprising that spokesmen of the less developed countries have been unenthusiastic about the environmental movement."[5]

Development economists now more often advocate a future that consists of greater sacrifices by wealthy nations so that developing economies can continue to raise per capita output. The United Nations Environmental Programme's *Global Environmental Outlook 2000* stated that "the global ecosystem is threatened by grave imbalances in productivity and in the distribution of goods and services," and it suggests that the solution to the poor nations' low standards of living lies in getting developed nations to cease their "excessive" consumption.[6] But can we really expect rich countries to cede poor countries a bigger piece of the current pie? As documented by Jared Diamond (2005), history suggests that war, oppression, and other forms of violence are more likely to decide who gets how much of the earth's riches.

6.2 Technological Change and Nature's Resources

Natural resources fall into two categories: (1) **renewable resources** and (2) **exhaustible resources**. Renewable resources are those that nature gradually replenishes after humans make use of them. Nature generates the oxygen that

---

[5] H. W. Arndt (1978), p. 135.
[6] Quoted in Vanessa Houlder (1999), "World on Environmental Collision Course," *Financial Times*, September 9.

humans breathe, for example. Evaporation, condensation, winds, and gravity distribute water throughout the world after humans put it to an almost infinite number of uses in agriculture, industry, and throughout their communities. Soils are replenished by the decomposition of organic material after humans harvest their crops. Natural processes are resilient, but nature's services are not unlimited.

If humans use nature's renewable resources too intensively, the amount of resources nature provides begins to decline. For example, the processes of evaporation, condensation, precipitation, and replenishment of the stores of fresh water take time and have strict capacity limits. In many parts of the world, falling water tables, dry lakes, and empty rivers reveal humanity's overuse of water. There is clearly a limit to how much water is available for human use at any one time. Similarly, when we cut down a forest, we can replant and nurture another to grow in its place. But, again, such restoration takes time. Given the rate of natural growth of trees, there is some maximum rate of recovery of board feet of lumber per year.

Another example of over-exploitation of nature's renewable services are the world's ocean fishing areas. Fish species that for centuries were a major source of protein for human consumption, such as cod and tuna, have nearly disappeared from areas where they were abundant. In short, the more intensively we use renewable resources, the more explicit and costly actions we must take to conserve the natural sphere and help nature replenish the resources we depend on for our social and economic existence. We could also improve the efficiency with which we use nature's services, such as eliminating waste during the harvesting, transport, storage, and transformation of nature's products and services into useful products. The human effort necessary to prevent a reduction in nature's renewable resources increases the more intensively we make use of these resources.

Nature's nonrenewable or exhaustible resources are the resources that, once used, are gone forever (or at least for a period of time that exceeds the human time perspective). Exhaustible resources include such things as petroleum, peat, iron ore, and tin. Once these products are taken out of the ground and used in production, they are no longer available in their original state. In sum, whether we look at renewable resources or exhaustible resources, the supply of natural resources is limited. Thus, the earth's ecosystem causes diminishing returns to the expansion of other factors of production in the economic sphere. But, recall that Solow's model suggests that diminishing returns can be overcome with technological change.

6.2.1 Technology and natural resources

The Solow growth model was illustrated in the previous chapter using a simple two-input production function

$$Y = f(L, K) \tag{6.1}$$

in which Y represents output, L is the labor supply, and K is the stock of physical capital. Solow's production function exhibits constant returns to scale and diminishing returns to individual factors. After adding depreciation, the model generated the hypothesis that long-run growth in per worker output cannot be achieved by means of investment in new capital alone if the other factor, L, is in fixed supply. Permanent growth in per worker output is possible if labor-augmenting technology, E, grows and expands the **effective supply** of labor, which we defined as the product of the physical supply of labor L and the efficiency factor E. Recall from the discussion of the Solow model in the previous chapter that in the case of an augmented production function with fixed L, variable K, and labor-augmenting technology E, or

$$Y = f[(L \cdot E), K] \tag{6.2}$$

the rate of growth of per worker output is equal to the rate of growth of E.

Since we have now expanded our perspective to include exhaustible resources and nature's capacity to continue providing renewable resources, we must examine what types of technological change are necessary to overcome the diminishing returns due to the physical limits of natural resources. To illustrate this case, suppose that inputs in the production function fall into three categories: the physical number of workers, L, the physical stock of capital equipment, K, and the sum of accessible non-renewable resources plus the sustainable flow of renewable services provided by our natural ecosystem, N. Each of these factors is multiplied by its efficiency factor, designated as E_L, E_K, and E_N, respectively. The economy's expanded production function is thus

$$Y = f(L \cdot E_L, K \cdot E_K, N \cdot E_N) \tag{6.3}$$

The technology-enhanced *effective factors* change in quantity when either their physical quantity changes or technology enhances their productivity, or both. Per capita output grows in the long run at the rate of change of E_L only if the other effective inputs grow proportionately to $L \cdot E_L$ so that no effective factor is subject to diminishing returns.

The rate of sustainable economic growth thus depends on whether humans can generate factor-augmenting technological changes to expand the effective stocks of all those factors of production that are fixed or limited in quantity. Of particular concern in this chapter is whether human society can generate new technologies to avoid the complete depletion of exhaustible resources or the destruction of some substantial portion of nature's capacity to provide its renewable services. Given the limits to exhaustible and renewable resources, the failure to generate technologies that raise $N \cdot E_N$ would cause diminishing returns to the expansion of the other effective factors, $L \cdot E_L$ and $K \cdot E_K$. We focus first on exhaustible resources.

6.2.2 Effective supply of exhaustible resources

Humans have demonstrated the ability to generate new knowledge and technology. According to William Baumol, Sue Ann Batey Blackman, and Edward Wolff (1989, p. 211):

> ... measured in terms of their prospective contribution to human welfare, the available quantity of our exhaustible and non-reproducible natural resources may be able to rise unceasingly, year after year. Rather than approaching exhaustion with continued use, their effective inventories may actually be growing and may never come anywhere near disappearance. In short, our society's growing per capita output, rather than constituting a case of profligacy in which society "lives off its capital," may in fact involve what amounts to a net saving of finite natural resources, so that their *effective stocks* are constantly expanded by the same family of technological developments that underlie the growth in real per-capita income since the Industrial Revolution.

Indeed, the supply of *effective* resources has been growing. Farm land that could produce only ten bushels of corn last century now produces several times as many bushels. The so-called **green revolution** has enabled China, India, and other countries to provide their growing populations with more food. Tree farms produced more marketable lumber than natural forests. Mining engineers developed technologies for reprocessing spent ores that were once considered waste. Meat production has been industrialized by switching from free-range feeding to feedlots. Each of the many technological changes seemed to generate more output from nature's services and resources.

Environmental stresses like global warming and the rapid loss of biodiversity make it clear, however, that technological change has not compensated for the use of all of nature's resources and services. Even the green revolution was not as productive as often suggested: among other things, the increased output came at the cost of pesticide poisoning, soil depletion, falling water tables, the destruction of rural communities, and appalling cruelty to animals. David Lobell, Woldram Schlenker, and Justin Costa-Roberts (2011) find that climate change, caused in part by energy-intensive industrialized agriculture, is already offsetting recent gains in corn and wheat yields. Clearly, the full set of technological changes needed to overcome all limits to growth has not been achieved. The next section begins with some examples of how, in principle, human society can overcome the fixed supply of exhaustible natural resources.

6.2.3 A model of effective exhaustible resource supply

To show how technological change can mitigate the problem of limited resources, we assume a very simple production function. Suppose that, unlike the more general production function (6.3) with several inputs, output is produced using a single exhaustible resource, H, according to:

$$Y = f(N) = 10 \cdot H \qquad (6.4)$$

This specific production function reflects a state of technology in which one unit of the natural resource can be transformed into ten units of output. Suppose also that we know for certain that there is a finite supply of 1,000 units of the natural resource on earth. At the current level of technology, therefore, the effective stock of resources stated in terms of what they can produce is 10,000 units of Y.

As a first example, suppose that the rate of technological change is zero. In this case, the best we can do each year is transform each unit of H into 10 units of Y. Suppose also that the demand for output Y is constant at 100 units per year. As detailed in Table 6.1, each year the economy produces 100 units of Y using 10 units of H. With constant technology and annual consumption of 100Y, after 100 years, production of Y comes to a halt because the initial stock of H is completely exhausted.

Table 6.1 Finite Stock of Resources with Constant Technology and Output

Year	Technology	Output	Usage	Physical Stock	Effective Stock
0	10	100	10	1,000	10,000
1	10	100	10	990	9,900
2	10	100	10	980	9,800
3	10	100	10	970	9,700
.	.	.	.	.	.
99	10	100	10	10	100
100	10	0	0	0	0

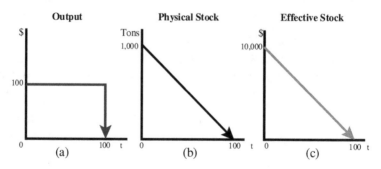

Figure 6.2 Limited Resources without Technological Progress

Figure 6.2 depicts the results from Table 6.1 in graphic form. Diagram (a) shows constant output until year 100, which in diagram (b) causes the physical stock of resources to decline at a constant rate. The effective stock of H also declines at a constant rate in diagram (c) since there is no technological change. When the resource runs out, the final output that was produced with the resource is no longer possible. This is the scenario that critics of economic growth fear.

6.2.4 Effective resource supply with technological change

Instead of the constant technology of the above example, suppose that technology improves at the rate of 5 percent per year so that producers of Y get 5 percent more output from each unit of the non-renewable natural resource than they got the prior year. If technology starts out at the level given by the production function (6.4), then this growing production function is

$$Y_t = 10(1.05)^t \cdot H, \tag{6.5}$$

where t is the number of years after the first year.

Table 6.2 Constant Output and 5 percent Rate of Technological Progress

Year	Technology	Output	Usage	Physical Stock	Effective Stock
0	10	100	10	1,000	10,000
1	10.5	100	9.52	990.5	10,400
2	11.03	100	9.07	981.4	10,820
3	11.58	100	8.64	972.8	11,261
4	12.16	100	8.23	964.5	11,724
↓	↓	↓	↓	↓	↓
99	1,252.39	100	0.08	801.6	1,003,914
100	1,315.01	100	0.08	801.5	1,054,010
↓	↓	↓	↓	↓	↓
∞	∞	100	0.00	800	∞

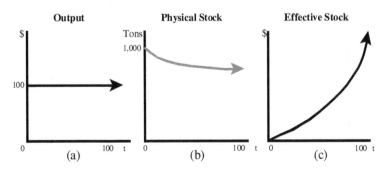

Figure 6.3 Limited Resources with 5 percent Technological Progress

Table 6.2 and Figure 6.3 detail the new situation if output is 100Y per year and technological change continually reduces the amount of H it takes to produce 100Y. Technology improves and increases effective stocks of the resource even as actual resources are used up. After 100 years, the physical stock of resources has fallen by 20 percent, but measured in terms of the output that they can be converted into, resources have effectively become more abundant. This increased abundance in effective resources is the result of technological change that, in this example, exceeds the rate of resource depletion, 5 percent to 1 percent. In the first year, the production of 100 units of Y requires expending 10 units of H, or 1 percent of the total existing supply of H. But, in each successive year technological breakthroughs effectively increase the resource by 5 percent for a net annual increase in effective H of 4 percent.

6.2.5 *Further examples: Effective supply with growth*

The above examples assume there is no output growth. Suppose now that output Y grows at 3 percent per year while technology grows at the same 5 percent rate assumed in Table 6.2. As Table 6.3 and Figure 6.4 illustrate, this example shows that as long as technology increases the effective stock resources faster than they are used up, the earth will not deplete its resources. The effective quantity of H increases despite output growth, albeit more slowly than in the previous example.

Table 6.3 Finite Resources with 3 percent Output Growth and 5 percent Technological Progress

Year	Technology	Output	Usage	Physical Stock	Effective Stock
0	10	100	10	1,000	10,000
1	10.5	103	9.81	990.2	10,397
2	11.03	106.09	9.62	980.6	10,811
3	11.58	109.27	8.44	971.1	11,242
↓	↓	↓	↓	↓	↓
100	1,315.01	1,921.86	1.46	560.3	736,757
↓	↓	↓	↓	↓	↓
∞	∞	∞	0.00	480	∞

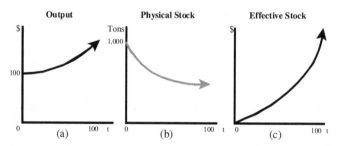

Figure 6.4 Limited Resources, 3 percent Growth and 5 percent Technological Progress

6.2.6 Which example is most realistic?

The above examples illustrate, first of all, that technological change can prevent the depletion of a finite set of non-renewable resource even though consumption grows each year. But, depending on the specific rates of output growth and technological change, economic collapse is also possible. Which of the above hypothetical examples best predicts how the world will actually deal with the exhaustion of resources over the next century or more? To answer this question, we need accurate estimates of (1) the stocks of resources, (2) the usage of resources in future years, and (3) the rate at which we will improve all of the technologies needed to address the many different shortages, stresses, and disasters we will face in the future. The future is uncertain and accurate predictions are impossible. What is clear, however, is that for output to continue growing, humanity must continue improving its technologies.

6.2.7 Technological change and exhaustible resources

The examples above suggest that output growth is sustainable if technological change increases the output produced per unit of exhaustible resources faster than the rate at which resources are depleted. Also, the physical inputs of exhaustible resources must decline over time. As illustrated in Figure 6.5, sustainable output growth from Y_1 to Y_2 to Y_3 requires technological change that shifts the production function from $f_1(H)$ to $f_2(H)$ to $f_3(H)$ so that the economy uses declining amounts of physical inputs of exhaustible resources from, say, H_1 to H_2 to H_3. The economic development question thus is: What will cause technology and resource use to change as shown in Figure 6.5?

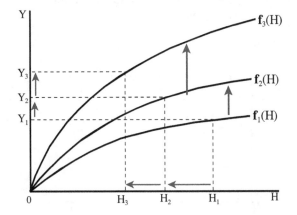

Figure 6.5 Sustaining Effective Resources Requires Technological Change

6.3 Resource Prices and Technological Change

Many orthodox economists argue that prices determined in free markets for natural resources provide incentives that ensure sustainable growth of output. They claim that when markets are efficient, current prices of commodities reflect future scarcities. Therefore, resource prices will induce producers and consumers to make choices that optimize long-run human well-being. To understand these arguments, this section reviews how orthodox economists rationalize their faith in resource markets.

6.3.1 Hotelling's rising prices, history's falling prices

Harold Hotelling (1931) showed that, all other things equal, the price of the exhaustible resource must rise over time. The intuition behind his model is that there will be no investments in projects to exploit natural resources unless the price that the investor can charge for a resource increases at a rate equal or greater than the rate of return to other potential investments available to investors. Specifically, Hotelling hypothesized that the price of an exhaustible resource is the expected price of the resource at some point in the future discounted to the present at the average rate of return on alternative investments.

Figure 6.6 depicts the curve of prices of an exhaustible resource over time. Starting at the intercept on the price axis, the curve rises exponentially over time to the level it is expected to command at some point in the future. For example, if the resource is expected to cost P_t at time t in the future, the discount rate necessary to make ownership of the resource attractive in comparison to other productive investments is reflected by the slope of the curve, and the present price will be P_0. Prices for periods between today and time t will lie along the curve connecting the prices P_0 and P_t.

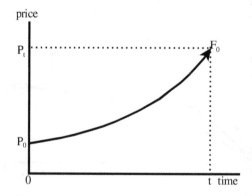

Figure 6.6 The Current Price P_0 is Related to Expected Future Prices

Figure 6.6 can be used to show how the price of a resource changes. Suppose, for example, that expectations of when the resource will reach the price of P_t rises by n years compared to earlier expectations. The entire line of discounted prices thus shifts to the right from P_0F_0 to P_1F_1, and the present price falls from P_0 to P_1. Or, suppose an alternative resource is invented, and its price is expected to be equal to F_2 when it is introduced at time t. In this case, the entire price curve shifts down, and the price of the first resource will fall to P_2. In sum, changes in current resource prices are due to changes in expected future resource prices.

Anyone who follows resource markets knows that the prices of natural resources fluctuate from year to year, sometimes quite a lot. Commodity prices certainly do not gradually move along a smooth curve such as the one shown in Figure 6.6. Figure 6.7 shows how changing predictions of future economic conditions, technologies, and the supplies of substitute resources cause current prices to change. The volatility of commodity prices suggests that the future is uncertain and predictions of future market conditions change frequently.

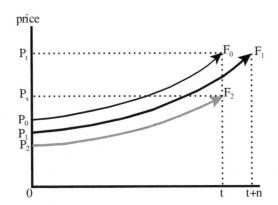

Figure 6.7 Changes in Expectations of Future Prices Change the Current Price

Figure 6.8 shows *The Economist* industrial commodity index for the years 1845-1999. The price index for a large set of commodities, mostly exhaustible, shows both volatility in the short run and a gradual decline in the long run. How do we reconcile Hotelling's theoretical result, that the price of an exhaustible resource must rise over time, with Figure 6.8, which shows that in real terms commodity prices have declined over time?

The explanation for the apparent contradiction between **Hotelling's pricing model** and the data on commodity price trends is contained in Figure 6.7. Hotelling's theoretical result is valid only if we know everything there is to know about future supplies and technology. Since the present price is linked to the expected future price of the resource, the present price will change if there is a change in expectations about the future price. The expected future price of a resource will thus change if there are unexpected discoveries of additional reserves of an exhaustible resource. Also, the price will change if there are unanticipated new technologies that increase, or decrease, the usefulness of the resource, such as a reduction in extraction costs or a technological breakthrough that increases the usefulness of substitute resources. The gradual price decline for exhaustible resources over 150 years suggests that the effective supplies of natural resources have increased over time.

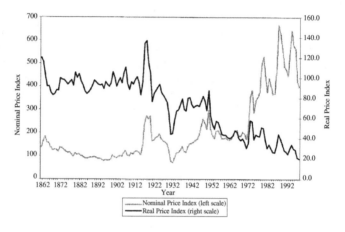

Figure 6.8 *The Economist* Industrial Commodity-Price Index
Source: Paul Cashin and C. John McDermott (2001), p. 11

This experience may now be causing the market to expect technological progress to continue into the future. Such expectations may keep current prices too low to stimulate the technological progress necessary to motivate the expected technological progress.

6.3.2 Do prices provide accurate signals?

If commodity prices are indeed unbiased predictors of future scarcity, then the gradual decline in prices of commodities shown in Figure 6.8 seems to suggest that economic forces may be generating enough technological change to make economic growth sustainable. Such a conclusion may not be warranted, however.

There are many reasons why resource markets fail to reflect the true price of natural resources and services. Extraction costs for exhaustible resources are often not fully accounted for, especially when mining activities generate harmful pollution and dangerous residues. Negative externalities are common in resource usage. Electric power plants often do not pay for the poor air quality from burning coal, lumber companies do not pay for the destruction of the natural habitat of millions of living organisms and species, and the owners of fishing boats are not charged for the long-run loss of fish stocks. Renewable resources, or what we will refer to as nature's services, are often not priced at all because there are no markets for many of nature's services. And, markets are seldom competitive to the point where prices accurately reflect underlying opportunity costs. In fact, some markets for natural resources are administered by near-cartels, as in the case of oil, or a few large purchasers dominate the markets, as in the case of most other major commodities.

One of so many tragic examples of the failure of Hotelling's model was the near-extinction of the American buffalo in the 1800s. As detailed by Scott Taylor (2011), a growing demand for buffalo skins in Europe motivated by the discovery of a new tanning technology, plus the lack of conservation policies in the United States, resulted in the nearly complete elimination of the buffalo population of North America over a period of just 10 years in the nineteenth century. There was no rise in prices or slowdown in the slaughter even as the buffalo population of 10–15 million was reduced to just a few hundred. A seemingly unlimited number of hunters entered the region to kill and skin the buffalos that wandered the Great Plains of the United States, intermediaries set up at various trading posts in the region to buy and ship the hides to Europe, and European tanners found ready markets for the sturdy buffalo leather. Writes Taylor (2011):

> Europe in the 19th century was the high income developed region, while America was a young developing country recently rocked by a bloody civil war caused by racial strife. In the 1870s, America was a large resource exporter with little or no environmental regulation while Europe was a high income consumer of U.S. resource products apparently indifferent to the impact their consumption had on America's natural resources. Written in this way it is apparent that the story of the buffalo has as much relevance today as it did 130 years ago. Many developing countries in the world today are heavily reliant on resource exports, and few, if any, have stringent regulations governing resource use. The slaughter on the plains tells us that waiting for development to foster better environmental protection can be a risky proposition: in just a few short years, international markets and demand from high income countries can destroy resources that otherwise would have taken centuries to deplete.

In short, orthodox theory generally does not accurately describe how exhaustible resource prices are actually set. The well-informed markets that economists often assume will set prices that accurately reflect all opportunity costs simply do not exist. Because they seldom accurately reflect true opportunity costs, market prices do not provide accurate signals for individual behavior or government policy making. Therefore, an efficient allocation of resources can only be achieved with the help of other measures such as taxes, subsidies, and explicit regulation of the economic sphere's interaction with the natural sphere.

6.4 Global Warming

The observed phenomenon of global warming offers a complex example of how accelerated growth of economic activity over the past two centuries is now causing serious damage to the earth's natural environment. Global warming suggests that even with rapid technological change in the economic sphere, humanity still faces diminishing returns in the natural sphere. In terms of equation (6.3) above, not all inputs in the production function were proportionately increased or enhanced by means of technological change over the past 200 years. In short, the technological changes that have effectively pushed back the limits to growth in the economic sphere of human existence actually caused the exploitation of natural resources to exceed the capacity of the natural sphere.

6.4.1 The issue of global warming

There is near-complete consensus among scientists that the earth's atmosphere is warming. There is also broad consensus that this global warming is caused by human economic activity, mostly in the form of **greenhouse gas (GHG)** emissions by industry, transport, power generation, and agricultural production. But, there is still uncertainty over what the exact consequences of global warming will be for humanity. Scientists do agree that there is a realistic possibility that a continuation of current trends in the growth of greenhouse gas emissions will jeopardize human life and many other forms of life on earth over the next century.

There is uncertainty about how much warming will occur as a result of past and current human activity because there may be delayed **feedback effects** from an initial increase in temperatures. Scientists suspect that the release of methane gases from the melting of the Arctic tundra and reduced reflection of the sun's heat with the melting of polar ice could cause a sudden steep upward spiral of temperatures. The uncertainty of the consequences of the clearly observable phenomenon of global warming has contributed to the complacency and inaction on the part of the world's governments.

The phenomenon of global warming is detailed in many documents, such as those by the OECD (2002), the European Union (2008), and the United Nations' Intergovernmental Panel on Climate Change (2007). In another noted report, Nicholas Stern (2008, p. 1) describes global warming as follows:

> Greenhouse gas emissions are externalities and represent the biggest market failure the world has seen. We all produce emissions, people around the world are already suffering from past emissions, and current emissions will have potentially catastrophic impacts in the future. Thus, these emissions are not ordinary, localized externalities. Risk on a global scale is at the core of the issue.

Global warming is a holistic issue. Climate is an integral component of our natural environment, and it determines such important natural services such as rainfall, temperatures, the amount of sunshine, wind intensity and direction, humidity, vegetation, and animal life. The climate is itself a very complex system whose specific characteristics in any one location at any one time are very difficult to predict. There is evidence suggesting that higher atmospheric temperatures will result in greater variations in general climatic conditions, as well as changes in rainfall, drought, seasonal changes, and the many other services provided by nature.

There is a possibility that global warming will have very costly, even catastrophic, consequences. Secondary effects from the warming of the atmosphere include rising ocean levels because of the melting of ice in the Arctic, Antarctic, and mountain glaciers. The Arctic Monitoring and Assessment Program (AMAP), the scientific body of the 12-nation Arctic Council, estimated in 2011 that sea levels will rise between 0.9 and 1.6 meters by 2100.[7] James Hansen (2007) argues that feedback effects will cause a much more rapid ice melt and oceans could rise by several meters by 2100. Entire countries, such as Bangladesh and the Netherlands, could be submerged. There is also the likelihood that rising ocean and soil temperatures in the arctic region, will release large amounts of GHGs stored on the ocean bottom and in the permafrost, which will cause an exponential rise in global warming beyond anything experienced on earth for at least 70 million years.

Humanity's response to the potentially disastrous consequences of global warming has been hampered by the special characteristics of the process of global warming. First of all, global warming is a slow process. Scientists attribute the greatest portion of current GHGs to post-World War II industrial production, agricultural expansion, and transportation, in short, the past 60 years of economic growth. The slow reaction of the climate to GHG accumulation also means that current GHG emissions will not have a noticeable effect in atmospheric temperatures for years. Therefore, people currently engaged in the activities that cause the release of GHGs into the atmosphere do not experience the consequences of their actions; it will be their children who experience the full effects of the warming of the atmosphere.

A second characteristic of global warming that delays human response is that the slow process has a lot of momentum. Global warming will not stop, much less reverse itself, for decades even if humans were to drastically cut GHG emissions today. So we face consequences from our GHG emissions that will not become apparent for many years. Yet, if we wait to act until we notice substantial climate change, it will be too late to avoid the potentially harmful long-run consequences of the climate change.

---

[7] AMAP (2011), "Arctic Pollution 2011," reported released May 6, 2011, available at http://arctic-council.org/working_group/amap.

Finally, human response has also been slowed by the fact that there is still great uncertainty about exactly what the long run effects of global warming will be. We have only data from the past and abstract models with which to predict future climate change. Yet, to avoid the possibility of future consequences that we cannot determine precisely, people, governments, and industries have to incur substantial costs to change economic and social activity today. It is no wonder that many governments have been slow to take serious action to deal with global warming. Despite the uncertainty about the details, however, there is almost no doubt at all among scientists that if economic and population growth continue to increase GHGs as they have, temperatures on Earth will rise to levels never before experienced by humans.

6.4.2 Evidence of global warming

Scientists have been aware of the potential for human activity to change the earth's climate for at least 100 years. Joseph Fourier (1827) described how the atmosphere trapped heat from the sun. John Tyndall (1861) identified the types of gases that trapped heat, and 100 years ago Svante Arrhenius (1896) calculated the possible effects of a doubling of GHGs. Among the various GHGs is carbon dioxide, which today accounts for about three-fourths of all GHGs in the atmosphere. GHGs also include methane, nitrous oxide, water vapor, and hydroflourocarbons. These GHGs accumulate in the atmosphere, so that annual emissions translate into a growing stock of GHGs in the atmosphere. The length of time that emissions remain part of the stock depends on a variety of factors, and some GHGs remain in the air longer than others. Over the last 100 years, carbon dioxide concentrations have risen from about 280 parts per million (ppm), the level they remained near for all the years of human existence, to 390 ppm in 2010.[8] Methane concentrations, which are many times more potent in capturing the sun's heat in the atmosphere, have more than doubled over the past century. Methane releases from the soil, the permafrost, and the ocean bottom play an important role in some of the feedback effects of carbon releases into the atmosphere. Methane mostly originates today from agriculture, especially modern factory farms and feedlot operations. By the mid-1980s, the evidence of global warming was quite convincing, and many scientists began to actively urge action to deal with global warming.

6.4.3 Projections of global warming

Predicting future global warming is difficult. But given the lagged reaction of global warming to current GHG emissions, we have no alternative but to use predictions of the future as part of our decision-making process.

---

[8] IPCC (2007); see also Justin Gillis (2010), "A Scientist, His Work and a Climate Reckoning," *New York Times*, December 21.

In 1990, the Intergovernmental Panel on Climate Change (IPCC), a United Nations sponsored working group of hundreds of scientists from around the world, issued a report assessing the current state of knowledge on global warming. The consensus of the IPCC scientists was that the continued growth of carbon emissions from human activities would raise temperatures by about 1°C by the year 2030. The report also predicted that current trends would probably double the concentration of carbon in the atmosphere in less than a century. It was estimated that such a doubling would eventually raise average temperatures in the world between 1.5° and 4.5°C (3–8°F). Such average temperatures would be unprecedented given the available climatic evidence for the last 800,000 years. The IPCC's 1990 conclusions echoed the warnings issued by James Hansen of NASA's Goddard Institute for Space in testimony before a U.S. Senate committee in 1988.

A 2007 IPCC report confirms the earlier projections of global warming:

> There is now "visible and unequivocal" evidence of the impacts of climate change, and consensus that human activities have been decisive in the warming observed so far: global average temperatures have risen by about 0.74°C since 1906, and the rise this century is projected to be between 1.8°C and 4°C.

The report also states that over the last 50 years, temperatures have risen by 0.13°C per decade, about twice the rate over the previous 50 years.

Nicholas Stern (2008, p. 5) summarizes all the available evidence as follows:

> There seems little doubt that, under BAU [business as usual], the annual increments to stocks would average somewhere well above 3 ppm CO_2e [carbon dioxide equivalent], perhaps 4 or more, over the next century. That is likely to take us to around, or well beyond, 750 ppm CO_2e by the end of the century. If we manage to stabilize there, that would give us around a 50–50 chance of a stabilization temperature increase above 5°C [9°F].

Table 6.4 presents Stern's summary of scientific estimates of global warming without taking feedbacks into consideration.

Table 6.4 Likelihood of Exceeding a Temperature Increase by 2100

Stabilization Level (in ppm CO_2e)	2^oC	3^oC	4^oC	5^oC	6^oC	7^oC
450	78	18	3	1	0	0
500	96	44	11	3	1	0
550	99	69	24	7	2	1
650	100	94	58	24	9	4
750	100	99	82	47	22	9

Source: Nicholas Stern (2007), Box 8.1, p. 220.

6.4.4 More uncertainty: Feedback

The 2007 report also discusses some of the feedbacks that are likely to accompany the rise in temperatures. For example, some scientists have conducted experiments suggesting that a 2°C rise in temperatures is likely to cause permafrost melting in the Arctic, which would release large amounts of carbon and methane now stored in the frozen ground. Such feedback could, under quite plausible assumptions, accelerate global warming towards an uncontrollable vicious cycle in which warming breeds more warming. Under such a scenario, not included in the probabilities in the IPCC report, temperatures could rise by 10°C (18°F) or more.

Carbon is also stored in the oceans, and some will be released into the atmosphere if water temperatures rise. Like the melting permafrost, there is the possibility of a spiraling of carbon emissions and temperature rises. Other scientists have reported similar spiraling feedback from the increased water vapor that a few degrees of global warming would create. The feedback processes are the most difficult to predict, since they are nonlinear in nature and, most likely, subject to thresholds. Most studies, like the Stern Report and the IPCC (2007) report, have therefore focused only on the direct consequences of rising GHG emissions. But, the potential for feedback effects increases the risk of continued growth of GHG emissions.

6.4.5 Stabilizing temperatures

In judging the likelihood of stabilizing atmospheric temperatures at each of the levels given in Table 6.4, keep in mind that in 2010 there were already 390 parts per million (ppm) of GHGs in the atmosphere. Also, at current trends, human activity is raising carbon concentrations by about 3 ppm per year. Therefore, under business as usual, 450 ppm will be reached sometime around 2030. Stabilization at 450 ppm will very likely raise temperatures by at least 2°C, which some scientists have suggested as the threshold at which the permafrost is likely to begin melting and releasing methane gas.

Stern (2007) reports that to stabilize the stock of carbon-equivalent GHGs at 450 ppm, we will have to begin reducing emissions of GHGs now and continue reducing them until they reach a level in 2050 that is 70 percent less than their 2007 level. That is, despite continued economic growth and population growth, human activity and human technology will have to emit just 30 percent as many GHGs into the atmosphere. Since the world's population is expected to rise by nearly 50 percent over this period, per capita emissions will have to fall to just 20 percent of 2010 levels. And, if current rates of economic growth continue, emissions per dollar of GDP will have to fall by over 90 percent. This will require large changes in technology and the way humans live.

6.5 The Loss of Biodiversity

Global warming is not the only complex environmental change brought about by the growing number of humans and the growing consumption of each of those humans. The human "footprint" on Earth is altering other aspects of our natural environment in ways that are likely to reduce the services of nature that humans have enjoyed in the past. These other impacts of the human footprint are not any easier to deal with than the anthropogenic climate change described in the previous section. This section focuses on **biodiversity**, that is, the number of different species of plants, animals, and micro-organisms that exist on earth. Biodiversity also encompasses the genetic variations and traits within species as well as assemblage of these species within ecosystems. Scientists are concerned about biodiversity because the rate at which individual species are becoming extinct has accelerated precipitously over the past century.

According to Robert May's (2010) survey of the causes of species losses, the loss of plant and animal species is closely related to climate change. This finding is not surprising given that climate plays a large role in the survival, or demise, of living organisms. One million species could be lost over the next 50 years if global warming progresses as predicted under the *business as usual* assumption in the Stern Report.[9] The loss of plant and animal species will feed back into more rapid global warming; forests are important carbon sinks, and their decline will increase the amount of carbon released into the atmosphere.

The loss of plant and animal variety is a distinct phenomenon from global warming because it is driven by many other impacts of humans' heavy footprint on Earth. Humans occupy more space on Earth and use more of the resources and services nature provides. More space for humans means less space for other animals and plants. The development of agriculture, which played such a large role in the growth of the human population, necessarily replaced diverse natural forests, grasslands, and wetlands with areas devoted to growing just a small variety of food crops. Modern agricultural technologies have extended the practice of monoculture, which adds to the dangerous homogeneity of plant and animal species raised by farmers across the earth. Most of the world grows the same varieties of corn, wheat, rice, fruits, and vegetables, and it raises a small number of species of cows, pigs, chickens, and sheep.

The alleged gains in efficiency from replacing nature's vast variety and redundancy of species with those species that grow most efficiently must be counterbalanced by the increased risk of losses of animal and plant species critical for human existence. The Irish potato blight of 1846, which resulted in one million people starving, was the consequence of the lack of plant diversity. Today, genetic engineering and cloning could make animal species so nearly identical across the world that one type of new bacteria or virus could wipe out a

---

[9] As reported in Vanessa Houlder (2004), "Over 1 Million Species Will Be 'Wiped Out' by Global Warming," *Financial Times*, January 8.

huge portion of the world's meat or dairy supplies. The loss of biodiversity means the economy and human society are increasingly putting all their eggs in one basket. The biotech industry is also developing genetically engineered animals and crops that provide inputs for industrial and pharmaceutical products. We have little understanding of what could happen if these new animals and plants cross-breed and cross-fertilize with the existing species that we depend on for food.

6.5.1 The issue of biodiversity

Plant and animal species continually become extinct. The process of evolution makes certain of that. However, there is evidence that the rate of species extinction has accelerated sharply, and as a consequence, the overall level of biodiversity is declining very rapidly. According to the most conservative estimates, over the past century, the rate of extinction is at least 100 times as fast as the long-run rate over the past few million years. The biologist, Edward O. Wilson (2002) estimates the true rate is probably 1,000 to 10,000 times the historical rate.

A problem with estimates like Wilson's is that we are not very certain of their accuracy. To date, scientists have distinguished only about 1.5 million species of living organisms, but educated guesses suggest there are probably 10 million, maybe even as many as 100 million, species on our planet. We can only tabulate the extinctions of those species that we monitor carefully, which is just a very small fraction of the 1.5 million species that scientists have identified and classified over the past 250 years. Scientific estimates of the loss of biodiversity, therefore, are based on just a minute sample of the total number of species living on earth. As is the case of all sampling methods, the full picture can only be presented as a range of outcomes. Since our sample is small, the ranges are large, and because we know little about the full sample, we cannot compute probabilities of possible outcomes.

Andrew Balmford and William Bond (2005) conclude their survey of the scientific literature as follows:

> Information on changes in the status of species, size of populations, and extent and condition of habitats is patchy, with little data available for many of the taxa, regions and habitats of greatest importance to the delivery of ecosystem services. However, what we do know strongly suggests that, while exceptions exist, the changes currently underway are for the most part negative, anthropogenic in origin, ominously large and accelerating.

The evolutionary processes of all species have been changed by the growing human footprint on Earth. A species that was successful in reproducing while living in the company of one set of organisms may find itself at a disadvantage when its fellow organisms evolve and become more successful in competing for food and space. A reminder of the interdependence of all living species, the sudden rise in extinctions of so many living species suggests how human evolution has progressed to the point where humans are altering the evolutionary processes of many other living organisms on Earth. In fact, the Nobel Prize-winning atmospheric chemist Paul Crutzen regards the influence of human behavior on the natural environment so significant as to constitute a new geological era, which he calls the **Anthropocene**.

Like global warming, specific estimates of the acceleration of rate of the decline in biodiversity are *uncertain*. Also like global warming, there is uncertainty about what the precise consequences of the rapid loss of so many species will mean for human well-being. But, also like global warming, scientists are almost certain that the process is real and that it will have adverse effects on humanity's well-being. As mentioned earlier, the loss of bio-diversity adds to the risk of human survival. The loss of some species could trigger declines of many other species, some of which are crucial to human survival or economic well-being.

6.5.2 The services of nature

According to the ecologist Gretchen Daily, "Nature's services are the conditions and processes through which natural ecosystems support and fulfill human life."[10] Because this definition covers essentially all renewable natural resources as well as the great variety of things nature provides on an ongoing basis, such as air, water, heat, soil replenishment, and waste recycling, it is useful to categorize these services. The Millennium Ecosystem Assessment (2005) splits nature's services into five categories:

> *Provisioning Services* — These are the products that nature provides to us directly, such as food, spices, water, air, warmth, vitamin D through sunlight, firewood, and myriad other natural things that humans consume. When humans were hunters and gatherers, they derived a large share of their existence directly from nature's services. Today, the world's people still depend on the direct provisions provided by nature, although our high degree of industrialization and urbanization increasingly separates us by at least one stage of production from most of nature's services. Yet, our expanded industrial and service economies depend more than ever on nature's raw materials, energy sources, climate, scenery, land, and other directly supplied natural services. And the growing number of poor people in less developed countries still depend directly on many of nature's services, such as fresh food, water, shelter, fuel, and cultural activities, for their survival.

---

[10] Quote from a Stanford University news release, February 6, 1997.

Regulating Services — Nature regulates our climate, recycles our waste, and maintains our relationships with all other living species. For example, natural forests, oceans, and soils sequester much of the carbon that humans emit into the air with their campfires, automobiles, and power plants. Most human waste is converted into fertile soil, minerals, and other organic materials that are again recycled through the ecosystem. Forests and other growth help to absorb rain into the ground for storage and later use, and they also prevent flooding and soil erosion. Forests also play a critical role in preventing global warming because they are the most important carbon sink. Furthermore, the complex interactions among all living organisms in nature maintain a balance that normally prevents one species from destroying all others, including humans. For example, nature provides an effective pest and disease control by regulating the relative quantities of bacteria, viruses, and other carriers that might infect humans.

Supporting Services — These provide the basic infrastructure of life. Supporting services include the capture of energy from the sun to produce complex organic compounds, soil formation, and the cycling of water and nutrients in terrestrial and aquatic ecosystems. Nature purifies water through evaporation and precipatation, it cleans the air through wind, gravity, and carbon capture. Over 100,000 different animal species, such as bats, bees, flies, moths, birds, and butterflies, provide pollination services for foods that comprise one-third of the human diet.

Cultural Services — Nature provides the environment in which humans live and create their cultures. In fact, nature helps to shape and preserve those cultures by providing the setting, the scenery, and the natural locations that are revered by cultures. In modern societies, nature provides the scenery, the warm beaches, and the mountain tops that humans travel to see. Nature also provides the inspiration for the scientific discoveries that advances human knowledge.

Preserving Services — The diversity and **redundancy** of the ecosystem provides insurance against future uncertainties.[11] If one species fails, it does not imply an immediate imbalance that threatens humans because there are many other species that provide similar services and can take up the slack. The great diversity of living organisms in the ecosystem reduces the risk of instability in the natural environment.[12] Biodiversity also gives humans more options to live the way they prefer in terms of climate, scenery, and food consumption, for example.

---

[11] See, for example, B. H. Walker (1992) and S. Naeem (1998).
[12] See, for example, D. Tilman, C. L. Lehman, and C. E. Bristow (1998).

This short set of examples only provides a brief summary of a very broad range of services that nature provides humanity. Since humanity came into being after the ecosystem, or nature, had been providing these and similar services for hundreds of millions, even billions, of years, humans tend to take nature's services for granted. Gretchen Daily challenges us to think about the importance of these services by asking what services we would bring with us if we were to begin life on the moon, an environment that currently does not support life. Obviously we would need air and water. But, Daily details many other things we would have to bring:

> Tackling the problem systematically, a hypothetical moon colonist could first choose from among all the species exploited directly for food, drink, spices, fiber and timber products, medicines, various industrial products (such as waxes, lac, rubber and oils) and so on. Even being selective, this list could amount to hundreds, even thousands of species.
>
> The space ship would be filling up before the colonists even began adding the species crucial to supporting those at the top of the list: the bacteria, fungi and small animals that help make soil fertile and break down waste and dead organic matter; the birds, bats and insects that pollinate the flowers; the grasses, herbs and trees that hold the soil in place, regulate the hydrological cycle, supply food for animals and so on.
>
> Soil organisms are crucial to the chemical conversion and physical transfer of essential nutrients to higher plants. The abundance of soil organisms is absolutely staggering: Under a square-yard of pasture in Denmark, for instance, the soil was found to be inhabited by roughly 50,000 small earthworms and their relatives, 50,000 insects and mites, and nearly 12 million roundworms. A pinch of soil may also contain over 30,000 protozoa, 50,000 algea, 4,000,000 fungi and unknown numbers of types of bacteria, with billions of individuals in each species.[13]

Daily's mental exercise forces us to recognize the vast range of services that we require from nature for our survival. Of course, the fact that we are dependent on so many of nature's services is nothing more than a logical reflection of the fact that humans evolved in a complex ecosystem. We are one living creature among millions of species, and we are part of the ever-changing balance among all of the components of nature's complex ecosystem. Humans have been on earth about 200,000 years, but life has been evolving for a couple of billion years. The biologist E. O. Wilson (2002) ends his description of Earth's millions of living organisms with: "They don't need us, but we need them."

6.5.3 The value of biodiversity

In Chapter 2, we mentioned that a team of environmentalists and economists headed by Robert Constanza (1997) estimated that in 1997 the value of the

---

[13] This quote is from a Stanford University news release, February 6, 1997.

goods and services provided by our natural environment was somewhere between $16 and $54 trillion, or a median of $33 trillion, per year. Since measured world GDP for 1997 was about $18 trillion, we can conclude that a full accounting of the value of what nature provides us every year is approximately twice current measures of world GDP. This estimate means that what the complex ecosystem, or what we call the natural sphere, provides for us is worth more to us than everything that humans produce on earth. In other words, humans themselves provide for only a portion, about a third, of their own sustenance on earth. Our most popular economic measures, of course, do not recognize this. Nor do humans seem to recognize the importance of the ecosystem for human welfare as they continue depleting nature's nonrenewable resources and its capacity to provide natural services.

Note that these estimates of the value of nature's services are highly uncertain. Several methods have been employed by researchers to estimate the value of nature's services.[14] In some cases, researchers can calculate the cost of services that humans would have to incur in order to provide nature's services themselves, such as waste treatment or water purification. In other cases, where the loss of biodiversity has already occurred, researchers can directly calculate the loss of benefits, such as the decline in the catch of ocean fish or the loss of tourist revenue when natural scenery is destroyed. Economists can also indirectly calculate the value of scenery, good climate, and soil quality by looking at how much more people pay for land located in scenic areas, warm climates, and fertile regions, versus less scenic, pleasant, and fertile areas. Health costs associated with deteriorating environments also provide useful information. However, it is very difficult to account for every single natural service that sustains human life.

Not only would better estimates of the values of nature's services be helpful, but we also need such estimates on a periodic basis so that we can see how the natural environment is coping with humanity and how environmental policies are working. Policymakers also need more precise information on what types of technological change are needed to make economic growth GDP sustainable. Chapter 18 returns to the question of how society should address threats like global warming and biodiversity loss.

6.6 The Solow Model and Renewable Resources

The Solow model from the last chapter relates output to investment in capital. This model roughly represents activity in the economic sphere. Earlier in this chapter, the expanded production function (6.3) shows output as a function of labor, capital, and natural resources. And Figure 6.5 above related exhaustible

---

[14] Many of these methods are detailed in S. C. Farber, Robert Constanza, and M. A. Wilson (2002).

resources to output in order to illustrate how output growth can be sustained in the face of a fixed quantity of exhaustible resources. We thus need a production function that includes both capital in the economic sphere and renewable resources in the natural sphere.

Humanity's exploitation of renewable natural resources is not unrelated to its exploitation of exhaustible resources. In fact, Jeffrey Krautkraemer (1998) argues that nature's capacity to supply services such as carbon sinks, clean water, and fertile soils is directly endangered by the pollution from using exhaustible resources such as carbon fuels. This suggests that the finite nature of exhaustible resources like carbon fuels may be a less pressing issue than the deterioration of the ecosystem that provides nature's renewable resources. Krautkraemer suggests, for example, that our economic growth will come to a halt because drastic climate change will disrupt our economy long before exhaustible resources like oil run out. We thus focus here on renewable resources, or nature's services.

6.6.1 An enhanced Solow model

Suppose that the economic sphere of human existence can be represented by the production function

$$Y = f(K \cdot E_K, S \cdot E_S) \qquad (6.6)$$

in which output Y is produced using capital, K, and renewable resources, S. The E's represent factor specific technologies, so that the production function shows the *effective* stock of physical capital $K \cdot E_K$ and nature's effective capacity to generate its services $S \cdot E_S$. We take the other factors, like labor, as given.

We could illustrate this version of the Solow model in a three dimensional diagram, or we can break our analysis down into two parts, each consisting of two dimensions. The latter approach is more convenient given that we are limited to two dimensions on the pages of this book. We begin with the natural dimension of the model, in which output Y is related to the amount of nature's services S. Then we will also show the Solow model's traditional economic dimension, in which output Y is related to the stock of capital K. Both physical capital and the ecosystem are subject to depreciation, but the depreciation functions are not exactly the same.

The services that the ecosystem provides are gradually replenished after humans make use of them. Therefore, the quantity of nature's services is limited by nature's capacity to replenish itself. For example, if humanity's economic output puts CO_2 into the air faster than the natural system can dissipate it, then the atmosphere deteriorates and the benefits provided by the natural climatic conditions diminish. Similarly, if human production uses water faster than natural processes replenish the water, then less water will be available in the future. A notable example is the shrinking of the Aral Sea in Central Asia to one third its original size when new irrigation projects diverted too much water.

In general, the more intensively humans use renewable resources, the more likely that nature will not be able to keep up and the more likely that humans must carry out intentional conservation efforts to support and restore nature's capacity to provide its services. Conservation involves such things as planting trees, stocking rivers with fish, repairing shorelines and beaches, filtering waste water, using catalytic converters on automobile exhaust systems, etc.   If humanity overuses nature's services without also engaging in the necessary conservation to sustain the ecosystem, the ecosystem's capacity to provide services declines.

Figure 6.9 shows the natural sphere of the economy. The production function in the natural sphere has a diminishing slope under the assumption that there are diminishing returns to inputs of natural resources, all other inputs such as capital and labor stocks equal. There is also a "depreciation" function, which we call the **conservation cost curve**, in recognition of the need to *conserve* nature's capacity to provide renewable services.

The conservation cost curve is not a linear function, like the depreciation function Solow assumed for physical capital. Nature's capacity to provide its services may not be stressed at all at low levels of use, for example at human economic output between Y_1 to Y_2 in Figure 6.9. Humanity can increase its use of nature's services from S_1 to S_2 at virtually zero marginal cost. However, when human society increases its economic output to Y_3, there is a noticeable stress on the natural ecosystem. Conservation activities with an economic cost of $c(S_3) > 0$ are required to sustain such resource use. If the marginal cost of conservation is greater than the marginal gain in output, then human production is not welfare maximizing.

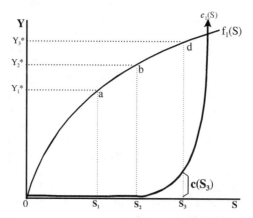

Figure 6.9 Economic Growth in the Natural Sphere

Figure 6.10 presents a two-sphere Solow model with the natural and economic spheres depicted side by side. Suppose that technological progress in the economic sphere raises output from Y_1 to Y_2 at new steady state that requires an increase in the capital stock from K_1 to K_2. This enhanced Solow model shows that this increase in economic output requires more inputs of natural services such as rainfall, oxygen, dissipation of air pollutants, absorption of water runoff, and so forth. The left-hand diagram shows that in the case of raising output from Y_1 to Y_2, there are zero marginal conservation costs (the conservation cost curve is horizontal) for the economy's use of the ecosystem's capacity. With no noticeable effect of economic growth on nature's services, people may come to believe they can essentially ignore the natural sphere and that nature's services will always be forthcoming at no cost.

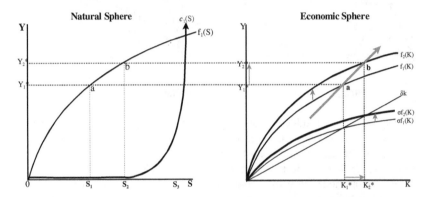

Figure 6.10 Economic Growth in the Natural and Economic Spheres

Now, suppose that humanity develops more new technologies that further expand its ability to raise output in the economic sphere. But also suppose that humanity does not see the sharply rising conservation cost curve in the left-hand side natural sphere diagram, so that it continues investing only in the new capital called for in the steady state as shown in the economic sphere. The right-hand side diagram, by itself, suggests further economic growth is perfectly possible if there is technological change and an accompanying increase in the capital stock in the economy.

As illustrated in Figure 6.11, suppose that another shift in the production function to $f_3(K)$ increases output from Y_2 to Y_3. Ignorant of the environmental consequences, in part because there was no noticeable effect from expanding economic output in the past, the economy implicitly assumes that the required natural services will again be available. The conservation cost curve shows, however, that sustaining the use of nature's services when exploitation rises above S_2 requires costly conservation activities, such as air pollution controls, water purification plants, soil conservation, irrigation projects, recycling, and so forth. Output Y_3 requires nature's services equal to S_3, and unless conservation efforts costing $c_1(S_3)$ are undertaken, such exploitation of nature will begin to destroy nature's capacity to provide its services in the future.

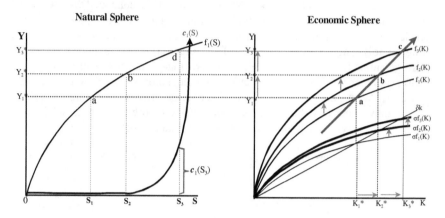

Figure 6.11 Economic Growth when the Natural Sphere is Stressed

Suppose that, indeed, the required expenditures of $c_1(S_3)$ are not undertaken because humanity prefers to ignore the required conservation costs. This causes the conservation cost curve, which reflects the cost of nature's services, to shift to the left, as shown in Figure 6.12. The decline in nature's capacity to provide renewable resources also causes the production function shown in the economic dimension to decline because a reduction in one of the inputs not shown in the two dimensions of the economic sphere reduces the marginal product of capital across the board. The environmental devastation in the natural sphere causes the production function in the economic sphere to fall back to $f_2(K)$, and output thus falls back to Y_2.

The decline in production is not a one-time phenomenon if decisions in the economic sphere continue to ignore the consequences of economic activity on the natural sphere. Because of the deterioration of nature's productive capacity and the leftward shift of the conservation cost curve, costly conservation activities are now necessary at levels of exploitation of nature's services below S_2, the level at which nature used to be able to replenish itself without human help. Unless human society now engages in real conservation activities costing $c_2(S_2)$, there will be further deterioration of nature's capacity to provide water, air, warmth, carbon sinks, flood control, etc., and the conservation cost curve will shift further to the left to $c_3(S_1)$. Output will fall further, perhaps back to Y_1, because the decline in nature's services further diminishes the production function in the economic sphere. Investment falls because the environmental disaster reduces the production function, income, and saving, and the capital stock in the economic sphere thus declines to an even lower steady state.

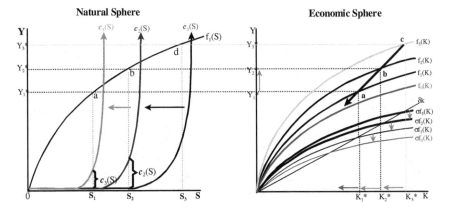

Figure 6.12 From Economic Growth to Economic Decline

It is important to note that the collapse described above can be avoided if society provides for the necessary conservation of nature's capacity to provide its services. But even with the required allocation of society's resources to conservation, the growth of output in the economic sphere must stop. Under the best of circumstance, the two-sector Solow model also has a steady state. Permanent growth is not sustainable with a finite supply of nature's services in the absence of technological change in both the economic and natural spheres.

6.6.2 There must be technological change in both spheres

In the previous chapter, the Solow model concluded that, in the face of diminishing returns and real costs to maintain constantly depreciating capital stocks, continued growth in output is possible only if there is technological progress that enables producers to get more output out of a given set of inputs. This conclusion is equally relevant when the natural environment is included in the Solow model. Figure 6.13 illustrates that, had there been improvements in how human society transforms nature's renewable resources into output, it could have increased output to Y_3 without triggering a devastating collapse of output. Specifically, if there had been technological progress in both the economic and natural spheres, and the production function had shifted out from $f_1(S)$ to $f_2(S)$ in the natural sphere in tandem with the shift from $f_2(K)$ to $f_3(K)$ in the economic dimension, then output could have increased to Y_3 without requiring any additional use of nature's services beyond S_2. Hence, the multi-dimensional Solow model shows that technological change can keep society's stress on the ecosystem at levels where nature can sustain its services.

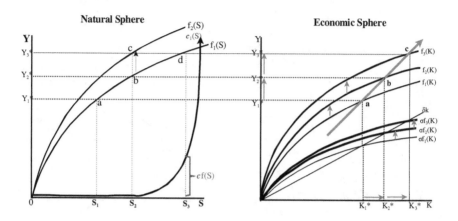

Figure 6.13 Technological Change in Both Spheres

The technological changes required in the natural sphere are different from technological changes that occur in the economic sector, however. Raising the efficiency in using nature's services involves such things as farming more intensively, substituting drip irrigation for more traditional methods that flood entire fields, and generating electricity with solar or wind power so that fewer greenhouse gases are emitted into the air. More subtle technological changes that enable society to achieve more welfare-enhancing output from the eco-system are improvements in food storage, improving transportation and packaging to reduce product losses and spoilage, and new farming methods such as crop rotation and no-till planting. More generally, humanity will have to change the way it lives and produces. People will need to use more public transport and fewer private vehicles, they will have to produce fewer material products and more services, and they will have to consume more collectively provided public goods and fewer individually owned private goods. These types of technological change are very difficult because they imply changing human cultures and conventional perceptions of the meaning of life. This takes time.

6.6.3 Summarizing the conclusions of the enhanced Solow model

The expanded Solow model thus provides broader insight into the process of economic growth than the single-sector model presented in the previous chapter. The expanded model permits us to exploit the Solow model's focus on diminishing returns, the steady state, depreciation of society's productive resources, and the importance of technological change in the natural sphere of human existence. The dynamic interactions between the economic and natural spheres could cause an economic collapse if environmental damage is not perceived and mitigated quickly.

6.7 A Strategy for the Future

This chapter focused on the natural sphere that humans inhabit along with the social and economic spheres. This chapter takes a major step in the analysis of economic development by expanding the popular Solow model of economic growth to include natural resources and nature's services to the production function. First, a simple model was developed to show how technological change can, in principle, overcome the barrier to economic development presented by the fixed supply of exhaustible resources on our Spaceship Earth. Second, the two major environmental problems of global warming and the loss of biodiversity were introduced and described. These two problems represent the destruction of nature's capacity to provide services critical to human existence.

Available evidence shows that humans are indeed failing to make all the investments in conservation to prevent a deterioration in the ecosystem's capacity to provide its services. Nor are we generating the necessary new ideas, new knowledge, or new technologies that increase the efficiency with which the economies of the world use exhaustible resources and nature's renewable but limited services. Recall the estimates by Mathis Wackernagel *et al.* (2002) and the World Wildlife Fund (2008) that humanity's use of the capacity of the global biosphere exceeds sustainable levels. The growing number of humans and the rise in their per capita production of material goods and services are damaging the ecosystem that provides the natural services that we need for our existence. The worst-case scenario illustrated above with the enhanced two-sphere Solow model above seems to be actually occurring now.

6.7.1 Net domestic product

A major problem for policymaking is the lack of information on what is really happening in the natural sphere. Some economists have used what information is available on resource depletion to adjust gross domestic product (GDP). One such measure, called **net domestic product (NDP)**, is estimated by subtracting from GDP the value of exhaustible resources used up. Estimating the depletion of natural resources is difficult, however. Martin Weitzman (1999) estimated the cost of resource depletion by assuming resource prices accurately reflect opportunity costs of effective alternatives plus extraction costs. He concluded that use of the fourteen most important exhaustible resources "causes us overall to lose the equivalent of about 1 percent of average consumption each year."[15] Thus, exhaustible resources will run out unless resource-enhancing technological change increases the effective supplies of those resources by more than 1 percent per year.

---

[15] Martin L. Weitzman (1999), p. 705.

The needed amount of technological change is greater than Weitzman estimates because he covers only 14 major minerals whose prices were easily available. Resource use also includes disposal costs (waste) and the damage to nature's capacity to provide renewable resources. Complex natural resources such as biodiversity and climate change must also be included.

In 1999, a team of scientists from Cambridge and Sheffield Universities in the United Kingdom estimated that it would cost about $300 billion per year, or about 1 percent of world GDP, just to conserve the planet's biodiversity.[16]   The Intergovernmental Panel on Climate Change (2007) estimated it would cost between 1 and 2 percent of world GDP to reduce greenhouse gas emissions and stop global warming. When all costs of compensating for natural resource use are accounted for, NDP is most likely four or five percent less than GDP. Given 2010 world GDP of about $75 trillion, the costs of resource depletion would be about $3 trillion per year, not an inconsequential amount of humanity's economic resources. Of course, as explained above, not spending this money to compensate for resource depletion and for the maintenance of the ecosystem will likely be much more costly to humanity in the long run.

6.7.2 The graphic cost of resource depletion

Figure 6.14 illustrates GDP and NDP. Suppose the global economy grows at the rate of 4 percent per year. Such a rate of growth implies that a real per capita GDP of 100 in year 1 will grow to 711 in 50 years. But, suppose also that the true costs of compensating for the use of non-renewable resources, the loss of biodiversity, the negative externalities that accompany production, and the effects of global warming add up to 5 percent of GDP. The growth path of net domestic product, NDP, will thus lie 5 percent below the growth path of GDP, as in Figure 6.14.

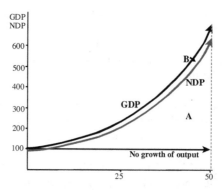

Figure 6.14 NDP versus GDP

---

[16] As reported in Vanessa Houlder (1999), "Game of High Stakes in a World Being Bled Dry," *Financial Times*, September 23.

The total cost of finding new technologies, carrying out conservation activities, and introducing alternatives to replace, enhance, and save the earth's scarce resources over the 50 year period is the area labeled B between the GDP and NDP growth paths. The true gains from economic growth are thus equal to the area A, which is less than the cumulative estimate of the gains from the growth of traditional GDP, which is the sum of the areas A and B. But, comparing areas A and B in Figure 6.14 suggests that the gains from economic growth are still quite large in the long run, much greater than the cost of mitigating the destruction of nature's resources and services.

Perhaps the costs of mitigating climate change and stopping the rapid loss of biodiversity are much greater than 5 percent of GDP. It is also likely that the rate of growth of economic production will have to be slowed, if for no other reason than the need to divert savings from capital investment to creating technological change to preserve the natural sphere. Building public transportation, installing alternative energy systems, and changing lifestyles will require a lot of resources. In short, the NDP curve may be much flatter and lie far below the GDP curve.

Figure 6.14 is misleading in another important way: The GDP curve is inaccurately shown as continuing upward. In fact, if resources are not conserved or effectively enhanced through technological progress, and society fails to apply some of its resources to mitigate the environmentally destructive effects of GDP growth, output will eventually stop growing and, in the case of a complete collapse of human civilization, approach zero.

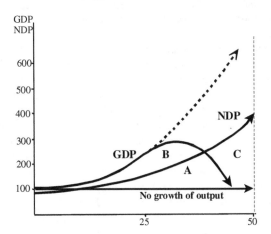

Figure 6.15 Gains from Growth vs. Costs of Depletion

Figure 6.15 more accurately represents the alternative growth paths that society really faces. One is the sustainable but substantially slower growth of path of NDP. The other is the unsustainable growth path of GDP. In the case of NDP, the early opportunity costs of conservation, technological change, and lower consumption seem like a rather steep price to pay for long-run sustainability. No doubt, people will be tempted to postpone or even ignore the most realistic estimates of the future consequences of business as usual. But, if foresight prevails, the costs in terms of lost consumption equal to B are more than compensated by the area C that would not be attainable if the unsustainable growth path of GDP were pursued and output indeed collapsed. The NDP growth path is sustainable because it represents net output after allocating resources for the research, innovation, and application of new technologies necessary to effectively replace those non-renewable resources used up and to change lifestyles so that nature's capacity to provide services is not depleted.

6.7.3 *Refining the definition of sustainable development*

There is thus more than one role for technological change in the process of economic growth. Because natural resources in their current physical state are finite, we need technological innovation to (1) increase the *effective* stocks of exhaustible resources and (2) keep humanity's use of nature's services within levels that sustain nature's capacity to maintain those services.

In Chapter 1, we defined **sustainable development** as

> The long-run process of economic change and development that maximizes the needs and aspirations of the current generations without sacrificing the ability of future generations to meet their needs and aspirations.

The evidence that current economic activity already exceeds nature's capacity to maintain its effective resources and services suggests that the global economy is on an unsustainable growth path.

The economist Herbert Stein is often cited as having said that "if something is not sustainable, it will stop." The two specific examples of global warming and species loss suggest that economic development may not just stop, but humanity may experience a reversal of economic development in the near future. The enhanced two-sphere Solow model shows what happens when market economies focus all attention on the economic decisions made in the economic (Y and K) dimension and permit stresses in the natural sphere to go unattended. In his book entitled *Collapse*, Jared Diamond (2005) describes many failed societies throughout history, such as Easter Island, the Pitcairn Islands, the ancient Anasazi civilization in today's Southwest U.S., Mayan civilization in Central America, and Viking settlements in Greenland. In each case, humans did not conserve their natural environment, and ultimately the stresses between the economy, society, and nature undermined entire societies.

Some economists, businesspeople, and policymakers argue that economic growth's pressure on the earth's resources will directly stimulate the technological changes necessary to mitigate the stresses. They effectively argue that economic growth creates incentives for the technological change that can sustain it. Specifically, greater resource scarcity raises prices, which then induce people to seek new supplies, better substitutes, and more efficient production methods that economize on scarce resources. In short, "necessity is the mother of invention."

Ecologists, environmental economists, and many development economists are not so optimistic about humanity's ability to deal with potential disasters in the natural sphere. The complexity of our economic, social, and natural environments, and of the system that links them, obscures the relationships between economic growth and the natural environment. Furthermore, the global dominance of capitalist economic systems, which focus almost exclusively on economic relationships in established markets, do not generate incentives to solve environmental problems that are not immediately reflected in market outcomes. Experience clearly shows that existing markets in the economic sphere have not led to the development and application of all the new technologies and lifestyle changes necessary to avoid climate change and biodiversity losses. Today, there simply are no markets whose prices accurately reflect true resource scarcities. Where far-sighted collective action is needed, human psychology instead leads people to focus on immediate economic problems. Recall our discussion in Chapter 3 on how the human brain's automatic and emotional responses are much quicker than its more rational deliberative responses.

The hedonic treadmill may also be to blame for the short-sighted quest for more environmentally-damaging economic output. Chapter 3 also described the evidence showing humans as social animals who greatly value their group status. These two observations led the writer and environmental editor of the French newspaper *Le Monde*, Hervé Kempf, to conclude that the clash between the economic and natural spheres is largely caused by the growing conspicuous consumption of the wealthy class. Kempf (2007) directly blames the rich for their high levels of resource-using consumption. But he also (p. xiii) draws on Thorsten Veblen's (1899) *Theory of the Leisure Class* to write:

> The oligarchy also exercises a powerful indirect influence as a result of the cultural attraction its consumption habits exercise on society as a whole, and especially on the middle class. People aspire to lift themselves up the social ladder, which happens through imitation of the superior class's consumption habits. Thus, the oligarchy diffuses its ideology of waste throughout the whole society.

The **hedonic treadmill** was described in Chapter 3 as the process whereby status-conscious people work very hard to get ahead of, or at least to not fall behind others, but instead end up generating economic growth that leaves their relative status unchanged. Recall, also, that Michael Prowse (2003) suggested the only gainers from the hedonic treadmill are wealthy capitalists, who use technological change and the hard work of hedonically-trapped workers to maintain the high profits that put them at the top of the income distribution.

Interestingly, Kempf also describes society's elite for having "no dream other than technology."[17] After the discussion of the Solow model in its various forms, this chapter also seems to have narrowed its prescriptions for the future to the need for new technologies, albeit a very wide range of new technologies and broad changes across all dimensions of the human existence. But can technological change really enable a sustainable economic development that includes continued economic growth?

The Industrial Revolution, and the capitalist system that enabled it, have transformed new ideas, knowledge, technology into the simplistic expansion of material consumption and physical convenience. Fundamentally, technological change can only be viewed as technological progress if it leads to greater human happiness. Human happiness remains an elusive goal, of course. But it is almost certain that true **technological progress** that enhances human well-being includes changes in social institutions, governance structures, the distribution of opportunities and wealth, and the organization of our daily lives. Narrowly-focused technological change in the economic sphere that ultimately causes a sharp decline in living standards or, worse, a collapse of human society does not constitute technological progress or economic development.

The next two chapters discuss technological change in detail. These chapters will show that humanity's past success in generating and applying new knowledge may not have enabled it to sustainably manage its increasingly large economic and social footprints in the natural sphere.

---

[17] Hervé Kempf (2007), p. xiii.

Key Terms and Concepts

Anthropocene
Biodiversity
Conservation cost curve
Cultural Services
Ecological footprint
Effective factor supplies
Exhaustible resources
Feedback effects
Global hectares (gha)
Global warming
Greenhouse gases (GHGs)
Hedonic treadmill
Hotelling's pricing model
Limited resources

Monocultural farming
Net domestic product (NDP)
Preserving Services
Provisioning Services
Redundancy of natural systems
Regulating Services
Renewable resources
Scarcity
Spaceship Earth
Supporting Services
Sustainable economic development
Technological progress
Unlimited wants

Questions and Problems

1. Why is the economic sphere not completely inside the human society sphere in Figure 6.1? Explain.
2. The textbook states that Paul Ehrlich's description of the future turned out to be much too pessimistic. Do you agree with that? Or do you think Ehrlich's 1970 predictions were accurate? Explain why or why not.
3. The discussion of sustainable economic development has used the words, "overdevelop," "underdevelop," "de-develop," and "semi-develop." Explain what each of these words mean in light of everything you have read in this chapter.
4. Is there a way to recover exhaustible resources, such as, metals?
5. Technological progress not only improves the efficiency of capital, labor, and natural resources and services, it can even replace some of these factors. Can you give some examples?
6. Are we experiencing technological progress with our technological change?
7. Is it realistic to assume a constant rate of increase in technological progress?
8. What is missing in the model of increasing effective supplies of resources with positive technological change? Discuss.
9. Must we stop economic growth in order to avoid an environmental collapse or human extinction?
10. Review the cases in Section 6.2.3, and then analyze the case of 2 percent output growth and 2 percent technological change. Explain your results.
11. Write a brief essay based on the two-sphere Solow model to explain why economic growth may not only cease but may actually reverse itself and leave people worse off than they were in the recent past.

12. Is the Hotelling model of resource pricing correct? Why might prices not rise in the future, as the model predicts? Begin your answer by explaining the Hotelling model, its assumptions, and its predictions.

13. Write an essay explaining why humans seem to have such difficulty accepting the scientific evidence on global warming and biodiversity loss. (Hint: focus on the nature of these two phenomena, especially their complexity, their long-term nature, and the difficulties of perceiving their consequences in our capitalist market economy.)

14. Is the economic development of the past 200 years sustainable? Explain your answer in detail using the models, concepts, and evidence presented in this chapter.

15. Explain precisely why Hervé Kempf blames "the rich" for global warming.

16. Has humanity ever faced such daunting environmental problems as global warming and biodiversity loss before? Explain.

17. Explain precisely the Solow model of the natural sphere in Figure 6.9. What are the model's assumptions and predictions?

18. Explain how Figure 6.5 is related to earlier Figures 6.2, 6.3, and 6.4.

19. Does Figure 6.14 justify ignoring the depreciation of our natural resources and ecosystem? Explain precisely why or why not.

20. What do scientists mean by feedback effects when they examine the potential outcomes from greenhouse gas emissions or biodiversity losses. Explain and provide examples.

21. Write a brief essay on why the Solow model and its reliance on diminishing returns makes it useful for analyzing the natural sphere of human existence. (Hint: Diminishing returns set in because some inputs are fixed in quantity.)

22. About two decades ago, Saudi Arabia decided to invest in irrigation infrastructure to tap the aquifers beneath its deserts in order to grow wheat. Today, the country is self-sufficient in wheat, but the aquifers are nearly depleted after 20 years of pumping. Saudi authorities knew that the ancient aquifer was not being replenished by nature anymore. Why did they go ahead with their project knowing that it could not last much more than a couple of decades? (Hint: Draw on the material from Chapter 3 on human behavior.)

References

AMAP (2011), "Arctic Pollution 2011," reported released May 6, available at http://arctic-council.org/working_group/amap.

Arndt, H. W. (1978), *The Rise and Fall of Economic Growth*, Chicago: University of Chicago Press.

Arrhenius Svante (1896), "On the Influence of Carbonic Acid and Air upon the Temperature of the Ground," *Philosophical Magazine* 41(2):237–272.

Balmford, Andrew, and William Bond (2005), "Trends in the State of Nature and Their Implications for Human Well-Being," *Ecology Letters* 8:1281–1234.

Baumol, William J., Sue Anne Batey Blackman, and Edward N. Wolff (1989), *Productivity and American Leadership: The Long View*, Cambridge, MA: MIT Press.

Boulding, Kenneth E. (1966), "The Economics of the Coming Spaceship Earth," in H. Jarrett (ed.), *Environmental Quality in a Growing Economy, Resources for the Future*, Baltimore: Johns Hopkins Press.

Cashin, Paul, and C. John McDermott (2001), "The Long-Run Behavior of Commodity Prices: Small Trends and Big Variability," IMF Working Paper WP/01/68, May.

Costanza, Robert, *et al.* (1997), "The Value of the World's Ecosystem Services and Natural Capital," *Nature* 387:253–260.

Daly, Herman E. (1998), "Uneconomic Growth," Clemens Lecture 11, Saint John's University, October 25.

Diamond, Jared (2005), *Collapse: How Societies Choose to Fail or Succeed*, New York: Penguin Books.

Ehrlich, Paul (1968), *The Population Bomb*, New York: Ballantine Books.

Ehrlich, Paul (1972), in Sue Titus Reid and David L. Lyon (eds.), *Population Crisis — An Interdisciplinary Perspective*, Glenview, Illinois: Foresman.

European Union (2008), *The Economics of Ecosystems & Biodiversity: An Interim Report*, downloaded from the EU website.

Farber, S. C., Robert Constanza, and M. A. Wilson (2002), "Economic and Ecological Concepts for Valuing Ecosystem Services," *Ecological Economics* 41:375–392.

Fourier, Joseph (1827), "Mémoire sur les températures du globe terrestre et des espaces planétaires," *Mémoires de l'académie royale des sciences* 7:569–604.

Fuller, R. Buckminster (1963), *Operating Manual for the Spaceship Earth*, New York: E. P. Dutton.

Hansen, James E. (2007), "Scientific Reticensce and the Sea Level Rise," *Environmental Research Letters* 2(2):1–6.

Hotelling, Harold (1931), "The Economics of Exhaustible Resources," *Journal of Political Economy* 39:137–175.

Howarth, Robert W., Renee Santoro and Anthony Ingraffea (2011), "Methane and the Greenhouse-Gas Footprint of Natural Gas from Shale Formations: A Letter," *Climatic Change* 106(4):679–690.

Intergovernmental Panel on Climate Change (2007), *IPCC Report on Global Warming*, New York: United Nations.

Kempf, Hervé (2007), *How the Rich Are Destroying the Earth*, White River Junction, VT: Chelsea Green Publishing Co., p. xiii.

Krautkraemer, Jeffrey (1998), "Nonrenewable Resource Scarcity," *Journal of Economic Literature* 36(4):2065–2107

Liu, Jiangguo *et al.* (2007), "Complexity of Coupled Human and Natural Systems," *Science* 317(September):1513–1516.

Lobell, David, Woldram Schlenker, and Justin Costa-Roberts (2011), "Climate Trends and Global Crop Production Since 1980," *Science*, online May 5, 2011.

May, Robert M. (2010) "Ecological Science and Tomorrow's World," *Philosophical Transactions of the Royal Society* 365:41–47.

Meadows, Donella H., *et al.* (1972), *The Limits to Growth*, New York: Universe Books.

Millennium Ecosystem Assessment (2005), "Living Beyond our Means: Natural Assets and Human Well-Being," Statement from the Board, Washington DC: World Resources Institute.

Naeem, S. (1998), "Species Redundancy and Ecosystem Reliability," *Conservation Biology* 12:39–45.

OECD (2002), *Working Together towards Sustainable Development*, Paris: OECD.

Prowse, Michael (2003), "Why Capitalism Will Never Permit Us to Live A Life of Leisure," *Financial Times*, August 9/10.

Rees, Martin (2005), *Our Final Hour: A Scientist's Warning*, New York: Basic Books.

Stern, Nicholas (2007), *The Economics of Climate Change*, Cambridge, U.K.: Cambridge University Press.

Stern, Nicholas (2008), "The Economics of Climate Change," *American Economic Review* 98(2):1–37.

Taylor, Scott (2011), "Buffalo Hunt: International Trade and the Virtual Extinction of the North American Bison," *American Economic Review*, forthcoming.

Tilman, D., C. L. Lehman, and C. E. Bristow (1998), "Divers," *The American Naturalist* 151:177–282.

Tomkins, Richard (2003), "Economic Progress Was Quite Nice While It Lasted," *Financial Times*, January 1.

Turner, R. K., J. Paavola, P. Cooper, S. Farber, V. Jessamy, and S Georgio (2003), "Valuing Nature: Lessons Learned and Future Directions," *Ecological Economics* 46:493–510.

Tyndall, John (1861), "On the Absorption and Radiation of Heat by Gases and Vapours," *Philosophical Magazine* 22:169–194, 273–285.

United Nations Population Fund (2010), *The State of World Population 2010*, New York: UNFPA; available at www.unfpa.org.

Veblen, Thorstein (1899), *The Theory of the Leisure Class*, New York: Modern Library.

Wackernagel, Mathis, *et al.* (2002), "Tracking the Ecological Overshoot of the Human Economy," *Proceedings of the National Academy of Sciences* 99:9266–9271.

Walker, B. H. (1992), "Biodiversity and Ecological Redundancy," *Conservation Biology* 6:18–23.

Weitzman, Martin L. (1999), "Pricing the Limits to Growth from Minerals Depletion," *Quarterly Journal of Economics* 114(2):691–706.

Wilson, Edward O. (2002), *The Future of Life*, New York: Alfred A Knopf, Inc.

World Wildlife Fund (2008), *Living Planet Report 2008*, Gland, Switzerland: World Wildlife Fund for Nature.

CHAPTER 7

Technological Change:
What Is It and How Do We Model It?

Knowledge is the only instrument of production not subject to diminishing returns.
(John Maurice Clark)

Solow's neoclassical model of economic growth shows that when some inputs into the economy's productive processes are fixed or not easily expanded, then long-run economic growth is possible only if technological progress overcomes diminishing returns to capital and the other factors of production that are variable. The multi-sphere Solow model from the previous chapter emphasizes the need for technological change across the natural sphere as well as the economic sphere because many resources and natural services are fixed in quantity. The size of the human population and the level of human production threaten to reverse the last 200 years' economic growth, unless humanity changes the way it uses nature's resources and services.

In light of the importance and variety of human technology, economists have developed models to explain technological change. Unlike the Solow model, which assumed that technological change was determined *exogenously* outside the model, these new models are often referred to as **models of endogenous technological change**. They are so named because they *endogenize* the process of technological change; that is, technology is one of the variables determined within the model. In this chapter, we will begin examining some of the recent and popular new endogenous growth models. However, we first need to clarify what we mean by **technology** and **technological change**. We cannot explain a process if we do not first define what we are explaining.

In the popular press, the term *technology* is often used to describe the efficiency with which the factory uses inputs, such as labor, machines, and raw

279

materials, to produce output. Sometimes, we equate technology with the development of some new machine or product. For example, the computer is viewed as a direct reflection of the cutting edge of current human technology, and we refer to the computer industry as a "high tech" industry. However, equating technology with specific products or industries ignores the many other forms of human knowledge and technologies that enhance human life. This chapter defines and explains a much more general concept of technology.

Chapter Goals

1. Define the principle terms and concepts used in the study of technology.
2. Explain how economists have measured technology, and highlight the problems with the most common measures.
3. Present the key features of technological change, such as the S-curve, path dependency, and geographic concentration of technological development.
4. Explain the combinatoric nature of knowledge and path dependency.
5. Discuss Thomas Kuhn's paradigm shifts and how his ideas qualify the standard view of the advancement of knowledge and technology.
6. Explain the learning by doing model of technological change and why economists questioned its basic logic.

7.1 Introduction to Technology and Technological Change

In the field of economic development, **human technology** is generally defined as the knowledge, techniques, procedures, operating rules, methods, tools, and instructions that humans draw on to transform factors of production into the goods and services they consume. Orthodox economics usually represents technology with a simple **production function**. In this case, technological change is illustrated as a shift in the production function.

Figure 7.1 illustrates an improvement in technology with the upward shift of the production function from $y = f(k)$ to $y = g(k)$, where y is output per worker and k is the amount of capita per worker. Note that when technology improves, output rises from y_1 to y_2 even if physical capital per person, k, remains the same.

The simple production function $y = f(k)$ may not represent technology very well. First of all, there are many more factors of production than capital. For example, the previous chapter showed that the services of nature are also in the economy's aggregate production function. There are also human capital and exhaustible natural resources. The stock of physical capital should really be divided into many very different categories, such as tools, machines, communications equipment, transportation equipment, buildings, infrastructure,

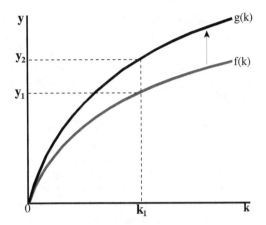

Figure 7.1 The Production Function and Technological Progress

and so forth. In general, a production function shown in terms of only y and k will shift when the other inputs, say the services of nature, increase or decrease. For example, the upward shift of y = f(k) in Figure 7.1 could have been the result of an increase in natural resources, the growth of the labor force, or an increase in human capital like education. Therefore, a shift in the production function in the k and y plane may not represent technological change at all; it could be the result of changes in the availability of other productive factors.

Changes in the effective availability of factors of production can be the result of factor-specific technological change. For example, in Chapter 5 we defined *labor* as the product of the number of workers, L, and labor-augmenting technology, E. You saw in the previous chapter that natural resources can be *effectively* increased with improved technology. That is, the input N in the production function was itself directly a function of some specific resource-enhancing technology.

Finally, it is not obvious that we can interpret y, the per worker output of goods and services, as a proxy for human well-being. Chapters 2 and 3 showed there is much more to human well-being than the personal consumption of material goods. Also complicating matters is the fact that technology affects the structure of the economy, and the structure determines the distribution of income. Also, changes in human knowledge affect individuals' productivity and how groups of people work together. These are all important determinants of human happiness and satisfaction with life.

In sum, the concept of technology cannot be accurately represented by a simple production function. Technological change can operate through the overall production function or directly on an individual factor of production. More specifically, technological change affects (1) the human production process, (2) the effective quantities of physical capital and natural inputs that humans can make use of, and (3) how humans perceive that production affects their well-being. That is an awful lot of information for one curve in a two-dimensional space. Nevertheless, the production function helps us conceptualize technology in a way that may be useful for understanding economic growth models.

7.1.1 Technological change and the production function

For further illustration, suppose human society's aggregate production relates output Y to three aggregate categories of inputs called labor, capital, and nature's services (natural resources), or, respectively, L, K, and S. Suppose, furthermore, that each of these three categories of inputs consists of physical objects, such as, for example, human beings, units of capital equipment, and tons of natural resources, each multiplied by a set of ideas, knowledge, instructions, and methods that enhance the productivity of each of the physical objects, which we designate as E_L, E_K, and E_S. The production function, therefore, can be written as

$$Y = f(L \cdot E_L, K \cdot E_K, S \cdot E_S) \qquad (7.1)$$

As now stated, technology enters this function through E_L, E_K, and E_S as well as in the form of the function $f(\ldots)$. That is, technological change can alter the quantity of each of the technology-augmented factors, and it can alter the overall production function that describes how society can transform a whole set of technology-augmented factors into final output. In holistic terms, technology can change how each of the components function, but it can also change the way the overall system functions.

In an article written nearly three decades ago, Robert Solow (1960) argues for linking technological change to specific factors of production. Computers are a good example of how technology and equipment are linked. The new computer technologies that have changed the way we do almost everything did not develop independently from the development of the computers that the new technologies were embodied in. The state of the art mainframe IBM computer in 1970 was capable of 12.5 million instructions per second (MIPS). At the turn of the millennium, personal computers are capable of nearly 200 MIPS. This improvement in technology did not occur separately from the development of equipment. There is no way that present knowledge can make that 1970 IBM computer run much faster. Today's hardware is needed to compute at 200 MIPS. We might also mention that the improvement in the technology embodied in new computer hardware is much greater than the mere increase in MIPS. The IBM mainframe computer cost $4.7 million dollars in 1970; today's personal computers cost less than $1,000! Thus, one clearly needs to look at the hardware in order to correctly measure the true rate of technological progress.

Per real dollar spent on hardware, one MIPS in 1970 cost 62,322 times as much as it does today.[1]

Buildings, structures like bridges and airports, as well as transportation equipment like trains and aircraft also reflect new ideas and methods. It would not have been possible to apply the assembly line process in the small artisan workshops that preceded the factory system. Whole new buildings were necessary.

This reasoning extends to labor and human capital. New ideas cannot be put into practice unless people learn about them and are trained to apply and use them. In effect, human labor is augmented by embodying the huge set of knowledge and techniques that exist outside the human body. Because modern societies have developed such a large stock of external technology, it can take more than 25 years of family upbringing, formal education from kindergarten through university, several years of work experience, and a lengthy exposure to society's culture to equip a person to contribute to society's productive activities. Natural resources and nature's services are also augmented by human technology. Nature provides the soil, rainfall, accumulated minerals, and atmospheric climate that produces the food humans grow, but most farmland has been altered to make it compatible with humans' agricultural technologies.

Technological change has altered, and continues to alter, the characteristics of labor, capital, and nature. The question of how much more should we alter our physical inputs is hotly debated today. Most societies actively discuss how much and what kind of education they should provide to their children, how much land use patterns should be regulated, whether dams should be built in rivers, and even whether it is permissible to genetically engineer living creatures so they conform more closely to what the food industry wants. You might say that technology, or the way humans do things, is changing who we are as human beings and how we live our lives.

From this brief introduction, it is clear that the definition of technology is not easy to pin down. Its depiction as a shift in the production function is clearly simplistic. But what is technology then?

7.1.2 A more holistic definition of human technology

The growth economist Paul Romer (1993) broadens the definition of technology so that it applies to all sectors of the economy:

> The word technology invokes images of manufacturing, but most economic activity takes place outside of factories. Ideas include the innumerable insights about packaging, marketing, distribution, inventory control, payments systems, information systems, transactions processing, quality control, and worker

---

[1] This information on technological change in the computer industry is from Michael Gort, Jeremy Greenwood, and Peter Rupert (1999).

motivation that are all used in the creation of economic value in a modern economy. If one looks carefully at the details of the operations of a corporation like Frito-Lay, one sees that there are as many subtle ideas involved in supplying potato chips to a consumer as there are in making computer chips. In addition, the ideas involved in supplying potato chips are probably more important for successful development in the poorest countries.[2]

Indeed, when we interpret the Solow model and what it implies about technology, we are interested in more than the cutting edge technology of a few industries like electronics, biotechnology, or information technology. Developing economies need technological change, but they more often than not need routine technologies to upgrade all parts of their economies. Also important are their government institutions and education systems to transfer what is already known to those who must apply new technologies. Technology is a very broad concept, which is why Romer's likes to use the term **ideas** rather than the more traditional *technology*. But, even Romer's description of technology may still not be broad enough.

To better grasp the scope of *human technology*, we first focus on the *human* portion of the term. Here it is useful to compare humans to other animal species. What most distinguishes humans from other animal species is, on the one hand, the extraordinary amount of knowledge and specialized techniques that they apply to their daily routine of going about life and, on the other hand, how much of their knowledge and techniques were developed separately from the evolution of the physical human being. That is, we humans draw on a huge body of ideas, knowledge, techniques, methods, procedures, and other forms of behavior that is passed on from person to person through culture, language, and various codified means rather than genetically or from parental nurturing.

For non-human animals, a much higher portion of their knowledge and technology is "hard-wired" in the instinctive and automatic processes of the brain, passed on through gene. Therefore, changes in the way most animals live, how they interact with each other, and how they deal with their natural environment occur largely through the slow process of evolution. Some knowledge is passed on tacitly through emulation and observation, but such transfer of knowledge is also largely restricted to biological relationships. The biologist Edward O. Wilson (1975) describes the techniques and practices that nonhuman animals pass on through genes and tacit interaction as technology "bound by a tight biological leash."

Humans, on the other hand, have rapidly changed their technologies, and we can observe such changes over the course of one lifetime. This rapid human technological change over the past 200 years, which appeared in the form of basic scientific advances, the design of new tools and machines, entire new products and entire new industries to produce them, new economic and political

---

[2] Paul Romer (1993), p. 543.

systems, and new institutions to intentionally guide human behavior, clearly was not the direct result of the transfer of genes and tacit interactions with close associates.

Katherine Nelson and Richard Nelson (2002, p. 720) describe the accumulation of technology outside the process of evolution as a uniquely human characteristic:

> Humans today cannot run much faster or shout much louder than humans of a century — or fifty centuries — ago, nor are our eyes any better. But we can get where we are going far faster by bike, by car, or by airplane. We can communicate over long distances by flags, telegraph, wireless, and now e-mail. We can see the galaxies an incredible distance away, and also the smallest molecules, through the technologies we have progressively developed over time. The biological leash has become longer and longer, so that today our species knowledge capabilities in many arenas appear very loosely attached to our biological makeup.

Human technology has gotten a life of its own, so to speak, to where it is able to survive separately from humans.

This is not to say that the evolution of the human brain is not an important determinant of human technology. In fact, the evolutionary process has given the human brain a very large capacity to store and process knowledge, and this capability has certainly been a major factor in developing human technology. It was the human mind that led to the development of the various tools for accumulating knowledge outside the brain. Most important has been the development of human social institutions:

> ... the minds of individual human actors are extended through the collective memories of the community as well as through the artifacts and symbols — especially spoken and written language — of their social worlds.[3]

Humans have developed a social structure and methods of communications that permit the accumulation of knowledge. Humans hold some of their technologies in the form of social culture that is passed from generation to generation by communicating through spoken language, writing, and formal learning processes. Today, humans increasingly hold knowledge in the form of written instructions that can be accessed and read by anyone at any time.

We define *human technology* as this entire set of techniques, knowledge, methods, procedures, and culture that exist outside and separately from the human brain. The instinctive knowledge that is passed biologically from generation to generation is part of the basic factor of production known as labor. The external human technology that is internalized through formal education and tacit interaction with other human beings is included, along with life experience and training, in the factor of production that we call **human capital**.

---

[3] Katherine Nelson and Richard R. Nelson (2002), p. 721.

In sum, the accumulated stock of human technology is very diverse. Human technology includes the techniques and processes that humans use to produce specific products. It also includes the social culture that influences how humans interact within their societies, the communications systems humans created to pass techniques, methods, and social rules of behavior along to others, and the techniques and systems that permit the external storage and accumulation of technologies. Technology therefore includes everything from social behaviors and norms learned from others to the information stored on internet servers.

7.1.3 The diversity of technological change

Because technology is diverse, it takes many types of activities to improve technology. Obviously, basic inventions, such as the wheel, electricity, or the transistor, have enabled the world economy to provide us with higher standards of living. Also important are specific applications of such inventions, such as the automobile, the light bulb, and the computer. And, we must not forget specific enhancements of new concepts and applications, such as a hybrid automobile, an energy-saving light emitting diode, or the mini laptop computer. It should be clear, however, that the efforts that lead to an expansion of general knowledge, such as the wheel and electricity, may be very different from the efforts that lead to new applications of existing knowledge, such as the automobile or the light bulb. Different again are the efforts by one firm to produce a new type of automobile or light bulb, or to improve the quality and reduce the costs of producing automobiles and light bulbs. Much more different are efforts to improve how the economic system allocates resources, encourages productive activity, stimulates entrepreneurs, and directs savings to the most profitable investment projects. And most important are the new abstract ideas and complex technologies we need to organize our societies and make economic development sustainable across the economic, social, and natural environments.

Research to generate new technology is often divided into **basic research** and **applied research**. The common belief is that basic scientific research precedes the use of that knowledge in practical applications, and many justifications for government funding of science are based on this perception. Those of us who spend most of our careers on university campuses like to believe that we provide the basic knowledge that serves as the foundation for successful practical projects throughout the economy and society. Technological change may also come from experimentation and tinkering by engineers employed to keep the factory working, amateur inventors motivated by personal curiosity, entrepreneurs seeking to make a fortune with a "better mousetrap," or workers seeking to make their dull job easier. Such applied innovation often occurs before basic research finds the full explanation for what was discovered.

A good example of innovation preceding basic scientific research is provided by steel producers in the second half of the nineteenth century. Steel makers' experiments greatly lowered the costs of making steel. One of the processes developed, known as the Bessemer process, eventually lowered the cost of producing steel more than ten-fold, thus making steel a viable material for a vast new array of products. Steel producers also discovered, through trial and error, that minute variations in inputs greatly affected the quality and durability of steel. These results stimulated the science of metallurgy. According to Nathan Rosenberg, an economic historian who has devoted his career to studying the development of technology, "even well into the twentieth century, metallurgy can be characterized as a sector in which the technologist 'got there first,' that is, developed powerful technologies, or alloys, in advance of systematized guidance by science."[4] This debate about what comes first, basic research or applied research, is reminiscent of the "chicken or egg" debate. Just as the chicken and the egg are part of the same process of life, so the different types of innovation, discovery, invention, and applied research are all part of the process of technological change.

The implementation of new ideas has been investigated by economic historians. For example, Carlo Cipolla (1978) traces the development and applications of the time clock over the centuries, and he makes it clear that the practical growth effects of new technologies often lagged behind the initial discoveries by centuries. Similarly, Alan Macfarlane and Gerry Martin (2002) found that the discovery, development, and applications of glass spanned millennia. Dick Teresi's (2002) *Lost Discoveries* describes many more new ideas and inventions that were not put to practical use for centuries. All of these works make it clear that there is often a long lag between the discovery of a new idea and when that idea is actually applied to where it enhances human welfare. There is technological change only when new knowledge is put to use.

Technology may be **codified** in the sense that it is written down in the form of specific instructions, a recipe, a blueprint, in a textbook, or on the internet. This is the external knowledge that we referred to earlier. But according to Michael Polanyi (1958), a lot of knowledge is **tacit knowledge** that is passed on "by example from master to apprentice."[5] The passing on, or **diffusion**, of technology is important for increasing economic growth, so it important to study how much technology and knowledge can be codified and how much is inherently non-codified. Tacit non-codified knowledge is usually more difficult to pass along than codified technologies.

Regardless of how we classify it, it is clear that technological change is a complex and diverse process. This makes modeling technological progress difficult. Can we come up with one model to explain the discovery of the Pythagorean theorem, the development of modern commercial banking, the

---

[4] Nathan Rosenberg (1994), p. 20.
[5] Michael Polanyi (1958), p. 53.

application of the "just-in-time" parts supply system, and the formulation of quantum physics? Each of these improvements in knowledge had its own motivation. Designing a single model that captures the incentives for creating each of these types of knowledge and technology is probably impossible.

7.1.4 A historical view of technology

Our level of technology today clearly exceeds what people knew one-hundred years ago, one-thousand years ago, or ten-thousand years ago. A simple approach to measuring technological change has been to count the number of innovations or new ideas. In fact, several growth models of endogenous technological change are based on this approach. But, some ideas have turned out to have a greater long-run economic impact than others. The discovery of fire changed the welfare of humanity more than the invention of the hula hoop. But can we accurately distinguish the momentous discoveries from the merely important ones, and the important ones from the less important ones? It is not easy to rank the importance of individual technological breakthroughs over the course of human history.

We gain some insight into the impact of new technologies by reviewing the history of population growth. Recall from Chapter 4 that the Malthusian model accurately described economic growth before 1800, when improvements in the world economy's capacity to produce were usually reflected directly in population growth rather than economic growth. There were several sudden shifts in population growth during the long course of human history. One such shift in population growth occurred between 10,000 and 5,000 BCE, when the rate of population growth increased twenty-fold, from 0.003 percent per year to 0.06 per cent per year. This change coincides with the development of agriculture and animal husbandry, which shifted the human economic environment from hunting and gathering to more permanent settlements based on the cultivation of land and the raising of animals in enclosed areas. Agriculture greatly increased the number of people the economy could support.

Historians have pointed to other major shifts in technology. Permanent settlements ultimately led to more sophisticated, if not always pleasant, forms of government. Large groups of people turned into nations, and this affected how the process of specialization and trade developed. The improvement in the means of transportation played important roles in advancing specialization and trade, as evidenced by sailing ships with large crews 3000 years ago, the construction of permanent roads 2000 years ago during the Roman Empire and canal systems 1000 years ago in China.

The origin of systematic research and development activity is distinguished by some as a major technological advance. An early example of systematic goal-oriented research and development is the establishment of the school of navigation by Portugal's Henry the Navigator back in the fifteenth century. King Henry established the school and research laboratory to develop better navigation methods and instruments in order to aid Portugal's efforts to extend trade routes to the Far East. Located at the southernmost point of Portugal in a place called Sagres, the government-funded institution is perhaps the first example of what we today often call a "research laboratory." Portuguese explorers and traders went on to use many of the new products and technologies to sail to distant lands and open up new trade routes. Sagres was a precursor to Thomas Edison's famous late nineteenth century research laboratory in Menlo Park, New Jersey, that developed electric lighting, electricity generation, the phonograph, the electric railroad, and thousands of other new products that used electricity as a power source.

Many other major technological discoveries and inventions come to mind. The discovery of fire more than 50,000 years ago permitted people to live in hostile climates, see at night, and improve the taste and safety of food. The discovery of the wheel permitted improvements in transportation and tools. The development of writing enabled the codification and much easier communication of new technology. Table 7.1 presents a list of important ideas from the past 1,000 years published in a special 2000 Millennium edition of *The Wall Street Journal*. No doubt, you can think of other technological breakthroughs that had important impacts for humanity.

7.1.5 *Ranking technological breakthroughs*

Nathan Rosenberg (1994, p. 15), the economic historian quoted earlier, suggests that "a major innovation is one that provides a framework for a large number of subsequent innovations, each of which is dependent upon, or complementary to, the original one." Paul Romer has described the powerful ideas that generate many further ideas as **meta-ideas**. This criterion certainly applies to the invention of agriculture, which in turn led to permanent settlements, urbanization, animal husbandry, water management, the wheel, steam power, democracy and many other characteristics of human life.

Table 7.1 A Time Line of Great Ideas

1046	China's Bi Sheng devises first movable-type printing system with clay characters.	1250	China starts manufacturing guns.
		1266	St. Thomas Aquinas pens "Summa Theologica," attempting to reconcile theology with economic conditions.
1050	Arabs bring decimal system to Spain.		
1086	Shen Kua's magnetic compass for navigation, China.	1275–1292	Marco Polo visits China.
		1280	Spinning wheel, Chinese invention, brought to Germany.
1100s	Hebrew scholar Maimonides analyzes linkages between wealth and charity.		
		1329	Korea uses foundry to print books with metal type.
1155	Map of western China is oldest known printed map.		
		1421	Florence grants first recorded patent, for a barge with hoisting gear.

1450s	Gutenberg perfects interchangeable type printing press.
1492	Leonardo de Vinci draws a flying machine.
1498	Toothbrush, using hog bristles, appears in China.
1500s	Holland protects rights of inventors to their creations.
1502	Peter Henlein of Nuremberg uses iron parts and coiled springs to build portable timepiece.
1530	Opium, known as laudanum, used as a pain reliever.
1572	Dutch use carrier pigeons during Spanish siege.
1602	Galileo invents the thermometer.
1610	Bagel invented in Krakow, Poland.
1620	Dutch-born Cornelius Drebbel tests submarine, cruises 15 feet under Thames in London, England.
1642	Blaise Pascal of France invents calculating machine to ease the drudgery of tax-collector father, but finds no takers.
1671	Germany's Gottfried Wilhelm Leibnitz devises mechanical calculator to add, divide and multiply.
1691	Paris prints first directory of street addresses.
1701	Jethro Tull creates horse-drawn mechanical drill to plant seeds in rows.
1709	Britain passes first copyright act.
1710	Umbrellas become popular in London.
1730	German A. Ketterer invents cuckoo clock.
1741	First professor of economics, Uppsala, Sweden.
1743	First known elevator installed at Versailles for Louis XV.
1755	Jean-Jacques Rousseau writes "Discourse on the Origin of Inequality," denounces private property as root of evil.
1759	Dr. Samuel Johnson denounces advertisements as overexaggerated and false.

1760	Belgian creates roller skates by replacing blades of ice skates with wheels.
1765	Eberhard puts erasers on pencils.
1776	Adam Smith publishes *his Wealth of Nations*.
1803	Jean Baptiste Say pens "A Treatise on Political Economy," says management is a factor of production.
1816	French chemist Joseph N. Niepce develops the first photographic negative.
1818	Mary Wollstonecraft Shelley writes "Frankenstein," an attack on industrialization.
1827	John Herschel proposes contact lenses.
1835	Natural gas is used for cooking.
1848	Karl Marx and Friedrich Engels predict the end of capitalism in *Communist Manifesto*.
1850	Australia's James Harrison designs ice-making machine.
1873	Color photographs are devised.
1879	Thomas Edison patents electric light bulb, one of his 1,093 patents.
1882	The first electric iron is patented.
1883	Britain's Francis Galton develops the questionnaire.
1885	Karl Friedrich Benz invents first operable auto with internal combustion engine.
1886	American housewife Josephine Corcoran patents first dishwashing machine.
1889	Brassiere is invented in Paris.
1894	Italian Gugliemo Marconi builds first radio equipment.
1903	Orville Wright becomes first man to fly in an airplane, traveling 120 feet in 12 seconds as his brother Wilbur watches.
1907	Britain urged to adopt daylight saving time to conserve fuel and provide more hours to train soldiers.
1910	French hairdresser devises the permanent wave.
1936	John Maynard Keynes publishes "The General Theory of Employment, Interest and

		1957	Space race begins with Soviet Union's launch of Sputnik.
	Money," advises governments to increase money supply to overcome Depression.	1977	American Ann Moore patents Snugli baby carrier, based on slings she saw African women use.
1946	Former civil engineer Louis Reard designs bikini.		
1947	Transistor invented by three physicists at Bell Laboratories, enabling the miniaturization of complex circuitry and the development of microchips.	1980	U.S. Supreme Court rules that "live human-made microorganism is patentable," creating biotech industry.
1949	George Orwell writes "1984," asserting technology is instrument of tyranny.	1983	Internet created as a network connecting computers, mostly for university academics to communicate and exchange information.
1949	Simone de Beauvoir writes "The Second Sex," inspiring feminist movement.	1991	"Leadership Secrets of Attila the Hun," by Wess Roberts becomes a bestseller.
1951	Britain's J. Lyons & Co. Uses world's first business calculator to calculate payrolls and optimum blends of tea.	1997	Scottish researchers clone a sheep.

Source: *The Wall Street Journal* (1999), January 11, p. R14.

7.2 Measuring Technological Change

Robert Solow used his growth model to design a clever way to directly measure technological change. This section details Solow's convenient measure, which you were already introduced to in Chapter 5 when we discussed East Asian economic growth.

7.2.1 The sources of growth equation

Solow's popular procedure for measuring technological change starts with the production function and compares the growth of inputs with the growth of output. Then, if output grows faster than a weighted average of inputs, the differential is assumed to represent the portion of output growth due to an improvement in technology.

Specifically, it is common to assume that the production function takes a convenient functional form known as the Cobb-Douglas equation (detailed in the Appendix of Chapter 5):

$$Y = AK^{\alpha} L^{1-\alpha} \tag{7.2}$$

The variables Y, K, and L in (7.2) represent output, the capital stock, and the labor force, respectively. The constant A is assumed to represent the level of technology. Without getting into too much mathematical detail here, we should point out that if we assume that $0 < \alpha < 1$, then the exponents α and $1 - \alpha$ add up to one even though each individual exponent is less than one. This ends up ensuring that the Cobb-Douglas production function exhibits constant returns to scale and decreasing returns to any single factor. The variable A is not the same as the "labor-augmenting" technology that we assumed earlier in equation (5.14) in Chapter 5. Rather, it is more accurate to think of A as "all-factor augmenting" technology, or more specifically, **total factor productivity (TFP)**. TFP represents the efficiency with which the entire production function transforms the whole set of physical factors of production into final output. It depends on many things, including the stock of human knowledge, the efficiency with which economic, political, and social institutions encourage productive activity and effort, and the management skills of producers and entrepreneurs. In short, A is a broad, all-inclusive definition of technology.

Equation (7.2) leads to a very convenient method for calculating the rate of technological change in the economy. First, we restate equation (7.2) in a more convenient form by making use of two mathematical rules. One is that the growth rate of the product of two variables is the sum of the growth rates of each variable. In terms of the growth notation we have been using, $g_{(A+B)} = g_A + g_B$. The other rule is that the growth rate of y^x is equal to x times the growth rate of y, or $x \cdot g_y$. Applying these mathematical rules to equation (7.2) gives us:

$$g_Y = g_A + \alpha g_K + (1-\alpha)g_L \qquad (7.3)$$

Equation (7.3) is usually called a **sources of growth equation** because it neatly decomposes the rate of growth of real output into the sum of (1) a weighted average of the growth rates of the productive factors plus (2) the rate of growth of total factor productivity. Solow assumed that the latter represented the change in the technology with which the economy converted inputs into output.

Rearranging equation (7.3), we arrive at a measure of the growth of A, or total factor productivity, our proxy for economy-wide technological change:

$$g_A = g_Y - [\alpha g_K + (1 - \alpha)g_L] \qquad (7.4)$$

That is, the rate of technological change, is simply the difference between the rate of growth of total output and the weighted average of the growth of factor inputs. The variable g_A is often referred to as the **Solow residual**; the term *residual* is appropriate because the estimate is the part of measured GDP growth that is not accounted for by the weighted average growth of the physical factors of production.

7.2.2 Estimates of the Solow residual

In his original article, Solow found the *residual* to be very large, which led him to conclude that the growth of U.S. GDP could not be explained very well by the growth of factor inputs. This finding, of course, confirmed what Solow determined with his logical model, namely, that in the long run, it takes technological change to generate economic growth.

There have been many more estimates of total factor productivity growth using Solow's methodology. Recall the estimates of total factor productivity for the largest developed economies and the four **Asian tigers** over the period 1960–1990. Those estimates showed that the growth of total factor productivity accounted for about half of the growth of real GDP in France, Germany, Italy, and the United Kingdom, and between a quarter and one-third of GDP growth in Hong Kong and Taiwan. Table 7.2 presents Victor Elías' estimates of total factor productivity for seven Latin American countries over the period 1950–1985. Elías was interested in showing how Latin American growth varied during the post-World War II period. His estimates are interesting because they suggest that not only does total factor productivity differ from country to country, but it varies widely from one decade to another in each country. In fact, the variation in total factor productivity from one decade to another is quite large. Mexico's growth in total factor productivity varied from 4.4 percent in the 1940s to −2.4 percent in the early 1980s. With the economy's overall technology effectively becoming less efficient, it is no wonder the growth of Mexican real per capita GDP was negative in the 1980s.

Table 7.2 Total Factor Productivity Growth — Latin America

Years	Argentina	Brazil	Chile	Mexico	Peru
1940–50	3.1%	n.a.	1.9%	4.4%	0.5%
1950–60	0.8	3.6	0.7	1.0	−2.6
1960–70	0.2	1.4	1.3	1.2	1.0
1970–80	−0.3	1.1	1.0	0.1	−0.5
1980–85	−2.9	−1.0	−2.7	−2.4	−2.6

Source: Victor J. Elías (1992).

7.2.3 Inaccuracies in measuring inputs and output

Because total factor productivity is measured as a residual, its estimates are only as good as the data on inputs and output. Good data are not always available, and variations in the methods to proxy the missing data result in many differences in published estimates of total factor productivity. The factor shares α and $1-\alpha$ are normally calculated from national income data. The growth of output is usually represented by the growth of real GDP. The number of workers should be adjusted for human capital (education, age, experience, etc.), hours worked, and unemployment in order to accurately capture the true input of human capital. Human capital should be included as a separate factor of production; by omitting it, the residual between output and inputs is too large.

Table 7.3 Total Factor Productivity Growth — Mexico

Years	Elías	Maddison & Assoc.	Fuess and Van den Berg	Growth of Real GDP per Capita
1950–60	1.0	3.2	-	6.05
1960–70	1.2	2.5	2.12	7.03
1970–80	0.1	1.2	−0.97	9.83
1980–85	−2.4	−0.5	−2.62	1.66

Sources: Victor J. Elías (1992); Scott M. Fuess, Jr. and Hendrik Van den Berg (1997); Angus Maddison and Associates (1992; and Instituto Nacional de Estadística, Geografía e Informática (1994), Part I, pp. 401–403.

The failure to adjust the labor data can severely bias estimates of total factor productivity. In Table 7.3, for example, there are three different measures of total factor productivity growth for Mexico. Note, specifically, the differences between the total factor productivity growth estimates for Mexico by Victor Elías, who adjusts his measure of total labor for changes in human capital, and those calculated in a study by Angus Maddison and Associates, who use simple numbers of workers without adjustments for human capital. Because the level of education has been improving in Mexico, the human capital-enhanced labor force has grown more rapidly than the simple number of workers. Elías is left with smaller residuals because he expands the labor force by a factor representing the level of education.

Data on capital stocks may be even less accurate than labor force data. Data on capital stocks are published on a regular basis only for some developed economies, and that data is of questionable accuracy. Researchers therefore commonly proxy the capital stock by the ratio of investment to GDP, but because such a measure ignores depreciation and the intensity with which capital is used, it is not a very accurate measure of the productive stock of capital. Clearly, most capital wears out over time, and if we simply added investment each period we would soon end up with a gross overestimate of the stock of capital actually in use. Because there is little or no information on capital stocks, most researchers have used the **perpetual inventory method** to produce estimates of capital stocks for developing economies.[6] This method estimates the stock of capital by adding new investment each period and subtracting from the capital that portion estimated to have depreciated. Accurate information on actual depreciation simply does not exist, not even in the most

---

[6] See, for example, the estimates for Latin America by Andre Hofman (1992).

advanced developed economies. Depreciation is often simply assumed to be a nice round number like 5 percent.

Unfortunately, even accurate measures of the amount of capital that is scrapped each year would still not give us an accurate picture of the true productive stock of capital. We also need to know how intensively the capital stock is used. For example, a bus company usually operates a varied fleet of buses, some new and some old. The older buses use more fuel, and they require more maintenance; hence, they are used only during peak hours and special events. The older buses run perhaps just two hours per day, while the newer buses operate throughout the day. The electric power industry provides another example of varying intensities of use of capital equipment. The most efficient power plants are used for twenty-four hours, while the older, less efficient plants are operated only during the peak hours. Hence, even if we accurately count all the capital equipment in the economy, the variable intensities with which different parts of the capital stock are used still prevent us from gaining an accurate measure of the true productive stock of capital.

The calculation of the Solow residual also requires an accurate measure of output growth. But, as discussed in earlier chapters, common measures of output growth, such as gross domestic product (GDP), are not accurate measures of true output. GDP does not include household activity, even if such activity produces welfare-enhancing output. Nor does GDP capture all illegal and "informal" activity, which can be quite substantial in many developing economies.

In Scott Fuess and Hendrik Van den Berg (1997), we sought more accurate estimates of total factor productivity growth in Mexico by adjusting output, capital stocks, and labor for estimated informal and household activity. Table 7.3 presents these estimates. Note how our estimates differ from those of both Elías and Maddison and Associates. The three sets of total factor productivity growth estimates agree on the trends, namely that Mexico's total factor productivity declined at an alarming rate in the second half of the 1900s, but the exact estimates differ quite a bit.

7.2.4 Sustainable technological progress

Another shortcoming of the Solow residual is its failure to capture the effects of factor use and output growth of the natural environment. Effectively, GDP measures only activity in the economic sphere and ignores changes in the natural environment. Economists do not normally put nature's services in the production function as we did in the last chapter, nor do they account for all negative environmental externalities of production when they measure GDP. Therefore, if the use of natural resources and nature's services are not included among the weighted average of inputs in equation (7.4) and GDP overstates true production because the increasingly rapid depletion of natural resources is not factored in, then the Solow residual will overstate the true rate of technological change.

Estimates such as those by Wackernagel *et al.* (2002) and World Wildlife Fund (2008) showing that humanity's exploitation of natural resources now exceeds the earth's capacity to replenish its renewable resources suggests that economists have indeed been overstating economic growth and technological change. In short, true output has not grown as fast as GDP suggests, and the growth of productive inputs has been faster than the traditional measures of capital and labor suggest. Herman Daly (1998) convincingly argues that the last 200 years' technological change is grossly overstated: economic growth has depended much more on the exploitation of nature's services and resources and less on technological advances than standard growth accounting lets on.

In sum, estimates of technological change are not very accurate. The common practice of using the sources of growth equation to estimate the Solow residual provides at best a suggestive indicator of the trend in technological change. The difficulty in measuring technological change constitutes a huge problem in development economics given the importance of technology for economic development.

7.3 Common Characteristics of Technological Change

Technological change is a shift in ideas, products, methods, systems, processes, designs, theories, etc. that change the way humans go about performing specific tasks, operating their economies, organizing their social systems, or interacting with nature. However, despite the diversity of what we call technology, a number of characteristics are common to many or even most types of technological change. This section describes some of the widely observed characteristics of technology that should probably be reflected in models of technological change.

7.3.1 The S-curve of technology diffusion

A frequently observed characteristic of technological change is that it tends to occur continuously in a long series of small steps. For example, in the early stages of the development of agriculture, societies continued to gather and hunt. Only gradually did human societies switch entirely to the cultivation of the land. And, despite the thousands of years that have passed, hunting and gathering are still in some form undertaken today.

The introduction of new technologies seems to often follow an **S-curve** like the one in Figure 7.2. New ideas spread slowly at first, then are applied more quickly, but it takes a long time for a new technology to win over the last potential users and reach full 100 percent acceptance. The S-curve became popular in the early 1950s after Bruce Ryan and Neal Gross (1943), two sociologists who worked at the Iowa Agricultural Experiment Station, found an S-pattern in the adoption of new hybrid corn by farmers in Iowa. The economists Svi Griliches (1957, 1958) later confirmed the S-curve pattern for the adoption of hybrid seed corn and Edwin Mansfield (1961) found S-curves for the diffusion of new technologies across individual firms as well as across industries.

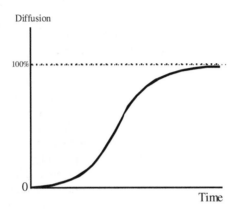

Figure 7.2 The S-Curve

Many explanations for the observed S-curve pattern have been offered. There is wide agreement that before any choices about acquiring new technology can be made, resources must be expended to understand and evaluate the technologies available. This takes time and involves a cost. The introduction of new technologies also requires the acquisition of new plants and equipment. Hence, firms are often reluctant to abandon still serviceable manufacturing plants using older technologies. The uncertainty of technological change also may lead potential users of technology to wait for further developments before they make the costly jump to a new path of technology. Psychological and cultural resistance to change no doubt also play a role.

An example of the S-curve pattern for technology adoption is the long period between the discovery of electricity and its major economic impact. A generator and electric lights were demonstrated in 1876 at Philadelphia's Centennial Exposition. It took six years before Thomas Edison opened the first commercial generator to power electric lights in the Wall Street district of New York. And, it was not until the turn of the century that electricity was readily available in all United States cities and towns. Only in the 1930s, 60 years later, did the Rural Electrification Act provide the financing to bring electric power to all rural areas of the U.S. Still, rural areas in many countries of the world lack electric power today. Similarly, the patent for the internal combustion engine was filed in 1877. But it was not until the late 1920s, fifty years later, that half of all households in the richest country of the world, the United States, owned an automobile. Today, a very small percentage of households in the United States still does not have an automobile. However, there are still many countries in the world where almost no one owns an automobile. The birth of the computer is often set in the late 1940s, when Bell Laboratories invented the first semiconductor, the transistor, and IBM built its Selective Sequence Electronic Calculator. It took about fifty years for half the homes in the United States to have a computer.

Today, a small percentage of households still does not have a computer. Figure 7.3 shows S-curves for a number of new products. While these examples all suggest that the spread of technology is far from quick, there is evidence suggesting that the process has gradually accelerated over time. It took millennia for farming and animal husbandry to replace hunting and gathering, but the more recent development of electricity has reached most corners of the world in about a century. More recently, Diego Comin and Bert Hobijn (2003), studied the diffusion of twenty different technologies across 23 countries over the period 1788–2001, and they found that the speed of diffusion has accelerated sharply since World War II. They also concluded that human capital and a country's social and economic institutions determine the rate of diffusion. Their findings also confirm that it still takes a considerable amount of time for technology to shift to a new location or industry.

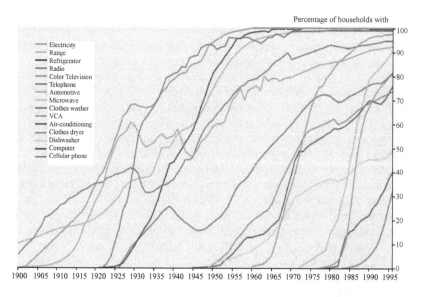

Figure 7.3 Further Examples of the S-Curve
(From The Federal Reserve Bank of Dallas, 1998)

7.3.2 *The slow application of electricity in manufacturing*

The factory system is one of the major technological developments of the past 1,000 years, and it completely changed the way economies went about producing goods.   After its initial development in the eighteenth century, however, the efficiency of factories improved very slowly during most of the 1800s. Then, with the introduction of electric motors in the late 1800s, factory production suddenly began to achieve large efficiency gains as factories began replacing steam power with electric power.

The earliest factories operated mostly on water power, which is why so many early factories were situated along rivers. But gradually the steam engine was used more often to power machinery. Both of these sources of power, the water wheel or the steam engine, meant that individual machines had to be linked to the single power source by large shafts. Figure 7.4 illustrates how individual machines were connected by large belts to a shaft in the ceiling. All machines on the factory floor turned when the shaft turned, whether they were being used or not. If one of the belts broke, which occurred frequently given the materials of the time, the entire factory came to a halt. The systems were also very dangerous because none of the machines could be stopped individually.

The first electric motors were relatively large and were designed to simply replace water wheels or steam engines. The picture of the belt system in Figure 7.4, taken in 1923, was in fact being driven by a large electric motor. The electric motor was used because it was easier to operate and more reliable than water power or steam power, but it still operated the same system of shafts and belts because it was costly to change the entire design of the factory. With time, industrial engineers came to see that machines driven by their own motors would provide more flexibility than centralized power systems. Electric motors could be made in various sizes, speeds, and gear ratios to cater to the needs of each individual part of the production process. They could also be adjusted to the talent of the operator, thus making factory machinery much safer. But the shift to individual motors was slow. In 1900, only 3 percent of U.S. factories used machines driven by individual electric motors controlled by individual machine operators. Even by 1920, fewer than one-third of U.S. factories had individually-controlled electric machines.

John Wert, a manager at the Maytag Company of Newton, Iowa in 1921, recalled that when electric motors were introduced "people said, 'They won't last, belt driven is better.'"[7] But, eventually electric motors proved to be exceptionally durable, and factories began to design production around machines powered by individual electric motors. The efficiency of factories improved rapidly with the new technology. At Mr. Wert's Maytag Company,

---

[7] As quoted in Bob Davis and David Wessel (1998), "At Dawn of Electricity, Feuds and Hype," *Wall Street Journal*, April 6, p. A17.

Figure 7.4 A Photo of The Belt-Driven Maytag Factory, Newton Iowa, 1923
(Photo: Courtesy of Maytag)

the productivity of workers producing washing machines improved by 48 percent after the introduction of individually-driven electric machines in the Newton factory in 1926. The economic historian Paul David estimates that at least half of the 5 percent annual productivity gains in U.S. industry in the 1920s were due to the rapid increase in applying electric power. By 1929, over half of all factories had converted as competition forced manufacturers to match the gains in efficiency of their competitors. According to David, "It takes decades for powerful innovations to boost an economy, but the delayed payoff can be immense."[8]

7.3.3 Technological change is not always technological progress

The example of the spread of electric power actually gives us only a partial view of that new technology. The discussion above focused only on how electric power was applied by the manufacturing industry. The spread of electric power was a much broader process, of course. One of the S-curves in Figure 7.3 represents the spread of electric power in general, and a number of the other S-curves in Figure 7.3 represent the adoption of home appliances that run on electricity, such as the radio, refrigerator, electric washer, and other home appliances. We could have also included the use of electricity for lighting, communications, and transportation. All of these technological changes are often assumed to represent improvements in human well-being. But what about

---

[8] As quoted in Davis and Wessel (1998), op. cit.

the power plants that produce the electricity that runs all the machines and home appliances?

Coal, oil, natural gas, nuclear, and hydro power are the most often used sources of power for electricity generation. Of these four sources, three emit carbon into the atmosphere. Nuclear power can contaminate wide areas, as the meltdowns in Chernobyl and Fukushima have demonstrated, and the problem of storage of spent nuclear fuel has not yet been solved. Hydroelectric power requires the construction of dams and other systems to divert water from its natural rivers to large lakes that flood large areas. In short, electricity generation alters the natural environment. The damage such power plants do to the environment must be seen as part of the broad range of technological changes brought about by the development of electricity and the application of electric power in factories, homes, and throughout human society.

In terms of the overall production function, there is little doubt that the development of electric power has enhanced both labor and physical capital. Better lighting, communications, air conditioning, individually controlled machinery, all of these things have made labor more productive. The assembly line, office equipment, teaching aids, and transportation are all more efficient because of electric power. But, the carbon emissions of electric power plants are contributing to global warming, which threatens to cause climate changes that will diminish the services of nature that humans have come to depend on. Hence, in the general production function $Y = f(L \cdot E_L, K \cdot E_K, S \cdot E_S)$, the technology levels E_L and E_K have improved or progressed, but the services of nature have not been augmented. If expectations about GHG emissions prove correct and the earth experiences substantial climate change, then E_S will decline. Such a decline in the effective supply of nature's services would lower the marginal products of the effective stocks of labor and capital and, possibly, more than offset the gains that the technological change of electric power provided by augmenting labor and capital.

7.3.4 The geographic diffusion of technology is also slow

Regional economists have found evidence showing that the application of new technologies are slow to spread geographically. The concentration of information technology firms in Silicon Valley, financial firms in London, and the automobile industry in Detroit are examples of how the application of new technologies tends to *agglomerate* close to where they were initially developed. Edward Glaeser *et al.* (1991) offered a simple explanation for agglomeration: "... intellectual breakthroughs must cross hallways and streets more easily than oceans and continents."

A century ago, the microeconomist Alfred Marshall devoted an entire chapter of his popular economics textbook to the "Concentration of Specialized Industries in Particular Localities." Marshall (1920) attributed concentration to three factors: (1) the availability of specialized labor, (2) the development of specialized suppliers of intermediate goods and services, and (3) the flows of technology between the industries. More recently, economists from the field of regional economics have hypothesized models that explain the development of cities, urban concentration, and the differences in the economic development across regions of a country. Richard Florida (2005) writes:

> Ideas flow more freely, are honed more sharply, and can be put into practice more quickly when large numbers of innovators, implementers, and financial backers are in constant contact with one another, both in and out of the office. Creative people cluster not simply because they like to be around one another or they prefer cosmopolitan centers with lots of amenities, though both those things count. They and their companies also cluster because of the powerful productivity advantages, economics of scale, and knowledge spillovers such density brings.[9]

We already know, of course, that human production as measured by GDP is much more geographically concentrated in the high-income countries than the overall human population, which is dispersed across rich and poor countries. Florida (2005) uses data on copyrights, patents, and scientific citations to show that creative and innovative activity is still much more concentrated than human production of goods and services. In fact, data on the residences of the most often cited scientists and scholars suggests that innovation and creativity occurs not just in a very small number of countries, but in a small number of cities within those countries. Concludes Florida (2005, p. 50): "As far as global innovation is concerned, perhaps a few dozen places worldwide really compete at the cutting edge." China and India, countries that are often described as *emerging economies*, barely register on Florida's map of innovation. This is not to say that Chinese and Indians are not creative. To the contrary, AnnaLee Saxenian (2002) finds that Chinese and Indian entrepreneurs started over one-third of new firms in Silicon Valley, the U.S. center of the information technology revolution. But that is precisely Florida's point: creative and innovative people tend to concentrate in certain geographic regions. In the language of regional economics, creative activity tends to agglomerate.

The **geographic agglomeration** of innovative activities further explains the S-curve. If it takes more time for new ideas to be applied in regions distant from where the ideas were first developed than in nearby regions, then for the world as a whole an S-curve pattern will accurately describe the global diffusion of technology. Recall from above that the spread of electricity and automobiles has been much slower across all countries of the world than within the United States, where these products originated.

---

[9] Richard Florida (2005), "The World Is Spiky," *Atlantic Monthly*, October, p. 50.

7.3.5 Technological change as a combinatoric process

New knowledge is built on current knowledge by *combining* existing ideas into new ideas. According to Martin Weitzman (1996, p. 12): "An abstract case could be made that *all* innovations, being expressions of human imagination, are in a sense combinatoric." The observation that the creation of new knowledge is a **combinatoric process** is very important for our understanding of technological change. The fact that each addition to human technology is derived from earlier technologies means the dynamic process of technological change follows certain patterns. For one thing, a combinatoric process can be explosive.

Table 7.4 shows a simple example of a combinatoric process of technological change. The example assumes that in each successive period of time, the number of new ideas created is equal to the number of all possible combinations of pairs of ideas created in the previous period. Under these assumptions, when the initial stock of knowledge in an economy consists of, say, four ideas, numbered 1 through 4 in Table 7.4, all the possible combinations of the initial four ideas result in six new ideas. Thus, after one period of innovation, this combinatoric process has expanded four ideas into six new ideas, which implies a total stock of knowledge equal to 10 ideas, an increase of 150 percent over the previous stock of four ideas. In the third round of innovation, the combinatoric process will increase the 6 new ideas A through F into 15 even newer ideas and an accumulation of 25 ideas in total. In the fourth round, the previous period's 15 new ideas are combined into 105 new ideas. In the fifth period, there are 5,460 combinations of the previous period's 105 new ideas. Of course, if combinations between old ideas and new ideas are also possible in each period, then the number of ideas would have grown even faster. In this case, period three would be able to combine 10 ideas, not the 6 shown in Table 7.4, for example. The explosive nature of a combinatoric process suggests that technological change is likely to accelerate over time.

History suggests that, despite its potentially explosive nature, technological change often slows down. Sometimes it stops altogether, and it can even turn negative. Knowledge can be forgotten or lost if resources are not explicitly employed to teach each successive generation the knowledge accumulated by earlier generations. Also, not all combinations of previous ideas produce useful new ideas. Finally, societies must maintain appropriate conditions that permit the combinatoric process to work. For example, vested interests must not be allowed to prevent new ideas from being applied, or people with different ideas must be encouraged, not socially and politically intimidated as different people often are. Discouragement of creativity by vested interests, social conservatives, and various forms of hierarchical oppression have been serious barriers to technological change throughout history. Despite these various concerns, it remains clear that, all other things equal, the greater the stock of knowledge,

Table 7.4 A Combinatoric Growth Process[1]

(new idea = a combination of two old ideas)

			New Ideas	Accumulated Ideas	Percentage Growth
Period 1	Begin with		4	4	
Period 2	$4!/(2! \cdot 2!)$	=	6	10	150%
Period 3	$6!/(4! \cdot 2!)$	=	15	25	150%
Period 4	$15!/(13! \cdot 2!)$	=	105	130	420%
Period 5	$105!/(103! \cdot 2!)$	=	5,460	5,590	4,200%

Period 1	Period 2		Period 3		
1	1,2 = A	2,3 = D	A,B	B,C	C,E
2	1,3 = B	2,4 = E	A,C	B,D	C,F
3	1,4 = C	3,4 = F	A,D	B,E	D,E
4			A,E	B,F	D,F
			A,F	C,D	E,F

[1] The number of combinations for n ideas taken r at a time is $n!/[(n-r)! \cdot r!]$; we take n as the number of ideas generated in the previous period and combine them 2 at a time, so r = 2. The symbol "!" represents a product of descending integers beginning with the number preceding the !, e.g., 5! = $5 \cdot 4 \cdot 3 \cdot 2 \cdot 1 = 120$.

the more combinations are possible. All other things equal, technological change should be more easily sustained as more knowledge is acquired.

7.3.6 Technological change can be path dependent

The combinatoric nature of knowledge helps to explain why technological change often seems to be a **path dependent** process in which each new step follows previous steps. Path-dependency implies that technologies depend on the level of technology already accumulated. Path dependency also means even momentous technological advances, such as the development of agriculture, the wheel, the factory system, or electricity, were just steps between previously acquired knowledge, experiments, and technological change and subsequent discoveries and inventions.

The gradual, combinatoric nature of technological change is evidenced by the fact that there is some dispute over who exactly is responsible for many of humanity's greatest discoveries and inventions. It is common knowledge that Alexander Graham Bell finalized the design for his successful telephone while sitting on a log over the Grand River near his parents' house in Brantford, Ontario, mulling over what he had up to that point discovered about sound. Yet, the same day that Alexander Graham Bell filed a patent application for the telephone, another inventor named Elisha Gray also filed a similar application. Malcolm Gladwell (2008, p. 56) writes about the frequency of **simultaneous discovery**:

In order to get one of the greatest inventions of the modern age... we thought we needed the solitary genius. But if Alexander Graham Bell had fallen into the Grand River and drowned that day back in Brantford, the world would still have had the telephone, the only difference being that the telephone company would have been nicknamed Ma Gray, not Ma Bell.[10]

Similarly, it is not entirely clear whether the Wright brothers were really the first ones to fly. Brazilians pride themselves on what they accept as the undisputed fact that their compatriot, Alberto Santos Dumont, was the first to fly a heavier-than-air craft entirely on its own power. Both the Wright brothers and Santos Dumont were working on aircraft, and while the Wright brothers were the first to lift off the ground, they used a catapult to start their aircraft while Santos Dumont took off on wheels under its own power. Different definitions of what constituted self-powered flight determine who was the first to fly.

Charles Darwin and Alfred Russel Wallace are both credited with discovering evolution. And there were four independent discoveries of sunspots in 1611 by Galileo in Italy, Scheiner in Germany, Fabricius in Holland, and Harriott in England. Newton and Leibnitz both discovered calculus. In economics, Roy Harrod and Evsey Domar both derived the identical growth model from John Maynard Keynes' prominent macroeconomic model published less than a decade earlier. These, and many other simultaneous discoveries effectively confirm that technological progress is a path dependent, step-by-step process. It is difficult to attribute even one of the steps to any particular person because so many people are walking along the same path.

We earlier described the resistance to changing from belt-driven to motor-driven machinery in U.S. industry. Previous technologies are often difficult to abandon. This resistance to change is not necessarily irrational, even though historical accounts sometimes suggest as much. The fact is that it is often costly to change methods, designs, and equipment. These factors suggest that there is a speed limit on the path of technological change.

An interesting example of how hard it is to change technology is the popular layout of the keys on your computer keyboard. The current layout is known as "QWERTY," in reference to the six keys at the upper left-hand side of the keyboard. The current layout was settled on, after considerable debate and experimentation, by early typewriter manufacturers. Early typewriters were unpowered, mechanical machines, and each key activated levers that pushed a reverse mold of a letter or symbol toward a roller that contained a sheet of paper. These levers obviously had to be activated in succession; if the typist hit two at once, they would get tangled and stuck near the point where they hit the paper. The layout of the key board was designed to minimize the likelihood of levers hitting each other even as experienced typists became able to type very fast.

---

[10] See also Matt Richtel (2008), "Edison... Wasn't He the Guy Who Invented Everything?," *New York Times*, March 30, on the confusion about who invented well-known products.

Those characters that were often typed in succession were placed some distance away from each other so mechanical collisions were less likely. But, today we have electronic keyboards, and the only criterion for a keyboard layout is the speed that the typist can hit the keys in succession. There is some dispute over whether the QWERTY design is indeed the most efficient for typing speed. Yet, no one has begun producing keyboards with another layout. Why not? People are used to it, and they have invested in learning the layout. If there is a gain in efficiency from an alternative layout, it would probably be very small at best. After several attempts at introducing allegedly more efficient layouts, no one is marketing an alternative keyboard today. Apparently, the fixed cost of retraining must be too great relative to what would, at best, be a very small long-run gain. The QWERTY layout was the best option when the typewriter was first developed, and, given all the costs and benefits, it remains the best option today. If we could start from scratch today, we might choose a different path. But technology never starts from scratch.

On a broader scale, the United States has been reluctant to adopt the metric system. China and Japan have no plans to change their cumbersome systems of writing. And people continue to speak their native languages, even though communications would be easier if we had just one language in the world. Ominously, the world today seems to be locked into technologies that require the use of fossil fuels that add to the greenhouse gases in the atmosphere. There are obvious alternative technologies available, but there are few incentives and high costs for someone to apply them. Most cars sold today still use an internal combustion engine fueled by gasoline. Most of our electric power plants use coal, the dirtiest fossil fuel in terms of greenhouse gas emissions. When this book was being written in 2011, there were several hundred new coal-fired power plants under construction throughout the world. It is costly to change paths and switch to using cleaner energy.

7.3.7 Technology is a nonrival good

One reason why we should not become too pessimistic about humanity's ability to generate new ideas and technologies in the future is that the production function of ideas and technology is different from the production function of most goods and services produced in an economy. Most conventional products are **rival goods**. An example of a rival good is a new coat: if one person wears it, someone else cannot wear that same coat. Only one person at a time can wear it. If another person wants a coat, she is going to have to make one, purchase one, or borrow one from someone who has an extra one. Ideas, technology, and knowledge, on the other hand, are at least partially **nonrival**. If one person comes up with an idea, develops a better procedure, designs a new method, or discovers some new bit of knowledge, another person can make use of the idea, procedure, method or knowledge without eliminating the innovator's or discoverer's use of their finding. Put more simply, we do not have to "reinvent the wheel" every time we need another wheel.

The nonrival nature of knowledge and technology means that the marginal cost of using a new idea or applying a particular new technology is very low or, sometimes, close to zero. This has the important implication that once a certain type of knowledge was available, competitive market forces would drive its price toward zero. But, at such a low price, why would anyone devote the effort, resources, and time to create new knowledge?

Even though they are nonrival and marginal applications are nearly costless, the price of the technology could be kept high if the technology is **excludable** in the sense that the creator of a new idea may be able to prevent people from using it. Excludability gives creators the power to limit supply and charge for the use of their ideas. **Patents** and **copyrights** are legal arrangements that give the creator of an idea, product, or process exclusive use for a given number of years. They effectively make *nonrival* ideas legally *excludable*. There are many other ways to exclude others from using a new idea. For example, the unique way that a new idea is incorporated into a product may give the innovator some market power with which to recoup the costs of innovation. It often also takes time for others to copy new ideas and apply them, especially more complex modern technologies. Some things may be impossible to copy exactly, such as the formula for Coca Cola. The Coca Cola Company opted to keep its formula secret rather than revealing its formula on gain a patent application.

From an overall welfare perspective, however, the issue of incentives for technology creation is not as simple as making technology excludable. It is probably true that, all other things equal, the excludability of ideas increases the incentive to produce new ideas and technologies. However, all other things are never equal. Because technological change is a combinatoric path-dependent process, excludability may reduce the number of potential combinations that future innovators can exploit. Excludability is thus a double-edged sword: It stimulates the quest for new knowledge by permitting the creators of knowledge to profit, but, by slowing the use of the innovation by others, it can stifle the creation of further knowledge. For this reason, patent laws usually limit the length of time that an exclusive patent remains in effect.

7.3.8 Paradigm shifts

The finding of an S-curve in the application of new technology suggests that technological change does not occur at a constant pace. Romer's meta-ideas suggests that some ideas are more powerful in stimulating further ideas than others. On the other hand, the combinatoric nature of technological change suggests a smooth continuous process. Evidence from science and industry shows that the growth of human knowledge and technology can follow a great variety of paths. Thomas Kuhn (1962) in fact suggested that science occasionally jumps to a completely new path.   Kuhn introduced the term **paradigm shift** into the literature.

The word **paradigm** is derived from the Greek word *paradeigma*, which means "pattern" or "example."   In his 1962 book *The Structure of Scientific Revolutions*, Thomas Kuhn defined a paradigm as a set of practices that define a scientific discipline.   Neoclassical economics serves as the dominant paradigm in mainstream economics today, for example.   According to Kuhn, the paradigm tells practitioners what they should observe and study, the types of questions that they should seek answers to, how they should go about answering those questions, and how they should interpret their findings.   Kuhn's placement of the paradigm at the center of the scientific process was very controversial, and his book started a major debate on how scientific knowledge is accumulated.

Thomas Kuhn (1962) argued that science did not progress according to the scientific method we detailed in Chapter 1 and that it was not a uniform process that generated a continuous stream of new ideas.   Rather, Kuhn described science as an episodic process consisting of periods of **normal science** interrupted by occasional spurts of **revolutionary science**.   Normal science consists of relatively routine activities that are closely controlled by the reigning paradigm that tells scientists, including social scientists like economists, how they should conduct their research and how they should frame their conclusions. As a practical example of how a paradigm influences research, most economics graduate programs are run by professors who instill in their students a specific culture that points them to what questions to ask, the methods with which to answer those questions, and how to present their answers.   Graduate programs often explicitly state their mission as teaching their students "to think like economists."   This phrase has become a code word for the willingness to adhere to the currently dominant Neoclassical School of economic thought.

Kuhn described how a scientific discipline's restrictive paradigm eventually causes some of its practitioners to run into **anomalies**, which are findings that do not conform to the paradigm's conclusions.   In economics, for example, the statistical finding that some of the countries that opened their borders to free trade did not grow faster, as neoclassical models of international trade suggest, is a clear anomaly.   Kuhn also described how disciplines usually ignore anomalies or find ways to explain them away.   Practitioners who insist that anomalies point out that another paradigm is called for are often marginalized and ignored, and most practitioners continue to ask and answer the questions that fall within the parameters of the dominant paradigm.   These mainstream scientists may believe they are objectively following the scientific method.   But, as the French sociologist Pierre Bourdieu (1990) argued, scientists are blinded by their culture, or in Kuhnian terms, their paradigm.   Bourdieu called for *reflexivity*, by which he meant that social scientists should reflect on their own field's culture so that they could overcome the restrictions it imposed on their work. Bourdieu effectively wanted to push scientists to look at the world outside the dominant paradigm.

Revolutionary science occurs when a critical mass of practitioners in a discipline deals with the anomalies that their paradigm-restricted research cannot explain by developing an alternative paradigm that does explain the anomalies. When the new paradigm becomes the accepted culture in the discipline, a paradigm shift is said to have occurred. At that point, textbooks are rewritten and the history of thought is revised to position the new paradigm as the logical result of objective researchers following the scientific method. Kuhn claimed, however, that the sharp discontinuous break between paradigms often results in a new paradigm being no more accurate or fruitful for the scientific advancement of knowledge than the older paradigm.

Giovanni Dosi (1982) applied Kuhn's thinking to the economic sphere:

> ... changes in the economic environment are a permanent feature of the system: those changes often simply stimulate technical progress... *along* one technological trajectory. Again in parallel with epistemology we can call it the "normal" technological activity. "Extraordinary" technological attempts (related to the search for new technological directions) emerge either in relation to new opportunities opened-up by scientific developments or to the increasing difficulty in going forward on a given technological direction (for technological or economic reasons or both.)[11]

Kuhn's vision of the evolution of scientific knowledge conflicted with the common belief that the scientific method generates the continuous growth of knowledge that continually improves our understanding of the economic, social, and natural spheres of human existence. Keep Kuhn's ideas in mind when you read about Schumpeter's model of technological change in the next chapter.

7.3.9 Summarizing the characteristics of technology

Now, having discussed the characteristics of technology, we can begin examining the models that explain technological change. Before proceeding, let's review the main characteristics of technology and technological change:

- Technology is a complex and varied set of ideas, knowledge, institutions, procedures, methods, and organizational forms.

- Technology is advanced by a variety of innovative activities ranging from highly organized scientific research to casual tinkering.

---

[11] Giovanni Dosi (1982), p. 157.

- Technology is difficult to measure and quantify because it consists of ideas and knowledge derived from a great variety of innovative activities.

- Technology is at least partially *nonrival*, and it is not completely *excludable*.

- Technological change is a *combinatoric* process that builds on earlier ideas.

- Because new ideas depend on accumulated knowledge, technological change is likely to be a *path-dependent* process.

- But, technology's time path does not have a constant slope; it can speed up and slow down.

- Technological change may be subject to *paradigm shifts* that interrupt *normal scientific activity* guided by a dominant paradigm.

- Paradigms facilitate ordinary science, but they can delay *revolutionary science*; the latter generates *meta-ideas*.

These characteristics of technology have been incorporated into the models of technological change that economists have built over the past two decades. The next section and the entire next chapter examine some of these new models.

7.4 Technological Change As An Externality: Learning By Doing

Early attempts at building models of technological change tried to explain the upward shifts of the production function as an **externality**, or an incidental by-product, of some other variable in the model. A favored approach was to hypothesize that new technologies appeared as an externality to production. These models are often called **learning by doing models**. By doing their job, people gradually learn and discover ways to work more efficiently. Thus, technological change is an unintended by-product, or externality, of production.

The externality approach is convenient because it permits us to endogenize technological change without abandoning the orthodox and static neoclassical model of production and its convenient assumption of perfect competition. The second and now more popular approach in mainstream neoclassical economics is to model technological change as the result of intentional research and development activities that require the application of scarce and costly resources. The second approach requires that the assumption of a perfectly competitive market be dropped. If we model innovation as a process that uses scarce resources and incurs real costs, then innovation becomes a type of investment that incurs up-front costs in order to generate uncertain future returns. To cover these costs, there must be long-run excess income over and above the costs of production. But excess profits do not occur in neoclassical economics' hypothesized competitive markets.

It is more difficult to model imperfectly competitive markets that permit the generation of profits. We devote the entire next chapter to models of intentional and costly innovative activities, and we discuss the motivations for such activities. In the remainder of this chapter, however, we focus on the attempts to model technological change as an inadvertent by-product of human economic activities such as production. These **externalities models** permitted neoclassical economists to maintain the assumption of perfect competition in models that provided logical explanations for technological change.

7.4.1 Learning by doing and technological change

Adam Smith (1776 [1976], pp. 13–14) suggested that one of the benefits of the division of labor is that people learn to work more efficiently when they focus on one or just a few tasks:

> Men are much more likely to discover easier and readier methods of attaining any object, when the whole attention of their minds is directed towards the single object, as is more likely to occur with increased specialization.

In more modern terminology, specialization increases the amount of learning by doing. In its simplest form, this concept essentially says that the more people work at something, the more efficient they become at doing their task. This is a case of human capital accumulation. This is why employers usually prefer experienced workers over novices. People who specialize and work at something for a long time may better understand the system in which they work, and they may be more likely to generate ideas that increase efficiency for everyone. That is, they not only become more efficient themselves, but they come up with new production methods, better product designs, new product ideas, and other forms of technology that is of use to other workers, firms, and the economy in general. For example, Douglas Irwin and Peter Klenow (1994) studied the extent of learning by doing in the semiconductor industry, an industry often distinguished for its rapid cost declines. They found that for dynamic random access memory semiconductors (DRAMS) costs had declined by 16 to 24 percent for each doubling of output. Similar percentage declines in costs have been found in many industries, and its graphical representation has a well-known name: the **learning curve**. A general version of the learning curve is given in Figure 7.5, which relates per unit costs of production of a

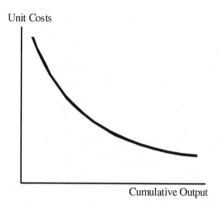

Figure 7.5 The Learning Curve

certain product to its cumulative production. Most studies have found that costs decline proportionately to their levels, so in absolute terms they fall at a declining rate.

The learning by doing process is usually described in such a way that it seems to generate technological change at no cost to the economy. Some observers concluded that it was the gaining of experience in production that led to declines in per unit costs. Economists liked this narrative because it permitted them to model technological change under traditional neoclassical assumptions of competitive markets that prevented excess profits and industrial concentration. This was too easy to be true, however. Detailed studies of suspected cases of learning by doing provided a more accurate picture of innovation.

7.4.2 The Liberty Ship program

Learning by doing models were initially inspired by studies of World War II production of military equipment. During the war, the United States quickly organized the large scale production of armaments and war equipment. Soon after the United States entered the war at the end of 1941, aircraft, ships, and tanks rolled out of factories at rates never before seen in the world. These factories were usually converted from producing consumer and other standard industrial products. The huge production levels have provided economists with an excellent opportunity to document learning by doing over a relatively short period of time. Also, very detailed data on the production were available because the government's cost-plus contracts with the privately-owned factories required detailed records of costs. The data became public after the war and provided economists with a unique opportunity to study mass production costs.

Figure 7.6 One of two preserved Liberty Ships, the SS John M. Brown.
(Photo by Project Liberty Ship, downloaded from Wikipedia)

One of the most interesting cases was the production of Liberty ships, the well-known mid-sized cargo ships that were the mainstay of the United States merchant marine fleet that supplied U.S. forces overseas during World War II. Begun in 1941, the program eventually involved 16 shipyards that built 2,580 ships of the exact same design in less than four years. Never before had ships of a single design been produced in such quantities over such a short period.

The shipyards that built the Liberty ships used a modular approach to shipbuilding, constructing different parts of each ship in different areas of the shipyard and then hauling the finished portions of the ship to the dry dock, where they were fitted onto the keel. Instead of using rivets to attach the shell plates, all parts were welded together. Specialization of tasks was taken to levels never before experienced in shipbuilding. The results were astounding, and toward the end of World War II some yards were completing each ship in less than thirty days. Leonard Rapping's (1965) well-known study of the Liberty Ship program found that the number of hours of labor required per ship fell by 12 to 24 percent for each doubling of output, on average. Such increases in labor productivity implied an average annual increase in labor productivity of 40 percent over the four years of the program. Apparently, with each additional ship produced, workers and managers learned to do things more efficiently. The Liberty Ship study was also enhanced by similar findings in other World War II defense industries. In an equally famous study, Alan Alchian (1963) took data from 22 aircraft factories during World War II and derived a learning curve nearly identical to Rapping's.

7.4.3 How is learning related to doing?

More recent studies using production data have qualified the early research on learning by doing. Peter Thompson (2003) reexamined the data on the Liberty Ship program that Rapping (1965) had studied, and he noticed from the detailed government records that production methods became substantially more capital intensive over time. This finding implies that there was a deliberate change in production technology as Liberty Ship production took place. Thompson reasoned that the innovation and investment was motivated by explicit incentives in the government contracts, which included bonus payments when shipbuilders accelerated output, improved quality, or lowered costs. When he includes the effects of the newly-developed equipment and the switch to more capital-intensive technologies into the analysis, he finds his adjustment reduces the estimated size of the unexplained learning effect by fifty percent. Thompson also detailed how the whole production process became increasingly modular over time, and he noticed from the data that the welding process became less and less labor intensive as automated welding equipment was gradually installed over the 1942–1945 period. Thompson thus concluded that the efficiency gains in the Liberty Ship program were to a substantial degree the result of intentional efforts to raise productivity. Only a portion of the efficiency gains could have been the result of unintended externalities from learning by doing.

In yet another study of the aircraft industry, Lanier Benkard (1999) concludes that some, but not all, learning carries over from one generation of aircraft to another. Benkard argues that *learning* can only be accurately explained if *forgetting* is included in the model. As time passes, accumulated learning "depreciates." Thus, a process of *learning by doing and forgetting* may be a more accurate description of efficiency gains in the aircraft industry. Kazuhiro Mishima (1999) re-examined the records at one of the 22 World War II B-17 factories that Alan Alchian (1963) had studied after the war, the Boeing Plant No. 2 in Seattle, Washington. He found that (p. 175):

> The agent of learning is the core managers of control functions in the plant, that is, those who *coordinate* various aspects of the plant operation to ensure that work in progress flows smoothly.... The hardware of production has little to do with learning in airframe fabrication and assembly.

Mishima concludes that the learning came not from the production workers but from the managers who organized the production. The organization and coordination of the complex processes for manufacturing sophisticated ships and airplanes were gradually improved as production took place. The acquisition of more specialized equipment was part of the improved organization, similar to what Thompson (2003) found for the Liberty Ship program.

There are also more general studies of learning by doing from different periods of history. These studies reveal that, throughout history, most *doing* does not seem to have been accompanied by much *learning*. In a study of production in different geographic locations during the latter half of the nineteenth and the early twentieth centuries, Dhamoos Sutthiphisal (2006) finds that the specific industries producing in different countries generate very different amounts of new technology. One example he provides is the shoe industry in the latter half of the twentieth century. In most low wage countries, the accumulated production experience in the shoe industry did not result in much new shoe-making technology, but in the United States shoe-making technology developed rapidly. Sutthiphisal found a strong statistical correlation between innovation in a particular industry and the availability of highly educated labor in general and highly skilled people in that industry in particular. His results suggest that models of technological change should seek to relate technological change to specific economic conditions, institutional arrangements, and specific incentives for producers to engage in innovative activities. By itself, doing is unlikely to be enough to sustain economic growth.

7.5 Summary and Observations

One of the first models of technological change that economists developed to explain the exogenous technology variable in the Solow growth model is the learning by doing model. This model assumes that externalities are generated as an unperceived by-product of production, and thus technological change is assumed to be a costless process. The assumption of costless external technological change avoids the difficult issue of how to pay for the up-front costs of innovation in models that assume perfect competition and the absence of profits in excess of production costs. There is little evidence to suggest that much new technology actually "just happens" as an external by-product of some other economic activity, however. The assumption of costless technological change is unsatisfactory for a general model of technological change. Like the Solow model, externalities models do not explain what would lead owners of industry to develop better machines or to improve their production procedures.

Detailed studies of the World War II data on government-sponsored war related manufacturing show that accumulated production does not miraculously result in technological improvements. Technological change occurs when *better* machines are installed, not just when *more* machines are installed. And because the U.S. government made bonus payments to firms who reduced costs and improved quality, many firms intentionally engaged in research and development to improve their production methods.

The question of how an economy creates new ideas and technologies is more important than ever. Global warming, accelerating biodoversity losses, stagnant real incomes for large groups of people, the continuation of extreme poverty in many countries, and other undesirable outcomes in the social and natural spheres of human existence further make it clear that new technologies do not automatically appear when and where they are needed. The clear failure of technology to neutralize economic growth's destruction of the natural environment means that humanity will have to take explicit measures to conserve nature or to change the way humans produce, consume, and live on Earth. We cannot wait for new ideas and technologies to just happen.

The finding that knowledge and technology are not free creates a problem for neoclassical economists: They cannot explain technological change using models that assume perfect competition in production. In fact, markets often do not work well, and finance is often not available for private individuals and firms to undertake costly innovations. Alternatives to free markets may be necessary if humanity is to generate all the required technological changes across all three of the spheres of human existence. For example, government institutions such as universities and research laboratories, funded through taxation, can muster the resources necessary for developing new technologies, systems, methods, procedures, institutions, and ideas necessary for sustainable economic development.

On the other hand, in many cases innovators can employ costly resources to generate new ideas, designs, strategies, procedures, and know-how provided they can earn sufficient profit from production to cover these up-front development costs. For example, if new products or methods can be used by innovators to gain monopoly power in the market, say by developing a superior product or lowering production costs, then they could effectively pay for the up-front costs of innovation with the profits that exceed the costs of production. This idea lies behind a popular model of technological change developed by Joseph Schumpeter, which is highlighted in the next chapter. It turns out the Schumpeter's model can be generalized to give us useful insight into the process of innovation in many circumstances.

Key Terms and Concepts

Applied research
Anomalies
Asian tigers
Basic research
Codified knowledge
Combinatoric process
Copyright
Diffusion of technology
Excludable products
Externalities models
Externality
Geographic agglomeration
Human capital
Human technology
Ideas
Learning by doing models
Learning curve
Meta-ideas
Models of endogenous technological
    change

Nonrival good
Normal science
Paradigm
Paradigm shift
Patent
Path dependency
Perpetual inventory method
Production function
Revolutionary science
Rival good
S-curve
Simultaneous discovery
Solow residual
Sources of growth equation
Tacit knowledge
Technological change
Technology
Total factor productivity (TFP)

Questions and Problems

1. Section 7.1.1 stated that physical capital is diverse and should be split into many distinct categories rather than being lumped together in physical capital. How many distinct categories of capital can you think of, and what are the unique characteristics of each that warrant their separate classification?
2. Explain why the application of new ideas tends to follow an S-curve pattern.
3. Explain precisely how a mathematical *production function* is transformed into a *sources of growth equation*, and how the latter is then used to derive a practical formula for estimating *total factor productivity*. Explain the advantages and disadvantages of using these estimates as proxies for technological change.
4. Define a meta-idea. Make a short list of meta-ideas. Explain your choices in light of the definition of a meta-idea.
5. Write a brief essay on Thomas Kuhn's concept of a paradigm shift. What are the full implications of Kuhn's hypothesis on paradigm shifts? Do paradigms speed up the accumulation of knowledge, or do they slow down the process? Explain.
6. Precisely explain what Thomas Kuhn meant by *normal science* and *revolutionary science*. How did Kuhn use these two concepts to explain the accumulation of knowledge?

7. Among the most popular models of endogenous technological change is the *learning by doing model*. Explain this model, and discuss its relevance. (Hint: review the evidence related to the Liberty ship program.)

8. Explain the link between the combinatoric nature of knowledge accumulation and the observed path dependency of technological change.

9. Define a rival good as opposed to a nonrival good. Present some examples of each. In which category do ideas, knowledge, and technology fall? Explain.

10. Why do research activities tend to occur mostly in just a few geographic regions of the world? Provide several possible explanations for the *agglomeration* of innovative and scientific activity.

11. Why does production so often become more efficient with experience? Explain the shape of the *learning curve*. Why does it flatten out?

12. Why do governments award patents and copyrights to people who develop new ideas, create new technologies, and originate works of art? Explain.

13. Why are there so many cases of simultaneous discovery? Explain how humans have accumulated such an exceptional amount of knowledge and technology compared to other living species.

14. Explain why human technology is unique among living species. How does human technology differ from the procedures, techniques, and methods used by other living species?

15. In light of the learning by doing model, can you think of any examples of where productivity improved simply because people learned from their experience? (Hint: Think about costly activities or inputs that have helped the learning process along.)

References

Alchian, Alan (1963), "Reliability of Progress Curves in Airframe Production," *Econometrica* 31(1):87–97.

Benkard, C. Lanier (1999), "Learning and Forgetting: The Dynamics of Aircraft Production," NBER Working Paper No. W7127, May.

Bourdieu, Pierre (1990), *In Other Words: Essays toward a Reflexive Sociology*, Palo Alto, California: Stanford University Press.

Cipola, Carlo M. (1978), *Clocks and Culture 1300–1700*, New York: Norton.

Comin, Diego, and Bart Hobijn (2003), "Cross-Country Technology Adoption: Making the Theories Face the Facts," *Federal Reserve Bank of New York Staff Reports* 169:June.

Daly, Herman E. (1998), "Uneconomic Growth," Clemens Lecture 11, Saint John's University, October 25.

Dosi, Giovanni (1982), "Technological Paradigms and Technological Trajectories: A Suggested Interpretation of the Determinants and Directions of Technical Change," *Research Policy* 11(3):147–162.

Elías, Victor J. (1992), *Sources of Growth, A Study of Seven Latin American Countries*, San Francisco: ICS Press.

Florida, Richard (2005), "The World Is Spiky," *Atlantic Monthly*, October.

Fuess, Scott M., Jr., and Hendrik Van den Berg (1997), "Transactions Activities and Productivity Growth in Mexico," *The Journal of Developing Areas* 31(1):387–398.

Gladwell, Malcolm (2008), "In the Air: Who Says Big Ideas Are Rare?" *The New Yorker*, May 12.

Glaeser, Edward, H.D. Kallal, José A. Scheinkman, and Andre Schleifer (1991), "Growth in Cities," NBER Working Paper 3787, July.

Gort, Michael, Jeremy Greenwood, and Peter Rupert (1999), "How Much of Economic Growth Is Fueled by Investment-Specific Technological Progress?," *Economic Commentary*, March 1, Federal Reserve Bank of Cleveland.

Griliches, Zvi (1957), "Hybrid Corn: An Exploration of the Economics of Technical Change," *Econometrica* 25(4):501–522.

Griliches, Zvi (1958), "Research Costs and Social Returns: Hybrid Corn and Related Innovations," *Journal of Political Economy* 66(5):419–431.

Hofman, Andre A. (1992), "Capital Accumulation in Latin America: A Six Country Comparison for 1950–1989," *Review of Income and Wealth* 38(4):365–401.

Instituto Nacional de Estadística, Geografía e Informática (1994), *Estadísticas Históricas de México*, Part I, Aguacalientes, Mexico: INEGI.

Irwin, Douglas A. and Peter J. Klenow (1994), "Learning by Doing Spillovers in the Semiconductor Industry," *Journal of Political Economy* 102(6):1200–1227.

Kuhn, Thomas (1962), *The Structure of Scientific Revolutions*, Chicago: University of Chicago Press.

Macfarlane, Alan, and Gerry Martin (2002), *Glass*, Chicago: University of Chicago Press.

Maddison, Angus, and Associates (1992), *The Political Economy of Poverty, Equity, and Growth, Brazil and Mexico*, Washington, DC: World Bank.

Mansfield, Edwin (1961), "Technical Change and the Rate of Imitation," *Econometrica* 29(4):741–766.

Marshall, Alfred (1959 [1920]), *Principles of Economics, 8th edition*, London: MacMillan & Co. Ltd.

Mishima, Kazuhiro (1999), "Learning by New Experiences: Revisiting the Flying Fortress Learning Curve," in Naomi Lamoreaux, Daniel Raff, and Peter Temin (eds.), *Learning by Doing in Markets, Firms, and Countries*, Chicago: University of Chicago Press, pp. 145–184.

Nelson, Katherine, and Richard R. Nelson (2002), "On the Nature and Evolution of Human Know-How," *Research Policy* 31:719–733.

Polanyi, Michael (1958), *Personal Knowledge, Towards a Post Critical Philosophy*, London: Routledge.

Rapping, Leonard (1965), "Learning and World War II Production Functions," *Review of Economics and Statistics* 47:81–86.

Richtel, Matt (2008), "Edison... Wasn't He the Guy Who Invented Everything?" *New York Times*, March 30.

Romer, Paul (1993), "Idea Gaps and Object Gaps in Economic Development," *Journal of Monetary Economics* 32:543–573.

Rosenberg, Nathan (1994), *Exploring the Black Box, Technology, Economics, and History*, Cambridge, U.K.: Cambridge University Press.

Ryan, Bruce, and Neal C. Gross (1943), "The Diffusion of Hybrid Seed Corn in Two Iowa Communities," *Rural Sociology* 8:15–24.

Saxenian, AnnaLee (2002) "Silicon Valley's New Immigrant High-Growth Entrepreneurs," *Economic Development Quarterly* 16(1):20–31.

Shrage, Michael (2002), "Wal-Mart Trumps Moore's Law," *Technology Review*, March.

Solow, Robert M. (1960), "Investment and Technological Progress," in Kenneth Arrow, Samuel Karlin, and Patrick Suppes (eds.), *Mathematical Models in the Social Sciences*, Stanford: Stanford University Press, pp. 89–104.

Smith, Adam (1776 [1997]), *An Inquiry into the Nature and Causes of the Wealth of Nations*, Chicago: University of Chicago Press.

Sutthiphisal, Dhanoos (2006), "Learning-by-Producing and the Geographic Links between Invention and Production: Experience from the Second Industrial Revolution," NBER working Paper 12469, August.

Temple, Jonathan (1998), "Equipment Investment and the Solow Model," *Oxford Economic Papers* 50:39–62.

Teresi, Dick (2002), *Lost Discoveries*, New York: Simon and Shuster.

Thomas, J. J. (1992), *Informal Economic Activity*, The University of Michigan Press, Ann Arbor.

Thompson, Peter (2003), "How Much Did the Liberty Shipbuilders Learn? New Evidence for an Old Case Study," *Journal of Political Economy* 109(1):103–137.

Wackernagel, Mathis, *et al.* (2002), "Tracking the Ecological Overshoot of the Human Economy," *Proceedings of the National Academy of Sciences* 99:9266–9271.

Weitzman, Martin L. (1996), "Hybridizing Growth Theory," *American Economic Review* 86(2):207–212.

Wilson, Edward O. (1975), *Sociobiology: The New Synthesis*, Cambridge, MA: Harvard University Press.

Wilson, Edward O. (2002), *The Future of Life*, New York: Alfred A Knopf, Inc.

World Wildlife Fund (2008), *Living Planet Report 2008*, Gland, Switzerland: World Wildlife Fund for Nature.

CHAPTER 8

Dynamic Models of Technological Change

The problem that is usually being visualized is how capitalism administers existing structures, whereas the relevant problem is how it creates and destroys them.

(Joseph Schumpeter[1])

The learning by doing model of the previous chapter is a step up from the Solow model's assumption of exogenous technological change. But, it is only a small step because it still tells us little about why and how human society goes about changing its technologies. The clever mathematical constructs of externality models and their compatibility with familiar models of competitive markets may satisfy the abstract intellectual desires of growth theorists, but holistic economists and social scientists need models that provide useful insight into how a real human society and its imperfect markets and faulty institutions can achieve sustainable economic development.

Chapter 6 explained that sustainable development depends on many very different types of technological change across the economic, social, and environmental spheres of human existence. So far, humanity has had difficulty generating all the knowledge and technologies needed to avoid doing lasting damage to the natural environment. The previous chapter concluded that it was unlikely that people would learn to change the technology and methods needed to sustain their economic, social, and natural systems by just doing their daily work. We clearly need a more realistic framework for analyzing technological change than the learning by doing model.

It is surprising that orthodox economists would ever make the assumption that new ideas and technologies are accidental and unnoticed byproducts of some other intentional economic activity. After all, mainstream neoclassical economists normally focus on incentives to explain the observed economic

---

[1] Joseph Schumpeter (1934), p. 34.

behavior of people. Recent research on innovation and technological change in fact clearly shows that the creation and application of new ideas, knowledge, methods, and technologies are costly activities that require costly resources, long-term planning, and sustained effort. As Thomas Edison is alleged to have remarked, innovation and invention are "10 percent inspiration and 90 percent perspiration."

The intentional nature of technological change was captured by Joseph Schumpeter at the start of the twentieth century in a dynamic model that makes costly research and development (R&D) activity an explicit choice by profit-maximizing businesses. Schumpeter's (1934 [1912]) model of technological change has recently been embraced by economists seeking to explain the technological progress that the Solow model leaves unexplained. Philippe Aghion and Peter Howitt (1992), Gene Grossman and Elhanan Helpman (1991), and Paul Romer (1990) are among those who have developed models of endogenous technological change and growth based on Schumpeter's ideas.

In this chapter, we present a general version of a **Schumpeterian model** of technological change. We present this model verbally and graphically. The Appendix presents a mathematical version of the model in order to provide you with an example of how growth economists usually present models. Even though Schumpeter sets up his model in the context of a profit-maximizing private firm, the dynamic framework can be generalized to fit circumstances

---

Chapter Goals

1. Review the evidence showing that innovation is a costly activity that requires future profit or some other source of income to justify the up-front costs.
2. Introduce Joseph Schumpeter's thoughts on economic change and technological progress.
3. Discuss the role of Schumpeter's entrepreneur in the innovative process.
4. Present a simplified graphic model that captures most of Schumpeter's dynamic model of creative destruction.
5. Explain innovative competition and how it contrasts with traditional price competition.
6. Discuss the dangers of protection and obstruction for the process of technological change.
7. Explain why international transfers of technology and knowledge are important for spreading economic development.
8. Review the role of technology in dealing with environmental barriers to economic development, and use the Schumpeter model to examine how these barriers can be dealt with.

across all the three spheres of human existence. The model can be used to show why innovation and technological progress occurs more easily in the economic sphere than in the social and natural environments. It can also be used to help explain how humanity can generate the urgently needed technologies in the natural sphere.

8.1 Schumpeter's Ideas on Technological Change

Research on technology shows that innovative activities are costly because they require scarce resources. If nothing else, innovation takes time, and time has opportunity costs. In general, innovative activities, or what in business is referred to as R&D (research and development), also require tools, equipment, a locale, and a substantial amount of prior knowledge. The latter input into the innovative process is often referred to as human capital. These resources have alternative uses, such as producing the things people already know how to make or investing in currently available machinery, tools, and infrastructure. That is, innovation has an opportunity cost.

UNESCO estimates that at the turn of the century research and development expenditures in the United States averaged 2.55 percent of GDP. A similar percentage was reported for Switzerland, and slightly higher portions of GDP were spent on research and development in Japan, Korea, and Sweden.[2] Such huge sums of money would not have been spent if new ideas and technologies were automatic or free. The main implication of the costly nature of innovation is that it can be carried out only if there is some way of dealing with the opportunity costs of the resources required.

Recall from the last chapter that the re-examination of the evidence on learning by doing during World War II production confirms that technological change was intentional and often the result of costly investments in research and new equipment and tools. Thompson's (2003) calculations suggest that just the new investments in the production facilities of the firms producing the Liberty Ships accounted for much of the efficiency gains during the three years of Liberty Ship production and "reduces the estimated size of the learning effect by fifty percent."[3] Jacob Schmookler's (1966) classic study of innovation in U.S. industry documented that inventions and discoveries were the result of profit-seeking behavior and not driven only by individual curiosity or accidental discoveries. More recently, Daron Acemoglu and Joshua Lim (2003) statistically confirmed a close relationship between innovation in the pharmaceutical industry and firms' market size and prospective profits. An

---

[2] As reported in The World Bank (2002), *World Development Indicators*, Washington, DC: World Bank, Table 5.11, pp. 322–324.
[3] Peter Thompson (2003), p. 133.

OECD study on industrial productivity notes that most investment in new equipment by producers is intentionally undertaken in order to acquire the technology embodied in the acquired capital.[4] In short, technological progress is not an accident or a free by-product of human production.

8.1.1 Endogenous growth models and perfect competition

Models of technological change must accurately reflect the costly and deterministic nature of innovation. Research, experimentation, analysis, planning, designing production equipment, and all the other activities related to the creation and application of new ideas, products, methods, procedures, and organization, require real and costly resources. Innovation is really an investment undertaken to achieve expected future gains. Since decisions must be made, models of the process of innovation must specify how and why innovators are motivated and enabled to incur the up-front costs of innovation.

In a market economy, the need to recover the up-front costs of innovation makes the assumption of perfect competition inappropriate. Perfectly competitive markets cause competition to drive the price in each market to the level where total revenue just covers the costs of production. The problem for innovation is that in such a competitive equilibrium, there is nothing left to cover the up-front costs of research and development, experimentation, market research, and all the other activities necessary for successful innovation. In the absence of "excess profits," there are no incentives for private firms to innovate.

Schumpeter hypothesized that innovators carry out their research, experiments, tests, planning, and other activities in order to generate "excess" profit that, hopefully, exceeds the up-front costs. Schumpeter recognizes that innovations, such as engineering a better product, designing a more attractive product, or improving production methods to lower production costs, give innovators an advantage over the competition and permits them to charge prices above their marginal production costs. Schumpeter described technological progress as a dynamic process of profit-driven **technological competition**, in which innovators continually apply costly resources to create new products, change production methods, reduce costly inputs, and change product characteristics to gain a competitive advantage over existing producers. As a result, society often benefits from the new technologies. Schumpeter's model has proven to be very useful because the general idea that costly innovation generates "excess benefits" defines a general dynamic optimization problem that can be used to explain many innovative situations in addition to the R&D activities of private enterprises operating in market economies.

---

[4] OECD (1997), *Technology and Industrial Performance*, Paris: Organisation for Economic Co-Operation and Development.

8.1.2 Joseph Schumpeter, a radical economist

During the first half of the twentieth century, mainstream economics focused on resource allocation using comparative static *all other things equal* analysis. So when Joseph Schumpeter (1912, 1934) described capitalism as a dynamic system that continually generates technological change, he was viewed as something of a radical. Because his ideas did not fit into the static neoclassical modeling framework, he was largely ignored by mainstream economists. The dominant neoclassical view of the market system was that it is inherently *stable*, always moving towards a stationary equilibrium. Schumpeter, however, described the capitalist system as an **evolutionary process** that never reverts to a stationary equilibrium. He criticized contemporary orthodox economists: "The problem that is usually being visualized is how capitalism administers existing structures, whereas the relevant problem is how it creates and destroys them."[5] He saw an ever-changing economy in which innovative activities continually set in motion changes that cause more disruptive innovations.

Schumpeter described the capitalist economy as a "perennial gale of **creative destruction**" in which each firm sought to gain an advantage in the marketplace through innovation. Each innovation, such as a more attractive design, a lowering of production costs, a new product, a new source of supply of inputs or raw materials, or an improved management method, was pursued because it held the possibility of generating higher profit for the innovating firm. Such *creative* activity also *destroyed* the market power that other firms had gained by means of their earlier innovations. Hence, the gains from innovation tend to be only temporary because the creative innovations of competitors will, sooner or later, destroy each innovator's newly-conquered market power. This process of creative destruction was, according to Schumpeter, the source of economic development and the increases in living standards observed in the early twentieth century.

Schumpeter's concept of *competition* was radically different from the price competition that traditional microeconomics positioned as the driving force of economic efficiency. Schumpeter argued that there was ferocious competition among firms, but it was technological competition, not price competition. This competition to develop new products and production processes in fact increased profits, but it was precisely these monopoly profits that induced innovators to incur the up-front costs of innovation. However, monopolies would not be permanent because technological competition generated only temporary profits. All profits, argued Schumpeter, were eventually eliminated by the creative destruction of competing innovators. Schumpeter effectively rejected the conclusion of standard microeconomic theory that monopoly profit is a form of market failure that creates costly **deadweight losses** for society and shifts

---

[5] Joseph Schumpeter (1934), p. 84.

income from workers to the owners of private capital. Provocatively, Schumpeter wrote that profits were, in fact, necessary for the economy to grow and raise standards of living. This was not a popular position to take at the beginning of the twentieth century. Income distribution had recently become much more unequal, and there was growing resentment of the so-called *robber barons* of big industry. Few mainstream economists equated monopolies with rising living standards at the start of the twentieth century.

Actually, Schumpeter's technological competition among large imperfectly competitive business firms does not always lead to welfare-improving technological change. Competitive technological change implies doing things differently in order to earn profit, not necessarily doing things that enhance human welfare. Innovative marketing activities such as advertising and building a firm's image may not add much to human well-being. Creating new products that appeal only to people's sense of status or vanity does not improve human welfare in the long run, nor does the common practice of changing new products only superficially while also engineering obsolescence into products in order to force consumers to spend on new products.

8.1.3 Creative destruction and the entrepreneur

Central to Schumpeter's process of creative destruction is the **entrepreneur**, the person who initiates, organizes, and manages the process of innovation. According to Schumpeter, the entrepreneur is the person who recognizes and grasps the opportunities for introducing a new product, changing a firm's management organization, exploiting a new market, finding a new source of raw materials, cutting the costs of production, or motivating the labor force. Entrepreneurs are the people who see the economic potential of inventions, who guide and organize the innovative process that employs inventors, and who arrange for the funds to finance the enterprise. The entrepreneur is the one who has the ambition, the vision of profit, and the organizational skills to bring a project to fruition. Most importantly, the entrepreneur is the organizer who can see the potential of profit through the haze of uncertainty that obscures the future:

> Carrying out a new plan and acting according to a customary one are things as different as making a road and walking along it... How different a thing this [entrepreneurship] is becomes clearer if one bears in mind the impossibility of surveying exhaustively all the effects and counter-effects of the projected enterprise... As military action must be taken in a given strategic position even if all the data potentially procurable are not available, so also in economic life action must be taken without working out all the details of what must be done. Here the success of everything depends on intuition, the capacity of seeing things in a way which afterwards proves to be true, even though it cannot be established at the

moment, and of grasping the essential fact, discarding the unessential, even though one can give no account of the principles by which this is done.[6]

Schumpeter's distinction between **risk** and **uncertainty** is similar to what John Maynard Keynes (1936) highlighted as the cause of macroeconomic in stability. *Risk* is the variation among a known set of outcomes with known probabilities, which assumes a great deal of knowledge about the process generating the variations. *Uncertainty*, on the other hand, is the situation in which not even all the possible outcomes, much less their probabilities, are known. Uncertainty implies completely unimaginable things could happen. The future is much better characterized by uncertainty, not risk. The entrepreneur is not just a manger of risk, but also an adventurer willing to face the unknown.

Schumpeter also attached great importance to the social and economic cultures within which entrepreneurs operate. Since the rate of technological change of an economy depends on how aggressively and competently entrepreneurs employ resources to innovate, the incentives and barriers they face are critical to the process of economic development. Among the critical institutions are society's attitude toward business success, the prestige of business activity, how well the education system prepares potential entrepreneurs, and how much freedom entrepreneurs have to pursue their ambitions. Schumpeter actually referred to entrepreneurs as "social deviants" who often clash with tradition and certainly act counter to the wishes of vested business and social interests. Schumpeter pointed out that entrepreneurs are often immigrants and minority groups, such as the Jews in Europe, expatriate Chinese in Southeast Asia, and Indians throughout the British Empire. Natives are often more bound by tradition, more aware of when they are stepping on others' toes, and more easily intimidated by vested interests. Schumpeter pointed out that the Chinese who were entrepreneurial in Singapore, Malaysia, and Trinidad had not been nearly as entrepreneurial in their native societies. More generally, Schumpeter argued that societies that tolerate people who break with tradition, think differently, and challenge vested interests will have higher levels of technological progress than societies that demand conformity.

It should be noted that Schumpeter was not the first to elevate the entrepreneur to a position of importance in the economy. The early French economist Richard Cantillon wrote in 1730 that producers in an economy consisted of two classes: hired people who received fixed wages and entrepreneurs with non-fixed, uncertain returns. Because other French Physiocrats, such as François Quesnay and Jean-Baptiste Say, also discussed entrepreneurs, the French word *entrepreneur* (one who "undertakes" or "takes in hand") has become part of the international language of economists. Recall, also, from Chapter 4 that in his 1776 *Wealth of Nations*, Adam Smith had described the "men of speculation" who carried out new ventures.

---

[6] Joseph Schumpeter (1934), p. 85.

Karl Marx included entrepreneurs in the capitalist bourgeoisie, whose contributions to technological change he explicitly recognized. Marx wrote: "The bourgeoisie cannot exist without constantly revolutionizing the instruments of production..."[7] The entrepreneur disappeared from the economics literature in the late nineteenth century when neoclassical economics dominated the field. Schumpeter reintroduced the entrepreneur to economics in the twentieth century.

8.1.4 Case study: Entrepreneurs in China

Research in the social sciences has approached the subject of entrepreneurship from three directions. First, economists have often examined the economic conditions and institutional arrangements that best enable entrepreneurial activities. Credit constraints in the financial sector, lack of property rights, dangers of war and civil strife, and government regulatory arrangements are most often mentioned as constraining entrepreneurial activity.

Sociologists, on the other hand, have studied how social conditions affect entrepreneurship. Societies that encourage risk-taking, tolerate differences, and encourage wealth accumulation will breed more entrepreneurial activity than those that protect vested interests, discourage risk-taking, and frown on being different. Social forces that encourage, or discourage, would-be entrepreneurs also operate at the cultural level or through family, friends, religious organization, or ethnic groups.

Psychologists have studied the individual characteristics of entrepreneurs. They have distinguished such personal traits as high risk tolerance, belief in one's ability to control life's outcomes, and self-confidence as keys to explaining successful entrepreneurship. Most studies have focused on just one of these approaches. Joseph Schumpeter combined all of these approaches to explaining entrepreneurship, never hesitating to discuss government regulation, poor credit markets, social pressures, and risk aversion in combination.

Simeon Djankow, Yingyi Qian, Gérard Roland, and Ekaterina Zhuravskaya (2006) use a more holistic statistical model that controls for all three sets of influences on entrepreneurship to examine the determinants of entrepreneurial activity in China. China is an interesting case study because it is a country in the process of shifting from a communist economic regime to a more capitalist structure. It is also a very fast-growing economy. Djankov *et al.* analyze the results of a detailed survey of over 2,000 entrepreneurs and non-entrepreneurs in five Chinese cities. They found that, all other things equal, Chinese entrepreneurs were much more likely to have family members and childhood friends who were also entrepreneurs. This suggests that, as Schumpeter suggested, social climate is important for entrepreneurship. Chinese entrepreneurs had substantially greater tolerance for risk, and they were

---

[7] Karl Marx (1948), p. 7.

more willing to work long and hard. Entrepreneurs were also more likely than non-entrepreneurs to report that political freedom was important to them. Interestingly, entrepreneurs' replies to the survey shows that they were not more happy in life than the non-entrepreneurs responding to the same survey.

Chinese entrepreneurs were much more optimistic about dealing with the government bureaucracy. Where 45 and 44 percent of non-entrepreneurs responded that corruption and crime, respectively, were serious problems, only 17 and 9 percent of entrepreneurs thought so. This suggests that entrepreneurs are more likely to have found practical ways of dealing with or avoiding the corruption and crime. Or, perhaps entrepreneurs more often benefit from the corruption and crime that other Chinese only see from the outside. The study does not show that corruption influences who becomes an entrepreneur; it only reveals that those who have become entrepreneurs are better able to live with it.

All in all, Chinese entrepreneurs fit the general profile Schumpeter provides. They are relatively ambitious, hard working, adaptable, and less risk averse. While they are not necessarily happier, Chinese entrepreneurs are relatively more driven to fulfill the business and financial goals they set for themselves.

8.1.5 The routinization of entrepreneurship

Not everyone agrees with Schumpeter's praise of social deviants. According to the historian David Hollinger, "the celebration of misfits promotes a worrisome anti-intellectualism and presents a distorted picture of the innovation process."[8] The historian of science Thomas Kuhn (1962), on the other hand, implicitly gave social deviants an important role in science. Recall from the previous chapter that Kuhn described science as "nothing more than long periods of boring conformist activity punctuated by outbreaks of irrational deviance."[9] **Normal scientific research**, the routine hard work of refining, improving, and expanding knowledge within the confines of a dominant paradigm, is only occasionally interrupted by revolutionary **paradigm shifts**. It takes cultural deviants to lay the groundwork for a paradigm shift.

Schumpeter's writings contained some contradictions. In his writings he recognized that much of the R&D activity had to be organized and carefully managed, not unlike large-scale production. In his later writings, Schumpeter discussed the "mechanization of progress," by which he meant the gradual migration of research and development from independent entrepreneurs to the more bureaucratic corporations in which R&D was a routine activity. In the same classic work where he emphasized the role of the entrepreneur in dealing with uncertainty, Schumpeter (1934, pp. 85–86) also wrote:

---

[8] Quoted in G. Zachary Pascal (2007), "Genius and Misfit Aren't Synonyms, or Are They?" *New York Times*, June 3.
[9] Thomas Kuhn (1962).

The more accurately... we learn to know the natural and social world, the more perfect our control of facts becomes; and the greater the extent, with time and progressive rationalisation, within which things can be simply calculated, and indeed quickly and reliably calculated, the more the significance of this function [entrepreneurship] decreases.

Richard Langlois (1987) attributes this contradiction between Schumpeter's praise of entrepreneurs and his praise of the *routinization* of innovation that reduced the role of entrepreneurs to Schumpeter's implicit acceptance of technological change as a process that continuously improves humanity's understanding of its natural, social, and economic circumstances.   That is, humans would improve the way they innovate just as their earlier innovative activities improved agricultural and industrial processes.

Later in his career, Schumpeter predicted that improvement in technology and knowledge that entrepreneurs made possible would ultimately undermine capitalism.   Schumpeter (1942, p. 185) wrote that "... the modern corporation, although the product of the capitalist process, socializes the bourgeois mind; it relentlessly narrows the scope of the capitalist motivations; not only that, it will eventually kill its roots."   He specifically saw former innovators using their wealth to push government to obstruct new entrepreneurs. Like Marx, therefore, Schumpeter came to see that the evolving economy did not simply repeat the past or follow simple models of economic behavior. Rather, the dynamic process of economic development continually evolves, and inconsistencies may arise that weaken the system.

William Baumol (2002) views the routinization of innovative activities with less alarm than Schumpeter. According to Baumol, innovation accelerated so much over the past century precisely because it has become "a regular and even ordinary component of the activities of the firm."[10]   He sees it continuing indefinitely into the future precisely because it has become a well-established routine rather than an exceptional activity.

This discussion reminds us once again that innovation can take many forms. Perhaps policymakers must take care to motivate and enable both **social deviance** and **routinization**. They must encourage risk taking and social change while, at the same time, maintaining social stability for the diligent workers who carry out routine scientific and production tasks in between the revolutionary paradigm shifts. Economic policies must also address the monetary rewards for innovation, and this inevitably requires policies that address how the gains from innovation are shared. On the one hand, it is a fact that the entrepreneur only gets rich when others do much of the routine work to make the paradigm shift a success. On the other hand, there must be incentives for the entrepreneur to shift the paradigm in the first place. It is often difficult to set an income policy that is compatible with both objectives or society's traditional social morals and norms.

---

[10] William J. Baumol (2002), p. 4.

8.1.6 The role of the financial sector

Schumpeter distinguished the critical role of an economy's financial sector in enabling the economy to engage in costly innovation and, therefore, to generate technological change. Without a financial sector to accumulate savings, to channel the savings to the most capable entrepreneurs, to monitor projects, to spread the risk of innovation, and to do all this at a reasonable cost, innovation is not possible. The British economist John Hicks (1969) famously stated that the Industrial Revolution could not have occurred without the concurrent development of banking and financial markets.

Schumpeter's concern with the role of the financial sector contrasts with many growth models that ignore financial intermediation and simply assume that savings are channeled to productive investment without cost or delay. History reminds us that financial sectors have often failed to link savers and innovators. Schumpeter, of course, lived through the Great Depression of the 1930s and was keenly aware of how a collapse of the financial sector quickly stops most investment and innovative activity.

8.1.7 Progress versus change

The concept of *creative destruction* captures another fundamental characteristic of economic development, which is that, in an economy with scarce resources, doing something new necessarily means that some current activity can no longer be done. As Dwight Lee and Richard McKenzie (1993) write in their book entitled *Failure and Progress, The Bright Side of the Dismal Science*:

> ... an understanding of scarcity keenly focuses attention on the fundamental and pervasive cause of failure: people's absolute inability to have everything that is desirable and the pervasive necessity of their making choices... Failures occur frequently because the successes that are occurring in the economy deny resources to the ventures that fail. When the automobile was invented, many producers of horse-drawn buggies could not continue to operate. Resources were diverted into the production of cars, as buggy makers were no longer able to offer buggies at prices that were attractive to consumers and pay the wages and input prices necessary to compete against automobile producers for resources.[11]

While it may be true that, in the long run, economic development *reduces* scarcity and increases the economy's capacity to convert its scarce resources into welfare-enhancing output, it does not *eliminate* scarcity. For example, at the start of the twentieth century, not only did the resources needed to produce automobiles have to be taken away from other productive activities such as building horse-drawn wagons and making buggy whips, but the process of

---

[11] Dwight R. Lee and Richard B. McKenzie (1993), p. 17.

innovation itself requires resources and, therefore, an additional reduction in output elsewhere in the economy. In sum, the opportunity cost of innovation is (1) the output that could have been produced with the resources used to generate new ideas and technologies and (2) the cost of the disruption of the status quo (structural change). These two fundamental costs of technological change have been built into most recent models of technological change.

8.1.8 Final thoughts on creative destruction

Towards the end of his career, Schumpeter became less optimistic about the process of creative destruction. We already mentioned his fear that innovation would become less dynamic if it becomes a routine activity in large corporations. He also feared innovators would use their profits not to engage in more innovation, but to lobby the government to lock in certain technologies and to protect them from new innovations.

Examples of the latter include the active lobbying by traditional fossil fuel producers, such as the oil industry, the automobile industry, coal-fired electricity plants, and corn ethanol producers to stop the application of carbon taxes or subsidies for alternative energy sources such as wind and solar power or energy conservation requirements for autos and buildings. In sum, creative destruction is necessary for technological progress, but it will be actively resisted by those who fear creative destruction will have negative consequences for them.

8.2 The Schumpeterian R&D Model

There are many models of endogenous technological change based on Schumpeter's ideas. The best known model is by Paul Romer (1990), who used Schumpeter's ideas to develop a more general mathematical model of the growth of technology. Romer's mathematical "Schumpeterian" model of technological change incorporates the following five fundamental ideas:

1. Innovations are generated by intentionally employing costly (scarce) resources to create new products, ideas, methods, etc.

2. Innovators must compete with producers to employ the economy's scarce, and thus costly, resources.

3. Innovation creates new products and techniques that are better, cheaper, more attractive, and more convenient than existing products, which makes them more desirable than existing products and techniques.

4. Just as their own innovations destroyed earlier innovations, innovators know that later innovations will eventually replace their innovations.

5. Innovators and their financiers weigh the costs of innovation and the discounted expected gains from innovation.

These five ideas describe an ongoing process in which individuals, firms, organizations, universities, or governments employ society's scarce resources to generate new knowledge, ideas, methods, forms of economic organization, and other changes in the way humans do things. This section introduces a simplified graphic version of the Romer model.

8.2.1 Imperfect competition and profits

In the traditional microeconomic model of a firm, an imperfectly competitive producer faces a downward-sloping demand curve. Such a downward-sloping demand curve implies an even steeper MR curve, as shown in Figure 8.1. The profit-maximizing producer increases production up to the point where marginal revenue (MR) equals marginal cost (MC). For simplicity, Figure 8.1 assumes the marginal cost of production is constant, which means the marginal cost (MC) curve is a horizontal line at price w. The profit-maximizing output is thus q, which is sold at price p. The difference between the product price and the marginal cost, (p-w), is the markup μ. Total profit in excess of variable production costs equals the shaded box in Figure 8.1, the product of quantity q and the markup μ. Successful entrepreneurs whose innovations give them market power and a downward-sloping demand curve, can set a price above the marginal cost of production w and, therefore, recover the cost of innovation.

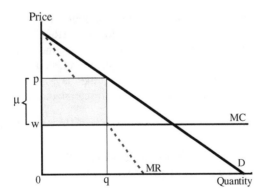

Figure 8.1 Monopoly Profit

The traditional diagram in Figure 8.1 is not dynamic because it does not show how long the firm can continue to reap profits. In Schumpeter's dynamic model of creative destruction, total profits from innovation have a time dimension; profit continues and society enjoys the benefits of an innovation until a new innovation *destroys* the old innovation.

8.2.2 Costly innovation must be paid for

The models of endogenous technological change usually model technological progress as the stream of products $x_1, x_2,..., x_n$, where each new product replaces the product preceding it because it is in some way superior to its predecessor. The models generally assume that innovators engage in innovative activity up to the point where the expected marginal gains from innovation equal the marginal costs of innovation. Suppose that the world consumes one product, denoted as x_t, at time t, and that the innovator who created x_t reaps a profit because the innovation made x_t preferable to x_{t-1}. This latter assumption implicitly includes the assumption that all consumers are identical (they are not distributed all along a downward-sloping demand curve) and that the markup is marginally less than the increase in value provided by the latest innovation (so that consumers no longer demand any more x_{t-1} after the creation of x_t).

In the Schumpeterian environment of *creative destruction*, profit from innovation depends on (1) the profit markup μ, (2) the level of production X, which is the quantity of the product x_t produced during one period of time, say one day, and (3) the number of periods (days) τ that the innovator can produce and enjoy the profit markup before the market power is *destroyed* by a subsequent innovation. Thus, profit π is equal to

$$\pi = \mu X \tau \qquad (8.1)$$

The level of production, X, depends on how many resources are devoted to production rather than research and development (R&D) activities. That is, daily production of x_t is directly related to the economy's total amount of productive factors and resources, R, and inversely related to the fraction of those resources devoted to innovation, n, during the day. Specifically, the total resources devoted to innovative activity, N, during the day are equal to

$$N = nR \qquad (8.2)$$

Suppose for simplicity, but no loss of generality, that one unit of resources R *produces* one unit of output x_t. Total production during the day is therefore:

$$X = (1 - n)R \qquad (8.3)$$

8.2.3 *The resource cost of innovation*

The rate of innovation can be found by solving a maximization problem that takes into consideration the costs of innovation and the expected benefits of innovation. Innovating firms seeking to create a new product x_{t+1} must purchase labor and other productive resources in competition with the producers who demand those same resources to produce the most recently-developed product, x_t. The opportunity cost of innovation is, therefore, the loss of some products x_t caused by taking scarce resources from production and using them in innovative activities.

The cost of resources will be lower, all other things equal, the more factors and resources, R, are available in the economy. But, all other things equal, the cost of resources rises with the level of innovative activity. The price of resources, w, is therefore a function of N and R as follows:

$$w = g(\overset{+}{N}, \overset{-}{R}) \qquad (8.4)$$

The signs over the independent variables show their directions of influence, that is, the signs of their partial derivatives with respect to w.

The process of innovation is uncertain, and devoting resources to R&D activity does not guarantee that something useful will actually be created. Nor is there normally a neat time schedule that says how long it will take before R&D activity will actually result in a successful creation. It is difficult to incorporate some unknown level of uncertainty into the maximization problem that we are setting up, so we must make some simplifying assumptions. Suppose that new products are developed according to an R&D process that has a known average outcome around which actual outcomes vary. Suppose, furthermore, that the average time it takes to come up with a new product or technology is a direct function of the amount of resources devoted to innovative activity and that the exact timing of any one R&D project fluctuates randomly around the average timing predicted by the amount of resources devoted to R&D activity in the economy. To keep things simple at this point of modeling the long-run development process, we assume that we can legitimately solve for the average number of innovations per period of time. We thus effectively assume that we can predict the future correctly *on average* and that the model generates an *expected* future value.

Another convenient simplifying assumption is that each innovator is a perfect competitor in the markets for resources used in the innovative process. Thus, each profit-maximizing entrepreneur employs resources to the point where marginal expected cost of innovation is equal to the expected future profits from innovation. The economy's average cost and profit functions are therefore viewed as their marginal functions by each of the competitive individual innovators. The model also conveniently assumes that innovators are risk-neutral so that they do not require a premium to induce them to undertake the inherently uncertain innovative activities.

Suppose that it takes on average β units of productive resources to produce one innovation per time period. Thus, with total productive resources, N, employed in innovative activity the the expected number of innovations per period, **q**, is then

$$\mathbf{q} = N/\beta \qquad (8.5)$$

Figure 8.2 provides a graphic illustration of the relationship between the amount of resources devoted to innovation, N, and the average quantity of innovations **q** generated per day. A brief note on the assumption of a linear R&D function is in order. There is no obvious reason why the R&D function would be linear. Good reasons can be found to assume the function is non-linear, perhaps subject to diminishing returns. On the other hand, the function could enjoy increasing returns if innovation is a combinatoric process of some sort; the more researchers are probing new ideas and communicating their findings, the easier it is for everyone to make progress toward finding new ideas, products, methods, etc. However, it is reasonably certain that the R&D function is an increasing function of the resources entrepreneurs devote to innovation. We therefore simplify and assume that the positive function is linear. This does not in any way reduce the generality of the qualitative results derived from the model.

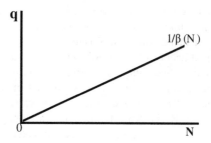

Figure 8.2 The Innovation Function

The average cost of innovation, CoI, that entrepreneurs expect to incur in generating an innovation is therefore

$$\mathrm{CoI} = w\beta \qquad (8.6)$$

This function specifies that the more research is undertaken, the more labor and other resources need to be hired. If the total supply of productive factors and resources are fixed at R, increasing innovation increases total demand for factors and resources, which drives up the prices of factors and resources. Hence, the cost of innovation, CoI, increases as innovative activity increases.

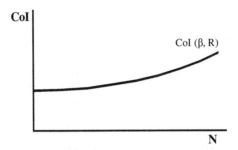

Figure 8.3 The Cost of Innovation

Figure 8.3 shows a typical upward-sloping CoI curve relating marginal costs of innovation to the amount of factors and resources used in innovation, N. All other things equal, the CoI curve shifts up when β, the amount of resources needed to generate an innovation, increases, and it will shift down if R, the total supply of resources, increases. In general notation, the cost of innovation is

$$CoI = h(\overset{+}{N}, \overset{-}{R}, \overset{+}{β}) \tag{8.7}$$

Whether it is worthwhile to incur the costs of innovation of course depends on the gains from innovative activity, which we will examine next.

Note that we are engaged in a standard modeling process. We begin with assumptions, and we set the parameters of the model. After we state all our assumptions and the parameters of the model, we will seek to generate logical conclusions by maximizing profit subject to the assumed parameters of the model. This exercise will clarify the key elements of the Schumpeterian model and Paul Romer's (1990) mathematical model of endogenous technological change. Since the model is often used by economists, it is important to understand the critical details and assumptions. Upon completing the process, we will discuss the strengths and weaknesses of the model.

8.2.4 The present value of innovation

Now that we have defined the cost of achieving an innovation, the next step in our maximization problem is to find the gain from innovation. In accordance with equation (8.1), $π = μXτ$, the expected profit from an innovation is a positive function of the average markup $μ$, the amount of output produced, X, and the length of time $τ$ that an innovator expects to enjoy the monopoly profit. The length of time $τ$ depends on how fast new innovations are created. Since we have assumed that it takes β units of resources to generate an innovation, it follows from equation (8.5) that the number of days that an innovator expects to enjoy his/her profit is equal to

$$E(\tau) = 1/\mathbf{q} = \beta/N \qquad (8.8)$$

For example, if it takes 100 days until a new innovation destroys the current product's market position, $\mathbf{q} = .01$.

According to equation (8.8), expected future profit is a direct function of β, a result that, at first glance, may seem counterintuitive. Keep in mind, however, that we are only defining the gains from innovation. The cost of innovation function has already been specified above in equation (8.5), and the costs of innovation rise as β increases. But, precisely because the cost of innovation rises with β, a higher β makes new innovation more costly and thus increases the time an innovator is likely to enjoy the profits of each innovation.

Expected future profit also depends on the amount of production X, which competes for the use of resources. The more resources that are used for innovation, the fewer are available for producing profitable products created by previous innovations. Hence, there are two reasons why the present value of an innovation is inversely related to N: (1) a higher N leads to a faster destruction of prior creations and (2) a higher N reduces the amount of resources available to produce profit-generating output. An increase in total resources, on the other hand, permits more future production X, which implies profits rise with R.

Finally, because innovations require *current* expenditures on research and development (R&D) that must be paid for from *future* profits, expected future profits must be discounted. The higher the interest rate, r, the more rapidly future earnings are discounted, and the lower is the PVI.

In general, the present value of future profit from innovation, denoted as PVI, takes on the following general form:

$$PVI = f(\overset{+}{\mu}, \overset{+}{R}, \overset{-}{N}, \overset{+}{\beta}, \overset{-}{r}) \qquad (8.9)$$

A more specific relationship can be derived by defining the right-hand variables in (8.1) more precisely. According to equations (8.1), (8.3), and (8.7), the expected profit, $E(\pi)$, accruing to an innovation is

$$E(\pi) = \mu X/\mathbf{q} = \mu(R - N)(\beta/N) \qquad (8.10)$$

The present value of innovation thus consists of a series of future profits, each one discounted to the present. Hence, the PVI takes on the form:

$$PVI = \sum_{j=1}^{(\beta/N)} 1/(1+r)^j \mu(R-N)(\beta/N) \qquad (8.11)$$

As shown in Figure 8.4, PVI declines as more resources are applied to innovative activity and the process of creative destruction speeds up, all other things equal. Equation (8.9) suggests that increases in the profit markup μ, the stock of productive resources R, and resource cost of innovation β cause the PVI curve to shift up. A rise in the interest rate r lowers the curve.

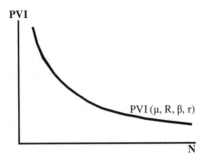

Figure 8.4 The PVI Curve

8.2.5 The equilibrium level of R&D activity

The top portion of Figure 8.5 combines Figures 8.3 and 8.4. The intersection of the CoI and PVI curves determines the equilibrium amount of resources that competitive entrepreneurs devote to innovative activity, $N = R - X$. The bottom half of Figure 8.5 is simply the Figure 8.2 turned upside down and conveniently attached along the horizontal axis that it shares with Figures 8.3 and 8.4. The $1/\beta$ curve translates the equilibrium level of N into the number of innovations per day. Given the values of the parameters that determine the CoI and PVI curves in the upper half of Figure 8.5 and the productivity of the innovative process as given by β, the economy produces **q** innovations per day.

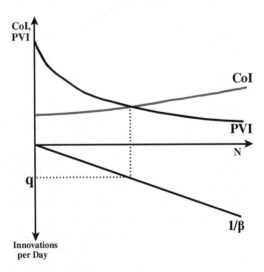

Figure 8.5 Equilibrium Innovation

8.2.6 The changes in μ, r, R, and β and innovation

The graphic model in Figure 8.5 can be manipulated to find the effects of changes in μ, R, β or r on the number of innovations **q**. For example, Figure 8.6 shows that, *all other things equal*, an increase in in the markup μ shifts the PVI curve up to PVI_1, as suggested by equation (8.11). As a result, the equilibrium N, the number of resources devoted to innovative activity, increases.   The increase in N, in turn, raises the number of innovations per day to q_1. Although we do not show the diagram here, you should be able to diagram the effect of an increase in the discount (interest) rate r.   This lowers the PVI curve and, therefore, reduces the average number of innovations per day.

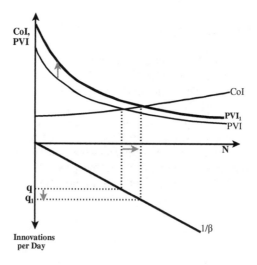

Figure 8.6 The Effects on Innovation of an Increase in μ

Figure 8.7 illustrates how a change in R affects innovation through shifts in both the CoI and PVI curves. For example, an increase in R lowers w, which, according to equation (8.6), shifts the CoI curve down to CoI_1, causes the equilibrium value of N to increase, and thus increases the number of innovations to q_1. However, an increase of R also shifts up the PVI curve because an increase in productive resources implies more production of new products and, therefore, more profits, all other things equal. This effect increases N further, and thus the number of innovations rises further to q_2.

A change in β is even more complex because it affects all the curves in Figure 8.5. Suppose, for example, that β declines, which implies an increase in the efficiency with which the economy generates and applies new ideas. First of all, a decrease in β shifts the 1/β line relating N and **q** clockwise, as shown in Figure 8.8. Second, the CoI curve shifts down, as suggested by equation (8.6).

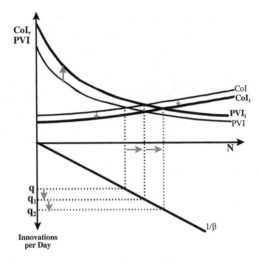

Figure 8.7 The Effects on Innovation of an Increase in **R**

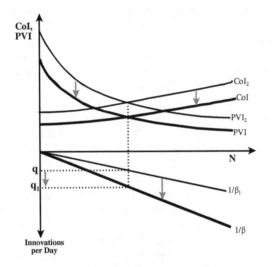

Figure 8.8 The Effects on Innovation of a Decrease in β

Finally, equation (8.9) indicates that the PVI curve also shifts down; all other things equal, if it gets less costly to innovate, then creative destruction occurs more frequently and any given innovation enjoys profits for a shorter period of time. The net result of these shifts appears to be ambiguous because a fall in β not only reduces the marginal cost of innovation, but it also reduces expected profits because the lower costs of innovation imply that the destruction side of the creative destruction process occurs more quickly. The net effect on innovation of a decline in β is likely to be positive, however. As detailed the Appendix at the end of this chapter, reasonable specifications of the PVI and CoI curves suggests that they exactly offset each other, leaving the shift of the $1/\beta$ line as the net contributor to the change in innovation. Thus, we could conclude that, under the plausible conditions, an improvement in the efficiency of innovation (a decline in β) raises the amount of innovation in the economy.

8.2.7 Some further observations

In summary, the Schumpeterian R&D model of technological change developed here can be represented as

$$\mathbf{q} = f(\overset{+}{\mu}, \overset{+}{R}, \overset{-}{r}, \overset{-}{\beta}) \qquad (8.12)$$

In words, all other things equal, the number of innovations in an economy is greater (1) the larger is the profit markup at which the successful innovator can sell her innovative new product, (2) the greater is the supply of resources available to innovators and producers, (3) the more highly innovators value future gains relative to current costs, and (4) the more efficient are innovators in employing the economy's scarce resources toward generating new innovations.

Equation (8.12) suggests that the amount of innovation depends on the total amount of resources. The higher the supply of resources, the lower is the opportunity cost of employing resources for R&D activity and, all other things equal, the less costly it is to innovate. This suggests that wealthier and/or larger societies will, all other things equal, experience more frequent technological changes than poor and/or small countries. The model seems to predict that the United States will grow faster than Bolivia.

There is no evidence that suggests a direct relationship between population size and economic development or between population size and per capita output, however. Many small countries have grown very rapidly, and many very large countries have had below-average growth performances. Luxembourg's per capita real income is twenty times that of India, and the city states of Hong Kong and Singapore have grown much faster than any large African or Latin American country. One possible reason why small countries can grow rapidly despite having a small stock of entrepreneurs and thinkers is that technology moves across borders. A country does not need to invent the wheel in order to have wagons or water wheels. The Schumpeter model may also not capture all aspects of technological change.

8.2.8 Land-grant universities and extension agents

The agricultural sector is often used as an example of a highly competitive industry. In an industry with millions of small farmers, each farmer is effectively a price taker. The R&D model of innovation would lead us to conclude that the agricultural sector engages in little innovation because individual farmers and firms have no way of capturing the profits of their innovations. Specifically, μ would be equal to zero. Yet, in countries like the United States, agriculture is noted for its high level of technology. Did individual farmers generate this technology? By and large, farmers applied new technology rapidly, but they did not themselves develop most of the new technologies. The development was done by imperfectly competitive, profit-seeking firms in the private chemical and agricultural machinery industries that supplied fertilizers, seeds, and tractors to the farmers. And, there has been a very successful program of government-funded universities and agricultural extension services engaged in research and the dissemination of new technologies.

Justin Smith Morrill, a member of the U.S. House of Representatives, introduced a law, known as the Morrill Act of 1862, that established the system that allocated large amounts of land the government had taken from Native Americans to each state for the establishment of universities to provide advanced education to large numbers of people who would not normally attend universities. The states usually sold the land and used the revenues to establish universities. Many of these *land-grant* universities became centers for agricultural research. They also trained large numbers of people who directly or indirectly spread the new technologies being developed at the land-grant universities. In the United States today, the average farmer is more educated than industrial workers.

The 1887 Hatch Act provided funds for the establishment of agricultural experiment stations at each of the land-grant universities. These stations conducted extensive research and employed people to spread the new technologies among farmers throughout each state. These measures soon began to increase agricultural productivity. Subsequent legislation channeled more funds to agricultural research and to extension services to introduce the new technologies to farmers.

The land-grant universities of the United States consider outreach to all citizens, farmers, and businesses of their state to be a major responsibility. Faculty members, especially in the sciences and agricultural fields, often devote as much of their time to research and serving the general public as they do teaching at the university. Growth economists, like Paul Romer, have pointed to the U.S. land-grant university as one of the most important institutions created to stimulate technological change. The tax-funded land-grant university effectively operated as the U.S. agricultural sector's R&D department.

James Adams and Roger Clemmons (2008) examined the origins of private research successes by examining citations in scientific papers. They found that industrial science draws heavily on past scientific research both inside and outside the firm. They report that "as time goes by, the share of knowledge flows from outside the firm increases. In turn, the contributions of outside scientific knowledge that is contributed by universities exceeds that of other firms."[12] Thus, it appears that research universities provide critical scientific knowledge to all industries, not just the agricultural sector of the economy. Note that land-grant universities and other public research organizations still fit in the Schumpeterian model; research is still movtivated by expected future gains, and the costly research is paid for before the gains are realized.

8.3 The Long-Run Trend in the Costs of Innovation

Figure 8.5 in the previous section seems to suggest that the quantity of innovations, q; remains constant over time. This conclusion is the result of the comparative static graphic model we have developed. This model settles at a stable equilibrium. In general, such a conclusion is not correct. A constant quantity of innovations equal to q each period actually implies that the *rate* of technological change slows down in the long run as the accumulated technology grows. A constant *rate* of technological change requires that the *number* of innovations per year increase in proportion to the rising level of technology.

8.3.1 How to avoid a technology slowdown

There are two ways in which the slowdown in technological progress can be avoided. First of all, the graphic model presented above assumes that total demand for output remains constant even as technological progress occurs. This was done to avoid the complexity of solving dynamic models in which everything changes over time. Realistically, if technological progress causes real output growth, then real incomes and product demand will increase. Recall that the Solow model suggests that the growth of real income will be equal to the rate of technological progress in the long run. Thus, demand for output and profits from innovation are likely to rise in proportion to technology, and the incentive to innovate will increase over time, thus ensuring that the development process will not weaken over time.

The slowdown in the rate of technological progress can also be avoided if the cost of research and development declines as technology expands. Paul Romer (1990) suggested that it gets easier to create new ideas the more ideas we already have to build on:

---

[12] James D. Adams and J. Roger Clemmons (2008), p. 27.

... every generation has underestimated the potential for finding new recipes and ideas. We consistently fail to grasp how many ideas remain to be discovered/the difficulty is the same one we have with compounding. Possibilities do not add up. They multiply.[13]

For example, the eighteenth century discovery of the steam engine led to many unforeseen developments. First used to pump out flooded mines, the steam engine was then applied to other stationary applications such as milling and sawing. Only in the nineteenth century did the steam engine lower the cost of hauling goods and people over land and water. Eventually, steam engines were used to generate electricity, which replaced many of the direct uses of steam in factories as well as enabling the introduction of labor-saving home appliances. In short, ideas multiply as each new idea breeds other ideas. But Romer also seems to imply that technological change is likely to accelerate the more knowledge is accumulated. Romer's suggestion that ideas multiply reflects the belief, common in the scientific community, that the more we discover, the more we find out how much we do not yet know and the more potential research projects beckon for our attention. Despite centuries of scientific discoveries, the editor of the scientific journal *Nature*, John Maddox still wrote at the turn of this century: "What stands out is that there is no field of science that is free from glaring ignorance, even contradiction."[14]

In his Schumpeterian model, Romer assumes that cost of research and development β is a variable that is related to the level of technology. Since technology improves over time, he thinks it is reasonable to assume that it becomes easier to create new products as more knowledge accumulates. In other words, β gets smaller as technology improves. Romer's assumption is equivalent to shifting the curve $1/\beta$ in the bottom half of Figure 8.5 to gradually become steeper so that the quantity of new innovations per period of time grows over time.

8.3.2 Measuring R&D

An important question for the R&D model discussed above is whether innovation becomes easier or harder as the number of innovations grows. While few people today believe what the director of the United States Patent Office believed at the turn of the twentieth century, namely that "we must certainly have discovered everything there is to discover by now," a number of economists have suggested that a slowdown in new discoveries is likely. They present some evidence to support their contention. There have been several

---

[13] From Romer's website www.stanford.edu/~promer?Econgro.htm.; also published as Romer (1998).
[14] As quoted in *The Economist* (1999), "A Survey of the 20th Century, On the Yellow Brick Road," September 11, p. 43.

studies that sought to measure innovation and the efforts made to innovate. It is, of course, extremely difficult to measure actual innovation and the resources expended to generate new ideas. The estimates of total factor productivity that we discussed in the previous chapter have been widely used as measures of the rate of innovation. Some studies have used the number of patents issued as a measure of ideas and innovation. As for the resources used to generate innovation, studies have used data on the number of people employed in research and development departments of firms and other research organizations. Data on these measures, total factor productivity, the number of patents, and the number of researchers employed, do not support the widely-accepted hypothesis that new ideas become easier to create as we accumulate knowledge.

In France, Germany, Japan, the United Kingdom, and the United States, the number of scientists and engineers engaged in research and development activities has grown two to four-fold over the past thirty years.[15] Expenditures on R&D activities by private firms in these countries show increases of similar magnitude. But, despite the apparent increase in research activity, the number of new patents issued each year has not shown any tendency to increase. The measured rate of productivity growth has remained in the range of 1 to 3 percent for 200 years. Higher rates prevailed for 25 years after World War II, but then fell back to the middle of the historical range for the remainder of the century. F.M. Scherer (1999) asks, "Is there some law of nature requiring that scientific and technical effort increase at 4 to 5 percent a year in order to maintain annual productivity growth... averaging 2 percent?"[16] Such increases in effort cannot be sustained forever. The reported increase in R&D expenditures with constant results suggests that it is getting harder and harder to create new ideas, not easier as Romer assumed.

Scherer's interpretation of the data is only as accurate as the data he interprets, however. For one thing, the number of patents issued does not necessarily reflect actual innovative activity or the number of new ideas created. And, remember that not all new ideas improve human welfare; some serve to increase the income of some at the expense of others. Some are simply useless from a welfare perspective. The difficulty lies in measuring knowledge, ideas, and everything else that can reasonably be considered *technology*. If that is not a difficult enough problem to overcome, the criteria for issuing patents are certainly not uniform across countries and they have changed over time. The motivation for seeking a patent may have changed as well, since the time and cost of applying is considerable, and the Harvard economist Zvi Griliches

---

[15] See, for example, Paul S. Segerstrom (1998) or Zvi Griliches (1990) for a description of this data and its sources.

[16] F.M. Scherer (1999), p. 48.

(1990) suggests that the quality of patent applications has changed to where only the better ideas are presented for patents.[17] That is, the percentage of new ideas that are patented may have gone down. If Griliches is correct, then the number of patents understates the number of new ideas actually created.

The number of scientists and engineers employed in research and development is not a very accurate measure of research effort either. Modern economies are much more specialized than they were in the past, and thus more people are classified as *researchers* today than in the past. That does not mean that there is necessarily more research activity, however. Based on alternative measures of accumulated knowledge and the resources applied to innovation, the scientist Thomas Barlow (2001) in fact reports that while 25 years ago knowledge increased at a rate that doubled the total stock of human knowledge every 14 years, today the stock of knowledge doubles every five years.[18]

8.3.3 The knowledge burden

Benjamin Jones (2009) distinguishes an important reason why Scherer's finding of a slowdown in research productivity may be accurate: The higher the level of human technology, the more learning would-be innovators must go through before they reach the cutting edge of knowledge where the next innovation is to be found. Jones looks at data on Nobel Prize winners and other data on great inventors, and he finds that the average age at which inventors are most productive has increased consistently over the past century. Specifically, he finds that, compared to a century ago, "innovators are much less productive at younger ages, beginning to produce major ideas 8 years later at the end of the twentieth century than they did at the beginning."[19] Of course, the longer average lifespan of modern humans could offset the later start, but Jones' data suggests that the later start is not compensated for by increasing productivity later in life. Jones (2009, p. 1) concludes that "individual innovators are productive over a narrowing span of their life cycle, a trend that reduces — other things equal — the aggregate output of innovators." To explain this apparent slowdown in new ideas, in an accompanying paper to the one cited above Jones (2010) builds a model that exhibits what he calls the **knowledge burden mechanism**. This burden acts on innovative investments in much the same way that depreciation rises proportionally to the capital stock in the Solow growth model. It is not difficult to imagine a model in which the knowledge burden slows, or even stops, the rate of technological change.

---

[17] See also Zvi Griliches (1998) for a complete compilation of Griliches vast work on productivity growth and R&D expenditures.

[18] Thomas Barlow (2001), "The Great Thing about Frivolous Research," *Financial Times*, August 4/5.

[19] Benjamin F. Jones (2009), p. 1.

8.3.4 Finding the right combinations

Romer may actually be too pessimistic about the expansion of knowledge and ideas. Recall from Section 7.3.3 in the previous chapter that a **combinatoric growth process** is even more explosive than a multiplicative growth process. It is the combinatoric nature of innovation that drove Merck & Co., one of leading pharmaceutical companies, to build a huge new chemistry and drug discovery building on an attractive office campus in Pennsylvania. The size of the new building surprised many people, but not those familiar with combinatoric processes. Merck built the large building in order to bring together a greater number of diverse scientists from different fields. In the words of the mathematician Henri Poincaré: "To create consists precisely in not making useless combinations and in making those which are useful.... Among chosen combinations the most fertile will often be those formed of elements drawn from domains which are far apart."[20]

Interestingly, Martin Weitzman's (1996) optimism about the combinatoric nature of technological change leads him to signal the concern that, in the long-run, our biggest problem will not be a lack of potential ideas, but our inability to pursue the exploding number of potential ideas. As the saying in the R&D sector goes, "You never run out of ideas — you just run out of time." Weitzman worries that we will have to make choices, and we will often make wrong choices. Our future economic development will become increasingly path dependent because the number of alternative paths not taken expands much faster than the economy.

Weitzman may be too pessimistic about long-run technological change, however. Why wouldn't our improved technologies expand our capacity to evaluate and apply new ideas grow in the same combinatoric fashion as the set of potential new ideas? Technological advances in information technology will enable researchers to comb the ever-increasing set of potential combinations for the most fruitful ones. Our technical capacity to process information is expanding, and even though there will be more potentially viable paths to follow in the future, we will also have the technology to explore many more paths.

8.3.5 Case study: Finding the right combinations in Peru

Recall Poincaré's words above: "Sometimes the most distant ideas combine into the most useful new ideas." Sometimes the useful ideas are distant in terms of time, not space, as the following case illustrates.

Sally Bowen (1999) describes how nearly 1,500 years ago, the Indians of the Andes mountains in what is now Peru built elaborate terraces and irrigation ditches in order to grow a variety of crops in the mountainous areas they

---

[20] Henri Poincaré (1908), "Mathematical Creation," reprinted in Brewster Ghiselin, ed. (1952), *The Creative Process*, Berkeley: University of California Press.

inhabited. The Inca and Huari Indians used an ingenious combination of clay and cactus mixture to bond stones together, a mixture that was quite pliable and resistant to the constant earthquakes that rock the region. New irrigation ditches made with cement have suffered frequent cracking and therefore lose a lot of precious water. The terraces, which cover an estimated 2 million hectares (5 million acres) of the Andes region, have largely eroded, and without irrigation they are not very useful anyway, permitting only one crop every five or ten years in the very poor, dry soil.

The modern combination of chemical fertilizers and poor, eroded soil does not perform as well as the now-forgotten combination of water supplied by irrigation canals to well-maintained terraces. A new program, funded by a foreign aid organization from the United Kingdom, is now attempting to reintroduce the old methods, albeit with a few new twists. By convincing the very poor farmers in the Andean highlands to repair the ancient terraces and irrigation canals according to the old technology, but then introducing a rotation of different crops based on modern knowledge about how different crops affect the soil and enhance soil nutrients, two crops per year are possible. The vegetables, such as kava, beans, and lentils, have added some vegetable protein to the diets of the farmers, who have traditionally grown only corn and potatoes. By the year 2000, 14 kilometers of irrigation ditches were restored, as well as 200 hectares of abandoned terraces. Old ideas can still be put to use; in this case, the combination of modern agronomy and ancient irrigation canals is a good new idea.

8.3.6 Protectionism and creative destruction

For the process of *creative destruction* to work, there must be *destruction* as well as *creation*. If an initial creation is not followed by a second creation, which implies the destruction of the first creation's advantage, then there will be no permanent growth in real output. Innovators have an incentive to try to prevent others from *destroying* their temporary advantage in the market, and in many societies the political environment permits them to slow the creative destruction process.

As the economic historian Joel Mokyr (1990, p. 301) writes:

> The enemies of technological change were not the lack of useful new ideas, but social forces that for one reason or another tried to preserve the status quo.

Stephen Parente and Edward Prescott (2000) propose that policymakers should establish rules, regulations, and procedures to prevent past innovators from obstructing future innovators. Anti-trust laws may be necessary not only to prevent monopolies but also to prevent current industry leaders from blocking new innovators.

8.3.7 The Holmes and Schmitz model

In the Schumpeterian tradition, Thomas Holmes and James Schmitz (1995, 1998) hypothesize that a certain country has two imperfectly competitive manufacturers who engage in Schumpeterian competition, each trying to establish technological superiority. Technological leadership enables a firm to earn a monopoly profit from production after effectively *destroying* its competition with its *creativity*. The *technological follower*, unable to profitably produce its obsolete product, then devotes all available resources to research and development in order to recapture technological leadership. The leading firm, on the other hand, must decide how many resources to allocate to the production that generates the profit with which to recoup its past investment in creating new technology and how much to allocate to research to create further innovations that will generate new profits after its current innovation is creatively destroyed. Or, government planners must decide how much tax revenue to allocate to universities for research and how much to use for building infrastructure to support production and distribution.

Holmes and Schmitz add an important wrinkle to the standard Schumpeterian model, however. They permit the technological leader to allocate resources to a *third* activity: *obstructing* the efforts of the technological follower to regain leadership. The decision to produce, research, or obstruct depends on the potential payoffs from each form of activity. Resources are allocated to R&D so long as the expected payoff is at least as great as the opportunity cost. Obviously, the more resources that are devoted to R&D, the faster is the rate of technological change. If resources are used to obstruct the follower, then R&D activity by competing firms slows.

Holmes and Schmitz model an economy in which foreign suppliers of manufactured goods can be subject to import tariffs. Consumers are assumed to have specific preferences over domestic manufactured goods, foreign manufactured goods, and domestic services provided. The latter are provided by a competitive domestic service sector, the manufactured goods are provided by a single leading producer who has most recently innovated successfully. Only one manufactured product is supplied by a domestic firm, depending on which firm has most recently innovated and has the leading product all consumers prefer. Holmes and Schmitz assume a positive elasticity of substitution between domestic and foreign manufactures, which means that demand for domestic manufactures will be higher if foreign products are denied entry into the domestic market or if the foreign products are highly taxed.

In the Holmes and Schmitz model, the degree to which domestic manufacturers engage in research or obstruction of each other's research depends on the relative payoffs to each form of activity. Holmes and Schmitz also show that there will be less obstruction under free trade than under restricted trade. The intuition for this conclusion is straightforward. In a protected domestic economy, the technological leader enjoys greater returns to innovation when it only has to compete with the domestic service sector for consumer dollars, and, hence, the payoff to obstructing other domestic manufacturers' research efforts is higher. In an open economy, when the manufacturer also has to compete with foreign firms, obstructing domestic competition has little effect on future profits. Worldwide competition would have to be obstructed, and that is much more difficult and costly. Hence, it becomes more useful to innovate than to expend resources obstructing the domestic competitor, and the domestic economy gains a more rapid rate of technological change under free trade. Of course, as mentioned above, domestic firms may find it profitable to lobby for trade barriers to keep foreign technology out of the country.

In a Schumpeterian framework, protectionism is a dynamic concept, driven by the interest of earlier innovators to prevent future innovators from creatively destroying their profits. Joseph Schumpeter's writing suggest that he was not always very optimistic about governments' ability to resist protectionism even in his dynamic creative destruction framework. Among other things, past innovators currently enjoy the profits of their past accomplishments, and this gives them a real advantage to influence government policies, regulations, and financial incentives in ways that obstruct future innovators. Potential future innovators do not yet know whether they will be profitable in the future; they have enough trouble raising resources to innovate much less paying for the access to government officials to defend themselves against obstructionist policies. There is, therefore, always the danger that vested interests will raise barriers to the creative destruction process. And, without continued creative destruction, technological change slows down or stops altogether.

There are also cases where new paradigms lobby to destroy existing paradigms where the new paradigms are not necessarily welfare improving. The growth of the automobile industry at the expense of the railroads is such a case in point. By means of massive advertising, political alliances with construction companies, real estate developers, and oil companies, the U.S. automobile industry managed to bias government policy towards building roads, shutting down public rail transportation, and subsidizing suburban sprawl that would require personal transport like the automobile. The classic example was General Motors' lobbying to close the Los Angeles urban rail network in the late 1940s. Even today, when the full costs of the carbon-intensive U.S. economy are well understood, it is still difficult to overcome the political and economic clout of the automobile, oil, and real estate industries. Technological protectionism is still a common business strategy.

8.3.8 Protectionism and paradigm shifts

Protectionism and the intentional obstruction of innovation can also be analyzed from the perspective of paradigms and paradigm shifts described by Thomas

Kuhn (1962) and Giovanni Dosi (1982). Recall from the previous chapter that Kuhn suggested science was an episodic process that consisted of periods of normal science in which scientists worked within a specific research program, or paradigm, that were interrupted by occasional scientific revolutions that substantially changed the paradigm or research program.   Pierre Bourdieu (1990) lent support with his discussion of how the **culture** of a field tends to protect the dominant paradigm.   There are very strong psychological and sociological forces at work to maintain a given path of technological change, even when the process is obviously slowing down and becoming more difficult.

Dosi focuses on private business innovation, and he finds additional economic forces at work in protecting the dominant paradigm and effectively obstructing revolutionary innovations that shift paradigms.   Dosi argues that once a new technological paradigm becomes dominant in an industry, oligopolies and even monopolies tend to develop through mergers and acquisitions or simple technical superiority.   Richard Nelson and Sidney Winter (1982) describe how the dominant technological paradigm, and the technologies generated under it, in fact cause a dynamic growth of powerful oligopolies. Once these large firms internalize the dominant technological paradigm and enjoy an advantage in developing further technologies within that paradigm, they have every incentive to stop future paradigm shifts.   Their control of the paradigm and its related technologies also tends to give them the wealth to engage in the political action to protect the paradigm that is the source of their income.

We thus see today's oil companies lobbying very hard to stop government programs to develop alternative energy sources.   They also lobby against government mandated fuel efficiency standards, subsidies for buying electric automobiles, and government funded mass transportation projects.   Oil companies want to prevent a shift in the technological paradigm from carbon fuels to alternative non-carbon energy sources.

In summary, the smooth technological change suggested by the abstract Romer/Schumpeter model needs to be qualified. Innovation is not only a costly process that requires the use of scarce resources, but there are various economic, social, and natural forces at work that impede the process.   The barriers to innovation include the difficulty in applying the scientific method in the real world where information is limited and innovators have strong incentives to protect their previously-conquered innovative advantages.   These issues will be examined again in later chapters that discuss institutions, international economic policies, the distribution of income, and environmental policies.

8.3.9 When is technological change progress?

The steps of the scientific method and the combinatoric nature of technological change seem to suggest that technological change is always a positive development, either increasing our knowledge, improving some product or procedure, or enhancing the overall economic or social system. However, there have been many new technologies that have proven to be harmful for human life. Technological change is not always equivalent to **human progress** in the sense that it unequivocally improves the well-being of humans. Human progress implies an improvement in human happiness or satisfaction with life.

We can just imagine how, for example, the discovery of fire by one of our ancestors hundreds of thousands of years ago permitted them to protect themselves against the cold, but we can also imagine some of our ancestors asphyxiated in their caves because they did not properly ventilate the smoke. Today, nuclear power is often touted as a source of clean energy, but the Hiroshima nuclear genocide, the Chernobyl nuclear meltdown, and the Fukushima multiple meltdowns triggered by the 2011 earthquake and tsunami in Japan make it clear that nuclear power can also intentionally or inadvertently kill large numbers of human beings. The discovery of petroleum as a source of energy provided humanity with many benefits, but the resulting growth of carbon emissions have now set in motion climate changes that threaten human life as we have known it for the past 100,000 years.

Estimates such as Mathis Wackernagel *et al.* (2002) showing humanity's footprint exceeds the capacity of the global ecosystem imply that true technological change, duly accounting for the reductions in the services of nature as well as the gains in human production, has recently been negative, not positive as suggested by the growth of measured GDP. In other words, the technological changes we experienced recently do not all constitute human progress. Some new technologies that increase output in the economic sphere actually damage one or more of the spheres humans also live in and depend on for their survival.

8.4 Technology and Developing Economies

The many empirical and theoretical studies of economic change and development have made it clear that the huge differences in per capita output across countries are, in large part, due to differences in the accumulation and application of knowledge, ideas, methods, procedures, and social institutions. Because diminishing returns and depreciation prevent low-income economies from catching up to high-income countries by means of factor accumulation alone, only faster and more positive technological change in lower-income economies can bring about convergence of per capita output in the world in the long run. Chapter 6 pointed out that in the long run continued expansion of production requires that such output growth be sustainable, that is, compatible with the natural and social spheres.

8.4.1 *Endogenous technological change and convergence*

The Schumpeterian and Romer models of endogenous technological change do not suggest that technological change will necessarily be any faster or more welfare enhancing in countries with low levels of accumulated technology than in countries that have already achieved high levels of technology.   The Schumpeterian R&D model suggests that technological change depends on the costs and gains from innovation. The costs of innovation are likely to be higher in countries that are poorly endowed with the resources necessary to generate new knowledge, have less human capital, and have accumulated less knowledge on which to build the combinatoric process of knowledge expansion. Also, the gains from innovation are likely to be smaller in low income countries. Perhaps we should not be surprised by the divergence of income levels throughout the world, therefore.

On the other hand, poor countries may be able to take advantage of the *nonrival* nature of technology. Recall that knowledge, ideas, methods, and all other forms of technology can be used by many people in many countries once they have been created in any one country. Developing economies are spared the expense of having to "reinvent the wheel," so to speak. In fact, one reason the Solow model has often been interpreted as predicting convergence is that it was assumed that, in the long run, technology's nonrival nature implies that it will be equally available everywhere.

Unfortunately, even the most casual observer is likely to notice that technology has not spread uniformly throughout the world. There are two main reasons for the lack of complete **technology transfers** to all parts of the world. First of all, there are barriers to the free flow of ideas and knowledge. Secondly, existing technology is not entirely free; there are very real costs involved in acquiring and applying ideas and knowledge.

The most obvious barriers to technology and knowledge transfers between countries are the many explicit and implicit barriers to reading, discussing, and studying foreign ideas.   An extreme case is the North Korean government's policy of keeping its citizens completely in the dark about what goes on outside the country and prohibiting contact with foreigners. More common are the rules imposed by religious authorities to discourage their followers from reading certain books and discussing "blasphemous" ideas that do not fit traditional approved beliefs. Culture more generally plays a subtle but significant role in preventing the spread of knowledge and technology. Many people effectively self-censor when it comes to new or foreign ideas because they are uncomfortable with the unfamiliar and the unknown. Recall Pierre Bourdieu's (1990) warning that no one can escape their culture and fully adhere to the scientific method when they confront choices among ideas, concepts, methods, and knowledge.   On the other hand, some societies reward new ideas and technologies, and they honor those who innovate.

Often, there are explicit and implicit costs to acquiring existing knowledge from elsewhere. The acquisition of technology may require the costly purchase of the equipment or machinery that embodies the technology. Similarly, it takes time and money to travel or study overseas, where the knowledge is available. There may be explicit prohibitions on foreign investment, which is recognized as one of the important channels through which knowledge moves between countries. Some available knowledge is protected by patents, which means other users have to pay license fees to apply the patented knowledge. International commerce has traditionally been an important channel for the exchange of ideas and know-how, but there are still many barriers to international trade. As discussed later in Chapters 14 and 16, international trade has a great number of consequences. Also, the world's lowest-income countries, who have the greatest need to import foreign technology, have often restricted international trade. At the same time, some of the highest-income countries often restrict trade in the types of products that would result in technology flows to poor countries.

8.4.2 Can technology transfers close the gap?

It is difficult to see how there ever can be an economic convergence across countries unless low-income countries take advantage of many of the ideas that others have already created. Original research is expensive, requiring many specialized inputs that are likely to be especially scarce in low-income economies. If it is indeed less costly and easier to adapt existing technologies than it is to develop a new technology from scratch, then economies with lower levels of technology may be able to grow faster.

To some extent, the increasing willingness of many developing countries to open their borders to foreign trade and investment reflects the growing realization that it is more difficult to generate technological change when the country is economically isolated. After three decades of near isolation under its communist government, China now permits its citizens to study overseas, acquire foreign books and newspapers, and communicate on the Internet. Among developing countries, China is now the largest destination of foreign business investment.

Also important for the spread of knowledge are the improvements in international communications. Table 8.1 shows the number of telephone lines, cellular phones, and Internet users per thousand people. The differences across countries and regions are large. For example, there is only one cell phone user and one Internet user for every one thousand Ethiopians, but there are 910 cell phone users and 534 Internet users for every one thousand Finns. If the spread of technology and knowledge depends on communications, it will be difficult for poor countries to catch up to the rest of the world in technology.

Table 8.1 Communications and Technology: 1990 and 2003

	Telephone Lines (Per 1,000 people)		Cellular Subscribers (Per 1,000 people)		Internet Users (Per 1,000 people)	
	1990	*2003*	*1990*	*2003*	*1990*	*2003*
World	**81**	**184**	**1**	**226**	**1**	**120**
High income OECD countries	**439**	**567**	**9**	**705**	**3**	**480**
Australia	456	542	11	719	0	567
Finland	534	492	52	910	4	534
France	495	566	5	696	1	366
Germany	441	657	4	785	1	473
Japan	441	472	7	679	0	483
United States	547	624	21	546	8	556
Central & Eastern Europe	**120**	**232**	**0**	**287**	**0**	**-**
Czech Republic	158	360	0	965	0	308
Hungary	96	349	0	769	0	232
Poland	86	307	0	451	0	323
Russian Federation	140	253	0	249	0	-
Developing countries	**29**	**113**	**0**	**134**	**0**	**53**
East & Southeast Asia	*18*	*172*	*0*	*212*	*0*	*80*
China	6	209	0	215	0	63
Malaysia	89	182	5	442	0	344
Singapore	346	450	17	852	0	509
South Korea	308	538	2	701	0	610
Thailand	24	105	1	394	0	111
Viet Nam	1	54	0	34	0	43
Latin America & Carib.	*89*	*165*	*0*	*239*	*0*	*-*
Chile	68	221	1	511	0	272
Cuba	31	64	0	3	0	9
Mexico	65	160	1	295	0	120
Venezuela	76	111	0	273	0	60
Arab States	*79*	*94*	*4*	*118*	*0*	*49*
Egypt	30	127	0	84	0	44
Iran	40	220	0	51	0	72
Lebanon	155	200	0	234	0	143
Syria	41	-	0	68	0	35
South Asia	*7*	*47*	*0*	*24*	*0*	*18*
India	6	46	0	25	0	17
Bangladesh	2	5	0	10	0	2
Myanmar (Burma)	2	7	0	1	0	1
Sub-Saharan Africa	*5*	*9*	*0*	*54*	*0*	*-*
Cote d'Ivoire	6	14	0	77	0	7
Ethiopia	3	6	0	1	0	1
Congo	7	2	0	94	0	4
Namibia	39	66	0	116	0	34
Nigeria	3	7	0	26	0	6

Source: United Nations (2005), *Human Development Report 2005*, UNDP: New York; Table 13.

From another perspective, cell phones may represent a technology that makes it easier for developing countries to improve their communications. For instance, Table 8.1 shows that in some Eastern European countries, e.g., the Czech Republic and Hungary, phone usage has caught up with the most developed countries not because these countries increased the number of traditional land lines, but because they expanded cell phone capacity.   In general, low-technology countries can skip intermediate technological paradigms and jump to the most efficient new technologies. Late developers are not as path-dependent as those countries that had to develop new technologies from scratch and without a good understanding of the costs and benefits of the available paths.   Latecomers have an advantage. For the time being, however, Table 8.1 suggest that most exchanges of ideas and information continue to occur within and among those countries that have already achieved high levels of technological progress.

8.5 Technology and the Natural Environment

Technological change can, in principal, mitigate the severe stress that economic growth is causing in the natural environment. New technologies are already available to reduce carbon emissions, for example, and further research will uncover more new ways to mitigate global warming, the loss of fish stocks in the oceans, reverse the destruction of rain forests, and other destructive practices.   Better agricultural practices and the replacement of wasteful production of biofuels like corn ethanol by other sources of energy could be achieved relatively quickly. Wind and solar energy can be greatly expanded almost immediately. Automobiles that are twice as fuel efficient as current vehicles are ready for production. Yet, despite the urgency and the impressive record of recent human innovation, efforts to develop and apply new technologies to deal with long-run environmental problems such as global warming and the loss of biodiversity are strongly resisted by many groups in most countries.

Such resistance is, in part, due to the cost of research and innovation. After ignoring the environmental costs of emitting carbon into the atmosphere or converting more and more natural habitat to farmland, no one is enthusiastic about beginning to pay those costs. The multi-dimensional Solow model from Chapter 6 showed that to prevent the growth of output in the economic sphere from eventually reversing, humanity must either engage in costly conservation of the ecosystem or pursue costly efforts to increase the efficiency with which human economic and social activity uses nature's resources. In the latter case, the Schumpeterian model makes it clear that if producers and consumers do not have to pay the costs of the environmental damage they cause, then there is no incentive for private innovators to develop the technologies that can reduce those costs. It is difficult to see how humanity can avoid environmental disasters without accepting a role for government policy.

This is not to say that prices could not change human behavior and stimulate conservation and innovation in the natural sphere. Conventional economic theory hypothesizes that shifts in the relative prices of factors of production motivate technological innovation that economizes on the use of the relatively more expensive factor(s). Empirical evidence shows that innovation indeed does respond to price shifts. For example, high energy prices during the 1970s strongly stimulated the development of energy-saving technologies.

8.5.1 Making environmentally friendly technology "profitable"

Global warming and the resulting climate change become apparent very slowly and with a lag, as explained in Chapter 6. The precise climate changes that current human actions are likely to cause are also uncertain. Hence, current price signals would not be very accurate, even if we had markets where the future consequences of current greenhouse gas emissions were priced. We do not have such markets, of course, so for the time being greenhouse gas emissions are unpriced externalities that individual producers and consumers pay little attention to.

Scientific data and models are available, however, and policymakers can use them to design taxes, subsidies, regulations, and direct assistance to producers, consumers, and innovators to ensure that environmental technologies are developed and applied. That is, government policy can be used to set the size and lifetime of the profit box for entrepreneurs, as in Figure 8.1, that reflect the true social gains from innovations so as to bring human activity more closely in line with the capacity of the natural environment. The government could use taxes to raise the costs of production that does not apply the new methods, procedures, alternative inputs, or conservation methods that innovation introduces. Alternatively, government policymakers could subsidize innovative activities and application of the innovations in accordance with the size and lifetime of the profit box in Figure 8.1. More direct incentives, such as limits on production that causes greenhouse gas emissions or a ban on the consumption of products produced by greenhouse gas emitting industries, could also provide strong incentives for creating less environmentally damaging technologies.

Governments will have to take more direct roles in generating new technologies, especially in generating the more basic scientific research that is necessary for dealing with complex and holistic global environmental problems. Recall how tax-funded land grant universities in the U.S. have advanced agricultural technology. The high risk and long payouts to basic scientific research calls for more funding for government research agencies, universities, and international organizations. Global problems like climate change, conserving the Earth's ecosystem, and the developing technologies that reduce the human footprint on the natural environment are not readily translated into profit boxes for private enterprises. Therefore, we need a collective response to what are effectively large profit boxes for all of humanity.

8.5.2 Making inter-generational decisions

Environmental issues like global warming and biodiversity are also challenging for the simple reason that they are long-term in nature. The difficulty of predicting the future, as discussed earlier in Chapter 6, is just one of the problems policymakers face. There is also the problem of how to value the welfare of future generations relative to the welfare of current generations. Equation (8.11) reminds us that the PVI is the discounted stream of future gains from innovation. A non-zero discount rate, no matter how small, will inevitably make gains in the distant future worth very little. For example, a discount rate of 5 percent per year means that a \$100 gain 100 years from now is worth a mere \$0.75 today. Why should humans today devote several percent of their per capita GDP to developing new technologies to mitigate global warming when the gains will not show up for a century? The size of the discount rate is an important issue because those who will gain from today's expenditures in the distant future are not alive to lobby for their interests. When it comes to making choices that impact the distant future, should current human beings discount the welfare of future generations at all?

In the case of corporations and business entrepreneurs, it seems quite reasonable for a firm to engage in costly R&D activity only when the returns will appear within in a few years. In such a short-term case, a discount rate of 5 percent seems reasonable, given the average cost of borrowing money to carry out research projects. But, the Schumpeterian model is general enough to apply to technologies to deal with the threats and barriers to human survival. Clearly, humanity faces a challenge in translating the future state of humanity into costly investment decisions. We will return to these questions in Chapter 18, where we discuss what environmental policies are needed to make future economic growth sustainable.

8.5.3 Environmental costs and true economic development

Political and business leaders often claim that environmental regulations, restrictions on carbon emissions, pollution controls, protection of endangered species, and other environmental regulations slow economic growth. They are correct, if short-run GDP growth is society's goal. Sustainable growth across all three spheres of human existence is likely to result in slower economic growth in the economic sphere. As illustrated by the multi-dimensional Solow model in Chapter 6, we have measured economic growth, or GDP growth, as the growth of production in the economic sphere. In today's high income countries, such growth duly accounted for the depreciation costs, and it also seems to have motivated enough costly research and development to continually shift the production function higher in the Y and K dimension. Unfortunately, humanity has ignored the costs of conservation and innovation in the natural sphere.

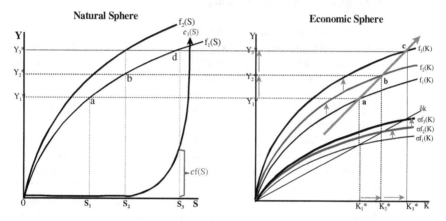

Figure 8.9 Economic Growth when the Natural Sphere Is Stressed

Figure 8.9, which is repeated from Chapter 6, shows that humanity got something of a free ride with regard to the **renewable services** of nature produced in the natural sphere. Up to the level of output Y_2 the natural sphere was able to produce the necessary amounts of fresh air, clean water, flood control, pollination, and other services to the economic sphere without damaging the ecosystem. However, if there is no improvement in the efficiency with which humanity uses nature's services, the growth of output to Y_3 requires conservation costs equal to cf(S) if future output is to be sustained. Alternatively, output can be sustainably increased to Y_3 if humanity engages in costly innovations that raise the production function in the natural dimension to $f_1(S)$ to $f_2(S)$.

To get to Y_3, human society incurs the costs of investment to cover depreciation and the growth of the capital stock to move the economy to the new steady state where output equals Y_3, and it also must cover the costs of the innovative activities that shifted the production function to $f_3(K)$. To make growth to Y_3 sustainable, human society must, therefore, increase its saving and investment to cover the additional conservation and/or innovative costs in the natural sphere. Society is likely to settle for some combination of increased saving and reduced, but sustainable, growth. For example, as more savings are allocated towards dealing with improving the efficiency with which society uses nature's resources in the natural sphere of human existence, saving devoted to new investment in factories, machines, roads, and other forms of physical capital in the economic sphere will be reduced, as will savings devoted to research and development of new production technologies. Hence, the growth of GDP, that is output in the economic sphere, will not grow as fast. Figure 8.10 illustrates one possible outcome of a shift in savings towards innovation in both the economic and natural spheres rather than only to investment in the economic sphere. In this case, economic growth would take the economy to point d and an output level of Y_2^*.

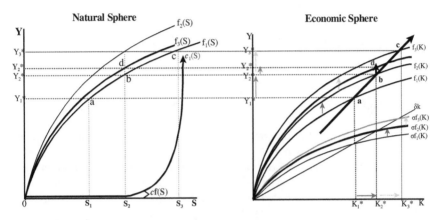

Figure 8.10 Economic Growth with Investment in the Natural Sphere

8.5.4 The Jevons effect complicates adjustment

Figure 8.10 refers only to the services of nature, the renewable resources, in the natural sphere. Recall from Chapter 6 that the physical inputs of **exhaustible resources**, H, must decline over time in order to avoid depletion of exhaustible resources. Figure 8.11 repeats the important Figure 6.5 from Chapter 6; this diagram shows the relationship between output Y and exhaustible resources H, taking all other inputs as given. The use of exhaustible resources can decline over time if technological change raises the efficiency of production and shifts the production function $Y = f(H)$ in Figure 8.11 up fast enough. Figure 8.11 illustrates how sustainable output growth from Y_1 to Y_2 to Y_3 is possible when technological change shifts the production function for exhaustible natural resources from $f_1(H)$ to $f_2(H)$ to $f_3(H)$ so that the economy uses declining amounts of physical inputs of exhaustible resources from, say, H_1 to H_2 to H_3.

Technological change per se does not guarantee sustainable output growth, however. The uncomfortable fact is that there has been very rapid technological change over the past 200 years, but the exploitation of exhaustible resources has expanded, not declined as Figure 8.11 illustrates. The noted nineteenth century economist W. Stanley Jevons (1865) explained why technological change will often fail to reduce resource use. Jevons explained that when technological

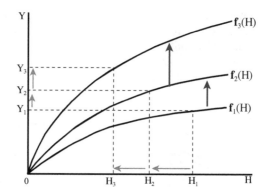

Figure 8.11 Technological Change Can Reduce the Use of Exhaustible Resources

improvements lower the amount of resources needed to produce goods and services, economic growth is stimulated and, in the end, more resources are used. This phenomenon is now called the **Jevons effect** or the **rebound effect**.

Jevons developed his argument around the use of coal. He argued that the Industrial Revolution was based on coal and the vast technological advances that found ever more efficient uses of coal to power machinery, transportation, and new materials. But, the result of all this technological progress would be the exhaustion of England's supply of coal. Economic growth was, therefore, both caused by technological change and ultimately condemned by technological progress. This puts the Schumpeterian model in an interesting perspective. Indeed, the Jevons effect has been observed for many exhaustible resources. The world uses much more iron ore today than it did 100 years ago, even though steel mills are much more efficient today at transforming ore into final materials. And today's more efficient gasoline motors have not prevented sharp increases in worldwide consumption of oil.

Sustainability thus requires humanity to generate not merely technological change, but a sufficiently high rate of technological change across all spheres of human existence to overcome the Jevons effect. Sustainable economic development may, therefore, require very substantial diversions of resources towards innovation. GDP may grow much more slowly. But, growth will be sustainable.

8.6 Conclusions and a Critique

This chapter has described Paul Romer's "Schumpeterian" model in which technological change is the result of intentional investment in research and development motivated by the expectation of future gains. These gains can take the form of profits accruing to private firms who gained market power through their innovations. They may also consist of an increase in the general welfare of society, which motivate government innovation, research carried out by universities, and other collective institutional arrangements to organize scientific and practical research and innovation. The fundamental idea behind the Schumpeterian model of technological change is that it takes costly resources to generate new ideas and knowledge. Resources are scarce, and therefore innovation must compete with other uses for society's resources, such as production and investment in tools and machines incorporating current technologies. The Schumpeterian world therefore faces an intertemporal maximization problem whose solution requires the comparison of the potential marginal gains from devoting resources to innovation and the marginal opportunity costs of taking those resources away from current production. This chapter makes it clear that output growth will be fastest in those societies whose natural and social environments permit individual and collective behavior that generates efficient solutions to this complex maximization problem. Sustainable economic development requires the maximization problem to be framed holistically to take into consideration the economic, social, and natural spheres in which humanity resides.

The Romer/Schumpeter model of technological change is often presented as a successor to the Solow model. It is better to see the former as complementing, not substituting, the Solow model because it explains the technological change that the Solow model takes as a given. At the same time, the Schumpeterian model ignores many variables, which is to be expected given the focus on the complex process of technological change. The Solow model's emphasis on diminishing returns and the need for maintaining balance among the effective inputs provides a good counterweight to the Schumpeterian model's rather optimistic view of technological change as an unlimited source of future economic growth. The multi-dimensional Solow model provides a sober reminder that sustainable growth requires an extremely complex variety of technological changes across all three spheres of human existence. Finally, the process of economic growth is not the smooth process that both models suggest, which means we have to look further to get an accurate representation of the complex process of economic development.

This chapter concludes Part II of the textbook. You have now familiarized yourself with a broad range of models and ideas that comprise the theory of economic growth and development. These models, when properly selected to fit the circumstances, help you understand and analyze the process of economic change and development. The next section addresses the details surrounding the principal variables contained in the models you have studied, such as population growth, investment in physical capital, education and human capital, and the role of government and other institutions. We will, of course, take the usual holistic approach, which means we will extend the analysis across a variety of models developed by economists over the past 200 plus years. We will also borrow from the accumulated knowledge of other fields, and continually move between the system and its parts. After taking into account the many details and complexity of human existence, you will appreciate how well the models we have studied explain economic development.

Key Terms and Concepts

Combinatoric growth process
Creative destruction
Culture
Deadweight losses
Entrepreneur
Evolutionary process
Exhaustible resources
Human progress
Jevons effect
Knowledge burden mechanism
Learning curve

Normal scientific research
Paradigm shifts
Rebound effect
Renewable services
Risk
Routinization of innovation
Schumpeterian model
Social deviance
Technological competition
Technology transfers
Uncertainty

Questions and Problems

1. Is it easier to expand current knowledge when we already know a lot, or does it become more and more difficult to think of new ideas after more ideas have already been thought of? Answer this question using material from this chapter, but feel free to add your own thoughts on the matter, provided of course that they exhibit logical reasoning.

2. If someone invented a new automobile that runs on dirt, but no one bought it, would this be considered technological progress? Discuss.

3. There are many examples of open source computer programs and operating systems. The best known ones are Java and Linux. Some think that open source coding for computer programs and operating systems is not the most efficient way of furthering technology because there are no obvious incentives for people to contribute their best efforts to improving these computer technologies. Discuss whether technology is more easily advanced through open source cooperation or private profit-motivated research.

4. Explain how the concepts of nonrival goods, excludability, and intellectual property rights are related to the process of technological progress.

5. Teddy Roosevelt once said: "The only thing worse than a regulated monopoly is an unregulated monopoly." Would Joseph Schumpeter agree with Roosevelt? Explain.

6. The text states that "our models of endogenous technological change do not give developing economies any distinct advantage or disadvantage in generating

technological progress." In other words, the endogenous models of technological change do not predict "convergence" as the Solow model seems to do. But, the text also points out that convergence becomes possible if ideas move from the more advanced to the less technologically-advanced economies. Discuss how the international flow of ideas and technology can be enhanced. What prevents the international transfer of technology?

7. Equation 8.9 in the main text represents the Schumpeterian R&D model. It lists the main variables that drive technological innovation and, hence, economic growth. Describe each of the variables and the direction of influence as given by the sign of the variable in the functional relationship.

8. The growth economist Paul Romer developed an *externality* model of economic growth before he published his well-known 1990 Schumpeterian R&D model of technological change. Romer writes, "When I look back on my work on growth, my greatest satisfaction comes from having rejected the first round of external effects models that I tried." Discuss some possible reasons why Romer is more satisfied with his 1990 Schumpeterian model.

9. In Sections 8.3.3, Benjamin Jones distinguishes an important reason why Scherer's finding of a slowdown in research productivity may be accurate: he refers to this reason as the *knowledge burden mechanism*. Explain and evaluate Jones' model.

10. Can you design a model of new ideas in which the production of new technology is not only dependent on the stock of existing technology, but also that the production of new ideas requires proportionately higher levels of education before new innovation becomes possible? Hint: Recall the Solow model in which higher levels of output require ever-larger stocks of capital that must be maintained and renewed.

11. Holmes and Schmitz expand the Schumpeterian model to include the option of obstructing innovation as well as the usual two options of producing or innovating. Do you think this is a realistic expansion of the model? Can you think of ways in which innovation is obstructed?

12. What motivation would anyone have to obstruct innovation? After all, isn't technological progress a good thing for everyone? Discuss.

13. Suppose that the government passes a law mandating that all automobiles be able to drive at least 50 miles per gallon of gasoline. What does the Jevons effect suggest will happen to total gasoline usage? Explain the Jevons effect in your answer. What other policies might work better to reduce the consumption of gasoline?

14. Some research concludes that subsidies for research and development have little effect in generating new technologies to mitigate global warming without being accompanied by specific requirements that the technology be applied or that taxes internalize the cost of carbon emissions. Wouldn't the availability of alternatives to carbon-based energy be enough to reduce carbon emissions?

15. One of the five fundamental ideas of Schumpeterian models of technological progress listed in section 8.2 is: "Innovation creates new products and techniques that are better, cheaper, more attractive, and more convenient than existing products, which makes them more desirable than existing products and techniques." Do you think this description covers all innovations in a capitalist economy? Discuss.

Appendix 8.1:   Mathematical Proof of the Positive Effect of β

Specifically, in Section 8.3.6 the equilibrium level of N occurs where the PVI and CoI curves, given by equations (8.6) and (8.11), intersect.   That is, in equilibrium the following equality holds:

$$\sum_{j=1}^{(\beta/N)} 1(1+r)^j \mu(R-N)(\beta/N) = w\beta \tag{A1.1}$$

Dividing each side of equation (A8.1) by β gives us the equilibrium condition:

$$\sum_{j=1}^{(\beta/N)} 1(1+r)^j \mu(R-N)(1/N) = w \tag{A1.2}$$

At the margin, the changes in PVI and CoI induced by a change in β are equal to the partial derivatives ∂PVI/∂β and ∂CoI/∂β, respectively.   Since β enters into both the CoI and PVI equations as a simple multiplicative factor, the partial derivatives of CoI and PVI with respect to β are, respectively

$$\partial PVI/\partial\beta = \sum_{j=1}^{(\beta/N)} 1(1+r)^j \mu(R-N)(1/N) \tag{A1.3}$$

and

$$\partial CoI/\partial\beta = w \tag{A1.4}$$

Equation (A1.2) determined that the right hand sides of (A1.3) and (A1.4) are equal, and, therefore, the two partial derivatives are equal.   That is, a decrease in β causes *equal* shifts in the CoI curve and the PVI curve at the equilibrium level of N.   Hence, the offsetting effects keep N unchanged after a decline in β in Figure 8.8, and the shift in the **q** = (1/β) curve in the bottom portion of the diagram determines the net effect of a decline in β on innovation. This led us to conclude that, under the plausible conditions, an improvement in the efficiency of innovation, that is, a decline in β, will raise the amount of innovation in the economy.

Appendix 8.2: A Mathematical Version of the Schumpeterian Model

Growth models are normally presented in mathematical form, not the graphic form of this chapter. In this appendix, we present a simple mathematical growth model that follows logic similar to that of the graphic model of the previous section, albeit with one important difference. Rather than making the assumption that each successive innovation (new product) replaces earlier innovations (products), the model in this appendix assumes that innovation consists of new products that are added to the existing stock of products. This model treats technological change as a continual accumulation of knowledge rather than the pure process of creative destruction in which new products eliminate and replace old products. In the growth literature, these two types of models are referred to as "quality ladder" models and "expanding variety" models, respectively. For example, in their advanced graduate-level textbook on economic growth, Robert Barro and Xavier Sala-i-Martin (2004) devote separate chapters to these two groups of models of endogenous technological change. The dichotomy between the two types of models is not as great as it seems; as shown below, the conclusions of the models are nearly identical. This is why they are used interchangeably in the growth literature.

Innovation and Profit

Suppose that each act of innovation consists of creating a new firm that produces a new product. We start with n firms in the economy, each producing one of n different products. Suppose also that one unit of labor is required to produce a product; this implies that the marginal (and average) cost of producing each good is equal to the wage rate, w. Because each product is different, each producer enjoys some degree of market power so that each firm faces a downward-sloping demand curve. For simplicity, suppose that each firm faces an identical demand curve, which means that each firm sets the same price equal to

$$p = w(1/\gamma) \tag{A2.1}$$

where $0 < \gamma < 1$ and the price markup $p - w = \mu = [(1 - \gamma)/\gamma]w$. Since $w = p\gamma$, profit per unit is $p(1 - \gamma)$. Because entrepreneurs face downward-sloping demand curves, they can set a price above the marginal cost of production w and, potentially, recover the cost of innovation.

The total value of output is GDP, and therefore total profits in the economy are equal to

$$\Pi = GDP(1 - \gamma) \tag{A2.2}$$

The profit of any one of the n identical firms is

$$\pi = [GDP(1 - \gamma)]/n \tag{A2.3}$$

The present value of the earnings of a successful innovation is equal to the discounted stream of future profits, or

$$PV = \sum_{j=0}^{\infty} \rho^i \pi_{t=I} \tag{A2.4}$$

where ρ is the discount factor $1/(1 + r)$, where r is the interest rate, and the $\pi_{t=i}$ are the future profits in each future time period t. The present value of all future profits can be thought of as the stock market or equity value of the firm.

The Equilibrium Level of Entrepreneurial Activity

Entrepreneurs will innovate and enter the market so long as the present value of future profits, PV, exceeds the current cost of product development. Suppose that β is equal to the units of labor required to develop each new product. The cost of developing a new product is thus $w\beta$. Assuming that there is a fixed number of workers in the economy, the more workers are hired by firms to develop new products, the higher will be w, the opportunity cost of those workers' marginal product in producing goods. Innovation will stop expanding when the discounted future earnings from producing the nth good are exactly equal to the cost of creating the nth good. Putting together the costs and profits from innovation, the *innovation profit,* defined as θ, is

$$\theta = PV - w\beta \tag{A2.5}$$

If there is competitive innovation, meaning that all prospective entrepreneurs can demand resources for innovation and, if successful, market their new products, then $\theta = 0$ and

$$PV = \beta w \tag{A2.6}$$

Equation (A2.6) represents the equilibrium condition for innovation profits. This equilibrium condition is similar to the intersection of the CoI and PVI curves in Figure 8.5.

The Equilibrium Rate of Technological Progress

We assume that firms live forever, but their profits are gradually eroded by the entry of new firms with new products. In the case of an endless flow of future profits, the discounted value of future profits can be approximated by π/r, where π is the average future profit and r is the interest rate. If the growth of products is zero, or $g = 0$, the total stock market valuation of a firm is

$$(PV) = [GDP(1 - \gamma)]/nr \qquad (A2.7)$$

where r is the rate of interest and n is the total number of firms and products. The total capitalization of the economy's stock market is thus

$$n(PV) = [GDP(1 - \gamma)]/r \qquad (A2.8)$$

If innovation is profitable, the number of products increases, however. For simplicity, suppose that (1) total output, or GDP, stays the same when new firms develop new products and (2) each new firm has to share a fixed amount of labor in the economy. Thus, the profit of any single firm $[GDP(1 - \mu)]/n$ will decrease if the number of firms increases. Specifically, profit will continually decline by the growth rate of new products/firms $g = \Delta n/n$. If $g > 0$, then the market valuation of *existing* firms is

$$n(PV) = [GDP(1 - \gamma)]/(r + g) \qquad (A2.9)$$

The equilibrium rate of innovation, g, can be found manipulating the above results. First, combining (A2.1) and (A2.6) gives us

$$p = w/\gamma = PV/\gamma\beta \qquad (A2.10)$$

Using (A2.9), equation (A2.10) can be rewritten as

$$p = PV/\gamma\beta = [GDP(1 - \gamma)]/\gamma\beta n(r + g) \qquad (A2.11)$$

Since it takes one unit of labor to produce each unit of output of old and new products, the total amount of labor devoted to production is exactly equal to the total quantity of output of products, which is equal to GDP/p. The amount of labor devoted to research and development is equal to the number of new products, ng, times the amount of labor required to create a new product, or βng. If the quantity of labor available in the economy is R, then the growth rate of new products must be compatible with

$$\beta ng + GDP/p = R \qquad (A2.12)$$

Using equation (A2.11) to substitute for p in equation (A2.12) yields

$$\beta ng + [\gamma\beta n(r + g)/(1 - \gamma)] = R \qquad (A2.13)$$

Multiplying all terms in (A2.13) by $(1 - \gamma)$ and dividing everything by βn:

$$g(1 - \gamma) + \gamma r + \gamma g = R(1 - \gamma)/\beta n \qquad (A2.14)$$

Equation (A2.14) can be further simplified to:

$$g + \gamma r = R(1 - \gamma)/\beta n \qquad (A2.15)$$

Isolating g, the growth of new products, on the right-hand side of the equation gives us a result that is very similar to the graphic Schumpeterian model of the previous section:

$$g = [R(1 - \gamma)/\beta n] - \gamma r \qquad (A2.16)$$

That is, the growth rate of new products, which is really intended as a proxy for the creation of new ideas and technology, depends directly on R and inversely on γ, β, n, and r.

The partial derivatives of g with respect to R, γ, β, n, and r are: $\partial g/\partial R = (1 - \gamma)/\beta n > 0$, $\partial g/\partial \gamma = -R/\beta n - r < 0$, $\partial g/\partial r = -\gamma < 0$, $\partial g/\partial \beta = -[R(1 - \gamma)]/(\beta)^2 n < 0$, and $\partial g/\partial n = -[R(1 - \gamma)\beta]/(\beta n)^2 < 0$. The signs of the derivatives suggest that the rate of technological change depends directly on the amount of productive resources R and inversely on γ, β, n, and r. Note that γ is inversely related to $\mu = [(1 - \gamma)/\gamma]w$, or $\partial\mu/\partial\gamma = [-w(1 - \gamma)/\gamma^{-2} - w/\gamma] < 0$. Given the result above that $\partial g/\partial \gamma < 0$ and the chain rule $\partial g/\partial \mu = (\partial g/\partial \mu) \cdot (\partial \mu/\partial \gamma)$, it follows that $\partial g/\partial \mu > 0$. Hence, the results here are compatible with the graphic Schumpeterian model in which we found that innovation was positively influenced by expected profits/gains.

How the Model Avoids a Technology Slowdown

The mathematical model above concludes that $\partial g/\partial n < 0$. That is, all other things equal, as technological change increases the number of products, n, the rate of technological change slows down. The slowdown in the rate of technological change can be avoided if the cost of research and development decline as technology expands. For example, Romer (1990) specifically assumes that cost of research and development β is not a constant, but a variable related to the size of the economy. That is, he assumes that it becomes easier to create new products as more products are created and as knowledge accumulates. In terms of the mathematical model, Romer assumed that

$$\beta = c/n \qquad (A2.17)$$

where c is a constant. Clearly β declines the larger is n. Substituting (A2.17) into (A2.16) yields

$$g = R(1 - \gamma)/c - \gamma r \qquad (A2.18)$$

The variable n is no longer a determinant of the rate of growth. In this equation, if R, γ, and r are constants, then the growth rate of new and better products will also be constant. Thus, there is no obvious tendency for the rate of innovation, or technological change, to slow over time. But note that the constancy of g depends on the specific assumption of declining costs of research and development as specified in equation (A8.17). Romer's assumption is equivalent to shifting the curve $1/\beta$ in the bottom half of Figure 8.5 to gradually become steeper so that the quantity of new innovations per period of time grows over time.

It is not clear whether this mathematical model provides a realistic explanation of the true process of innovation and technological progress. You can see many relationships that may appear reasonable. The mathematics guarantees that the conclusions are logically correct *given the initial assumptions behind the model.* You can also see how a clever model such as this can seduce the user into complacency. This elegant model provides answers to difficult questions, and its elegance makes the explanation even more compelling. You will have to judge for yourself whether the Schumpeterian model is accurate enough to use for shaping economic policy.

References

Aghion, Philippe, and Peter Howitt (1992), "A Model of Growth through Creative Destruction," *Econometrica* 60:323–51.

Acemoglu, Daron, and Joshua Lim (2003), "Market Size and Innovation: Theory and Evidence from the Pharmaceutical Industry," MIT Department of Economics Working Paper 03–33, September.

Adams, James D., and J. Roger Clemmons (2008), "The Origins of Industrial Scientific Discoveries," NBER Working Paper No. 13823, February.

Barro, Robert, and Xavier Sala-i-Martin (2004), *Economic Growth*, 2nd ed., Cambridge, MA: MIT Press.

Baumol, William J. (2002), *The Free Market Innovation Machine*, Princeton, NJ: Princeton University Press.

Bell, R.M., and D. Scott-Kemmis (1990), "The Mythology of Learning by Doing in World War II Airframe and Ship Production," *Explorations in Economic History* 27.

Bourdieu, Pierre (1990), *In Other Words: Essays Toward a Reflexive Sociology*. Stanford, CA: Stanford University Press.

Bowen, Sally (1999), "Inca Canals Flow Afresh," *Financial Times*, October 11, 1999.

Djankow, Simeon, Yingyi Qian, Gérard Roland, and Ekaterina Zhuravskaya (2006), "Who Are China's Entrepreneurs?" *American Economic Review* 96(2):348–352.

Dosi, Giovanni (1982), "Paradigms and Technological Tranjectories: A Suggested Interpretation of the Determinants and Directions of Technological Change," *Research Policy* 11(3):147–162.

Griliches, Zvi (1990), "Patent Statistics as Economic Indicators: A Survey," *Journal of Economic Literature* 28(4):1681–1707.

Griliches, Zvi (1998), *R&D and Productivity, The Econometric Evidence*, Chicago: University of Chicago Press.

Grossman, Gene M., and Elhanan Helpman (1991), *Innovation and Growth in the Global Economy*, Cambridge, Massachusetts: MIT Press.

Hicks, John (1969), *A Theory of Economic History*, Oxford, U.K.: Clarendon Press.

Holmes, Thomas J., and James A. Schmitz (1995), "Resistence to New Technology and Trade Between Areas," *Federal Reserve Bank of Minneapolis Quarterly Review* 19(1):2–17.

Holmes, Thomas J., and James A. Schmitz (1998), "A Gain from Trade: More Research, Less Obstruction," Federal Reserve Bank of Minneapolis, Staff Report No. 245.

Jevons, William Stanley (1865), *The Coal*, London: Macmillan and Co.; http://www.econlib.org/library/YPDBooks/Jevons/jvnCQ.html.

Jones, Benjamin F. (2009), "The Burden of Knowledge and the Death of the 'Renaissance Man': Is Innovation Getting Harder?" *Review of Economic Studies* 76(1):283–317.

Jones, Benjamin F. (2010), "Age and Great Invention," *Review of Economics and Statistics* 92(1):1–14.

Kuhn, Thomas (1962), *The Structure of Scientific Revolution*, Chicago: University of Chicago Press.

Langlois, Richard N. (1987), "Schumpeter and the Obsolescence of the Entrepreneur," Paper presented at the History of Economics Society annual meeting, June 21, Boston.

Lee, Dwight R., and Richard B. McKenzie (1993), *Failure and Progress, The Bright Side of the Dismal Science*, Washington, D.C.: The Cato Institute.

Marx, Karl, and Frederick Engels (1848 [1948]), The Communist Manifesto, New York: International Publishers.

Mokyr, Joel (1990), *The Lever of Riches*, New York: Oxford University Press.

Mokyr, Joel (2002), *The Gifts of Athena*, Princeton, NJ: Princeton University Press.

Nelson, Richard R., and Sidney G. Winter (1982). *An Evolutionary Theory*, Cambridge, MA: Harvard University Press.

OECD (1997), *Technology and Industrial Performance*, Organisation for Economic Cooperation and Development, Paris.

Parente, Stephen L., and Edward C. Prescott (2000), *Barriers to Riches*, Cambridge, MA: MIT Press.

Popp, David (2002), "Induced Innovation and Energy Prices," *American Economic Review* 92(1):159–170.

Romer, Paul M. (1990), "Endogenous Technological Change," *Journal of Political Economy* 98(5):S71–S102.

Romer, Paul M. (1993), "Idea Gaps and Object Gaps in Economic Development," *Journal of Monetary Economics* 32:543–573.

Romer, Paul M. (1994), "The Origins of Endogenous Growth," *Journal of Economic Perspectives* 8(1):3–22.

Romer, Paul M. (1998), "Economic Growth," in David R. Henderson (ed.), *The Fortune Encyclopedia of Economics*, New York: Warner Books.

Scherer, F. M. (1999), *New Perspectives on Economic Growth and Technological Innovation*, Washington, D.C.: Brooking Institution Press.

Schmookler, Jacob (1966), *Invention and Economic Growth*, Cambridge, MA: Harvard University Press.

Schumpeter, Joseph (1912), *Theorie der Wirtschaftliche Entwicklung*, Leipzig: Duncker & Humbolt.

Schumpeter, Joseph (1934), *The Theory of Economic Development*, Cambridge, MA: Harvard University Press.

Schumpeter, Joseph (1942), *Capitalism, Socialism, and Democracy*, New York: Harper and Brothers.

Segerstrom, Paul S. 1998), "Endogenous Growth without Scale Effects," *American Economic Review* 88:1290–1310.

Thompson, Peter (1999), "How Much Did the Liberty Shipbuilders Learn? New Evidence for an Old Case Study," mimeo, May.

Thompson, Peter (2003), "How Much Did the Liberty Shipbuilders Learn? New Evidence for an Old Case Study," *Journal of Political Economy* 109(1):103–137.

Wackernagel, Mathis, *et al.* (2002), "Tracking the Ecological Overshoot of the Human Economy," *Proceedings of the National Academy of Sciences* 99(14):9266–9271.

Weitzman, Martin L. (1996), "Hybridizing Growth Theory," *American Economic Review* 86(2):207–212.

Weitzman, Martin L. (1998), "Recombinant Growth," *Quarterly Journal of Economics* 113(2):331–60.

PART III

Key Elements of Economic Development

The discussion of the models of economic development and technological change detailed in Part II brought out many relationships among key economic and social variables that shape a country's economic development. This part of the book details some of those variables and discusses their roles in the process of economic development.

Chapter 9 focuses on population growth. The Solow model obscured the role of population growth by putting all variables in per capita terms, but it was able to generate the specific conclusion that faster population growth translates into a lower steady state level of per capita income. The Schumpeterian models of technological change gave people a direct role in the innovative process; the larger the population, the faster technological change. Chapter 9 discusses the conflict between population growth as a source of congestion that slows economic development and population growth as a source of resources for generating technological change. Chapter 10 discusses human capital, which is the stock of "embodied" knowledge, experience, and learning that increases the effective supply of labor separately from the growth of the physical population.

Chapter 11 discusses the financial sector of the economy. This is the sector that is responsible for channeling savings to investors and innovators. The financial sector is a critical element in the process of economic development. Its task is difficult to carry out because lending and borrowing imply intertemporal exchanges in which one party receives a payment today in exchange for a payment or many payments in the future. The volatility of modern economies is often traced to the many failures in the financial sector of the economy. Underdeveloped economies often have poorly performing financial sectors, and the 2007–2009 global economic recession made it clear that the financial sector is a weak link even in highly developed economies.

Chapters 12 and 13 cover institutions, which are all the formal rules, laws, and regulations, and informal culture, norms, and customs that guide and motivate individuals to behave within complex social systems. Chapter 12 provides a general introduction to institutions, both formal and informal, and Chapter 13 focuses on the formal institution of government. The economic role of government is under intense debate in many countries, and Chapter 13 discusses the reasons why government is necessary in a complex modern economy. Building effective governance structures as an economy develops is a challenge given the potential for government to be hijacked by special interests.

CHAPTER 9

Population Growth

Thus, if developing areas are to grow economically, it seems clear that they must first deal with the population problem.

(From a U.S. Department of Energy Brochure, 1976)[1]

It is more likely that one ingenious curious man may rather be found among 4 million than among 400 persons.

(William Petty, 1682)[2]

Nearly all models of economic growth give population growth a prominent role. However, the different models do not agree on what that role is. Some of the growth models show that population growth is detrimental to economic growth. Others show population growth as a major contributor to growth. For example, recall from Chapter 4 that Thomas Malthus and other Classical economists predicted eternal poverty because any growth in real income causes population growth, which then invariably ends up undermining the growth in per capita output. The Solow model suggests that, all other things equal, population growth has an adverse effect on the *level* of the economy's growth path because the steady state level of output declines as population growth rises. Fundamentally, population is the denominator in the formula for per capita income; all other things equal, the greater the population, the lower is per capita income.

Models of endogenous technological change, such as the Schumpeterian model from the previous chapter, specify technological progress as a positive function of the amount of productive resources engaged in R&D activity. There is no doubt that people, and the human capital they embody, are the fundamental

---

[1] Quoted in Julian L. Simon (1996), p. 402.
[2] William Petty was a seventeenth century English intellectual who contributed to the early development of the social science of economics as well as liberal social philosophy in general.

source of innovation. Not surprisingly, therefore, models of technological change conclude that a growing population increases R&D activity and, therefore, economic growth. Determining which of these viewpoints of population growth is correct is the question that occupies us in this chapter.

The debate about population growth is a very active one in the field of economic development. For example, the organization Population Action International, states unequivocally that "The evidence is overwhelming that the current trend towards smaller families and slower population growth is beneficial to the well-being of both our planet and its people."[3] On the other hand, the economist Julian Simon (1996) wrote that "the ultimate resource is people – skilled, spirited, and hopeful people who will exert their wills and imaginations for their own benefit, and inevitably they will benefit not only themselves but the rest of us as well."[4]

Recall from Table 1.1 in Chapter 1 that both economic growth and population growth accelerated sharply after 1800. It is hard to believe that the simultaneous surges in population and per capita output are purely coincidental. But the fact that two variables move in tandem does not necessarily mean that one variable *causes* or is *caused by* the other. Also, the close correlation of population growth and economic growth only lasted for about 150 years of human history. Before 1800, population growth and economic development were not so clearly linked. As predicted by the Malthusian model, population grew slowly but living standards did not noticeably improve over time.

Over the past 50 years, the natural growth of population has actually been *negatively* related to economic growth in many of the world's most developed countries. The points in Figure 9.1 relate population growth and economic

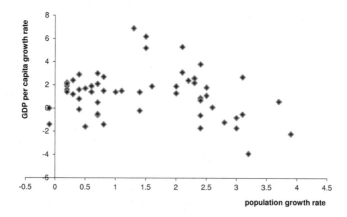

Figure 9.1 Population Growth and Economic Growth: 1973–2000

---

[3] Population Action International (1998).
[4] Julian L. Simon (1996), p. 589.

growth over the last quarter of the twentieth century for a broad sample of the world's economies, and it is very difficult to distinguish any clear relationship. The scatter does not point to any clear relationship between population growth and economic growth. The relationship must be more complex than the Classical Malthusian, Solow, or Schumpeterian models suggest.

Chapter Goals

1. Present the conflict between population growth's congestive effects and its creative effects.
2. Describe the trends in population growth over the past 100,000 years.
3. Present the fundamental mechanics of demographic change driven by variations in birth and death rates.
4. Explain the population transition over the past three centuries.
5. Discuss some models that have been suggested for explaining the population transition and the recent slowdown in population growth.
6. Contrast the long-run effects of population growth with the short-run effects of changes in the population profile and dependency ratio.
7. Examine projections of future population growth.

9.1 The Many Views of Population Growth

One view of population growth is that it increases the number of mouths to feed and, therefore, constitutes a burden on humanity. The second view focuses on people as a creative resource that drives technological progress. Your conclusion about population growth will be very different depending on which of these two effects of population growth you think is stronger.

In trying to decide between these two opposite perspectives, many economists and other social scientists have detailed many more causes and effects of population growth. For example, population growth increases the scale of human society and, therefore, the scale of the human economy. If economic production is subject to economies of scale, and the Industrial Revolution made it clear that manufacturing often benefitted from economies of scale, then a world with more people will provide a higher per capita level of output, all other things equal, than a world with fewer people. More holistic views of population growth have considered all of these effects plus the enlargement of humanity's footprint on the natural environment. The large expansion of human economic activity is having substantial direct and indirect feedback effects on the earth's ecosystem. The fact that these feedback effects diminish long-run human well-being has led holistic economists to propose policies to limit population growth.

9.1.1 Population growth's congestive effects

The Classical (Malthusian) model of population growth and the assumption of diminishing returns suggests that output will grow more slowly than the population. Given that there is a fixed amount of land, diminishing returns causes each additional person to have a lower marginal product of labor and, hence, population growth reduces the average per capita output of the economy. Thus, population growth causes congestion that reduces the ability of the economy to increase production per capita.

The Solow model similarly arrives at the conclusion that population growth causes congestion. Recall from Chapter 5 that when the rate of population growth rises in the Solow model, all other things equal, the economy's steady-state levels of capital and output decline. The reason for this fall in the steady state is that an economy with a growing population must save and invest part of its output to equip the additional members of the workforce and maintain its level of per capita output. The faster the population grows, the larger the proportion of output that must be devoted to providing new members of labor force with capital.

The Classical model and the Solow model are both biased in their view of population growth, however, because they deal only with the so-called **congestion problem** and, therefore, they can only conclude that people are a burden. Neither model sees people as a resource for producing new ideas. Also, the Classical and Solow models ignore the effects of population growth on the overall natural environment and any feedback that might impact human well-being.

9.1.2 People as the source of technological progress

Models of technological progress predict a very different result. The externalities models of technological progress suggest that population growth increases the production that generate technology externalities, for example. Even if investment occurs merely to equip new workers, such investment is assumed to still generate new ideas and increase the amount of knowledge available to the economy. In the case of learning by doing, even when output increases for no other reason than that more people working, technology will still be enhanced because people are learning.

The Schumpeterian models of intentional costly R&D activity provide a favorable view of population because they specify people as innovators. The more people there are, the more new ideas will be created to everyone's benefit. This view is summed up very well by Simon Kuznets (1973), who asks the general question: "Why, if it is man who was the architect of economic and social growth in the past and responsible for the vast contributions to knowledge and technological and social power, a larger number of human beings need result in a lower rate of increase in per capita product?"[5] Population growth's **creative effect** from increasing the number of potential innovators could overcome diminishing returns from running up against fixed quantities of other inputs.

9.1.3 Population growth, economies of scale, and congestion

Even without generating new ideas, population growth increases the scale of the economy, which permits firms, industries, and the entire economy to exploit **economies of scale**. Economies of scale refers to the case where output rises faster than inputs as the economy shifts to large-scale production. Population's effect on economies of scale was emphasized by Julian Simon (1992, p. 397):

> In addition to the acceleration of progress in knowledge-creation and technology... a larger population also achieves economies of scale. A larger population implies a larger total demand for goods; with larger demand and higher production come division of labor and specialization, larger plants, larger industries, more learning by doing, and other related economies of scale. Congestion is a temporary cost of this greater efficiency, but it does not seem to present an ongoing difficulty in the context of production.

Simon, therefore, sees the economies of scale that population growth makes possible as overcoming the congestion costs associated with population growth.

The economic historian Ester Boserup (1965, 1981) concluded from her extensive research on technological change in Scandinavian agriculture that the very congestion created by population growth directly creates the incentives that cause technological progress. She argues that congestion is not a long-run problem because it creates incentives for people to create the technological progress that ultimately ends up raising living standards. It is interesting to note that Boserup came up with her very different hypothesis in 1965 after looking at the same historical evidence as Thomas Malthus had looked at more than 150 years earlier. Malthus took technological progress to be an *exogenous*, and fortuitous, occurrence that would raise living standards and thus *cause* population growth, which, according to his model, then reverses the standard of living because of diminishing returns. Boserup saw population growth as the exogenous force that causes the congestion that becomes an endogenous stimulus for the technological changes that ultimately raise human well-being. As the saying goes, "necessity is the mother of invention."

---

[5] Simon Kuznets (1973), p. 3.

9.1.4 The changing effect of growth on population

Until recently, population growth conformed to the Malthusian and Classical hypotheses that rising incomes cause population growth to rise as well. Economic growth brought improved nutrition, better sanitation, and modern health care, which lowered infant mortality and increased longevity. However, contrary to what the Classical economists predicted, incomes have not fallen all the way back to subsistence levels; they instead rose over the past two centuries.

Since 1960, all high income economies have experienced declines in their birth rates. Were it not for immigration, many high income countries would today have declining populations. Population growth has also slowed in developing countries, most notably in the East Asia where economic growth accelerated the most.

It is not clear whether population growth will continue to slow, however. The currently observed negative correlation between income and population growth is an anomaly in human history, as the next section shows.

9.2 A Brief Demographic History

The human race, in its present form (*homo sapien sapiens*), appeared on Earth less than 300,000 years ago. Virtually all the other species currently living on the earth had already existed for a long time when the human race evolved. For example, winged insects have been around for 225 million years, grasshoppers for 215 million years, and birds for 140 million years. In their relatively short time of existence, humans have multiplied very rapidly. Table 9.1 gives us the detailed figures on world population growth over the past 300,000 years of human history.

Table 9.1 contains data compiled by Michael Kremer (1993) from a variety of estimates from economic historians and authoritative anthropological and historical studies. Kremer's data also closely matches the picture presented by the noted economic historian, Robert Fogel (1999), whose historical account of population clearly illustrate the gradual increase in the world's population before 1800 and the explosive growth during the last two centuries.

Table 9.1 shows that, by today's standards, population growth was extremely slow until about 10,000 BCE. Humans lived as predators, hunting, fishing, and gathering to obtain food. In the words of the historian W. Howells (1959): "Man lived as a really primitive hunter and gatherer of wild fruits and vegetables for all but one per cent of his known existence."[6] Then, starting in the Middle East, between 10,000 and 7000 BCE, farming and animal husbandry

---

[6] W. Howells (1959), p. 143.

were developed. These new technologies greatly increased the capacity of our planet to support the human population. These technological breakthroughs also radically changed the way humans lived. The population historian Carlo Cipolla called the development of farming the "first great economic revolution."[7] By 5000 BCE, farming had spread to, or had been independently invented in, nearly all of the rest of the world. The population growth rate rose more than ten-fold between 10000 BCE and 4000 BCE.

Table 9.1 The History of the World's Population[1]

Year	Population (Millions)	Growth Rate (Annual %)	Year	Population (Millions)	Growth Rate (Annual %)
−300000	1	-	1300	360	−0.03
−25000	3	0.0031	1400	350	0.19
−10000	4	0.0045	1500	425	0.25
−5000	5	0.034	1600	545	0.0
−4000	7	0.069	1650	545	0.23
−3000	14	0.066	1700	610	0.33
−2000	27	0.061	1750	720	0.45
−1000	50	0.14	1800	900	0.58
−500	100	0.14	1850	1,200	0.40
−200	150	0.06	1900	1,625	0.83
1	170	0.06	1920	1,813	0.92
200	190	0.0	1940	2,213	1.28
400	190	0.03	1950	2,516	1.82
600	200	0.05	1960	3,019	2.02
800	220	0.09	1970	3,693	1.87
1000	265	0.19	1980	4,450	1.81
1100	320	0.12	1990[2]	5,284	1.70
1200	360	0.0	2000[3]	6,057	1.30
			2010[4]	6,909	1.18

[1] Except for 1990, 2000, and 2010, all data is from Michael Kremer (1993), Table 1, p. 683.
[2] The World Bank (1992), World Development Report 1992, Washington, DC: World Bank.
[3] Human Development Report 2002 (2002), New York: UNDP, TABLE 5, p. 165.
[4] United Nations, Department of Economic and Social Affairs; www.unpopulation.org.

The development of farming led to the establishment of more permanent settlements and the gradual disappearance of nomadic societies. Permanent settlements were necessary for people to fully exploit the new technologies of farming and animal husbandry. Permanent settlements soon led to the first true urban areas. Beginning in the Fertile Crescent of the Middle East, in what is today Iraq, urban settlements supported increasing numbers of people who lived without hunting, gathering, or growing their own food. Permanent settlements also led to a more defined geographic distribution of the world's population.

[7] Carlo Cipolla (1962), p. 18.

People began identifying each other by the geographic location in which they resided. Permanent borders between groups of people were established and defended. Nations eventually came into being as political structures developed to govern the regional societies. These new and larger societies contrasted sharply with the much smaller groups of people that engaged in migratory lifestyles during the hunting and gathering stage of human development.

Urbanization implied higher levels of specialization compared to primitive hunter-gatherer societies. The increased specialization increased the amount of exchange that occurred between people.   Society became much more complex. This increased specialization and complexity must have enabled more people to survive and raise their offspring to maturity because Kremer's data suggests that population growth accelerated by a full order of magnitude around the year 5,000 BCE.

Table 9.2 shows that during the period 1500–1820 increased world output was still almost entirely accounted for by population growth. The Classical model of population growth thus still described the world fairly accurately. But some time around 1800, the world entered a phase of rapidly-rising living standards. In line with the Malthusian model, population growth accelerated, but technological progress outpaced even the faster population growth. Notice how population growth not only rose, but continued to accelerate throughout the nearly two-hundred year period, just as economic growth did. It took about 100 years, from 1820 to 1929, to double the world's population from about 1 billion to 2 billion. But, it took only 60 years to nearly triple world population from about 2.5 billion people in 1950 to nearly 7 billion in 2010.

Table 9.2 World Population, Real GDP, and Per Capita GDP: 1500–2003

Year	World Population (millions)	GDP Per Capita (billions 1990 $)	Period	Population	GDP Per Capita (Annual % growth rates)
0	231	445			
1000	267	436	0–1000	0.01	0.00
1500	425	565	1000–1500	0.10	0.05
1820	1,068	651	1500–1820	0.29	0.04
1870	1,260	895	1820–1870	0.33	0.64
1913	1,772	1,539	1870–1913	0.79	1.64
1929	2,047	1,806	1913–1929	0.90	1.00
1950	2,512	2,138	1929–1950	0.97	0.80
1973	3,896	4,123	1950–1973	1.91	2.86
2003	6,852	6,432	1973–2003	1.50	1.41

Source: Angus Maddison (2006), *Historical Statistics for the World Economy: 1–2003 AD*, Statistical Appendix; this document was downloaded on August 19, 2006 from the website (http://ggdc.net/maddison/) maintained by the Groningen Growth & Development Centre at the University of Groningen, Netherlands. Growth Rates are from Angus Maddison (2003), *The World Economy: Historical Statistics*, Paris: OECD, Table 8b.

Table 9.3 shows the growth rates of population for an assortment of countries and regions for the period 0-2003. Notice that the population growth rates vary quite a bit across regions, countries, and time periods. In the 1800s, the highest population growth rates occurred in countries that received waves of immigrants, such as Argentina, Australia, New Zealand, and the United States. During 1950–1973, Latin America had the highest population growth rates. These high rates were the result of large decreases in death rates and, in many cases, higher birth rates. Today, Africa has the highest rates of population growth. The next section explains how birth rates and death rates interact to generate these net population growth rates.

Table 9.3 Average Annual Population Growth Rates: 0–2003

	0–1000	1000–1500	1500–1820	1820–1870	1870–1913	1913–1950	1950–1973	1973–2003
Western Europe	0.00	0.16	0.26	0.69	0.77	0.42	0.71	0.32
Austria	0.03	0.21	0.16	0.59	0.94	0.07	0.39	0.26
Belgium	0.03	0.25	0.28	0.79	0.95	0.32	0.52	0.19
Denmark	0.07	0.10	0.20	0.99	1.07	0.97	0.71	0.23
Finland	0.07	0.40	0.43	0.81	1.28	0.76	0.66	0.37
France	0.03	0.17	0.23	0.42	0.18	0.02	0.96	0.48
Germany	0.02	0.25	0.23	0.91	1.18	0.13	0.63	0.15
Italy	-0.03	0.15	0.20	0.65	0.68	0.64	0.66	0.19
Netherlands	0.04	0.23	0.28	0.88	1.25	1.35	1.24	0.62
Norway	0.07	0.08	0.37	1.17	0.80	0.78	0.84	0.46
Sweden	0.07	0.06	0.48	0.96	0.70	0.60	0.65	0.31
Switzerland	0.00	0.15	0.35	0.58	0.88	0.53	1.39	0.44
U.K.	0.09	0.03	0.26	0.88	0.91	1.57	0.62	0.69
Portugal	0.02	0.10	0.37	0.55	0.75	0.94	0.27	0.41
Spain	0.00	0.11	0.18	0.57	0.52	0.88	0.94	0.50
Eastern Europe	0.03	0.15	0.31	0.77	0.92	0.26	1.01	0.32
Former USSR	0.06	0.17	0.37	0.97	1.33	0.38	1.44	0.54
Western Offshoots	0.05	0.07	0.44	2.86	2.07	1.25	1.54	1.09
United States	0.06	0.09	0.50	2.83	2.08	1.21	1.45	1.06
Latin America	0.07	0.09	0.07	1.25	1.63	1.96	2.73	1.96
Mexico	0.07	0.10	-0.04	0.67	1.13	1.75	3.11	2.05
Asia (excl. Japan)	0.00	0.09	0.07	1.25	1.63	1.96	2.73	1.96
China	0.00	0.11	0.41	-0.12	0.47	0.61	2.10	1.33
India	0.00	0.08	0.20	0.38	0.43	0.45	2.11	2.05
Japan	0.09	0.14	0.22	0.21	0.95	1.32	1.14	0.55
Africa	0.07	0.07	0.15	0.40	0.75	1.64	2.37	2.69
World	*0.01*	*0.10*	*0.27*	*0.40*	*0.80*	*0.93*	*1.93*	*1.62*

Source: Angus Maddison (2003), Table 8a, p. 257.

9.3 The Components of Population Growth

The population grows if the number of people born exceeds the number of people who die. Specifically, the change in the population, ΔP, is

$$\Delta P = B - D \tag{9.1}$$

where B is the number of births and D is the number of deaths. The rate of growth of the population is therefore

$$\Delta P/P = (B - D)/P = B/P - D/P \tag{9.2}$$

The variables B/P and D/P, the number of births and deaths relative to the total population, are known as the **birth rate** and **death rate**, respectively. Equation (9.2) states that the rate of population growth equals the birth rate minus the death rate.

For example, suppose that the population P equals 1,000,000. Suppose, also, that in one year 20,000 people are born and 10,000 people die. In this case, according to equation (9.1), the population registers a net increase of 10,000. And, according to equation (9.2), the population growth rate is

$$\Delta P/P = g_P = 20,000/1,000,000 - 10,000/1,000,000 = .02 - .01 = .01. \tag{9.3}$$

That is, the population grows at a rate of 1 percent per year.

The history of population growth can thus be split into a history of birth rates and a history of death rates. Clearly, events such as war, famine, and plagues cause a sudden increase in the death rate, which then translates into a sudden decline in the rate of population growth. On the other hand, the ends of wars, famines, and plagues tend to cause a sudden increase in population growth by *both* increasing the birth rate and decreasing the death rate. Recall, also, that the Malthusian/Classical population function hypothesizes that an increase in income per capita raises the rate of population growth by increasing the birth rate and decreasing the death rate. That is, the model hypothesizes that higher incomes not only reduce deaths from poor health or starvation, but by keeping people alive longer adults have more children and are also better able to care for those children.

For most of human history, birth rates and death rates were closely in balance, as evidenced by the very low population growth rates. Over the last 200 years, however, birth rates have substantially exceeded death rates in most countries in most years. The next sections details some of the interesting patterns of change. These patterns demand a more complete explanation than the Malthusian/Classical model provides.

9.3.1 Historical examples

We can gain a better understanding of what causes the population to change if we analyze birth rates and death rates separately. Table 9.4 presents birth rates and death rates for England and Wales. Figure 9.2 shows the same birth, death, and net population growth rates in graphic format. The pattern is clear: In England and Wales, the death rate declined from 1750 to 1850 but the birth rate did not. Toward the end of the 1800s, both the death and birth rates declined, but the absolute difference between the two rates remained about the same. In the twentieth century the death rate declined still further, but the birth rate declined very rapidly, nearly falling as much as the death rate. As a result of this *delayed* decline in the birth rate, population growth rose from less than 0.5 percent to over 1.0 percent in the latter half of the 1700s, remained at over

Table 9.4 Birth Rates, Death Rates, and Net Natural Population Growth: England & Wales, Finland, France, Norway, Sweden, and Mexico, 1750–2002

		1750	*1800*	*1850*	*1900*	*1950*	*2000*
England	Birth Rate	.035	.034	.034	.027	.017	.011
& Wales	Death Rate	.030	.023	.023	.015	.013	.011
	Net	.005	.011	.011	.012	.004	.000
Finland	Birth Rate	.0453	.0384	.0363	.0310	.0245	.011
	Death Rate	.0286	.0247	.0282	.0177	.0101	.010
	Net	.0167	.0137	.0121	.0133	.0144	.001
France	Birth Rate	.0350	.0317	.0261	.0201	.0206	.013
	Death Rate	n.a.	.0263	.0241	.0195	.0127	.009
	Net	.005	.0054	.0020	.0006	.0079	.004
Norway	Birth Rate	.0344	.0282	.0325	.0267	.0191	.013
	Death Rate	.0250	.0241	.0173	.0141	.0091	.010
	Net	.0094	.0041	.0152	.0126	.0100	.003
Sweden	Birth Rate	.0371	.0314	.0318	.0256	.0164	.010
	Death Rate	.0263	.0244	.0217	.0146	.0100	.009
	Net	.0108	.0070	.0101	.0110	.0064	.001

Mexico	*1896*	*1907*	*1920*	*1930*	*1940*	*1950*	*1960*	*1970*	*1980*	*1990*	*2000*
Birth Rate	.0304	.0318	.0314	.0495	.0443	.0456	.0461	.0442	.0350	.0258	.0213
Death Rate	.0310	.0321	.0253	.0267	.0228	.0161	.0115	.0101	.0063	.0062	.0047
Net	−.0006	−.0003	0.0061	.0228	.0215	.0293	.0346	.0341	.0267	.0195	.0166

Source: Carlo M. Cipolla (1962), Table 16, pp. 80–81. The 2000 numbers are for the United Kingdom; The World Bank (2002), *2002 World Development Indicators*, Washington, D.C.: World Bank, Table 2.1, pp. 48–51. For Mexico: Instituto Nacional de Estadística, Geografía e Informática (1994), *Estadísticas Históricas de México*, Volume I, Table 1.14, p. 65; 2000 data downloaded from United Nations website http://data.un.org/.

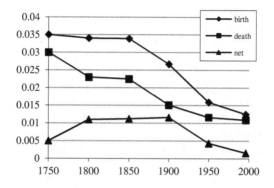

Figure 9.2 Population Growth in England: 1750–2000

1.0 percent throughout the 1800s, and then again fell to less than 0.5 percent after 1950. During the 1990s the natural rate of population growth approached zero.

Do other countries show similar patterns? There are only a few countries for which we have detailed birth and death rates going back as far as the 1700s; listed in Table 9.4 are the birth and death rates for Finland, France, Norway, and Sweden. We do find patterns for the Scandinavian countries that are similar to England and Wales. France, on the other hand, shows a somewhat different pattern: France's population growth remained much lower over the 1800–1992 period because its birth rate declined more rapidly. But France's pattern is unique among this group of six countries.

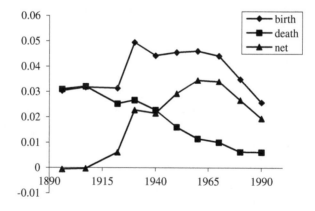

Figure 9.3 Natural Population Growth: Mexico

Among developing economies we frequently observe yet another pattern. As shown in Figure 9.3, Mexico's population was virtually stagnant at the beginning of the twentieth century as a high death rate matched the birth rate. Then, beginning in the 1920s, the birth rate increased, probably stimulated by the end of the 1910–1920 civil war and the acceleration of economic growth, while the death rate declined. The net natural rate of population growth increased drastically, from about zero in 1900 to a peak of nearly 3.5 percent per year in the early 1960s. Recently, the birth rate has declined rapidly in Mexico, and even though the death rate has also continued to fall, the rate of population growth fell to under 2 percent per year in the 1990s.

9.3.2 Demographic transition

The tables and figures above describe a pattern of demographic change that has come to be known as the **demographic transition**. The majority of countries that are today classified as developed followed a fairly uniform pattern. First, the death rate begins to decline, which causes the rate of population growth to rise. Then the birth rate also begins to decline while the death rate declines further. When the birth rate declines as fast as the death rate, population growth reaches its peak rate. Eventually, the death rate reaches low levels and it cannot decline much more, but the birth continues to decline. Eventually, the birth rate approaches the death rate. Population growth slows down and may, as in some European countries today, stop. Figure 9.4 shows the demographic transition's pattern.

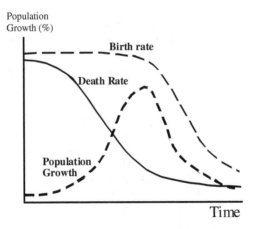

Figure 9.4 The Demographic Transition

The demographic transition is related to economic growth. As Malthus foresaw, increases in income tend to improve nutrition and sanitation, the increases in agricultural productivity and international trade of commodities reduce the frequency of famine, and technological advances in the field of medicine and public health directly reduce the death rate. Indeed, life expectancy increased rapidly beginning in the 1800s. The noted demographer Massimo Livi-Bacci (1997, p. 118) designates this decline in the death rate as a monumental development in human history:

> ... life lengthened and the hierarchical sequence of death, dictated by age, became firmly rooted. Out of the disorder of earlier times, due to random and unpredictable mortality, the processes of life became orderly.

This "orderliness" is a necessary ingredient for economic development, according to Livi-Bacci. The greater certainty of reaching an advanced age and the much lower likelihood that children would fail to reach the age of reproduction raised the returns to investment in education and other forms of human capital. Lower likelihood of unexpected mortality encouraged all other types of investment as well for the simple reason that the investor was more likely to reap the benefits from sacrificing current consumption. Livi-Bacci described the high rates of infant mortality before the twentieth century as inefficient because so many costly births and costly child rearing did not result in productive adults.

The reduction of infant mortality also diminished the need for families to have large numbers of children in order to guarantee continuation of the family line, sufficient labor on the farm, or old-age care for parents. Thus, the decline in death rates itself helped to stimulate the reduction in birth rates that generally followed.

In Figure 9.5, we show a stylized comparison of demographic transitions of today's developed countries and developing economies. The curves show the demographic transition nearly complete in the developed countries of Europe, Japan, and North America, while the transition in the developing economies began later and is still running its course. Population growth in the developing economies has begun to slow, but it is still quite fast by historical standards. Notice that the height of the population growth curve for today's developed economies never went much beyond one percent, but the developing economies surpassed two percent. Many economies in Africa and the Middle East still have population growth rates over two percent.

The curves for individual countries vary quite a bit in terms of height, length, and curvature. Birth rates and death rates are influenced by a wide variety of economic, social, institutional, religious, and political factors, and these factors are far from uniform across countries and over time. In fact, the process of economic development changes all the economic, social, institutional, cultural, and political factors that influence population growth. But, there are general patterns that do seem to hold across the many different countries.

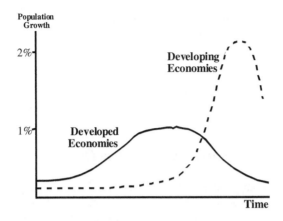

Figure 9.5 Comparison of Demographic Transitions

Time will tell if the countries that are still in their transformations will actually complete the process and return to having constant, albeit much larger, populations. For example, the philosophical dispute over birth control is still far from settled, and widespread shifts in the use of contraceptives and other birth control methods would have a major effect on future birth rates. At the same time, the growing income inequalities and the reduced social role of government in many societies could restore the desire for people to have more children as a form of social insurance at old age. The future is difficult to predict, especially for a complex phenomenon like population growth. Perhaps, the future will bring completely different patterns than Figures 9.4 and 9.5 suggest.

9.3.3 Patterns of population growth: Summary

Based on what we have learned about the history of population growth in this and the previous section, we can conclude the following:

- World population growth has gradually increased over the very long run, with large jumps in the growth rate at about 5000 BCE and 1800 CE.

- The death rate is inversely related to economic growth.

- The relationship between economic growth and the birth rate is unclear; countries may increase birth rates at one stage of economic growth, but birth rates tend to fall as per capita incomes rise to very high levels.

- Population growth seems to fit the Malthusian model until about 1800.

- Since 1800, population growth has been accompanied by a more rapid growth of GDP, and GDP per capita increased by a factor of ten.

- World population growth has slowed since 1960.

The following section will focus on several recent attempts to model these observed complex patterns of population growth and economic growth.

9.4 Explaining the Patterns of Population Growth

None of the growth models we have discussed so far provide an accurate explanation for the economic and demographic trends that we have observed in the world. A number of economists have built growth models that endogenize population growth along with other key determinants of economic growth. These models attempt to more holistically explain the demographic patterns that we have observed in the world.

9.4.1 Kremer's model of long-run economic growth

Michael Kremer (1993) observed a close correlation between population growth and economic growth over the centuries, and he built a simple model to explain the apparent positive relationship between the two. He modeled population growth as having *both* congestion effects and creative effects. On the one hand, Kremer followed Thomas Malthus by assuming that population growth increases whenever per capita output rises and that this increase in population combines with diminishing returns to fixed resources to prevent long-run gains in per capita income. But Kremer went beyond Malthus by also assuming that population growth provides the resources with which the economy develops new technologies. He, therefore, effectively endogenized both population growth and technological progress.

First, Kremer assumed that the process of creating new knowledge and applied technologies are related to the size of the population according to

$$\Delta A = qPA \qquad (9.4)$$

In which q, the research productivity per person, is a constant greater than zero, P is the population, and A is the stock of accumulated knowledge and technology. Kremer thus related the growth of technology directly to the size of the population augmented by the stock of knowledge. The intuition behind equation (9.4) is that the more minds there are in the world, the more new ideas will be created. But, the assumption that the *change* in knowledge is positively related to the amount of accumulated knowledge implies that the more we know, the more ideas for further investigation we perceive. Recall from Chapters 7 and 8, the discussion of whether technological progress is a diminishing, multiplicative, or combinatoric process.

Manipulating equation (9.4), Kremer arrived at

$$\Delta A/A = g_A = qP \tag{9.5}$$

which says that the rate of growth of technology is proportional to the size of the population. So, if the research productivity of every person in the economy remains constant, then the rate of technological progress will increase as the world becomes more populated. Population growth is thus *creative*.

Kremer then assumes that Malthus' long-run view of the world is correct. He thus assumes that the world's production function is of the Cobb-Douglas type discussed in Chapter 5 with diminishing returns, namely,

$$Y = AP^{\alpha}N^{1-\alpha} \tag{9.6}$$

where, in addition to those variables already defined in equation (9.4), Y is output, N is land (natural resources), and $0 < \alpha < 1$. Per capita income equals

$$Y/P = y = A(P^{\alpha}/P)N^{1-\alpha} = AP^{\alpha-1}N^{1-\alpha} \tag{9.7}$$

Note the negative exponent, $(\alpha - 1) < 0$, for P. This means that an increase in population, all other things equal, causes Y/P to decline. In this sense, population growth is *congestive*.

Kremer also follows Malthus in assuming that the population grows whenever per capita income is above subsistence per capita income, designated as y_S, and that it decreases whenever it falls below y_S. Thus, long-run per capita output is constant at y_S, which thus implies that in the long run

$$y_S = AP^{\alpha-1}N^{1-\alpha} \tag{9.8}$$

Diminishing returns, fully captured by the Cobb-Douglas production function (9.6), guarantees that there is a unique steady state level of population, P*, associated with each level of A, the fixed level of N, and the long-run level of y_S. That is

$$P^* = (A/y_S)^{1/(1-\alpha)}N = ZA^{1/(1-\alpha)} \tag{9.9}$$

where, under the Malthusian assumptions of fixed resources and constant long-run subsistence per capita output, Z is a constant equal to $(1/y_S)^{1/(1-\alpha)}N$. Kremer thus concludes that in the long run the steady state level of population is directly (positively) related to the level of technology.

Because the absolute size of the population is a function of the level of technology, the growth rate of population is also a function of the growth rate of technology. Specifically, converting equation (9.9) to logarithms and differentiating with respect to time, the now familiar exercise of converting a levels relationship into a relationship among growth rates gives us

$$g_{P*} = [1/(1 - \alpha)]g_A \qquad (9.10)$$

Since we know from equation (9.5) that $g_A = qP$, we can rewrite (9.10) as

$$g_{P*} = [q/(1 - \alpha)]P \qquad (9.11)$$

Therefore, the rate of population growth depends directly on the research productivity of people, q, and inversely on the relative importance of natural resources in the production function. The constant $(1 - \alpha)$ determines the strength of diminishing returns to land. In sum, the more new ideas are generated by people and the less onerous are diminishing returns, the faster the growth in the earth's capacity to support human life and the faster the population grows.

Kremer's simple model illustrates two things: (1) continually increasing populations are sustainable because technological progress permits the earth to support more and more people, and (2) it is the increase in population itself that endogenously generates the technological progress that enables the population to grow at ever faster rates. The second point is reminiscent of the hypotheses of Ester Boserup, which was that the congestion caused by population growth itself directly creates incentives that lead to technological fixes that relieve the pressures on society's limited resources.

The value of Kremer's simple model is that it describes the link between technological progress and the growth of population as a bi-directional one, and thus apparently reconciles the opposing congestion and creativity views of population growth. Kremer claims that equation (9.11) accurately describes the evolution of the rate of population growth over the centuries and millennia. But his Malthusian model is clearly not compatible with the growth in per capita output over the past 200 years or the slowdown in population growth over the past several decades.

Nor does Kremer really address the relationship between humans and their natural environment. His specification of the constant $(1 - \alpha)$ to represent the strength of diminishing returns to land eliminates the possibility that the relationship between the human population and the natural environment varies depending on the size of the human population or their level of consumption. This observation points to a second weakness of the Kremer model: it aggregates all economic activity into a single variable, and it is not sufficiently holistic to deal with the all three spheres of human existence, namely the economic, social, and environmental spheres.

It is, of course, much more difficult to model transitions, such as the Industrial Revolution and the demographic transition, than it is to model smooth and continuous long-run trends.   In the next two sections, we describe two models that attempt to endogenously generate transitions in economies' growth paths such as we have experienced since 1800.

9.4.2 Galor and Weil's model of human capital accumulation

Oded Galor and David Weil (1998, 1999) developed a model that explains three phases of the relationship between population growth and economic growth: (1) the Malthusian period up to 1800 when the population grew but per capita output was nearly stagnant, (2) the Post-Malthusian period after 1800 when *both* population and per capita output grew more rapidly, and (3) the modern growth period when in the more developed economies and many middle-income countries of the world per capita output growth accelerated but population growth slowed.   Galor and Weil's model endogenously determined the rates of population growth, technological progress, and economic growth, and the interactions between these variables generate the transitions between the three phases of economic growth.

Galor and Weil assumed a direct relationship between the size of the **human capital-augmented population** and the rate of technological progress according to the function

$$g_A = f(H \cdot P) = f(Q) \tag{9.12}$$

In equation (9.12), P represents the number of people, H is an index of average human capital per person, and $Q = H \cdot P$ is the population augmented by its human capital.   Galor and Weil assumed the relationship between the rate of technological progress and human capital to be a positive one. They also assumed that technological progress caused economic growth, and in the tradition of the Malthusian model, economic growth was assumed to cause the population growth.

Galor and Weil assumed another relationship that was critical to their model's ability to generate transitions from one phase of growth to another, namely that the return to human capital r_H rises as technology grows.   That is, they hypothesized that technological progress made investment in human-capital more profitable, and parents therefore would provide their children with more formal instruction and other forms of human capital as their incomes rose.

In Galor and Weil's model, the population grew gradually over time, and because the rate of technological progress was directly related to the size of the population, technological progress also accelerated, just like in Michael Kremer's model above. Unlike the traditional Malthusian/Classical framework, however, in Galor and Weil's model a virtuous cycle emerges: Technological progress raises the return to human capital, which then increases investment in human capital, and this in turn causes the human capital-augmented population to expand, which further accelerates technological change. This virtuous cycle eventually leads to the first transition from the Malthusian to the Post-Malthusian phase of economic growth when the gradual rise in human capital eventually increases technological change enough for it to overcome diminishing returns and generate positive gains in per capita output. This phase was reached around 1800 in the more developed economies of Europe and North America.

As the return to human capital increased, Galor and Weil hypothesized that parents would not only use their increased per capita income to pay for increased investment in their children, but they would also expand their *per child* investment in human capital by having fewer children. The increased investment per child would then continue to raise the size of the human capital-augmented population, technological progress would continue to grow, and because the growth of the population slows, the growth of per capita output would grow even more rapidly. Galor and Weil call this the **modern growth period.**

Galor and Weil thus generated the two phases of the demographic transition, something that neither the Malthusian model nor the Kremer model were able to do. They did so by linking population growth to technological progress and investment in human capital. Data on family size, per capita GDP levels, and education expenditures are more or less consistent with the Galor and Weil hypothesis in many countries.

9.4.3 Jones' model of the production function of ideas

Charles Jones (1999) built a different model that also generates a transition from a Malthusian regime to a modern growth regime. Jones hypothesized, as did Kremer and Galor and Weil, that the number of new ideas produced is directly related to the size of the population. Jones also assumed that the death rate is inversely related to per capita output because higher incomes provide better nutrition, sanitation, and health. However, he diverged from other models by hypothesizing that the birth rate was the result of a long-run maximization exercise by parents assumed to have preferences for both children and higher consumption. Specifically, he assumed that the production function for consumption goods shifted with technological change, but the production function of children remained constant. Thus, economic growth lowered the cost of consumption goods relative to the cost of children. Finally, Jones assumed that some productive resources were fixed in quantity; therefore, there were diminishing returns and the Malthusian regime would dominate until technological change enabled the economy to overcome the diminishing returns.

Jones' assumption that technological change accelerates as the growing population produces more new ideas caused his model to generate the gradually rising rate of population growth that occurred over the thousands of years of human history up to 1800.   His model generated a transition because of the assumption that people's preferences between consumption and children shift: at low levels of income, people use increases in income to have both more consumption and more children, but at higher levels of income, people substitute ever-cheaper consumption goods for costly children.   Thus, Jones' model predicts that the birth rate eventually falls, and per capita output growth will accelerate because the slower growing population eats up less and less of the more rapidly growing total output.

9.4.4 Leibenstein's model of the marginal child

Harvey Leibenstein (1974) also hypothesized that childbearing is a rational choice by parents who weigh the marginal benefits and marginal costs of each additional child.   Among the costs of children are food, clothing, and shelter. Direct education and entertainment are also costs, as are the parents' opportunity costs of spending time to teach, entertain, and supervise children.   Parents could use the time to earn income and enjoy leisure.   In higher income economies, more expensive food is eaten, the clothing is fancier, housing is nicer, the education required to ensure success in life takes more years, and the opportunity cost of lost earnings is greater.   Leibenstein thus reasoned that the cost of an additional child (or **marginal child** in Leibenstein's neoclassical terminology) rises with per capita income.

Leibenstein further reasoned that the cost of children increases with the number of children in the family.   One or two children easily fit into a house, but more children may require moving to a larger home, which implies a large additional cost.   With more children, parenting occupies more time and may prevent one of the parents from holding a job, with large opportunity costs. Parenting simply becomes more difficult as the number of children increases.

While the costs rise, the benefit of an additional child decreases with income.   Leibenstein reasoned that children do provide joy and companionship, as well as income and support when parents reach old age.   The **pension motive** for having children is more important in poor countries and for poor people than it is in the developed economies and for high-income families.   The higher parents' income, the less the gains from the pension motive for having children. In fact, nearly all higher income countries have government organized pension systems that serve as a more efficient and secure substitute to the family as the principal provider of the older members of society.   The gains from the pension motive is also likely to decline as the number of children increases.   Finally, Leibenstein assumed the joy from additional children diminishes as well.   In sum, Leibenstein builds a theoretical case for an inverse relationship between per capita income and fertility based on the assumptions that (1) the cost of an additional, or marginal, child *rises* with income and the number of children, and (2) the benefits an additional child *falls* with income and the number of children.

9.4.5 Why birth rates have declined

Each of the models discussed above provided data to support their conclusions. But aggregate data can be misleading because population growth is such a complex variable. There have been many detailed case studies that add more specific evidence. For example, Mark Rosenzweig (1990) examined the behavior of parents in different regions of India as new grain varieties were adopted by local farmers during the period 1961–1971. Rosenzweig traced the spread of this new agricultural technology and then matched it with data on birth rates and schooling in each region to see if the technological progress lowers birth rates or increases investment in human capital. He found that parents' decisions about how many children to have and how much schooling to provide each of them were correlated with the adoption of new technology. The fact that these conclusions are based on data from India several decades ago, before India began its current growth spurt, suggests that even modest technological progress in a poor country can stimulate a demographic transition toward slower population growth.

There is evidence that birth rates decrease as parents become more educated. For example, in Bangladesh non-governmental organizations (NGOs), which are often funded by foreign sources, have focused on educating women. According to one newspaper report, these NGOs are credited, or blamed, for reducing the birth rate from 6.1 births per woman in 1980 to 3.4 births in 1998.[8] Another background report on a small Indonesian village states that the sharp increase in mandatory education in Indonesia in 1977 was explicitly intended, at least in part, to reduce the birth rate. "A prime goal was to educate women--smart women had fewer babies."[9] These examples suggest that more educated parents make different decisions about how many children to have than less educated parents. It is not clear whether the decisions are due to a better understanding of their options or simply a shift in behavior after girls go to school. Evidence suggests that countries with high rates of population growth have, on average, the lowest levels of education.

There may be other important forces that can further explain the observed inverse relationship between economic growth and population growth in the more developed countries of the world. For example, a number of studies have shown that economic growth reduces fertility because higher standards of living and higher levels of education increase birth control. Also, higher standards of

---

[8] *The Economist* (1998), "The Other Government in Bangladesh," July 25, p. 42.
[9] James P. Sterba, (1998), "A Village Transformed by Suharto's Politics Now Frets and Waits," *The Wall Street Journal*, July 22, pp. A1 and A8.

living increase the cost of raising children, who require greater amounts of education and a longer period of nurturing in order to successfully enter the workforce in technologically advanced economies. Many writers have pointed to the fact that most high income countries have social insurance and retirement systems that support people when they reach old age as a factor in reducing birth rates. In these countries, parents no longer need their own children to support them at old age. Also, increased income brings more opportunities for saving and storing wealth, which further reduces the need for parents to invest in children in order to ensure support at old age.

9.4.6 Concluding thoughts on the population transition

The models by Jones and Galor and Weil depicted population as having a positive effect on technological progress. The latter focused on human capital while the former focused on changing consumption patterns to generate a population transition. Leibenstein brought in other factors likely to influence. These studies were included here as interesting examples of the extensive literature on population produced by many social scientists. Note that they represent the neoclassical tradition of mainstream economics in that they assume rational behavior that reacts to observations within the rather limited perspective of the economic sphere of human existence. In reality, population growth is influenced by a huge set of variables that interact across the economic, social, and natural spheres. Fundamentally, population growth is a biological process.

It is not clear how rational parents really are. Lawrence Finer and Stanley Henshaw (2006) found that in 2001 almost half of all pregnancies in the United States were unintended. If 50 percent of pregnancies in a country with one of the highest levels of education and relative freedom to make personal decisions are unplanned, then how rational is human reproduction really? Worldwide, estimates of the proportion of pregnancies that are unintended are similar to Finer and Henshaw's findings for the United States.[10]

The fact is that humans evolved within social and natural environments, and their behavior reflects the incentives and constraints of those environments. The Classical model of population growth is similar to how biologists seem to view the process of evolution, which is that species will increase their numbers when their economic environments sustain more people. Thomas Malthus framed his theory of population growth in those terms, namely that when incomes rise, that is, when economic conditions are favorable, people will have more offspring. The recent slowdown in population growth is difficult to reconcile with the Malthusian population model, however, and the previous sections presented some alternative models from the mainstream neoclassical paradigm that hypothesize purely rational behavior. Heterodoxy suggests that

---

[10] See for example Alan Gutmacher Institute (1999) and United Nations (2007).

we should think of more general models that incorporate the complex mixture of automatic, emotional, and cognitive processes that drive the human brain and influence human behavior.

The recent slowdown in population growth suggests that human society indeed does find ways to adjust population growth to reflect natural environmental restraints. As Indian women demonstrated, people's cognitive brain capacity does enable them to react to changes in their social and natural environment by shifting to fewer and better educated children. But, history suggests that the demographic transition is a slow process, with biological and cultural forces maintaining a strong influence over human reproduction. The next section describes an interesting counter-example.

9.4.7 China's policy of birth planning

Many countries have instituted policies to reduce population growth, but few have done so as aggressively as China has over the past four decades. In 1971, the Chinese government instituted policies to induce couples to postpone marriages, wait longer between children, and have fewer children. The central government of China set birth targets for each of the administrative districts of the country, and local officials were charged with meeting those targets. The central government launched a promotional campaign, contraceptives were made available, and family planning was expanded. Even though the program was officially described as "voluntary," local officials, anxious to fulfill their targets, often applied pressure for couples to have abortions. Birth rates fell from three percent in 1970 to less than two percent by the end of the decade, but that decline was seen as insufficient.

In 1979, the so-called *one child* campaign was announced. Chinese couples were strongly urged to have just one child, and strong incentives were put in place. For example, public housing in cities was available only to couples with one child, and there was discrimination against the heads of larger families in government employment. Abortion and sterilization were among the methods of contraception provided by the government. The one child policy often clashed with the traditional desire of couples to have a son. Pressured to have only one child, infanticide and late-term abortions were not uncommon as couples tried to avoid having just one daughter. Even though the one-child policy was not as strongly enforced in the rural areas, and many exceptions were allowed, there are now 70 million families with just one child, or "little emperor" as the often-pampered single children are sometimes called. And, the rate of population growth slowed to just 1.2 percent by the late 1990s.

The one-child policy is now being relaxed. Apparently, the government thinks that recent economic growth has moved China along its demographic transformation to where, even with a relaxing of the policies to limit families to one child, population growth is likely to remain near its current low level.

As a result of the sudden and substantial reduction in its birth rate brought on by the one-child policy, China now benefits from a favorable population profile. There are relatively few children compared to the working age population, which is very large given the spurt in births and the reductions in infant mortality beginning some 50 years ago. This favorable age structure of the population no doubt contributes to China's rapid economic growth today. However, the sudden reduction in the birth rate that occurred 20 years ago is now sharply reducing the growth of the working age population just when increasing numbers of Chinese are reaching retirement age.

China thus faces a severe ageing problem in the future. Its ratio of workers to retired people will fall even more rapidly than it is now falling in most other high income countries at the end of their demographic transition. It will be interesting to see how the Chinese government and the Chinese people respond to the changing demographic situation. Will Chinese population growth accelerate again?

9.5 The Short-Run Effects of Shifts in Population Growth

In the above analysis we examined the long-run trends in population growth. The short-run consequences of population growth can be very different and equally consequential, however. We could argue, as we have done in the past, that our emphasis on long-term economic development permits us to ignore short-run effects. But, the short-run is not very short when it comes to population growth. With life expectancies surpassing seventy years in most countries, even short-run changes in population growth have effects that last a long time.

9.5.1 Population profile

In order to better understand the implications of changes in population growth, we begin by describing the **population profile**. We illustrate a population profile in Figure 9.6. Note that along the vertical axis we classify the population by age groups spanning 20 years in this case. Along the bottom of the diagram we measure the percentage of the total male and female populations represented by each of the age groups. The diagram shows that about 30 percent of the population is between 0 and 20, 25 percent is between 20 and 40, 20 percent between 40 and 60, 15 percent between 60 and 80, and 10 percent is older than 80.

The population profile in Figure 9.6 has a typical pyramid shape, which reflects the common situation where the younger age groups contain more members than older age groups. Younger age groups tend to be larger for the

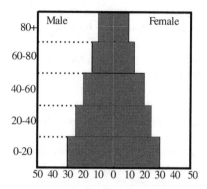

Figure 9.6 The Population Profile

simple reason that some people in each age group die before they reach the older groups. The pyramid shape is accentuated when there is population growth: with more people being born than passing away, there are more young people than older people.

The very rapid population growth seen in some developing countries is a recent phenomenon. Population growth rates exceeding three percent per year, for example, were the result of a sharp decline in infant mortality combined with a rise in birth rates over the past several decades. A large and sudden increase in population growth causes the population profile to take an extreme pyramid shape, such as in Figure 9.7.

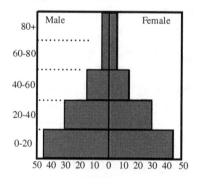

Figure 9.7 A Sudden Rise in Population Growth

On the other hand, the population profiles of the developed countries where the rate of population growth is near zero are like the pattern in Figure 9.8. A very low death rate means that most people live to an old age, and a low birth rate means that people are added to the population only about as fast as old people pass away. Hence, for such countries, the population profile no longer has the typical pyramid shape. There are roughly equal numbers of people in each of the first four age groups; only in the oldest group, eighty years old and above, are the numbers smaller as the death rate for that group is substantially higher than for the other age groups.

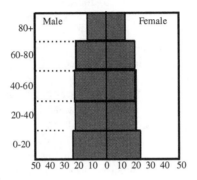

Figure 9.8 Developed Country Population Profile

Another very interesting case is that of countries such as China, which saw their death rates plummet many decades ago, but only experienced falling birth rates in the most recent decades. For such countries, the middle age groups have the largest numbers of people. The oldest age group is still very small, because its numbers reflect still high child mortality rates over half a century ago. Its youngest age group is small because China's strict policies on family size were instituted just three decades ago. The middle groups are large because low death rates and high birth rates caused a surge in the number of people born and surviving. Figure 9.9 depicts this situation.

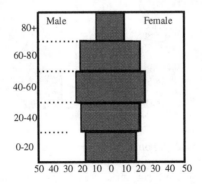

Figure 9.9 China's Current Population Profile

9.5.2 *The dependency ratio*

In order to better understand how demographic change can affect aggregate economic behavior, we set up a simple example of how changing population growth rates affect the population profile. Suppose that in a certain country called Demographia, all people live to the age of 80, roughly the average life expectancy in most developed countries. Suppose, furthermore, that people spend their first twenty years at home and in school, learning and adapting to life. Then, they work for the next forty years. The final twenty years, from age 60 to their death at age 80, is spent in retirement. People are thus in the labor force for half of their lives.

Suppose also that the total population of Demographia is 800,000 people. The rate of population growth is zero, the result of a birth rate of 12.5 births per thousand people each year and an equal death rate of 12.5 deaths per thousand people each year. Thus, there are 10,000 babies each year to replace the 10,000 people that die. If this process has been occurring for at least 80 years, then the demographic structure of the population of Demographia looks like the left-hand side profile in Figure 9.10. Each twenty-year group contains exactly the same 25 percent of the total population, the result of constant population growth and the fact that everyone lives exactly 80 years. The unique example of zero population growth with constant and equal birth and death rates means there are equal numbers of people in each age group, 200,000 to be exact. Also, the labor force remains a constant 50 percent of the total population. Hence, the percentage of the population not working, which is often referred to as the **dependency ratio**, is a constant 50 percent of the population.

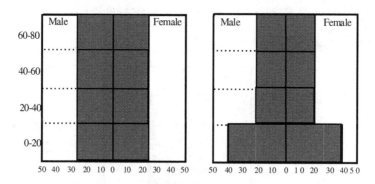

Figure 9.10 A Population Surge 20 and 60 Years Later

Now, suppose that the birth rate increases from a constant 10,000 per year to 20,000 per year, perhaps because of a decline in infant mortality or changing lifestyles that lead people to value children more highly. For the time being, there are still only 10,000 deaths each year because there are still only 10,000 people that reach the age of eighty each year. The population thus begins to increase, and there is a positive rate of population growth. This initially causes an increase in the number of children, and for the first twenty years after the change in the birth rate, there is no increase in the number of people working. After exactly twenty years, the population profile looks like the right-hand side profile in Figure 9.10. There are now 400,000 people aged twenty or younger, but there are still just 200,000 people in each of the remaining age groups. The total population is now 1,000,000, and the dependency ratio increases to 60%, as only 400,000 out of 1,000,000 people are at working age.

Now, let's assume that after those twenty years of doubled birth rates, the birth rate in our simple example falls back to just 10,000 births per year. Note that with a population of 1,000,000, 10,000 births implies a birth rate of 10 per thousand, a lower rate than when there were 10,000 births and the population was 800,000. After another twenty years the population profile will look like the left-hand profile in Figure 9.11. Now the dependency ratio falls to 40 percent.

Sixty years after the 20-year surge in births ended, and with annual births back at 10,000 per year, the population profile looks like the right-hand side profile of Figure 9.11. Now, 40 percent of the population is over 60 and retired. The dependency ratio is 60 percent again, just as it was when the larger generation was in its infancy. This case is similar to the situation many developed economies find themselves in, with a shrinking number of working people to support the increasing numbers of retired people. We see, therefore, how a temporary surge in population growth creates a ripple effect through the population profile for the next eighty years. This ripple effect of "baby-boomers" first raises, then lowers, and then again raises the economy's dependency ratio. Only after eighty years does the population profile again look like the left-hand profile in Figure 9.10.

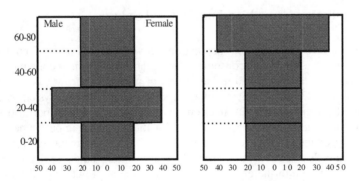

Figure 9.11 Alternative Population Profiles and Dependency Ratios

9.5.3 The importance of the population profile

The reason that a country's population profile matters is that different age groups play different roles in the economy. For example, the youngest age group produces little and requires a considerable investment in human capital by family or formal educational institutions. The oldest age group also contributes relatively less to production, but requires substantial family and formal medical attention. The middle age groups are at what we call **working age**, and they provide the bulk of society's labor effort and creativity.

The population profile is likely to influence saving and investment. People at working age need to save for future retirement and the reduced capacity to work and support themselves at old age. Therefore, the larger the proportion of the population that is of working age, all other things equal, the more people will be saving and the fewer are "dissaving." Economies with a greater share of its population in the working ages, as in the two profiles on the left-hand sides of Figures 9.10 and 9.11, respectively, will tend to have a higher rate of saving, all other things equal, than an economy with profile such as those on the right-hand sides of the two Figures. A high dependency ratio increases the burden on society to provide education, as there are relatively few working people to raise children and pay the taxes for schools.

In sum, many economic variables are related to the population profile, and therefore many variables will change as a country's population profile changes. These variables determine an economy's rate of growth. And, since population transitions such as those illustrated in Figures 9.10 and 9.11 can take nearly 100 years, the changes in population profiles have effects on economic development that linger for a long time.

9.6 Population Growth and the Natural Sphere

The economics literature on population growth focuses almost entirely on people's roles as workers, consumers, and innovators in the economic sphere. Little attention has been paid to the effects of population growth on the natural sphere. Yet, it should be obvious that the destruction of the ecosystem is caused not only by increased output and consumption by individuals, but also by the growing number of individuals. This combination of growing output per worker and the growing number of workers has not been appreciated in orthodox growth models. This section partially rectifies this omission by examining population growth in the enhanced two-sector Solow growth model introduced in Chapter 6.

9.6.1 Population growth in the natural sphere

In Chapter 5, we used the Solow model to show that population growth lowers the steady state level of output in the economic sphere. To show the effect of population growth on the natural sphere, we assume there is no long-run output growth because technological change is zero. We begin with the Solow model in per worker terms and the assumption that population grows at a positive rate, or $\omega > 0$. Figure 9.12 repeats the two-sector Solow model detailed in Chapter 6. First, as explained in Chapter 5, population growth shifts the depreciation function in the Solow model in the economic sphere up from δk to $(\delta + \omega)k$, which lowers the economy's steady state in the economic sphere from y_1^* and k_1^* to y_2^* and k_2^*, respectively, compared to zero population growth.

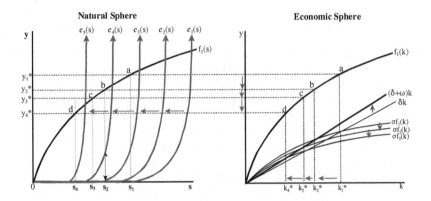

Figure 9.12 Economic Growth, Population Growth, and Stress in the Natural Sphere

In the natural sphere, the growth of the population causes the conservation function to shift to the left. The reason for this shift is the fact that the ecosystem has the capacity to provide an absolute level of services, but with a growing population a constant per capita consumption of nature's services implies an increased absolute level of consumption. Hence, in the diagram's *per capita* terms, the point at which the ecosystem begins to degrade shifts to the left as population grows.

Population growth first shifts the conservation function from $c_1(s)$ to $c_2(s)$ and then $c_2(s)$ to $c_3(s)$, for example. Note that the per worker output level of y_2^* can be maintained at zero marginal cost in the natural sphere even after these shifts in the conservation function. However, when population growth continues and the conservation function shifts to $c_4(s)$, the steady state at y_2^* is no longer sustainable, at least not without devoting some of society's resources to conservation activity. But with society using some of the savings generated in the economic sphere to carry out conservation efforts in the natural sphere, the investment function will be lower in the economic sphere. The economy thus shifts to, say, the lower steady state per worker output at y_3^*. But if population growth continues, even the lower per capita income of y_3^* eventually becomes unsustainable.

What this example shows then is that if society ignores the long-run effects of population growth, even policies that stabilize per capita resource use at current sustainable levels will not prevent a long-term environmental and economic collapse.   Scientists who study the evolutionary process are, of course, quite aware of how populations of living species fluctuate and how those fluctuations are driven by over-population relative to the available resources necessary for the species' survival. Figure 9.12 shows that humanity is not yet immune to such fundamental evolutionary demographic patterns.

9.6.2 Technological change and population growth in the natural sphere

Since technological change has offered a possible solution to earlier examples of unsustainability, we should examine whether technological progress can avoid the downward spiral shown in Figure 9.12.   Figure 9.13 first shows technological change that shifts the production function in the economic sphere from $f_1(k)$ to $f_2(k)$. All other things equal, the steady state shifts to point e on the new production function, where per worker output is y_2^* and the capital stock is k_2^*, the latter funded by a higher savings function $\sigma f_2(k)$. But this steady state level of output in the economic sphere is not sustainable without devoting resources to conservation because per worker output y_2^* requires inputs of nature's services per worker of s_1 at a level that damages nature's ecosystem. Just as in the example of Figure 9.12 above, additional savings need to be applied to either conservation or technological change in the natural sphere.

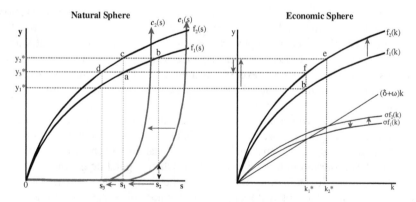

Figure 9.13 Population Growth, Technological Change, and Stress in the Natural Sphere

Suppose that the people in this hypothetical society collectively through their government decide to take measures that channel savings towards innovation in the natural sphere. If such additional resources redirected towards technological change push the production function for nature's services up to $f_2(s)$, then the natural sphere permits the higher level of economic output y_2^* to be produced with the sustainable level of nature's services per worker, s_1.

However, if population growth continues, this new steady state eventually becomes unsustainable because the conservation function shifts to the left. Note that as the conservation function shifts from $c_1(s)$ to $c_2(s)$, the per worker use of nature's services s_1 require conservation expenditures or further expenditures to generate technological change in the natural sphere. A constant rate of population growth thus requires continual technological change in the natural sphere to keep the production function of nature's services shifting up fast enough to keep the economy on the flat part of the leftward-shifting per capita conservation function. In sum, the combination of per capita output growth and population growth requires savings and investment in technological change in both the economic and natural spheres, as well as expenditures to replace depreciated capital and to equip new members of society with physical and human capital.

The two-sector Solow model suggests that the burden of population growth is substantially greater than the single-sector Solow model lets on. And, this two-sector Solow model still ignores the social costs of economic growth and change. It is likely, in fact, that population growth strains the social sphere as well as the economic and natural spheres. Economists have yet to devote much thought to population growth's environmental and social effects, however. Most studies of sustainable growth focus on reducing emissions from economic production. Little attention is given to the sheer growth of the number of human footprints. The power of compounding is great: the continuation of the 2000 population growth rate for 700 years would result in each person having just one square meter of land to stand on. It will take either some very substantial technological changes (intergalactic migrations?) or the potentially simpler measures to end population growth to avoid such an impossible situation.

9.7 Summary and Some Conjectures

Population growth is, apparently, holistic in that it is related to humans' social and natural environments in complex ways, and the population function is not likely to be stable with regard to any one small set of deterministic variables.

Economists have, nevertheless, developed models to explain population growth and population growth's relationship to economic growth. For example:

- The Classical and Solow models of growth suggest that population growth is congestive and detrimental to economic growth.

- The models of technological progress show population growth as a positive factor for growth because people are a source of innovation.

- New models have been suggested showing how society transitions from an initial stage of slow economic and demographic change to a second stage of economic *and* population growth, and finally to a third stage of continued economic growth but slowing of population growth.

This chapter has also used the enhanced two-sector Solow model to explain why human sustainability depends on the interactions between economic growth and population growth. In the meantime, the human population continues to grow.

9.7.1 Projected future population growth

Table 9.6 shows the United Nations' population figures for the years 1950 through 2000 and projections up to 2050. The table shows projections for the world as well as for the developed countries and the less developed countries separately. These population projections are based on various plausible assumptions about future fertility and death rates. The United Nations provides medium, high, and low estimates, as well as the projected future population under the assumption that 2005 birth and death rates remain constant until 2050. Notice that the medium, high, and low projections are all below the population growth that would occur if current birth and death rates continued until 2050. In other words, the United Nations is assuming that the current tendency for birth rates to decline will continue in the future.

According to United Nations population projections, the world's population growth will occur entirely in less developed countries. As a result of the expected zero growth of population in developed economies between now and 2050, today's less developed countries will account for almost 87 percent of the world's population by 2050. Developing economies accounted for 68 percent of the world's population in 1950. Of course, development economists hope that many of the countries classified as less developed economies will be developed economies by 2050. The analysis in the previous section of this chapter suggests that the expected population growth makes it very difficult to substantially raise per capita consumption for so many people.

Table 9.5 World Population Projections — 1950–2050
(millions of people)

Actual:	World			Developed Countries[1]		Less Developed Countries
1950	2,535			813 (32%)		1,721
1960	3,031			916 (30%)		2,115
1970	3,698			1,008 (27%)		2,690
1980	4,451			1,083 (24%)		3,368
1990	5,294			1,149 (22%)		4,145
2000	6.124			1,194 (20%)		4,929
2010	6.896			1,236 (18%)		5,660

Projections:	Medium	High Fertility	Low	Constant	Developed Medium	Less Developed Projections
2020	7,667	7,966	7,363	7,919	1,253 (16%)	6,413
2030	8,317	8,913	7,727	8,996	1,260 (15%)	7,053
2040	8,823	9,829	7,871	10,265	1,256 (14%)	7,566
2050	9,191	10,756	7,791	11,857	1,245 (13%)	7,946

Source: United Nations (2007), "The 2006 Revision Database," Department of Economic and Social Affairs; downloaded from www.unpopulation.org. The 2010 population figure downloaded in May of 2011 from the interactive United Nations website at www.unpopulation.org.
[1] Percentage is equal to the ratio of developed country population to world total.

Table 9.6 underscores why some economists and many other social scientists have advocated more direct policies for reducing birth rates and overall population growth. If current birth rates remain unchanged until 2050, then the world's population will nearly double from the 2000 level. The United Nations' low projection is for world population growth to stop altogether by 2050. This zero population growth (ZPG) will come to pass if birth rates slow even faster than they are currently slowing. Such a sharp deceleration in population growth has, so far, occurred only in a few countries that have reached high levels of GDP per capita.

9.7.2 Consequences of future population growth

Because birth rates declined most in countries that experienced the fastest economic growth, many authors have suggested that the answer to the population problem is more economic growth. There are two practical concerns with this suggestion. First, many countries with the highest population growth rates are precisely those who do not seem to be able to achieve rapid economic growth. Population growth may, therefore, be part of a vicious cycle that traps countries in poverty: High population growth makes economic growth difficult, and population growth thus remains high, which makes growth difficult, etc. Second, humanity's ecological footprint is the sum of population and economic growth, so the more rapid economic growth may not reduce population growth enough to shrink the footprint.

A holistic perspective suggests we do not have time to await the gradual slowdown in population growth and economic growth before dealing with the environmental stresses created by the growing human footprint on Earth. At current trends, it will take perhaps another century for population growth to stabilize. There are also some indications that in the first decade of the twenty-first century birth rates appear to be increasing again in New Zealand, the United States, and a number of high income countries in Europe. Mikko Myrskylä, Hans-Peter Kohler and Francesco Billari (2009) show that in many high income countries there is again a positive relationship between population growth and economic development when they quantify development using the *Human Development Index* (See Section 2.2.4 in Chapter 2) rather than GDP per capita. Their analysis suggests that "at advanced HDI levels, further development can reverse the declining trend in fertility."

The 7 billion people already alive today must quickly generate the new knowledge and technologies that make our growing population and its growing consumption levels compatible with the natural environment. The demographic transition is unlikely to quickly relieve environmental stresses. Rajendra Pachauri, the chair of the Intergovernmental Panel in Climate Change (IPCC) is not upbeat about the renewed rise in birth rates in high consumption countries: "We can't support lifestyles even remotely like those in Europe and North America."[11]

9.7.3 Further issues

There are many interesting population issues that we did not cover in this chapter. For example, the role of immigration in determining a country's population growth was not discussed. In fact, immigration is playing an increasingly important role in determining individual countries' rates of population growth. In some countries, immigration adds or subtracts as much as a full percentage point to population growth. Because immigration is an integral part of the process known as *globalization*, it is covered in Part IV of the textbook.

Holistically, people are producers, innovators, and consumers. Evolution "hard-wired" us to do all three of those things because they proved to be useful for survival. Humans have also developed the capacity and social structures to add to the basic abilities and capacities we are born with. That is, we can learn and improve from experience. The next chapter extends this discussion of population by focusing on human capital, which comprises the education, experience, training, learning by doing, and all the other things that enhance the productive capacity of individual people after birth. For example, by going to school and studying we become more productive and, because knowledge is

---

[11] Quoted in Julia Whitty (2010), "The Last Taboo," *Mother Jones*, May/June.

combinatoric, more innovative. At the end of the textbook, we will also discuss how human beings might be able to learn to live and consume in ways that are more compatible with our social and natural environments.

Key Terms and Concepts

Birth rate
Congestion problem
Creative effect of population
Death rate
Demographic transition
Dependency ratio
Economies of scale
Human capital

Human capital-augmented population
Marginal child
Modern growth period
Pension motive
Policy of birth planning
Populaton profile
Working age

Questions and Problems

1. Describe the demographic transition over the past three centuries, breaking the process down into birth rates and death rates.
2. Explain precisely how the enhanced Solow model describes the long-run consequences of steady population growth. (Hint: Distinguish between the effects of per capita output growth and the absolute capacity of the ecosystem.)
3. There seems to be some optimism among development economists that the current slowing of population growth will eventually stabilize the world population. Is such optimism warranted? Explain why or why not. (Hint: Bring into your answer some of the explanations of the demographic transition, such as Oded and Galor, Leibenstein, and others.)
4. Use a series of population profiles to explain the demographic and economic consequences of China's "policy of birth planning." Be sure to use concepts such as the dependency ratio, working age, and the creative effect of population.
5. Discuss Ester Boserup's hypothesis that congestion motivates its own solutions. Do you agree with Boserup? Explain.
6. A fictional television personality on a popular comedy television show once commented on his marriage plans as follows: "We plan to have at least a dozen children in the hope that one of them will find the solution to the population problem." Explain the logic behind this statement.
7. In what ways is population growth congestive? Provide some examples, and offer some specific solutions to this congestion problem.
8. In China, rapid population growth was slowed using strict government-imposed restrictions on births. In few other countries have governments taken such an active role in slowing population growth. Is it possible to stop population growth in other ways as effectively as China's top-down regulation? Discuss.

9. Write an essay addressing the question: Does humanity have time to let the demographic transition run its course? (Hint: Use the enhanced two-sector Solow model to explain the long-run effects of population growth on growth in the economic and natural spheres.)
10. After everything you have read in this chapter on the economic effects of population growth, what is your assessment of Thomas Malthus' model of economic development discussed in Chapter 4? Was Malthus too pessimistic, as many growth economists contend?

References

Alan Guttmacher Institute (1999), *Sharing Responsibility: Women, Society and Abortion Worldwide*, New York: Alan Guttmacher Institute.

Boserup, Ester (1965), *The Conditions of Agricultural Growth*, London: Allen and Unwin.

Boserup, Ester (1981), *Population and Technological Change*, University of Chicago Press, Chicago.

Cipolla, Carlo (1962), *The Economic History of World Population*, Baltimore: Penguin Books.

Finer, Lawrence B., and Stanley K. Henshaw (2006), "Disparities in Rates of Unintended Pregnancy in the United States, 1994 and 2001," *Perspectives on Reproductive and Sexual Health* 38:90–96.

Fogel, Robert (1999), "Catching Up with the Economy," *American Economic Review* 89(1):1–21.

Galor, Oded, and David N. Weil (1999), "From Malthusian Stagnation to Modern Growth," *American Economic Review* 89(2):150–154.

Howells, W. (1959), *Mankind in the Making*, New York.

Jones, Charles I. (1999), "Was the Industrial Revolution Inevitable? Economic Growth Over the Very Long Run," mimeo, May 26, 1999, Version 1.5.

Kremer, Michael (1993), "Population Growth and Technology Change: One Million B.C. to 1990," *Quarterly Journal of Economics* 108:681–716.

Kuznets, Simon (1973), *Population, Capital and Growth*, New York: Norton.

Leibenstein, Harvey (1974), "An Interpretation of the Economic Theory of Fertility: Promising Path or Blind Alley?," *Journal of Economic Literature* 12:457–479.

Livi-Bacci, Massimo (1997), *A Concise History of World Population*, 2nd Ed., Oxford: Blackwell.

Maddison, Angus (2003), *The World Economy: Historical Statistics*, Paris: OECD.

Maddison, Angus (2006), *Historical Statistics for the World Economy: 1–2003AD*, downloadable from the website (http://ggdc.net/maddison/) maintained by the Groningen Growth & Development Centre at the University of Groningen, Netherlands.

Myrskylä, Millo, Hans-Peter Kohler, and Francesco Billari (2009), "Advances in Development Reverse Fertility Declines," *Nature* 460:741–743.

Population Action International (1998), *Fact Sheet, What Birth Dearth? Why World Population Is Still Growing*, Washington, D.C.

Rosenzweig, Mark R. (1990), "Population Growth and Human Capital Investments: Theory and Evidence," *Journal of Political Economy* 98(5):S38–S70.

Simon, Julian L. (1992), *Population and Development in Poor Countries*, Princeton, NJ: Princeton University Press.

Simon, Julian L. (1996), *The Ultimate Resource 2*, Princeton, NJ: Princeton University Press.

Simon, Julian L. (1992), "An Integration of the Invention-Pull and Population-Push Theories of Economic-Demographic History," in Julian Simon (ed.), *Population and Development in Poor Countries*, Princeton, NJ: Princeton University Press.

United Nations (2007), *World Population Prospects: The 2006 Revision*, New York: Population Division of the Department of Economic and Social Affairs of the United Nations Secretariat.

CHAPTER 10

Human Capital: Humans' Acquired Abilities

Educate part of the community and the whole of it benefits.

(Amartya Sen)[1]

Human capital is the know-how that people acquire through education, training, experience, and socialization. Human capital consists of the ideas, knowledge, techniques, methods, procedures, and social norms that people internalize through culture, language, education, informal instruction, and many other tacit or codified means. Human capital is distinct from the "hard-wired" portion of human knowledge that is embodied in the evolved instinctive and automatic processes of the brain.

The most distinctive aspect of human capital is that it also consists of know-how acquired from a huge disembodied stock of ideas, knowledge, and technologies that humanity has built up over time. Humans stand out among living beings for having developed the means to accumulate and pass on knowledge to successive generations outside the purely biological process of evolution or the processes of parenting and socialization by means of personal interaction. According to Katherine Nelson and Richard Nelson (2002):

> ... the minds of individual human actors are extended through the collective memories of the community as well as through the artifacts and symbols — especially spoken and written language — of their social worlds.

Human capital is the term used to describe the accumulated external set of human knowledge, technology, culture, and ideas, created and carried forward by earlier generations of humans that individuals internalize in order to enhance their ability to function within their economic, social, and natural environments.

---

[1] As quoted in *The Economist* (1999), "No School, No Future," March 27, p. 45.

Like all **capital**, human capital is a resource created in the economy by means of an investment process. Economists often model education as an investment in a productive resource, for example. Also like physical capital, human capital is subject to **depreciation** and **obsolescence**. People continually forget the knowledge and human technologies they have previously internalized. And, as technological change occurs, some accumulated knowledge and experience may no longer be of use. In the long run, old people die and the young people who replace them must be supplied with knowledge from humanity's store of knowledge. Humans must, therefore, continually invest in new human capital to maintain the per capita stock of human capital.

The rapid growth in per capita GDP in many East Asian countries has brought human capital, and specifically **education**, to the forefront of the economic growth and development literature. Hong Kong, Korea, Singapore, and Taiwan, among other Asian economies, invested heavily in education in order to increase human capital. According to a World Bank (1993) study:

> In nearly all the rapidly growing East Asian economies, the growth and transformation of systems of education and training during the past three decades has been dramatic. The quantity of education children received increased at the same time that the quality of schooling, and of training in the home, markedly improved. Today [1993], the cognitive skill levels of secondary school graduates in some East Asian economies are comparable to, or higher than, those of graduates in high-income economies.[2]

Notwithstanding the World Bank's apparent certainty, the exact role of human capital in the development process remains to be settled. It is not easy to define or measure human capital, and interpretations of research results are not conclusive. Economists often focus on education, which is the method modern

---

Chapter Goals

1. Define human capital.
2. Focus on education, which is the process through which a modern society transfers a major part of its general technology to its members.
3. Analyze education as an "investment" in human capital the same way as an investment in physical capital.
4. Model human capital as one of the key resources applied to the creation of new technology in the Schumpeterian R&D model.
5. Examine how education and other teaching/learning processes generate enough positive technological change to overcome diminishing returns.
6. Discuss the relationship between education and child labor.

---

[2] The World Bank (1993), p. 43.

societies use to equip their citizens with human capital, although there are many other ways humans embody knowledge, experience, and culture. This chapter describes the roles of human capital and education in the process of economic development.

10.1 Definition of Human Capital

Human capital is sum total of knowledge, ideas, cultural norms, experience, habits, talent, beliefs, and learned mental processes that a person internalizes in his or her natural genetically-designed human body over the course of a lifetime. Human capital consists of information stored in the human memory that can be drawn on when there is a perceived need to make a choice or decision. Much of this stored information comes from past interactions with a person's natural and social environments.

Human capital consists, in part, of what we call experience. Human experience reflects both specific life experiences and the more general culture in which one is brought up. But there is much more to human capital than mere memories or upbringing. A large portion of what we call human capital consists of accumulated knowledge derived from thinking about and making sense of past interaction with our natural and social environments. This process of accumulation of knowledge is referred to as the **learning** process. Therefore, human capital consists of experience and learning. Human societies also organize some amount of formal learning activities, which we normally refer to as education.

Human capital has been defined as the stored information in the cognitive portion of the human brain that humans use to make deliberative decisions. However, such a definition would not be entirely accurate. Recall from Chapter 3 that the human brain operates as a combination of automatic, emotional, and cognitive processes. Different parts of the brain dominate under different circumstances, and the allocation of brain capacity toward dealing with different circumstances is part of the learning process. Experiments show that in the case of an unknown problem, many more areas of the brain activate than in the case of known problems. Human behavior is therefore guided by a learning process that involves many parts of the brain. More likely, learning is the process of reorganizing the brain to more effectively respond to specific circumstances and problems. Recall the psychological study on how floor traders in financial exchanges learn to deal with the apparent confusion, and how experienced traders are more relaxed and better able to separate important price shifts from the "noise" of continuous trading. In sum, human capital consists of the internalization of experience and a complex learning process that trains the brain to more efficiently deal with life circumstances.

The fact that people learn from personal experience does not mean that learning is a purely individual activity. Human societies, in fact, take many measures to influence the learning process of each member of society through informal and formal social activities, which we refer to as **socialization** and **education**, respectively. This chapter focuses on formal education because it is more easily increased than the informal processes of socialization, and is a favorite policy target for development economists.

10.2 Education

In growth models, economists often proxy human capital with indicators such as years of education or the numbers of people earning educational degrees of various levels. The amount of education and human capital are not identical, of course, since human capital is acquired by many means other than formal education. Nor does educational activity always increase productive human capital. Studies have revealed huge differences in the quality of education around the world, and some formal education consists of cultural or political indoctrination that is destructive rather than productive. Finally, education is a **flow** while human capital is a **stock**, and stocks depreciate over time.

But, as is so often the case in development economics, accurate data do not exist. Since economists must use something to quantify human capital in their research, they often use available data on expenditures on education, the percentage of children attending school, or the average years of schooling as proxies (stand-ins) for the total stock of human capital. This is not correct, of course, since human capital consists of much more that knowledge acquired by means of formal education. But, how do we measure habits and practical experience retained for future reference somewhere in people's brains?

Still, formal education is useful to study for the simple reason that it is a major government activity in every country. There is a broad consensus among social scientists that education is critical for sustaining a modern society.

10.2.1 Trends in education

Table 10.1 provides detailed data for school attendance in countries around the world. Table 10.1 shows the **enrollment ratios**, which are the ratios of total students at each level of schooling to the total population at the ages when students normally attend those levels of schooling. Note that in some countries the ratios exceed 100 percent; that usually indicates that people outside the normal age groups attend school, as in the case where older people go back to school to make up for gaps in their past education or when people return to school after losing a job or becoming dissatisfied with their career path.

Table 10.1 Enrollment Ratios in Education: 1991–2005
(School attendance as a percentage of school age population)

	Primary Education				Secondary Education				Tertiary Education			
	1991		2005		1991		2005		1991		2005	
	Male	Female	Male	Female	Male	Female	Male	Female	Male	Female	Male	Female
Developed Economies												
Australia	108	108	104	104	81	84	152	144	36	43	64	80
Austria	101	101	106	106	105	98	105	100	36	32	46	55
Belgium	99	101	104	103	101	102	112	108	40	49	56	70
Bulgaria	99	96	103	101	74	77	106	101	30	33	41	47
Canada	105	103	100	99	101	101	119	116	85	105	53	72
Czech Rep.	104	97	102	100	93	90	95	97	18	14	44	52
Denmark	98	98	98	99	106	127	108	113	46	52	83	101
Finland	99	99	100	99	106	127	108	113	46	52	49	64
France	109	108	111	110	96	101	116	116	37	43	49	64
Germany	102	102	101	101	99	97	101	99	-	-	-	-
Greece	99	98	101	101	95	93	103	101	37	36	83	95
Hungary	102	95	99	97	78	79	96	96	14	14	53	78
Ireland	102	103	108	106	96	105	108	118	31	28	52	67
Italy	104	104	103	102	83	83	100	99	33	31	56	76
Japan	100	100	100	100	101	98	101	102	36	23	59	52
Netherlands	101	104	108	106	124	115	120	117	43	36	58	63
N. Zealand	102	102	102	102	89	91	119	127	42	48	66	99
Norway	100	100	98	98	101	105	114	114	39	46	63	97
Poland	99	98	98	98	80	83	100	99	19	25	53	74
Portugal	122	116	117	112	62	71	94	104	20	26	49	64
Romania	91	91	108	106	92	92	85	86	10	09	40	50
Spain	109	108	108	105	101	108	121	127	35	38	60	74
Sweden	100	100	97	97	88	92	103	103	29	35	64	100
Switzerland	90	91	102	101	102	96	98	91	33	18	52	43
U.K	109	106	107	107	88	88	104	107	33	29	50	70
U.S.	104	102	99	99	91	93	94	95	66	82	69	97
Developing Economies												
Asia:												
Bangladesh	-	-	107	111	-	-	47	48	-	-	08	04
China	130	120	113	112	55	42	74	74	04	02	21	20
Hong Kong	102	103	108	101	78	82	89	85	-	-	32	31
India	111	84	123	116	55	53	63	50	08	04	13	09
Indonesia	-	-	119	115	50	41	63	63	-	-	19	15
Iran	115	104	100	122	65	49	83	78	14	07	23	25
Korea	105	105	105	104	91	88	93	93	51	25	110	69
Malaysia	96	95	96	96	56	58	72	81	-	-	28	36
Nepal	133	85	118	108	43	21	49	42	08	03	08	03
Pakistan	-	-	99	75	33	16	31	23	04	02	05	04
Philippines	110	109	113	112	69	72	81	90	22	32	25	31
Singapore	105	102	-	-	70	65	-	-	-	-	24	17
Sri Lanka	110	105	102	101	68	73	82	83	06	03	-	-
Thailand	100	103	98	91	-	-	77	75	-	-	19	13
Vietnam	110	103	98	91	-	-	77	75	-	-	19	13

Table 10.1 (Continued)

	Primary Education 1991		Primary Education 2005		Secondary Education 1991		Secondary Education 2005		Tertiary Education 1991		Tertiary Education 2005	
	Male	Female	Male	Female	Male	Female	Male	Female	Male	Female	Male	Female
Africa:												
Algeria	103	88	116	107	67	53	80	86	-	-	17	24
Botswana	98	104	107	105	40	47	72	75	04	03	05	05
Burkina Faso	44	28	64	51	09	05	16	12	01	00	03	01
Burundi	77	65	91	78	07	04	15	11	01	00	03	01
Cameroon	98	92	126	107	32	23	49	39	-	-	07	03
Chad	72	32	92	62	11	02	23	08	-	-	02	00
Congo	123	111	91	84	54	39	42	35	68	02	06	01
Egypt	100	83	104	97	79	62	89	82	20	11	-	-
Ethiopia	36	24	101	86	15	11	38	24	01	00	04	01
Ghana	80	68	90	87	42	27	47	40	02	00	07	04
Kenya	96	92	114	110	32	24	50	48	-	-	03	02
Libya	108	101	108	106	-	-	90	107	-	-	54	59
Mali	32	19	74	59	09	05	29	18	01	00	03	02
Mauritius	109	109	102	102	54	56	89	88	05	03	15	19
Morocco	76	52	111	99	41	29	54	46	13	08	12	10
Nigeria	96	77	111	95	29	21	37	31	-	-	13	07
Niger	32	19	54	37	08	04	10	07	-	-	01	01
South Africa	109	108	106	102	64	75	90	97	13	11	14	17
Sudan	55	42	65	56	23	18	35	33	03	03	-	-
Tunisia	120	107	111	108	50	39	80	88	10	07	25	35
Uganda	76	64	119	119	14	08	21	17	02	01	04	03
Zimbabwe	108	105	97	95	54	42	38	35	07	03	05	03
Latin America:												
Argentina	116	117	113	112	-	-	83	89	-	-	54	76
Brazil	159	150	146	135	-	-	101	111	11	12	21	27
Chile	102	100	106	101	70	75	90	91	-	-	49	47
Colombia	102	104	113	111	46	55	74	82	14	14	28	31
Costa Rica	103	102	110	111	43	46	77	82	15	17	23	28
Cuba	100	98	104	99	84	96	93	94	18	25	46	78
El Salvador	80	81	115	111	23	28	62	64	-	-	17	21
Guatemala	86	75	118	109	-	-	54	49	-	-	11	08
Honduras	106	110	113	113	29	37	58	73	10	08	13	20
Mexico	113	109	110	108	52	52	78	83	17	12	24	24
Nicaragua	92	97	113	110	40	49	62	71	08	08	17	19
Paraguay	108	105	106	103	30	32	63	64	-	-	21	28
Peru	120	116	113	112	69	68	91	92	-	-	33	34
Uruguay	108	107	110	108	-	-	98	113	-	-	27	55
Venezuela	94	97	106	104	29	40	70	79	-	-	38	41
Caribbean:												
Guyana	94	93	133	131	76	81	101	103	-	-	06	13
Jamaica	102	101	95	94	64	67	86	89	08	06	12	26
Surinam	103	105	120	120	94	95	102	102	-	-	09	15
Trinidad	97	96	102	99	78	82	79	82	07	06	11	14

Table 10.1 (Continued)

	Primary Education				Secondary Education				Tertiary Education			
	1991		2005		1991		2005		1991		2005	
	Male	Female	Male	Female	Male	Female	Male	Female	Male	Female	Male	Female
Middle East												
Bahrain	110	110	105	104	67	53	80	86	16	20	22	50
Israel	96	100	109	110	85	92	93	92	34	35	50	66
Jordan	100	101	95	96	62	65	87	88	22	24	38	40
Kuwait	62	59	99	97	43	43	92	98	-	-	11	29
Lebanon	107	104	108	105	-	-	85	93	-	-	47	54
Qatar	104	97	106	106	81	86	101	99	12	40	10	33
Saudi Arabia	79	68	91	91	49	39	89	86	11	10	23	34
Syria	106	95	127	121	56	41	70	65	21	14	-	-
Turkey	103	95	96	91	59	37	83	68	16	09	36	26
U.A.E.	116	89	85	82	63	73	62	66	04	14	12	39
Yemen	94	33	101	75	-	-	62	31	-	-	14	05
Transition Economies												
Azerbaijan	111	110	97	95	87	88	84	81	28	19	16	14
Georgia	97	97	93	94	96	94	82	83	34	40	45	47
Kazakhstan	90	89	110	108	97	101	100	97	-	-	44	62
Mongolia	96	98	92	94	77	88	86	98	10	18	33	54
Tajikistan	92	90	103	99	-	-	89	74	27	17	26	09
Albania	111	100	106	105	84	72	79	77	07	07	15	23
Belarus	110	94	103	100	-	-	95	96	48	53	53	72
Russia	109	109	129	128	91	96	93	91	46	58	60	82
Ukraine	89	89	107	107	96	98	92	85	46	47	63	75

Source: UNESCO (2007), downloaded from the UNESCO website http://www.stats.uis.unesco.org on September 22, education Tables 5 and 14.

Note also that the differences across countries do not correlate perfectly with differences in income levels. The transition economies, for example, have low per capita incomes, but they have high levels of education, a legacy from when they were part of the U.S.S.R. Note also that the differences for higher education are generally greater than the cross-country differences for primary education. In general, though, the poorest countries have the lowest levels of education. If education is indeed a critical input for innovation, then these differences in educational attainment are disturbing. The countries that need to grow the fastest in order to catch up to the rest of the world are those with the lowest levels of education.

10.2.2 Gender and education

Table 10.1 also shows that the levels of education attained by men sometimes differ from those attained by women. For example, the absolute difference between the mean years of schooling for men and women is virtually zero in the developed economies, with women obtaining more formal education than men in many countries, especially at the tertiary level. This may reflect the large numbers of women who earn degrees in nursing or teacher education. On the other hand, in Africa a much higher percentage of men attend school than do women. In some African countries, women receive virtually no formal education at all. Note the very low percentages of women in Burkina Faso and Niger, for example, who attend primary school.

Africa is not alone in its unequal education of men and women, however. In Middle Eastern and South Asian countries such as Yemen, Afghanistan, and Pakistan women attend school at much lower rates than do men. In Latin America and the Caribbean, levels of education are for the most part well above the average for developing economies, and in some Latin American countries, the educational gender gap is inverted, with women attending school longer than men, on average.

All in all, the picture on gender and education is a mixed one. There are still huge gender differences in education in many countries of the world. In many other countries levels of education have been raised, and the gender gap in education is being reduced. This is a problem that appears to have solutions, even if those solutions have not been implemented everywhere.

10.2.3 Convergence in educational opportunities

Table 10.1 shows that, with some exceptions, a higher percentage of young people are attending elementary and secondary school as well as institutions of higher learning than in the past. Additional evidence of convergence in education is provided in Table 10.2, which compares the generation that is aged 45 through 54 with the generation that is twenty years younger, aged 25 through 34 for member countries of the high-income Organization for Economic Cooperation and Development. Notice that for almost all countries, the percentage of people with a secondary education has risen from one generation to the next.

The average for the OECD countries is a 15 point increase in the percentage of people with a secondary education from one generation to the next, from 55 percent to 71 percent. The single greatest increase is for Korea, where the percentage rose from 39 percent to 86 percent. Countries such as Greece and Spain also showed very substantial improvements in their levels of educational attainment. The countries with the highest percentages of their populations with secondary education showed the smallest gains. The United States stands out with its essentially unchanged level from one generation to another. Of course, the United States had the highest percentage of its population with a secondary education, and its percentage is still very high.

Table 10.2 Percentage of Adults with Secondary Education and Higher — 1994–1995

Country: Age Group:	25–34	45–54	Difference
Australia	57	51	6
Austria	81	66	15
Belgium	70	47	23
Canada	84	71	12
Czech Republic	91	83	8
Finland	83	59	23
France	86	62	24
Germany	89	84	5
Greece	64	34	29
Ireland	64	36	28
Italy	49	28	21
Korea	86	39	47
Netherlands	70	56	13
Norway	88	79	9
Poland	88	68	20
Portugal	31	16	14
Spain	47	18	29
Sweden	88	69	18
Switzerland	88	79	9
United Kingdom	86	72	15
United States	87	86	0
Average of OECD Countries	71	55	15

Source: Table A2.2, OECD (1998), *Human Capital Investment, An International Comparison*, Paris: OECD, p. 99.

While these data suggest that among the more developed economies of the world there has definitely been a convergence of educational opportunities, there is little evidence that such a convergence is occurring among all economies of the world.   Education levels remain low in many parts of the world. According to the United Nations Children's Fund (UNICEF), in sub-Saharan Africa spending per child on education in the late 1990s has been about half what it was twenty years earlier. It is also estimated that some 40 million children in sub-Saharan Africa receive absolutely no schooling, a number that will rise to 70 million by the year 2015 if current rates of schooling continue.

The educational outcomes shown in Table 10.3 suggests that there is substantial variation in skills across countries. These variations are not neatly correlated with the amount of money invested in education. For example, the United States has one of the highest percentages of its population with "low" reading skills, and it is the only developed country in which younger people exhibit a lower reading ability than their parents. Yet U.S. per-student expenditures on education are the highest in the world, and U.S. students spend among the largest number of years in school among high income countries.

Table 10.3 Reading Skills, 1994–1995, Selected Countries[1]

Country	Age Groups with Low Reading Skills			Reading Skills In Agriculture		Reading Skills In Manufacturing	
	16–65	16–25	46–55	Low	High	Low	High
Australia	44.9	38.1	51.1	49.7	13.2	48.0	16.9
Belgium	39.6	23.6	48.3	56.1	10.1	38.4	16.5
Canada	42.9	32.6	54.0	44.4	22.7	45.6	23.2
Germany	41.7	34.2	42.4	57.7	23.5	35.0	21.5
Ireland	57.0	49.9	65.9	65.3	9.1	50.7	12.9
Netherlands	35.9	22.9	48.3	29.7	22.1	34.8	21.5
New Zealand	50.6	47.5	54.9	56.1	10.6	57.5	12.3
Poland	76.1	65.3	82.6	86.9	2.3	78.3	6.7
Sweden	25.1	19.7	26.6	27.9	27.8	21.7	38.6
Switzerland[F]	45.1	33.6	47.9	63.2	10.7	50.4	11.0
Switzerland[G]	47.2	32.8	54.8	60.6	7.9	48.3	19.3
United Kingdom	50.4	44.4	52.7	49.1	12.1	43.8	21.8
United States	49.6	55.5	49.6	42.0	32.0	53.3	16.2

Source: Tables A2.3, A2.4, OECD (1998), Human Capital Investment, An International Comparison, Paris: OECD, Centre for Educational Research and Innovation, pp. 99–100.
[1] The reading test results were categorized into five literacy groups: "low" groups 1 and 2, "medium" group 3, and "high" groups 4 and 5. The "low" groups include people with reading skills below the average for developed countries.

Table 10.3 also shows that reading skills differ across industries as much as they differ across countries. In the case of agriculture, reading skills in the United States are among the highest in the developed world. Only the Netherlands and Sweden have relatively fewer people with low reading skills employed in the agricultural sector. But, the U.S. manufacturing labor force ranks among the lowest in terms of the reading skills of its workers, despite the country's very high graduation rates from secondary education.

10.2.4 Summary of the state of education in the world

The overall state of education in the world is, at the same time, encouraging and discouraging. On the one hand, levels of education have been increasing at a rapid rate. More and more countries are reaching the very high rates of education that only a few highly developed economies were able to achieve in the past. Incredible gains have been made by some countries. Taiwan, for example, raised its average number of years of education from less than three years in the early 1950s to nearly 12 years in 2005. But, in many countries of Africa, South Asia, and the Middle East levels of education remain low.

In addition to the need for human capital to create and adopt new technologies, there may be a need to expand education simply to keep up with the growing complexity of the modern economic and social spheres that humans live in. An important, but so far unanswered, question is whether the increase in education that we observe in the world is keeping pace with the complexity of the modern world. More fundamentally, if human capital is not keeping up with the effective growth of other productive inputs, then people become a source of diminishing returns to per worker investment in physical capital. Below-par education may, therefore, impact growth directly by reducing technological innovation and indirectly by lowering the returns to investment.

10.3 The Costs and Benefits of Education

We have already discussed externalities and diminishing returns as the important issues related to education and human capital. This focus is obvious when education is incorporated into the standard models of economic growth. But, the role of education has often been analyzed using the more traditional cost-benefit analysis economists have applied to many areas of economic policy. This section explains what this approach can tell us about education.

10.3.1 Net returns to education

Cost-benefit analysis is a complete accounting of all costs and benefits over time. Cost-benefit analysis is often undertaken to analyze the value of investment projects. Investment projects normally involve an initial outlay and future returns, although more complex projects can involve additional future payments as well as returns. Cost-benefit analysis thus requires a complete intertemporal accounting of gains and losses. A simple example of cost-benefit analysis is presented in the **time profile of investment** in Figure 10.1 and Table 10.4.

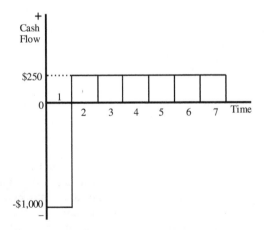

Figure 10.1 Time Profile of Investment

Table 10.4 Cost-Benefit Example

Discount Factor $1/(1+.1)^n$		*Expenses:*	*Income:*
Year One	1.000	$-\$1,000(1.00) = -\$1,000$	$ 0
Year Two	.909		$\$250(.909) = \$227$
Year Three	.826		$\$250(.826) = \$207$
Year Four	.751		$\$250(.751) = \$188$
Year Five	.683		$\$250(.683) = \$171$
Year Six	.621		$\$250(.621) = \$155$
Year Seven	.564		$\$250(.564) = \$141$
Sum:		$-\$1,000$	$\$1,089$

1. Net Present Value = $1,089 - $1,000 = $89; 2. Benefit-Cost Ratio = $1,089 / $1,000 = 1.089; 3. Internal Rate of Return = 13 percent.

Suppose that a hypothetical investment project requires an initial outlay of $1,000 in the first year and provides returns of $250 for the years two through seven. The common method in economics for judging this project is to compare all the positive cash flows and the negative cash flows, properly discounted to the present time. The first $250 in income in year two must be divided by $(1 + r)$, where r is the rate of discount or interest rate. The second $250 in year three must be divided by $(1 + r)^2$, the third $250 by $(1 + r)^3$, and so forth. If, for example, the discount rate is 10 percent per year, then the first $250 needs to be divided by 1.1, the second by $1.1^2 = 1.21$, $1.1^3 = 1.33$, etc. Table 10.4 gives the complete accounting of expenses and income.

Table 10.4 shows three measures, based on these results, that can be used to judge the profitability of investment projects: the Net Present Value (NPV), the Benefit-Cost Ratio (BCR), and the Internal Rate of Return (IRR). The NPV is the net value of all discounted payments and receipts. The hypothetical project depicted in Figure 10.1 has a net return of $89 when the rate of discount is 10 percent. The BCR is often the more useful for comparing alternative projects because, as the ratio of costs and benefits, it is independent of the size of the project. The BCR is simply the ratio of the sum of all discounted receipts relative to the discounted costs. The IRR is the rate of discount that would cause the discounted value of future returns to equal the cost of the project. Note that in the project in Table 10.4, the IRR is 13 percent. The IRR is the measure that most interests us here because the returns to education are most often presented as an IRR.

Figure 10.2 presents a typical pattern of costs and returns to education. Schooling is costly, even if it is carried out at home or on the job. At a minimum, education requires time, which implies that it has an opportunity cost. Usually, someone must do the parenting and teaching, and after basic life skills are learned, classrooms, books, and other costly teaching materials are increasingly required. Figure 10.2 compares two cases: a child who begins work at age 10 and another who continues in school before going to work at age 16. Both cases involve parenting and educational costs equal to area A. The years of extra schooling involve the opportunity cost of what the potential worker could earn (area B) plus the costs of providing the specific learning (area E). The line ae represents the earnings over time of someone who does not continue in school after the age of 10. Note that we draw this line as an upward-sloping one to reflect the gradual increase in experience that enhances a worker's performance over time. Total lifetime earnings of someone who begins work at age 10 are thus equal to the areas B + C. On the other hand, someone who continues in school between the ages of 10 and 16 incurs an extra opportunity cost B (lost income from work) and schooling costs E, but then, upon entering the labor force, enjoys an earnings stream represented by the line df. Total lifetime earnings of a more educated worker are C plus D. If the discounted value of the area D exceeds the discounted values of the areas E plus B, then the return to the extra education between ages 10 and 16 is positive. The larger is the area D relative to areas B and E, the higher is the rate of return to education.

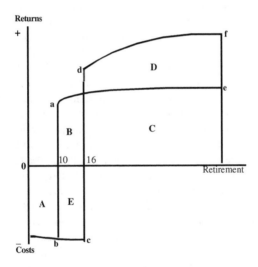

Figure 10.2 Returns to Education

10.3.2 Private versus social returns to education

Figure 10.2 contains a serious ambiguity: The costs and benefits of education to the individual, called the private costs and benefits, are usually different from the costs and benefits to society. Clearly, in our analysis of whether the return to education is high or low, we want to determine the social costs and benefits. But, because it is often easier to calculate the costs and benefits for an individual, many studies have focused on the private costs and benefits of education. Also, the private costs and benefits are more likely to motivate people's individual decisions to pursue education.

The private costs of education are the sum of (1) opportunity costs of not working plus (2) any specific costs incurred, such as school tuition, fees, books, transportation, etc. The benefits are the extra income earned, over and above the income the individual would have earned had he not acquired the education. These private costs and benefits may differ from society's costs and benefits for several reasons. First, all or part of the costs of schooling may be paid for by the government, and privately paid tuition may cover just a portion of the actual costs of running a school or university. Often, education is provided to people free of charge, which means society collectively bears the entire direct cost of providing education, leaving the individual only with the opportunity cost of not working. That is, in terms of Figure 10.2, the individual may incur no area E cost, but society certainly does incur such a cost. Neoclassical labor economists would conclude that this situation leads to inefficient excess demand for education by individuals to the point where social costs exceed social benefits.

Second, the extra earnings that accrue to an individual with a diploma may not accurately reflect the marginal gain to society from the extra education. There is widespread evidence across many societies that a diploma is often used as a screening or signaling device to separate the more talented from the less talented workers, not because the education leading up to the diploma makes workers more productive, but because it is believed that the potentially more productive workers are more likely to attend school. Other economists have suggested that diplomas are often used as a rationing device in economies that suffer high rates of unemployment. Faced with many applicants for few jobs, employers raise educational requirements to the point where supply equals demand and the scarce jobs to those with the highest qualifications, regardless of whether those qualifications are really necessary to perform the job or not. Thus, from an individual perspective, just as in the screening or signaling case, education pays off because a better job is obtained. But, from society's perspective the education does not really add to output because the scarce jobs could be performed just as well by people without the superfluous diploma. For this reason, private benefits may overstate the benefits to society from education, which will, all other things equal, also result in inefficient excess demand for education.

Private and social costs also differ because of externalities. These externalities can include many different things, including Adam Smith's suggestion that educated people are more responsible citizens and the common argument that educated people have a greater ability to learn new methods. Educated individuals may also find it easier to transfer to new jobs, and such flexibility facilitates the structural changes an economy must undergo during the development process. More educated people are also more likely to pass knowledge on to others, both at work and at home. Such inter-generational transfers of knowledge, ideas, and technologies clearly make education much more productive from society's point of view than from the individual's. And education may provide important human capital for innovation. In sum, it is likely that the education of a person benefits more than just that person. The external effects of education are very difficult to measure, and many of the suggested externalities to education are widely disputed. Few studies attempt to capture any but the most obvious externalities. We will have more on externalities late in the chapter.

Two of the sources of discrepancies between private and social costs and benefits of education are not controversial, and they can be approximated with even limited amounts of data. These are the direct costs of education and the opportunity costs of education. The public costs of education can be found in government budgets, and the direct private costs can be estimated from data used to compile the national accounts. Private schools' costs are included in the national product, as are the production of books and school materials. Opportunity costs can be estimated using data on wages and other labor income.

10.3.3 *Estimates of the returns to education*

The importance of human capital, or E_L, over basic labor, L, within the factor we call effective labor, or $L{\cdot}E_L$, can be measured by how overall wages change when human capital increases. For example, studies by George Psacharopoulos (1994) and Psacharopoulis and Harry Patrinos (2002) estimate that education augments basic labor by 7.7 to 12 percent for each year of education. To put these estimates into perspective, suppose the income for basic labor is equal to 100. Then, in developed economies where people achieve, on average, 12 years of education the return to the combination of labor and human capital will be at least $100(1.077)^{12} = 244$ and possibly as much as $100(1.12)^{12} = 390$. In high income countries, therefore, the contribution of the human capital component of effective labor, $(L{\cdot}E_L)$, to output may be more than three times as large as the contribution of basic labor, L.

In poorer developing countries, education accounts for a much smaller percentage of labor income. However, that does not make education less important in less developed countries. For one thing, this means that gains in per capita income will depend substantially on increasing education. The gains from education are further enhanced by the findings that, because education is relatively scarce in less developed countries, the marginal private and social returns to education are higher in poor countries.

Table 10.5 presents several recent estimates on the private and social returns to education for a variety of countries. The table also separates the returns to the three main levels of education. Note how the social returns to education decline as the level of education rises. In general, the returns to

Table 10.5   Average Estimated Rates of return to Education

	Social			Private		
	Primary	Secondary	Higher	Primary	Secondary	Higher
Psacharopoulos and Patrinos Survey:						
Low-income countries (< $755)	21.3	15.7	11.2	35.8	19.9	26.0
Middle-income countries	18.8	12.9	11.3	27.4	18.0	19.3
High-income countries (> $9,266)	13.4	10.3	9.5	25.6	12.2	12.4
Sub-Saharan Africa	25.4	18.4	11.3	37.6	24.6	27.8
Asia	16.2	11.1	11.0	20.0	15.8	18.2
Europe/Middle East/North Africa	15.6	9.7	9.9	13.8	13.6	18.8
Latin America/Caribbean	17.4	12.9	12.3	26.6	17.0	19.5
OECD countries	8.5	9.4	8.5	13.4	11.3	11.6
World	18.9	13.1	10.8	26.6	17.0	19.0
Schutz Survey:						
Africa	27	19	14	45	28	33
Asia	18	14	12	34	15	18
Latin America	35	19	16	61	28	26
High-Income Countries	13	10	8	19	12	11

Sources: George Psacharopoulos and Harry Anthony Patrinos (2002), Tables 1 and 2; and T. Paul Schutz (1988), p. 543.

primary education are higher than the returns to **secondary** and **higher education**. Table 10.5 also shows that the returns to education are also much higher in low income countries than they are in high income countries.

The costs of higher education are much higher per pupil than in primary and secondary education, and this drives down the social rates of return to university education. Higher education requires highly-educated professors, research laboratories, and large libraries. The very high return to lower education in developing countries also makes sense because the costs of providing primary education are relatively low, the opportunity costs of going to school for young children are low, and overall levels of education in low-income countries are low.

Table 10.5 also highlights the differences between private and social rates of return. The high private rates of return to higher education, relative to the social returns, reflect the fact that higher education is usually subsidized by governments. Universities are often seen as centers of research that have positive externalities for the rest of the economy. There is also the belief that university education provides greater technological externalities than primary or secondary education. And, in many countries subsidies for universities are the result of special interest politics. Because they require good elementary and secondary educations, university educations are often available only to middle and upper class students who had the means to pay for earlier education.

The role of education in the rapid growth episodes of East Asia may, therefore, be due to the better allocation of education spending across the different levels of schooling. According to the World Bank study cited earlier:

> In most of the economies of East Asia, public investments in education were not only larger than elsewhere in absolute terms — they were also better. They responded more appropriately to coordination failures in the market for education. Emphasis on universal, high-quality primary education had important payoffs both for economic efficiency and for equity. The excess demand for secondary and tertiary education, generated by rapid attainment of universal primary education, was met largely by a combination of expansion of a public secondary system with meritocratic entrance requirements and a self-financed private system. This stands in stark contrast to many other low- and middle-income economies, which have stressed public subsidies to university education."[3]

As East Asian economies reach the highest levels of development, they may find it necessary to invest more in higher education.

Table 10.6 Annual Private Rates of Return to Education — 1995[1]

Country	Women Secondary	Women University	Men Secondary	Men University	Return to Business Capital
Australia	12.5	6.7	7.5	10.4	13.6
Canada	16.1	28.5	12.5	16.5	19.3
Czech Republic	13.8	7.0	22.0	8.7	-
Denmark	11.8	9.2	10.4	11.0	10.7
Finland	8.1	14.3	10.4	14.8	9.4
France	14.1	12.7	14.2	14.1	15.0
Germany	5.5	8.2	5.7	10.9	13.7
Ireland	28.8	17.4	18.6	14.0	14.4
Italy	9.5	4.6	10.4	9.9	15.9
Netherlands	24.4	10.5	14.1	10.8	17.9
New Zealand	11.2	10.3	12.8	11.6	18.5
Norway	17.3	13.3	11.3	11.6	7.6
Portugal	32.4	28.3	33.3	27.3	-
Sweden	9.9	5.3	10.9	8.2	14.2
Switzerland	22.1	5.2	19.0	5.5	4.2
United Kingdom	19.1	19.1	14.3	12.7	11.8
United States	22.9	12.6	26.3	12.6	18.3
Average	*16.4*	*12.5*	*14.9*	*12.4*	*13.6*

Source: Table A4.4, OECD (1998), Human Capital Investment, An International Comparison, Paris: Organisation for Economic Cooperation and Development, Centre for Educational Research and Innovation; p. 113.
[1] Estimated at different levels over a working lifetime for employed persons only.

---

[3] The World Bank (1993), p. 203.

The returns to each level of education are different for high-income countries than they are for low-income countries. Table 10.6 shows estimated rates of private returns to education in developed economies. Note in Table 10.6 that the rates of return to education in developed economies are more similar across secondary and university levels, and the returns are more similar to the returns of other types of investment in developed economies. This implies developed economies have exploited educational opportunities to a greater extent, and they have invested relatively efficiently at the various levels of education. An efficient allocation of educational investment should show similar rates of return across all levels, genders, and all types of investment.

In sum, the results of the cost-benefit studies on education show that:

- Both private and social returns to education are usually higher for the lower levels of education than they are for higher education; and

- Returns to education are usually higher in lower-income countries than in higher-income countries.

The evidence suggests that low-income countries should devote more of their scarce resources to expanding elementary education for both women and men.

10.3.4 Developing country expenditures on education

Education and learning require intentional efforts to teach, instruct, train, inform, and absorb information. Table 10.7 shows that in the developed economies, government expenditures on education are equal to about 5.5 percent of GDP. In developing countries, on average, government expenditures on education average 4.5 percent of the lower GDPs. These are large sums of money.

10.3.5 The statistical evidence on education is not entirely clear

The question is, therefore, whether countries are spending efficiently on education. One way to examine this is to statistically test the relationship between education and growth. As mentioned at the start of this chapter, the spectacular growth of the East Asian economies, which invested heavily in education, renewed interest in the role of education in the growth process. But, establishing that it was indeed the increase in education that caused the economic growth in East Asia has proven to be difficult. In general, empirical studies on education and economic growth have provided conflicting results.

It is very difficult to measure human capital, education, and, of course, economic development. In this light, even the very positive estimates of the returns to education must be questioned. While it is relatively easy to measure

Table 10.7 Public Expenditures on Education as a Percentage of GDP

	1980	2000–07		1980	2000–07		1980	2000–07
Developed Economies			**Asia:**			Senegal	-	5.1
Australia	5.5	4.7	Bangladesh	1.5	2.4	South Africa	-	5.1
Austria	5.6	5.4	China	2.5	1.9	Tanzania	4.4	6.8
Belgium	6.1	6.1	Hong Kong[1]	2.8	3.3	Tunisia	5.4	8.1
Bulgaria	4.5	4.1	India	2.8	3.2	Uganda	1.2	3.8
Canada	6.9	4.9	Indonesia	1.7	3.5	Zambia	4.5	1.4
Czech Rep.	-	4.6	Iran[1]	3.6	4.8	Zimbabwe	6.6	4.6
Denmark	6.9	7.9	Korea	3.7	4.2			
Finland	5.3	5.9	Malaysia	6.0	4.5	**Latin America:**		
France	5.0	5.6	Nepal	1.8	3.8	Argentina	2.7	4.9
Germany	-	4.4	Pakistan	2.0	2.9	Brazil	3.6	5.2
Greece	-	4.0	Philippines	1.7	2.6	Bolivia	4.4	6.3
Hungary	4.7	5.4	Singapore	2.8	2.8	Chile	4.6	3.4
Ireland	-	4.9	Sri Lanka	2.7	3.2	Colombia	1.9	3.9
Italy	-	4.3	Thailand	3.4	4.9	Costa Rica	7.8	5.0
Japan	5.8	3.4	Vietnam	-	5.3	Cuba		9.7
Netherlands	7.6	5.5				Dom. Rep.	2.2	2.2
N. Zealand	5.8	6.9	**Africa:**			El Salvador	3.9	3.6
Norway	7.2	6.2	Algeria	7.8	5.1	Guatemala	-	3.2
Poland	-	4.9	Botswana	-	8.1	Haiti	1.5	1.4
Portugal	3.8	5.3	Burkina Faso	2.6	4.6	Honduras	3.2	-
Romania	3.3	4.4	Burundi	-	7.2	Mexico	4.7	4.8
Russia	-	3.9	Cameroon	3.2	2.9	Nicaragua	3.4	3.1
Spain	-	4.4	Chad	-	1.9	Panama	4.8	3.8
Sweden	9.0	6.7	Congo	2.6	1.8	Paraguay	1.5	4.0
Switzerland	5.0	5.3	Côte d'Ivoire	-	4.5	Peru	3.1	2.7
U.K.	5.6	5.6	Egypt	5.7	3.8	Uruguay	2.3	2.8
U.S.	6.7	5.5	Ethiopia	-	5.5	Venezuela	4.4	3.7
			Gabon	2.7	3.8			
Developing Economies			Ghana	3.1	5.4	*Developed*		
Middle East			Kenya	6.8	7.0	*Economies[1]*	5.6	5.5
Israel	7.9	6.4	Mauritania	-	4.4			
Jordan	-	4.9	Morocco	6.1	5.7	*Developing*		
Syria	4.6	3.9	Namibia	-	6.5	*Economies[1]*	3.9	4.5
Turkey	2.8	2.9	Nigeria	-	0.9			
			Niger	3.1	3.7			

Source: Data for 1980 is from: World Bank (1998), *World Development Report 1998–1999*, Washington D.C., Table 6, pp. 200–201. Data for 2000–2007 is from *Human Development Report 2010*, New York: United Nations Development Programme, Table 15, pp. 202–205.

the differences in income and productivity between a literate person and an illiterate person, one cannot help but wonder how economists measure the returns to society from advanced university educations, some of which equip people to generate the meta-ideas that shift paradigms and mitigate big problems like global warming.

It is apparent from this brief discussion of the empirical evidence that the relationship between education and economic growth is not as clear and neat as we would like. And we have not even yet discussed more complex externalities and the social role of education! Perhaps our growth models can help.

10.3.6 Diminishing returns and human capital

Human capital, and hence investments in human capital such as education, can be analyzed using an expanded production function. Specifically, we can use the general production function introduced in Chapter 7, the one that relates society's aggregate output Y to three aggregate categories of inputs, labor L, capital K, and nature's services S, each augmented by factor-specific technologies E_L, E_K, and E_S:

$$Y = f(L \cdot E_L, K \cdot E_K, S \cdot E_S) \qquad (10.1)$$

Human capital enters this function through E_L directly when human technology is embodied through education and other forms of learning, or indirectly by serving as an input in the process that generates the general technologies that shift the entire production function f(.). Human capital can increase economic growth in two ways, therefore.

As explained in Section 7.4 of Chapter 7, per capita output grows as long as there is some positive increase in labor-augmenting technology, or when the growth of y = Y/L exceeds the growth of y = Y/(L·E_L) and the growth of E_L > 0. Permanent growth of labor-augmenting technology requires a permanent growth of human capital and labor-augmenting technological progress, as well as the permanent growth of the effective supplies of physical capital and nature's services, the other two elements of the production function depicted in equation (10.1).

Note that if the supply of nature's services cannot be increased in the long run, then the Solow model will conclude that permanent growth in per worker output is only possible if the economy increases the stock of natural resource-augmenting technology E_S. Hence, human capital's role as an input into the process of technological change is critical for continued economic growth in a resource-constrained world. To evaluate this potential role for human capital, we again need to call on a model of technological change.

10.3.7 Human capital and R&D activity

Human capital is potentially an important contributor to the creation of new technology because, as we have discussed in Chapters 7 and 8, the creation of new ideas, knowledge, methods, and other forms of technology requires inputs of productive resources. It has often been suggested that innovative and R&D activities require highly knowledgeable and educated labor. Because knowledge creation is a combinatoric process that combines existing ideas to create new ideas, the most successful innovators are likely to be those people who most thoroughly grasp the current state of knowledge and understanding. Supporting this contention is the fact that most R&D activity occurs in firms, universities, and government agencies located in the developed economies where human capital is relatively abundant.

If indeed human capital plays a critical role in the innovative process, then we can substitute human capital for resources in the Schumpeter model of technological change. Figure 10.3 repeats Figure 8.7 from Chapter 8, which showed how an increase in resources increased innovation, except that Figure 10.3 defines N as the amount of human capital used in the innovative process of the economy. The model shows that if education increases total human capital, the price of productive resources falls, and the CoI curve shifts down to CoI_1. By itself, this causes the equilibrium value of human capital, the amount of society's human capital applied to innovation, to increase, and the number of innovations to increase to q_1. The increase in human capital is also likely to shift up the PVI curve because the increased productivity of workers increases wages and/or profits. This effect increases N further, and thus the number of innovations rises further to q_2.

The growth of technology thus depends on the overall cost of labor plus the cost of education. If labor markets are competitive, the cost of educated labor will, in equilibrium, be the wage for uneducated labor plus the cost of

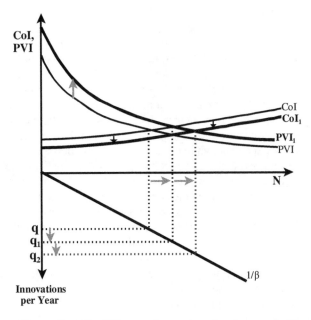

Figure 10.3 The Effects on Innovation of an Increase in H

education. Firms engaged in competitive innovation will seek workers with human capital up to the point where the price of educated labor becomes so high that the marginal gain from innovation is overtaken by the rising cost of innovating. The lower the cost of education, the greater the number of educated R&D workers and the greater the rate of technological change. The challenge for economists is to accurately assess the costs and benefits of education, and more broadly human capital, in the processes of innovation and technological change. It is unlikely that existing estimates of the returns to education capture education's dynamic effects, which suggests they understate the overall returns to human capital and investments in education.

10.4 The Optimal Supply of Education with Externalities

Once we accept that human capital is a productive resource for both production and innovation, we are left with the important question of who should pay for the investment in human capital. This question is complicated by the fact that the social return to education is most likely greater than the private return. Also, when human capital augments the supply of labor, other factors of production capture part of the gains in productivity. That is, the employer of a worker generally captures part of the return to human capital. So, should the employer pay for education and training workers? Or, should the employee pay? Often, society pays collectively.

From a neoclassical perspective, it is beneficial for society to pay to educate people as long as the gains from the increased innovation and production exceed the cost of the education. It would be worthwhile for a private employers to provide the human capital through training, evening classes, or on-the-job instruction as long as the extra gains from innovation or the increased productivity in production exceed the basic wage for workers without such education. From their perspective, workers themselves should be willing to acquire additional education provided the jobs that require the extra education pay more than enough to cover the cost of schooling.

In general, however, the gains from one person's education do not accrue equally to employers, workers, other factors of production, or society as a whole. Education and the many other forms of human capital have externalities, which means that there are many gains and losses to people other than those directly involved in the productive activities and innovative activities where the human capital is employed. In other words, there are likely to be market failures in the pricing and employment of human capital. This is why education is so often provided by government. Employers and the workers themselves do not, in general, acquire education and enhance their human capital up to the point where the marginal gains to society as a whole equal the marginal costs to society as a whole.

10.4.1 Human capital and externalities

One approach is to specify human capital, or specifically education, as having positive externalities. Recall the quote at the start of this chapter by Amartya Sen: "Educate part of the community and the whole of it benefits." Like the externalities to physical investment discussed in Chapter 5, externalities to human capital can help the economy overcome diminishing returns and, therefore, potentially generate permanent economic growth.

This idea that education generates positive externalities is by no means new. Over 200 years ago, many of the classical economists argued strongly for government's active support of education on the grounds of the positive externalities that society would gain from a more educated labor force and populace. Adam Smith reflected such progressive contemporary thought when he wrote that when it educates its people, a country:

> ... derives no inconsiderable advantage from their instruction. The more they are instructed, the less liable they are to the delusions of enthusiasm and superstition, which, among ignorant nations, frequently occasion the most dreadful disorders... In free countries, where the safety of government depends very much upon the favourable judgement which people may form of its conduct, it must surely be of the highest importance that they should not be disposed to judge rashly or capriciously concerning it.[4]

Smith effectively argues that the growth of human capital in a society can, through its various effects on human behavior, influence economic growth in much more complex ways than by simply increasing the amount of productive resources in the production function.

Adam Smith also saw education as a necessary response to the tendency for people to become too specialized and focused on one aspect of life. Recall from Chapter 4 that Adam Smith described the division of labor, or specialization, as the fundamental characteristic of economic growth. Smith recognized a downside to this specialization:

> In the progress of the division of labour, the employment of the far greater part of those who live by labour... comes to be confined to a few very simple operations.... The man whose whole life is spent in performing a few simple operations, of which the effect too are, perhaps, always the same, has no occasion to exert understanding, or to exercise his invention in finding out expedients for removing difficulties which never occur.[5]

Smith was concerned about the likely emergence of tunnel vision by an increasingly specialized labor force, which would not be compatible with the

---

[4] Adam Smith (1776 [1976]), Book V, p. 309.
[5] Adam Smith (1776 [1976]), *op. cit.,* Book V, pp. 302–303.

growing complexity of industrial society. Education and learning are essential for understanding the increasingly complex economies and societies that specialization would create. Since Smith's time, education has been associated with lower crime rates, greater political participation in political activity, and less oppressive social, economic, and political institutions. Chapter 3 presented evidence showing that education and learning contribute directly to human happiness and well-being.

Smith noted an ironic contrast between primitive and advanced human societies: In a less advanced society, "there is a good deal of variety in the occupations of every individual, there is not a great deal in those of the whole society.... In a civilized state, on the contrary, though there is little variety in the occupations of the greater part of individuals, there is an almost infinite variety in those of the whole society."[6] If Smith was already concerned with the level of specialization achieved in his lifetime during the late eighteenth century, we can only surmise that our modern society is, therefore, in even greater danger that specialization of human activity will discourage people from acquiring a holistic understanding of their world. Like the confusion surrounding the near-meltdown of the Three Mile Island nuclear power plant described in Chapter 1, few people today understand how our economic and social system really works. The confusion surrounding the policy debate on how to deal with the global financial meltdown in 2008–2009 further underscores how the education systems of most countries are not preparing people to deal with the complexity of their economic and social spheres. The high levels of specialization in a modern society reduce its ability to address the increasingly complex problems it faces, as Smith feared, "unless government takes some pains to prevent it."[7] Therefore, according to Smith, the icon of the laissez-faire free market school of economics, society must publicly fund and provide education.

10.4.2 A case of multiple equilibria

The evidence discussed earlier suggests that education is both a cause and a result of economic growth. One implication of such a bi-directional relationship is that the economy may have more than one stable equilibrium. Development economics has developed many models that generate **multiple equilibria** because of non-linearities, structural rigidities, or complex relationsips among variables. For example, the large externalities associated with education generate alternative equilibrium growth rates, including a growth path where economic growth is very slow or nonexistent. Like a **vicious cycle**, low levels of education cause the economy to grow slowly, the slow growth leads people to acquire little education, which in turn retards the creation of new ideas, which slows growth, and so the cycle continues. Or, the economy could settle on a

---

[6] Adam Smith (1776 [1976]), *op. cit.,* Book V, p. 304.
[7] Adam Smith (1776 [1976]), *op. cit.,* Book V, p. 303.

rapid growth path, caught in a **virtuous cycle** in which rising levels of education cause the economy to grow rapidly, which causes people to acquire more education, improves the economy's capacity to produce new ideas, raises the rate of economic growth, and so on. Both outcomes are possible because education and growth reinforce each other.

A specific example of vicious and virtuous cycles can be constructed using our cost-benefit diagram from Figure 10.2. In Figure 10.4 below we assume, for simplicity, that all people have identical abilities and preferences, and thus that the curves apply to all people. If very few people invest in education, there is no economic growth, and the future earnings curves are aU and bE for uneducated and educated workers, respectively.

Suppose that economic growth is enhanced by the positive externalities from raising the level of education of the entire population. That is, if the majority of people acquire education, rather than just a few individuals, economic growth increases and the future earnings curves of both the few uneducated and the majority of educated workers rise. That is, suppose that the increase in returns to labor from the increase in economic growth triggered by the rise in overall education shifts the curves for both uneducated and educated people from aU to aU' and bE to bE', respectively. These assumptions reflect Adam Smith's belief that if there are too many uneducated people in society, the economy does not function very well. But, for people to have the incentive to acquire education, the future private gains must outweigh the short-run private costs.

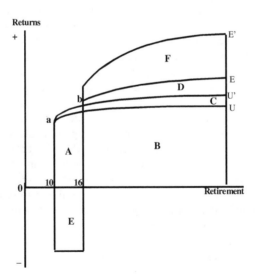

Figure 10.4 Returns to Education with Growth

We have drawn Figure 10.4 in such a way that the private costs of education, areas, opportunity costs A plus education costs E, are greater than the gain in future earnings from education if there is no economic growth, the areas C + D. But, the curves are also drawn so that the gains from education are greater than the private costs of education if the great majority of people receive an education and there is economic growth. We effectively assume that

$$(C + D) < (A + E) < (C + D + F) \qquad (10.2)$$

It should be clear that, so long as the rate at which people discount the future is not too high, the acquisition of education by a majority of people and the resulting economic growth is beneficial for society. Specifically, total income when most people acquire education (and the economy grows) exceeds total income when people do not acquire education by more than the cost of providing everyone with an education.

It should be apparent that the decision whether to invest in education depends on whether people believe that there will be economic growth. Because society will be better off in the case of growth, the optimal outcome is for everyone to go to school. But, if cultural traditions or the unavailability of schooling keeps a majority of people uneducated, there will not be enough educational externalities to generate economic growth and no one else will gain from their schooling. Thus, every individual will reason that it is not in their best interest to pay for an education, and society settles in the no-growth equilibrium. If somehow a few more people could be convinced to go to school or a few more schools are built and staffed, so that a slight majority of people go to school, then the positive-growth equilibrium could be achieved. In fact, if everyone was convinced that a majority of people will go to school and the economy will grow, then everyone will want to go to school and all of society achieves the maximum gains in welfare.

There is a clear role for society to act collectively through government action in this situation. For example, the government could simply require all children to attend school. This is, of course, what the governments in most countries do. In many developing countries, rules for mandatory schooling are not always rigorously enforced, but increasingly even developing countries are finding incentives to induce people to send their children to school because all people in society gain if everyone acquires education. Coercive methods may not be agreed to for older youths or adults, even though higher education also has very positive externalities for human society. Other incentives are necessary to induce people to acquire socially-beneficial education.

10.4.3 Why private education falls short of social needs

In many countries, education and training are also provided privately by employers. The amount of employer training is unlikely to be socially optimal, however, because employers can never be sure that they will receive the full benefits of the education they provide their workers. Since education is an up-front investment, a trained worker can quit and go to work for another employer, taking the newly embodied knowledge with her. In this case, either the new employer or the worker, or both, gain the full benefits of the worker's human capital while the original employer paid for the human capital. This is a classic case of a market failure caused by the impossibility of establishing property rights over the invested human capital; since human capital is embodied in human beings, such property rights would imply a form of slavery if they were held by anyone other than the person in which the human capital was internalized. Hence, employers are careful to invest in their workers' human capital only to the extent that they can reasonably expect to reap benefits from the investment.

In practice, we do find that employers often limit educational expenses to programs that provide job-specific human capital that is not of great use in other jobs. Why would firms pay for costly general education that can be easily applied elsewhere? There are cases where employers provide more general education, like an MBA or other degree programs, in order to motivate employees, but, in most cases firms are unlikely to provide their workers with a social optimal level of education.

In addition to the uncertainty of multiple potential social equilibria, there are other reasons why workers themselves may not invest in human capital up to the point where the marginal gains in future discounted income are just equal to the marginal costs of acquiring more human capital. Investment requires that up-front costs be covered, however, and people may be constrained from acquiring the necessary financing for education, even if it promises to pay off handsomely in the future. In fact, private markets for financing of education often fail to provide a society with the optimal amount of investment. In the case of education, it is difficult to pledge collateral to prospective lenders; indentured servitude is illegal in most countries. Governments often get involved in enabling private financing of education by guaranteeing the privately provided loans and enforcing repayment through the tax system and the courts. Also, private employers often sponsor education in return for legal obligations to work for the employer for some set amount of time. Apprenticeships often set obligations for both workers and employers.

These, and many other, reasons explain why, as Table 10.7 shows, government provides most of the world's formal education. There are many ways that government provides and promotes learning. Most often, government has become the direct provider of education. Whether government-provided education is optimal from an economic perspective remains an open, and hotly debated, question.

Another complicating factor is the presence of conflicting incentives and pressures faced by governments. Government may not provide education at a socially optimal level, even if that optimal level could be calculated. For example, many governments use schools for ideological indoctrination and to spread political propaganda as well as to teach skills, scientific understanding, and productive knowledge. Also, public education bureaucracies may organize education for their own benefit rather than for the benefit of students or the economy as a whole. And other special interests may also influence the government to provide levels of education that are not economically efficient, such as university educations to the children of the politically well-connected at the expense of primary education for the children of the rest of the people in the economy.

Note also that government funding of education does not eliminate all the costs faced by students. Even with free education, students still face the opportunity cost of going to school, which can be considerable in some countries where families live at subsistence levels and the earnings of children are important to the family's very existence. Free education only eliminates the direct costs of education for prospective purchasers of human capital. This is an important point, because many writers have asked how it is possible that people do not send their children to school when the school is absolutely free. In the case of mandatory school attendance, students are in effect forced to pay the opportunity cost of schooling, not to mention other remaining costs such as school supplies, books, uniforms, etc.

Some developing country governments have come up with interesting ways to address this latter problem. For example, Santiago Levy (2006) analyzes Mexico's PROGRESA program, which pays rural families a monthly subsidy when they send their children to public schools in order to compensate them for the opportunity cost of education.

10.4.4 Further difficulties in setting education policy

In the real world, it is difficult for government policies to fine tune to such a degree that the government provides only the education that private individuals or firms cannot provide. A common solution has been to have the government provide most education. But, it should be apparent that the above market failures provide no blanket justification for all education to be government provided. Families can and do finance much of the total cost of education, and virtually all of the opportunity cost. The response of families to improved returns to education has been exactly as our theory predicts; as economic growth raises the returns to educated labor, families send their children to school for more years. Recall the study on India that found rural families responded to better economic opportunities by raising fewer and better-educated children.

Another interesting result of the likely under-investment in education is that, if indeed education facilitates R&D activity, developing economies potentially stand to gain much from increasing their levels of education. It is often suggested that it is easier to adopt an existing idea than to come up with a completely new idea. That is, original research is much more costly than the adaptation of existing technologies. Since the developing economies have much lower levels of technology than the developed economies, they are in a position to increase their levels of technology by copying and adapting existing technologies rather than engaging in the difficult task of pushing back the frontiers of knowledge. If it takes less human capital to adapt an existing idea than it takes to create a new one, investments in education in the developing economies could provide for much faster economic growth than education investments in the developed countries. In other words, the marginal effect of human capital in the R&D production function is greater in developing economies than it is in highly-developed economies. The generally higher returns to education in developing economies could certainly reflect the differences in the cost of generating technological change at different stages of development.

Interestingly, the lower costs of adaptation versus the costs of creating new ideas also means that the huge expenditures on education in the developed countries provide positive externalities for developing economies. Educating more people in Canada and Japan, for example, increases creativity in those countries and ultimately increases economic growth throughout the world as technology spreads. Of course, developing countries do need to let the ideas flow in from abroad, and they must provide the basic education and institutions necessary for people to be able to adapt foreign ideas and for the economy to absorb new technology.

10.4.5 The roles of education in the economic and social spheres

Return for a moment to the discussion in Section 10.5.1 above on Adam Smith's concern about how economic specialization would discourage people from acquiring a holistic understanding of their increasingly complex economies and societies. It is not possible for people to function in a democracy without some understanding of the broad costs and consequences of government policies. Smith's argument for public education must be qualified by the fact that not all education promotes social responsibility and political participation.

In general, the forms of education most useful to employers in the economic sphere are not the same as those needed to sustain the social system or maintain harmony between the social and natural spheres. And the type of education that maximizes human happiness is probably different again. Some education is intended to teach people specific tasks and procedures, some seeks to entertain the human mind's natural inquisitiveness, and some socializes people so they can function within their societies. More ominously, some education indoctrinates and sustains unequal social structures. Many of the arguments about what education should consist of center around an inherent conflict in education: education can be oppressive as well as liberating. Education can be used to distort and shape people's thinking for specific purposes. Not all education promotes critical thinking. Much of what we call formal education consists of processes whereby teachers pass on facts and ideas without criticism or discussion.

According to the well-known Brazilian educator Paulo Freire, education is a form of oppression when it imposes a particular perspective on students. Freire (1970) criticized contemporary education in his native Brazil and most other countries for following the **banking model of education**. This model describes formal education as a process in which teachers tirelessly deposit knowledge in their students, who patiently accumulate the deposited knowledge for later withdrawals to tide them through life and work. According to Freire (1970), this model "transforms students into receiving objects. It attempts to control thinking and action, leads men and women to adjust to the world, and inhibits their creative power." Freire (1970, Chapter 2) argued that this concept of education justifies **narrative education**, which:

> ... leads students to memorize mechanically the narrated account. Worse yet, it turns them into "container," into "receptacles" to be "filled" by teachers. The more completely she fills the receptacles, the better a teacher she is. The more meekly the receptacles permit themselves to be filled, the better students they are.

Note that our models in this chapter essentially reflect the banking model.

Freire (1970, Chap. 2) advocated **problem-posing education** that lets students develop their ability to think critically and begin to examine their existence in the world:

> Banking education (for obvious reasons) attempts, by mythicizing reality, to conceal certain facts which explain that human beings exist in the world; problem-posing education sets itself the task of demythologizing. Banking education resists dialogue; problem-posing education regards dialogue as indispensible to the act of cognition which unveils reality.

Freire's ideas were seen as revolutionary, and the Brazilian military government jailed him briefly after the 1964 coup and drove him into exile in Chile. His thoughts on education were not really much more radical than Smith's call for public education to offset the mind-numbing effects of the division of labor. Nor were they much different from the still-popular writings of the turn of the century American educator John Dewey (1897, p. 77):

With the advent of democracy and modern industrial conditions, it is impossible to foretell definitely just what civilization will be twenty years from now. Hence it is impossible to prepare the child for any precise set of conditions. To prepare him for the future life means to give him command of himself; it means so to train him that he will have the full and ready use of all his capacities...

Clearly, such education is necessary for democracy to function and enable societies to deal with complex issues. However, it is difficult to see how private employers would be willing to directly initiate and fund education that encourages independent thinking and the questioning of existing economic and social systems. In fact, even in democracies taxpayers often complain about taxes being used to fund government education that does not match what they think are the labor market's needs.

10.5 Child Labor and Human Capital

The International Labour Office (2006) estimated that, in 1995, nearly 200 million children between the ages of 5 and 14 worked full-time. Nearly all of these children live in developing economies. There has been a growing concern over **child labor** in recent years, even though there is evidence that the number of children working is declining in most countries of the world. Many children that work are exploited and paid below-market rates.

10.5.1 Child labor throughout history

Child labor has been common throughout human history. Only in the last one or two centuries has child labor come to be seen as something that should be universally discouraged and even banned outright. Until this last century, nearly all children routinely performed tasks that contributed to the survival of the family and the community. The children of farm families actively participated in the family enterprise. Farm chores were generally viewed as a virtuous activity that taught responsibility and passed skills from parents to children. The Industrial Revolution changed the way children worked, however. Rather than working and learning with their parents in their homes or on their farms, when families moved to towns and cities, children began to work in factories.

It was in the countries where the Industrial Revolution first took root, most notably in England, that child labor was first explicitly restricted. In the early 1800s, laws were passed setting a minimum age for employment in factories. An interesting law regulating child labor was enacted in 1837 in the state of Massachusetts, the leading industrial state in the United States at that time. This law prohibited firms from employing children under the age of 15 who had not attended school for at least three months during the previous year. Most criticism of child labor today still reflects the fear that work and education are conflicting choices.

Increases in standards of living over the past 200 years have been accompanied by a decline in child labor. For example, in 1861, 37 percent of all children between the ages of 10 and 14 in England and Wales worked. Kaushik Basu (1998) reports that census data from the nineteenth century show similar rates of labor force participation by children occurred at that same time in the United States, Belgium, and Japan.[8]   Today, child labor is virtually unknown in these countries. Notably, in developing economies child labor is also diminishing quite noticeably. Table 10.8, based on International Labour Organisation (ILO) data, shows that child labor is declining everywhere. Even in Ethiopia, fewer 10–14 year old children are working full time today than was the case only few years ago. Italy's rate in 1950 was twice as high as India's today. Nevertheless, some countries still have a large portion of their children working rather than attending school. Of course, we do not known how accurate these data are, especially given that the subject is controversial and potentially embarrassing to governments.

The employment of young children has largely disappeared in the countries where the Industrial Revolution originated. But, during the twentieth century the practice of employing children in factories and workshops of various types became commonplace in many developing economies as manufacturing globalized and shifted from the high-income to the low-wage countries. The question thus arises whether child labor will also disappear in these countries. Early industrialized countries enacted laws and regulations limiting child labor, which suggests today's developing countries may want to do the same. On the other hand, a number of studies suggest that it was economic and social development that really brought child labor to an end in today's developed economies. For example, Peter Scholliers (1995) examines detailed historical data on the Ghent, Belgium, cotton industry and concludes that child labor diminished quite independently of laws or regulations. On the other hand, Martin Brown, Jens Christiansen, and Peter Philips (1992) find that in the U.S. fruit canning industry both laws and economics played a role in reducing child labor. There is a wide variety of evidence that makes it difficult to reach clear conclusions about the causes of child labor and the best policies to deal with it.[9]

10.5.2 The economics of child labor

In cases where schools are available, child labor implies that the children, or their families, find it more advantageous for them to work than to attend school. Recall our discussion on the returns to education. It is more advantageous to work than to go to school if the current costs of education are higher than the

---

[8] Kaushik Basu (1998), p. 18.

[9] A set of case studies in Hugh Cunningham and Piero Paolo Viazzo, eds. (1996) detail the many costs and benefits of child labor. There is no consensus on whether laws or economic growth are responsible for the end of child labor.

increase in expected future income that education provides. The higher the cost of education and the lower the eventual benefits, the more likely that children will work instead of going to school.

Table 10.8 Labor Force Participation Rate, Children 10–14 Years of Age 1950–2009

	1950	1960	1970	1980	1990	1995	2000–2009
World	28%	25%	22%	20%	15%	13%	-
Africa	38%	36%	33%	31%	28%	26%	29%
Latin America	19%	17%	15%	13%	11%	10%	9%
Asia	36%	32%	28%	23%	15%	13%	12%
Europe	6%	4%	2%	0%	0%	0%	0%
Ethiopia	53%	51%	49%	46%	43%	42%	53%
Brazil	24%	22%	20%	19%	18%	16%	4%
India	35%	30%	26%	21%	17%	14%	12%
Italy	29%	11%	4%	2%	0%	0%	0%

Source: 1950 through 1995: ILO (1996), Economically Active Population: Estimates and Projections, ILO, Geneva; 2000–2009 from UNICEF (2011), *State of the World's Children*, New York: United Nations Children's Fund, Table 9.

The returns to education are likely to be directly related to economic growth, as we illustrated graphically in a case study above. In fact, existing evidence clearly shows that the incidence of child labor is inversely related to per capita real GDP. Data from the International Labour Office of the ILO (2006) and UNICEF (2011) shows that the labor force participation rate for children aged 10–14 years declines rapidly with increases in countries' per capita real GDP. For example, the data in Table 10.8 shows that in the early twenty-first century in one of the very poorest countries of the world, Ethiopia, over 50 percent of all 10–14 year-old children were in the labor force. This compares with the 2000–2009 averages of 29 percent for all of Africa, 4 percent for Brazil, the largest country in Latin America, and effectively zero percent for Europe. The more recent study by the ILO suggests that the percentages have declined only slightly in Africa but substantially in Latin America. Yet, there are still nearly 200 million children aged 14 or younger working in developing countries.

Child labor is not a simple function of per capita real income, however. There are other causes of child labor. One obvious problem in many developing economies is the lack of schools. Table 10.7 gave the percentages of GDP spent on education, and the numbers were not much lower for developing economies compared to the most developed economies. However, the levels of real GDP differ enormously across countries, and the same percentage of real GDP accounts for about 15 times as much real expenditure in a European country as it does in a Sub-Saharan country. The actual expenditures on education are, in fact, very low in developing economies. It should not be surprising that in many developing countries there are not enough teachers, school buildings, and books available to educate all students seeking schooling.

Extreme poverty can also be a barrier to education because it leaves families no option but to send their children out to work. The cost-benefit model of educational choice that we have been using assumes that people will bear the short-run cost of education if the long-run benefits exceed the costs. But, poverty implies that there may be no way to bear the short-run costs. Starvation in the short-run implies no long-run at all! Charles Swanson and Kenneth Kopecky (1999) use the cost-benefit model described earlier in this chapter to hypothesize that life expectancy plays a role in determining the level of education. They indeed find ample evidence that the longer people expect to use the skills and knowledge acquired through schooling, the higher the return to that schooling and the more schooling they will seek.

10.5.3 Policies to deal with child labor

The cost-benefit model of education suggests that economic growth will reduce the incidence of child labor. But, economic growth may not be enough to induce all children to substitute education for work. Additional policy actions may be called for, especially if child labor is a sub-optimal economic outcome caused by discrimination or market failures. Laws and regulations were used in industrial countries in the past century, and quite a few developing countries have also passed legislation dealing with child labor.

Many of the recent calls for curbs on child labor have come from groups in developed countries, not from within the developing economies where the child labor occurs. This makes the current policy environment very different from the nineteenth century, when domestic political pressures led to domestic laws and regulations to deal with child labor. Given this concern with child labor in other countries, the suggested policies are different as well. Some groups have called for international organizations to take up the issue. For example, the United Nations and its subordinate organizations like the ILO and UNESCO have already been very active in extending labor laws to include restrictions on child labor. The World Trade Organization (WTO) has been actively lobbied to include labor standards in its trade regulations. Other groups that have less patience to deal with international organizations have simply called for their own governments to act by, for example, banning the importation of products supposedly produced with child labor.

10.6 Summary and Conclusions

This chapter examined the role of human capital and education in raising people's standards of living. The strong interest in education was stimulated by the economic success of the East Asian tigers, countries that greatly increased their levels of education and achieved very high rates of economic growth. Although there is broad agreement that the large investments in education were one of the causes of the rapid rates of economic development in East Asia, it is probably also true that the rapid economic growth stimulated demand for education. With a brighter future, people become more interested in investing in their futures by accumulating human capital.

Statistical evidence suggests that there is a bi-directional relationship between education and economic growth; education causes growth to increase and the increased growth in turn increases the demand for education. This bi-directional causality between education and economic growth has some interesting implications. One is that the economy may get caught in vicious or virtuous cycles because the bi-directional causality creates multiple growth equilibria, some at low rates of growth, others at high rates of growth. There appear to be vicious cycles in Africa, where both growth and education are very low, and virtuous cycles in East Asia, where investment in human capital and economic growth are both very high. Clearly, the relationship is complex and many more variables play a role in determining the exact influence of investments in human capital and education on the process of economic development.

Models from earlier chapters suggest that education can stimulate economic development through several channels. On the one hand, education can be viewed as a form of investment in human capital, in which case the Solow growth model leads to the conclusion that education is subject to diminishing returns and depreciation, and it is, therefore, only capable of causing short-run and medium-run economic growth. Even so, education and additional human capital can bring substantial short-run growth if levels of education are raised substantially.

The experience of East Asian countries is often interpreted as proving that education accelerates economic growth by expanding human capital. But Asian growth was not only the result of enhancing labor. The broad based economic development in Asia was also the result of substantial restructuring of economies and societies, which constituted a more general form of technological change. Education is likely to have played a role in making such broad economic and social change possible because investment in education generates externalities that permit the economy to overcome diminishing returns. Also, education provides the human capital needed for innovative activities; and once it has generated new knowledge, it helps to spread the new ideas and knowledge to more people around the world.

Finally, Adam Smith (1776), Paulo Freire (1970), and many others have pointed out that education enhances humans' ability to think abstractly and holistically. That is, education not only teaches facts and procedures, but it teaches people how to think. Education is critical for holistic thinking because it opens new perspectives that enable people to better understand their circumstances. But for education to fulfill its holistic role, it must be problem-posing, not merely education of the top-down narrative kind. Perhaps the prevalence of narrative education helps to explain the mixed statistical results on the role of education. School attendance does not teach people to think; creativity and holistic thinking depend on the style and quality of teaching the student encounters inside the school.

Key Terms and Concepts

Banking model of education
Capital
Child labor
Cost-benefit analysis
Depreciation
Education
Enrollment ratio
Flow of education
Human capital
Learning
Multiple equilibria

Narrative education
Obsolescence
Primary education
Problem-posing education
Secondary education
Socialization
Stock of human capital
Tertiary (higher) education
Time profile of investment
Vicious cycle
Virtuous cycle

Questions and Problems

1. Define human capital.
2. At the start of Section 10.2, the text states: "... education is a **flow** while human capital is a **stock**, and stocks depreciate over time." Explain and discuss.
3. Table 10.1 shows that the levels of education attained by men often differ from those attained by women. Do you see any patterns? Can you explain those patterns?
4. Is human capital becoming more evenly distributed in the world? Use evidence from this chapter and any other sources you can find to answer this question.
5. Table 10.2 shows that in almost all countries, the percentage of people with a secondary education has risen from one generation to the next. Which country has not experienced an increase? What would explain the differences across countries?
6. Use the logic of Figure 10.2 to explain why education is a welfare-enhancing activity for a society to undertake. Also, use the model to explain why there may be a limit to how much a society should invest in education if long-run welfare maximization is the goal.
7. The logic that underlies the intertemporal cost-benefit analysis illustrated in Table 10.4 and Figures 10.1 and 10.2 may not include all the true costs and benefits of education. Discuss.

8. Is there a role for government in providing education? Explain. (Hint: Discuss the evidence of differences between social and private returns to education.)
9. The text states: "It is likely that the education of a person benefits more than just that person." Explain.
10. Summarize the returns to education presented in Table 10.5. What patterns do you see? What might explain those patterns?
11. Economists from Adam Smith to Amartya Sen have advocated government provision of education. Why do you think many modern-day politicians are advocating cuts in public education today? Compare the arguments for public education by Smith and Sen with those made by some current politicians.
12. Explain Adam Smith's argument, discussed in Section 10.5.1, that the growing division of labor mandates more public investment in education.
13. Explain the possibility of multiple equilibria in the model shown in Figure 10.4. (Hint: Explain how the presence of externalities causes individual incentives to fail in pushing the overall economy to an efficient outcome.)
14. Examine Table 10.7. What stands out from these numbers? Do poor countries spend a greater part of their governments' revenues on education than high-income countries do? What do these numbers imply for future economic development? Discuss.
15. What exactly is the role of education? Discuss the various view presented in this chapter.
16. Does education promote economic development? Discuss why or why not. (Hint: Place education in the models you have studied in earlier chapters.)
17. Define child labor. Why is child labor a problem for economic development? Discuss.

References

Basu, Kaushik (1998), "Child Labor: Cause, Consequence, with Remarks on International Labor Standards," Working paper, December 5.

Benhabib, J., and M. Spiegel (1994), "The Role of Human Capital in Economic Development: Evidence from Aggregate Cross-Country Data," *Journal of Monetary Economics* 34(2):143–174.

Borensztein, Eduardo, Juan De Gregorio, and Jung-Wha Lee (1998), "How Does Foreign Direct Investment Affect Economic Growth?," *Journal of International Economics* 45:115–135.

Brown, Martin, Jens Christiansen, and Peter Philips (1992), "The Decline of Child Labor in the US Fruit and Vegetable Canning Industry: Law or Economics," *Business History Review* 66(4):723–770.

Cunningham, Hugh, and Piero Paolo Viazzo, eds. (1996), *Child Labor in Historical Perspective, 1800-1985: Case Studies from Europe, Japan, and Colombia*, UNICEF, Florence.

Denison, Edward F. (1985), *Trends in American Economic Growth, 1929–1982*, Washington, D.C.: The Brookings Institution.

Dewey, John (1897), "My Pedagogic Creed," *School Journal* 54 (January):77–80.

Freire, Paulo (1970), *Pedagogy of the Oppressed*, New York: Continuum.

International Labour Office (1996), *Economically Active Population: Estimates and Projections*, Geneva: ILO.

International Labour Office (2006), *Global Child Labour Trends, 2000 to 2004*, ILO, Geneva, April.

Levy, Santiago (2006), *Progress Against Poverty: Sustaining Mexico's Progresa-Oportunidades Program*, Washington, D.C.: Brookings Institution.

Nelson, Katherine, and Richard R. Nelson (2002), "On the Nature and Evolution of Human Know-How," *Research Policy* 31:719–733.

Psacharopoulos, George (1994), "Returns to Investment in Education: A Global Update," *World Development*, September:1325–1343.

Psacharopoulos, George, and Harry Anthony Patrinos (2002), "Returns to Investment in Education: A Further Update," World Bank Policy Research Working Paper No. 2882, September.

Scholliers, Peter (1995), "Grown-ups, Boys, and Girls in the Ghent Cotton Industry, The Voorman Mills, 1935–1914," *Social History* 20.

Shutz, T. Paul (1988), "Education Investments and Returns," in Hollis Chenery and T.N. Srinivasan, *Handbook of Development Economics*, Amsterdam: North Holland.

Smith, Adam (1776 [1976]), *An Inquiry into the Nature and Causes of the Wealth of Nations*, Chicago: The University of Chicago Press.

Swanson, Charles E., and Kenneth J. Kopecky (1999), "Lifespan and Output," *Economic Enquiry* 37(2):213–225.

World Bank (1993), *The East Asian Miracle, Economic Growth and Public Policy*, Washington, D.C.: The World Bank.

CHAPTER 11

The Financial Sector of the Economy

I wish somebody would give me some shred of evidence linking financial innovation with a benefit to the economy.

(Paul Volcker)[1]

The following subheading recently appeared in the weekly news magazine *The Economist*: "To sustain rapid rates of growth, the world needs to save more."[2] Some growth models make the same point. For example, the Harrod-Domar growth model discussed in Chapter 4 hypothesizes a simple linear relationship between saving and growth. The Solow model shows that, all other things equal, a higher saving rate results in a higher steady state level of output.

It is not saving, per se, that causes economic growth, however. A World Bank study of East Asia's rapid growth in per capita GDP concluded that East Asia's high savings rates since the 1960s were more an *outcome* of high growth rates than a *cause*.[3] Dani Rodrik, after studying the huge World Bank data base on saving, likewise concluded that "[i]ncreases in saving appear to be the outcome of economic growth, not a fundamental determinant of it."[4] Rodrik(1998, p. 30) in fact makes a provocative suggestion for achieving a higher rate of economic growth:

> The policy implication is clear: policies geared towards raising domestic saving do not deserve priority when designing economic programs. As our case studies demonstrate, the key to generating virtuous cycles of high growth-high

---

[1] Dave Kansas and David Weidner (2009), "Volcker Praises the ATM, Blasts Finance Execs, Experts," *Wall Street Journal*, December 8.
[2] *The Economist* (1995), "Rattling the Piggy Bank," May 6.
[3] The World Bank (1993).
[4] Dani Rodrik (1998), "Saving Transitions," working paper prepared as part of the World Bank research project on saving, July, p. 30.

investment-high saving is to kindle the animal spirits of entrepreneurs by increasing the expected profitability of their activities. Enhancing production and investment incentives seems preferable to working on saving incentives.

Rodrik effectively says that saving only makes funds available for investment and innovation. By itself, saving does not *cause* investment and innovation.

This chapter outlines the many reasons why a society's willingness to refrain from current consumption does not automatically translate into productive investment or innovation. Equally important, it seeks to explain why the availability of productive investment or innovative projects does not always lead a society to reduce its current consumption and fund those projects.

This chapter focuses on the **financial sector** of an economy, whose task it is to channel society's savings to investment projects and innovative activities. In most economies, the financial sector consists of banks, insurance companies, stock markets, bond markets, central banks, government regulators, and many other formal institutions. In less developed economies, and most developed economies, the financial sector is also likely to consist of informal financial arrangements such as street money lenders, pawn shops, check discounters, and trusting friends and family. Regardless of a country's level of economic development, the financial sector often fails to carry out its task of channeling sufficient savings to maintain its capital stock, finance its most promising new projects, and fund the innovation necessary to sustain economic development.

In general, financial transactions are difficult to carry out. Savers and investors are usually distinct groups of people facing different incentives.

Chapter Goals

1. Explain the difference between saving and investment, and the motivations that lead people to save and invest.
2. Show how different economies exhibit very different savings behaviors.
3. Explain the role of the financial sector of the economy as one of channeling savings to investment.
4. Explain the reasons intertemporal exchanges are prone to failure.
5. Specifically explain information asymmetries, moral hazard, and adverse selection.
6. Discuss the risk of default in intertemporal transactions.
7. Explain government remedies for financial market failures, such as government institutions that enforce contracts, property registries that permit the use of collateral, and regulations that mandate information be provided to both sides of financial transactions.
8. Discuss microfinance and its successes and failures.
9. Explain why crony capitalism misdirects financial sectors' allocation of society's savings to projects across the three spheres of human existence.

Innovators, or what Schumpeter called "social deviants," are often even farther separated from savers. And, many hands are always ready to grab the savings entrusted to the financial system. The 2008–2009 global financial crisis revealed that financial sectors are prone to systemic failures and fraud that disrupt the flow of savings to investment and cause severe economic depressions.

11.1 Saving

Saving, which is the act of not consuming all of one's wealth, has varied greatly over time and across countries. This fact undermines the assumption of a constant savings rate made by the Harrod-Domar and Solow growth models. In fact, the differences in saving rates across regions seem to have gotten larger over the past two decades. Table 11.1 shows that in 2008 savings rates varied from over 50 percent of GDP in China to minus 27 percent in Zimbabwe. There was also considerable variation between 1980 and 2008 for each country. For example, while India nearly doubled its savings rate from 17 percent to 32 percent, El Salvador's savings rate fell from 14 to −2 percent.

Table 11.1
Gross Domestic Saving and Investment as a Percentage of GDP, 1980 and 2008

		Gross Domestic Saving		Gross Domestic Investment	
		1980	*2008*	*1980*	*2008*
Developed	Australia	24%	26%	25%	28%
Economies	Austria	27	26	29	24
	Canada	25	19	24	21
	France	23	17	24	19
	Italy	24	19	27	19
	Japan	31	21	32	20
	Netherlands	22	26	22	18
	Spain	21	22	23	24
	Sweden	19	23	21	17
	United States	19	11	20	14
Africa:	Cote d'Ivoire	20	19	27	11
	Ethiopia	3	4	9	22
	Ghana	5	9	6	20
	Kenya	18	8	29	21
	Madagascar	−1	9	15	33
	Mauritius	10	11	21	21
	Morocco	14	25	24	36
	Mozambique	−24	2	0	21
	South Africa	36	19	28	19
	Tunisia	24	23	29	27
	Zambia	19	26	23	22
	Zimbabwe	14	−27	17	2

Table 11.1 (Continued)

		Gross Domestic Saving		Gross Domestic Investment	
		1980	*2000*	*1980*	*2000*
Asia:	Bangladesh	2	17	15	24
	China	35	52	35	48
	Hong Kong	34	30	35	23
	India	17	32	21	36
	Indonesia	38	34	24	31
	Korea	24	30	32	26
	Malaysia	33	36	30	14
	Nepal	11	8	18	30
	Pakistan	7	11	18	19
	Philippines	24	16	29	15
	Singapore	38	47	46	29
	Sri Lanka	11	18	34	40
	Thailand	23	32	29	22
Latin	Argentina	24	26	25	21
America:	Brazil	21	16	23	17
	Chile	17	27	21	19
	Colombia	20	20	19	23
	Costa Rica	16	21	27	20
	Dominican Republic	15	7	25	15
	Ecuador	26	21	26	32
	El Salvador	14	−2	13	13
	Mexico	25	21	27	22
	Paraguay	18	10	32	16
	Peru	32	26	29	22
	Uruguay	12	19	17	18
	Venezuela	33	23	26	25
Middle	Egypt	15	12	28	19
East:	Jordan	−8	−7	37	15
	Saudi Arabia	62	37	22	26
	Turkey	11	14	18	15
Eastern	Bulgaria	39	18	34	26
Europe:	Hungary	29	23	31	22
	Latvia	33	18	26	19
	Poland	23	20	26	20
	Romania	35	24	40	31
	Russia	22	26	22	19
World:		24	22	24	22
Low Income Countries:		16	18	20	22
Middle Income Countries:		28	25	27	25
High Income Countries:		23	21	24	21

Sources: 1980 figures are from The World Bank, *World Development Report 1998–1999*, Washington, D.C., 1998, Table 13, pp. 214–215; 2008 figures are from IMF (2011), *World Economic Outlook*, Washington, D.C.: International Monetary Fund, April.

Table 11.1 also makes it clear that countries' rates of domestic saving and domestic investment are seldom identical. For example, China raised its saving rate from 35 percent in 1980 to 52 percent in 2008, while its rate of investment rose from 35 to 48 percent. In 2008, China invested 4 percent of its savings overseas. Table 11.1 shows that many African countries invested more than they saved in 2008. Domestic saving can differ from domestic investment if there are international financial inflows or outflows. In Africa, foreign loans, foreign investment, remittances from overseas migrants, and foreign aid often made up the difference between domestic saving and domestic investment.

11.1.1 The population profile and saving

The variation in savings rates across countries has stimulated much research into the determinants of saving. A popular economic model of saving is the life-cycle model of saving. This model suggests that saving occurs because individuals try to smooth out their lifetime consumption, which means, among other things, that young working people save for their retirement later in life. Indeed, a well-known study by Nathanial Leff (1969, pp. 893–894) covering a large number of developing economies found that during the 1960s "dependency ratios — and ultimately high birth rates — are among the important factors which account for the great disparity in aggregate savings rates between developed and underdeveloped countries." Recall from Chapter 9 that the dependency ratio is the share of non-working people in the total population, and the ratio can be illustrated using a population profile.

Figure 11.1 shows two population profiles, just like the ones we discussed in Chapter 9. The population profile in the left-hand box of Figure 11.1 represents a society that has been experiencing an acceleration in population growth over the past century, and there are many more young people than old people. Because of the large young 0–20 year old group, the productive 20–40 and 40–60 year age groups comprise less than half of the population, and therefore the economy's *dependency ratio* is over 50 percent. People who do not earn any income cannot save, which suggests that this society saves less than the society depicted in the right-hand diagram of Figure 11.1.

Notice that in the right-hand diagram of Figure 11.1 the working age population is relatively large compared to the non-working young and very old. This society has a lower dependency ratio than the first economy. In fact, this society's largest age group is the 40–60 year group, which is usually the highest income group that also tends to save the most. This group has already raised its children and is most aware of the need to save for retirement.

The society depicted in the right-hand diagram of Figure 11.1 will in the future save much less because that same 40–60 year age group will in 20 years reach retirement and be replaced by the smaller group below it. And, that smaller group will, 20 years after that, be replaced by the even smaller group below it.

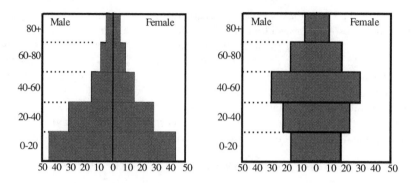

Figure 11.1 Population Profiles and Saving

In the future, therefore, the second society will save less. On the other hand, the society on the left may save more in the future if it is able to reduce its birth rate. In fact, if it reduces its birth rate, the left-hand society will in two generations have a population profile like the society shown in the right-hand diagram in Figure 11.1. In sum, changes in birth and death rates bring gradual changes in countries' age profiles. Therefore, if the population profile and the dependency ratio are indeed important determinants of a country's savings rate, then differences in savings rates will shift only gradually over time.

11.1.2 Changing profiles and savings rates: The evidence

Projections of population growth indicate that the region of the world where age profiles will change the most in the next half-century is Asia. The East Asian countries of Japan, China, and the Asian tigers have all greatly reduced their birth rates to bring them more in line with their low mortality rates. Countries like China, Korea, and Taiwan have life expectancies that approximate those of the most developed countries; Japan has the highest life expectancy of any country in the world. Thus, the sharply reduced birth rates combined with the very low mortality rates means that the populations of the East Asian countries are becoming much older on average. At the present time, their population profiles look like the right-hand side of Figure 11.1. But, by the year 2025, the number of people over the age of 60 will be three times as large as today, and there will be *fewer* working-age people than there are today. The population profiles will become top-heavy, wider at the top than at the middle and the bottom. The population profile model suggests that the rate of saving in East Asia will decline in the future.

A set of country studies edited by James Poterba (1994) for the National Bureau of Economic Research shed doubt on the **life cycle theory of saving** and the relevance of population profiles for predicting saving behavior. For example, Table 11.2 provides evidence from one of these studies showing that in most countries people save even after retirement. In two countries, Italy and Japan, the saving rate among elderly households exceeds 30 percent of income. Even in countries with social insurance and retirement benefits, the saving rate of people approaching retirement is high. Perhaps saving in China, Taiwan, and other Asian countries will not decline when their dependency ratios increase.

The population profile is just one of many determinants of saving. Many countries with identical population age profiles exhibit very different savings behavior. Culture, expectations about the future, taxes, and the scope of government also influence saving behavior.

Table 11.2 Age-Specific Personal Saving Rates (percent): OECD Countries

Age Group	Canada	Germany	Italy	Japan	United Kingdom	United States
<30	0.0	9.8	10.0	17.9	5.0	−2.2
30–34	3.0	9.8	20.0	27.4	8.0	7.1
35–39	3.0	10.6	26.0	31.8	12.0	9.4
40–44	5.0	10.2	22.0	31.8	12.0	9.8
45–49	5.0	10.2	23.0	28.5	11.0	11.2
50–54	8.0	10.4	31.0	31.5	10.0	13.9
55–59	11.0	11.0	32.0	34.5	13.0	16.6
60–64	9.0	12.2	34.0	31.7	6.0	8.6
65–69	6.0	9.2	36.0	32.0	2.0	7.1
70–74	6.0	9.7	31.0	33.8	9.0	1.1
>74	8.0	10.2	n.a.	31.1	n.a.	n.a.

Source: James M. Poterba (1994), "Introduction," in Poterba (ed.), *International Comparisons of Household Saving*, Chicago: The University of Chicago Press, NBER Project Report, p. 8.

11.1.3 Research using the World Bank saving data base

The World Bank has put together a data base on saving that covers 112 developing and 22 developed countries beginning in 1960.[5] This data has spurred a series of recent statistical studies confirming that overall saving is positively correlated with (1) real per capita income, (2) the rate of economic growth, and (3) government saving (budget surpluses). Correlation says nothing about the direction of causality, of course. In fact, statistical tests that seek to uncover the direction of causality suggest that economic growth determines saving, not the other way around.

---

[5] This evidence was first published in working papers such as, for example, Norman Loayza, Humberto Lopez, Klaus Schmidt-Hebbel, and Luis Serven (1998), "Saving in the World: Stylized Facts," working paper taken from the World Bank Internet site, November; Norman Loayza, Klaus Schmidt-Hebbel, and Luis Serven (1999), "What Drives Saving across the World?," working paper from World Bank Internet site, September.

The World Bank data also show that in the case of per capita income and saving, it is income levels that drive saving at the lower levels of per capita income. For the more developed economies, however, differences in the levels of per capita income do not seem to explain differences in saving rates. As expected, saving is also found to be negatively correlated with the dependency ratios. Thus, the current high rates of saving in the East Asian economies may be due, at least in part, to their low dependency ratios. Cultural factors may also be at play in the case of Asia, however. Table 11.2 above showed that saving is amazingly constant across age groups in Japan, suggesting that age structure plays little role in that country's high rate of saving. But, Japan may be an exception. East Asian tigers such as Taiwan, South Korea, and Singapore went through their population transition in the 1970s, and their populations had begun to age rapidly after 2010. So far, East Asia's high savings rates have not yet begun to fall. Sub-Saharan Africa offers a different example; it has yet to begin its population transition.

The World Bank data appears to refute the hypothesis put forward by some development economists, namely that a large share of national income for the relatively wealthy would increase overall national saving. World Bank data shows that saving is higher, all other things equal, in countries with more equal distributions of income and wealth. To many economists' surprise, the World Bank data failed to confirm hypothesized correlations between the rate of saving and interest rates, the terms of trade, and the rate of inflation.

11.1.4 *Saving for the environment: What the evidence implies*

The World Bank's main conclusions on saving cover only saving done explicitly through the formal financial sectors of countries around the world. But, what about saving the environment and nature's services? Here the World Bank's conclusions may be misleading.

For example, the finding that recorded savings are positively correlated with real per capita income may not be accurate once we take the natural environment into consideration. Even as people refrain from consuming some proportion of their rising incomes, those same rising incomes over the past 200 years depleted natural resources and diminished the Earth's capacity to provide natural services. Similarly, the World Bank's finding of a positive correlation between saving and income growth must be adjusted to account for the equally positive correlation between economic growth and resource depletion. The **environmental debt** reported by, for example, Wackernagel *et al.* (2002) and the World Wildlife Fund (2008) means that the world's savings are not as great as the data suggests. Some of the reported savings should have been allocated to reducing that environmental debt.

11.2 The Fundamental Role of the Financial Sector

Economist and Nobel laureate John Hicks stated flatly that the Industrial Revolution would not have happened without the concurrent development of financial markets. According to Hicks (1969), the Industrial Revolution was characterized by a sharp rise in the use of machinery and other capital goods, and thus large investment in fixed real assets was required in order to realize the Industrial Revolution's gains in productive efficiency. Such investment required the mobilization of large amounts of savings, which would have been impossible without the creation of liquid financial assets. Hicks' thus concluded that the development of the financial sector and financial markets is a key determinant of economic growth over the past 200 years.

Recall Paul Volcker's quote at the start of this chapter, however. There are in fact many cases in which the financial sector failed to perform its function of efficiently allocating savings to investment and innovation. In general, the decision to save does not automatically result in investment and innovation. Saving is the act of *not consuming* and thus not demanding goods and services. Real **investing**, on the other hand, consists of using real resources to create new **capital** or to develop new technology. The incentives that influence saving are not the same as those that motivate investment. And the incentives that stimulate innovation are different again. Also, the people who are motivated to save are, in general, not the same people or entrepreneurs who carry out the investment and innovative activities. It is the financial sector's task to channel the funds made available by savers to those who have the most productive investment projects. This is not an easy task.

Corruption and unethical behavior are major causes of the financial sector's repeated failures to efficiently allocate savings to investment and innovative activities. Anyone studying the financial sector should keep in mind the brief interview of the famous American bank robber Willy Sutton, in which a reporter asked him why he robbed banks. Willy's reply was: "Because that's where the money is." In fact, in today's ever wealthier global economy, enormous amounts of money flow through the financial sector. It would be naïve to not expect that many people, groups, businesses, governments, and bank officials themselves will expend great effort and ingenuity to get their hands on that money.

11.2.1 Financial failure is a constant

Recent economic downturns in several Asian and Latin American economies have been blamed on the poor performances of their financial sectors. The 1997 financial crisis in Asia, introduced in Chapter 1, was the result of poorly performing banks. The allocation of loans to favored industries by banks that belonged to the same conglomerates that owned the industries in South Korea,

Indonesia, Malaysia, and Thailand, and elsewhere diluted the quality of financial institutions' loans. Known as **crony capitalism**, cozy relationships between banks and borrowers meant that large numbers of non-performing loans had effectively already pushed many large banks close to insolvency by 1997. External financial pressures thus pushed the financial system into actual bankruptcy, causing the devastating 1997 financial crisis and recession.

The collapse of the Mexican economy in 1995 was also due in large part to the fragility of the Mexican financial sector. Mexican banks had heavily leveraged themselves by means of foreign borrowing. When the financial collapse caused the economy to fall into a long recession, Mexican taxpayers were forced to cover losses from bad loans by the nation's commercial banks equal to about 15 percent of GDP. In Russia, unknown billions of U.S. dollars of savings were simply stolen from the banking system and "laundered" through assorted foreign bank accounts and businesses operated by various *new oligarchs* who were able to exploit the economic and political chaos that followed the collapse of the Soviet Union.

Fraud, incompetent management, and inefficient allocation by financial sectors are not unique to developing or Eastern European transition economies, of course. The failures of savings and loan banks in the United States in the 1980s led to a massive government injection of capital to restore the failed banks' balance sheets. In total, this government intervention cost U.S. taxpayers over $200 billion at the time. Between 2007 and 2009, world financial markets were rocked by a new wave of bank failures, failures of derivatives markets, and even the failure of insurance companies, all triggered by the collapse of a real estate bubble perpetrated by irresponsible bank behavior in the United States. Governments in the United States, Europe, Japan, and elsewhere responded to the 2007–2009 financial crisis with injections of public funds as the complexity of the more "developed" financial sectors in the developed countries quickly extended the failures in the U.S. real estate market throughout the world. Global markets for securitized assets and the other derivatives froze, clearly refuting claims by many orthodox economists that financial innovation had made the financial sector safer and more stable. The globalization of financial markets did not stabilize markets; to the contrary, the ease with which money and assets crossed borders only meant that the crisis, which started in the United States, quickly spread throughout the world. In early 2009, all of the world's economies were either in recession or seeing their GDP growth declining rapidly toward recessionary levels. 2009 was the first year since World War II that the aggregate real economy activity in the world declined.

In September of 2008, the U.S. Congress hastily approved $700 billion for the Secretary of the Treasury to use for buying up bad debt in the hope that this would reverse a sharp contraction in bank lending that was having real consequences for the economy. Such purchases were correctly criticized as an attempt to solve the financial crisis without diluting stockholders' equity in the banks. That is, the arrangement was an attempt to use taxpayer obligations to bail out private banks, with the justification of also saving the economy. The United Kingdom and other European governments, to their credit, took the more direct route of saving the economy by taking over unsound banks before restoring their balance sheets. Such intervention favored taxpayers over the stockholders of the financial firms, since with a public takeover the taxpayers benefit if the financial sector ultimately becomes profitable again.

We are now getting ahead of the analysis, however. The next subsection presents a simple model of a financial sector that will help to explain the issues we have described above.

11.2.2 A simple model of the financial sector

Savers are individuals, households, firms, or governments who do not use all of their current income to acquire consumption goods but instead carry their income over to later periods. Investors are those who seek to create productive capital. It is very unlikely that each saver also has investment opportunities that can exactly absorb desired saving in any given period of time. Many savers do not have the managerial ability, the foresight, the technical know-how, or the entrepreneurial zeal to invest their savings themselves. On the other hand, those with the best ideas for productive investments are unlikely to possess the savings necessary to carry out their projects. This mismatch of people who wish to save and people who wish to invest establishes the need for financial markets and financial intermediaries through which savers and investors can exchange current purchasing power for future purchasing power.

In order to illustrate the source of demand for savings, suppose that an individual can invest in several different projects. One opportunity might bring an expected return of, say, 25 percent; that is, by investing $1,000 in this project, the investor will receive $250 per year in output or money. There may be another opportunity that offers 20 percent on an investment of $2,000, another that offers 15 percent on an investment of $2,500, a fourth that offers 12.5 percent on an investment of $2,000, a fifth that offers 7.5 percent on $500, and so forth. How many of these projects the individual invests in depends on the interest rate at which he or she can borrow and lend. If, say, it is possible to borrow or lend at an interest rate of 10 percent, then even with no personal savings to draw on the investor can profitably invest in projects 1 through 4 by borrowing a total of $7,500. The net gain is the difference between the total returns of the investments and the cost of borrowing. This net gain is shown in Figure 11.2 as areas a, b, c, and d, the area above the 10 percent interest line for each investment.

The market rate of interest defines the opportunity cost of funds. If, for example, our investor has $15,000 in accumulated wealth, he or she will still only invest in the first four productive projects with returns above 10 percent

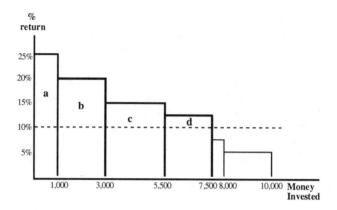

Figure 11.2 Potential Investments for the Individual Saver

and lend the remaining $7,500 to others at the market interest rate of 10 percent. Investing in the fifth and sixth projects would not be worthwhile because the opportunity cost of the 10 percent return available elsewhere in the financial markets exceeds the projects' returns of 7.5 and 5 percent, respectively. Our investor would do better by channeling the $7,500 to the other investors who have projects or personal uses whose returns exceed 10 percent.

11.2.3 *Extending the analysis to the whole economy*

The individual behavior illustrated in Figure 11.2 needs to be modified if we look at the capital market of an entire economy. Instead of an individual investor/borrower facing a given market rate of interest at which a seemingly infinite amount of wealth can be lent or borrowed, the total demand for savings will be the sum of all the individual investors' projects. Total demand for savings can be represented by a smooth downward-sloping curve instead of the step-wise pattern in Figure 11.3.

As shown in Figure 11.3, equilibrium in the financial market is at the intersection of the downward-sloping demand-for-funds curve, D, and the supply-of-savings curve, S. Remember, the area under D represents the total returns to the economy's investment projects. The supply curve of saving essentially reflects people's opportunity cost of foregone consumption. The upward-sloping supply of savings curve drawn in Figure 11.3 thus implies that a higher rate of interest is necessary to induce people to save more. This may not be correct, however, and there is evidence that higher interest rates may have an *income effect* that leads people to actually spend more when they earn higher interest rates on their savings. The supply curve of savings could be vertical or even backward-bending. But, the basic conclusion that the market interest rate and the volume of lending and borrowing are determined by the intersection of

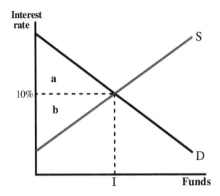

Figure 11.3 Supply and Demand for Savings

the supply and demand curves for loanable funds remains generally valid. We thus follow orthodox convention and use the standard upward-sloping supply curve for our illustration in Figure 11.3.

Equilibrium in Figure 11.3 occurs at the market rate of interest of 10 percent, where total investment is I. Investors receive returns equal to the height of the demand-for-loanable-funds curve, while they must pay 10 percent for borrowed funds; they earn a surplus equal to the area **a**. Similarly, savers earn a surplus over and above their perceived value of foregone consumption equal to the area **b**. This exchange of purchasing power between today and some future time period, or what we generally call **intertemporal exchange**, is thus beneficial to both lenders and borrowers.

11.3 Market Failures in the Financial Sector

Welfare-maximizing intertemporal exchanges, such as those depicted in Figure 11.3, cannot always be completed. Financial markets often do not carry out what would be mutually-beneficial intertemporal exchanges. Among the reasons for such **market failures** are (1) **financial repression** by governments, (2) *crony capitalism* by lenders, and (3) the unique characteristics of intertemporal markets that make it inherently difficult to complete welfare-enhancing intertemporal transactions even when there is no fraudulent or biased manipulation of banks and markets. Financial repression consists of the regulations, taxation, and legal codes that restrict how the financial sector channels savings to investors. Crony capitalism is the preferential treatment that banks give certain customers, often because of prior relationships or common ownership of banks and firms that seek loans. The remainder of this chapter details several unique features of intertemporal markets that make it difficult for them to achieve the outcome illustrated in Figure 11.3.

11.3.1 The possibility of default

Intertemporal exchanges involve the exchange of something today for something else at a later time. The fundamental problem inherent in any intertemporal exchange is that, in the absence of moral restrictions, legal penalties for failing to fulfill an agreed-to transaction, or concerns about the long-run consequences of dishonest behavior, one party to the agreement has a real incentive to accept a payment or good now and then not deliver on the future obligation. If a **default** on an agreed-to future payment or future delivery of a good or service is likely, the party that has to incur the earlier cost will not enter into such a transaction. The transaction will not take place even though it would be beneficial to both parties if they could commit to carrying out fully the terms of the intertemporal transaction.

This perverse incentive is surmountable, however, as evidenced by the many intertemporal transactions that *are* routinely carried out in most economies. Societies have established mechanisms to prevent people from reneging on intertemporal agreements. Most countries use the threat of compensatory payments, fines, confiscation of goods or wealth, or even imprisonment to force people to honor intertemporal agreements and contracts. It takes a fairly sophisticated legal system to enforce banking contracts, although many societies have found innovative ways to enable intertemporal transactions subject to adverse incentives. The next sub-section describes an interesting case from Taiwan.

11.3.2 Contract enforcement in Taiwan

Taiwan is one of the four Asian tigers that achieved phenomenal rates of economic growth over the past four decades. Unlike another Asian tiger, South Korea, which actively promoted the creation of large industrial conglomerates (known as **chaebol**), the Taiwanese economy has been characterized by the rapid growth of large numbers of small firms. Many of these small firms have successfully grown to become major exporters of manufactured goods. The entrepreneurs that founded these small businesses required financing, and the Taiwanese financial sector performed the task of channeling saving to productive investors quite well.

The financial sector that had developed in the fast-growing Taiwanese economy was a mix of highly-regulated banks and largely unregulated **curb lenders**. The term *curb* is often used to refer to less formal financial markets because the earliest informal lenders often operated on the curb in front of formal, regulated banks. Banks have been government-owned in Taiwan, and they have been run in a very bureaucratic fashion. The banks took few risks and dealt mostly with well-established borrowers that had sufficient collateral to cover their loans. The low interest-rate ceiling imposed by the government caused demand for credit to exceed supply, and the already risk-averse bureaucrats became even more prone to lend only to the most secure borrowers. Entrepreneurs with good ideas but little collateral had to find their financing elsewhere. It is estimated that small and medium firms financed up to 65 percent of their investment internally through family sources and retained earnings, which suggests that when business opportunities exist, the absence of a modern financial industry may not be as great a barrier to innovation as the financial industry claims. The remainder of investment was largely financed through curb markets.

Lenders in Taiwan's informal curb markets were often businesses that did have access to credit from the government-owned banks. For example, a large firm that enjoyed a good reputation and had investments in plant and equipment that could serve as collateral would obtain a low-interest loan from a government bank, and this firm would then extend credit to smaller suppliers and customers. Effectively, large firms accepted the potential risks of default by small and medium firms, and the government banks made loans to large firms knowing full well that some of the borrowed funds would be passed on to their suppliers and customers. This *dual* system of finance was able to function because the government supported the curb market with a critical piece of legislation, the Negotiable Instruments Law, enacted in 1955. This law made it a crime, punishable by as much as two years in prison, to bounce a postdated check. According to Tyler Biggs (1991), by enforcing the law that made bouncing a postdated check a serious crime enforced by the existing criminal justice system, the government in effect made the curb market for trade financing viable.

Taiwan's dual financial sector of formal banks and informal curb markets is giving way today to a more sophisticated multi-layered financial industry. This is only natural as the Taiwanese economy develops. Nevertheless, Taiwan offers a very good example of how borrowers and lenders can take advantage of existing institutions and culture to create alternative channels for savings to finance productive investment projects without a massive reorganization of the financial sector of the economy.

11.3.3 Enforceable contracts do not eliminate all risk

There are many problems in carrying out intertemporal exchanges that have nothing to do with theft and dishonesty. For example, a borrower responsible for a future payment or producer committed to a future delivery of some good or service may simply be unable to make the required payment or delivery, despite every intention to honor the contract. Perhaps the investment project for which an entrepreneur borrowed other people's savings simply does not generate the expected earnings because of unforeseen shifts in business conditions. Maybe economic conditions in the economy change unexpectedly, causing expected earnings to fall short of what is needed to meet the future obligation. Perhaps the future obligation requires more hard work, effort, or sacrifice than was thought necessary when the obligation for future payment or delivery of some service was entered into. The future is difficult to predict, and it is easy to miscalculate a borrower's ability to repay or a supplier's ability to deliver on future obligations. The most honest, law-abiding borrower may fail to meet a future obligation because of unforeseen circumstances. Intertemporal trades therefore involve uncertainty and risk even when informal or explicit legal institutions deal effectively with intentional defaults on future obligations.

The risk inherent in intertemporal exchanges can prevent welfare-enhancing transactions from being concluded. First of all, potential lenders may be **risk-averse**, which means they prefer a certain outcome to an uncertain one. On the margin, risk-averse lenders will prefer to lend to the project with the more certain payoff even if the expected payoff of the more certain project is less than the expected payoff of the less certain project. For society as a whole, the average risk is low because it is spread across a large number of projects, and it would usually be preferable to undertake the projects with the highest expected payoffs. But, any single potential lender, facing a finite set of potential projects, will clearly have to take into consideration the specific risks of each project.

The way to lead individual investors to allocate their savings in a way that maximizes the returns for society as a whole is to reduce individual risks to the level that society faces. This is where **financial intermediaries** such as banks, mutual funds, or pension funds play such an important role. Intermediaries can reduce risk to individual savers by *pooling* savings and lending to a diverse set of investment projects. Traditional banks, for example, engage in **risk pooling** by combining the savings of many depositors and lending the funds to a great variety of borrowers, such as car buyers, credit card users, home purchasers, and many different businesses. Mutual funds provide savers with the opportunity to hold a share of a diversified portfolio of stocks or bonds even though they contribute only a small amount of money to the fund. The benefits for economic growth are obvious: while individual savers would not risk all of their wealth on a single risky but promising entrepreneur, financial intermediaries eliminate risk to individual savers by making pooled savings available to a large sample of entrepreneurs with potentially high-return but risky projects.

Pooling risky borrowers is not as simple as it may seem, however. There is still the problem that savers, intermediaries, and purchasers of assets do not have all the information they need to accurately assess the risks and returns of the projects proposed by prospective borrowers, issuers of stock, sellers of bonds, or entrepreneurs with prospective investment projects. In most cases, potential borrowers usually know more about an investment project and their ability to repay than do lenders. When information is not equally available to both sides of a transaction, information is said to be **asymmetric**. Asymmetric information generally causes markets to fail to efficiently allocate savings to investment projects.

11.3.4 The adverse selection problem

Asymmetric information creates an **adverse selection** problem. To illustrate this problem, suppose first that two apparently equal people walk into a bank and claim to have $1,000 projects that promise an average return of 20 percent. Should the bank indiscriminately give each of them the requested funds if the going interest rate is 10 percent? Or, should the bank refuse one or the other request for a loan? Your answer will depend on the risk associated with each project, of course. Suppose that the first prospective borrower's project is guaranteed to yield a 20 percent return no matter what happens. But the second borrower's expected 20 percent return is the average of two equally-likely outcomes, one with a 140 percent return but the other resulting in the complete loss of the entire investment. There is thus a 50 percent chance that the borrower ends up with $2,400 and a 50 percent chance that the borrower loses everything. On average, the borrower ends up with $1,200, indeed a 20 percent return on the $1,000 investment. The bank sees the situation very differently: in the case of the 140 percent, it still gets only $1,100 back, its original $1,000 plus the 10 percent interest rate charged on the loan. The borrower gets to keep $2,400 − $1,100 = $1,300. In case of total failure, on the other hand, the lender loses $1,000 but the borrower ends up with no more or less than she started out with. The borrower expects to earn $650, or ($1,300 + $0)/2. But for the bank the expected outcome is highly negative; the average of a 10 percent or $100 gain and a $1,000 loss is a loss. Thus, the bank should only give a loan to the first borrower who will definitely repay the loan.

What if information is asymmetric and the second borrower falsely claims to have a project like the first borrower's? Banks attempt to gather as much information as possible in order to evaluate borrowers' claims and accurately evaluate prospective investments. Asymmetric information remains a problem, however, even for experienced banks. Even venture capital firms who actually participate in the management of new firms, pension funds with staffs of investment experts, and other financial intermediaries that specialize in gathering information never manage to overcome all informational asymmetries.

The adverse selection problem stems from the likelihood that prospective borrowers like the second one are more likely than the first type of borrower to seek loans rather than use their own money. Loans effectively permit borrowers to spread the risk of their project to the lender. Thus, like the insurance company that finds most customers for flood insurance live in areas most prone to flooding, banks will find that the riskiest borrowers are likely to be the most frequent seekers of loans. If banks assume each prospective customer is an average investor with an average likelihood of failure, they will underestimate the true likelihood of failure by the people who actually enter their bank to apply for loans.

Adverse selection is not easily solved, however. Raising interest rates in order to cover the potential losses from giving loans to risky borrowers may be self-defeating. As interest rates are raised to cover suspected risks, some of the less risky but lower return projects are no longer viable. The more interest rates are increased, the fewer safe projects seek loans and the higher the percentage of risky borrowers. Unless the bank can overcome the problem of asymmetric information, it may simply not be profitable to be in the banking business. Many insurance companies simply do not insure homes in a floodplain.

In a famous article, Joseph Stiglitz and Andrew Weiss (1981) pointed out that the optimal way for banks to deal with the adverse selection problem is to randomly *ration* loans at an interest rate below the rate that clears the market. It is better to keep the interest rate low in order to be sure that borrowers include many of the less risky kind. Raising interest rates to cover risk may be futile as high interest rates only make the population of would-be borrowers more risky on average. But, such rationing means the market does not achieve the market clearing equilibrium in Figure 11.3.

11.3.5 The moral hazard problem

Another problem that hinders financial transactions is **moral hazard**, which refers to the likelihood that once borrowers have acquired a loan, they will behave differently than they would have without the loan. The insurance industry of course deals with this problem all the time. For example, a person with fire insurance may feel less of a need to buy a fire alarm than the person without insurance; hence, a fire becomes more likely when insurance is in place. Similarly, a firm may take more risks after acquiring a large loan because, after all, it is other people's money that is at risk.

To prevent moral hazard, lenders have to monitor the activities of borrowers. Hence, banks usually require progress reports on projects for which they lend money, bank officials may schedule periodic meetings with borrowers, and in many countries bank officials sit on the boards of directors of major borrowers. Venture capital firms take very active roles in the operations of the projects and companies in which they invest, often sitting on the board or participating in the day-to-day operations. Lenders must make sure that borrowers do not get careless with the borrowed money, and that they continue to operate in a manner that ensures repayment of loans.

11.3.6 Government regulation and the information problem

There is a well-defined role for government policy to assist financial markets and intermediaries. In a developed economy such as the United States, the

Securities and Exchange Commission (SEC), the government agency that overseas stock and bond markets, requires that firms that issue stock or bonds make public a certain amount of financial information on a regular basis. Similar agencies exist in most countries, although the specific reporting requirements differ greatly. Most countries require extensive information from firms offering stock in their companies. In most countries the government agencies that supervise banks require that banks make public their financial statements so that depositors and other holders of bank liabilities can judge the bank's ability to meet its obligations. Government-mandated information can thus mitigate, at least in part, the asymmetric information problem and permit financial markets and financial intermediaries to function where they otherwise would fail to complete many intertemporal transactions.

In the United States, the recent financial collapse was ignited by an informational failure: U.S. investment banks created and sold worldwide large numbers of securities backed by mortgages issued by local U.S. banks. These securities enabled banks to quickly finance their lending in the global securities market, which funneled funds from all over the world to the booming U.S. real estate market. While this was initially hailed as a sign of how globalization improved the efficiency of the world financial industry, the realization that these mortgage-backed securities were not worth what everyone thought they were worth ended up undermining the balance sheets of virtually all financial firms across the globe. As it turns out, this was an informational failure enabled by poor government oversight, extensive fraud at various levels of management, and excessive complexity that obscured what was going on. Of interest here is the failure of the ratings agencies, the private firms who, for a fee, perform analysis of securities and institutions and issue a rating of the risk and financial worth. These ratings agencies rated securities backed by large pools of mortgages as perfectly safe and fully worth the sum of the underlying mortgages. Further investigation shows that the ratings firms were clearly biased by the fact that they were paid for the ratings by the very investment banks who sold the securities. Worse, these investment banks also did other types of business with the ratings firms, which gave the latter every incentive to treat their customers kindly. Hence, buyers of the securities were misinformed.

It can be argued, of course, that it is the business of banks and other financial intermediaries to acquire the information necessary to complete intertemporal transactions and that government interference is not necessary. But, even if they could acquire the necessary information, intermediaries may not have an incentive to do so because the information that they acquire quickly becomes a public good. For example, suppose that after a bank devotes a large amount of resources to investigate the viability of a borrower's project, it decides to grant a loan to the borrower. Other banks and investors can then use the bank's decision to help them decide whether to lend to that firm, buy its stock, or buy its bonds. They effectively use the first bank's hard-found information free of charge. The other intermediaries, because they would not have to incur the costs of investigating the borrower, could offer intermediation services at a lower price and take business away from the first bank. The first bank may, therefore, decide to not devote resources to information gathering and, instead, wait for other banks to reveal information. If all intermediaries behave in this fashion, society as a whole will spend too little on gathering information, and savings will not be as efficiently allocated to investment and innovative projects. This situation is reminiscent of the case of under-investment in activities to create new **nonrival** technologies, discussed in Chapter 7. Here it is the *nonrival* nature of information that tends to result in *under*-investment in information.

11.3.7 Property rights and collateral: A role for government

Government can enhance the financial sector's ability to channel savings to investment projects in other ways. An important role for government is to establish the institutions and procedures that allow borrowers to pledge their property as **collateral** for loans. Collateral is some real or financial asset of value in the possession of the borrower that the lender can claim in the case of a default. Collateral reduces the risk to the lender, because something else of equal or greater value will be obtained if the borrower defaults. Equally important, collateral sends a strong signal that the borrower really intends to repay the loan, because a default leads to the loss of collateral property worth as much or more than the repayment of the loan. Collateral can thus overcome the information asymmetry between borrower and lender, make fraud unprofitable, address the adverse selection and moral hazard problems, lower the cost of financial intermediation, and enable more mutually beneficial financial transactions to be completed.

Collateral for loans is normally classified as either **personal property**, which consists of *tangible* things, such as real estate, structures, inventory, equipment, livestock, and tools, or **intangibles** such as accounts receivable and contracts to supply future goods or services. Collateral is not always available, however. In many countries, the legal system makes it difficult to use intangible assets as collateral for loans because (1) collateral cannot be easily defined, (2) lenders cannot easily establish exclusive rights to specific collateral, and (3) the enforcement of collateral arrangement is costly or unpredictable. The use of collateral requires that property rights be well defined. And, of course, there is not much property, tangible or intangible, in very poor economies.

A comparison of lending to cattle ranchers in the United States and Uruguay by Heywood Fleisig (1996) illustrates the legal institutions necessary for collateral. At the time of the study, small cattle ranchers in Uruguay were having difficulty obtaining credit. In many countries, a bank can lend to cattle ranchers and claim, say, 200 of the rancher's 1,000 cows as collateral for a

$200,000 loan. The bank would only have to check a central registry to make sure that at least 200 of the rancher's cows were not yet pledged as collateral to other lenders. In Uruguay, on the other hand, the lender had to identify each individual cow as collateral. Thus, while in many countries the lender could claim $200,000 worth of cows if the borrower defaults, in Uruguay the lender had to find the exact 200 cows specified in the contract. If the specific cows died, the lender had little recourse.

Further complicating the use of collateral for farm loans was the fact that Uruguay had no indexed registry of collateral. There was nothing to prevent a rancher from pledging the same cows for any number of loans or other financial transactions. In the case of default, the lender was never sure that others would not come forward to demand the same cows. In order for collateral to be a practical solution to the asymmetric information problem, there must be centralized **registries of collateral** whose records are open to public scrutiny.

Finally, the process of claiming collateral often took more than two years in Uruguay because the lender had to follow lengthy legal procedures before the courts would authorize the lender to take possession of the cattle pledged as collateral. Over a period of two years the cattle can die, disappear, or get sick. According to Fleisig (1996, p. 45): "Not surprisingly, under these conditions, lenders demand collateral that is sure to outlast a lengthy adjudication process — in other words, real estate." But, if real estate is the only collateral accepted by lenders because it is the only collateral that can safely cover the losses of default, then only owners of land can borrow from banks. If land is very unequally distributed, as is precisely the case in many Latin American countries like Uruguay, the many tenant farmers simply cannot get loans to finance the purchase of cattle or any other movable equipment or machinery that, under the right institutions, could serve as its own collateral.

11.3.8 Financial intermediaries also face perverse incentives

Government regulation and supervision of the financial sector is not an easy task. It requires government officials to have the same talent and training as bankers, securities dealers, and financial managers they oversee. Such talent is especially scarce in developing economies. The 1990s financial crises in Asia, Mexico, and Russia were in large part due to poor government supervision and regulation of the banking sector. The 2008 world financial crisis was entirely a result of lax government regulation and oversight, which itself was the result of the intentional dismantling of the U.S. financial regulation after years of relentless lobbying by the private financial industry. These financial crises serve to remind us that financial intermediaries and markets introduce potential market failures of their own. When savers entrust intermediaries with their money, there are incentives for intermediaries to engage in self-interested activities that are not in the best interest of the savers.

An individual bank is continually tempted to invest in more risky assets in order to maximize the expected difference between earnings and the costs of capturing funds from savers. And, if the excessively-risky assets do not work out and the bank can no longer meet its obligations, it is the depositors who suffer the losses. The possibility of bank failures has led many countries to provide depositors with **deposit insurance**, which compensates depositors when a bank fails. But such insurance leads to adverse selection of financial intermediaries because, just as in the case of the more risky borrower in the example earlier, the banks with the riskier projects are likely to offer the highest interest rates on deposits. Thus, deposit insurance can result in risky banks growing faster than less risky banks, and the likelihood of bank failure increases.

11.3.9 Financial intermediaries versus financial markets

In most developed countries, and in an increasing number of developing economies, we observe a variety of **financial markets** and **financial intermediaries** functioning simultaneously. Stock markets exchange financial assets whose value can be easily judged by most savers, as in the case of stocks of well-known firms and corporations. **Centralized exchanges**, like most stock exchanges, where all buyers and sellers interact to exchange standardized assets are quite inexpensive to operate and provide clear price and volume information to prospective buyers and sellers. **Over-the-counter markets** in which a few private firms hold inventories of assets for sale are used to exchange foreign currencies, most bonds, and nearly all more sophisticated financial assets and derivatives. The private firms offering to buy and sell financial assets over-the-counter generally charge more for their services because they face higher inventory and marketing costs. And because buyers and sellers do not see any transactions other than their own, these markets are not nearly as transparent as centralized exchanges. The firms who operate in over-the-counter markets exercise market power and generally reap substantially higher profits which more than compensate for their higher costs. Centralized stock markets and over-the-counter bond markets coexist with intermediaries like banks, pension funds, and insurance companies in what we broadly term the financial sector of the economy. The more developed the financial sector, the greater the variety of financial markets and intermediaries that make up the sector.

Ross Levine (1997) found that the higher the per capita output in an economy, (1) the larger is the banking sector as measured by the amount of bank assets relative to GDP, (2) the larger is the value of stock traded on the stock markets relative to GDP, (3) the greater are the assets of other (non-bank) financial institutions relative to GDP, and (4) the greater is "financial depth" as measured by the total value of money and financial assets relative to GDP. Thus, all parts of the financial sector tend to grow as economies grow, although they do not all grow proportionally. At the same time, the growth of the financial sector is an important contributor to economic development. Financial markets and intermediaries facilitate the flow of savings to investment projects despite the different motivations, abilities, needs, and knowledge of savers and investors. In many cases, the liquidity of financial markets and the pooling of assets and liabilities by specialized intermediaries reduce risk. However, the financial sector often also adds to risk. There is debate over how the financial sector should be organized and regulated in a developing economy.

11.4 Microfinance

Common wisdom says that the cost of monitoring the performance of investment projects, relative to the size of their loans, is very high for banks that lend small amounts of money to a large number of borrowers. This high cost of monitoring small loans is often given as a reason why banks prefer to lend to large businesses and projects rather than small entrepreneurs and small businesses. Such a bias in favor of well-established, large firms and against small upstarts constitutes a serious failure of financial intermediaries in allocating savings to the most productive investment projects. In recent years, however, a number of innovative financial intermediaries have come up with ways of monitoring many small borrowers. After all, many small borrowers have productive investment projects and some successful small borrowers do eventually become large borrowers. Banks do, therefore, have an incentive to serve small borrowers.

Today, there are thousands of banks and financial organizations making loans of less than $1,000 to some 75 million borrowers in over 100 developing countries. These **microfinance institutions (MFIs)** have adopted various mechanisms to reduce fixed costs of lending and monitoring. Their success has led many conventional banking organizations to enter the market for microfinance and make loans ranging from $50 to $1,000 for relatively short periods to very poor borrowers. Microfinance is seen as a promising solution to world poverty, and the founder of one of the pioneering MFIs, the Grameen Bank of Bangladesh, was awarded the Nobel Peace Prize in 2006.

11.4.1 The Grameen Bank of Bangladesh

In 1972, Muhammad Yunus returned to his native Bangladesh after receiving a PhD in economics and teaching for several years in the United States. As Yunus (2003) describes his life, when he returned to Bangladesh to take up a teaching position there, he came to realize that a major economic barrier to economic progress in Bangladesh was the lack of access to credit by poor Bangladeshis. Women had virtually no access to bank borrowing of any type. After experimenting with various schemes to provide small loans to rural women entrepreneurs, in 1983 Yunus obtained a government charter to put into effect what he thought was a workable model for a microfinance bank. After 25 years of operation, the Grameen Bank of Bangladesh provides a successful example of how to overcome some of the problems associated with loaning to small businesses and people with very little income or wealth.

Today, the Grameen Bank lends over $400 million per year to small borrowers. Most of the borrowers are women who work in what is traditionally a very male-oriented society. The majority of the loans are for less than $100, although the average loan is much larger. To make and monitor so many small loans, the Grameen Bank instituted a scheme to induce borrowers to behave in a manner that keeps them actively pursuing the activities for which they were lent money: (1) small cells of borrowers jointly assume responsibility for the repayment of the loans of all members of the cell and (2) weekly meetings of all borrowers serve as a collective monitoring mechanism where peer pressure can be exerted.

The peer pressure can obviously become obsessive, as each member of the cell badgers the other cell members about everything from their lifestyles to their business practices. But, the peer pressure does seem to work, at least for a time. First time borrowers have a 98 percent repayment rate. The cells imply that monitoring of borrowers is in part carried out by fellow borrowers and, hence, at no direct cost to the Grameen Bank. The repayment rate falls for second and third time borrowers, however. Perhaps people eventually stop responding to peer pressure.

Grameen Bank incurs other costs not normally incurred by mainstream banks, however. The Grameen Bank organizes regular meetings to promote good business behavior and actively push borrowers to break with many traditional forms of Bangladeshi social behavior. Grameen borrowers are very persistently encouraged to engage in family planning, to participate in a national program of tree planting, and to give up traditional practices such as providing dowries when daughters marry.

The Grameen Bank has received much praise for seeking to change institutions that, according to many social scientists, inhibit entrepreneurship and economic growth. But, the Grameen Bank has also been criticized. For example, Jeffrey Tucker (1995) argues that it is more like a cult than a bank. He points to the Grameen Bank's losses early in its existence, the fact that the bank took in few deposits, and its reliance on donations and cheap loans from foreign organizations to fund its lending activity. Critics of Grameen Bank also point to its weekly meetings where the borrowers chant a narrative of rather ideological principles called the "Sixteen Decisions." In recent years, however, the Grameen Bank's balance sheet has become increasingly solvent, and in the early twenty-first century it was capturing deposits to cover nearly all its loans.

Operating in a traditional, male-oriented society such as Bangladesh will inevitably result in any bank catering largely to women with small businesses to be perceived as radical or disruptive. Success stories abound, however. One woman who used a Grameen Bank loan to acquire a cellular phone in 1999 provided the first phone service in her small village. "My life is getting better," she claims. "People consider me a person of honor."[6] Given its goal of raising living standards, not making a profit, the Grameen Bank's reliance on donations during its early years cannot be used as evidence of its failure as a bank.

Much has been learned about micro-finance, and other groups in other countries have gone on to show that lending to small farmers and entrepreneurs can in fact be quite profitable. For example, the Village Bank division of Bank Rakyat Indonesia has made over 2 million small loans in rural villages averaging about $500 dollars each. Its profits from microfinance grew to where they covered the losses from loans that its parent, Bank Rakyat, made to large industrial borrowers.[7]

Now, the high profitability of microfinance may be undermining the purposes of the new system. In Nicaragua, there were recently public protests of a local microfinance led by a group called *No Pago* (I won't pay), which was protesting recent arrests of some microborrowers for failing to pay their debts. The microfinance firm blamed the Nicaraguan President Daniel Ortega for fanning the flames of discontent with the private microfinance banks because he wants to promote a new government-run credit agency for small farmers. But the protestors complain that the interest rates on private microfinance loans are too high, often over 18 percent per year.[8] There are reports of similar complaints in other countries. For example, in Bosnia microfinance rates often top 30 percent per year, and loans are poorly monitored. In fact, there are indications that in Bosnia the microfinance industry has gradually morphed in to a high-interest predatory consumer lending industry.[9]

11.4.2 The Grameen model is not new

The Grameen Bank's use of peer pressure to guarantee loan repayment is not a new banking technology. Avner Greif (1995) points out that Medieval Europe used such a system to support long-distance commerce. The growth of trade among "strangers" over long distances is difficult to explain by the usual conclusions of game theory in economics. For a repeated game format to generate behavior that mimics trust, the individuals in the game have to face repeated contacts with the same players, so that the fear of retaliation in the future for current cheating is strong enough to discourage current cheating. But, individual merchants in Medieval Europe seldom dealt with each other more

---

[6] Miriam Jordan (1999), "It Takes a Cell Phone, A New Nokia Transforms a Village in Bangladesh," *The Wall Street Journal*, June 25.

[7] Jacob Yaron, McDonald Benjamin, and Stephanie Charitonenko (1998).

[8] Elyssa Pachico (2009), "'No Pago' Confronts Microfinance in Nicaragua," Research report for the North American Congress on Latin America, October 28.

[9] Phil Cain (2010), "Microfinance Meltdown in Bosnia," *Aljazeera.net*.

than once and yet routinely shipped goods to each other under the expectation that payment would be forthcoming. Greif's examination of historical records uncovered various schemes that resembled Grameen Bank's method of having all borrowers in a community share each other's obligations.

For example, Greif uncovered the case of a merchant from Genoa in Northern Italy who was late in making a payment for goods shipped by a trader from Tripoli in Northern Africa. Tripoli sent a notice to Genoa, and the Genoese trader immediately sent the payment to Tripoli, explicitly requesting the North African trader to not hold any other Genoese for ransom. Apparently, the tardy Genoese trader had come under pressure from other Genoese traders to make the payment because there was an informal system in place whereby merchants from the same city were held responsible for the unpaid debts of their fellow citizens, much like the fellow members of one of Grameen's groups are held responsible for individual loans to each member of the group. Greif found many instances of *community responsibility* for individual debts, and he argues that, by converting the enforcement of inter-community debt into an intra-community enforcement system, trade was able to flourish despite the lack of sophisticated international legal institutions.

Modern regulatory systems to oversee banks and financial markets reflect the ages-old principle of community responsibility for financial transactions. Modern central banks, financial regulatory agencies, and other government agencies effectively exercise the community's pressure to make bankers and issuers of financial assets behave honestly. Without such oversight, fraud and mismanagement inevitably runs rampant and the financial system fails. The ill-advised financial deregulation during the 1980s and 1990s enabled the fraudulent and irresponsible behaviors that caused the 2007–2009 global recession. Once again, humanity was reminded that individually-motivated behavior is not compatible with systemic stability. Financial intermediaries and markets require community oversight and monitoring.

11.4.3 Nacional Monte de Piedad

In 1450 in Perugia, Italy, the Franciscan religious order established the Monte de Pietá movement, which organized pawn shops that provided zero interest loans. Loans were given in exchange for collateral deposited physically with the Monte de Pietá (literal translation: deposit of mercy). In place of interest payments, which were illegal under the rules of the Catholic Church at that time, borrowers were strongly encouraged to make a contribution to the church. The institution, therefore, was both a source of revenue to the church and a less onerous competitor to the private lenders that often charged exorbitant fees to desperate debtors. The movement spread throughout Roman Catholic Europe, and in 1774 it arrived in New Spain, or Mexico.

Pedro Romero de Terreros, the owner of several colonial enterprises in New Spain including the Real del Monte silver mine in Hidalgo, contributed a small fortune to the founding of Sacro y Real Monte Pio de Animas (The Sacred and Royal Pawn Institution for Souls). Now called the Nacional Monte de Piedad, the institution still functions today, managed from its headquarters on the northwest corner of the Zócalo, the huge central plaza in Mexico City. The institution was set up to (1) make small low-cost loans to people in need of emergency assistance, and (2) to use its accumulated profits for funding charitable organizations. A few years after its establishment, its board authorized the charging of interest on loans, a controversial decision at the time.

The Monte de Piedad survived Mexico's independence from Spain in the early nineteenth century, when it dropped the "Real" from its name, and the separation of church and state after the Mexican Revolution in the early twentieth century, when it became simply the **Nacional Monte de Piedad**. But its basic purpose has changed little, which is to offer small low-interest loans on pawned items to poor segments of Mexican society. By the early twenty-first century, the Nacional Monte de Piedad has grown into a large microfinance organization with over 150 branches throughout Mexico serving 750,000 borrowers totaling nearly 1 billion Mexican pesos (about US$75 million). The enterprise handles over 30 million pawned items each year in its warehouses. According to the latest information, Nacional Monte de Piedad charges 4 percent interest per month, and borrowers have 17 months to repay and recover their pawned goods. Commercial pawn shops in Mexico charge over 10 percent per month. After some years of poor financial results, Nacional Monte de Piedad recently resumed making grants to charitable organizations, one of its original purposes when it was founded in 1774. The institution now offers small mortgages and home improvement loans to poor families, an expansion of services made possible by the improvement of Mexican institutions that define property and collateral.

11.4.4 The future of microfinance

The financial sector of an economy can only be analyzed from a holistic perspective that includes social and cultural factors as well as the usual economic institutions that mainstream economics has focused on. The mainstream economics perspective tends to lead economic advisors to recommend that developing countries must import Western institutions if they are to ever have a modern financial sector. Such advice has led to many failures in developing countries, at which point there are the inevitable claims that the banking system or newly imposed financial markets failed because of "poorly developed institutions." The examples of the curb markets in Taiwan, the Grameen Bank in Bangladesh, and the Monte de Piedad in Mexico make it clear that the financial sector can function in what Western economists see as "deficient" institutional environments.

By matching the needs of the curbside lenders to the existing legal structure in Taiwan, the simple definition of large penalties for bouncing a check made curbside lending viable and relatively efficient.   More important, the measure created a channel for money to flow from the formal banking sector to the curbside lenders.   Grameen bank adopted an ages-old principle of linking obligations to groups rather than individuals, and thus mobilizing existing social relationships to do the expensive task of monitoring borrowers, to make microfinance economically viable.   The Nacional Monte de Piedad, of course, represents a simple way of overcoming weak property rights and the costly legal process required for repossessing collateral by having people physically deposit collateral with the lender.   In each case, a holistic identification of a country's culture, community structure, and other social institutions enabled viable banking institutions to function.

Recent experience suggests that the high-income Western countries have themselves also failed to respect their own cultural and social environments when they reformed their banking regulations, government oversight, and legal procedures over the past three decades.   The 2008 financial crisis is a direct result of the failure of regulators to recognize that financial liberalization would be incompatible with the West's culture of individual greed and the myopic corporate quest for profits taught at leading business colleges.   Interestingly, the United States has had trouble creating microfinance institutions despite the alleged efficiency of its economic institutions.   Mark Schreiner and Gary Woller (2003) hypothesize that in the U.S. the poorest workers are *relatively* less trained and talented, compared to the rest of the population, than the poorest workers are in most poor developing countries.   The higher level of economic development in the United States means that the costs of entry into new businesses is much higher in the United States and much too costly for micro loans to play a definitive role.   Richard Taub (1998) argues that microfinance for small entrepreneurs in the United States most often generates service jobs, unlike developing economies where many new entrepreneurs engage in producing goods.   Service firms are more difficult to analyze and monitor for lenders.   There is also likely to be a large adverse selection problem in countries like the United States, where small borrowers often have access to credit through established banks and credit unions.   Small borrowers in rich countries with viable projects often have collateral and can, therefore, obtain relatively inexpensive financing.   Thus, in developed countries, the borrowers who end up seeking micro-finance loans may be exceptionally risky or dishonest.

11.5 Systemic Failures in the Financial Sector

Several decades ago, two prominent financial economists, Ronald McKinnon (1973) and Edward Shaw (1973) attributed the poor performance of investment and growth in developing economies to **financial repression**, which was defined as government rules, regulations, and institutional structures that restrict or prevent savers and borrowers from freely carrying out their desires to exchange assets. In many cases, regulations and institutions prevent the market failures detailed above. However, government interference in the financial sector may be designed to benefit some savers or investors at the expense of others.

Financial repression is reported to have earned governments in developing economies revenue equal to 2 percent of GDP.[10] The gains to governments come in the form of lower interest payments on government debt, higher profits by government-owned banks, direct taxes on banks and other financial institutions and markets, the free collection of taxes and bills for the government by banks, and interest-free loans to the government in the form of required deposits at the central bank. Other examples of financial repression are the intentional efforts by governments to redirect savings to certain sectors of the economy believed to be critical to economic development. Sometimes, special interests are able to induce the government to force the financial sector to direct savings their way.

11.5.1 Interest rate ceilings

A common form of financial repression is a ceiling on interest rates. Recall from earlier in the chapter that the curbside lenders in Taiwan arose, in part, because the government imposed interest rate ceilings on its banks and thereby made bank financing difficult to obtain for small firms. Figure 11.4 illustrates the case of an interest rate ceiling. The supply curve S of savings relates the amount of loanable funds offered at each rate of interest. The demand curve for loanable funds is labeled D. The demand curve for loanable funds reflects an ordering of potential investment projects, ranked in a declining order of their expected rates of return.

In Figure 11.4, the interest rate that would equate supply and demand is i. If an interest rate ceiling is imposed, say at i_{MAX}, then the market for loanable funds will not clear. At i_{MAX}, the demand for loanable funds exceeds supply by the amount $Q_M Q_F$, which is the quantity of projects that would be profitable at i_{MAX} but are not carried out because supply of loanable funds is only Q_M. Figure 11.4 also shows the interest rate ceiling requires some form of rationing among potential borrowers, who cannot all be satisfied. If the rationing process is economically efficient, all the borrowers along the demand curve segment from **a** to **b** would be selected; this guarantees that the projects with the highest returns would be undertaken with the limited availability of savings Q_M. But,

---

[10] See Alberto Giovannini and Martha de Melo (1993) and M.J. Fry, C.A.E. Goodhart, and A. Almeida (1996).

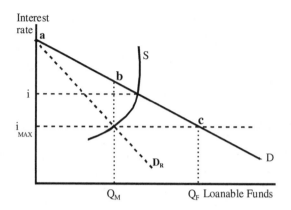

Figure 11.4 The Effect of an Interest Rate Ceiling

note that *all* projects along the demand curve down to point **c** are profitable when the interest rate is i_{MAX}. If, under the interest rate ceiling, a rationing process ends up giving funds to borrowers with investment projects whose return is below those from the segment **ab**, while excluding some of the borrowers from the segment **ab**, the overall returns from investment will be even lower. Most actual rationing schemes tend to do an imperfect job of selecting projects, not least because a repressed market is often the result of political lobbying on behalf of borrowers in the lower half of the segment **bc** who could not afford loans at the market rate i.

Governments have often forced banks and other financial institutions to direct funds toward specific industries or sectors of the economy. For example, after World War II many developing nations instituted measures to promote manufacturing and heavy industry to replace traditional sectors like agriculture, and these measures usually included mandates for banks to lend to the favored new sectors. One result of limiting lending to specific types of investments is to shrink the demand for loanable funds. Suppose demand is restricted to D_R in Figure 11.4, then the end result is similar to our earlier example of an interest rate ceiling. Overall returns to investment fall, as the last industrial or housing projects will have returns close to i_{MAX}, while at least some projects in commerce, agriculture, mining, and other sectors will have returns above i_{MAX}.

11.5.2 Human psychology and self-imposed repression

There is another important reason why intertemporal markets fail: people often do not make rational intertemporal decisions. Psychology and experimental economics have found that people often make bad choices, inconsistent choices, and completely irrational choices when they make intertemporal decisions.

For one thing, research from psychology and experimental economics has shown that people exhibit a bias favoring the status quo. This means that starting points influence subsequent choices, even though rational behavior would suggest that choices should be based exclusively on expected future outcomes alone. That is, sunk costs should not influence marginal decisions concerning action to determine future outcomes. Cass Sunstein and Richard Thaler (2004) found that in the United States, 14 percent of workers who were automatically enrolled in a plan to deduct a percentage of their paycheck for deposit in a tax-exempts savings plan chose to opt out of the plan, but only 49 percent of workers chose such a plan when they were required to explicitly indicate to their employers that they wanted to join such an automatic savings plan. Clearly, if people were fully rational it would make no difference whether people were automatically enrolled but could opt out or they were not automatically enrolled but could opt in by simply telling their employer they wanted the deductions into the savings plan made for them. People are strongly influenced by the status quo to the detriment of their long-run welfare, however, as discussed in detail in Chapter 3.

People are also highly influenced by how information about the future is presented to them. For example, Sunstein and Thaler (2004) also describe how people are more likely to agree to a risky medical procedure when they are told there is a 90 percent chance of success than when they are told there is a 10 percent chance of failure. Sunstein and Thaler conclude that because the framing of a situation affects people's behavior, providing more information only helps if the information is presented in a fully neutral fashion.

There are many other ways in which human behavior tends to repress intertemporal markets. For example, people tend to accept the information they already have as accurate and thorough when in fact it isn't, and even when it is accurate, they tend to give it too much weight by ignoring other readily available information. People tend to be overconfident about how well they understand their circumstances, and they fail to seek better information or take broader perspectives. That is to say, people avoid holism, preferring to view the world from a single familiar perspective. In the case of forward-looking decisions, which are inherently uncertain, limiting information can be especially costly in terms of long-run welfare.[11]

There are many studies showing that people consistently fail to accurately estimate risk and probabilities. A simple example is the fact that many more people are afraid of flying than of driving, yet everyone knows that per mile traveled, a person is ten times as likely to be killed on the road. And, people do not consistently discount the future. For example, when people are faced with the choice of $1,000 cash today versus $1,050 next week, most people will take the $1,000 cash. Yet, when faced with a choice of $1,000 exactly one year

---

[11] Richard W. Kopcke, Jane Sneddon Little, and Geoffrey M.B. Tootell (2004), p. 23.

from now and $1,050 one year plus one week from now, almost everyone opts for the $1,050.

All of these violations of human rationality imply that financial markets, and the financial sector in general, are not likely to maximize intertemporal welfare. There may actually be a role for government regulation and other institutional arrangements. Among the possible institutional arrangements could be provisions that require people to confirm their stated choices more than once, giving them time to think over the problem. Another solution might be to require more information to be presented to people making long-run choices.

In summary, the models showing how an expansion of intertemporal exchanges is beneficial for long-run human welfare depend critically on how well people react to the opportunity to engage in intertemporal exchange. Unfortunately, we still have much to learn before we can accurately predict when people are likely to behave rationally and when they are likely to behave in accordance with their evolved automatic and emotional brain processes. Yet, without this knowledge, it is difficult to accurately design the institutions necessary to maximize intertemporal human welfare, even if we could efficiently overcome the efforts of special interests to shape institutions in their favor. In short, we are likely to continue facing failures in the financial sector. Sustainable development becomes more difficult to achieve when the financial sector fails.

11.5.3 Culture and the financial sector: Islamic finance

The charging of interest on loans has been viewed with disapproval in many societies, and laws against **usury** still exist in many countries today. Usury is defined as an "exorbitant" rate of interest, but exactly what rate is "exorbitant"? In some societies, there are religious rules against charging any interest at all. Recall from the discussion of Mexico's Nacional Monte de Piedad that its predecessors from Europe had been founded to offer loans with no interest because the Roman Catholic Church banned interest payments in the Middle Ages. Today, some cultures still reject interest charges on loans as immoral. For example, Islamic scholars interpret **shariah law** (divine Islamic law) as prohibiting the charging of predetermined, guaranteed interest rates. It is interesting to investigate how this form of financial repression is being dealt with by some 100 financial institutions in 45 different countries that practice what has come to be called **Islamic finance** or **sharia-compliant finance**.[12] There are now stock funds based in non-Islamic countries that invest only in companies that comply with Islamic principles, and even the world's major multinational banks engage in Islamic banking to attract savers and borrowers seeking shariah-compliant banking.

---

[12] There are many accounts of Islamic finance; see, for example, Zamir Iqbal (1997), "Islamic Financial Systems," *Finance & Development*, June, or Timur Kuran (1995).

The belief that predetermined and guaranteed rates of interest go against Islamic principles is based on the prophet Mohammad's prohibition of **riba**, or "an excess." Many Muslims believe that social justice requires borrowers and lenders to share rewards as well as losses, which will not be the case if one participant in an intertemporal transaction has to pay interest regardless of the success or failure of the project for which the money was borrowed. Thus, savings accounts that pay a predetermined rate of interest are not allowed, but mutual funds in stocks that pay dividends according to company performance may well be acceptable. Of course, if the companies that pay the dividends benefit from loans at fixed interest rates obtained in non-shariah compliant financial markets, those dividends may not comply with shariah. Therefore, Islamic finance is difficult to define and carry out.

In many ways, Islamic finance is not different from the way financial markets work in most parts of the world. Islamic finance would efficiently allocate savings to the highest-return projects since that would be the preference of both lenders and borrowers. Clearly, lenders will be highly motivated to carefully examine potential projects and to monitor the management of the projects as well. Moral hazard and adverse selection could prevent mutually-beneficial transactions from being carried out. There might be a conflict with regard to the risk of potential ventures, with lenders preferring less risk and borrowers preferring more risky ventures because it is not entirely their money that is at risk. Lenders and borrowers that do not wish to share risk equally may be discouraged from engaging in intertemporal transactions at all. And, because Islamic finance does not permit one party to an intertemporal exchange to carry all the risk, Islamic banks find it more difficult to offer savers shorter holding periods relative to the payoff periods of the banks' assets.

The recent expansion of Islamic mutual funds that invest in stocks, commodities, and leasing contracts suggests that some of the difficulties inherent to Islamic finance can be overcome. For example, some securitization of carefully selected investments has permitted some reductions in risk through pooling while still, in principle, following Islamic law. And, the equal sharing of risk can actually enhance intertemporal transactions by preventing some of the instability that has plagued financial sectors in many developing countries caused by one side of the transaction carrying too much of the risk and thus being perceived as too risky to trust. Under Islamic finance rules, savers and investors are more likely to share the same concerns and interests. Also, the closer synchronization of payoff periods and holding periods reduces the chance that financial institutions cannot meet their obligations.

The sharing of profits and losses by lenders and borrowers is actually quite appropriate for financing new entrepreneurs. The venture capital funds that have been so important in promoting new enterprises in the United States behave in much the same way as Islamic finance requires: if a new entrepreneur fails, the venture capital fund writes the project off, but if the venture succeeds, the lender takes a large portion of the profits. For ventures that have a high probability of failure, but which pay handsome rewards in the case of success, the standard fixed-interest loan is not very attractive: the lender suffers the loss of most if not all the principal if the project fails, but gains only a measly interest return while the entrepreneur captures most of the large gain in the case of success. This may be why banks traditionally favor lending to well-established firms and individuals over lending to riskier entrepreneurs with new projects. The Islamic financial institution may be more likely to favor riskier but potentially highly-profitable projects because it will share in the profits.

Islamic banks face a serious adverse selection problem, however. Timur Kuran (1995), in his assessment of Islamic finance, finds that most Islamic banks have gone to great lengths to charge fees that are in most ways very similar to interest rates; under 5 percent of loans made by Egyptian Islamic banks are reported to have been true risk-sharing arrangements. One reason why Islamic banks seek ways to approximate fixed interest rates is that the banks fear "that industrialists with high expected returns will borrow from conventional banks (to maximize their returns in the likely event of success), while those with low expected returns will favor profit and loss sharing (to minimize their losses in the likely event of failure)."[13]

There are other problems that Islamic finance has not been able to solve. One problem is that it imposes barriers to transactions between Muslims and non-Muslims. Because most of the world does not follow Islamic finance rules and principles, international investment by Islamic financial institutions is difficult. In fact, in many countries where Islam is the dominant religion, such as Egypt, Indonesia, and many Persian Gulf states, the financial sectors do not normally practice Islamic finance. Islamic banks are thus faced with deciding whether they can lend to firms that also carry some conventional debt, and Islamic stock funds must decide whether they can include stock in companies that have issued conventional fixed-interest bonds. In sum, Islamic finance holds some advantages over other financial systems, and it suffers from some disadvantages. Its biggest barrier is its incompatibility with other financial systems, which places it at a severe disadvantage in the increasingly global economy with its predominantly Western financial rules. On the positive side, Islamic finance was largely immune to the 2007–2009 financial crisis. Also, Islamic finance has grown very rapidly, and even large global banks in London and other major financial centers have begun to offer shariah-compliant products.

11.5.4 Crony capitalism: Private financial repression

South Korea was one of the fast-growing East Asian economies that suffered a slowdown in economic growth in 1997 and 1998 that was triggered by a

---

[13] Timur Kuran (1995), p. 162.

financial crisis. Analysts have blamed the Korean crisis on *crony capitalism*, a term that was often used to refer to the South Korean banks' practice of channeling savings to a select group of favored large firms while ignoring entrepreneurs, small businesses, and other potentially more productive investment projects. The South Korean financial sector consists mainly of large private banks. These banks were closely related to, or even owned by, the major South Korean industrial conglomerates, known as *chaebol*.

The South Korean government had actively favored the development of the chaebol, and the system that came to be known as *crony capitalism* was effectively encouraged.[14] The chaebol, such as the Hyundai, Samsung, Daewoo, LG, and SK group, among others, were thought to be better able to carry out South Korea's goal of becoming a major industrial force in the world than free competition among smaller firms. The chaebol expanded rapidly with the ample bank financing; they raised very few investment funds through the sale of bonds or stock. Since they were well known to the banks, loans to the chaebol required little investigation or monitoring, and so long as the large conglomerates performed reasonably well, the banks stood to make a good profit, especially because with the large pool of captive savers the banks did not have to pay high rates of interest to capture funds.

The close relationship between the banks and the conglomerates was destined to cause problems because savings were not being actively channeled to the highest-return investments. The ease with which they could borrow also meant that the chaebol did not have to invest very carefully. When, after the exchange rate crisis and financial crunch in 1997, the chaebol stopped growing and it became apparent that many chaebol investment projects were not profitable, many banks found themselves with many nonperforming loans. The banks at first ignored bad loans, preferring to roll over the loans or even lend more to the conglomerates. More bad investments were made on top of existing unprofitable investments. But, as the East Asian financial crisis in 1997 caused capital to flee South Korea, the banks were unable to continue lending to their preferred customers. The South Korean economy went into a tailspin, many banks finally had to admit they made bad loans, and the South Korean government had to spend taxpayer money to restore the financial sector to solvency.

The phenomenon of crony capitalism looks a lot like financial repression. In fact, we can use Figure 11.4 to describe the phenomenon. Suppose that the total demand for loans from the chaebol and all other investors and innovators are given by the demand curve D, and the portion of demand for funds from the crony chaebol consists of the curve D_R. By lending only to the cronies at the lower interest rate, the banks are still profitable because savers have no option but to put their savings in the banks, total lending to the chaebol is equal to Q_M

---

[14] This account is based, in part, on Anne O. Krueger and Jungho Yoo (2001).

at the low interest rate i_{MAX}. There are no funds left to lend to the many other non-chaebol projects lying between the points **a** and **b** on the total demand curve for funds. These projects have returns that are greater than the chaebol projects along the bottom half of their demand curve for funds, D_R. Hence, crony capitalism does the same damage as an interest rate ceiling with directed investment because it keeps borrowing costs low for selected cronies.

The South Korean case of crony capitalism was exacerbated by the fact that the chaebol conglomerates were so closely related to the banks, which in turn had near monopoly power to capture savings in the country. But note that crony capitalism is actually a logical outcome of all commercial banks' standard operating procedures. Because banks have to judge borrowers, and they must expend resources in order to acquire information with which to judge potential borrowers, it is very likely that, all other things equal, they will favor past known borrowers over new unknown borrowers. For familiar borrowers, after all, much of the investigative work has already been done, and the past lending provided the bank with even more difficult-to-obtain, borrower-specific information. A new borrower requires much more work, and if the borrower has less of a track record, the borrower is perceived as being more risky. Hence, even the most rational and objective bankers will tend to favor loans to past clients over loans to unknown new clients. Of course, personal relationships, corporate relationships, and corruption will bias banks even further towards making loans to existing customers.

11.6 Crony Capitalism and the Natural Environment

As described above, crony capitalism inefficiently channels savings to society's investment projects and innovative activities. As a result, society's productive capital is not being maintained or expanded at the lowest cost in terms of foregone current consumption. And, the growth of output is reduced because some higher return projects are not undertaken. Elements of crony capitalism occur under many circumstances.

Recall the discussion in Chapter 6 showing that the process of economic development is undermined when financial intermediaries and financial markets favor familiar investors and innovators in the economic sphere but ignore investments and innovative actions in the collectively-owned natural sphere. Investment and innovation in the natural sphere are critical for human well-being, but financial institutions have not been designed for channeling savings to the types of investment and innovation necessary to deal with complex environmental problems. Crony capitalism should, therefore, be seen more holistically as not only a problem of bias within the economic sphere, but as bias across spheres. The complexity of human existence and the cost of information will cause financial intermediaries and financial markets to favor their familiar customers within the familiar economic sphere.

11.6.1 The financial system's bias towards the economic sphere

The enhanced Solow model in Chapter 6 included both the economic and natural dimensions of human existence. That model showed that if there is no technological innovation in both the economic and natural spheres, economic growth in the economic sphere eventually causes conservation deficit in the natural dimension of the model because the increased economic output also demands a higher level of nature's services. Chapter 6 concluded that failing to conserve the ecosystem slows growth in the economic sphere, all other things equal.

Crony capitalism that favors the economic sphere will, like the financial crises caused by crony capitalism in Korea and elsewhere, cause the entire holistic system to fail. Figure 11.5 illustrates this latter scenario. If savings are not channeled to conservation or developing and applying natural resource-saving technologies, a level of output in the economic sphere of Y_3 is not sustainable. Recall from Chapter 6 how the destruction of the ecosystem soon reduces nature's services to well below the S_3 level nature could earlier provide. The financial sector's failure to channel resources towards maintaining the natural environment eventually makes it impossible for nature to provide services at even the Y_2 and Y_1 levels. Despite continued financial flows to investment and innovation in the economic sphere, the production function in the economic sphere falls when nature's services decline. No growth at all would have been preferable to the unsustainable economic growth that ultimately collapsed output below even Y_1.

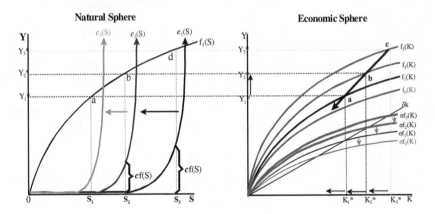

Figure 11.5 Decline under Crony Capitalism that Favors the Economic Sphere

In short, cronyism towards the economic sphere generates higher economic growth in the short run, but because the natural sphere supplies natural services required for human production and existence, damage to the ecosystem will eventually reverse economic growth. And, unless resources are quickly allocated towards conservation and/or applying new resource-saving technologies, GDP will fall below what it would have been if savings had been allocated towards conservation and technological change rather than the more familiar investment and R&D in the economic sphere. The crony capitalism that characterized the South Korean economy was rightfully criticized for its role in causing the severe recession. Studies suggesting that humanity's use of nature's services now substantially exceeds the capacity of the global biosphere suggests that a large number of mostly developed economies are guilty of much more costly cronyism towards their economic spheres.

11.6.2 The conflicting consequences of financial deregulation

Many governments in both developed and developing countries have used warnings about crony capitalism to justify deregulation of their financial sectors. There is little convincing evidence that such deregulation has resulted in faster economic growth, however. First, deregulation is unlikely to raise growth by raising the saving rate. As shown earlier in this chapter, the volume of saving may not respond to a change in the rate of interest, which means that scrapping interest rate ceilings will, generally, not increase saving. John Williamson and Molly Mahar (1999) examined deregulation episodes in 24 countries during the 1990s, and they found that the overall rate of saving was not significantly affected. A World Bank study reaches the same conclusion: Analysis of eight specific episodes of financial deregulation "failed to find a systematic effect on saving."[15] The effect was apparently negative in South Korea and Mexico, positive in Ghana and Turkey, and negligible in Chile, Indonesia, Malaysia, and Zimbabwe. The evidence also suggests that financial liberalization stimulates consumption more than it does savings in the short run.

Of course, if financial liberalization or an improvement in the performance of the financial sector does not increase saving, financial liberalization may still cause a gain in per capita output. Recall Schumpeter's claim that a well-developed financial sector was a critical institution if entrepreneurs were to successfully engage in a process of creative destruction. So even if saving does not increase, a more efficient allocation of savings towards entrepreneurs could increase economic growth without any increase in saving.

Robert King and Ross Levine (1993) published an influential article that supported financial deregulation as a step towards faster economic growth in developing countries. The relationship between the development of stock markets and economic growth was analyzed by Ross Levine and Sara Zervos (1996). In the same year, the World Bank devoted almost two entire issues of the *World Bank Economic Review* to articles showing why *deepening* the

---

[15] The World Bank (1999), p. 2.

financial sector to include more financial markets and alternative types of financial institutions raises economic growth. The strongly positive light in which these articles presented the financial sector provided a justification for the World Bank's push for financial liberalization in developing countries.

The enthusiasm for financial liberalization waned with the turmoil of the 2007–2009 financial collapse in the United States and most other developed economies. This financial collapse was a direct result of deregulation and unregulated financial innovation that fed stock and real estate bubbles, excessive debt, and, fundamentally, the failure of the world's major banking and financial institutions. If the United States and Europe cannot get bank deregulation right, can the developing countries that participate in the international financial system avoid financial collapse?

The most worrisome aspect of the 2007–2009 financial collapse is that it occurred separately from the growing environmental debt that the same global financial system's cronyism also contributes to. Global warming, the loss of biodiversity, the growing scarcity of water, and other clear signs of ecological failures abound. Even if the financial authorities find ways to prevent further financial collapses, the continued cronyism of the financial sector towards the economic sphere continues to push us towards environmental collapses that are likely to have much more devastating and lasting social and economic consequences.

11.7 Summary and Conclusions

The main reason why economists are interested in finding the determinants of saving is that they believe saving to be an important cause of economic growth. But, the evidence on the relationship between the rate of saving and the rate of economic growth is not clear, nor is the precise role of saving in the broader process of economic development. While the saving and economic growth are correlated, detailed analysis suggests that economic growth is more often the *cause* of higher saving, but higher saving does *not cause* permanently higher economic growth. Of course, economic growth is not an accurate measure of sustainable economic development, so most of the statistical studies relating saving and growth tell us very little about how saving is related to fundamental economic development.

What is certain is that the world's financial sectors are failing to efficiently channel savings to socially productive investment and innovation. Nowhere is this more apparent than in the case of financing projects to deal with global warming. Action to reduce carbon emissions is urgently needed because global warming is a slow persistent process that can only be reversed over a period of several decades, not days, months, or even years. The gains from the various projects to develop alternative energy technologies, to reduce the human activities that generate the greatest amount of carbon emissions, and to shift industry and agriculture to less carbon-intensive production methods will not be seen for decades. And even then, they will appear only as hypothetical gains over uncertain estimates of what otherwise would have occurred. The financial sector of the modern global economy is simply not designed to handle such uncertain long-term intertemporal transactions for which there are no obvious immediate profits.

Economic, social, and political institutions are needed to guide the individual actions that collectively deal with these complexities. At the very minimum, government must create incentives that lead private financial institutions, savers, investors, and innovators to carry out the long-run intertemporal transactions associated with investment and innovation in the natural sphere. Realistically, it will take a sophisticated mix of taxes, subsidies, regulations, grants, and direct involvement by government to allocate savings across all three spheres of human existence.

There is no guarantee that governments will create the necessary incentives and institutions, however. Government failures are as ubiquitous as market failures because government is as much a human institution as are markets. In The next part of the book examines in detail the role of institutions in economic development.

Key Terms and Concepts

Adverse selection
Asymmetric information
Capital
Centralized exchange
Chaebol
Collateral
Crony capitalism
Curb lenders
Default
Deposit insurance
Environmental debt
Financial failures
Financial intermediary
Financial market
Financial repression
Financial sector
Grameen Bank
Intangible assets
Intertemporal exchange

Investment
Islamic finance
Life-cycle model of saviing
Market failure
Microfinance institutions (MFIs)
Moral hazard
Nacional Monte de Piedad
Nonrival information
Over-the-counter markets
Personal property
Registry of collateral
Riba
Risk aversion
Risk pooling
Saving
Saving rate
Shariah-compliant finance
Shariah law
Usury

Questions and Problems

1. Explain why economists link saving to the age structure of the population. (Hint: See the use of population profiles to explain saving in the text.)

2. How different are saving rates across the different countries of the world? Are these differences related to the different levels of per capita GDP in the countries? Analyze and discuss.

3. An examination of the relationship between saving and economic development suggests that "economic growth determines saving, not the other way around." How might economic growth influence saving? Explain as many possible channels of causality as you can.

4. Does the rate of saving vary with the distribution of income? What do you think the relationship is?

5. At the start of Section 11.3, the text states: "Among the reasons for such market failures are (1) financial repression by governments, (2) crony capitalism by lenders, and (3) the unique characteristics of intertemporal markets that make it inherently difficult to complete welfare-enhancing intertemporal transactions even when there are is not intentional manipulation of banks and markets." What are those "unique characteristics of intertemporal markets"? Explain.

6. In order for a market to function efficiently and to benefit both sellers and buyers, all information regarding the product being exchanged must be available to all actual and prospective market participants. How do information asymmetries cause interntemporal markets to fail? Explain.

7. Define precisely how adverse selection can distort a financial market. Provide an example.

8. Banks are often described as institutions that reduce risk by pooling savings. On the other hand, banks have been accused of making the economic system more risky. Discuss and explain this apparent contradiction.

9. Explain how Grameen Bank overcame the moral hazard problem on small loans. Is its approach practical in all countries?

10. Governments have often regulated the financial sector of their economies. Why is such regulation deemed necessary? (Hint: Explain why financial markets often fail and how government rules and regulations can prevent those failures.)

11. Why is it difficult for banks to provide small loans to poor people in less developed countries? (Hint: Explain the costs of banking and the lack of institutions critical to banking in many developing countries.)

12. How does Islamic finance differ from conventional Western finance? What advantages does Islamic finance have? What disadvantages does it have?

13. What is "crony capitalism?" Explain, and provide some examples from the chapter.

14. Why does the textbook refer to the financial sector's reluctance and inability to provide financing to projects in the natural sphere as a form of crony capitalism? Explain crony capitalism and how the term applies to the lack of adequate investment in conservation and innovation in the natural sphere.

15. Define environmental debt. Does humanity have an environmental debt? Explain why or why not.

References

Biggs, Tyler S. (1991), "Heterogeneous Firms and Efficient Financial Intermediation in Taiwan," in Michael Roemer and Christine Jones (eds.), *Markets in Developing Countries*, San Francisco: ICS Press.

Fleisig, Heywood (1996), "Secured Transactions: The Power of Collateral," *Finance & Development* June:44–46.

Fry, M.J., C.A.E. Goodhart, and A. Almeida (1996), *Central Banking in Developing Countries: Objectives, Activities and Independence*, London: Routledge.

Giovannini, Alberto, and Martha de Melo (1993), "Government Revenue from Financial Repression," *American Economic Review* 83:953–963.

Greif, Avner (1995), "Markets and Legal Systems: The Development of Markets in Late Medieval Europe and the Transition from Community Responsibility to an Individual Responsibility Legal Doctrine," Working Paper, April 18.

Hicks, John (1969), *A Theory of Economic History*, Oxford: Clarendon Press.

Iqbal, Zamir (1997), "Islamic Financial Systems," *Finance and Development*, June.

King, Robert G., and Ross Levine (1993), "Finance, Entrepreneurship, and Growth: Theory and Evidence," *Journal of Monetary Economics* 32:513–542.

Krueger, Anne O., and Jungho Yoo (2001), "Chaebol Capitalism and the Currency-Financial Crisis in Korea," NBER Conference Paper, February.

Kopcke, Richard W., Jane Sneddon Little, and Geoffrey M.B. Tootell (2004), "Conference Overview, How Humans Behave: Implications for Economics and Economic Policy," *New England Economic Review*, Federal Reserve Bank of Boston.

Kuran, Timur (1995), "Islamic Economics and the Islamic Subeconomy," *Journal of Economic Perspectives* 9(4):155–173.

Leff, Nathanial H. (1969), "Dependency Rates and Savings Rates," *American Economic Review* 59(5):893–894.

Levine, Ross and Sara Zervos (1996), "Stock Market Development and Long-Run Growth," *The World Bank Economic Review* 10(2):323–339.

Levine, Ross (1997), "Financial Development and Economic Growth: Views and Agenda," *Journal of Economic Literature* 35(2):688–726.

Loayza, Norman, Humberto Lopez, Klaus Schmidt-Hebbel, and Luis Serven (1998), "Saving in the World: Stylized Facts," Working Paper taken from the World Bank Internet site, November.

Loayza, Norman, Klaus Schmidt-Hebbel, and Luis Serven (1999), "What Drives Saving across the World?," Working Paper from World Bank Internet site, September.

McKinnon, Ronald (1973), *Money and Capital in Economic Development*, Washington, D.C.: Brookings Institution.

Pachico, Elyssa (2009), "'No Pago' Confronts Microfinance in Nicaragua." Research report for the North American Congress on Latin America; 28 October.

Poterba, James M. (1994), "Introduction," in James Poterba (ed.), *International Comparisons of Household Saving*, Chicago: The University of Chicago Press.

Shaw, Edward S. (1973), *Financial Deepening in Economic Development*, New York: Oxford University Press.

Schreiner, Mark, and Gary Woller (2003), "Microenterprise Development Programs in the United States and in the Developing World," *World Development* 31(9):1567–1580.

Stiglitz. Joseph E., and Andrew Weiss (1981), "Credit Rationing in Markets with Imperfect Information," *American Economic Review* 71(3):393–410.

Sunstein, Cass R., and Richard H Thaler (2004), "Libertarian Paternalism Is Not an Oxymoron," paper presented at the 48th Economic Conference of the Federal Reserve Bank of Boston, June 2003.

Taub, Richard P. (1998), "Making the Adaptation Across Cultures and Societies: A Report on an Attempt to Clone the Grameen Bank in Southern Arkansas," *Journal of Developmental Entrepreneurship* 3(1):353–369.

Thaler, Richard H., and Schlomo Benzarti (2004), "Save More Tomorrow: Using Behavioral Economics to Increase Employee Saving," *Journal of Political Economy* 2004.

Tucker, Jeffrey (1995), "The Micro-Credit Cult," *The Free Market* (Ludwig Von Mises Institute) 13(11):7–8.

Wackernagel, Mathis, *et al.* (2002), "Tracking the Ecological Overshoot of the Human Economy," *Proceeding of the National Academy of Sciences* 99(14):9266–9271.

Williamson, John, and Molly Mahar (1999), "A Survey of Financial Liberalization," *Princeton Essays in International Finance*, No. 211.

World Bank (1993), *The East Asian Miracle*, A World Bank Policy Research Report, New York: Oxford University Press.

World Bank (1999), "Why Do Savings Rates Vary across Countries?," *World Bank Policy and Research Bulletin* 10(1).

World Wildlife Fund (2008), *Living Planet Report 2008*, Gland, Switzerland: World Wildlife Fund for Nature.

Yaron, Jacob, Benjamin McDonald, and Stephanie Charitonenko (1998), "Promoting Efficient Rural Financial Intermediation," *The World Bank Research Observer* 13(2):147–170.

Yunus, Muhammad, with Alan Jolis (2003), *Banker to the Poor*, New York: Persius Books.

CHAPTER 12

Institutions and Sustainable Development

The social world is accumulated history, and if it is not to be reduced to a discontinuous series of instantaneous mechanical equilibria between agents who are treated as interchangeable particles, one must reintroduce into it the notion of capital and with it, accumulation and all its effects.

(Pierre Bourdieu, 1986)[1]

The past 200 years' rapid growth of per capita production, commonly measured by gross domestic product, represents only a very brief episode in human history. Humanity has been changing the way it lives and organizes itself for much longer. The human population has grown for much of the past 200,000 years of its existence, although there is evidence that the latest species of homo sapiens flirted with extinction on various occasions. And, while the increasing numbers of humans gradually spread to all corners of the world, they have also been expanding the size of the societies in which they interact with other human beings on a regular basis. Economically, human societies are increasingly characterized by specialization and exchange. The expansion of social and economic interaction among ever larger groups of people has been especially rapid over the past 10,000 years. Human society has become very complex.

In small hunter and gatherer societies, permanent personal relationships governed nearly all human interaction. Beginning about 10,000 years ago, however, humans began to find ways to interact with much larger and dispersed groups of people. Humans increasingly interacted with total strangers. This expansion of human societies coincided with technological advances in the supply of food. When the first human farmers began growing crops in the Fertile Crescent in what is today Iraq, human society began to be radically

---

[1] Pierre Bourdieu (1986), p. 241.

transformed as well. Evidence now suggests that agriculture and animal husbandry were developed independently in several other locations around the world, and the various technologies were then passed from group to group across the regions of the world. Almost everywhere, humans stopped living in small bands of hunters and gatherers and began farming. This changed human societies in fundamental ways. Among other things, the switch from hunting and gathering to farming meant that the process of human technological change became more complex. Humans shifted from developing tools such as spears and fire that enabled them to more efficiently hunt and gather to developing technologies and institutions that governed much larger human societies. The adoption of agriculture and animal husbandry meant humans lived in permanent settlements rather than nomadic groups. Villages, towns, cities, and nations came to characterize human society.

The growth in the size of human communities has been a slow process. It has taken 10,000 years to transform hunter-gatherer societies into today's globalized community. Dealing with strangers is not easy for humans, whose instincts and emotions have been hard-wired through the millions of years of evolution of humans and their ancestors while living in small groups of hunters and gatherers. Experimental economics and game theory show that exchanges with unfamiliar people on a one-time basis are much more difficult to carry out than repeated exchanges with an unchanging group of relatives and fellow clan members. Specialization leaves people vulnerable to decisions and actions of more and more strangers. History provides a seemingly endless set of examples of exploitation, theft, slavery, rape, murder, war, and other destructive human behaviors. Today, after several thousand years of increasing specialization and exchange among strangers, people are still fearful of foreigners, people from different ethnic backgrounds, and anyone they have not met before.

Yet, despite the inherent dangers, humans have somehow figured out how to deal constructively with more and more people beyond their immediate families and clans, as evidenced by the high degree of interdependence among the world's nearly 7 billion people today. The critical technology that humans developed to manage their larger and increasingly complex societies consisted of developing social and economic institutions. **Institutions** are the wide range of formal rules, governing structures, and informal norms, cultures, and customs that guide and motivate individuals to behave within complex social systems. Complex systems like human society cannot function well if the parts, the individual people, rely purely on their evolved instincts. Institutions are the technology that governs the whole system. They reflect humans' ability to think abstractly and contemplate the bigger picture.

This chapter explains the role of institutions in human society. The next chapter focuses specifically on the formal government institutions that humans have put in place. Since the economy is but a small component of the social system, which, in turn, is a component of the even larger natural environment, these chapters focus on more than just those institutions that enable economic interactions among strangers. Our holistic approach demands that we analyze how institutions shape the relationships between the economy, society, and the natural environment, the whole system that humans are part of. The complexity of these relationships poses an enormous challenge to humanity. Will the human capacity for abstract thinking be able to overcome individual instincts and generate the social institutions necessary for survival in our current complex existence?

Chapter Goals

1. Discuss the broad reasons why human society needs institutions to guide its economic, social, and ecological interactions.
2. Explain that interdependence in today's world is only partly dealt with through formal markets supported by market institutions.
3. Discuss the potential of conflict between formal and informal institutions.
4. Explain the tragedy of the commons.
5. Discuss the role of culture in human society and how culture guides human economic activity.
6. Present Pierre Bourdieu's sociological framework for analyzing culture.
7. Use Bourdieu's framework for explaining why culture enables complex economic and social systems to function despite uncertainty and limited understanding of our human existence.
8. Use Bourdieu's ideas to explain why it is difficult to reform institutions.
9. Make it clear that institutions are critical for economic development.
10. Review Bourdieu's discussion of how culture shapes people's perspectives and distorts economists' analysis of economic development.

12.1 The Role of Institutions in Human Society

In his insightful book, *The Company of Strangers*, Paul Seabright (2010) refers to the transition from traditional small hunting and gathering communities to the increasing dependence on strangers over the past ten thousand years as a "great experiment." Despite the inherent dangers, people have tried to find ways to deal constructively with people beyond their immediate families and clans. They were motivated to do this because there are very real gains from dealing with strangers.

There are three fundamental advantages from expanding the number of people that comprise a human society:

- Gains from specialization.

- Reductions in risk resulting from unpredictable adverse outcomes.

- Faster expansion of knowledge.

Each of these has contributed to increasing human population and living standards.

The gain from specialization was detailed by Adam Smith (1776) over two centuries ago in *An Inquiry into the Nature and Causes of the Wealth of Nations*, where he referred to it as the "division of labour." Specialization, in turn, requires people to exchange their production, or in the words of Adam Smith, the division of labor depends on people's "propensity to truck, barter, and exchange one thing for another."[2] Because specialization, exchange, and economic growth are interrelated, Smith effectively concluded that international trade positively influences economic growth. But such trade means dealing with more people, many of whom will be strangers. According to Smith, therefore, economic growth means people must learn to deal with strangers.

The second advantage of expanding economic interaction beyond immediate families and clans is that it creates opportunities to reduce the various risks that threaten our lives and our well-being. To the extent that people face risks that are, at least in part, specific to them rather than to all of society, cooperation among people can reduce individual risks. For example, when one isolated community's crops fail, it starves. If communities can devise a mechanism whereby they provide each other with food in such emergencies, people are likely to survive longer together than they would on their own. Modern societies have developed a whole range of institutions, markets, and organizations that effectively enable distrustful individuals and complete strangers to effectively help each other deal with unfortunate events and outcomes. The insurance industry, the bond markets, private charities, international banking, foreign trade, the enforcement of contracts, and government transfer programs are modern institutions that enable individuals and communities to deal with unexpected catastrophes.

The third advantage of living in larger societies is that the advancement of knowledge becomes easier and more efficient. Humans have evolved to become a species that has an extraordinary ability to think abstractly, reason logically, and expand knowledge. We have enhanced our ability to expand knowledge by developing language, writing, record keeping, formal systems of logic, and, of course, the scientific method. With the ability to communicate abstract knowledge, one person's discovery becomes more easily available to others. The widespread embrace of the scientific method has made the advancement of

---

[2] Adam Smith (1776 [1976]), Book I, p. 17.

knowledge more efficient and consistent. However, advances in human development also depend on interactions with growing numbers of people.

As pointed out in Chapter 7, knowledge and technology are **nonrival goods** that can be used by many people at the same time. If everyone lives in isolation, then every person has to effectively reinvent the wheel before they can construct a wagon. But if people communicate and observe, a new technology has to be invented only once. Not coincidentally, throughout history the most advanced societies were those that had the most contact with other societies. The more people linked themselves together by exploiting language, writing, and newer forms of communication, the more rapidly innovation occurred. Recall the words of the seventeenth century intellectual William Petty: "it is more likely that one ingenious curious man may rather be found among 4 million than among 400 persons."[3]

12.1.1 Dependence on strangers is problematic

Interaction with strangers can be dangerous. Despite the potential mutual gains from cooperating with others, there are real incentives for individuals and groups to exploit, rob, oppress, enslave, and kill others. After all, it is really much easier to let someone else work to grow a field of grain and then steal it when it is ready. It is often more convenient to get others to do the hard work rather than doing it ourselves. It is also tempting to renege on agreements and to misrepresent one's side of a negotiated bargain. Human evolution has not equipped humans with the behavioral attributes necessary for optimally exploiting the mutual gains from cooperating with each other.

Matt Ridley (1996) details how the evolutionary process over the past several million years, when humans and their ancestors lived in hunter/gatherer societies, left today's humans with inherited traits that are most appropriate for cooperating within small groups of individuals. Experimental economics has designed games in which people interact with others under a variety of rules and circumstances. These experiments have confirmed that a **tit-for-tat** strategy in a repeated game ends up looking like cooperative behavior that Ridley describes for small groups of humans. But tit-for-tat strategies work only in repeated games, that is, in games where the same people face each other repeatedly year after year, as would members of the same family or clan. Cooperation breaks down very quickly in one-time game experiments when people do not know each other and expect to never see each other again after the game is played. This is why evolution made people instinctively fearful of strangers.

The globalization of economic activity over the past few centuries shows that humans have, nevertheless, discovered ways to deal with strangers despite their evolved instincts. Deepak Lal (1998, p. 10) writes:

---

[3] Petty, William (1682[1899]), p. 474.

The cooperative gains that result from the increasing division of labor in a more complex civilization would not have been available without some mechanism for dealing with the increased potential for defection when social interactions became anonymous and sporadic.

The fundamental capacity that has enabled humans to overcome their instinctive fears of strangers and has enabled them to reap the benefits of ever more extensive human interactions is described by Paul Seabright:

> It is only in the last ten thousand years that human beings have had to come to terms on a significant scale with the impact of strangers, and it is only in the last two hundred or so that this impact has become a dominant fact of everyday life. To manage the hazards imposed on us by the actions of strangers has required us to deploy a different skill bequeathed to us by evolution for quite different purposes, the capacity for abstract symbolic thought.[4]

As discussed in Chapter 3, the evolution of the human brain enables people to do more than just *automatically* or *instinctively* react to circumstances. Humans have come to understand enough about the social sphere they inhabit to shape it and change it. Specifically, their intelligence and capacity for abstract thought to design institutions, rules, procedures, laws, financial incentives, punishments, and more subtle forms of communication enable humans, who are hard-wired by evolution to fear strangers, to deal in a cooperative manner with total strangers.

12.1.2 Getting the institutions right

The economic historian Douglass North (2005) reminds us that the creation of institutions and the shaping of incentives to stimulate cooperative behavior "has been a trial and error process of change with lots of errors, endless losers, and no guarantee that we will continue to get it right in spite of the enormous accretion of knowledge over those centuries."[5] One need only look back at the twentieth century and its two World Wars, the Great Depression, holocaust, death marches, gulags, ethnic discrimination, and persistent poverty to understand that humanity often still gets the institutions very wrong.

According to North, the inconsistencies between people's objectives and society's actual outcomes are caused by (1) the lack of accurate information on our physical, social, and economic environment, and (2) the resistance to change. As detailed in Chapter 3's discussion of human behavior, people instinctively prefer the status quo to change because such tendencies proved to be a successful survival strategy in the distant past. Furthermore, knowledge about our complex physical and social environments is woefully incomplete,

---

[4] Paul Seabright (2010), p. 315.
[5] Douglass C. North (2005), p. 15.

and even perfectly logical and abstract thinking will not give us the optimal institutional arrangements we need. North (2005, pp. 15–16) writes:

> Throughout human history there has always been a large residual that defied rational explanation — a residual to be explained partly by non-rational explanations embodied in witchcraft, magic, religions; but partly by more prosaic non-rational behavior characterized by dogmas, prejudices, "half-baked" theories. Indeed despite the... assertion by eminent theorists that it is not possible to theorize in the face of uncertainty, humans do it all the time; their efforts range from ad hoc assertions and loosely structured beliefs such as those encompassed in the labels "conservative" and "liberal" to elegant systematic ideologies such as Marxism or organized religions.

Sociologists call these ad hoc assertions and loosely structured beliefs **culture**.

Institutions are normally classified as either **formal institutions** or **informal institutions**. The former are those rules, regulations, laws, and government structures that are intentionally designed and imposed to guide human behavior. They can be changed as fast as the political system, the bureaucracies that manage the political system, and the other interests that influence society's social, political, and economic organizations are able to act. The informal institutions are the traditions, morals, norms, beliefs, accepted myths, mannerisms, and common social behaviors. These institutions are part of a society's culture, the symbolic structures that humans create to give their activities significance and importance.

12.1.3 Not all institutions are equally flexible

All institutions, because they are human-made, are subject to revision and change. But all institutions never change in unison. Deepak Lal (1998) argues that culture inevitably lags behind the ever-changing realities of our natural and social environments. The fact that knowledge precedes, and often greatly outpaces, cultural change helps to explain the common clash between intellectuals and social conservatives and between universities and their surrounding communities. Culture also often lags behind formal laws, regulations, and procedures, which is why people often complain about their government's regulations and workers often resist new work procedures. Traditionally, the only things that changed more slowly than human culture were the natural environment and the hard-wired processes of the human brain.

The differences in the rates of change of reality, knowledge, formal institutions, culture, and human instinct almost guarantee that when humans' economic and social environments change more rapidly, their cultural beliefs and evolutionary hard-wired behavioral systems fall further behind. This is why the interaction with strangers in today's growing and internationally integrated or "globalized" economy is becoming increasingly tenuous. Unless humans accelerate their acquisition and application of knowledge, the inevitable social and economic changes may create institutional inconsistencies that undermine the process of economic development.

The classification of the institutions according to their stability and speed of adjustment is useful for understanding human society's dynamic economic, social, and natural environments. All the parts of the system, as well as the whole system, continually change as each is impacted by, and impacts, the system and its parts. Table 12.1 lists institutions above the natural environment and human evolution in terms of their expected speed of change. Formal institutions change faster than informal institutions.

Table 12.1 The Flexibility of the Sources of Economic and Social Change
(Listed in Order of Most Changeable to Least Changeable)

1. Economic Activity
2. Technology
3. *Formal Institutions*
4. *Informal Institutions — Culture*
5. The Natural Environment
6. Human Evolution

You may question the position of the natural environment near the bottom of the list, especially in light of the rapid changes in climate, land use, and biodiversity we are seeing today. Today, humanity's footprint on Earth seems to be changing the natural sphere more rapidly than human culture can change to deal with it, which leaves only the evolutionary process of the human brain as the slowest moving process. Still, such natural changes are relatively slow. In fact, it is the slowness of nature's anthropogenic transformation that makes it so difficult to convince people that environmental degradation is a human-made problem that needs attention. Throughout most of history, the fundamental characteristics of the natural environment were taken as a given, something humans had to adapt to and could not influence.

12.1.4 The relationship between formal and informal institutions

Formal institutions can change more rapidly than informal institutions. The former can be decreed, the latter are normally passed on from generation to generation in a slow-moving socialization process. These variable degrees of flexibility of institutions means formal and informal institutions can become incompatible. In the words of the economist Victor Nee (1998; pp. 86–87):

> Formal rules are produced and enforced by organizations such as the state and firm to solve problems of collective action through third-party sanctions, while informal norms arise out of networks and are reinforced by means of ongoing social relationships. To the extent that members of networks have interests and preferences independent of what rulers and entrepreneurs want, the respective contents of informal norms and formal organizational rules are likely to reflect opposing aims and values... When the formal rules of an organization are perceived to be congruent with the preferences and interests of actors in subgroups, the relationship between formal and informal norms will be closely coupled. The close coupling of informal norms and formal rules is what promotes high performance in organizations and economies... Close coupling of informal and formal constraints results in lower transaction costs...

Examples of how formal and informal incentives collide can be easily found in the various attempts to convert communist economies to market economies after the fall of the U.S.S.R. The so-called economic transition from communism to more market driven economies has been much more difficult than most people foresaw. It is one thing to privatize government-owned assets and enact laws that mandate markets, it is quite another to create a well-functioning market economy. The new rules mandate market-compatible behavior, but the informal habits, traditions, and networks lead people to behave in ways that are not compatible with an efficient market economy. The mafia-like business networks that have arisen in Russia, and which thwart the transition to a competitive market economy, closely reflect pre-transition networks. As North (1987, p. 422) wrote: "While the rules may change overnight, individual responses will be much more complex and slow to adapt." Economic growth is therefore limited by people's ability to adapt to the new institutions that are necessary in order to carry out more complex transactions. Russia's attempts to install new institutions to support a market economy have proven to be anything but easy. In fact, the Russian economy contracted instead of growing after the allegedly inefficient system of central planning was abandoned. An interesting contrast is provided by China, where the formal rules have been adjusted more slowly, and a vibrant private economy has developed along with the continued dominance of the centralized communist government.

The huge informal or **black markets** that exist in many developing economies are examples of the conflict between formal rules and culture. The widespread smuggling that occurs in most developing economies that restrict international trade similarly reflects the conflict between formal and informal norms and rules. In many societies, smuggling is socially acceptable even though the formal laws of the country prohibit the importation of goods. Some economists, most popularly Hernando de Soto (1989), have observed that black markets are able to carry out transactions that formal institutions prevent in formal markets, and they argue that informal institutions can actually mitigate the damage done by poorly designed formal institutions. But realistically, there are few examples of pirates, smugglers, and Robin Hoods who actually improve overall human well-being by flaunting formal laws and political structures. Most pirates stole and pillaged for their own benefit. Successful societies are those that find ways to make their entire range of institutions more favorable for sustainable economic development.

12.1.5 The complexity and inconsistencies of change

There is ample historical evidence of how the increase in social complexity often causes actual reversals in economic production for lack of institutional support. In fact, it is possible to argue that all episodes of globalization and the expansion of cooperation with strangers were eventually reversed. For example, people from three continents increasingly traded with each other and migrated to each other's territories during the time of the Roman Empire, but then the world again broke up into more isolated regions. After the western half of the Roman Empire broke up into small states, Europe entered a period that we now refer to as the Dark Ages. And the late nineteenth century globalization was effectively reversed during the economic turmoil following World War I, culminating with the sharp decline in international trade, investment, and migration during the Great Depression of the 1930s. China provides another example: China was the most advanced economy of the world in the year 1000, when it traded with other countries throughout the Far East and the Asian subcontinent. But, its economy stagnated for the remainder of the last millennium when its leaders opted to isolate the country from foreign influences. These refusals by people to continue expanding their dependence on strangers were a result of normal human behavior in the face of existing formal and informal institutions.

In sum, humans and their capacity for abstract reasoning have not consistently been able to build the new institutions needed to support the complexity of changing social environments. New institutional structures lag behind the changes brought by economic activity and technological change. And, formal institutions that represent humans' best efforts to think abstractly and manage the complexities of their existence often clash with slow-moving informal institutions. New laws that do not fit well within a country's culture are unlikely to be obeyed, and regulations that mandate behavior that is different from what people have traditionally done will tend to have little impact. The limits to our ability to build institutions may be the most critical limit on how fast human society can develop.

12.2 Human Behavior and Institutions

Institutions can be good or bad for human well-being. For example, government leaders can pass legislation that bans cigarette advertising and smoking in public places, with the collective result that society's overall death rate falls and the average person lives longer. This institutional change is arguably a good thing for humanity. But note that the new institution of a smoking ban attempts to counteract "bad" informal institutions, such as tradition, personal habits, and the commercial practice of dishonest advertising that encouraged people to smoke.

A complex human society requires an elaborate set of institutions to maintain some level of order and organization. But complex systems can function at many different levels of efficiency. And, the complexity of human society means that, in general, shifts in institutions can cause both large improvements in human well-being or huge deteriorations in living standards. History is filled with examples of entire societies that disintegrated because institutions were not able to motivate individual behaviors that generated sustainable systemic outcomes.

12.2.1 Individual rationality does not guarantee social success

The fact that the overall outcome of an economic or social system is not the simple sum of its parts means that economic failures are not necessarily the result of irrational behavior on the part of the individuals that make up the society. Even if people are fully rational at all times, good economic and social outcomes are still not guaranteed. Unfortunately, perfectly rational behavior may contribute to famines, poverty, crime, war, and economic stagnation.

Suppose that there is an economy where all people live by farming their five-acre plots of land. Suppose, furthermore, that five acres of land are sufficient, given the good climate of the country, to grow enough food to live a healthy life, attend to family, and enjoy cultural activities. But, in order to get the most out of the five acres, each farmer must work eight hours every day planting, cultivating, weeding, harvesting, and processing the harvest. Suppose, finally, that this economy has no government, no laws, no law enforcement, and no cultural constraints. In other words, this is an "everyone for themselves" society. If everyone is fully rational and able to assess their environment, each person may conclude that they face two options in life: (1) work eight hours every day to grow enough to eat, or (2) goof off most of the year and, at the end of the growing season, steal a weaker neighbor's harvest. For a physically strong person, both options yield the same expected income. On the other hand, rational but physically weak individuals also face two options: (1) work eight hours every day to grow enough to eat only to end up with no food because a stronger neighbor will steal the harvested crop, or (2) goof off most of the year and then starve. Strong rational welfare-maximizing individuals will opt to steal a weak neighbor's harvest and enjoy leisure for most of the year. The weak rational farmers expect that they will have their harvest taken from them, and they decide it is not worth their while to spend the entire growing season working eight hours per day planting, cultivating, watering, weeding, etc. only to have someone else take the fruits of their labor. Thus, what economists would classify as rational individual behavior by both strong and weak farmers results in everyone starving because no one grows food.

This example illustrates the possibility for conflict between individual welfare and the overall welfare of all fully rational members of society. As rational beings, the strong chose the easiest route, and the weak chose their own best response to the inevitable by not producing either. Society as a whole had only one choice in order to maximize overall welfare, and that was for everyone to farm their plot of land and produce food, but that best outcome is not achievable without some collective form of action. The sum total of individual behaviors, even individually rational behaviors, does not automatically lead to the optimal social outcome.

You might question whether people would really permit their society to self-destruct in this manner. Unfortunately, history is full of such examples. For example, in Somalia in the early 1990s, mass starvation occurred because Somalian farmers did not plant their fields in the face of widespread violence and theft by private militias controlled by various warlords. Not even foreign food aid could prevent starvation because the private militias stole most of the food shipments just as they stole farmers' production. The problem was that the institutions that guided *individual* Somalian's were incompatible with overall human welfare.

12.2.2 The tragedy of the commons

The theft-versus-production example is an extreme case of what has been referred to the **tragedy of the commons**, introduced to the economics literature by Garret Hardin (1968). The term *commons* refers to collectively-owned resources, such as land, water, or forest, that each individual member in a community can use for their benefit. The term *tragedy* of course refers to a sequence of events that end with an unwelcome and undesirable, but inevitable, result. Common ownership can end in tragedy if unconstrained individuals do not act in ways that sustain the long-run health of a commonly-used resource.

The fish stocks in the oceans provide a current example of the tragedy of the commons. No one owns the oceans or the fish, and fishing activity is currently regulated, if at all, only in national waters by the individual nations that border the oceans. The stocks of the most popular types of fish are all being depleted, or, as in the case of cod, have effectively already been depleted. A. Rogers and D. Laffoley (2011) even suggest that the rate of deterioration is still accelerating. Individual fishers, fishing firms, and fishing cooperatives have responded to the reduction in their catches by improving technologies that permit them to fish even more intensively for the dwindling number of fish. Soon, we will no longer have tuna, cod, haddock, or many other familiar fish that have been major portions of people's diets in many countries. You can surely imagine the tragic situation of a captain of a fishing boat:

he knows he is contributing to the depletion of fish stock that makes his work less productive, but he sees no alternative but to go out and fish because it would make no difference if he stopped fishing while everyone else continued fishing.

The earth's atmosphere provides another obvious example of how individuals, firms, and entire nations continue to increase greenhouse gas emissions even though almost everyone involved knows that this is causing the earth's climate to change. The problem of the commons is that individuals, firms, or even national governments have little direct incentive to stop actions that, collectively, are harmful to the future of the commons. Many opponents of restrictions on greenhouse gas emissions justify their opposition by asking: "What good does it do for us to undertake costly carbon-reducing measures when China and India will just continue expanding their emissions?" In short, the problem of the commons is yet another example where uncoordinated individual behavior, no matter how individually rational, cannot bring about an optimal long-term outcome for society as a whole.

What is needed to deal with the problem of the commons is a community-wide set of institutions to compel individuals in a community to act in ways that preserve the commons. To deal with the fishing and environmental issues above, we need international agreements on fishing capacity and greenhouse gas emissions, duly enforced by a permanent international monitoring organization. Many U.S. political leaders question the wisdom of the United States agreeing to reduce carbon emissions when other countries hesitate to reduce their abuse of our common atmosphere. But, without the United States, by far the largest contributor to the accumulated anthropogenic greenhouse gas concentrations already in the atmosphere, agreeing to reduce its emissions, why should much poorer developing countries commit to doing so?

Hardin (1968, p. 1245) suggests the following possible strategies for dealing with commonly owned lands:

> We might sell them off as private property. We might keep them as public property, but allocate the right to enter them. The allocation might be on the basis of wealth, by the use of an auction system. It might be on the basis of merit, as defined by some agreed-upon standards. It might be by lottery. Or it might be on a first-come, first-served basis, administered to long queues. These, I think, are all the reasonable possibilities. They are all objectionable. But we must choose — or acquiesce in the destruction of the commons...

Hardin's options are detailed in Nobel-laureate Elinor Ostrom's (2005) analyses of how to deal with the commons. Ostrom warns against searching for a one-size-fits-all solution. After analyzing a very large number of potential tragedies and humans' efforts to deal with them, she identifies four types of **membership rules**, nine types of **personal characteristic rules**, and thirteen **relationship rules**. The first consists of rules that define how one gains access to the commons, such as a membership fee, a government authorization, or a peer vote. The second refers to personal characteristics, such as gender, age, education, or skills that culture uses to define rights and privileges. The third category of rules includes criteria based on a person's relationship to the commons, such as a property right, a formal membership, or length of prior use. Note that these rules fall into the two categories that we have referred to as formal institutions and informal institutions.

According to Ostrom (2009), small groups are often better able than large groups to organize themselves and avoid a tragic end to the use of a common resource. The likelihood of successful commons management depends on the size of the commons, the importance of the commons for survival, the predictability of the effects of overuse, the number of users, the social organization of the users, and the quality of leadership. These factors differ greatly across countries, time periods, and specific groups within countries. Ostrom's research shows that not all commons have tragic outcomes. However, Ostrom warns that with increased population pressure, increased resource use, and the increased complexity of human technologies, the tragedy of the commons may become more difficult to deal with. In more general terms, it may not get any easier to act collectively to establish the right types of institutions to avoid future tragedies. Humanity's recent failures to deal with climate change and biodiversity support Ostrom's fears for the future.

12.2.3 Game theory and the tit for tat strategy

The field of economics has used experiments based on game theory to provide useful insight into how humans can establish rules under which they can overcome adverse individual incentives and the tragedy of the commons. Game theory looks at how specific sets of rules and strategies increase or decrease the gains from economic and social interaction among groups of people.

Especially interesting are the results from a game tournament organized by the economist Robert Axelrod (1984), in which game theorists were invited to play each other in the *Prisoner's Dilemma* game. This game involves a pair of prisoners accused of having jointly committed a serious crime, but the authorities do not have definitive proof. Each prisoner is isolated from the other and offered the following choice: (1) confess and implicate the other in exchange for a prison sentence of one year, or (2) admit nothing and hope that the other prisoner does not select the first option. In the latter case, the prisoner will go free for lack of evidence if the other prisoner also remains silent and does not confess. However, if one prisoner does confess and testifies against the other, the silent prisoner will be sentenced to ten years behind bars. For the prisoners, the optimal outcome is achieved if both remain silent. But if the two prisoners do not trust each other to remain silent, the optimal strategy for each is to confess and thus avoid the onerous ten year prison term.

Note that the outcome of the prisoners' dilemma game is likely to differ depending on whether the players play once or repeatedly. In a repeated game, the players have time to build, or destroy, trust. Axelrod's tournament consisted of repeated games, a series of 200 repetitions to be exact. The player who accumulated the least amount of jail time over the total all of the series of 200 games played with each of the other players was declared the winner of the tournament. The winner of the tournament was Anatol Rapoport, a prominent mathematical psychologist, who played the game according to the strategy known as **tolerant tit for tat**:

1. Unless provoked, cooperate with your fellow prisoner and remain silent.

2. If the other implicates you, retaliate by doing exactly the same thing to the other player in the next round.

3. After retaliating in kind, forgive and cooperate again in the subsequent round.

The term *tit for tat* implies that a player responds by doing to the other exactly what the other did to her in a previous round. Thus, one player's silence and refusal to confess triggers similar behavior by the other player the following round. A violation of trust leads the other player to punish the uncooperative player by confessing and implicating the first player in the following round, which pushes both players to worse outcomes. The game is *tolerant* because, after one tit-for-tat punishment, a player forgives the other's lack of cooperation and goes back to *not confessing* and thus risking the worst outcome in the hope that the retaliation made the other player see the futility in not cooperating.

The tolerant tit for tat strategy's win at the tournament surprised many participants. They had expected that tolerant tit for tatters would be exploited and repeatedly made to serve ten year jail sentences. Those who were surprised should, perhaps, have realized that the prevalence of tolerant tit for tat rules across all cultures throughout history suggests that strategy has indeed been found to work in many contexts.

Evolutionary biologists have, in fact, discovered many animal species follow the rules of tolerant tit for tat. There is also ample evidence showing that humans are hard-wired to not only accord some degree of trust to others, but also to retaliate when others do not cooperate and then, at a later date, to forgive and move on. For example, most people naturally smile when they meet a stranger for the first time, which is a sign that they are naturally inclined to start the game with a cooperative strategy. At the same time, people feel anger when someone takes advantage of their tolerance; for example, psychologically people get very angry when someone cuts into a waiting line, cheats on an exam that they did not cheat on, or violates what they perceive as the "rules of the game."

Such anger serves a useful purpose; if there was no "tit for tat" retaliation, violations would quickly escalate, and all would suffer. However, to keep society in a cooperative mode, retaliation to violations of the social rules of the game must be proportional to the violation. Overreaction causes a conflict to escalate, which makes a return to mutually beneficial cooperation more difficult.

Psychological studies also show that humans have an innate biological tendency to forget and forgive others. The fact that evolution has instilled in people a willingness to forgive others suggests that this is a useful social behavioral characteristic for maintaining group cohesion and permanence. In nature, numbers are important for survival of the group.

The tit for tat strategy is also recognized in international law, which adheres to the principle that countries cannot initiate war, but they are justified in retaliating against those who violate that principle. The tit for tat strategy also effectively describes Cold War nuclear policy, where the United States and the U.S.S.R. each promised to refrain from using its weapons so long as the other also refrained. It worked because the consequences of first strike and retaliation were so awful and both sides clearly saw that an attack would be devastating to everyone because each side was fully committed to retaliating in the case of a violation.

History also warns against the alternative strategy of retaliating disproportionately to a deviation from the tolerant tit for tat strategy. When the retaliation exceeds the damage done by the initial deviation from cooperation, the overreaction will tend to be perceived as the sum of a "fair" response plus a new violation that must then be retaliated against. Hence, disproportionate retaliation tends to escalate a conflict. An historical example of excessive retaliation is the imposition of reparations payments on Germany by Britain and France at the end of World War I. It was not entirely clear that Germany was more to blame for the war than many of the countries allied with the declared victors, yet Germany was forced to pay the victors' war debts. Hitler exploited this injustice in his political campaigns and, ultimately, he used the issue to gain domestic political support for rearmament and eventual war. Interestingly, the willingness of the allied countries to forgive and invite their adversaries Germany and Japan into the Western coalition after World War II resulted in a long period of cooperation and peace among major countries that continues through today.

After the September 11, 2001 destruction of the World Trade Center in New York by terrorists, the U.S. government also used people's instinctive desire for retaliation to gain support for a disproportionate response in the form of an invasion and occupation of Iraq, a country not connected to the Trade Center bombing. It should not be surprising, therefore, that a violent and deadly insurgency arose in Iraq after the U.S. invasion. It remains to be seen if the violence in Iraq will subside or whether the United States' violation of the tolerant tit-for-tat strategy leaves Iraq with continued violence.

The 2009 Israeli attack on Gaza, which killed 1,350 Gazans, represents another violation of the tit-for-tat strategy. The Israeli attack was allegedly in retaliation for home-made rocket attacks by some unkown but small number of Gazans which killed no one.[6] Tit-for-tat game strategy suggests that Israel's disproportionate response of killing 1,359 Gazans was intended to escalate the conflict.

12.2.4 Results of the 2004 tournament

The Prisoner's Dilemma tournament was repeated in 2004, on the twentieth anniversary of Akerlof's original tournament. The rules were changed somewhat: participants were allowed to enter more than one player in the competition so that players could form coalitions and carry out pre-arranged joint strategies with other players. A team from Southampton University in the United Kingdom entered the computer tournament with a large set of players, one of which won the tournament while most of its teammates ended up at the bottom of the standings.[7] This time the winner was not a tolerant tit for tatter.

The Southampton players preformed as a team. They were programed to perform certain initial moves that enabled them to recognize each other. One assumed the role of "master", the rest were "slaves" programmed to sacrifice themselves for the benefit of the masters. Whenever a slave player did not recognize the other player as a Southampton player, it would immediately play the role of spoiler and do a lot of damage to the other player by repeatedly not cooperating. When it recognized its "master," it would repeatedly allow the master to exploit them. The lesson to be drawn from the 2004 competition is that when players do not play the game as equals, such as when there is oppression or enslavement by some players, a small number of players can achieve a higher score than they could by playing a tolerant tit-for-tat strategy, but such a win for the master comes at a devastating expense to both opponents and slaves.

Colonial conquests in the eighteenth and nineteenth centuries provide examples of the strategy of forced subservience and oppression of some players in the game. Colonial powers often forced leaders in colonies to sacrifice the interests of the colonials and, instead, serve the interests of the colonists. The colonists gained cheap resources, a captive market for their industries, soldiers for their colonial armies, and relatively high incomes for their home populations. While it may have been rational for the European colonial powers to colonize and oppress, the overall worldwide gains from interaction between nations and people certainly were not optimized under the economic strategy of colonization.

---

[6] FAIR (2009), "The Blame Game in Gaza," Media Advisory by Fairness & Accuracy in Reporting, January 1.
[7] Report in Wendy M. Grossman (2004), "New Tack Wins Prisoner's Dilemma," *Wired*, October 13.

In applying these results to the real world today, we are tempted to ask to what extent transnational corporations (TNCs) and international financial institutions are designed to behave like colonialists. TNCs use their economic and political clout to gain military protection and to shape institutions in their favor, thus effectively assembling a team of international players who act as masters and slaves to promote the interests of the masters (TNCs) at the expense of labor, smaller competitors, and consumers.

12.2.5 Sometimes people are irrational

We have noted in previous chapters that people do not always behave in accordance with the rules of logic, or what economists would refer to as rational behavior. The prefrontal cortex of the human brain, where deliberative and rational thought originates, does not control all our actions and decisions. Much of what we do and decide is determined by the automatic and emotional sections of the brain, and, sometimes, even the rational prefrontal cortex makes mistakes because it is overwhelmed by the complexity it faces or because its shortcut methods prove inaccurate. One conclusion from the research on human behavior is that institutional rules and government coercion can improve lifetime welfare by prodding people to suppress their basic emotional processes and behave as models of intertemporal maximization suggest.

Recall the research from psychology and experimental economics discussed in Chapter 3 showing that people exhibit a bias favoring the status quo. This means that starting points influence subsequent choices, even though rational behavior would suggest that choices should be based exclusively on expected future outcomes alone. This was reinforced in the previous chapter, where we cited research on how people make long-term decisions. For example, Richard Thaler and Schlomo Benzarti (2004) found that a savings plan that automatically increases workers' contributions to a retirement plan but allows workers to opt out of the increase increases actual savings by much more than a savings plan that requires workers to explicitly click a box to request that they be enrolled in the plan. If people were fully rational, it would make no difference for the rate of savings whether people were automatically enrolled with an option to opt out or they had to click a box to become enrolled. Institutions can be changed to improve overall economic outcomes.

If it is found that the former option brings human society greater well-being in the long-run, a formal government institution such as a law requiring increased contributions to workers' savings plans could be put in place. There might also be a role for government to carry out the research to determine which option is more welfare enhancing. Other possible government interventions include regulations requiring people to confirm their stated choices more than once, thus motivating them to think over the problem. There could be a requirement that carefully worded information be provided to people making long-run choices.

In summary, institutions raise human welfare when (1) they help to overcome the disconnect between rational individual behavior and overall outcomes (the Somalia case and failures of the commons) and (2) they move people toward behaving more rationally when automatic and emotional processes in the brain are likely to overrule the deliberative processes. The challenge is to accurately predict how institutional changes will actually lead people to behave so that new institutions will actually promote behaviors that improve people's overall welfare.

It is important to keep in mind that all human activity is already influenced by many formal and informal institutions. **Institutional reform** therefore consists of either tweaking existing institutions or replacing them with new institutions, not putting institutions in place where there were none. This means that changes in institutions can worsen as well as improve economic and social outcomes. Examples above showed how institutions were reformed so that they alter human behavior in some way that increased human well-being. However, the process of institutional reform can be co-opted by special interests in order to shift wealth, power, or social status in their favor at the expense of others. Sometimes institutional reform is initiated by groups who explicitly seek to gain at the expense of others. For example, a political coup that deposes a democratic government brings institutional change, but it would be tough to argue that such change constitutes positive *reform*.

12.3 Institutions and Exchange

Douglass North and other economists of the *New Institutionalist* school argue that institutions are important for economic development because they affect the *cost* of conducting the exchanges required for increasing specialization. North (1987, pp. 419–420) warns against the neoclassical economic assumption that markets for goods and factors of production always work smoothly and costlessly:

> What economists have not realized until recently is that exchange is not costless. Economists still misunderstand the costs involved in exchange, regarding exchange as costless (as the standard neoclassicists assume) or unproductive (as in the classical notion of unproductive labor), or contending that such costs exist but are passive, and therefore not important, or are neutral with respect to their consequences for economies... In fact the costs of transacting are the key to the performance of economies.

North approaches economic history as the study of how people have been able to reduce transaction costs and, therefore, engage in more and increasingly complex transactions.

12.3.1 Transactions costs and economic efficiency

In the early stages of economic development, when there were hunter-gatherer societies, exchange took place mostly in small communities with common ideologies and a common set of rules and traditions. Exchange was almost exclusively **personal** in the sense that individuals were engaged in repeated dealings with each other and had a great deal of knowledge about each other and the products being transacted. Cheating, deceiving, or failing to pay were rare because the inherent tendencies for people to retaliate would prevent future welfare-enhancing transactions. But as economic growth occurred, communities became larger, exchanges became more complex, and exchanges began to extend to people in other communities and other regions. **Impersonal exchange** became the norm, and people had less and less knowledge about each other or the products being exchanged. Exchanges were increasingly likely to be one-time occurrences rather than repeated transactions between the same people. Exchanges also were increasingly intertemporal, with all the inherent difficulties discussed in Chapter 11. In today's complex and wealthy societies, sustainable development requires sophisticated institutions.

North distinguishes four variables that determine transaction costs: (1) the cost of measuring the value of goods and services to be exchanged, (2) the size of the market, (3) the cost of enforcement, and (4) ideology and convictions. The first variable is related to the costs of information about goods and services being traded, as well as information about the transactors, their honesty, their ability to pay, and the likelihood that they will honor an agreement. The second variable has to do with how impersonal a market is; the larger the market, the more likely that transactions occur between people who do not know each other and that two people will never transact again in the future. This means there is no past experience to draw on and no need to establish a reputation with the other transactor. The third variable reminds us that when transactions become impersonal, as they do in large markets, a body of law, courts, and the coercive power of some authority to enforce judgments becomes necessary for carrying out complex transactions. The fourth variable is related to culture or informal institutions. North suggests transactions are easier in impersonal markets if people share a conviction about the justice and appropriateness of the society and economic system within which they are acting. Unfortunately, "specialization and division of labor produce divergent perceptions of reality and hence contrasting and conflicting views of fairness and justice of institutional arrangements."[8]

Economists often model markets as operating costlessly, bringing buyers and sellers together to engage in mutually beneficial exchanges. But markets are not costless. For one thing, markets require management, administration, record keeping, and other costly activities. Also, markets require a broad set of

---

[8] Douglass North (1987), p. 424.

formal and informal institutions to function properly. First of all, there must be some level of trust between total strangers. Institutions such as third party guarantees, well-understood and transparent procedures, judicial enforcement of contracts and standards, accurate information on products and services, and legal recourse in cases of fraud or deception. For example, James Anderson and Douglas Marcouiller (1999) calculate that Latin America's international trade would be 34 percent greater if its legal institutions were as supportive of trade as those of the European Union. Trade among the developed economies of Europe, which on average have better legal systems and law enforcement, is just easier than trade with developing economies such as those in Latin America. Most of the institutions that support markets are costly to operate and maintain. Legal systems require courts, judges, lawyers, and police enforcement.

12.3.2 The evolution of markets

Much has been written about the advantages of letting markets guide people's economic decisions. But, exactly what do we mean by a market? A market is often defined as any situation where would-be buyers and sellers come together voluntarily to attempt to exchange goods, services, assets, promises, or formal contracts that they *expect* to be mutually-beneficial. A self-sufficient peasant who eats the corn that he himself grows does not engage in a market transaction. The government's collection of taxes is not a market transaction because the payment of taxes is not voluntary. The definition of a market does not say that all market transactions end up being beneficial to everyone who voluntarily entered into a market transaction. As anyone who has ever bought something that they later regretted having spent their money on knows, not every transactions turns out as expected. The definition of a market transaction requires that participation is voluntarily and there is an *expectation* of gaining from the transaction.

This definition covers a great variety of markets, from retail specialty shops to international financial markets. Markets can be perfectly competitive (a very large number of buyers and sellers of homogeneous commodities) or they can be monopolistic (small numbers of buyers and/or sellers and differentiated products). The procedures followed in markets fall into one of three categories: (1) one-to-one negotiation, often referred to as **haggling**, (2) a non-negotiable **menu** of prices posted by the seller for the would-be buyer to take or to leave, or (3) some type of **auction** process. Some markets combine posted prices and haggling. The costs of bringing together a large number of potential buyers for a specific product has made auctions prohibitively expensive to operate, which is why most goods and services are transacted in the first two types of markets. Auction markets seem to be economical only in certain situations. For example, homogeneous goods such as commodities that are transacted in large quantitites make it worthwhile for people to assemble to try to acquire the product. Commodity markets have often used auctions to set prices. Auctions are also used to sell works of art or antiques, which also attract large numbers of buyers willing to take the time to try to acquire an expensive one-of-a-kind product. But, imagine having to attend an auction and go through a lengthy bidding procedure to acquire each and every product you use!

Auction markets have some distinct advantages over menu markets and haggling. Menu markets have the disadvantage of revealing only a single price, which means buyers and sellers cannot use the market to determine the complete demand and supply of the good in question. Haggling does permit people to interact to a much greater extent and reveal much more about their wants and costs. But, haggling is a one-on-one activity and there is no way of knowing whether the two people doing the haggling are the ones willing to sell for the least and pay the most. Thus, both menu markets and haggling can lead to inefficient outcomes where transactions do not maximize supplier and buyer surplus. Auctions can overcome these shortcomings by soliciting bids from a large group of people. Markets are also costly in that inventories have to be held, time is expended in making the sale, and customers must acquire knowledge about the products they are acquiring. Retail and wholesale activity normally accounts for several percent of GDP even in the least complex economies. This cost does not add to human welfare directly; it is a cost of enabling transactions that may, or sometimes may not, be welfare-enhancing.

The Internet is lowering the costs of transacting through auction markets. The improved efficiency of on-line auctions over traditional markets has been noticed by the many United States industries that are moving toward web auctions to purchase supplies and industrial parts, for example. The likely outcome of Internet auctions is that many transactions that could not be carried out will now be completed. According to William Sahlman of Harvard Business School, one likely result will be that prices of second-hand items will rise, while the price of new items will fall, in large part because the auctions make second-hand markets viable and thus provide competition for newly produced products.[9]

Internet auctions still face some practical and institutional problems, however. Products still must be physically shipped to buyers. Payment must be arranged. There are also problems of trust: Does the buyer send payment first, or does the seller ship the item first? What if the buyer is disappointed in the product because it does not match the description provided during the on-line auction? Worldwide auctions require new institutions such as free trade, convenient international financial markets, some way of confirming ability to pay, product characteristics, and compensation in the case of a breach of contract between people in different parts of the world. But, just as institutions evolved to permit the growth of markets and efficient exchange in the past, there

---

[9] As reported in The Economist (1999), "The Heyday of the Auction," *The Economist*, July 24, p. 68.

are potentially substantial gains from finding the right institutions to reduce the transactions costs of markets.

12.3.3 Most human exchanges and negotiations do not involve markets

Economists often assume that all transactions among humans pass through some type of market. This is not an accurate assumption. Institutional economists have shown that in general markets are neither free nor always easy to use, and for this reason many exchanges among individual human beings take place outside markets. Most of the exchanges people make occur within the family, among friends, within a business or corporate organization, or between individuals and nature. These non-market transactions seldom involve an explicit price or immediate compensation.

When we enjoy nature's services like sunshine, we generally just take it by positioning ourselves where the service is available; there is no "market" transaction. In the case of water, we may need to install a pump or an irrigation ditch, but as far as the actual exchange from nature to our use, there is seldom a market or a record of the transaction. Only when humans create ownership of nature's services by establishing formal property rights, can we speak of a market. The difficulty in establishing and enforcing property rights over nature's services and all natural resources means that humans will continue to mostly just "take" nature's services as they find convenient.

Most of the world's manufactured goods and an increasing proportion of the world's services are produced in private businesses that carry out a huge number of exchanges within their organization according to set procedures and explicit commands rather than in open markets. One of the reasons for the growth of business corporations is that so many transactions between workers, managers, support services, marketing services, research and development, distribution, and all the other functions that create, produce, and distribute products are best carried out within a single business organized along a set of procedures rather than on open markets. Could Toyota produce an automobile if engineers, designers, office staff, assembly workers, maintenance staff, quality control staff, warehouse workers, product managers, copy editors in marketing, and each of the remaining thousands of workers had to individually negotiate with each other all day long for every task performed or service exchanged? The continual flow of interactions between the tens of thousands of workers throughout Toyota's organization are more efficiently carried out according to work rules, specific instructions, memos, direct orders, and established routines. Also, rather than make a payment at each transaction point, it is much easier to work under the understanding that workers who perform a huge number of different actions during the week will be paid a specific amount at the end of the week. The prominence of large producers in most economic sectors suggests that this internalization of transactions is efficient under many circumstances.

The split between market transactions and internally managed transactions within business organizations is always in flux. Today, even as multinational corporations spread their business organizations across borders, they are simultaneously also increasingly outsourcing to other firms many functions that were previously performed within the company. Current management theory suggests that business firms keep within their organization only those activities they consider to be their *core competencies*, and all other activities should be *outsourced*, that is, purchased from other firms that have competencies in those activities. This suddenly popular business philosophy seems to contradict previously popular tendencies for firms to integrate all stages of production.

The focus on core competencies contrasts with Henry Ford's Ford Motor Company in the early twentieth century, which tried to internalize every activity needed to produce an automobile. Ford built a steel mill next to its Detroit factory, and acquired a rubber plantation in Brazil to supply a tire factory. Ford Motor Company eventually learned that it was more efficient to purchase steel from U.S. Steel and tires from Firestone through market transactions, and focus on what it knew best, which was to assemble and distribute automobiles. These management changes suggest that the ratio of internal administrative transactions to external market transactions is growing in favor of market transactions. That is not quite the case, however, because corporations are also spreading across national borders, effectively bringing in-house more international transactions that are related to their core competencies.

In sum, the total production of goods and services by households, firms, government, cooperatives, and nature involves some market transactions. But markets account for just a small portion of the total interpersonal and nature-to-human transactions that occur. Yet, all of these transactions are critical to human well-being, and institutions determine if and how all of these transactions are carried out. Institutions shape family behavior, social interactions, business organization, markets, government, and all other human organizations within which humans interact and exchange services. The level of a country's economic development depends on how efficiently all transactions are carried out, not just how efficiently the subset of market transactions are carried out.

12.3.4 Social capital

All channels through which interpersonal transactions and exchanges are carried out, from formal markets to informal family relationships, require some set of institutions to guide interpersonal transactions. We have already noted some of the institutions that support market transactions. Exchanges among friends, family, and acquaintances are often described as depending on **social capital**. In contrast to specific formal institutions such as a judicial system to enforce contracts and prevent theft, social capital refers to the informal institutions that effectively create and maintain networks of personal relationships that facilitate inter-personal transactions.

An interesting case of trade in the Mediterranean region after the fall of Rome clarifies the difference between formal institutions and social capital. Medieval traders faced serious problems of theft and poor contract enforcement because the fall of the Roman Empire effectively eliminated formal institutions that could establish trust between long-distance traders in the Mediterranean region. Avner Greif (1989a) investigated old documents to reconstruct how merchants in the eleventh century Mediterranean operated. He found that merchants organized into peer organizations or networks, within which each member found it to be in his best interest to operate according to established rules that ensured the best outcome for the group.

Greif concluded that coalitions of merchants were necessary for trade: "Agency relations in the period under study were characterized by asymmetric information, since the revenues the agent received depended upon circumstances that were not directly observed by the merchant."[10] Hence, in a standard market, where "faceless" buyers, sellers, and firms interact in anonymity, an overseas agent would be tempted to misreport the price of the transaction and embezzle some of the revenue. Since everyone knows that an anonymous agent has an incentive to cheat, merchants would be reluctant to hire such an agent in the first place, and trade could not take place. But, how is a merchant then to sell overseas without personally going with his merchandise to the foreign market? An institution is needed to compel honest behavior.

In the absence of a strong legal structure for enforcing contracts, reputation can serve as an enforcement mechanism, provided reputation is important to one's long-run well-being. This is where the coalition comes in: Greif found that a network of Jewish traders known as the Maghribi, operated under the following implicit rules: (1) each coalition merchant will employ only coalition merchants to serve as their agents abroad, (2) all members agree to immediately stop dealing with any member who is caught cheating another member, and (3) all members will be free to cheat (punish) any member who is caught cheating one of the members. This implicit contract "enables merchants to employ agents for assignments which both parties know ahead of time will be of short duration. Since an agent who considers cheating a specific merchant risks his relations with *all* the coalition members, the agent's lifetime expected utility is rather robust with respect to the length of his associations with a specific merchant."[11] The Maghribi traders bought and sold their goods throughout the Middle East and Mediterranean region despite the lack of formal legal institutions to support formal contractual arrangements.

This example shows that informal institutions, such as social networks, can substitute for formal institutions. Informal arrangements often enable exchanges

---

[10] Avner Greif (1989a), p. 865.
[11] Avner Greif (1989a), p. 878.

when markets do not function well or do not exist at all. Of course, there are many examples where social capital and other informal institutions do not work well either. In fact, in another work, Greif (1989b) shows that Mediterranean trade greatly expanded in later centuries when formal institutions, such as legal codes, commercial courts to arbitrate contracts, and public registries of legal claims, augmented or replaced social capital and other informal institutions in the major trading centers. But the fact remains that trades and other inter-personal transactions can occur under various combinations of formal and informal institutions. The next section discusses informal institutions that fall under the broader definition of culture.

12.4 Culture

Informal institutions include most of the social norms, perspectives, myths, procedures, symbols, and social habits that we call **culture**. Culture is usually defined as the set of common patterns of human activity in a society and the symbolic structures that people value and identify themselves with. According to the United Nations Educational, Scientific and Cultural Organization (UNESCO):

> ... culture should be regarded as the set of distinctive spiritual, material, intellectual and emotional features of society or a social group, and that it encompasses, in addition to art and literature, lifestyles, ways of living together, value systems, traditions, and beliefs.[12]

Like all institutions, cultural traditions, myths, religions, norms of behavior, manners, artistic expressions, and symbols influence individual human behavior. Culture causes socially-inclined individuals to conform to others who embrace the same culture, which enhances social cohesion and enables complex economic systems and human societies to function.

In the ranking the adjustability and flexibility of the components of social change, we earlier showed informal institutions, and thus culture, to be rather sluggish compared to economic outcomes, technology, or even the more formal government and organizational institutions like laws, regulations, and business procedures. This is not to say that culture does not change. In modern societies, where people are more often affected by the changes in economic outcomes, technology, and political structures, culture tends to change more rapidly. Increased international contacts among people have also accelerated the rate of cultural change. Nevertheless, economic outcomes, technological change, and formal institutions are often constrained by the slow adjustment of culture.

---

[12] UNESCO (2002), "Universal Declaration on Cultural Diversity." Alfred Kroeber and Clyde Kluckhorn (1952) compiled a list of 164 definitions of culture from a survey of the literature.

There are many categories of culture. People often refer to French culture, American culture, or Japanese culture, implicitly suggesting that culture is linked to nations or nationality. Many cultural symbols and traditions transcend nations, however. Think of Buddhist culture, seafaring culture, Caribbean culture, etc. On the other hand, many subcultures exist within a national society. For example, we routinely refer to a variety of subcultures such as corporate culture, academic culture, cowboy culture, hip hop culture, and vegetarian culture, among many, many others. An individual can participate in more than one culture. For example, with the increased specialization in our workforce, most people simultaneously embrace well-defined professional cultures as well as one or more social cultures. Immigrants often embrace more than one national or ethnic culture. Increasingly, societies must deal not only with the incompatibility between formal and informal institutions, but also incompatibilities between informal institutions.

12.4.1 Case study: A culture clash and exploitation

The meeting of people with different cultures can result in misunderstanding and conflict. For example, when the Dutch West India Company settled the Hudson Valley in what is today New York State, they first established Fort Orange near present-day Albany and settled 30 Dutch families nearby. A war with the Native Americans soon followed, as the natives did not take kindly to new settlers occupying what they saw as their territory. The Dutch then sought a more secure location, and they settled at the tip of what is today Manhattan Island. In order to avoid future conflicts with the Native Americans, the Dutch offered to buy the island.

The Dutch gave the Native-Americans trinkets and other items worth 60 Dutch guilders at the time of the transaction, 1626. Such a sum would be worth about $400 today. Of course, legend has it that the Dutch paid $24 for Manhattan Island, but this latter sum was due to a nineteenth century U.S. Ambassador to the Netherlands, who calculated that 60 Dutch guilders in 1600 were about equal to 24 U.S. dollars in 1839. The problem with this famous transaction was that the Native-Americans did not think they were selling the island. The European concept of land ownership was unknown in the Western Hemisphere before the Europeans arrived; the Native-Americans believed they were merely letting the Dutch use the land. This misunderstanding is readily apparent in the writing of one of the patroons, as the early Dutch landowners in the colony were called: "It was [the Native-Americans'] custom, when a new governor came... that there should be a gratuity given them, thereby to continue the friendship between ye Indians and our nation."[13] The Native-Americans saw their consent to let the Dutch inhabit certain territories as a friendship that had to

---

[13] Quoted in Stuart Ferguson (1999), "Going Dutch: Manhattan for Sale," *The Wall Street Journal*, November 19, p. W10.

be continually nurtured with gifts. The Dutch officials in New Amsterdam, on the other hand, saw the 60 guilders as payment for the permanent transfer of property ownership.

In sum, because Dutch and Native-American cultures did not view property rights from the same perspective, it was difficult to engage in mutually-beneficial exchanges with the newly-arriving European settlers. This is not to infer that the Europeans might not simply have stolen land if the natives had presented neatly registered deeds of ownership of all their lands. But, a fair exchange was certainly not going to be possible given that the Native Americans did not share the same culture with the Dutch.

12.4.2 Cultures and subcultures

The above example of a clash between two completely alien cultures suggests that cultures exist separately from each other. That was certainly the case when European culture first met Native American culture. In general, however, the lines between cultures are not clear, nor can individuals be easily defined by any one culture or subculture. The early twentieth century sociologist Max Weber (1978) wrote that society cannot be analyzed in terms of specific and clear classes or ideologies because individual status in society often cuts across traditional concepts of classes or subcultures. This is increasingly the case in internationally integrated societies with many immigrants. The French sociologist Pierre Bourdieu (1977, 2000) has suggested more detailed concepts to enable social scientists to better distinguish the cultures and subcultures that influence the behavior of an individual.

Bourdieu begins by defining a **field** as the social or intellectual arena within which people spend much of their working hours and within which they focus their efforts to advance their primary social interests. While people are usually consciously part of a broad national culture, as they go about their daily activities they pay attention only to their immediate social environment, or field. They thus strongly embrace the field's particular culture. Often, a field is one's work, which means that people embrace a culture that is identified with a particular job, industry, or profession. For academics, the term *field* is especially appropriate, because so much of one's life is spent within a well-defined intellectual field. Your author identifies himself as an economist, and, yes, I own a tweed sports coat with leather elbow patches. Bourdieu's concept of field is more general than an academic field; he describes how young people tend to embrace the culture of their school environment, members of the military similarly adopt military culture, and frequent patrons of coffee shops embrace certain rules of behavior that are not found in either fast food restaurants or high-end restaurants. Bourdieu also refers to these cultures as fields.

Bourdieu develops two additional concepts in order to better define culture. First of all, when people embrace the culture that permeates a field they identify with, they adopt a certain set of dispositions, or what Bourdieu defines as **habitus**. Bourdieu borrows this concept from earlier social thinkers including Aristotle and Max Weber. Specifically, habitus' is a set of subjective but persistent perceptions, customs, conventions, norms, and forms of outward behavior and expression. The habitus determines both a person's disposition and how (s)he is perceived within the field. A person develops these subjective dispositions of the habitus in response to the objective field (s)he participates in. A soldier whose field is the military is likely to adopt a habitus characterized by a willingness to engage in aggressive behavior, the unquestioned acceptance of rank and authority, and a strong affirmation of nationalism. A small businessperson's habitus is more likely to be characterized by an admiration for enterprising people and a focus on monetary rewards.

In order to psychologically deal with the combination of an *objective* field and a *subjective* habitus, thinking people have developed complex conceptions of reality often referred to as *beliefs*. Bourdieu calls these **doxa**. Doxa are the fundamental, deep-founded, mostly unproven set of beliefs that a person comes to rely on for survival within a particular field. These are the "half-baked theories" that Douglass North referred to earlier in this chapter when we sought to explain how people deal with the inevitable lack of full understanding of their complex existence. Psychologically and neurologically, doxa are the patterns that people come to see as normal and that they use as reference by which to judge their circumstances. Bourdieu argues that doxa serve to rationalize, justify, and, therefore, legitimize the particular objective arrangement of the field and the subjective habitus of those who participate successfully in a field.

Bourdieu argues that the habitus, augmented by the doxa, give cultures their persistence and permanence. Habitus and doxa, that is culture, change slowly even in the face of substantial changes in actual economic outcomes, social shifts, or changes in the natural environment. Incompatibilities between reality and people's perceptions and beliefs are, therefore, common in rapidly changing economic, social, and natural environments. Accordingly, humans have difficulty dealing with changing circumstances. More broadly, human societies have difficulty in dealing with systemic shifts, especially when those shifts involve more than one sphere of human existence.

12.4.3 Symbolic violence — The iron hand of culture

Sociologists view culture, or what Bourdieu specified as the interactive combination of the field, habitus, and doxa, as having a great deal of power to shape human behavior. Many sociologists, in fact, argue that culture can be oppressive because it effectively enforces and perpetuates unjust hierarchical social structures. Doxa and habitus combine to justify, and thus strengthen, the existing social structure. The dominant doxa and habitus effectively perpetuate the privileges of those who dominate the social sphere by making their position of dominance a self-evident and universally accepted fact of life even by those at the lower rungs of the hierarchy.

To better understand the oppressive nature of culture, Bourdieu introduced another cultural concept: **cultural capital**. Cultural capital consists of acquired behavioral characteristics, material goods, and formal certifications that give a person status in a specific field or in society in general. Cultural capital differs from social capital, discussed earlier. Social capital refers specifically to personal relationships within networks that enable people to engage in economic transactions. Cultural capital has to do with status and power in society. Bourdieu breaks cultural capital down into detailed categories.

First there is **inherited cultural capital**, which includes specific traditions and culture that can take considerable time to transfer and absorb, such as habits developed during upbringing, language and dialect, social mannerisms, and personal relationships. Cultural capital also includes objects, such as a musical instrument, a home, or an intellectual's library of books. Bourdieu calls this **objectified cultural capital**, and it is important for solidifying a person's status in a field or broader society. For example, the manager of a bank is obligated to drive a nice car to work because being seen getting off the bus at the corner of the block would undermine her status in the eyes of those below her, equal to her, and above her in the hierarchy. Finally, there is what Bourdieu calls **institutionalized cultural capital**, which are institutional recognitions of cultural capital held by individuals, such as diplomas, awards, certifications, and other official credentials. All of these forms of capital shape outcomes when people interact, exchange, bargain, cooperate, jointly perform tasks, or use public goods in the commons. Cultural capital is a source of power, quite apart from a person's real economic, physical, or intellectual capabilities.

The concept of power is fundamental to cultural capital. When a holder of cultural capital uses this power against someone who holds less cultural capital, and seeks to alter that person's actions or social position, the former is said to exercise **symbolic violence**. Exploitation, oppression, and harassment are overt forms of symbolic violence, but symbolic violence also often takes on more implicit forms. For example, a boss' frown or look of disapproval often suffices to make some employees come in to work without pay on Saturday. The subtle ways on which people deal with each other communicates approval, disproval, support, and condemnation. Symbolic violence among adults is fundamental to the perpetuation of gender, ethnic, and age inequalities.

Bourdieu (2001) shows that symbolic violence leads people to act against their own interest because the prevailing doxa establish cultural capital to be a legitimate determinant of the social hierarchy. The objects of symbolic violence are often complicit in their own subordination because they adjust their doxa to match the social field they inhabit. Symbolic violence is, in many ways, much more powerful than physical violence because it is embedded in the way individuals see themselves and their society. Symbolic violence is supported by people's vision of the legitimacy of the social order.

Cultural capital serves to perpetuate and legitimize inequalities caused by the unequal distribution of economic capital such as wealth, ownership of resources, market power, or social capital such as business connections and family relations. For example, working class children come to see the educational success of their upper- and middle-class peers as a legitimate reflection of their greater ability or their harder work. In truth, many diplomas are little more than institutionalized cultural capital that is a direct result of a class-based inequitable distribution of inherited cultural and economic capital. Similarly, in many societies males are perceived to hold more cultural capital than women, and the dominant doxa effectively empowers males to communicate their wishes or desires for women to alter their behavior in ways that may not be in their own best interest.

People legitimize social capital and power because they desire protection, stability, security, and dignity. For example, workers will accept and convince themselves that their abusive boss is really a nice guy and that they claim to "understand" why he acts the way he does even though there is little real evidence for such an understanding. The truth is, most likely, that they cannot afford to lose the income, the healthcare benefits, or the social status that go along with their job. And thus social inequality is maintained.

There is today about as much inequality in the world as there was when Karl Marx predicted that increasing economic inequality would cause a social revolution. These unequal economic outcomes are the result of not only the unequal distributions of economic capital, but also the unequal distribution of cultural capital. **Economic capital** resides in the ownership and control of the means of production in society. In a modern society, economic capital often consists of financial assets as well as real tangible assets. Economic capital is the result of a gradual process of accumulation, which means that a change in the distribution of economic capital can be brought about in two ways: (1) a sudden redistribution of accumulated economic capital through taxation, theft, government confiscation, or social revolution, or (2) a gradual shift in how economic capital is accumulated by changing income flows. The former are difficult to carry out because they invariably clash with the distribution of cultural capital, whose distribution cannot be quickly changed given that it is created through education, social experience, family upbringing, and gradual acclimatization. Thus, only the second option of a gradual shift in accumulated economic capital and accompanying differentiated accumulation of cultural capital may be possible. This may explain why there have been so few class revolutions, and economic revolutions have often failed. An economic revolution, to be successful, must be accompanied by a cultural revolution, which requires a sharp change in the doxa and individuals' habitus developed in line with the doxa. In short, culture may be the greatest constraint on the course of economic and social change. The cultures of the many fields with which humans identify themselves often block the economic, political, and technological changes necessary to achieve sustainable economic development.

12.4.4 The blinding influence of culture

Economics has not integrated the role of informal institutions like culture into the analysis of economic development and change. Bourdieu's observation that habitus and doxa combine to perpetuate the culture of a field helps us understand why economists so often continue to apply models that have been shown to be inaccurate and unsupported by objective evidence. For example, economists' assumptions about the competitive structure of markets and these markets' role in maintaining efficient equilibria in a market economy are part of the doxa of the field of economics. This doxa justifies neoclassical economists' habitus of boiling all policy arguments down to cost/benefit analysis based on a social welfare function that equates welfare to the monetary value of material consumption. Any observer of human behavior knows that conclusions based on such models are biased, yet most economists do not question their neoclassical models because within their field they are continually reassured by their well-learned doxa and the habitus of every other economist they interact with that the models are appropriate. Such biases are common to all cultures and subcultures, of course, but it is inexcusable for scientists to ignore such biases in their own work.

Most social scientists would probably admit that they often subjectively evaluate their own social environment, but they would probably also claim that when it comes to performing their professional duties as scientists they behave *objectively*. Bourdieu (1988, 2005) argues, however, that everyone is influenced by their habitus when they judge observable phenomena. It is difficult for social scientists to analyze the world without being under the influence of their field's *subjective* culture. Bourdieu thus called for a "sociology of sociology," in which sociologists use their own methods to distinguish how their own analysis is biased by their familiar habitus and doxa, not to mention the symbolic violence of their peers.

In general, culturally-induced intellectual bias takes several forms, among which are the bias in subject matter, bias in the selection of evidence, and bias in the interpretation of observations and experimental results. For example, economists tend to focus exclusively on market activities, use data generated by markets, and to interpret the observed results from a market perspective. Hence, most economic research analyzes activities included in measured GDP, uses market prices and quantities to quantify human economic activity, and judges outcomes in terms of market prices. There are relatively few economic studies of household activity, and economic outcomes seldom examine human happiness, social changes, or stresses on the ecosystem. Of those types of studies that there are, it stands to reason that feminist economists have led the way given that feminine economists are most aware of symbolic violence in the field of economics. One of the most egregious logical errors committed by economists is to justify these biases by claiming topics such as human happiness, species depletion, gender discrimination, and class conflict are "non-economic" issues beyond the scope of economics.

The likelihood of bias within an intellectual field is one of the reasons why, in this textbook, we explicitly promote holistic scientific analysis that emphasizes systemic, multi-disciplinary, and evolutionary relationships. Multi-disciplinary views are preferable to the narrow disciplinary approach usually taken by economists and other social scientists. By looking at issues from the perspective of more than one field, social scientists are less likely to be blinded by their own field's particular doxa and socially-imposed habitus.

12.5 The Importance of Institutions for Economic Development

Now that you understand the concept of institutions and the role they play in guiding human behavior, it is instructive to go back to our growth models and examine how institutions affect the types of behavior that are especially important for sustainable economic development. The models of economic growth made it clear that technological change is the key to sustained economic growth. Hence, we should focus specifically on how institutions influence the creation, dissemination, and adaptation of new ideas.

12.5.1 Institutions and innovation

Innovation requires many of the same institutions that favor investment, such as enforcement of contracts and protection from fraud. But, innovation and creation of new ideas require other institutions as well. There are both formal and informal institutions that can promote, or discourage, innovation. Policymakers cannot spur innovation by simply changing some laws, regulations, and rules. People have to want to accept the new rules and regulations, and they have to see innovation as an attractive form of behavior. Specifically, people must have the freedom to think and promote new ideas. Hence, societies whose institutions suppress free expression, discourage different ways of doing things, or punish people who question established views are unlikely to generate many new ideas or take advantage of ideas already available from other societies. It would also be useful if institutions encourage the free flow of ideas from abroad. International trade and investment should not be restricted too severely, and the flow of people, either as immigrants or visitors, should not be entirely closed. Schumpeter would certainly also insist on institutions that establish a stable financial sector that efficiently channels savings to innovators and entrepreneurs. To some extent, economic success should be rewarded, and failure should not be entirely prevented: the process of *creative destruction* must be sustained.

Paul Romer advocates government policies that encourage the search for new ideas, but he admits that this is not easy to do. Romer (1998) suggests the following:

> ... most economists support three government policies designed to encourage the production, transmission, and implementation of ideas: universal subsidies for education, competitive grants for basic research, and patents and copyrights, which offer temporary monopoly profits on ideas. Economists also recognize, however, that such policies may not provide adequate incentives to discover the many small applied ideas needed to convert a basic idea such as the transistor into a product such as computer memory, or to convert a new product such as the videocassette recorder (which was first produced in the United States) into an inexpensive consumer good.

Institutions and policies that encourage the creation and spread of useful new ideas are themselves the most important ideas of all. Romer would call such institution-creating ideas **meta-ideas** because they stimulate many more new ideas. Britain's formal establishment of patents and copyrights in the eighteenth century probably qualifies as a meta-idea. Also, the establishment of land-grant universities and agricultural extension services in the United States in the 19th century are clearly meta-ideas. The laws and regulations that maintain a healthy and sound financial sector also qualify, such as those implemented during the Great Depression in the United States and resulted in nearly forty years without a major financial crisis. It is not clear what we call the ideas that supported the recent deregulation of most countries' financial sectors, which promptly sank the world into the 2007–2009 global recession and set back investment and innovative activity for several years.

12.5.2 Institutions and sustainability

Schumpeter's emphasis on institutions and their close relationship with innovation and entrepreneurship should warn us of the potential conflicts between economic growth and sustainable development. To begin with, recall that Bourdieu (1988, 2005) argued that social scientists, like economists, effectively analyze the world subject to the dominant habitus and doxa associated with their field. The dominant culture of economics, unfortunately, restricts economic analysis to the economic sphere of human existence. Holistically, the study of the relationship between institutions and economic development must consider how the institutions that affect economic growth simultaneously affect human society and the natural environment.

Recall the augmented two-sphere Solow model from Chapters 6, 8, and 11 showing how, in the case of renewable natural resources, the growth of economic output can only be sustained if there is technological change in the natural sphere as well as the economic sphere. Schumpeter's original focus on entrepreneurship in the economic sphere is, therefore, incomplete. We must take the Schumpeterian model into a much more general framework of analysis that includes social institutions such as culture, political institutions, government policy, and society's capacity to take collective action to deal with complex long-run issues. The profit motive that drove outcomes in the original Schumpeterian model must be replaced by the more general long-run concept of sustainable economic development. It takes a rather complex set of formal and informal institutions to ensure that there is innovation across all spheres of human existence. Sustainable economic development in a modern society requires foresight and the recognition of a collective responsibility for the welfare of humanity. Chapter 18 will examine policies and institutions for long-run sustainable economic development in more detail.

12.6 Nation Building: Defying the Strength of Institutions

Institutional change seems to have played a major role in enabling the acceleration of economic growth over the past two centuries. For example, improvements in the institutions that support finance enabled the creation of large business ventures and investment projects. Innovation was stimulated by economic and political systems that tolerated change and provided people with more personal freedom and better protection of their property. The Enlightenment and the embrace of the scientific method no doubt played a role in accelerating innovation in the last two centuries.

In hindsight, it is clear that it is not easy to establish economically-efficient and socially-compatible institutions. Over the past 100 years, institutional development did not prevent two world wars, a Great Depression, concentration camps and death marches, many financial crashes and economic failures, many regional wars, and frequent cruelty by humans against other humans. The 2007–2009 Great Recession, caused by the dismantling of banking regulation and government oversight, is just the latest reminder that institutions can deteriorate and cause economic development to stop or even reverse itself. While humanity has indeed often sought to reform its formal institutions in order to deal with its increasingly complex economies and societies, it clearly has not yet mastered the process. Sluggish informal institutions often got in the way of success. This section looks at the many attempts over the past two centuries to rebuild entire institutional structures that were ambitiously referred to as **nation building**.

Over the past two centuries, political leaders of many countries whose armies attacked and invaded other countries often claimed to be engaged in nation building. Historians define nation building as the use of military power to enable a process of institutional and political reform to stabilize society and perhaps even establish a democratic government. World War I and World War II, which were unprecedented in their destruction and human carnage, were followed by serious attempts at nation building. Other alleged attempts at nation building include Cuba and the Philippines after the Spanish-American war, South Korea after the Korean War, Haiti during the 1990s, and, most recently, Afghanistan and Iraq after invasions by the United States. Historians still debate the true motives for these wars, but political leaders repeatedly claimed that the noble cause of nation building was what led them, very reluctantly of course, to authorize military action.

12.6.1 *The Paris Conference and the failure of nation building*

The classic attempt by the world's most powerful nations to "build nations" was the 1919 **Paris Conference** at the end of World War I. It was President Wilson of the United States, the country that helped to turn what appeared to be an inevitable stalemate into a victory for the Allied countries, which included France, Britain, Italy, and Japan. The Paris Peace Conference produced not only the armistice treaty with Germany, signed at Versailles in 1919, but it also included enormously complex negotiations to reorder the world after the collapse of the Austrian-Hungarian and Ottoman Empires. New borders were drawn all over central Europe and the Middle East. The one-sided nature of the Versailles Treaty forced Germany to admit guilt for a war that was, without question, the result of much more complex forces and alliances for which all participants shared blame. This heavy-handed and, to Germany, demeaning treaty served to foment a resentment that was exploited by Adolph Hitler to achieve his rise to power in Germany in the 1930s. For this reason, the Paris Conference is often criticized for laying the foundation for World War II.

The world's leaders cannot be blamed for rushing into the many agreements that emerged from the Paris Conference; they spent half a year in Paris deciding on the terms. As described in great detail by Margaret MacMillan (2001), the world's governments effectively resided in Paris for much of 1919. U.S. President Woodrow Wilson, Britain's Prime Minister David Lord George, France's Georges Clemenceau, Italy's Vittorio Orlando, and the many other national leaders actively participated in the long meetings that set the details of the final agreements. Given the enormous task they gave themselves, their ultimate failure should not be surprising. Worse yet, the eventual costs of the mistakes made at Paris make the long period of negotiation even more difficult to justify. Richard Holbrooke (2001, p. ix), who recently served in several U.S. governments that engaged in nation building, described Paris as follows:

> As the peacemakers met in Paris, new nations emerged and great empires died. Excessively ambitious, the Big Four set out to do nothing less than fix the world, from Europe to the far Pacific. But facing domestic pressures, events they could not control, and conflicting claims they could not reconcile, the negotiators were, in the end, simply overwhelmed; and made deals and compromises that would echo down through history.

Many of the borders drawn became the focus of conflicts, such as those that defined Poland, Yugoslavia, Modern Turkey, Iraq, and Palestine.

It was U.S. President Woodrow Wilson who convinced the world's leaders that the Paris Conference would correct for past injustices and pave the way for a better world in the future. Wilson's rhetoric was highly moralistic, and he effectively tried to push contemporary world leaders to engage in a complete political reform of the world. Wilson was not as practical as he was idealistic, however, nor was he particularly adept at diplomacy. He made strong enemies at home, and he quickly lost support for his program in the U.S. In Paris, he was unable to push matters in the directions he had foreseen. In the end, American voters rejected his proposals and elected isolationist Republican administrations throughout the 1920s.

12.6.2 The failure of Paris did not deter further nation building

Nation building has been revived many times after World War II. In fact, the Cold War period 1950–1990 included a birth of many new nations as the visual remnants of pre-twentieth century colonialism were dismantled. There are over 200 countries in the world today, the majority of them created over the past 50 years. There have been some successes among these more recent attempts at nation building. But, there have been many failures. So far World War III has not erupted, but there have been many regional wars and military conflicts. At the time of this writing, wars, occupations, and other military actions were occurring in Afghanistan, Iraq, Palestine, Pakistan, Sudan, Yemen, Libya, among many other countries. Many of these countries were part of the deliberations of the Paris Conference in 1919. Some of the recent conflicts are the result of new attempts at nation building, such as the creation of Israel in 1948.

James Payne (2006) compiled a list of intentional attempts by the United States and Great Britain to build nations. He defines *nation building* as involving (1) a military invasion to depose an existing government, and (2) a deliberate attempt to establish a democratic form of government. This definition excludes the peacekeeping missions intended merely to pacify a country in civil war, punitive missions to punish a foreign government but not to change that government, and the establishment of overseas military bases for regional protection or other strategic reasons. This definition also excludes the typical examples of colonialism, where the colonial power was clearly motivated by plunder and economic advantage rather than the welfare of the country being attacked.

Table 12.2 Nation-Building Military Occupations by Great Britain and the United States, 1850–2000

British Occupations		*United States Occupations*	
Botswana 1886–1966	*success*	Austria 1945–1955	*success*
Brunei 1888–1984	failure	Cuba 1898–1902	failure
Burma 1885–1948	failure	Cuba 1906–1909	failure
Cyprus 1914–1960	failure	Cuba 1917–1922	failure
Egypt 1882–1922	failure	Dominican Rep. 1911–1924	failure
Fiji 1874–1970	*success*	Dominican Rep. 1965–1967	*success*
Ghana 1886–1957	failure	Grenada 1983–1985	*success*
Iraq 1917–1932	failure	Haiti 1915–1934	failure
Iraq 1941–1947	failure	Haiti 1994–1996	failure
Jordan 1921–1956	failure	Honduras 1924	failure
Kenya 1894–1963	failure	Italy 1943–1945	*success*
Lesotho 1884–1966	failure	Japan 1945–1952	*success*
Malawi 1891–1964	failure	Lebanon 1958	failure
Malaysia 1909–1957	*success*	Lebanon 1982–1984	failure
Maldives 1887–1976	*success*	Mexico 1914–1917	failure
Nigeria 1861–1960	failure	Nicaragua 1909–1910	failure
Palestine 1917–1948	failure	Nicaragua 1912–1925	failure
Sierra Leone 1885–1961	failure	Nicaragua 1926–1933	failure
Solomon Is. 1893–1978	*success*	Panama 1903–1933	failure
South Yemen 1934–1967	failure	Panama 1989–1995	*success*
Sudan 1899–1956	failure	Philippines 1898–1946	*success*
Swaziland 1903–1968	failure	Somalia 1992–1994	failure
Tanzania 1920–1963	failure	South Korea 1945–1961	failure
Tonga 1900–1970	*success*	West Germany 1945–1952	*success*
Uganda 1894–1962	failure		
Zambia 1891–1964	failure		
Zimbabwe 1888–1980	failure		

Source: From James L. Payne (2006), pp. 603–604.

Payne details 51 cases of *nation building* by Great Britain and the United States between 1850 and 2000 (See Table 12.2). This sample thus ignores the very early British colonies like the United States, Canada, and the Caribbean, as well as the most recent cases of Iraq and Bosnia. Payne classifies only 14 of the 51 cases as "successes" in the sense that a democratic government remained solidly in place after the British or U.S. occupation ended. Payne concludes that "nation building by force is generally unsuccessful. A president who went around the world invading countries in order to make them democratic would probably fail most of the time."[14]

The weakness of nation building may be greater than Payne's high proportion of failures suggests, however. First of all, there has been a general trend toward democracy in the world over the past 150 years, and some of the countries that were invaded would probably have become democracies without the invasion. Payne points to South Korea, a country that fell into a dictatorship after the U.S. occupation in 1950. U.S. interference in South Korea's governing structure ended in 1961, when General Park Chung-Hee grabbed dictatorial powers. In 1985, democratic elections were held without outside force or invasion.

It is also likely that in the successful cases of Austria (1945–1955) and Italy (1943–1945), the occupiers actually had no explicit plans to introduce democracy, even though democracy took hold. At the close of World War II, Austria was occupied jointly by the U.S.S.R. and the United States. The Soviet Union brought the exiled Socialist leader Karl Renner to Austria in the hope he would take over the government. The United States was distrustful of the socialist, and they refused to recognize the Renner government. Within six months, and to the surprise of both the Soviet Union and the United States, Renner put in place a democratic political system. Neither the United States nor the Soviet Union thus "built" Austria as they intended.

The case of Italy was similar. When U.S. occupation forces helped to turn Italians against the fascist Mussolini government in 1943, the British wanted to build a constitutional monarchy in Italy. Italian sentiment was against that, and attempts by the occupying British forces to influence the provisional Italian government greatly weakened it. Giancarlo Pasquino (1986) argues that it was fortunate the "Americans did not have a specific policy for Italy, or any clear-cut design for the shaping of the Italian political system."[15] The Italian voters overwhelmingly voted against a constitutional monarchy in 1946, and Italy has been a full democracy ever since. Many, if not all, of Payne's 14 successes may not have been intentional cases of "nation building" at all. It is also clear from the 14 successful cases of democratization that the countries benefitted greatly from earlier institutional development as well as fortuitous circumstances. The failures often exhibited sharp conflicts between the desires of the invading forces and the traditional economic and social structures. The idea that U.S. forces can build a democratic government and a growing modern economy in Afghanistan is probably delusional. Informal institutions such as tribalism, religion, and the predominance of non-market economic interactions will take generations to overcome. Not even a ten-year occupation, against the will of the country, can expect to have much of a nation building effect. One must conclude that there must have been other motivations for the U.S invasion.

---

[14] James L. Payne (2006), p. 604.
[15] Giancarlo Pasquino (1986), p. 60.

12.6.3 Is gradual change more successful?

The results of sudden shifts in formal government institutions have also been consistently disappointing in the so-called transition countries of the former U.S.S.R. and Eastern Europe. Long economic depressions followed the fall of the Soviet Union and the dismantling of the communist institutions. In fact, the consequences transcended the economic sphere, and life expectancy in many of the former Soviet Republics fell to where it is now substantially below what it was in 1990. The poorly-functioning institutions that were well-established could not be quickly replaced by better institutions. Imposing a market system on societies where market systems had never functioned proved impossible because informal cultures that developed during earlier political regimes continued to guide individual behavior. Corruption exploded, government institutions ceased providing critical services before new institutions could be set up to replace them, and centrally planned business networks were dismantled. On the other hand, the more gradual shift from central planning to capitalist markets in China seems to be more sustainable, especially because the Chinese changes in economic policies have, so far, not undermined the established political power base.

Recall also the example of Taiwan in Chapter 11, which discussed the economy's financial sector. Taiwan's banking system was split between a formal banking sector that served large businesses, and an informal "curb market" for loans that served small, informal businesses. Rather than overhauling the entire banking industry, as development experts prescribed, the Taiwanese government passed a law permitting the post-dating of checks and making it a major crime to "bounce" such a post-dated check when it came due. This made it safe for large firms to channel financing from their banks to their small suppliers in the informal sector, thus effectively extending formal bank financing to the informal economy.

The examples of successful gradual institutional changes and failed large institutional changes do not imply that governments have only modest institutional roles to fulfill. Note that Taiwan's small institutional change that strengthened the informal curb market still required the government to make legal changes and provide law enforcement. In general, the success humanity has achieved in raising standards of living over the past 200 years is a direct result of intentional efforts to impose new formal government institutions to deal with the complexity of interdependent modern economies. The trick is to keep the new formal institutions compatible with the slow moving informal cultures and traditions so that they induce gradual change rather than causing destructive conflicts. These changes are usually better made by indigenous leaders and not by foreign invaders.

12.7 Summary and Conclusions

This chapter has focused on institutions, which are the laws, social norms, traditions, religious beliefs, and other formal and informal rules that shape the behavior of individuals and groups in society. Mainstream economics has studied institutions from within the economic sphere of human existence. It has, therefore, focused on how formal and informal institutions induce people to engage in productive and innovative activities that add to total economic output. The Schumpeterian model of innovation, by relating profit and costly innovative activities, follows that tradition.

A more holistic view of institutions begins with the premise that people are not hard-wired to behave in ways that optimize the long-run sustainable welfare of humanity in a modern society. Human instincts date back to ancestors who faced very different social and natural circumstances than humans face today. Hard-wired instincts are important because they determine most human behavior. Holism also recognizes the role of informal institutions such as culture. Informal institutions, like hard-wired human behaviors, also lag behind the real changes that occur in people's economic, social, and natural spheres. Ironically, economic and social disasters can be caused by perfectly rational behavior reacting to the incentives provided by sluggish lagging institutions. Finally, because the economic system is part of the broader social and natural spheres of human existence, the economic system is not a linear sum of its parts. Therefore, the overall economic outcomes can vary greatly under different institutional constraints. In short, a complex modern human society requires a rather complex adjustment of economic and social institutions to induce individual and firm behavior that achieves a high level of sustainable economic development. Success is not guaranteed.

This chapter focused on how quickly formal and informal institutions can be modified to meet the challenges faced by complex modern societies. Special attention was given to the broad set of informal institutions commonly referred to as culture. The quote at the start of the chapter by Pierre Bourdieu suggests institutions are like a form of capital that is accumulated gradually over time. That is, they have momentum, and they change slowly subject to new influences that arrive gradually and erratically. Because it changes relatively slowly, at least compared to economic outcomes and more formal institutions like government policies and regulations, culture effectively introduces a "fixed input" that can cause diminishing returns to investment and innovative activities. Further complicating matters is the inevitable fact that culture biases our perspectives, which means humans struggle to deal efficiently with the complex problems they face.

Many of the institutions necessary for a modern economy to carry out the many complex transactions that support its high degree of specialization require collective decisions. This usually requires some type of governance structure, a "third party" with some degree of coercive power. Humans must nurture their own government institutions; the default mode in the absence of a modern governance structure seems to be either chaos or volatile standoffs between small groups and gangs reminiscent of the hunter-gatherer period when humans evolved many of their hard-wired behaviors.

Just as all institutions, a formal governance structure can improve human well-being, or it can reduce it. The required third party can be a hereditary monarch, a rigid theocracy, a democratically-elected parliamentary system, or a military dictatorship imposed by a foreign power. A government is a compromise between the need for an enforcer of necessary formal institutions and the hijacking of the power of government to benefit some people at the expense of others. Given the expanding role that government has come to play in modern economies, we clearly need to examine the economic role of government and government institutions in much more detail. That is the topic of the next chapter.

Key Terms and Concepts

Auction	Institutionalized cultural capital
Black markets	Membership rules
Cultural capital	Menu prices
Culture	Meta-ideas
Doxa	Nation building
Economic capital	Nonrival goods
Field	Objectified cultural capital
Formal institutions	Paris Conference
Habitus	Personal characteristic rules
Haggling	Personal transactions
Impersonal exchange	Relationship rules
Informal institutions	Social capital
Inherited cultural capital	Symbolic violence
Institution	Tit for tat
Institutional reform	Tragedy of the commons

Questions and Problems

1. Discuss the reasons why human society needs institutions to guide interactions across the economic, social, and natural spheres. Doesn't rational behavior by all people guarantee good economic, social, and ecological outcomes?

2. Explain Paul Seabright's three ways in which people gain from interacting with larger numbers of people. Can you think of additional ways in which people gain from dealing with strangers?

3. To what extent is the unprecedented level of interdependence in today's world realized by means of formal markets supported by market institutions? Present evidence to support your answer.

4. Table 12.1 ranks the main categories of phenomena that change human existence over time. Explain the ranking, and then find examples that conform with the ranking. Can you find examples that contradict the ranking?

5. Discuss the potential of conflict between formal and informal institutions. Can you provide some examples of where new laws or regulations are not followed because they clash with traditional ways of doing things?

6. Explain the markets that link the economic sphere and the natural sphere. Do they exist? What formal and informal institutions could enable more sustainable interaction between the economic and natural spheres?

7. Explain the tragedy of the commons. What types of institutions can protect the commons?

8. Discuss the role of culture in human society and how culture guides human economic activity.

9. Describe Pierre Bourdieu's sociological framework for analyzing culture. Specifically, define the concepts of field, habitus, and doxa. Can you think of examples of each?

10. Use Bourdieu's framework for explaining why culture enables complex economic and social systems to function despite uncertainty and limited understanding of our human existence.

11. We have mentioned earlier in the textbook Thomas Kuhn's hypothesis that most science consists of routine and well-structured activities, and that only occasionally is there revolutionary science that shifts science onto a new path. Use Bourdieu's sociological concepts of habitus and doxa, as well as cultural capital and symbolic violence to explain Kuhn's hypothesis.

12. Why did Bourdieu insist that social scientists should engage in analyzing the biases in their fields? Why is a commitment to follow the scientific method not sufficient for objective scientific research?

13. Pierre Bourdieu uses the concept of symbolic violence to describe the power of culture to oppress people as well as to perpetuate social structures. Do you agree that culture gives some people power over others? Explain and provide examples to support your answer.

14. Write an essay on why institutions are critical for economic development.

15. Explain Bourdieu's discussion of how culture shapes people's perspectives and distorts economists' analysis of economic development.

16. Why does nation building so often fail? Provide some examples from history. (Hint: Be sure to build your answer around this chapter's discussion of formal and informal markets.)

17. Can the introduction of new formal institutions, such as new laws, regulations, or government agencies, bring about substantial change in how our economy and society functions? Explain your answer based on what you have learned about institutions, and provide real world examples to support your answer.

18. Explain James Payne's definition of nation building. What is the difference between nation building and colonialism?

Appendix 12.1: Empirical Studies of Institutions and Economic Growth

Most studies of the role of institutions in inducing economic growth and development have followed familiar statistical procedures. For example, statistical tests of the "causes" of economic growth most often used regression equations based on the *sources of growth* equation

$$g_Y = r + \alpha g_K + (1 - \alpha)g_L \qquad (A1.1)$$

which says that the rate of growth of real output is the sum of (1) the weighted average of growth rates of the factors of production capital, g_K, and labor, g_L, plus (2) the rate of technological change, r. This equation was then augmented by adding institutional variables and other potential explanatory variables, say Z, to create the regression equation,

$$g_Y = a_0 + a_1 g_K + a_2 g_L + a_3 Z \qquad (A1.2)$$

With data on the growth of Y, K, L, and Z, the values of the constant a_0 and the coefficients of the explanatory variables, a_1, a_2, and a_3, equation (A1.2) can be estimated using least squares or other modern statistical linear regression methods. The variable r in equation (A1.1), the "constant" a_0 in the regression equation (A1.2), represents the rate of total factor productivity growth, which is the amount of economic growth not explained by the growth of the actual factors of production. If the addition of one or more Z variables to the regression equation reduces estimates of the value of a_0, then we can conclude that the Z's help to explain growth of output.

Finding the Right Z Variable to Represent Institutions

The regression equation (A1.2) is especially appropriate for testing the importance of certain institutions for the efficient functioning of an economy. The improvement in the institutional framework that guides economic activity is as much an improvement in "technology" as a new machine or a better management method. In fact, institutional innovations such as patents and land grant universities were distinguished as "meta-ideas" in the chapter above.

Xavier Sala-i-Martin (1997) performed one of the more often quoted studies of institutions. Sala-i-Martin includes many variables that determine the economic "climate," that is, the institutional environment that guides individual actions. Among other things, Sala-i-Martin finds that all five of his religious variables, namely the fraction of the population that is Buddhist, Catholic, Confucian, Muslim, and Protestant, are significantly related to economic growth. But, the five do not all have the same sign: countries whose populations are predominantly Buddhist, Confucian, and Muslim have faster growing economies, *ceteris paribus*, while countries whose people are predominantly Catholic or Protestant grow more slowly. In terms of Pierre Bourdieu's split of culture into field, habitus, and doxa, Sala-i-Martin's religious variables quantify the doxa and habitus. Variables related to formal institutions, include political variables such as the number of revolutions and coups, war, an index of the rule of law, lack of political rights, and an index of civil liberties. All have the expected signs, namely violence reduces growth and more freedom and protection of rights enhances growth. Institutions related to international trade and finance also seem to matter, as evidenced by the significance of variables such as the number of years the economy has been open to trade, the black market foreign exchange premium (a measure of how much exchange restrictions distort the exchange rate), and another index of exchange rate distortions. It is hard to make much economic sense out of the variables related to geographic location, but clearly some regions have performed better than other regions; notably, Latin America and Sub-Saharan Africa have more than their share of low-growth economies. Such regional variables represent the entire set of formal and informal institutions within each region that are not explicitly represented in Sala-i-Martin's other variables.

Robert Hall and Charles Jones (1997, 1999) proceed directly to test the hypothesis that differences in levels of economic success across countries are driven primarily by the institutions and government policies that frame the economic environment in which people produce and transact. They regress the *levels* of per capita income for a large cross-section of countries on several alternative measures of the institutional environment. First, they develop an index that reflects how well government policies encourage productive activity over transfer activity. Next, they measure the openness of the economy to international trade. Third, they use a measure of the extent to which the economy is "organized according to capitalist characteristics." Hall and Jones also use two other less- obvious measures of institutions, namely the percentage of the population that speaks a major international language such as English or Spanish and the distance the country is located from the equator.

Hall and Jones find that the institutional variables are able to explain most (over 75 percent) of the variation in levels of per capita income across countries of the world. They thus conclude that if institutions were all the same across countries, the relative differences in per capita incomes would be less than one-fourth of what we now observe. They conclude: "... differences in levels of economic success across countries are driven primarily by the institutions and government policies that frames the economic environment in which people produce and transact."[16]

Keefer and Knack (1997) also run a series of regressions in which they test the statistical significance of institutional variables on economic growth. They use three sets of qualitative measures of institutions: measures of the security of property and contractual rights, measures of the rule of law, and measures of the quality of government bureaucracy. Two sets of measures were developed by independent international investor risk services, *International Country Risk Guide* and *Business Environment Risk Intelligence*, and the third set of indexes was developed by political scientists. To measure the security of property, the authors use specific indexes of the *risk of expropriation, the risk of repudiation of contracts by government, the risk of nationalization,* and *contract enforceability*. In order to measure the effective adherence of the government to the rule of law, the authors use an index of *executive constraints*, or limits on the arbitrary power of the executive branch of government. Finally, they measure the quality of bureaucracies by using specific indexes of *bureaucratic delays, corruption in government*, and *bureaucratic quality*. Keefer and Knack find that a country's ability to reduce the relative gap with developed economies is significantly related to each of the institutional variables tested.

Stanley Fischer (1993) focused on the relationship between macroeconomic policies, such as monetary policy and fiscal policy, and economic growth. He used three variables to represent the macroeconomic policies of governments: the rate of inflation, the budget deficit, and distortions in the foreign exchange markets. The first two obviously proxy the soundness of monetary and fiscal policy, and the latter is directly related to international trade and investment policies. Fischer finds that "... a stable macroeconomic environment, meaning a reasonably low rate of inflation and a small budget deficit, is conducive to sustained economic growth."[17] Fischer further claims that additional statistical tests show that causality runs from macroeconomic policy to growth. Fischer emphasizes that his tests suggest that macroeconomic policy influences growth mostly because inflation and budget deficits reduce investment and productivity growth.

In general, regression studies of economic growth suggest institutions matter a lot. Still, these studies have been far from definitive because they use simple GDP growth as a measure of economic development. The use of GDP growth as the dependent variable in the regression equation may help to explain why capitalist institutions were often statistically significant. It is not clear how sustainable economic development should be quantified. Also, many of the institutional variables are rough proxies for formal and/or informal institutions, as in the case of regional variables and general classifications of religions, languages, education levels, etc. While it is clear that economic development is

---

[16] Hall and Jones (1997), p. 173.
[17] Stanley Fischer (1993), p. 509.

not simply determined by changes in capital, labor, and technological change, there is still much work to be done before statistical analysis can give us solid confirmation of the importance of specific institutions for sustainable economic development.

References

Anderson, James E., and Douglas Marcouiller (1999), "Trade, Insecurity, and Home Bias: An Empirical Investigation," NBER Working Paper W7000, March.

Axelrod, Robert (1984), *The Evolution of Cooperation*, New York: Basic Books.

Bourdieu, Pierre (1977), *Outline of a Theory of Practice*, Cambridge, U.K.: Cambridge University Press.

Bourdieu, P. (1986) "The Forms of Capital," in J. Richardson (ed.), *Handbook of Theory and Research for the Sociology of Education*, New York: Greenwood, 241–258.

Bourdieu, Pierre (1988), *Homo Academicus*, Cambridge: Polity Press.

Bourdieu, Pierre (2000), *Pascallian Meditations*, Cambridge, U.K.: Cambridge University Press.

Bourdieu, Pierre (2001), *Masculine Domination*, Cambridge: Polity Press.

Bourdieu, Pierre (2005), *Science of Science and Reflexivity*, Chicago: University of Chicago Press.

De Soto, Hernando de Soto (1989), *The Other Path*, New York: Harper and Row.

Fischer, Stanley (1993), "The Role of Macroeconomic Factors in Growth," *Journal of Monetary Economics* 32:485–512.

Greif, Avner (1989a), "Reputation and Coalitions in Medieval Trade: Evidence on the Maghribi," *Journal of Economic History* 49(4):857–882.

Grief, Avner (1989b), "Cultural Beliefs and the Organization of Society: A Historical and Theoretical Reflection on Collectivist and Individualist Societies," *Journal of Political Economy* 102:912–950.

Hall, Robert E., and Charles I. Jones (1997). "Levels of Economic Activity Across Countries," *American Economic Review* 87(2):173–177.

Hall, Robert E., and Charles I. Jones (1999), "Why Do Some Countries Produce so Much More Output per Worker than Others?," *Quarterly Journal of Economics* 114(1):83–116.

Holbrooke, Richard (2001), "Foreword" in Margaret MacMillan (2001), *Paris 1919: Six Months That Changed the World*, New York: Random House.

Hardin, Garrett (1968), "Tragedy of the Commons," *Science* 162:1243–1248.

Keefer, Philip, and Stephen Knack (1997), "Why Don't Poor Countries Catch Up? A Cross-National Test of an Institutional Explanation," *Economic Inquiry* 35(3): 590–602.

Kroeber, Alfred, and Clyde Kluckhorn (1952), *Culture: A Critical Review of Concepts and Definitions*, Cambridge, MA: The Museum.

Lal, Deepak (1998), *Unintended Consequences: The Impact of Factor Endowments, Culture, and Politics on Long-Run Economic Development*, Cambridge, MA: MIT Press.

MacMillan, Margaret (2001), *Paris 1919: Six Months That Changed the World*, New York: Random House.

Nee, Victor (1998), "Norms and Networks in Economic and Organizational Performance," *American Economic Review* 88(2):85–88.

North, Douglass C. (1987), "Institutions, Transactions Costs and Economic Growth," *Economic Inquiry* 25:419–420.

North, Douglass C. (2005), *Understanding the Process of Economic Change*, Princeton, NJ: Princeton University Press.

Ostrom, Elinor (2005), *Understanding Institutional Diversity*, Princeton, NJ: Princeton University Press.

Ostrom, Elinor (2009), "A General Framework for Analyzing Sustainability of Social-Ecological Systems," *Science* 325(5939):419–422.

Pasquino, Gianfranco (1986), "The Demise of the First Fascist Regime and Italy's Transition to Democracy: 1943–1948," in Guillermo O'Donnell, Philippe C. Schmitter, and Laurence Whitehead (eds.), *Transitions from Authoritarian Rule: Southern Europe,* Baltimore: Johns Hopkins University Press.

Payne, James L. (2006), "Does Nation Building Work?," *The Independent Review* 10(4):599–610.

Petty, William (1682), "Another Essay in Political Arithmetic," in Charles Henry Hull, ed. (1899), *The Economic Writings of Sir William Petty*, Cambridge, U.K.: Cambridge University Press.

Ridley, Matt (1996), *The Origins of Virtue*, New York: Penguin Books.

Rogers, Alex D., and D. d'A. Laffoley (2011), "Summary Report of the International Earth System Expert Workshop on Ocean Stresses and Impacts, Oxford: International Program on the State of the Ocean (IPSO).

Romer, Paul M. (1998), "Economic Growth," from David R. Henderson (ed.), *The Fortune Encyclopedia of Economics*, New York: Warner Books.

Sala-i-Martin, Xavier (1997), "I Just Ran Two Million Regressions," *American Economic Review* 87(2):178–183.

Seabright, Paul (2010), *The Company of Strangers, A Natural History of Human Life*, *2nd Ed.*, Princeton, NJ: Princeton University Press.

Smith, Adam (1776 [1976]), *An Inquiry into the Nature and Causes of the Wealth of Nations*, Chicago: University of Chicago Press.

Thaler, Richard H., and Schlomo Benzarti (2004), "Save More Tomorrow: Using Behavioral Economics to Increase Employee Saving," *Journal of Political Economy*, 2004.

Thomas, J. J. (1992), *Informal Economic Activity*, Ann Arbor: University of Michigan Press.

Weber, Max (1978), *Economy and Society*, Berkeley: University of California Press.

CHAPTER 13

Formal Government Institutions

There are no cases of complex high income societies that do not have an elaborate structure of government.

(Douglass C. North, 1987)

Government plays a large role in most economies of the world. Most of the growth of that role occurred over the past century. As Figure 13.1 makes clear, government spending in the fourteen most developed economies of the world has grown from less than 10 percent of GDP at the start of the twentieth century to nearly 50 percent of total output at the start of the twenty-first century. Of the 14 countries, the United States was lowest with 33 percent, which was still nearly a ten-fold increase from 3.9 percent in 1870. At the very end of the twentieth century, Sweden was highest at 65 percent, up from 5.7 percent in 1870. Even developing countries have seen their share of government expenditures rise, although not to the levels experienced in the most developed economies. The Brazilian government's expenditures are over 30 percent of GDP.

The graph in Figure 13.1 is somewhat misleading in that it depicts total government expenditures, not government consumption of national output. A great share of government expenditures are transfer payments, that is, taxes and other revenue passed on to people, organizations, and business firms as retirement payments, subsidies, unemployment benefits, etc. Average government consumption was just under twenty percent at the start of the twenty-first century. And government affects economic activity by means of regulations, laws, and other institutions, and this influence does not show up as expenditures or transfers. Overall, governance structures at various levels are influential institution in all countries.

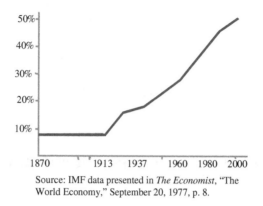

Source: IMF data presented in *The Economist*, "The
World Economy," September 20, 1977, p. 8.

Figure 13.1 Government Spending as a percent of World GDP

   In all countries there are many levels of governance that operate
simultaneously.   For example, there are national governments, state or
provincial governments, regional governments, and municipal governments.
There are many other governance structures erected to supervise education
systems, organize agricultural production, build and operate infrastructure
projects such as seaports, airports, railroads, utilities, and communications, and
carry out charitable activities.   These various levels of governance, in turn,
operate many specific institutions, such as the schools and universities that issue
the diplomas and certificates that enhance the cultural capital discussed in the
previous chapter or the judicial systems that enforce contracts and build trust for
intertemporal transactions discussed in Chapter 11. Some governance structures
are closely related to a society's culture and traditions, as for example mosques,
churches, sports clubs, and mutual aid societies, and they might be viewed more
as informal institutions.   However, it is fair to say that most governance
structures are formal institutions that were intentionally designed and created to
carry out collective tasks or to explicitly shape people's behavior and actions.
   Douglass North (1987), the economic historian quoted at the start of
this chapter, argues that uncoordinated and ungoverned individual actions do
not, in general, lead to the best possible economic and social outcomes in
complex societies and economies. Of course, formal government institutions do
not guarantee optimal outcomes either. Government institutions often fail to
achieve their fundamental purpose of inducing the human actions that maximize
social well-being. Governments can misallocate society's resources with poorly
designed regulatory and tax policies, a likely outcome when the powers of
government are controlled by special interest groups. Because government is
granted coercive power, government has the power to steal on behalf of special
interests, oppress some individuals and groups at the request or insistence of
others. It can carry out wars and other forms of violence that destroy life and

property. There are both welfare-enhancing government institutions and destructive government institutions.

In this chapter, formal government institutions are examined in detail. Regardless of where the arguments about the size of government eventually lead, there are many reasons for giving the government a role in human societies. As Douglass North wrote, "there are no cases of complex high income societies that do not have an elaborate structure of government."[1]

Chapter Goals

1. Discuss the economic roles of government.
2. Begin with Adam Smith's basic functions of government.
3. Explain the extent of Smith's ideas on government to make it clear that his invisible hand did not mandate an end to government.
4. Examine the many additional reasons why modern complex economies and societies need collective government actions, including the presence of externalities, monopoly power in markets, economic inequality, and macroeconomic stability.
5. Discuss the concept of economic rights and the case for collective (government) responsibility to provide society's members with jobs, basic income, health, and social participation.
6. Explain why governments often fail, and detail damaging activities such as as rent-seeking, corruption, and the shift of economic activity to informal markets and social arrangements.
7. Detail the formal economic institution of intellectual property rights, which includes patents and copyrights.

13.1 The Economic Roles of Government

Few social scientists argue that a complex economy with high levels of specialization and exchange can function without laws, rules, and the enforcement of those laws and rules. Most people recognize that government needs some degree of coercive power in order to restrict and direct individual behavior and actions. But there are many disagreements on precisely what it is that governments should do and what their role in the economy should be. In many countries, governments are doing much more than just facilitating transactions and protecting people from doing harm to each other. In other countries, governments do not try to fulfill even those basic roles. What, exactly, should governments do to maximize human well-being and sustain the economies and societies that humans have developed?

---

[1] North (1987), p. 421.

13.1.1 Adam Smith's basic functions of government

Adam Smith is often described as suggesting a simplistic governance policy of *laissez faire*, which means making society's economic decisions on the basis of market-determined prices and quantities. However, Smith had a much more holistic view of government than many of his supporters claim or his critics give him credit for. Smith not only explicitly addressed the need for establishing the institutions necessary for markets to function, but he advocated many other roles for government.

Specifically, Smith (1776 [1976], Book II, pp. 208–209) gave government:

> ... three duties to attend to; three duties of great importance, indeed, but plain and intelligible to common understandings: first, the duty of protecting the society from the violence and invasion of other independent societies; secondly, the duty of protecting, as far as possible, every member of the society from the injustice or oppression of every other member of it, or the duty of establishing an exact administration of justice; and, thirdly, the duty of erecting and maintaining certain public works and certain public institutions, which it can never be for the interest of any individual, or small number of individuals, to erect and maintain; because the profit could never repay the expense to any individual or small number of individuals, though it may frequently do much more than repay it to a great society.

Each of these "three duties" of government deserves some discussion.

Smith's recognition of government's duty to protect society from aggression of other countries did not mean he was an advocate of maintaining a large military force. He feared a permanent military force would end up being used to further the specific aims of government officials or those who gained the favor of the government:

> Men of republican principles have been jealous of a standing army as dangerous to liberty. It certainly is so, wherever the interest of the general and that of the principal officers are not necessarily connected with the support of the constitution of the state.[2]

History offers many examples of inappropriate use of military power by government.

Smith also recognized the need to protect individuals from threats, harassment, and oppression by others. Specialization and exchange will not evolve fairly or efficiently if some parties to the transactions have the power to intimidate or dominate others. Thus, Smith argued that governments had a duty to protect, as far as possible, every member of the society from the injustice, oppression, and defrauding by other members of society.

---

[2] Adam Smith (1776 [1976]), Book II, p. 229.

Smith pointed out that most crime involves attempts to steal property and wealth. He thus included among government's duties the protection of property as well as the enforcement of contractual agreements and the right to restitution in the case of fraud and other forms of willful deception. He noted that the intentional nonpayment of debt constituted theft just as much as taking some tangible good without paying for it. He also argued that without the protection of property and the enforcement of contracts, markets would not work well. Many people would stop voluntarily paying for things if they could simply steal them with impunity, as evidenced even today in the case of the natural environment.

Smith advocated additional roles for government that went beyond the protection of person and property, such as the maintenance of law and order, and the protection from foreign threats. He also explicitly discussed government's role in erecting and maintaining welfare-enhancing public works and public institutions that would otherwise not be created or maintained by individuals or small groups of individuals. These are what we today call **public goods**.

The classic example of a public good is the lighthouse. It is difficult to prevent people from using a lighthouse by observing its signal at night and thereby avoiding a shipwreck on a rocky coast. In this sense, the lighthouse is a **nonrival good** that can be consumed by more than one person at a time without diminishing the benefit to any one user. The problem is that a lighthouse is also largely **non-excludable** in that it is difficult to prevent someone from observing its signal, regardless of whether they pay for the lighthouse's service. Therefore, private individuals or groups would probably not find it profitable to erect lighthouses on their own. And, because the marginal cost of providing a nonrival good to one more user is essentially zero, economic efficiency requires that the service be provided free of charge to each marginal (additional) user. But, who will build and pay for the lighthouse then? There is potentially a role for government here. A government could provide the service free of charge and cover the cost of providing the service through taxation. Such taxation might be directed at shipowners who directly use the lighthouse's services. Or, it could be argued that the entire population should be taxed because the lighthouse's support of shippers and fishing boats ends up benefitting everyone in the form of more reliable shipping services and cheaper food.

There are many other examples of public goods. National defense, which Adam Smith singled out as an activity for government to perform, is also a nonrival and non-excludable good. The park in the center of the city, police protection, fire prevention, and the national weather service are other candidates for government involvement. But, in line with his reputation for favoring markets Adam Smith (1776 [1976], Book II, p. 245) cautioned against government provision of services that can be provided by private enterprises:

> That the erection and maintenance of the public works which facilitate the commerce of any country, such as good roads, bridges, navigable canals, harbours,

&c. must require very different degrees of expence in the different periods of society, is evident without any proof. It does not seem necessary that the expence of those public works should be defrayed from that public revenue, as it is commonly called, of which the collection and application are in most countries assigned to the executive power. The greater part of such public works may easily be so managed, as to afford a particular revenue sufficient for defraying their own expence, without bringing any burden upon the general revenue of society.

The mere fact that projects are large does not make them public goods or require that the government actively take a role in providing them. Smith is, therefore, often interpreted as suggesting government should limit its provision of activity to providing true public goods that would not be provided in the proper quantities by private individuals or firms.

In modern societies public goods cover most networks in communications, transportation, and information. It is inefficient to operate more than one telephone network, highway system, or internet. There would be needless duplication of capital investment, and there would be potentially even more costly exclusions of potential users to each duplicate network. There is, therefore, a strong case for collective government provision and unrestricted use of public network infrastructures.

13.1.2 Externalities and government policy

Externalities are a common problem in economics. Market prices may not accurately reflect the true marginal costs and marginal utilities of goods and services. What we mean here by *true* are the costs and utilities for society not just those for the individual decision makers. Markets do not always set prices that account for all the costs and benefits of a product. Examples of externalities abound, and most principles of economics textbooks typically discuss negative externalities such as those associated with pollution, noise, and congestion. Chapter 6 detailed the detrimental effects of human activity on the natural sphere, which are seldom internalized in market prices. Some externalities are positive. For example, farmers earn their income from the food they produce, but they also enhance the scenery by preserving green areas in increasingly urban societies. Many European governments have explicitly recognized the scenic and cultural benefits of maintaining traditional farms in the face of commercial pressure to convert farmland to other uses, and they subsidize farmers to sustain their activities.

Positive externalities can enhance economic development. For example, Chapter 10 showed that the benefits that society gained from people's education exceeded the gains to the individual who acquired the education. Preventive healthcare similarly exhibits positive externalities in the form of a more productive workforce and higher disposable income.

Standard economic analysis suggests that an activity generating the externalities should be subsidized by the government. For example, the finding that education has positive external effects on the rate of technological change suggests that education should be subsidized. The learning by doing model similarly suggests that production should be subsidized since nearly everyone in the economy benefits from the learning process. But, accurate subsidization is difficult. How large are the externalities? Who exactly gains from the externalities? Do some types of investment or production generate more externalities than others? We seldom have accurate answers to these questions. Nevertheless, governments in nearly all countries use tax revenue to finance public education. Many governments also subsidize healthcare and investment in infrastructure projects.

13.1.3 Externalities and the holistic nature of human welfare

A holistic approach to sustainable economic development effectively seeks to internalize what mainstream economic analysis leaves as externalities. Mainstream economics focuses on markets, and markets normally capture only the direct benefits of most production. Markets normally miss many of the more subtle indirect and systemic gains or losses from human economic activities like production, consumption, and innovation. For example, economic analysis, and the statistical analysis to test that economic analysis, will usually describe a specific type of productive economic activity, say electricity generation, as directly causing an increase in human welfare by increasing GDP and income. The more electricity is produced, the higher is GDP, and the better off humanity is. Such analysis effectively assumes that all the other factors that influence human welfare, such as community relationships, nature's services, or personal health, are determined through other channels and not in any way related to the particular productive activity. Economists normally leave the analysis of communities, the ecosystem, and health issues to sociologists, ecologists, and medical researchers.

Figure 13.2 illustrates the relationships as orthodox economists often hypothesize them in their practical studies and analyses. Recall that this view of human society as consisting of a set of separate components is called *scientific reductionism*. This approach reflects the belief that we can add up the various direct influences of the different changes in economic, social, ecological, and health conditions to determine the overall change in human welfare. Holism, on the other hand, recognizes that systems are complex arrangements of parts. Those parts interact in complex ways to determine the overall outcome, which is human welfare in this example.

Figure 13.3 more accurately reflects the influence of electricity generation on human welfare. Figure 13.3 suggests that an increase in electricity production indeed has a positive direct effect on human welfare. But there are

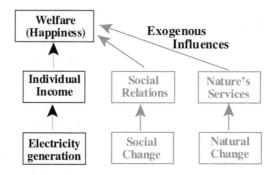

Figure 13.2 The Scientific-Reductionist Perspective

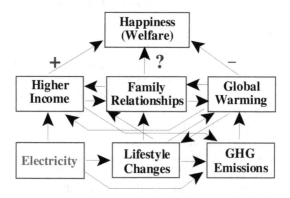

Figure 13.3 The Holistic Perspective

also many indirect effects, such as the effects of electricity on people's lifestyles, as in the case of new home appliances, the telephone, radio, television, the Internet, and every other product and service powered by electricity. The generation of electricity in coal-fired power plants also increases the greenhouse gas (GHG) emissions that contribute to global warming, and these changes are likely to diminish human happiness in the future because the natural environment will differ from that in which humans evolved. Changes in human lifestyles affect personal and family relationships, and some of those changes also affect GHG emissions and global warming.

There are many relationships that ultimately link the generation of electricity to human happiness. You can, no doubt, think of more channels through which one influences the other. Figure 13.3 notes that while the direct effect is likely to be positive for human welfare, the social consequences are more ambiguous, and the GHG emissions caused by electricity generation and economic growth in general are likely to generate negative welfare effects.

Unlike economists who model in a scientific reductionist manner, holistic analysis views these indirect effects not as externalities but as real effects worthy of attention in the economist's frame of analysis.

In sum, markets are likely to reflect the direct costs and benefits of electricity but miss many of the indirect effects of electricity on human welfare. The prices set in electricity markets are, therefore, unlikely to provide the signal that leads producers and users of electricity to generate and use the socially-optimal amount of electricity that maximizes long-run human happiness. The holistic approach and the explicit recognition of the indirect effects (the externalities) make it clear that there is a role for government action to ensure society produces an optimal amount of electricity, optimal in the sense that all the effects of generating electricity are factored into the decision process.

13.1.4 Imperfect competition and government policy

Another reason laissez-faire and free markets do not produce optimal outcomes is that free markets are never perfectly competitive, as economic models assume.   This means market prices do not accurately reflect underlying opportunity costs, and this creates welfare losses compared to the perfect competition idealized market outcome.

A diagram of a monopoly market is given in Figure 13.4. A monopoly is not a price taker; rather, a monopoly faces a downward-sloping demand curve and has some choice over what price to set. By setting its price given by the quantity where marginal revenue equals marginal cost, the monopolist maximizes profit, which will equal the shaded area defined by the points pfew. There is of course a **deadweight loss** equal to the triangle fae, which represents the potential gains in welfare that would accrue to society if production were expanded beyond q. Society could recover the deadweight loss if, say, the government somehow forces the monopoly to charge price w and produce the quantity s. Alternatively, the government could directly operate the monopoly industry and charge w and supply s. Or the government could enact anti-trust laws that explicitly prohibit one firm from dominating an industry in an attempt to maintain enough competition to keep the price closer to w and, therefore, production closer to s. This latter approach will not be successful if the market is inherently monopolistic because the size of a one efficient producer is large enough to supply the whole market or when there are important network effects that mandate a single provider.

The regulation of a monopoly may, according to the Schumpeterian model, reduce the rate of technological change. Government policy may, therefore, tolerate some degree of market power so that the industry has incentives to generate technological improvements. In this case, there would be a role for government to ensure that Schumpeterian competition and creative destruction are maintained and innovators do not perpetuate their acquired market power.

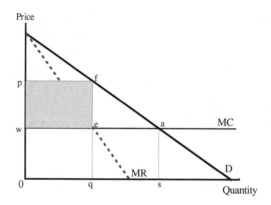

Figure 13.4   Monopoly Profit

13.1.5 Intertemporal decisions

Intertemporal markets often fail to reflect the full social costs and benefits of borrowing and lending over time. As discussed in Chapter 11, there are roles for government to play to improve the performance of financial markets and financial intermediaries. When markets face severe informational problems, as occurred in the early 2000s when financial markets were undermined by new financial instruments that no one understood well enough to value accurately, the government can play a "third party" role of forcing the parties directly involved in transactions to reveal more information than they would reveal voluntarily. The government can also enforce the requirement that the information revealed be correct and complete. The 2007–2008 financial collapse made it clear that the government of the United States and the governments of most other major economies had not performed this oversight role appropriately.

A government-operated judicial system that enforces contracts can help to eliminate many of the moral hazard problems inherent in intertemporal transactions by letting signatories to contracts recover damages when the terms of the contract are not met.   Recall also from Chapter 11 that another government institution, formal property rights, allows borrowers to pledge collateral in order to overcome moral hazard and information problems that plague intertemporal transactions.

Finally, there may be a role for the government to promote procedures and rules that help to overcome people's psychological tendencies to irrationally favor the status quo over alternatives and the short run over the long run. In these cases, the government effectively uses its coercive powers to nudge people towards acting in their own long-run interest.

13.1.6 Macroeconomic stability

Holism recognizes that the relationship between the whole system and its component parts is not an unchanging linear set of relationships along the lines of Walras' late nineteenth century general equilibrium model discussed in Chapter 4. Ever since the Great Depression, most national governments have assumed some responsibility for maintaining full employment, price stability, and economic growth. Most countries today operate active central banks, adjust fiscal policies to reflect domestic and international macroeconomic conditions, and authorize government agencies to carry out oversight of the financial industry to prevent excessive risk taking and potential financial breakdowns.

However, a government's ability to maintain economic stability is limited by its knowledge of macroeconomics, its relationships to other economies of the world, and its internal politics. While there has not (yet) been a repetition of the Great Depression, there have been many financial crises in many countries, continual and large fluctuations in employment, prices, and output, a worrisome growth of international imbalances in trade and investment flows, and the Great Recession in many developed economies from 2007 to 2009. Even more difficult is the task of providing continued economic development that is demanded of developing country governments.

13.1.7 Achieving a just distribution of society's production

Governments in most countries use taxes, subsidies, assistance programs, and myriad other means to redistribute wealth and income among individuals, households, corporations, and groups of people. In the previous chapter, we discussed the potentially damaging consequences of institutions that transfer income and wealth from some members of society to others. Often, the relatively wealthy use their economic power to capture the government's coercive power and use it for their special interests. On the other hand, there are valid justifications for altering the distribution of income and wealth in society, especially if the current stock of wealth and related flows of income are the result of past injustices.

Recall from Chapter 3 that an additional dollar, peso, or yuan of income for a wealthy person does not add as much to their happiness as that same dollar, peso, or yuan added to the income of a poor person living in the same society. Therefore, total national happiness may increase when income or wealth is transferred from relatively wealthy households to relatively poor households. This observation does not, by itself, justify taking something from a wealthy person and giving it to a poor person. But, if we also recognize that much of a person's income depends on inherited economic, social, and cultural capital as well as a large dosage of luck, then redistribution of income to those who did not enjoy the same inherited advantages and luck becomes a perfectly justifiable government policy. The difficulty again lies in the details because it is difficult to calculate the precise gains due to pure luck and endowment as opposed to personal effort and learning.

Interestingly, the alleged proponent of the **invisible hand of markets**, Adam Smith, agreed with some distribution of wealth from the rich to the poor:

> The necessaries of life occasion the great expense of the poor... The luxuries and vanities of life occasion the principle expense of the rich, and a magnificent house embellishes and sets off to the best advantage all the other luxuries and vanities which they possess... It is not very unreasonable that the rich should contribute to the public expense, not only in proportion to their revenue, but something more than in that proportion.[3]

In most developed countries today, income tax rates are designed to be **progressive**, meaning high-income earners are taxed a higher proportion of their income than low-income earners. Resistance, lobbying, and political control by the wealthy in most of these countries have reduced these progressive income tax rates and pushed governments to give exemptions from paying the taxes. Less developed countries usually depend less on income taxes and more on easier-to-collect direct sales taxes, import taxes, and excise taxes, which are less progressive.

13.1.8 Government leadership in changing the institutional structure

In the previous chapter, we noted that informal institutions, such as traditions, religions, or social mores, change very slowly. Hence, when there are substantial changes in the social and natural environments, there is a role for government to push for changes in the formal institutional environment in order to compensate for the inevitable conflict between reality and the sluggish informal institutions. Note that we are not arguing here that informal institutions generally adversely affect overall national welfare. In fact, many traditions, religious ideas, and social customs continue to provide positive incentives for socially-optimal behavior despite rapid changes in our social and natural environments. Cultural rules against stealing, cheating, lying, and hurting other people mostly raise the welfare of populations and, therefore, support economic development. However, because many traditions, religious principles, and social customs directly or indirectly favor the status quo, they tend to lose their effectiveness in the face of *changing* economic, social, and natural environments.

Institutions that make change difficult, no matter how compatible they are with people's preferences in the short run, constrain economic development and long-run human welfare. Economically-efficient change may, therefore, require the use of authority and coercion by the government to change and enforce

---

[3] Adam Smith (1776 [1976]), Chapter 2, Part V.

formal institutions such as laws, regulations, and oversight to counteract entrenched informal institutions. Given the greater flexibility with which formal government institutions can be changed, relative to informal institutions like culture and traditions, there is a role for government to lead in designing society's institutional structure. For example, entrenched cultures often support economic and social discrimination against women, minorities, or foreigners. Cultural capital perpetuates inequalities that not only clash with progressive concepts of fairness and justice, but they often cause inefficient economic outcomes that lower total output in the economy. Discrimination against people with new ideas and entrepreneurial traits is clearly detrimental to long-run sustainable economic development, and marginalizing people who might have new ideas and entrepreneurial traits is equally detrimental. Laws and regulations against discrimination and other forms of cultural oppression can therefore improve the performance of the economy and raise the welfare of otherwise excluded groups.

Culture, traditions, and lifestyles that developed over generations are hindering society's ability to prevent the environmental deterioration that has accompanied the world's recent rapid economic growth. The apparent rapid acceleration of global warming and loss of biodiversity suggest that we cannot afford to wait generations for human activity to become less environmentally damaging. Therefore, immediate changes in government laws, regulations, and oversight are required to shift incentives to induce individuals to live and work in ways that are more environmentally friendly. Of course, changes in formal government institutions may clash with sluggish informal institutions dating back many generations. In many countries today we are witnessing sharp conflicts between ecological reality and people's preference to continue living in ways that deplete the earth's resources. But these difficulties do not diminish the need for collective actions, based on abstract thinking and scientific study, and instituted by means of formal government institutions.

13.1.9 There are no human rights without economic rights

Closely related to Adam Smith's discussion of government's role in protecting person and property from domestic and foreign threats is the general consensus among most people that government should support basic human rights such as freedom of speech, freedom of beliefs, freedom from discrimination on the basis of gender or ethnic background, and freedom from all forms of oppression. Economists often focus only on economic rights, such as free competition, free trade, free labor markets, and the protection of personal property. Again, there is a tendency for mainstream economists to limit their analysis to government's economic role to the provision of economic freedoms, although a few have pursued broader analyses linking an economy's performance to broader human rights. There has been a lively debate about whether democracies experience faster economic growth than dictatorships.

The justification for government involvement in the economy is not limited to the question of whether human rights are good for economic growth, however. The political granting of basic human rights like free speech, the right to vote, freedom of religion, the right to organize workers into a labor union, etc. are meaningless if people's economic existence is threatened or restricted. A starving person desperate for income is not free to speak her mind or negotiate on an equal basis in a labor market, regardless of what the law states. As President Franklin D. Roosevelt said in his 1944 State of the Union address to the U.S. congress:

> This Republic had its beginning, and grew to its present strength, under the protection of certain inalienable political rights — among them the right of free speech, free press, free worship, trial by jury, freedom from unreasonable searches and seizures. They were our rights to life and liberty.
>
> As our nation has grown in size... — as our industrial economy expanded — these political rights proved inadequate to assure us equality in the pursuit of happiness. We have come to a clear realization of the fact that true individual freedom cannot exist without economic security and independence. "Necessitous men are not free men." People who are hungry and out of a job are the stuff of which dictatorships are made.

President Roosevelt's wife, Eleanor Roosevelt, had urged her husband to include the quoted words in his address, and she worked tirelessly after his death to have economic rights incorporated into the *United Nations Universal Declaration of Human Rights* after World War II.

The Universal Declaration was approved by the United Nations General Assembly on December 10, 1948, by a vote of 48 in favor, 0 against, with 8 abstentions. Only six Soviet Republics, the apartheid state of South Africa, and Saudi Arabia did not vote to approve the document. The Declaration includes basic human rights such as:

> Article 3: Everyone has the right to life, liberty and security of person.
>
> Article 4: No one shall be held in slavery or servitude; slavery and the slave trade shall be prohibited in all their forms.
>
> Article 5: No one shall be subjected to torture or to cruel, inhuman or degrading treatment or punishment.
>
> Article 6: Everyone has the right to recognition everywhere as a person before the law.

But, in line with Roosevelt's linking of human rights to economic rights, the Universal Declaration of Human Rights also includes articles such as:

Article 23: Everyone has the right to work, to free choice of employment, to just and favourable conditions of work and to protection against unemployment.

Article 24: Everyone has the right to rest and leisure, including reasonable limitation of working hours and periodic holidays with pay.

Article 25: Everyone has the right to a standard of living adequate for the health and well-being of himself and of his family, including food, clothing, housing and medical care and necessary social services, and the right to security in the event of unemployment, sickness, disability, widowhood, old age or other lack of livelihood in circumstances beyond his control.

Article 26: Everyone has the right to education. Education shall be free, at least in the elementary and fundamental stages. Elementary education shall be compulsory. Technical and professional education shall be made generally available and higher education shall be equally accessible to all on the basis of merit.

The full *Universal Declaration of Human Rights* is an Appendix to this chapter.

In 1948 many governments accepted the Declaration and transformed it into government policies in their countries. The United Nations *Declaration* greatly extended the economic role of government. Today, sixty years later, many government leaders still do not accept that human rights require economic rights such as employment, healthcare, education, and shelter.

13.1.10 Summarizing the motivations for collective government action

In sum, there are many justifications for government activity that go well beyond Adam Smith's basic three government functions. Market failures due to externalities, incomplete information, and imperfect competition are the norm rather than the exception. As a background report by the World Bank for its 1997 *World Development Report* states: "Markets are almost always incomplete, and information is always imperfect."[4] Holism also reminds us that economies can fail to generate satisfactory outcomes; individual parts operating without regard for the overall system can cause economic depressions, starvation, and social revolutions. Conventional economic analysis often reaches conclusions about the role of government without taking the complexities of human society and the externalities into consideration. Furthermore, happiness studies and psychology show that the well-being of individuals justifies a redistribution of income and wealth within a market system. And, finally, the complexity of modern human societies cannot seriously claim to promote human rights without also guaranteeing the economic rights that enable people to exercise their freedoms. It is difficult to imagine a person can be free without also having access to education, work, income, and healthcare.

---

[4] Pedro Belli (1997).

However, history shows that governments do not always do a very good job of handling the many tasks that they take on. Many governments are not even successful in carrying out all three of Smith's basic functions, much less all the other actions justified by the broad range of concerns detailed above. In the real world, we unfortunately face the uncomfortable reality of both imperfect markets and imperfect government institutions to deal with market failures and the complexity of human society.

13.2 Government Failures

The fact that the market system does not always function efficiently to allocate society's scarce resources does not automatically justify government action in the economy. The government can also fail to achieve its goals, and intervention in markets by the government is not always successful in improving a market failure. Government can do more harm than good. War, corruption, government-sponsored oppression, redistribution from the poor to the well-connected, and protection of vested interest against the creative destruction of innovators are but a few examples of common government failures. Finding the *visible hands* of government that lead to optimal solutions may be just as difficult as finding the institutions that enable the *invisible hand* of perfect competition and complete markets.

13.2.1 Why government may fail to accomplish its goals

There are many reasons why government fails to generate welfare-enhancing economic outcomes when it interjects itself into the economy. Among them are (1) the lack of information, (2) the self-interest of government leaders and bureaucrats, and (3) the hijacking of government power by special interests. The first source of failure is not difficult to comprehend. Government often tries to do things when it simply does not have enough information or understanding of the situation to make good choices. For example, when markets set a price that is thought to misrepresent the true costs of a product or service, there is often disagreement on what those true costs really are. Recall the discussion in the previous section on the many direct and indirect effects of generating electricity. In principle, the government could correct for such a market failure, but if the government actually sets another "wrong" price an improvement in welfare is not guaranteed.

The second source of government failure reflects the reality that government is operated by human beings who have their own interests, beliefs, and ideas. Government officials can be lazy, dishonest, or overzealous. Some government officials or employees have their own political agenda or beliefs that they seek to impose. More common is the problem of bureaucratic momentum that makes change or new policies difficult to carry out. Just like private businesses that fail to adjust to changing markets, government agencies organized to carry out one set of tasks often cannot adjust to new circumstances or new tasks assigned to them.

The third reason why government may fail to improve economic outcomes is that: "With a state inevitably comes a struggle to control it in the interests of one of the parties."[5] The growth economist Paul Romer writes that "if the government has important discretionary power over economic affairs, members of the government can all too easily divert that power from its intended public purpose and put it to private use."[6] The difficulty of controlling government is not a new problem; note the 2,000-year old Latin saying *Quis custodies ipsos custodes*? — Who will oversee the overseers?

13.2.2 Rent seeking

An important step to understanding government failure is the recognition that government is not an infallible organization that always does what is best for the nation, the economy, or humanity. In reality, government is made up of people, just like any organization, and those people are as much interested in their own welfare as anyone else. Government officials and bureaucrats, like all people, tend to do the best they can for themselves and those people they are concerned about, given the constraints within which they operate. If using its coercive power to take from individual A in order to give to individual B will be advantageous to them, then government officials may indeed attempt to bring about such a transfer, even if overall national welfare is negatively affected. Government officials are continually offered incentives to act in ways that favor special interests.

The things that people do in order to effectively take wealth from others, rather than producing it from scratch, are generally referred to as **rent seeking**. Rent seeking can be as simple as theft, or it can consist of lobbying activites to induce government to pass legislation that favors one industry over other industries. The term was first coined by Anne Krueger (1974) in an influential paper in which she investigated the welfare effects of import restrictions in Turkey. The basic concept that Krueger called rent-seeking had actually been described earlier by Gordon Tullock (1967), who devoted a career to analyzing situations where incentives lead individuals or firms to apply scarce and costly resources to influence government to bring about transfers in their favor. Krueger observed that in Turkey many very talented individuals spent most of their working hours lobbying the government officials who had the power to issue import permits. These rent-seekers were talented people who were quite capable of engaging in productive activity, but they elected to lobby for favors

---

[5] Douglass North (1987), p. 425.
[6] Paul M. Romer (1998).

instead. Why? The Turkish government's import restrictions created a scarce commodity, import permits, which let favored importers capture rents equal to the difference between foreign prices and protected domestic prices.

From the perspective of individual entrepreneurs, it was perfectly rational to seek the rents that the import permits provided. But, the rent-seeking activity was a waste of resources from the perspective of Turkey's overall welfare. The import quota created an abnormal return to an activity that added nothing to Turkey's output of welfare-enhancing goods and services but nevertheless used up resources that could have been used to produce welfare-enhancing goods. Krueger calculated that the total cost of rent seeking in Turkey in the early 1970s could have been as much as 14 percent of the national product.

13.2.3 An example of rent seeking

In economics, the term **rent** refers to the return to a factor that exceeds its opportunity cost, or what is necessary to keep that factor employed in its current function as opposed to some other application. You may recall from your microeconomics course that in perfect competition each factor receives exactly the value of its marginal product, and the price of a good is exactly equal to the sum of the costs of all the factors and resources used to produce it. In the case of perfect competition, the only time there is economic rent is when a factor is in fixed supply, such as in the case of land. But, economic rent can also occur when the market exhibits some degree of monopoly power or when some restriction prevents an otherwise-competitive market from clearing at the competitive equilibrium. Resource-using *rent-seeking* activities like lobbying, public relations, networking, and other ways of courting favors from government, often seek to enhance monopoly power, reinforce a market failure to one's own advantage, or prevent a competitive market outcome.

A simple example of how rent-seeking activity can change a market outcome in favor of one group, to the detriment of another, is given in Figure 13.5. The supply curve for spaghetti is drawn as a horizontal line, which implies that the spaghetti industry operates under constant marginal costs. The demand curve for spaghetti is downward-sloping as usual, reflecting the fact that each additional box of spaghetti consumed adds less to welfare than did the previous box. In a competitive market, where there are large numbers of potential buyers and many producers, the equilibrium price will be equal to P_C. The producers earn just enough on each box of spaghetti to pay the variable costs of producing that box. Total variable costs are equal to the rectangle A, which is the product of the marginal cost of each box of spaghetti and the quantity of spaghetti. There are no excess profits above the cost of the resources and factors needed to produce the spaghetti.

Suppose now that, instead of a large number of competitive suppliers who take the price as given, there is just one monopoly supplier of spaghetti. A monopolist would be foolish to sell spaghetti at price P_C. By charging a higher

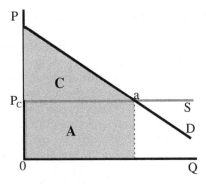

Figure 13.5 The Welfare Gains from a Market for Spaghetti

price, the monopolist can earn a profit. As shown in Figure 13.6, the price that maximizes profit is the price that results in the quantity where the marginal revenue curve intersects the horizontal marginal cost curve. The monopolist's profit-maximizing price is, therefore, P_M.

Comparing the competitive equilibrium and the monopoly equilibrium, consumers of spaghetti were much better off under the competitive equilibrium. In the competitive case, the entire area caP_C represents **consumer surplus**, which is the total benefits received by consumers over and above the cost of the spaghetti. A monopolist gains profit by restricting supply, raising the price to P_M, and appropriating the box B from the consumer surplus area in Figure 13.6. Monopoly power thus effectively transfers part of the welfare of consumers to a monopoly producer with the market power to set the price. The box B is the rent sought by the monopolist, but consumers lose areas B and L. Area L is thus the deadweight loss; the monopolist gains less than consumers lose, and the economy produces less welfare when the monopolist sets the price at P_M.

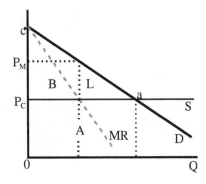

Figure 13.6 An imperfectly-competitive market

Suppose now that we are back in the situation described in Figure 13.5, with a large number of competitive producers. But, suppose also that these producers are rational and they understand how a monopolist would behave. They might be led to engage in rent-seeking activity and seek institutions that would effectively force them to behave collectively the way a monopolist would behave. One possible institutional change the spaghetti producers could introduce is to create some type of industry organization that has the exclusive right to market spaghetti in the country. Such an organization, or **cartel**, could acquire a reduced supply from each firm, sell the smaller amount of spaghetti at the monopoly price, and then distribute the "monopoly" profits to each of the producers.

The cartel has to find some way to enforce this cartel, however, because once the cartel is successful in raising prices, there is a strong incentive for individual firms to supply more product to the market outside the cartel arrangement because, once the cartel succeeds in reducing supply, the price received by each supplier is above the marginal cost of production. Enforcement of the limits on supply by each producer may require a substantial staff of monitors, inspectors, and auditors. So long as the costs of enforcement are less than the size of the box B, the cartel improves the well-being of the producers, but the costs to society are nevertheless likely to be higher than just the standard deadweight loss because enforcement costs use up part of the profit box B.

An attractive strategy of the competitive suppliers would be to convince the government to step in and enforce the cartel. Unlike the would-be private cartel, the government has coercive power backed up by armed police, courts, and prisons. The spaghetti producers association could lobby the government to enforce a minimum price of P_M or maximum output levels for each firm. Producers might be willing to devote some portion of the potential rent, area B in Figure 13.6, to pay for the lobbyists, the bribery, the campaign contributions, or the public relations campaign to get the government to agree to the scheme. This lobbying cost may be cheaper for the producers than enforcing the cartel themselves because government officials might be willing to commit publically-funded police and investigators in exchange for a small bribe or campaign contribution. The bribed government officials do not pay for the enforcement, and taxpayers are seldom aware of precisely where their taxes are spent.

Another approach to capturing the potential monopoly rent in box B of Figure 13.6 is for a small group of spaghetti producers to band together and lobby or convince the government to prohibit production of spaghetti by anyone except them. Or, they could lobby or bribe to gain passage of a law that sets arbitrary standards for spaghetti production that they know many producers cannot meet, thereby limiting production to a smaller number of producers.

You might ask why any government would do any of these things and how it could get away with such schemes. The fact is that governments routinely favor specific producers over consumers. In Europe, Japan, and many other countries, for example, food prices are propped up through government intervention in agricultural markets. One reason for this government support of farmers and the food industry is that these producers have done a very good job of lobbying, that is, rent-seeking.

13.2.4 A final comment on rent seeking

Rent seeking is widespread. Since most economic policies, including taxes, subsidies, government regulations, and the provision of public goods involve a redistribution of some sort, most government policy decisions can trigger some form of rent seeking activity. Pranab Bardhan (1993) surveys articles on the relationship between democracy and economic growth, and he describes the conflict between encouraging citizen activism and preventing rent seeking as "one of the fundamental organizational dilemmas of democratic development... how to reconcile the demands of an open polity for legitimacy and accountability... with the necessary insulation of the policy process from the marauding lobbies of distributive politics."[7] The use of resources to influence government, whether for a blatant grab of someone else's wealth, as in the case of the spaghetti cartel, or simply to let the government know how you feel about an issue, inevitably uses scarce resources and thus has real opportunity costs.

13.2.5 The comparative advantage of government

In order to determine the proper role of the government in the economy, Anne Krueger (1990), suggests that the split in economic activity among markets and government should also follow the logic of comparative advantage. Her reasoning is based on her experience in working in developing economies, where the managerial and administrative skills needed for the government to carry out the difficult tasks asked of it are very scarce. This scarcity of human resources implies that:

> ... undertaking any activity in the government sector is costly because it places an even greater drain on scarce administrative and organizational resources; not only will scarce talent be drained from the private sector, but administration of other governmental activities is likely to be weakened... Government is a non-market organization, and it generally must do things on a large scale. It should follow that activities such as maintenance of law and order (including especially enforcement of contract), provision of information (such as agricultural research and extension) and provision of basic public services which are inherently large-scale in scope

---

[7] Pranab Bardhan (1993), p. 47.

(such as roads and communications) are those in which the government is at no disadvantage in providing services on a large scale and where private agents may face a disadvantage in attempting to do so.[8]

In other words, even if there are many legitimate potential roles for the government to play in the economy, the government generally does not have enough resources or the expertise to do all things. Thus, government, like households, businesses, and society as a whole, needs to make choices; it should concentrate on doing those things it can do comparatively well. Pursuing idealized government programs and actions that have no chance of succeeding in practice make no more sense than expecting a monopolized and institutionally hampered partial market system to efficiently allocate society's resources.

13.3 Corruption

Rent-seeking activities include a variety of legal ways to induce government officials to tilt the institutions of government in one's favor. In many democracies, campaign contributions are perfectly legal and actively encouraged. Lobbying activity by special interest groups to make their interests known to politicians and policy makers is also an accepted form of political activity in most countries.

Some rent-seeking activities are considered to be illegal. Most countries ban bribery, threats, and kickbacks to influence government activity. Such activities are classified as forms of **corruption**, which is the illegal use of public institutions for private benefit. Public officials may also use their powers to tax, spend, regulate, or oversee for their own gain rather than for the purpose their power was granted. Government is operated by individual people with the same mixtures of strengths, weaknesses, and self-serving motivations that characterize all people. These individuals are guided by the same formal and informal institutions that they are charged with counteracting as government officials.

13.3.1 Casual evidence of corruption

Corruption has received increased attention in the press and official circles in recent years. Indicative of the types of news we have seen is the following report that appeared some years ago in *The Wall Street Journal*:

SHANGHAI, China — China disclosed Tuesday that $25.8 billion has disappeared from state grain-purchase funds in the past six years, one of the most dramatic

---

[8] Anne O. Krueger (1990), pp. 16–17.

admissions of official ineptitude and corruption since the country's economic reforms began two decades ago.

Between April 1992 and the end of March this year, state loans advanced to buy grain totaled 543.1 billion yuan ($63.61 billion), but grain agencies can only account for purchases and stocks valued at 329.1 billion yuan, the state-run China Business Times reported. A nationwide audit by China's Finance Ministry and the country's central bank found that more than 80 billion yuan allocated for grain purchases had been diverted to hotel and luxury-housing projects, stocks and futures trading or to purchases of cars and mobile phones, the newspaper said.[9]

The sheer magnitude of the money involved is astounding. Clearly, some people have gotten very wealthy diverting funds destined for one purpose to their own personal benefit. There is also the question of whether the Chinese government should have been spending its citizens' money to purchase grain in the first place, but the fact is that it was and it failed miserably to perform its intended task.

Corruption is not exclusively a characteristic of developing economies, of course. For example, the U.S. occupation of Iraq after its 2003 invasion has been rife with corruption, the scope of which is suggested by the apparent "disappearance" of as much as $18 billion in cash distributed by the U.S. administration there.[10] Corruption in Iraq did not begin with the U.S. invasion of Iraq, however. Paul Volcker's probe into the *Oil-for-Food Program* administered by the United Nations in Iraq between the 1991 Gulf War and the 2003 U.S. invasion uncovered widespread corruption on the part of private firms in many countries, government officials of many developed countries, and United Nations administrators.[11] The U.S. invasion of Afghanistan has also been plagued by the disappearance of great sums of money targeted by the U.S. for specific military and economic development projects. The U.S. occupation has been further plagued by the resurgence of the opium trade, a result of U.S. support of local warlords, who have effectively been empowered to regain their former prominence in the world opium trade.[12]

Corruption does not require the confusion of war to permit it to thrive, however. From the May 29, 2009, issue of *Ethics Newsline*, published by the Institute for Global Ethics, reported that in India $580 million flowed to judges each year, obviously with the intention of influencing court outcomes. This is a very substantial sum in a low income country. Corruption has also flourished in

---

[9] Craig S. Smith (1998), "China Says $25.8 Billion for Grain Is Missing," *The Wall Street Journal*, Tuesday, October 14, p. A15.

[10] Aljazeera News (2011), "Missing Iraq cash 'as high as $18bn'," Aljazeera English website, June 19, available at http://english.aljazeera.net/news/middleeast/2011/06/2011.

[11] Claudio Gatti and Mark Turner (2004), "Dealing with Saddam's Regime: How Fortunes Were Made in Iraq through the UN's Oil-for-Food Programme," *Financial Times*, April 8.

[12] See, for example, Philip Shishkin and David Crawford (2006), "In Afghanistan, Heroin Trade Soars Despite U.S. Trade," *The Wall Street Journal*, January 18.

the former Soviet Union, where the collapse of communist regimes left an institutional vacuum. For example, a journalist for *The Economist* reported recently how, while driving to an important meeting at the Kremlin in Moscow, he was stopped by a policeman. The reporter negotiated a modest bribe, but when he looked in his wallet he found the smallest bill he had was 1,000 rubles, about $30. This was much more than the usual bribe for questionable traffic stops, but the policeman quickly proposed that for 1,000 rubles he would forgive the traffic violation and also escort the reporter through traffic to the Kremlin. With police car's siren blaring and lights flashing ahead of him, the journalist easily made his appointment.[13]

Judicial systems are not immune to corruption in developed countries. The *New York Times* reports that in 2004, after a $9.3 million campaign for a judge in a Southern state, the elected judge voted to reverse a $430 million breach of contract verdict against State Farm Insurance. Not coincidentally, employees, lawyers, and others affiliated with the company had made a combined $350,000 in campaign contributions to the very same judge just months earlier.[14] Research also showed that in the state of Ohio over a 12 year period, there were 215 cases where state judges were assigned to cases that involved campaign contributors. In only nine cases did the judges recuse themselves from the proceedings. The judges voted in favor of the contributor in over 70 percent of the remaining cases.

Another incredible story of government corruption also comes from the United States.[15] In early 2009, two juvenile court judges in the state of Pennsylvania were found to have taken $2.6 million in bribes from privately-operated prisons in Pennsylvania in exchange for sending more people to prison. The two judges routinely ignored calls for leniency from prosecutors and sentenced thousands of youths accused minor crimes or misdemeanors to extended stays in one of the newly constructed private prisons in their district. One girl was sentenced to 11 months in prison for a schoolyard fight in which no one was hurt. Another was sentenced to 3 months imprisonment for posting a mildly insulting message on a Web site. This horrendous case of corruption seriously harmed children and in some cases may have resulted in irreversible mental impacts because of the poor treatment of young inmates in for-profit private prisons. Left out of the news reports was the fact that Pennsylvania legislators had only recently decided to shift to private prisons, allegedly because government was less efficient than private firms in providing prison services. Do you suppose the lawmakers who voted to privatize state prisons might have been influenced by rent seeking by the private prison providers?

---

[13] *The Economist* (2006), "How to Grease a Palm," December 21.

[14] Dorothy Samuels (2006), "Judges for Sale," *New York Times*, December 12.

[15] Reported by Amy Goodman (2009), "Jailing Kids for Cash," *Democracy Now!*, February 17.

Table 13.1 Transparency International's Corruption Perception Index — 2007[1]

Country	Rank	Index	Country	Rank	Index	Country	Rank	Index
Denmark	1	9.4	Saint Vincent	30	6.1	"		
Finland	1	9.4	Qatar	32	6.0	"		
New Zealand	1	9.4	Malta	33	5.8	Belarus	150	2.1
Singapore	4	9.3	Macao	34	5.7	Ecuador	150	2.1
Sweden	4	9.3	Taiwan	34	5.7	Kazakhstan	150	2.1
Iceland	6	9.2	UAE	34	5.7	Kenya	150	2.1
Netherlands	7	9.0	Dominica	37	5.6	Kyrgyzstan	150	2.1
Switzerland	7	9.0	Botswana	38	5.4	Liberia	150	2.1
Canada	9	8.7	Cyprus	39	5.3	Sierra Leone	150	2.1
Norway	9	8.7	Hungary	39	5.3	Tajikistan	150	2.1
Australia	11	8.6	Czech Rep.	41	5.2	Zimbabwe	150	2.1
United Kingdom	12	8.4	Italy	41	5.2	Bangladesh	162	2.0
Luxembourg	12	8.4	Malaysia	43	5.1	Cambodia	162	2.0
Hong Kong	14	8.3	South Africa	43	5.1	Cen.Africa	162	2.0
Austria	15	8.1	South Korea	43	5.1	Papua N. Gui.	162	2.0
Germany	16	7.8	Bahrain	46	5.0	Turkmenistan	162	2.0
Ireland	17	7.5	Bhutan	46	5.0	Venezuela	162	2.0
Japan	17	7.5	Costa Rica	46	5.0	Congo, Dem R.	168	1.9
France	19	7.3	Cape Verde	49	4.9	Eq. Guinea	168	1.9
United States	20	7.2	Slovakia	49	4.9	Guinea	168	1.9
Belgium	21	7.1	Latvia	51	4.8	Laos	168	1.9
Chile	22	7.0	Lithuania	51	4.8	Afghanistan	172	1.8
Barbados	22	6.9	Jordan	53	4.7	Chad	172	1.8
Saint Lucia	24	6.8	Mauritius	53	4.7	Sudan	172	1.8
Spain	25	6.7	Oman	53	4.7	Tonga	175	1.7
Uruguay	25	6.7	Greece	56	4.6	Uzbekistan	175	1.7
Slovenia	27	6.6	Namibia	57	4.5	Haiti	177	1.6
Estonia	28	6.5	Kuwait	58	4.3	Iraq	178	1.5
Portugal	28	6.5	Cuba	59	4.2	Myanmar	179	1.4
Israel	30	6.1	Poland	59	4.2	Somalia	179	1.4

Source: Transparency International, as taken from their website, transparency.org, on October 20, 2007.

[1] For the full table and countries ranked between 60 and 150, see www.transparency.org.

13.3.2 Measures of worldwide corruption

Berlin-based *Transparency International*, a non-profit organization founded to combat corruption around the world, every year ranks countries on a scale of zero to ten, with the most corrupt countries close to zero. These rankings are based on surveys of businesspeople, risk analysts, and the general public, so they are subjective. Transparency International makes their rankings public at www.transparency.org. The 2007 rankings are given in Table 13.1.

Note that, in general, more developed countries tend to be characterized by lower levels of corruption. All five Scandinavian countries are among the ten least corrupt countries in the list. Many poor African countries are at the bottom of the list. But there are some surprises. The United States' score is twentieth on the list. Perhaps it should not be so surprising that the 2007–2009 financial crisis was sparked by fraud in the U.S. mortgage market. Note also that the Asian tiger economies of Singapore and Hong Kong are ranked at very low levels of corruption, among many developed economies of Europe. Does this help to explain their economic success?

13.3.3 The conditions for corruption

The underlying cause of government corruption is the set of incentives that encourage people to rent seek or to refrain from rent seeking. Among these incentives are institutions, of course. So an important question is: Have the institutions that encourage corruption become more prominent in the world economy? Since government corruption is defined as *the abuse of public power for private benefit*, the incentives for government corruption are to be found in the ways that government is empowered to redirect income and wealth from some groups to others. Among those ways are:

> **Regulation** — Many governments, in accordance with some of the justifications given above, regulate many economic activities, such as setting prices, wages, the number of hours worked, the quantity of imports permitted, safety regulations, and the qualifications for professional licensing. Regulations can induce those who are being regulated to bribe officials to look the other way. For example, in Korea the bribery of building inspectors induced them to ignore the violation of building codes, and the substandard construction of a department store that later collapsed with a considerable loss of life.[16]

> **Authorizations and Permits** — In most countries, government has the power to authorize or deny citizens the right to do many things. Liquor licenses are needed for restaurants to serve alcoholic drinks to customers, driver's licenses are needed to drive a car, a building permit is required to build a house, a merchant's license is needed to open a store, etc. The rules for issuing such permits and authorizations are often imprecise and complicated. In Brazil, people known as *despachantes* (dispatchers) rent out their experience in dealing with the Brazilian government bureaucracy. Despachantes know which bureaucrats to deal with, the order in which the bureaucratic hoops must be jumped through, and, in some cases, who and how much to bribe. Despachantes are routinely employed to acquire simple documents such a passport, automobile registration, or a driver's license. The over 180,000 lobbyists working in Washington, DC, represent a more sophisticated U.S. version of Brazilian despachantes. Lobbyists work to gain government favors for entire industries and special interest

---

[16] As reported in Susan Rose-Ackerman (1997).

groups. The number of lobbyists has also grown greatly in Brussels, the home of the European Union.

Taxation — Governments tax in order to pay for the activities they perform and the transfer payments they make. Taxation is often complex. Income taxes require extensive documentation and records, sales taxes require invoices and sales slips, and employment taxes require extensive records on hours worked and wages paid. Property taxes require estimates of the value of the property being taxed. In many developing countries, taxpayers openly ignore requirements to pay taxes, secure in the fact that there will be no consequences. In many developed countries, taxpayers hire financial advisors to help navigate the complexities of tax laws and regulations, and it is seldom clear to what extent final tax payments are legal or not.

Transfers and Subsidies — Whenever government has the power to hand out money or goods, there are obvious incentives for corruption. While most government programs that provide people with payments, goods, or services have established criteria for deciding who receives government payments, such criteria are often vague, easily satisfied using falsified documents, or simply ignored.

Government Expenditures — Governments spend large amounts of money on construction projects, transportation equipment, military hardware, and other government purchases. Kickbacks on such government purchases constitute one of the main categories of government corruption. Because it is more difficult to demand kickbacks on maintenance and upkeep of existing equipment and infrastructure, we observe frequent building of new infrastructure rather than maintaining existing infrastructure in developing economies. According to Tanzi and Davoodi (1998): "In cases of extreme corruption, operation of and maintenance on the physical infrastructure of a country are intentionally neglected so that some infrastructure will need to be rebuilt, thus allowing corrupt officials the opportunity to extract additional commissions from new investment projects."[17] Perhaps it should not be surprising, therefore, that in the reconstruction of Iraq, the U.S. occupation administration quickly dismissed all of the Iraqi government maintenance and engineering agencies that had been holding the precarious electricity grid together. With the collapse of the system, the U.S. occupation administration could then justify awarding contracts to foreign companies to build completely new electricity distribution systems that

---

[17] Vito Tanzi and Hamid Davoodi (1998), p. 8.

were incompatible with the existing system.[18] The shift to using private contractors for providing routine maintenance and services for U.S. troops fighting wars overseas is troubling: if there are large profits to be made providing U.S. soldiers with meals, lodging, and transportation services, will these firms lobby for the United States to engage in more active wars?

Financial Repression — Financial repression in the form of interest rate ceilings, common in many countries that use low interest rates to effectively subsidize certain borrowers, implies that markets are not allowed to clear. Hence, some rationing scheme must be devised, which opens up the possibility for corruption. Illegal payments and other benefits are often made to obtain below-market interest rates. Such a below-market price almost guarantees that investment funds will be inefficiently allocated. The well-connected and the unscrupulous get the funds, not the poor or the entrepreneurs targeted by the programs. When living in São Paulo, Brazil, your author was offered a low-interest loan to build a weekend cabin by a bank loan officer recommended by the builder; the loan officer worked for a government-owned bank and made no secret of the fact that he was offering money diverted from a subsidized program intended to fund homes for low-income workers.[19]

Privatization of Government Assets — In recent years, governments have increasingly privatized public infrastructure and government-owned enterprises, especially in centrally-planned economies and developing economies that pursued rapid industrialization through direct government investment. Privatization offered opportunities for private buyers to acquire valuable resources at favorable prices, especially if they could influence the bidding process. There are many examples of former Communist Party officials in the countries that made up the former U.S.S.R. ending up with ownership of former government-owned enterprises and property, often for extremely low prices that bear no connection to the true worth of the assets. The richest man in the world in 2010, Carlos Slim of Mexico, made his multi-billion dollar fortune by using his political influence and, many contend, willingness to reward Mexican officials to let him buy the Mexican public telephone company along with the stipulation that the company would keep its monopoly status in the Mexican market. Slim provided better services, but he also increased prices drastically and became extremely wealthy.

---

[18] Michael Schwartz (2008), "Wrecked Iraq: What the Good News from Iraq Really Means," TomDispatch.com, downloaded on October 10.

[19] We sought regular financing instead. Later on we were defrauded by the builder, who took the downpayment and declared insolvency before completing the cabin.

13.3.4 How can corruption be reduced?

The discussion above makes it clear that there are many government activities that provide opportunities for corruption. These opportunities for wrong-doing must be taken in the context of other counteracting factors because we see great variation in the levels of corruption across countries, as suggested by the corruption index given in Table 13.1. John Mukum Mbaku (1996) attributed bureaucratic corruption to the rules and institutions bureaucrats operate under:

> Given the incentive system provided by existing rules, legal strategies and other forms of corruption cleanups are unlikely to be effective. In addition to the fact that manipulating outcomes within the rules is not an effective way to secure the outcomes desired by society, these strategies can only function effectively if the counteracting agencies and those who manage them are properly constrained by a rule of law and are free of corruption. Many of the police officers and judges who are called upon to cleanup corruption are themselves beneficiaries of the corrupt system of resource allocation...[20]

Hence, when informal institutions, namely the local culture, effectively approves of corruption, the best formal government institutions may not be able to prevent corruption.

It may be nearly impossible to eliminate all government corruption, however, for the simple reason that government has power. As the saying goes, "power corrupts." The corrupting influence of power is very nicely illustrated in an interview by George Lefcoe, a former commissioner at the Los Angeles County Regional Planning Commission, on why he retired:

> I really missed the cards from engineers I never met, the wine and cheese from development companies I never heard of, and, especially, the honeybaked ham from, of all places, Forest Lawn [Cemetery], even though the company was never an applicant before the commission when I was there.
>
> But because I missed them I think it was a good idea that I resigned. I do not think it is wise to stay in public office too long a time.
>
> My first Christmas as commissioner — when I received the ham — I tried to return it at once, though for the record, I did not, since no one at Forest Lawn seemed authorized to accept hams, apparently not even for burial. My guess is that none of the many public servants who received the ham ever had tried to return it.
>
> When I received another ham the next Christmas, I gave it to a worthy charity. The next year, some worthy friends were having a party so I gave it to them. The next year I had a party and we enjoyed the ham.
>
> In the fifth year, about the tenth of December, I began wondering, where is my ham?[21]

---

[20] John Mukum Mbaku (1995), p. 115.

[21] As reported in *The Wall Street Journal* (1998), "Notables & Quotables," December 18, p. A14.

Recall that psychological studies show that humans adapt to changing circumstances and, eventually, accept them as normal. Recall also Pierre Bourdieu's sociological description of the habitus, or set of acquired dispositions, that guides individual action within a field. The dominant role of habitus in shaping human behavior suggests that when corruption becomes the norm in a society, it is difficult to eliminate it. This is evident in the fact that Transparency International's ratings change very little from year to year. This apparent fact also underscores the importance of the whole set of informal and formal institutions for explaining economic behavior.

13.3.5 *Measuring the effect of corruption on growth*

Paolo Mauro (1995) tested the effect of corruption on economic growth. He uses information from *Business International*, a consulting group, to construct an index of corruption. Specifically, he uses the results of three separate surveys on (1) the integrity of the legal environment and the judiciary, (2) the regulatory environment and "red tape" faced by firms and entrepreneurs, and (3) the predominance of actual corruption and questionable payments. In his statistical regression analysis, Mauro finds that corruption is highly significant as an explanatory variable of economic growth. Further analysis shows that corruption works through investment; the higher is corruption, the lower is investment. The value of the corruption coefficient in Mauro's regressions is also quite high. For example, if Uruguay were to have the same regulatory environment, low level of red tape, and low level of corruption as the United Kingdom, then all other things equal it would have grown by over one-half of one percentage point faster. Hence, government institutions seem to substantially influence economic growth through their effect on corruption.

Mauro' study has been widely referenced in the economic development literature, but subsequent statistical studies have brought its conclusions into question. For example, Jakob Svensson (2005) examined a cross-section of developing countries and found no statistically significant relationship. M. T. Rock and H. Bonnett (2004) calculated four different indicators of corruption and then tested the statistical relationship between those indicators and GDP growth. They found that corruption slows growth in most developing countries, but in large East Asian emerging economies (China, Indonesia, South Korea, Thailand, and Japan) corruption is actually positively related to economic growth. As the Appendix to the last chapter explained, statistical studies of institutions are difficult and subject to misinterpretations. The relationship between corruption and institutions is too complex for simple statistical procedures to accurately measure it. Development economics will have to pursue other routes to understanding, such as more case studies and more holistic analyses of the economic effects of specific formal policies. Also, better data on institutions and economic development are needed. The contradictions in the statistical results could simply be the result of variations in the accuracy and scope of the data used.

13.4 Informal Activity: Making the Best of Bad Institutions

Hernando de Soto (1989), in his very influential book on economic development in Peru, describes the difficulties that migrants from the Andean highlands face when they arrive in the capital city of Lima in search of a better life. New migrants have difficulty finding inexpensive housing and well-paying work with legal employers. They almost invariably end up living and working in what is known as the **informal sector** of the economy.[22]

The migrants build housing using whatever materials they can find or purchase cheaply, and the structures usually violate official building codes. Moreover, the houses are often built on land that the migrants do not own; they often simply invade open space, sometimes as part of a large group of *invasores* who seek safety in numbers. The migrants usually find a job working for a small business or independent entrepreneurs who are not legally registered, do not contribute to government mandated retirement, unemployment, and other funds on behalf of the worker, and who often do not pay the official minimum wage. If the migrants cannot find a job, they do such things such as selling gum on a street corner, waiting outside supermarkets to carry groceries home for people, cleaning cars, simply begging, or engaging in any other activity that brings in some precious coins to put food on the table.

13.4.1 Informality is a widespread phenomenon

The situation in Peru, described by de Soto, is repeated in nearly all other developing economies. In these countries, the informal sector exists side by side with the **formal sector**, which is the part of the economy that operates according to the country's formal legal institutions. This coexistence of informal and formal sectors, with the formal sector providing much higher standards of living than the informal sector, has led many development economists to refer to developing economies as **dual economies**. But, this term is misleading in that it implies that an economy such as Peru's is really two separate economies, not a single integrated economy. Actually, the informal and formal sectors are closely related, and they operate under the same institutions. The coexistence of formal and informal sectors is what happens when people are constrained by poorly functioning institutions.

Informal activities and markets should not automatically be equated with poverty, exploitation, or marginalization, all terms which describe a *condition*;

---

[22] Other names are *shadow economy, underground economy*, and *black market*. We prefer the name *informal*, because it contrasts directly with the *formal sector*.

rather, informal activities exchanged in informal markets are a *process* that can generate a range of incomes, involves many independent entrepreneurs as well as factory workers, and can account for a very large share of an economy's total output. Nor does informal activity imply that there are illicit goods and services involved. The informal sectors in developing countries almost always produce goods and services that are similar, or even identical, to those produced in the formal sector, e.g., restaurant meals, haircuts, appliance repair services, and taxi rides are simultaneously supplied by formal and informal suppliers. Obviously, illicit services such as prostitution and the forgery of documents will, by definition, be produced in the informal sector since they are also illegal acts in most countries. The basic distinction between formal and informal activities depends not on the characteristics of the goods and services produced, but rather on whether the production process and the distribution of the products conform to formal legal and regulatory requirements.

13.4.2 Informal economic activity is a form of rent evasion

In the case of rent seeking activity, people attempt to influence the policies and institutions that create restrictions on individual economic behavior. Informal activity, on the other hand, is an attempt to carry out mutually-beneficial transactions *despite* rules, laws, or other institutions that restrict them. In effect, informal activity is **rent-evading activity**. The results of rent-evading activity depend on the institutions, or incentives, that establish the relative costs and benefits of engaging in formal and informal activity.

The formal and informal markets are closely linked. Suppose, for example, that an informal market develops because only a limited number of suppliers are awarded official permits to perform a service or supply a product, say taxi services. Depending on how many taxi permits are issued, some number of suppliers who cannot operate officially will be motivated to provide their services informally. If informal suppliers offer their services for less, some consumers will cross over to the informal market as well. Hence, in orthodox neoclassical terms, when an informal market arises, both supply and demand are diminished in the formal market, and there will be some equilibrium price difference between formal and informal markets.

The informal market may not carry out all the transactions that were prevented from taking place in the formal market by the regulation. The evasion of laws and regulations by consumers and/or suppliers may be more risky or more costly. Perhaps the taxi drivers risk going to jail if they get caught supplying services without a license. Or, consumers riding in informal taxis risk punishment. Hence, not all restricted supply in the formal market spills over to an informal market. Of course, if governments do not enforce the restrictions on formal taxi services, then most taxis will avoid getting the permits, and the informal market will dominate. In the extreme case where consumers are not at all reluctant to buy in the informal market, the price and licensing regulations would do the licensed suppliers no good at all because all demand would spill into the informal market and there would be no formal transactions. Informality, or rent-evasion, may thus actually help to limit the ability of some groups to use the government to gain a monopoly in the economy; if government institutions are not up to the task of enforcing the restrictions on competition, there will be little rent to be gained from rent-seeking.

13.4.3 Estimates of informal activity

Table 13.2 lists some recent estimates of informal activity for developed economies. Table 13.3 presents available estimates compiled from a variety of

Table 13.2 Informal Sector as a Percentage of GDP: Selected Developed Countries

Greece	28.5%	Finland	18.0%	Netherlands	13.0%
Italy	27.0	Denmark	17.9	New Zealand	12.6
Spain	22.5	Germany	16.3	Great Britain	12.5
Portugal	22.5	Canada	15.8	Japan	11.1
Belgium	22.0	Ireland	15.7	Austria	10.6
Sweden	19.1	France	15.0	Switzerland	9.4
Norway	19.1	Australia	14.1	United States	8.7

Source: Friedrich Schneider and Dominik H. Enste (2000), p. 80.

Table 13.3 Informal Economic Activity: Selected Developing Countries 1994/2000

Country	Informal Workers as % of Active Workers		
	All Workers	*Women*	*Men*
North Africa	48	43	49
Algeria	43	41	43
Tunisia	50	39	53
Egypt	55	46	57
Sub-Saharan Africa	72	84	63
Guinea	72	87	66
Kenya	72	83	59
South Africa	51	58	44
Latin America	51	58	48
Bolivia	63	74	55
Brazil	60	67	55
Chile	36	44	31
Costa Rica	44	48	42
El Salvador	57	69	46
Mexico	55	55	54
Asia			
Indonesia	78	77	78
Philippines	72	73	71
Thailand	51	54	49

Source: Prepared by Jacques Chames for the ILO (2002), *Statistics on the Informal Economy*, Geneva: ILO.

sources and presented by the International Labour Organisation (ILO). These are indirect estimates because there is no actual data available on informal activity. The reliability of the various indirect methods is questionable, but the numbers are large enough to leave little doubt that the informal sector is substantial in most developing economies. Estimates in Tables 13.2 and 13.3 range widely. Overall, informal activity is a lower percentage of economic activity in developed countries compared to less developed countries. Nevertheless, the ratio of informal activity to formal GDP is still high, with few developed countries' informal sectors estimated at less than 10 percent of their GDPs.

13.4.4 Informality is more prevalent in developing countries

Less developed economies tend to have more informal activity than more developed economies for several reasons. First, unequal political power and the persistence of colonial legal structures often means that formal institutions more often clash with the interests of the majority of people. Informality is often a very rational response to those poor institutions.

Second, lower levels of income make complying with rules, regulations, laws, and social norms relatively more costly. For example, a $10 fee for a vendor's permit is as much as a week's income for many of the informal street vendors in Africa, Latin America, or South Asia. Even a $50 fee in a developed country for the same type of permit would be equivalent to only a few hours' work. Where in the developed economy, people simply pay the $50, in a poor country people opt to sell on the street without getting the vendor's permit.

Third, because economic growth is a more recent phenomenon, many existing informal institutions evolved before rapid structural change and economic development occurred. Also, the cultural shock of going from a traditional subsistence economy to a moderate level of development may be much greater than the continual fine-tuning of institutions in an economy that is already highly developed. And in developed countries, cultures may actually glorify change and growth, so that people anticipate adjusting to, rather than resisting, changing circumstances.

13.4.5 Informality and development

The informal sector, by permitting some transactions to be carried out when restrictive institutions would otherwise prevent them from occurring, could be favorable to economic development. But informality has some costs of its own.

Perhaps the greatest cost of informality is that it restricts government's ability to tax and regulate. For government to perform the functions it must carry out in a complex modern economy, as described earlier in this chapter, it must tax. If taxation drives transactions into informal markets, beneficial government activities cannot be funded. For example, taxes fund public goods, fees cover real costs of government services, regulations prevent activities with negative externalities, and permits provide explicit guarantees of quality and competence. In many cases, informal products are of poor quality, and there are many cases of dangerous informal working conditions. For example, informal production of charcoal with double the amount of air pollution compared to regulated formal production does not raise human well-being.

The fact that informal economic activity is technically illegal imposes various costs on participants in informal activities. The government could stop the activity at any time, property may be seized, and people may be punished. Informal production and commerce is thus subject to greater risk. The lack of formal property rights often means that informal businesses have no access to the formal financial markets since they technically do not exist in the eyes of the law. Long-term contracts cannot be enforced in the courts and police protection is often not provided. The lack of formal property rights means potential borrowers have no collateral against which to borrow. As a result, long-term intertemporal transactions are more difficult in an informal market. In fact, evidence shows that informal production tends to be undercapitalized. Therefore, there is less investment and innovation in an informal sector of the economy. Also, with fewer opportunities for small producers and merchants to grow into larger businesses, economies of scale cannot be exploited.

On the positive side, Hernando de Soto (1989) argues that informal activity is a long-run force that can bring about improvements in a country's institutions. Specifically, de Soto describes how Peru's rigid laws and regulations serve to perpetuate the unequal ownership and incomes that have been a characteristic of Peru for centuries. De Soto sees the energy with which people pursue informal economic activities as evidence that they can force a change in the system. Informal activity undermines the gains from rent seeking activities such as lobbying for government regulations and other forms of protection against competition. Also, the informal sector creates a new special-interest group that is likely to lobby for change in the existing institutions. De Soto argues that the arrival of large numbers of people from rural areas of Peru and their organization in informal markets in the large capital city of Lima will ultimately result in a more dynamic and innovative economy.

De Soto's interpretation of informal activity is a new variation of historian Henri Pirenne's well-known hypothesis that the gradual movement of people from feudalistic rural communities to towns and cities in Medieval Europe caused structural economic changes that would, centuries later, enable the Enlightenment and the Industrial Revolution. Pirenne argues that the persistent clash between established interests in the small fortified towns and newly-arrived workers and artisans were the channels through which commerce grew and new ideas took hold. Pirenne (1925, p. 113) described the arrival of newcomers and their construction of suburban settlements outside the established fortified Medieval towns as follows:

Conflicts immediately arose. They were inevitable, in view of the fact that the newcomers, who were strangers, were hardly inclined to value the interests, rights and customs which inconvenienced them. Room had to be made for them as best as could be done, and as their numbers increased their encroachments became more and more bold.

De Soto argues that migration from the Peruvian highlands to Lima will similarly dislodge the privileged classes and stimulate economic change.

Today, 20 years after de Soto wrote about the informal sector in Peru, the economy as measured by GDP has grown substantially, but there is still much poverty and informality. It is still difficult for informal workers from the Andean highlands to break into the formal economy. But then it did take nearly a millennium for migrants and desperate informal workers to completely destroy feudalism and create Europe's modern wealthy economies.

13.4.6 Summarizing the consequences of informality

In sum, informal markets arise because regulation, taxation, or some other distortion in the formal market prevents some suppliers or consumers from completing mutually-beneficial transactions. Informal activities permit at least some of the mutually-beneficial production and transactions restricted by regulation, taxation, or discrimination in formal markets. They are also likely to attract some activities from the formal sector. When there are benefits to the regulations, taxes, and laws that the government introduced into the formal market, such as regulations to stop harmful activities or taxes to compensate for negative externalities, then the informal market clearly reduces overall welfare.

Finally, the presence of informal economic activities reflects incompatibilities between formal and informal institutions. These incompatibilities may reflect the power of some groups to use government to promote their specific interests. Because culture and other informal institutions change slowly, while the political process often pushes formal institutions ahead of culture's path, informality is likely in evolving societies. Informality is thus especially likely in societies where political institutions are easily corrupted and economic and social change is rapid.

13.5 The Institution of Intellectual Property Rights

After the long discussion of government institutional mandates and failures, this section focuses on one specific government institution: **patents** and **copyrights**. These are government-authorized property rights on intellectual creations, hence the general term **intellectual property rights** that is commonly used to describe them. Intellectual property rights are designed to provide a direct incentive for individuals and organizations to create new ideas, technologies, and knowledge, and are perfectly compatible with the Schumpeterian model of technological change. This formal government institution, therefore, appears to be growth-enhancing.

13.5.1 The history of patents and copyrights

Patents and copyrights as we know them today came into use in several countries in the 1700s. The British are often credited with inventing copyrights. In 1710, the British Parliament enacted a statute that prohibited the unauthorized printing, reprinting, or importing of books for a limited number of years following their first appearance. A patent law was also passed at that time in order to encourage inventiveness. But there is evidence that the ancient Greeks used patents to encourage innovation. While the practice was not used in the Roman Empire or elsewhere in the world at that time, references to patents again appear in the Middle Ages.[23] Records show that Venice granted a 10–year monopoly to inventors of silkmaking machines just after 1200. Almost three centuries later, in 1474, Venice passed a general patent statute that recognized patents as a right, not a government favor, to be awarded purely on merit. Galileo was awarded a patent. English kings occasionally awarded exclusive rights to inventors and writers called *letters patent*, but unlike the 1710 statute that authorized patents and copyrights according to objective criteria based on merit, these early patents were often just exclusive monopoly rights for politically connected friends or industries, not rewards for innovation or creativity.

After its independence from England, the founders of the United States explicitly wrote into the Constitution the government's power "to promote the progress of science and useful arts, by securing for limited times to authors and inventors the exclusive right to their respective writings and discoveries."[24] The Patent Act of 1790 and the Copyright Law of the same year were among the first legislative actions of the Congress of the United States following the ratification of the Constitution. Today, patent and copyright laws exist in most countries, although the details of the laws and the enforcement levels vary considerably from country to country.

13.5.2 The patent as a property right to an idea

A patent is, first of all, a formal recognition of a person, group of persons, or organization's invention, scientific discovery, or technological enhancement. Second, a patent assigns to that person, group of persons, or organization the exclusive right to apply the invention, discovery, or technique, or to sell the right

---

[23] Ramon A. Klitzke (1964).

[24] Article I, Section 8 of the Constitution of the United States.

to others. A copyright similarly gives authors, composers, movie producers, and other producers of creative works the exclusive right to decide how their books, symphonies, films, and other works are to be used and marketed. Intellectual property rights effectively make nonrival goods like ideas, designs, and musical melodies legally excludable, thus permitting their owners to extract rents from their use in production.

The economic rationale for patents and copyrights should be clear. Recalling our discussion of the Schumpeter model in Chapter 8, costly innovation and R&D activity cannot take place without some mechanism for recovering the up-front costs. The property rights accorded by a patent or copyright permit the owners of the intellectual property rights to recover their up-front costs in the form of monopoly rents.

13.5.3 The cost of protecting intellectual property rights

There are substantial enforcement costs involved with patents and copyrights because others may have strong incentives to steal valuable ideas. Ideas are nonrival goods, which implies that, save the costs imposed by patents and copyrights, their marginal cost to a new user is low. For patents and copyrights to effectively provide inventors and creators with rents, suspected theft must be investigated, and confirmed theft must be punished and original innovators must be compensated. This generally requires government institutions such as investigators, police, lawyers, and courts. Confirming patent or copyright infringement is not always easy, and enforcement requires fairly sophisticated institutions and talented people.

A further difficulty with patents and copyrights is deciding how long they should remain in force. On the one hand, the longer the patent or copyright, the greater the rewards to inventors, researchers, authors, and artists. On the other hand, longer periods of protection may make subsequent innovation more difficult because a patent makes the subsequent extension of discoveries and ideas more expensive. Recall the discussion of the combinatoric nature of knowledge: new ideas build on old ideas. Hence, intellectual property rights can restrict subsequent use of those ideas in the combinatoric processes that increase human knowledge.

The conflict between the need to cover the costs of creating new ideas and the potentially restrictive effect of property rights on the dissemination of new ideas throughout the economy is not as great as it seems, however. Property rights give inventors a monopoly in using a new idea, and they can also market that idea to others who can use it more productively than the original innovator. Naomi Lamoreaux and Kenneth Sokoloff (1999) contend that making ideas and creations marketable is as important a function of intellectual property rights as the creation of monopoly rights. The opportunity to trade patent rights increases the value of an innovation because the inventor does not have to also be a manufacturer, marketer, or entrepreneur in order to capture the profits from an innovation. Lamoreaux and Sokoloff argue that patent laws permit innovators to specialize in what they do best: innovate. This means innovators can exploit their comparative advantage in innovation without having to organize production to exploit the innovation. Making patents marketable also promotes the dissemination of ideas to those who are in the best position to exploit them. Some European countries have *required* patent holders to license their ideas to anyone willing to pay a reasonable license fee, thus enabling them to earn rent but not allowing them to absolutely restrict use of their valuable ideas.

13.5.4 International protection of intellectual property rights

The worldwide trade negotiations known as the "Uruguay Round," which created the World Trade Organization (WTO) in 1994 and has now been ratified by over 150 countries, set goals for establishing uniform rules for intellectual property rights to replace the widely diverse set of national rules that have developed over the past several hundred years. For example, the United States, provided patent holders with protection for 17 years following the issuance of the patent while some European countries offered protection for up to fifty years. Copyrights in the United States protects authors for 50 years after their death. Many developing economies and former communist countries had weak or nonexistent patent and copyright protection.

In some countries, a patent is awarded to the first person to register an idea. In other countries the patent is awarded to the first inventor of the idea. Obviously, it is easier to register the first person who comes to the patent office with a new idea; discovering who actually thought up the new idea first could be problematic. But that practical consideration was not what led countries to adopt the "first-to-register" procedure over the "true inventor" principle. The first-to-register procedure is a holdover from the days when countries encouraged the borrowing of foreign technology, and the first-to-register procedure, by rewarding the person who brought a new idea from abroad, encouraged the importation of new technology. The first-to-register procedure has led to international conflict because, not infrequently, the same technology has been patented by different people in different countries. Interestingly, the revision of U.S. patent law in 2011 to switch from the *first to innovate* principle to the *first to register* principle was allegedly intended to harmonize procedures across countries, but it could also trigger more industrial espionage. The switch could also benefit well organized corporate R&D departments at the expense of independent innovators located far from innovative centers.

All members of the World Trade Organization (WTO) have agreed to adhere to the Berne Convention, which establishes the basic rules for patent and copyright protection. The Berne Convention dates back to 1866 but has been updated and amended many times. For example, the WTO trade negotiations begun in the early 2000s also established that computer programs would, from now on, fall under the Berne Convention. As for patents, members of the WTO have agreed to provide patent protection for twenty years from the date of application for products and processes, with equal treatment for nationals and foreigners. Despite signing the WTO agreement, not all nations enforce the rules with equal vigor.

13.5.5 Patents as an example of the clash of formal and informal incentives

In order to understand the different views on ownership of ideas, it is useful to distinguish between **invention, discovery**, and **revelation**.[25] By *invention* we mean the act of creating new knowledge. A *discovery*, on the other hand, does not create anything new; it is the observation of something that was not noticed before. Discovery is not necessarily easier than invention; in both of these cases, considerable effort may have to be expended. Finally, a *revelation* is defined as new knowledge or a new idea that is not the result of a specific effort to invent or discover it. It just appears as a gratuitous event, unplanned and unanticipated.

From a growth perspective, it is clear that both invention and discovery need to be rewarded if they are to be carried out. They are costly activities that would not normally be undertaken unless there was some prospect of future gains. Revelation, by definition, is not an intentional, costly activity. Therefore, it requires no explicit motivation. But, the distinction between a revelation and an invention is not always clear. Suppose that a firm employs a number of researchers to find the formula for a certain new drug to prevent the common cold. While these researchers are experimenting and testing different chemical mixtures, they accidentally find the formula for artificial chocolate that is indistinguishable from the real thing. Is this a revelation, a discovery, or an invention? It is safe to say that many inventions and discoveries are revelations in the sense that the inventors and discoverers came upon unexpected findings; after all, the nature of invention and discovery is to uncover something that was not known before. Nevertheless, whether people regard new ideas as inventions, discoveries, or revelations is important for how societies reward the activities that create new ideas.

William Alford (1995) describes how China's Confucian heritage is incompatible with the ownership of ideas. According to Confucian beliefs, human knowledge is something that has already been discovered by the "Ancients," and current generations only have to interact with the past in order to gain this knowledge. To claim this knowledge as some individual's personal property is, therefore, improper since all knowledge is really just a revelation that can be found in the works of the past. Thus, when Britain attempted to

---

[25] This section closely follows John D. Mittelstaedt and Robert A. Mittelstaedt (1997).

impose intellectual property rights on China at the end of the nineteenth century, the informal institutions saw to it that such a formal foreign institution did not take hold. The Communist government, which denied most forms of private property, abolished intellectual property rights in 1949. Given the cultural heritage, it should be no wonder that despite the Chinese government's promise to the contrary, intellectual property rights are only weakly enforced in China today. At the same time, the increase in new patents awarded in developed economies seems to also clash with other existing formal institutions, as evidenced by the sharp rise in legal proceedings contesting patents.

Islamic countries tend to follow the Qur'an's (16:78) advice: "Allah brought you out of your mother's womb devoid of all knowledge, and gave you ears and hearts that you may give thanks." The common interpretation of these words is that knowledge is gained with the assistance of Allah, and the role of the inventor is thus diminished. Knowledge provided by God is a revelation, not a human invention. Many countries whose laws are based on the principles of Islam have not enacted patent or copyright laws, nor have they recognized the patents and copyrights issued by other countries.[26] Mittelstaedt and Mittelstaedt (1997) note, however, that this situation may be changing. In the late 1980s, the Islamic Fikh Councils (a Pan-Islamic entity that considers, among other things, the role of Islamic thought in the modern world) have supported intellectual property rights. But this is a new view, and even if the Fikh Councils recognize the need for incentives for innovation and the gains from participating in global institutions, strict enforcement of patents and copyrights in Islamic countries may take some time to become accepted.

It is also likely that the formal laws and regulations on intellectual property rights that are eventually established on a worldwide basis will end up reflecting some of the traditions of countries other than the major industrial nations. For example, Ziauddin Sardar (1977) points out that the teachings of Islam suggest that property should not be held in disuse and to the exclusion of others. Thus, if Islamic nations adopt patent and copyright laws, they are likely to insist that licensing of ideas be mandatory as it is in the patent laws of European countries. United States and Canadian patent law, on the other hand, permits the patent holder to hoard knowledge and keep anyone else from using it.

Of course, it was not very long ago that patents and copyrights were not protected in the Western world either. Plagiarism was not considered a crime in the Middle Ages, as "truth" was considered beyond the ownership of human beings. In his study of Chaucer, Donald Howard (1987) notes that in fourteenth century England it was still commonly accepted that "truth by whomever spoken, comes from God." That certainly sounds very similar to the statement we quoted earlier from the Qu'ran.

---

[26] Steven D. Jamar (1992).

The formal protection of intellectual property rights is, in fact, a relatively new institution everywhere in the world. It is an institution that will take some time to become accepted in societies with incompatible informal incentives. In fact, it can be argued that informal institutions are not fully compatible with intellectual property rights in any society today. Note how, in the most advanced economies with the most developed intellectual property rights, many people do not hesitate to download copyrighted materials from the Internet. Businesses routinely reverse engineer rivals' products in order to "discover" the technologies and ideas they contain rather than purchase the rights to specific technologies.

Another clash between culture and formal intellectual property rights involves the awarding of patents for basic knowledge about nature. For example, private firms have in recent years been allowed to patent discoveries about living species' genetic characteristics. Awarding someone the rights to the human genome is viewed by many scientists as equivalent to having permitted someone to patent gravity, the table of the elements, or the process of evolution. Some countries see this as overreaching by the United States and other countries where much scientific research is carried out. Many developing countries today argue that the WTO agreement on intellectual property rights needs to be renegotiated in order to ban the awarding of patents or copyrights for basic knowledge about the natural sphere.

13.6 Summary and Conclusions

Government can provide human society with the ever-changing array of formal institutions needed to keep human society operating efficiently as it grows in size and complexity. Creating government institutions to deal with complex systemic issues remains a very difficult and uncertain human endeavor, however. It is difficult to expand the role of government to deal with changing economic, social, and environmental circumstances because, like society as a whole, governments lack the resources to handle all tasks before them. Governments may also fail to achieve their stated goals because the people that make up the government lack sufficient information and understanding of our complex world. And, government officials' own interests often clash with the interests of the overall population whose interests they are charged with serving. There is also the problem of government power being diverted to promote the welfare of some individuals and groups at the expense of others.

As explained in the previous chapter, formal government institutions are likely to clash with society's slow-moving informal institutions. Such clashes manifest themselves in a variety of ways. Corruption flourishes when new government institutions lack respect because they do not reflect society's accepted norms and traditions. Informal activities grow when new formal institutions create incentives for excesses that are not restrained by existing informal institutions. Sometimes a government institutes new formal institutions with the specific intent to cause a clash with prevalent informal institutions. For example, slavery, gender discrimination, and child labor were institutions that were intentionally made illegal in most countries.

Some of the most damaging clashes between formal and informal institutions have occurred when people from different countries and cultures encountered each other. Even in today's integrated global economy, exporters, importers, and international investors routinely have to deal with incompatible formal institutions like legal systems based on different historical precedents, different concepts of governance, and different informal institutions such as cultures and social norms. These international clashes of cultures and politics have become more frequent as human society has developed the technologies to travel farther and communicate with more people. The next section of this textbook examines the expansion of international economic activities, or what is popularly called globalization, and what this internationalization of economic activity means for sustainable economic development.

Key Terms and Concepts

Cartel	Invention
Consumer surplus	Invisible hand of markets
Copyright	Non-excludable good
Corruption	Nonrival good
Deadweight loss	Patent
Discovery	Progressive tax
Dual economies	Public goods
Economic rent	Rent
Externalities	Rent-seeking
Formal sector	Rent-evading activity
Informal sector	Revelation
Intellectual property right	

Questions and Problems

1. Describe Adam Smith's three basic functions of government. Is his list complete, or are there more functions for government? Explain.
2. In economics, a public good is both nonrival and nonexcludable. Explain how the lighthouse example fits or doesn't fit this definition. Explain.

3. Define an externality. Why do externalities require corrective measures that usually involve government? How are externalities related to the complexity of human existence across the three spheres? Explain.

4. Provide a list of reasons, and their explanations, for collective action in the economy. Does your list justify the growth of government in modern economies? Support your answer with evidence and examples.

5. Write an essay to answer the following question: Can all human rights be effectively granted without also guaranteeing some economic rights?

6. Do you agree with the United Nations Universal Declaration of Human Rights? Explain why or why not.

7. Evaluate this statement: "The fact that the market system does not always function efficiently to allocate society's scarce resources does not automatically justify government action in the economy."

8. Explain in detail why government may not generate welfare-enhancing economic outcomes when it interjects itself into the economy.

9. Explain Anne Krueger's idea of comparative advantage in justifying how many economic activities government should undertake. Do you agree with her? What would you have the government do in a poor country? In a wealthy country?

10. Define rent-seeking activity. Provide some examples.

11. Use Figures 13.5 and 13.6 to explain how much rent-seeking could potentially occur. Explain your conclusions precisely in reference to the diagrams.

12. What are the conditions for corruption? Explain.

13. What role does culture play in enabling corruption? (Hint: Make use of Pierre Bourdieu's sociological concepts to explain how people might decide to engage in corrupt practices. What solutions to corruption does Bourdieu's framework of analysis suggest?)

14. There is much evidence that the privatization of government assets is often a corrupt process. How might privatization be corrupted? Wouldn't private self-interested behavior rule out corruption? Discuss.

15. Was George Lefcoe, the former commissioner at the Los Angeles County Regional Planning Commission quoted in the text, within his rights to accept the gift of a ham? What would you have done?

16. Is informal economic activity good for economic development? Discuss the pro's and con's of informal activity.

17. Can informal economic activity in less developed countries be ended? Explain how.

18. Write an essay to answer the following question: "Should less developed countries honor intellectual property rights that belong to people in developed economies?"

19. The world seems to be in agreement that 20 years is about right for the duration of a patent. Explain why that might be a reasonable length of time for a patent.

20. Copyrights on creative writing, movies, and art have been increased to over 100 years in some countries. Is this too long or about right? Explain your answer.

21. Why have religions often ruled against the idea of establishing property rights for ideas and knowledge? What are the moral issues associated with patents and copyrights? Discuss.

References

Alford, William P. (1995), *To Steal a Book is an Elegant Offense*, Stanford, CA: Stanford University Press.

Bardham, Pranab (1993), "Symposium on Democracy and Development," *Journal of Economic Perspectives* 7(3):45–50.

Belli, Pedro (1997), "The Comparative Advantage of Government: A Review," World Bank Policy Research Working Paper #1834, October, Washington, D.C.

De Soto, Hernando (1989), *The Other Path*, New York: Harper and Row.

Howard, Donald R. (1987), *Chaucer, His Life, His Works, His World*, New York: Ballentine Books.

International Labour Office (2002), *Statistics on the Informal Economy*, Geneva: ILO.

Jamar, Steven D. (1992), "The Protection of Intellectual Property under Islamic Law," *Capital University Law Review* 21:1079–1107.

Klitzke, Ramon A. (1964), "History of Patents Abroad," in Robert Calvert (ed.), *The Encyclopedia of Patent Practice and Invention Management*, New York: Reinhold Publishing Corporation.

Krueger, Anne O. (1974), "The Political Economy of the Rent-Seeking Society," *American Economic Review* 64:291–303.

Krueger, Anne O. (1990), "Government Failures in Development," *Journal of Economics Perspectives* 4(3):16–17.

Lamoreaux, Naomi R., and Kenneth L. Sokoloff (1999), "Inventive Activity and the Market for Technology in the United States, 1840–1920," NBER Working Paper No. W7107, May.

Mauro, Paolo (1995), "Corruption and Growth," *Quarterly Journal of Economics* 110: 681–712.

Mittelstaedt, John D., and Robert A. Mittelstaedt (1997), "The Protection of Intellectual Property: Issues of Origination and Ownership," *Journal of Public Policy & Marketing* 16(1):14–25.

Mukum Mbaku, John (1995), "Bureaucratic Corruption in Africa: The Futility of Cleanups," *Cato Journal* 16(1):99–118.

North, Douglass C. (1987), "Institutions, Transactions Costs and Economic Growth," *Economic Inquiry* 25(3):419–428.

Olson, Mancur (1982), *The Rise and Decline of Nations, Economic Growth, Stagflation, and Social Rigidities*, New Haven: Yale University Press.

Phongpaicht, Pasuk, and Sungsidh Piriyarangsan (1994), *Corruption and Democracy in Thailand*, Bangkok: Political Economy Centre, Faculty of Economics, Chulalongkorn University.

Pirenne, Henri (1927 [1969])), *Medieval Cities: Their Origins and the Revival of Trade*, Princeton, NJ: Princeton University Press.

Rock, M. T., and H. Bonnett (2004), "The Comparative Politics of Corruption: Accounting for the East Asian Paradox in Empirical Studies of Corruption, Growth and Investment." *World Development* 32(6):999–1017.

Romer, Paul M. (1998), "Economic Growth," in David R. Henderson (ed.), *The Fortune Encyclopedia of Economics*, New York: Warner Books.

Rose-Ackerman, Susan (1997), "The Political Economy of Corruption," Chapter 2 in Kimberly Ann Elliott (ed.), *Corruption and the Global Economy*, Washington, D.C.: Institute for International Economics.

Sardar, Ziauddin (1977), *Science, Technology and Development in the Muslim World*, London: Croom Helm, Ltd.

Schneider, Friedrich, and Dominik H. Enste (2000), "Shadow Economies: Size, Causes, and Consequences," *Journal of Economic Literature* 38(1):77–114.

Smith, Adam (1776 [1976]), *An Inquiry into the Nature and Causes of the Wealth of Nations*, Chicago: University of Chicago Press.

Svensson, Jakob (2005), "Eight Questions about Corruption," *Journal of Economic Perspectives* 19(3):19–42.

Tanzi, Vito (1998), "Corruption Around the World," *IMF Staff Papers* 45(4):559–594.

Tanzi, Vito, and Hamid Davoodi (1998), *Roads to Nowhere: How Corruption in Public Investment Hurts Growth*, Washington D.C.: International Monetary Fund.

Tullock, Gordon (1967), "The Welfare Costs of Tariffs, Monopolies, and Theft," *Western Economic Journal* 5:224–232.

PART IV

International Economic Integration

International trade grew twice as fast as output during the second half of the twentieth century, and since the 1980s, international investment has grown twice as fast as international trade. The proportion of the world's population living outside their country of birth has quadrupled over the past half century, from less than one percent to nearly four percent. From a historical perspective, this international economic integration, that is, the accelerated growth of international trade, international investment, international financial flows, and immigration, is unprecedented in scope and volume. The current episode of international economic integration is not entirely unique, however. There have been previous episodes of expansion of international trade, investment, finance, and migration.

For example, in the latter half of the nineteenth century some countries reached levels of international trade, international investment, and immigration even larger than we currently observe at the start of the twenty-first century. Both this, and the current, international integration episodes coincided with relatively high rates of growth of per capita production as measured by gross domestic product (GDP). For example, Figure IV-1 suggests that per capita GDP has been pulled along by the growth of international trade over the past 200 years, slowing only when trade contracts. These correlations have led many economists to conclude that international economic integration enhances human welfare.

Of course, the fact that two variables move in tandem does not necessarily imply that one *causes* the other. Beginning with Adam Smith and David Ricardo some 200 years ago, economists have developed strong, logical arguments showing that international trade and investment improve human welfare. The early twentieth century economist D. H. Robertson famously described nineteenth century international economic integration as follows: "The specializations of the nineteenth century were not simply a device for using to

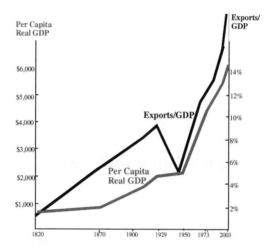

Figure IV-1 World Economic Growth and Trade

the greatest effect the labours of a given number of human beings; they were above all an engine of growth."[1]

Many people remain unconvinced by economists' arguments, however. Some elements of international economic integration constitute real threats to economic, social, and environmental welfare. In the words of Dani Rodrik, people fear that "in a fully integrated world economy, wages would be set in Shenzen [China], the price of capital determined in New York, and tax rates legislated in the Cayman Islands."[2] To understand the diversity of opinions, a broader holistic perspective on international economic integration is called for. Orthodox international economics does not provide such a perspective.

A holistic analysis of international economic integration

First of all, it is important to recognize that the rapid growth of international trade, investment, and migration over the past 200 years covers but a brief episode in human history. Specialization and exchange have actually been expanding since the origins of humanity more than one hundred thousand years ago. The spread of agriculture and animal husbandry transformed human societies from bands of hunters and gatherers into more complex organizations consisting of much larger groups of people living in permanent settlements. Villages grew into towns, cities, and, eventually, nations that operated under one political structure. In small hunter and gatherer societies, permanent personal

---

[1] D. H. Robertson (1938), "The Future of International Trade," *The Economic Journal* 48(189). p. 5.
[2] Rodrik, Dani (1998), "Symposium on Globalization in Perspective: An Introduction," *Journal of Economic Perspective* 12(4), p. 5.

relationships governed human interaction. But in larger communities humans had to find ways to interact with much larger and dispersed groups of "strangers." This growth in the size of human communities was a slow process because engaging in transactions with unfamiliar people on a one-time basis is much more difficult than dealing repeatedly with the same small group of relatives and fellow clan members.

In his book, *The Company of Strangers*, Paul Seabright refers to the transition from living in traditional small hunting and gathering communities to our current dependence on strangers from all over the world as the "great experiment" of the past 10,000 years.[3] Humans were motivated to deal with more people beyond their immediate familiar groups by the potential gains from dealing with strangers. According to Seabright, these gains from dealing with more strangers fell into three categories: (1) gains from specialization, (2) reductions in risks from unpredictable adverse outcomes, and (3) faster expansion of knowledge.

In any case, today's high standards of living would be impossible without extensive trade and many other forms of economic cooperation among large numbers of people. It is inherently difficult to trade and cooperate when people do not know each other, they cannot meet face to face when they deal with each other, they come from different cultures and backgrounds, and they know that they are unlikely to ever have to deal with each other again in the future. That is, there are many incentives for people to misbehave towards each other in a complex global society.

It is not easy to deal with strangers

Despite the good reasons for cooperating with each other, individuals also have strong incentives to exploit, steal from, enslave, and kill others. People are tempted to renege on agreements and misrepresent their side of the bargain. For example, it is really much easier to let someone else spend a season growing a field of grain and then steal it just when it is ready. Or, it may be more convenient to coerce others to do the hard work rather than doing it ourselves. The present complex global economy that Seabright called the "great experiment" has not evolved smoothly. Effectively, human evolution over the long period of hunting and gathering, plus earlier evolution of human ancestors, did not fully prepare us for dealing with strangers.

Niall Ferguson (2008) presents interesting observations on the world's few remaining isolated tribes of hunters and gatherers. There is no evidence that small groups were any less violent towards each other than modern societies were in the twentieth century. Ferguson writes: "When two groups of such primitive peoples chanced upon each other, it seems, they were more likely to

---

[3] Seabright, Paul (2010), *The Company of Strangers: A Natural History of Economic Life*, 2nd Ed., Princeton, NJ: Princeton University Press.

fight over scarce resources... than to engage in commercial exchange. Hunter-gatherers do not trade. They raid."[4]

Humans have had some success in dealing with the mismatch between evolved human instincts and the gains from cooperating with large numbers of total strangers in a complex integrated global economy. Seabright describes how humans developed institutions to "temper their appeals to the deep emotions, to family and clan loyalty, with just enough abstract reasoning to help *homo sapiens sapiens*, the shy, murderous ape, emerge from family bands in the savanna woodland in order to live and work in a world largely populated by strangers."[5] Seabright continues his discussion of the new global economy with a warning: "This experiment is still young, and needs all the help it can get."

As pointed out in Chapter 12, economic and social circumstances tend to change faster than we can adjust the human institutions necessary to deal with the growing complexities of human societies. Informal institutions like culture therefore lag far behind the ever-changing realities of our social and economic environments. Culture also tends to lag behind our accumulation of rational knowledge and understanding of the realities of our environment. When institutions fail, economic interaction between strangers can fail to provide the gains from dealing with larger groups of strangers that Seabright distinguishes.

A precautionary approach to international economic integration?

Not all economists agree with Seabright that the process of international economic integration deserves "all the help it can get." For example, Edward Herman (1999) provides a less benevolent description of international economic integration:

> Like free trade, globalization has an aura of virtue. Just as "freedom" must be good, so globalization hints at internationalism and solidarity between countries, as opposed to nationalism and protectionism, which have negative connotations. The possibility that cross-border trade and investment might be economically damaging to the weaker party, or that they might erode democratic controls in both the stronger and weaker countries, is excluded from consideration by mainstream economists and pundits. It is also unthinkable in the mainstream that the contest between free trade and globalization, on the one hand, and "protectionism," on the other, might be reworded as a struggle between "protection" — of transnational corporate rights — versus the "freedom" of democratic governments to regulate in the interests of domestic non-corporate constituencies.[6]

---

[4] Niall Ferguson (2008), *The Ascent of Money: A Financial History of the World*, London: Allen Lane, pp. 14–15.
[5] Paul Seabright (2010), op. cit., p. 257.
[6] Edward S. Herman (1999), "The Threat of Globalization," *New Politics* 7(2).

Herman's arguments go well beyond the traditional distrust of strangers that humans inherited from their ancestors. He recognizes the dangers of the increasingly powerful transnational corporations, the unequal military and economic power across countries, and the tendency for governments to manipulate the sentiments of their constituencies for political purposes.

International trade and international investment often occur under institutions and circumstances that permit one party to exploit another. When trade in a product or commodity is dominated by a small number of large multinational corporations, as is usually the case today, workers and farmers who produce goods are pressured into accepting lower wages and prices. And, at the other end of the exchange, final consumers are influenced and pressured into paying higher prices. Consumers are routinely deceived about the benefits and desirability of products with sophisticated advertising and marketing. More fundamentally, the shifts in production across borders affect economic and social structures in many ways. Wages and incomes change, the mix of a country's industries and jobs changes, foreign cultural influences become more prominent, business environments change, government economic policies no longer work the same way they do in closed economies, tax revenues are affected, technological change may take different directions, unemployment may rise, and life can become less secure and familiar. Unfortunately, today's dominant political and economic paradigms do not encourage the application of the precautionary principle to international economic integration.

The purpose of the three chapters of Part IV of the textbook is, first of all, to advance the understanding of international economics and the role international trade, investment, finance, and migration play in the development process. The four chapters that follow present some of the traditional models economists have used to explain international trade, investment, and migration. To address the legitimate accusation that economists' models are incomplete, the upcoming chapters also move well beyond the standard models to provide a more holistic explanation of international economic activity.

In short, international economic integration is a complex process with consequences, and causes, that extend well beyond what economists' standard models suggest. Peoples' views of international economic integration are determined by more than the few variables measured in economists' models. These observations about the complexity of international economic integration are not intended to suggest that the process is inherently good or bad. There are many positive aspects to the gradual replacement of isolated tribal, regional, and national societies by a more integrated global society in which humans from all parts of the world interact economically, politically, socially, and culturally. But the process of international economic integration does create stresses in the economy, society, and the natural environment. Skepticism about the benefits of international trade, foreign investment, or immigration is, therefore, not a sign of a lack of willingness to understand international economics. Rather, it is a reflection of the complexity of the issue; people who look at different parts of the problem reach different conclusions. Unlike traditional introductions to international economics, the following chapters provide a more holistic perspective from which to arrive at policies for dealing with the evolving international economic integration of human society.

CHAPTER 14

International Trade and Development

... the sea brought Greeks the vine from India, from Greece transmitted the use of grain across the sea, from Phoenicia imported letters as a memorial against forgetfulness, thus preventing the greater part of mankind from being wineless, grainless, and unlettered.
(Plutarch, 100 A.D.)

In 1820, just one percent of the world's output was exported beyond countries' borders. This is a tiny percentage, considering that during the previous three hundred years exploratory journeys had resulted in Europeans "discovering" the Western Hemisphere, opening trade with Africa, and finding a sea route to Asia to replace the Silk Road and other land routes cut off by war lords and hostile rulers in Central Asia. But trade did not grow much because until the nineteenth century, it remained difficult and expensive to transport goods.

Before 1800, goods were transported either by road or by water. Sailing ships were slow and completely at the mercy of the weather, they required large crews to man the sails, and on ocean journeys they were not very safe. Land transport before 1800 consisted of wagons pulled by horses or mules. In many countries roads did not exist, and goods were carried on the backs of animals and people. Another factor that restricted trade was poverty. Before 1800, the world was almost universally poor, which meant that there were few consumers who could pay to transport goods over long distances. This is not to say that the roots of the modern global economy do not extend further back than 1800. To the contrary, the modern globally integrated economy dates back to at least 1500, the voyages by European adventurers, and the spread of colonialism. It was during the colonial era that European merchants began to engage in both voluntary and forced trade with all parts of the world. But the rapid expansion of international trade had to wait until the nineteenth century. Over the past two centuries, the world's economies have become intimately connected to the point that no national economy is self-sufficient anymore.

This chapter begins our analysis of international trade and its contribution to modern economic development. The orthodox model of trade is presented and then qualified by introducing heterodox perspectives.

Chapter Goals

1. Discuss the rapid growth of international trade after 1800.
2. Present the neoclassical model of international trade, which is popularly referred to as the Heckscher-Ohlin (HO) model.
3. Explain the neoclassical model using the standard small-country diagram to derive some of the model's key conclusions.
4. Present the key conclusions of the HO model, and discuss how economists rely on these conclusions to justify free trade policies.
5. Discuss the weaknesses of the HO model and its assumptions.
6. Explain how some orthodox economists have qualified the conclusions of the HO model by considering adjustment costs, terms of trade shifts, and endogenous economic growth.
7. Detail how economies of scale and imperfect competition generate alternative conclusions about international trade.
8. Present the infant industry argument for protection.
9. Explain how environmental externalities alter the HO model's conclusions about free trade.

14.1 The Growth of International Trade

International trade began to grow rapidly in the 1800s when transport costs fell and economic development raised incomes and demand for foreign products. From just 1 percent of GDP in 1800, international trade grew to nearly 5 percent of GDP by 1870 and 8 percent at the start of the twentieth century. This section presents some important details of this growth of trade.

14.1.1 New transport technologies

During the course of the nineteenth century, ocean transport was revolutionized by the iron steamship, which was much safer, easier to operate, and, of course, not dependent on the winds. Steamships were not only faster than sailing ships, they could adhere to fixed schedules. The introduction of the screw propeller and steel hulls further reduced shipping times and increased the size of ships. Also, without the need for masts to hold sails, steamships could be designed to better meet specific needs, such as the transport of passengers, iron ore, and grain. The cost of shipping coal between continents fell by 70 percent between 1840 and 1910.[1]   Steam engines on board enabled the development of refrigerated ships to carry chilled and frozen foods.   By the 1870s frozen beef was regularly supplied from North America, Argentina, and Australia to Europe. The opening of the Suez and Panama Canals lowered transport costs further.

Railroads revolutionized land transportation.   Refrigeration permitted railroads to carry fresh and frozen foods across large distances.   Because railroads effectively eliminated water transport's great comparative advantage and virtual monopoly on long-distance bulk transport, the transport industry became more competitive and shippers were forced to reduce their prices.[2]

Other evidence of the fall in transport cost are the sharp declines in the differences in prices of specific products in different parts of the world. In 1870 wheat prices in Liverpool, Great Britain, were 58 percent higher than in Chicago, the market where wheat shipments from the fertile U.S. Midwestern farm lands originated. The price gap had narrowed to 18 percent by 1895, and to 16 percent by 1912.[3]   The price gap for meat shrank somewhat later, as it was dependent on the development of refrigeration; the price gap for bacon in Chicago and Liverpool narrowed from 92 percent in the late 1800s to just 18 percent in 1913.   Also, between 1870 and 1913 the United States–British price gap for cotton textiles fell from 14 percent to near zero, the iron bar price gap from 75 to 21 percent, and the gap for cow hides from 28 to 9 percent.[4]   The opening of the Suez Canal and the introduction of steamships to the Indian trade reduced the price gap for cotton between Bombay and Liverpool from 57 percent to 20 percent, and the jute price gap from 35 to 4 percent.   Balance of payments data from the 1800s suggests that transport costs as a percentage of the value of goods exported fell from 30 percent in 1800 to about 3 percent around 1900, a 90 percent decline over the entire century.[5] It is estimated that transport costs declined by nearly 50 percent just from 1870 to 1910.[6]

By 1929, the year before the Great Depression began, about 9 percent of world production of goods was exported to other countries.   The Great Depression's protectionist trade policies and the turmoil of World War II cut the share of exports in world production nearly in half.   Only about 5 percent of total world production was exported in 1950.

Beginning after 1950, further technological breakthroughs in ocean shipping reduced the per ton cost of ocean freight dramatically, and by 1990 per ton costs were less than 30 percent of their 1920 level.   Containerization greatly reduced transshipment costs, or **cabotage**, which can be substantial for products that

---

[1] C. K. Harley (1988); Douglass North (1958).
[2] Thomas J. Holmes and James A. Schmitz, Jr. (1995).
[3] Philippe Aghion and Jeffrey G. Williamson (1998), p. 136.
[4] Aghion and Williamson (1998), p.136.
[5] Michael Mussa (2000).
[6] Kevin H. O'Rourke and Jeffrey G. Williamson (1999), p. 36.

must travel by a variety of land and sea modes to reach their destination. Not only is it costly and time-consuming to unload and reload goods, but transshipment points are where goods are most often damaged or stolen. By 2000, over 90 percent of ocean freight was moving by container. At the same time, air freight made the transportation of fresh flowers, fruit, vegetables, fish, and other perishables possible. Large jet aircraft like the Boeing 747 freighter permitted the outsourcing of critical components throughout the world even as companies sought quicker delivery times for their revolutionary just-in-time production systems. In 1965 just 6.2 percent of the value of all U.S. imports and 8.3 percent of exports traveled by air, but by 1998 those percentages were approaching 30 percent.[7]   David Hummels (1999) calculates that for trips of 5,000 kilometers, air freight rates fell by one-third over the 25 years between 1973 and 1998, and for trips of 9,000 kilometers, rates fell by nearly one-half.

14.1.2 Is trade an engine or handmaiden of growth?

The British economist D. H. Robertson (1938) labeled international trade as "the engine of growth." Given the influence of technological change on both growth and trade, Irving Kravis (1970) may have been closer to the truth when he wrote that trade is just a "handmaiden of growth." The culture of orthodox economics seems to embrace the "engine" hypothesis. In reality, it is always difficult to distinguish the direction of causality between two variables that seem to move together.

Table 14.1 shows that between 1950 and the end of the millennium, world GDP increased nearly eightfold while exports increased more than thirty-fold. Since 1800, the share of exports only contracted during the Great Depression when economic growth also collapsed. On the one hand, the role of transport technology in expanding international trade suggests that the close correlation between trade and GDP growth is the *result* of economic development. D. H. Robertson alleged, however, that trade was the *cause* of economic development. To make this claim, economists need to show how and why international trade directly *causes* the technological change that enables continual growth in output and substantial improvements in human welfare.

The main purpose of this chapter is to seek an answer to the question: Is globalization merely a characteristic of our increasingly complex human society on Earth, or is it a fundamental driving force of human progress? The short answer to this question is that trade is most likely both an engine and a handmaiden. Trade grows because it benefits from the technological improvements and income increases that are part of the development process. On the other hand, recall from Chapter 4 that Adam Smith (1776 [1976], p. 7) wrote in his *Wealth of Nations*:

---

[7] U.S. Bureau of the Census (1998), *Statistical Abstract of the United States.*

Table 14.1 World Exports and Per Capita Gross Domestic Product: 1820–2007

Year	World Exports (millions 1990$)	World GDP (millions 1990$)	Exports as % of World GDP	Per Capita $1990 GDP
Maddison's Real Per Capita Estimates:				
1820	7,255	694,442	1.0%	$667
1870	50,345	1,101,369	4.6	867
1913	212,425	2,704,782	7.9	1,510
1929	334,408	3,696,156	9.0	1,806
1950	295,621	5,336,101	5.5	2,114
1973	1,690,648	16,059,180	10.5	4,104
1998	5,817,080	33,725,635	17.2	5,709
International Monetary Fund's Nominal Figures:				
2004	11,069,000	40,671,000	27.2	6,250
2007	17,170,533	54,273,887	31.6	7,000

Source: Data for 1820 and 1929 are from Angus Maddison (1995), Tables E-2, p. 211, and I-4, p. 239. 1870, 1913, 1950, and 1998 are from Angus Maddison (2001), Tables F-3 and F-5, and Table C5-b. The 2004 figures are from the International Monetary Fund (2005), *World Economic Outlook*, April 2005, Washington, D.C.: IMF, Table 1, p. 201, and Table 20, p. 230; 2007 figures are from UNCTAD (2008), *Handbook of Statistics 2008*, New York: United Nations.

> The greatest improvements in the productive powers of labour, and the greater part of the skill, dexterity, and judgment with which it is any where directed, or applied, seem to have been the effects of the division of labour.

That is, the process of economic development and rising living standards imply an increase in specialization, which, in turn, requires increased trade. This suggests that policies to expand trade have the added benefit of promoting economic development.

Historical evidence also suggests, however, that removing trade barriers does not always bring economic development. Most countries that are rich today engaged in various forms of trade **protectionism** in the past. The United States, for example, maintained import tariffs between 20 percent and 40 percent for the entire nineteenth century when it was building its new industries to compete with Britain, the leader of the Industrial Revolution. More recently, experiments with free trade in Latin America have had mostly disappointing economic results. Recall the discussion of mercantilism in Chapter 4, the economic paradigm adopted by most European nations between 1500 and 1800. Mercantilists explicitly protected industry from foreign competition. The United States and Japan, which would become the two largest industrial economies after the middle of the twentieth century, also used high tariffs and explicit barriers to imports in order to protect their industrial firms over extended periods of time. In short, the relationship between international trade and economic development is a complex relationship. Depending on where, when, and how you observe the phenomenon, different conclusions are possible.

As is often the practice in this book, we begin with the relevant orthodox economic model. Given our discussion here, it will be obvious that the orthodox model of international trade cannot decide whether trade is an engine or a handmaiden. The answer to that question calls for holistic analysis that looks at the dynamic processes of economic development and globalization of economic activity from a systemic and inter-disciplinary perspective.

14.2 Orthodox Economic Analysis of International Trade

The most popular model of international trade, taught in almost all university economics courses around the world, is the **Heckscher-Ohlin (HO) model**. This model is named in honor of the two Swedish economists who first developed it early in the twentieth century. The model establishes the well-known principle of **comparative advantage**, which economists often use to justify free trade policies. The model also shows that increased trade causes shifts in the allocation of society's resources. These shifts alter people's incomes, and they change the structure of an economy. An economy that trades with other countries does not look the same as an economy that closes its borders to trade. The HO model captures some of these changes.

As will be explained below, the HO model shows that the welfare gains from international trade are derived from exchange and specialization. The model shows how trade lets a country concentrate on producing those goods and services which it is especially good at producing, regardless of how it values those goods, and how it can exchange those goods and services for things it values more highly and could only produce itself at a much higher cost. The HO model ignores many of the long-run and dynamic economic consequences of international trade. The model also ignores the influences and consequences of trade that occur in the social and natural spheres. Despite the shortcomings, in order to understand economists' arguments for free trade, we must understand the model on which they often base those arguments.

14.2.1 The production possibilities frontier

Suppose the economy of the country of Homeland has the resources and know-how to produce various combinations of two goods, food and clothing, as illustrated by the **production-possibilities frontier (PPF)** in Figure 14.1. You may remember the PPF from your principles of economics course. Homeland's resources and know-how permits it to produce any combination of clothing and food lying on or below the PPF. For example, combinations such as 200 pounds of food and 350 pieces of clothing or 300 pounds of food and 300 pieces of clothing can realistically be produced. Of course, a combination of products that lies below the PPF, such as the combination of 200 units of clothing and 200 units of food, could be also produced. But such a combination implies some type of inefficiency that prevents the economy from using all of its resources or its best technologies. On the other hand, any combination of food and clothing outside the PPF, such as point A at 350 pounds of food and 350 pieces of clothing, is not feasible given Homeland's resources and know-how. In short, the PPF illustrates the economic problem of scarcity: When the economy produces a combination on the PPF curve, an increase in output of one product necessitates a decrease in output of the other.

The PPF curve is typically drawn so that it has a bowed-out shape, as in Figure 14.1. Such a PPF curve is said to be *concave to the origin*. In economic terms, a concave PPF means that the production of food and clothing is characterized by **increasing costs**. The higher the level of production of a good, the greater are the marginal **opportunity costs** in terms of the other goods that could be produced. The PPF depends on the resources available to society and the level of technology with which society can transform its resources into final goods and services. An increase in productive resources, say by means of investment in more physical or human capital, or an improvement in technology, say an improvement in generating electricity, shift the curve out. On the other hand, a decline in productivity, such as the loss of nature's services because of overexploitation of the ecosystem, shifts the PPF inward.

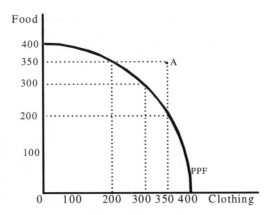

Figure 14.1 The Production Possibilities Frontier: Scarcity Requires Choices

14.2.2 Consumer demand and indifference curves

The PPF represents the supply side of the economy; it gives the possible combinations of food and clothing that the economy *could* produce. But, which of the many possible combinations of food and clothing will Homeland actually choose to produce? Which of the possible combinations of food and clothing lying on the PPF do people prefer? To answer these questions, the demand side of Homeland's economy must be added to the model.

The H-O model assumes people maximize their welfare by allocating their incomes among the alternative products so that each additional, or *marginal*, dollar spent adds the most to personal welfare. How consumers value one good relative to another is usually represented graphically by **indifference curves**, which are sets of combinations of goods that are valued equally by consumers, or to among which consumers are *indifferent*. Figure 14.2 illustrates a typical set of indifference curves for a simplified world of two goods. For example, the combinations of food and clothing represented by points k, m, n, and q all leave consumers equally well off, or indifferent, so they lie on the same indifference curve I_1.

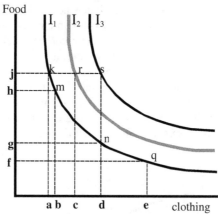

Figure 14.2 Indifference Curves

The combinations at points r and s in Figure 14.2 represent higher levels of welfare than the combination at k, for example, because they combine the identical amount of food at k with higher amounts of clothing, obviously a preferred situation for consumers. Hence, the combination r must lie on a higher indifference curve than k, and s must lie on an even higher indifference curve than r. The two points r and n are more difficult to compare because r combines a higher amount of food than at the combination n with a *lower* amount of clothing than at n. Logic suggests that r is preferable to n because consumers are indifferent between n and m, and the point r is clearly preferable to m. This reasoning leads to a simple conclusion: The higher the indifference curve, the higher the welfare associated with the combinations of goods on the curve.

The indifference curves in Figure 14.2 are drawn so that their slope gradually declines as clothing is substituted for food. The curves' shapes reflect the assumption that consumers value one good more highly the less of it they have relative to the other good. For example, if consumers select the combination k on the indifference curve I_1, which combines the quantity **a** of clothing and **j** of food, a decline in food consumption from, say, **j** to **h** requires that they be compensated with an increase in clothing from **a** to **b**. At the combination n, however, consumers require a larger increase in clothing consumption to fully compensate them for a reduction of food consumption. For example, a decline in food consumption from **g** to **f**, which is identical in quantity to the decline from **j** to **h**, requires a larger offsetting amount of clothing from **d** to **e**. The more people have of one good, the less valuable that good becomes in terms of the other good. The indifference curves thus reflect a preference for variety over a large quantity of just one thing.

One assumption of the HO model is that the indifference curves represent the aggregate preferences of the group of *all* consumers. This is a very questionable assumption for a model of international trade. Individuals have different preferences, and the **aggregate indifference curves** representing the whole social group must change their shapes when there is a redistribution of income. In the case of international trade, when there is a shift to free trade some groups increase their incomes while others lose income, and the aggregate indifference curves are unlikely to remain constant. And if trade is correlated with economic growth, a process which shifts demand for factors of production and redistributes income, this model's predictions of the gains from trade become even less accurate. But because economists lack an easy way to represent aggregate preferences in the face of structural economic changes, they routinely ignore these potential complications and assume aggregate indifference curves remain constant.

This is another example of the limits of models. Models are convenient simplifications, but they can generate inaccurate conclusions and predictions. The international trade model we are developing here will generate some strong conclusions, so keep in mind some of the questionable assumptions behind the model. You should be skeptical of the generality of the model's conclusions.

14.2.3 Combining the supply and demand sides of the economy

The welfare-maximizing production combination of food and clothing is found at the point where the PPF and the indifference curves have the same slope and just touch each other, as illustrated by the line p, at point A in Figure 14.3. Mathematically, the curves are said to be *tangent* at point A. The PPF illustrates how much production of one good must be reduced in order to make available the resources needed to produce one more unit of the other good. The indifference curve shows how much of one good people are willing to give up in exchange for one more unit of the other good. At the tangency between the PPF and indifference curves, the relative opportunity costs of producing food and clothing, respectively, are proportional to the relative marginal benefits from consuming food and clothing.

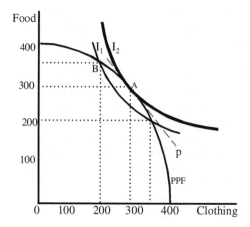

Figure 14.3 Equilibrium in the Closed Economy

The tangency point A is the best possible outcome because at each other point it is not possible to improve national welfare by reallocating productive resources and/or switching consumption expenditures. For example, take the point B in Figure 14.3, where the slope of the PPF is −1/2. At B the economy can produce two more units of clothing if it reduces food production by one pound. But, the slope of the indifference curve at point B is −2, which implies that consumers are quite willing to give up two pounds of food in exchange for one unit of clothing. Thus consumers clearly improve their welfare when the economy provides an additional unit of clothing at the opportunity cost of only half a pound of food. More such exchanges, and moving along the PPF in the direction of A, clearly adds to national welfare.

The concave PPF and the convex indifference curves imply that the trade-offs change as production shifts along the PPF toward A. Specifically, the marginal cost of clothing rises, and the marginal value of clothing falls as more clothing is substituted for food. Only when the economy provides consumers with the combination of food and clothing represented by the point A is the tradeoff permitted by the PPF exactly equal to the tradeoff people would be willing to accept. This tradeoff is represented by the price line p, whose slope represents the relative prices of food and clothing. If all markets are efficient in the sense that prices accurately reflect the relative preferences of consumers and the true marginal costs of producers, then it might be possible to assume that the economy will approach the point A. I_2 is the highest indifference curve consumers in Homeland can reach, given their productive capacity as represented by the PPF.

These results described here all assume that Homeland is an isolated economy. What happens if Homeland opens its borders to international trade?

14.2.4 The gain from international exchange

In general, the relative prices of goods in the rest of the world will not be the same as in the isolated Homeland economy illustrated in Figure 14.3. The quantities of productive factors and the levels of technology in other countries are unlikely to be identical in every country. If we can assume that the total world PPF is simply the sum of all the individual economies' PPFs, then, in general, the PPF of the combined world economy will tend to be shaped differently than Homeland's PPF. Consumer preferences are also unlikely to be the same everywhere. This means that the relative prices of food and clothing in the rest of the world will generally not be the same as in the Homeland economy. The resulting difference in relative prices at home and abroad is the source of the potential gains from international trade for Homeland.

To illustrate how differences in relative prices of food and clothing create potential gains from trade, suppose that in Homeland the slope of p at the point A in Figure 14.3 is exactly −1. A slope of −1 implies that consumers value a pound of food and a piece of clothing equally and that the economy can increase output of clothing by one piece if the resources made available by a one-pound reduction in food production are applied to clothing production instead. Suppose also that in the rest of the world the relative prices are reflected in a price line whose slope is −1/3, or −0.33. That is, in the rest of the world, a pound of food costs three times as much as a piece of clothing, perhaps because the rest of the world has a much better clothing manufacturing know-how (technology) than does Homeland or because the rest of the world has relatively more of the types of resources, such as workers and sewing machines, than Homeland does.

The relative prices of the two products in Homeland and the rest of the world determine the relative opportunity costs in each country. Notice that the opening of trade causes Homeland to specialize in the product for which it has the lower opportunity cost. Homeland is said to have a **comparative advantage** in producing food because its opportunity cost for food is less, just one-third, than that of the rest of the world. By the same logic, the rest of the world has a comparative advantage in producing clothes, since their opportunity cost for clothing is one-third that of Homeland.

A Homeland consumer who values a pound of food the same as a piece of clothing can go overseas and exchange a pound of food for three pieces of clothing. In fact, in the absence of transport costs and trade restrictions, everyone in Homeland will engage in such foreign transactions up to the point where they acquire so much clothing and give up so much food that their relative preferences for additional clothing and food reflect the 0.33 price ratio.

Suppose, finally, that Homeland is a very small economy and that world prices will not be affected by its entry into the world markets for food and clothing. That is, Homeland is assumed to be "a perfect competitor" in the huge world market. This assumption lets us conveniently treat the world price ratio of

0.33 as a constant that Homeland consumers and producers can take advantage of but cannot influence. In this case, Figure 14.4 illustrates the gain from international trade for Homeland. Suppose for the time being that Homeland continues producing 300 pounds of food and 300 pieces of clothing at point A. International trade would permit Homeland's consumers to acquire any combination of food and clothing along the **consumption possibilities line** CPL_1 that passes through A with a slope of −0.33. The slope of the CPL reflects the fact that the very small country of Homeland can exchange one pound of food for three units of clothing in the rest of the world. Given that the aggregate indifference curve has a slope of −1 at A, Homelanders find it advantageous to exchange a unit of food for an additional unit of clothing. Note that in an open economy consumers can move outside their PPF. But, they will move only as long as they gain from their foreign trades. As consumers exchange more and more food for clothing, they begin to value food and clothing differently, as suggested by the changing slope of the indifference curve. The substitution of clothing for food continues until the point B is reached; the tangent indifference curve at B means that the relative preferences are the same as the slope of CPL_1, and the value of clothing is 1/3 as much as that of food. Additional exchanges of food for clothing will not increase welfare. B is definitely a better outcome than consumption at A because a higher aggregate indifference curve is reached.

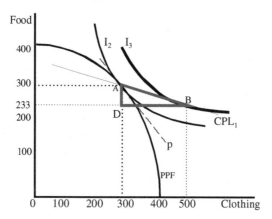

Figure 14.4 The Gain from Exchange

The **trade triangle** in Figure 14.1 represents the international trade that takes Homeland to its higher level of welfare. The triangle shows how much domestically-produced food, measured along its vertical height, is exported in exchange for imports of foreign clothing, measured along the horizontal width. In Figure 14.4, 67 units of Homeland's food are exchanged for 200 units of foreign clothing. The shift from I_2 to I_3 is the **gain from international exchange**.

14.2.5 The gain from international specialization

You may notice in Figure 14.5 that there is a way for Homeland to achieve even greater welfare gains from trade. Note that the world price ratio defines not only the trade-offs that consumers face, but it also defines the relative gains to producers from producing food or clothing since producers have the option, with free trade, to sell overseas as well as at home. It is no longer optimal for Homeland producers to produce the combination of food and clothing at point A, where the relative marginal opportunity cost of producing an additional unit of food is less than the world price of food, and the opportunity cost of producing an additional unit of clothing is greater than the world price of clothing. Profit-maximizing producers employ more factors to produce the relatively expensive food, and fewer to produce the relatively cheaper clothing.

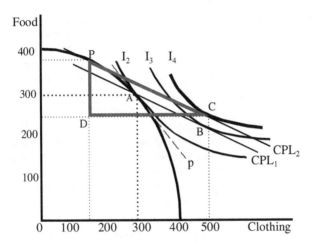

Figure 14.5 The Gains from Exchange and Specialization

Profit-maximizing producers shift production to point P, where the relative opportunity costs of producing food and clothing are the same as in the rest of the world. The value of production and real income is equal to the sum of goods produced at point P, and the consumption possibilities line for the economy is thus CPL_2, Welfare-maximizing consumption now occurs at point C on the higher indifference curve I_4. The gain in welfare from I_3 to I_4 is the **gain from specialization**. The volume of trade is greater when Homeland takes advantage of both the gain from exchange and the gain from specialization; compare the trade triangle in Figure 14.5 relative to the trade triangle in Figure 14.4. Also, the total gains from trade are greater; a higher indifference curve is reached.

Note that Homeland gains welfare by exporting the product for which it has a comparative advantage. That is, it specializes in and exports those products that it is relatively more efficient at producing. This comparative advantage may be the result of Homeland's relatively different endowments of factors of production and resources, or its unique technological capabilities. Examples of comparative advantage influencing trade would be tropical countries that export bananas and coffee, countries with large populations and small accumulated capital stocks that export labor-intensive products like clothing, and beautiful islands that specialize in tourism.

14.2.6 Welfare gains from trade according to the HO model

There have been many studies that estimated the gains from international trade, and nearly all have followed the reasoning that lies behind the static HO model detailed above. Some studies used specific welfare functions and production functions to model the supply and demand sides of the economy before introducing price changes expected from letting goods flow across the border. Others used supply and demand models for many categories of products to calculate the welfare effects of the trade-induced price shifts. The conclusion of all of these studies is that the gains from international trade are small.

One of the earliest studies by Giorgio Basevi (1966) estimated that trade restrictions cost the United States one-tenth of one percent of the value of its GDP. This was a surprising result, but mainstream economists found little to criticize since the study followed the logic of the well-accepted HO model. Robert Feenstra (1992) surveyed the whole set of pre-1990 studies on the costs of protection for the U.S. economy, and he estimated that the total loss to the United States from its protectionist tariffs and quotas across all industries was about $30 billion at 1986 prices, or about three quarters of one percent of U.S. GDP. U.S. protectionism also caused losses in other countries. Feenstra assumed that foreign losses were equal U.S. losses, which led him to conclude that the total cost of U.S. trade restrictions was about US$60 billion. This is a large number, but it is a very small percentage of total world income.

In Van den Berg and Lewer (2007), we surveyed all studies published in major economics journals that estimated the welfare gains from international trade according to the conceptual framework of the HO model. The estimates of the gains from international trade almost all fell in the 0.5 to 1 percent of GDP range. Such small percentages add up to hundreds of billions of dollars per year throughout the world, but relative to GDP such results do not translate into a strong case for free trade. Economic growth normally adds more than 1 percent to income in most economies every year. The estimated small gains from trade and mainstream economists' enthusiasm for free trade seem to be inconsistent.

14.2.7 An evaluation of the HO model and the gains from trade

The discussion above explains how the Heckscher-Ohlin model generates several important conclusions about international trade:

- International trade increases human welfare because it increases the total value of the goods and services consumed.

- Countries specialize according to their comparative advantage, which is why trade causes some national industries to grow and others to contract.

- Trade shifts a country's productive factors and resources from its import-competing industries towards its export industries.

- When an economy opens to trade, consumption patterns change because exported products become more expensive and import-competing goods become less expensive.

- Estimates of the gains from trade shown in the HO model are very small, on the order of one-half to one percent of GDP.

Whether the above conclusions about the effects of international trade are accurate depends on what real world evidence shows. Are the conclusions mere hypotheses or are they scientifically proven theories? Economists seem to have largely accepted the above conclusions, as evidenced by economists' survey responses on whether they support free international trade.[8] These conclusions of the HO model depend on the many specific assumptions made in building the model.

Among the HO model's many assumptions are:

- All industries have increasing costs, and markets are perfectly competitive.

- There are no increasing returns to scale.

- There are no externalities that cause prices to differ from opportunity costs.

- Preferences do not shift when production and consumption shift.

- The economy is always at full employment.

- There are no transition costs when resources shift between industries.

- Shifts in resources between industries are instantaneous and complete.

---

[8] See, for example, Robert J. Blendon, *et al.* (1997).

- Technology remains constant.

- Supplies of productive inputs like labor and capital are fixed in quantity.

- Trade is always balanced, and the value of exports always equals imports.

These assumptions are the starting point from which the HO model logically arrives at its conclusions. But because these assumptions are unrealistic, the model's conclusions have been questioned.

Another fundamental shortcoming of the H-O model is that it is *static*. It describes how, all other things equal, a nation is always better off trading with others as opposed to remaining self-sufficient. The model's static perspective is reflected in the assumptions that technology is constant and that the opening of trade does not change the supply of labor. Remember that over two centuries ago, Adam Smith linked specialization and exchange to the process of economic growth and development. Economic development is a **dynamic process** in which all other things *never* remain equal. The HO model does not accurately capture the effects of international trade in a growing, changing economy.

More generally, the model fails to consider popular concerns about globalization, such as the loss of jobs, the competitive struggles of industries facing import competition, the introduction of foreign cultures, the loss of national sovereignty to transnational firms that use trade to spread their organizations across national borders, the macroeconomic effects of the international investment flows that accompany trade, and the growing dependence on foreign products and natural resources. The next section examines the dynamic relationship between international trade and economic growth. Later sections of this chapter and the next two chapters take up these concerns about trade that the HO model does not address.

14.3 International Trade and Economic Growth

Economic growth is often depicted as an outward shift of the economy's PPF, as in Figure 14.6. If, for example, technological change lets the economy produce more food and clothing from its available productive resources, the PPF shifts out to where the economy can reach the indifference curve I_2 at the tangency point B. That same welfare level can be reached through international trade, as shown in the previous section and also depicted in Figure 14.6.

Notice that the combinations of goods consumed are different in each of the two cases in Figure 14.6: economic growth shifts the tangency between the PPF and the indifference curve I_2 to point B, while opening the economy to trade shifts the tangency between the CPL and I_2 to point C. In terms of overall welfare, trade and growth seem to achieve the same welfare gain.

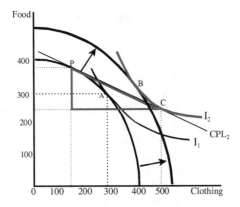

Figure 14.6 The Similarity between Trade and Growth

When we look at the huge discrepancies between per capita real income in the most developed countries and the less developed countries, international trade's one-time static improvement in real income does not seem very meaningful. Compare, for example, the two economies with identical populations depicted by the PPFs labeled A and B in Figure 14.7. For the economy B at the bottom left corner of Figure 14.7, a one-time improvement in welfare brought about by opening up to international trade does not do much to close the 1,000 percent difference in per capita income between it and the more developed economy A. For most people living in the less developed economies of Africa, Latin America, and Asia, economic development is not about moving from I_1 to I_2. Rather, what is needed are welfare gains on the order of moving from I_1 to I_{20}. Such a gain requires a persistent outward shift of the PPF that only continual growth of welfare-enhancing economic activity can bring about.

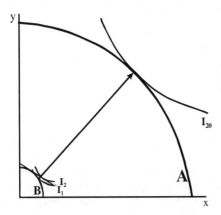

Figure 14.7 The Static Gain from Trade and the Dynamic Gain from Economic Growth

14.3.1 International trade and Schumpeter's model of innovation

The gain from international trade described in the HO model can be incorporated into the Solow growth model as a one-time upward shift in the economy's production function. Trade indeed is a gain in economic efficiency that increases the value of goods and services available from a given set of resources and technology. But, recall from previous discussions of the Solow model that such a shift in the production function brings only medium-term growth that stops when the economy arrives at its new steady state. Permanent growth requires continual technological progress.

The Schumpeterian model of technological change suggests several ways in which international trade might cause long-run economic development. Most obvious is international trade's ability to increase the gains from innovation by making new products available to more people in more countries. Thus, all other things equal, the profits from innovation are increased. Effectively, the integration of separate national markets into a single international market increases total demand faced by a prospective innovator. A second effect of the integration of separate economies is that the supply of productive resources can be more efficiently allocated to innovative activities.

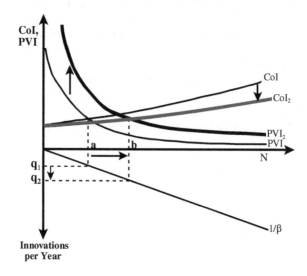

Figure 14.8 International Economic Integration and Innovation

Figure 14.8 uses the graphic version of the Schumpeter model, first presented in Chapter 8, to illustrate these two effects. By increasing the size of an economy through international trade, the greater profit from the enlarged market shifts the PVI curve to PVI_2, and the greater access to the world's productive resources shifts the CoI curve down to CoI_2. As a result, the amount of resources employed in R&D activities rises from a to b, which increases the likely number of innovations per year from q_1 to q_2. The Schumpeterian model of technological change thus seems to suggest that technological innovation an integrated world economy will, in the long run, be greater than the sum of real incomes of economies growing in isolation.

This analysis ignores changes that accompany the economic growth, however. First of all, income is distributed differently in the integrated economy than in isolated individual economies because resources are shifted from the import-competing industries to export industries in each country. Also, technological change shifts the demand for productive factors, which also shifts incomes among factor owners. Finally, the overall growth in income that often accompanies technological change also redistributes incomes because product prices shift in accordance with **income elasticities of demand**.

More problematic is the observation, noted in Chapter 7, that technological progress often centers in certain locations. The prospect of geographic agglomeration of innovative activity opens up the possibility that in a dynamic global economy not all economies enjoy welfare gains from expanding trade. Long-run incomes from innovation may rise in some countries and fall in others. In short, a dynamic perspective on international trade and growth does not support the HO model's conclusion that *all* countries gain from trade.

14.3.2 Trade and technology transfers

There are other channels through which international trade can affect the rate of technological change. One of these is trade's effect on international technology transfers, or more simply, the international exchange of ideas that Paul Seabright (2010) listed as one of the gains from dealing with strangers. International trade and accompanying activities like international marketing, market research, product planning, and foreign travel can help spread knowledge and technology.

Table 14.2 A Slowing Combinatoric Growth Process
(new idea = the unique combination of two old ideas)

		New Ideas	Accumulated Ideas	Percentage Growth
Period 1		3	3	
Period 2	$3!/(1! \cdot 2!)$	= 3	6	100%
Period 3	$3!/(1! \cdot 2!)$	= 3	9	50%
Period 4	$3!/(1! \cdot 2!)$	= 3	14	33%
Period 5	$3!/(1! \cdot 2!)$	= 3	15	25%

The number of combinations for n ideas taken r at a time is $n!/[(n-r)! \cdot r!]$, where n is the number of new ideas generated in the previous period and they are combined two at a time, so r = 2. The symbol "!" represents a product of descending integers, e.g., $5! = 5 \cdot 4 \cdot 3 \cdot 2 \cdot 1 = 120$.

Chapter 7 characterized technological change as a **combinatoric process**. An implication of such a process is that the more knowledge we have, the more likely it is we will find new combinations. For example, if the economy begins with just three ideas rather than the four ideas in the example from Chapter 7, then Table 14.2 shows the rate of technological change actually *decreases* over time. Not illustrated is the case of an initial stock of knowledge consisting of two useful ideas, in which technological change stops entirely after just two periods.

These examples of combinatoric processes are obviously unrealistic; the state of knowledge certainly consists of more than three ideas. On the other hand, not all combinations produce useful new ideas. Knowledge can also be forgotten. And, there may be institutional barriers against certain combinations, such as the ban on modern astronomy during the Inquisition or the formal and informal restrictions on stem cell research in the United States today. Recall, also, the discussion of Thomas Kuhn's (1962) hypothesis that scientific development and technological change are not continuous but episodic because innovation tends to be shaped by paradigms, or cultures, that restrict scientific work to a limited set of combinations.

In sum, the greater the stock of knowledge, the more combinations there are, and the less likely the process will stagnate. And, because casual observation suggests that technology is not the same in all countries, the integration of economies through trade is likely to reveal new fruitful combinations. Ideas from afar may be more likely to shift paradigms by making people more aware of revolutionary new paradigms.

14.3.3 Statistical evidence on trade and development

The arguments for protection suggest that there is some uncertainty about how international trade affects a country's economic development. This theoretical uncertainty has led many economists to estimate the net effect of international trade on human well-being using available data and statistical methods. Such statistical analyses have been done for many countries over many different time periods. Many have used **time-series** data consisting of many observations spread over various time periods for individual countries. Others carried out **cross-section** studies using sets of observations for many countries at a given point in time. More recently, **panel studies** that simultaneously apply time-series data for a cross-section of countries have become popular. The results of the statistical studies often suggest that trade liberalization is correlated with economic growth. But, because of the difficulty in distinguishing the many causes of economic growth, the statistical results have not definitively proven that trade is an engine of growth as Robertson (1938) suggested.

The results of statistical studies examining the relationship between international trade and economic growth often suggest that trade liberalization is positively related to economic growth.[9] And, the estimated effect of trade on growth often appears to be economically significant as well as statistically significant. On average, the cross-section and time-series studies suggest that the rate of growth of real GDP rises by about 0.20 percentage points for every 1 percentage point increase in the growth rate of international trade. That is, an economy whose exports and imports grow 5 percentage points faster than those of its more protectionist neighbor will grow about one percentage point faster than that neighbor, all other things equal. The power of compounding expands such an increase of one percentage point in annual growth into a per capita GDP that is 2.7 times as large as its neighbor's after one century. That is the difference between a developed economy's per capita income of $27,000 per capita and a middle-income developing economy's per capita income of $10,000.

Empirical studies of the relationship between foreign trade and economic growth most often estimated the parameters of linear statistical models of the form

$$G_{GDP} = a_0 + a_1 G_K + a_2 G_L + a_3 TRADE + a_4 Z + u \qquad (14.1)$$

where G_{GDP}, G_K, and G_L are the growth rates of real gross domestic product, capital stock, and labor force, respectively, TRADE represents the growth of trade, Z is a set of other variables thought to explain economic growth (such as institutional variables, distance from trade partners, trade policies, etc.), and u is the standard error term that describes the random variation around the regression relationship. A positive value of a_3 implies a positive relationship between trade and growth. This equation is popular among researchers because data to proxy the model's variables are readily available from national accounts and large data bases such as Angus Maddison's (1995, 2001, 2003) historical time series. The results from estimating the parameters of the model are problematic, however. The data are inaccurate, and estimates of the influence of the variables included in the model are biased by the omission of many other potentially influential variables from the model.

14.3.4 What does the statistical evidence suggest?

In Van den Berg and Lewer (2007) we surveyed the many statistical studies of the relationship between international trade and growth. We found 34 cross-section studies published in the leading economics journals. These studies included a total of 196 separate regressions using cross-section data for samples of countries in a regression model like equation (14.1). The average estimated value of the coefficient of the growth of real exports was 0.22. Since the

---

[9] Useful surveys of the empirical literature include Joshua Lewer and Hendrik Van den Berg (2003), Sebastian Edwards (1998), Robert Baldwin (2003), and Chapter 2 of Van den Berg and Lewer (2007).

variables in the regressions were stated in terms of growth rates, this coefficient estimate implies that for a one percentage point increase in the growth rate of trade, the economy's growth rate increased by about one fifth (0.22/1.00) of one percentage point.

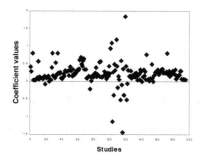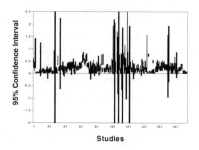

Figure 14.9 The Scatters and 95 percent Confidence Distributions of Coefficient Estimates for *196 Cross-Section* Regressions of Trade on Growth (Studies Shown in order of Date of Publication)

The graphic patterns of the 196 regressions shown in Figure 14.9 suggest quite a bit of variation across the 196 regression estimates. The left-hand diagram shows the estimated regression coefficients for the growth of exports from each of the 196 cross-section regressions, listed from left to right in order of publication date. Only 111 of the 196 coefficients fall between 0.15 and 0.45. The diagram on the right shows the 95 percent confidence intervals of the 196 point estimates. Nearly 90 percent of the coefficient values covered by the confidence intervals are positive, but most are very close to zero. Still, about 90 percent are statistically significantly different from zero, which seems to suggest the statistical evidence is fairly strong that there is a positive relationship between trade and growth.

In Van den Berg and Lewer (2007) we also summarize the results from statistical studies of individual countries over extended periods of time, or what are called time-series studies. The average estimated regression coefficient is nearly identical to the 0.22 found for the cross-section regressions. Also, the variation in the estimates is similarly quite large. Such large variations in the estimates suggest that many other variables also influence a country's growth of GDP. The variations in the confidence intervals suggest that studies also used different estimation methods.

14.3.5 Conclusions suggested by the statistical evidence

Francisco Rodriguez and Dani Rodrik (1999, 2001) find a very close correlation between iInternational trade and institutions like the quality of government programs, protection of human rights, culture, and many other social institutions. It is probably impossible for statistical programs to differentiate between the trade's effect on growth and the growth effects of the various institutions. The computed correlation between trade and growth may, therefore, not be due to the fact that an open economy grows faster because it trades more. Rather, the more rapid growth may be due to the institutional and policy variables that happen to also facilitate international trade. If this is the case, then free trade policies will not deliver economic development in countries where institutions prevent trade from improving technology, efficiency, or income distribution.

In a related study, Rodrik, Arvind Subramanian, and Francesco Trebbi (2002) find that the estimated coefficient for trade in a regression equation like (14.1) becomes statistically insignificant when variables representing institutions are included in the Z matrix of other influential variables. Variables quantifying how countries apply the rule of law, protect property rights, promote human rights, enforce patents, and regulate the economy are statistically more important for growth than opening the borders to trade. In a follow-up study, Roberto Rigobon and Rodrik (2005) controlled for the simultaneous effects of many more variables, and trade was found to actually have a negative impact on a country's average level of income.

Economists have long found negative correlations between trade and growth when they restricted their analysis to resource-exporting countries. Robert Auty (1993) and Jeffrey Sachs and Andrew Warner (1995) referred to the negative statistical relationship between trade and growth as the **resource curse**. Sachs and Warner summarize the *resource curse* as follows:

> The oddity of resource-poor economies outperforming resource-rich economies has been a constant motif of economic history. In the seventeenth century, resource-poor Netherlands eclipsed Spain, despite the overflow of gold and silver from Spanish colonies in the New World. In the nineteenth and twentieth centuries, resource-poor countries such as Switzerland and Japan surged ahead of resource-abundant countries such as Russia. In the past thirty years, the world's star performers have been the resource-poor Newly Industrializing Economies of East Asia — Korea, Taiwan, Hong Kong, Singapore — while... the oil-rich countries of Mexico, Nigeria, Venezuela, have gone bankrupt.

Differences in institutions no doubt help to explain the often-reported negative relationship between exports of natural resources and economic growth, what is often referred to as the resource curse. Some studies contend that it is actually resource trade that causes the poor economic institutions that impede economic development. For example, Carlos Leite and Jens Weidman (1999) present evidence that suggests resource exports increase political corruption. And, Thor Gylfasson and Gylfi Zoega (2002) find a positive correlation between resource exports and income inequality. Carlos Leite and JensWeidman (1999) and Timothy Azarchs and Tamar Khitarishvili (2010) find that some resource exports are more damaging to growth than others; fuel and ores are more often linked to economic declines than agricultural exports. Press accounts routinely link natural resource exports to social conflicts driven by competition for the economic rents created by export demand, especially the civil wars in African countries in recent decades. Other hypothesized causes of the resource curse are the long-term decline in commodity prices and the volatility of resource prices. Finally, oil and other resource exports may crowd out manufacturing and service activities that have greater technology spillovers.

Robert Baldwin (2003) sums up his survey of case studies and statistical studies on the relationship between international trade and growth as follows:

> It is true developing countries are often given the advice that decreasing trade barriers is a more effective way of achieving higher sustainable rates of growth than tightening trade restrictions. But... those giving such advice also emphasize the need, as a minimum, for a stable and non-discriminatory exchange-rate system and usually also the need for prudent monetary and fiscal policies and corruption-free administration of economic policies for trade liberalization to be effective in the long-run. It seems to me that the various country studies do support this type of policy advice and the cross-country statistical studies do not overturn this conclusion. But the recent critiques of the latter studies demonstrate that we must be careful in attributing any single economic policy, such as the lowering of trade barriers, as being a sufficient government action for accelerating the rate of economic growth.

The long-running debate over whether trade is "the engine of growth" or merely a "handmaiden of growth" has not yet been settled.

14.4 Why Free Trade May Not Benefit a Country

The HO model shows that a shift to free trade causes some industries to expand and others to contract. The comparative-static HO model, by comparing only the starting and end points of the process, ignores how an economy actually adjusts dynamically. The HO model assumes that when economies specialize they instantaneously and costlessly shift factors of production from declining industries to expanding industries. It also assumes that all factors of production are productive in all industries. In reality, there are **adjustment costs** when international trade causes the economy to specialize. Many resources must move, which takes time, transportation, and adjustments. Workers may have to endure temporary unemployment after losing their jobs as they search for new jobs in other industries. Those jobs may be located in other communities. Workers may lose some of their accumulated human capital, and they may need to learn new techniques, practices, and procedures. Capital equipment may be even more difficult to shift from one industry to another. A farm tractor cannot be used to manufacture clothing, which is exactly what the HO model assumes in the two-good, two-country example of food and clothing.

14.4.1 Adjustments to trade are costly

Recall that opening a closed economy to trade implies a shift from the self-sufficiency equilibrium at point A in Figure 14.6 to production at P and consumption at C. Such shifts in resource allocation do not normally occur without some temporary disruptions to employment and some sub-optimal consumption decisions. The economy incurs real costs, in terms of lost output, when workers have to move from one location to another, when equipment and buildings (capital) are abandoned in one industry and new investment must be undertaken in another industry, or when workers have to take time off from work in order to learn new skills.

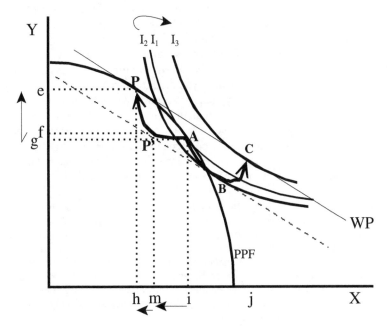

Figure 14.10 Adjusting to Free Trade

Figure 14.10 illustrates a potentially more realistic path of adjustment of an economy that shifts from self-sufficiency to free trade that includes some temporary unemployment. In this case, the trade-induced change in relative prices of X and Y causes the production to move inside the production possibilities frontier (PPF) from A to P along the path through point P', not along the edge of the PPF as suggested in Figure 14.6. The portion of the path between A and P' reflects a rapid fall in the production of X, from i to m, matched by only meager growth in the production of Y from g to f. The reason for such a path is that not all workers and other productive resources move immediately from one industry to the other. Even if consumers immediately allocate their incomes in the most efficient way possible, production at point P' caused by temporarily unemployed resources generates only enough real income to permit consumers to consume at point B in the lower indifference curve I_2. If consumers adjust slowly to the new prices and allocate their income according to past habits, they may not even reach I_2.

When, for example, people have sufficient human capital to perform other tasks and they have the financial wherewithal to cover the costs of moving to other parts of the country, then production can shift more quickly towards the export industry and the static welfare gains from trade can be achieved sooner. Also, if banks and financial markets quickly shift the flow of savings from financing investment in shrinking industries to financing investment in the expanding export industries, the gains from trade will appear sooner. In the real world, there will always be a substantial time lag in shifting physical capital from one sector to another. It simply takes time to build new factories, expand infrastructure, and produce the specialized equipment necessary in new industries. Hence, temporary unemployment and unused industrial capacity are likely when an economy suddenly opens its economy to international trade. The owners of specialized physical and human capital used only in the industry X, the declining industry in Figure 14.10, will suffer substantial losses in the long run as well because their capital may be permanently unemployed.

Adam Smith, who is so often quoted by free trade advocates, understood the costs of adjustment and the losses to the declining industries:

> The undertaker of a great manufacture, who, by the home markets being suddenly laid open to the competition of foreigners, should be obliged to abandon his trade, would no doubt suffer very considerably. That part of his capital which had usually been employed in purchasing materials and in paying his workmen, might, without much difficulty, perhaps, find another employment. But that part of it which was fixed in workhouses, and in the instruments of trade, could scarce be disposed of without considerable loss. The equitable regard, therefore, to his interest requires that changes of this kind should never be introduced suddenly, but slowly, gradually, and with a very long warning.[10]

Alan Blinder, President Clinton's advisor who helped sell the North American Free Trade Agreement (NAFTA) to a skeptical public in 1993, has now also recognized the cost of adjustment to trade. Blinder compares the scope of today's trade-driven shifting of jobs between different countries to the Industrial Revolution in its effects on "how and where people lived, how they educated

---

[10] Adam Smith (1976 [1976]), p. 494.

their children, the organization of businesses, the form and practices of governments."[11]

14.4.2 The example of NAFTA

An example of the complexity and difficulties associated with adjustment to a major surge in international trade is the case of the **North American Free Trade Agreement (NAFTA)** between Canada, Mexico, and the United States.[12] When it went into effect in 1995, NAFTA permitted U.S. agricultural firms to begin exporting grains and other processed and semi-processed foods to Mexico. These were the same foods that were widely grown and produced by several million small farmers in Mexico prior to free trade. The huge fertile Great Plains region gives the United States a natural comparative advantage in many farm products like grain. In addition, the U.S. government subsidizes agricultural production, which further adds to U.S. grain producers' advantage in overseas markets. The implementation of NAFTA quickly caused prices to fall, which devastated Mexico's traditional agriculture and had dire effects on employment and the overall health of rural communities in Mexico. The acceleration of Mexican immigration to the United States in recent years is a direct consequence of the destruction of Mexican agriculture by the surge of U.S. farm products into Mexico. Traditional Mexican farmers had little option but to leave the land and seek work in Mexico's cities, where unemployment was already high. Often, they opted to head north and cross the border, usually illegally, to take much higher-paying jobs in the United States.

Economists used the HO model to argue that Mexico's imports of U.S. agricultural products would be paid for by Mexican exports to the United States, and that Mexico's loss of jobs in agriculture would be matched by jobs in Mexican export industries. Plus, some economists added that technology transfers would make Mexican agriculture more efficient and profitable. NAFTA did provide a market for Mexican products in the United States, but Mexican exporters had to compete in the U.S. market with other foreign suppliers like China. This meant Mexican producers had to reduce costs quickly, which they did by minimizing labor inputs. The end result was that Mexican industry did not provide nearly enough new jobs for the Mexican farmers displaced by efficient U.S. agriculture, and wages in Mexico plunged as unemployed Mexican workers were willing to take any job they could get. This case suggests Adam Smith's advice should have been heeded: "changes of this kind should never be introduced suddenly, but slowly, gradually, and with a very long warning."

---

[11] Alan Blinder (2006). See also David Wessel and Bob Davis (2007), "Pain from Free Trade Spurs Second Thoughts," *Wall Street Journal*, March 28.
[12] This section follows David Bacon (2008) and Mamerto Péres, Sergio Schlesinger, and Timothy A. Wise (2008).

14.4.3 Shifts in the terms of trade

When a country reduces import tariffs or eliminates import quotas, a country often experiences a change in its **terms of trade**, which is the ratio of how much a country has to export in order to acquire a given amount of imports. The terms of trade reflects the cost of imports in terms of exports, and they are crucial for determining a country's gains from trade. Also, over time a country may find that shifts in world demand and supply substantially increase or decrease a country's welfare gains from trade. Less developed countries that export agricultural commodities may be especially vulnerable to adverse shifts in their terms of trade, and less reliance on international trade could be welfare enhancing in the long run.

Interestingly, the traditional HO model can be used to show how, in the case of a country large enough to influence international prices, the gains from increased international trade may be undermined by adverse price movements. One such case, which Jagdish Bhagwati (1958) called **immiserizing growth**, shows that even within the framework of the neoclassical HO model there are special circumstances under which international trade can cause the growth in output to reduce welfare.

Figure 14.11 illustrates how economic growth that is biased towards expanding a country's capacity to export can actually cause national welfare to decline. Suppose the economy's productive capacity is initially represented by the production possibilities frontier PPF_1. If the world's terms of trade are given by the line ToT_1, then the country open to trade can specialize by producing at the point P_1 and trading to consume at the consumption point A, thus reaching the indifference curve I_4. The country exports food in exchange for clothing at the terms of trade given by the slope of the line ToT_1. Then, suppose the economy grows and the production possibilities frontier shifts out to PPF_2. The diagram suggests that the economy's growth seems to have been concentrated in the economy's export sector, the food industry. This will often be the case in developing economies where the export sector is the only part of the economy that has ready access to financing. If, furthermore, the country is a major supplier of food to the world economy the price of food will decline. In Figure 14.11, the country's terms of trade are assumed to decline from ToT_1 to ToT_2 as exports of food increase. The diagram shows that this ToT decline can more than offset the positive welfare effect of an increase in productive capacity. Hence, after the growth in capacity and the increase in exports, the country consumes at the point B, which lies on a lower indifference curve. Had the country not been open to trade, the growth of production would have provided a gain in welfare, albeit the gain from point D on I_1 to point C on I_2, both lower levels of welfare than were achieved before and after immiserizing growth by the open economy.

Note that Figure 14.11 does *not* suggest that closing the economy to international trade necessarily increases national welfare. Comparing the consumption points A and B with C and D shows that a closed economy does not suffer immiserizing growth, but it never attains the levels of welfare achieved by an open economy before or after the immiserizing growth.

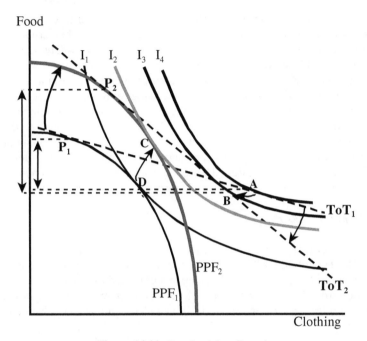

Figure 14.11   Immizerizing Growth

Miltiades Chacholiades (1990) lists the conditions that make immiserizing growth possible: (1) the exporting country's growth in productive capacity is concentrated in the sectors of the economy that export, (2) the price elasticity of demand for the export product is inelastic, (3) exports account for a large share of the country's GDP, (4) technological change is minimal, (5) the export country supplies a large portion of total world output, and (6) the export country does not restrict trade. Not all six of these conditions have to be satisfied for growth to be immiserizing. Even when demand is elastic, the other five conditions may still be strong enough to cause immiserizing growth.

There are a number of documented cases of immiserizing growth, mostly developing countries that dominated specific commodity markets where demand was relatively price inelastic. For example, in the early twentieth century, Brazil was the dominant supplier of coffee to the world, coffee accounted for a very large percentage of Brazilian GDP, the coffee industry's growth was based mostly on factor accumulation, not technological change, and demand for coffee is very price *inelastic*. Also, it takes 7 to 8 years before a newly planted coffee tree produces its first harvest of coffee beans. Hence, feedback from coffee prices to individual farmers is delayed. They do not know for many years whether they have planted too many or too few trees. Over-investment can go on for years.

Raúl Prebisch (1950) and Hans Singer (1950) argued that, in fact, differences in demand elasticities will inevitably cause the terms of trade for primary product exporters to decline. This idea is now widely referred to as the **Singer-Prebisch thesis**. A country that has a comparative advantage in producing products for which demand is inelastic will not benefit as much from international trade as a country that enjoys rising terms of trade for its exports. Developing economies are especially prone to suffering immiserizing growth because they tend to be exporters of raw materials and agricultural products for which demand does not respond quickly to price changes. Also, mining projects are major long-term investments, and agricultural production is often tightly linked to a country's culture. Hence, developing countries' economies are unable to quickly alter their structures in response to changing terms of trade.

14.4.4 Infant industries

The **infant industry** argument for trade protection was detailed back in 1791 by Alexander Hamilton, the first U.S. Secretary of the Treasury. In his *Report on Manufactures*, he urged the newly independent United States to protect its infant industries from British competition. The argument was further legitimized in the mid-1800s when John Stuart Mill included it in his popular economics textbook:

> The only case in which, on mere principles of political economy, protecting duties can be defensible, is when they are imposed temporarily (especially in a young and rising nation) in hopes of naturalizing a foreign industry, in itself perfectly suitable to the circumstance of the country. The superiority of one country over another in a branch of production often arises only from having begun it sooner. There may be no inherent advantage on one part, or disadvantage on the other, but only a present superiority of acquired skill and experience. A country which has this skill and experience yet to acquire, may in other respects be better adapted to the production than those which were earlier in the field... A protecting duty, continued for a reasonable time, will sometimes be the least inconvenient mode in which the nation can tax itself for the support of such an experiment.[13]

Mill then immediately qualified his endorsement of infant industry protection as follows:

---

[13] John Stuart Mill (1848), p. 922.

But the protection should be confined to cases in which there is good ground of assurance that the industry it fosters will after a time be able to dispense with it; nor should the domestic producers ever be allowed to expect that it will be continued to them beyond the time necessary for a fair trial of what they are capable of accomplishing.

The argument that there must be a reasonable probability that an industry will become profitable in the future for an industry to be awarded protection has come to be known as the **Mill criterion**. Later economists distinguished additional assumptions that implicitly lie behind the infant industry argument, namely that (1) there is some kind of learning by doing process that relates production costs to production experience, (2) only domestic production experience can help the learning process because technology and know-how cannot be easily acquired from abroad (technology is country-specific), and (3) know-how and technology cannot be easily acquired from other sectors of the economy.

While such a long list of qualifications was seen by orthodox economists as invalidating the infant industry argument for protection, many development economists and developing country policymakers accepted the qualifications as being satisfied in most less developed economies. They saw that the financial sector in their countries was not set up to provide funds to money-losing industries over the long periods of maturation that they would have to endure in developing economies. They also believed that industrialization per se would generate learning processes and technology transfers that could not be captured by the individual business owners or the financial sector. Finally, governments in poor countries seldom had access to tax systems that could generate sufficient funds to cover the costs of direct subsidies to infant industries. Hence, the indirect method of having consumers of imports effectively pay for the temporary cost of protection may indeed be the most efficient way to bring potentially profitable infant industries into existence in developing economies.

In the latest round of trade negotiations, the so-called Doha Round, a group of developing countries pushed for amending the rules of the World Trade Organization (WTO) to permit low-income economies to more openly and substantially protect their infant industries, as they were effectively permitted to do before the WTO rules came into effect in 1994. Under the 1947 General Agreement on Trade and Tariffs (GATT) that preceded the more formal current regulatory framework of the WTO, developing countries were given great leeway to protect their economies from import competition. Interestingly, economic historians have often pointed out that today's leading industrial economies, such as the United States, Germany, and Japan, protected their industrial sectors during the formative years with a wide array of tariffs, quotas, regulatory restrictions on imports, and strong appeals to nationalism. Today's largest newly industrializing countries, China and Brazil, in fact find many ways to continue protecting their infant industries from foreign competition.

14.4.5 Increasing returns to scale

The HO model assumes that all industries face rising costs when they expand their output. The production possibilities curve is bowed out to reflect such increasing opportunity costs as one industry expands at the expense of another. More generally, increasing costs reflect the assumption that aggregate production in an economy is subject to diminishing returns. As you recall, Classical economists like Thomas Malthus and David Ricardo built diminishing returns into their models, and Robert Solow assumed it in his growth model.

The assumption of increasing costs is needed to justify the assumption of perfect competition in the HO model. If costs declined with output, large firms would have an advantage over small ones, and perfect competition will be replaced by oligopolies and monopolies. Prices will no longer accurately reflect opportunity costs, and the owners of many firms will enjoy excess profits.

Adam Smith's (1776) example of a pin factory has been often used to illustrate how a large scale pin producer can produce many more pins per worker than a small workshop could. Today we describe such a pin factory as an **increasing returns to scale** industry because increasing the scale of operations reduces the cost per item produced.   Manufacturing tends to be carried out by a small number of large firms, not large numbers of competitive producers.

A production possibilities frontier (PPF) for an economy consisting of two increasing returns to scale industries, pizza and books, is given in Figure 14.12. The PPF is convex to the origin, with the diminishing slope reflecting the increasingly *smaller* amounts of one product that must be sacrificed in order to achieve ever *greater* amounts of the other.

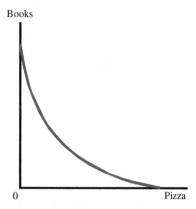

Figure 14.12 The PPF when Production is Subject to Increasing Returns to Scale

It can be shown that international trade still increases welfare when production is characterized by increasing returns to scale. Suppose that the two increasing returns to scale industries, books and pizza, have identical PPFs in two countries, A and B. The two-country diagram looks like Figure 14.13. Suppose also that consumer tastes can be represented by the orthodox indifference curves exhibiting preferences that vary depending on the relative quantities of books and pizzas. These assumptions conveniently eliminate differences in tastes, resource availability, or technology as potential influences on trade. In the absence of trade, each economy produces and consumes where its PPF is tangent to the indifference curve I_1. The relative prices of books and pizza would be the same in both countries at A and A*, respectively. Neither country appears to have a comparative advantage: the opportunity costs are the same in each country at 1 book equals 1 pizza. Welfare in each country is represented by the indifference curves I_1 and I_1*, respectively.

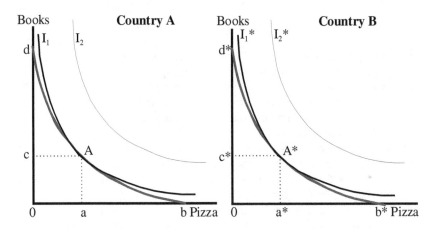

Figure 14.13 International Trade with Increasing Returns to Scale

But there are potential gains from trade because increasing returns to scale create a tradeoff: consumers prefer more variety to less variety, but the cost of each product is lower if consumers opt for less variety by consuming only one of the two goods. This tradeoff is less onerous when countries A and B agree to trade. For example, suppose each country agrees to specialize in producing just one of the two goods in order to exploit increasing returns to scale and exchanges books for pizzas or pizzas for books. In this case, consumers can enjoy the variety of both books and pizza as well as lower costs of each product.

In Figure 14.14 country A specializes in the production of books and produces at **d**, and country B produces only pizzas at **b***. If they set relative prices as given by the dashed lines and exchange books and pizzas, trade will be represented by the identical shaded trade triangles. The two countries consume the combinations of books and pizza B and B*, respectively, and reach the higher indifference curves I_2 and I_2*. International trade raises human welfare in

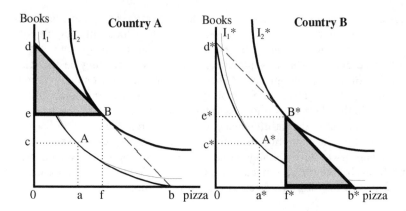

Figure 14.14 Specialization and Trade with Increasing Returns to Scale

each country even though A and B are initially identical in every way. Each country effectively gains a comparative advantage after the expansion of one increasing-returns-to-scale industry in each country lowers its costs below those of the same, but contracting, industry in the other country.

This example suggests that the direction of specialization by each of the two initially-identical economies is entirely arbitrary. Who specialized in what could have been decided by a coin toss. The model is not clear on why the two countries would settle for the terms of trade necessary to bring countries A and B to points B and B*, respectively. In practice, the first firm to expand and exploit increasing returns gains the comparative advantage.

Realistically, a case can be made that government action should be used to ensure that the country ends up specializing in those industries that will grow most rapidly or those that will enjoy favorable terms of trade in the future. For example, suppose that, unlike the nice equal outcomes in Figure 14.15, the relative prices at which the trade occurs will in the future bring the two identical countries very different gains from trading books and pizza. Figure 14.15 shows Country A gaining relatively less from trade than Country B. Outcomes like this are quite realistic because, as already discussed above, world prices depend on income elasticities and price elasticities. In this case, the country that ends up specializing in pizza production appears to shift to a higher indifference curve than the country that specializes in producing books. Because people value pizza more than books, the shifting terms of trade favored Country B, which luckily ended up specializing in pizza production and gaining the comparative advantage in that industry.

Research on trade under increasing returns to scale and imperfect competition has led many economists to conclude that international trade is likely to be welfare enhancing under many circumstances, but it is no longer possible to conclude that free trade is always the optimal policy for a national government to pursue in order to maximize its citizens' welfare. Perhaps, government interference can push the direction of international trade toward a more favorable outcome such as the point C* in Figure 14.15.

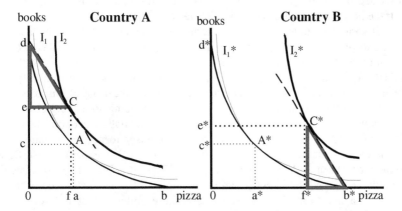

Figure 14.15 Unequal Gains from Trade with Increasing Returns to Scale

In a world where governments often actively support their exporters, a country whose government remains inactive would effectively default to inferior outcomes such as point C. Policies to protect and promote industries with the greatest growth potential are called **strategic trade policies**. In the example above, policies by the government of Country B to protect, subsidize, or otherwise encourage the growth of the pizza industry would constitute a strategic trade policy.

14.4.6 Manufacturing, agriculture, and technological change

The last two sections of this chapter have presented several alternative perspectives on international trade that do not match the HO model's assumptions:

- Trade influences, and is influenced by, economic growth and development.

- The shift to free trade requires costly shifts and losses of resources.

- Terms of trade change over time.

- There are potential gains from protecting infant industries.

- Increasing returns to scale industries spread gains from trade unequally.

Looked at from these perspectives, free trade is no longer necessarily the best policy for maximizing a country's long-run national welfare. Also, the gains and losses accruing to particular interest groups are no longer the same as those described by the HO model. Chapter 16 will present some historical examples of trade policies that reflected these alternative assumptions.

It should be noted that these alternative ideas are not new. In fact, they were part of the discussion of international trade before the Classical economists began to lay the foundations that later economists would transform into the HO model. The transition costs of international trade have been noticed by people for millennia, every time imports put some local producer out of business rather than leading the producer to quickly shift into producing something else. Also, increasing returns to scale were discussed by the Italian economist Antonio Serra in 1613.[14] Today's international economists forget that Adam Smith discussed the interaction between industrial sectors that experienced different economies of scale. For example, Smith (1776[1976], Book 1, p. 9) wrote that agriculture was not as likely to enjoy economies of scale such as he described for the pin industry: "The nature of agriculture, indeed, does not admit of so many subdivisions of labour, nor of so complete a separation of one business from another, as manufactures." As it turns out, Smith failed to anticipate the industrialization of modern agriculture, but his suggestion that different industries experience different degrees of economies of scale was a very important insight. The gains from international trade depend critically on whether or not countries specialize in industries that enjoy economies of scale. The HO assumption of constant returns to scale may lead to inaccurate conclusions about the general gains from international trade.

14.4.7 Enclaves, maquiladores, and spillovers

Whether international trade increases the rate of technological progress in a country depends on whether the acts of exporting and importing products spreads new knowledge and technology to the whole economy. Ever since the nineteenth century, when developing countries and colonies became major sources of raw materials for the industrializing countries of Europe and North America, development economists have been especially interested in determining whether trade generates **efficiency spillovers** to the rest of the developing countries' economies. Export industries in developing countries have often been criticized for not causing spillovers to the local economy.

An interesting case is nitrate mining in northern Chile in the late nineteenth century. Before the chemical industry began producing nitrate, this valuable component of agricultural fertilizers came from natural deposits of the mineral. The agricultural revolution in the 1800s greatly increased world demand for

---

[14] This fact is pointed out by Erik Reinert (2007).

nitrate, and the northern desert region of Chile was a primary source. Nitrate was also used for explosives, and the growing militarization in the world made that a growth market. Chile was endowed with vast deposits of nitrate.

In the 1870s, several large British mining firms established operations in the extremely arid and completely unpopulated desert region of northern Chile, just annexed by Chile after its late-nineteenth century war with Peru and Bolivia. These firms operated far out of sight of most Chileans, who lived in the central part of the country 1,000 miles to the south. The mining firms built their own port facilities and rail connections, and they employed relatively few Chileans in their capital-intensive industry. All equipment and supplies were imported from Britain. There were few opportunities for technology spillovers or transfers, and the huge profits derived from the very low production costs and the high world prices for nitrate accrued largely to the British stockholders of the mining firms. The nitrate industry was a classic example of an **enclave industry**, which is a foreign-owned industry that imports capital from and exports natural resources to the rest of the world without engaging in many other transactions in the domestic economy.

There are ways to turn isolated enclaves into industries with economy-wide externalities, however. In the late 1800s, the Chilean government was able to gradually extract larger and larger tax revenues from the highly profitable foreign nitrate firms, and these revenues permitted it to expand government services without having to levy many taxes on Chileans. This approach of using taxation to create spillovers to the local economy was later extended to the foreign-owned copper industry in Chile. The copper industry operated in remote regions high in the Andes Mountains. The government of Chile thus grew to be a large participant in the economy without developing a local tax base. In a way, this was a politician's dream come true: the government provided its constituents education, roads, utilities, and a myriad of other services without having to tax them. When the prices of copper exports collapsed during the Great Depression of the 1930s, the government ran into severe budgetary problems. Suddenly, higher taxes on domestic citizens and firms were needed to pay for the government services that had been funded by taxes on exports by the foreign mining firms.

The **maquiladora** plants along Mexico's border with the United States are sometimes viewed as a modern example of so-called enclave industries. Maquiladoras are largely foreign-owned assembly plants that take advantage of low Mexican wages without integrating fully into the Mexican economy. The Mexican government allowed these plants to import components, parts, and raw materials free of tariffs, provided all output was again exported. The U.S. government, under a special provision of its trade laws, permitted these plants to export back to the U.S. market with the payment of tariffs only on the value added in Mexico. Foreign managers often lived on the U.S. side of the border and commuted daily to Mexico. Critics argued that the rules governing the maquiladoras and the maquila industries practically guaranteed that they would be enclaves. The North American Free Trade Agreement (NAFTA) between Mexico, Canada, and the United States has not yet spread export production throughout Mexico, even though firms can now import parts and raw materials freely and then export or sell locally as the market demands. There is still a concentration of assembly industries along the U.S. border that use inexpensive Mexican labor to assemble products for the U.S. market.

14.5 The Environmental Impact of International Trade

One of the most serious shortcomings of orthodox economic models of international trade, such as the static HO model, is that they ignore trade's important external effects, or **externalities**, across the economic, social, and natural spheres. For example, international trade can be used to shift some polluting industries from rich to poor countries. Some environmentalists argue that trade merely moves polluting productive activities from one country to another, but it does not reduce global pollution. International trade actually adds to environmental destruction by using energy resources to move goods around the globe.

This section discusses some of the environmental consequences of international trade. Specifically, we analyze how international trade affects the greenhouse gas (GHG) emissions that contribute to global warming.

14.5.1 Shifting GHG emissions to less developed countries

Recall the description of the sale and shipment of the German Thyssen-Krupp steel mill to a Chinese steel producer in the Introduction to the first section of this textbook. We observed that air pollution was reduced in Germany after the plant shut down, but it increased in China where the plant was reassembled and operated. A by-product of the sale of the German steel plant to a Chinese firm is that the steel mill's GHGs and those of the power plant that supplies electricity to the steel mill are now emitted in China rather than Germany.

When it comes to a worldwide phenomenon like global warming, it does not matter where the steel is produced. However, with expanded international trade, emissions are generated when the steel and Chinese products made with the steel are shipped around the world rather than being produced closer to their end markets. Furthermore, the Chinese coal-fired power plants that provide most of the electric power to the transplanted steel plants emit more greenhouse gases than do current German power generators, which increasingly consist of natural gas plants and wind farms. Therefore, the international trade that this relocation of German steel plants enabled increased global GHG emissions.

The HO model of international trade is often used to explain that the shift of industries like steel and manufacturing to labor-abundant economies like China, India, and Brazil is a simple matter of comparative advantage. But comparative advantage is based on more than just factor endowments: differences in environmental policies across countries also determine relative production costs across countries. When costs are not accurately accounted for in all countries, trade will generally not reflect true comparative advantage. Transnational corporations often shift production to countries where environmental regulations are weakest or most easily ignored. The large variations in national environmental regulations have caused a "race to the bottom" in environmental regulation because governments fear they will lose industries, and jobs, to countries with more lax rules. For example, Arik Levinson and Scott Taylor (2008) examine production and imports across twenty industrial categories impacted by new environmental regulation in the U.S., and they find that about half the increase in U.S. imports of those products can be statistically explained by the increases in regulation.

14.5.2 Institutional failures in the global food distribution system

At the start of this chapter, we noted how declines in transportation costs expanded international trade. With lower transport costs, transnational food retailers like Wal-Mart, Tesco, Carrefour, and other large retailers have converted food distribution into global networks that keep consumers supplied with the full range of fresh foods year-round, supplied from producers spread throughout the world. These distributors and retailers have grown in size by increasingly shifting food production to countries where labor costs are lowest. For example, labor costs for processing codfish in Norway are $1.36 per pound, but they are only $0.36 in China. As a result, cod caught off Norway's shores is shipped to China for processing before being shipped back to Norway to be sold. But, this apparent exploitation of comparative advantage comes at a cost: greenhouse gas emissions from transporting food.

Shippers do not pay for all the costs of moving food around the world. For example, international shippers pay fewer taxes than domestic shippers do in most countries. The 1944 Convention on International Civil Aviation established that fuel for international air transport is exempt from national taxes. There is a similar international agreement for ocean shipping. These rules were put into effect allegedly to prevent taxes being used to restrict trade. But, such rules also prevent countries from imposing welfare-improving taxes that could internalize the cost of GHG emissions.

The European Union in 2008 proposed taxing airlines for their GHG emissions, and the measure is scheduled to go into effect in 2012. By getting transport services to pay the full cost of its GHG emissions, it is hoped that international trade in food will more accurately reflect the true cost of carrying goods. A carbon tax is a straightforward way to deal with the current bias favoring international trade. Of course, a carbon tax on transport will not capture the fact, for example, that grass-fed beef from New Zealand produces much fewer GHG emissions than feedlot-fed U.S. beef. If the transport tax stops U.S. imports from New Zealand in favor of home-produced beef, worldwide GHG emissions could actually rise. To avoid such a perverse result, the U.S. government must simultaneously tax U.S. feedlot operators for their GHG emissions. Trade taxes alone cannot bring efficient market outcomes; domestic prices must also accurately reflect true local production costs. Blocking imports on environmental grounds while ignoring the environmental destruction of domestic producers would be an especially egregious form of trade protectionism.

14.5.3 The GHGs embedded in trade

The monitoring of GHG emissions provides us with information on how many GHGs are being emitted and where the emissions occur. This information shows that the moving of a steel mill from Germany to China decreased emissions in Germany and increased emissions in China. Germany can then report progress in reducing their GHG emissions. However, the physical location of the actual sources of GHG emissions is not necessarily important for assigning national obligations for reducing GHG emissions. Since the net gains from trade as illustrated by most trade models, like the Heckscher-Ohlin model, looks at the gains from trade in terms of consumption, not production, a good case can be made that an individual country's GHG emissions should also be calculated in terms of final consumption rather than production. If the environmental consequences of a country's consumption determine the responsibility for global pollution, then moving a factory to China does not reduce Germany's damage to the eco-system.

A 2008 study for the U.K. Department for Environment, Food and Rural Affairs (DEFRA) carried out by research groups at the University of York in the U.K. and the University of Sidney in Australia, recalculated Britain's emissions according to its consumption rather than its production. Figure 14.16 describes how the study reclassified the origin of GHGs. The boxes labeled 1 through 6 locate production, and the arrowheads determine the location of consumption. If GHG emissions are attributed to production, the domestic economy's GHG emissions are equal to the sum of emissions produced in the boxes 1, 2, 5, and 6. On the other hand, if GHG emissions are attributed to final consumption, then the domestic economy's total GHG emissions are the sum of emissions produced in the boxes 1a, 1, 3, 5, and 6. The difference between these two sets, 1a + 3 − 2, is the excess of GHGs from consumption over GHGs from production. Table 14.3 presents Wiedman *et al.*'s estimates. Table 14.3 shows that GHG emissions from U.K. production did not increase between 1992 and 2004, but the United Kingdom's consumers clearly increased their GHG emissions.

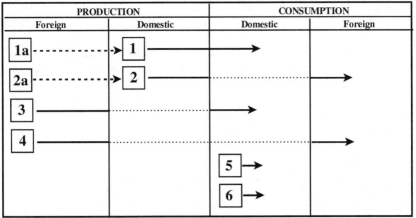

1 - UK emissions from production for domestic consumption
2 - UK emissions from production for export
1a - Imported emissions through intermediate inputs to UK production for domestic consumption
2a - Imported emissions through intermediate inputs tp UK production for export
3 - Imported emissions for UK domestic consumption
4 - Imported emissions for UK export
5 - UK emissions generated by households (excluding use of private automobiles)
6 - UK emissions generated by households from private use of automobiles

Figure 14.16 Comparing GHG Emissions from National Production versus Consumption (Figure from the U.K. Department for Environment, Food and Rural Affairs, DEFRA)

Table 14.3 CO$_2$ Emissions Embedded in the United Kingdom's International Trade

Year	UK Producer Emissions (1+2+5+6)	UK Consumer Emissions (1+1a+3+5+6)	Balance of Emissions Embedded in Trade (1a+3−2)
1992	620.0	647.2	26.8
1995	593.5	652.3	58.9
1998	606.3	680.3	73.9
1999	597.7	664.9	67.2
2000	609.0	680.7	71.7
2001	624.4	732.1	107.5
2002	609.7	730.1	120.4
2003	624.8	763.6	138.8
2004	630.6	762.4	131.8

Source: Table 2 in Wiedman, T., R. Wood, M. Lenzen, J. Minx, D. Guan, and J. Barrett (2008).

14.5.4 Another example of GHGs embedded in trade

The "race to the bottom" effect of international trade is also illustrated by the surge in U.S. exports of used automobiles to Mexico after the North American Free Trade Agreement (NAFTA) eliminated trade restrictions between the two countries in 1994. Before NAFTA went into effect, Mexico had banned the import of all used vehicles in order to protect its domestic automobile industry. Mexico now imports many automobiles ten years or older from the United States, where such cars have little value and are often scrapped or used very little. Between half a million and a million used U.S. vehicles were imported into Mexico each year between 2005 and 2008.[15] Because they are old, these vehicles, on average, emit more carbon and other GHGs than the average automobile on the road in the United States, but they emit less than the average vehicle on the road in Mexico. As a result, this used vehicle trade has caused average emissions per vehicle to decline in both the United States and Mexico but total emissions increased.

Lucas Davis and Matthew Kahn (2010) estimate that total global GHG emissions have actually increased because this trade gives new life to old vehicles that otherwise would have been scrapped. They report that this trade has caused no discernible decline in the number of vehicles on the road in the United States, but the availability of low-priced vehicles increased sales to Mexican consumers who would otherwise not acquire a motor vehicle. Also important to their calculations is the Massachusetts Institute of Technology Energy Laboratory's (2000) finding that for a lifetime driving distance of 300,000 kilometers, 93 percent of an automobile's carbon emissions come from fuel usage, and only 7 percent are caused producing the vehicle. Davis and Kahn's (2010, p. 60) conclusion is relevant for used steel mills as well as used cars:

> With durable goods, how and where goods are consumed is potentially more important than how and where they are produced... With global pollutants the location of consumption is irrelevant, but the magnitude of lifetime consumption is not. As a result, policies aimed at reducing greenhouse gas emissions may not achieve aggregate gains when fuel inefficient durable goods can be traded.

In general, because international trade can cause GHG emissions to increase, any calculation of the gains from trade must include the costs of the emissions.

14.6 Summary and Concluding Remarks

The models examined in this chapter suggest that international trade influences human welfare in a number of ways. The Solow model suggests that trade can only help achieve sustainable economic development if it enhances the process of technological change. The Schumpeterian model of technological change suggests that this could happen, for example, if the international market offers entrepreneurs greater profits for their innovative activities than the domestic market, or if trade relationships across borders help to spread ideas and expand the combinatoric process that advances human knowledge.

---

[15] Lucas W. Davis and Matthew E. Kahn (2010).

These conclusions are, of course, based on logical models built on assumptions that do not accurately reflect the real circumstances under which international trade is actually carried out. This chapter has shown that some of the assumptions made by both the orthodox models of international trade and the models of growth are unrealistic. For example, the Hechscher-Ohlin model of trade assumes that social welfare is the sum of individual welfare levels, that all production is good for human welfare, that market prices accurately reflect all opportunity costs, that there are no externalities like environmental damage, and that all transactions are voluntary. Proponents of free trade instinctively use the orthodox neoclassical paradigm to frame their arguments for free trade. Opponents of free trade policies, on the other hand, point to the many historical cases where people were hurt, and continue to be hurt, by the economic, social, and environmental changes that accompany the growth of international trade. This chapter discussed how international trade causes structural changes in the economy that affect individuals' employment and income in potentially adverse ways. Trade can also have adverse environmental effects. Of course, there are also many advantages to dealing with strangers, and there is ample historical evidence that should make us ponder before we build more walls between nations and societies.

International trade must be examined within a much more holistic framework that takes into consideration the relationships between the economy, human society, and the natural environment on Earth. Chapter 16 will discuss some broader perspectives of international trade. Before we can holistically examine international trade, however, we first need to examine other components of the process of international economic integration, namely international investment, international finance, and immigration. As the next chapter describes, these other forms of international economic activity are related to international trade in many complex ways.

Key Terms and Concepts

Adjustment costs	Gain from exchange
Aggregate indifference curves	Gain from specialization
Cabotage	Heckscher-Ohlin (HO) model.
Combinatoric process	Immiserizing growth
Comparative advantage	Income elasticities of demand
Consumption possibilities line	Increasing costs
Cross-section data	Increasing returns to scale
Dynamic process	Indifference curves
Efficiency spillovers	Infant industry
Enclave industry	Maquiladora
Externalities	Mill criterion

North American Free Trade Agreement
   (NAFTA)
Opportunity costs
Panel data
Production-possibilities frontier (PPF)
Protectionism

Resource curse
Singer-Prebisch thesis
Strategic trade policies
Terms of trade
Time-series data
Trade triangle

Chapter Questions and Problems

1. Why did international trade grow so fast during the nineteenth century? Discuss the evidence presented in the chapter.
2. Is international trade an engine of growth or a handmaiden of growth? Explain your answer.
3. List the assumptions of the Heckscher-Ohlin model. Why does the model make such assumptions? Discuss.
4. Is it valid to assume that all the individual welfare functions can be summed together to arrive at the social welfare function? What logical assumptions must be made about each individual function for the social welfare function to be the sum of the individual functions? Explain. Are these assumptions realistic?
5. Why are indifference curves drawn convex to the origin? Explain what this shape implies about people's tastes.
6. Why is the production possibilities frontier concave to the origin? Explain.
7. In a closed economy, what is the meaning of the tangency between the production possibilities frontier and the aggregate indifference curve? Explain precisely what the common slope at the tangency implies and why the tangency point constitutes a maximum.
8. What does a production point inside the production possibilities frontier imply? Explain.
9. Present the key conclusions of the HO model, and discuss how economists rely on these conclusions to justify free trade policies.
10. Discuss the weaknesses of the HO model and its assumptions.
11. The HO model is sometimes interpreted as showing that an economy can enjoy the gains from exchange without specializing, but it cannot enjoy the gains from specialization without trading with foreigners. Explain precisely using the small-country HO model.
12. Interpret Figure 14.5. What does it suggest about the gains from international trade?
13. Why are mainstream economists so enthusiastic about international trade as a way to raise living standards when economists' estimates of the gains from trade are so small? (Hint: Use Figure 14.7 to frame your answer.)
14. Explain why a comparative static model such as the Heckscher-Ohlin model cannot describe the relationship between international trade and economic growth. (Hint: Remember the "all other things equal assumption" that is applied when the model is used to explain the gain from trade.)

15. Explain the significance for the relationship between international trade and economic growth of the example presented in Table 14.1. (Hint: Recall Poincaré's quote in the text.)

16. Ponder Figure 14.9 for a few minutes, and then write down your impression. What does the diagram tell you about the statistical results? How confident are you that the finding that, on average, a one percent rise in the growth of trade is related to a 0.22 percent rise in the rate of growth of GDP implies that trade causes economic growth? Explain.

17. Contrast Figure 14.10 with the Heckscher-Ohlin model presented earlier in the chapter. Which is more realistic? Which presents a stronger case for free trade?

18. Under what circumstances is immiserizing growth a likely outcome? What should a country do if it finds itself in such a situation?

19. Present the infant industry argument for protection.

20. Is the infant industry argument a valid argument for protecting new industries in less developed countries? Explain in detail.

21. Does the increasing returns to scale model conclude that free trade is beneficial for all countries concerned? Explain.

22. How does the increasing returns to scale model of trade differ from the Heckscher-Ohlin model in its conclusions? Explain.

23. Should countries be judged on their carbon emissions according to their production or their consumption. Explain. What role does international trade play in this argument?

24. Explain how some orthodox economists have qualified the conclusions of the HO model by considering adjustment costs and terms of trade shifts.

25. The increasing returns to scale model of trade has been used by policymakers to justify strategic trade policies. Explain what such policies imply and why they might increase national welfare. (Hint: Use Figure 14.15 to explain your answer.)

26. Write a brief essay explaining how environmental externalities alter the HO model's conclusions about free trade.

References

Aghion, Philippe, and Jeffrey G. Williamson (1998), *Growth, Inequality and Globalization*, Cambridge, U.K.: Cambridge University Press.

Auty, Richard M. (1993), *Sustaining Development in Mineral Economies: The Resource Curse Thesis*, London: Routledge.

Azarchs, Timothy, and Tamar Khitarishvili (2010), "Disaggregating the Resource Curse: Is the Curse More difficult to Dispel in Oil States than in Mineral States?" Levy Institute Working Paper No. 641, December.

Bacon, David (2008), *Illegal People: How Globalization Creates Migration and Criminalizes Immigrants*, Boston: Beacon Press.

Baldwin, Robert E. (2003), "Openness and Growth: What's the Empirical Relationship?" in Robert E. Baldwin and L. Alan Winters (eds.), *Challenges to Globalization*, Chicago: University of Chicago Press.

Basevi, Giorgio (1966), "The United States Tariff Structure: Estimates of Effective Rates of Protection of U.S. and Industrial Labor," *Review of Economics and Statistics* 48(2):147–170.

Bhagwati, Jagdish (1958), "Immizerizing Growth: A Geometrical Note," *Review of Economic Studies* 25(2):201–205.

Blendon, Robert J., *et al.* (1997), "Bridging the Gap between the Public's and Economists' Views of the Economy," *Journal of Economic Perspectives* 11(3):105–118.

Blinder, Alan (2006), "Offshoring: The Latest Industrial Revolution?" *Foreign Affairs*, March.

Chacholiades, Miltiades (1990), *International Economics*, New York: McGraw-Hill.

Davis, Lucas W., and Matthew E. Kahn (2010), "International Trade in Used Vehicles: The Environmental Consequences of NAFTA," *American Economic Journal: Economic Policy* 2(4):58–82.

Edwards, Sebastian (1998), "Openness, Productivity and Growth: What Do We Really Know?," *Economic Journal* 108(1):383–398

Feenstra, Robert C. (1992), "How Costly is Protectionism?" *Journal of Economic Perspectives* 6:159–178.

Gylfasson, Thor, and Gylfi Zoega (2002), "Inequality and Economic Growth: Do Natural Resources Matter?" CESinfo Working Paper 712, April.

Harley, C.K. (1988), "Ocean Freight Rates and Productivity, 1840–1913: The Primacy of Mechanical Invention Reaffirmed," *Journal of Economic History* 48:851–876.

Holmes, Thomas J., and James A. Schmitz (1995), "Resistence to New Technology and Trade Between Areas," *Federal Reserve Bank of Minneapolis Quarterly Review* 19(1):2–17.

Hummels, David (1999), "Have International Transportation Costs Declined?," Working Paper, University of Chicago, September.

Kravis, Irving B. (1970), "Trade as a Handmaiden of Growth: Similarities between the Nineteenth and Twentieth Centuries," *Economic Journal* 80(32):850–872

Kuhn, Thomas (1962), *The Structure of Scientific Revolution*, Chicago: University of Chicago Press.

Leite, Carlos, and Jens Weidman (1999), "Does Mother Nature Corrupt?" IMF Working Paper 99/85, July.

Levinson, Arik, and Scott Taylor (2008), "Unmasking the Pollution Haven Effect," *International Economic Review* 49(1):223–254.

Lewer, Joshua J., and Hendrik Van den Berg (2003), "How Large Is International Trade's Effect on Economic Growth?" *Journal of Economic Surveys* 17(3):363–396.

Maddison, Angus (1995), *Monitoring the World Economy 1820–1992*, Paris: OECD.

Maddison, Angus (2001), *The World Economy, A Millennial Perspective*, Paris: OECD.

Maddison, Angus (2003), *The World Economy: Historical Statistics*, Paris: OECD.

Massachusetts Institute of Technology Energy Laboratory (2000), "On the Road in 2020: A Lifecycle Analysis of New Automobile Technologies," MIT Working Paper EL 00–003.

Mill, John Stuart (1848), *Principles of Political Economy*, London, U.K.: Longmans, Green.

Mussa, Michael (2000), "Factors Driving Global Economic Integration," paper presented at the Federal Reserve Bank of Kansas City symposium, Jackson Hole, WY, August 25.

North, Douglass (1958), "Ocean Freight Rates and Economic Development 1750–1913," *Journal of Economic History* 18:537–555.

O'Rourke, Kevin H., and Jeffrey G. Williamson (1999), *Globalization and History*, Cambridge, MA: MIT Press.

Pérez, Mamerto, Sergio Schlesinger, and Timothy A. Wise (2008), *The Promise and the Perils of Agricultural Trade Liberalization: Lessons from Latin America*, Washington, DC: Washington Office on Latin America and the Global Development and Environment Institute.

Reinert, Erik S. (2007), *How Rich Countries Got Rich and Why Poor Countries Stay Poor*, New York: Public Affairs.

Robertson, D.H. (1938), "The Future of International Trade," *The Economic Journal* 48(189):1–14.

Rodriguez, Francisco, and Dani Rodrik (1999), "Trade Policy and Economic Growth: A Skeptics Guide to the Cross-National Evidence," NBER Revised Working Paper, No. 7081.

Rodriguez, Francisco, and Dani Rodrik (2001), "Trade Policy and Economic Growth: A Skeptics Guide to the Cross-National Evidence," in Ben Bernanke and Kenneth S. Rogoff (eds.), *NBER Macroeconomics Annual 2000*, Cambridge, MA: MIT Press.

Prebisch, Raúl (1950), *The Economic Development of Latin America and Its Principle Problems*, Lake Success, NY: United Nations Economic Commission for Latin America.

Rodrik, Dani, Arvind Subramanian, and Francesco Trebbi (2002), "Institutions Rule: The Primacy of Institutions over Geography and Integration in Economic Development," *NBER Working Paper*, No. w9305, November.

Rigobon, Roberto, and Dani Rodrik (2005), "Rule of Law, Democracy, Openness, and Income: Estimating the Interrelationships," *The Economics of Transition* 13(3):533–564.

Sachs, Jeffrey, and Andrew Warner (1995b), "Natural Resource Abundance and Economic Growth," NBER Working Paper 5398, December.

Seabright, Paul (2004), *The Company of Strangers: A Natural History of Economic Life*, Princeton, NJ: Princeton University Press.

Singer, Hans W. (1950), "U.S. Foreign Investment in Underdeveloped Areas: The Distribution of Gains between Investing and Borrowing Countries, *American Economic Review* 40:473–485.

Smith, Adam (1776 [1976]), *An Inquiry into the Nature and Causes of the Wealth of Nations*, Chicago: University of Chicago Press.

UNCTAD (2008), *Handbook of Statistics 2008*, New York: United Nations.

Van den Berg, Hendrik, and Joshua J. Lewer (2007), *International Trade and Economic Growth*, Armonk, NY: M.E. Sharpe.

Wiedman, T., R. Wood, M. Lenzen, J. Minx, D. Guan, and J. Barrett (2008), *Development of an Embedded Carbon Emissions Indicator*, report to the UK Department for Environment, Food and Rural Affairs (DEFRA) by Stockholm Environment Institute at the University of York and Centre for Integrated Sustainability Analysis at the University of Sydney, June, 2008, DEFRA, London, U.K.

CHAPTER 15

International Investment, International Finance, and Economic Development

... the claims of enormous benefits from free capital mobility are not persuasive.
(Jagdish Bhagwati, 1998)

This chapter examines two more components of globalization: **international investment** and **international finance**. The former consist of international sales and purchases of physical capital. The latter covers international borrowing and lending in its many forms. International finance and international investment are often related, as when a transnational corporation based in one country pays for, or *finances*, the building of a new factory in another country. In general, every purchase or sale of physical capital, which requires an upfront payment in exchange for expected future returns, involves a financial calculation. International finance is not always linked to international investment, however. When a London bank lends to a Brazilian firm that is building a factory in Brazil, for example, there is international finance but no international investment since no foreigner acquires physical capital in Brazil.

Note that when there is no formal intertemporal exchange between two distinct parties, there may still be an implicit financial transaction. For example, a firm that funds overseas investment from cash flow *implicitly finances* its investment. Financial transactions need not involve investment at all. People and governments often lend and borrow to finance individual and collective consumption.

The previous chapter discussed how fast international trade has grown. In recent decades, international investment and financial flows between countries have grown even more rapidly than international trade. But this growth has fluctuated from year to year, and it has varied greatly across countries.

International investment reacts sharply to changes in the performance of economies and the availability of financing. In developing economies, years of high levels of international investment are often followed by years of near zero international investment. International financial flows are even more volatile. In many developing countries, largè net *inflows* of foreign money one year have been followed by large net *outflows* in subsequent years. The frequency of such **reversals** of financial flows are the reason why one of the orthodox economists and ardent advocates of free trade, Jagdish Bhagwati, follows the quote at the top of the previous page with the sentence: "Each time a crisis related to capital flows hits a country, it typically goes through the wringer." This chapter examines what he means by "wringer."

The volatility of international investment is, at least in part, related to the general difficulties in carrying out intertemporal exchanges, as already discussed in Chapter 11. The problems with informational asymmetries, enforcement of contracts, and monitoring of borrowers' performance are more difficult to deal with when assets are exchanged across national boundaries, between different autonomous political systems, and between different commercial and legal cultures. The rapid growth of international finance suggests that either modern finance has overcome the difficulties that plagued intertemporal transactions in the past or the gains from international investment and finance are now so large that they outweigh the potential dangers of sudden reversals of investment flows and the future difficulties in servicing foreign debt. As this chapter explains, the truth is more complex: the gains from international investment and financial transactions are indeed large for some firms and banks, but they are large in part because these firms have been able to pass the risk on to others.

As in the case of international trade, mainstream orthodox economics relies on neoclassical models that show there are gains from international investment and financial flows for all countries concerned. This chapter first presents a model that describes the efficient allocation of international investment, followed by a second model that describes the gains from international diversification. While these two models provide important insights, they are not entirely realistic because, among other things, they ignore many of the difficulties of intertemporal transactions that were discussed in Chapter 11. They also assume that all assets are interchangeable.

There are in fact substantial differences between different types of assets. The prices of some are much more volatile than others. Some assets are more often subject to default or non-payment than others. And, some can be more easily bought and sold, and are thus more **liquid**, than others. Also, international investment and finance can create foreign debt burdens for countries that undermine macroeconomic stability. Foreign debt creates currency mismatches that can translate foreign exchange movements into large balance sheet changes for indebted firms and banks that cause bankruptcies and financial crises. International borrowing and lending can also perpetuate poverty in developing countries because foreign ownership lets foreigners capture more economic surplus.

Finally, this chapter introduces transnational corporations (TNCs) and the foreign direct investment (FDI) that creates them. The growth of TNCs is substantially changing the international economic sphere and how it interacts with the social and natural spheres.

Chapter Goals

1. Discuss the difference between international investment and finance.
2. Present the neoclassical models of international investment and finance, which show that transactions respond to differences in returns as well as diversification opportunities.
3. Examine the possible effects of international investment and finance on economic growth and development.
4. Discuss international financial crises, their causes, and consequences.
5. Present the historical case study of Mexico and its 200 years of borrowing and defaults.
6. Detail the 1982 debt crisis that pushed most developing economies into recession and extended periods of economic stagnation.
7. Discuss the common threads across the many financial crises in developing economies during the past three decades.
8. Explain the Washington Consensus policies that the IMF imposed on debtor countries.
9. Discuss the role of uncertainty and foreign debt in international financial crises.
10. Explain the rise and dominance of transnational corporations in the global economy

---

15.1 The Economics of International Investment and Finance

An asset is anything that has value and forms part of the wealth or property of the asset's owner. A distinction is often made between **real assets**, like buildings, land, and factories, and **financial assets**, which are claims on future payments. Thus, an asset can take the form of tangible property, or it can be a verbal promise to pay "next month when I get my paycheck." In general, an asset is something that has value today because it is expected to have value in the future, either because it generates future returns or it can be redeemed or resold in the future. An asset is sometimes referred to as a **store of wealth**.

Among international trade in financial assets, or what we call international financial flows, are stocks, bonds, financial derivatives, bank deposits, bank loans, and international lending by governments and international agencies. A major share of real international investment consists of **foreign direct investment (FDI)**, which is overseas investment by transnational firms (TNCs) and the spread of business organizations across borders. Real assets traded internationally include such things as the building of factories, homes, and electric power grids, as well as the accumulation of inventories, commodities, and entire business organizations.

15.1.1 A traditional model of international investment

Recall the simple model of a financial market from Chapter 11, repeated here as Figure 15.1. This model depicts a supply and demand model of a country's financial market in which money is exchanged. The demand curve for savings, or **loanable funds**, is a downward-sloping curve that represents, in descending order according to their rates of return, the various real and financial investment opportunities for employing loanable funds. The downward sloping demand curve reflects a country's investment and innovative projects listed in descending order (as in Figure 11.3). The supply curve of savings or loanable funds is shown as an upward-sloping curve, which reflects the assumption that as people save more, the higher is the interest rate they can earn from lending their purchasing power to investors, innovators, and consumers.

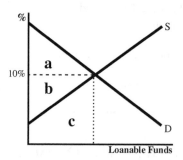

Figure 15.1 The Market for Loanable Funds

The equilibrium in the market for loanable funds occurs at the interest rate of 10 percent in Figure 15.1. The area under the demand curve, the sum of areas a, b, and c, represents the total returns to the descending order of financial and real investments along the loanable funds demand curve. The area under the supply of funds curve, area c, represents the opportunity cost of foregone consumption by savers. Both savers (suppliers) and borrowers (demanders) in the financial market enjoy net gains, or surpluses, from being able to engage in **intertemporal exchange**. In Figure 15.1, borrowers receive returns equal to the area below the demand for funds curve, while they must pay the equilibrium interest rate of 10 percent for borrowed funds. Borrowers therefore earn a **surplus** equal to the area a. Savers earn the difference between their perceived value of foregone consumption, as represented by the supply curve, and the 10 percent rate paid by borrowers, which is equal to the area b.

If it is beneficial to both borrowers and lenders within one country to engage in intertemporal exchanges of purchasing power, it is potentially even more beneficial for borrowers and lenders of all countries to exchange assets across their borders. Figure 15.2 shows a two-country version of the single-economy partial-equilibrium loanable funds market model from Figure 15.1. Suppose the world consists of two countries, Greece and Turkey, and the rates of return on financial assets in the two countries are 6 percent and 4 percent, respectively. The differences in rates create arbitrage opportunities.

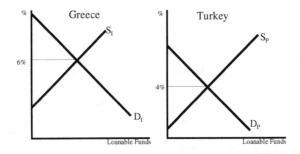

Figure 15.2 Two-Country Partial Equilbrium Investment Model

All other things equal, savers prefer to place their wealth where the returns are highest. Thus, if there are no restrictions on international financial flows, savings move from Turkey to Greece, as shown in Figure 15.3. The supply curve of funds to purchase assets in Greece shifts out from S_I to S_{I+F}, where the "F" in the subscript stands for the amount of foreign savings that move from Turkey to Greece. The supply of savings in Turkey shifts to the left by an equal amount, as given by the shift of S_P to S_{P-F}. The center diagram illustrates the international market for savings, which represents the "spillovers" from the domestic markets for savings, or loanable funds, when interest rates in the international market differ from the domestic equilibrium interest rates. The amount of savings that move from the low-interest market to the high-interest market is the amount of international finance, $I_I = 0k = eg = hj$.

As Figure 15.1 showed, savers gain the area between the market rate of return and the opportunity costs of saving given by the supply curve of savings, which means that Turkish savers gain the areas c and d in the right hand diagram of Figure 15.3. The shaded area c represents that part of the total returns that used to be captured by borrowers in Turkey but now, along with area d, accrue to Turkish savers. The net gain to Turkish citizens is the area d, the difference

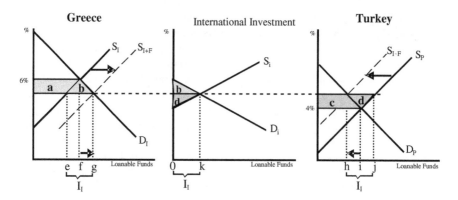

Figure 15.3 Two-Country Partial Equilbrium Investment Model

between (1) the additional returns earned by Turkish savers from being able to lend their savings in both Turkey and Greece, and (2) the higher returns that must be paid to savers by Turkish borrowers. Turkish borrowers have to compete with the higher returns on loans in Greece.   In Greece, savers in Greece lose the area a, but Greek borrowers find that the lower interest rate provides gains equal to the areas a and b. Thus, in each country the gainers gain more welfare than the losers lose, although the roles of savers and borrowers are reversed. The total amount of financing falls in Turkey, and it rises in Greece.

The partial equilibrium model of international finance presented here is a one-period model that ignores the returns to assets paid in later periods. Loans eventually have to be paid back. Also, in our example above we implicitly assumed that investment projects cannot move from one country to another by holding the demand curve in each country constant; recall that each demand curve represents the available investment and consumption opportunities in descending order. It is possible, even likely, that some investment projects will move from the high-interest country to the low-interest country in order to take advantage of lower borrowing costs. For example, a firm may look at available financing in deciding where to build its next factory. In this case, the demand curves for loanable funds shift with changes in interest rates.

The traditional model of international investment thus concludes that savings flow from the country with lower interest rates to another with a higher interest rate. As is typical of neoclassical models, the arbitrage process causes returns on financial and real assets to become equal across countries. There are distributional effects, but under the orthodox assumption of "representative" individuals the net welfare effects in both countries are deemed to be positive.

The model does not explain why there are differences in returns to financial assets across countries. Such differences may be the result of differences in intertemporal preferences, which can be due to differences in age, family responsibilities, wealth, and the willingness to bear risk. The differences in returns to international financial investment may also be the result of differences in the availability of factors of production, in the level of technology or in institutions that impact business outcomes. This model also fails to capture the dynamic effects of international financial flows, which may alter the preferences or productive capacities of countries by adding to physical capital stocks or letting consumers borrow at lower interest rates.

15.1.2 Risk and diversification

The simple model above predicts that financial flows between countries move in one direction only, from the economy where real and financial assets have low returns to the economy with high returns. Yet, data on the balance of payments for individual countries show that over the course of a given year there are many sales of real and financial assets to foreigners *and* purchases of foreign real and financial assets from foreigners. Financial flows move in both directions.

Bi-directional financial flows can be explained by a second important motivation for acquiring foreign assets known as **diversification**. All assets have some risk in the sense that no one is ever perfectly certain that the assets will hold their value and pay out the promised or expected returns. But risk varies greatly across different types of assets. Since wealth holders tend to be **risk averse**, relatively safe projects with lower expected returns are often financed ahead of more risky projects with higher expected returns. Effectively, diversification improves the tradeoff between risk and return by spreading wealth across a diverse set of assets. Because the diverse assets' values vary differently over time in response to economic conditions, the overall value of the whole set of assets fluctuates much less than the value of each of the individual assets in the *portfolio*. When the value of one asset falls, other assets may fall less or may even rise in value, thus keeping the average value of the portfolio from changing as much as any one individual asset does. Diversification allows more savings to flow to profitable but risky projects.

International finance increases opportunities for diversifying asset holdings because assets in different countries are less likely to be as closely correlated as assets within a single economy. Pooling assets from different countries thus reduces risk more than when diversification is limited to only domestic assets. The diversification motive explains why international investment in stocks and bonds has grown so much in the last 25 years. The acquisition of small amounts of many different financial assets is known as **portfolio investment**. Mutual funds of foreign stocks and bonds have proliferated, making it even easier for individuals to engage in international portfolio investment.

15.1.3 The long-run dynamic gains from international investment

The models of international investment and finance in the previous section do not provide a complete picture of what a country gains, or loses, when it opens its borders to international investment and financial flows. In order to highlight those potential long-run benefits of international investment for economic development, this section links international investment and finance to the Schumpeterian R&D model of technological progress as well as increasing returns to scale that occur in certain sectors of the economy.

Robert Lucas (1990) asked: Why doesn't most capital flow from rich to poor countries? According to the neoclassical paradigm, the fact that poor countries have much less capital than rich countries means that, all other things equal, the marginal return to capital should be much higher in poor countries than in rich countries. In practice however, international financial flows are mostly from high-income countries to other high income countries, not from high income countries to poor capital-scarce countries.

Lucas examined several possible explanations for the lack of foreign investment in countries with little capital: (1) technology is not as advanced in low-income economies, (2) people have more human capital as well as physical capital in the rich countries, and human capital is complementary to physical capital, (3) there are large risks associated with intertemporal transactions between countries because long-term contracts cannot be effectively enforced, and (4) there are explicit restrictions on international investment. Lucas argued that policies to increase the flow of savings to capital-scarce countries should focus on increasing human capital, eliminating barriers to capital flows, and improving institutions. Recall from Chapter 11 that the levels of investment and innovation depend not only on the availability of savings, but also on the profitability and motivation for carrying out investment and innovative projects.

A more holistic analysis of international investment suggests there is another process at work: shifting savings to countries where economies of scale are largest. Poor less developed economies with small capital stocks often have relatively low returns to capital because their economies consist of mostly diminishing returns industries, such as farming and tourism services, while high income countries specialize in higher-return industries that enjoy increasing returns to scale and are dominated by powerful corporations. In such a case, international investment flows increase the scale of the high-return industries in the wealthy countries, which further increases the wealth generated on those countries and worsens the international distribution of income.

15.1.4 Schumpeterian innovation and international investment

The Solow model shows that increased saving and investment can only bring the economy medium-term economic growth; permanent, continuous economic growth requires continual technological progress. Therefore, in order to examine the role of international investment on long-run economic growth we must examine how foreign investment and finance affect technological change.

Recall from Chapter 6 that the Schumpeterian model specifies innovation as an *intentional* and *costly* activity undertaken by profit-seeking entrepreneurs or welfare-maximizing policymakers. The Schumpeterian process of innovation was summarized in Chapter 8 by the equation:

$$q = f(\overset{+}{\pi}, \overset{-}{r}, \overset{+}{R}, \overset{-}{\beta}) \qquad (15.1)$$

The variable q is the amount of innovation, R represents the supply of resources in the economy, π is the profit or social welfare gain from innovating, β reflects the efficiency of R&D activities in terms of the resources necessary to generate innovations, and r is the discount rate that reflects society's valuation of future versus current income.

From this Schumpeterian perspective, international trade can be shown to have a positive influence on human welfare. First, trade spreads technology and encourages its application in more countries. International investment can reduce the cost of innovation, β, because it facilitates the flow of ideas. There is also evidence suggesting that the specific category of foreign direct investment is especially important as a channel for the flow of technology to developing countries. And, international trade can make more resources available, which according to equation (15.1) also enhances innovation and economic growth.

Some statistical studies have found a positive correlation between investment in productive equipment and countries' rates of economic growth.[1] There is evidence that the effect of equipment investment on economic growth is actually stronger in developing economies in the early stages of industrialization than it is in the more developed economies.[2] Foreign investment often involves the building of foreign factories, the acquisition of existing foreign firms and facilities, and the creation of marketing and distribution organizations in other countries, which are all activities that involve transfers of know-how abroad.

Statistical studies on technology flows are inconclusive, however, in part because it is probably impossible to measure technology flows with any degree of accuracy. Researchers use indirect indicators, such as the residual measure of **total factor productivity** discussed in Chapter 7, which you will recall is based on questionable measures of output, labor, and capital stocks. Others have used patent applications, which usually require applicants to state previous patents on which their ideas are based and thus permit economists to trace how ideas flowed from one country to another. But most technology does not involve formal patents, so these studies cannot settle the issue.

---

[1] Classic articles are Brad De Long and Lawrence Summers (1991) and De Long and Summers (1992).
[2] For example: Jonathan Temple (1998) and A.J. Aurbach, K.A. Hassett, and S.D. Oliner (1994).

15.2 International Financial Flows and Economic Crises

Before we can begin to calculate the benefits of international investment, we still need to examine Bhagwati's point that financial flows are potentially destabilizing.   This section analyzes some of the many financial crises in developing economies over the past 30 years that have been triggered by sudden reversals in international financial flows.

15.2.1 International finance in the nineteenth century

Financial flows between countries are not a recent phenomenon. Substantial amounts of international lending have in fact taken place for centuries, even millennia. For example, the central government of the Roman Empire collected taxes throughout the region to fund the government in Rome, which in turn transferred funds to pay for infrastructure projects throughout the empire. In the fifteenth century, the Medici family's banks lent large amounts to sovereign governments throughout Europe. Not coincidentally, international financial panics and defaults are not recent phenomena either.

International financial flows grew rapidly during the nineteenth century. In fact, measured as a fraction of GDP, by the end of the nineteenth century capital flows were often larger then than they are today. For example, over the period 1880–1914, annual *outflows* of savings averaged about 5 percent of GDP in the United Kingdom, reaching 9 percent in 1913. These numbers imply that the United Kingdom exported nearly half of its total savings, and many British savers stored a very large portions of their wealth in foreign assets, either directly in the form of bonds or indirectly through loans made by their banks to foreign governments and firms. But Britain was not unique; between 1880 and 1914, savings outflows approached 5 and 6 percent of GDP in France and Germany, respectively.

The major importers of savings in the world were the newly-populated countries such as Australia, Canada, the United States, and New Zealand. Also, Scandinavian countries such as Sweden and Norway were major importers of capital during the late 1800s. During the 1880s, inflows of foreign savings averaged nearly 10 percent of GDP in Australia. Savings inflows into Canada exceeded 6 percent of its GDP in the 1880s, averaged about 4.5 percent in the 1890s, rose to 7 percent in the first decade of the twentieth century, and reached 14 percent of Canadian GDP between 1910 and 1913. Foreign saving was equal to nearly 35 percent of total investment in New Zealand and Canada and nearly 25 percent in Australia and Sweden between 1880 and 1914. These were all rapidly-growing economies, and returns to investment there were high. There were also financial flows to less developed economies and colonies, most notably Argentina, South Africa, India, and Brazil, but not on the scale of the flows to the countries mentioned above. In contrast, financial flows today account for less than 5 percent of total investment in developing economies.

Most international lending in the nineteenth century was in the form of bonds intermediated by British investment banks. Michael Edelstein (1982) estimated that London investment houses earned fees of between 1.6 and 3.9 percentage points for their services. The investment banks negotiated the bonds' terms and promoted their sale. Sometimes the banks advanced funds to the issuers of the bonds in anticipation of the sale of the bonds. The investment banks also acted as principal negotiators on behalf of the bondholders when there were defaults. **Defaults** on foreign loans and bonds by firms and governments of developing economies occurred with some regularity, but on average the returns on foreign lending were at least as high as domestic lending for British banks and investors.[3]

15.2.2 The case of Mexico

Mexico provides an interesting case study of default and lending. Since its independence nearly 200 years ago, Mexico has gone through four episodes of foreign borrowing, default, and debt resolution.[4] The first episode began right after it gained its independence in 1821, when Mexico contracted the placement of bonds for £3.2 million ($16 million) through a London financial house. The Mexican government actually received only $6 million, the remainder going to various fees and withholdings in London accounts for future interest payments. A second private bond offering was contracted in London the following year, but this time Mexico had to pledge one-third of all of its customs revenue as security for this and the previous bonds. Lax customs collections caused Mexico to miss coupon payments on the bonds in 1827. In the 1830s, the Mexican government and bondholders agreed to let Mexico capitalize interest owed by issuing new bonds. But, after a year Mexico stopped servicing these new bonds.

During the Mexico–Texas war in 1834, Mexico attempted to negotiate what would today be referred to as a *debt-equity swap*: in exchange for writing off Mexico's debt, bondholders were offered land in Texas, Sonora, California, and elsewhere. This scheme had few takers, since Mexico was expected to lose those territories to the United States. Mexico was unable to engage in further borrowing as it fought wars against the United States and then suffered an invasion by France (which justified the invasion by claiming it was seeking restitution for unpaid Mexican debts). Mexico defeated the French forces and refused to settle its foreign debt. Only after the dictator Porfirio Díaz rose to power in the late 1800s did Mexico offer a settlement.

---

[3] For interesting accounts of past international investment flows see Eichengreen and Lindert, eds. (1989); Marichal (1989) discusses international investment flows to Latin America.
[4] This account of Mexico's history of foreign borrowing is based to a considerable degree on Aggarwal (1989).

Porfirio Díaz was an autocrat who was supported by business interests in Mexico and financial interests in the United States. In 1888, he offered a settlement in which foreign bondholders recovered all of their principal, and interest payments averaged 2.3 percent per year on the 1824 bonds and 1.1 percent on the 1825 bonds. This was a very favorable outcome for foreign bondholders given the time that had passed since the debt was contracted. In the same year of 1888, Mexico sold £10.5 million in new bonds to German capitalists. In 1901 oil was discovered in Mexico, and new financing was readily obtained in exchange for pledges of oil revenue.

Porfirio Díaz was apparently not as well liked by Mexicans as he was by foreign investors, and his autocratic regime was overthrown in 1911. The start of what would soon become the *Mexican Revolution* caused a massive outflow of capital to the United States by worried foreign investors and many Mexican business interests. The revolutionary government sought foreign funds to counter the capital flight, and loans of $10 million were obtained from American banks in 1911 and again in 1912. In 1913 the United States government, in disagreement with the socialist policies of the new revolutionary government, prohibited further lending to Mexico.

After the Revolution, bankers resumed negotiations with Mexico's new government to resume debt service. There was little progress as many Mexican politicians were opposed to negotiating with foreign bankers about the **odious debt** contracted by the autocratic regime of Porfirio Diaz.[5] In 1927, Mexico unilaterally suspended debt service on all outstanding foreign debt. Foreign banking interests sent a committee of economic and banking experts to examine Mexico's economic problems in detail, after which they offered to write off 94.5 percent of all unpaid interest provided Mexico continued future interest and principle payments. The Mexican Congress defiantly refused this offer. Only in 1942, with World War II underway and the United States anxious to eliminate all conflicts among allies, was a final agreement reached. With the help of U.S. government financial assistance, Mexico was allowed to settle its debt of over $500 million for about $50 million, or 10 cents on the dollar.

15.2.3 Global finance up to 1980

Globally, international financial flows diminished greatly after World War I and through the depression years of the 1930s. Even after World War II and well into the 1950s and 1960s, international financial flows as a percentage of overall economic activity were very small in comparison to the late 1800s. Direct government-to-government aid accounted for the major part of capital flows between developed and less developed economies in the 1950s and 1960s.

---

[5] The term *odious debt* has been used recently to refer to loans contracted by various African dictators during the past 25 years; current governments refuse to recognize loans that were stolen and often deposited in dictators' accounts in the very countries whose banks made the loans.

Private lending was actively restricted by both capital exporting and capital importing countries. Many developing countries pursued **import substitution policies** under which governments actively restricted imports in order to stimulate domestic industrial development. Developed country governments, in their concern to recover from World War II and to avoid a repeat of the 1930s depression, encouraged savings to stay at home during the 1950s and 1960s. Only towards the end of the 1960s did the developed economies in Europe and Japan begin to let their banks, insurance companies, and pension funds make foreign loans and the purchase other types of foreign assets.

Table 15.1 Capital Flows to Developing Countries (U.S. $ millions)

	1977–1982	*1983–1989*	*1990–1994*
All Developing Countries			
Total Net Capital Inflows	30.5	8.8	104.9
Net FDI[1]	11.2	13.3	39.1
Net Portfolio Investment	−10.5	6.5	43.6
Other[2]	29.8	−11.0	22.2
Asia			
Total Net Capital Inflows	15.8	16.7	52.1
Net FDI	2.7	5.2	23.4
Net Portfolio Investment	0.6	1.4	12.4
Other	12.5	10.1	16.3
Western Hemisphere			
Total Net Capital Inflows	26.3	−16.6	40.1
Net FDI	5.3	4.4	11.9
Net Portfolio Investment	1.6	−1.2	26.6
Other	19.4	−19.8	1.6
Other Developing Countries			
Total Net Capital Inflows	−11.6	8.7	12.7
Net FDI	3.2	3.7	3.8
Net Portfolio Investment	−12.7	6.3	4.6
Other	−2.1	−1.3	4.3

Source: Table 1.1 from International Monetary Fund (1995), *International Capital Markets, Developments, Prospects, and Policy Issues*, Washington, D.C., p. 33.
[1] FDI (Foreign direct investment) is private investment by transnational corporations to purchase or construct businesses in foreign countries.
[2] The "Other" category includes bank loans as well as foreign aid.

15.2.4 The resumption of private international lending (and borrowing)

When the **Organization of Petroleum Exporting Countries (OPEC)** cartel sharply raised the price of oil in 1973, the oil producing countries suddenly found themselves with huge international trade surpluses. The flip side of the coin was that oil importing countries suddenly saw their trade balances move into the red. The OPEC countries' aggregate trade surplus rose from zero in 1972 to a positive $60 billion in 1974 after the price of oil was raised from $4.00 per barrel to about $10 per barrel.

The sharp changes in countries' trade balances threatened to force the oil importing countries to slow down their pace of economic growth in order to reduce or even reverse the growth of oil consumption. To the relief of many policymakers, the international financial system recycled the petrodollars fairly easily. The surge in dollars earned by oil exporting countries swelled deposits at branches of large commercial banks in London and other major banking centers. The banks then lent the money to oil importing countries to offset their higher foreign payments for oil. As a result, there appeared to be no need for oil importing countries to adjust their economies for the higher oil prices, at least not right away. But oil importing countries began to accumulate foreign debt.

In OPEC countries with large populations, such as Iran, Nigeria, and Venezuela, there were many pressures for governments to spend the revenues earned by their state-owned oil companies. By the late 1970s the OPEC surplus had disappeared. But, the international credit markets remained flush with money even as the OPEC surplus dwindled because the central banks of most high-income economies expanded money supplies to avoid recessions triggered by the oil price supply shock. The monetary expansions caused inflation to accelerate, and the prices of coffee, iron ore, sugar, cotton, tobacco, soy beans, and other commodities rose nearly as much as oil. Even though inflation pushed nominal interest rates up, the loose monetary policies of the United States, Britain, and other industrial economies kept real interest rates on international loans very low. Thus, despite their heavy international borrowing, developing countries found that the ratio of debt service to export earnings did not grow very much. They were able to roll over existing loans, and they could even add new loans.

OPEC raised oil prices again in 1979 after the forced exile of the dictatorial Shah and the subsequent political turmoil in Iran. A barrel of oil reached $30, and the collective trade surplus of the OPEC countries rose from zero in 1978 to over $100 billion in 1980. The international banking system again began recycling the petrodollars. Between 1979 and 1981 Brazil added $16 billion, Argentina $11 billion, and Mexico $21 billion to their foreign debts.

15.2.5 The macroeconomics of international investment

When a country's citizens, firms, or government borrow money from foreigners, the country can consume and invest more than its economy produces. The sum of domestic expenditures, namely consumption plus investment plus government purchases, is referred to as **absorption**. Foreign borrowing allows a country to *absorb* more than it produces. For example, if the citizens, firms, and government of a country sell assets (borrow) abroad equal to five percent of their national product, they can run a trade deficit of five percent of GDP and absorb 105 percent of their national product.

When a country pays back its outstanding loans, a trade surplus must be generated and absorption must fall below 100 percent of domestic production. If interest and principal payments are, say, 5 percent of GDP, then in the absence of new borrowing absorption can be only 95 percent of national production. Reducing absorption reduces current national welfare.

15.3 The Aftermath of the 1982 Debt Crisis

The new surge in the recycling of petrodollars in 1979 was short-lived. By this time, central banks in major developed economies had stopped reacting to rising unemployment with expansionary monetary policies. Instead, they tightened money supplies to stop inflation. These tight monetary policies pushed interest rates to over ten percent and the United States, British, and other high-income economies into deep recessions. That left the OPEC surplus as the international financial markets' main source of new funds. Soon that source also dried up when the second oil price increase could not be maintained after the major oil consuming economies fell into recession. It took less than two years for the huge OPEC surplus of $100 billion to become a deficit of $10 billion. The end of international financial flows to developing countries had devastating consequences.

15.3.1 The high levels of debt in 1982

Table 15.2 details the debt of less developed countries in 1982. Brazil had the largest foreign debt, followed by Mexico, Argentina, Korea, Venezuela, and Egypt. Not all countries faced similar debt burdens. In terms of the ratio of debt to GNP (column 2), an indicator of a country's **ability to pay**, Costa Rica, Cote d'Ivoire, Egypt, Bolivia, the Sudan, Zambia, and Jamaica had accumulated the heaviest debt burdens by 1982. The ratio of interest payments to GNP (column 4) indicates the share of total national production that must in effect be transferred to foreigners in payment of past borrowing. For example, Costa Rican citizens' absorption of national production was only 85.2 percent because they transferred 14.8 percent of GNP to foreigners as interest payments.

Table 15.2 also shows foreign debt and interest payments as a percentage of exports (columns 3 and 5), which are indicators of a country's **foreign currency cash flow** with which it can service its foreign debt. In 1982, foreign debt exceeded 400 percent of exports in Argentina, Brazil, Egypt, Morocco, and the Sudan. The higher real interest rates in the early 1980s increased interest payments on foreign debt to 47.1 percent of 1982 export earnings in Brazil, 43.5 percent in the Sudan, and 40.5 percent in Chile. It is difficult to see how those countries could have met their debt obligations without further borrowing.

Table 15.2 Foreign Debt of 30 Selected Developing Economies in 1982
(US$'s in millions)

Country	(1) Gross External Debt (US$millions)	(2) Debt as a GNP	(3) % of 1982 Exports	(4) Interest as GNP	(5) % of Exports	(6) Long-Term claims of Private Banks (US$millions)
Algeria	$17,641	34.7%	108.4%	2.9%	9.2%	$4,439
Argentina	43.634	79.0	447.8	5.9	33.3	18,104
Bolivia	3,328	101.4	348.6	3.1	10.5	901
Brazil	92,961	34.6	405.3	4.0	47.1	57,605
Chile	17,315	68.7	333.9	8.3	40.5	12,100
Colombia	10,306	16.8	145.7	1.4	12.5	3,758
Costa Rica	3,646	157.1	306.3	14.8	28.9	1,190
Côte d'Ivoire	8,945	126.7	319.6	9.8	24.7	3,487
Ecuador	7,705	64.2	273.3	8.2	34.9	3,600
Egypt	29,526	121.1	422.8	4.3	15.1	923
India	27,438	12.6	190.2	0.0	0.3	1,800
Indonesia	25,133	24.4	108.6	1.6	7.0	6,848
Jamaica	2,846	97.6	219.9	6.5	14.6	467
Korea	37,330	48.4	125.3	4.9	12.8	11,346
Malaysia	13,354	37.5	70.2	1.2	2.2	7,589
Mexico	86,081	52.0	328.0	6.0	37.8	46,666
Morocco	12,536	83.4	422.0	5.1	25.9	2,744
Nigeria	12,954	12.4	89.6	1.1	8.3	5,531
Pakistan	11,638	35.1	339.6	1.0	9.2	624
Peru	10,712	37.8	229.1	3.7	22.2	3,061
Philippines	24,412	59.9	344.7	5.7	32.7	6,786
Sudan	7,218	101.1	823.5	5.3	43.5	1,276
Syria	6,187	43.6	241.0	0.9	4.9	0
Thailand	12,238	30.5	125.1	2.5	10.2	4,216
Turkey	19,716	36.2	238.7	3.0	19.7	4,873
Uruguay	2,647	27.9	79.7	1.7	4.8	1,276
Venezuela	32,158	32.9	145.7	1.2	5.5	14,800
Yugoslavia	19,900	30.3	126.9	2.6	11.0	12,004
Zaire	5,079	36.1	292.7	2.6	21.0	531
Zambia	3,689	99.9	332.0	5.1	17.0	132

Sources: Tables 2.1, 2.3, 2.4, 2.5, and 2.9 from William R. Cline (1995), *International Debt Reexamined*, Washington D.C.: Institute for International Economics, which were reportedly compiled from the World Bank's *World Debt Tables* and the International Monetary Fund's *International Financial Statistics* and *Balance of Payments Statistics Yearbooks*.

Table 15.2 shows that as a percentage of its national product, Korea's foreign debt was larger than Brazil's, 48.4 percent to 34.6 percent. But 1982 interest payments for Korea were just 12.8 percent of exports while Brazil used nearly half of its 1982 export earnings to cover its foreign interest payments. The reason for this difference in debt burdens was that Korea exported over four times as much of its total national production. Korea also paid a lower rate of interest on its outstanding debt because foreign banks translated its lower debt burden into a lower risk of default. Korea continued servicing its debt after the rise in interest rates in 1982. Brazil defaulted on its obligations.

There are other interesting cases in Table 15.2. For example, Egypt had one of the highest levels of foreign debt, 121.1 percent of GNP, but its interest payments in 1982 were only 4.3 percent of GNP. Its foreign borrowing consisted largely of low-interest and zero-interest loans from foreign governments and multilateral aid agencies. The last column of Table 15.2 shows that virtually none of Egypt's loans were from private commercial banks. When market interest rates were low in the 1970s, private bank loans seemed like a great bargain. But when tight monetary policies pushed market interest rates into double digits, Egypt was lucky to be carrying mostly low-interest, subsidized debt.

For most developing countries, the sudden rise in interest rates and the tight money conditions in the global money markets made further borrowing impossible. The servicing of the accumulated debt required a reverse transfer of purchasing power from developing countries to developed country banks. Developing countries suddenly had to reduce absorption and export more than they imported.

15.3.2 Reaching an agreement

Total private bank loans to developing country governments and agencies exceeded the capital of the world's major commercial banks in 1982. Massive defaults would seriously disrupt the financial sectors of the world's major economies at a time when governments of the high income countries were still dealing with the recessions and high unemployment triggered by the tight monetary policies instituted to reduce high inflation at the end of the 1970s.

The concern for the health of the private banking systems led developed country governments and central banks to actively join in the search for a solution to what came to known simply as *the debt problem*. The resulting negotiations thus became a **three-person game**, with foreign borrowers, lending banks, and developed country governments, each bargaining with the other two groups. Two international agencies, the **International Monetary Fund (IMF)** and the World Bank, were also called on to act on behalf of the developed country governments as will be detailed below. The governments in the debtor countries struggled to avoid major economic disruptions that would threaten their political legitimacy and support. They thus sought both a reduction in their debt obligations to the private foreign banks and financial assistance from developed country governments and international institutions like the IMF. Creditor banks, of course, sought to recover as much of their outstanding loans as possible. While they renegotiated the terms of their loans to the debtors, private creditor banks also lobbied their own governments to supplement what the debtor countries could realistically repay.

Negotiations continued through much of the 1980s, while the IMF provided some temporary financial assistance in exchange for promises of economic reforms by developing country governments. The debtors, creditors, and governments had to deal with many difficult issues that required substantial sacrifices by one or all of the participants in the negotiations:

- How much debt should be forgiven — all, some, or none?

- Who bears the costs of writing off debt?

- Should all debtors enjoy debt relief or just some?

- If just some, which debtor countries?

- How much debt should be rescheduled as opposed to forgiven?

- How much new lending should creditors provide to debtors?

- Should debtors change their economic policies, and how?

- How will policy changes affect the welfare of people in debtor countries?

- What is the role of international agencies?

- What is the role of developed country governments?

It proved very difficult to reach a consensus on these questions. With the help of their central banks, private banks avoided defaults, but growth ceased almost entirely in the debtor economies of Latin America and Africa. The 1980s came to be referred to as the **lost decade** in most developing countries.

At the very end of the decade, the U.S. introduced a framework for solving the debt crisis known as the **Brady Plan** (named for United States' Secretary of the Treasury Nicholas Brady). The essential elements of the Plan were:

- Countries that adopt IMF mandated economic reforms would have their debt loads reduced.

- The International Monetary Fund (IMF) would send its economists to monitor, judge, and certify debtor countries' reform programs.

- Creditors would write down outstanding debt to reflect the "market value" of the debt on the secondary market for sovereign debt.

- One or more developed country governments, the International Monetary Fund, or the World Bank would offer guarantees on the remaining debt so that creditors will be assured of future debt service.

The Brady Plan thus consisted of a combination of debt write-offs by the creditors, unpopular economic policies in debtor countries to improve their ability to repay the debt, and loan guarantees by developed country governments to spread the cost of settlement to taxpayers in wealthy countries. The problem debtors whose debt was nearly worthless on the secondary market would have most of their debt forgiven, while more sound economies had relatively less debt forgiven. This may seem unfair, but this outcome is typical of bankruptcy proceedings. Arguably, the poorest countries had gained few benefits from their foreign loans.

Creditors accepted a substantial reduction in expected future debt service payments, developing countries issued new **Brady bonds** whose principal was backed by U.S. Treasury notes and other sound assets offered by developed country governments. Developing countries agreed to undertake economic reforms under the supervision of the IMF.

The IMF played several roles in implementing the Brady Plan. In its traditional role as *central banker for central banks*, the IMF provided short-term credit to debtor country governments. More controversial was the IMF's push for **economic reforms** in debtor countries. The IMF's policy prescriptions included free trade, competitive foreign exchange rates, and the elimination of barriers to private financial inflows. The IMF also pushed for conservative monetary policies to reduce inflation, tax hikes and expenditure cuts to eliminate the government budget deficits, and the privatization of government assets, such as utilities, railroads, communications companies, and publicly-owned banks, allegedly to provide additional government income. Official statements by the IMF often claimed that these policies were necessary for debtor countries to resume the rapid rates of economic growth they had achieved during the 1950s and 1960s.

In fact, the reforms did not bring much growth even relative to the low levels of output during the severe 1980s recessions, but they did generate trade surpluses that provided the foreign exchange earnings for servicing the foreign debts. Many developing country officials questioned whether the economic policy changes they were being asked to make were even intended to increase economic growth. Some argued that the IMF's policies facilitated the takeover of domestic firms and banks by transnational corporations and international financial conglomerates. Foreign private investors also began acquiring privatized public utilities and infrastructure. The IMF's free market, free trade, and privatization policies came to be known as the **Washington Consensus** since the IMF and the U.S. government that controlled the IMF were both located in Washington DC.

15.3.3 Another crisis in Mexico

Mexico was the first country to sign a Brady Agreement in 1990. After its per capita GDP had not grown for a decade, the Mexican economy finally began to grow again in the early 1990s, albeit much more slowly than back in the 1950s and 1960s. It seemed as though the Brady Plan and the Washington Consensus policies were beginning to produce their predicted results. The Mexican government also made headway in reducing inflation by cutting monetary expansion, and this strengthened the value of the Mexican peso. The reduced inflationary expectations reduced the perceived exchange rate risk associated with investing in Mexico, which encouraged foreign investors to buy Mexican stocks and bonds. Mexican firms, banks, and government agencies were encouraged to borrow overseas from foreign banks. Both borrowers and lenders were further reassured by Mexico's IMF-induced policy reforms and the signing of the **North American Free Trade Agreement (NAFTA)**.

The improved economic performance was short-lived, however. 1994 was an election year, and the Mexican government sharply increased spending and the money supply. The ruling political party, the Institutional Revolutionary Party (PRI), had been in power since the 1920s, but more than a decade of slow economic growth had weakened its formidable political power. Rumors had it that the previous presidential election in 1986 had required a massive election fraud for the PRI to maintain power, and 1994 was also expected to be a very close election. The government's spending surge caused the economy to grow rapidly during 1994, but the rising government budget deficit and the money creation to finance the deficit undermined confidence in the government's commitment to stabilize the peso. Some economists and political pundits, in fact, criticized the government's attempt to keep the peso fixed in value to the dollar while simultaneously increasing public spending, expanding the money supply, and opening the borders to trade and investment as prescribed by NAFTA, which was just going into effect.

Many Mexican individuals and firms, as well as some foreign investors who had previously acquired Mexican assets, began exchanging peso-denominated assets for dollar-denominated assets outside the country. This **capital flight** grew throughout 1994, and the Mexican central bank spent nearly all of its $24 billion of dollar reserves purchasing the pesos being dumped on the foreign exchange market in what would prove a futile attempt to prevent the value of the currency from falling.[6] Capital flight reached panic proportions at the end of the year when Mexico's reserves were nearly exhausted. In December, with no dollar reserves left, the Mexican government could no longer spend dollars to buy pesos to keep the peso from depreciating, and without support the peso promptly lost half its value.

---

[6] Despite criticism of foreign investors, it was mostly domestic wealth that moved out of the country first, as documented by Frankel and Schmukler (1996).

The collapse of the peso caused a severe economic recession. Some analysts seemed surprised that the sharp depreciation of the peso did not immediately increase Mexican exports and employment. Instead, the peso depreciation bankrupted much of the Mexican banking sector and many industrial firms. The IMF-mandated deregulation and privatization of the Mexican banking sector, plus the prospects of NAFTA, had encouraged Mexican banks to borrow dollars in the United States and other global money markets in order to lend to their customers in Mexico, who were anxious to invest and expand business in the growing Mexican economy. Also, the sudden deregulation after decades of tight bank regulation left the Mexican banks unprepared to make business loans. Margins were small, and many bad loans were made by inexperienced bank personnel spurred by their managers to capture market share in the newly deregulated industry. So when the peso depreciated by 50 percent at the end of 1994, the liability side of bank balance sheets grew precipitously. Banks' foreign debt suddenly doubled in size in terms of pesos. The bank balance sheets were further weakened after the peso depreciation because many of the banks' customers had also borrowed overseas in order to expand to meet growing demand and the promise of further growth under NAFTA. Many bank customers defaulted on their Mexican bank loans.

At the end of 1994, the bankrupt banks stopped lending, and Mexico's per capita GDP fell by 10 percent in 1995. On the advice of the IMF, the Mexican government bailed out the banks by buying their foreign debt. Thus a substantial portion of private foreign debt became public foreign debt, and Mexican taxpayers ultimately would have to repay this debt. The transfer would effectively be made by reducing absorption drastically.

More troublesome was the fact that the 1994–1995 recession hit just as NAFTA opened Mexico's borders to imports. Recall from the previous chapter how cheap U.S. food products pushed Mexican farmers off the land and into the cities. With few jobs in the cities after the 1994 debt crisis, Mexican workers streamed across the U.S. border in search of work. In an economically integrated world, international trade, international investment, and international migration interact in complex ways.

15.3.4 The Asian crisis of 1997

Not long after the Mexican crisis, in 1997 the world economy was surprised in 1997 by a sudden massive outflow of money from several fast-growing East Asian economies. South Korea, Hong Kong, Singapore, and Taiwan, the so-called *Asian tigers*, had been the very fastest growing economies of the world since 1960. Several other East Asian countries, Indonesia, Thailand, and Malaysia, the so-called *new Asian tigers*, had also experienced very rapid economic growth rates over the decade prior to 1997. These East Asian economies were often held up as examples of successful developing economies.

The governments of most Southeast Asian countries had avoided the accumulation of large amounts of government debt, and government budgets were in balance.   Inflation was not high compared to most developing economies in the 1980s.   The Southeast Asian economies actively promoted exports and foreign trade.   Many of their manufacturers were **outward-oriented** and subject to some level of foreign competition.   Thus, according to the reasoning behind the Washington Consensus, a financial crisis should not have happened in these countries.   But a more holistic analysis reveals that the conditions for foreign exchange crises were clearly present.   The governments of most of the fast-growing Asian countries had fixed their exchange rates to the U.S. dollar, using reserves of foreign exchange to intervene when necessary to keep the market from raising or lowering the exchange rates.   By 1997, these controlled exchange rates exceeded what many investors suspected were the appropriate levels for balancing the supply and demand of foreign currencies in the long run.   The suspected **currency overvaluation** was, in part, due to an appreciation of the U.S. dollar relative to most other currencies after 1995.   Also important was China's depreciation in 1994.   China produced and exported many of the same labor-intensive manufactures that the new tigers were exporting.   There was also the fact that years of exceptional growth had raised wages and other costs relative to wages in the still much poorer Chinese and South Asian economies.

The governments of most East Asian countries had openly committed to fixing their currencies to the U.S. dollar, and they thus continued to use foreign reserves to buy their currencies and keep the value of their currencies from falling even as expectations of an exchange rate depreciation grew.   East Asian firms began to store their wealth in assets denominated in other currencies.   As much as $80 billion is reported to have flowed out of Indonesia, Korea, Malaysia, the Philippines, and Thailand in 1997 and 1998 to purchase foreign assets.[7]   These outflows sharply reversed the earlier inflows of foreign borrowing by Asian banks to fund real estate booms in their countries.   They used the foreign dollars and yen to provide mortgages denominated in national currencies.   Since the banks would have to repay their loans in dollars and yen, this set up a serious currency mismatch that would be problematic if the exchange rates ever changed.

Indeed, in 1997 the fixed exchange rates were abandoned because speculative outflows of domestic money caused the Asian central banks to run out of foreign exchange reserves.   They used the reserves to buy the domestic currencies that speculators were supplying to the markets in order to buy foreign currencies.   No one wanted to hold currencies that were increasingly expected to depreciate.   When the Asian central banks stopped intervening in the foreign exchange markets, the national currencies fell sharply in value relative to the

---

[7] Van Wincoop and Yi (2000).

major currencies of the world. Just as in Mexico, the sudden rise in foreign liabilities caused bank and firm balance sheets to deteriorate in many Asian countries bank lending ceased, investment stopped, and economic activity fell sharply in 1998. Real GDP fell by 13 percent in Indonesia, 11 percent in Thailand, and 8 percent in Malaysia. It took nearly 10 years for Indonesia' per capita GDP to get back up to its 1997 level.

15.3.5 Some common threads

In addition to the financial crises described above, there were financial crises and subsequent deep economic recessions in Russia, Brazil, Argentina, Turkey, and several other developing economies during the 1990s and early 2000s. The crises shared a number of common characteristics:

- Government agencies, banks, and private business firms had accumulated substantial amounts of foreign debt.

- Foreign debt was denominated in dollars and other foreign currencies, thus creating a mismatch between foreign obligations and the sources of funds that were usually domestic tax revenues and business earnings.

- Currency mismatches forced governments to try to keep exchange rates from changing by using foreign currency reserves to demand domestic currency.

- International economic conditions changed and the exchange rates that governments were trying to hold steady were no longer realistic.

- Fearing a future depreciation of the currency, investors increasingly shifted their wealth into foreign assets.

- Governments therefore had to use ever larger amounts of their reserves of foreign currencies to buy the excess supply of their currencies and prevent the exchange rates from changing.

- When the government ran out of foreign currency reserves, the domestic currency had to be allowed to depreciate sharply.

- The depreciation and the currency mismatches then combined to cause a financial crisis and, subsequently, a deep economic recession.

The triggers of this sequence of events varied. Often, changes in international economic and financial conditions, not shifts in domestic economic conditions and policies, caused exchange rates to fail to balance money inflows and outflows. It should also be noted that serious financial crises occurred only in countries where there were high levels of foreign debt. With large foreign debts denominated in foreign currencies, there were currency mismatches between the liabilities and assets of domestic banks, government agencies, and business firms that had accumulated the foreign debt.

In public pronouncements, government officials often blamed *speculators* for international financial crises. Technically, **speculation** refers to the act of taking a risky position in a market, as for example purchasing foreign assets in anticipation of future exchange rate depreciation. Once the prospect of a crisis and currency depreciation becomes likely, many banks, firms, and investors are likely to begin *speculating* against the local currency. Investors seeking to protect the real value of their wealth sell assets denominated in currencies they expect to depreciate and purchase assets in currencies more likely to appreciate. Importers of goods and services become speculators too when they protect themselves against a future depreciation by making advance purchases of foreign goods that would become more expensive if their currency depreciates. And, exporters keep their overseas receipts parked in foreign bank accounts in order to await the depreciation that will increase the amount of domestic currency earned from the overseas sale. Such widespread speculation by domestic and foreign investors, exporters, and importers increases demand for foreign currencies and reduces their supply. Central banks then have to spend even more reserves of foreign exchange to prevent their currency from depreciating. Panics become self-fulfilling prophecies when, after losing substantial amounts of foreign reserves countering the financial outflows, the central bank is forced to let the currency depreciate.

15.3.6 Foreign debt and currency mismatches

In each of the 1990s financial crisis triggered by a currency depreciation, we find that domestic banks, governments, and business firms had borrowed overseas in dollars and other major currencies while making domestic loans, collecting taxes, or earning income in domestic currency. Most developing countries have little choice but to borrow overseas in terms of dollars or other major currencies because foreign lenders will not carry the exchange rate risk.

In fact, international banking operates almost entirely in dollars, euros, yen, pounds, Swiss francs, and a few other major currencies. This gives the firms, banks, and governments in those major countries an inherent advantage over their counterparts in developing countries. For example, because the U.S.'s foreign obligations are entirely set in U.S. dollars, dollar depreciation causes no change in U.S. borrowers' dollar obligations to foreigners. It is the foreign lenders who, in terms of their currency, would suffer a loss in the value of their overseas assets when the dollar depreciates. In recent years, a few more private loans and bonds sold in international markets have been denominated in developing country currencies, but the interest rates paid have been very high. It costs a lot to induce foreigners to accept the risk of future foreign exchange rate changes. Currency mismatches thus remain a source of fragility in international finance.

15.3.7 Can financial crises be avoided?

After the 1997 Asian exchange rate crises in Asia, some developing countries intentionally began to build up stocks of foreign reserves. Their central banks printed domestic currency with which to purchase foreign currencies in the foreign exchange market to lower the value of their currency and generate persistent trade surpluses with other countries. These trade surpluses are the flip side of the recent large U.S. trade deficits of between $500 billion and $1 trillion per year during the early 2000s. Some see the undervalued currencies as a crude attempt to boost employment through exports. But, the accumulation of reserves by developing countries is also carried out by governments seeking to protect their economies from speculative attacks and financial crises in the future. Large reserves of foreign currencies enable countries to credibly fix exchange rates, regardless of other economic policies, because potential speculators would understand that governments can supply foreign currencies to offset even very large speculative financial outflows and thus prevent exchange rate changes.

Interestingly, the massive accumulation of reserves by China, Taiwan, South Korea, Brazil, and other developing countries is now viewed as a source of international financial instability, even though it protects individual currencies against speculative attacks. The United States, whose dollars serve as the reserve currency for most countries, is now such a large net debtor in the world that some economists fear foreign central banks will no longer want to acquire U.S. dollars for fear that the value of the dollar will fall and reduce the value of their accumulated reserves. The accumulation of foreign currency reserves has yet another cost: goods must be produced and exported without an offsetting import of useful goods from abroad, which means absorption must be less than 10 percent. So far, the government of China and other emerging economies apparently are willing to incur these costs.

One way to avoid this difficult choice between two costly and uncertain alternatives is to directly prevent banks, government agencies, and business firms from accumulating foreign debt and building currency mismatches in their balance sheets. John Maynard Keynes proposed such restrictions on international financial flows for the entire world at the end of World War II. Keynes had studied the many financial crises from before World War I and the inter-war period, and he was keenly aware that the fundamental mechanics of such crises were the same in most cases. His proposal in 1944 effectively anticipated the financial crises such as those experienced by developing countries over the last three decades. Were he still alive, he might also have resisted the Washington Consensus policies of opening economies to foreign trade, foreign investment, and foreign financial flows. In poor countries with small pools of savings, for example, the Washington Consensus policy of privatizing government assets often led domestic investment groups to leverage purchases of government assets using borrowed dollars, euros, or yen. Thus, both the demand for foreign debt and the means to acquire it were enabled by the IMF-sponsored economic reforms.

15.3.8 A note on exchange rate uncertainty

Exchange rates play a crucial role in the financial stability of indebted economies. Sudden shifts in exchange rates trigger balance sheet effects that cause defaults and financial crises, which in turn trigger deep economic recessions when the financial sector freezes its activities and stops funding investment and innovative activities. Unfortunately, when countries open their economies to international trade, international investment, and, above all, international finance, there is little possibility of preventing volatile exchange rate changes because large amounts of money can quickly move into or out of assets denominated in a specific currency.

Orthodox financial models depict the exchange rate as rationally determined by markets that take all available information into consideration. Hence, exchange rates, which are simply a ratio of the values of two assets, domestic money and foreign money, will tend be stable as long as everyone's rational assessments of the future remain stable. The evidence on foreign exchange markets does not support this rational expectations hypothesis, however. Evans and Lyons' (2005) found that news events explained only a very small part, less than 3 percent, of the immediate and subsequent variation in exchange rates, which calls into question the efficiency of foreign exchange markets. Other studies have documented great variations in the risk premium over time and across different pairs of currencies, which suggests that the foreign exchange market is influenced by variations in confidence. Finally, Peter Isard (2006) suggests that the foreign exchange market may simply not be fully rational, at least not as rationality is defined in macroeconomics.

Isard draws on the work of John Maynard Keynes (1936), who argued that the future cannot be objectively calculated in the way that orthodox economists hypothesize rational people calculate expectations. Keynes argued that participants in large financial markets have very limited information on which to base their decisions. Therefore, investors, traders, and everyone else have to set their expectations using partial information, not complete information as the rational expectations and efficient market hypotheses suggest:

> It is reasonable... to be guided to a considerable degree by the facts about which we feel somewhat confident, even though they may be less decisively relevant to the issue than other facts about which our knowledge is vague and scanty.[8]

Because they are constrained by time and the costs of acquiring information, people use what they already know and remember, rather than the complete information set assumed by the orthodox rational expectations hypothesis.

Keynes also observed that investors, lenders, and other economic actors tend to focus on the near past rather than the distant past in shaping their view of the future. This has been largely confirmed by psychological research. People generally discount the past, just as they tend to discount the future. People attribute low probabilities to outcomes that have not occurred recently, even though, fundamentally, these are as likely to occur as more familiar recent events. In short, we do not know everything we need to know, and what we do know and remember is relatively recent.

Second, Keynes disputed the notion that expectations are an objectively calculated weighted average of possible future outcomes. Keynes argues that no future economic outcome can ever be determined with certainty, and, therefore, the expected future exchange rate is not a number we can calculate objectively. In the words of Keynes (1936, p. 152):

> The actual results of an investment over a long term of years very seldom agree with the initial expectations. Nor can we rationalise our behaviour by arguing that to a man in a state of ignorance errors in either direction are equally probable, so that there remains a mean actuarial expectation based on equi-probabilities. For it can easily be shown that the assumption of arithmetically equal probabilities based on a state of ignorance leads to absurdities... our existing knowledge does not provide a sufficient basis for a calculated mathematical expectation.

In short, exchange rates are little more than poorly formulated guesses because people simply do not fully understand the complex economic and social processes that generate all conceivable economic outcomes. Keynes effectively viewed the future as *uncertain*, not risky, where **risk** is represented by the distribution of a set of outcomes with known probabilities. Under **uncertainty**, people have insufficient information or knowledge to calculate the probabilities of all possible outcomes, which makes it impossible to arrive at a single predicted outcome or expected value. In fact, in most cases people face a future in which all the possible outcomes are not even known the future contains many "unknown unknowns."

Peter Isard (2006, p. 5) writes that "Keynes was well aware that investor choices between foreign and domestic assets do not depend on interest rates and exchange rates alone." Paul de Grauwe (1989) described exchange rates as

---

[8] John Maynard Keynes (1936), p. 148.

near-rational, a term he borrowed from the behavioral economists George Akerlof and Janet Yellen (1987). Akerlof and Yellen's experimental economics research confirmed that in setting prices, people are strongly influenced by current prices in deciding on what price to charge or pay. De Grauwe argues that, in the absence of overwhelming evidence that some very different exchange rate is called for, exchange rates tend to remain relatively stable around some initial **anchor price** that more or less clears the market because people have gotten used to it.

The problem with using an *anchor*, or what Keynes called **convention**, to guide decisions is that, inevitably, the anchor comes lose when something upsets the "conventional" world view. Unexpected shifts in the supply or demand for foreign exchange can cause exchange rates to become very volatile after conventional beliefs turn out to have been wrong. Once confidence is eroded, the volatility may last for a long time before a new anchor value may take hold and confidence in new conventions grows.

The uncertainty of the future suggests economic policies should err on the side of caution. In order avoid Bhagwati's "wringer," countries should avoid accumulating large foreign debts. Those gains from international investment and lending shown in orthodox models implicitly assume a certain future without foreign exchange rate risk or sudden shifts in international financial flows. Another suggested course of action is that countries permit only certain types of foreign investment. For example, it is often suggested that foreign direct investment is the least volatile form of international investment and, therefore, the most beneficial for financing economic development projects.

15.4 Foreign Direct Investment

Foreign direct investment (FDI) is fundamentally different from the purchase of many other types of financial assets in that it involves active participation in the management and financial monitoring of a foreign business. Examples of FDI are the construction of factories overseas, the building of foreign marketing and distribution organizations, and the acquisition of controlling interests in existing foreign businesses. This latter form of FDI is referred to as **mergers and acquisitions (M&A)**; the first two examples of establishing new overseas businesses and facilities are called **greenfield investments**.

FDI is closely related to international trade. In the first decade of the 2000s, nearly 90 percent of U.S. imports and exports involved a transnational corporation (TNC) on at least one end of the transaction. Over one-third of international trade is **intra-firm trade**, which is trade between subsidiaries of the same TNC. In this case the same corporate managers control both the exporter in one country and the importer in another country.

15.4.1 The growth of FDI and TNCs

In 1960, FDI accounted for 6 percent of all international financial flows. In 1990, TNCs accounted for about 20 percent of all international financial flows, and by the 2000s FDI's share occasionally surpassed 30 percent. According to data from UNCTAD's (2007) *World Investment Report*, FDI grew three times as fast as overall investment worldwide. Table 15.3 provides more detail on the accumulated stock of FDI in each major industrial sector. The variation in growth rates suggests that FDI is more likely in some industries than others.

Vertical FDI occurs when a TNC builds or acquires foreign facilities that comprise one stage of its complete production process. An example of a vertical foreign direct investment is Ford's engine plant in Brazil, which supplies engine blocks to Ford assembly plants in Brazil, Europe, and the United States. Similarly, Toyota's wholesale organizations located in nearly every country of the world are vertically related to its manufacturing plants located in just a few countries.

Horizontal FDI, on the other hand, consists of FDI that duplicate facilities and operations that the TNC already owns and operates in other countries. The huge French retailer Carrefour, for example, operates distribution centers and chains of retail stores in a number of countries, and its investment in distribution, warehousing, and retail facilities is similar in every country. Ford and Toyota operate automobile assembly plants producing the same cars in several different countries.

TNC investments across developed economies are more often horizontal investments than FDI between more developed and less developed economies. TNCs in developing countries more often serve to vertically integrate the supply chain. Howard Shatz and Anthony Venables (2000) estimate that less than 4 percent of production by European affiliates of U.S. TNCs is sent back to the United States market, but 18 percent of U.S. affiliate production in developing economies is exported to the U.S. U.S. affiliates in Mexico send 40 percent of their output to their parent firms in the U.S. Shatz and Venables also confirm Brainard's (1997) finding that the spread of a TNCs production is more likely to be horizontal the higher are transport costs and trade barriers and the lower are economies of scale at the plant level. Vertical FDI is, therefore, driven by factor cost differences, a principal determinant of comparative advantage.

15.4.2 The history of TNCs

Businesses have operated in more than one country for centuries. Nearly 2,500 years ago, Sumerian merchants stationed employees abroad to sell goods or acquire foreign products. By 1600, private companies began setting up permanent operations in colonial regions protected by their governments' armies

Table 15.3: Estimated World FDI Stock, by Sector and Industry: 1990 and 2005[1]
(Billions of US$s)

	1990			2005		
	MDCs	LDCs	World	MDCs	LDCs	World
Primary	*161.5*	*2.2*	*163.8*	*584.1*	*35.4*	*618.6*
Agriculture, forestry, and fishing	5.2	0.3	5.6	4.3	1.6	5.9
Mining, quarrying, petroleum	156.3	1.9	158.2	577.4	33.8	610.2
Manufacturing	*793.6*	*6.4*	*800.0*	*2,655.3*	*117.4*	*2,774.3*
Food, beverages, tobacco	75.6	0.4	76.0	298.8	2.5	301.4
Textiles, clothing, leather	19.6	0.2	19.7	132.2	3.2	135.5
Wood and wood products	21.5	0.0	21.6	81.7	2.1	83.8
Publishing, printing, media	2.3	-	2.3	15.6	0.0	15.7
Coke, oil refining, nuclear	39.3	-	19.3	35.7	0.0	35.7
Chemicals	150.9	0.8	151.7	560.0	3.6	564.5
Rubber and plastic products	14.5	0.1	14.6	33.7	2.2	35.9
Non-metallic mineral products	13.1	0.2	13.3	35.3	0.8	36.2
Metal products	66.4	0.9	66.4	266.3	1.5	268.1
Machinery and equipment	42.0	0.0	42.1	108.9	0.5	109.5
Electrical and electronic equip.	97.5	1.0	98.5	240.6	9.0	149.6
Precision instruments	13.5	-	13.5	50.8	0.3	51.0
Motor vehicles, transport equip.	60.3	0.0	60.3	427.4	1.3	428.7
Other Manufacturing and unspec.	177.1	3.5	181.6	368.3	90.3	458.7
Services	*834.9*	*11.6*	*846.6*	*6,264.0*	*830.7*	*7,095.6*
Electricity, gas, water	9.6	-	9.6	96.5	6.8	103.7
Construction	18.2	0.2	18.4	73.1	8.7	81.1
Trade	139.9	1.9	141.8	631.1	107.2	738.4
Hotels and restaurants	7.1	-	7.1	96.2	8.6	104.8
Transport, storage, communic.	39.8	0.5	40.3	557.4	53.6	611.2
Finance	400.0	7.2	407.2	2,208.9	176.7	2,385.8
Real estate sales	-	-	-	1.7	-	1.7
Business activities	55.1	1.3	56.4	2,127.2	454.3	2,582.1
Public administration and defense	-	-	-	4.0	-	4.0
Education	0.4	-	0.4	0.4	-	0.4
Health and social services	0.9	-	0.9	1.2	-	1.2
Community, social services	3.4	-	3.4	19.5	1.7	21.2
Other services and unspecified	160.5	0.5	161.0	448.5	13.1	461.6
Total	*1,794.2*	*20.9*	*1,815.2*	*9,570.4*	*1,005.1*	*10,577.1*

Source: UNCTAD (2007), *World Investment Report 2007*, New York: United Nations Conference on Trade and Development, Annex Table A.1.11.
[1] United Nations classifications of more developed countries (MDCs) and less developed countries (LDCs); see UNCTAD website: www.unctad.org.

and navies. Mira Wilkins (1970) describes the 1606 settlement at Jamestown, Virginia, the first European settlement in what is today the United States, as FDI by the British-based Virginia Company. Investments by large colonial enterprises like the Dutch East India Company and the British East India Company were also a form of FDI. The modern independent TNC that moved outside colonial boundaries and set up operations in many foreign countries only came into being in the nineteenth century, however.

The Singer Company's opening of a sewing machine factory in Scotland in the late 1860s is often given as the earliest example of modern FDI. The I. M. Singer Company was formed in New York in 1851 after Isaac Singer was given a disputed patent for the bobbin, the technological breakthrough that made mechanical sewing possible.[9] Singer's early business plan was to set up manufacturing in Elizabeth, New Jersey, and to offer exclusive territories within the United States to local independent distributors. It soon found it more advantageous to organize its own marketing organization because the performance of independent distributors was mixed, at best. Overseas, the Singer Company had authorized a French company to manufacture its sewing machines in France for a royalty of 15 percent. The French firm was soon found to be under-reporting how many machines it manufactured in France in order to reduce its royalty payments. Singer therefore switched to expanding its own sales organizations overseas. By 1861, Singer had sales offices in Glasgow and London. When sewing machine sales outgrew its capacity to also supply European markets from its New Jersey factory, Singer decided in 1867 to open a factory in Glasgow, Scotland. By the end of the nineteenth century, Singer was operating a network of sales organizations, retail stores, distribution centers, and factories in more than 100 countries.[10]

In 1914, nearly three-fourths of U.S.-owned assets abroad were direct investments. This was not the case for other countries; a much larger proportion of British investment overseas consisted of bonds and bank lending. Early in the twentieth century, when the United States overall was a net debtor to the rest of the world, its FDI greatly exceeded foreigners' FDI in the United States. As recently as 1960, half of the world's accumulated stock of FDI was owned by U.S.-based TNCs.

Foreign TNCs began investing more heavily in the United States in the 1980s. They quickly made up for lost time, and in the year 2000, new foreign FDI in the United States was nearly twice as much as new U.S. FDI abroad.[11] Worldwide, in 2000 U.S. TNCs owned less than one-fourth of the world's accumulated stock of FDI, which is quite a drop from the 50 percent share in 1960. The growth of TNCs from other countries is evidenced by the fact that in the early 2000s about 10 percent of the accumulated stock of FDI was owned by TNCs based in developing countries.[12] Among such developing country FDI are

---

[9] Actually, there is evidence that Isaac Singer stole the idea, but he had enough money to employ lawyers to fight several court cases that ultimately gave the Singer Company ownership of the patent for the bobbin.

[10] Isaac Singer had another motivation for setting up a factory in Scotland: he was being prosecuted for bigamy in the United States, and he found it convenient to move to Scotland with one of his wives.

[11] Harlan W. King (2001), Maria Borga and Raymond J. Mataloni, Jr. (2001).

[12] Robert E. Lipsey (2001).

the recent purchases of IBM's personal computer business by the Chinese firm Lenovo, Ford's Jaguar division by the Indian firm Tata, and the Volvo by a Chinese state-owned automaker.

15.4.3 TNCs and international trade

In the 1980s, a study on the role of TNCs in U.S. foreign trade revealed that of the total U.S. exports of $212.2 billion in 1982, $203.4 billion (95.9 percent of the total) were made by U.S. TNC's and affiliates of foreign TNC's. At the same time, U.S. and foreign TNCs in the United States imported 77 percent of all goods imported into the United States. The data also highlighted the fact that a substantial portion of exports and imports were intra-firm trade. Specifically, the data showed that of total exports of $212.2 billion, $46.6 billion were by U.S. TNC's to their foreign affiliates and $20.2 billion were by U.S. affiliates of foreign TNC's to their own firms' home-country operations. That is, 31.5 percent of all U.S. goods exports were intra-firm transfers. For imports the situation was similar: 36.6 percent of all U.S. imports were intra-firm transfers.

More recent studies suggest that TNCs role in international trade has not diminished since the detailed study of the 1980s. According to a 1997 U.S. Department of Commerce study, the intra-firm trade shares of U.S. exports and imports of goods changed little during the 1980s and 1990s.[13] It is safe to say that TNCs today are involved in nearly all international trade.

15.4.4 TNCs and the spread of technology

TNCs carry out most of the world's private R&D and, therefore, control much of the world's industrial knowledge and technology. TNCs potentially play a major role in the dissemination of technology throughout the world. There is evidence that TNCs are well-positioned to spread knowledge because they are directly involved in the personal contacts, learning processes, and hands-on experiences that are required to pass along complex forms of information and knowledge.

Contrary to the common perception that technology transfers from abroad are a free source of knowledge, they are often quite costly. Applying existing technology normally involves a learning process and/or an adaptation of the technology to one's specific circumstances. Such learning and adaptations are not free. David Teece (1977) estimated the costs of technology transfers across countries in the chemicals, petroleum refining, and machinery industries, and he found that, on average, the cost of adopting foreign technologies was equal to 19 percent of total project costs. Edward Mansfield, Schwartz, and Wagner (1981) also found the costs of adopting existing technologies to be substantial; for 48

---

[13] William J. Zeile (1997), p. 23.

product introductions in the chemical, drug, electronics, and machinery industries in the United States, the estimated cost of imitation was equal to about 65 percent of the total cost of innovation.

Recall from Chapter 7 that Michael Polanyi (1958) described knowledge as mostly *tacit*, by which he means that it is passed on "by example from master to apprentice."[14] Jeremy Howels (2000, p. 53) defines tacit knowledge as "know-how that is acquired via the informal take-up of learned behavior and procedures." Technology is not normally transferred in the *codified* form of precise blueprints that are easily copied. Richard Nelson and Sidney Winter (1982) extend Polanyi's ideas by describing how the organizational structure of a firm influences how tacit knowledge is passed along and, more generally, how it shapes the path of technological change. More generally, Meric Gertler (2007, p. 90) argues that "tacit knowledge can be shared effectively between two or more people only when they also share a common social context: shared values, language, and culture." Since FDI extends business organizations across borders, the resulting TNCs extend a cultural environment of "shared values, language, and culture" in which tacit knowledge can more easily be passed across borders. In short, technology flows are likely to reflect earlier flows of FDI. A TNC enjoys a cost advantage in transferring technology because its organization already has people that understand the technology and have experience applying it.

TNCs are likely to provide a selective set of channels for the spread of knowledge, however. As noted above, FDI occurs more frequently in some industries than others. Also, FDI is managed with the firm's interests in mind, which means it only incurs the expense of spreading the tacit knowledge it needs to make its overseas investments operate efficiently. There is unlikely to be much technology transferred in the case of assembly operations built only to take advantage of low wage levels and lax labor regulations. On the other hand, there may be transfers of knowledge when a TNC shifts R&D activities overseas or when management personnel is transferred between different parts of a TNCs global operations.

15.4.5 Is FDI less volatile than other financial flows?

FDI is less volatile than most other types of international financial flows. FDI, it is argued, is more stable because it cannot be as quickly reversed as, for example, portfolio investments like stocks and bonds. FDI involves the acquisition of real assets that are not so easily bought and sold. Also, FDI implies an extension of business organizations across borders. It is difficult to quickly change a business organization, its supply channels, and its marketing channels. This image of FDI as a stable form of international investment may not be entirely accurate, however.

---

[14] Michael Polanyi (1958), p. 53.

While it is difficult to reverse past FDI quickly, new inflows of FDI can certainly be reduced to zero immediately. A sudden cessation of FDI inflows can also trigger an exchange rate crisis, especially if an economy was receiving large inflows of FDI that were offsetting large trade deficits that cannot be easily reversed. Also, FDI may be more mobile than many policymakers suspect. In a study of foreign-owned plants in Indonesia, Andrew B. Bernard and Fredrik Sjöholm (2003) find that foreign-owned plants are 20 percent more likely to close than domestic plants when the economy slows.

Another concern about FDI is that it can behave like a predator precisely when domestic firms are most vulnerable. At the time of an economic crisis, well-funded foreign firms can acquire assets in a country at what Paul Krugman (2000) labeled "fire-sale prices." Then, once the crisis has passed, the economy has recovered, and the exchange rate has reversed its decline, the foreign buyers of the domestic firms end up earning extremely high rates of return on their investments. Thus, FDI may actually increase the long-run costs of a financial crisis.

15.5 Why Have Transnational Corporations Grown?

The rapid growth of TNCs suggests that there are advantages for businesses to extend their organizations across national borders. Business economists point out that there are both costs and benefits of expanding business organizations across borders. There are also external costs and benefits associated with TNCs. We will focus on the short-run and long-run externalities later. In this section we look at why firms decide to expand across borders.

Most of the gains from FDI are related to the advantages of *internalizing* transactions within a single business organization as opposed to transacting with people and firms outside the organization. In general, if a business firm finds it is less costly to **internalize** transactions than to engage in "arms-length" transactions with other firms, managers will elect to allocate resources *administratively* rather than using market transactions. According to Richard Caves (1996, pp. 1–2):

> The Darwinian tradition holds that the most profitable pattern of enterprise organization should ultimately prevail: Where more profit results from placing plants under a common administrative control, multiplant enterprises will predominate, and single-plant firms will merge or go out of business. In order to explain the existence and prevalence of [TNCs], we require models that predict where the multiplant firm enjoys advantages from displacing the arm's-length market and where it does not. In fact, the prevalence of multiplant (multinational) enterprises varies greatly from sector to sector and from country to country.

In short, Caves argues that if a business firm believes that it can better take advantage of its unique assets, technology, reputation, and personnel in other national markets, it will opt to extend its business organization to those locations and become a TNC.

15.5.1 Why TNCs dominate the economic sphere

There are many other advantages to spreading a business organization across political borders. Among those recognized in the business literature are:

1. Comparative advantage — Some activities are better performed in other countries than at home. United Fruit did not try to grow bananas in the United States; they found it more advantageous to build banana plantations in Honduras and Costa Rica, where warm weather and good soil made banana production more productive.

2. The Hold-Up Problem — Outside suppliers of specialized inputs into a firm's production process are reluctant to make large investments to supply specialized parts and components to a single buyer. An outsourcing firm has an incentive to "renegotiate" the terms of the contract once the supplier is locked into this new supplier capacity. Suppliers can strengthen their hand by *holding up* their investments until the outsourcing firm agrees to contractual terms more favorable to the supplier. The growth of TNCs suggests that it is often easier for managers to squeeze their own foreign subsidiaries than it is to pressure outside suppliers.

3. Economies of scale — Firms may become more efficient at certain tasks the larger their operations become, and therefore a single firm spread throughout the world may be able to produce more efficiently than independent firms located in each of the countries of the world. A firm already in possession of a product design or a large research facility would be at a competitive advantage vis-à-vis a smaller local firm that must start from scratch to develop a product.

4. Exploiting core competencies — **Core competencies** are those activities that provide the firm with its highest markup and profit margins. Modern management theory advocates that firms outsource all activities except for their core competencies, which will guarantee the highest profits. FDI is a logical extension of a core competencies strategy. FDI enables the firm to expand its business overseas while keeping all its the core activities in house.

5. Exploiting reputations — Successful TNCs are often those firms that have established strong reputations and brands. The importance of reputation and brand recognition tends to favor large firms, which can devote more resources to establishing their brands in the market.

6. *Jumping trade barriers* — If a firm has a reputation, know-how, or fixed product development costs that can be profitably exploited in foreign markets, but trade barriers prevent the export of its products to other markets, then it may be profitable to invest in factories behind the tariff and quota walls that block trade.

7. *Avoiding taxes and regulations* — Differences in regulation and taxation may make business activities more profitable in some countries than others, and profit-motivated corporations will tend to exploit the differences.

8. *Diversification* — By spreading its production and marketing operations more evenly across countries, and thereby better balancing expenses and revenue in each currency, TNCs reduce their exposure to foreign exchange fluctuations.   Also, TNCs can reduce their financing costs because operations in many countries provide an alternative to a diversified portfolio of assets. Fang Cai and Francis Warnock (2004) present evidence suggesting that stock in TNCs throughout the world is valued more highly because purchasers of stock prefer TNCs' inherent reduction in business risk.

9. *Access to Financing* — Recent flows of capital to less developed economies suggest that TNCs are better able to deal with the difficulties of financing investment in economies where financial systems and institutions to enforce contracts are not as well developed. Because of their size, TNCs have access to foreign financing where domestic firms in less developed countries are not trusted enough to access the less expensive global financial markets.

10. *Reducing competition* — With the lowering of trade barriers, foreign competition increases. One way to reduce these competitive pressures is to acquire foreign competitors. Such mergers and acquisitions (M&A) explain a large portion of FDI in recent years.

11. *Enhancing innovative success* — Innovation is driven by a process that is subject to large economies of scale, yet it is also dependent on outside ideas. We normally see R&D activities concentrated at research centers, and we commonly see research activity concentrated in specific geographic regions like Silicon Valley. A TNC with operations in many countries may therefore have an advantage in accurately assessing technologies available overseas and thus better able to find an optimal combination of centralization (internal proximity) and dispersion (external proximity) for organizing its research activity. As Hélène Blanc and Cristophe Sierra (1999, p. 203) suggest, "[TNCs] increasingly tend to develop international intra-firm networks to exploit the 'locationally differentiated potential' of foreign centres of excellence."

12. Knowledge and technology are difficult to sell — Know-how is often unique to the firms that developed it or built up the experience that gradually produced the know-how. Thus, these firms must establish overseas units to reap the economic rewards of their accumulated know-how.

Note that the explanations for the growth of TNCs listed above are not mutually exclusive. Several may apply to each case of FDI. For example, the large inflow of FDI to Ireland over the past two decades has been driven by the desire to jump over the European Union's trade barriers and set up production inside the European Union, to take advantage of Ireland's low corporate taxes, and to exploit Ireland's lax regulatory structure. Whatever the particular reasons for the growth rise of individual TNCs in specific countries and regions, many factors have combined to make TNCs the dominant form of business organization in the world economy today.

15.5.2 TNCs are altering the economic and social spheres

When FDI and international trade are combined, as is increasingly the case, the growth of TNCs has many complex consequences. For example, labor organizations argue that TNCs and their ability to shift production across borders has weakened labor's market power. Labor unions have little power to push for wage increases when employers can easily shift production to non-union plants in other countries. The international mobility of capital also reduces governments' power to tax capital. If TNCs are indeed highly responsive to cost differences, attempts to increase corporate taxes will cause outflows of FDI. It thus becomes difficult for government to redistribute income from the owners of capital to poor or unemployed workers.

TNCs' market power permits them to gain ever higher shares of national income at the expense of consumers, workers, and resource suppliers. The growing international market power of TNCs is due to the rise in overseas mergers and acquisitions rather than greenfield investments. Thus, rather than increasing the overall productive capacity of countries or applying new ideas and technologies in other countries, FDI increasingly is used to concentrate existing productive capacity within fewer and larger TNCs.

TNCs have used their increasing wealth to capture the power of government. They have used this power to shape government institutions in their favor. In addition to pushing for more benevolent tax regimes, TNCs have actively supported political parties and government leaders who will reduce regulations that add to their operational costs. The reduced power of labor unions, mentioned above, was not entirely due to international competition; it was also the result of lobbying by business to change labor laws and make organizing workers more difficult. Furthermore, TNCs shape technology flows to their advantage, and they control who gets to use the technologies they develop. Business has lobbied hard to achieve the current global system of patents and copyrights, which establish global ownership of ideas, techniques, formulas, designs, and other forms of intellectual property.

TNCs not only use their power to influence market outcomes, but they use their wealth to lobbying and capture government power. They then use their political clout to directly undermine the institutions that serve to keep the market system competitive. Furthermore, as TNCs grow by substituting internally managed transactions for "arms-length" market transactions, they further reduce the scope of the market economy. The larger the firm, the more exchanges and transactions are done by memorandum, instructions, procedural rules, and direct commands; there are no voluntary decisions within an inherently autocratic and hierarchical TNC. Neoclassical market models do not apply to intra-firm transactions.

15.6 A Final Note

This chapter and the previous one examined three components of economic globalization: international trade, international investment, and international finance. The next chapter examines economic policies that deal with international trade, investment, and finance. It will be readily apparent from how governments have dealt with international trade, investment, and finance that international economic policies tend to reflect political and social issues. But politics aside, the next chapter will also show that government policies often reflect concerns related to economies of scale, industrial concentration, and technological innovation, conditions that are often assumed away in orthodox comparative static models of the neoclassical paradigm.

Key Terms and Concepts

Ability to pay	Core competencies
Absorption	Currency overvaluation
Anchor price	Default
Brady bonds	Diversification
Brady Plan	Economic reform
Capital flight	Financial assets
Convention	Foreign currency cash flow

Foreign direct investment (FDI)
Greenfield investments
Hold-Up Problem
Horizontal FDI
Import substitution policies
Internalization of transactions
International finance
International investment
International Monetary Fund (IMF)
Intertemporal exchange
Intra-firm trade
Liquidity
Loanable funds
Lost decade
Mergers and acquisitions (M&A)
North American Free Trade Area
(NAFTA)

Odious debt
Organization of Petroleum Exporting
Countries (OPEC)
Outward-orientation
Portfolio investment
Real assets
Reversals of financial flows
Risk
Risk aversion
Speculation
Store of wealth
Three person game
Total factor productivity
Uncertainty
Vertical FDI
Washington Consensus

Questions and Problems

1. Explain the following statement: International investment always involves international finance, but international finance may not be related to any form of international investment. (Hint: Define your terms first.)

2. Describe the orthodox model (Figures 15.1, 15.2, and 15.3) of international investment and finance in detail. Then explain what important aspects of international finance that this model ignores. (Hint: Recall the discussion of financial failures in Chapter 11.)

3. Recall Robert Lucas' question: Why doesn't capital flow from rich to poor countries? Discuss the relevance of this question and explain the answer to the question.

4. Foreign direct investment (FDI) is often split into greenfield investments and mergers and acquisitions (M&A). Explain the difference between the two categories of FDI. Provide international examples of each of these two types of FDI.

5. Explain the Brady Plan. Why did it take so long for the concerned parties to negotiate a settlement to the 1982 defaults?

6. Why was foreign debt so problematic in 1982? Why had so many countries accumulated so much foreign debt, and what happened in 1982 to bring the problem to a head? Put the debt into historical perspective as well as the usual economic perspectives.

7. Review the discussion of Mexico's foreign debt episodes, and distinguish the similarities and differences between Mexico's various defaults on foreign debt. Why did foreign banks and investors keep lending after each successive default?

8. The period 1950–1970 was characterized by relatively little international borrowing by developing economies, yet economic growth was quite rapid compared to more recent decades when borrowing was much greater. Does this mean that there is a

reverse relationship between international borrowing/lending and economic growth? Explain your answer using historical evidence and economic models.

9. Why did the exchange rate crises turn into financial crises in Mexico and East Asia? Why did the sharp decline in the value of the national currency not trigger a boom in exports that stimulated the overall economy, as some exchange rate models suggest, but instead caused a sharp downturn in investment and economic activity? Could the financial crises have been avoided?

10. The chapter notes that less developed countries have increasingly sought to protect themselves from exchange rate crises by accumulating large amounts of foreign reserves. Is the accumulation of foreign reserves a cost-effective way to insure against speculative attacks and currency crises? Carefully weigh the pros and cons of accumulating large foreign exchange reserves. (Hint: Explain how a country accumulates foreign reserves and what this means for domestic absorption.)

11. What were the common threads across the financial/economic crises in Mexico, Asia, and the many less developed countries in 1982?

12. Under the Brady Plan, debtor countries agreed to carry out a variety of economic "reforms" under supervision of the IMF allegedly in order to improve their ability to service their foreign debt. Despite undertaking many of the required reforms, Mexico again suffered a currency collapse and financial crisis in 1994. Did any of the economic reforms contribute to the new crisis? (Hint: Review the reforms and the description of the causes of Mexico's 1994 crisis.)

13. Describe the Washington Consensus. Explain the post-1982 circumstances that enabled the International Monetary Fund to impose the Washington Consensus on many developing country governments. Has the Washington Consensus been successful in restoring rapid economic growth in developing economies?

14. Was the IMF's recommendation of privatization of domestic firms and banks a good idea? Did the privatization generate enough funds for debtor countries to service their debt? Explain.

15. Why was the 1982 debt crisis so difficult to resolve? (Hint: Describe the "game" that characterized the negotiations between the interested parties.)

16. Explain why multinational enterprises have grown to become so dominant in nearly all of the world's economies? (Hint: Discuss the unique advantages of an international business organization over other forms of business organization.)

17. The focus on core competencies seems to mandate both a downsizing of a firm and the expansion of the firm overseas. Is this a contradiction? (Hint: Discuss the concept of core competencies and then show how spreading a business across borders expands the gains from its core competencies.)

18. Explain how a transnational corporation (TNC) can circumvent taxes and government regulations. Does this give TNCs an advantage over purely national firms? Discuss.

19. Explain why purchasing the stock of a transnational corporation (TNC) may be less risky than purchasing shares of the local firm? (Hint: Discuss portfolio diversification and show how a TNC is effectively a diversified portfolio.)

20. Do you think Bhagwati's opinion that countries should not borrow overseas at all is valid? Explain.

21. Explain why uncertainty generates instability in the international economic/financial system. Explain why long-run intertemporal decisions are uncertain. (Hint: Discuss the difference between risk and uncertainty.)

22. The large inflow of FDI to Ireland over the past two decades has been driven by the desire to jump over the European Union's trade barriers and set up production inside the European Union, to take advantage of Ireland's low corporate taxes, and to exploit Ireland's lax regulatory structure. How has this strategy worked out? Explain.

References

Aggarwal, Vinod K. (1989), "Interpreting the History of Mexico's External Debt Crises," in Barry Eichengreen and Peter H. Lindert (eds.) *The International Debt Crisis in Historical Perspective*, Cambridge, MA: MIT Press.

Akerlof, George, and Janet.Yellen (1987), "Rational Models of Irrational Behavior, *American Economic Review* 77(2):197–217.

Archibugi, Danielle, and Jonathan Michie (1995), "The Globalization of Technology: A New Taxonomy," *Cambridge Journal of Economics* 19:121–140.

Aurbach, A.J., K.A. Hassett, and S.D. Oliner (1994), "Reassessing the Social Returns to Equipment Investment," *Quarterly Journal of Economics* 109:789–802.

Barba Navaretti, Giorgio, and Anthony J. Venables (2004), *Multinational Firms in the World Economy*, Princeton, NJ: Princetón University Press.

Bernard, Andrew B., and Fredrik Sjöholm (2003), "Foreign Owners and Plant Survival," NBER Working Paper 10039, October.

Berger, Philip, and Eli Ofek (1995), Diversification's Impact on Firm Value," *Journal of Financial Economics*.

Bhagwati, Jagdish (1998), "The Capital Myth," *Foreign Affairs*, May/June.

Blanc, Hélène, and Cristophe Sierra (1999), "The Internationalization of R&D by Multinationals: A Trade-off between External and Internal Proximity," *Cambridge Journal of Economics* 23:187–206.

Borensztein, E., J. De Gregorio, and J-W. Lee (1998), "How Does Foreign Direct Investment Affect Economic Growth?," *Journal of International Economics* 45:115–135.

Borga, Maria, and Raymond J. Mataloni, Jr. (2001), "Direct Investment Positions for 2000, Country and Industry Detail," *Survey of Current Business* 91(7):16–29.

Brainard, S. Lael (1997), "An Empirical Assessment of the Proximity-Concentration Trade-off between Multinational Sales and Trade," *American Economic Review* 87(4):520–544.

Cai, Fang, and Francis E. Warnock (2004), "International Diversification at Home and Abroad," Board of Governors of the Federal Reserve System, discussion paper 793, Washington, D.C., February.

Caves, Richard E. (1996), *Multinational Enterprise and Economic Analysis*, Cambridge, U.K.: Cambridge University Press.

De Grauwe, Paul (1989), *International Money: Postwar Trends and Theories*, Oxford: Oxford University Press.

De Long, J. Bradford, and Lawrence H. Summers (1991), "Equipment Investment and Economic Growth," *Quarterly Journal of Economics* 106(2):445–502.

De Long, J. Bradford, and Lawrence Summers (1992), "Equipment Investment and Economic Growth: How Strong is the Nexus?," *Brookings Papers on Economic Activity* (1):57–199.

Edelstein, Michael (1982), *Overseas Investment in the Age of High Imperialism: The United Kingdom, 1850–1914*, New York: Columbia University Press.

Eichengreen, Barry, and Peter H. Lindert, eds. (1989), *The International Debt Crisis in Historical Perspective*, Cambridge, MA: MIT Press.

Evans, Martin D., and Richard K. Lyons (2005), "Do Currency Markets Absorb News Quickly?," *Journal of International Money and Finance* 24(2):197–217.

Frankel, Jeffrey A., and Sergio L. Schmukler (1996), "Country Fund Discounts and the Mexican Crisis in December 1994: Did Local Residents Turn Pessimistic Before International Investors?," International Finance Discussion Paper #563, Board of Governors of the Federal Reserve System, September.

French, Kenneth R., and James M. Poterba (1991), "Investor Diversification and International Equity Markets," *American Economic Review* 81(2):222–226.

Gertler, Meric S. (2007) "Tacit Knowledge in Production Systems: How Important is Geography?," in Polenske K.R. (ed.), *The Economic Geography of Innovation*, Cambridge, U.K.: Cambridge University Press, pp. 87–111.

Howells, Jeremy (2000), *Knowledge, Innovation and Location*, London: Manchester University Press.

Isard, Peter (2006), "Uncovered Interest Parity," IMF Working Paper WP/06/96, April.

Keynes, John Maynard (1923), *Tract on Monetary Reform*, London: MacMilllan.

Keynes, John Maynard (1936), *General Theory of Employment, Interest, and Money*, London: MacMillan.

King, Harlan W. (2001), "The International Investment Position of the United States at Yearend 2000," *Survey of Current Business,* July:7–15.

Krugman, Paul (2000), "Fire-Sale FDI," in Sebastian Edwards (ed.), *Capital Flows and the Emerging Economies: Theory, Evidence, and Controversies*, Chicago: University of Chicago Press, pp. 43–60.

Lipsey, Robert E. (2001), "Foreign Direct Investment and the Operations of Multinational Firms: Concepts, History, and Data," NBER Working Paper 8665, December.

Lucas, Robert E., Jr. (1990), "Why Doesn't Capital Flow from Rich to Poor Countries?," *American Economic Review* 80(2):92–96.

Mansfield, E., M. Schwartz, and S. Wagner (1981), "Imitation Costs and Patents: An Empirical Study," *Economic Journal* 91:907–18.

Marichal, Carlos (1989), *A Century of Debt Crises in Latin America*, Princeton, NJ: Princeton University Press.

Moran, Theodore H. (1998), *Foreign Direct Investment and Development*, Washington, D.C.: Institute for International Economics.

Nelson, Richard. R., and Sidney G. Winter (1982), *An Evolutionary Theory of Economic Change*, Cambridge, MA: Harvard University Press.

Polanyi, Michael (1958), *Personal Knowledge: Towards a Post Critical Philosophy*, London: Routledge.

Romer, Paul (1993), "Idea Gaps and Object Gaps in Economic Development," *Journal of Monetary Economics* 32:543–573.

Shatz, Howard J., and Anthony J. Venables (2000), "The Geography of International Investment," in G.L. Clark, M. Feldman, and M.S. Gertler (eds.), *The Oxford Handbook of Economic Geography,* Oxford, U.K.: Oxford University Press.

Teece, David J. (1977),"Technology Transfer by Multinational Firms: The Resource Cost of Transferring Technological Know-How," *Economic Journal* 77(1):49–87.

Temple, Jonathan (1998), "Equipment Investment and the Solow Model," *Oxford Economic Papers* 50:39–62.

Tobin, James (1958), "Liquidity Preference as Behavior Towards Risk," *Review of Economic Studies*, February.

UNCTAD (2007), *World Investment Report 2007*, New York: United Nations Conference on Trade and Development.

Van Wincoop, Eric, and Kei-Mu Yi (2000), "Asia Crisis Postmortem: Where Did the Money Go and Did the United States Benefit?," Federal Reserve Bank of New York *Economic Policy Review*, September, 51–70.

Wilkins, Mira (1970), *The Emergence of Multinational Enterprise: American Business Abroad from the Colonial Era to 1914*, Cambridge, MA: Harvard University Press.

Zeile, William J. (1997), "U.S. Intrafirm Trade in Goods," *Survey of Current Business* 87(2).

CHAPTER 16

International Economic Policy:
Heterodox Approaches

United Fruit gave the world not just bananas but also "banana republics."
(Peter Chapman, *Financial Times*)[1]

Chapter 14 began with the Heckscher-Ohlin model of international trade, and the previous chapter presented a simple two-country model of international investment. These models are not holistic because they ignore many interrelationships between the economic, social, and natural spheres. Also, their static nature prevents them from accurately representing a dynamic process like economic development. Because they miss most of the long run consequences of international trade, investment, financial flows, and migration, these models are not useful for designing international economic policies.

International economic policy must recognize that, unlike what orthodox economic models assume, international trade, international investment, and international finance are not carried out in perfectly competitive market structures. Many transactions are carried out within corporate structures, as explained in the previous chapter. Nor are economic outcomes the result of rational decisions by well-informed individuals. Where there are markets, the market power of the participants generally leads to prices that do not accurately reflect opportunity costs. Product, labor, and financial markets are almost always dominated by a small number of large transnational corporations. Furthermore, the government policies and institutions that influence markets are shaped by the lobbying activities of the same transnational corporations that have the greatest market power and profits to buy the government's support. Beyond the uncompetitive markets in which people buy products and sell their

---

[1] Peter Chapman (2007), "Rotten Fruit," *Financial Times*, May 5/6.

labor, most human interactions and transactions do not occur in anything that can be represented as a market in which suppliers and demanders objectively weigh their numerous alternative options. Rather, most decisions occur within the home and the workplace, which means love, custom, culture, procedure, and bosses' instructions guide most human decisions.

International trade, investment, finance, and migration comprise the complex process of international economic integration. This process is actually an integral part of the dynamic process of economic development. Drawing on well-established ideas, this chapter's discussion will suggest that international economic integration often concentrates wealth and economic power. It is not necessarily the *equalizing* process that orthodox economic models predict. Heterodox perspectives of globalization lead to very different conclusions about economic policies. The orthodox conclusions that free trade and free financial flows maximize human welfare are no longer credible when increasing returns to scale, industrial concentration, and dynamic growth processes are taken into consideration. Heterodox policy prescriptions differ sharply from orthodox policy recommendations, such as those of the Washington Consensus.

The first section below discusses **colonialism**, the international economic system in which some countries used their military power to control the economic and political organization of other countries. The reality of colonialism is not compatible with the assumptions of the HO model of trade. Also, the colonial experience helps us understand why so many Third

---

Chapter Goals

1. Discuss mercantilism and its overseas manifestation, colonialism.
2. Present a case study of Brazil and its adoption if import substitution industrialization (ISI) in the twentieth century.
3. Explain agglomeration and its relationship to increasing returns to scale.
4. Explain the rationale for ISI, and evaluate how well ISI worked in developing economies.
5. Detail the ideas behind ISI, such as dependency theory and structuralism.
6. Discuss the role of Raúl Prebisch and the United Nations Commission for Latin America in advancing ISI policies throughout the developing world.
7. Discuss immigration and its role in an agglomerating global economy.
8. Describe and analyze the role of transnational corporations in the agglomerating global economy.
9. Assess the current global economic system and contrast it with earlier episodes of colonialism and mercantilism.
10. Discuss the evidence on the effectiveness of foreign aid.
11. Reassess neoclassical models of international economic activity from heterodox perspectives of international economic integration.

World governments have resisted free international trade and financial flows. This chapter details the widespread adoption of **import substitution industrialization (ISI)** policies after World War II. The chapter concludes with an examination of the direct government-to-government assistance programs, **foreign aid**, and their effectiveness in shaping economic development.

16.1 Mercantilism and the Colonial System

When Adam Smith (1776) was writing about why free trade was beneficial for human well-being, most international trade was being carried out within colonial empires. Trade was among very unequal trading partners, and it was subject to many restrictions imposed by colonizing governments. When Smith criticized **mercantilism** and advocated unregulated free trade, he was effectively criticizing colonialism and calling for a political regime change.

Historian Charles Wilson (1963) broadly described mercantilism as "all the devices, legislative, administrative, and regulatory, by which societies still predominantly agrarian sought to transform themselves into commercial and industrial societies."[2] Mercantilism was a system of government regulation and control over economic activity to protect and favor the government's commercial allies and financial supporters, usually merchants, artisans, and industrialists. Mercantilism was an integral force in shifting Europe away from the fragmented small administrative units that characterized feudalism to the centralized nation-states of nineteenth and twentieth century Europe. The economic historians Robert Eckelund and Robert Tollison (1981) describe mercantilism as a **rent-seeking society** in which commercial interests bid for, and gain control of, government mechanisms that provide them with special privileges and monopoly power. Their definition is useful, but mercantilism is a much more complex phenomenon with many social and political implications.

In sixteenth century Europe, mercantilism solidified the power of national monarchs over the local aristocracies established during earlier feudal societies. When the same alliances between central governments and commercial interests were extended overseas, mercantilism turned into colonialism. Colonialism was effectively a joint government-private conquest of foreign territory and resources. European monarchs embraced colonialism as an alternative source of tax revenue to the tributes by domestic feudal lords. Instead of bargaining over the mutual obligations inherent in feudal relationships, central monarchs found it more convenient to align themselves with the newly emerging commercial interests in overseas ventures. By offering commercial interests military and administrative support, monarchs were able to extract a substantial share of the profits from the overseas ventures. Mercantilism was, therefore, a system in

---

[2] Charles Wilson (1963), p. 26.

which government institutions were designed to serve the interests of private commerce and industry. This section uses the example of Brazil, a colony of Portugal, to detail the process whereby European governments imposed mercantilism on the world.

16.1.1 The example of Brazil

It is difficult to generalize across many individual historical events, but there were many common characteristics across the different colonial empires constructed by the European powers that sent their navies and armies overseas to pursue the commercial interests of monarchs and allied elites.   For illustration, we focus below on the interesting case of Brazil, currently one of the large emerging economies. Since its "discovery" by the Portuguese explorer Pedro Cabral in 1500, Brazil's economic development was largely driven by international trade. But, it will become clear that Brazil's experience cannot be accurately assessed using the orthodox Heckscher-Ohlin (HO) model of trade.

When Pedro Cabral claimed Brazil as a Portuguese territory in 1500, he was the captain of a ship funded by the King of Portugal to sail around the horn of Africa to trade for spices in India. Government funding of such voyages was granted on the condition that the Portuguese Crown be paid a substantial tax on the eventual profits of the venture. The Crown often awarded merchants monopoly privileges in overseas territories, and it provided the navies and armies to protect the merchants in overseas territories. With the local Portuguese countryside and village economies still controlled by traditional local aristocracies, overseas commerce was a convenient new source of revenue with which the Portuguese royal family could fund the armies, bureaucrats, and personal wealth necessary to consolidate their national governments. In the fifteenth century, King Henry "the Navigator" of Portugal had taken an especially active role in promoting overseas commercial ventures.

Unlike other larger European monarchies like Spain, England, and France, Portugal was a small country. It initially sought trading posts in Africa and the East Indies rather than territorial control of overseas lands. In the case of Brazil, however, there were few products to trade for in the vast jungle territory; Brazil's most valuable early resource export was Brazilwood (pau brasil), which was processed to produce a red dye used in the textile industry. But this product ultimately proved to be of little value beyond giving the new territory its name. The Portuguese, therefore, adopted what was quickly becoming a common colonization strategy, and it awarded large tracts of land (capitânias) to Portuguese adventurers (donatários) willing to go to Brazil, invest in their properties, and attract colonists. In exchange for the land titles and near free reign in the allotted lands, the crown demanded a share of the revenues generated by the private investments. According to William Glade (1969, p. 156), this system made early Brazilian colonization "a business venture, combined with aspects of private subgovernment." The donatários became the elite that would for the next five centuries dominate Brazil's society, economy, and political system.

The Portuguese donatários introduced new crops from elsewhere in the Portuguese empire, such as Middle Eastern sugar cane that they already cultivated profitably in Portugal's Azores and Cabo Verde islands in the Atlantic. Sugar grew well in Brazil, but it was a labor-intensive crop most efficiently produced on large plantations. Labor was in short supply in the Brazilian capitânias because there were few Portuguese settlers, the introduction of European diseases killed the greater portion of natives, and those natives still alive fled into the interior of the huge country to escape disease and hard labor. Brazilian landowners began importing slave labor from Portuguese outposts in Africa, thus initiating the Atlantic slave trade. By 1600, Brazil was the world's leading sugar producer, and slaves greatly outnumbered the Portuguese in Brazil.

The **sugar cycle** of Brazilian development was centered in what is today the Northeast region of the country, where Cabral touched land and the early capitânias were established. Brazilian plantation society was characterized by huge income inequalities and little lasting economic development, although substantial riches were accumulated by the plantation owners. Brazilian sugar production declined in the late seventeenth century when other European colonial powers introduced sugar to their own colonies in the Caribbean and elsewhere. Most colonial empires explicitly restricted foreign trade to trade between the mother country and its overseas colonies whenever possible, and Brazil's mother country, Portugal, offered a very small market for sugar. The Northeast region of Brazil, where sugar production was centered, stagnated economically. It remains the poorest region of Brazil today, 400 years later.

Around 1700, gold and diamonds were discovered in the interior of Brazil, in a region that is today the state of Minas Gerais. A gold rush ensued, and nearly half of the world's output of gold during the eighteenth century came from Minas Gerais. Some sugar planters from the Northeast moved their slaves to Minas Gerais to work in the gold mines, but the region was mostly settled by eager new arrivals from Portugal and elsewhere. The gold rush generated more diverse economic development in Minas Gerais than the sugar cycle did in the Northeast because gold mining was based on individual operations. Demand for food and transportation stimulated farming. Raising the mules to carry supplies in and products out of the interior region to the coastal city of Rio de Janeiro became a major support activity.

The gold boom led to a more direct Portuguese government presence in Brazil because tax revenues now had to be collected from many small miners and farmers, not just a few well-known plantation owners. To facilitate tax collection and reduce evasion, Portuguese bureaucrats and soldiers intentionally limited transport to a single mule trail between Rio and Minas Gerais. Also, all ships leaving Brazil had to sail together in convoys accompanied by government escorts back to Portugal, allegedly for protection against pirates but mostly to prevent smuggling and tax evasion. All trade from Brazil was also required to pass through Portuguese merchants authorized by the Crown. Smuggling nevertheless grew, and the economically-oppressive measures fueled resentment among the miners, farmers, and the local Brazilian business elite. The first uprising against the colonial government occurred in Minas Gerais in the late 1700s. It was difficult for a small country like Portugal to control a large colonial territory like Brazil, especially since Portugal held many other colonial lands in Africa and Asia, such as Angola, Mozambique, Goa, Timor, and Macao.

The spread of slavery, the awards of huge territories to a privileged few, the tight regulation of trade, and the inefficient procedures to avoid tax evasion resulted in an inefficient economic system in Brazil. Colonialism did not maximize the total potential gains from international trade and investment. Most notably, the system did not spread the economic benefits equitably among colonialists and colonies.

16.1.2 Mercantilism after Brazil's political independence

Brazil gained a sudden increase in stature when, in 1807, the Portuguese royal court fled Napoleon's Iberian invasion and made Brazil's small capital city of Rio de Janeiro the de facto capital of the entire Portuguese empire. The wealthy Brazilian families that held an estimated two-thirds of the colony's wealth at the start of the nineteenth century declared independence after the Napoleonic wars ended and the Portuguese Crown returned to Lisbon. They did not want to see Brazil restored to its status as a distant colony. The Brazilian elite that arose in the Portuguese mercantilist-colonial system opted to establish a new monarchy rather than the usual republican form of government selected by the newly independent former Spanish colonies in Latin America. The Brazilian elite convinced the son of the Portuguese king to remain as Emperor of Brazil. This is why Brazil's independence cry was "I'm staying" (Eu fico).

The elite quickly replaced that first emperor, Dom Pedro I, with his 5-year old son in 1831 when the former was suspected of still being loyal to Portugal. An appointed regent ruled in the young emperor's place until 1840, when Dom Pedro II assumed the Brazilian throne. Brazil remained a monarchy until 1889. It did not abolish slavery until 1888. The country was effectively ruled by a somewhat shaky coalition of elite commercial and agricultural families as a type of **plutocracy**. Only in 1889 was a republican form of government adopted after years of debate within the elite about slavery and the monarchy. The shift in government finally occurred because of the growing economic influence of the new commercial elite, the coffee barons.

Coffee had been introduced to Brazil from the Middle East early in the eighteenth century. Coffee trees require a temperate climate but they cannot withstand frost. The delicate combination of cool but never cold weather is often met in the higher altitudes of tropical countries. The vast coastal highlands of Brazil were close to ideal for coffee cultivation. Independence had ended the Portuguese trade restrictions, so Brazilian coffee producers could trade with everyone. Then the iron steamship cut transport costs from Rio de Janeiro to Europe by over 70 percent between 1840 and the early twentieth century.[3] Brazilian coffee production and exports grew rapidly with worldwide demand from the increasingly numerous and wealthy middle class consumers in Europe and the United States. Coffee cultivation spread from the Parayba valley near Rio de Janeiro southward into the large state of São Paulo and westward into the former mining region of Minas Gerais. The port of Santos, just below the São Paulo plateau, became the world's largest coffee port.

The coffee boom put huge amounts of capital into the hands of the coffee farmers of the state of São Paulo. Coffee farming required large amounts of labor, and because the importation of slaves was strongly opposed by its largest trade partner, Great Britain, Brazil began encouraging immigration from Portugal, Italy, Spain, Germany, and most other parts of Europe. The entire southern part of Brazil, down to the state of Rio Grande do Sul on the Uruguayan border, became a melting pot of European immigrants. Brazil's diversity was further enhanced by later immigrations from Japan and the Middle East, as well as continual internal migration of Brazilians from the relatively poor Northeast region to the more developed south. British foreign investment in Brazil's infrastructure followed, and soon railroads fanned out from the port of Santos and the nearby city of São Paulo into the vast interior of the state. By 1900, Brazil produced half the world's coffee, and coffee accounted for 80 percent of the country's export earnings.

The wealth accumulation by São Paulo coffee producers laid the basis for Brazilian industrialization. Already in the first decade of the twentieth century, the growing immigrant population was creating a viable market for locally produced textiles, clothing, footwear, woodworking, and processed foods. Most of the new industries were established in the city of São Paulo. The role of coffee as an engine of growth was only diminished by the volatility of coffee prices and, by the early 1900s, persistent overproduction as other countries, such as Colombia and Mexico, expanded production. The politically powerful coffee interests in São Paulo pushed the Brazilian government to guarantee prices and purchase excess stocks. The boom and bust nature of coffee production was apparent after World War I, as prices rose in the 1920s as the world economy recovered from the war but then collapsed by two-thirds at the start of the Great

---

[3] C. K. Hartley (1988); Douglass North (1958).

Depression. Brazil's political response to this latest coffee bust would radically change the process of economic development in Brazil.

In sum, during the nineteenth century Brazil's integration into the world economy accelerated through the expansion of coffee production in the southern part of the country. A new class of merchants arose that gained their domestic political power from the huge profits derived from coffee exports. The *coffee barons* used their political clout to push the government, and the taxpayers, to protect them from adverse climate and market conditions. This mercantilistic collaboration between the government and coffee producers enabled the country to fund much of its early industrialization from export earnings rather than from foreign borrowing.

16.1.3 Brazil in the 1930s

At the beginning of the Great Depression, the prices of primary products fell precipitously. Celso Furtado (1963) estimates that Brazil's terms of trade fell by about 50 percent, which meant that 1930 exports of coffee and other primary products only purchased half as many real imports as in 1929. Brazil was able to balance its foreign payments only by severely devaluing its currency and making imports much more expensive relative to domestic products. Exactly as exchange rate theory predicts, this shift in relative prices of imports to domestic products led domestic consumers to substitute domestic goods for foreign goods. Brazilian trade thus remained in balance despite the collapse of export earnings because it suddenly became economical to produce many products in Brazil that, before 1929, had been imported from abroad.

The boom in Brazilian industrial production was only partially caused by the devaluation's effect on import prices, however. Domestic demand was also stimulated by the Brazilian government's very expansionary fiscal and monetary policies. These policies were actually an unintentional by-product of traditional domestic mercantilist rent-seeking. As noted, coffee producers were a very powerful political force in Brazil. So when coffee prices fell sharply, the Brazilian government responded by providing huge subsidies that maintained domestic coffee farmers' incomes despite the fall in international prices. To fund these subsidies, the Brazilian government printed money. Therefore, in 1930 Brazil unintentionally carried out precisely the expansionary monetary and fiscal policies later advocated by John Maynard Keynes (1936) to reduce the Depression's high unemployment in Britain, the United States, and elsewhere. In the words of Celso Furtado (1963, p. 212):

> It is therefore quite clear that the recovery of the Brazilian economy which took place from 1933 onward was not caused by any external factor but by the pump-priming policy unconsciously adopted in Brazil as a by-product of the protection of coffee interests.

Industrial production in Brazil by 1933 had recovered its 1929 level. That year, 1933, marked the deepest point of the Great Depression in most developed countries of the world. By 1937, when much of the world was still trying to recover from the Great Depression, Brazil's industrial production was 50 percent greater than it was in 1929. Overall Brazilian real GDP was 20 percent greater in 1937 compared to 1929. Most of the new industries were located in São Paulo, where the coffee wealth was concentrated.

16.1.4 From accidental to planned industrialization

The good economic performance during the 1930s influenced Brazilian policymakers in the 1940s. World War II increased demand for raw materials, and Brazil's exports to the United States expanded rapidly during the war years. Even after the war, demand for Brazil's traditional exports was strong, fueled by the world economy's recovery from the war. Because of the growing exports, the value of the Brazilian currency had to rise relative to other currencies for its balance of payments to remain in balance. This rise in the value of the currency increased the prices of Brazilian goods relative to foreign goods, the exact opposite of what occurred in the 1930s. The government and the many new industrialists feared that the process of import substitution would be reversed. There was concern that the many new industries would be unable to survive a cheapening of imports from the traditional industrial countries interested in using exports to help their economies recover from the war.

The new industrialists, the labor unions whose members worked in the new industries, and other commercial interest in the urban areas of southern Brazil lobbied for government support. The Brazilian government decided to institute trade restrictions to offset the improved terms of trade that were undermining Brazilian industries' ability to compete with imports. These explicit trade barriers after World War II were very different from the general depreciation of Brazil's currency that brought about the import substitution in the 1930s, however. In 1948 Brazil passed a **law of similars**, which authorized a complete ban of all imports of "similar" products as soon as any domestic firm could show it was capable of supplying any specific product to the domestic market.

Under the law of similars, imports of a product, whether it cost twice as much or five times as much to produce in Brazil as it did in the rest of the world, would be protected. The law also provided permanent protection, unlike an exchange rate that is subject to future change. Thus, the law of similars and the broad protection it gave to all domestic producers went well beyond the traditional **infant-industry** argument for protection detailed in Chapter 14 because it completely severed the links between comparative advantage and domestic production. It awarded domestic producers eternal subsidies by Brazilian consumers, who were forced to pay the high prices charged by producers protected from foreign competition. Economists are still debating whether this was a good policy choice.

16.2 Interpreting Brazil's Colonial and Post-Colonial Experiences

Brazil's choice of explicit trade and investment restrictions after World War II was not arrived at casually or accidentally. Of course, domestic politics played a role, but the country's colonial and post-colonial experiences weighed heavily in the political process that led to the policy shifts. A feature of colonialism that did not escape many Brazilian intellectuals was that trade relationships did not become more equitable when formal colonial links were severed. Brazil and virtually all other former colonies remained exporters of raw materials and importers of industrialized products even after political independence.

There was ample evidence showing that trade and investment between European countries and their colonies had not been beneficial for the colonies. When per capita incomes rose persistently in Europe and the United States during the 1800s and early 1900s, most developing countries and colonies remained poor.[4] This is the historical period when incomes across countries diverged sharply and the persistent split between developed and less developed countries was created. In the case of Brazil, it was only when the country effectively cut itself off from international trade by means of its 1930 devaluation that the country experienced rapid industrialization and moved away from its colonial role of supplier of raw materials to the world's more industrialized countries. The real reason for Brazil's law of similars was the strong sentiment against returning to the pre-World War I trade regime.

16.2.1 Dependency theory

Many Latin American economists called for developing countries to sever all economic ties with their former colonial masters. Their particular interpretation of colonialism came to be known as **dependency theory**. This perspective was well elaborated by the German-born and American-educated economist Andre Gunder Frank (1967), who built on the works of Marx and the socialist economist Paul Baran (1957).

Frank challenged the idea that developing countries were in an early stage of development that developed countries had already passed through. He argued that twentieth century poor countries were in a unique state, called **underdevelopment**, which the rich countries never experienced. Currently rich countries never passed through a stage where they had to co-exist with much wealthier and more highly industrialized countries:

> ... even a modest acquaintance with history shows that underdevelopment is not original or traditional and that neither the past nor the present of the underdeveloped countries resembles in any important respect the past of now

---

[4] Paul Bairoch (1993).

developed countries. The now developed countries were never *under*developed, though they may have been *un*developed. It is also widely believed that the contemporary underdevelopment of a country can be understood as the product or reflection solely of its own economic, political, social, and cultural characteristics or structure. Yet historical research demonstrates that contemporary underdevelopment is in large part the historical product of past and continuing economic and other relations between satellite underdeveloped countries and the now developed metropolitan countries. Furthermore, these relations are an essential part of the structure and development of the capitalist system on a world scale as a whole.[5]

Frank saw the world economy as a continually evolving system, one that was very different from the one that existed in the past. The contemporary system was dominated by the large wealthy economies, and that domination forced the underdeveloped countries to remain in a subservient economic state.

Frank was not unique in recognizing that countries are part of a global economic system. Orthodox trade theory also looks at countries in an integrated world economy. But Frank and the other dependency theorists disputed the claim by orthodox models that economic interdependence would make poor countries richer. Frank (1978, p. 101) argued that interdependence actually *prevented* less developed economies from developing:

> When we examine this metropolis-satellite structure, we find that each of the satellites, including now-underdeveloped Spain and Portugal, serves as an instrument to suck capital or economic surplus out of its own satellites and to channel part of this surplus to the world metropolis of which all are satellites. Moreover, each national and local metropolis serves to impose and maintain the monopolistic structure and exploitative relationship of this system... as long as it serves the interest of the metropoles which take advantage of this global, national, and local structure to promote their own development and the enrichment of their ruling classes.

Rather than serving as an engine of growth, dependency theorists like Frank described trade as a channel through which rich **center countries** exploited poor **peripheral countries** and perpetuated the unequal distribution of world income.

16.2.2 The Structuralist School

Dependency theory is often identified with **structuralism**, a popular philosophical trend in Latin America after World War II. Dependency theorists, like structuralists, explicitly rejected orthodox economics' fundamental assumption that economic outcomes are the result of free choices made by individuals who rationally strive to maximize their individual welfare.

---

[5] Andre Gunder Frank (1978), p. 100.

Structuralists argued that human behavior is holistically influenced by culture, institutions, and psychological factors that combine to perpetuate the status quo. Structuralists further emphasized that international trade creates and then perpetuates unequal economic and social structures. For example, Brazilian sugar exports in the sixteenth and seventeenth centuries created a plantation society whose slavery and unequal income led to an inequality of wealth and ownership that still distorts incomes in Brazil today. Thus, where modern economic analysis assumes smooth functions and continuous marginal adjustments to price signals in efficient interpersonal markets, structuralists argued that developing economies were plagued by structural rigidities, such as culture and institutions, that ruled out smooth adjustments. Structuralists were convinced that if developing countries followed their current comparative advantages, they would be locked into exporting primary products for centuries, unable to adjust to falling commodity prices or opportunities for exploiting economies of scale in other industries.

The **Structuralist school** of economics was related to a French philosophical movement headed by the anthropologist Claude Lévi-Strauss. This philosophical movement was also called *structuralism*, and it replaced existentialism as the dominant philosophical paradigm in France in the late 1940s and 1950s. Like the Structuralist School of economics, philosophical structuralists rejected the idea that humans make choices entirely according to their free will. Rather, they saw human behavior being shaped by various *structures* or, in terms of our holistic language, *systems*. They concluded that human economic behavior could only be explained if the social, cultural, political, natural, and economic structures were understood. Structuralist economists saw human economic behavior as tightly bound by the broader economic and social systems within which people lived. Developing countries, they claimed, found themselves in a mercantilist economic system that defined their economy's trade and industrial structures.

These philosophical and economic ideas helped to push most developing country governments to take the route that Brazil took after World War II. Structuralism was also well received in newly-independent countries in Africa and Asia, who had little desire to continue the trade channels through which the colonialists had exploited them. Today, it is the agglomeration of economic activity that points to a need for protectionist policies to permit developing economies to promote the development and growth of industries that enjoy economies of scale.

16.3 The Agglomeration of Economic Activity

At the start of this textbook, we pointed out that technological change and economic development alter the structures of economies and societies. Highly developed economies produce a very different mix of goods and services than do underdeveloped economies. For one thing, as economies grow and become richer, agricultural output shrinks as a percentage of the value of total output. At the same time, the industrial sector tends to grow rapidly during the early phases of economic growth, but as economies reach the highest levels of development, industrial activity again shrinks as a proportion of total output and the services and innovative sectors become larger. High income countries also tend to use very different production methods. In short, people living in the rich economies generally work at different jobs and consume different baskets of goods and services in comparison to people living in economies that generate only low per capita levels of output.

One of the characteristics of economic development is the movement of productive resources, including people, toward cities and countries where most of the manufacturing and innovative activities occur. Manufacturing and innovation are characterized by economies of scale, which make it advantageous for these activities to concentrate. Earlier chapters discussed how past economic development was closely related to the rise of urban settlements, a process that has now reached the point where over half the world's population lives in cities. In this section, we discuss the technological changes and economic development that have resulted in a greater geographic concentration of economic activity. Economists have referred to this process as **agglomeration**.

16.3.1 The causes of agglomeration

Nearly a century ago, Alfred Marshall (1920) devoted an entire chapter of his popular economics textbook to the "Concentration of Specialized Industries in Particular Localities." Marshall attributed geographic concentration to three factors: (1) the availability of specialized labor, (2) the development of specialized suppliers of intermediate goods and services, and (3) the flows of technology between the industries.[6] Other economists have generated further hypotheses for why economic activities agglomerate in specific geographic locations. The driving force of most agglomeration models are transportation costs and the various costs of transferring technology between people.

Agriculture is, by nature, linked to the land. Agriculture, therefore, tends to disperse throughout the world in accordance with the natural conditions of the land and the availability of other factors that complement the land in producing agricultural products. Agriculture requires other services, especially as technology improves and incomes rise, which is why towns and cities developed and spread out wherever agricultural activity flourished. But it was the Industrial Revolution that gave towns and cities a much stronger reason to exist:

---

[6] For a general introduction to spatial economics, see Walter Isard (1975) or Edgar M. Hoover and Frank Giarratani (1984). Ellison, Glaeser, and Kerr (2010) examine data from the United States and United Kingdom and conclude that all three of Marshall's factors indeed influence agglomeration.

urban agglomerations were the best location for factories that needed large numbers of workers and outside suppliers of inputs and support services.

Paul Krugman (1991) attributes the agglomeration of industrial activity to **increasing returns to scale**. In manufacturing it is more efficient to produce a large amount of output in one large factory than to produce the same amount of output in a large number of small factories scattered throughout the economy. Krugman hypothesizes that the rate at which industrial activity agglomerates depends on the cost of transportation and the scope of increasing returns to scale. When transport costs are high, economies of scale cannot be fully exploited because industry remains scattered around the country to service the dispersed population engaged in agricultural activities and the service activities related to agriculture. However, technological change and economic development cause transport costs to fall, lower transport costs permit increasing returns to scale to be further exploited, and industrial activity increasingly agglomerates. As an example of the contemporary importance of economies of scale and geographic agglomeration, Donald Davis and David Weinstein (2003) used detailed cost data on Japanese firms to conclude that Japan's real GDP would be 20 percent lower if production were evenly distributed throughout the country rather than concentrated as it is in certain towns and cities.

Industrial activity is not the only economic activity that agglomerates. Industrial firms require more and more outside support services as their output grows, and therefore firms that service industry also agglomerate in the same places where industry agglomerates. And because the workers at the factories spend a large portion of their income where they live, consumer services also agglomerate in the same locations where industrial activity agglomerates and employs people. Krugman's story of agglomeration is incomplete, however, because economies of scale differ across agriculture, industry, services, *and* innovative activity, not just the first three of these economic categories.

16.3.2 The agglomeration of innovative activity

The concentration of information technology (IT) firms in California's Silicon Valley, financial firms in London, and the biotech industry in the Boston area are examples of how new technologies spur new activities in certain geographic areas. Data on research expenditures by region and the addresses listed on patent applications suggest that innovative activity is in fact centered in a small number of developed economies, while very little measurable new technology is developed in developing economies.[7] Even within developed countries, most innovative activities occur in just a few metropolitan areas.

---

[7] See, for example, the data on R&D expenditures as a percentage of GDP given in UNESCO (2002), *Statistical Yearbook*, Geneva: UNESCO, or in World Bank (2002), *World Development Indicators*, Washington, DC: World Bank, Table 5.11, pp. 320–322.

The geographic concentration of innovative activity is partially driven by the geographic concentration of the resources most important for innovative activities. Countries with large numbers of highly educated people tend to have a comparative advantage in generating new ideas and technologies. Since innovation is combinatoric and builds on existing knowledge, those people most likely to combine existing ideas into new ideas are those who have access to, and a good understanding of, existing knowledge. There is, therefore, a virtuous cycle at work: The regions that have the resources most important for innovative activity accumulate more knowledge, which in turn makes further technological progress more likely.

The explanation of the geographic concentration of innovation still requires another condition to be satisfied, however. Recall the nonrival nature of technology; once an idea is conceived, it becomes available to everyone else. This nonrival nature of knowledge suggests that knowledge should be nearly free and, therefore, will be passed from one economy to another so that, in the end, it will not matter for subsequent technological change where any one innovation takes place. However, when Adam Jaffe, Manuel Trajtenberg, and Rebecca Henderson (1993) compared the locations of the owners of patents with citations of those patents in later patent applications, they found that "[l]ocalization fades over time, but only very slowly."

Recall from Chapter 7 Richard Florida's (2005) examination of copyrights, patents, and scientific citations, and his finding that creative and innovative activity was much more concentrated than the manufacturing or services industries. Wrote Florida (2005, p. 50): "As far as global innovation is concerned, perhaps a few dozen places worldwide really compete at the cutting edge." One reason for the agglomeration of innovative activity is that the adoption and application of existing technologies is not free. Recall the S-curve introduced in Chapter 7, which depicted the gradual dissemination of knowledge over time and space. And even when knowledge is **nonrival**, firms have many ways to keep "trade secrets" from reaching their competitors. Today, the institution of intellectual property rights enables firms to make knowledge and technology excludable. Recall also from the last chapter Michael Polanyi's (1958) point that the tacit nature of most knowledge and technology means adoption requires costly and time-consuming person-to-person interactions. Technologies therefore tend to remain within corporate structures. And when new variations of technologies arise outside the firm, mergers and acquisitions (M&A) are often used to bring new technologies back into the corporate structures of the dominant firms.

16.3.3 The changing patterns of economic activity

Agglomeration is unlikely to result in all economic activity becoming concentrated into a single small region, like some type of black hole.

Agglomeration is limited by the resources available in any given geographic location. For example, space is a resource that is obviously limited, as is the ecosystem's capacity to maintain clean air and water in densely populated areas with intensive economic activity. More generally, if there are not unlimited amounts of labor, capital, and infrastructure in a region, the agglomeration of innovative activity must take resources away from other economic activities, such as production and investment. As a result, the cost of manufacturing in an innovative region will rise relative to the costs of manufacturing elsewhere. On the other hand, as workers' wages rise, new migrants will be attracted, and the population will grow to meet the increased demand for labor. But because space is a fixed resource, land prices will rise and land-intensive activities become more costly. Also, increased congestion will require people to spend more scarce time getting around the crowded region, and the existing capital infrastructure will be strained. The rising costs of agglomeration will then drive away and disperse those activities least subject to increasing returns to scale as well as those least constrained by transport costs. Urban areas will therefore tend to become either industrial centers or innovative centers, not both. Limited resources thus imply that the world will experience **specialized agglomeration**.

Casual observation suggests this indeed is happening. Some regions have become known as *high tech* centers, such as San Francisco, Boston, Austin, and San Diego in the United States, while others have become industrial centers, such as the state of São Paulo in Brazil and the coastal region of China. Communications and computer technologies developed in California's Silicon Valley enabled customer services to concentrate in Bangalore, India. Centuries of experience still gives London an advantage in financial services and banking. The above examples show that the process of agglomeration can cross national boundaries.

The economies of scale in industrial production and innovative activities, and the greater economies of scale in the latter compared to the former, are fundamental to the process of international economic integration. Agglomeration increases regional and national specialization, which means agglomeration leads to more regional and international trade. Agglomeration, of course, also tends to bring about a concentration physical investment. And, because investment is increasingly in the form of private foreign direct investment, the integrated global economy is increasingly dominated by transnational business organizations that concentrate their manufacturing, marketing, management, and R&D activities in different countries.

Finally, the geographic agglomeration of economic activity can only occur if workers move out of the dispersed agricultural sector to the industrial and services activities that agglomerate in urban areas. The flow of people from rural agricultural communities to growing towns and cities has been going on for thousands of years in most parts of the world, of course. However, rapid industrialization caused the process to greatly accelerate over the past 200 years. And, now, the process is global as the agglomerative nature of innovative activities pulls talented immigrants toward the world's innovative centers. Anna Lee Saxenian (1994, 2002) describes how Chinese and Indian entrepreneurs started over one-third of new firms in Silicon Valley, the U.S. center of the information technology revolution.

Fundamentally, even if immigrants do not directly enhance innovative activity, there will still be migration from regions and nations where diminishing returns tends to reduce the rewards for labor and towards those regions and nations where increasing returns boost wages.[8] The apparent fact that immigrants actually enhance the increasing returns to scale in innovative centers only hastens the migration of people. The next subsection examines the role of immigration in the process of economic development and agglomeration.

16.3.4 Immigration and agglomeration

International migration, or **immigration**, has grown rapidly over the past half century, and it is now a major determinant of population growth in many countries. Immigration increased rapidly towards the end of the twentieth century. Canada, Australia, New Zealand, and the United States, received large inflows of immigrants from Europe throughout the post-World War II period. Australia and Canada each received more than 2 million immigrants between 1946 and 1964. A number of Western European countries, which had supplied so many people to the rest of the world from 1600 to 1900, themselves began to receive large inflows of immigrants from elsewhere in Europe and from North Africa after 1960. Even Ireland, which sent over 4 million immigrants to the Western Hemisphere in the second half of the nineteenth century, began receiving large inflows of immigrants toward the end of the twentieth century. Because of this immigration, in 2004 Ireland's population exceeded 4 million for the first time since 1871.[9] Some 8 million Germans expelled from Eastern Europe after World War II settled in West Germany, and over one million ethnic French moved back to France during Algeria's war of independence in the late 1950s. The collapse of the Soviet Union and the other communist governments in Eastern Europe has, since 1990, resulted in immigration from Eastern Europe to the high-income Western European economies. Over 1 million immigrants legally enter European countries each year, and perhaps another 500,000 asylum seekers and unauthorized immigrants enter each year as well.[10] Immigration has greatly changed many European societies, as suggested by the high percentages of foreigners living in each country, as shown in Table 16.1. Switzerland's

---

[8] The relationship between diminishing returns and migration was noted by Alfred Marshall (1890 [1920]) over a century ago. He devoted a whole chapter of his poplar *Principles of Economics* textbook to the interactions between diminishing returns and increasing returns and their role in shifting population from rural to urban areas.

[9] Tom Hundley (2004), "Booming Ireland Sees Population swell to 130-Year High," *Chicago Tribune*, December 4.

[10] *The Economist* (1998), "Millions Want to Come," April 4.

population and labor force is about 25 percent foreign, and Luxembourg's labor force is over one-third foreign born.

People do not immigrate only to the developed countries of Europe and North America. There are an estimated 7 million Pakistanis, Filipinos, Indians, Palestinians, Egyptians, and other foreigners working in Saudi Arabia. Perhaps another 5 million foreigners live and work as construction workers, domestics, and day laborers in the other oil-rich Gulf states on the Arabian Peninsula.[11] Rapidly-growing Asian economies such as Singapore, Malaysia, and Thailand also have attracted immigrants from populous countries such as Indonesia, Bangladesh, Philippines, and India. An estimated one in four factory workers in Malaysia are foreigners.[12]

Table 16.1 Foreign-Born Population and Labor Force: 2004

% of:	Population	Labor Force
Europe:		
Austria	3.0	15.3
Belgium	11.5	11.4
Denmark	6.3	5.9
France	10.0	11.3
Germany	13.0	12.2
Ireland	1.0	10.0
Italy	2.5	5.9
Luxembourg	33.1	45.0
Netherlands	10.6	11.1
Spain	5.3	11.2
Sweden	12.2	13.3
Switzerland	23.5	25.3
United Kingdom	9.3	9.6
Japan	1.2	1.0
Traditional Immigrant Destinations:		
Australia	23.6	24.9
Canada	18.0	17.8
United States	12.8	15.1

Source: OECD (2006), *International Migration Outpook*, Paris: OECD, Chart 1.4 and Table 1.8.

Like all aspects of the international economic integration, immigration is intimately related to many variables in the economic, social, and natural spheres. This complexity is reflected in the words of the Swiss novelist Max Frisch: "We

---

[11] Robin Allen (2000), "A Time Bomb in the Desert," *Financial Times*, June 10/11.
[12] Peter Waldman (1998), "Grim Farewell for Asia's Foreign Workers," *The Wall Street Journal*, January 9.

wanted workers, and people came."[13] The movement of people not only moves labor from one country to another, but it also moves cultures, consumers, innovators, children, parents, human capital, interdependencies, and all the other things that are "people." Immigration upsets political systems, changes social relationships, and results in cultural clashes. But, it can also stimulate new ideas and cultural changes that benefit societies that receive immigrants.

Evidence suggests that immigrants are largely driven by income difference across countries. Since these differences have grown over the past century, it should not be surprising that immigration has also grown despite some efforts by countries to restrict the international flow of people. Note in Table 16.1 that foreigners account for a surprisingly large portion of the people living in most high income countries today. It is estimated that about 3 percent of the world's people live outside their country of birth. The number of immigrants in developing countries is not well documented, although recent census data suggests the number of foreigners in some emerging economies is rising. The 2010 Chinese Census counted over half a million foreigners living and working in the country. There are probably many more "informal" immigrants from North Korea and other neighboring countries working in China.

The increase in immigration can be explained by agglomeration. As an increasing percentage of economic activity concentrates in specific areas, regions, and countries, more people are needed to work in the growing industries. The link between agglomeration and immigration is the presence of economies of scale in both manufacturing and innovative activities, the two categories of economic activity that are central to modern capitalist economies.

Joseph Schumpeter emphasized the role of entrepreneurs in the process of creative destruction. The entrepreneur sees opportunities for introducing new products, changing a firm's organization, exploiting new markets, finding new sources of raw materials, cutting the costs of production, or motivating workers. Schumpeter (1934, p. 155) considered the entrepreneur to be a "social deviant" because his or her attitude was different from the average member of society:

> The reaction of the social environment against one who wishes to do something new... manifests itself first of all in the existence of legal and political impediments. But neglecting this, any deviating conduct by a member of a social group is condemned, though in greatly varying degrees according as the social group is used to such conduct or not.

Schumpeter pointed out that immigrants often become entrepreneurs because they are less attached to the traditions of society and, therefore, less reluctant to innovate. Further highlighting the potential contribution of immigrants to

---

[13] Max Frisch is a noted twentieth century Swiss novelist and writer; his words are quoted from Colin Nickerson, Globe Staff (2006), "A Lesson in Immigration: Guest Worker Experiments Transformed Europe," *Boston Globe*, April 19.

innovation is Thomas Kuhn's (1962) discussion of revolutionary *paradigm shift*, which suggests that such shifts in technology require some degree of social deviance.

Barry Chiswick (2000) found that the self-selection of immigrants in terms of personal characteristics favorable to economic development is more pronounced "the greater the out of pocket (direct) costs of migration and return migration, the greater the effect of ability on lowering the costs of migration, and the smaller are the wage differences by skill in the lower income origin than in the higher income destination." The fact that international migration is difficult and risky implies that immigrants are likely to be less risk averse and more adventuresome than the average person in their countries of origin. If immigrants are really more entrepreneurial, more willing to sacrifice now for future gains, better educated, and more ambitious than the average population of the country they leave behind, then the source country is likely to suffer both immediate and long-term losses. On the other hand, when new immigrants are more ambitious, educated, entrepreneurial, and forward-looking, the destination country will gain more from their arrival.

Immigrants carry ideas and technologies with them to their destination countries, and they effectively expand the stock of knowledge and ideas in the destination country. For example, Carlo Cipolla (1978) describes how immigrants helped to develop the famous Swiss clock and watch industry. The clock and watch industry played a particularly important leadership role in developing Swiss technology and precision engineering. That the clock industry came to be centered in Geneva Switzerland is a bit of a historical accident, an accident related to immigration. Many early clock makers were French, but a large percentage of the early French clock makers, who were highly literate and often interested in various aspects of science, were also active in the Reformation movement. When the Roman Catholic monarch of France expelled the *Huguenots*, as French Protestants were called, a small number of Protestant French clock makers went to Geneva at the invitation of John Calvin, the religious leader of that Swiss city. According to Cipolla (p. 64), in the clock industry's infancy in 1500, "to destroy or to build up the industry it was enough to dismiss or attract a few dozen craftsmen." In Geneva, the Swiss watch industry was founded by "the inflow of a handful of refugees–to the injection of a small but precious amount of human skills."

16.3.5 *Immigrants and the brain drain*

If immigrants can contribute to the process of economic development in countries receiving immigrants, it would seem logical that economic development suffers in the country immigrants leave behind. In fact, development economists and sociologists have argued that immigrants' native countries may suffer large losses because those who leave are often the countries' most educated people. For example, during the past three decades, over 70 percent of newly-trained physicians in Pakistan left the country, and over 60 percent of Ghana's doctors emigrated to other, usually more developed, countries. There are more Haitian physicians practicing medicine in the United States than in Haiti. It was estimated that in 1987, about 30 percent of Sub-Saharan Africa's educated population had immigrated to other parts of the world.[14] In fact, immigration policies in many developed economies are designed to accomplish precisely such an outcome. Canada and Australia, for example, award immigrant visas according to a point system that rewards education and skills. Economists have labeled the departure of large numbers of educated and talented people from poor countries as the **brain drain**.

The brain drain can be a problem for source countries for two reasons:

- Educated and skilled immigrants leave with human capital that was partially paid for by people remaining in the source country.

- Educated people are necessary for creating and adapting technology, so long-run economic development may slow with the departure of educated people.

But, if highly talented people are a benefit to the source countries, why are they so poorly compensated at home and why do they seek work overseas?

One reason for the brain drain is that professional and technical skills are not always fully rewarded in emigrants' home countries. Bad economic policies in poor countries may leave educated people with absolutely *no* opportunities at home. A relevant example is Egypt, where the 2011 political protests were carried out mostly by educated young people who had no jobs or opportunities to use their education in Egypt. Often, technology is so much less developed in poor economies that the returns to all factors, even the scarce ones, are lower. Also, human capital needs more and better factors to work with if it is to earn the returns that it can earn in developed economies. For example, a physician is very scarce in Malawi, but if she has no hospital or medicines to dispense, she cannot be very productive. That same doctor, in a fully equipped hospital and with pharmacies stocked with the necessary medicines, adds much more to human health in a developed country.

The brain drain is also promoted by immigration policies in developed countries. It is usually much easier for an educated person to get an immigrant visa than an uneducated worker. Countries like Canada, Australian, New Zealand, and others give priority to highly educated immigrants. Thus, it is the most educated Africans that have the best opportunity to get through the rigid barriers to immigration that most developed economies have in place. The

---

[14] Aaron Siegel (1993), *An Atlas of International Migration*, London: Hans Zell Publishers.

discussion of agglomeration helps to explain why high income economies favor educated immigrants: all countries seek to stimulate their innovative sectors, and innovation requires talented and well-informed people.

16.3.6 Immigrants and agglomeration again

In general, the agglomeration of high-paying jobs in innovative centers causes a brain drain that slows economic growth elsewhere. Immigration, therefore, is an integral part of the agglomerative process of economic development. Before the twentieth century, immigration largely reflected a reallocation of labor from land-scarce countries to land-abundant and resource-abundant countries. In the eighteenth and nineteenth centuries, colonialism was driven by Europe's search for raw materials for its growing industries. European immigrants moved to the colonies and land-abundant countries like the Argentina, Brazil, Canada, Australia, and the United States. In other cases, European colonists exploited labor in the colonies to produce raw materials on plantations and in mines, sometimes moving labor from one colony to another if labor and resources were not both equally abundant.

By the twentieth century, however, trade in primary commodities was not as lucrative, as commodity prices fell relative to the prices of manufactures. Economic activity began to agglomerate and industrial economies grew much richer than traditional agricultural economies. Today, the demand for labor is falling in the primary sectors. Modern mining technologies are highly capital-intensive, and agriculture has been industrialized as well. As described by Vandana Shiva (2005), large-scale monoculture is rapidly replacing traditional small scale agriculture even in labor abundant countries like India. The growing number of unemployed people in former colonies and other raw material supplying economies increasingly see migration to the centers of agglomeration as their only route to survival. Native communities remain poor, or even suffer declines in income. In sum, agglomeration makes economic development a very unequal process as concentrations of capital, labor, and human capital only increase the economic divergence across regions.

16.4   Import Substitution Industrialization (ISI)

In both rich and poor countries, governments have applied international trade and international investment policies that explicitly recognize the agglomerative nature of economic activity. Recall that after World War II, Brazil and many other developing country governments instituted explicit policies to escape from their colonial periphery status by promoting their own agglomerating industrialization. The alternative, in their view, was to accept marginalization by remaining suppliers of natural resources and agricultural products to the agglomerated centers of industry and innovation located in wealthy countries. The protectionist policies adopted by less developed countries, like Brazil, came to be known as import substitution industrialization (ISI).

ISI policies consisted of a wide range of trade bans, quotas, tariff, and administrative mechanisms, like Brazil's Law of Similars, designed to protect domestic industries so that they could effectively defy comparative advantage and *substitute* domestic industrial production for formerly-imported goods. ISI policies were based on the belief that economic growth could be accelerated by actively directing economic activity away from the traditional agricultural and resource sectors and toward manufacturing.

16.4.1 Import substitution policies

The proponents of ISI believed that expansion of manufacturing would lead to a more rapid growth of technology and technology spillovers in developing economies than would the continuation of their traditional specialization in producing raw materials such as foods and minerals. Henry Bruton's (1998) description of ISI after World War II points out that at the time many development economists emphasized the **dualistic** coexistence in less developed countries of large traditional agricultural sectors and smaller *modern* sectors that looked more like those sectors in developed countries. Bruton argues that development economists thus came to view economic development as a process of shrinking the traditional sector, and the institutions that guided it, and promoting the growth of the modern industrial sector. They argued that developing economies could only become fully developed economies by completing the shift from the traditional activities to modern economic activities.

While he no doubt captures some of the spirit of the support for ISI, Bruton's often-quoted description of ISI does not fully reflect the sophistication of the arguments its proponents presented. You have already read about the dependency theorists and the structuralists. Other important intellectual supporters of ISI policies were the development economists Arthur Lewis (1954), Gunnar Myrdal (1956), and John Fei and Gustav Ranis (1964). The advocacy of ISI policies by the United Nations Economic Commission for Latin America (ECLA) was also very important. The director of ECLA, the Argentinean economist Raúl Prebisch (1950, 1959), presented a detailed rationale for ISI policies in Latin America and other developing regions of the world.

Prebisch began by pointing out that in a world with free trade, developing economies' comparative advantage in trade fell in primary production like agriculture and mining. He then drew on evidence showing that the income elasticity of demand for primary products was inelastic and demand for such products would not grow in proportion to world income. On the other hand, demand for the industrial products that the wealthier developed countries produced had an income elasticity of demand greater than one. Prebisch therefore predicted that underdeveloped countries' **terms of trade**, or the ratio of how much a country can import with its earnings from exports, would gradually decline. Prebisch extended D.H. Robertson's (1938) description of trade as an "engine of growth" by arguing that the declining terms of trade of underdeveloped countries would result in international trade serving as a greater engine of growth for the industrialized countries than for the primary product exporters in the third world. Underdeveloped or undeveloped countries would thus fall farther behind industrialized countries if they continued to produce according to their current comparative advantage.

For most of the twentieth century, commodity prices indeed trended downward, the occasional oil price spike notwithstanding. Recall the graph in Figure 6.5 in Chapter 6 showing the persistent, if unsteady, downward trend in commodity prices over the course of the twentieth century. To make matters worse, the decline in primary product prices has been accompanied by a growing gap between the prices received by primary product producers and the prices paid by the end users of primary products. Incomes in producer countries were thus even more depressed than the terms of trade suggest. For example, Jacques Morisset (1998) examined the differences between raw primary product prices in exporting countries and prices of the processed primary products in import markets (beef cows/beef, coffee beans/coffee, crude oil/fuel oil, crude oil/gasoline, rice/rice, sugar/sugar, and wheat/bread) between 1975 and 1994. He concluded that "the spread between world commodity prices and domestic consumer prices has increased over time, by about 100 percent on average for the seven commodities analyzed here for 1975–1994."[15]

Morisset examined possible explanations for this rapid expansion of the differential between export prices of raw materials and prices in the final export markets, including changes in trade policies, transport and insurance costs, and marketing and processing costs. But he finds none of these are supported by the evidence. He argues that the most likely explanations are the increased demand for processed food products in high-income countries and the growing concentration of the food processing industry in the hands of a small, and shrinking, number of large transnational corporations. The latter trend has enabled a few large corporations to simply take a greater share of the gains from exchange. These findings are troubling because they suggest that even the low measured income elasticity of demand for primary products overstates the expected growth of primary product demand. With this capture of the surplus by a few corporate intermediaries, it even becomes possible for rising demand to raise end-user prices without raising primary prices.

---

[15] Jacques Morisset (1998), p. 520.

Another characteristic of commodity prices is their year-to-year volatility. Primary product prices have fluctuated rather wildly around the long-term downward trend. Christopher Blattman, Jason Hwang, and Jeffrey Williamson (2004) use statistical analysis to show that it is the volatility of export prices, not persistent price declines, that most significantly depresses economic growth in developing countries. We, of course, warn against accepting statistical results too quickly, but it is certainly true that economies deal with gradual changes much more easily than sudden, unpredictable changes. Therefore, an economy might be better off diversifying its export earnings across more and different products in order to stabilize the "engine of growth."

The second strand of Prebsich's argument for ISI policies came from the Structuralist and Dependency Theory schools of economic thought. Prebisch noted how the colonial system had shaped the structure of Latin American economies and most other developing economies. He called for policies to change the economic structure imposed by comparative advantage and the foreign firms that dominated international trade. The ISI policies he advocated would expand the manufacturing sector by pulling resources away from traditional economic activities like agriculture and mining. ISI policies that closed a country's borders and intentionally defied its comparative advantage were seen as a necessary short-run cost to force a long-run structural change in the economy. Structuralists like Prebisch claimed that the structural changes forced by ISI policies would pay off in the form of faster long-run economic development.

The popularity of ISI policies in the developing world was also due to their political viability in many developing countries. For example, in most Latin American developing countries, the national government was supported by an implicit coalition of traditional families in rural areas, urban businesses, and urban workers. Under ISI policies, it was the latter two groups that gained from the trade protection at the expense of consumers and farmers in general, and these two groups were powerful enough to form a dominant coalition. ISI policies made them even more powerful, and the coalition became solidly entrenched in many third world countries. ISI was also acceptable to the intellectual elite of Latin America, whose Marxist and Dependency Theory perspectives made them suspicious of international trade with capitalist economies. At the same time, the lingering nationalism fueled by fascist-leaning leaders such as Juan Perón in Argentina and Getúlio Vargas in Brazil during the Great Depression was also compatible with policies that cut traditional ties to the rest of the world.

16.4.2 An assessment of import substitution policies

Table 16.2 shows that while international trade grew as a percentage of overall economic activity in most of the world between 1950 and 1973, in Latin

America and South Asia, where countries most actively embraced import substitution, trade declined as a percentage of GDP. On the other hand, in East Asian economies such as Taiwan and South Korea trade grew relative to these countries' rapidly growing GDPs. Pro-trade economists and international institutions like the World Bank and the International Monetary Fund actively argued that the East Asian countries' openness to trade and superior growth performances "proved" that free trade was a better development policy than ISI. The true results of ISI are not so easy to assess, and simple comparisons between Latin America and East Asia do not help much.

In defense of ISI, the large competitive industrial sectors in countries like Brazil, South Africa, Mexico, and India owe their development to protectionism. But it is not possible to say that ISI policies successfully brought sustainable economic development to the third world. There is still a third world, after all. One of ISI's failures is that it stimulated economic changes that were not sustainable. As the discussion of the 1982 debt crisis in Chapter 15 makes clear, the financial crises throughout the developing world in the 1980s and 1990s were, in part, the result of imbalances that developed when ISI policies were in effect.

When in the early 1980s most countries that had adopted ISI policies stopped growing, the so-called *Asian tigers* that had opted to intentionally promote their export industries were able to sustain high rates of economic growth. In a widely-distributed report, the World Bank attributed the East Asian success to a combination of policies that they labeled as **export orientation** in order to sharply differentiate them from the ISI policies adopted by other developing countries.[16] Note in Table 16.2 how international trade grew as a share of GDP in countries such as Taiwan, Korea, and the other Asian tigers. More thorough analysis reveals, however, that East Asian economic growth was probably not the result of openness to trade. In fact, the East Asian economies actively protected their new infant industries even as other policies encouraged these protected firms to export.

In one example, Wan-wen Chu (1997) traces the experience of the Taiwanese bicycle industry. The assembly of bicycles began right after World War II in Taiwan, but this business was threatened when trade with Japan was opened up in 1949. The government of Taiwan quickly banned imports, and soon restricted even the import of parts to just 12 critical components. Behind the wall of protection, bicycle parts manufacturers set up shop in Taiwan, and several bicycle manufacturers expanded into large, efficient manufacturers during the 1950s. In the 1960s output began to decline as incomes grew and Taiwanese began to buy motorcycles instead of bicycles. The Taiwanese government offered incentives for the bicycle manufacturers to export their products, and by 1972 bicycle exports just to the United States reached 1 million units.

---

[16] World Bank (1993), *The East Asian Miracle*. New York: Oxford University Press.

Table 16.2 Merchandise Exports as Percentage of GDP

	1929	*1950*	*1973*	*1992*
Western Europe	13.3	9.4	20.9	29.7
Canada	15.8	13.0	19.9	27.2
United States	3.6	3.0	5.0	8.2
Argentina	6.1	2.4	2.1	4.3
Brazil	7.1	4.0	2.6	4.7
Mexico	14.8	3.5	2.2	6.4
Total Lat. America	9.7	6.2	4.6	6.2
China	1.7	1.9	1.1	2.3
India	3.7	2.6	2.0	1.7
Indonesia	3.6	3.3	5.0	7.4
Japan	3.5	2.3	7.9	12.4
Korea	4.5	1.0	8.2	17.8
Taiwan	5.2	2.5	10.2	34.4
Thailand	6.6	7.0	4.5	11.4

Source: Angus Maddison (1995), *Monitoring the World Economy 1820–1992*, Paris: OECD, Table 2.4, p. 38.

Taiwanese bicycle producers benefitted from a surge in foreign demand for bicycles. As described by David Herlihy (2004), the period from 1970 to 1973 saw U.S. demand for adult bicycles grow from less than one million per year to 8 million in 1973. U.S. industry traditionally produced children's bicycles, the only people who rode bicycles in automobile-oriented U.S. society. The sudden growth of the adult bicycle market provided a fortuitous opportunity to Taiwanese producers and their government's industrial policies. The Taiwanese government's commitment to industrial policy is further evidenced by its reaction when the 1974 economic recession in the United States reduced the market to back below 1 million units: the government stepped in with financial assistance in the hope that the decline in U.S. demand was only temporary. The government also subsidized investments necessary to meet new U.S. safety regulations. These policies were rewarded when U.S. demand grew again later in the 1970s.

Chu shows that the Taiwanese bicycle industry could never have reached the efficient levels of production had it produced only for its domestic market. Chu (p. 68) concludes that the success of the industry was due to Taiwan's ISI policies and protection from foreign competition:

The history of the industry indicates that the causes of growth were several. The progress made under import-substitution, and the favorable factors on both the overall and industry level in Taiwan, made it the choice of production site when international capital wanted to move sourcing offshore. All three — import-substitution, a favourable environment, and globalisation of production, were necessary conditions for the growth of the bicycle sector.... Accumulated learning during the import-substitution period enabled the bicycle industry to expand its capacity quickly, and it enjoyed a high rate of parts self-sufficiency in the early 1970s. Thus, import-substitution is not really a waste, as the neoclassical school has asserted.

Taiwan is today still a supplier of high end adult bicycles to the United States and world markets. Most lower priced bicycles are now made in China, often in factories owned by or supported by Taiwanese firms. As the outward-oriented ISI policies were designed to accomplish, Taiwanese industry has moved up the value scale. But the foundation was built behind protection and government subsidies, both typical ISI policies.

The lesson of ISI policies is that, under many circumstances, they work very well to change the structure of a developing economy. But, as the next case makes clear, ISI is limited by the size of the domestic economy. For example, Brazil had a large market that could support a great variety of industries operating under increasing returns to scale, but smaller economies do not have that privilege. Hence, the combination of ISI and export promotion, such as Taiwan followed with bicycles, is a logical extension of the concept of ISI in small countries. Taiwan is, therefore, not a refutation of the ISI model; it represents a case of pragmatic adjustment of the model.

16.4.3 An extreme example of ISI[17]

Import substitution policies often failed to meet economic development goals. For example, the Chilean government decided in the very early 1960s that domestic production of automobiles was to be promoted. Chilean policymakers envisioned that in the first several years domestically produced automobiles would consist mostly of imported components, but domestic producers were to be gradually pressured to use ever increasing amounts of domestic components by also prohibiting the importation of parts and components. This latter measure was intended to insure that the new domestic automobile assembly industry would generate **spillovers** to the local economy by providing incentives for the establishment of parts suppliers and other new manufactures of glass, tires, upholstery, etc.

Unfortunately, other political priorities interfered. For domestic political reasons, the Chilean government required the automobile assembly plants to set up in the northern city of Arica, one thousand kilometers north of the central region where nearly all of Chile's ten million inhabitants lived. This measure was intended to provide a boost to an isolated region of the country where the

---

[17] This account of the Chilean automobile industry in the 1960s is largely based on an article by Leland L. Johnson (1967), "Problems of Import Substitution: The Chilean Automobile Industry," *Economic Development and Cultural Change*, Vol. 15, pp. 202–216.

opposition political party had recently exploited the poor economic situation to gain a majority in local elections. Thus, ISI policies were mixed with regional development objectives, which further raised the cost of producing automobiles on a small scale in a small country like Chile.

Complicating matters further was the Chilean government's regulation of foreign exchange dealings. All requests to exchange Chilean escudos for foreign currency had to be directed to the Central Bank, and it often took months before the exchange was approved. The uncertainty about whether foreign exchange would be available for imports of auto parts and components turned what should have been a year-round industry into a seasonal industry. Each of the automobile factories in Arica would, at the beginning of the year, request foreign exchange in order to import parts to build automobiles. In the meantime, the factories had to wait with their orders for domestically produced parts such as batteries, tires, and windshields. Only towards the end of the year would they have all of the needed parts to begin manufacturing, so most cars were produced over a brief period at the end of the year. When the inventory of parts was used up, production stopped until, at the end of the next year, there would be another flurry of automobile manufacturing. Workers were hired only temporarily and then fired. Thus the protected industry did not generate new permanent employment in Arica.

The Chilean automobile industry in the 1960s was characterized by small assembly plants. Twenty different assembly plants produced just 8,180 cars in 1963 and 7,558 cars in 1964. No manufacturer operated a large plant because no one had much faith in the permanence of the government's programs to (1) protect the infant auto industry and (2) to force the industry to stay in Arica. It was rumored that the government was holding conversations with foreign firms to build a modern car factory near Santiago. Assembly industries in Arica arranged with foreign automobile manufacturers to supply kits of parts for local assembly in what were little more than large warehouses in Arica. The assembly process was very slow and labor-intensive, and the final price of an automobile was about eight times the cost of the imported components. A car that cost about $2,500 in the United States cost over $8,000 in Chile.

In evaluating the policies that led to Chile's inefficient automobile industry, it is clear that none of the goals of the conflicting policies were met. There was little learning by doing because very few workers were permanently employed in Arica and the methods used in the assembly operations were rather backward and required little learning. The volume of production was too small to encourage Chilean production of specialized components and parts.

16.4.4 Lessons from ISI

The lesson from Chile is that even when free trade is not optimal, protectionism does not always improve matters. Specifically, ISI must be selectively applied.

It made no sense for a small country like Chile to promote an automobile industry, but it is also true that the much larger country of Brazil today has a very efficient and integrated automobile industry, thanks largely to ISI policies of the past.

Another lesson from the experience with ISI is that the period of protection must be used to build flexibility into the structure of the domestic economy. The example of the Taiwanese bicycle industry shows that a protected industry must face incentives to adjust as the country's economy develops and as world markets evolve.   Today, mass market bicycle manufacturing is centered in China, not Taiwan, and Taiwanese firms operate many of the Chinese plants, providing management and marketing expertise.   As described above, the remaining Taiwanese bicycle industry builds top of the line products and components that command high prices in the global market.   More important, other high-tech industries like computers, computer chips, and biotechnology are growing in Taiwan.   Alice Amsden and Wan-wen Chu (2003) detail the measures for nurturing high tech industries in Taiwan, such as the 1992 *Development of Critical Components and Products Act* that covered government assistance to the electronics industry.   These new industries and the government's assistance thus repeated the pattern of successful temporary role of ISI in the process of economic development.

   Whether ISI policies are successful or not thus depends on how the policies are applied.   As Henry Bruton (1989, p. 1641) concludes:

> The idea that some form of protection is in order to enable a country to establish its place in the world economy, in order to establish an economy that is flexible and resilient, is a fundamental idea. To get the form of this protection right and to get the changes that take place behind this protection to produce this kind of economy, is what import substitution is all about.

Not everyone will agree with even Bruton's nuanced conclusion.   Many opponents of globalization would prefer permanent barriers to trade, and most neoclassical free market proponents would prefer to throw open the borders and wait for private business to make economic development happen.

   The fact is that today's most developed countries used protection from trade to shape their economies.   Recall Alexander Hamilton's arguments for infant industry protection, which the United States effectively applied throughout the nineteenth century and, some would say, still applies selectively today.   Similarly, nineteenth century Germany, twentieth century Japan, the European Union after World War II, and most other developed economies at one time or another used policies similar to the ISI policies applied by developing countries after World War II.

   Erik Reinert (2007) argues that the composition of *exports* determines how the gains from international economic integration are distributed. Joshua Lewer and your author (2003) found that the composition of *imports* also matters, with imports of capital goods having a much greater effect on output growth than consumer imports. This should not be surprising in light of Jeremy Greenwood *et al.*'s (1997) finding that 60 percent of the growth of U.S. output was due to technological changes that were embodied in new capital equipment and equipment-specific software. Michelle Cavallo and Anthony Landry (2010) calculated that U.S. output growth was aided by the relative decline in the price of capital imports. These findings are important for developing economies in that they remind us that even exporters of industrial products may see their terms of trade deteriorating.

Past trends in supply and demand elasticities for the different categories of products do not determine future trends, of course. The next section looks at some important structural trends likely to influence the future gains and losses from international economic integration.

16.5 Trade, FDI, and Agglomeration: Modern Mercantilism?

Up to this point in our discussion of alternative views of international economic integration, it is safe to conclude that mainstream economic theory does not capture the broad fundamental changes in international economic integration very well. The process of agglomeration, the shift of productive factors to certain regions, and the increasingly dominant role of transnational corporations cannot be addressed by orthodox international economics. Interestingly, international economic policies and public sentiment may be more accurate than economists' prescriptions and models.

When Adam Smith (1776) complained about the mercantilist policy of favoring exports over imports and their advocacy of trade barriers to achieve a positive trade balance, he countered with a suggested model of international trade that largely ignored the international economic system of his time: colonialism. The mercantilists that Smith criticized were not simple self-centered protectionists; mercantilism is a more complex phenomenon that consists of the use of government power to further private commercial interests in exchange for commercial support of the government leadership. Smith's arguments for free trade became central to mainstream economics, but the real world continued to function as a mercantilist system.

16.5.1 The recent evolution of mercantilism

We now have an international economic system that, compared to the past, is highly specialized and *agglomerated*. Key dynamic activities such as creative activities, research and development are centered in a few countries of the world, the same countries where the most educated people reside and work, and where the management of the world's transnational corporations is concentrated.

Therefore, a disproportionate share of wealth is agglomerated in these same countries and regions of the world.

A second characteristic of modern economic development is that the agglomerated wealth creation is increasingly managed and controlled within large private transnational corporations (TNCs). As noted earlier, TNCs are responsible for most of the world's international trade and international investment. By means of the brain drain, they accumulate the most educated and most talented people to perform the management, research, and marketing activities that enable TNCs to prosper and grow. Transnational financial firms carry out most of the world's international financial transactions and operate the world's financial markets. TNCs also carry out the bulk of all private innovative activities.

National governments are increasingly eclipsed in size and wealth by transnational business and financial organizations. This is not to say that national political leaders no longer have power. Politicians in most countries still have substantial power, and they can still play one commercial interest group against another in order to extort the funding and support they need to remain in political power. In this sense, things have not changed much since the mercantilists first engaged in colonialism. But, the TNCs seem to be getting the upper hand in the private-public relationships that characterize modern mercantilism. Globalization means that commercial interests no longer bargain with one national government about how much they will pay governments for their protection and favoritism. As TNCs, the world's commercial elites can take their taxes, political contributions, and employment elsewhere if a government's terms are not to their liking. The largely unregulated international financial corporations have spurred a "race to the bottom" by continually shifting their financial activities to the most favorable regulatory jurisdictions.

Transnational business organizations increasingly control the power of national governments and use that power to shape the world to conform to their commercial interests. National governments' many other constituencies, such as farmers, labor unions, bureaucrats, small businesses, intellectuals, ethnic groups, and other traditional organized groups, are losing the influence they had gained under the spread of democracy and democratic institutions during the nineteenth and twentieth centuries.

This is a potentially dangerous development. Business organizations are inherently autocratic organizations that tolerate little internal dissent from their single-minded pursuit of profits. The profit motive, relentlessly pursued by its autocratic management structure, does increase their wealth, which they use to gain a greater control of mercantilistic commercial-government alliances. It thus become less likely that international trade, investment, finance, and migration will be managed to maximize human welfare or spread the gains from international economic integration equitably.

16.5.2 *TNCs and international economic policy*

The international economic integration being carried out by private transnational corporations directly weakens national governments' power to control economic activity. For example, the increasingly complex relationship between FDI, international trade, and migration is making it almost impossible for national governments to use their power over exchange rates and trade policies to alter international trade flows. With foreign components often exceeding 25 percent of the total value of the final domestic product in any one country, a depreciation of the domestic currency will not stimulate as great an increase in domestic production because that would require increased imports of parts and components that become more expensive after the depreciation.

The international aircraft industry provides an example of how FDI has changed the relationship between the trade balance and the value of the dollar. Note this revealing newspaper story:

> Aircraft engines and engine parts, a category that has experienced a 24 percent increase in imports in the latest 12 months, are also affected by global sourcing, but in a more complex way. General Electric in the United States and Snecma of France, for example, jointly manufacture the jet engine for Boeing's 373 and Airbus's 320. G.E. makes the "hot section" at its plant in Cincinnati, while Snecma manufactures the giant fans in France. They ship these components to each other and each partner does the final assembly of the engines for its customers. In addition, G.E. makes smaller jet engines for the commuter planes that Bombardier makes in Canada and Embraer makes in Brazil. These are exported to those countries, but 24 percent of the value of the engines is composed of components imported from Japan. The upshot is that exports of engines and engine parts are rising, but so are imports.[18]

The transnational corporate networks of factories, distribution systems, marketing operations, and supply chains structurally locks in trade patterns. In effect, past investment by TNCs drives the global economy.

Policymakers in national governments are not the only ones who are challenged by the ascendancy of TNCs. Economists must also adjust. A quarter century ago, Peter Drucker warned of a new era for economists studying international economics:

> We... have no theory for an international economy that is fueled by world investment rather than by world trade. As a result, we do not understand the world economy and cannot predict its behavior or anticipate its trends."[19]

---

[18] Louis Uchitelle (2005), "Made in the U.S.A. (Except for the Parts)," *New York Times*, April 8.

[19] Peter F. Drucker (1987), "From World Trade to World Investment," *Wall Street Journal*, May 26.

Despite this warning, little has changed in the field of international economics. But looking at Drucker's words more holistically, he actually understates the complexity of the current global economy because he ignores international R&D activities. As is made clear by the earlier discussion of agglomeration, the international economy is substantially shaped by where innovative activity agglomerates. Routinized innovative activity is concentrated in private firms, and they are increasingly spreading such activity across borders to capture the economies of scale in the world's actual and prospective innovative centers.

16.5.3 Further concerns about TNCs

FDI is intimately mixed up with the disruptive processes of economic growth, such as the shifting of jobs across borders, the stagnation of workers' wages in many developed economies, and the repeated sharp changes in the prices of commodities. Robert Lipsey (2002, p. 60) notes that:

> The association of FDI with more trade and faster growth would not necessarily please critics of multinationals. Trade links reduce the freedom of action of a country's government domestically, if not that of its people. Fast growth involves disruptions and the destruction of the value of old techniques of production and old skills. Those who value stability over economic progress will not be convinced of the worth of the gifts brought by foreign involvement. That is especially true if the gains are captured by small elements of the population or if no effort is made to soften the impact of the inevitable losses.

Obviously, the costly promotion of FDI must be based on solid evidence of positive externalities and long-run growth in true human well-being. However, cost-benefit studies seldom take into account all of the dynamic long-run economic, social, and environmental consequences of the spread of transnational business organizations.

16.5.4 Neocolonialism?

The inequality and oppression of colonialism has been thoroughly documented by historians. Private European firms openly used their nations' military might to extend their operations in the colonies. They did not engage in idealized arms-length voluntary market transactions, nor did they follow the rules of their own civilized societies in their interactions with people in the colonies. Today, it seems incredible that most people in eighteenth and nineteenth century European countries were so blind to the horrors of colonialism.

We offer here some excerpts from Joseph Conrad's short novel *Heart of Darkness*. This is a story, written at the close of the nineteenth century, about an English captain hired by a colonial enterprise to sail a river boat to an ivory trading post deep in the Belgian Congo. The manager of the distant outpost of the TNC was named Kurtz, who Conrad describes as not only "an emissary of pity, and science, and progress," but also an egotistical tyrant: "'my ivory, my station, my river, my —' everything belonged to him." Conrad also noted that "Kurtz had been educated partly in England... His mother was half-English, his father was half-French. All Europe contributed to making Kurtz...."[20]

Especially interesting is the English river boat captain's description of a company report that Kurtz had written. The following passage from the book, which consists of the captain repeating and describing the lofty language of the report, is insightful:

> "By the simple exercise of our will we can exert a power for the good practically unbounded," etc. etc. From that point he soared and took me with him. The peroration was magnificent, though difficult to remember, you know. It gave me the notion of an exotic Immensity ruled by an august Benevolence. It made me tingle with enthusiasm. This was the unbounded power of eloquence — of words — of burning noble words. There were no practical hints to interrupt the magic current of phrases, unless a kind of note at the foot of the last page, scrawled evidently much later, in an unsteady hand, may be regarded as the exposition of a method. It was very simple, and at the end of that moving appeal to every altruistic sentiment it blazed at you, luminous and terrifying, like a flash of lightning in a serene sky: "Exterminate all the brutes!"[21]

In short, stated good intentions do not prevent bad behavior. Today, the lofty language of corporate mission statements continue to provide cover for less lofty actions of employees who face difficult day-to-day struggles to satisfy the firm's fundamental objective of profit.

It is easy to dismiss Conrad's novel as pertaining to another era. Surely no one like Kurtz could get away with such brutal behavior today! There is ample evidence, however, that suggests little has changed. Some of today's TNCs are run by modern-day Kurtz's.

In June of 2009, the Royal Dutch Shell Oil Company agreed to a $15.5 million settlement in U.S. court over alleged killings of opponents to its oil operations in Nigeria. Among the dead were the environmentalist and writer Ken Saro-Wiwa, who had organized a worldwide campaign to stop Shell's projects on the Ogoni tribe's lands in Nigeria. According to company documents obtained by lawyers representing the families and reported in 2009 by the London Newspaper *The Independent*, Shell had written to the local governor requesting "the usual assistance" after Ogoni activists blocked the laying of a pipeline in 1993.[22] One death resulted when government soldiers disrupted the

---

[20] Joseph Conrad (1899 [2003]), p. 92.

[21] Joseph Conrad (1899 [2003]), p. 92.

[22] Andy Rowell (2009), "Secret Papers 'Show How Shell Targeted Nigeria Oil Protests'," *The Independent*, June 14.

protests. A few days later, Shell went to the country's military leadership to "request support from the army and police." The military's subsequent clampdown on the Ogoni resulted in about 2,000 deaths and 30,000 homeless, numerous reported cases of rape, plunder, and theft by the brutal forces of Nigeria's military government. Shell Oil's global website in 2011 provided the following mission statement:

> Our Shell General Business Principles contain the core values of honesty, integrity and respect for people. We apply these through our Code of Conduct and provide training to help staff and contractors meet our standards. If violations occur then we take appropriate action.[23]

A more subtle case of modern colonialism is the Canada-based Pacific Rim Mining Company and its use of provisions of the Central American Free Trade Agreement (CAFTA) to protect its interests overseas. CAFTA was signed and ratified by the governments of Canada, the United States, the Dominican Republic, and five Central American countries in 2008. Specifically, Pacific Rim Mining appealed to CAFTA rules that state governments cannot take over foreign investments without full compensation. In this case, the sovereign government of El Salvador is being sued in the mandatory arbitration court in order to stop El Salvador's operating ban on a mine that was shown to pollute local water supplies. Under CAFTA, El Salvador must compensate a foreign investor if its policies, even when they are instituted to promote the general welfare of its citizens, reduces the value of the foreign investment.[24]

CAFTA is typical of recent trade agreements between rich and poor countries in that they include provisions to protect foreign investment. TNCs routinely lobby their governments during the negotiations of regional trade agreements to get provisions that give them power over national governments of the countries where they operate their business organizations. International agreements such as CAFTA, therefore, represent a modern version of colonialism whereby TNCs use their own relatively large and powerful national governments to push for international agreements that further their business interests in other countries. Note that this is not fundamentally different from the colonial powers who directly established authority in the colonies in order to protect the interests of the private groups that exploit the colonies' resources. In public, the push by developed countries for regional free trade agreements with poor countries is presented as a legitimate pursuit of better global institutions, "a power for the good practically unbounded" in Conrad's words. The quest for

---

[23] Downloaded from www.shell.com on June 26, 2011.

[24] Cyril Mychalejko (2010), "Canadian Company Threatens El Salvador with Free Trade Lawsuit over Mining Project," www.UpsideDownWorld, org.

such free trade agreements is further justified by using the simplistic Heckscher-Ohlin model to show that free trade benefits all countries. The actual agreements are laced with special provisions, among many others, to protect the property of TNCs against government regulations in the poor countries that are routine in the more democratic wealthy countries.

16.6 Foreign Aid

Not all financial flows across borders are motivated by private trade, investment, or financial transactions. Developing countries often receive grants and loans from developed-country governments, which are loosely referred to as **foreign aid** or **overseas development assistance (ODA)**. Foreign aid made up the largest share of capital flows to developing countries in the 1950s and 1960s. Today, foreign aid is less important for most developing countries because other forms of international investment have grown. Still, for many very low-income countries foreign aid remains an important source of foreign currency with which to pay for needed foreign goods and services.

It is not clear whether foreign aid helps nations improve their economic conditions. Foreign aid is often mixed with military aid, and even non-military aid is often designed to serve economic interests in the donor countries rather than the interests of the recipient countries. Some foreign aid is stolen.

16.6.1 Foreign aid and GDP growth

Statistical evidence suggests that foreign aid has little or no effect on GDP growth in developing countries. In Sub-Saharan Africa, where foreign aid accounts for about 50 percent of investment and 40 percent of imports, per capita output has declined over the past 20 years. ODA's ineffectiveness in Africa can be explained by many aspects of the ODA regimes that are place. For example, high income countries have for decades provided food for poor countries, not because of their compassion for starving people, but because politically-motivated farm subsidies had to be justified to the developed country taxpayers. Paying domestic farmers high prices to produce too much food seemed less objectionable if the food was later sent to feed starving people in some distant country. The Kenyan writer, Binyavangu Wainaina (2007), recalls U.S. food aid to Africa as follows:

> When free American maize [corn] turned up in Kenyan schools in the 1980s, it arrived in bags and presented itself at school dining tables: steaming yellow, not white like the maize flour we knew as a staple... We saw the sacks unloaded and started to speculate. I must confess that I hated school food anyway, and that yellow maize porridge tasted not much worse than everything else we were forced

to eat. But our speculation was powerful. It is American animal feed. And it started tasting a bit too earthy. It has been treated with contraceptive chemicals. And it started to taste metallic. It was sent to us because it has gone bad already. And it started to smell funny.

Soon, in the Njoro High School dining hall, vast amounts of yellow porridge went directly into the bins. Our teachers, normally violent fascists in matters of discipline, looked the other way. We had food fights with the porridge every evening, and the floor would be littered with the clumpy remnants of America's love.[25]

Gifts are not appreciated when recipients suspect the donor's self-interest is the primary motivation for the gift.

Ragur Rajan and Arvind Subramanian (2006) identify another channel through which the growth effect of foreign aid is undermined: Inflows of foreign aid cause a country's exchange rate to appreciate, which reduces exports. These authors distinguish foreign aid's adverse effect on a recipient country's exports of labor-intensive products, precisely the types of industrial products for which developing economies have a comparative advantage. African economist Dambisa Moyo describes ODA's adverse effect on trade from the perspective of domestic producers: "When aid arrives in the form of a hundred thousand mosquito nets, the [local] net-maker is out of business, and one-hundred and sixty people (employees and dependents) are now aid-dependent."[26]

Foreign aid also often fails to benefit the poorest people of the world. The 10 countries that are home to the poorest *two-thirds* of the world's population have, over the past five decades, received less than *one-third* of all foreign aid. And, when aid does flow to the countries with the lowest per capita incomes, it seldom reaches the poorest people in those countries. Peter Boone (1995) investigated foreign aid for education in sub-Saharan Africa during the 1980s, and he found that U.S.$1 went to each primary school pupil, $11 to each secondary student, and $575 in foreign aid was spent on the average university student. Of course, universities are more costly to operate than primary schools, but the inequality in the distribution of foreign aid is much greater than the per pupil cost difference. To understand the discrepancy, we have to remember that most students who attend universities in Sub-Saharan Africa come from relatively wealthy families. Only wealthy families can afford to send their children to the elite private elementary and high schools that adequately prepare students for university entrance exams. Hence, the running joke among experienced development economists that foreign aid is "poor people in rich countries helping rich people in poor countries."

---

[25] Reprinted in *Harper's Magazine*, June 2007, p. 22.
[26] "Aiding and Abetting: An Interview with Dambisa Moyo," *Guernica*, April, 2009.

16.6.2 Domestic capabilities and foreign aid

The capacity of the recipient country to use foreign aid productively is the key to successful foreign aid. Craig Burnside and David Dollar (1997, 2000) focused on the importance of recipient countries' economic policies. Specifically, Burnside and Dollar created an economic policy index based on a country's (1) trade policy, (2) fiscal policy, and (3) inflation. The index was calculated annually over a 24 year period for 54 developing countries; this let Burnside and Dollar do both time-series analysis for individual countries and cross-section comparisons. On the basis of their index, they divided countries into those with a *sound policy environment* and those with a *poor policy environment*. Not surprisingly, the countries with sound policies, as a group, enjoyed much higher rates of economic growth than the group of countries with poor economic policies. Within the group of countries with sound policies, those that received relatively more foreign aid also grew more rapidly than the low-aid countries within the group, over 3.5 percent compared to 2 percent per year. But, within the group of countries with poor economic policies, foreign aid had no noticeable effect on growth rates. Burnside and Dollar (1997, p. 6) conclude:

> Aid can be a powerful tool for promoting growth and reducing poverty. To do this effectively, it should be given to countries that are already helping themselves by putting growth-enhancing policies into place. In the Cold War period, donors, and bilateral donors in particular, did not do this effectively. The aid that went to countries with poor policies was wasted, although it could have helped growth and poverty reduction in countries with sound policy environments.

Burnside and Dollar estimate that if over the past 25 years aid had been allocated only to countries with sound policies rather than to the actual mix of sound- and poor-policy countries, overall GDP growth of developing countries would have increased by one-third.

16.6.3 Developed countries' commitment to aid

The year 2005 was designated as the "Year of Development," and at a widely publicized summit in Gleneagles, Scotland, the leaders of the world's developed economies pledged to sharply increase foreign aid. Three years earlier, in 2002, those same leaders or their predecessors, at a summit in Monterrey, Mexico, had made similar pledges to increase development aid. Some leaders point to the rise in development aid from about $60 billion per year in during the years 2000 through 2002 to over $100 billion during the years 2005 through 2007 to prove that they were indeed serious during those summits and that 2005 was indeed a "year of development."

The United States made foreign aid payments of $27.6 billion in 2006, which is not a small number. But, from another perspective, U.S. foreign aid is just two-tenths of one percent of its GDP. Such a small amount of foreign aid may reflect the belief that foreign aid accomplishes little or nothing. On the other hand, the small transfers of wealth could simply reflect Americans' lack of interest in people in poor countries. The low percentage of GDP accounted for by official foreign aid does not reflect the belief that government to government aid is the problem, because private aid flows to developing countries are very low too. Private aid flows by U.S.-born citizens add at most one twentieth of one percent to overall U.S. aid flows to poor countries.

Wojciech Kopchuk, Joel Slemrod, and Shlomo Yitzaki (2002) carry out an interesting exercise to estimate the importance that Americans and the citizens of other high-income countries assign to the welfare of foreigners in poor countries relative to the welfare of their own fellow citizens. The authors first estimate the amount of domestic redistribution that occurs through high-income donor countries' own domestic tax systems, and then they compare that estimate to the amount of redistribution that occurs across borders through foreign transfers. Kopchuk, Slemrod, and Yitzaki conclude that observed international aid flows suggest people in a rich country like the United States value the welfare of foreigners at most $1/6^{th}$ as much as their fellow national citizens, and possibly as little as $1/2000^{th}$ as much. The estimates vary greatly across alternative assumptions about how to calculate human welfare. But in any case, people in rich countries do not seem to care much about people in poor countries.

Arguably, much of what we call foreign aid is really (a) military training and equipment for subservient political regimes, (2) subsidies to donor country commercial interests in developed countries, as in the case of food aid and foreign infrastructure projects, (c) hollow gestures to lead concerned people to think their political leaders are really trying to do good in the world, and (d) simple graft that enriches certain firms and individuals in both the donor and receiving countries. Kopchuk *et al.* (2002) effectively explain why ODA takes the forms that it does.

16.7 Concluding Remarks

Orthodox economists tend to look favorably on the rapid growth of international trade, international investment, international finance, and international migration. If challenged, most orthodox economists would probably reply that they base their advocacy of open borders on solid proven analysis accumulated over three centuries of theoretical and empirical research. Economists' views may be influenced by the fact that growing international economic integration has coincided with the rapid growth of material wealth over the 200 years. For example, Maddison (2003) shows that while world trade expanded from less than one percent of output to about one quarter of all goods produced, the world's average per capita GDP increased by a factor of ten. Many alternative measures of human welfare also point to a clear improvement in human welfare. For example, life expectancy in the world has tripled since 1800, infant mortality has become rarer in most countries, education levels have risen almost everywhere, nutrition has become more constant, more people have access to safe water than ever before, and labor saving technologies have been developed to reduce physical toil in almost all types of human work.

However, as we have repeated often, correlation does not prove causality. This rosy picture of international trade, investment, finance, and immigration is undermined by many facts about economic life in the global economy. International economic integration has also coincided with growing economic inequality, both within countries and across countries.   These growing discrepancies in incomes can be measured in terms of such indicators as poverty rates, health crises, hunger, oppression, discrimination, and unemployment. And, recall the happiness studies, behavioral economics' experiments, psychological experiments, and neuroscientific studies that have concluded that individual happiness is largely determined by one's relative status in society rather than absolute wealth.   Therefore, it is likely that the expanding income disparities within and across countries over the past 200 years have at least partially offset the welfare enhancing effect of the growth of average per capita material well-being.   Also throwing doubt on the rosy picture of globalization is the 2007–2008 Great Recession.   Financial stability, unemployment, and income losses have been a consistent recurrence over the past two centuries, and the integrated economy now quickly transmits economic shocks in any country to all other economies.   Finally, international economic integration over the past several centuries has also coincided with colonization, slavery, deadly wars, neocolonialism, and a sharp division of the world into "haves" and "have nots."

Orthodox international economists are constrained by a neoclassical model that assumes the world consists of 7 billion socially isolated but somehow fully informed individuals that interact with each other every moment of the day in a massive set of efficient and competitive markets. History suggests that the real welfare gains the world has achieved occurred while government policies recognized that the real world does not consist exclusively of competitive markets where rational and fully-informed individuals carry out all their interpersonal transactions. The rise of TNCs and their heavy lobbying activity in the countries where they operate makes it clear that we still inhabit a world economy that is to a considerable degree mercantilist in nature. There are few competitive markets, and government policies favor the home countries and owners of TNCs. Yet, mainstream economists continue to view the world through their neoclassical paradigm.   Joseph Stiglitz wrote that "Changing paradigms is not easy. Too many have invested too much in the wrong models."[27]

This chapter pointed out that many economic activities are subject to increasing returns to scale. Economic activity, therefore, tends to concentrate within larger business organizations. At the same time, international economic integration increasingly encourages business organizations to spread across countries. The process of international economic integration does not, therefore, necessarily lead to more competition and more efficient market outcomes.

International economic integration is fostering the growth of transnational corporations (TNCs), which already dominate business in most countries. By spreading technology, shaping consumer demand, and integrating economic activity, TNCs shape the societies we live and work in. Through lobbying, advertising, merchandising, tax manipulation, and the effective control of the commercial news media, TNCs have tremendous political power, not unlike the colonial era private enterprise described by Joseph Conrad. TNCs have the power to exterminate those they see as brutes, so to speak. Yet, because TNCs provide most of the better-paying jobs and virtually all of the products we crave, restricting the profit-oriented TNCs in our globalized lives will not be easy.

Note that these observations do not imply that some well-orchestrated conspiracy is underway. The last three chapters have shown that there are natural economic, technological, and social reasons for the dominance of economic activity in the hands of TNCs. Mercantilist alliances between commercial interests and governments are an evolving and gradual process carried out in accordance with self-interest, evolving institutions, and a variety of constraints imposed by economic, social, and natural circumstances. But, it is clear that we are experiencing a major shift in the institutions of our complex economic and social systems.

The fact that we face an evolving system rather than an orchestrated conspiracy does not make reality easier to deal with. The modern equivalent of ISI would now have to do more than protect the domestic growth of manufacturing industries. Since the 1970s, the prices of manufactured consumer goods have been declining with the rapid expansion of manufacturing throughout East Asia, and ISI countries like Brazil pushed for more local production of capital goods in the hope of capturing a greater share of profits to capital. The terms of trade for manufactured capital goods have also deteriorated in recent decades, which suggests that the agglomeration of manufacturing is no longer as great a determinant of national wealth.[28] Today, for underdeveloped countries to gain a greater share of the growth and

---

[27] Joseph Stiglitz (2010), "Needed: A New Economic Paradigm," *Financial Times*, August 20.
[28] See, for example, Michelle Cavallo and Anthony Landry (2010).

development of the internationally integrated economy they must capture and transfer to their citizens a greater portion of the global earnings of TNCs.

Greater equality in the internationally integrated economy, therefore, requires new policies that give people in developing economies more control over the organization and ownership of the TNCs that dominate the global economy. Some governments indeed have pursued such policies. Recall from the previous chapter, that the number of TNCs based in less developed countries has grown, and many of these new TNCs are government-owned or government-supported. Another approach is to force TNCs to transfer more technology and engage in innovative activities in developing economies. China now routinely pressures foreign TNCs to expand research and development activities in China.[29]

Simply requiring TNCs to perform more research and development activities in poor countries is not necessarily a useful policy in all developing countries, however. Donald Bartlett and James Steele (2011) write that even though medical research has indeed shifted to developing countries, this international integration of research often takes on the look of colonial exploitation of foreign resources (people). Pharmaceutical TNCs increasingly carry out their tests of new drugs in India, Bangladesh, and other low income countries because it is cheaper and regulations on human experiments are not as rigorous. In the end, however, TNCs still own the technology, and their stockholders and managers located in rich countries still capture the gains from technological change.

In sum, humanity faces the difficult challenge of managing a global economic system comprised almost entirely of large profit-motivated business organizations that operate across national political jurisdictions. It is not yet clear whether democracy can flourish in such a world, much less whether modern mercantilism will maximize the welfare of the world's seven billion members. There are obvious dangers to the concentration of economic power in the hands of largely unaccountable business organizations that are managed by people who have been given incentives that appeal directly to personal greed and status within narrow corporate cultures. Without viable democratic control over institutions and government policies, the international economic system will create many more of the banana republics mentioned in this chapter's opening quote.

---

[29] Waldmeir, Patti (2011), "Beijing Presses Motor Groups to Share Technology," *Financial Times*, February 19.

Key Terms and Concepts

Agglomeration	Mercantilism
Brain drain	Nonrival good
Center countries	Overseas development assistance
Colonialism	(ODA)
Dependency theory	Peripheral countries
Dualistic economy	Plutocracy
Export orientation	Rent-seeking activity
Foreign aid	Specialized agglomeration
Immigration	Spillovers
Import substitution	Structuralism
industrialization (ISI)	Structuralist school
Increasing returns to scale	Sugar cycle
Infant-industry	Terms of trade
Law of similars	Underdevelopment

Questions and Problems

1. Define mercantilism and explain how mercantilism morphed into colonialism in the sixteenth and seventeenth centuries. (Hint: Explain why European monarchs found colonial enterprises politically useful.)

2. Explain how Portugal colonized the territory that eventually became the country of Brazil. What kind of an economy did this form of colonization create?

3. Discuss how Brazil "stumbled" on to the import substitution industrialization (ISI) policies that ultimately converted the traditional commodity exporter into an industrial exporter. (Hint: Be sure to define ISI policies, and then relate global economic conditions in the 1930s to Brazil's economic performance.)

4. Describe Brazil's law of similars. Explain the advantages and disadvantages of such blanket protection of domestic production.

5. What did Andre Gunder Frank mean when he described third world countries as underdeveloped rather than undeveloped? How were his ideas related to Structuralism and Dependency Theory?

6. Structuralism and the Neoclassical paradigm are often described as polar opposites. Is this an accurate description? Explain.

7. Why does economic activity tend to agglomerate? Explain.

8. Describe how primary production, services, manufacturing, and innovative activities differ in their propensity to agglomerate geographically. How is the process of agglomeration shaped by how each of these four categories of economic activity evolve over time?

9. Why does the regional economist Richard Florida conclude that "the world is spiky?" Explain.

10. Explain the role of immigration in the process of agglomeration. Can agglomeration advance if immigration is banned?
11. Evaluate the policies of import substitution industrialization (ISI). Should governments of less developed countries still pursue ISI policies?
12. If highly talented people are such a benefit to the source countries, why are they so poorly compensated at home and why do they seek work overseas?
13. From a human welfare perspective, explain the advantages and the disadvantages of the growth of transnational corporations (TNCs). Overall, are TNCs a good thing for human societies? Discuss.
14. What effect do foreign direct investment (FDI) and the transnational corporations (TNCs) it creates have on international trade? Discuss. (Hint: Combine traditional trade theory and the principle of comparative advantage from Chapter 14 with Peter Drucker's ideas and the discussion of agglomeration from this chapter.)
15. What would be the effect of an international agreement among governments to enforce a strict set of anti-trust laws forbidding cross-border mergers and acquisitions that reduce the number of competitors in the global market?
16. Does a transnational corporation's pursuit of profit ensure its behavior and actions benefit humanity? (Hint: Explain how the goal of profit defines TNC behavior and how that behavior shapes economic outcomes under neoclassical assumptions and alternative assumptions such as economies of scale.)
17. Why are transnational corporations (TNCs) criticized more often than domestic corporations? Why do a TNC's priorities clash with national interests? Discuss.
18. In this chapter, transnational corporations (TNCs) are compared to the nineteenth-century colonial enterprises that benefited from their governments' military control of foreign countries and often exploited foreign workers and resources. Is this a fair comparison? Discuss. (Hint: Don't hesitate to criticize the textbook; the conclusion of the chapter was very strong and intended to stimulate discussion of a controversial issue.)
19. Does overseas development aid (ODA) generate economic development? Discuss.
20. Is today's global economy still characterized by mercantilism? Discuss.

References

Amsden, Alice, and Wan-wen Chu (2003), *Beyond Late Development: Taiwan's Upgrading Policies*, Cambridge, MA: MIT Press.

Bairoch, Paul (1993), *Economics and World History: Myths and Paradoxes*, Chicago: University of Chicago Press.

Baldwin, Robert E. (2003), "Openness and Growth: What's the Empirical Relationship?" in Robert E. Baldwin and L. Alan Winters (eds.), *Challenges to Globalization*, Chicago: University of Chicago Press.

Baran, Paul (1957), *The Political Economy of Growth*. New York: Monthly Review Press.

Bartlett, Donald L., and James B Steele (2011), "Deadly Medicine," *Vanity Fair*, January.

Blattman, Christopher, Jason Hwang, and Jeffrey Williamson (2004), "The Impact of the Terms of Trade on Economic Development in the Periphery, 1870–1939: Volatility and Secular Change," NBER Working Paper 10600, July.

Boone, Peter (1995), "Politics and the Effectiveness of Foreign Aid," *European Economic Review* 40(2): 289–329.

Bruton, Henry (1989), "Import Substitution," Chapter 30 in H. Chenery and T. N. Srinivasan (eds.), *Handbook of Development Economics*, Vol. 2. Amsterdam: Elsevier.

Bruton, Henry J. (1998), "A Reconsideration of Import Substitution," *Journal of Economic Literature* 31:903–936.

Burnside, Craig, and David Dollar (1997), "Aid Spurs Growth in a Sound Policy Environment," *Finance & Development* 34(4):4–7.

Burnside, Craig, and David Dollar (2000), "Aid, Policies, and Growth," *American Economic Review* 90(4):848.

Cassen, Robert, and Associates (1994), *Does Aid Work?*, Oxford: Clarendon Press.

Cavallo, Michelle, and Anthony Landry (2010), "The Quantitative Role of Capital Goods Imports in US Growth," *American Economic Review: Papers and Proceedings* 100(May):78–82.

Chiswick, Barry R. (2000), "Are Immigrants Favorably Self-Selected? An Economic Analysis," in Caroline D. Brettell and James F. Hollifield (eds.), *Migration Theory: Talking Across Disciplines*, New York: Routledge, pp. 61–76.

Chu, Wan-wen (1997), "Causes of Growth: A Study of Taiwan's Bicycle Industry," *Cambridge Journal of Economics* 21:55–72.

Cipolla, Carlo (1978), *Clocks and Culture, 1300–1700,* New York: W.W. Norton.

Conrad, Joseph (1899 [2003]), *Heart of Darkness,* New York: Barnes and Noble Classics.

Davis, Donald R., and David E. Weinstein (2003), "Why Countries Trade: Insights from Firm-Level Data," *Journal of the Japanese and International Economies* 17:432–447.

Eckelund, Robert B., and Robert Tollison (1981), *Mercantilism as a Rent Seeking Society*, College Station, Texas: Texas A&M University Press.

Ellison, Glenn, Edward L. Glaeser, and William R. Kerr (2010), "What Causes Industry Agglomeration? Evidence from Coagglomeration Patterns," *American Economic Review* 100(3): 1195–1213.

Fei, John C. H., and Gustav Ranis (1964), *Development of the Labor Surplus Economy,* Homewood, IL: Richard Irwin.

Florida, Richard (2005), "The World Is Spiky," *Atlantic Monthly,* October.

Frank, Andre Gunder (1967), *Dependent Accumulation and Under-Development*, London: MacMillan.

Furtado, Celso (1963), *The Economic Growth of Brazil: A Survey from Colonial Times to Modern Times,* Berkeley: University of California Press.

Glade, William P. (1969), *The Latin American Economies: A Study of Their Institutional Evolution.* New York: American Book.

Grimwade, Nigel (1989), *International Trade: New Patterns, Production and Investment*, London: Routledge

Greenwood, Jeremy, Zvi Hercowitz, and Per Krussel (197), "Long-Run Implications of Investment-Specific Technological Change," *American Economic Review* 87(3):342–362.

Harley, C. K. (1988), "Ocean Freight Rates and Productivity, 1840–1913: The Primacy of Mechanical Invention Reaffirmed," *Journal of Economic History* 48:851–876.

Herlihy, David V (2004), *Bicycle*, New Haven, CN: Yale University Press.

Hoover, Edgar M., and Frank Giarratani (1984), *An Introduction to Regional Economics*, New York: Alfred A. Knopf.

Isard, Walter (1975), *Introduction to Regional Science*, Englewood Cliffs, NJ: Prentice-Hall.

Jaffe, Adam B., Manuel Trajtenberg, and Rebecca Henderson (1993), "Geographic Localization of Knowledge Spillovers as Evidenced by Patent Citations," *Quarterly Journal of Economics* 108(3):577–598.

Johnson, Leland L. (1967), "Problems of Import Substitution: The Chilean Automobile Industry," *Economic Development and Cultural Change* 15:202–216.

Keynes, John Maynard (1920), *The Economic Consequences of the Peace*, London: Harcourt, Brace and Howe.

Kopchuk, Wojciech, Joel B. Slemrod, and Shlomo Yitzaki (2002), "Why World Distribution Fails," *European Economic Review* 49(4):1051–1079.

Kravis, Irving B. (1970), "Trade as a Handmaiden of Growth: Similarities between the Nineteenth and Twentieth Centuries," *Economic Journal* 80(32):850–872.

Krueger, Anne O. (1980), "Trade Policy as an Input to Development," *American Economic Review* 70(2):288–292.

Krugman, Paul R. (1991), "Is Free Trade Passé?," *Journal of Economic Perspectives* 1(2):131–142.

Kuhn, Thomas (1962), *The Structure of Scientific Revolutions*, Chicago: University of Chicago Press.

Lewer, Joshua, and Hendrik Van den Berg (2003), "How Large Is International Trade's Effect on Economic Growth?" *Journal of Economic Surveys* 17(3):363–396.

Lewis, W. Arthur (1954), "Economic Development with Unlimited Supplies of Labor," *Manchester School* 22(2):139–191.

Lipsey, Robert E. (2002), "Home and Host Country Effects of FDI," NBER Working Paper 9293, October.

Maddison, Angus (2003), *The World Economy: Historical Statistics*, Paris: OECD.

Marshall, Alfred (1890 [1920]), *Principles of Economics, 8th edition*, London: MacMillan & Co. Ltd.

North, Douglass (1958), "Ocean Freight Rates and Economic Development 1750–1913." *Journal of Economic History* 18(1958):556–573.

Polanyi, Michael (1958), *Personal Knowledge, Towards a Post Critical Philosophy*, London: Routledge.

Morisset, Jacques (1998), "Unfair Trade? The Increasing Gap between World and Domestic Prices in Commodity Markets during the Past 25 Years," *The World Bank Economic Review* 12(3):503–523.

Miyagiwa, K. (1991), "Scale Economies in Education and the Brain Drain Problem," *International Economic Review* 32(3):743–759.

Myrdal, Gunnar (1956), *Economic Theory and the Underdeveloped Regions*, London: G. Duckworth & Co.

Prebisch, Raúl (1950), *The Economic Development of Latin America and Its Principal Problems*, Lake Success, NY: United Nations Department of Social Affairs.

Prebisch, Raúl (1959), "Commercial Policy in the Underdeveloped Countries," *American Economic Review*, Papers and Proceedings 49(2):251–273.

Rajan, Raghuram G., and Arvind Subramanian (2006), "What Undermines Aid's Impact on Growth?", Paper presented at the Trade and Growth Conference, Research Department, International Monetary Fund, Washington, D.C., January 9.

Reinert, Erik S. (2007), *How Rich Countries Got Rich and Why Poor Countries Stay Poor*, New York: Public Affairs.

Robertson, D.H. (1938), "The Future of International Trade," *The Economic Journal* 48(189):1–14.

Saxenian, AnnaLee (1994), *Regional Advantage: Culture and Competition in Silicon Valley and Route 128*, Cambridge, MA: Harvard University Press.

Saxenian, AnnaLee (2002), "Brain Circulation: How High-Skill Immigration Makes Everyone Better Off," *The Brookings Review* 20(1):28–31.

Schumpeter, Joseph (1934), *The Theory of Economic Development*, Cambridge, MA: Harvard University Press.

Shiva, Vandana (205), *India Divided*, New York: Seven Stories Press.

Siegel, Aaron (1993), *An Atlas of International Migration,* London: Hans Zell Publishers.

Smith, Adam (1776 [1976]), *An Inquiry into the Nature and Causes of the Wealth of Nations*, Chicago: University of Chicago Press.

Svensson, Peter (1998), "Strategic Trade Policy and Endogenous R&D-Subsidies: An Empirical Study," *Kyklos* 51(2):259–275.

Wainina, Binyavanga (2007), "Glory," *Bidoun*, Spring (Reproduced in *Harper's Magazine*, June 2007, p. 22).

Wilson, Charles (1963), *Mercantilism*, London: Routledge & Kegan Paul,

World Bank (1993), *The East Asian Miracle.* New York: Oxford University Press.

Waldmeir, Patti (2011), "Beijing Presses Motor Groups to Share Technology," *Financial Times*, February 19.

Wong, K.-Y., and C.K. Yip (1999), "Education, Economic Growth, and Brain Drain," *Journal of Economic Dynamics and Control* 23(5–6):699–726.

PART V

Development Issues

Early in March of 1811, several hundred knitters assembled in the town square of Nottingham, England, not far from the forest from where Robin Hood supposedly carried out his raids to "steal from the rich and give to the poor." This time, the mob met to plan an attack on a factory that had installed new machines that did the work that the knitters had been accustomed to doing. The workers feared for their jobs. That evening, the mob destroyed about 60 new "stocking frames" in a nearby factory. In November of that year, a similar mob saw one of their members shot to death by factory guards during an attack on a hosiery factory. This group was allegedly led by a "rabble rouser" who went by the name of Ned Lud. These rebellious workers soon came to be known as *Luddites*. The following year, another such raid on a factory resulted in two

workers being shot to death, as factory owners began hiring armed guards to protect their factories. In 1813, 17 men were hanged after being convicted of "machine breaking."[1]

The luddites were skilled textile workers who were angry because their wages were threatened by new machinery that could be operated by cheaper unskilled workers and even children in place of the skilled workers. By the beginning of the nineteenth century, that machinery was

Frame Breaking - 1812
(Picture in public domain)

---

[1] Malcolm I. Thomis (1970), *The Luddites: Machine Breaking in Regency England*, Hampton, Connecticut: Archon Books.

739

eroding the workers' income.   The idea that technological progress was dangerous to human welfare was not only embraced by workers who were being directly replaced by the new machines that British factories were installing during the Industrial Revolution.   Many other people throughout British society saw industrialization as a threat to their way of life.   Perhaps people's perceptions of technological progress and economic growth reflected a fear of the unknown.

Writers and artists found ways to creatively express people's fears and real experiences in the Industrial Revolution.   About the same time that Ned Lud was inciting his fellow workers in a rage against the machines, Mary Shelley was writing *Frankenstein, or the Modern Prometheus*, the well-known tale of technological progress run amok.   Charles Dickens painted vivid pictures of the urban poor in England during the nineteenth century.   You are already familiar with how Thomas Malthus and other Classical economists, contemporaries of Ned Lud, presented their negative view of economic growth: attempts to raise living standards were futile because the resulting population growth would drive incomes right back to the same subsistence levels of consumption that had characterized all of human history up to that point.   A few decades after Lud and Malthus, Karl Marx concluded that the continued replacement of workers by machines, which he saw as inevitable in a capitalist society, would eventually trigger a social revolution.

There were many reasons why many people did not see the increase in material output as a good thing.   First of all, the rise in material output was not equally shared by all members of society; the distribution of income became much less equal as machines, or capital equipment, became a more important component of the economy's productive processes.   Many people experienced no increase in income at all, and some, like the unemployed Luddites, lost their source of income altogether.   Also, the Industrial Revolution brought economic and social changes that were not captured by measures like GDP.   In addition to the disruptive shift of population from rural communities to urban areas, there were the longer working hours, specialization in monotonous tasks, and the increased uncertainty of employment.   The process of economic change inherent in the switch to the factory system included changing professions, moving to another community, abandoning acquired human and social capital, the dehumanization of work, and the forced shift to a new way of life.

The Industrial Revolution's expansion of measured GDP was built on the exploitation of exhaustible natural resources like coal, which initiated the process of climate change that is now imposing real costs on humanity.   The environmental costs of industrialization were largely ignored by the public, but the deterioration in public health was quite obvious.   Urban populations became more vulnerable to diseases, nutrition worsened for poor urban dwellers who no longer had access to land to grow food, and factory jobs were often dangerous and grueling.   In sum, the Industrial Revolution made many people better off, and some became very wealthy, but many others were forced to work much harder and live in much more precarious economic conditions. The lingering environmental effects are now forcing economists to further recalculate the costs and benefits of the Industrial Revolution.

Mark Twain famously quipped: "I'm all for progress; it's change I don't like." Arthur Lewis, the noted development economist, wrote:

> It is because economic growth has both its gains and its losses that we are all almost without exception ambivalent in our attitudes toward economic growth. We demand the abolition of poverty, illiteracy and disease, but we cling desperately to the beliefs, habits and social arrangements which we like, even when these are the very cause of the poverty which we deplore.[2]

The conflict between development and change is explicit in Joseph Schumpeter's model of *creative destruction*, which describes the process of technological change as a continual series of new economic activities replacing old economic activities. Sustainable economic development *reduces* scarcity in the long run, but in the short run it does not eliminate scarcity. Choices still need to be made.

The Luddites who resisted economic change were not the misguided crackpots they are accused of being. The final two chapters of this textbook show that the opposition to economic change is in many cases firmly based in reality. Chapter 17 examines how economic development affects the distribution of income and wealth. Recall from Chapter 3 that human beings largely judge their well-being relative to other fellow humans. Therefore, economic changes may increase or decrease human welfare, depending on how the changes in economic structure affect the distribution of income and wealth.

Chapter 18 examines how humanity is dealing, or more accurately, *not* dealing with the conflict between economic development and the natural environment. An important question to be answered is whether sustainable economic development is even possible. Can humanity continue to increase its numbers and per capita real output without triggering a potentially deadly clash with nature?

International economic and social integration has occurred, off and on, throughout history since humans walked out of Africa. Nevertheless, the current acceleration of the processes of economic and social change is alarming to many observers. Development economists, other social scientists, and observers across the intellectual spectrum are increasingly questioning whether the economic, social, and environmental changes are really going to improve human well-being. It is by no means certain that humanity will be able to muster enough abstract thinking and collective action to deal with the new complexities of our human existence.

---

[2] Arthur Lewis (1955), *The Theory of Economic Growth*, Homewood, IL: Irwin, p. 430.

CHAPTER 17

The Distribution of Income and Wealth

... a society is well-ordered when it is not only designed to advance the good of its members but when it is also effectively regulated by a public conception of justice.

(John Rawls, 1971, pp. 4–5)

The costs and benefits of economic change and development are seldom shared equally throughout society. The very unequal distribution of income and the even less equal distribution of accumulated wealth make it very clear that the past 200 years of rapid economic development and change was anything but an egalitarian process. We noted in the introduction to this section of the textbook that the Luddites raged against the machines because the costs and benefits of the Industrial Revolution were not shared equally throughout society. While some people became much wealthier, others were forced to work much harder and live in much more precarious economic conditions. Human beings are not comfortable with inequality, as explained in Chapter 3.

In this chapter, we focus on how the gains and losses from economic growth and development are distributed. The overall distributional effects of the changes associated with economic development depend on how (1) short-run transition costs, (2) shifts in current earnings to labor, (3) long-run effects on the returns to accumulated human, physical, and financial capital, (4) broader social effects, and (5) long-run environmental effects are allocated across society. This chapter will show that, in general, the costs and benefits of economic change and development are not allocated equally within countries or across countries. A final assessment of the distributional consequences of economic change requires economists to decide on what the preferred distribution of society's economic benefits and costs are. Also critical to assessing distributional costs is the question of how a society achieves its preferred distribution. Fortunately, the holistic approach of this textbook has prepared you to grapple with difficult questions such as these.

Chapter Goals

1. Discuss how economic growth and structural change inevitably causes the distribution of income to change.
2. Explain the costs associated with structural change.
3. Examine the various measures of income distribution as well as wealth distribution.
4. Specifically, explain the Gini coefficient and the Lorenz curve.
5. Discuss the historical data on the distribution of income.
6. Explain the Kuznets hypothesis and its historical validity.
7. Analyze the concept of economic equality, and specifically explain Rawls' "veil of ignorance."
8. Discuss the concept of economic rights and how they relate to the concept of equal opportunity.
9. Explain the concepts of absolute and relative poverty.
10. Discuss the evidence on poverty over time and across countries.

17.1 Economic Development and Structural Change

In the long run, economic development can only be sustained if an economy, and the society within which it is embedded, expand their knowledge and change their technologies. Technological change almost always reallocates the economy's resources. Technological change is seldom "neutral" in the sense that the marginal contributions to output increase proportionately for all inputs. Also, as per capita incomes rise, different sectors of the economy and industries within each sector will grow at different rates because the income elasticities of demand vary across products and services. Furthermore, since the increased specialization that accompanies growth will generally also cause international trade to grow, resources will shift toward those sectors of an economy that enjoy an international comparative advantage. Here we focus on the last two of these three structural changes in a growing economy.

17.1.1 An orthodox explanation of structural change

Each industry in an economy has its own particular technologies. Neoclassical economists would say that each industry has its particular production function. This means that for given availability and relative prices of factors of production, each industry will use the factors in different proportions. Therefore, if different industries grow at different rates, the demand for inputs and factors of production will not change uniformly either, and the relative rates of return to the factors of production will change. The owners of some factors gain more than others. Some may even suffer a loss in real income. Ned Lud may not have understood the long-run benefits of technological progress and economic growth, but he correctly observed that the technological changes embodied in new textile machines were reducing the demand for his labor!

To better grasp the structural effects of technological change, suppose, first, that an economy enjoys **balanced growth**. Balanced growth implies that everything increases by the same proportion, as illustrated in Figure 17.1, in which the production-possibilities frontier PP shifts out by the same percentage, say 50 percent, in all directions to P'P'. If, for example, income elasticities of demand for both product X and product Y are exactly one, which means consumption of both X and Y also increases by exactly 50 percent, then the actual goods produced also increase by 50 percent. After balanced growth, the economy is simply a magnified version of the pre-growth economy.

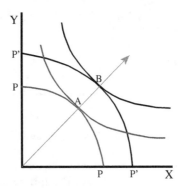

Figure 17.1 Balanced Growth

Such balanced growth is very unlikely to occur in the real world, however. First of all, resources do not generally grow in equal proportions. Physical and human capital grow as a result of investment; labor grows because the population grows and the propensity to work changes. It is unlikely that economic factors will cause the population to grow at exactly the same rate as the capital stock. Nor is technology likely to increase the efficiency with which resources are converted into output equally in both X and Y industries. In general, technology tends to be *biased* toward one or the other industry, and the production-possibilities frontier does not shift symmetrically in all directions.

17.1.2 Unbalanced growth

Figure 17.2 illustrates the effect of unbalanced changes in technology. This diagram is similar to the one depicted in Figure 17.1, except that technological change causes output in the X industry to grow more rapidly than the output in Y. Figure 17.2 continues to assume that the income elasticities of demand for both goods are equal to one. In neoclassical analysis, this implies there is a perfectly symmetrical schedule of indifference curves (the dotted curves) so that if the relative prices of X and Y stay the same, consumers will select quantities of X and Y in constant proportion for all levels of income. Assuming the demand side of the economy stays the same when technology changes is the common "all other things equal" assumption that makes it easier to distinguish the effects on consumption after a change in technology.

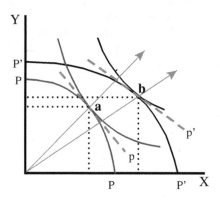

Figure 17.2 Unbalanced Growth

With technological change improving efficiency in the X industry faster than in the Y industry, Figure 17.2 shows PPF shifting out disproportionately in favor of the industry X. As a result, output of X grows relatively more than output Y, and the relative price of X falls with the uneven shift of the PPF, as evidenced by the different slopes of the dashed price lines p and p', which causes consumers to shift consumption toward X.

In general, **unbalanced technological change** is the likely outcome of innovative activity. Recall our discussion of technological progress in Chapter 7; the uncertainties of the combinatoric process and the irregularities of technology diffusion between industries and countries make balanced technological change a near impossibility. In general, the irregular progress of technological change causes unbalanced growth across an economy's sectors, and this will also tend to cause unbalanced changes in the welfare of workers, owners, suppliers, and entrepreneurs in each of those sectors.

17.1.3 Unequal income elasticities of demand

In the simple two-product models of production above we made the convenient assumption that the income elasticities of demand were the same for both products. But consumers do not generally continue acquiring all products and services in the same proportion as their incomes vary with economic change. Specifically, income elasticities of demand are different for different products.

The **income elasticity of demand** for product X is defined as:

$$\eta_x = \frac{\Delta Q_x/Q_x}{\Delta Y/Y} \tag{17.1}$$

where ΔQ_X is the change in the quantity demanded of X, Q_X is the absolute quantity of X demanded prior to a change in income, ΔY is the change in income, and Y is the level of income prior to the change. η_x is the proportional change in quantity demanded of X relative to the proportional change in income. In general, in an economy with many products, the income elasticities differ from one product to another.

Table 17.1 presents income elasticities of demand for a sample of products from a classic 1970 study. For example, a one percent rise in income causes consumers in the United States to increase spending on going to the movies by 3.41 percent, and to decrease spending on flour by 0.36 percent. It should not be surprising that demand for foreign travel increases rapidly as people's incomes rise. The demand for most food products does not increase in proportion to income (chicken being the one exception). Flour, a product with a negative income elasticity of demand, is called an **inferior good**.

Table 17.1 Income Elasticities of Demand

Product	Income Elasticity	Product	Income Elasticity
Motion pictures	3.41	Gasoline	1.36
Foreign travel	3.09	Chicken	1.06
Medical insurance	2.02	Tobacco products	0.86
Electricity (household)	1.94	Beef	0.45
Stationery	1.83	Pork	0.18
Jewelry and watches	1.64	Flour	−0.36

Sources: Hendrik S. Houthakker and L.S. Taylor (1970), *Consumer Demand in the United States, Analysis and Projections*, Cambridge, MA: Harvard University Press, except for chicken, beef, and pork, which are from M.K. Wohlgenant and W.F. Hahn (1982), "Dynamic Adjustment in Monthly Consumer Demand for Meats," *American Journal of Agricultural Economics*, August.

The relationship between demand and income was studied by Ernst Engel, a nineteenth century statistician. **Engel's law** states that the income elasticity of food is low, and thus the proportion of a country's income spent on food declines as per capita income rises. On the other hand, the share in consumption of luxury goods increases as income rises. Engel's law implies that if, for example, X is pork and Y is jewelry, then the indifference curves change shape as we move out from the origin.

Figure 17.3 assumes that there is balanced growth in output, which permits us to see clearly how the production mix changes because of differences in income elasticities of demand. The industry that produces the product with the higher income elasticity of demand, the jewelry industry in this case, will expand more rapidly than the pork industry. Compare the increase in pork output, from a to b, to that of jewelry, from c to d, as the economy grows and moves from equilibrium at A to a new equilibrium at A'.

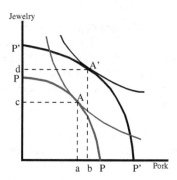

Figure 17.3 Variations in Demand Elasticities

Table 17.2 classifies economic activity into four categories. Agriculture shrinks as a percentage of GDP as per capita income rises. Part A shows a sample of 16 developed countries, and their value added in agriculture shrank from 39 percent in 1870 to a mere 2 percent in 2000. A more diverse sample of economies in Part B shows that countries with the highest per capita incomes are also the countries where agriculture accounts for the smallest percentage of GDP. In only two countries did agriculture increase its share of GDP: Nigeria and Congo. These two countries suffered sharp declines in per capita output during the 1980s and 1990s because of, respectively, corruption and civil war, which above people back to the land for survival.

In general, unbalanced technological change and diverse income elasticities of demand cause the structure of an economy to change as economic development occurs. The above discussion can be summarized as follows:

- Economic growth implies an increase in real per capita income, and because income elasticities of demand differ across products, an increase in income tends to change the mix of products demanded.

- Technological progress generally differs from one industry to another, at least in the short and medium run, which means economic growth changes the structure of the supply side of the economy.

- The growth of each factor is different, since each is driven by different motivations and institutions, which means that factor growth also changes the structure of the production side of the economy.

- The demand side of the economy also changes as a result of income adjustments after shifts in factors across industries.

Table 17.2 Shares of GDP by Major Sector

A. 16 Developed Countries[1]	*Agriculture*	*Industry*	*Services*
1870	39%	26%	35%
1900	28	31	41
1950	15	41	44
2000	4	29	68

B. Individual Countries[2]		*Agriculture*		*All Industry[4]*	*Manufacturing*		*Services*	
Country	*GDP per capita[3]* *(2000 U.S.$)*	*1980*	*2000*	*1980* *2000* *(%'s)*	*1980* *2000*		*1980*	*2000*
United States	29,340	3	2	33	27	22	18	64	71
Japan	23,180	4	2	42	40	29	30	54	58
France	22,320	4	2	34	26	24	19	62	72
United Kingdom	20,640	2	2	43	31	27	21	55	67
Australia	20,130	5	3	36	26	19	14	60	68
Korea	12,270	15	6	40	43	28	26	45	51
Argentina	10,200	6	7	41	37	29	25	52	56
Mexico	8,190	8	5	33	27	22	20	59	68
Malaysia	6,990	22	12	38	48	21	34	40	40
South Africa	6,990	7	4	50	38	23	24	43	57
Brazil	6,160	11	8	44	36	33	23	45	56
Thailand	5,840	23	11	29	40	22	29	48	49
Philippines	3,540	25	17	39	32	26	22	36	52
China	3,220	30	18	49	49	41	37	21	33
Jamaica	3,210	8	7	38	35	17	16	54	58
Indonesia	2,790	24	16	42	43	13	26	34	41
Zimbabwe	2,150	16	18	29	24	22	17	55	58
India	1,700	38	25	24	30	16	19	39	45
Ghana	1,610	58	37	12	25	8	5	30	38
Pakistan	1,560	30	25	25	25	16	17	46	50
Bangladesh	1,100	34	23	24	28	16	18	42	49
Nigeria	820	21	32	46	41	8	5	34	27
Congo, Dem. Rep.	750	25	58	33	17	14	-	42	25

[1] From Angus Maddison (1989), *The World Economy in the Twentieth Century*, Paris: OECD, Table 1.4, p. 20; 2000 data from World Bank (2002), *World Development Indicators*, World Bank: Washington, D.C., Table 4.2, pp. 208–210.
[2] From World Bank (2000, 2002), *World Development Indicators*, Washington, D.C.: World Bank; Table 4.2.
[3] These per capita GDP figures are adjusted by the World Bank for purchasing power parity; see World Bank (1996), *World Development Report*, Washington, D.C.: World Bank.
[4] Manufacturing is a component of All Industry, thus the numbers in the previous columns include manufacturing. All Industry is the sum of manufacturing, mining, construction, and utilities.

17.1.4 The costs of structural change

A change in jobs often requires people to change locations. Changing jobs tends to involve a period of unemployment and, sometimes, anxiety. Also, a new job may require different job skills, and thus some of the human capital accumulated from past job experience may become obsolete. Owners of physical capital can also be adversely affected by shifts in output in the economy, of course. Having one's savings tied up in machines that are suddenly no longer needed constitutes a very real loss of wealth. In short, structural change can cause a fall in welfare for some people, firms, or even entire sectors of the economy.

From a distributional perspective, individuals and groups of individuals will generally not share evenly in the eventual gains from economic growth. In fact, even when economic development and change raises *average* per capita output, some people may actually end up worse off if their specialized skills become obsolete or their industry's output declines. As shown above, economic growth and development shifts the demand for inputs such as labor, capital, and human capital. Because different industries have different production functions and thus demand factors in different proportions, the relative prices of inputs will change. Demand for some productive factors may actually fall with economic growth, even though overall demand for goods increases.

The changing structure of the economy is not the only reason why the distribution of income shifts as an economy develops. Development is a complex process, and many other changes occur that redistribute real incomes. For one thing, recall the growth of transnational corporations in the previous chapter. These shifts in the management and ownership of business have contributed to the growing income inequality because they led to more industrial acquisitions, outsourcing to lower wage regions and countries, and the undermining of worker rights to organize and bargain collectively. Wages to labor have actually fallen in many countries despite the growth of GDP. Also, the destruction of the ecosystem, a well-documented by-product of economic growth, shifts welfare away from the poor who rely disproportionately on nature's services for survival towards those who exploit nature's services and resources for profit.

17.2 Measuring the Distribution of Income

It is not true that economic growth *must* increase income inequality. However, because structural shifts in the economy change relative incomes, economic growth has often been associated with increasing **income inequality**.

The degree of income inequality is commonly measured by comparing the proportion of total national income captured by different income groups. The most popular measure of income distribution divides the population into even-sized groups according to their incomes and then ranks the groups beginning with the group of people with the lowest incomes. We can then observe what portion of total income is captured by each of those income groups.

17.2.1 First look at inequality

Table 17.3 divides the population of each country into quintiles, or groups each consisting of 20 percent of the total population, ranked from the group with lowest incomes to those with the highest incomes. For example, in Bolivia in 2002 the lowest quintile of households earned just 1.5 percent of total GDP. The second quintile earned 5.9 percent of national income. Thus, the poorest 40 percent of Bolivian households earned 7.4 percent of total national income. The third quintile earned 10.9 percent of national income, so 60 percent of all Bolivian households still earned less than 20 percent of national income. Also, the third quintile of households earned an average income that is only half the national average. Note that the fourth quintile still earns less than the national average. The top quintile of households captures 63.0 percent of Bolivia's GDP.

In South Korea, the lowest 20 percent of households earn 7.9 percent of national income, the second 20 percent earn 13.6 percent of national income. In South Korea, the second quintile enjoys a substantially higher percentage of national income than does the third quintile in Bolivia. In South Korea, the fourth quintile, or 20 percent, enjoys above-average income with its 23.1 percent share, and the average South Korean household in the highest income quintile earns less than twice the national average. Income inequality is much lower in South Korea than in Bolivia.

17.2.2 The Lorenz curve

On the graphs in Figures 17.4 and 17.5, we depict the population quintiles, ranked by income levels from the lowest to the highest, beginning at the left side and extending along the horizontal axis. The percentage of income earned is depicted along the vertical axis. For Bolivia, the point a represents the first quintile, matching 20 percent of households measured along the horizontal axis and 1.5 percent of total GDP along the vertical axis. The points b, c, and d represent the 2nd, 3rd, and 4th quintiles, respectively. The curve connecting these points is called the **Lorenz curve**. The more curved is the Lorenz curve, the less equal is the distribution of income. A dotted straight line, such as the line 0T, represents a hypothetical perfectly equal income distribution, where each quintile earns exactly 20 percent of total national income. The closer the Lorenz curve lies to 0T, the more equal the income distribution. Figure 17.4 shows Bolivia's and South Korea's Lorenz curves. As suggested by Table 17.3, South Korea's Lorenz curve lies above Bolivia's curve.

Table 17.3 Income Distribution for Selected Countries

Country	Survey Year	Gini	Lowest 10%	Lowest 20%	Second 20%	Third 20%	Fourth 20%	Highest 20%	Highest 10%
Albania	2004a	31.1	3.4	8.2	12.6	17.0	22.6	39.5	24.4
Algeria	1995a	35.3	2.8	7.0	11.6	16.1	22.7	42.6	26.8
Argentina	2004c	51.3	0.9	3.1	7.6	12.8	21.1	55.4	38.2
Armenia	2003a	33.8	3.6	8.5	12.3	15.7	20.6	42.8	29.0
Australia	1994c	35.2	2.0	5.9	12.0	17.2	23.6	41.3	25.4
Austria	2000c	29.1	3.3	8.6	13.3	17.4	22.9	37.8	23.0
Azerbaijan	2001a	36.5	3.1	7.4	11.5	15.3	21.2	44.5	29.5
Bangladesh	2000a	33.4	3.7	8.6	12.1	15.6	21.0	42.7	27.9
Belarus	2002a	29.7	3.4	8.5	13.2	17.3	22.7	38.3	23.5
Belgium	2000c	33.0	3.4	8.5	13.0	16.3	20.8	41.4	28.1
Benin	2003a	36.5	3.1	7.4	11.3	15.4	21.5	44.5	29.0
Bolivia	2002c	60.1	0.3	1.5	5.9	10.9	18.7	63.0	47.2
Bosnia & Herz.	2001a	26.2	3.9	9.5	14.2	17.9	22.6	35.8	21.4
Botswana	1993a	60.5	1.2	3.2	6.0	9.7	16.0	65.1	51.0
Brazil	2004c	57.0	0.9	2.8	6.4	11.0	18.7	61.1	44.8
Bulgaria	2003a	29.2	3.4	8.7	13.7	17.2	22.1	38.3	23.9
Burkina Faso	2003a	39.5	2.8	6.9	10.9	14.5	20.5	47.2	32.2
Burundi	1998a	42.4	1.7	5.1	10.3	15.1	21.5	48.0	32.8
Cambodia	2004a	41.7	2.9	6.8	10.2	13.7	19.6	49.6	34.8
Cameroon	2001a	44.6	2.3	5.6	9.3	13.7	20.4	50.9	35.4
Canada	2000c	32.6	2.6	7.2	12.7	17.2	23.0	39.9	24.8
Chile	2003c	54.9	1.4	3.8	7.3	11.1	17.8	60.0	45.0
China	2004c	46.9	1.6	4.3	8.5	13.7	21.7	51.9	34.9
Hong Kong	1996c	43.4	2.0	5.3	9.4	13.9	20.7	50.7	34.9
Colombia	2003c	58.6	0.7	2.5	6.2	10.6	18.1	62.7	46.9
Costa Rica	2003c	49.8	1.0	3.5	8.2	13.1	21.2	54.1	37.4
Côte d'Ivoire	2002a	44.6	2.0	5.2	9.1	13.7	21.3	50.7	34.0
Croatia	2001a	29.0	3.4	8.3	12.8	16.8	22.6	39.6	24.5
Czech Republic	1996c	25.4	4.3	10.3	14.5	17.7	21.7	35.9	22.4
Denmark	1997c	24.7	2.6	8.3	14.7	18.2	22.9	35.8	21.3
Dominican Rep.	2004c	51.6	1.4	4.0	7.8	12.1	19.3	56.7	41.1
Ecuador	1998c	53.6	0.9	3.3	7.5	11.7	19.4	58.0	41.6
Egypt.	2000a	34.4	3.7	8.6	12.1	15.4	20.4	43.6	29.5
El Salvador	2002c	52.4	0.7	2.7	7.5	12.8	21.2	55.9	38.8
Estonia	2003a	35.8	2.5	6.7	11.8	16.3	22.4	42.8	27.6
Ethiopia	2000a	30.0	3.9	9.1	13.2	16.8	21.5	39.4	25.5
Finland	2000c	26.9	4.0	9.6	14.1	17.5	22.1	36.7	22.6
France	1995c	32.7	2.8	7.2	12.6	17.2	22.8	40.2	25.1
Georgia	2003a	40.4	2.0	5.6	10.5	15.3	22.3	46.4	30.3
Germany	2000c	28.3	3.2	8.5	13.7	17.8	23.1	36.9	22.1
Ghana	1998–99a	40.8	2.1	5.6	10.1	14.9	22.9	46.6	30.0
Greece	2000c	34.3	2.5	6.7	11.9	16.8	23.0	41.5	26.0
Guatemala	2002c	55.1	0.9	2.9	7.0	11.6	19.0	59.5	43.4
Guinea	2003a	38.6	2.9	7.0	10.8	14.7	21.4	46.1	30.7
Guinea-Bissau	1993a	47.0	2.1	5.2	8.8	13.1	19.4	53.4	39.3
Haiti	2001c	59.2	0.7	2.4	6.2	10.4	17.7	63.4	47.7
Honduras	2003c	53.8	1.2	3.4	7.1	11.6	19.6	58.3	42.2
Hungary	2002a	26.9	4.0	9.5	13.9	17.6	22.4	36.5	22.2
India	2004–05a	36.8	3.6	8.1	11.3	14.9	20.4	45.3	31.1

Table 17.3 (Continued)

Country	Survey Year	Gini	Lowest 10%	Lowest 20%	Second 20%	Third 20%	Fourth 20%	Highest 20%	Highest 10%
Indonesia	2002a	34.3	3.6	8.4	11.9	15.4	21.0	43.3	28.5
Iran	1998a	43.0	2.0	5.1	9.4	14.1	21.5	49.9	33.7
Ireland	2000c	34.3	2.9	7.4	12.3	16.3	21.9	42.0	27.2
Israel	2001c	39.2	2.1	5.7	10.5	15.9	23.0	44.9	28.8
Italy	2000c	36.0	2.3	6.5	12.0	16.8	22.8	42.0	26.8
Jamaica	2004a	45.5	2.1	5.3	9.2	13.2	20.6	51.6	35.8
Japan	1993c	24.9	4.8	10.6	14.2	17.6	22.0	35.7	21.7
Jordan	2002–03a	38.8	2.7	6.7	10.8	14.9	21.3	46.3	30.6
Kazakhstan	2003a	33.9	3.0	7.4	11.9	16.4	22.8	41.5	25.9
Kenya	1997a	42.5	2.5	6.0	9.8	14.3	20.8	49.1	33.9
Korea, Rep.	1998c	31.6	2.9	7.9	13.6	18.0	23.1	37.5	22.5
Kyrgyz Rep.	2003a	30.3	3.8	8.9	12.8	16.4	22.5	39.4	24.3
Lao PDR	2002a	34.6	3.4	8.1	11.9	15.6	21.1	43.3	28.5
Latvia	2003a	37.7	2.5	6.6	11.2	15.5	22.0	44.7	29.1
Lesotho	1995a	63.2	0.5	1.5	4.3	8.9	18.8	66.5	48.3
Lithuania	2003a	36.0	2.7	6.8	11.6	16.0	22.3	43.2	27.7
Macedonia	2003a	39.0	2.4	6.1	10.8	15.5	22.2	45.5	29.6
Madagascar	2001a	47.5	1.9	4.9	8.5	12.7	20.4	53.5	36.6
Malawi	2004–05a	39.0	2.9	7.0	10.8	14.8	20.7	46.6	31.8
Malaysia	1997c	49.2	1.7	4.4	8.1	12.9	20.3	54.3	38.4
Mali	2001a	40.1	2.4	6.1	10.2	14.7	22.2	46.6	30.2
Mauritania	2000a	39.0	2.5	6.2	10.6	15.2	22.3	45.7	29.5
Mexico	2004a	46.1	1.6	4.3	8.3	12.6	19.7	55.1	39.4
Moldova	2003a	33.2	3.2	7.8	12.2	16.5	22.1	41.4	26.4
Mongolia	2002a	32.8	3.0	7.5	12.2	16.8	23.1	40.5	24.6
Morocco	1998–99a	39.5	2.6	6.5	10.6	14.8	21.3	46.6	30.9
Mozambique	2002–03a	47.3	2.1	5.4	9.3	13.0	18.7	53.6	39.4
Namibia	1993c	74.3	0.5	1.4	3.0	5.4	11.5	78.7	64.5
Nepal	2003–04a	47.2	2.6	6.0	9.0	12.4	18.0	54.6	40.6
Netherlands	1999c	30.9	2.5	7.6	13.2	17.2	23.3	38.7	22.9
New Zealand	1997c	36.2	2.2	6.4	11.4	15.8	22.6	43.8	27.8
Nicaragua	2001a	43.1	2.2	5.6	9.8	14.2	21.1	49.3	33.8
Niger	1995a	50.5	0.8	2.6	7.1	13.9	23.1	53.3	35.4
Nigeria	2003a	43.7	1.9	5.0	9.6	14.5	21.7	49.2	33.2
Norway	2000c	25.8	3.9	9.6	14.0	17.2	22.0	37.2	23.4
Pakistan	2002a	30.6	4.0	9.3	13.0	16.3	21.1	40.3	26.3
Panama	2003c	56.1	0.7	2.5	6.6	11.4	19.6	59.9	43.0
Papua N. Guin.	1996a	50.9	1.7	4.5	7.9	11.9	19.2	56.5	40.5
Paraguay	2003c	58.4	0.7	2.4	6.3	10.8	18.6	61.9	46.1
Peru	2003c	52.0	1.3	3.7	7.7	12.2	19.7	56.7	40.9
Philippines	2003a	44.5	2.2	5.4	9.1	13.6	21.3	50.6	34.2
Poland	2002a	34.5	3.1	7.5	11.9	16.1	22.2	42.2	27.0
Portugal	1997c	38.5	2.0	5.8	11.0	15.5	21.9	45.9	29.8
Romania	2003a	31.0	3.3	8.1	12.9	17.1	22.7	39.2	24.4
Russia	2002a	39.9	2.4	6.1	10.5	14.9	21.8	46.6	30.6
Rwanda	2000a	46.8	2.1	5.3	9.1	13.2	19.4	53.0	38.2
Senegal	2001a	41.3	2.7	6.6	10.3	14.2	20.6	48.4	33.4
Serbia & Mon.	2003a	30.0	3.4	8.3	13.0	17.3	23.0	38.4	23.4
Sierra Leone	1989a	62.9	0.5	1.1	2.0	9.8	23.7	63.4	43.6

Table 17.3 (Continued)

Country	Survey Year	Gini	Lowest 10%	Lowest 20%	Second 20%	Third 20%	Fourth 20%	Highest 20%	Highest 10%
Singapore	1998c	42.5	1.9	5.0	9.4	14.6	22.0	49.0	32.8
Slovak Republic	1996c	25.8	3.1	8.8	14.9	18.7	22.8	34.8	20.9
Slovenia	1998a	28.4	3.6	9.1	14.2	18.1	22.9	35.7	21.4
South Africa	2000a	57.8	1.4	3.5	6.3	10.0	18.0	62.2	44.7
Spain	2000c	34.7	2.6	7.0	12.1	16.4	22.5	42.0	26.6
Sri Lanka	2002a	40.2	3.0	7.0	10.5	14.2	20.4	48.0	32.7
Swaziland	2000–01c	50.4	1.6	4.3	8.2	12.3	18.9	56.3	40.7
Sweden	2000c	25.0	3.6	9.1	14.0	17.6	22.7	36.6	22.2
Switzerland	2000c	33.7	2.9	7.6	12.2	16.3	22.6	41.3	25.9
Tajikistan	2003a	32.6	3.3	7.9	12.3	16.5	22.4	40.8	25.6
Tanzania	2000–01a	34.6	2.9	7.3	12.0	16.1	22.3	42.4	26.9
Thailand	2002a	42.0	2.7	6.3	9.9	14.0	20.8	49.0	33.4
Trinidad & Tob	1992c	38.9	2.2	5.9	10.8	15.3	23.1	44.9	28.8
Tunisia	2000a	39.8	2.3	6.0	10.3	14.8	21.7	47.3	31.5
Turkey	2003a	43.6	2.0	5.3	9.7	14.2	21.0	49.7	34.1
Turkmenistan	1998a	40.8	2.6	6.1	10.2	14.7	21.5	47.5	31.7
Uganda	2002a	45.7	2.3	5.7	9.4	13.2	19.1	52.5	37.7
Ukraine	2003a	28.1	3.9	9.2	13.6	17.3	22.4	37.5	23.0
U. K.	1999c	36.0	2.1	6.1	11.4	16.0	22.5	44.0	28.5
U. S.	2000c	40.8	1.9	5.4	10.7	15.7	22.4	45.8	29.9
Uruguay	2003c	44.9	1.9	5.0	9.1	14.0	21.5	50.5	34.0
Uzbekistan	2003a	36.8	2.8	7.2	11.7	15.4	21.0	44.7	29.6
Venezuela, RB	2003c	48.2	0.7	3.3	8.7	13.9	22.0	52.1	35.2
Vietnam	2004a	34.4	4.2	9.0	11.4	14.7	20.5	44.3	28.8
Yemen, Rep.	1998a	33.4	3.0	7.4	12.2	16.7	22.5	41.2	25.9
Zambia	2004a	50.8	1.2	3.6	7.9	12.6	20.8	55.1	38.8
Zimbabwe	1995–96a	50.1	1.8	4.6	8.1	12.2	19.3	55.7	40.3

a. Refers to expenditure shares by percentiles of population, ranked by per capita expenditure. b. Urban data. c. Refers to income shares by percentiles of population, ranked by per capita income. Source: World Bank (2007), *2007 World Development Indicators* (2007), Washington, D.C.: World Bank.

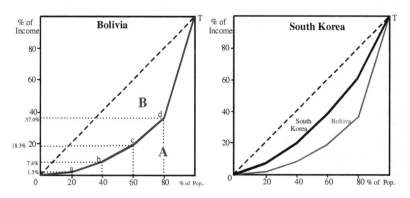

Figure 17.4 The Lorenz Curves for Bolivia and South Korea

There is a convenient numerical measure of income inequality called the **Gini coefficient** that is derived from the Lorenz curve diagram. It is calculated by comparing the region B in Figure 17.4 to the total area under the straight line 0T, which is the area A + B. Specifically, the Gini coefficient is equal to B/(A + B). The smaller the Gini coefficient, the more equal the income distribution. In Figure 17.4, we compare the Lorenz curves for Bolivia and South Korea, and we see that the Lorenz curve for the latter lies much closer to the line 0T. Thus, South Korea's Gini coefficient is lower than Bolivia's: 31.6 compared to 60.1. Table 17.3 has recent Gini coefficients for many countries.

The simplicity of the Gini coefficient suggests that it may not be a very accurate representation of how a society shares its real output and income. The Gini coefficient suffers many of the same shortcomings as GDP and other quantitative measures of complex economic phenomena, as we will see below.

17.2.3 Longitudinal data

Another difficulty in measuring income inequality is that standard measures of income inequality such as the Gini coefficient measure the distribution of income across people or households at a given point in time. For true equality, we should compare incomes over people's lifetimes, not in a single calendar year, because income tends to vary over the life cycle. The accumulation of human capital from experience increases income as people get older. Starting salaries are lower than mid-career salaries. Young entrepreneurs who are just starting their businesses have lower incomes than older successful entrepreneurs. Also, older people will have accumulated more assets that provide further income. Thus, even if all people have identical lifetime earnings, a Gini coefficient calculated using annual income in a given calendar year will signal some degree of income inequality.

Income distribution statistics are almost always based on census data that examines household income at certain intervals, usually once every ten years, but it does not follow the income of specific households over time. In the hypothetical case where all households have the same lifetime income but incomes vary over a person's lifetime, each census would show that there was income inequality. However, if we could follow each household over time, we could calculate each family's lifetime income and use that to estimate the Gini coefficient. Such **longitudinal data** tracing family income over time is seldom available.

Fortunately, there are some useful case studies. For example, there is data available on lifetime income for a sample of families in Peru. A study by Javier Herrera in the Peruvian capital city, Lima, followed 421 households across the years 1990–1996. This study came after an earlier study of 721 Peruvian households over 1985–1990.[1] Table 17.4 below summarizes the data from

---

[1] This evidence is reported in detail in Gary S. Fields (2001).

Herrera and the earlier study for Peru. Notice that there was quite a bit of **income mobility** even over a mere 5 or 6 years in that many families moved from one quintile to another. Over half of all households in the bottom quintile had moved to a higher quintile at the end of the period in each table. During both periods, a slightly higher percentage of households that started out in the third, or middle, quintile was likely to fall back to a lower quintile than to move up to a higher quintile at the end of the period.

Table 17.4 Peru: Mobility Across Income Quintiles

1985 quintile	Peru: 1985–1990 Percent in each quintile in 1990					1990 quintile	Peru: 1990–1996 Percent in each quintile in 1996				
	1st	2nd	3rd	4th	5th		1st	2nd	3rd	4th	5th
1st	48.3%	24.1	16.6	6.2	4.8	1st	43.5%	30.6	15.3	8.2	2.4
2nd	29.9	23.6	25.0	11.8	9.7	2nd	22.6	15.5	29.8	23.8	8.3
3rd	11.8	25.7	29.2	25.0	8.3	3rd	22.6	25.0	22.6	19.1	10.7
4th	7.6	15.3	17.4	32.6	27.1	4th	7.4	23.8	20.2	25.0	23.8
5th	2.8	11.1	11.8	24.3	50.0	5th	4.8	4.8	11.9	23.8	54.8

Source of original data: Javier Herrera (1999), "Ajuste Económico, Desigualdad, y Movilidad," DIAL (July).

Gary Fields (2001) presents data on income mobility over time for Malaysia, Chile, China, Cote d'Ivoire, and India. This data is not as thorough as the data for Peru, but similar conclusions stand out. Generally, the distribution of income measured over a longer period of time is more equal than the distribution of annual income. The data for China is least encouraging in that it finds that there was little change in the income of the rural poor and that income mobility for the lowest-income groups was not great in rural areas.

Longitudinal studies similar to the one on Peru are urgently needed for more countries. We need to compare the income mobility in different countries and relate it to different institutions, different social systems, and different degrees of economic and personal freedom.   If there is little variation in incomes between the young and the old and if income mobility is much lower in many less developed economies with large traditional economic sectors, the Gini coefficients will not accurately describe the differences in lifetime income distribution across countries.

17.3 Long-Term Trends in the Distribution of Income

Is income distributed more equally today than, say, 200 years ago? Many writers have inferred that income distribution must have been more equal before the Industrial Revolution than it has been since the world began its growth surge 200 years ago. After all, there is an absolute minimum subsistence level of output below which the real per capita income of a sustainable society cannot fall.   Therefore, if the average per capita income prior to the Industrial Revolution was only slightly above that lower bound, how wide could the dispersion of incomes have been?   On the other hand, historical evidence suggests that during the past several millennia, societies headed by monarchs were notoriously unequal, with the monarchs and their immediate administrations often gaining half of the nation's production while nearly everyone toiled at subsistence levels of income.

17.3.1   The distribution of income in the distant past

Because of the widespread poverty throughout history, the Gini coefficient for pre-Industrial Revolution times was probably quite high.   At the height of the Roman Empire, about half of all people were slaves and or indentured servants whose lives were controlled by somebody else.   Obviously, slaves did not earn income, and slave owners had little incentive to provide much more than the bare minimum consumption to keep their investment alive and working, although some slave owners may have provided some added benefits as incentives for enslaved people to work harder.   Slavery and other forms of extreme oppression were also common in many other parts of the world 2,000 years ago, including Africa, Asia, and the Americas.   And, even though the very slow positive rate of population growth throughout human history suggests that average per capita income must have been slightly above subsistence, high mortality rates suggest that many individual people ended up with incomes below subsistence.   There is also plenty of evidence that small privileged groups had incomes and wealth that exceeded the average by huge multiples.   Kings, emperors, pharaohs, popes, tribal chiefs, army generals, and other political and religious rulers enjoyed lifestyles quite different from ordinary people.

In comparing current economic inequalities with medieval England, Champernowne and Cowell (1998, p. 52) suggest that "in some respects the underlying inequality of social and economic power was much greater then: the pre-industrial medieval lord had much wider powers in his right to tie workers to the land, his control over appointments and through other forms of patronage." Various sources of historical data on income enable Champernowne and Cowell to compile a simple index of inequality that suggest the distribution of income in the fifteenth century was less equal than in the twentieth century.   They also present evidence that income in medieval Augsburg was more equal than income in that same German region in the sixteenth century, but it was less equal than the distribution of income in twentieth century Germany.

Europe was not unique in its economic inequality.   When the Spanish arrived in the Western Hemisphere 500 years ago, they found that the Aztec and Inca Empires in present-day Mexico and Peru, respectively, had rigid hierarchies not very different from what they themselves had.   For example, the Aztec Emperor was both the political and religious leader of his nation, much like the Monarch of Spain who represented the Church as well as the political organization of Spain. The Aztec emperor lived in rather ostentatious surroundings compared to the subsistence incomes enjoyed by most Aztecs, who in turn enjoyed better standards of living than the many neighboring peoples who had been subjected by the conquering Aztecs.

Eleventh century Ghana was ruled by the Caliph Tenkaminen. According to one historical account, "If gold nuggets are discovered in the country's mines, Tenkaminen reserves them for himself and leaves the gold dust for his subjects."[2] He imported glass windows from Northern Africa for his palace, he wore silk from the Far East, and his horses were decorated with gold rings. Ghengis Khan, who conquered most of China, Iran, Iraq, Korea, and nearly all of Russia in the twelfth century, is alleged to have said that "[t]he greatest joy is to conquer one's enemies, to pursue them, to seize their property, to see their families in tears, to ride their horses and to possess their daughters and wives."[3] Suryavarman II, the ruler of Cambodia in the twelfth century, built one of the largest religious monuments of all time, Angkor Wat. When he traveled, he rode in a throne on top of an elephant, accompanied by hundreds of young women carrying his gold and silver on open platters for everyone to see. These examples all suggest extreme inequality.

17.3.2 Estimating historical Gini coefficients

We can show the Lorenz curves for the ancient empires, as we do for Tenkaminen in Figure 17.5. With the king and his close associates taking half

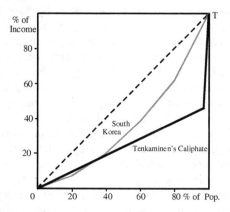

Figure 17.5 Inequality in modern South Korea and eleventh century Ghana

---

[2] Rachel Emma Silverman (1999), "Rich and Richer, Fifty of the Wealthiest People of the Past 1,000 Years," *The Wall Street Journal*, Monday, January 11, p. R6.
[3] Silverman (1999), op. cit.

of the nation's income and the remaining 99 percent of the population equally sharing the same subsistence level of income, as historical accounts suggest, the Gini coefficient is greater than that of South Korea or most developed economies today.

Branko Milanovic (2006) brings together a wide variety of historical information about Byzantium (roughly the eastern half of the Mediterranean area) during the rule of Basil II from 976 and 1025 C.E. He examines evidence of income differences in the rural areas, where 90 percent of the population lived, and urban areas. He finds evidence showing that large landowners comprised just 1 percent of the rural population but enjoyed income 7 times that of the remaining small farmers, landless tenants, and slaves, who all lived at or just above bare subsistence. Incomes in the Byzantine cities were higher, on average; artisans and craftsmen earned 5 times the subsistence level of income. However, this class of workers comprised just half of the urban population and thus 5 percent of the total population of Byzantium. Other urban workers, beggars, soldiers, and marginals lived at less than double the subsistence level. Byzantine nobles, on the other hand, enjoyed incomes 100 times subsistence, but they comprised less than one-half of 1 percent of the population. Putting all this information together, Milanovic calculates a Gini coefficient for Byzantium in the year 1000 of a little less than .45. This is lower than Ginis for today's developing countries like Brazil and South Africa, but larger than the Ginis of nearly all of the more developed countries today.

The Gini coefficient for Byzantium is surprisingly high given that per capita real income in Byzantium was about $750 in today's prices. How high can the Gini be with nearly everyone close too subsistence income? Milanovic actually estimates adjusted Gini coefficients called **maximum feasible Gini** coefficients. He argues that the standard Gini coefficient is inaccurate because the requirement that all living people enjoy at least subsistence income limits the possible variation in income. According to Milanovic (2006; p. 468):

> In one case, at a very low average income, even a relatively modest Gini will mean that the surplus is appropriated by a tiny fraction of the population. Inequality would have been at its feasible peak. An increase in inequality [as measured by the Gini] as income goes up is therefore compatible, somewhat paradoxically, with a (socially) less concentrated acquisition of income: the underlying social reality may be less inegalitarian even if the Gini coefficient is greater.

Milanovic, Peter Lindert, and Jeffrey Williamson (2007) estimate adjusted Gini coefficients, effectively raising estimated Gini coeffficients for poor countries in order to account for the bias imposed by the fact that there is effectively a floor under the incomes for most people living at subsistence income. They re-estimate Gini coefficients for 14 historical societies, including the Roman Empire in the year 14 CE. Table 17.5 presents their estimates of the principal economic measures in addition to their Gini estimates. Note that

Milanovic, Lindert, and Williamson also use their evidence on social classes and income levels to estimate the maximum feasible Gini coefficients. All in all, Table 17.5 suggests that income inequality within individual countries is not generally more or less today than it was in the past.

Table 17.5 Gini Coefficients for 14 Historical Countries

Country — Date (Millions)	Population	GDP/capita	Gini Max.	Feasible Gini	Today's Gini
Roman Empire — 14	55.0	844	39.4	52.8	Italy (2000): 35.9
Byzantium — 1000	15.0	710	41.0	43.6	
Holland — 1561	1.0	1,129	56.0	64.5	Netherlands (1991): 31.5
England & Wales — 1688	5.7	1,418	45.0	71.7	U.K. (1999): 37.4
Holland — 1752	2.0	2,035	63.0	80.3	Netherlands (1991): 31.5
Moghul India — 1750	182.0	530	48.9	46.3	India (1994): 27.9
Old Castille — 1752	2.0	745	52.5	24.5	Spain (1990): 32.5
Nueva España — 1790	4.5	755	63.5	47.0	Mexico (2000): 53.8
England & Wales — 1801	30.0	2,006	51.5	80.0	U.K. (1999): 37.4
Bihar (India) 1807	3.3	533	32.8	35.5	India (1994): 27.9
Kingdom of Naples — 1811	5.0	752	28.4	46.8	Italy (2000): 35.9
Brazil — 1872	10.2	721	43.3	33.5	Brazil (2002): 58.8
China — 1880	377.5	540	24.5	25.9	China (2001): 41.6
British India — 1947	346.0	617	49.7	35.5	India (1994): 37.9

Source: Branko Milanovic, Peter H. Lindert, and Jeffrey G. Williamson (2007), "Measuring Ancient Inequality, NBER Working Paper 13550, October, Tables 1 and 2, pp. 76–77.

17.3.3 The distribution of wealth

The Gini coefficient has been used to measure the world distribution of *wealth* as well as the distribution of *income*. Income distribution is more often studied because annual income data are more readily available than estimates of accumulated wealth, but from the perspective of economic inequality, it may be more useful to look at the distribution of accumulated wealth. **Wealth** is defined as the accumulated value of assets and capital in people's possession. Therefore, income is the *flow* of new purchasing power acquired, and when these flows are adjusted for expenditures and depreciation of accumulated assets, they indicate how the *stock* of accumulated wealth changes. It is the accumulated set of assets, not annual income, that has most often been equated with economic power.

Many societies have suffered internal conflicts over the distribution of ownership of land. The Mexican Revolution (1910–1920) was fought, in large part, over the very concentrated ownership of land by a small number of families and the Church. Recently, political parties representing indigenous populations in Bolivia and Ecuador won elections because they favored redistribution of land and wealth. In Brazil, the "sem-terras" (landless) movement has often engaged in occupations of land in order to demand a redistribution of land. Violent clashes have left many injured and dead over the past 10 years.

On a more abstract level, Marxist economists argue that the capitalist system results in incomes becoming increasingly unequal over time. Because the growing ranks of the workers, the **proletariat**, live at bare subsistence, they cannot save, and, therefore, the distribution of wealth grows increasingly unequal over time. Recall from Chapter 4 how Marx reasoned that the owners of the means of production, the **bourgeoisie**, gain an increasingly larger share of the economy's income as they invest in ever greater amounts of capital in an ultimately futile effort to maintain profits by reducing labor costs. As a result, labor income is reduced as growing unemployment creates a "reserve army of the unemployed" that pushes wages to subsistence.

Marx predicted a social revolution in which the proletariat collectively took ownership of all wealth. Marxist revolutions occurred, among other places, in Russia in the early twentieth century, China in the middle of the twentieth century, and Cuba in 1958. These revolutions did not bring "workers paradises," but income and wealth distributions in communist states were much more equal than those of market economies. Even after introducing "market reforms," Gini coefficients in the former communist states of the Soviet Union and Eastern Europe are still relatively low compared to capitalist economies (see Table 17.3).

Table 17.6 shows the Gini coefficients for *wealth* for a small number of countries for which we have reasonable wealth data. This data does not entirely support Marx's hypothesis. While the wealth Ginis are substantially higher than the income Ginis for the same countries, as Marx predicted would happen in capitalist economies, Table 17.6 does not show a uniform relationship between

Table 17.6 Comparing Wealth and Income Shares: 2000 *(Adjusted for PPP)*

	Lowest 50%	90%	Top 10%	Wealth Gini	Income Gini	Ratio of Ginis for Wealth and Income
Australia	9.0	56.0	45.0	0.622	0.352	1.77
Canada	47.0	53.0	-	0.663	0.326	2.03
China	14.4	58.6	41.4	0.550	0.469	1.17
France	-	39.0	61.0	0.730	0.327	2.23
Germany	3.9	55.7	44.4	0.671	0.283	2.37
India	8.1	47.1	52.9	0.667	0.368	1.81
Indonesia	5.1	34.6	65.4	0.763	0.343	2.22
Italy	7.0	51.5	48.5	0.609	0.360	1.69
Japan	13.9	60.7	39.3	0.547	0.249	2.20
Korea, South	12.3	56.9	43.1	0.579	0.316	1.83
Spain	13.2	58.1	51.7	0.565	0.347	1.63
Switzerland	-	28.7	71.3	0.803	0.337	2.38
U.K.	5.0	44.0	56.0	0.697	0.360	1.94
U.S.A.	2.8	30.2	69.8	0.801	0.408	1.96
World	*1.6*	*29.9*	*71.1*	*0.802*	*0.660*	*1.22*

Source: James B. Davies, Susanna Sandstrrom, Anthony Shorrocks, and Edward N. Wolff (2006), "The World Distribution of Household Wealth," WIDER Report, December 5, Tables 9, 10.

income inequality and wealth inequality. Note that China has the lowest wealth Gini among the countries listed, but it has the highest income Gini. Perhaps this is due to the fact that wealth accumulation has only begun in China after its recent shift to a market economy. Switzerland, on the other hand, has the highest wealth Gini, but one of the lower income Ginis.

17.4   The Relationship between Growth and Income Distribution

United Nations data and the curves in Figure 17.6 show no clear time-series trend in the relationhip between output growth and the distribution of income. The Gini coefficients for the many countries listed in Table 17.3 does not suggest an obvious cross-sectional relationship between output per capita and income inequality either. Some development economists have, nevertheless, suggested that growth and inequality are related.

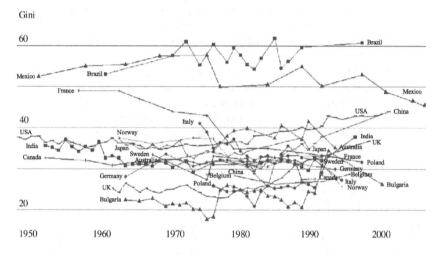

Figure 17.6 Trends in National Gini Coefficients: 1950–2006

17.4.1 The Kuznets curve

Simon Kuznets is best known for his work on national income accounts around the world. His observations on economic growth and the distribution of that growth across societies led him to hypothesize that the relationship between income inequality and a country's per capita income varied over the course of economic development. He hypothesized that in the early stages of economic growth, increases in per capita income are concentrated in some sectors of the economy or regions of a country. Later, when the economy changes structure and adopts new technologies, welfare gains spread to all sectors and regions.

Kuznets (1955) went so far as to claim that income inequality was necessary for generating the increases in savings required to finance greater investment. This same argument was echoed by other economists of the time, including Arthur Lewis (1954) and Nicholas Kaldor (1956), who believed that families with very low incomes saved less than families with high incomes. The conclusion was that societies with relatively equal distributions and very low per capita incomes would generate less savings, and thus investment, than societies with equally low per capita incomes and small groups of relatively wealthy families. These authors effectively suggested that income inequality was a necessary condition that an economy had to pass through on the path to economic development.

In Figure 17.7, the Gini coefficient is measured along the vertical axis and the level of real per capita output is measured on the horizontal axis. The **Kuznets hypothesis** is represented by a humped curve like KK in Figure 17.7. Figure 17.6 plots the estimated Gini coefficients for a large number of countries, both developed and developing, over the period 1950–2000. There are few curves in Figure 17.6 that look like Kuznets hypothesized them to be shaped. However, most Ginis change little as countries increase their GDP per capita. Most countries that started out in 1950 with high Gini coefficients still had relatively high Ginis in 2000. Countries with relatively equal distributions of income mostly maintained their equal distributions as they developed. France and Norway noticeably reduced their Ginis over the period shown, and China, the U.K., Brazil, and the United States exhibit rising Ginis. This evidence on individual countries does not support the Kuznets hypothesis.

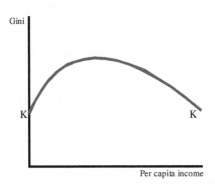

Figure 17.7 The Kuznets Curve

17.4.2 Trends in World income inequality: The global Gini

While the data reviewed above suggest that inequality within countries has not shown any tendency to become more unequal, many writers have argued that for the world as a whole income has indeed become more unequally distributed. Their argument is straight forward: Since Gini coefficients for individual countries have not showed any tendency to improve, and average incomes across countries have diverged substantially since 1800, it is obvious that worldwide income inequality must have become more unequal. Lant Pritchett (1997) has accurately entitled his account of the past 200 years as "Divergence, Big Time!"

A number of authors have combined national income data into a world distribution of income and estimated **global Gini coefficients**. In his appropriately entitled book, Surjit Bhalla (2002), *Imagine There's No Country*, adjusts the income levels of groups in all countries according to the purchasing power of the national currencies and creates a global set of income groups. He also looks at consumption levels rather than income levels because income is not always well measured. He then uses this aggregate world data to estimate Gini coefficients for 1950, 1960, 1970, 1980, 1990, and 2000. His results show the global Gini coefficient remained between 60 and 70 over the period 1950–2000.

Sudhir Anand and Paul Segal (2008) survey Bhalla's study along with several other studies on global income distribution, which seem to have arrived at results similar to Bhalla's. Table 17.7 shows the estimates of the Global Gini by the studies surveyed by Anand and Segal. Notice that between 1960 and 2000, according to the Gini coefficient, the distribution of income across the world's 6 billion-plus citizens has not become less equal. In fact, when we consider that during those four decades average per capita income rose substantially, the *maximum feasible Gini* must have risen as well. Therefore, the world's income distribution may have become more equal.

The results in Table 17.7 are somewhat robust because each of the authors uses different methods to aggregate national income distribution data into a global measure and different original data sets for different sized groups within countries. Yet, the final estimates are quite similar. Anand and Segal conclude

Table 17.7 Global Income Gini Coefficients: 1960–2000

Author(s)	1960	1970	1980	1990	2000
Bhalla 1	0.66	0.69	0.68	0.67	0.65
Bhalla 2	0.63	0.66	0.67	0.66	0.63
Bourguignon and Morrison	0.635	0.650	0.657	0.657[1]	
Chotikapanich, Valenzuela, and Rao	0.658	0.648			
Dikhanov and Ward		0.668	0.682	0.686	0.683[2]
Dowrick and Akmal 1			0.659	0.636[3]	
Dowrick and Akmal 2			0.698	0.711[3]	
Milanovic 2005				0.622[4]	0.641[4]
Sala-i-Martin		0.653	0.660	0.652	0.637

[1] 1992; [2] 1999; [3] 1993; [4] 1988 and 1998
Source: Data from Table 1 in Sudhir Anand and Paul Segal (2008).

that "there is insufficient evidence to determine the direction of change in global interpersonal inequality in recent decades." On the other hand, the estimated Gini coefficients are quite high, and they show no sign of getting smaller.

17.4.3 Does inequality reduce growth?

Instead of asking whether economic growth increases inequality, economists have also examined whether inequality affects the rate of economic growth. Several empirical studies have found that income distribution can help to explain the rate of growth. These studies estimated statistical regression equations with the Gini coefficient as one of the independent variables hypothesized to explain economic growth, as in the following model:

$$\text{Growth} = a_0 + a_1 X_1 + \dots + a_n X_n + a_{n+1}\text{Gini}, \tag{17.2}$$

in which X_1 through X_n are n other explanatory usually hypothesized to affect economic growth, such as investment, education, institutions, etc. The variable "Growth" is usually represented by real GDP per capita. Most studies find the coefficient a_{n+1} to be significantly negative. That is, countries with less equal distributions of income, *other things equal*, tend to grow more slowly.

Kevin Murphy, Andrei Shleifer, and Robert Vishny (1989) suggest a simple reason why more equal distributions foster economic growth: Increasing returns to scale require a large middle class of consumers, and an economy with a more equal distribution of income will tend to have a larger middle class. Philip Keefer and Stephen Knack (1995) predict a positive correlation between income equality and growth because they believe income inequality causes greater uncertainty about the permanence of property rights. According to Keefer and Knack, "It is through this uncertainty, which creates inefficiencies in production and reduces investment, that inequality slows growth."

Variations on Keefer and Knack's model were developed by Torsten Persson and Guido Tabellini (1994), Alberto Alesina and Dani Rodrik (1994), and Roberto Perotti (1995). These authors hypothesize that inequality will motivate government to engage in redistributive activity. The first two papers appeal to the "median voter" model of political science. According to that model, a high degree of income inequality makes it more likely that the median voter, the person in the middle of the distribution, will favor some form of redistribution of income or wealth. Perotti suggests that violence is more likely with a less equal income distribution. Civil war, theft, confiscation, and other violent activities in which some groups take property from others are the most violent forms of redistribution and, probably, the most damaging to economic growth. However, statistical studies do not consistently find income inequality to be a statistically significant explanatory variable for violent political events.

17.4.4 Technological progress and income inequality

The Industrial Revolution that began in eighteenth century England and Scotland is often seen as the foundation of the rapid economic growth of the past 200 years. The Industrial Revolution is usually described as a period when inventions of textile machinery, more efficient steam power, and new machines of all types greatly increased worker productivity. It was surprising, therefore, when Knick Harley (1993) calculated that productivity growth actually declined during the early phase of the Industrial Revolution. Harley found that output per worker was growing at 0.4 percent around the middle of the eighteenth century, but then it declined to just 0.2 percent over a period of forty years. Eventually, productivity growth picked up, and some 70 or so years after the start of the Industrial Revolution, somewhere around the third and fourth decades of the nineteenth century, output per worker began to grow at 0.5 percent. More important for our focus in this chapter, Peter Lindert and Jeffrey Williamson (1983) observed that at the start of the Industrial Revolution the slowdown in the growth of per worker output was accompanied by a sharp increase in income inequality.

Jeremy Greenwood and Mehmet Yorukoghu (1997) and Greenwood (1999) gathered historical evidence from many sources to demonstrate that this pattern of productivity growth and income inequality is not unique to the original Industrial Revolution. It is a pattern that has repeated itself several times, including during the recent rapid growth of information technology (IT). First there is a surge in new technology and a variety of new equipment and methods are introduced, and rather than an increase in the growth of per worker output, there is a slowdown in worker productivity, and incomes become less equal. Eventually, after a generation or more the process reverses itself as the new inventions are absorbed, the new technologies become more familiar, machines increasingly incorporate the new technologies and permit untrained workers to effectively use them, worker productivity again rises, and income inequality falls back to where it was before the surge in technology began. Greenwood and Yorukoghu attribute this pattern of technology growth, per worker output, and income inequality to the high costs of adopting new technology. Specifically, it takes highly skilled labor to apply new technology. Because skilled labor is scarce and because investment in human capital is a slow process, the difference between the income of skilled workers and average workers, or the **skill premium**, must rise with an increase in technological progress.

Boyan Jovanovich (1997) estimates that the costs of applying new technologies exceed the initial invention costs by as much as 20 to 1, and they can equal as much as 10 percent of GDP. Recall the S-curves discussed in Chapter 7; the slow rate at which new technologies are adopted suggests that there must be high adoption costs. To these invention costs and the direct costs of applying the new technologies we must also add the cost of the broader changes in the structure of the economy that accompany major technological breakthroughs. Among other things, there are the costs of obsolescence of the old technologies and the equipment that embodies those technologies. The change in the structure of the economy may very well also reward the more educated workers, who tend to be more adaptable and more able to take on new tasks. If this is true, then the so-called *skill premium* increases when technological change and economic growth accelerate.

17.4.5 How to reduce inequality in a growing economy

One obvious question that arises in light of Greenwood and Yorukoghu's explanation of how economies behave after the introduction of major new technologies is the following: How has it been possible for an economy like Taiwan's to prevent its distribution of income from becoming less equal while it adapted vast amounts of new technology, experienced rapid economic development, and went through substantial structural changes? On the other hand, the fastest-growing economy in the 1990s and early 2000s, China, has been not been able to prevent sharp increases in income and wealth inequality.

Nancy Birdsall, David Ross, and Richard Sabot (1995) find that education and the expansion of trade served to prevent East Asian economies like Taiwan from moving along a Kuznets curve toward greater income inequality. Specifically, the very rapid increase in education, from an average of less than three years in the 1950s to an average of 10 years by the late 1990s, prevented the skill premium from rising very much. The growth in demand for skills was effectively matched by the growth in supply of higher skills. At the same time, Taiwan's selective application of import substitution industrialization permitted comparative advantage to drive international trade in protected industrial goods. Taiwan first exported mostly labor-intensive goods during the early stages of its rapid growth. This reduced the strain on the demand for skills. Some models of international trade suggest that exports of labor-intensive goods raise the wages of basic labor and reduce the returns to scarce skills and capital, which is an inequality-reducing outcome in a labor abundant country.

In contrast, Brazil, a country whose Gini coefficient is among the highest in the world, invested much less in education than did Taiwan; the average Brazilian today has less than half as many years of education as the average citizen of Taiwan. Therefore, as Brazil's import-substitution policies led to the introduction of new technologies and the growth of skill-intensive industries that produced the goods that had previously been imported, the demand for skills greatly outgrew the supply of skills. According to Gary Fields (1980), the skill premium in Brazil increased by 50 percent during the 1960s.

There are, of course, other historical reasons why Brazil's income distribution is very unequal. The early Portuguese invasion resulted in a few favored families gaining ownership to most of the land, and the persistence of slavery until 1889 further perpetuated inequality. But, recent economic growth seems to have worsened the situation over the past 50 years.

17.5 What Is the Most Desirable Distribution of Income?

You might ask yourself: If you had magical powers and could impose any distribution of wealth and income you choose on the economy where you live, what kind of a distribution would you choose? You might be tempted to take a lot for yourself, leaving little for the rest of the population. But, in this case, you had better also give something to a substantial number of people with guns, tanks, and prisons to protect you from all the hungry people with little left to lose. On the other hand, you might opt to do exactly the opposite and give everybody an equal share of the total economic pie. But, if it is true that humans have some choice over their own destiny, then a perfectly equal distribution of income and wealth would eliminate what orthodox neoclassical economic theory assumes is the key incentive for people to work, save, and innovate. We need to clarify the options.

17.5.1 Elements of a "just society"

Most people can probably agree that justice demands that everyone have an equal opportunity to pursue their interests and to better themselves and heir families. Most people also will agree that racial, gender, and/or ethnic discrimination are not just. Similarly, oppression, theft, coercion, and threats of violence are not just. Discrimination and oppression are generally the result of unequal levels of power in society, the result of one person's power over those with less power. While there is little disagreement in the abstract about equal opportunity and unequal levels of power, in practice there are sharp disagreements about what equal opportunity means or what constitutes an oppressive position of power.

No one is precisely certain about what equal opportunity looks like or how we can tell whether people really interact under their own volition, completely free from personal or cultural oppression. All we can observe are the outcomes of human activity and interaction, and we must reverse-engineer the processes that generated those outcomes. Complicating such exercises is the general view that unequal outcomes do not necessarily imply an unjust process. Whether society is just depends on people's perception of their social system.

Some argue that economic and social outcomes must be truly random, that is, completely beyond the control of anyone, for them to be "just." But even if economic outcomes accurately reflect people's individual capabilities and preferences, is that a just outcome? Are preferences and capabilities randomly distributed, or are they, at least in part, determined by heredity or society itself? Neither sociology nor economics finds evidence that individual human capabilities are completely random. In a complex interdependent society; human capital and personal capabilities are determined by culture and wealth, which, in turn, are determined by many people other than the individuals themselves.

It can also be argued that even pure luck is not just. Are events and economic outcomes that are beyond the control of humanity also beyond the responsibility of humanity towards those individuals impacted by those events? The popularity of insurance and social safety nets suggest that societies in fact often assume responsibility for helping those members who are adversely affected by events beyond their control. Sometimes, societies even help those whose "bad luck" is obviously partly their own fault. Most developed countries tax the general population in order to provide healthcare to everyone, regardless of whether they lived healthy lives or they drank heavily and ate unhealthy foods their entire lives. Most cultures have some provision for compassionate responses to others' suffering no matter what the cause of that suffering.

Finally, many cultures also equate equality with *equal effort*. That is, the distribution of income or wealth should, at least partially, reflect effort and work. Of course, it is difficult to distinguish effort, capability, and lifestyle preferences from pure luck or inheritance. The issue is greatly complicated by the fact that a social system, in the form of culture, sets norms and informal institutions. People then use that culture to shape their "judgments" of people's behavior and the associated outcomes. There are great differences across cultures, which no doubt explains the large differences in how societies deal with income and wealth inequality. One example of how cultural differences determine how societies view individual outcomes are the very different rates of incarceration across countries, ranging from 26 per 100,000 in Mauratania and Nepal to 611 and 738 in Russia and the United States, respectively. Even accounting for substantial differences in culture, these numbers suggest that people in these countries also hold different opinions on whether personal behavior is controlled by the individual or the result of social and economic conditions that are a collective outcome beyond the control of an individual.

17.5.2 Rawls' "veil of ignorance"

The **social-contractionist philosophy** of John Rawls (1971) provides a reasonable definition of a just society and what a just society's distribution of income might look like. In seeking to define what makes a society just, Rawls reasoned that a truly unbiased definition of social justice can only be arrived at from behind a **veil of ignorance** that hides one's own personal characteristics, background, culture, and circumstances. That is, a just society is the one people would design if, hypothetically, they did not know their actual social class, race, gender, sexual orientation, level of wealth, education, talent, and other personal and social characteristics. Rawls reasoned that, from behind their veil of ignorance, people would be especially concerned about the conditions of the least well-off people in a society because they realize that they could be one of those unfortunate people.

So, what kind of a society and institutions would someone design if they had no idea who they are and in what conditions they would live in? Rawls' criteria for a just society seem to give society the role of providing personal freedom and equal opportunities in acquiring education, wealth, and social status. Furthermore, Rawls' criteria imply that society should provide assistance for the unfortunate and the unlucky who, for reasons not entirely of their own doing, are prevented from taking advantage of all the opportunities. Modern societies are likely to use their government to achieve such social justice.

From behind Rawls' veil of ignorance, many people are likely to decide that a just society would probably seek "equal outcomes for equal effort," thus leaving individuals the freedom to choose how much effort they want to expend. Equal outcomes for equal effort requires not only equal opportunity in its fullest sense (including equal preparation and endowment), but in a complex social and natural environment, it implies social insurance like unemployment insurance and disability insurance, progressive taxation, collective government services, and direct government transfers to compensate for uncontrollable adverse individual outcomes. In short, Rawls argues that a **just society** strives for equal opportunity, and to the extent that outcomes are determined in part by forces beyond the control of individuals, for mechanisms by which the lucky compensate the unlucky.

17.5.3 Can humanity achieve a just society?

Rawls' perspective on social justice represents what people might choose if they indeed chose their future from behind a veil of ignorance. But people live in a real world, and their views are strongly influenced by the formal and informal institutions of their society. Humans are also hard-wired by evolution to behave in ways that contradict Rawls' criteria for social justice.

Recall the research on human behavior, which we discussed in Chapter 3. For one thing, people's preferences depend on their status quo. Recall that Daniel Kahneman and Amos Tversky (2000) found people disproportionately value their current status quo over other possibilities. In one of their many experiments, they found that people value the object A that they have over the object B that they do not possess, but when they find themselves in possession of object B while object A belongs to someone else, a surprising number of people then claim to prefer the object B to object A. Kahneman and Tversky refer to this phenomemnon as the **endowment effect**, which makes people **loss averse**. Like so many living creatures that exhibit **territoriality**, people will fight harder to hold on to what they have than to acquire something new. Numerous studies show that people need an extra inducement to get them to abandon their status quo and embrace change. It should not be surprising, therefore, that people seldom willingly surrender positions of power. The human capacity for abstract thought, so well described by Paul Seabright (2010), means that people quickly find mental justifications for the status quo; even when objective analysis makes it clear that they in effect enjoy an advantage over others, people find ways to justify that privilege. As the sociologist Pierre Bourdieu (1977, 2001) suggests, societies are likely to develop informal institutions, or culture, that justify social hierarchies. In practice, it is very difficult for any society to view justice from behind a Rawlsian veil of ignorance.

Further reinforcing the tendency for societies to distribute their income and wealth unequally is the fact that people are very conscious of their status in society. Recall from the discussion of the happiness studies in Chapter 3 that data for high-income developed countries shows that people's average level of happiness does not change as real per capita income grows, but at any point in time, people with high incomes are happier, on average, than people with relatively lower incomes living in the same country. That is, people are much more conscious of their relative income status than they are of their absolute income, provided their basic needs for living without hunger and physical suffering are satisfied. Figure 17.8 illustrates the finding of happiness studies: individuals' relative levels of happiness rise and fall with income in each year, but the entire relationship between income and happiness shifts as average per capita income in society rises over time. Hence, average happiness does not rise with personal income, but any individual that experiences a sudden rise or fall in relative income experiences a rise or fall in life satisfaction or happiness.

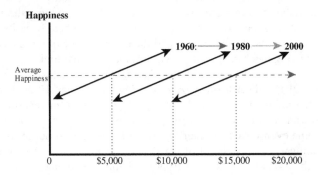

Figure 17.8 Life Satisfaction: Relative vs. Average Happiness

The importance of relative income for human happiness reflects income's role in signaling a person's status in a modern capitalist economy. Recall from Chapter 3 that happiness studies confirm a positive relationship between happiness and people's sense of belonging and being valued. An egalitarian society in which people are consistently and openly valued is likely to come closer to maximizing human welfare than an unequal monetized society in which income is widely accepted as a measure of one's worth.

17.5.4 Inequality as a report card grade for a market economy

A practical reason why a high degree of inequality is worrisome in a modern capitalist economy is that large differences in rewards for work and prices for production should elicit a response by workers and producers that eliminate those differences. That is, large inequalities should trigger arbitrage activities to exploit the differences. For example, if the price of good A is very high relative to the cost of producing it, resources should flow to the A industry, and the subsequent increase in output will bring prices more into line with costs, thus eliminating the exceptional profits. Differences in prices and income are necessary, but people's responses to those price and income differences will automatically tend to keep those differences from getting too large. Similarly, neoclassical economics often hypothesizes that a high return to education will induce more people to seek education, and the increase in educated people will in turn reduce the marginal return to education. Neoclassical analysis might seek to explain the failure of self-interested behavior to reduce income inequality by looking for possible barriers, regulations, or transactions costs that prevent people from responding to the price incentives.

A more holistic inter-disciplinary analysis suggests that there are numerous factors that limit human behavior. In many economies there are barriers to entry for new competitors, regulations that prohibit certain activities, price controls, and other arbitrary forms of protection and punishment. In these cases prices cannot perform their task of providing the incentives to lead people to do what others value. Labor markets are also distorted by discrimination, the power of employers over prospective employees, employment-linked benefits such as retirement funds and health insurance, and the complex role of wages as a short-run market clearing mechanism and a long-run motivational tool.

Formal and informal institutions that distort markets exist for many reasons. Recall the discussion of *rent seeking* in Chapter 13. A capitalist system of private ownership tends to transform into a mercantilist system because government institutions are captured by the wealthy seeking to shift national income even further in their favor. The growing influence of lobbyists in most political centers is clear evidence of mercantilism's ascendancy throughout the world, as is the growth of private financing of political campaigns. The prominent role of advertising, which is really nothing more than propaganda paid for by private firms, in shaping modern culture is indisputable. Thus, a highly unequal distribution of income in a market economy tells us that market institutions are not functioning well and that, perhaps, collective government action is needed to enable arbitrage to work.

Informal institutions and culture also reduce markets' ability to reduce inequalities. Many forms of discrimination are obscured in traditions, social norms, and seemingly innocent laws, but they nevertheless prevent people from doing what fundamental economic incentives would otherwise encourage them to do. Recall Pierre Bourdieu's concepts of symbolic violence and cultural oppression discussed in Chapter 12. Markets cannot generate just outcomes if informal institutions and culture barriers restrict voluntary market participation or economic conditions limit choices.

17.5.5 *The relationship between economic equality and social justice*

When Rawls concludes that people would choose an egalitarian economic structure from behind a hypothetical veil of ignorance he is effectively arguing that the basic human rights that underlie social justice are inoperative without basic economic rights. The idea that economic rights are necessary to enable the fundamental human rights that most nations of the world claim to espouse is not as radical as some of Rawls' critics contend. The basic idea goes back at least to the Enlightenment. At the midpoint of the last century, nearly all governments of the world explicitly accepted the idea in a United Nations declaration.

Chapter 13 described U.S. President Franklin D. Roosevelt's State of the Union address to Congress in 1944. In this address, Roosevelt went beyond the traditional list of human rights such as "the right of free speech, free press, free worship, trial by jury, freedom from unreasonable searches and seizures" and called for **economic rights**:

> As our nation has grown in size and stature, however — as our industrial economy expanded — these political rights proved inadequate to assure us equality in the pursuit of happiness. We have come to a clear realization of the fact that true individual freedom cannot exist without economic security and independence. "Necessitous men are not free men." People who are hungry and out of a job are the stuff of which dictatorships are made. In our day these economic truths have become accepted as self-evident. We have accepted, so to speak, a second Bill of Rights under which a new basis of security and prosperity can be established for all — regardless of station, race, or creed.

Roosevelt detailed what economic rights he thought would be necessary for people to enjoy fundamental human rights such as free speech, freedom of thought, political freedom, and freedom of religion:

- The right to a useful and remunerative job in the industries or shops or farms or mines of the nation; The right to earn enough to provide adequate food and clothing and recreation;

- The right of every farmer to raise and sell his products at a return which will give him and his family a decent living;

- The right of every businessman, large and small, to trade in an atmosphere of freedom from unfair competition and domination by monopolies at home or abroad;
- The right of every family to a decent home;

- The right to adequate medical care and the opportunity to achieve and enjoy good health;

- The right to adequate protection from the economic fears of old age, sickness, accident, and unemployment;

- The right to a good education.

Roosevelt's ideas helped to shape subsequent U.S. legislation, but not all his economic rights are yet firmly established in the United States. Other countries have come much closer to meeting the economic rights outlined by Roosevelt.

After his death, Roosevelt's wife Eleanor campaigned to incorporate economic rights into the 1948 United Nations *Universal Declaration of Human Rights*. Among the economic rights in the United Nations Declaration are:

Article 22: Everyone, as a member of society, has the right to social security and is entitled to realization... of the economic, social and cultural rights indispensable for his dignity and the free development of his personality.

Article 23: (1) Everyone has the right to work, to free choice of employment, to just and favourable conditions of work and to protection against unemployment; (2) Everyone, without any discrimination, has the right to equal pay for equal work; (3) Everyone who works has the right to just and favourable remuneration ensuring for himself and his family an existence worthy of human dignity, and supplemented, if necessary, by other means of social protection; (4) Everyone has the right to form and to join trade unions for the protection of his interests.

Article 25: (1) Everyone has the right to a standard of living adequate for the health and well-being of himself and of his family, including food, clothing, housing and medical care and necessary social services, and the right to security in the event of unemployment, sickness, disability, widowhood, old age or other lack of livelihood in circumstances beyond his control.

Article 26: Everyone has the right to education. Education shall be free, at least in the elementary and fundamental stages. Elementary education shall be compulsory. Technical and professional education shall be made generally available and higher education shall be equally accessible to all on the basis of merit...

The *Universal Declaration* was adopted by the United Nations General Assembly on 10 December 1948 by a vote of 48 in favor, 0 against, with 8 abstentions. By including such a broad range of political, social, and economic rights, the world's political leaders effectively approved Rawls' definition of a just society in 1948.

17.6 Poverty

The condition in which people do not enjoy all the basic economic rights is often described as **poverty**. More than half a century after it adopted the *Universal Declaration of Human Rights*, the General Assembly of the United Nations in 2000 adopted a declaration of which the eleventh and twelfth principles are:

> *11.* We will spare no effort to free our fellow men, women and children from the abject and dehumanizing conditions of extreme poverty, to which more than a billion of them are currently subjected. We are committed to making the right to development a reality for everyone and to freeing the entire human race from want.

> *12.* We resolve therefore to create an environment — at the national and global levels alike — which is conducive to development and to the elimination of poverty.

The term *poverty* was thus brought into the discussion of economic rights. This section's discussion of poverty will make it clear that the 2000 Declaration is, in effect, an admission that the world's governments have failed to implement the 1948 Universal Declaration of Human Rights.

17.6.1 Defining poverty

Poverty has been used as both a relative term and an absolute term. A person or family can be considered to be *poor* or living in *poverty* if their access to goods and services is low relative to most other people in the economy. Alternatively, poverty has been used to describe an absolute standard of living, usually at or near minimum subsistence.

To illustrate the difference between relative and absolute poverty, suppose that the economy grows by 100 percent over a decade and that the distribution of income stays the same. In this case, everyone's income must have increased by the same 100 percent over what it was 10 years earlier. Absolute poverty must have been reduced by the economic growth because the doubling of all incomes must have raised at least some of the people living below the absolute poverty line out of poverty. But, relative poverty will not have changed at all with such a uniform doubling of income for everyone in the economy. Each person is still in the same relative position they were in before the growth.

In practice, poverty is often defined by a **poverty line**, which is a level of income that is deemed to provide people with a satisfactory standard of living. In most developed economies, these poverty lines are continually redefined upward, often tracking the average level of per capita GDP fairly closely. In other words, most developed economy governments, with the apparent approval of their voters, seem to have opted to define poverty on relative terms. In the highest-income economies, people defined as being *poor* often have automobiles, central heating, modern medicine, and access to schooling for their children. In the distant past, no one, not even kings, had homes with central heating, nor did they have the foods and medical care that today give even poor people life expectancies of over 70 years in many countries of Europe, North America, and elsewhere in the world. Perceptions of what constitutes poverty, at least in relative terms, has changed over time.

17.6.2 *Poverty throughout the world*

The percentage of the world's people living in absolute poverty has fallen over the past 50 years in both relative and absolute terms. Yet, the persistence of substantial poverty around the world suggests that economic growth has not been nearly fast enough, nor has it raised the incomes of the poorest segments of societies fast enough to eliminate poverty.

Table 17.8 gives several different poverty lines. For developing economies, the World Bank uses $1 and $2 per day per person. Note that this classification is based on U.S. dollars adjusted for real purchasing power. For developed economies, the United Nations Development Programme (UNDP) uses $14 U.S. dollars per day per person to define poverty. The data for the broad set of countries are not quite comparable, but the prevalence of absolute poverty in the developing economies is underscored by the fact that the percentage of people living on daily incomes of less than $14 in the developed countries is usually less than the percentage of people with incomes of less than $1 and $2 in developing countries.

For those people who are concerned about relative incomes, $2 per day may not be as devastating in a country where everyone earns $2 per day than it would be in a country where the average per capita income is $50 per day. Recall the comparisons of Mbwebwe Kabamba, the Congolese surgeon, and Enos Banks, the unemployed former miner living in a trailer in Kentucky. Income may not be the best determinant of poverty, which is a relative concept that varies across societies.

The New Economics Foundation (NEF), a British research organization that seeks to address economic issues using heterodox analytical approaches, presents many further shortcomings of simple $1 per day measures beyond the obvious fact that they do not capture the welfare effects of hierarchy and distribution. In their study entitled "How Poor Is Poor?", NEF urges a poverty line based on economic rights, such as those in the *United Nations Declaration of Human Rights*, rather than simple isolated economic outcomes such as per capita GDP.   If indeed human well-being depends not less on material consumption than the active participation in one's society, then a simple $1 cutoff is rather meaningless, especially over time.   An economy could raise everyone's income above $1 per day while increasing the incomes of an elite group by a much greater percentage and restricting further income opportunities to the rest of society.   Would this really constitute the elimination of poverty?

Table 17.8 Regional Poverty Estimates

Region:	1981	1984	1987	1990	1993	1996	1999	2001
People Living on Less than $1 a day (millions):								
East Asia & Pacific	596	562	426	472	415	287	282	271
China	634	425	308	375	334	212	223	212
Europe & Central Asia	3	2	2	2	17	20	30	17
Latin America & Carib.	36	46	45	49	52	52	54	50
Mid.East & N. Africa	9	8	7	6	4	5	8	7
South Asia	475	460	473	462	476	461	429	431
Sub-Saharan Africa	164	198	219	227	242	271	294	313
Total	1,482	1,277	1,171	1,218	1,208	1,097	1,096	1,089
Excluding China	848	852	863	844	873	886	873	877
People Living on Less than $2 a day (millions):								
East Asia & Pacific	1,170	1,109	1,028	1,116	1,079	922	900	864
China	876	814	731	825	803	650	627	594
Europe & Central Asia	20	18	15	23	81	98	113	93
Latin America & Carib.	99	119	115	125	136	117	127	128
Middle East & N. Africa	52	50	53	51	52	61	70	70
South Asia	821	859	911	958	1,005	1,029	1,039	1,064
Sub-Saharan Africa	288	326	355	382	410	447	489	516
Total	2,450	2,480	2,478	2,654	2,764	2,674	2,739	2,735
Excluding China	1,574	1,666	1,747	1,829	1,961	2,024	2,111	2,142
Share of People Living on Less than $2 a Day (%):								
East Asia & Pacific	84.8	76.6	67.7	69.9	64.8	53.3	50.3	47.4
China	88.1	78.5	67.4	72.6	68.1	53.4	50.1	46.7
Europe & Central Asia	4.7	4.1	3.3	4.9	17.2	20.7	23.8	19.7
Latin America & Carib.	26.9	30.4	27.8	28.4	29.5	24.1	25.1	24.5
Mid. East & N. Africa	28.9	25.2	24.2	21.4	20.2	22.3	24.3	23.2
South Asia	89.1	87.2	86.7	85.5	84.5	81.7	78.1	77.2
Sub-Saharan Africa	73.3	76.1	76.1	75.0	74.6	75.1	76.1	76.6
Total	66.7	63.7	60.1	60.8	60.2	55.5	54.4	52.9
Excluding China	58.8	58.4	57.5	56.6	57.4	56.3	55.8	54.9

Source: World Bank (2005), *World Development Indicators*, Washington, D.C.: World Bank; Table 5.2.

17.6.3 Growth may not reduce poverty

In much of the popular literature, economic growth and poverty reduction are assumed to be synonymous. Indeed, measures of poverty and economic growth seem to suggest that growth does reduce poverty. Available measures may not reflect real living conditions, however. Economists know little about how very poor people actually live. As described recently by Abijit Banerjee and Esther Duflo (2007), when the reality of life in poverty is analyzed in detail, it becomes clear that the growth of output measured in terms of GDP per capita does not correlate closely with a poor person's sense of happiness or life satisfaction.

Banerjee and Duflo summarize the results of surveys of the extremely poor in 13 countries. They find, first of all, that poor people living on less than $1 per day devote between 50 and 75 percent of their incomes to food. Surprisingly, in some countries the extremely poor have radios and televisions; for example, in Nicaragua nearly half of the extremely poor have televisions. In India no extremely poor people have televisions. On the other hand, in India and Pakistan the extremely poor spend a substantial percentage of their low incomes on assorted festivals and social events. It seems that social relationships play a much greater role in the lives of Indian and Pakistani poor than in the lives of poor Nicaraguans. Life satisfaction and happiness are, therefore, not likely to be the same in Nicaragua, India, and Pakistan either.

The surveys also report that the extremely poor in Mexico spend 8.1 percent of their less than $1 per day income on tobacco and alcohol, the poor in India spend 4 percent on tobacco and/or alcohol, but in Peru and Guatemala, the poor spend virtually nothing on tobacco and alcohol. Banerjee and Duflo (2007, p. 146) suggest that perhaps "the poor in these countries prefer other intoxicants," which suggests that surveys such as these described by Banerjee and Duflo still do not accurately measure either poverty or living conditions. In Peru, the poor often chew coca leaves as a stimulant.

Studies on poverty also tend to ignore the fact that nature's services represent a much higher percentage of daily consumption for the poor than for richer people, Since world economic growth has been consistently reducing nature's services such as fresh water, forest resources, hunting grounds, soil replenishment, and clean air, the livelihoods of many of the world's poorest people are deteriorating with economic growth. Global warming is projected to reduce agricultural production and raise temperatures to uncomfortable levels within this century. Rich societies and rich people within poor societies will be able to isolate themselves from the consequences of global warming much more effectively than the poor who rely on nature more directly.

We also often observe measured GDP per capita growing because of "conspicuous consumption" on the part of those at the top of the world's income distribution. Better communications and increased immigration flows have made people everywhere much more aware of living conditions elsewhere in the world. Therefore, the divergence of incomes across countries may have reduced the life satisfaction or happiness of people in the poorest parts of the world, even though there has been some positive growth of measured output everywhere. Because relative income is more important for happiness than absolute income, unequal economic development combined with better communications can translate into fewer happy people.

17.7 Further Thoughts on Poverty and Income Equality

When the United Nations General Assembly passed its Millennium Declaration in 2000 and agreed to work toward eliminating poverty in the world, it also reconfirmed a specific set of development targets. Among these targets were:

> *Target 1:* Halve, by 2015, the proportion of people whose income is less than $1 a day
>
> *Target 2:* Halve, by 2015, the proportion of people who suffer from hunger
>
> *Target 3:* Ensure that, by 2015, children everywhere, boys and girls alike, will be able to complete a full course of primary schooling
>
> *Target 4:* Eliminate gender disparity in primary and secondary education preferably by 2005 and in all levels of education no later than 2015
>
> *Target 5:* Reduce by two-thirds, between 1990 and 2015, the under-five mortality rate
>
> *Target 6:* Reduce by three-quarters, between 1990 and 2015, the maternal mortality ratio
>
> *Target 7:* Have halted by 2015 and begun to reverse the spread of HIV/AIDS
>
> *Target 8:* Have halted by 2015 and begun to reverse the incidence of malaria and other major diseases
>
> *Target 9:* Integrate the principles of sustainable development into country policies and programs and reverse the loss of environmental resources
>
> *Target 10:* Halve, by 2015, the proportion of people without sustainable access to safe drinking water and basic sanitation

These targets remind us that the distribution of income and the levels of poverty are not easily represented by the measures we have presented. Neither the specification of minimum levels of GDP per capita nor the Gini coefficient constructed using the same income and GDP data can do justice to the complex economic, social, psychological, and environmental issues surrounding concepts such as poverty, happiness, or the distribution of society's costs and benefits.

The targets for health and education are appropriate because health and education are both outcomes of the current economic system and means toward improving those outcomes in the future. Incapacitated and uneducated people have little chance of improving their economic and social conditions. Poverty is directly influenced by the distribution of health and education.

Targets for environmental conditions are also appropriate because the poor are relatively more dependent on nature's services. The poor also have fewer means to protect themselves against environmental degradation. The global warming and loss of biodiversity caused largely by today's most developed countries threatens poor countries, and the poor within those countries, disproportionately. The relationship between the natural environment and the issues of poverty and inequality is even more complex than these observations suggest, however. In the next chapter we again focus on sustainable growth, and we will specifically examine potential policies for achieving a sustainable human society. Successful policies will need to address both social and natural imbalances.

Terms and Concepts

Balanced growth	Lorenz curve
Bourgeoisie	Loss aversion
Economic rights	Maximum feasible Gini
Endowment effect	Poverty
Engel's law	Poverty line
Gini coefficient	Proletariat
Global Gini coefficients	Skill premium
Income elasticity of demand	Social-contractionist philosophy
Income inequality	Territoriality
Income mobility	Unbalanced growth
Inferior good	Unbalanced technological change
Just society	Veil of ignorance
Kuznets hypothesis	Wealth
Longitudinal data	

Questions and Problems

1. Explain how economic growth and structural change cause the distribution of income to change.
2. The textbook explains that wealth is a *stock* that accumulates over time and income is the *flow* that feeds the stock of wealth. What does this relationship suggest about the ease with which inequalities in wealth and income can be changed?
3. Explain the Gini coefficient and how it is derived from the Lorenz curve.

4. Discuss the historical data on the distribution of income. Are modern societies more unequal than societies of centuries past?
5. Describe the Kuznets hypothesis and evaluate its historical validity.
6. Explain the difference between human rights and economic rights. Are they, or are they not, related?
7. What is the more valid measure of human equality: the distribution of opportunities or the distribution of actual income? Discuss.
8. How is income inequality related to economic development? Explain as many links as you can think of.
9. Does income inequality affect economic growth or does economic growth affect inequality? Discuss.
10. Explain John Rawls' "veil of ignorance." Is this a good way to judge equality? Explain.
11. Write an essay answering the following question: Is it possible to have human rights such as freedom of speech and personal safety in the absence of certain economic rights?
12. Discuss the concept of economic rights and how they relate to the concept of equal opportunity.
13. Explain the concepts of absolute and relative poverty. Which are more important for measuring economic development?
14. The text concludes that countries with relatively equal distributions of income mostly maintained their equal distributions as they developed. On the other hand, the data suggests that France and Norway reduced their Gini coefficients over the period shown, and China and United States exhibit rising Ginis. Why do you think these trends differ across countries?
15. What is the difference between income and wealth? Explain.
16. Is economic growth influenced by the income distribution? What has been proposed as reasons for any influence if indeed there is some?
17. Do wages always reflect worker productivitiy? Why is this question important for explaining the distribution of income?
18. There is a common saying: "You get what you deserve." Discuss this saying in light of Rawls' veil of ignorance.

Appendix 17.1: Inequality of Lifetime Per Capita Income

Chapter 2 described expected individual lifetime welfare (EILW), a measure that gives a more accurate picture of individual human welfare. The EILW can also provide better answers to the question of whether human welfare is becoming more or less equal across the countries of the world. The rate of absolute convergence of real per capita income across countries or regions can be found by estimating the regression

$$\ln(y_{t+n}) - \ln(y_t) = a + b \ln(y_t) \qquad (17A.1)$$

in which y_t is real per capita income in year t. If the coefficient b is negative, we can conclude that real per capita incomes converged over the period from year t to year t + n. The *speed of convergence* is equal to $\lambda = -\ln(1 + b)/n$, and the often-reported *half-life*, t^*, of the absolute income gap is the solution to $e^{-\lambda t^*} = 0.5$, or $t^* = -\ln(0.5)/\lambda$. The half-life is the time it takes for half of a substance, the difference between current inequality and full equality in this case, to cease to exist in its current form. Table 17A.1 presents regression estimates and, when they were negative, the speed of convergence for both per capita real GDP and the EILW for the countries included in Table 2.6 in Chapter 2.

Table 17A.1 makes it clear that average individual welfare across countries diverged sharply during the 1800s. It makes little difference whether per capita real GDP or the EILW is used to compare welfare across countries. The coefficients from regressing subsequent growth on the initial levels of per capita real GDP and the EILW are positive and nearly identical for the period 1820–1900. Life expectancy and real per capita GDP both grew more rapidly, on average, in the countries with the higher EILWs.

In the twentieth century there are substantial differences between what real per capita GDP and the EILW tell us about the convergence of average individual welfare. For the period 1900–1950, note that the coefficient for the EILW is considerably smaller than for the regression relating the growth and initial levels of annual real per capita real GDP. Thus, individual welfare appears to have diverged less rapidly during the first half of the twentieth century than annual per capita real GDP data indicate.

During the second half of the twentieth century, the coefficient of the speed of convergence is positive. Furthermore, the relatively more rapid convergence of the EILW, compared to annual real per capita GDP, suggests that individual welfare probably converged more rapidly than comparisons of real per capita GDP show. The more rapid convergence of the EILW is the result of the relatively more rapid improvements in life expectancy in the developing economies. The half-life of the differences in welfare across the sample of

Table 17A.1
Convergence of Expeceted Individual Lifetime Welfare for 12 Countries: 1820–1998

		1820–1900	*1900–1950*	*1950–1998*
Real Per Capita GDP:				
	Regression coefficient:	0.65800	0.13160	−0.18756
	Speed of Convergence:	−0.00632	−0.00247	0.00433
EILW:				
	Regression coefficient:	0.63230	0.08720	−0.27650
	Speed of Convergence:	−0.00612	−0.00167	0.00674

countries is only about 100 years in the case of the EILW but it is about 160 years for annual per capita real GDP. The convergence of expected individual lifetime welfare is not as slow as annual per capita real GDP. This is encouraging because evidence suggests people value longevity more highly than added income.

References

Alesina, Alberto, and Dani Rodrik (1994), "Distributive Politics and Economic Growth," *Quarterly Journal of Economics* 112:465–90.

Anand, Sudhir, and Paul Segal (2008), "What Do We Know about Global Income Inequality?" *Journal of Economic Perspectives* 46(1):57–94.

Banerjee, Abhijit, and Esther Duflo (2007), "The Economic Lives of the Poor," *Journal of Economic Perspectives* 21(1):141–167.

Bhalla, Surjit S. (2002), *Imagine There's No Country*, Washington, D.C.: Institute for International Economics.

Birdsall, Nancy, David Ross, and Richard Sabot (1995), "Inequality and Growth Reconsidered," Research Memorandum No. 142, Center for Development Economics, Williams College.

Bourdieu, Pierre (1977), *Outline of a Theory of Practice*, Cambridge, U.K.: Cambridge University Press.

Bourdieu, Pierre (2001), *Masculine Domination*, Cambridge, U.K.: Polity Press.

Champernowne, D. G., and F. A. Cowell (1998), *Economic Inequality and Income Distribution*, Cambridge, U.K.: Cambridge University Press.

Fields, Gary S. (1980), *Poverty, Inequality, and Development*, Cambridge, U.K.: Cambridge University Press.

Fields, Gary S. (2001), *Distribution and Development: A New Look at the Developing World*, Cambridge, MA: MIT Press.

Greenwood, Jeremy (1999), "The Third Industrial Revolution: Technology, Productivity, and Income Inequality," *Economic Review* 35(1), Cleveland Federal Reserve Bank.

Greenwood, Jeremy, and Mehmet Yorukoghu (1997), "1974," *Carnegie-Rochester Conference Series on Public Policy* 46:49–95

Harley, C. Knick (1993), "Reassessing the Industrial Revolution: A Macro View," in Joel Mokyr (ed.), *The British Industrial Revolution: An Economic Perspective*, Boulder, Colorado: Westview Press.

Jovanovich, Boyan (1997), "Learning and Growth," in David Kreps and Kenneth F. Wallis (eds.), *Advances in Economics and Econometrics*, Vol. 2, New York: Cambridge University Press.

Kahneman, Daniel, and Amos Tversky (2000), *Choices, Values and Frame*, Cambridge, U.K.: Cambridge University Press.

Kaldor, Nicholas (1956), "Alternative Theories of Distribution," *Review of Economic Studies* 23:83–100.

Keefer, Stephen, and Stephen Knack (1995), "Polarization, Property Rights and the Links between Inequality and Growth," Working Paper No. 153, Center for Institutional Reform and the Informal Sector, University of Maryland at College Park, April.

Kuznets, Simon (1955), "Economic Growth and Income Inequality," *American Economic Review* 45(1):1–28.

Lewis, Arthur W. (1954), "Economic Development with Unlimited Supplies of Labour," *The Manchester School* 22:139–91.

Lindert, Peter H., and Jeffrey G. Williamson (1983), "Reinterpreting Britain's Social Tables, 1688–1913," *Explorations in Economic History* 20(1):94–109.

Maddison, Angus (1989), *The World Economy in the 20th Century*, Paris: OECD.

Milanovic, Branko (2006), "An Estimate of Average Income and Inequality in Byzantium Around Year 1000," Review of Income and Wealth 52(2):449–470.

Milanovic, Branko, Peter H. Lindert, and Jeffrey G. Williamson (2007), "Measuring Ancient Inequality," NBER Working Paper 13550, October.

Murphy, Kevin, Andrei Shleifer, and Robert Vishny (1989), "Income Distribution, Market Size, and Industrialization," *Quarterly Journal of Economics* 104:537–564.

Perotti, Roberto (1995), "Income Distribution, Democracy, and Growth: An Empirical Investigation," Presented at NBER-CREI Conference on Growth, Barcelona, Spain, March, 1995

Persson, Torsten, and Guido Tabellini (1994), "Is Inequality Harmful for Growth?" *Economic Review* 57:787–806.

Pritchett, Lant (1997), "Divergence, Big Time," *Journal of Economic Perspectives* 11(3):3–17.

Rawls, John A. (1971), *A Theory of Justice*, Cambridge, MA: Harvard University Press.

Seabright, Paul (2004), *The Company of Strangers: A Natural History of Economic Life*, Princeton, NJ: Princeton University Press.

Thomis, Malcolm I. (1970), *The Luddites: Machine Breaking in Regency England*, Hampton, Connecticut: Archon Books.

CHAPTER 18

Policies for Sustainable Economic Development

I couldn't forgive him or like him but I saw that what he had done was, to him, entirely justified. It was all very careless and confused. They were careless people...they smashed up things and creatures and then retreated back into their money or their vast carelessness, or whatever it was that kept them together, and let other people clean up the mess they had made...

(F. Scott Fitzgerald, *The Great Gatsby*)

Earth's ecosystem is under severe pressure from the growth of the human population and humanity's expanding economic production. There is vast evidence that humanity's exploitation of the Earth's natural services now exceeds the Earth's capacity to sustain those services. As pointed out earlier, Mathis Wackernagel *et al.* (2002) estimated that humanity's exploitation of the Earth's **renewable natural resources** corresponded to 70 percent of capacity in 1961, but grew to 120 percent in 1999. The World Wildlife Fund (2008, p. 2) estimates that "humanity's demand on the planet's living resources... now exceeds the planet's regenerative capacity by about 30 percent."

Technological advances are not sustaining the effective stocks of **non-renewable natural resources** either. In the case of petroleum, evidence suggests that humanity is approaching, or has already approached, **peak extraction**. The International Energy Agency (2010) documents how additional supplies of crude oil are increasingly costly to find, extract, and process. New finds are not keeping up with depletion of existing fields. New technologies can provide alternative energy sources, but so far new technologies have led to more carbon fuels like tar sands oil, shale gas, and "clean" coal. The world's fastest growing emerging economies, Brazil, China, India, and Russia, are still building infrastructures based on the consumption of carbon fuels.

It is also clear that humanity's efforts to compensate for the stress on nature's services and the depletion of non-renewable resources have often made things worse. The so-called **green revolution** that is credited with rapidly increasing the amount of food produced per acre during the latter half of the twentieth century has caused numerous new stresses in the social and natural spheres. The rapid substitution of machines for people in agriculture destroyed traditional rural communities and displaced hundreds of millions of people. The green revolution thus not only expanded grain production, it also expanded urban slums, illegal immigration, and income inequality.

The Green Revolution is causing massive environmental damage. Modern agriculture contributes more to global warming than do transportation or electric power generation. The green revolution was essentially carbon-intensive technological change consisting of more fertilizers made from oil and natural gas, increased use of machinery powered by diesel fuel, irrigation powered by carbon fuels, and carbon-based transportation systems. The green revolution also consisted of a massive shift towards **monoculture**, the ubiquitous large-scale capital-intense production of single crops covering vast territories formerly devoted to much more varied agricultural production. Monoculture is the main contributor to species depletion and the loss of biodiversity. Monoculture is motivated by economies of scale from substituting large equipment for labor, heavy applications of chemical fertilizers and insecticides in place of more labor-intensive and varied exploitation of the land, and linking farms to industrial food processing operations in which machinery and assembly-line methods process standardized and uniform products. The negative externalities of these energy intensive methods on the social and natural spheres are ignored in the calculations of costs and benefits of the green revolution.

Humanity's response to the increased pressure on the Earth's petroleum reserves has centered on developing biofuels, such as ethanol, produced from corn, sugar cane, and other crops that require vast amounts of land and water. Biofuels have also contributed to the expansion of monoculture. For example, in Brazil the production of sugar cane, which serves as the raw material for producing ethanol, has pushed cattle and other types of agriculture into the Amazon basin, the huge region that is Earth's largest carbon sink.

Efforts to exploit other sources of petroleum, such as the development of the tar sands in Alberta, Canada, are much more environmentally damaging than conventional oil production. Converting tar sands into petroleum requires large amounts of natural gas and other energy to "melt" the tar. Thus creating crude oil from tar sands adds new carbon emissions to the already large carbon emissions from using a liter of gasoline. The processing of the Alberta tar sands also threatens to make one of Canada's largest river basins uninhabitable.

Equally damaging is the rapid expansion of natural gas production by means of the newly developed process of hydraulic fracturing (popularly called **fracking**). Natural gas is widely touted as a lower-carbon fuel, and it is being increasingly used as a substitute for coal in electric power plants because gas plants emit about half as much carbon into the air per unit of energy as coal-fired power plants do. Fracking has made available gas from shale deposits that were long considered unexploitable, and the price of natural gas plummeted in 2010 in anticipation of this technology. The process requires the pressurized injection of highly toxic chemicals into shale formations, and there is already vast evidence of water contamination in areas where fracking has been carried out. Robert Howarth, Renee Santoro, and Anthony Ingaffea (2011) show that natural gas captured by means of hydraulic fracturing emits just as many greenhouse gases as burning coal to generate an equivalent amount of electricity. Specifically, they found (p. 679): "Natural gas is composed largely of methane, and 3.6 percent to 7.9 percent of the methane from shale-gas production escapes to the atmosphere in venting and leaks over the lifetime of a well." Methane is a much more potent greenhouse gas than carbon. In sum, finding more Earth-friendly substitutes for coal and oil is, so far, proving to be very difficult.

The growth of economic activity has also fueled social conflicts and oppression. For example, growing demand for energy has triggered wars over oil and supply routes in Kuwait, Iraq, Libya, and Georgia, as well as numerous threats of war against oil producers like Iran, Venezuela, and Ecuador. The continued violence in the Niger Delta of Nigeria is driven by the extreme poverty that exists side by side with the oil industry. There have been civil wars in more than a dozen African countries over the control of assorted natural resources. Large countries such as China, the United States, Russia, and others are actively engaged in a military arms race in order to expand and maintain their control over the world's scarce resources. Several countries, among them Iran, Pakistan, and North Korea, have developed or are accused of seeking to develop nuclear weapons to protect themselves and their resources. The disruption of societies by foreign nations seeking control over natural resources is not a new phenomenon, of course. Resource wars characterized the colonization of Latin America, Africa, and Asia starting 500 years ago. Despite having been led to believe that colonization is a thing of the past, the same quest for control of Earth's natural resources has only taken on new appearances.

Human society is on a dynamic path of economic, social, and environmental change that is simply not sustainable. Humans are not generating enough new ideas, knowledge, and technology to mitigate the damage their growing consumption of resources is causing across all spheres of human existence. The scientist James Lovelock appropriately reminds us that "it is not the Earth that is threatened, but civilization."[1] Yet, there is no political consensus on how to address the threats of global warming, biodiversity losses, the growing inequality of incomes and wealth, and the social disruption of human communities. Just as F. Scott Fitzgerald describes the behavior of the

---

[1] Quoted from a conversation by the French journalist/writer Hervé Kempf (2007), p. 3.

wealthy protagonists in his novel, *The Great Gatsby*, the world's rich societies of the world refuse to acknowledge the costs of their carelessness.

This chapter outlines the case for ending the human-made stresses on the natural environment. It details the potential costs of reducing the environmental and social stresses that economic and population growth have caused. The chapter concludes with ideas on how humanity will manage the shift from its unsustainable path of economic growth to sustainable economic development.

Chapter Goals

1. Discuss the hesitant political support for costly policies to address environmental problems like global warming and biodiversity losses.
2. Explain why uncertainty and missing information actually strengthen the case for precautionary mitigation policies.
3. Review the reasons why sustainable growth requires technological change in the natural sphere to sustain nature's services to the economic sphere.
4. Explain the cap and trade scheme to limit carbon emissions.
5. Present case studies that illustrate how indirect schemes to cut carbon emissions can fail to accomplish their goals.
6. Explain the Jevons effect.
7. Describe the efforts in Ecuador and Bolivia to establish the rights of Mother Earth and limit humans' ability to exploit nature at will.
8. Discuss whether economic growth is sustainable and what future societies might reorganize themselves to prevent the collapse of the natural sphere.

18.1 The Urgent But Difficult Case for Environmental Policies

In 2009, the Copenhagen Conference where a new international agreement to replace the expiring Kyoto Protocol on Climate Change was to have been negotiated was a failure. Most notable was the agreement between President Obama of the United States and the leaders of the largest developing economies, China and India, to effectively let each country do whatever it wanted. President Obama was being lobbied by U.S. oil companies, automakers, and the politically powerful U.S. Chamber of Commerce to undermine international agreement on environmental rules. The leaders of China and India were interested in maximizing the growth of their economies, and they were opposed to harsh restrictions on carbon emissions or limits on the use of carbon fuels. The 2007–2009 financial crisis and economic recession made political leaders from countries that had earlier pushed for more stringent environmental policies willing to accept defeat in Copenhagen. A follow-up meeting one year later in Cancun, Mexico brought equally little progress.

Human psychology, as discussed in Chapter 3, makes such short-sightedness towards the ominous long-run trends perfectly understandable. Culturally, economic growth is so firmly established as the premier policy objective in the minds of economists and policymakers that any discussion on environmental problems is simply uncomfortable. The world needs a major paradigm shift, but to date there has not been enough dissent in the political and economic cultures that would to empower such a paradigm shift.

18.1.1 *Dealing with uncertainty: The example of global warming*

The issue of global warming is greatly complicated by the uncertainty over how the higher greenhouse gas (GHG) concentrations in the atmosphere will affect the climate and the overall natural environment. We do not know exactly how far atmospheric temperatures will rise or what the consequences of the resulting climate changes will be. Also, we are not sure how humans will cope with the changing climate. Robert Pindyck (2006) describes the situation as follows:

> In a world of certainty, the design of environmental policy is relatively straightforward, and boils down to maximizing the present value of the flow of social benefits minus costs. But the real world is one of considerable uncertainty — over physical and ecological impact of pollution, over the economic costs and benefits of reducing it, and over the discount rates that should be used to compute present values. The implication of uncertainty are complicated by the fact that most environmental policy problems involve highly nonlinear damage functions, important reversibilities, and long time horizons.

Given these difficulties, how do policy makers address uncertain threats?

First, it is important to grasp the difference between **risk** and **uncertainty**. Risk is what insurance companies normally deal with, namely a set of potential outcomes with well-defined probabilities that permit a fairly accurate calculation of expected values and probability that some future outcome will fall within a specific range of all possible outcomes. In the case of global warming, we are not sure of the probabilities with which each of the possible outcomes will occur in the future. Scientists do not even know what all the possible outcomes are.

Sometimes, uncertainty is used as a justification for not acting. Statements such as "we need to study the matter further before deciding" and "we should wait until all the evidence has been examined" are widely accepted as reasonable strategies. Waiting until all the evidence has been examined is almost certainly not the correct strategy in the case of potentially catastrophic events like global warming. To explain why, we begin with Figure 18.1.

This diagram shows a distribution of outcomes characterized by the standard normal distribution function f(x), a function you are no doubt familiar with if you have taken an elementary statistics course. The normal distribution

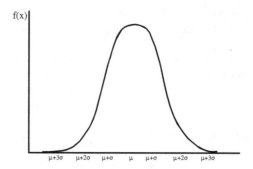

Figure 18.1 A Standard Normal Distribution

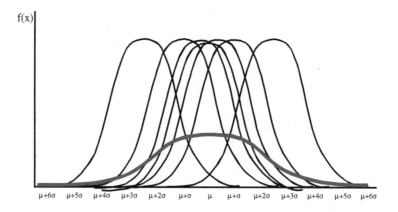

Figure 18.2 A Distribution of Standard Normal Distributions

is centered on the mean outcome μ, and nearly all outcomes fall between the mean and plus or minus three standard deviations, σ, from the mean. The standard deviation is the average difference between the mean outcome and each actual observed outcome.

Martin Weitzman (2007) notes that when there is uncertainty about the exact shape and position of the probability distribution of possible outcomes, the probability distribution of the events in question becomes flatter with fatter tails. To understand what he means by this, suppose that we are not certain about which of a whole group of distributions, shown in Figure 18.2, represents the phenomenon we are interested in. Figure 18.2 shows a "distribution of distributions", the thicker line, that includes all possible outcomes across all of the possible distributions. Notice how the aggregate distribution is much flatter and has "fatter" tails than any individual normal distribution. That means that extreme outcomes are relatively more likely. For example, for a normal distribution centered on μ, there is virtually no chance that an outcome lying more than three standard deviations from the expected mean will occur. However, with uncertainty about the exact location of the distribution of outcomes, an outcome that lies four standard deviations from the expected mean clearly has a meaningful likelihood of occurring, as evidenced by the distance between the thicker aggregate distribution and the horizontal axis at $\mu + 4\sigma$ and $\mu - 4\sigma$. As the Oxford University economist Paul Klemperer writes: "The continuing scientific uncertainty about the pace of climate change should make us more concerned, not less."[2]

Martin Weitzman (2007) provides more details about how a state of uncertainty affects our objective judgment of the future:

> The tiny probabilities of nightmare impacts of climate change are all such crude ballpark estimates that there is a tendency... to dismiss them on the "scientific" grounds that they are much too highly speculative to be taken seriously because they are statistically indistinguishable from zero... [T]he exact opposite is in fact true... the more speculative and fuzzy are the tiny tail probabilities of high-impact extreme events, the less ignorable and the more serious is the situation for an agent whose welfare is measured by present discounted expected utility.

In his paper, Weitzman assumes an orthodox intertemporal welfare function to show that, under a variety of plausible discount rates, catastrophic environmental events with very small likelihoods should be actively avoided as long as abatement costs are no more than a few percent of the value of human life. Weitzman accepts current estimates that the costs of lowering carbon emissions back to historical levels are probably not more than a few percent of annual GDP, and he thus rejects the "wait-and-see" approach to global warming.

18.1.2 The costs of controlling global warming

The Intergovernmental Panel on Climate Change (2007) estimated that it would cost between 1 and 2 percent of world GDP to reduce greenhouse gas emissions enough to avoid global warming, and the Stern Report (2007) also suggests a cost of 1 percent of GDP for mitigating the effects of global warming.[3] Nicholas Stern (2008) later increased his cost estimate to closer to 2 percent of global GDP because updated evidence suggested that global warming was progressing more rapidly than a consensus of scientists had thought a few years earlier.

The costs of stopping global warming cover a variety of ways in which we would have to change human activity on earth. About two-thirds of the GHGs in the atmosphere are derived from energy use in industry, transportation, heating and cooling our homes, and in growing our food. The remaining GHGs

---

[2] Paul Klemperer (2008), "If Climate Sceptics Are Right, It Is Time to Worry," *Financial Times*, February 29.

[3] IPCC (2007), Nicholas Stern (2007, 2008).

are the result of waste management and the destruction of forests and other natural environments as a result of changes in human land use. GHG emissions can be reduced by switching to new sources of energy that emit fewer GHGs, such as replacing coal-fueled electricity generation with solar, wind, and yet-to-be-invented non-toxic sources of energy. The ultimate costs of reducing GHG emission will also depend on how well humans develop new technologies that improve the ratio of output relative to GHG-emitting inputs in generating energy, powering transportation, and producing industrial output. Among these new "technologies" will be new forms of social and economic organization. We will have to change the way humans live and work. GHG emissions will have to be reduced by shifting demand to products that require less energy input, such as smaller energy-efficient homes, more efficient and fewer appliances, more vegetarian diets, smaller and more efficient automobiles, and public transportation. Humans will also have to maintain forests that absorb carbon, store more water, and protect the living species that provide valuable services to humanity and that form critical links in the ecological system.

Not all of the measures to reduce GHG emissions are costly. For example, raising the efficiency of automobile engines, improving insulation in buildings and homes, replacing incandescent light bulbs actually cost less than conventional products, and a vegetarian diet requires far fewer natural resources to produce food while most likely also reducing medical expenses later in life. Humans are locked into many habits that make no economic sense at all. Figure 18.3 shows that a substantial portion of the measures needed to reduce GHG emissions to levels that will stabilize GHGs at 550ppm (parts per million) are not net costs.[4] The gains from actions that actually reduce costs keep the total costs of all the required reductions in GHGs to about 1 percent of world GDP.

As you contemplate Figure 18.3, keep in mind that it assumes the optimal mitigation strategy is to limit the rise in GHGs in the atmosphere to 550 ppm. Bill McKibben (2008) and many other scientists and environmentalists argue for bringing the concentration of GHGs back to 350 parts per million. Allowing the atmosphere to accumulate up to 550 ppm would most likely raise temperatures more than 2 degrees Celsius, which means feedback mechanisms could be triggered that could raise temperatures by many more degrees very quickly.

It is very difficult to predict the future course of technological change and, therefore, the precise costs of stabilizing the earth's temperatures at any given level. But it seems reasonable to assume that at this point in time we face mitigation costs equal to about 2 percent of annual GDP. The safer goal of stabilization at 350ppm will likely cost more than that. Of course, the final cost of preventing global warming will also depend on how efficient the mitigation

---

[4] Per-Anders Enkvist, Tomas Nauclér, and Jerker Rosander (2007), "A Cost Curve for Greenhouse Gas Reduction," *The McKinsey Quarterly* 1:35–45.

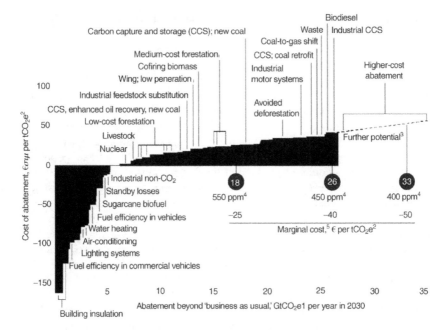

Figure 18.3 Global Warming Abatement Costs
Source: McKinsey and Vattenfall, *The McKinsey Quartely*, 2007, Number 1.

policies are. Later in the chapter, we will compare alternative policies to motivate new technologies, conservation, and lifestyle changes.

18.1.3 The other example: Biodiversity

As Chapter 6 showed, global warming is not the only barrier to continued economic growth that humanity faces. Scientists have documented a sharp acceleration in the rate of extinction of the Earth's plants, animals, and micro-organisms. What we call **biodiversity** encompasses not only the number of species, but also the specific genetic variations within species and the assemblage of the species within ecosystems.

GHG emissions and global warming are related to the loss of plant and animal species. Carbon directly affects living organisms, and because global warming affects the earth's climate, species survival rates are affected. For example, when carbon dioxide is released into the air, about a third ends up in the oceans; when this CO_2 dissolves in the water it forms a weak acid and increases the acidity of the oceans. About a third of carbon emitted into the air is absorbed by plants, soil, and other land ecosystems. The remainder stays in the atmosphere. If the current growth of carbon emissions continues, the acidity of the oceans will increase enough to push many marine organisms into extinction before the end of this century. The Earth will lose its reef-building corals, for example. The *Stern Report* (2007) projects a loss of 1 million species over the next 50 years if global warming progresses as predicted under "business as usual" by the Stern Report.[5]

The loss of plant and animal species also affects global warming. Forests are important carbon sinks, and their decline will increase the amount of carbon released into the atmosphere. Despite these and many other close relationships, however, it is useful to view the loss of biodiversity as distinct from global warming because it is driven by some distinct aspects of human activity.

The fundamental problem is that the growth of the human population and its per capita economic production has led humans to occupy much more space on earth and use more of the resources and services nature provides. More space for humans means less space for other animals and plants. The development of agriculture, which has played a very large role in the growth of the human population, replaced diverse natural forests, grasslands, and wetlands with areas devoted to growing a small variety of food crops. Also, as already noted, economies of scale have extended the practice of monoculture. The direct economic efficiency of monoculture is derived from exploiting only the most efficient plant and animal species for human consumption. But, as explained in Chapter 6, the resulting loss of biodiversity reduces the **redundancy in nature** and destroys resources that are important to human existence.

18.1.4 The momentum of our current path

The discussions of global warming and biodiversity should have revealed some important similarities of these two issues. In both cases we are dealing with slow-moving processes whose consequences will appear only years from now. In both cases, we also are dependent on scientific predictions, which, in turn, are dependent on our imperfect knowledge and models of very complex systems. Global warming and the loss of biodiversity are both anthropogenic. The scientific consensus is that the rapid acceleration of species losses and global warming are very real, even if we cannot calculate the exact rates of change. And, finally, there is a scientific consensus that both global warming and the accelerating losses of biodiversity could prove disastrous for humanity.

Neither global warming nor the loss of biodiversity are being addressed very well by the governments that represent the collective population that makes up human society. The poor response is not the result of a lack of information. For example, in 1992 an international summit of nations produced the **Convention on Biological Diversity**, which committed nations to take measures to slow, and eventually stop, the decline in plant and animal species. This treaty

---

[5] As reported in Vanessa Houlder (2004), "Over 1 Million Species Will Be 'Wiped Out' by Global Warming," *Financial Times*, January 8.

was ratified by 187 nations and the European Union. Only the United States, Iraq, the Vatican, Somalia, Andorra, and Brunei did not commit to the treaty. In 2002, the signatories of the 1992 treaty met for a 10-year assessment of progress towards reducing biodiversity loss. Since the scientific evidence showed that biodiversity losses were still accelerating, the Conference negotiated a Strategic Plan in which member countries committed to achieving a significant reduction in biodiversity loss by 2010. But, while more evidence of biodiversity losses continues to mount, there has been little real international cooperation or action towards reversing biodiversity loss.

With regard to global warming, recall from Chapter 6 that Joseph Fourier described the greenhouse effect in 1827.[6] John Tyndall identified the types of gases that trapped heat in 1861, and Svante Arrhenius calculated the possible effects of a doubling of GHGs in 1896.[7] And yet, nearly two centuries after Fourier, some of those who stand to lose from putting an end to their environmentally disastrous consumption are still actively contesting this scientific knowledge.[8]

Some critics of increased environmental regulation accept scientific knowledge but claim, instead, that the costs of regulations will be too high in terms of lost economic growth. The exact costs of mitigating environmental problems are not known with certainty. The big unknown on the cost side of the policy debate is the future path of technological change. How much will it cost to develop the new technologies and change the way we do things so that we reduce GHG emissions? Can we produce those new technologies quickly? The Schumpeterian model suggests that technological change can be accelerated with the appropriate incentives, but even then the process of technological change is impossible to predict accurately. We could have a major technological breakthrough next year that effectively stops global warming, or we could find that the warming process is already much farther along and already irreversible.

This brings us back to Weitzman's point above that uncertainty does not justify inaction on global warming. To put Weitzman's argument into a clearer perspective, note first that people routinely deal with uncertainty and make decisions based on partial information and understanding. For example, when we decide to insure our house against fire or our car against theft, in both cases the probability of each event is very small and, probably, not fully known. Yet, in each case, we are willing to part with a consequential sum of money to avoid

---

[6] Joseph Fourier (1827), "Mémoire sur les températures du globe terrestre et des espaces planétaires," *Mémoires de l'académie Royale des Sciences* 7:569–604.
[7] John Tyndall (1861), "On the Absorption and Radiation of Heat by Gases and Vapours," *Philosophical Magazine* 22:169–194, 273–285; Svante Arrhenius (1896), "On the Influence of Carbonic Acid and Air upon the Temperature of the Ground," *Philosophical Magazine* 41(2):237–272.
[8] See, for example, Jane Meyer (2010), "Covert Operations," *The New Yorker*, August 30.

the catastrophic loss of such a large asset. In the cases of global warming and biodiversity, human existence is in play. How much should we humans be willing to pay to insure a sustainable future existence?

To answer this question, we first need to define the value of our existence. As Kip Viscusi's (1993) survey of studies of the **value of life** concludes, economists and the legal courts have put the value of a human life in the United States at about $7 million, on average, in 2009 dollars. Since average per capita GDP in the United States is about $45,000, a human life there is worth about $150 per dollar of per capita GDP. We can calculate the value of life for the whole world; the global average per capita GDP in 2009 prices is about U.S.$10,000 and there were 6.7 billion people in that year. Therefore, the total value of human life on earth in 2009 was 6.7 billion people x U.S.$10,000 x U.S.$150 = about $10 quadrillion (or, 10 million billion). This amount is 7,500 times 2009 world GDP of $67 trillion. Hence, if we must spend 2 percent of GDP per year to stop global warming, we are effectively being asked to make a payment of about $25 per $100,000 of insured value to insure our most valuable asset, life, against an uncertain possibility of total loss. People spend much higher rates to insure their homes and cars. Yet, the world's political leaders are reluctant to spend such a small premium to insure the future survival of humanity.

The quote from *The Great Gatsby* at the start of the chapter reflects one possible explanation for the lack of action. Those who wield power, the wealthy, are the ones who through their excessive consumption are disproportionately responsible for damaging the ecosystem. But they can, or they think they can, continue to use their wealth to protect themselves from the damage they cause. The poor, who consume much less, are expected to suffer most of the consequences. For example, according to a representative for the Maasai tribe in Kenya, who lost 5 million cattle to drought in the first decade of the twenty-first century: "The Maasai community does not drive 4 x 4s or fly off on holidays in airplanes. We have not caused climate change, yet we are the ones suffering."[9] It seems as though the reluctance of our political leaders to stop global warming and biodiversity losses stems from the disproportional economic and political influence of the special interests who are the root of the environmental problems.

18.2 Environmental Policy

Chapter 6 pointed out that technological change can mitigate the severe stress that economic growth is causing in the natural environment. Some technologies that reduce carbon emissions are already available but have not yet been widely applied. More environmentally sustainable agricultural methods are available to

---

[9] Quoted in Naomi Klein (2009), "Climate Rage," *Rolling Stone*, November 11.

replace energy-intensive monoculture. The wasteful production of biofuels like corn ethanol, which require huge inputs of energy from other sources, could be terminated immediately with little loss of net energy. Wind and solar energy can be greatly expanded almost immediately. Automobiles that can drive twice the distance per liter of fuel compared to current vehicles are already in production, and there are hybrid vehicles on the market that increase fuel efficiency even more. Further research will surely uncover more new ways to mitigate global warming, reverse the loss of fish stocks in the oceans, end the need to cut down rain forests, and reduce the need for so many other destructive practices. Yet, despite the urgency and the impressive record of recent human innovation, efforts to develop and apply new technologies to deal with long-run environmental problems such as global warming and the loss of biodiversity are strongly resisted by many politically powerful groups.

The resistance to change is, in part, due to the cost of research and innovation. After ignoring the environmental costs of emitting carbon into the atmosphere or converting more and more natural habitat to farmland for many years, no one is enthusiastic about paying those costs now, especially if those who are asked to pay are not the same people and firms that got away with not paying for their environmental damage in the past. The Schumpeterian model and its focus on the costly nature of innovation make it clear that if producers and consumers do not have to pay the costs of the environmental damage they cause, then private innovators will not develop the costly technologies that can reduce those costs. Ways will have to be found to "internalize" the negative externalities, to make prices more accurately reflect the true underlying costs. Since few if any markets internalize environmental costs, there is a clear role for more direct collective action by governments.

18.2.1 Environmental costs and economic growth

Business leaders often argue that environmental regulations, restrictions on carbon emissions, pollution controls, protection of endangered species, and other environmental regulations will slow economic growth. The fallacy of this argument can be understood using the logic of the multi-dimensional Solow model in Chapter 6. Recall that sustainable growth across all three spheres of human existence will likely result in slower economic growth in the economic sphere. Those who only look at the economic sphere see little cause for alarm about the future sustainability of economic growth. In most high income countries, GDP growth seems to have been sufficient to cover the depreciation of the physical capital stock in the economic sphere. Also, the potential for future profits seems to have motivated enough costly research and development to continually shift the production function higher in economic sphere. But, the narrow focus on the economic sphere ignores the environmental and social costs.

Figure 18.4 shows how, until recently, humanity enjoyed a free ride in the natural sphere.   Up to the hypothetical output level Y_2, humanity's environmental footprint is not noticeable. Only when the growth of economic output passes Y_2 does economic production incur real natural costs. When output reaches Y_3, conservation costs equal to $cf(S_3)$ are required in order to sustain the output of nature's services, S. Without such conservation efforts, economic output will decline because nature's services decline. The World Wildlife Fund (2008) study detailed at the start of this chapter suggests that human society recently has passed the point S_2.

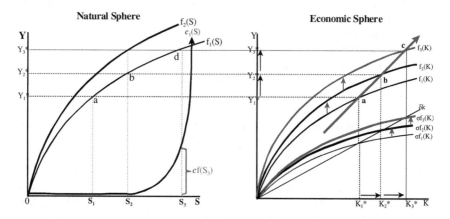

Figure 18.4 Economic Growth when the Natural Sphere Is Stressed

Alternatively, output can be sustainably increased to Y_3 if humanity engages in costly innovations that raise the production function in the natural dimension from $f_1(S)$ to $f_2(S)$. To sustain output at Y_3, human society must cover the costs of investment to cover depreciation and the growth of the capital stock to move the economy to the new steady state where output equals Y_3 in the economic sphere, and it also must cover the costs of the innovative activities that shifted the production function to $f_2(S)$ in the natural sphere. To make growth to Y_3 sustainable, saving and investment must be increased to cover depreciation and innovation in both the economic and natural spheres.

Figure 18.5 illustrates a potential path of sustainable development. The economy moves to an equilibrium at output Y_4, which is greater than Y_2 but smaller than Y_3. Y_4 is the result of a slower rate of technological change in the economic sphere, where the production function shifts only as far as $f_4(K)$. It is also the result of a lower amount of saving applied in the economic sphere, one that supports only the level of capital investment K_2^*. This lower production and investment in the economic sphere frees up savings to generate either enough innovation in the natural sphere to shift the production function there from $f_2(S)$ to $f_4(S)$ *and* to cover the conservation cost cf(S). In sum, by diverting resources towards actions that mitigate environmental degradation, GDP grows more slowly. But this slower rate of growth is sustainable because costs in both the economic and natural spheres are covered.

Will humanity indeed save more, consume less, and innovate in both spheres in order to achieve sustainable growth to Y_3? There may be resistance by those who view their existence as taking place exclusively in the economic sphere because the growth of output in the economic sphere will not be as fast. Holism suggests that, for the well-being of humanity, such resistance must be overcome.

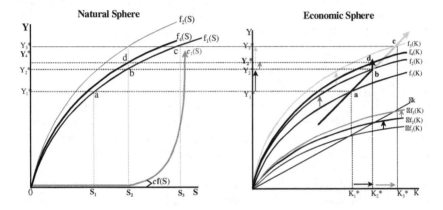

Figure 18.5 Economic Growth with Investment in the Natural Sphere

18.2.2 *The available policy tools*

Many policies for reducing GHG emissions have been suggested. Nations around the world have begun to implement some of these policies, albeit in a rather uncoordinated and inconsistent manner. First, there are outright **prohibitions** or **limits** on GHG emissions, which may be applied across the board throughout the economy or to specific industries or users. For example, more than a decade ago the U.S. state of California mandated that a certain percentage of motor vehicles in the state emit no GHGs at all. Economists more often argue for applying **GHG taxes** to all sectors of the economy. A GHG emissions tax effectively increases the cost of emitting GHGs and, therefore, provides an incentive to find alternatives to the GHG emitting activity. Policymakers have recently favored **cap and trade** schemes, under which some maximum amount of GHG emissions is determined and permits for that amount of emissions are issued, after which a carbon exchange market sets a price for the permits. In practice, under such a cap and trade system, the permits have usually been distributed free of charge to previous GHG emitters in order to overcome business and political resistance to restrictive GHG policies.

Finally, private industry and business often argue for *voluntary* and **self-regulation** schemes. Such programs rely on the good will and social responsibility of business and corporate organizations. Given normal business ethics, the autocratic nature of corporate structures, the single-minded focus on profits in the private sectors of most economies, and the potential for a policy "race to the bottom" in the competitive global economy, it is unrealistic to expect voluntary programs and self-regulation to reduce GHG emissions.

Politically, policy makers in government must make the difficult decisions on who will pay to reduce GHG emissions. Should current emitters bear the full cost? Should the costs be spread among the users of the products whose production generated the emissions? Should the entire society share in the costs?

18.2.3 Taxes versus quantitative restrictions

A tax on GHG emissions provides the government with revenues paid by the firms that produce the emissions and the users of the firms' products. Figure 18.6 illustrates how such revenue is generated and who ends up effectively paying the tax. In this example of the electricity market, Figure 18.6 assumes that this is a rising cost industry, as evidenced by the upward-sloping supply curve, and that the market is not perfectly competitive, as evidenced by the downward-sloping demand curve. The private supply curve S_P for electricity reflects only the costs of production directly paid by the power industry, such as coal, transportation of the coal, capital equipment, financial costs, salaries, and wages. In Figure 18.6, the cost of electricity will be P_P if there is no GHG emissions tax, and the quantity of electricity demanded will be equal to Q_P.

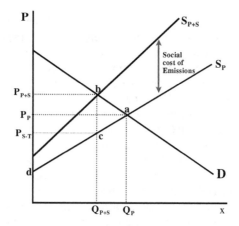

Figure 18.6 Taxes versus Quantitative Restrictions

But if the true costs of production are greater because there are the external costs associated with climate change caused by the industry's GHG emissions, the supply curve that reflects the full costs S_{P+S} lies above the private supply curve. Suppose that scientific studies have determined that the damage from GHG emissions increases in proportion to the amount of electricity generated. In this case, the true social supply curve will lie above and be more steeply sloped than the private supply curve. If the government sets a tax exactly equal to the estimated external social costs of the GHG emissions associated with the industry's output, and if the industry simply adds the tax to the price of electricity, then the industry supply curve will be the curve S_{P+S}. The price of electricity then rises to P_{P+S}, and the quantity supplied falls to Q_{P+S}. The decline in electricity production reduces GHG emissions. Notice that the price to consumers of electricity does not rise by the full amount of the tax, and producers effectively absorb part of the tax at their price P_{S-T}. The profit of the electricity industry falls, consumers pay a higher price, and the government gains tax revenue equal to the difference between P_{P+S} and P_{S-T} times the amount of electricity sold. These distortion-reducing government tax revenues could be used to replace other distorting taxes for a secondary net gain to the economy.

Neither the industry nor the consumers of electricity will be happy about the GHG tax, of course. The government could use its tax revenue to compensate the industry and/or the consumers, but such indirect compensation is seldom as politically convenient as not enacting the tax to begin with. From a holistic perspective, it is obvious that society will pay the equivalent of the tax in the form of global warming later if it does not levy the market-correcting tax and reduce its GHG emissions now. The willingness of a society to institute a GHG tax is thus related to people's understanding of the intertemporal costs and benefits. If a society is not convinced that GHG emissions cause global warming or that global warming will cause costly damage in the future, then it is unlikely that policymakers will introduce GHG taxes. Of course, knowledge does not guarantee good policies; special interests may still derail legislation through lobbying, propaganda, and corruption.

A cap and trade system is, in many ways, similar to the GHG tax illustrated in Figure 18.7. Suppose that, instead of a GHG tax-augmented supply curve, the government simply supplies a fixed amount of GHG emission permits equal to the quantity $S_{C\&T}$, as shown in Figure 18.7. This vertical line effectively becomes the supply of electricity curve when the price exceeds P_C. The intersection between this effective supply curve and the demand curve leads to a price at $P_{C\&T}$. At this quantity of electricity supplied, the marginal private cost is P_C, and the GHG emission permit is worth the difference between the sale price of electricity and the private production cost, or $P_{C\&T} - P_C$. If the authorities set the *cap* correctly, the price at which the permits are *traded* in the market equals the marginal cost of the global warming caused by the permitted GHGs.

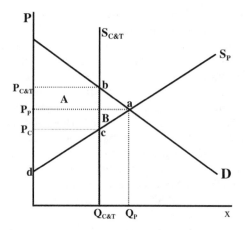

Figure 18.7 Cap and Trade

There is an important difference between a GHG tax and a cap and trade system, however. A tax directly puts revenue in the hands of the government, but the increase in income to holders of the emission permits accrue to those lucky or corrupt enough to receive the scarce permits. Only when the government auctions the permits are the tax and the cap and trade scheme effectively identical in that all revenue accrues directly to the government. A competitive auction would raise the price for the permits pretty close to $P_{C\&T}$ - P_C. On the other hand, if the government awards the permits free of charge, then the polluters gain the extra revenue from the higher price. Recent cap and trade schemes in Europe have distributed permits for free to current polluters; most likely the free distribution of the permits was seen as an incentive for polluters to go along with the scheme to reduce electricity production. Or, the scheme could have been simply the result of political lobbying.

Finally, the government could simply mandate a minimum price for electricity equal to $P_{C\&T}$. This case would benefit producers at the expense of consumers, as in the case where GHG emission permits are handed free of charge to the electricity producers in the example just above. So, in general, the three schemes described here, namely the GHG tax, a cap and trade system, and a regulated price, are all designed to set a price that effectively internalizes the environmental externalities. All three raise the price of the product whose production causes environmental damage, and they all reduce the level of the damaging production. They differ in how they allocate the costs of the policy between producers, consumers, and the government. The political attractiveness of each of these schemes therefore also differs.

Given the gains and losses to consumers, producers, and government budgets, it is not hard to imagine the rent-seeking activity that will accompany the formulation of public policies to reduce GHG emissions. Current producers will, no doubt, try to stop the government from imposing any scheme to raise prices or reduce output. But, failing that, those producers who currently pollute will lobby for a cap and trade regime in which they are given emission permits without charge. Consumers may also oppose new policies that raise the prices they pay for goods and services if they are unaware or insensitive to how damage in the natural sphere affects them. If emissions must be dealt with, consumers would most likely prefer a tax or an auction system under cap and trade, with the government revenue distributed back to them to offset the higher prices of the goods and services they buy. This scheme was recently proposed in the United States.

18.2.4 The political economy of environmental policy

The United States is one of just two countries that did not ratify the Kyoto Agreement and 1997 Protocol. In 2008, the U.S. Senate failed to pass even a modest law called the *Lieberman-Warner Climate Security Act*, which provided for 4 to 6 percent reduction in 2020 GHG emissions compared to 1990 levels. This contrasts with the European Union and individual European countries, which have already committed to much greater reductions ranging from 20 percent to 36 percent. The European Union has been moving towards a full cap and trade system, although most of the permits were given to polluters free of charge. During the first round of the system, European governments issued so many permits that the price of carbon emissions fell to near zero. In other words, the cap and trade program did not really restrict carbon emissions.

At the time of the December 2009 Copenhagen meeting mentioned earlier, the consensus among countries seemed to favor the cap and trade approach. A direct tax on the sources of carbon emissions was not being actively considered by the governments of the world's major economies. Table 18.1 shows some of the recent offers from individual countries.

Table 18.1 Short- and Long-Term Carbon Reduction Targets (Compared to 1990)

	2020	*2050*	*Notes*
IPCC	−25–40%	−80–95%	Developed countries
European Union	−20–30%	−60–80%	The higher reductions go into effect if there is an international agreement
United Kingdom	−26–32%	−60%	
Germany	−36%	−40%	if EU commits to −30%
Netherlands	−30%		
U.S. (Senate Bill)	−4–6%	−50%	

Source: 1SKY Education Fund

Many environmentalists oppose cap and trade schemes. They greatly prefer a **carbon tax** or direct regulation of carbon emissions. First of all, they argue that cap and trade establishes an effective property right over the atmosphere, and human nature suggests such property rights will not easily be surrendered once granted. If the rights to emit carbon are awarded to firms and countries according to current emissions, as carbon permits have indeed usually been awarded in most countries, then a cap and trade system effectively constitutes what the environmental organization *Rising Tide* calls a "massive resource grab." The commons is privatized and very unequally distributed under a cap and trade system. Since the wealthy nations emit most carbon, such a privatization will benefit the rich countries most.[10]

Another fear about cap and trade is that the market for carbon permits will be unstable and, therefore, fail to provide clear incentives for firms to invest in alternative energy systems, conservation, and new products. Also, if prices fluctuate excessively, consumers are less likely to permanently change their consumption patterns. Furthermore, there are fears about how the carbon markets will be operated. Will they turn into typical financial markets, where speculators and gamblers dominate short term trading, much like they do in stock markets and foreign exchange markets? Will the world's financial firms run the carbon markets as over-the-counter markets that they control and manipulate for their profit?

Most worrisome is how carbon permits will be allocated and their overall quantities determined. The recent experience of the European Union is sobering. Early in the 2000s, the EU initiated a cap and trade scheme, but as mentioned above, it issued too many permits and caused their price to fall to zero. Also, the issuing of carbon permits requires a rather elaborate monitoring system to keep track of who emits how much carbon, reconciles the emissions with the permits issued, and punishes violations. Critics of cap and trade correctly foresaw massive violations, corruption, and large scale failures in government oversight of the European carbon trading scheme.

A carbon tax is simpler than a cap and trade scheme. Most carbon fuels are already taxed, and providers of carbon fuels are concentrated and easily identified. As Figure 18.7 shows, by taxing the supplier, the tax is effectively shared by users and producers, prices rise, and quantity consumed falls. A tax can be more easily adjusted in the face of shifts in supply and demand in order to maintain the long-run target prices needed to motivate innovation and conservation. Economists prefer carbon taxes to cap and trade schemes that award permits to current polluters because the former are effectively free sources of revenue for the government. Economists often echo the words of Worldwatch Institute's David Roodman (1999, p. 173):

---

[10] For more on this issue, see Larry Lohman (2006), "Carbon Trading: A Critical Conversation on Climate Change, Privatization, and Power," *Development Dialogue* 48, September.

... tax burdens are already substantial in most countries. So there are plenty of taxes that could be cut with the money raised from environmental taxes. A tax shift would result — not a tax increase. Today, nearly 95 percent of the $7.5 trillion in tax revenues raised each year worldwide comes from levies on payrolls, personal income, corporate profits, capital gains, trade, and built property, all of which are essentially penalties for work and investment. It violates common sense to tax heavily the activities societies generally want while taxing lightly the activities they do not want.

Carbon taxes thus offer an efficient way to close budget deficits or to substitute other taxes that distort and create deadweight losses. The revenue from a carbon tax can also be directly allocated towards conservation projects and innovative new technologies to shift the production functions in the economic and natural spheres.

The case for carbon taxes is made more difficult by the high cost of carbon energy's externalities. Carbon taxes that fully capture the full cost of using carbon fuels will be very costly for energy users. In the case of coal, for example, a study on Appalachian coal mining by Paul Epstein *et al.* (2011) estimated the social costs of coal's likely effects on climate change, public health, mercury contamination, fatalities from the mining, transport, and use of coal, government subsidies, and the lost value of mined land. Public health costs were calculated using the standard value of a statistical life of $7.5 million used by the U.S. Environmental Protection Agency. This value is about the same as Viscusi's (1993) survey that we discussed earlier in this chapter. After putting all the costs together, Epstein *et al.* (2011) conclude:

> ... the best estimate for the total economically quantifiable costs, based on a conservative weighing of many of the study findings, amount to some $345.3 billion, adding close to 17.8¢/kWh of electricity generated from coal... These and the more difficult to quantify externalities are borne by the general public.

The average residential price of electricity in the United States is about 12¢/kWh. A tax on coal that fully reflects the externalities from its use would thus about triple coal's price. Such a price increase would immediately make alternative sources of energy like wind power and solar power and projects to reduce energy usage like better building insulation, public transportation, and prohibitions on further urban sprawl fully viable. It is no wonder the coal industry, the railroads that carry the coal, and other carbon fuel producers and users lobby so hard to discredit scientific studies and to simply hold up new policies. The fact is that carbon-intensive technologies are so thoroughly embedded in modern economies means that an energy paradigm shift away from carbon fuels will impose huge costs on established producers and consumers. It is easier to continue to ignore the externalities.

18.3 Cases of Environmental Policy Failures

The above discussion of carbon taxes and the alternative cap and trade program suggests that measures that raise prices are not easy to design and apply within a political system that must contend with opposing interests and their continual attempts to subvert the policies in their favor. This section examines several attempts to put into effect seemingly clever attempts to improve the relationship between human society and the natural environment without raising prices.

18.3.1 Hoy No Circula: A case of policy failure

Mexico City is well known for its air pollution. The city of over 20 million residents is the industrial center of the Mexican economy. Air pollution was already a problem as long ago as the 1960s. By 1990, over 2 million automobiles and nearly 1 million buses and trucks circulated within the metropolitan area, adding substantially to the city's dirty air that was already polluted by the concentration of Mexico's industry in the same metropolitan area. The air pollution problem of Mexico City was made worse than in similar developing country urban centers by the city's high altitude, which implies thinner air, and the surrounding mountains served to trap dirty air in the central valley of Mexico where the city is located.

Action to clean the air was increasingly called for, and in 1989 the government responded by effectively trying to "ration" air: it devised a plan to reduce the number of cars on the road by prohibiting each vehicle from circulating on one of the five weekdays. Named the **Hoy No Circula** plan, or the "not driving today" plan, it mandated that cars whose license plate numbers started with 0 or 1 could not be driven on Mondays, those whose numbers started with 2 or 3 could not be driven on Tuesdays, and so on. There were no restrictions on the weekend. The rules were easy to enforce because the license plate numbers were easily visible to the police, and fines were set high. What seemed like a simple way to reduce the number of cars and the pollutants they emitted did not work; the number of cars and pollution both increased.

This surprising outcome showed that rationing is often an inefficient device for achieving a quantitative goal. To illustrate this, we set up a simple example that assumes the amount of pollution produced by a car is roughly proportional to the amount of gasoline used. Note that one alternative to rationing is to increase the tax on gasoline and increase the cost of driving directly. Suppose that, as in Figure 18.8, the demand for gasoline is the downward-sloping line D. High on the demand curve are the most important trips for which people would be willing to pay a high price for gasoline. At the lower end are the least important trips, the ones that are not worthwhile making unless the price of gasoline is very low. Thus, if the price of gasoline rises from, say, 2 pesos to 3 pesos per liter because the gasoline tax is raised by 1 peso per liter, then the amount of gasoline demanded, and also the number of kilometers driven, declines from b to a. We assume here that the supply curve is horizontal, which is quite realistic because in Mexico all gasoline is supplied by the state-owned oil company Pemex, and the price of gasoline is an administered policy variable only vaguely related to marginal supply costs. The government would presumably "tax" gasoline by instructing Pemex, the Mexican national oil company, to raise the price by 1 peso per liter. Pollution hopefully also declines by the same percentage as the quantity of gasoline declines, or ab/0b. The total welfare loss to consumers from the price increase is equal to the area L.

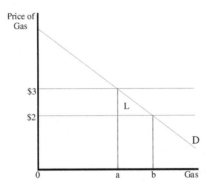

Figure 18.8 A Tax on Gasoline

In Figure 18.9, we illustrate the random one-day-per-week rationing of cars. Since license plate numbers are not in any way correlated with the utility that drivers get from driving, the rationing scheme is as likely to prevent someone at the high end of the demand curve from driving as it is from restricting someone at the lower end of the curve. Just for illustrative purposes, suppose that the drivers whose license plate numbers start with 6 and 7, and cannot drive on Thursday, are in three groups located at three different parts of the demand curve. Together, they consume one-fifth of the pre-rationing quantity of gasoline, so that the three horizontal distances cd, ea, and fb are equal to ab in Figure 18.9.

Note that the total welfare loss is greater for the rationing scheme than it was for the tax scheme by the amount of the shaded areas; the sum of the areas s, t, u, v, w, and x is equal to the area L in Figure 18.8. Compared to taxation, the shaded areas thus represent the extra loss of welfare from rationing due to the fact that the rationing scheme does not distinguish between those who greatly benefit from driving and those that have only marginally positive gains from driving, those who have easy alternatives to driving and those who do not, and those who enjoy driving and those who do not.

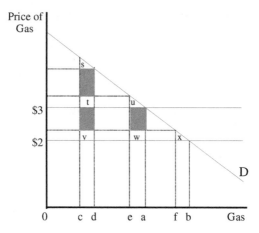

Figure 18.9 Rationing travel by date

The rationing scheme was also viewed as "unfair" because some people appeared to sacrifice more than others.   Some people had good public transportation nearby, others did not. Some people worked four-day workweeks and their rationed day happened to be their day off. A sense of unfairness, of course, makes people less inclined to cooperate and go along with the spirit of the formal rules. Recall the conflict between formal and informal institutions in Chapter 13. As a result of all these factors, a general awareness of the need to combat what clearly were welfare-reducing levels of pollution was not sufficient to prevent individual actions from undermining the plan.

Gunnar Eskeland and Tarhan Feyzioglu (1997) analyzed the *Hoy No Circula* program in detail. They first estimated what gasoline consumption in Mexico City would have been without the *Hoy No Circula* regulations by relating historical gasoline use to past income and then extrapolating that relationship into the future. They found that actual gasoline consumption increased much more rapidly than could be justified by income increases and changes in the price of gasoline. Eskeland and Feyzioglu examined three possible reasons for the surprising positive relationship between the *Hoy No Circula* regulations and gasoline consumption: (1) more weekend driving, (2) reduced congestion, and (3) an increase in the number of cars. While it would seem likely that people would make up for some of the lost automobile weekday trips on the weekend, when driving was unrestricted.   But Eskeland and Feyzioglu found little evidence of increased weekend driving. The congestion effect was positive: the reduction of one-fifth of the legal car population on any given weekday reduced the time that it took to reach a destination on Mexico City's chronically congested highways and streets, and this led people who otherwise would not have driven to drive. Eskeland and Feyzioglu found that the reduction in the number of cars on the road was only 0.4 cars for every car removed from the road by the *Hoy No Circula* regulations. But, if weekend driving did not noticeably increase and the congestion effect only partially offset the direct effect of the regulations on the number of cars on the road, then why did gasoline consumption *rise* after 1989? The answer lay with the third cause: the number of cars registered in Mexico City increased sharply after 1989.

Prior to 1989, because of its relatively high per capita income levels, Mexico City had been a net exporter of used cars to the rest of the country. During the 1980s, an average of 74,000 vehicles were transferred by Mexico City residents to residents of other areas of Mexico each year. But, during the period 1990–1993, Mexico City residents acquired an average 85,000 vehicles per year from the rest of the country. The Hoy No Circula program motivated people to buy inexpensive used cars to drive on the days their regular new automobiles were idled by the rationing scheme. The effect on air pollution was even worse than the numbers of cars suggest because old cars emit much more carbon. Thus, what seemed like a clever measure to reduce the number of cars on the road without imposing a politically unpopular tax failed dismally. This example from Mexico shows that there are probably no easy ways to avoid imposing the costs of environmental damage on those who cause the damage.

A policy of directly raising the cost of driving all cars, as with an increase in the gasoline tax, would in all probability have been more effective in reducing pollution. Certainly, there would have been no shift to less fuel-efficient old cars; in fact, people probably would have accelerated purchases of fuel-efficient, low-polluting new cars.

18.3.2 Clean coal technology

It is widely accepted that technological change could possibly overcome the negative effects of energy usage. This explains why special interests have used the appeal of technology to actually prevent fundamental changes on environmental policies. For example, the coal industry and the electric power industry that is the major user of coal in its power plants have together mounted a global public relations campaign to convince the public that there are new technologies that can eliminate the devastating GHG emissions of coal-fired electric power plants. The new technology touted by the coal industry is technically referred to as **carbon capture and storage**. The technology essentially involves isolating carbon dioxide before it is emitted into the atmosphere, compressing it, and pumping it deep underground where it is supposed to remain forever. So far, there have only been a few relatively small projects to capture and store carbon, and there is no consensus on the viability of the process.

Coal is currently the dirtiest of all fossil fuels. In the countries responsible for most of the world's carbon emissions, such as Australia, China, India, and the United States, coal accounts for over half of the electric generating capacity. China continues to build new coal plants. In many countries, there is strong public opposition to building new coal-fired power plants. The purpose of the coal industry's propaganda campaign is to counter the scientific evidence and the efforts by environmental groups to organize support for closing existing coal-fired power plants and prevent the construction of new coal-fired plants. The power industry's publicity campaign openly admits that the new technologies are "not yet ready," but it suggests that they will soon be ready to install in existing and new coal-fired power plants. The electric power industry is effectively arguing that there is no reason to stop building coal-fired power plants because technology will soon be available to make them carbon neutral.

Prospects for carbon capture are, in fact, not very good, and even under best of possible outcomes the process introduces new uncertainties. Early in 2008, the U.S. government stopped funding the construction of a test project for a large coal-fired test plant in Illinois because, apparently, costs were exceeding initial estimates by a large margin. In 2009, the project was restarted as President Obama, who was a Senator from Illinois before becoming President, had touted clean coal during his presidential campaign. BP, the British oil company, recently abandoned plans for a carbon storage project in Australia when it encountered problems containing carbon permanently underground. Carbon dioxide is a deadly gas, and underground storage is complicated by the natural occurrence of earthquakes and the normal shifting of soils and rock formations. The sudden release of large amounts of carbon dioxide could kill huge numbers of people if the gas spread through populated areas.

In late 2008, the Swedish energy company Vattenfall began operating a coal-fired electric power plant in eastern Germany that promised zero carbon emissions by means of carbon capture.[11] This first carbon-free coal plant is small in scale, however, providing only enough power for about 25,000 homes in eastern Germany.

There are several other large-scale carbon storage projects underway, one of which is the Sleipner carbon injection project that captures carbon emissions from the production of natural gas in the North Atlantic off the coast of Norway. Sleipner is run by the Norwegian state-owned company StatoilHydro, and consists of returning carbon back into the massive Utsira rock formation under the ocean near to where Statoil is currently pumping up oil and natural gas. On their web site, Statoil claims there has been no leakage since the project went on stream in 1996. Several scientists have questioned that statement, however. Peter Haugan of the Institute of Geophysics at the nearby University of Bergen, Norway, argues that: "It's not possible to prove that all injected CO_2 is still

---

[11] Chris Bryant (2008), "Vattenfall Fires Up CO2-Free Power Station," *Financial Times*, September 10.

there."[12] More disturbingly, counter to earlier predictions that the pressurized carbon would seep upward through the rock formation at a rate of at most 1 meter per year, recent tests have shown that the gas has moved up at a rate of 10 meters per year, and much of the carbon is now lodged near the top rather than the bottom of the Utsira formation. At another injection project on the Utsira formation, workmen in 2008 noticed oily water on the surface. The injection was stopped, and further tests found that some undisclosed amount of oil and gas had escaped through an ocean floor crater.

Carbon capture and storage has also been found to take substantial extra energy to pressurize the sequestered carbon and to inject it into the ground, even when reliable underground storage areas can be found. Second, carbon storage requires the transport of carbon from where it is produced to storage areas. The claim that the Utsira formation under the North Atlantic could store all of Europe's carbon emissions for hundreds of years implies a vast system of pipelines to move the carbon to the undersea storage areas. These costs effectively eliminate coal's cost advantage over most other alternative energy sources. According to Statoil, the Sleipner carbon capture and storage project does not make economic sense even with the very high carbon tax currently applied by the Norwegian government.[13] A small project in West Virginia that sequesters a small percentage, less than 2 percent in the initial phase, of a power plant's carbon emissions nearly doubles the price of electricity produced.[14] In sum, given the dangers and the costs of carbon capture and storage, this technology remains highly speculative. Policies that permit the construction of coal-fired electric generation plants are, therefore, equally speculative.

18.3.3 Carbon offsets

The discussion above comparing carbon trading versus carbon taxes was straightforward, and the difference between the two options were clear. In principle, carbon emissions can be reduced to 350ppm either way, provided policymakers apply the appropriate tax or set the appropriate number of permits. But the choice between permits and taxes has been muddied by another scheme introduced into the Kyoto Protocol at the insistence of the United States and several other developed countires: **carbon offsets**.

Offsets are credits that current carbon emitters pay to new carbon-reducing projects to "offset" their emissions. For example, suppose a coal-fired power plant in the United Kingdom emits more carbon than it is permitted to emit under a cap and trade system. As is the practice in Europe, the U.K. power plant was probably given a certain number of permits for free, but let's suppose that

---

[12] Quoted in Greenpeace International (2009), "Reality Check on Carbon Storage," Policy paper posted on www.greenpeace.org.

[13] *The Economist* (2009), "Trouble in Store," March 5, 2009.

[14] David Biello (2009).

there were not enough free permits to cover this year's emissions. The plant could reduce its emissions by installing new equipment, using alternative fuels, or simply cutting back on electricity production. Or, it could buy offsets from some completely unrelated industrial, agricultural, or mining conservation project elsewhere in the world that is certified as a carbon-reducing project. Such a project could be a new plantation of trees in Indonesia, a new scrubber on a powerplant in India, or, as reported in a recent investigative article, a project in Brazil that "planned to collect fruit and vegetable waste from grocery stores and street markets and compost that waste into organic fertilizer, which could then be sold to farms." Apparently this latter project avoids creating climate-changing methane gasses normally produced with composting by using microorganisms to break down the waste. The investor in this project sold credits equal to the expected reduction in the carbon-equivalent value of its expected methane reductions relative to traditional composting methods.[15] Effectively, carbon offsets serve as an incentive to discourage carbon emissions and encourage projects that reduce emissions. The difficulty is creating an institutional structure that identifies emitters and projects that reduce carbon in the atmosphere and transfers the funds from one group to the other.

Offset projects such as the one in Brazil are overseen by the United Nations. The **Kyoto Protocol**, which was negotiated under the auspices of the United Nations, authorized the program called the **Clean Development Mechanism (CDM)**.[16] The system is described as follows by the investigative reporter Mark Shapiro (2010, p. 32):

> Never before has the United Nations presided over the issuing of securities, and carbon offsets are unlike any securities ever created: because such gases emerge not just from factories and automobiles but from felled trees, animal and agricultural waste, and innumerable other sources from every corner of the earth, the supply of promises to reduce greenhouse-gas emissions is potentially infinite. And unlike traditional commodities, which sometimes during the course of their market exchange must be delivered to someone in physical form, the carbon market is based on the lack of delivery of an invisible substance to no one. In an attempt to compensate for this intangibility, the United Nations has certified twenty-six firms worldwide to "validate" the promises of emissions reducers and then to "verify," often years later, that those reductions actually occurred.

The developer of the Brazilian composting project was the Irish carbon investment firm *EcoSecurities*, and it contracted with the Swiss firm *SGS Group* to validate the project. SGS has been in business for over 100 years conducting product inspections, such as determining the moisture level in a shipment of

---

[15] Mark Shapiro (2010), "Conning the Climate," *Harper's Magazine*, February, p. 32.
[16] It was actually the United States that insisted on a cap and trade system with offsets at Kyoto; after getting the measures into the agreement, the U.S. refused to ratify the protocol and left it up to everyone else to implement the idea.

barley or confirming the absence of toxic chemicals in children's clothing. Now it is also one of only two major firms validating carbon credit schemes.

The Rio de Janeiro office of SGS determined that the composting project would result in 67,000 tons of carbon not being emitted into the atmosphere, which at the going price of $22 per ton, created credits worth about $1.5 million that EcoSecurities could sell to carbon emitters like the U.K. coal-fired power plant. SGS reached its conclusions by using technical formulas for carbon emissions reductions that may not have been relevant for the particular project being analyzed, and it also assumed that the project would not have been carried out without the U.K power plant's purchase the carbon credits of $1.5 million.

There are serious doubts about how accurate validators' estimates are and whether the projected emissions reductions actually materialize. Follow-up studies by numerous organizations and researchers suggest that overestimation of carbon reductions are the norm. Lambert Schneider (2007) and the U.N.'s Intergovernmental Panel on Climate Change (2007) found that projects often do not materialize, and many more are canceled before their projected future carbon reductions are all carried out. Schneider also found that as many as 40 percent of the projects would have been undertaken without the subsidies derived from selling offsets; hence, the offsets did not reduce carbon emissions. In late 2009, the country of Papua New Guinea sacked its climate change minister for validating as many as $100 million offsets for non-existent projects. Incredibly, under the rules of the Kyoto Protocol, offsets remain valid even if projects fail to materialize or turn out to be much less beneficial than projected. Mark Shapiro (2010) reports that negotiators at Kyoto did appreciate the uncertainties of carbon offsets, but they feared that doubts about the true value of offsets would effectively kill the prospects for an offset market. Therefore, they eliminated future doubts by letting purchasers of the credits use them for up to 21 years even, according to one World Wildlife Federation official, "when nothing in effect is being done to reduce emissions."[17]

The environmental group Rising Tide North America (2009) wrote: "Perversely, factories in India and China have sold offset credits for implementing modest clean ups required by law throughout the Global North, and then have used their "emissions reduction" revenue to expand the same, highly-polluting industries."[18] Fiona Harvey (2007) of the *Financial Times* reported on several such outcomes. For example, some €4.6 billion of carbon credits were sold for the installation of less than €100 million in capital expenditures at chemical plants in India and other developing economies to

---

[17] Mark Shapiro (2010), "Conning the Climate," *Harper's Magazine*, February, p. 38.

[18] Rising Tide North America (2009), "Hoodwinked in the Hothouse; False Solutions to Climate Change," pamphlet downloaded from www.risingtide.org, November.

reduce the greenhouse gas known as HFC-23.[19] The carbon credits, therefore, were huge windfalls for these industries, and may have contributed to the expansion of these industries in developing countries rather than in developed countries where the HFC-23 gas is already regulated.

Despite the shortcomings of the U.N.'s Clean Development Mechanism, the program is being expanded. In 2010, the U.N. began accepting carbon capture technologies, which were described above as unproven and of questionable validity, as a justification for carbon credits, thus making such projects more profitable for their developers while potentially providing the world with more unrealized carbon reductions. The corruption of good ideas for financial gain is both discouraging and destructive. Should environmentalists oppose these so-called "market mechanisms" to reduce carbon emissions in favor of equally corruptible direct government regulation?

18.3.4 Species losses and international policy

In March of 2010, negotiators from 120 countries came together in Doha, Qatar under the auspices of the Convention on International Trade in Endangered Species of Wildlife, Fauna, and Flora (CITES). CITES is a United Nations body, and it is the only body currently authorized to ban trade in endangered animals and plants. It was expected that the conference would approve bans on trade in several high-profile pending extinctions, such as the bluefin tuna, elephants, polar bears, and hammerhead sharks. But when it came time to vote, none of these cases were approved for greater protection.

Monaco had introduced a motion to ban the international trade of the Atlantic bluefin tuna, which is dangerously close to extinction. Once an unwanted by-product from cod fishing sold to the cat food industry, bluefin tuna is today in high demand as sushi restaurants have become popular around the world. The bluefin sushi market is worth billions of dollars in Japan, and one exceptionally coveted 262 kilogram fish recently sold for $175,000 in Tokyo's Tsukiji fish market. Lobbying at Doha was intense, and the fishing and restaurant lobbies were successful in preventing any ban on bluefin tuna trade. Monaco's motion was rejected 68 to 20, despite evidence that the Atlantic bluefin tuna is close to extinction. The proponents of a trade ban to let bluefin tuna stocks recover were no match for the well-funded lobbyists from Japan, Canada, and other fishing nations that simply wanted to continue fishing and supplying the growing demand for sushi. The renowned marine biologist Sylvia Earle described the pending extinction as follows:

---

[19] Fiona Harvey (2007), "Billions Lost in Kyoto Carbon Trade Loophole," *Financial Times*, February 8; See also Fiona Harvey and Stephen Fidler (2007), "Industry Caught in Carbon 'Smokescreen' *Financial Times*, April 25.

We have 10 years, no more, it is happening now in our time. If we do nothing and continue the way we are, it will be all over... When the world is down to the last tuna, someone will be willing to pay a million dollars to eat it.[20]

Industries which only consider their own interests in the economic sphere still seemed to be able to win the day at the 2010 CITES meeting. The power of special interests will have to be overcome if the rapid rate of species depletion is to be slowed or reversed. Conservation is not costless, and somehow agreement will have to be reached on who is to bear the costs of restricting human exploitation of the ecosystem.

18.3.5 The Jevons effect

Conservation and technological change in the natural sphere is made more difficult by the **Jevons effect** of technological change. As pointed out in 1865 by W. Stanley Jevons, improvements in the efficiency with which exhaustible resources are used tend to lead to their increased use, not decreased use. Recall from Chapter 6 that the depletion of exhaustible resources can only be avoided if technological change lowers the physical consumption of the resources. But, over the past century, we have seen technology raise both the efficiency with which humans transform resources into final goods and the volumes of those resources they put into the productive processes of the economy. The expanded use of energy resources like coal and oil, as well as the greater cultivation of land and exploitation of minerals, all stimulated by very substantial technological breakthroughs in how to apply those resources, have enabled today's high levels of material consumption. But we clearly have not slowed the physical use of natural resources.

Jevons' suggestion in 1865 that British industry would soon deplete the supply of coal despite the greater efficiency with which the coal was used in production has been expanded into a more complete hypothesis about how technological improvements increase the use of exhaustible energy resources by Daniel Khazzoom (1980), L. Brookes (1990), and Harry Saunders (1992): Energy efficiency gains result in increases in energy use. Saunders called this hypothesis, that improvements in energy efficiency end up increasing energy consumption the **Khazzoom-Brookes postulate**. The main mechanism that generates this paradoxical outcome is economic growth. Efficiency gains make energy less expensive and increase its usefulness, and this stimulates economic growth, which, in turn, increases demand for energy further. As a result, energy use today is much higher than it was in the past, and the accompanying carbon emissions are thus also higher. In its "International Energy Outlook 2010," the U.S. Department of Energy predicts energy usage to rise further as large developing

---

[20] Quoted in Nick Clark (2010), "Little Celebration as CITES Ends," Aljazeera.net, March 26.

economies like Brazil, China, and India grow.[21]   Energy usage from 2010 through 2035 is predicted to grow by 1.4 percent per year, or by almost exactly 50 percent in 25 years.

A possible policy response to the prediction that economic growth will outrun the technological efficiency of energy and increase the overall use of energy resources is to institute measures that raise energy prices. Taxes that raise the market price of resources are potentially an efficient approach in this case. By forcing markets to reflect the full cost of externalities and the approaching scarcity of energy resources, governments can thwart the Jevons effect and invalidate the Khazzoom-Brookes postulate.

18.3.6 Subsidies for research versus energy taxes

Critics of policies for taxing or explicitly restricting environmentally damaging economic and social activities often suggest that, instead of raising producers' and consumers' costs with taxes and regulations, government should directly promote technological change. This approach seems reasonable and perfectly in line with conclusions reached earlier in this chapter as well as in Chapters 6, 8, and 11 with the two-dimensional Solow model. Unfortunately, as the policymakers in Mexico City discovered, policies that avoid directly raising costs are unlikely to be effective in stopping environmental degradation.

There are effectively two separate issues that policymakers must address when they design policies to promote new environmentally-friendly technologies that shift the production function up in the natural sphere. First, markets for new knowledge are imperfect and spillovers to others make it difficult for innovators to capture the full benefits of their innovations. Secondly, market economies are not set up to properly value innovations that shift up the production function in the natural sphere. It is these dual market failures, the failure to provide incentives to innovators and the failure to accurately value environmental damage, that lead David Popp (2004) to examine how subsidies to R&D activities can effectively move society to a sustainable growth path. He concludes that without specific carbon taxes or direct regulations that internalize environmental costs, R&D subsidies to compensate for knowledge spillovers will not be effective in shifting up the natural sphere's production function. This is not to say that subsidies are not effective in raising R&D levels, but the new technologies will only be applied if the subsidies are accompanied by a carbon tax or other mechanisms that fully and accurately internalize environmental externalities and thus make business as usual more costly. R&D subsidies help to overcome knowledge market failures, but it takes direct measures to motivate the actual application of the new

---

[21] U.S. Department of Energy (2010), "International Energy Outlook 2010 — Highlights," Report DOE/EIA-0484(2010), May 25.

technologies in the natural sphere. Paying engineers to design a better wind turbine for generating electricity will not lead to projects that actually use the new technology. New projects exploiting the new technology will only occur if the price of electricity reflects the true costs to society and traditional generation is made more costly.

Hence, politically less controversial subsidies for developing alternative energy technologies cannot substitute for the politically divisive direct carbon taxes that raise prices for producers and consumers. One could be tempted to conclude that calls for subsidies and other direct government support for research are actually efforts by vested interests to actually avoid the real changes necessary to address climate change or species depletions. Working on nuclear technologies or high-speed rail technologies does not directly impact the coal industry or the airline industry. Only a carbon tax on coal plants and airline fuel consumption will shift electricity users to other sources or air passengers to trains.

18.4 What Technologies Do We Need for Sustainability?

This chapter has made a case for actively dealing with environmental problems that threaten human survival. The previous section further explained that such policies must set incentives and establish mandates that directly lead to the application of new technologies that make human activity sustainable in all spheres of human existence. This section discusses how such new technologies are likely to change life for most humans and how economists need to change their understanding of what economic development means.

Deciding to act is only a first step. Actually putting in place policies that will reverse the rise in carbon emissions or preserve the ecosystem is a very difficult task for the fragmented world of independent countries and diverse interests. Environmental policies must make the costs that were being ignored explicit, and this means the policies will impose new burdens on people, governments, and firms. There will thus always be people, groups, and business firms who oppose the environmental policies. Even if a consensus for action can be built, there will inevitably be arguments over how the burden should be shared. In sum, it will be difficult to undertake the policies needed to stop global warming, resource depletion, and destruction of the ecosystem. This section adds another difficulty: the technological changes needed to make life sustainable imply radical shifts in human lifestyles and humanity's economic and social systems.

18.4.1 Sustainability in all three spheres and economic interests

Holistically, it is difficult to see how anyone will gain from permitting the natural sphere to deteriorate to where is causes the collapse of human society.

Even the special interests who lobby to be permitted to continue their damaging economic activities will eventually suffer losses. For example, Sushi restaurants will suffer when the Atlantic bluefin tuna go extinct. Therefore, all interests should welcome measures to protect the long-run sustainability of human society. Surely measures will be taken before Bluefin tuna become extinct, won't they?

Recall the case of the American buffalo, however. The buffalo were hunted on the open plains by individual hunters who were free to shoot as many as they could, and within ten years the population of several million buffalos was reduced to a few hundred. This example shows that in the absence of the collective establishment and enforcement of institutions, individual people ignore the holistic consequences of their actions. Often, they simply do not understand the full consequences of their actions. Sometimes they understand, but they have no available governance structure through which to translate their concerns into a just collective response. Think of the lawlessness of the open plains of the United States right after the Native Americans had been forced off their land and into reservations. Whose buffalo were the individual hunters shooting? If one of them decided to stop shooting, would things have changed?

The recent 2007–2009 global economic crisis provides a different example of how humanity struggles to deal with systemic problems that require holistic analysis and collective responses by diverse groups. The economic crisis made it clear that the international financial system is unstable and that a few private banks in one country can cause a global economic recession. In this case, we have to ask why those bankers did not realize that their careless lending and fraudulent creation of complex financial derivatives endangered the well-being of the entire world's population. And for those who did, why did they not care?

The discussion of human psychology and sociology in Chapter 3 described why human society creates cultures that people use to guide them through the incomprehensible complexity of human existence. These cultures, which Pierre Bourdieu referred to as subjective habitus and doxa, enable people to survive in their particular field. These cultures and our automatic behavioral tendencies elevate the status quo over alternative scenarios, and this makes it difficult for humans to deal with complexities they only partially understand. The situation is even more difficult when collective action is required. So bankers keep making bad loans, hunters keep shooting buffalos, and political leaders avoid policy shifts needed for humanity's long-run survival.

Humanity faces many difficult problems. We have discussed many in this textbook: growing economic inequality and poverty (discussed in Chapter 17), global warming (Chapter 6), biodiversity loss (Chapter 6), peak oil (this chapter), financial instability (Chapters 11 and 15), the perverse incentives of modern corporations (Chapter 15), overpopulation (Chapter 9), growing natural resource shortages (Chapters 6 and 18), and the social conflicts related to resource shortages and environmental deterioration (Chapters 16 and 18). How do we solve these systemic and global problems if we cannot muster a collective response?

The British astronomer Martin Rees (2003) unhesitatingly claims that when you add the spread of nuclear and biological technologies to the many unsustainable trends such as those listed above, the pending conflicts suggest a mathematical probability that humans will survive until the end of this century of only about 50 percent. James Lovelock, whose Gaia hypothesis we discussed back in Chapter 1, paints an equally discouraging future for humanity. Recall that Lovelock's Gaia (Mother Earth) hypothesis states that the planet Earth functions as a large homeostatic organism that actively adjusts its internal natural conditions in order to survive in the universe. Lovelock (2006) writes that the earth has a serious fever that will, within the next 100 years, drastically change human civilization: "We are responsible and will suffer the consequences: as the century progresses, the temperature will rise 8 degrees centigrade in temperate regions and 5 degrees in the tropics." Lovelock also questions humanity's ability to undo the damage it has done:

> By failing to see that the Earth regulates its climate and composition, we have blundered into trying to do it ourselves, acting as if we were in charge. By doing this, we condemn ourselves to the worst form of slavery. If we choose to be the stewards of the Earth, then we are responsible for keeping the atmosphere, the ocean and the land surface right for life. A task we would soon find impossible-and something before we treated Gaia so badly, she had freely done for us.[22]

Lovelock makes a very important point when he states humanity cannot control the earth's environment. Indeed, humanity seems to have developed an overly optimistic belief in its ability to devise new technologies to deal with whatever barriers to further growth that may arise.

Humanity has reached the stage of economic development where it can destroy critical elements of the natural environment, and it has even set off several uncontrollable processes that threaten humanity's very existence. Despite having achieved such prominence in nature, humanity clearly does not have enough understanding or technology to completely control its existence. Humanity seems to have blundered into an ecological catastrophe: powerful enough to do damage, but clueless on how to fix the damage done.

Recall that we concluded section 1.4.4 in Chapter 1 by describing the scientific method as an efficient process for advancing knowledge. We also noted, however that science has not given us quick answers to everything. Knowledge creation is a costly activity that is constrained by society's limited resources. We wrote that a "scientist modestly accepts that science is a work in progress, and it always will be." Scientists thus have to accept that knowledge is incomplete. More important, humanity has to understand that science can

---

[22] James E. Lovelock (2006).

sometimes only provide partial answers to some of society's most serious problems. Decisions have to be made in various states of uncertainty.

In reference to the current state of nature and humanity's large footprint on Earth, we know that our population growth, economic growth, and technological change are doing potentially irreversible damage to the natural sphere that we depend on for our existence. This path is clearly not sustainable, yet we are not sure what alternative path we should follow. In fact, humanity seems to be unwilling to even consider the option of slowing down. When the 2007–2009 financial crisis slowed economic growth, every political leader spoke only of restoring economic growth. "Learned ignorance" suggests that humanity should stop and ask for directions before continuing on. The **precautionary principle** is called for. We should avoid unknown paths that we have reason to believe may be dangerous until we are better prepared to protect ourselves from the suspected dangers.

This is not to suggest that humanity's situation is hopeless. Humanity in fact has enough understanding of its three spheres of existence to not only greatly improve its chances of survival but to even achieve further economic development that enhances human happiness. James Lovelock (2006) suggests a plausible path forward:

> We should be the heart and mind of the Earth, not its malady. So let us be brave and cease thinking of human needs and rights alone, and see that we have harmed the living Earth and need to make our peace with Gaia. We must do it while we are still strong enough to negotiate, and not the broken rabble led by brutal war lords. Most of all, we should remember that we are a part of it, and it indeed is our home.

Lovelock effectively calls for humanity to recognize that they must coexist with nature. Humanity cannot conquer nature as if it were just another foreign colony. The Earth will outlast humanity. It is humanity that is endangered. The planet has already issued many warnings to the rowdy group of human tenants, but as Hervé Kempf (2007) reminds us, the rowdiest (richest) are too absorbed in their drunken consumption to hear the warnings.

18.4.2 The rights of nature

Even though many people in the countries where technology has advanced the most do not appear to understand how their technology is changing humanity's relationship with the natural sphere, people in poor countries often do understand. People in poor countries are much more dependent on nature for their survival. Thus, when people in poor countries obtain a greater voice under more democratic institutions, they tend to opt for a more sustainable relationship with nature. In 2008, Ecuador included an explicit recognition of rights of the Earth in a new constitution. Specifically, the Ecuadorian Constitution gives

Mother Nature "the right to exist, persist, maintain and regenerate its vital cycles, structure, functions and its processes in evolution."

Another Andean country, Bolivia, in 2010 passed a comprehensive law declaring the Rights of Mother Earth (Ley de Derechos de la Madre Tierra). Article 3 of this law defines the meaning of Mother Earth:

> Mother Earth is a living dynamic organism that is an indivisible community of all life systems and humanity, interrelated, interdependent and complementary, who share a common destiny.[23]

Note that this definition recognizes the holistic nature of human existence within the economic, social, and natural spheres. The basic principles explicitly stated in the Ley de Derechos de la Madre Tierra are:

1. Harmony between the dynamic economic and social processes of humanity and the evolving natural processes of nature.
2. Precedence of the interests of collective society over individual rights.
3. Sustenance of the ecosystem.
4. Peace with nature and the obligation to preserve that peace for future generations of humans.
5. Restrictions on the commercialization and privatization of nature.
6. Cultural integration of nature into all aspects of Bolivian society through dialogue, learning, and respect.

The law explicitly defines Mother Earth's rights to:

1. Life and regeneration.
2. Biodiversity
3. Clean water
4. Clean air
5. Stability and balance
6. Restoration and regeneration
7. Existence free of human contamination

The law also gives Nature legal status, defended by a new cabinet level department to actively represent Nature. It further defines the collective responsibilities of the Bolivian people and their government towards Mother Nature.

It will be interesting to observe how this law changes the economic development of Bolivia, a country constrained by poverty and extremely unequal distribution of wealth. Sheer human desperation will tempt people and the government to violate nature the way humans have always done.

---

[23] Translation from Spanish by your author.

Encouragingly, when Bolivians were able to gain a voice in their democratic system, the overwhelming majority opted for coexistence rather than exploitation by voting for passage of the *Ley de Derechos de la Madre Tierra*. This example is important as an example for other countries because Bolivia by itself cannot change humanity's relationship with nature. Sustainable economic development requires many more laws preserving the rights of nature.

18.4.3 Changing the culture of consumption

Ecuador and Bolivia' successes notwithstanding, few countries appear willing to change their relationship with nature. This lack of will reflects the fear that the rights of Mother Nature translate into a reduction in humanity's consumption of Earth's resources. It seems impossible to cut consumption with the world's population heading towards 10 billion humans by the end of the twenty-first century. Also, we still have the legitimate goal of providing all humans with living standards that satisfy basic needs; recall that happiness improves with income up to about U.S.$10,000, after which it flattens out.

Perhaps technology will improve the efficiency with which humanity uses Earth's resources and it will be possible to give the expected additional three million people consumption levels equal to what better-off European and North American humans now enjoy without increasing the physical exploitation of Earth. But remember that current levels of production are already doing irreversible damage to the ecosystem. We need to reduce the consumption of the services of nature before the ecosystem collapses. The natural sphere can only be preserved with a reduction in material production in the economic sphere. Therefore, humanity must find a way to enjoy life with levels of material consumption that are a small fraction of what people now consume. Lifestyle changes are part of the paradigm shift to sustainability.

There have been calls for reductions in human consumption in the past. For example, Paul Ehrlich (1968) urged developed economies to "de-develop" so that the developing economies of the world could "semi-develop." Ehrlich's call has been mocked by many writers who saw the world continuing to raise consumption for increasing numbers of people. Still, Ehrlich was not so far off in his prediction that human economic development would become unsustainable; estimates of historical resource consumptions by Mathis Wackernagel *et al.* (2002) suggest that humanity's exploitation of Earth's renewable natural resources surpassed 100 percent of capacity during the 1980s, less than twenty years after Ehrlich wrote. The exploitation reached 120 percent of the earth's sustainable capacity in 1999.

Many authors today call for an end to the quest for continued economic growth. Peter Victor (2008), Lester Brown (2009), Valerie Fournier (2008), among others, argue that lifestyles must accommodate a low-consumption culture. As you already know from reading Chapter 1, a future of modest economic growth was forecast back in 1930 by John Maynard Keynes. Keynes is best known for his macroeconomic model that helped to design policies for avoiding economic depressions, but he often took a much longer perspective in his writing. In his famous essay, Keynes (1930) contemplated how humans would deal with an advanced society without economic growth:[24]

> Thus we have been expressly evolved by nature — with all our impulses and deepest instincts — for the purpose of solving the economic problem. If the economic problem is solved, mankind will be deprived of its traditional purpose.
>
> Will this be a benefit? If one believes at all in the real values of life, the prospect at least opens up the possibility of benefit. Yet I think with dread of the readjustments of the habits and instincts of the ordinary man, bred into him for countless generations, which he may be asked to discard within a few decades.
>
> Thus for the first time since his creation man will be faced with his real, his permanent problem — how to use his freedom from pressing economic cares, how to occupy the leisure, which science and compound interest will have won for him, to live wisely and agreeably and well.

Keynes' fear that people would have trouble making "readjustments of habits and instincts" was well founded. Capitalist societies continue to actively design policies to generate output growth despite unprecedented levels of material wealth. His positive visions have not come to pass. In 1930, the first year of the Great Depression, Keynes (1930) showed a remarkable optimism:

> I feel sure that with a little more experience we shall use the new-found bounty of nature quite differently from the way in which the rich use it to-day, and will map out for ourselves a plan of life quite otherwise than theirs. For many ages to come the old Adam will be so strong in us that everybody will need to do some work if he is to be contented. We shall do more things for ourselves than is usual with the rich today, only too glad to have small duties and tasks and routines. But beyond this, we shall endeavor to spread the bread thin on the butter — to make what work there is still to be done to be as widely shared as possible. Three-hour shifts or a fifteen-hour week may put off the problem for a great while. For three hours a day is quite enough to satisfy the old Adam in most of us!

While there are some groups calling for shorter workweeks, politicians in almost every country of the world, less developed and developed, still talk about increasing GDP. Amazingly, in 2011 one of the candidates seeking the Socialist Party's nomination to run for President in France was criticized by the other socialist candidates for having been part of a previous government that reduced the legal French workweek from 40 to 35 hours. The idea of a fifteen hour workweek is not embraced by even the most radical groups on the fringe of current social thought in 2011.[25]

---

[24] Keynes' original essay and related essays are in Lorenzo Pecchi and Gustavo Piga, eds. (2008).

[25] The New Economics Foundation, a radical British think tank, calls for a 21-hour workweek. See *www.neweconomics.org*.

18.4.4 How to change the culture of growth

The environmental economist Jeroen van den Bergh (2010) examines the practical effects of a range of policies to reduce the use of Earth's resources. He begins by stating that "GDP represents the largest information failure in the world." The focus on GDP causes us to not only judge economic performance using a measure that does not represent economic well-being, but because it does not count many of nature's services, GDP obscures the consequences of economic activity on the natural sphere. Van den Bergh also warns against focusing on the growth of output when designing policies for sustainable development. No matter how well it is measured, simply reducing any one type of output will simply cause resource use to expand elsewhere. Recall the response of Mexican drivers to rationing. Emphasis on working hours is more useful because it addresses resource use across the board. Also, van den Bergh reinforces Popp's (2002, 2004) point that sustainability requires policies to directly reduce ecologically harmful human activities. He calls for carbon taxes and other taxes to cover environmental externalities, as well as bans on commercial advertising that promote the consumption of status goods that do nothing for long-term well-being.

Politically, the sheer scope of the economic and social changes needed to convert human society from a high-resource using system to a sustainable low-resource using system is daunting. There is much uncertainty about who will gain and lose from the paradigm shift, and those with wealth are lobbying very hard to make sure the shift benefits them. This leads the feminist economist Patricia Perkins (2010) to remind her fellow economists that women have in many ways been treated as free resources, not unlike the natural environment. For example, women work for free outside the economic system more often than men. Policies for achieving sustainability must, therefore, address all potential misallocations, not only the exploitation of natural resources. Reducing the exploitation of nature's services could result in greater exploitation of women, who were already marginalized in the labor market. This will certainly happen if the economy has trouble reducing overall working hours in the face of higher resource costs.

Jeroen van den Bergh (2010) also argues that a sustainable global economy, which may or may not include actual growth in economic output, is only possible with an international commitment.

> Global environmental problems cannot be tackled by voluntary action and grassroots initiatives. An effective international agreement... is critical for any effective national environmental policies and strategies. For only then countries can implement safe climate policies without harming their competitive position, which will contribute to the social-political acceptability of such policies in these countries.... The main and unresolved problem is of course how to get democratic-political support for an effective international climate agreement.

Opposition to environmental policies is strong, as we should expect given that meaningful policies clash with well-established commercial interests. Business interests are already actively working to preserve their privileges, either by convincing people the environmental issues are not important or, if the costs must be borne, pushing those costs onto others. Recall the quote from F. Scott Fitzgerald in his classic novel *The Great Gatsby*, posted at the start of the chapter:

> They were careless people... they smashed up things and creatures and then retreated back into their money or their vast carelessness, or whatever it was that kept them together, and let other people clean up the mess they had made...

Those in power do not recognize the damage they do, nor do they much care even when they suspect they may have caused a problem.

The world's wealthy countries are unlikely to surrender their privileges voluntarily. Recall also how in 2009, the presidents of the world's two largest carbon emitters, The United States and China, combined to prevent a meaningful climate agreement to succeed the earlier Kyoto Agreement. The so-called emerging economies like China and Brazil are still quite aware of their past colonial status, and they are not inclined to agree to new rules that internalize all environmental costs. After all, why can't they too exploit nature just like the rich countries did and continue to do?

It is encouraging to see that voters in poor democratic countries like Bolivia and Ecuador have rejected this short-sighted approach to the natural sphere. Hopefully, their approach serves as the critical mass of scientific dissent that triggers the paradigm shift that preserves humanity's place on Earth.

Key Terms and Concepts

Biodiversity
Cap and trade
Carbon capture and storage
Carbon offsets
Carbon tax
Clean Development Mechanism (CDM)
Convention on Biological Diversity
Fracking
GHG tax
Green revolution
Hoy No Circula
Jevons effect
Khazzoom-Brookes postulate

Kyoto Protocol
Limits on GHGs
Monoculture
Non-renewable natural resources
Peak extraction
Precautionary principle
Prohibitions
Redundancy in nature
Renewable natural resources
Risk
Self-regulation
Uncertainty
Value of life

Questions and Problems

1. Why, despite very clear and specific scientific evidence of their severity, is there such weak support for policies to address environmental problems like global warming and biodiversity? Explain.
2. Does *uncertainty* strengthen or weaken the case of active environmental policies? Explain.
3. People spend much higher rates to insure their homes and cars. Yet, so far, people seem reluctant to spend such a small premium to insure the future of humanity. Why is that?
4. Explain Martin Weitzman's argument that uncertainty should make us more cautious than we would be in dealing with conventional risk. (Hint: Discuss the difference between risk and uncertainty, and show how uncertainty affects the traditional distribution of potential outcomes.)
5. Review the discussion of the costs of stopping global warming, and supplement the evidence presented in this chapter with outside research. Is it worth incurring the estimated costs? Explain your reasoning.
6. Explain the cap and trade scheme to limit carbon emissions. (Hint: Use diagrams such as Figures 18.6 and 18.7 to illustrate your explanation.)
7. This chapter presents some cases of how indirect schemes to cut carbon emissions can fail to accomplish their goals. What are the common threads across the policy failures? How could the failures have been prevented.
8. Why are many environmental groups opposed to cap and trade schemes combined with offsets? (Hint: Explain the market rationale behind the scheme, and then explain where the market-based scheme breaks down.)
9. Explain the Jevons effect. How is the Khazzoom-Brookes postulate related to the Jevons effect?
10. Section 18.1.4 ends with the following question: Can the wealthy United States, which produced the greatest share of the GHGs in the atmosphere and stimulated mass consumption around the world, simply ignore the consequences of its past actions and refuse to contribute to the costs of mitigating global warming while it continues to promote its resource-using lifestyle around the world? Write an essay answering this question.
11. Given that policies to reduce carbon emissions are costly, who should pay those costs? Should current emitters bear the full cost? Should the costs be spread among the users of the products whose production generated the emissions? Should the entire society share in the costs? Explain your answer.
12. Was the green revolution a true technological revolution or just more intensive use of underpriced exhaustible resources for short-term gains? Discuss.
13. The corruption of good ideas for financial gain is both discouraging and destructive. Should environmentalists oppose these so-called "market mechanisms" to reduce carbon emissions in favor of equally corruptible direct government regulation?
14. In the case of the near extinction of the American buffalo, why was the resource so quickly destroyed? (Hint: Explain whose buffalo the individual hunters shooting, and why if one of them decided to stop shooting, nothing would have changed other than that individual hunter would not have earned any income from selling hides.)

15. Can the wealthy United States, which produced the greatest share of the GHGs in the atmosphere and stimulated mass consumption around the world, simply ignore the consequences of its past actions and refuse to contribute to the costs of mitigating global warming while it continues to promote its resource-using lifestyle around the world?

16. The textbook states: "Those who wield power, the wealthy, are the ones who through their excessive consumption are disproportionately responsible for damaging the ecosystem. But they can use their wealth to protect themselves from this damage." Do you think this is true? Are there some damages that simply cannot be fixed with money?

17. Discuss John Maynard Keynes' prediction of fifteen hour workweeks by the start of the twenty-first century. Write a brief essay explaining why Keynes' prediction has not come to pass.

18. What might economic development that sustains all three spheres of human existence look like? Write a description of a sustainable society, paying careful attention to how such a society satisfies sustainability in the economic, social, and natural spheres.

References

Arrhenius, Svante (1896), "On the Influence of Carbonic Acid and Air upon the Temperature of the Ground," *Philosophical Magazine* 41(2):237–272.

Biello, David (2009), "Burying Climate Change: Efforts Begin to Sequester Carbon Dioxide from Power Plants," *Scientific American*, September 22.

Brookes, L. (1990), "The Greenhouse Effect: The Fallacies in the Energy Efficient Solution." *Energy Policy* 18:199–201.

Brown, Lester (2009), *Plan B 4.0: Mobilizing to Save Civilization*, New York: Norton.

Ehrlich, Paul (1968), *The Population Bomb*, New York: Ballantine Books.

Enkvist, Per-Anders, Tomas Nauclér, and Jerker Rosander (2007), "A Cost Curve for Greenhouse Gas Reduction," *The McKinsey Quarterly* 1:35–45.

Epstein, Paul R., Jonathan J. Buonocore, Kevin Eckerle, Michael Hendryx, Benjamin M. Stout III, Richard, Heinberg, Richard W. Clapp, Beverly May, Nancy L. Reinhart, Melissa M. Ahern, Samir K. Doshi, and Leslie Glustrom (2011), "Full Cost Accounting for the Life Cycle of Coal," in "Ecological Economics Reviews," Robert Costanza, Karin Limburg, and Ida Kubiszewski (eds.), *Annals of the New York Academy of Science* 1219:73–98.

Eskeland, Gunnar S., and Tarhan Feyzioglu (1997), "Rationing Can Backfire: The 'Day without a Car' in Mexico City," *The World Bank Economic Review* 11(3):383–408.

Fitzgerald, F. Scott (1925), *The Great Gatsby*, New York: Scribner.

Fourier, Joseph (1827), "Mémoire sur les températures du globe terrestre et des espaces planétaires," *Mémoires de l'académie royale des sciences* 7:569–604.

Fournier, Valerie (2008), "Escaping from the Economy: The Politics of Degrowth," *International Journal of Sociology and Social Policy* 28(11/12):528–545.

Greenpeace International (2009), "Reality Check on Carbon Storage," Policy paper posted on www.greenpeace.org.

Howarth, Robert W., Renee Santoro, and Anthony Ingraffea (2011), "Methane and the Greenhouse-Gas Footprint of Natural Gas from Shale Formations: A Letter," *Climatic Change* 106(4):679–690.

Intergovernmental Panel on Climate Change (2007), *IPCC Report on Global Warming*, New York: United Nations.

International Energy Agency (2010), *World Energy Outlook 2010*, Paris: OECD/IEA.

Kempf, Hervé (2007), *How the Rich Are Destroying the Earth*, White River Junction, VT: Chelsea Green Publishing Co.

Keynes, John Maynard (1930), "Economic Possibilities for our Grandchildren," in *Essays in Persuasion*, New York: W.W. Norton & Co., [1963], pp. 358–373.

Khazzoom, J. Daniel (1980). "Economic Implications of Mandated Efficiency Standards for Household Appliances." *The Energy Journal* 11(2):21–40.

Klemperer, Paul (2008), "If Climate Sceptics Are Right, It Is Time to Worry," *Financial Times*, February 29.

Klein, Naomi (2009), "Climate Rage," *Rolling Stone*, November 11.

Lohman, Larry (2006), "Carbon Trading: A Critical Conversation on Climate Change, Privatization, and Power," *Development Dialogue* 48, September.

Lovelock, James E. (1972), "Gaia as Seen through the Atmosphere," *Atmospheric Environment* 6(8):579–580.

Lovelock, James E. (2006), "The Earth Is About to Catch a Morbid Fever that May Last as Long as 100,000 Years," *The Independent*, January 16.

McKibben, Bill (2008), *Deep Economy: The Wealth of Communities and the Durable Future*, New York: St. Martin's.

Pecchi, Lorenzo, and Gustavo Piga, eds. (2008), *Revisiting Keynes: Economic Possibilities of our Grandchildren*, Cambridge, MA: MIT Press.

Perkins, Patricia E. (2010), "Equitable, Ecological Degrowth: Feminist Contributions," Paper presented at the 2nd Conference on Economic Degrowth, March 26.

Popp, David (2002), "Induced Innovation and Energy Prices," *American Economic Review* 92:160–180.

Popp, David (2004), "R&D Subsidies and Climate Policy: Is There a Free Lunch?" NBER Working Paper 10880, October.

Pyndyck, Robert S. (2006), "Uncertainty in Environmental Economics," NBER Working Paper No. 12752, December.

Rees, Martin (2003), *Our Final Hour: A Scientist's Warning: How Terror, Error, and Environmental Disaster Threaten Humankind's Future In This Century — On Earth and Beyond*, New York: Basic Books.

Rising Tide North America (2009), "Hoodwinked in the Hothouse; False Solutions to Climate Change," pamphlet downloaded from www.risingtide.org, November.

Roodman, David Malin (1999), "Building a Sustainable Society," in Lester R. Brown, Christopher Flavin, Hillary French (eds.), *State of the World 1999, a Worldwatch Institute Report on Progress toward a Sustainable Society*, New York: Norton.

Saunders, Harry D. (1992), "The Khazzoom-Brookes postulate and neoclassical growth," *The Energy Journal*, October 1.

Schneider, Lambert (2007), "Is the CDM Fulfilling its Environmental and Sustainable Development Objectives? An Evaluation of the CDM and Options for Improvement," report prepared for the World Wildlife Federation by the German Institute for Applied Ecology, November 5.

Shapiro, Mark (2010), "Conning the Climate," *Harper's Magazine*, February, 31–39.

Stern, Nicholas (2007), *The Economics of Climate Change*, Cambridge, U.K.: Cambridge University Press.

Stern, Nicholas (2008), "The Economics of Climate Change," *American Economic Review* 98(2).

Tyndall, John (1861), "On the Absorption and Radiation of Heat by Gases and Vapours," *Philosophical Magazine* 22:169–194, 273–285.

Van den Bergh, Jeroen (2010), "Five Types of 'Degrowth' and a Plea for 'Growth'," Paper presented at the 2nd Conference on Economic Degrowth, March 26.

Victor, Peter A. (2008), *Managing without Growth: Slower by Design, Not Disaster*, Cheltenham, U.K.: Edward Elgar.

Viscusi, Kip (1993), "The Value of Risks to Life and Health," *Journal of Economics Literature* 31(4):1912–1946.

Wackernagel, Mathis, *et al.* (2002), "Tracking the Ecological Overshoot of the Human Economy," *Proceedings of the National Academy of Sciences* 99:9266–9271.

Weitzman, Martin (2007), "Structural Uncertainty and the Value of Statistical Life in the Economics of Catastrophic Climate Change," NBER Working Paper No. 13490, October.

World Wildlife Fund (2008), *Living Planet Report 2008*, Gland, Switzerland: World Wildlife Fund for Nature.

Name Index

Subject Index

Geographic Index

CPSIA information can be obtained
at www.ICGtesting.com
Printed in the USA
LVHW082121240720
661243LV00044B/62

9 789814 374644